CODE OF FEDERAL REGULATIONS

Title 5
Administrative Personnel

Parts 1 to 699

Revised as of January 1, 2018

Containing a codification of documents
of general applicability and future effect

As of January 1, 2018

Published by the Office of the Federal Register
National Archives and Records Administration
as a Special Edition of the Federal Register

Table of Contents

Cite this Code: CFR

To cite the regulations in this volume use title, part and section number. Thus, 5 CFR 1.1 *refers to title 5, part 1, section 1.*

Explanation

The Code of Federal Regulations is a codification of the general and permanent rules published in the Federal Register by the Executive departments and agencies of the Federal Government. The Code is divided into 50 titles which represent broad areas subject to Federal regulation. Each title is divided into chapters which usually bear the name of the issuing agency. Each chapter is further subdivided into parts covering specific regulatory areas.

Each volume of the Code is revised at least once each calendar year and issued on a quarterly basis approximately as follows:

Title 1 through Title 16..........as of January 1
Title 17 through Title 27..........as of April 1
Title 28 through Title 41..........as of July 1
Title 42 through Title 50..........as of October 1

The appropriate revision date is printed on the cover of each volume.

LEGAL STATUS

The contents of the Federal Register are required to be judicially noticed (44 U.S.C. 1507). The Code of Federal Regulations is prima facie evidence of the text of the original documents (44 U.S.C. 1510).

HOW TO USE THE CODE OF FEDERAL REGULATIONS

The Code of Federal Regulations is kept up to date by the individual issues of the Federal Register. These two publications must be used together to determine the latest version of any given rule.

To determine whether a Code volume has been amended since its revision date (in this case, January 1, 2018), consult the "List of CFR Sections Affected (LSA)," which is issued monthly, and the "Cumulative List of Parts Affected," which appears in the Reader Aids section of the daily Federal Register. These two lists will identify the Federal Register page number of the latest amendment of any given rule.

EFFECTIVE AND EXPIRATION DATES

Each volume of the Code contains amendments published in the Federal Register since the last revision of that volume of the Code. Source citations for the regulations are referred to by volume number and page number of the Federal Register and date of publication. Publication dates and effective dates are usually not the same and care must be exercised by the user in determining the actual effective date. In instances where the effective date is beyond the cut-off date for the Code a note has been inserted to reflect the future effective date. In those instances where a regulation published in the Federal Register states a date certain for expiration, an appropriate note will be inserted following the text.

OMB CONTROL NUMBERS

The Paperwork Reduction Act of 1980 (Pub. L. 96–511) requires Federal agencies to display an OMB control number with their information collection request.

Many agencies have begun publishing numerous OMB control numbers as amendments to existing regulations in the CFR. These OMB numbers are placed as close as possible to the applicable recordkeeping or reporting requirements.

PAST PROVISIONS OF THE CODE

Provisions of the Code that are no longer in force and effect as of the revision date stated on the cover of each volume are not carried. Code users may find the text of provisions in effect on any given date in the past by using the appropriate List of CFR Sections Affected (LSA). For the convenience of the reader, a "List of CFR Sections Affected" is published at the end of each CFR volume. For changes to the Code prior to the LSA listings at the end of the volume, consult previous annual editions of the LSA. For changes to the Code prior to 2001, consult the List of CFR Sections Affected compilations, published for 1949-1963, 1964-1972, 1973-1985, and 1986-2000.

"[RESERVED]" TERMINOLOGY

The term "[Reserved]" is used as a place holder within the Code of Federal Regulations. An agency may add regulatory information at a "[Reserved]" location at any time. Occasionally "[Reserved]" is used editorially to indicate that a portion of the CFR was left vacant and not accidentally dropped due to a printing or computer error.

INCORPORATION BY REFERENCE

What is incorporation by reference? Incorporation by reference was established by statute and allows Federal agencies to meet the requirement to publish regulations in the Federal Register by referring to materials already published elsewhere. For an incorporation to be valid, the Director of the Federal Register must approve it. The legal effect of incorporation by reference is that the material is treated as if it were published in full in the Federal Register (5 U.S.C. 552(a)). This material, like any other properly issued regulation, has the force of law.

What is a proper incorporation by reference? The Director of the Federal Register will approve an incorporation by reference only when the requirements of 1 CFR part 51 are met. Some of the elements on which approval is based are:

(a) The incorporation will substantially reduce the volume of material published in the Federal Register.

(b) The matter incorporated is in fact available to the extent necessary to afford fairness and uniformity in the administrative process.

(c) The incorporating document is drafted and submitted for publication in accordance with 1 CFR part 51.

What if the material incorporated by reference cannot be found? If you have any problem locating or obtaining a copy of material listed as an approved incorporation by reference, please contact the agency that issued the regulation containing that incorporation. If, after contacting the agency, you find the material is not available, please notify the Director of the Federal Register, National Archives and Records Administration, 8601 Adelphi Road, College Park, MD 20740-6001, or call 202-741-6010.

CFR INDEXES AND TABULAR GUIDES

A subject index to the Code of Federal Regulations is contained in a separate volume, revised annually as of January 1, entitled CFR INDEX AND FINDING AIDS. This volume contains the Parallel Table of Authorities and Rules. A list of CFR titles, chapters, subchapters, and parts and an alphabetical list of agencies publishing in the CFR are also included in this volume.

An index to the text of "Title 3—The President" is carried within that volume.

The Federal Register Index is issued monthly in cumulative form. This index is based on a consolidation of the "Contents" entries in the daily Federal Register.

A List of CFR Sections Affected (LSA) is published monthly, keyed to the revision dates of the 50 CFR titles.

REPUBLICATION OF MATERIAL

There are no restrictions on the republication of material appearing in the Code of Federal Regulations.

INQUIRIES

For a legal interpretation or explanation of any regulation in this volume, contact the issuing agency. The issuing agency's name appears at the top of odd-numbered pages.

For inquiries concerning CFR reference assistance, call 202–741–6000 or write to the Director, Office of the Federal Register, National Archives and Records Administration, 8601 Adelphi Road, College Park, MD 20740-6001 or e-mail *fedreg.info@nara.gov.*

SALES

The Government Publishing Office (GPO) processes all sales and distribution of the CFR. For payment by credit card, call toll-free, 866-512-1800, or DC area, 202-512-1800, M-F 8 a.m. to 4 p.m. e.s.t. or fax your order to 202-512-2104, 24 hours a day. For payment by check, write to: US Government Publishing Office – New Orders, P.O. Box 979050, St. Louis, MO 63197-9000.

ELECTRONIC SERVICES

The full text of the Code of Federal Regulations, the LSA (List of CFR Sections Affected), The United States Government Manual, the Federal Register, Public Laws, Public Papers of the Presidents of the United States, Compilation of Presidential Documents and the Privacy Act Compilation are available in electronic format via *www.ofr.gov.* For more information, contact the GPO Customer Contact Center, U.S. Government Publishing Office. Phone 202-512-1800, or 866-512-1800 (toll-free). E-mail, *ContactCenter@gpo.gov.*

The Office of the Federal Register also offers a free service on the National Archives and Records Administration's (NARA) World Wide Web site for public law numbers, Federal Register finding aids, and related information. Connect to NARA's web site at *www.archives.gov/federal-register.*

The e-CFR is a regularly updated, unofficial editorial compilation of CFR material and Federal Register amendments, produced by the Office of the Federal Register and the Government Publishing Office. It is available at *www.ecfr.gov.*

OLIVER A. POTTS,
Director,
Office of the Federal Register
January 1, 2018

THIS TITLE

Title 5—ADMINISTRATIVE PERSONNEL is composed of three volumes. The parts in these volumes are arranged in the following order: Parts 1–699, 700–1199 and part 1200–end. The contents of these volumes represent all current regulations codified under this title of the CFR as of January 1, 2018.

For this volume, Cheryl E. Sirofchuck was Chief Editor. The Code of Federal Regulations publication program is under the direction of John Hyrum Martinez, assisted by Stephen J. Frattini.

Title 5—Administrative Personnel

(This book contains parts 1 to 699)

NOTE: Title 5 of the United States Code was revised and enacted into positive law by Pub. L. 89–554, Sept. 6, 1966. New citations for obsolete references to sections of 5 U.S.C. appearing in this volume may be found in a redesignation table under Title 5, Government Organization and Employees, United States Code.

CHAPTER I—OFFICE OF PERSONNEL MANAGEMENT

SUBCHAPTER A—CIVIL SERVICE RULES

SUBCHAPTER B—CIVIL SERVICE REGULATIONS

Office of Personnel Management

SUBCHAPTER A—CIVIL SERVICE RULES

PART 1—COVERAGE AND DEFINITIONS (RULE I)

AUTHORITY: 5 U.S.C. 3301, 3302.

SOURCE: 28 FR 10022, Sept. 14, 1963, unless otherwise noted.

§ 1.1 Positions and employees affected by the rules in this subchapter.

The rules in this subchapter shall apply to all positions in the competitive service and to all incumbents of such positions. Except as expressly provided in the rule concerned, the rules in this subchapter shall not apply to positions and employees in the excepted service.

§ 1.2 Extent of the competitive service.

The competitive service shall include: (a) All civilian positions in the executive branch of the Government unless specifically excepted therefrom by or pursuant to statute or by the Office of Personnel Management (hereafter referred to in this subchapter as OPM) under § 6.1 of this subchapter; and (b) all positions in the legislative and judicial branches of the Federal Government and in the Government of the District of Columbia which are specifically made subject to the civil service laws by statute. OPM is authorized and directed to determine finally whether a position is in the competitive service.

§ 1.3 Definitions.

As used in the rules in this subchapter:

(a) *Competitive service* shall have the same meaning as the words "classified service", or "classified (competitive) service", or "classified civil service" as defined in existing statutes and executive orders.

(b) *Competitive position* shall mean a position in the competitive service.

(c) *Competitive status* shall mean basic eligibility to be noncompetitively selected to fill a vacancy in a competitive position. A competitive status shall be acquired by career-conditional or career appointment through open competitive examination upon satisfactory completion of a probationary period, or may be granted by statute, executive order, or the Civil Service Rules without competitive examination. A person with competitive status may be promoted, transferred, reassigned, reinstated, or demoted without taking an open competitive examination, subject to the conditions prescribed by the Civil Service Rules and Regulations.

(d) An employee shall be considered as being in the competitive service when he has a competitive status and occupies a competitive position unless he is serving under a temporary appointment: *Provided*, that an employee who is in the competitive service at the time his position is first listed under Schedule A, B, or C shall be considered as continuing in the competitive service as long as he continues to occupy such position.

(e) *Tenure* shall mean the period of time an employee may reasonably expect to serve under his current appointment. Tenure shall be granted and governed by the type of appointment under which an employee is currently serving without regard to whether he has a competitive status or whether his appointment is to a competitive position or an excepted position.

§ 1.4 Extent of the excepted service.

(a) The excepted service shall include all civilian positions in the executive branch of the Government which are specifically excepted from the requirements of the Civil Service Act or from the competitive service by or pursuant to statute or by OPM under § 6.1 of this subchapter.

(b) *Excepted service* shall have the same meaning as the words "unclassified service", or "unclassified civil service", or "positions outside the competitive civil service" as used in existing statutes and executive orders.

(c) *Excepted position* shall have the same meaning as "unclassified position", or "position excepted by law", or "position excepted by executive order", or "position excepted by Civil Service Rule", or "position outside the competitive service" as used in existing statutes and Executive orders.

PART 2—APPOINTMENT THROUGH THE COMPETITIVE SERVICE; RELATED MATTERS (RULE II)

AUTHORITY: 5 U.S.C. 3301, 3302.

SOURCE: 28 FR 10023, Sept. 14, 1963, unless otherwise noted.

§ 2.1 Competitive examinations and eligible registers; suitability and fitness for civil service employment.

(a) OPM shall be responsible for:

(i) Open competitive examinations for admission to the competitive service that will fairly test the relative capacity and fitness of the persons examined for the position to be filled.

(ii) Standards with respect to citizenship, age, education, training and experience, physical and mental fitness, and for residence or other requirements that applicants must meet to be admitted to or rated in examinations.

(iii) Standards of suitability based on character and conduct for appointment to a position in the competitive service, for appointment to a position in the excepted service where the incumbent can be noncompetitively converted to the competitive service, and for career appointment to a position in the Senior Executive Service.

(iv) Minimum standards of fitness based on character and conduct for appointment in any other position in the excepted service of the executive branch, except for (A) positions in any element of the intelligence community as defined in the National Security Act of 1947, as amended, to the extent they are not otherwise subject to OPM appointing authorities, and (B) positions where OPM is statutorily precluded from prescribing such standards."

(b) In addition to the names of persons who qualify in competitive examinations, the names of persons who have lost eligibility on a career or career-conditional register because of service in the armed forces, and the names of persons who lost opportunity for certification or who have served under career or career-conditional appointment when OPM determines that they should be given certification, may also be entered at such places on appropriate registers and under such conditions as OPM may prescribe.

(c) Whenever the Office of Personnel Management (1) is unable to certify a sufficient number of names to permit the appointing officer to consider three eligibles for appointment to a fourth-class postmaster position in accordance with the regular procedure, or (2) finds that a particular rate of compensation for fourth-class postmaster positions is too low to warrant regular competitive examinations for such positions, it may authorize appointment to any such position or positions in accordance with such procedure as may be prescribed by OPM. Persons appointed under this paragraph may acquire competitive status subject to satisfactory completion of a probationary period prescribed by OPM.

[28 FR 10023, Sept. 14, 1963, as amended by E.O. 13764, 82 FR 8115, Jan. 23, 2017]

§ 2.2 Appointments.

(a) OPM shall establish and administer a career-conditional appointment system for positions subject to competitive examinations which will permit adjustment of the career service to necessary fluctuations in Federal employment, and provide an equitable and orderly system for stabilizing the Federal work force. A competitive status shall be acquired by a career-conditional appointee upon satisfactory completion of a probationary period, but the appointee shall have career-conditional tenure for a period of service to be prescribed by regulation of OPM. When an employee has completed the required period of service his appointment shall be converted to a career appointment without time limitation: *Provided*, That his career-conditional appointment shall not be converted to a career appointment if the limitation on the number of permanent employees in the Federal civil service established under paragraph (b) of this section would be exceeded thereby. Persons selected from competitive civil service registers for other than temporary appointment shall be given career-conditional appointments: *Provided*, That career appointments shall be given to the following classes of eligibles:

(1) Persons whose appointments are required by statute to be made on a permanent basis;

(2) Employees serving under career appointments at the time of selection from such registers;

(3) Former employees who have eligibility for career appointments upon reinstatement; and

(4) To the extent permitted by law, persons appointed to positions in the field service of the U.S. Postal Service for which salary rates are fixed by the act of July 6, 1945, 59 Stat. 435, as heretofore or hereafter amended and supplemented.

(b) Under the career-conditional appointment system there shall be a limit on the number of permanent employees in the Federal civil service which shall be the ceiling established by section 1310 of the Supplemental Appropriation Act, 1952 (65 Stat. 757), as amended. In the event section 1310, supra, is repealed, OPM is authorized to fix such limitation on the number of permanent employees in the Federal civil service as it finds necessary to meet the needs of the service.

(c) OPM may determine the types, duration, and conditions of indefinite and temporary appointments, and may prescribe the method for replacing persons holding such appointments.

§2.3 Apportionment.

Subject to such modifications as OPM finds to be necessary in the interest of good administration, appointments to positions in agencies' headquarters offices which are located within the metropolitan area of Washington, DC, shall be made so as to maintain the apportionment of appointments among the several States, Territories, and the District of Columbia upon the basis of population.

§2.4 Probationary period.

Persons selected from registers of eligibles for career or career-conditional appointment and employees promoted, transferred, or otherwise assigned, for the first time, to supervisory or managerial positions shall be required to serve a probationary period under terms and conditions prescribed by the Office.

[45 FR 4337, Jan. 22, 1980]

PART 3—NONCOMPETITIVE ACQUISITION OF STATUS (RULE III)

Sec.

AUTHORITY: 5 U.S.C. 3301, 3302.

SOURCE: 28 FR 10023, Sept. 14, 1963, unless otherwise noted.

§3.1 Classes of persons who may noncompetitively acquire status.

(a) Upon recommendation by the agency concerned, and subject to such noncompetitive examination, time limits, or other requirements as OPM may prescribe the following classes of persons may acquire a competitive status without competitive examination:

(1) A person holding a permanent position when it is placed in the competitive service by statute or executive order or is otherwise made subject to competitive examination.

(2) A disabled veteran who, in a manner satisfactory to OPM, has completed a course of training in the executive branch of the Government prescribed by the Administrator of Veterans' Affairs in accordance with the act of March 24, 1943 (57 Stat. 43).

(3) An employee who has served at least two years in the immediate office of the President or on the White House Staff and who is transferred to a competitive position at the request of an agency.

(4) An employee who was serving when his name was reached for certification on a civil service register appropriate for the position in which he was serving: *Provided,* That the recommendation for competitive status is made prior to expiration of the register on which his name appears or is made during a period of continuous service since his name was reached: *Provided further,* That the register was being used for appointments conferring competitive status at the time his name was reached.

(b) Upon recommendation by the employing agency, and subject to such requirements as the Office of Personnel Management may prescribe, the following classes of handicapped employees may acquire competitive status without competitive examination:

(1) A severely physically handicapped employee who completes at least two years of satisfactory service in a position excepted from the competitive service.

(2) A mentally retarded employee who completes at least two years of satisfactory service in a position excepted from the competitive service.

(3) An employee with a psychiatric disability who completes at least 2 years of satisfactory service in a position excepted from the competitive service.

[28 FR 10023, Sept. 14, 1963, as amended by E.O. 12125, 3 CFR, 1979 Comp., p. 375; 65 FR 41868, July 7, 2000]

§3.2 Appointments without competitive examination in rare cases.

Subject to receipt of satisfactory evidence of the qualifications of the person to be appointed, OPM may authorize an appointment in the competitive service without competitive examination whenever it finds that the duties or compensation of the position are such, or that qualified persons are so rare, that, in the interest of good civil-service administration, the position cannot be filled through open competitive examination. Any person heretofore or hereafter appointed under this section shall acquire a competitive status upon completion of at least one year of satisfactory service and compliance with such requirements as OPM may prescribe. Detailed statements of the reasons for the noncompetitive appointments made under this section shall be published in OPM's annual reports.

§3.3 Conversion of appointments.

Any person who acquires a competitive status under this part shall have his appointment converted to career-conditional appointment unless he meets the service requirement for career appointment prescribed under §2.2(a) of this subchapter.

PART 4—PROHIBITED PRACTICES (RULE IV)

Sec.

AUTHORITY: 5 U.S.C. 3301, 3302.

§4.1 Prohibition against political activity.

No person employed in the executive branch of the Federal Government, or any agency or department thereof, shall use his official authority or influence for the purpose of interfering with an election or affecting the result thereof. No person occupying a position in the competitive service shall take any active part in political management or in political campaigns, except as may be provided by or pursuant to statute. All such persons shall retain the right to vote as they may choose and to express their opinions on all political subjects and candidates.

[28 FR 10024, Sept. 14, 1963]

§4.2 Prohibition against racial, political or religious discrimination.

No person employed in the executive branch of the Federal Government who has authority to take or recommend any personnel action with respect to any person who is an employee in the competitive service or any eligible or applicant for a position in the competitive service shall make any inquiry concerning the race, political affiliation, or religious beliefs of any such employee, eligible, or applicant. All disclosures concerning such matters shall be ignored, except as to such membership in political parties or organizations as constitutes by law a disqualification for Government employment. No discrimination shall be exercised, threatened, or promised by any person in the executive branch of the Federal Government against or in favor of any employee in the competitive service, or any eligible or applicant for a position in the competitive service because of his race, political affiliation, or religious beliefs, except as may be authorized or required by law.

[28 FR 10024, Sept. 14, 1963]

§4.3 Prohibition against securing withdrawal from competition.

No person shall influence another person to withdraw from competition for any position in the competitive service for the purpose of either improving or injuring the prospects of any applicant for appointment.

[28 FR 10024, Sept. 14, 1963, as amended at 45 FR 4337, Jan. 22, 1980]

PART 5—REGULATIONS, INVESTIGATION, AND ENFORCEMENT (RULE V)

AUTHORITY: 5 U.S.C. 3301, 3302; E.O. 12107.

SOURCE: 45 FR 4337, Jan. 22, 1980, unless otherwise noted.

§5.1 Civil Service regulations.

The Director, Office of Personnel Management, shall promulgate and enforce regulations necessary to carry out the provisions of the Civil Service Act and the Veterans' Preference Act, as reenacted in title 5, United States Code, the Civil Service Rules, and all other statutes and Executive orders imposing responsibilities on the Office. The Director is authorized, whenever there are practical difficulties and unnecessary hardships in complying with the strict letter of the regulation, to grant a variation from the strict letter of the regulation if such a variation is within the spirit of the regulations, and the efficiency of the Government and the integrity of the competitive service are protected and promoted. Whenever a variation is granted the Director shall note the official record to show:

(a) The particular practical difficulty or hardship involved, (b) what is permitted in place of what is required by regulations, (c) the circumstances which protect or promote the efficiency of the Government and the integrity of the competitive service, and (d) a statement limiting the application of the variation to the continuation of the conditions which gave rise to it. Like variations shall be granted whenever like conditions exist. All such decisions and information concerning variations noted in the official record shall be published promptly in a Federal Personnel Manual Letter or Bulletin and in the Director's next annual report.

§5.2 Investigation and evaluations.

The Director may secure effective implementation of the civil service laws, rules, and regulations, and all Executive orders imposing responsibilities on the Office by:

(a) Investigating the qualifications, suitability, and fitness of applicants for positions in the competitive service, positions in the excepted service where the incumbent can be noncompetitively converted to the competitive service, career appointments to positions in the Senior Executive Service, and any other positions in the excepted service of the executive branch for which the Director has standard-setting responsibility under Civil Service Rule II.

(i) The Director may require appointments to be made subject to investigation to enable the Director to determine, after appointment, that the requirements of law or the Civil Service Rules and Regulations have been met.

(ii) The Director may cause positions to be designated based on risk to determine the appropriate level of investigation, and may prescribe investigative standards, policies, and procedures.

(iii) The Director may prescribe standards for reciprocal acceptance by agencies of investigations and adjudications of suitability and fitness, except to the extent authority to apply additional fitness standards is vested by statute in an agency.

(b) Evaluating the effectiveness of: (1) Personnel policies, programs, and operations of Executive and other Federal agencies subject to the jurisdiction of the Office, including their effectiveness with regard to merit selection and employee development; (2) agency compliance with and enforcement of applicable laws, rules, regulations and office directives; and (3) agency personnel management evaluation systems.

(c) Investigating, or directing an agency to investigate and report on, apparent violations of applicable laws, rules, regulations, or directives requiring corrective action, found in the course of an evaluation.

[45 FR 4337, Jan. 22, 1980, as amended by E.O. 13197, 66 FR 7853, Jan. 25, 2001; E.O. 13764, 82 FR 8115, Jan. 23, 2017]

§ 5.3 Enforcement.

(a) The Director is authorized to ensure enforcement of the civil service laws, rules, and regulations, and all applicable Executive orders, by:

(1) Instructing an agency to separate or take other action against an employee serving an appointment subject to investigation when the Director finds that the employee is disqualified or unsuitable for Federal employment. Where the employee or the agency appeals the Director's finding that a separation or other action is necessary, the Director may instruct the agency as to whether or not the employee should remain on duty and continue to receive pay pending adjudication of the appeal: *Provided*, That when an agency separates or takes other action against an employee pursuant to the Director's instructions, and the Director, on the basis of new evidence, subsequently reverses the initial decision as to the employee's qualifications and suitability, the agency shall, upon request of the Director, restore the employee to duty or otherwise reverse any action taken.

(2) Reporting the results of evaluation or investigations to the head of the agency concerned with instructions for any corrective action necessary, including cancellation of personnel actions where appropriate. The Director's findings resulting from evaluations or investigations are binding unless changed as a result of agency evidence and arguments against them. If, during the course of any evaluation or investigation under this section, the Director finds evidence of matters which come within the investigative and prosecutorial jurisdiction of the Special Counsel of the Merit Systems Protection Board, the Director shall refer this evidence to the Special Counsel for appropriate disposition.

(b) Whenever the Director issues specific instructions as to separation or other corrective action with regard to an employee, including cancellation of a personnel action, the head of the agency concerned shall comply with the Director's instructions.

(c) If the agency head fails to comply with the specific instructions of the Director as to separation or other corrective action with regard to an employee, including cancellation of a personnel action, the Director may certify to the Comptroller General of the United States the agency's failure to act together with such additional information as the Comptroller General may require, and shall furnish a copy of such certification to the head of the agency concerned. The individual with respect to whom such separation or other corrective action was instructed shall be entitled thereafter to no pay or only to such pay as appropriate to effectuate the Director's instructions.

[45 FR 4337, Jan. 22, 1980, as amended by E.O. 13764, 82 FR 8115, Jan. 23, 2017]

§ 5.4 Information and testimony.

When required by the Office, the Merit Systems Protection Board, or the Special Counsel of the Merit Systems Protection Board, or by authorized representatives of these bodies, agencies shall make available to them, or to their authorized representatives, employees to testify in regard to matters inquired of under the civil service laws, rules, and regulations, and records pertinent to these matters. All such employees, and all applicants or eligibles for positions covered by these rules, shall give to the Office, the Merit Systems Protection Board, the Special

Counsel, or to their authorized representatives, all information, testimony, documents, and material in regard to the above matters, the disclosure of which is not otherwise prohibited by law or regulation. These employees, applicants, and eligibles shall sign testimony given under oath or affirmation before an officer authorized by law to administer oaths. Employees are performing official duty when testifying or providing evidence pursuant to this section.

PART 6—EXCEPTIONS FROM THE COMPETITIVE SERVICE (RULE VI)

AUTHORITY: 5 U.S.C. 3301, 3302.

SOURCE: 28 FR 10025, Sept. 14, 1963, unless otherwise noted.

§6.1 Authority to except positions from the competitive service.

(a) OPM may except positions from the competitive service when it determines that (A) appointments thereto through competitive examination are not practicable, or (B) recruitment from among students attending qualifying educational institutions or individuals who have recently completed qualifying educational programs can better be achieved by devising additional means for recruiting and assessing candidates that diverge from the processes generally applicable to the competitive service. These positions shall be listed in OPM's annual report for the fiscal year in which the exceptions are made.

(b) OPM shall decide whether the duties of any particular position are such that it may be filled as an excepted position under the appropriate schedule.

(c) Notice of OPM's decision granting authority to make appointments to an excepted position under the appropriate schedule shall be published in the FEDERAL REGISTER.

[28 FR 10025, Sept. 14, 1963, as amended by E.O. 11315, 3 CFR, 1966–1970 Comp., p. 597; E.O. 12043, 43 FR 9773, Mar. 10, 1978; E.O. 13562, 75 FR 82587, Dec. 30, 2010]

§6.2 Schedules of excepted positions.

OPM shall list positions that it excepts from the competitive service in Schedules A, B, C, and D, which schedules shall constitute parts of this rule, as follows:

Schedule A. Positions other than those of a confidential or policy-determining character for which it is not practicable to examine shall be listed in Schedule A.

Schedule B. Positions other than those of a confidential or policy-determining character for which it is not practicable to hold a competitive examination shall be listed in Schedule B. Appointments to these positions shall be subject to such noncompetitive examination as may be prescribed by OPM.

Schedule C. Positions of a confidential or policy-determining character shall be listed in Schedule C.

Schedule D. Positions other than those of a confidential or policy-determining character for which the competitive service requirements make impracticable the adequate recruitment of sufficient numbers of students attending qualifying educational institutions or individuals who have recently completed qualifying educational programs. These positions, which are temporarily placed in the excepted service to enable more effective recruitment from all segments of society by using means of recruiting and assessing candidates that diverge from the rules generally applicable to the competitive service, shall be listed in Schedule D.

[E.O. 13562, 75 FR 82587, Dec. 30, 2010]

§6.3 Method of filling excepted positions and status of incumbents.

(a) The head of an agency may fill excepted positions by the appointment of persons without civil service eligibility or competitive status and such persons shall not acquire competitive status by reason of such appointment: *Provided,* That OPM, in its discretion, may by regulation prescribe conditions under which excepted positions may be filled in the same manner as competitive positions are filled and conditions under which persons so appointed may acquire a competitive status in accordance with the Civil Service Rules and Regulations.

(b) To the extent permitted by law and the provisions of this part, and subject to the suitability and fitness requirements of the applicable Civil Service Rules and Regulations, appointments and position changes in the excepted service shall be made in accordance with such regulations and practices as the head of the agency concerned finds necessary.

[28 FR 10025, Sept. 14, 1963, as amended by E.O. 13764, 82 FR 8115, Jan. 23, 2017]

§6.4 Removal of incumbents of excepted positions.

Except as may be required by statute, the Civil Service Rules and Regulations shall not apply to removals from positions listed in Schedules A, C, or D or from positions excepted from the competitive service by statute. The Civil Service Rules and Regulations shall apply to removals from positions listed in Schedule B of persons who have competitive status.

[28 FR 10025, Sept. 14, 1963, as amended by E.O. 13562, 75 FR 82587, Dec. 30, 2010]

§6.5 Assignment of excepted employees.

No person who is serving under an excepted appointment shall be assigned to the work of a position in the competitive service without prior approval of OPM.

§6.6 Revocation of exceptions.

OPM may remove any position from or may revoke in whole or in part any provision of Schedule A, B, C, or D. Notice of OPM's decision making these changes shall be published in the FEDERAL REGISTER.

[E.O. 11315, 3 CFR, 1966–1970 Comp., p. 597, as amended by E.O. 12043, 43 FR 9773, Mar. 10, 1978; E.O. 13562, 75 FR 82587, Dec. 30, 2010]

§6.7 Movement of persons between the civil service system and other merit systems.

Whenever OPM and any Federal agency having an established merit system determine it to be in the interest of good administration and consistent with the intent of the civil service laws and any other applicable laws, they may enter into an agreement prescribing conditions under which persons may be moved from one system to the other and defining the status and tenure that the persons affected shall acquire upon such movement.

§6.8 Specified exceptions.

(a) Positions in the Department of the Interior and in the Department of Commerce whose incumbents serve as the principal representative of the Secretary in their respective regions shall be listed in Schedule C for grades not exceeding grade GS–15 of the General Schedule, and shall be designated Noncareer Executive Assignments for positions graded higher than GS–15. Incumbents of these positions who are, on February 15, 1975, in the competitive service shall not be affected by the foregoing provisions of this section.

(b) Positions in the Community Services Administration and ACTION whose incumbents serve as regional director or regional administrator shall be listed in Schedule C for grades not exceeding GS–15 of the General Schedule and shall be designated Noncareer Executive Assignments for positions graded higher than GS–15. Incumbents of these positions who are, on November 29, 1977, in the competitive service shall not be affected by the foregoing provisions of this subsection.

(c) Within the Department of Agriculture, positions in the Agriculture Stabilization and Conservation Service the incumbents of which serve as State Executive Directors and positions in the Farmers Home Administration the incumbents of which serve as State Directors or State Directors-at-Large shall be listed in Schedule C for all grades of the General Schedule.

[E.O. 11839, 40 FR 7351, Feb. 19, 1975, as amended by E.O. 11887, 40 FR 51411, Nov. 5, 1975; E.O. 12021, 42 FR 61237, Dec. 2, 1977; 47 FR 4227, Jan. 29, 1982]

PART 7—GENERAL PROVISIONS (RULE VII)

Sec.

AUTHORITY: 5 U.S.C. 3301, 3302.

SOURCE: 28 FR 10025, Sept. 14, 1963, unless otherwise noted.

§7.1 Discretion in filling vacancies.

In his discretion, an appointing officer may fill any position in the competitive service either by competitive appointment from a civil service register or by noncompetitive selection of a present or former Federal employee, in accordance with the Civil Service Regulations. He shall exercise his discretion in all personnel actions solely on the basis of merit and fitness and without regard to political or religious affiliations, marital status, or race.

§7.2 Reemployment rights.

OPM, whenever it determines it to be necessary, shall prescribe regulations governing the release of employees (both within the competitive service and the excepted service) by any agency in the executive branch of the Government for employment in any other agency, and governing the establishment, granting, and exercise of rights to reemployment in the agencies from which employees are released.

[28 FR 10025, Sept. 14, 1963. Redesignated by E.O. 13197, 66 FR 7853, Jan. 25, 2001]

§7.3 Citizenship.

(a) No person shall be admitted to competitive examination unless such person is a citizen or national of the United States.

(b) No person shall be given any appointment in the competitive service unless such person is a citizen or national of the United States.

(c) OPM may, as an exception to this rule and to the extent permitted by law, authorize the appointment of aliens to positions in the competitive service when necessary to promote the efficiency of the service in specific cases or for temporary appointments.

[E.O. 11935, 41 FR 37301, Sept. 3, 1976. Redesignated by E.O. 13197, 66 FR 7853, Jan. 25, 2001]

PART 8—APPOINTMENTS TO OVERSEAS POSITIONS (RULE VIII)

Sec.

AUTHORITY: 5 U.S.C. 3301, 3302.

SOURCE: 28 FR 10025, Sept. 14, 1963, unless otherwise noted.

§8.1 Additional authority of OPM.

In addition to authorizing the recruitment and appointment of persons to overseas positions under regulations issued under the preceding Rules, OPM may, by the regulations prescribed by it, authorize the recruitment and appointment of persons to such positions as provided in §8.2. As used in this part, *overseas positions* means positions in foreign countries and in other areas beyond the continental limits of the United States, except as provided in §8.4.

§8.2 Appointment of United States citizens.

United States citizens may be recruited overseas for appointment to overseas positions in the competitive service without regard to the competitive requirements of the Civil Service Act. Persons so recruited who meet the qualification standards and other requirements of OPM for overseas positions may be given appointments to be known as "overseas limited appointments." Such appointments shall be of temporary or indefinite duration, and shall not confer the right to acquire a competitive status. OPM may authorize overseas limited appointments for United States citizens recruited within the continental limits of the United States whenever it determines that it is not feasible to appoint from a civil-service register. Persons serving under appointments made pursuant to this section are hereby excluded from the operation of the Civil Service Retirement Act of May 29, 1930, as amended, unless eligible for retirement benefits by continuity of service or otherwise.

§8.3 Appointment of persons not citizens of the United States.

Persons who are not citizens of the United States may be recruited overseas and appointed to overseas positions without regard to the Civil Service Act.

§ 8.4 Positions excepted from the application of this part.

This part shall not apply to positions in Hawaii, Puerto Rico, the Virgin Islands, and Alaska, and on the Isthmus of Panama.

PART 9—WORKFORCE INFORMATION (RULE IX)

SOURCE: E.O. 13197, 66 FR 7853, Jan. 25, 2001, unless otherwise noted.

§ 9.1 Definition.

As used in this rule, 'Executive agency' means an Executive department, a Government corporation, and an independent establishment, as those terms are defined in chapter 1 of title 5, United States Code, but does not include the Federal Bureau of Investigation, the Central Intelligence Agency, the Defense Intelligence Agency, the National Imagery and Mapping Agency, the National Security Agency, and, as determined by the President, any Executive agency or unit within an Executive agency which has as its principal function the conduct of foreign intelligence or counterintelligence activities.

§ 9.2 Reporting workforce information.

The Director of the Office of Personnel Management may require all Executive agencies to report information relating to civilian employees, including positions and employees in the competitive, excepted, and Senior Executive services, in a manner and at times prescribed by the Director. The Director shall establish standards for workforce information submissions under this section, and agencies shall ensure that their submissions meet these standards consistent with the Privacy Act. The Director may exempt from this section a specific agency or group of employees when the Director determines that an exemption is appropriate because of special circumstances.

PART 10—AGENCY ACCOUNTABILITY SYSTEMS; OPM AUTHORITY TO REVIEW PERSONNEL MANAGEMENT PROGRAMS (RULE X)

SOURCE: E.O. 13197, 66 FR 7853, Jan. 25, 2001, unless otherwise noted.

§ 10.1 Definitions.

For purposes of this rule—

(a) 'Agency' means an Executive agency as defined in Rule IX, but does not include a Government corporation or the General Accounting Office; and

(b) 'Merit system principles' means the principles for Federal personnel management that are set forth in section 2301(b) of title 5, United States Code.

§ 10.2 Accountability systems.

The Director of the Office of Personnel Management may require an agency to establish and maintain a system of accountability for merit system principles that

(1) Sets standards for applying the merit system principles,

(2) Measures the agency's effectiveness in meeting these standards, and

(3) Corrects any deficiencies in meeting these standards.

§ 10.3 OPM authority to review personnel management programs and practices.

The Office of Personnel Management may review the human resources management programs and practices of any agency and report to the head of the agency and the President on the effectiveness of these programs and practices, including whether they are consistent with the merit system principles.

SUBCHAPTER B—CIVIL SERVICE REGULATIONS

PART 110—POSTING NOTICES OF NEW OPM REGULATIONS

AUTHORITY: 5 U.S.C. 1103.

SOURCE: 69 FR 33535, June 16, 2004, unless otherwise noted.

§ 110.101 What are OPM's Notice and Posting System responsibilities?

OPM will issue a notice that will provide information for Federal agencies, employees, managers, and other stakeholders on each of its new proposed, interim, and final regulations. Each notice will transmit:

(a) A posting notice that briefly explains the nature of the change, and provides a place for Federal agencies to indicate where the full text of the FEDERAL REGISTER notice will be available for review.

(b) A copy of the notice of rulemaking that appears in the FEDERAL REGISTER or a link to a Web site where the notice of rulemaking appears.

§ 110.102 What are Agency responsibilities?

(a) Agencies will make regulations available for review by employees, managers, and other interested parties. Federal agencies receiving the notices of rulemaking described in § 110.101(b) will make those regulations available for review upon request. Each agency will complete the posting notice described in § 110.101(a) indicating where and how requests to review these materials should be made.

(b) Agencies will determine posting locations and, if desired, develop supplemental announcements. Agencies will display completed posting notices in a prominent place where the notices can be easily seen and read. Agencies will choose the posting location that best fits their physical layout. Agencies may supplement these postings with announcements in employee newsletters, agency Web sites, or other communication methods. The basic requirement to post the notice continues, however, even if supplemental announcement methods are used.

(c) Agencies will post notices of the new regulations even if the FEDERAL REGISTER comment date has passed. The public comment period on proposed regulations begins when a notice of proposed rulemaking is published in the FEDERAL REGISTER, not with the posting of the notice described in § 110.101(a). The purpose of posting notice is solely to inform agency personnel of changes. Agencies are required to post the posting notice even if the formal deadline for comments shown in the preamble of the FEDERAL REGISTER notice of rulemaking has passed. Agencies should make every reasonable effort to minimize delays in distributing the notice described in § 110.101 to their field offices.

(d) No fixed posting period. There are no minimum or maximum time limits on displaying the notice described in § 110.101(a). Each office receiving a notice for posting should choose the posting period which provides the best opportunity to inform managers and employees of regulatory changes based upon office layout, geographic dispersion of employees, and other local factors.

PART 151—POLITICAL ACTIVITY OF STATE OR LOCAL OFFICERS OR EMPLOYEES

AUTHORITY: 5 U.S.C. 1302, 1501–1508, as amended, Reorganization Plan No. 2 of 1978, section 102, 92 Stat. 3783, 3 CFR 1978 Comp. p. 323; and E.O. 12107, section 1–102, 3 CFR 1978 Comp. p. 264.

SOURCE: 35 FR 16783, Oct. 30, 1970, unless otherwise noted.

GENERAL PROVISIONS

§ 151.101 Definitions.

In this part:

(a) *State* means a State or territory or possession of the United States.

(b) *State or local agency* means:

(1) The executive branch of a State, municipality, or other political subdivision of a State, or an agency or department thereof; or

(2) The executive branch of the District of Columbia, or an agency or department thereof.

(c) *Federal agency* means an executive agency or other agency of the United States, but does not include a member bank of the Federal Reserve System;

(d) *State or local officer or employee* means an individual employed by a State or local agency whose principal employment is in connection with an activity which is financed in whole or in part by loans or grants made by the United States or a Federal agency but does not include—

(1) An individual who exercises no functions in connection with that activity.

(2) An individual employed by an educational or research institution, establishment, agency, or system which is supported in whole or in part by—

(i) A State or political subdivision thereof;

(ii) The District of Columbia; or

(iii) A recognized religious, philanthropic, or cultural organization.

(e) *Political party* means a National political party, a State political party, and an affiliated organization.

(f) *Election* includes a primary, special, and general election.

(g) *Nonpartisan election* means an election at which none of the candidates is to be nominated or elected as representing a political party any of whose candidates for Presidential elector receives votes in the last preceding election at which Presidential electors were selected.

(h) *Partisan* when used as an adjective refers to a political party.

(i) *Elective office* means any office which is voted upon at an election as defined at § 151.101(f), above, but does not include political party office.

[40 FR 42733, Sept. 16, 1975, as amended at 79 FR 25484, May 5, 2014]

PERMISSIBLE ACTIVITIES

§ 151.111 Permissible activities.

(a) All State or local officers or employees are free to engage in political activity to the widest extent consistent with the restrictions imposed by law and this part. A State or local officer or employee may participate in all political activity not specifically restricted by law and this part, including candidacy for office in a nonpartisan election and candidacy for political party office.

[40 FR 42733, Sept. 16, 1975]

PROHIBITED ACTIVITIES

§ 151.121 Use of official authority; coercion; candidacy; prohibitions.

A State or local officer or employee may not—

(a) Use his official authority or influence for the purpose of interfering with or affecting the result of an election or a nomination for office; or

(b) Directly or indirectly coerce, attempt to coerce, command, or advise a State or local officer or employee to pay, lend, or contribute anything of value to a political party, committee, organization, agency, or person for a political purpose.

(c) Be a candidate for elective office if the salary of the employee is paid completely, directly or indirectly, by loans or grants made by the United States or a Federal agency.

[40 FR 42733, Sept. 16, 1975, as amended at 79 FR 25484, May 5, 2014]

§ 151.122 Candidacy; exceptions.

Section 151.121(c) does not apply to—

(a) The Governor or Lieutenant Governor of a State or an individual authorized by law to act as Governor;

(b) The Mayor of a city;

(c) A duly elected head of an executive department of a State, municipality, or the District of Columbia, who is not classified under a merit or civil service system of a State, municipality, or the District of Columbia;

(d) An individual holding elective office;

(e) Activity in connection with a nonpartisan election; or

(f) Candidacy for a position of officer of a political party, delegate to a political party convention, member of a National, State, or local committee of a political party, or any similar position.

[40 FR 42733, Sept. 16, 1975, as amended at 40 FR 47101, Oct. 8, 1975; 79 FR 25484, May 5, 2014]

PART 175—OPM MANDATORY REVIEW OF CLASSIFIED DOCUMENTS

AUTHORITY: E.O. 12065, 43 FR 28949.

§175.101 Policy.

The Office of Personnel Management bases its procedures for handling national security information on Executive Order 12065, "National Security Information," and Information Security Oversight Office Directive No. 1 concerning national security information.

[45 FR 995, Jan. 4, 1980]

§175.102 Requests for the declassification of documents.

Any Federal agency, Government employee or member of the public has the right to request a mandatory review of any classified document, held by the Office of Personnel Management, which was classified for national security purposes by the Civil Service Commission. The Office of Personnel Management does not have the authority to classify documents.

(a) Requests for mandatory declassification review should be addressed to the Director, Office of Management, or the designee of the Director, who will act on requests within 60 days. Requests need not be made in any special form but shall, as specified in section 3-501 of the Executive order, reasonably describe the information.

(b) Based upon the review, the document, or any reasonably segregable portion thereof that no longer requires protection under the Executive order, shall be declassified and released unless withholding is otherwise warranted under applicable law.

(c) No OPM official will refuse to confirm the existence or non-existence of any document requested under the Freedom of Information Act or the mandatory review provisions of the Executive order, unless the fact of its existence or non-existence would itself be classifiable under the Executive order. OPM Administrative Manual chapter 22, covering OPM policies and procedures relating to classified information or material is available for inspection by the public in the OPM Library, room 5H27, 1900 E. St., NW., Washington, DC, or in one of the 10 OPM regional offices in the following cities: Atlanta, Boston, Chicago, Dallas, Denver, New York, Philadelphia, St. Louis, San Francisco and Seattle.

[45 FR 995, Jan. 4, 1980]

PART 177—ADMINISTRATIVE CLAIMS UNDER THE FEDERAL TORT CLAIMS ACT

AUTHORITY: 28 U.S.C. 2672; 28 CFR 14.11.

SOURCE: 65 FR 44945, July 20, 2000, unless otherwise noted.

§177.101 Scope of regulations.

The regulations in this part apply only to claims presented or filed with the Office of Personnel Management (OPM) under the Federal Tort Claims Act, as amended, for money damages against the United States for injury to or loss of property or personal injury or death caused by the negligent or wrongful act or omission of an officer or employee of OPM while acting within the scope of his or her office or employment.

§ 177.102 Administrative claim; when presented; appropriate OPM office.

(a) For purposes of the provisions of 28 U.S.C. 2401(b), 2672, and 2675, a claim is deemed to have been presented when OPM receives from a claimant, his or her authorized agent or legal representative, an executed Standard Form 95 (Claim for Damage, Injury or Death), or other written notification of an incident, accompanied by a claim for money damages stating a sum certain (a specific dollar amount) for injury to or loss of property, personal injury, or death alleged to have occurred as a result of the incident.

(b) All claims filed under the Federal Tort Claims Act as a result of the alleged negligence or wrongdoing of OPM or its employees will be mailed or delivered to the Office of the General Counsel, United States Office of Personnel Management, 1900 E Street NW, Washington, DC 20415–1300.

(c) A claim must be presented to the Federal agency whose activities gave rise to the claim. A claim that should have been presented to OPM, but was mistakenly addressed to or filed with another Federal agency, is presented to OPM, as required by 28 U.S.C. 2401(b), as of the date the claim is received by OPM. When a claim is mistakenly presented to OPM, OPM will transfer the claim to the appropriate Federal agency, if ascertainable, and advise the claimant of the transfer, or return the claim to the claimant.

(d) A claimant whose claim arises from an incident involving OPM and one or more other Federal agencies, will identify each agency to which the claim has been submitted at the time the claim is presented to OPM. OPM will contact all other affected Federal agencies in order to designate the single agency that will investigate and decide the merits of the claim. In the event a designation cannot be agreed upon by the affected agencies, the Department of Justice will be consulted and will designate an agency to investigate and determine the merits of the claim. The designated agency will notify the claimant that all future correspondence concerning the claim must be directed to that Federal agency. All involved Federal agencies may agree to conduct their own administrative reviews and to coordinate the results, or to have the investigation conducted by the designated Federal agency. But, in either event, the designated agency will be responsible for the final determination of the claim.

(e) A claim presented in compliance with paragraph (a) of this section may be amended by the claimant at any time prior to final agency action or prior to the exercise of the claimant's option under 28 U.S.C. 2675(a). Amendments must be in writing and signed by the claimant or his or her authorized agent or legal representative. Upon timely filing of an amendment to a pending claim, OPM will have 6 months in which to make a final disposition of the claim as amended and claimant's option under 28 U.S.C. 2675 (a) will not accrue until 6 months after the filing of an amendment.

§ 177.103 Administrative claim; who may file.

(a) A claim for injury to or loss of property may be presented by the owner of the property, his or her authorized agent or legal representative.

(b) A claim for personal injury may be presented by the injured person, his or her authorized agent or legal representative.

(c) A claim based on death may be presented by the executor or administrator of the decedent's estate or by any other person legally entitled to assert a claim under the applicable State law.

(d) A claim for loss totally compensated by an insurer with the rights to subrogate may be presented by the insurer. A claim for loss partially compensated by an insurer with the rights to subrogate may be presented by the insurer or the insured individually, as their respective interests appear, or jointly. When an insurer presents a claim asserting the rights to subrogate, he or she will present with the claim appropriate evidence that he or she has the rights to subrogate.

(e) A claim presented by an agent or legal representative must be presented in the name of the claimant, be signed by the agent or legal representative, show the title or legal capacity of the person signing, and be accompanied by evidence of his or her authority to present a claim on behalf of the claimant as agent, executor, administrator, parent, guardian, or other representative.

§177.104 Investigations.

OPM may investigate, or may request any other Federal agency to investigate, a claim filed under this part.

§177.105 Administrative claim; evidence and information to be submitted.

(a) *Death.* In support of a claim based on death, the claimant may be required to submit the following evidence or information:

(1) An authenticated death certificate or other competent evidence showing cause of death, date of death, and age of the decedent.

(2) Decedent's employment or occupation at time of death, including his or her monthly or yearly salary or earnings (if any), and the duration of his or her last employment or occupation.

(3) Full names, addresses, birth date, kinship, and marital status of the decedent's survivors, including identification of those survivors who were dependent for support from the decedent at the time of death.

(4) Degree of support afforded by the decedent to each survivor dependent on him or her for support at the time of death.

(5) Decedent's general physical and mental condition before death.

(6) Itemized bills for medical and burial expenses incurred by reason of the incident causing death, or itemized receipts of payment for such expenses.

(7) If damages for pain and suffering before death are claimed, a physician's detailed statement specifying the injuries suffered, duration of pain and suffering, any drugs administered for pain, and the decedent's physical condition in the interval between injuries and death.

(8) Any other evidence or information which may have a bearing on either the responsibility of the United States for the death or the amount of damages claimed.

(b) *Personal injury.* In support of a claim for personal injury, including pain and suffering, the claimant may be required to submit the following evidence or information:

(1) A written report by the attending physician or dentist setting forth the nature and extent of the injury, nature and extent of treatment, any degree of temporary or permanent disability, the prognosis, period of hospitalization, and any diminished earning capacity. In addition, the claimant may be required to submit to a physical or mental examination by a physician employed by OPM or another Federal agency. On written request, OPM will make available to the claimant a copy of the report of the examining physician employed by the United States, provided the claimant has furnished OPM with the report referred to in the first sentence of this subparagraph. In addition, the claimant must have made or agrees to make available to OPM all other physician's reports previously or thereafter made of the physical or mental condition that is the subject matter of his or her claim.

(2) Itemized bills for medical, dental, and hospital expenses incurred, or itemized receipts of payment for such expenses.

(3) If the prognosis reveals the necessity for future treatment, a statement of expected expenses for such treatment.

(4) If a claim is made for loss of time from employment, a written statement from his or her employer showing actual time lost from employment, whether he or she is a full-or part-time employee, and wages or salary actually lost.

(5) If a claim is made for loss of income and the claimant is self-employed, documentary evidence showing the amount of earnings actually lost.

(6) Any other evidence or information which may have a bearing on either the responsibility of the United States for the personal injury or the damages claimed.

(c) *Property damage.* In support of a claim for injury to or loss of property, real or personal, the claimant may be required to submit the following evidence or information:

(1) Proof of ownership of the property.

(2) A detailed statement of the amount claimed with respect to each item of property.

(3) An itemized receipt of payment for necessary repairs or itemized written estimates of the cost of such repairs.

(4) A statement listing date of purchase, purchase price, and salvage value, where repair is economical.

(5) Any other evidence or information which may have a bearing on either the responsibility of the United States for the injury to or loss of property or the damages claimed.

§ 177.106 Authority to adjust, determine, compromise, and settle.

(a) The General Counsel of OPM, or his or her designee, is delegated authority to consider, ascertain, adjust, determine, compromise, and settle claims under the provisions of 28 U.S.C. 2672, and this part. The General Counsel, in his or her discretion, has the authority to further delegate the responsibility for adjudicating, considering, adjusting, compromising, and settling any claim submitted under the provisions of 28 U.S.C. 2672, and this part, that is based on the alleged negligence or wrongful act or omission of an OPM employee, with the exception of claims involving personal injury. All claims involving personal injury will be adjudicated, considered, adjusted, compromised and settled by the Office of the General Counsel.

§ 177.107 Limitations on authority.

(a) An award, compromise, or settlement of a claim under 28 U.S.C. 2672, and this part, in excess of $25,000 can be effected only with the prior written approval of the Attorney General or his or her designee. For purposes of this paragraph, a principal claim and any derivative or subrogated claim will be treated as a single claim.

(b) An administrative claim may be adjusted, determined, compromised, or settled under this part, only after consultation with the Department of Justice when, in the opinion of the General Counsel of OPM, or his or her designee:

(1) A new precedent or a new point of law is involved; or

(2) A question of policy is or may be involved; or

(3) The United States is or may be entitled to indemnity or contribution from a third party and OPM is unable to adjust the third party claim; or

(4) The compromise of a particular claim, as a practical matter, will or may control the disposition of a related claim in which the amount to be paid may exceed $25,000.

(c) An administrative claim may be adjusted, determined, compromised, or settled under 28 U.S.C. 2672, and this part, only after consultation with the Department of Justice when, OPM is informed or is otherwise aware that the United States or an employee, agent, or cost-type contractor of the United States is involved in litigation based on a claim arising out of the same incident or transaction.

§ 177.108 Referral to Department of Justice.

When Department of Justice approval or consultation is required, or the advice of the Department of Justice is otherwise to be requested, under § 177.107, the written referral or request will be transmitted to the Department of Justice by the General Counsel of OPM or his or her designee.

§ 177.109 Final denial of claim.

Final denial of an administrative claim must be in writing and sent to the claimant, his or her attorney, or legal representative by certified or registered mail. The notification of final denial may include a statement of the reasons for the denial. But, it must include a statement that, if the claimant is dissatisfied with the OPM action, he or she may file suit in an appropriate United States district court not later than 6 months after the date of mailing of the notification.

§ 177.110 Action on approved claim.

(a) Payment of a claim approved under this part is contingent on claimant's execution of a Standard Form 95 (Claim for Damage, Injury or Death); a claims settlement agreement; and a Standard Form 1145 (Voucher for Payment), as appropriate. When a claimant is represented by an attorney, the Voucher for Payment will designate both the claimant and his or her attorney as payees, and the check will be delivered to the attorney, whose address is to appear on the Voucher for Payment.

(b) Acceptance by the claimant, his or her agent, or legal representative, of an award, compromise, or settlement made under 28 U.S.C. 2672 or 28 U.S.C. 2677 is final and conclusive on the claimant, his or her agent or legal representative, and any other person on whose behalf or for whose benefit the claim has been presented, and constitutes a complete release of any claim against the United States and against any employee of the Federal Government whose act or omission gave rise to the claim, by reason of the same subject matter.

PART 178—PROCEDURES FOR SETTLING CLAIMS

Subpart A—Administrative Claims—Compensation and Leave, Deceased Employees' Accounts and Proceeds of Canceled Checks for Veterans' Benefits Payable to Deceased Beneficiaries

Subpart B—Settlement of Accounts for Deceased Civilian Officers and Employees

SOURCE: 62 FR 68139, Dec. 31, 1997, unless otherwise noted.

Subpart A—Administrative Claims—Compensation and Leave, Deceased Employees' Accounts and Proceeds of Canceled Checks for Veterans' Benefits Payable to Deceased Beneficiaries

AUTHORITY: 31 U.S.C. 3702; 5 U.S.C. 5583; 38 U.S.C. 5122; Pub. L. No. 104-53, 211, Nov. 19, 1995; E.O. 12107.

§ 178.101 Scope of subpart.

(a) *Claims covered.* This subpart prescribes general procedures applicable to claims against the United States that may be settled by the Director of the Office of Personnel Management pursuant to 31 U.S.C. 3702, 5 U.S.C. 5583 and 38 U.S.C. 5122. In general, these claims involve Federal employees' compensation and leave and claims for proceeds of canceled checks for veterans' benefits payable to deceased beneficiaries.

(b) *Claims not covered.* This subpart does not apply to claims that are under the exclusive jurisdiction of administrative agencies pursuant to specific statutory authority or claims concerning matters that are subject to negotiated grievance procedures under collective bargaining agreements entered into pursuant to 5 U.S.C. 7121(a). Also, these procedures do not apply to claims under the Fair Labor Standards Act (FLSA). Procedures for FLSA claims are set out in part 551 of this chapter.

§ 178.102 Procedures for submitting claims.

(a) *Content of claims.* Except as provided in paragraph (b) of this section, a claim shall be submitted by the claimant in writing and must be signed by the claimant or by the claimant's representative. While no specific form is required, the request should describe the basis for the claim and state the amount sought. The claim should also include:

(1) The name, address, telephone number and facsimile machine number, if available, of the claimant;

(2) The name, address, telephone number and facsimile machine number,

if available, of the agency employee who denied the claim;

(3) A copy of the denial of the claim; and,

(4) Any other information which the claimant believes OPM should consider.

(b) *Agency submissions of claims.* At the discretion of the agency, the agency may forward the claim to OPM on the claimant's behalf. The claimant is responsible for ensuring that OPM receives all the information requested in paragraph (a) of this section.

(c) *Administrative report.* At OPM's discretion, OPM may request the agency to provide an administrative report. This report should include:

(1) The agency's factual findings;

(2) The agency's conclusions of law with relevant citations;

(3) The agency's recommendation for disposition of the claim;

(4) A complete copy of any regulation, instruction, memorandum, or policy relied upon by the agency in making its determination;

(5) A statement that the claimant is or is not a member of a collective bargaining unit, and if so, a statement that the claim is or is not covered by a negotiated grievance procedure that specifically excludes the claim from coverage; and

(6) Any other information that the agency believes OPM should consider.

(d) *Canceled checks for veterans' benefits.* Claims for the proceeds of canceled checks for veterans' benefits payable to deceased beneficiaries must be accompanied by evidence that the claimant is the duly appointed representative of the decedent's estate and that the estate will not escheat.

(e) *Where to submit claims.* (1) All claims under this section should be sent to the Program Manager, Office of Merit Systems Oversight and Effectiveness, Room 7671, Office of Personnel Management, 1900 E Street NW., Washington, DC 20415. Telephone inquiries regarding these claims may be made to (202) 606–7948.

(2) FLSA claims should be sent to the appropriate OPM Oversight Division as provided in part 551 of this chapter.

[62 FR 68139, Dec. 31, 1997, as amended at 65 FR 40967, July 3, 2000]

§ 178.103 Claim filed by a claimant's representative.

A claim filed by a claimant's representative must be supported by a duly executed power of attorney or other documentary evidence of the representative's right to act for the claimant.

§ 178.104 Statutory limitations on claims.

(a) *Statutory limitations relating to claims generally.* Except as provided in paragraphs (b) and (c) of this section or as otherwise provided by law, all claims against the United States Government are subject to the 6-year statute of limitations contained in 31 U.S.C. 3702(b). To satisfy the statutory limitation, a claim must be received by the Office of Personnel Management, or by the department or agency out of whose activities the claim arose, within 6 years from the date the claim accrued. The claimant is responsible for proving that the claim was filed within the applicable statute of limitations.

(b) *Claims under the Fair Labor Standards Act.* Claims arising under the FLSA, 29 U.S.C. 207, *et seq.*, must be received by the Office of Personnel Management, or by the department or agency out of whose activity the claim arose, within the time limitations specified in the FLSA.

(c) *Other statutory limitations.* Statutes of limitation other than that identified in paragraph (a) of this section may apply to certain claims. Claimants are responsible for informing themselves regarding other possible statutory limitations.

§ 178.105 Basis of claim settlements.

The burden is upon the claimant to establish the timeliness of the claim, the liability of the United States, and the claimant's right to payment. The settlement of claims is based upon the written record only, which will include the submissions by the claimant and the agency. OPM will accept the facts asserted by the agency, absent clear and convincing evidence to the contrary.

§ 178.106 Form of claim settlements.

OPM will send a settlement to the claimant advising whether the claim may be allowed in whole or in part. If OPM requested an agency report or if the agency forwarded the claim on behalf of the claimant, OPM also will send the agency a copy of the settlement.

§ 178.107 Finality of claim settlements.

(a) The OPM settlement is final; no further administrative review is available within OPM.

(b) Nothing is this subpart limits the right of a claimant to bring an action in an appropriate United States court.

Subpart B—Settlement of Accounts for Deceased Civilian Officers and Employees

AUTHORITY: 5 U.S.C. 5581, 5582, 5583.

§ 178.201 Scope of subpart.

(a) *Accounts covered.* This subpart prescribes forms and procedures for the prompt settlement of accounts of deceased civilian officers and employees of the Federal Government and of the government of the District of Columbia (including wholly owned and mixed-ownership Government corporations), as stated in 5 U.S.C. 5581, 5582, 5583.

(b) *Accounts not covered.* This subpart does not apply to accounts of deceased officers and employees of the Federal land banks, Federal intermediate credit banks, or regional banks for cooperatives (see 5 U.S.C. 5581(1)). Also, these procedures do not apply to payment of unpaid balance of salary or other sums due deceased Senators or Members of the House of Representatives or their officers or employees (see 2 U.S.C. 36a, 38a).

§ 178.202 Definitions.

(a) The term *deceased employees* as used in this part includes former civilian officers and employees who die subsequent to separation from the employing agency.

(b) The *term money due* means the pay, salary, or allowances due on account of the services of the decedent for the Federal Government or the government of the District of Columbia. It includes, but is not limited to:

(1) All per diem instead of subsistence, mileage, and amounts due in reimbursement of travel expenses, including incidental and miscellaneous expenses which are incurred in connection with the travel and for which reimbursement is due;

(2) All allowances upon change of official station;

(3) All quarters and cost-of-living allowances and overtime or premium pay;

(4) Amounts due for payment of cash awards for employees' suggestions;

(5) Amounts due as refund of salary deductions for United States Savings bonds;

(6) Payment for all accumulated and current accrued annual or vacation leave equal to the pay the decedent would have received had he or she lived and remained in the service until the expiration of the period of such annual or vacation leave;

(7) The amounts of all checks drawn in payment of such compensation which were not delivered by the Government to the officer or employee during his or her lifetime or of any unnegotiated checks returned to the Government because of the death of the officer or employee; and

(8) Retroactive pay under 5 U.S.C. 5344(b)(2).

§ 178.203 Designation of beneficiary.

(a) *Agency notification.* The employing agency shall notify each employee of his or her right to designate a beneficiary or beneficiaries to receive money due, and of the disposition of money due if a beneficiary is not designated. An employee may change or revoke a designation at any time under regulations promulgated by the Director of the Office of Personnel Management or his or her designee.

(b) *Designation Form.* Standard Form 1152, Designation of Beneficiary, Unpaid Compensation of Deceased Civilian Employee, is prescribed for use by employees in designating a beneficiary and in changing or revoking a previous designation; each agency will furnish the employee a Standard Form 1152 upon request. In the absence of the prescribed form, however, any designation, change, or cancellation of beneficiary witnessed and filed in accordance with the general requirements of this part will be acceptable.

(c) *Who may be designated.* An employee may designate any person or persons as beneficiary. The term *person or persons* as used in this part includes a legal entity or the estate of the deceased employee.

(d) *Executing and filing a designation of beneficiary form.* The Standard Form 1152 must be executed in duplicate by the employee and filed with the employing agency where the proper officer will sign it and insert the date of receipt in the space provided on each part, file the original, and return the duplicate to the employee. When a designation of beneficiary is changed or revoked, the employing agency should return the earlier designation to the employee, keeping a copy of only the current designation on file.

(e) *Effective period of a designation.* A properly executed and filed designation of beneficiary will be effective as long as employment by the same agency continues. If an employee resigns and is reemployed, or is transferred to another agency, the employee must execute another designation of beneficiary form in accordance with paragraph (d) of this section. A new designation of beneficiary is not required, however, when an employee's agency or site, function, records, equipment, and personnel are absorbed by another agency.

§ 178.204 Order of payment precedence.

To facilitate the settlement of the accounts of the deceased employees, money due an employee at the time of the employee's death shall be paid to the person or persons surviving at the date of death, in the following order of precedence, and the payment bars recovery by another person of amounts so paid:

(a) First, to the beneficiary or beneficiaries designated by the employee in a writing received in the employing agency prior to the employee's death;

(b) Second, if there is no designated beneficiary, to the surviving spouse of the employee;

(c) Third, if none of the above, to the child or children of the employee and descendants of deceased children by representation;

(d) Fourth, if none of the above, to the parents of the deceased employee or the survivor of them;

(e) Fifth, if none of the above, to the duly appointed legal representative of the estate of the deceased employee; and

(f) Sixth, if none of the above, to the person or persons entitled under the laws of the domicile of the employee at the time of his or her death.

§ 178.205 Procedures upon death of employee.

(a) *Claim form.* As soon as practicable after the death of an employee, the agency in which the employee was last employed will request, in the order of precedence outlined in § 178.204, the appropriate person or persons to execute Standard Form 1153, Claim for Unpaid Compensation of Deceased Civilian Employee.

(b) *Claims involving minors or incompetents.* If a guardian or committee has been appointed for a minor or incompetent appearing entitled to unpaid compensation, the claim should be supported by a certificate of the court showing the appointment and qualification of the claimant in such capacity. If no guardian or committee has been or will be appointed, the initial claim should be supported by a statement showing:

(1) Claimant's relationship to the minor or incompetent, if any;

(2) The name and address of the person having care and custody of the minor or incompetent;

(3) That any moneys received will be applied to the use and benefit of the minor or incompetent; and

(4) That the appointment of a guardian or committee is not contemplated.

§ 178.206 Return of unnegotiated Government checks.

All unnegotiated United States Government checks drawn to the order of a decedent representing money due as defined in § 178.202, and in the possession of the claimant, should be returned to the employing agency concerned. Claimants should be instructed to return any other United States Government checks drawn to the order of a decedent, such as veterans benefits, social security benefits, or Federal tax refunds, to the agency from which the checks were received, with a request for further instructions from that agency.

§ 178.207 Claims settlement jurisdiction.

(a) *District of Columbia and Government corporations.* Claims for unpaid compensation due deceased employees of the government of the District of Columbia shall be paid by the District of Columbia, and those of Government corporations or mixed ownership Government corporations may be paid by the corporations.

(b) *Office of Personnel Management.* Each agency shall pay undisputed claims for the compensation due a deceased employee. Except as provided in paragraph (a) of this section, disputed claims for money due deceased employees of the Federal Government will be submitted to the Office of Merit Systems Oversight and Effectiveness, in accordance with § 178.102 of subpart A. For example:

(1) When doubt exists as to the amount or validity of the claim;

(2) When doubt exists as to the person(s) properly entitled to payment; or

(3) When the claim involves uncurrent checks. *Uncurrent checks* are unnegotiated and/or undelivered checks for money due the decedent which have not been paid by the end of the fiscal year after the fiscal year in which the checks were issued. The checks, if available, should accompany the claims.

(c) *Payment of claim.* Claims for money due will be paid by the appropriate agency only after settlement by the Office of Merit Systems Oversight and Effectiveness occurs.

[62 FR 68139, Dec. 31, 1997, as amended at 65 FR 40967, July 3, 2000]

§ 178.208 Applicability of general procedures.

When not in conflict with this subpart, the provisions of subpart A of this part relating to procedures applicable to claims generally are also applicable to the settlement of account of deceased civilian officers and employees.

PART 179—CLAIMS COLLECTION STANDARDS

Subpart A—General Provisions and Administration

Subpart B—Salary Offset

Subpart C—Administrative Offset

Subpart D—Administrative Wage Garnishment

AUTHORITY: 31 U.S.C. 952; 5 U.S.C. 1103; Reorganization Plan No. 2 of 1978; 5 U.S.C. 5514; 5 CFR part 550 subpart K; 31 U.S.C. 3701; 31 U.S.C. 3711; 31 U.S.C. 3716; 31 U.S.C. 3720A.

Subpart A—General Provisions and Administration

§ 179.101 General collection standards.

The general standards and procedures governing the collection, compromise, termination, and referral to the Department of Justice of claims for money and property that are prescribed in the regulations issued jointly by the General Accounting Office and the Department of Justice pursuant to the Federal Claims Collection Act of 1966 (4 CFR part 101 *et seq.*), apply to the administrative claim collection activities of OPM.

[33 FR 12406, Sept. 4, 1968]

§ 179.102 Delegation of authority.

(a) The Chief Financial Officer and his or her delegates are designated by the Director and authorized to perform all the duties for which the Director is responsible under the Debt Collection Act of 1982 and Office of Personnel Management regulations with the exception of debts arising from the Civil Service Retirement and Disability Fund, the Employees' Life Insurance Fund, the Retired Federal Employees Health Benefits Act (74 Stat. 849), and the Employees Health Benefits Fund. However, the Chief Financial Officer and his or her delegates will request a review by the General Counsel or his or her designee for all claims processed (in amounts of $2500 or more) for compromise, suspension, and termination of collection action.

(b) The Associate Director for Retirement and Insurance and his or her delegates are designated by the Director and authorized to perform all the duties for which the Director is responsible under the Debt Collection Act of 1982 and Office of Personnel Management regulations on debts caused by payments from the Civil Service Retirement and Disability Fund (subchapter III of chapter 83 or chapter 84), claims under the provisions of the Federal Employees' Life Insurance Fund (chapter 87), the Retired Federal Employees Health Benefits Act (74 Stat. 849), the Employees Health Benefits Fund (chapter 89), the Panama Canal Construction Annuity Act (58 Stat. 257), and, the Lighthouse Service Widows' Annuity Act (64 Stat. 465).

[59 FR 35216, July 11, 1994]

Subpart B—Salary Offset

SOURCE: 59 FR 35216, July 11, 1994, unless otherwise noted.

§ 179.201 Purpose.

The purpose of the Debt Collection Act of 1982 (Pub. L. 97–365), is to provide a comprehensive statutory approach to the collection of debts due the Federal Government. These regulations implement section 5 of the Act which authorizes the collection of debts owed by Federal employees to the Federal Government by means of salary offset, except that no claim may be collected by such means if outstanding for more than 10 years after the agency's right to collect the debt first accrued, unless facts material to the Government's right to collect were not known, and could not reasonably have been known, by the official or officials who were charged with the responsibility for discovery and collection of such debts. These regulations are consistent with the regulations on salary offset published by the Office of Personnel Management (OPM) on July 3, 1984 (49 FR 27470) in 5 CFR part 550, subpart K.

§ 179.202 Scope.

(a) These regulations provide procedures for the collection of monies from a Federal employee's pay by salary offset to satisfy certain debts owed the Government.

(b) These regulations apply to all collections by the Director of OPM (except collections involving debts because of payments made from the Civil Service Retirement and Disability Fund, payments made under the Retired Federal Employees Health Benefits Act (74 Stat. 849), the Panama Canal Construction Annuity Act and the Lighthouse Service Widows' Annuity Act and payments or premiums relating to the Federal Employees' Life Insurance Fund or the Federal Employees Health Benefits Fund) from:

(1) Federal employees who owe debts to OPM; and

(2) OPM employees who owe debts to other agencies.

(c) These regulations do not apply to debts or claims arising under the Internal Revenue Code of 1954, as amended (26 U.S.C. 1 *et seq.*); the Social Security Act (42 U.S.C. 301 *et seq.*); the tariff laws of the United States; or to any case where collection of a debt by salary offset is explicitly provided for or prohibited by another statute (e.g., travel advances in 5 U.S.C. 5705 and employee training expenses in 5 U.S.C. 4108).

(d) Section 179.207 does not apply to any adjustment to pay arising from an employee's election of coverage or a change in coverage under a Federal benefits program requiring periodic deductions from pay, if the amount to be recovered was accumulated over four pay periods or less.

(e) Nothing in these regulations precludes the compromise, suspension, or termination of collection actions, where appropriate, under the standards implementing the Federal Claims Collection Act (31 U.S.C. 3711 *et seq.*, 4 CFR parts 101–105, 38 CFR 1.900 *et seq.*).

(f) Nothing in these regulations precludes an employee from requesting a waiver of the debt under applicable statute; under the standards and procedures specified by the Federal Claims Collection Standards (FCCS); or waiver of salary overpayment under 5 U.S.C. 5584, 10 U.S.C. 2774, or 32 U.S.C. 716, by submitting a subsequent claim to the General Accounting Office in accordance with procedures established by the General Accounting Office.

§ 179.203 Definitions.

As used in this subpart the following definitions shall apply:

Agency means:

(1) An Executive Agency as defined by section 105 of title 5, United States Code;

(2) A military department as defined by section 102 of title 5, United States Code;

(3) An agency or court of the judicial branch including a court as defined in section 610 of title 28, United States Code, the District Court for the Northern Mariana Islands and the Judicial Panel and Multidistrict Litigation;

(4) An agency of the legislative branch, including the U.S. Senate and the U.S. House of Representatives; and

(5) Other independent establishments that are entities of the Federal Government.

Certification means a written debt claim, as prescribed by § 179.209, that is received from a creditor agency and which requests the paying agency to offset the salary of an employee.

Claim See debt.

Creditor agency means an agency of the Federal Government to which the debt is owed. For purposes of this part *creditor agency* includes OPM, unless otherwise noted.

Debt means money owed by an employee of the Federal Government to an agency of the Federal Government, from sources which include loans insured or guaranteed by the United States and all other amounts due the Government from fees, leases, rents, royalties, services, sales of real or personal property, overpayments, penalties, damages, interests, fines and forfeitures (except those arising under the Uniform Code of Military Justice) and all other similar sources.

Delinquent means the failure to pay an obligation or debt by the date specified in the initial notification or applicable contractual agreement, unless other payment arrangements have been agreed to by OPM and the debtor by that date, or if, at any time thereafter, the debtor fails to satisfy the obligations under a payment agreement with the creditor agency.

Director means the Director of OPM or his or her designee.

Disposable pay means that part of current basic pay, special pay, incentive pay, retired pay, retainer pay, or, in the case of an employee not entitled to basic pay, other authorized pay remaining after the deduction of any amount required by law to be withheld. OPM shall allow the following deductions, and any others required by law to be withheld, in determining disposable pay subject to salary offset;

(1) Federal employment taxes;

(2) Amounts mandatorily withheld for the U.S. Soldiers' and Airmen's Home;

(3) Fines and forfeitures ordered by a court martial or by a commanding officer;

(4) Federal, state or local income taxes no greater than would be the case if the employee claimed all dependents to which he or she is entitled and such additional amounts for which the employee presents evidence of a tax obligation supporting the additional withholding;

(5) Amounts withheld from benefits payable under title II of the Social Security Act where the withholding is required by law;

(6) Amounts deducted for Medicare;

(7) Health insurance premiums;

(8) Normal retirement contributions as explained in 5 CFR 581.105(e) (e.g., Civil Service Retirement deductions, Survivor Benefit Plan or Retired Serviceman's Family Protection Plan); and

(9) Normal life insurance premiums (e.g., Serviceman's Group Life Insurance and basic Federal Employee's Group Life Insurance premiums) exclusive of optional life insurance premiums.

Employee means a current employee of OPM or other agency, including a current member of the Armed Forces or Reserve of the Armed Forces of the United States.

FCCS means the Federal Claims Collection Standards jointly published by the Department of Justice and the General Accounting Office of 4 CFR 101.1 *et seq.*

Hearing official means an individual (including an administrative law judge) responsible for conducting any hearing with respect to the existence or amount of a debt claimed, and rendering a decision on the basis of such hearing. A hearing official may not be under the supervision or control of the Director of OPM when OPM is the creditor agency.

Notice of intent to offset or *notice of intent* means a written notice from a creditor agency to an employee that states the creditor agency's determination that the employee owes a debt to the creditor agency and apprises the employee of certain administrative rights.

Notice of salary offset means a written notice from the paying agency to an employee after a certification has been issued by the creditor agency, informing the employee that salary offset will begin at the next officially established pay interval.

Office means the central and regional offices of the Office of Personnel Management.

Paying agency means the agency of the Federal Government which employs the individual who owes a debt to an agency of the Federal Government. In some cases, OPM may be both the creditor agency and the paying agency.

Payroll office means the payroll office in the paying agency which is primarily responsible for the payroll records and the coordination of pay matters with the appropriate personnel office with respect to an employee. Payroll office, with respect to OPM, means the central payroll office.

Salary offset means an administrative offset to collect a debt under 5 U.S.C. 5514 by deduction(s) at one or more officially established pay intervals from the current pay account of an employee, without his or her consent.

Salary Offset Coordinator means an official, designated by the Director of OPM, who is responsible for coordinating debt collection activities for OPM.

Waiver means the cancellation, remission, forgiveness, or non-recovery of a debt allegedly owed by an employee to OPM or another agency as permitted or required by 5 U.S.C. 5584, 10 U.S.C. 2774, 32 U.S.C. 716, or any other law.

§ 179.204 Applicability of regulations.

These regulations are to be followed for all OPM collections (except those involving retirement, life, and health insurance debts for recovery by the Associate Director for Retirement and Insurance) in instances where:

(a) OPM is owed a debt by an individual currently employed by another agency;

(b) OPM is owed a debt by an individual who is a current employee of OPM; or

(c) OPM currently employs an individual who owes a debt to another Federal agency. Upon receipt of proper certification from the creditor agency, OPM will offset the debtor-employee's salary in accordance with these regulations.

§ 179.205 Waiver requests and claims to the General Accounting Office.

These regulations do not preclude an employee from requesting waiver of an overpayment under 5 U.S.C. 5584, 10 U.S.C. 2774, 32 U.S.C. 716, or in any way questioning the amount or validity of a debt by submitting a subsequent claim to the General Accounting Office in accordance with the procedures prescribed by the General Accounting Office. These regulations do not preclude an employee from requesting a waiver pursuant to other statutory provisions pertaining to the particular debt being collected.

§ 179.206 Notice requirements before offset.

(a) Deductions under the authority of 5 U.S.C. 5514 shall not be made unless the creditor agency provides the employee with written notice that he/she owes a debt to the Federal government a minimum of 30 calendar days before salary offset is initiated. When OPM is the creditor agency, this notice of intent to offset an employee's salary shall be hand-delivered at work, or sent by registered mail, return receipt requested, to the employee's most current address that is available to the Office and will state:

(1) That the creditor agency has reviewed the records relating to the claim and has determined that a debt is owed, the amount of the debt, and the facts giving rise to the debt;

(2) The creditor agency's intention to collect the debt by means of deduction from the employee's current disposable pay account until the debt and all accumulated interest are paid in full;

(3) The amount, frequency, beginning date, and duration of the intended deductions;

(4) An explanation of OPM's policy concerning interest, penalties and administrative costs including a statement that such assessments must be made unless excused in accordance with the FCCS, 4 CFR 101.1 *et seq.* (§ 179.214);

(5) The employee's right to inspect and copy all records of the office pertaining to the debt claimed, or to request and to receive copies of such records if personal inspection is impractical;

(6) If not previously provided, the opportunity to establish a schedule for the voluntary repayment of the debt through offset or to enter into an agreement to establish a schedule for repayment of the debt in lieu of offset (4 CFR 102.2(e)). The agreement must contain terms agreeable to the Office and must be in such form that it is legally enforceable. The agreement must:

(i) Be in writing;

(ii) Be signed by both the employee and the creditor agency;

(iii) Specify all the terms of the arrangement for payment; and

(iv) Contain a provision accelerating the debt in the event of a default by the debtor, but such an increase may not result in a deduction that exceeds 15 percent of the employee's disposable pay unless the employee has agreed in writing to the deduction of a greater amount (5 CFR 550.1104(i)).

(7) The right to a hearing conducted by an impartial hearing official (an administrative law judge, or alternatively, a hearing official not under the supervision or control of the Director) with respect to the existence and amount of the debt claimed, or the repayment schedule (*i.e.*, the percentage of disposable pay to be deducted each pay period), so long as a petition is filed by the employee as prescribed in § 179.207;

(8) The method and time period for requesting a hearing;

(9) The name, address and phone number of an official or employee of the Office who may be contacted concerning procedures for requesting a hearing;

(10) The name and address of the office to which the petition for a hearing should be sent;

(11) That a timely and properly filed petition for hearing will stay the commencement of collection proceedings (a timely filing must be received in the office specified under paragraph (a)(10) of this section within 15 calendar days after receipt of such notice of intent to offset);

(12) That the Office will initiate certification procedures to implement a

salary offset (which may not exceed 15 percent of the employee's disposable pay) not less than 30 days from the date of receipt of the notice of debt, unless the employee files a timely petition for a hearing;

(13) That a final decision on the hearing (if a hearing is requested) will be issued at the earliest practical date, but not later than 60 days after the filing of the petition requesting the hearing, unless the employee requests and the hearing official grants a delay in the proceedings;

(14) That any knowingly false or frivolous statements, representations, or evidence may subject the employee to;

(i) Disciplinary procedures appropriate under chapter 75 of title 5, United States code; part 752 of title 5, Code of Federal Regulations; or any other applicable statute or regulations;

(ii) Penalties under the False Claims Act, sections 3729 through 3731 of title 31, United States Code, or any other applicable statutory authority; and

(iii) Criminal penalties under sections 286, 287, 1001, and 1002 of title 18, United States code, or any other applicable statutory authority;

(15) Any other rights and remedies available to the employee under statutes or regulations governing the program for which the collection is being made;

(16) That unless there are applicable contractual or statutory provisions to the contrary, amounts paid on or deducted for the debt, which are later waived or found not owed to the United States, will be promptly refunded to the employee; and

(17) That proceedings with respect to such debt are governed by section 5 of the Debt Collection Act of 1982 (5 U.S.C. 5514).

(b) The Office is not required to comply with paragraph (a) of this section for any adjustment to pay arising from:

(1) An employee's selection of coverage or a change in coverage under a Federal benefits program requiring periodic deductions from pay, if the amount to be recovered was accumulated over four pay periods or less; or

(2) An employee's consent to make voluntary withholdings from his or her current pay account.

§ 179.207 Hearing.

(a) *Request for hearing.* Except as provided in paragraph (b) of this section, an employee who desires a hearing concerning the existence or amount of the debt or the proposed offset schedule must send such a request to the office designated in the notice of intent (§ 179.207(a)(10)). The request (or petition) for hearing must be received by the designated office not later than 15 calendar days following the employee's receipt of the notice. The employee's request (or petition) must:

(1) Be signed by the employee;

(2) Fully identify and explain with reasonable specificity all the facts, evidence and witnesses, if any, that the employee believes support his or her position; and

(3) Specify whether an oral or paper hearing is requested. If an oral hearing is desired, the request should explain why the matter cannot be resolved by review of the documentary evidence alone (4 CFR 102.3(c)).

(b) *Failure to timely submit.* (1) If the employee files a petition for a hearing after the expiration of the 15 calendar day period provided for in paragraph (a) of this section, the Office may accept the request if the employee can show that the delay was the result of circumstances beyond his of her control or failure to receive actual notice of the filing deadline (unless the employee had actual notice of the filing deadline).

(2) An employee waives the right to a hearing, and will have his or her disposable pay offset in accordance with the Office offset schedule, if the employee:

(i) Fails to file a timely request for a hearing unless such failure is excused; or

(ii) Fails to appear at an oral hearing of which he or she was notified unless the hearing official determines that failure to appear was due to circumstances beyond the employee's control.

(c) *Representation at the hearing.* The creditor agency may be represented by legal counsel. The employee may represent himself or herself or may be represented by an individual of his or her choice and at his or her expense.

(d) *Review of Office records related to the debt.* (1) An employee who intends to inspect or copy creditor agency records related to the debt, as provided by § 179.207(a)(5), must send a letter to the official designated in the notice of intent to offset stating his or her intention. The letter must be received within 15 calendar days after the employee's receipt of the notice.

(2) In response to a timely request submitted by the debtor, the designated official will notify the employee of the location and time when the employee may inspect and copy records related to the debt.

(3) If personal inspection is impractical, arrangements shall be made to end copies of such records to the employee.

(e) *Hearing official.* The Office may request an administrative law judge to conduct the hearing, or the Office may obtain a hearing official who is not under the supervision or control of the Director of OPM.

(f) *Obtaining the services of a hearing official when OPM is the creditor agency.* (1) When the debtor is not an OPM employee and the Office cannot provide a prompt and appropriate hearing before a hearing official furnished pursuant to another lawful arrangement, the Office may contact an agent of the paying agency designated in 5 CFR part 581, appendix A, or other individual designated by the paying agency, and request a hearing official.

(2) When the debtor is an OPM employee, the Office may contact any agent of another agency designated in 5 CFR part 581, appendix A, or otherwise designated by that agency, to request a hearing official.

(g) *Procedure*—(1) *General.* After the employee requests a hearing, the hearing official shall notify the employee of the form of the hearing to be provided. If the hearing will be oral, the notice shall set forth the date, time and location of the hearing. If the hearing will be paper, the employee shall be notified that he or she should submit arguments in writing to the hearing official by a specified date after which the record shall be closed. This date shall give the employee reasonable time to submit documentation.

(2) *Oral hearing.* An employee who requests an oral hearing shall be provided an oral hearing if the hearing official determines that the matter cannot be resolved by review of documentary evidence alone (e.g., when an issue of credibility or veracity is involved). The hearing is not an adversarial adjudication and need not take the form of an evidentiary hearing. Oral hearings may take the form of, but are not limited to:

(i) Informal conferences with the hearing official, in which the employee and agency representative will be given full opportunity to present evidence, witnesses, and argument;

(ii) Informal meetings with an interview of the employee; or

(iii) Formal written submissions with an opportunity for oral presentation.

(3) *Paper hearing.* If the hearing official determines that an oral hearing is not necessary, he or she will make a determination based upon a review of the available written record (4 CFR 102.3(c) (2) and (3)).

(4) *Record.* The hearing official must maintain a summary record of any hearing provided by this subpart (4 CFR 102.3(c)(1)(ii)). Witnesses who testify in oral hearings will do so under oath or affirmation.

(h) *Date of decision.* The hearing official shall issue a written opinion stating his or her decision, based upon documentary evidence and information developed at the hearing, as soon as practicable after the hearing, but not later than 60 days after the date on which the petition was received by the creditor agency, unless the employee requests a delay in the proceedings. In such case the 60-day decision period shall be extended by the number of days by which the hearing was postponed.

(i) *Content of decision.* The written decision shall include:

(1) A statement of the facts presented to support the origin, nature, and amount of the debt;

(2) The hearing official's findings, analysis, and conclusions including a determination whether the debtor's petition for hearing was baseless and resulted from an intent to delay creditor agency collection activity and whether the Office should pursue other actions

against the debtor as provided by 5 CFR 550.1104(d)(11); and

(3) The terms of any repayment schedules, if applicable.

(j) *Failure to appear*. In the absence of good cause shown (e.g., illness), an employee who fails to appear at a hearing shall be deemed, for the purpose of this subpart, to admit the existence and amount of the debt as described in the notice of intent. If the representative of the creditor agency fails to appear, the hearing official shall proceed with the hearing as scheduled and make his/her determination based upon the oral testimony presented and the documentary evidence submitted by both parties. With the agreement of both parties, the hearing official shall schedule a new hearing date. Both parties shall be given reasonable notice of the time and place of the new hearing.

§ 179.208 Certification.

(a) OPM salary offset coordinator shall provide a certification to the paying agency in all cases where:

(1) The hearing official determines that a debt exists;

(2) The employee fails to contest the existence and amount of the debt by failing to request a hearing; or

(3) The employee fails to contest the existence of the debt by failing to appear at a hearing.

(b) The certification must be in writing and must state:

(1) That the employee owes the debt;

(2) The amount and basis of the debt;

(3) The date the Government's right to collect the debt first accrued;

(4) That the Office's regulations have been approved by OPM pursuant to 5 CFR part 550, subpart K;

(5) The date on which payment(s) is due;

(6) If the collection is to be made in installments, the number of installments to be collected, the amount of each installment or percentage of disposable pay, and the commencement date of the first installment, if a date other than the next officially established pay period is required; and

(7) The date(s) of any action(s) taken under 5 U.S.C. 5514(b).

§ 179.209 Voluntary repayment agreement as alternative to salary offset.

(a)(1) In response to a notice of intent, an employee may propose to repay the debt by making voluntary installment payments as an alternative to salary offset. An employee who wishes to repay a debt without salary offset shall submit in writing a proposed agreement to repay the debt. The proposal shall admit the existence of the debt, and the agreement must be in such form that it is legally enforceable. The agreement must:

(i) Be in writing;

(ii) Be signed by both the employee and the creditor agency;

(iii) Specify all the terms of the arrangement for payment; and

(iv) Contain a provision accelerating the debt in the event of default by the debtor, but such an increase may not result in a deduction that exceeds 15 percent of the employee's disposable pay unless the employee has agreed in writing to deduction of a greater amount (5 CFR 550.1104(i)).

(2) Any proposal under paragraph (a) of this section must be received by the official designated in the notice of intent within 30 calendar days after receipt of the notice.

(b) The creditor agency will review a timely and properly submitted repayment proposal by the employee debtor and notify the employee whether the proposed written agreement for repayment is acceptable. It is within the creditor agency's discretion to accept a repayment agreement instead of proceeding by offset.

(c) If the creditor agency decides that the proposed repayment agreement is unacceptable, the employee will have 15 days from the date he or she received notice of that decision to file a petition for a hearing or a special review as provided by § 179.210.

(d) If the creditor agency decides that the proposed repayment agreement is acceptable, the alternative arrangement must be in writing, signed by both the employee and the creditor agency designee and meet the other requirements of this section for a voluntary repayment agreement.

§ 179.210 Special review.

(a) An OPM employee subject to salary offset or a voluntary repayment agreement, may, at any time, request a special review by the Office of the amount of the salary offset or voluntary payment, based on materially changed circumstances such as, but not limited to, catastrophic illness, divorce, death, or disability.

(b) In determining whether an offset would prevent the employee from meeting essential subsistence expenses (food, housing, clothing, transportation and medical care), the employee shall submit a detailed statement and supporting documents for the employee, his or her spouse, and dependents indicating:

(1) Income from all sources;

(2) Assets;

(3) Liabilities;

(4) Number of dependents;

(5) Expenses for food, housing, clothing and transportation;

(6) Medical expenses; and

(7) Exceptional expenses, if any.

If an OPM employee requests a special review under this section, the employee shall file an alternative proposed offset or payment schedule and a statement, with supporting documents (§ 179.210(b)), stating why the current salary offset or payments result in an extreme financial hardship to the employee.

(c) The Director shall evaluate the statement and supporting documents, and determine whether the original offset or repayment schedule imposes an extreme financial hardship on the employee. The Director shall notify the employee in writing of such determination, including, if appropriate, a revised offset or repayment schedule.

(d) If the special review results in a revised offset or repayment schedule, the OPM salary offset coordinator shall provide a new certification to the payroll office.

§ 179.211 Notice of salary offset.

(a) Upon receipt of proper certification from a creditor agency, the OPM payroll office will send the OPM employee, identified in the certification as the debtor, a written notice of salary offset. Such notice shall, at a minimum:

(1) State that OPM has received a properly certified debt claim from a creditor agency;

(2) Contain a copy of the certification received from the creditor agency;

(3) Advise the employee that salary offset will be initiated at the next officially established pay interval; and

(4) State the amount of the claim and amount of deductions.

(b) The payroll office shall provide a copy of the notice to the creditor agency and advise such agency of the dollar amount to be offset and the pay period when the offset will begin.

§ 179.212 Procedures for salary offset.

(a) The Director or his or her designee shall coordinate salary deductions under this subpart.

(b) OPM payroll office shall determine the amount of an employee's disposable pay and implement the salary offset.

(c) Deductions shall begin effective the pay period following receipt by OPM's payroll office of proper certification of the debt (§ 179.208).

(d) *Types of collection*—(1) *Lump-sum payment.* A debt will be collected in a lump sum if possible. If an employee is financially unable to pay in one lump sum or the amount of the debt exceeds 15 percent of disposable pay for an officially established pay interval, collection must be made in installments.

(2) *Installment deductions.* Installment deductions will be made over a period not greater than the anticipated period of employment and, except in rare circumstances, not to exceed 3 years. The size and frequency of installment deductions will bear a reasonable relation to the size of the debt and the employee's ability to pay. The amount deducted for any period will not exceed 15 percent of the disposable pay from which the deduction is made unless the employee has agreed in writing to the deduction of a greater amount.

(3) *Lump-sum deductions from final check.* A lump-sum deduction exceeding the 15 percent disposable pay limitation may be made from any final salary payment pursuant to 31 U.S.C. 3716 in order to liquidate the debt, whether the employee is being separated voluntarily or involuntarily.

(4) *Lump-sum deductions from other sources.* When an employee subject to salary offset is separated from OPM and the balance of the debt cannot be liquidated by offset of the final salary check, the Office, pursuant to 31 U.S.C. 3716, the FCCS and OPM's implementing regulations, may offset the balance of the debt against any financial payment due the employee from the U.S. Government.

(e) *Multiple debts.* In instances where two or more creditor agencies are seeking salary offset, or where two or more debts are owed to a single creditor agency, OPM payroll office may, at its discretion, determine whether one or more debts should be offset simultaneously within the 15 percent limitation.

(f) *Precedence of debts owed to OPM.* For OPM employees, debts owed to the Office generally take precedence over debts owed to other agencies. In the event that a debt to the Office is certified while an employee is subject to a salary offset to repay another agency, the OPM payroll office may decide whether to have that debt repaid in full before collecting its claim or whether changes should be made in the salary deduction being sent to the other agency. If debts owed the Office can be collected in one pay period, the payroll office may suspend the salary offset to the other agency for that pay period in order to liquidate the office debt.

(g) When an employee owes two or more debts, the best interests of the Government shall be the primary consideration in determining the order of debt collection. The OPM payroll office, in making this determination, will be guided primarily by the statute of limitations that affects the collection of the debt(s).

§ 179.213 Coordinating salary offset with other agencies.

(a) *Responsibility of OPM as the creditor agency.* (1) The Director or his or her designee shall coordinate debt collections with other agencies and shall, as appropriate:

(i) Arrange for a hearing or special review upon proper petitioning by a Federal employee; and

(ii) Prescribe, upon consultation with the General Counsel, such additional practices and procedures as may be necessary to carry out the intent of this regulation.

(2) The designated salary offset coordinator will be responsible for:

(i) Ensuring that each notice of intent to offset is consistent with the requirements of § 179.206;

(ii) Ensuring that each certification of debt that is sent to a paying agency is consistent with the requirements of § 179.208;

(iii) Obtaining hearing officials from other agencies pursuant to § 179.207(f); and

(iv) Ensuring that hearings are properly scheduled.

(3) *Requesting recovery from current paying agency.* Upon completion of the procedures established in these regulations and pursuant to 5 U.S.C. 5514, the Office must:

(i) Certify, in writing, to the paying agency that the employee owes the debt, the amount and basis of the debt, the date on which payment(s) is due, the date the Government's right to collect the debt first accrued, and that the Office's regulations implementing 5 U.S.C. 5514 have been approved by the Office of Personnel Management;

(ii) Advise the paying agency of the amount or percentage of disposable pay to be collected in each installment and the number and commencing date of the installments (if a date other than the next officially established pay period is required);

(iii) Advise the paying agency of the action(s) taken under 5 U.S.C. 5514(b) and give the date(s) and action(s) was taken (unless the employee has consented to the salary offset in writing or signed a statement acknowledging receipt of the required procedures and the written consent or statement is forwarded to the paying agency);

(iv) Submit a debt claim certification containing the information specified in paragraphs (a)(3)(i), (a)(3)(ii) and (a)(3)(iii) of this section and an installment agreement (or other instruction on the payment schedule), if applicable, to the employee's paying agency; and

(v) Submit the debt claim, as provided in § 179.208, to the employee's paying agency for collection if the employee is in the process of separating, and has not received a final salary check, or other final payment(s) from the paying agency. The paying agency must certify the total amount of its collection on the debt and send a copy of the certification to the employee and another copy to the creditor agency. If the paying agency's collection does not fully satisfy the debt, and the paying agency is aware that the debtor is entitled to payments from the Civil Service Retirement and Disability Fund or other similar payments that may be due the debtor employee from other Federal Government sources, the paying agency will provide written notification of the outstanding debt to the agency responsible for making such other payments to the debtor employee. The written notification shall state that the employee owes a debt (including the amount) and that the provisions of this section have been fully complied with. The Office must submit a properly certified claim to the agency responsible for making such payments before the collection can be made.

(4) *Separated employee.* If the employee is already separated and all payments due from his or her former paying agency have been paid, the Office may request, unless otherwise prohibited, that money due and payable to the employee from the Civil Service Retirement and Disability Fund (5 CFR 831.1801 *et seq.* or 5 CFR 845.401 *et seq.*) or other similar funds, be administratively offset to collect the debt (31 U.S.C. 3716 and the FCCS).

(5) *Employee transfer.* When an employee transfers from one paying agency to another paying agency, the Office is not required to repeat the due process procedures described in 5 U.S.C. 5514 and this subpart to resume the collection. The Office will submit a properly certified claim to the new paying agency and will subsequently review the debt to make sure the collection is resumed by the new paying agency.

(b) *Responsibility of the Office as the paying agency*—(1) *Complete claim.* When the Office receives a certified claim from a creditor agency, deductions should be scheduled to begin at the next officially established pay interval. Before deductions can begin, the employee must receive written notice from the Office including:

(i) A statement that the Office has received a certified debt claim from the creditor agency;

(ii) The amount of the debt claim;

(iii) The date salary offset deductions will begin, and

(iv) The amount of such deductions.

(2) *Incomplete claim.* When the Office receives an incomplete certification of debt from a creditor agency, the Office must return the debt claim with notice that procedures under 5 U.S.C. 5514 and 5 CFR 550.1101 *et seq.* must be followed and a properly certified debt claim received before action will be taken to collect from the employee's current pay account.

(3) *Review.* The Office is not authorized to review the merits of the creditor agency's determination with respect to the amount or validity of the debt certified by the creditor agency.

(4) *Employees who transfer from one paying agency to another.* If, after the creditor agency has submitted the debt claim to the Office, the employee transfers from OPM to a different paying agency before the debt is collected in full, the Office will certify the total amount collected on the debt. One copy of the certification will be furnished to the employee and one copy to the creditor agency along with notice of the employee's transfer.

§ 179.214 Interest, penalties and administrative costs.

The office shall assess interest, penalties and administrative costs on debts owed pursuant to 31 U.S.C. 3717 and 4 CFR part 101.1 *et seq.* Penalties and administrative costs will be assessed on all delinquent debts.

(a) In cases of default on a previous repayment agreement, the Office reserves the right to set a new interest rate which reflects the current value of funds to the Treasury at the time a new repayment agreement is executed.

(b) The Office, on a case-by-case basis, may waive all interest accrued on debts paid in full within 60 days of the due date if there is no indication of fault or lack of good faith on the part of the debtor.

(c) The Office may waive, in whole or in part, the collection of interest, penalties, and/or administrative costs assessed under this section under the criteria specified in part 103 of 4 CFR, chapter II, relating to the compromise of claims (without regard to the amount of the debt).

(d) The Office may waive, in whole or in part, the collection of interest, penalties, and/or administrative costs assessed under this section if the Office determines that collection of these charges would be against equity and good conscience or not in the best interests of the United States.

(e) The Office shall waive the accrual of interest pending consideration of a request for reconsideration, administrative review, or waiver of the underlying debt under provisions of a permissive statute providing for such review related to the debt.

(f) The Office shall waive interest on repayment agreements when the amount of interest accruing equals or exceeds the amount of installments the debtor can reasonably afford and there is no indication of fault or lack of good faith on the part of the debtor.

§ 179.215 Refunds.

(a) The Office shall promptly refund any amounts deducted under the authority of 5 U.S.C. 5514 when:

(1) The debt is waived or otherwise found not to be owing the United States (unless expressly prohibited by statute or regulation); or

(2) An administrative or judicial order directs the Office to make a refund.

(b) Unless required or permitted by law or contract, refunds under this subsection shall not bear interest.

§ 179.216 Request for the services of a hearing official when the creditor agency is not OPM.

(a) The Office will provide a hearing official upon request of the creditor agency when the debtor is employed by the Office and the creditor agency cannot provide a prompt and appropriate hearing before a hearing official furnished pursuant to another lawful arrangement.

(b) The salary offset coordinator will secure qualified personnel to serve as hearing officials.

(c) Services rendered under this section will be provided on a fully reimbursable basis pursuant to the Economy Act of 1932, *as amended*, 31 U.S.C. 1535.

§ 179.217 Non-waiver of rights by payments.

An employee's involuntary payment of all or any portion of a debt collected under this subpart must not be construed as a waiver of any rights which the employee may have under 5 U.S.C. 5514 or any other provision of contract or law unless there are statutory or contractual provisions to the contrary.

§ 179.218 Additional administrative collection action.

Nothing contained in this subpart is intended to preclude the use of any other administrative remedy which may be appropriate.

Subpart C—Administrative Offset

SOURCE: 59 FR 35214, July 11, 1994, unless otherwise noted.

§ 179.301 Scope of regulations.

These regulations apply to the collection of debts owed to the United States arising from transactions with OPM other than those involving payments made from the Civil Service Retirement and Disability Fund (the Fund), or where a request for an offset from OPM's administrative accounts—other than the Fund—is received by OPM from another Federal agency. Regulations for other agencies to request OPM's Retirement and Insurance Group to recover a debt from the Fund are provided at subpart R of part 831 and subpart D of part 845 of title 5, Code of Federal Regulations. These regulations are consistent with the Federal Claims Collection Standards on Administrative Offset issued jointly by the Department of Justice and the General Accounting Office as set forth in 4 CFR 102.3.

§ 179.302 Definitions.

Administrative offset, as defined in 31 U.S.C. 3701(a)(1), means withholding money payable by the United States Government to, or held by the Government for, a person to satisfy a debt the person owes the Government.

Person, includes a natural person or persons, profit or non-profit corporation, partnership, association, trust, estate, consortium, or other entity which is capable of owing a debt to the United States Government except that agencies of the United States, or of any State or local government, shall be excluded.

§ 179.303 General.

(a) The Director or his or her designee, after attempting to collect a debt from a person under section 3(a) of the Federal Claims Collection Act of 1966, as amended (31 U.S.C. 3711(a)), may collect the debt by administrative offset subject to the following:

(1) The debt is certain in amount; and

(2) It is in the best interest of the United States to collect the debt by administrative offset because it is less costly and speeds payment of the debt;

(b) The Director, or his or her designee, may initiate administrative offset with regard to debts owed by a person to another agency of the United States Government, upon receipt of a request from the head of another agency, or his or her designee, and a certification that the debt exists and that the person has been afforded the necessary due process rights.

(c) The Director, or his or her designee, may request another agency that holds funds payable to an OPM debtor to offset the debt against the funds held and will provide certification that:

(1) The debt exists; and

(2) The person has been afforded the necessary due process rights.

(d) If the 6-year period for bringing action on a debt provided in 28 U.S.C. 2415 has expired, then administrative offset may be used to collect the debt only if the costs of bringing such action are likely to be less than the amount of the debt.

(e) No collection by administrative offset shall be made on any debt that has been outstanding for more than 10 years unless facts material to the Government's right to collect the debt were not known, and reasonably could not have been known, by the official or officials responsible for discovering and collecting such debt.

(f) These regulations do not apply to:

(1) A case in which administrative offset of the type of debt involved is explicitly provided for or prohibited by another statute.

(2) Debts owed to OPM by other agencies of the United States or by any State or local government.

§ 179.304 Notification procedures.

Before collecting any debt through administrative offset, a notice of intent to offset shall be sent to the debtor by certified mail, return receipt requested, at the most current address that is available to OPM. The notice shall provide:

(a) A description of the nature and amount of the debt and the intention of OPM to collect the debt through administrative offset;

(b) An opportunity to inspect and copy the records of OPM with respect to the debt;

(c) An opportunity for review within OPM concerning OPM's determinations with respect to the debt; and

(d) An opportunity to enter into a written agreement for the repayment of the amount of the debt.

§ 179.305 Agency review.

(a) A debtor may dispute the existence of the debt, the amount of the debt, or the terms of repayment. The request to review a disputed debt must be received by the OPM official identified in the notification within 30 calendar days of the debtor's receipt of the written notice described in § 179.304.

(b) If the debtor requests an opportunity to inspect or copy OPM's records concerning the disputed claim, 10 business days will be granted for the review. The time period will be measured from the time the request for inspection is granted or from the time the copy of the records is received by the debtor.

(c) Pending the resolution of a dispute initiated by the debtor, transactions in any of the debtor's account(s) maintained in OPM may be temporarily suspended to the extent of the debt that is owed. Depending on the type of transaction, the suspension could preclude payment, removal, or transfer, as well as prevent the payment of interest or discount due thereon. Should the dispute be resolved in the debtor's favor, the suspension will be lifted immediately.

(d) During the review period, interest, penalties, and administrative costs authorized under the Federal Claims Collection Act of 1966, as amended, will continue to accrue.

§ 179.306 Written agreement for repayment.

A debtor who admits liability but elects not to have the debt collected by administrative offset will be afforded an opportunity to negotiate a written agreement for the repayment of the debt. If the financial condition of the debtor does not support the ability to pay in one lump-sum, reasonable installments may be considered. No installment arrangement will be considered unless the debtor submits a financial statement, executed under penalty of perjury, reflecting the debtor's assets, liabilities, income, and expenses. The financial statement must be submitted within 10 business days of OPM's request for the statement. At OPM's option, a confess-judgment note or bond of indemnity with surety may be required for the installment agreement. Notwithstanding the provisions of this section, any reduction or compromise of a claim will be governed by 4 CFR part 103 and 31 U.S.C. 3711.

§ 179.307 Administrative offset.

(a) If the debtor does not exercise the right to request a review within the time specified in § 179.305 or, if as a result of the review, it is determined that the debt is due and no written agreement is executed, then administrative offset shall be ordered in accordance with these regulations without further notice.

(b) Request for offset to a Federal agency: The Director or his or her designee may request that funds due and payable to a debtor by a Federal agency be administratively offset in order to collect a debt owned to OPM by that debtor. In requesting administrative offset OPM, as creditor, will certify in writing to the Federal agency holding funds of the debtor:

(1) That the debtor owes the debt;

(2) The amount and basis of the debt; and

(3) That OPM has complied with the requirements of 31 U.S.C. 3716, its own administrative offset regulations, and the applicable provisions of 4 CFR part 102 with respect to providing the debtor with due process.

(c) Request for offset from a Federal agency: When administrative offset is authorized, any Federal creditor agency may request OPM to make an administrative offset from any OPM funds that are due and payable to a creditor agency's debtor. OPM shall initiate the requested administrative offset only upon:

(1) Receipt of written certification from the creditor agency:

(i) That the debtor owes the debt;

(ii) The amount and basis of the debt;

(iii) That the agency has prescribed regulations for the exercise of administrative offset; and

(iv) That the agency has complied with its own administrative offset regulations and with the applicable provisions of 4 CFR part 102, including providing any required hearing or review.

(2) A determination by OPM that collection by offset against funds payable by OPM would not otherwise be contrary to law.

§ 179.308 Accelerated procedures.

OPM may make an administrative offset against a payment to be made to the debtor prior to the completion of the procedures required by §§ 179.304 and 179.305 if failure to take the offset would substantially jeopardize OPM's ability to collect the debt, and the time before the payment is to be made does not reasonably permit the completion of those procedures. Such prior offset shall be promptly followed by the completion of those procedures. Amounts recovered by offset but later found not to be owed to OPM shall be promptly refunded.

§ 179.309 Additional administrative procedures.

Nothing contained in this chapter is intended to preclude the use of any other administrative remedy which may be available.

Subpart D—Administrative Wage Garnishment

AUTHORITY: 15 U.S.C. 46; 31 U.S.C. 3720D; 31 CFR 285.11(f).

§ 179.401 Administrative wage garnishment.

General. OPM may use administrative wage garnishment to collect debts in accordance with the requirements of 31 U.S.C. 3720D and 31 CFR 285.11, including debts it refers to the Bureau of the Fiscal Service, Department of the Treasury, for cross-servicing pursuant to 31 U.S.C. 3711. This part adopts and incorporates all of the provisions of 31 CFR 285.11 concerning administrative wage garnishment, including the hearing procedures described in 31 CFR 285.11(f). This section does not apply to collection of debt by Federal salary offset, under 5 U.S.C. 5514, the process by which OPM collects debts from the salaries of Federal employees.

[79 FR 29072, May 21, 2014]

PART 180—EMPLOYEES' PERSONAL PROPERTY CLAIMS

AUTHORITY: Sec. 3, 78 Stat. 767, as amended; 31 U.S.C. 241.

SOURCE: 43 FR 47163, Oct. 13, 1978, unless otherwise noted.

§ 180.101 Scope and purpose.

(a) The Military Personnel and Civilian Employees' Claims Act of 1964, 31 U.S.C. 240 to 243, authorizes the Director, Office of Personnel Management to settle and pay (including replacement in kind) claims of officers and employees of OPM, amounting to not more than $15,000, for damage to or loss of personal property incident to their service. Claims are payable only for such types, quantities, or amounts of tangible personal property (including money) as the approving authority shall determine to be reasonable, useful, or proper under the circumstances existing at the time and place of the loss. In determining what is reasonable, useful, or proper, the approving authority will consider the type and quantity of property involved, circumstances attending acquistion and use of the property, and whether possession or use by the claimant at the time of damage or loss was incident to service.

(b) The Government does not underwrite all personal property losses that a claimant may sustain and it does not underwrite individual tastes. While the Government does not attempt to limit possession of property by an individual, payment for damage or loss is made only to the extent that the possession of the property is determined to be reasonable, useful, or proper. If individuals possess excessive quantities of items, or expensive items, they should have such property privately insured.

§ 180.102 Claimants.

(a) The following are proper claimants:

(1) Officers and employees of OPM;

(2) Former officers and employees of OPM whose claims arose out of incidents which occurred before their separation;

(3) The authorized agent or legal representative of persons in §§ 180.102(a)(1) and 180.102(a)(2);

(4) Survivors of persons in §§ 180.102(a)(1) and 180.102(a)(2) in the following order of precedence:

(i) Spouse,

(ii) Children,

(iii) Father or mother, or both,

(iv) Brothers or sisters, or both.

(b) A claim may not be presented by or for the benefit of a subrogee, assignee, conditional vendor, or other third party.

§ 180.103 Time limitations.

A claim must be presented in writing within 2 years after it accrues, except during war or armed conflict. If war or armed conflict occurs within the 2-year period following accrual, when claimant shows good cause, the claim may be presented within 2 years after the cause ceases to exist but not more than 2 years after termination of the war or armed conflict. A claim accrues when loss or damage is or should have been discovered by claimant even though such loss or damage occurred at a prior time.

§ 180.104 Allowable claims.

(a) A claim may be allowed only if:

(1) The damage or loss was not caused wholly or partly by the negligent or wrongful act of the claimant, claimant's agent, a member of claimant's family, or claimant's private employee (the standard to be applied is that of reasonable care under the circumstances);

(2) The possession of the property damaged or lost and the quantity possessed is determined to have been reasonable, useful, or proper under the circumstances; and

(3) The claim is substantiated by proper and convincing evidence.

(b) Claims which are otherwise allowable under this part shall not be disallowed solely because the property was not in the possession of the claimant at the time of the damage or loss or solely because the claimant was not legal owner of the property for which the claim is made. For example, borrowed property may be the subject of a claim.

(c) Subject to the conditions in § 180.104(a) and the other provisions of this part, any claim for damage to or loss of personal property incident to service with OPM may be considered and allowed. The following are examples of the principal types of claims which may be allowed. These examples are not exclusive and other types of claims may be allowed unless excluded by § 180.106:

(1) *Property damaged or lost in quarters.* Claims may be allowed for damage to or loss of property located at:

(i) Quarters within the 50 States and the District of Columbia that were assigned to the claimant or otherwise provided in kind by the United States;

(ii) Quarters outside the 50 States and the District of Columbia that were occupied by the claimant, whether or not they were assigned or otherwise provided in kind by the United States, except when the claimant is a local inhabitant; or

(iii) Any warehouse, office, working area, or other place (except quarters) authorized or apparently authorized for the reception or storage of property.

(2) *Transportation or travel losses.* Claims may be allowed for damage to or loss of property incident to transportation or storage pursuant to orders, or in connection with travel under orders, including property in custody of a carrier, an agent or agency of the Government, or the claimant.

(3) *Motor vehicles.* Claims may be allowed for automobiles and other motor vehicles damaged or lost in oversea shipments provided by the Government. "Shipments provided by the Government" means via Government vessels, charter of commercial vessels, or by Government bills of lading on commercial vessels, and includes storage, unloading, and off-loading incident thereto. Other claims for damage to or loss of automobiles and other motor vehicles may be allowed only when use of the vehicle on a non-reimbursable basis was required by the claimant's supervisor.

(4) *Mobile homes.* Claims may be allowed for damage to or loss of mobile homes and their contents under the provisions of § 180.104(c)(2). Claims for structural damage to mobile homes, other than that caused by collision, and damage to contents of mobile homes resulting from such structural damage must contain conclusive evidence that the damage was not caused by structural deficiency of the mobile home and that it was not overloaded. Claims for damage to or loss of tires mounted on mobile homes may be allowed only in cases of collision, theft, or vandalism.

(5) *Money.* Claims for money in an amount that is determined to be reasonable for the claimant to possess at the time of the loss are payable:

(i) Where personal funds were accepted by responsible Government personnel with apparent authority to receive them for safekeeping deposit, transmittal, or other authorized disposition, but were neither applied as directed by the owner nor returned;

(ii) When lost incident to a marine or aircraft disaster;

(iii) When lost by fire, flood, hurricane, or other natural disaster;

(iv) When stolen from the quarters of the claimant where it is conclusively shown that the money was in a locked container and that the quarters themselves were locked;

(v) When taken by force from the claimant's person.

(6) *Clothing.* Claims may be allowed for clothing and accessories worn on the person which are damaged or lost:

(i) During the performance of official duties in an unusual or extraordinary-risk situation;

(ii) In cases involving emergency action required by natural disaster such as fire, flood, hurricane, or by enemy or other belligerent action;

(iii) In cases involving faulty equipment or defective furniture maintained by the Government and used by the claimant as required by the job situation; or

(iv) When using a motor vehicle.

(7) *Property used for benefit of the Government.* Claims may be allowed for damage to or loss of property (except motor vehicles) used for the benefit of the Government at the request of, or with the knowledge and consent of, superior authority or by reason of necessity.

(8) *Enemy action or public service.* Claims may be allowed for damage to or loss of property as a direct consequence of:

(i) Enemy action or threat thereof, or combat, guerilla, brigandage, or other belligerent activity, or unjust confiscation by a foreign power or its nationals;

(ii) Action by the claimant to quiet a civil disturbance or to alleviate a public disaster; or

(iii) Efforts by the claimant to save human life or Government property.

(9) *Marine or aircraft disaster.* Claims may be allowed for personal property damaged or lost as a result of marine or aircraft disaster or accident.

(10) *Government property.* Claims may be allowed for property owned by the United States only when the claimant is financially responsible to an agency of the Government other than OPM.

(11) *Borrowed property.* Claims may be allowed for borrowed property that has been damaged or lost.

§ 180.105 Claims not allowed.

(a) A claim is not allowable if:

(1) The damage or loss was caused wholly or partly by the negligent or wrongful act of the claimant, claimant's agent, claimant's employee, or a member of claimant's family;

(2) The damage or loss occurred in quarters occupied by the claimant within the 50 States and the District of Columbia that were not assigned to the claimant or otherwise provided in kind by the United States;

(3) Possession of the property lost or damaged was not incident to service or not reasonable or proper under the circumstances.

(b) In addition to claims falling within the categories of § 180.105(a), the following are examples of claims which are not payable:

(1) *Claims not incident to service.* Claims which arose during the conduct of personal business are not payable.

(2) *Subrogation claims.* Claims based upon payment or other consideration to a proper claimant are not payable.

(3) *Assigned claims.* Claims based upon assignment of a claim by a proper claimant are not payable.

(4) *Conditional vendor claims.* Claims asserted by or on behalf of a conditional vendor are not payable.

(5) *Claims by improper claimants.* Claims by persons not designated in § 180.102(a) are not payable.

(6) *Small items of substantial value.* Claims are not payable for money or for small articles of substantial value, such as watches or expensive jewelry, when shipped with household goods or as unaccompanied baggage.

(7) *Articles of extraordinary value.* Claims are not payable for expensive articles of gold, silver, other precious metals, paintings, antiques other than bulky furnishings, relics, and other articles of extraordinary value when shipped with household goods by ordinary means or as unaccompanied baggage at normal released valuation. Claims for such articles are payable when their loss is incident to shipment by expedited mode in accordance with current joint travel regulations. This prohibition does not apply to articles in the personal custody of the claimant or articles properly checked, provided that reasonable protection or security

measures have been taken by the claimant.

(8) *Articles acquired for other persons.* Claims are not payable for articles intended directly or indirectly for persons other than the claimant or members of the claimant's immediate household. This prohibition includes articles acquired at the request of others and articles for sale.

(9) *Property used for business.* Claims are not payable for property normally used for business or profit.

(10) *Unserviceable property.* Claims are not payable for wornout or unserviceable property.

(11) *Violation of law or directive.* Claims are not payable for property acquired, possessed, or transported in violation of law, regulation, or other directive. This does not apply to limitations imposed on the weight of shipments of household goods.

(12) *Intangible property.* Claims are not payable for intangible property such as bank books, checks, promissory notes, stock certificates, bonds, bills of lading, warehouse receipts, baggage checks, insurance policies, money order, and traveler's checks.

(13) *Government property.* Claims are not payable for property owned by the United States unless the claimant is financially responsible for the property to an agency of the Government other than OPM.

(14) *Motor vehicles.* Claims for motor vehicles, except as provided for by § 180.104(c)(3), will ordinarily not be paid. However, in exceptional cases, meritorius claims for damage to or loss of motor vehicles may be recommended to the Office of the General Counsel for consideration and approval for payment.

(15) *Enemy property.* Claims are not payable for enemy property, including war trophies.

(16) *Losses recoverable from carrier.* Claims are not payable for losses, or any portion thereof, which have been recovered or are recoverable from a carrier, except as permitted under § 180.106.

(17) *Losses recoverable from insurer.* Claims are not payable for losses, or any portion thereof, which have been recovered or are recoverable from an insurer, except as permitted under § 180.106.

(18) *Losses recoverable from contractor.* Claims are not payable for losses, or any portion thereof, which have been recovered or are recoverable under contract, except as permitted under § 180.106.

(19) *Fees for estimates.* Claims are not normally payable for fees paid to obtain estimates of repair in conjuction with submitting a claim under this part. However, where, in the opinion of the approving authority, the claimant could not obtain an estimate without paying a fee, such a claim may be considered in an amount reasonable in relation to the value or the cost of repairs of the articles involved, provided that the evidence furnished clearly indicates that the amount of the fee paid will not be deducted from the cost of repairs if the work is accomplished by the estimator.

(20) *Items fraudulently claimed.* Claims are not payable for items fraudulently claimed. When investigation discloses that a claimant, claimant's agent, claimant's employee, or member of claimant's family has intentionally misrepresented an item claimed as to cost, condition, cost to repair, etc., the item will be disallowed in its entirety even though some actual damage has been sustained. However, if the remainder of the claim is proper it will be paid. This does not preclude appropriate disciplinary action if warranted.

§ 180.106 Claims involving carriers and insurers.

(a) Claimants must comply with the following before presenting claims involving a carrier or insurer:

(1) Whenever property is damaged or lost while being shipped pursuant to authorized travel orders, the owner must file a written claim for reimbursement with the carrier according to the terms of its bill of lading or contract before submitting a claim against the Government. The claimant may present a claim to the Government immediately after making demand on the carrier.

(2) Whenever property which is damaged or lost incident to the claimant's service is insured in whole or in part,

the claimant must make a written demand against the insurer for reimbursement under the terms and conditions of the insurance coverage. Such demand should be made within the time limit provided in the policy and prior to the filing of a claim against the Government. The claimant may present a claim to the Government immediately after making demand on the insurer.

(b) If the claimant fails to make the required demand on the carrier or insurer or make reasonable efforts to collect the amount recoverable, the amount payable under the provisions of these regulations shall be reduced by the maximum amount recoverable. However, no deduction will be made if the circumstances of the claimant's service were such as to preclude timely filing of the claim with the carrier or insurer and it is determined that a demand would have been impracticable or unavailing in any event.

(c) When a claim is paid by OPM, the claimant will assign to the United States, to the extent of any payment on the claim accepted by claimant, all rights, title, and interest in any claim against any carrier, insurer, or other party arising out of the incident on which the claim against the United States is based. On request, the claimant also will furnish such evidence as may be required to enable the United States to enforce the claim.

(d) After payment of a claim by the United States, if the claimant receives any payment from a carrier, contractor, insurer, or other third party, the claimant will pay the proceeds to the United States to the extent of the payment received by the claimant from the United States.

§ 180.107 Claims procedure.

(a) *Filing a claim.* Claims not exceeding $500 shall be filed with the appropriate bureau or regional director. Claims in excess of $500 shall be filed with the Office of the General Counsel, Office of Personnel Management, 1900 E Street NW., Washington, DC 20415. Claims shall be in writing, using G.C. Form 33 when available, and shall contain as a minimum:

(1) Name, address, and place of employment of the claimant;

(2) Place and date of the damage or loss;

(3) A brief statement of the facts and circumstances surrounding the damage or loss;

(4) Cost, date, and place of acquisition of each piece of property damaged or lost;

(5) Two itemized repair estimates, or value estimates, whichever is applicable;

(6) Copies of police reports, if applicable;

(7) A statement from the claimant's supervisor that the loss was incident to service;

(8) A statement that the property was or was not insured;

(9) With respect to claims involving thefts or losses in quarters or other places where the property was reasonably kept, a statement as to what security precautions were taken to protect the property involved;

(10) With respect to claims involving property being used for the benefit of the Government, a statement by the claimant's supervisor that the claimant was required to provide such property or that the claimant's providing it was in the interest of the Government; and

(11) Other evidence as may be required.

(b) *Single claim.* A single claim shall be presented for all lost or damaged property resulting from the same incident. If this procedure causes a hardship, the claimant may present an initial claim with notice that it is a partial claim, an explanation of the circumstances causing the hardship, and an estimate of the balance of the claim and the date it will be submitted. Payment may be made on a partial claim if the approving authority determines that a genuine hardship exists.

(c) *Claims investigator.* When a claim is filed, the appropriate associate or regional director, or the General Counsel, shall appoint a claims investigator to evaluate the claim and make a recommendation as to its disposition. Where the cost to repair damaged property does not exceed $100 per item and the claims investigator has inspected the damaged property, the claimant and the approving authority may agree upon a reasonable amount to be claimed for repair of an individual item in lieu of an independent estimate by a qualified repairman. In such a case, the claims investigator and the approving authority will certify that the property has been examined and that the amount claimed is a reasonable allowance for the cost of the repairs.

(d) *Loss in quarters.* Claims for property loss in quarters or other authorized places should be accompanied by a statement indicating:

(1) Geographical location;

(2) Whether the quarters were assigned or provided in kind by the Government;

(3) Whether the quarters are regularly occupied by the claimant;

(4) Name of the authority, if any, who designated the place of storage of the property if other than quarters;

(5) Measures taken to protect the property; and

(6) Whether the claimant is a local inhabitant.

(e) *Loss by theft or robbery.* Claims for property loss by theft or robbery should be accompanied by a statement indicating:

(1) Geographical location;

(2) Facts and circumstances surrounding the loss, including evidence of the crime such as breaking and entering, capture of the thief or robber, or recovery of part of the stolen goods; and

(3) Evidence that the claimant exercised due care in protecting the property prior to the loss, including information as to the degree of care normally exercised in the locale of the loss due to any unusual risks involved.

(f) *Transportation losses.* Claims for transportation losses should be accompanied by the following:

(1) Copies of orders authorizing the travel, transportation, or shipment or a certificate explaining the absence of orders and stating their substance;

(2) Statement in cases where property was turned over to a shipping officer, supply officer, or contract packer indicating:

(i) Name (or designation) and address of the shipping officer, supply officer, or contract packer;

(ii) Date the property was turned over;

(iii) Inventoried condition when the property was turned over;

(iv) When and where the property was packed and by whom;

(v) Date of shipment;

(vi) Copies of all bills of lading, inventories, and other applicable shipping documents;

(vii) Date and place of delivery to the claimant;

(viii) Date the property was unpacked by the carrier, claimant, or Government;

(ix) Statements of disinterested witnesses as to the condition of the property when received and delivered, or as to handling or storage;

(x) Whether the negligence of any Government employee acting within the scope of his employment caused the damage or loss;

(xi) Whether the last common carrier or local carrier was given a clear receipt, except for concealed damages;

(xii) Total gross, tare, and net weight of shipment;

(xiii) Insurance certificate or policy if losses are privately insured;

(xiv) Copy of the demand on carrier or insured, or both, when required, and the reply, if any;

(xv) Action taken by the claimant to locate missing baggage or household effects, including related correspondence.

(g) *Marine or aircraft disaster.* Claims for property losses due to marine or aircraft disaster should be accompanied by a copy of orders or other evidence to establish the claimant's right to be, or to have property, on board.

(h) *Enemy action, public disaster, or public service.* Claims for property losses due to enemy action, public disaster, or public service should be accompanied by:

(1) Copies of orders or other evidence establishing the claimant's required presence in the area involved, and

(2) A detailed statement of facts and circumstances showing an applicable case enumerated in § 180.104(c)(8).

(i) *Property used for benefit of Government.* Claims for property loss when the property was used for the benefit of the Government should be accompanied by:

(1) A statement from the proper authority that the property was supplied by the claimant in the performance of

official business at the request of, or with the knowledge and consent of, superior authority or by reason of necessity; and

(2) If the property being used for the benefit of the Government was damaged or lost while not in use, evidence that the loss occurred in an authorized storage area.

(j) *Money*. Claims for loss of money deposited for safekeeping, transmittal, or other authorized disposition, should be accompanied by:

(1) Name, grade, and address of the person or persons who received the money and any others involved;

(2) Name and designation of the authority who authorized such person or persons to accept personal funds, and the disposition required; and

(3) Receipts and written sworn statements explaining the failure to account for funds or return them to the claimant.

(k) *Motor vehicles in transit*. Claims for damage to motor vehicles in transit should be accompanied by a copy of orders or other available evidence to establish the claimant's lawful right to have the property shipped and evidence to establish damage in transit.

[43 FR 47163, Oct. 13, 1978, as amended at 44 FR 76747, Dec. 28, 1979]

§ 180.108 Settlement of claims.

(a) *Authority*. Associate Directors and Regional Directors are authorized to settle and pay any claim not exceeding $500 and arising under this part. The General Counsel is authorized to settle and pay any claim not exceeding $15,000 and arising under this part. Unless cognizable under § 180.104(c)(3), claims for damage to or loss of motor vehicles may be settled and paid only by the General Counsel.

(b) *Redelegation*. The approving authorities may establish such procedures and make such redelegations as may be required to fulfill the objectives of this part.

(c) *Cost or value*. The amount awarded on any item of property will not exceed the cost of the item (either the price paid in cash or property) or the value at the time of acquisition if not acquired by purchase or exchange. The amount payable will be determined by applying the principles of depreciation to the adjusted dollar value or other base price of property lost or damaged beyond economical repair; by allowing the cost of repairs when an item is economically repairable, provided the cost of repairs does not exceed the depreciated value of the item; and by deducting salvage value, if appropriate.

(d) *Depreciation*. Depreciation in value of an item is determined by considering the type of article involved, its cost, condition when damaged beyond economical repair or lost, and the time elapsed between the date of acquisition and the date of damage or loss.

(e) *Appreciation*. There will be no allowance for appreciation in the value of the property except that the cost of the item may be adjusted to reflect changes in the purchasing power of the dollar before depreciation is computed. Appreciation will not be allowed solely because the loss occurred or the claimant now resides in an area remote from the place of purchase of the property.

(f) *Expensive articles*. Allowance for expensive items (including heirlooms and antiques) or for items purchased at unreasonably high prices will be based on the fair and reasonable purchase price for substitute articles of a similar nature.

(g) *Acquisition*. Allowance for articles acquired by barter will not exceed the cost of the articles tendered in barter. No reimbursement will be made for articles acquired in black market or other prohibited activities.

(h) *Replacement*. Replacement of damaged or lost property may be made in kind whenever appropriate.

(i) *Amount allowable*. Subject to the limitations of §§ 180.108(c) through 180.108(h), the amount allowable in settlement of a claim is either:

(1) The depreciated value immediately prior to damage or loss of property damaged beyond economical repair or lost, less any salvage value; or

(2) The reasonable cost of repairs when property is economically repairable, provided that the cost of repairs does not exceed the depreciated value.

(j) *Notification*. The approving authority shall notify the claimant in writing of the action taken on the claim and, if the claim is disapproved or only partially approved, the reasons therefor.

(k) *Carrier or insurer.* In the event a claim submitted against a carrier or insurer under §180.106 had not been settled before settlement of a claim against the Government under this part, the approving authority shall notify such carrier or insurer to pay the proceeds of the claim to OPM to the extent OPM has made payment to the claimant.

(l) *Review.* The action of the approving authority is final; however, the decision may be reconsidered if the claimant so requests and submits a written explanation why reconsideration is appropriate.

(m) *Attorney's fees.* No more than 10 per centum of the amount paid in settlement of each individual claim submitted and settled under this subpart shall be paid or delivered to or received by any agent or attorney on account of services rendered in connection with that claim and the same shall be unlawful, any contract to the contrary notwithstanding. Any person violating this or any other provision of sections 240 to 243 of title 31, United States Code, shall be deemed guilty of a misdemeanor and upon conviction thereof shall be fined in any sum not exceeding $1000.

[43 FR 47163, Oct. 13, 1978, as amended at 44 FR 76747, Dec. 28, 1979]

PART 185—PROGRAM FRAUD CIVIL REMEDIES

Sec.

AUTHORITY: 28 U.S.C. 2461 note; 31 U.S.C. 3801–3812.

SOURCE: 60 FR 7891, Feb. 10, 1995, unless otherwise noted.

§185.101 Purpose.

This subpart implements the Program Fraud Civil Remedies Act of 1986, Public Law 99–509, 6101–6104, 100 Stat. 1874 (October 21, 1986), codified at 31 U.S.C. 3801–3812. Section 3809 requires each authority head to promulgate regulations necessary to implement the provisions of the statute. The subpart establishes administrative procedures for imposing civil penalties and assessments against persons who make, submit, or present, or cause to be made, submitted, or presented, false, fictitious, or fraudulent claims or written statements to authorities or to their agents, and specifies the hearing and appeal rights of persons subject to allegations of liability for such penalties and assessments. The moneys collected as a result of these procedures are deposited as miscellaneous receipts in the Treasury of the United States.

§ 185.102 Definitions.

For the purposes of this part—

ALJ means an Administrative Law Judge in the authority appointed pursuant to 5 U.S.C. 3105 or detailed to the authority pursuant to 5 U.S.C. 3344.

Authority means the Office of Personnel Management (OPM).

Authority head means the Director of the Office of Personnel Management or the Director's designee.

Benefit is very broad, and is intended to cover anything of value, including but not limited to any advantage, preference, privilege, license, permit, favorable decision, ruling, status or loan guarantee.

Claim means any request, demand, or submission—

(a) Made to the authority for property, services, or money (including money representing benefits, grants, loans or insurance);

(b) Made to a recipient of property, services, or money from the authority or to a party to a contract with the authority:

(1) For property or services if the United States—

(i) Provided such property or services;

(ii) Provided any portion of the funds for the purchase of such property or services; or

(iii) Will reimburse such recipient or party for the purchase of such property or services; or

(2) For the payment of money (including money representing grants, loans, insurance, or benefits) if the United States:

(i) Provided any portion of the money requested or demanded; or

(ii) Will reimburse such recipient or party for any portion of the money paid on such request or demand; or

(c) Made to the authority which has the effect of decreasing an obligation to pay or account for property, services, or money.

Complaint means the administrative complaint served by the reviewing official on the defendant under § 185.107.

Defendant means any person alleged in a complaint under § 185.107 to be liable for a civil penalty or assessment under § 185.103.

Government means the United States Government.

Individual means a natural person.

Initial decision means the written decision of the ALJ required by § 185.110 or § 185.137, and includes a revised initial decision issued following a remand or a motion for reconsideration.

Investigating Official means the Inspector General or the Inspector General's designee.

Knows or has reason to know means that a person, with respect to a claim or statement:

(a) Has actual knowledge that the claim or statement is false, fictitious, or fraudulent;

(b) Acts in deliberate ignorance of the truth or falsity of the claim or statement; or

(c) Acts in reckless disregard of the truth or falsity of the claim or statement.

Makes shall include the terms presents, submits, and causes to be made, presented, or submitted. As the context requires, making or made, shall likewise include the corresponding forms of such terms.

Person means any individual, partnership, corporation, association, or private organization, and includes the plural of that term.

Representative means an attorney who is in good standing of the bar of any State, Territory, or possession of the United States or of the District of Columbia or the Commonwealth of Puerto Rico or other individual designated in writing by the defendant.

Reviewing Official means the General Counsel of OPM or the General Counsel's designee. For the purposes of § 185.105 of these rules, the General Counsel personally, or members of the General Counsel's immediate staff, shall perform the functions of the reviewing official provided that such person or persons serve in a position for which the rate of basic pay is not less than the minimum rate payable under section 5376 of title 5 of the United States Code. All other functions of the reviewing official, including administrative prosecution under these rules, shall be performed on behalf of the

General Counsel by members of the Office of the General Counsel.

Statement means any representation, certification, affirmation, document, record, or accounting or bookkeeping entry made:

(a) With respect to a claim or to obtain the approval or payment of a claim (including relating to eligibility to make a claim); or

(b) With respect to (including relating to eligibility for):

(1) A contract with, or a bid or proposal for a contract with; or

(2) A grant, loan, or benefit from, the authority, or any State, political subdivision of a State, or other party, if the United States Government provides any portion of the money or property under such contract or for such grant, loan, or benefit, or if the Government will reimburse such State, political subdivision, or party for any portion of the money or property under such contract or for such grant, loan, or benefit.

§ 185.103 Basis for civil penalties and assessments.

(a) In addition to any other remedy that may be prescribed by law, any person shall be subject to a civil penalty of not more than $10,781, where the person makes a claim and knows or has reason to know that the claim:

(1) In false, fictitious, or fraudulent;

(2) Includes, or is supported by, any written statement which asserts a material fact which is false, fictitious, or fraudulent;

(3) Includes, or is supported by, any written statement that:

(i) Omits a material fact;

(ii) Is false, fictitious, or fraudulent as a result of such omission; and

(iii) Is a statement in which the person making such statement has a duty to include such material fact; or

(4) Is for payment for the provision of property or services which the person has not provided as claimed.

(b) Each voucher, invoice, claim form, or other individual request or demand for property, services, or money constitutes a separate claim.

(c) A claim shall be considered made to the authority, recipient, or party when such claim is actually made to an agent, fiscal intermediary, or other entity, including any State or political subdivision thereof, acting for or on behalf of the authority, recipient, or party.

(d) Each claim for property, services, or money is subject to a civil penalty regardless of whether such property, services, or money is actually delivered or paid.

(e) If the Government has made any payment (including transferred property or provided services) on a claim, a person subject to a civil penalty under paragraph (a)(1) of this section may also be subject to an assessment of not more than twice the amount of such claim or that portion thereof that is determined to be in violation of paragraph (a)(1) of this section. Such assessment shall be in lieu of damages sustained by the Government because of such claim.

(f) Any person who makes a written statement that:

(1) The person knows or has reason to know:

(i) Asserts a material fact which is false, fictitious, or fraudulent; or

(ii) Is false, fictitious, or fraudulent because it omits a material fact that the person making the statement has a duty to include in such statement; and

(2) Contains, or is accompanied by, an express certification or affirmation of the truthfulness and accuracy of the contents of the statement may be subject, in addition to any other remedy that may be prescribed by law, to a civil penalty of not more than $10,781 for each such statement.

(g) Each written representation, certification, or affirmation constitutes a separate statement.

(h) A statement shall be considered made to the authority when such statement is actually made to an agent, fiscal intermediary, or other entity, including any State or political subdivision thereof, acting for or on behalf of the authority.

(i) No proof of specific intent to defraud is required to establish liability under this section.

(j) In any case in which it is determined that more than one person is liable for making a claim or statement under this section, each such person may be held liable for a civil penalty under this section.

(k) In any case in which it is determined that more than one person is liable for making a claim under this section on which the Government has made payment (including transferred property or provided services), an assessment may be imposed against any such person or jointly and severally against any combination of such persons.

[60 FR 7891, Feb. 10, 1995, as amended at 81 FR 46828, July 19, 2016]

§ 185.104 Investigation.

(a) If an investigating official concludes that a subpoena pursuant to the authority conferred by 31 U.S.C. 3804(a) is warranted, he or she may issue a subpoena.

(1) The subpoena so issued shall notify the person to whom it is addressed of the authority under which the subpoena is issued and shall identify the records or documents sought;

(2) The investigating official may designate a person to act on his or her behalf to receive the documents sought; and

(3) The person receiving such subpoena shall be required to tender to the investigating official, or the person designated to receive the documents, a certification that

(i) The documents sought have been produced;

(ii) Such documents are not available and the reasons therefor; or

(iii) Such documents, suitably identified, have been withheld based upon the assertion of an identified privilege.

(b) If the investigating official concludes that an action under the Program Fraud Civil Remedies Act may be warranted, the investigating official shall submit a report containing the findings and conclusions of such investigation to the reviewing official.

(c) Nothing in this section shall preclude or limit an investigating official's discretion to refer allegations directly to the Department of Justice for suit under the False Claims Act or other civil relief, or to defer or postpone a report or referral to the reviewing official to avoid interference with a criminal investigation or prosecution.

(d) Nothing in this section modifies any responsibility of an investigating official to report violations of criminal law to the Attorney General.

§ 185.105 Review by the reviewing official.

If, based on the report of the investigating official under § 185.104(b), the reviewing official determines that there is adequate evidence to believe that a person is liable under § 185.103, the reviewing official shall transmit to the Attorney General a written notice of the reviewing official's intention to have a complaint issued under § 185.107. Such notice shall include:

(a) A statement of the reviewing official's reasons for issuing a complaint;

(b) A statement specifying the evidence that supports the allegations of liability;

(c) A description of the claims or statements upon which the allegations of liability are based;

(d) An estimate of the amount of money, or the value of property, services, or other benefits, requested or demanded in violation of § 185.103;

(e) A statement of any exculpatory or mitigating circumstances that may relate to the claims or statements known by the reviewing official or the investigating official; and

(f) A statement that there is a reasonable prospect of collecting an appropriate amount of penalties and assessments.

§ 185.106 Prerequisites for issuing a complaint.

(a) The reviewing official may issue a complaint under § 185.107 only if:

(1) The Department of Justice approves the issuance of a complaint in a written statement described in section 3803(b)(1) of title 31 of the United States Code, and

(2) In the case of allegations of liability under § 185.103(a) with respect to a claim, the reviewing official determines that, with respect to such claim or a group of related claims submitted at the same time such claim is submitted (as defined in paragraph (b) of this section), the amount of money, or the value of property or services, demanded or requested in violation of § 185.103(a) does not exceed $150,000.

(b) For the purposes of this section, a related group of claims submitted at the same time shall include only those claims arising from the same transaction (e.g., grant, loan, application, or contract) that are submitted simultaneously as part of a single request, demand, or submission.

(c) Nothing in this section shall be construed to limit the reviewing official's authority to join in a single complaint against a person, claims that are unrelated or were not submitted simultaneously, regardless of the amount of money, or the value of property or services, demanded or requested.

§ 185.107 Complaint.

(a) On or after the date the Department of Justice approves the issuance of a complaint in accordance with section 3803(b)(1) of title 31 of the United States Code, the reviewing official may serve a complaint on the defendant, as provided in § 185.108.

(b) The complaint shall state the following:

(1) The allegations of liability against the defendant, including the statutory basis for liability, an identification of the claims or statements that are the basis for the alleged liability, and the reasons why liability allegedly arises from such claims or statements;

(2) The maximum amount of penalties and assessments for which the defendant may be held liable;

(3) Instructions for filing an answer, including a specific statement of the defendant's right to request a hearing and to be represented by a representative; and

(4) The fact that failure to file an answer within 30 days of service of the complaint will result in the imposition of the maximum amount of penalties and assessments without right to appeal, as provided in § 185.110.

(c) At the same time the reviewing official serves the complaint, he or she shall serve the defendant with a copy of these regulations.

§ 185.108 Service of complaint.

(a) Service of a complaint must be made by certified or registered mail or by delivery in any manner authorized by Rule 4 of the Federal Rules of Civil Procedure. Service is complete upon receipt.

(b) Proof of service, stating the name and address of the person on whom the complaint was served, and the manner and date of service, may be made by:

(1) Affidavit of the individual serving the complaint by delivery;

(2) A United States Postal Service return receipt card acknowledging receipt; or

(3) Written acknowledgment of receipt by the defendant or his or her representative.

§ 185.109 Answer.

(a) The defendant may request a hearing in the answer filed with the reviewing official within 30 days of service of the complaint.

(b) In the answer, the defendant:

(1) Shall admit or deny each of the allegations of liability made in the complaint;

(2) Shall state any defense on which the defendant intends to rely;

(3) May state any reasons why the defendant contends that the penalties and assessments should be less than the statutory maximum; and

(4) Shall state the name, address, and telephone number of the person authorized by the defendant to act as defendant's representative, if any.

(c) If the defendant is unable to file an answer meeting the requirements of paragraph (b) of this section within the time provided, the defendant may, before the expiration of 30 days from service of the complaint, file with the reviewing official a general answer denying liability and requesting a hearing, and a request for an extension of time within which to file an answer meeting the requirements of paragraph (b) of this section. The reviewing official shall file promptly with the ALJ the complaint, the general answer denying liability, and the request for an extension of time as provided in § 185.110. For good cause shown, the ALJ may grant the defendant up to 30 additional days within which to file an answer meeting the requirements of paragraph (b) of this section. The ALJ shall decide expeditiously whether the dependent shall be granted an additional period of time to file such answer.

§ 185.110 Default upon failure to file an answer.

(a) If the defendant does not file an answer within the time prescribed in § 185.109(a), the reviewing official may refer the complaint to the ALJ.

(b) Upon the referral of the complaint, the ALJ shall promptly serve on the defendant in the manner prescribed in § 185.108, a notice that an initial decision will be issued under this section.

(c) The ALJ shall assume the facts alleged in the complaint to be true and, if such facts establish liability under § 185.103, the ALJ shall issue an initial decision imposing the maximum amount of penalties and assessments allowed under the statute.

(d) Except as otherwise provided in this section, by failing to file a timely answer the defendant waives any right to further review of the penalties and assessments imposed under paragraph (c) of this section and the initial decision shall become final and binding upon the parties 30 days after it is issued.

(e) If, before such an initial decision becomes final, the defendant files a motion with the ALJ seeking to reopen on the grounds that extraordinary circumstances prevented the defendant from filing an answer, the initial decision shall be stayed pending the ALJ's decision on the motion.

(f) If, on such motion, the defendant can demonstrate extraordinary circumstances excusing the failure to file a timely answer, the ALJ shall withdraw the initial decision in paragraph (c) of this section, if such a decision has been issued, and shall grant the defendant an opportunity to answer the complaint.

(g) A decision of the ALJ denying a defendant's motion under paragraph (e) of this section is not subject to reconsideration under § 185.138.

(h) The defendant may appeal to the authority head the decision denying a motion to reopen by filing a notice of appeal with the authority head within 15 days after the ALJ denies the motion. The timely filing of a notice of appeal shall stay the initial decision until the authority head decides the issue.

(i) If the defendant files a timely notice of appeal with the authority head, the ALJ shall forward the record of the proceeding to the authority head.

(j) The authority head shall decide expeditiously whether extraordinary circumstances excuse the defendant's failure to file a timely answer based solely on the record before the ALJ.

(k) If the authority head decides that extraordinary circumstances excused the defendant's failure to file a timely answer, the authority head shall remand the case to the ALJ with instructions to grant the defendant an opportunity to answer.

(l) If the authority head decides that the defendant's failure to file a timely answer is not excused, the authority head shall reinstate the initial decision of the ALJ, which shall become final and binding upon the parties 30 days after the authority head issues such decision.

§ 185.111 Referral of complaint and answer to the ALJ.

Upon receipt of an answer, the reviewing official shall file the complaint and answer with the ALJ.

§ 185.112 Notice of hearing.

(a) When the ALJ receives the complaint and answer, the ALJ shall promptly serve a notice of hearing upon the defendant in the manner prescribed by § 185.108. At the same time, the ALJ shall send a copy of such notice to the reviewing official or his or her designee.

(b) Such notice shall include:

(1) The tentative time and place, and the nature of the hearing;

(2) The legal authority and jurisdiction under which the hearing is to be held;

(3) The matters of fact and law to be asserted;

(4) A description of the procedures for the conduct of the hearing;

(5) The name, address, and telephone number of the representative of the Government and of the defendant, if any; and

(6) Such other matters as the ALJ deems appropriate.

§ 185.113 Location of hearing.

(a) The hearing may be held:

(1) In any judicial district of the United States in which the defendant resides or transacts business;

(2) In any judicial district of the United States in which the claim or statement in issue was made; or

(3) In such other place as may be agreed upon by the parties and the ALJ.

(b) Each party shall have the opportunity to present argument with respect to the location of the hearing.

(c) The hearing shall be held at the place and at the time ordered by the ALJ.

§ 185.114 Parties to the hearing.

(a) The parties to the hearing shall be the defendant and OPM.

(b) Except where the authority head designates another, OPM shall be represented by the members of the Office of the General Counsel.

(c) Pursuant to section 3730(c)(5) of title 31, United States Code, a private plaintiff under the False Claims Act may participate in these proceedings to the extent authorized by the provisions of that Act.

§ 185.115 Separation of functions.

(a) The investigating official, the reviewing official, and any employee or agent of the authority who takes part in investigating, preparing, or presenting a particular case may not, in such case or a factually related case:

(1) Participate in the hearing as the ALJ;

(2) Participate or advise in the initial decision or the review of the initial decision by the authority head, except as a witness or a representative in public proceedings; or

(3) Make the collection of penalties and assessments under section 3806 of title 31, United States Code.

(b) The ALJ shall not be responsible to or subject to the supervision or direction of the investigating official or the reviewing official.

§ 185.116 Ex parte contacts.

No party or person (except employees of the ALJ's office) shall communicate in any way with the ALJ on any matter at issue in a case, unless on notice and opportunity for all parties to participate. This provision does not prohibit a person or party from inquiring about the status of a case or asking routine questions concerning administrative functions or procedures.

§ 185.117 Disqualification of reviewing official or ALJ.

(a) A reviewing official or ALJ in a particular case may disqualify himself or herself at any time.

(b) A party may file with the ALJ a motion for disqualification of a reviewing official or an ALJ. Such motion shall be accompanied by an affidavit alleging personal bias or other reason for disqualification.

(c) Such motion and affidavit shall be filed promptly upon the party's discovery of reasons requiring disqualification, or such objections shall be deemed waived.

(d) Such affidavit shall state specific facts that support the party's belief that personal bias or other reason for disqualification exists and the time and circumstances of the party's discovery of such facts. It shall be accompanied by a certificate of the representative of record that it is made in good faith.

(e) Upon the filing of such a motion and affidavit, the ALJ shall proceed no further in the case until he or she resolves the matter of disqualification in accordance with this section.

(1) If the ALJ determines that a reviewing official is disqualified, the ALJ shall dismiss the complaint without prejudice.

(2) If the ALJ disqualifies himself or herself, the case shall be reassigned promptly to another ALJ.

(3) If the ALJ denies a motion to disqualify, the authority head may determine the matter only as part of his or her review of the initial decision upon appeal, if any.

§ 185.118 Rights of parties.

Except as otherwise limited by this part, all parties may:

(a) Be accompanied, represented, and advised by a representative;

(b) Participate in any conference held by the ALJ;

(c) Conduct discovery as provided under § 185.122;

(d) Agree to stipulations of fact or law, which shall be made a part of the record;

(e) Present evidence relevant to the issues at the hearing;

(f) Present and cross-examine witnesses;

(g) Present oral arguments at the hearing as permitted by the ALJ; and

(h) Submit written briefs and proposed findings of fact and conclusions of law after the hearing.

§ 185.119 Authority of the ALJ.

(a) The ALJ shall conduct a fair and impartial hearing, avoid delay, maintain order, and assure that a record of the proceeding is made.

(b) The ALJ has the authority to:

(1) Set and change the date, time, and place of the hearing upon reasonable notice to the parties;

(2) Continue or recess the hearing in whole or in part for a reasonable period of time;

(3) Hold conferences to identify or simplify the issues, or to consider other matters that may aid in the expeditious disposition of the proceeding;

(4) Administer oaths and affirmations;

(5) Issue subpoenas requiring the attendance of witnesses and the production of documents at depositions or at hearings;

(6) Rule on motions and other procedural matters;

(7) Regulate the scope and timing of discovery;

(8) Regulate the course of the hearing and the conduct of representatives and parties;

(9) Examine witnesses;

(10) Receive, rule on, exclude, or limit evidence;

(11) Upon motion of a party, take official notice of facts;

(12) Upon motion of a party, decide cases, in whole or in part, by summary judgment where there is no disputed issue of material fact;

(13) Conduct any conference, argument, or hearing on motions in person or by telephone; and

(14) Exercise such other authority as is necessary to carry out the responsibilities of the ALJ under this part.

(c) The ALJ does not have the authority to find Federal statutes or regulations invalid.

§ 185.120 Prehearing conferences.

(a) The ALJ may schedule prehearing conferences as appropriate.

(b) Upon the motion of any party, the ALJ shall schedule at least one prehearing conference at a reasonable time in advance of the hearing.

(c) The ALJ may use prehearing conferences to discuss the following:

(1) Simplification of the issues;

(2) The necessity or desirability of amendments to the pleadings, including the need for a more definite statement;

(3) Stipulations and admissions of fact or as to the contents and authenticity of documents;

(4) Whether the parties can agree to submission of the case on a stipulated record;

(5) Whether a party chooses to waive appearance at an oral hearing and to submit only documentary evidence (subject to the objection of other parties) and written argument;

(6) Limitation of the number of witnesses;

(7) Scheduling dates for the exchange of witness lists and of proposed exhibits;

(8) Discovery;

(9) The time and place for the hearing; and

(10) Such other matters as may tend to expedite the fair and just disposition of the proceedings.

(d) The ALJ may issue an order containing all matters agreed upon by the parties or ordered by the ALJ at a prehearing conference.

§ 185.121 Disclosure of documents.

(a) Upon written request to the reviewing official, generally prior to the filing of an answer, the defendant may review any relevant and material documents, transcripts, records, and other materials that relate to the allegations set out in the complaint and upon which the findings and conclusions of the investigating official under § 185.104(b) are based, unless such documents are subject to a privilege under Federal law. Upon payment of fees for duplication, the defendant may obtain copies of such documents.

(b) Upon written request to the reviewing official, the defendant, may also obtain a copy of all exculpatory information in the possession of the reviewing official or investigating official relating to the allegations in the complaint, even if it is contained in a document that would otherwise be privileged. If the document would otherwise be privileged, only that portion containing exculpatory information must be disclosed.

(c) The notice sent to the Attorney General from the reviewing official as described in § 185.105 is not discoverable under any circumstances.

(d) The defendant may file a motion to compel disclosure of the documents subject to the provisions of this section. Such a motion may only be filed with the ALJ following the filing of an answer pursuant to § 185.109.

§ 185.122 Discovery.

(a) The following types of discovery are authorized:

(1) Requests for production of documents for inspection and copying;

(2) Requests for admissions of the authenticity of any relevant document or of the truth of any relevant fact;

(3) Written interrogatories; and

(4) Depositions.

(b) For the purpose of this section and § 185.123, the term *documents* includes information, documents, reports, answers, records, accounts, papers, and other data and documentary evidence. Nothing contained herein shall be interpreted to require the creation of a document.

(c) Unless mutually agreed to by the parties, discovery is available only as ordered by the ALJ. The ALJ shall regulate the timing of discovery.

(d) Motions for discovery are to be handled according to the following procedures:

(1) A party seeking discovery may file a motion with the ALJ. Such a motion shall be accompanied by a copy of the requested discovery, or in the case of depositions, a summary of the scope of the proposed deposition.

(2) Within 10 days of service, a party may file an opposition to the motion and/or a motion for protective order as provided in § 185.125.

(3) The ALJ may grant a motion for discovery only if he or she finds that the discovery sought:

(i) Is necessary for the expeditious, fair, and reasonable consideration of the issues;

(ii) Is not unduly costly or burdensome;

(iii) Will not unduly delay the proceeding; and

(iv) Does not seek privileged information.

(4) The burden of showing that discovery should be allowed is on the party seeking discovery.

(5) The ALJ may grant discovery subject to a protective order under § 185.125.

(e) Depositions are to be handled in the following manner:

(1) If a motion for deposition is granted, the ALJ shall issue a subpoena for the deponent, which may require the deponent to produce documents. The subpoena shall specify the time and place at which the deposition will be held.

(2) The party seeking to depose shall serve the subpoena in the manner prescribed in § 185.108.

(3) The deponent may file with the ALJ within 10 days of service a motion to quash the subpoena or a motion for a protective order.

(4) The party seeking to depose shall provide for the taking of a verbatim transcript of the deposition, which it shall make available to all other parties for inspection and copying.

(f) Each party shall bear its own costs of discovery.

§ 185.123 Exchange of witness lists, statements and exhibits.

(a) At least 15 days before the hearing or at such other time as may be ordered by the ALJ, the parties shall exchange witness lists, copies of prior statements of proposed witnesses, and copies of proposed hearing exhibits, including copies of any written statements that the party intends to offer in lieu of live testimony in accordance with § 185.133(b). At the time the above documents are exchanged, any party that intends to rely on the transcript or deposition testimony in lieu of live testimony at the hearing, if permitted by the ALJ, shall provide each party with a copy of the specific pages of the transcript it intends to introduce into evidence.

(b) If a party objects, the ALJ may not admit into evidence the testimony of any witness whose name does not appear on the witness list or any exhibit not provided to the opposing party as provided above unless the ALJ finds good cause for the failure or that there is no prejudice to the objecting party.

(c) Unless another party objects within the time set by the ALJ, documents exchanged in accordance with paragraph (a) of this section shall be deemed to be authentic for the purpose of admissibility at the hearing.

§ 185.124 Subpoenas for attendance at hearing.

(a) A party wishing to procure the appearance and testimony of any individual at the hearing may request that the ALJ issue a subpoena.

(b) A subpoena requiring the attendance and testimony of an individual may also require the individual to produce documents at the hearing.

(c) A party seeking a subpoena shall file a written request therefor not less than 15 days before the date fixed for the hearing unless otherwise allowed by the ALJ upon a showing of good cause. Such request shall specify any documents to be produced and shall designate the witnesses and describe the address and location thereof with sufficient particularity to permit such witnesses to be found.

(d) The subpoena shall specify the time and place at which the witness is to appear and any documents the witness is to produce.

(e) The party seeking the subpoena shall serve it in the manner prescribed in § 185.108. A subpoena on a party or upon an individual under the control of a party may be served by first class mail.

(f) A party or the individual to whom the subpoena is directed may file with the ALJ a motion to quash the subpoena within 10 days after service or on or before the time specified in the subpoena for compliance if it is less than 10 days after service.

§ 185.125 Protective order.

(a) A party or a prospective witness or deponent may file a motion for a protective order with respect to discovery sought by an opposing party or with respect to the hearing, seeking to limit the availability or disclosure of evidence.

(b) In issuing a protective order, the ALJ may make any order which justice requires to protect a party or person from annoyance, embarrassment, oppression, or undue burden or expense, including one or more of the following:

(1) That the discovery not be had;

(2) That the discovery may be had only on specified terms and conditions, including a designation of the time or place;

(3) That the discovery may be had only through a method of discovery other than that requested;

(4) That certain matters not be the subject of inquiry, or that the scope of discovery be limited to certain matters;

(5) That discovery be conducted with no one present except persons designated by the ALJ;

(6) That the contents of discovery or evidence be sealed;

(7) That a sealed deposition be opened only by order of the ALJ;

(8) That a trade secret or other confidential research, development, commercial information, or facts pertaining to any criminal investigation, proceeding, or other administrative investigation not be disclosed or be disclosed only in a designated way; or

(9) That the parties simultaneously file specified documents or information enclosed in sealed envelopes to be opened as directed by the ALJ.

§ 185.126 Evidence.

(a) The ALJ shall determine the admissibility of evidence.

(b) Except as provided in this part, the ALJ shall not be bound by the Federal Rules of Evidence. However, the ALJ may apply the Federal Rules of Evidence where appropriate, e.g. to exclude unreliable evidence.

(c) The ALJ shall exclude irrelevant and immaterial evidence.

(d) Although relevant, evidence may be excluded if its probative value is substantially outweighed by the danger of unfair prejudice, confusion of the issues, or by considerations of undue delay or needless presentation of cumulative evidence.

(e) Although relevant, evidence may be excluded if it is privileged under Federal law.

(f) Evidence concerning offers of compromise or settlement shall be inadmissible to the extent provided in Rule 408 of the Federal Rules of Evidence.

(g) The ALJ shall permit the parties to introduce rebuttal witnesses and evidence.

(h) All documents and other evidence offered or taken for the record shall be open to examination by all parties, unless otherwise ordered by the ALJ pursuant to § 185.125.

§ 185.127 Fees.

The party requesting a subpoena shall pay the cost of the fees and mileage of any witness subpoenaed in the amounts that would be payable to a witness in a proceeding in United States District Court. A check for witness fees and mileage shall accompany the subpoena when served, except that when a subpoena is issued on behalf of the authority, a check for witness fees and mileage need not accompany the subpoena.

§ 185.128 Form, filing and service of papers.

(a) *Form.* Documents filed with the ALJ shall include an original and two copies. Every pleading and paper filed in the proceeding shall contain a caption setting forth the title of the action, the case number assigned by the ALJ, and a designation of the paper (e.g., motion to quash subpoena). Every pleading and paper shall be signed by, and shall contain the address and telephone number of the party or the person on whose behalf the paper was filed, or his or her representative.

(b) *Filing.* Papers are considered filed when they are mailed. Date of mailing may be established by a certificate from the party or its representative or by proof that the document was sent by certified or registered mail.

(c) *Service.* A party filing a document with the ALJ shall, at the time of filing, serve a copy of such document on every other party. Service upon any party of any document other than those required to be served as prescribed in § 185.108 shall be made by delivering a copy or by placing a copy of the document in the United States mail, postage prepaid and addressed, to the party's last known address. When a party is represented by a representative, service shall be made upon such representative in lieu of the actual party.

(d) *Proof of service.* A certificate of the individual serving the document by personal delivery or by mail, setting forth the manner of service, shall be proof of service.

§ 185.129 Computation of time.

(a) In computing any period of time under this part or in an order issued thereunder, the time begins with the day following the act, event, or default, and includes the last day of the period, unless it is a Saturday, Sunday, or legal holiday observed by the Federal Government, in which event it includes the next business day.

(b) When the period of time allowed is less than 7 days, intermediate Saturdays, Sundays, and legal holidays observed by the Federal Government shall be excluded from the computation.

(c) Where a document has been served or issued by placing it in the mail, an additional 5 days will be added to the time permitted for any response.

§ 185.130 Motions.

(a) Any application to the ALJ for an order or ruling shall be by motion. Motions shall state the relief sought, the authority relied upon, and the facts alleged, and shall be filed with the ALJ and served on all other parties.

(b) Except for motions made during a prehearing conference or at the hearing, all motions shall be in writing. The ALJ may require that oral motions be reduced to writing.

(c) Within 15 days after a written motion is served, or such other time as may be fixed by the ALJ, any party may file a response to such motion.

(d) The ALJ may not grant a written motion before the time for filing responses thereto has expired, except upon consent of the parties or following a hearing on the motion, but may overrule or deny such motion without awaiting a response.

(e) The ALJ shall make a reasonable effort to dispose or all outstanding motions prior to the beginning of the hearing.

§ 185.131 Sanctions.

(a) The ALJ may sanction a person including any party or representative for the following reasons:

(1) Failure to comply with an order, rule, or procedure governing the proceeding;

(2) Failure to prosecute or defend an action; or

(3) Engaging in other misconduct that interferes with the speedy, orderly, or fair conduct of the proceeding.

(b) Any such sanction, including but not limited to those listed in paragraphs (c), (d), and (e) of this section, shall reasonably relate to the severity and nature of the failure or misconduct.

(c) When a party fails to comply with an order, including an order for taking a deposition, the production of evidence within the party's control, or a request for admission, the ALJ may

(1) Draw an inference in favor of the requesting party with regard to the information sought;

(2) In the case of requests for admission, deem each matter of which an admission is requested to be admitted;

(3) Prohibit the party failing to comply with such order from introducing evidence concerning, or otherwise relying upon, testimony relating to the information sought; and

(4) Strike any part of the pleadings or other submissions of the party failing to comply with such request.

(d) If a party fails to prosecute or defend an action under this part commenced by service of a notice of hearing, the ALJ may dismiss the action or may issue an initial decision imposing penalties and assessments.

(e) The ALJ may refuse to consider any motion, request, response, brief or other document which is not filed in a timely fashion.

§ 185.132 The hearing and burden of proof.

(a) Where requested in accordance with § 185.109 the ALJ shall conduct a hearing on the record in order to determine whether the defendant is liable for a civil penalty or assessment under § 185.103 and, if so, the appropriate amount of any such civil penalty or assessment considering any aggravating or mitigating factors.

(b) The authority shall prove defendant's liability and any aggravating factors by a preponderance of the evidence.

(c) The defendant shall prove any affirmative defenses and any mitigating factors by a preponderance of the evidence.

(d) The hearing shall be open to the public unless otherwise closed by the ALJ for good cause shown.

§ 185.133 Determining the amount of penalties and assessments.

(a) In determining an appropriate amount of civil penalties and assessments, the ALJ and the authority head, upon appeal, should evaluate any circumstances that mitigate or aggravate the violation and should articulate in their opinions the reasons that support the penalties and assessments they impose. Because of the intangible costs of fraud, the expense of investigating such conduct, and the need to deter others who might be similarly tempted, double damages and a significant civil penalty ordinarily should be imposed.

(b) Although not exhaustive, the following factors are among those that may influence the ALJ and the authority head in determining the amount of penalties and assessments to impose with respect to the misconduct (*i.e.*, the false, fictitious, or fraudulent claims or statements) charged in the complaint;

(1) The number of false, fictitious or fraudulent claims or statements;

(2) The time period over which such claims or statements were made;

(3) The degree of the defendant's culpability with respect to the misconduct;

(4) The amount of money or the value of the property, services, or benefit falsely claimed;

(5) The value of the Government's actual loss as a result of the misconduct, including foreseeable consequential damages and the costs of investigation;

(6) The relationship of the amount imposed as civil penalties to the amount of the Government's loss;

(7) The potential or actual impact of the misconduct upon public confidence in the management of Government programs and operations;

(8) Whether the defendant has engaged in a pattern of the same or similar misconduct;

(9) Whether the defendant attempted to conceal the misconduct;

(10) The degree to which the defendant has involved others in the misconduct or in concealing it;

(11) Where the misconduct of employees or agents is imputed to the defendant, the extent to which the defendant's practices fostered or attempted to preclude such misconduct;

(12) Whether the defendant cooperated in or obstructed an investigation of the misconduct;

(13) Whether the defendant assisted in identifying and prosecuting other wrongdoers;

(14) The complexity of the program or transaction, and the degree of the defendant's sophistication with respect to it, including the extent of the defendant's prior participation in the program or in similar transactions;

(15) Whether the defendant has been found, in any criminal, civil, or administrative proceeding to have engaged in similar misconduct or to have dealt dishonestly with the Government of the United States or of a State, directly or indirectly;

(16) The need to deter the defendant and others from engaging in the same or similar misconduct; and

(17) The potential impact of the misconduct on the rights of others.

(c) Nothing in this section shall be construed to limit the ALJ or the authority head from considering any other factors that in any given case may mitigate or aggravate the offense for which penalties and assessments are imposed.

§ 185.134 Witnesses.

(a) Except as provided in paragraph (b) of this section, testimony at the hearing shall be given orally by witnesses under oath or affirmation.

(b) At the discretion of the ALJ, testimony may be admitted in the form of a written statement or deposition. Any such written statement must be provided to all others parties along with the last known address of such witness, in a manner which allows sufficient time for other parties to subpoena such witness for cross-examination at the hearing. Prior written statements of witnesses proposed to testify at the hearing and deposition transcripts shall be exchanged as provided in § 185.123(a).

(c) The ALJ shall exercise reasonable control over the mode and order of interrogating witnesses and presenting evidence so as to—

(1) Make the interrogation and presentation effective for the ascertainment of the truth,

(2) Avoid needless consumption of time, and

(3) Protect witnesses from harassment or undue embarrassment.

(d) The ALJ shall permit the parties to conduct such cross-examination as may be required for a full and true disclosure of the facts.

(e) At the discretion of the ALJ, a witness may be cross-examined on matters relevant to the proceedings without regard to the scope of his or her direct examination. To the extent permitted by the ALJ, cross-examination on matters outside the scope of direct examination shall be conducted in the manner of direct examination and may proceed by leading questions only if the witness is a hostile witness, an adverse party, or a witness identified with an adverse party.

(f) Upon motion of any party, the ALJ shall order witnesses excluded so that they cannot hear the testimony of other witnesses. This rule does not authorize exclusion of the following:

(1) A party who is an individual;

(2) In the case of a party that is not an individual, an officer or employee of the party designated by the party's representative; or

(3) An individual whose presence is shown by a party to be essential to the presentation of its case, including an

individual employed by the Government engaged in assisting the representative for the Government.

§ 185.135 The record.

(a) The hearing shall be recorded and transcribed. Transcripts may be obtained following the hearing from the ALJ at a cost not to exceed the actual cost of duplication.

(b) The transcript of testimony, exhibits and other evidence admitted at the hearing, and all papers and requests filed in the proceeding constitute the record for the decision by the ALJ and the authority head.

(c) The record may be inspected and copied (upon payment of a reasonable fee) by anyone, unless otherwise ordered by the ALJ pursuant to § 185.125.

§ 185.136 Post-hearing briefs.

The ALJ may require the parties to file post-hearing briefs. In any event, any party may file a post-hearing brief. The ALJ shall fix the time for filing such briefs, not to exceed 60 days from the date the parties receive the transcript of the hearing or, if applicable, the stipulated record. Such briefs may be accompanied by proposed findings of fact and conclusions of law. The ALJ may permit the parties to file reply briefs.

§ 185.137 Initial decision.

(a) The ALJ shall issue an initial decision based only on the record, which shall contain findings of fact, conclusions of law, and the amount of any penalties and assessments imposed.

(b) The findings of fact shall include a finding on each of the following issues:

(1) Whether the claims or statements identified in the complaint, or any portions thereof, violate § 185.103.

(2) If the person is liable for penalties or assessments, the appropriate amount of any such penalties or assessments considering any mitigating or aggravating factors that he or she finds in the case, such as those described in § 185.133.

(c) The ALJ shall promptly serve the initial decision on all parties within 90 days after the time for submission of post-hearing briefs and reply briefs (if permitted) has expired. The ALJ shall at the same time serve all parties with a statement describing the right of any defendant determined to be liable for a civil penalty or assessment to file a motion for reconsideration with the ALJ or a notice of appeal with the authority head. If the ALJ fails to meet the deadline contained in this paragraph, he or she shall notify the parties of the reason for the delay and shall set a new deadline.

(d) Unless the initial decision of the ALJ is timely appealed to the authority head, or a motion for reconsideration of the initial decision is timely filed, the initial decision shall constitute the final decision of the authority head and shall be final and binding on the parties 30 days after it is issued by the ALJ.

§ 185.138 Reconsideration of initial decision.

(a) Except as provided in paragraph (d) of this section, any party may file a motion for reconsideration of the initial decision within 20 days of receipt of the initial decision. If service was made by mail, receipt will be presumed to be 5 days from the date of mailing in the absence of contrary proof.

(b) Every such motion must set forth the matters claimed to have been erroneously decided and the nature of the alleged errors. Such motion shall be accompanied by a supporting brief.

(c) Responses to such motions shall be allowed only upon request of the ALJ.

(d) No party may file a motion for reconsideration of an initial decision that has been revised in response to a previous motion for reconsideration.

(e) The ALJ may dispose of a motion for reconsideration by denying it or by issuing a revised initial decision.

(f) If the ALJ denies a motion for reconsideration, the initial decision shall constitute the final decision of the authority head and shall be final and binding on all parties 30 days after the ALJ denies the motion, unless the initial decision is timely appealed to the authority head in accordance with § 185.139.

(g) If the ALJ issues a revised initial decision, that decision shall constitute the final decision of the authority head and shall be final and binding on the parties 30 days after it is issued, unless it is timely appealed to the authority head in accordance with § 185.139.

§ 185.139 Appeal to authority head.

(a) Any defendant who has filed a timely answer and who is determined in an initial decision to be liable for a civil penalty or assessment may appeal such decision to the authority head by filing a notice of appeal with the authority head in accordance with this section.

(1) A notice of appeal may be filed at any time within 30 days after the ALJ issues an initial decision. However, if another party files a motion for reconsideration under § 185.138, consideration of the appeal shall be stayed automatically pending resolution of the motion for reconsideration.

(2) If a motion for reconsideration is timely filed, a notice of appeal shall be filed within 30 days after the ALJ denies the motion or issues a revised initial decision, whichever applies.

(3) If no motion for reconsideration is timely filed, a notice of appeal must be filed within 30 days after the ALJ issues the initial decision.

(4) The authority head may extend the initial 30-day period for an additional 30 days if the defendant files with the authority head a request for an extension within the initial 30-day period and shows good cause.

(b) If the defendant files a timely notice of appeal with the authority head and the time for filing motions for reconsideration under § 185.138 has expired, the ALJ shall forward the record of the proceeding to the authority head.

(c) A notice of appeal shall be accompanied by a written brief specifying exceptions to the initial decision and reasons supporting the exceptions.

(d) The representative for OPM may file a brief in opposition to exceptions within 30 days of receiving the notice of appeal and accompanying brief.

(e) There is no right to appear personally before the authority head.

(f) There is no right to appeal an interlocutory ruling by the ALJ.

(g) In reviewing the initial decision, the authority head shall not consider any objection that was not raised before the ALJ unless the objecting party can demonstrate extraordinary circumstances causing the failure to raise the objection.

(h) If any party demonstrates to the satisfaction of the authority head that additional evidence not presented at such hearing is material and that there were reasonable grounds for the failure to present such evidence at such hearing, the authority head shall remand the matter to the ALJ for consideration of such additional evidence.

(i) The authority head may affirm, reduce, reverse, compromise, remand or settle any penalty or assessment determined by the ALJ in any initial decision.

(j) The authority head shall promptly serve each party to the appeal with a copy of the decision of the authority head and a statement describing the right of any person determined to be liable for a penalty or assessment to seek judicial review.

(k) Unless a petition for review is filed as provided in section 3805 of title 31, United States Code, after a defendant has exhausted all administrative remedies under this part and within 60 days after the date on which the authority head serves the defendant with a copy of the authority head's decision, a determination that a defendant is liable under § 185.103 is final and not subject to judicial review.

[60 FR 7891, Feb. 10, 1995; 60 FR 22249, May 5, 1995]

§ 185.140 Stays ordered by the Department of Justice.

If, at any time, the Attorney General or an Assistant Attorney General designated by the Attorney General transmits to the authority head a written finding that continuation of the administrative process described in this part with respect to a claim or statement may adversely affect any pending or potential criminal or civil action related to such claim or statement, the authority head shall stay the process immediately. The authority head may order the process resumed only upon receipt of the written authorization of the Attorney General or of the Assistant Attorney General who ordered the stay.

§ 185.141 Stay pending appeal.

(a) An initial decision is stayed automatically pending disposition of a motion for reconsideration or of an appeal to the authority head.

(b) No administrative stay is available following a final decision of the authority head.

§ 185.142 Judicial review.

Section 3805 of title 31, United States Code, authorizes judicial review by an appropriate United States District Court of a final decision of the authority head imposing penalties and/or assessments under this part and specifies the procedures for such review.

§ 185.143 Collection of civil penalties and assessments.

Sections 3806 and 3808(b) of title 31, United States Code, authorize actions for collection of civil penalties and assessments imposed under this part and specify the procedures for such actions.

§ 185.144 Right to administrative offset.

The amount of any penalty or assessment which has become final, or for which a judgment has been entered under § 185.142 or § 185.143, or any amount agreed upon in a compromise or settlement under § 185.146, may be collected by administrative offset under section 3716 of title 31, United States Code, except that an administrative offset may not be made under section 3716 against a refund of an overpayment of Federal taxes, then or later owing by the United States to the defendant.

§ 185.145 Deposit in Treasury of the United States.

All amounts collected pursuant to this part shall be deposited as miscellaneous receipts in the Treasury of the United States, except as provided in section 3806(g) of title 31, United States Code.

§ 185.146 Compromise or settlement.

(a) Parties may make offers of compromise or settlement at any time.

(b) The reviewing official has the exclusive authority to compromise or settle a case under this part at any time after the date on which the reviewing official is permitted to issue a complaint and before the date on which the ALJ issues an initial decision.

(c) The authority head has exclusive authority to compromise or settle a case under this part at any time after the date on which the ALJ issues an initial decision, except during the pendency of any review under § 185.142 or during the pendency of any action to collect penalties and assessments under § 185.143.

(d) The Attorney General has exclusive authority to compromise or settle a case under this part during the pendency of any review under § 185.142 or of any action to recover penalties and assessments under section 3806 to title 31, United States Code.

(e) The investigating official may recommend settlement terms to the reviewing official, the authority head, or the Attorney General, as appropriate. The reviewing official may recommend settlement terms to the authority head, or the Attorney General, as appropriate.

(f) Any compromise or settlement must be in writing.

§ 185.147 Limitations.

(a) The notice of hearing with respect to a claim or statement must be served in the manner specified in § 185.108 within 6 years after the date on which such a claim or statement is made.

(b) If the defendant fails to file a timely answer, service of a notice under § 185.110(b) shall be deemed a notice of hearing for purposes of this section.

(c) the statute of limitations may be executed by written agreement of the parties.

PART 210—BASIC CONCEPTS AND DEFINITIONS (GENERAL)

Subpart A—Applicability of Regulations; Definitions

AUTHORITY: 5 U.S.C. 1302, 3301, 3302; E.O. 10577, 3 CFR, 1954–1958 Comp. p. 218.

Subpart A—Applicability of Regulations; Definitions

§ 210.101 Applicability of various parts of regulations.

(a) *General.* In most parts, the applicability of the part is stated specifically in the part or is otherwise apparent from the substance of the part.

(b) *Parts 315 through 339.* Parts 315 through 339 of this chapter apply to all positions in the competitive service and to all incumbents of those positions; and, except as specified by or in an individual part, these parts do not apply to positions in the excepted service or to incumbents of those positions.

[33 FR 12407, Sept. 4, 1968, as amended at 44 FR 45587, Aug. 3, 1979]

§ 210.102 Definitions.

(a) The definitions in paragraph (b) of this section apply throughout this chapter, except when a defined term is specifically modified in or specifically defined for the purpose of a particular part.

(b) In this chapter:

(1) *Appointing officer* means a person having power by law, or by lawfully delegated authority, to make appointments to positions in the service of the Federal Government or the government of the District of Columbia.

(2) *OPM* means the Office of Personnel Management.

(3) *Days,* unless otherwise defined or limited, means calendar days and not workdays. In computing a period of time prescribed in this chapter, the day of the action or event after which the designated period of time begins to run is not to be included. The last day of the period so computed is to be included unless it is a Saturday, a Sunday, or a legal holiday in which event the period runs until the end of the next day which is neither a Saturday, a Sunday, nor a legal holiday.

(4) *Demotion* means a change of an employee, while serving continuously within the same agency:

(i) To a lower grade when both the old and the new positions are under the General Schedule or under the same type graded wage schedule; or

(ii) To a position with a lower rate of pay when both the old and the new positions are under the same type ungraded wage schedule, or are in different pay method categories.

(5) *Eligible* means an applicant who meets the minimum requirements for entrance to an examination and is rated 70 or more in the examination by OPM.

(6) *Employee* means a civilian officer or employee.

(7) *Metropolitan area of Washington, DC.,* means the District of Columbia; Alexandria, Fairfax, and Falls Church Cities, Va.; Arlington, Fairfax, Loudoun, and Prince William Counties, Va.; and Charles, Montgomery, and Prince Georges Counties, Md.

(8) *Noncompetitive action* means a promotion, demotion, reassignment, transfer, reinstatement, or an appointment based on prior service.

(9) *Overseas* means outside the continental United States, but does not include Alaska, Guam, Hawaii, the Isthmus of Panama, Puerto Rico, or the Virgin Islands.

(10) *Position change* means a promotion, demotion, or reassignment.

(11) *Promotion* means a change of an employee, while serving continuously within the same agency:

(i) To a higher grade when both the old and the new positions are under the General Schedule or under the same type graded wage schedule; or

(ii) To a position with a higher rate of pay when both the old and the new positions are under the same type ungraded wage schedule, or are in different pay method categories.

(12) *Reassignment* means a change of an employee, while serving continuously within the same agency, from one position to another without promotion or demotion.

(13) *Reemployed annuitant* means an employee whose annuity under subchapter III of chapter 83 of title 5, United States Code, was continued on reemployment in an appointive position on or after October 1, 1956.

(14) *Register* means a list of qualified applicants compiled in order of relative standing for certification.

(15) *Reinstatement* means the noncompetitive reemployment for service as a career or career-conditional employee of a person formerly employed in the competitive service who had a

competitive status or was serving probation when he was separated from the service.

(16) *Status quo employee* means an employee who failed to acquire a competitive status when the position in which he was serving was placed in the competitive service by a statute, Executive order, or Civil Service rule, which permitted his retention without the acquisition of status.

(17) *Tenure* means the period of time an employee may reasonably expect to serve under his current appointment. It is granted and governed by the type of appointment under which an employee is currently serving without regard to whether he has a competitive status or whether his appointment is in a competitive position or in an excepted position.

(18) *Transfer* means a change of an employee, without a break in service of 1 full workday, from a position in one agency to a position in another agency.

[33 FR 12407, Sept. 4, 1968, as amended at 34 FR 19495, Dec. 10, 1969; 38 FR 22535, Aug. 22, 1973]

PART 211—VETERAN PREFERENCE

Sec.

AUTHORITY: 5 U.S.C. 1302, 2108, 2108a.

SOURCE: 81 FR 83109, Nov. 21, 2016, unless otherwise noted.

§ 211.101 Purpose.

The purpose of this part is to define veterans' preference and the administration of preference in Federal employment. (5 U.S.C. 2108, 2108a)

§ 211.102 Definitions.

For the purposes of preference in Federal employment, the following definitions apply:

(a) *Veteran* means a person who has been discharged or released from active duty in the armed forces under honorable conditions, or who has a certification as defined in paragraph (h) of this section, if the active duty service was performed:

(1) In a war;

(2) In a campaign or expedition for which a campaign badge has been authorized;

(3) During the period beginning April 28, 1952, and ending July 1, 1955;

(4) For more than 180 consecutive days, other than for training, any part of which occurred during the period beginning February 1, 1955, and ending October 14, 1976;

(5) During the period beginning August 2, 1990, and ending January 2, 1992; or

(6) For more than 180 consecutive days, other than for training, any part of which occurred during the period beginning September 11, 2001, and ending on August 31, 2010, the last day of Operation Iraqi Freedom.

(b) *Disabled veteran* means a person who has been discharged or released from active duty in the armed forces under honorable conditions performed at any time, or who has a certification as defined in paragraph (h) of this section, and who has established the present existence of a service-connected disability or is receiving compensation, disability retirement benefits, or a pension because of a statute administered by the Department of Veterans Affairs or a military department.

(c) *Sole survivor veteran* means a person who was discharged or released from a period of active duty after August 29, 2008, by reason of a sole survivorship discharge (as that term is defined in 10 U.S.C. 1174(i)), and who meets the definition of a "veteran" in paragraph (a) of this section, with the exception that he or she is not required to meet any of the length of service requirements prescribed by paragraph (a).

(d) *Preference eligible* means a veteran, disabled veteran, sole survivor veteran, spouse, widow, widower, or parent who meets the definition of "preference eligible" in 5 U.S.C. 2108.

(1) Preference eligibles other than sole survivor veterans are entitled to have 5 or 10 points added to their earned score on a civil service examination in accordance with 5 U.S.C. 3309.

(2) Under numerical ranking and selection procedures for competitive service hiring, preference eligibles are

entered on registers in the order prescribed by § 332.401 of this chapter.

(3) Under excepted service examining procedures in part 302 of this chapter, preference eligibles are listed ahead of persons with the same ratings who are not preference eligibles, or listed ahead of non-preference eligibles if numerical scores have not been assigned.

(4) Under alternative ranking and selection procedures, *i.e.*, category rating, preference eligibles are listed ahead of individuals who are not preference eligibles in accordance with 5 U.S.C. 3319.

(5) Preference eligibles, other than those who have not yet been discharged or released from active duty, are accorded a higher retention standing than non-preference eligibles in the event of a reduction in force in accordance with 5 U.S.C. 3502.

(6) Veterans' preference does not apply, however, to inservice placement actions such as promotions.

(e) *Armed forces* means the United States Army, Navy, Air Force, Marine Corps, and Coast Guard.

(f) *Active duty* or *active military duty:*

(1) For veterans defined in paragraphs (a)(1) through (3) and disabled veterans defined in paragraph (b) of this section, means active duty with military pay and allowances in the armed forces, and includes training, determining physical fitness, and service in the Reserves or National Guard; and

(2) For veterans defined in paragraphs (a)(4) through (6) of this section, means full-time duty with military pay and allowances in the armed forces, and does not include training, determining physical fitness, or service in the Reserves or National Guard.

(g) *Discharged* or *released from active duty* means with either an honorable or general discharge from active duty in the armed forces. The Department of Defense is responsible for administering and defining military discharges.

(h) *Certification* means any written document from the armed forces that certifies the service member is expected to be discharged or released from active duty service in the armed forces under honorable conditions not later than 120 days after the date the certification is submitted for consideration in the hiring process, at the time and in the manner prescribed by the applicable job opportunity announcement. Prior to appointment, the service member's character of service and qualifying discharge or release must be verified through a DD form 214 or equivalent documentation.

[81 FR 83109, Nov. 21, 2016, as amended at 81 FR 94909, Dec. 27, 2016]

§ 211.103 Administration of preference.

Agencies are responsible for making all preference determinations except for preference based on a common law marriage. Such a claim must be referred to OPM's General Counsel for decision.

PART 212—COMPETITIVE SERVICE AND COMPETITIVE STATUS

AUTHORITY: 5 U.S.C. 1302, 3301, 3302; E.O. 10577, 3 CFR, 1954–1958 Comp., p. 218.

SOURCE: 33 FR 12408, Sept. 4, 1968, unless otherwise noted.

Subpart A—Competitive Service

§ 212.101 Definitions.

In this chapter:

(a) *Competitive service* has the meaning given that term by section 2102 of title 5, United States Code, and includes:

(1) All civilian positions in the executive branch of the Federal Government not specifically excepted from the civil service laws by or pursuant to statute, by the President, or by the Office of Personnel Management, and not in the Senior Executive Service; and

(2) All positions in the legislative and judicial branches of the Federal Government and in the government of the District of Columbia specifically made subject to the civil service laws by statute.

(b) *Competitive position* means a position in the competitive service.

(5 U.S.C. 2102)

[33 FR 12408, Sept. 4, 1968, as amended at 45 FR 62413, Sept. 19, 1980]

§ 212.102 Authority to make determinations.

OPM determines finally whether a position is in the competitive service.

Subpart B [Reserved]

Subpart C—Competitive Status

§ 212.301 Competitive status defined.

In this chapter, competitive status means an individual's basic eligibility for noncompetitive assignment to a competitive position. Competitive status is acquired by completion of a probationary period under a career-conditional or career appointment, or under a career executive assignment in the former executive assignment system, following open competitive examination, or by statute, Executive order, or the Civil Service rules, without open competitive examination. An individual with competitive status may be, without open competitive examination, reinstated, transferred, promoted, reassigned, or demoted, subject to conditions prescribed by the Civil Service rules and regulations.

[33 FR 12408, Sept. 4, 1968, as amended at 57 FR 10123, Mar. 24, 1992]

Subpart D—Effect of Competitive Status on Position

§ 212.401 Effect of competitive status on position.

(a) An employee is in the competitive service when he has competitive status and is in a competitive position under a nontemporary appointment.

(b) An employee in the competitive service at the time his position is first listed under Schedule A, B, or C remains in the competitive service while he occupies that position.

PART 213—EXCEPTED SERVICE

Subpart A—General Provisions

Subpart B [Reserved]

Subpart C—Excepted Schedules

SCHEDULE A

SCHEDULE B

SCHEDULE C

SCHEDULE D

AUTHORITY: 5 U.S.C. 3161, 3301 and 3302; E.O. 10577, 3 CFR 1954–1958 Comp., p. 218; Sec. 213.101 also issued under 5 U.S.C. 2103. Sec. 213.3102 also issued under 5 U.S.C. 3301, 3302, 3307, 8337(h), and 8456; E.O. 13318, 3 CFR 1982 Comp., p. 185; 38 U.S.C. 4301 *et seq.;* Pub. L. 105–339, 112 Stat 3182–83; E.O. 13162; E.O. 12125, 3 CFR 1979 Comp., p. 16879; and E.O. 13124, 3 CFR 1999 Comp., p. 31103; and Presidential Memorandum—Improving the Federal Recruitment and Hiring Process (May 11, 2010).

Sec. 213.101 also issued under 5 U.S.C. 2103.

Sec. 213.3102 also issued under 5 U.S.C. 3301, 3302, 3307, 8337(h), and 8456; 38 U.S.C. 4301 *et seq.*; and Pub. L. 105–339, 112 Stat. 3182–83.

SOURCE: 46 FR 20147, Apr. 3, 1981, unless otherwise noted.

Subpart A—General Provisions

§ 213.101 Definitions.

In this chapter:

(a) Excepted service has the meaning given that term by section 2103 of title 5, United States Code, and includes all positions in the executive branch of the Federal Government which are specifically excepted from the competitive service by or pursuant to statute, by the President, or by the Office of Personnel Management, and which are not in the Senior Executive Service.

(b) *Excepted position* means a position in the excepted service.

(5 U.S.C. 2103)

§ 213.102 Identification of positions in Schedule A, B, C, or D.

(a) As provided in 5 U.S.C. 3302, the President may prescribe rules governing the competitive service. The rules shall provide, as nearly as conditions of good administration warrant, for—

(1) Necessary exceptions of positions from the competitive service; and

(2) Necessary exceptions from the provisions of sections 2951, 3304(a), 3321, 7202, and 7203 of title 5, U.S. Code.

(b) The President delegated authority to the Office of Personnel Management (OPM) in Civil Service Rule VI to except positions from the competitive service when OPM determines that:

(1) Appointments thereto through competitive examination are not practicable; or

(2) Recruitment from among students attending qualifying educational institutions or individuals who have recently completed qualifying educational programs can better be achieved by devising additional means for recruiting and assessing candidates that diverge from the processes generally applicable to the competitive service.

(3)(i) Upon determining that any position or group of positions, as defined in § 302.101(c), should be excepted indefinitely or temporarily from the competitive service, the Office of Personnel Management will authorize placement of the position or group of positions into Schedule A, B, C, or D, as applicable. Unless otherwise specified in a particular appointing authority, an agency may make Schedule A, B, C, or D appointments on either a permanent or nonpermanent basis, with any appropriate work schedule (*i.e.*, full-time, part-time, seasonal, on-call, or intermittent).

(ii) When OPM establishes eligibility requirements (e.g., residence, family income) for appointment under particular Schedule A, B, or D exceptions, an individual's eligibility for appointment must be determined before appointment and without regard to any conditions that will result from the appointment.

(c) For purposes of making any such determinations, *positions* includes:

(1) Those that are intended to be removed indefinitely from the competitive service because the nature of the position itself precludes it from being in the competitive service (e.g., because it is impracticable to examine for the knowledge, skills, and abilities required for the job); and

(2) Those that are intended to be removed temporarily from the competitive service to allow for targeted recruiting and hiring from among a particular class of persons, as defined by the Office of Personnel Management, with the opportunity for the persons selected for those positions to convert to the competitive service at a later date.

[77 FR 28213, May 11, 2012]

§ 213.103 Publication of excepted appointing authorities in Schedules A, B, C, and D.

(a) Schedule A, B, C, and D appointing authorities available for use by all agencies will be published as regulations in the FEDERAL REGISTER and the Code of Federal Regulations.

(b) Establishment and revocation of Schedule A, B, and C appointing authorities applicable to a single agency shall be published monthly in the Notices section of the FEDERAL REGISTER.

(c) A consolidated listing of all Schedule A, B, and C authorities current as of June 30 of each year, with assigned authority numbers, shall be published annually as a notice in the FEDERAL REGISTER.

[47 FR 28902, July 2, 1982, as amended at 62 FR 18505, Apr. 16, 1997; 77 FR 28213, May 11, 2012]

§ 213.104 Special provisions for temporary, time-limited, intermittent, or seasonal appointments in Schedule A, B, C, or D.

(a) When OPM specifies that appointments under a particular Schedule A, B, C, or D authority must be temporary, intermittent, or seasonal, or when agencies elect to make temporary, intermittent, or seasonal appointments in Schedule A, B, C, or D, those terms have the following meaning:

(1) *Temporary appointments,* unless otherwise specified in a particular Schedule A, B, C, or D exception, are made for a specified period not to exceed 1 year and are subject to the time limits in paragraph (b) of this section. Time-limited appointments made for more than 1 year are not considered to be temporary appointments, and are not subject to these time limits.

(2) *Intermittent positions* are positions in which work recurs at sporadic or irregular intervals so that an employee's tour of duty cannot be scheduled in advance of the administrative workweek.

(3) *Seasonal positions* involve annually recurring periods of employment lasting less than 12 months each year.

(b) Temporary appointments, as defined in paragraph (a)(1) of this section, are subject to the following limits:

(1) *Service limits.* Agencies may make temporary appointments for a period not to exceed 1 year, unless the applicable Schedule A, B, C, or D authority specifies a shorter period. Except as provided in paragraph (b)(3) of this section, agencies may extend temporary appointments for no more than 1 additional year (24 months of total service). Appointment to a successor position (*i.e.,* a position that replaces and absorbs the original position) is considered to be an extension of the original appointment. Appointment to a position involving the same basic duties, in the same major subdivision of the agency, and in the same local commuting area is also considered to be an extension of the original appointment.

(2) *Restrictions on refilling positions under temporary appointments.* Except as provided in paragraph (b)(3) of this section, an agency may not fill any position (or its successor) by a temporary appointment in Schedule A, B, C, or D if that position had previously been filled by temporary appointment(s) in either the competitive or excepted service for an aggregate of 2 years, or 24 months, within the preceding 3-year period. This limitation does not apply to programs established to provide for systematic exchange between a Federal agency and non-Federal organizations.

(3) *Exceptions to the general limits.* The service limits and restrictions on refilling positions set out in this section do not apply when:

(i) Positions involve intermittent or seasonal work, and employment in the same or a successor position under one or more appointing authorities totals less than 6 months (1,040 hours), excluding overtime, in a service year. The service year is the calendar year that begins on the date of the employee's initial appointment in the agency. Should employment in a position filled under this exception total 6 months or more in any service year, the general limits set out in this section will apply to subsequent extension or reappointment unless OPM approves continued exception under this section. An individual may be employed for training for up to 120 days following initial appointment and up to 2 weeks a year thereafter without regard to the service year limitation.

(ii) Positions are filled under an authority established for the purpose of enabling the appointees to continue or enhance their education, or to meet academic or professional qualification requirements. These include the authorities set out in paragraphs (r) and (s) of § 213.3102 and paragraphs (a), (b), and (c) of § 213.3402, and authorities granted to individual agencies for use in connection with internship, fellowship, residency, or student programs.

(iii) OPM approves extension of specific temporary appointments beyond 2 years (24 months total service) when necessitated by major reorganizations or base closings or other rare and unusual circumstances. Requests based on major reorganization, base closing, restructuring, or other unusual circumstances that apply agencywide must be made by an official at the headquarters level of the Department or agency. Requests involving extension of appointments to a specific position or project based on other unusual circumstances may be submitted by the employing office to the appropriate OPM service center.

[59 FR 46897, Sept. 13, 1994, as amended at 59 FR 64841, Dec. 16, 1994; 62 FR 18505, Apr. 16, 1997; 62 FR 55725, Oct. 28, 1997; 62 FR 63628, Dec. 2, 1997; 77 FR 28213, May 11, 2012]

Subpart B [Reserved]

Subpart C—Excepted Schedules

SCHEDULE A

§ 213.3101 Positions other than those of a confidential or policy-determining character for which it is impracticable to examine.

Upon specific authorization by OPM, agencies may make appointments under this section to positions which are not of a confidential or policy-determining character, and which are not in the Senior Executive Service, for which it is not practicable to examine. Examining for this purpose means application of the qualification standards and requirements established for the competitive service. Positions filled under this authority are excepted from the competitive service and constitute Schedule A. For each authorization under this section, OPM shall assign an identifying number from 213.3102 through 213.3199 to be used by the appointing agency in recording appointments made under that authorization.

[46 FR 20147, Apr. 3, 1981, as amended at 46 FR 45323, Sept. 11, 1981, 59 FR 64841, Dec. 16, 1994; 62 FR 19900, Apr. 24, 1997]

§ 213.3102 Entire executive civil service.

(a) Positions of Chaplain and Chaplain's Assistant.

(b) [Reserved]

(c) Positions to which appointments are made by the President without confirmation by the Senate.

(d) Attorneys.

(e) Law clerk trainee positions. Appointments under this paragraph shall be confined to graduates of recognized law schools or persons having equivalent experience and shall be for periods not to exceed 14 months pending admission to the bar. No person shall be given more than one appointment under this paragraph. However, an appointment which was initially made for less than 14 months may be extended for not to exceed 14 months in total duration.

(f)–(h) [Reserved]

(i) Temporary and less-than-full time positions for which examining is impracticable. These are:

(1) Positions in remote/isolated locations where examination is impracticable. A remote/isolated location is outside the local commuting area of a population center from which an employee can reasonably be expected to travel on short notice under adverse weather and/or road conditions which are normal for the area. For this purpose, a population center is a town with housing, schools, health care, stores and other businesses in which the servicing examining office can schedule tests and/or reasonably expect to attract applicants. An individual appointed under this authority may not be employed in the same agency under a combination of this and any other appointment to positions involving related duties and requiring the same qualifications for more than 1,040 workings hour in a service year. Temporary appointments under this authority may be extended in 1-year increments, with no limit on the number of such extensions, as an exception to the service limits in § 213.104.

(2) Positions for which a critical hiring need exists. This includes both short-term positions and continuing positions that an agency must fill on an interim basis pending completion of competitive examining, clearances, or other procedures required for a longer appointment. Appointments under this authority may not exceed 30 days and may be extended for up to an additional 30 days if continued employment

is essential to the agency's operations. The appointments may not be used to extend the service limit of any other appointing authority. An agency may not employ the same individual under this authority for more than 60 days in any 12-month period.

(3) Other positions for which OPM determines that examining is impracticable.

(j) Positions filled by current or former Federal employees eligible for placement under special statutory provisions. Appointments under this authority are subject to the following conditions.

(1) *Eligible employees.* (i) Persons previously employed as National Guard Technicians under 32 U.S.C. 709(a) who are entitled to placement under §353.110 of this chapter, or who are applying for or receiving an annuity under the provisions of 5 U.S.C. 8337(h) or 8456 by reason of a disability that disqualifies them from membership in the National Guard or from holding the military grade required as a condition of their National Guard employment.

(ii) Executive branch employees (other than employees of intelligence agencies) who are entitled to placement under §353.110 but who are not eligible for reinstatement or noncompetitive appointment under the provisions of part 315 of this chapter.

(iii) Legislative and judicial branch employees and employees of the intelligence agencies defined in 5 U.S.C. 2302(a)(2)(C)(ii) who are entitled to placement under §353.110.

(2) *Employees excluded.* Employees who were last employed in Schedule C or under a statutory authority that specified the employee served at the discretion, will, or pleasure of the agency are not eligible for appointment under this authority.

(3) *Position to which appointed.* Employees who are entitled to placement under §353.110 will be appointed to a position that OPM determines is equivalent in pay and grade to the one the individual left, unless the individual elects to be placed in a position of lower grade or pay. National Guard Technicians whose eligibility is based upon a disability may be appointed at the same grade, or equivalent, as their National Guard Technician position or at any lower grade for which they are available.

(4) *Conditions of appointment.* (i) Individuals whose placement eligibility is based on an appointment without time limit will receive appointments without time limit under this authority. These appointees may be reassigned, promoted, or demoted to any position within the same agency for which they qualify.

(ii) Individuals who are eligible for placement under §353.110 based on a time-limited appointment will be given appointments for a time period equal to the unexpired portion of their previous appointment.

(k) Positions without compensation provided appointments thereto meet the requirements of applicable laws relating to compensation.

(l) Positions requiring the temporary or intermittent employment of professional, scientific, or technical experts for consultation purposes.

(m) [Reserved]

(n) Any local physician, surgeon, or dentist employed under contract or on a part-time or fee basis.

(o) Positions of a scientific, professional, or analytical nature when filled by bona fide members of the faculty of an accredited college or university who have special qualifications for the positions to which appointed. Employment under this provision shall not exceed 130 working days a year.

(p)–(q) [Reserved]

(r) Positions established in support of fellowship and similar programs that are filled from limited applicant pools and operate under specific criteria developed by the employing agency and/or a non-Federal organization. These programs may include: internship or fellowship programs that provide developmental or professional experiences to individuals who have completed their formal education; training and associateship programs designed to increase the pool of qualified candidates in a particular occupational specialty; professional/industry exchange programs that provide for a cross-fertilization between the agency and the private sector to foster mutual understanding, an exchange of ideas, or to bring experienced practitioners to the agency; residency programs through which participants gain experience in a Federal clinical environment; and programs that require a period of Government service in exchange for educational, financial or other assistance. Appointments under this authority may not exceed 4 years.

(s) Positions with compensation fixed under 5 U.S.C. 5351–5356 when filled by student-employees assigned or attached to Government hospitals, clinics or medical or dental laboratories. Employment under this authority may not exceed 4 years.

(t) [Reserved]

(u) *Appointment of persons with intellectual disabilities, severe physical disabilities, or psychiatric disabilities*—(1) *Purpose.* An agency may appoint, on a permanent, time-limited, or temporary basis, a person with an intellectual disability, a severe physical disability, or a psychiatric disability according to the provisions described below.

(2) *Definition.* "Intellectual disabilities" means only those disabilities that would have been encompassed by the term "mental retardation" in previous iterations of this regulation and the associated Executive order, Executive Order 12125, dated March 15, 1979.

(3) *Proof of disability.* (i) An agency must require proof of an applicant's intellectual disability, severe physical disability, or psychiatric disability prior to making an appointment under this section.

(ii) An agency may accept, as proof of disability, appropriate documentation (e.g., records, statements, or other appropriate information) issued by a licensed medical professional (e.g., a physician or other medical professional duly certified by a State, the District of Columbia, or a U.S. territory, to practice medicine); a licensed vocational rehabilitation specialist (State or private); or any Federal agency, State agency, or an agency of the District of Columbia or a U.S. territory that issues or provides disability benefits.

(4) *Permanent or time-limited employment options.* An agency may make permanent or time-limited appointments under this paragraph (u)(4) where an applicant supplies proof of disability as described in paragraph (u)(3) of this section and the agency determines that the individual is likely to succeed in the performance of the duties of the position for which he or she is applying. In determining whether the individual is likely to succeed in performing the duties of the position, the agency may rely upon the applicant's employment, educational, or other relevant experience, including but not limited to service under another type of appointment in the competitive or excepted services.

(5) *Temporary employment options.* An agency may make a temporary appointment when:

(i) The agency determines that it is necessary to observe the applicant on the job to determine whether the applicant is able or ready to perform the duties of the position. When an agency uses this option to determine an individual's job readiness, the hiring agency may convert the individual to a permanent appointment in the excepted service whenever the agency determines the individual is able to perform the duties of the position; or

(ii) The work is of a temporary nature.

(6) *Noncompetitive conversion to the competitive service.* (i) An agency may noncompetitively convert to the competitive service an employee who has completed 2 years of satisfactory service under this authority in accordance with the provisions of Executive Order 12125, as amended by Executive Order 13124, and § 315.709 of this chapter, except as provided in paragraph (u)(6)(ii) of this section.

(ii) Time spent on a temporary appointment specified in paragraph (u)(5)(ii) of this section does not count towards the 2-year requirement.

(v)–(w) [Reserved]

(x) Positions for which a local recruiting shortage exists when filled by inmates of Federal, District of Columbia and State (including the Commonwealth of Puerto Rico, the Virgin Islands, Guam, American Samoa, and the Trust Territory of the Pacific Islands) penal and correctional institutions under work-release programs authorized by the Prisoner Rehabilitation Act of 1965, the District of Columbia Work Release Act, or under work-release programs authorized by the States. Initial appointments under the authority may not exceed 1 year. An initial appointment may be extended for one or more periods not to exceed 1 additional year each upon a finding that the inmate is still in a work-release status and that a local recruiting shortage still exists. No person may serve under this authority longer than 1-year beyond the date of that person's release from custody.

(y) [Reserved]

(z) Not to exceed 30 positions of assistants to top-level Federal officials when filled by persons designated by the President as White House Fellows.

(aa) Scientific and professional research associate positions at GS–11 and above when filled on a temporary basis by persons having a doctoral degree in an appropriate field of study for research activities of mutual interest to appointees and their agencies. Appointments are limited to persons referred by the National Research Council under its post-doctoral research associate program, may not exceed 2 years, and are subject to satisfactory outcome of evaluation of the associate's research during the first year.

(bb) Positions when filled by aliens in the absence of qualified citizens. Appointments under this authority are subject to prior approval of the Office except when the authority is specifically included in a delegated examining agreement with the Office.

(cc)–(ee) [Reserved]

(ff) Not to exceed 24 positions when filled in accordance with an agreement between OPM and the Department of Justice by persons in programs administered by the Attorney General of the United States under Public Law 91–452 and related statutes. A person appointed under this authority may continue to be employed under it after he ceases to be in a qualifying program only as long as he remains in the same agency without a break in service.

(gg)–(kk) [Reserved]

(ll) Positions as needed of readers for blind employees, interpreters for deaf employees and personal assistants for handicapped employees, filled on a full time, part-time, or intermittent basis.

(5 U.S.C. 3301, 3307, 8337(h); 5 U.S.C. 3301, 3302; E.O. 12364, 47 FR 22931)

[47 FR 28902, July 2, 1982]

EDITORIAL NOTE: For FEDERAL REGISTER citations affecting § 213.3102, see the List of CFR Sections Affected, which appears in the Finding Aids section of the printed volume and at *www.fdsys.gov*.

§ 213.3199 Temporary organizations.

Positions on the staffs of temporary organizations, as defined in 5 U.S.C. 3161(a). Appointments may not exceed 3 years, but temporary organizations may extend the appointments for 2 additional years if the conditions for extension are related to the completion of the study or project.

[68 FR 24605, May 8, 2003]

SCHEDULE B

§ 213.3201 Positions other than those of a confidential or policy-determining character for which it is not practicable to hold a competitive examination.

(a) Upon specific authorization by OPM, agencies may make appointments under this section to positions which are not of a confidential or policy-determining character, and which are not in the Senior Executive Service, for which it is impracticable to hold open competition or to apply usual competitive examining procedures. Appointments under this authority are subject to the basic qualification standards established by the Office of Personnel Management for the occupation and grade level. Positions filled under this authority are excepted from the competitive service and constitute Schedule B. For each authorization under this section, OPM shall assign a number from 213.3202 through 213.3299 to be used by the appointing agency in recording appointments made under that authorization.

(b) [Reserved]

[46 FR 20147, Apr. 3, 1981, as amended at 47 FR 57655, Dec. 28, 1982; 53 FR 15353, Apr. 29, 1988]

§ 213.3202 Entire executive civil service.

(a)–(i) [Reserved]

(j) Special executive development positions established in connection with Senior Executive Service candidate development programs which have been approved by OPM. A Federal agency may make new appointments under this authority for any period of employment not exceeding 3 years for one individual.

(k)–(l) [Reserved]

(m) Positions when filed under any of the following conditions:

(1) Appointment at grades GS–15 and above, or equivalent, in the same or a different agency without a break in service from a career appointment in the Senior Executive Service (SES) of an individual who:

(i) Has completed the SES probationary period;

(ii) Has been removed from the SES because of less than fully successful executive performance, failure to be recertified, or a reduction in force; and

(iii) Is entitled to be placed in another civil service position under 5 U.S.C. 3594(b).

(2) Appointment in a different agency without a break in service of an individual originally appointed under paragraph (m)(1).

(3) Reassignment, promotion, or demotion within the same agency of an individual appointed under this authority.

(n) Positions when filled by preference eligibles or veterans who have been separated from the armed forces under honorable conditions after 3 years or more of continuous active military service and who, in accordance with the provisions of Pub.L. 105–339, applied for these positions under merit promotion procedures when applications were being accepted from individuals outside its own workforce. These veterans may be promoted, demoted, or reassigned, as appropriate, to other positions within the agency but would remain employed under this excepted authority as long as there is no break in service. No new appointments may be made under this authority after November 30, 1999.

(o) [Reserved]

[47 FR 28904, July 2, 1982]

EDITORIAL NOTE: For FEDERAL REGISTER citations affecting § 213.3202, see the List of CFR Sections Affected, which appears in the Finding Aids section of the printed volume and at *www.fdsys.gov*.

SCHEDULE C

§ 213.3301 Positions of a confidential or policy-determining nature.

(a) Upon specific authorization by OPM, agencies may make appointments under this section to positions which are policy-determining or which involve a close and confidential working relationship with the head of an agency or other key appointed officials. Positions filled under this authority are excepted from the competitive service and constitute Schedule C. Each position will be assigned a number from § 213.3302 to § 213.3999, or other appropriate number, to be used by the agency in recording appointments made under that authorization.

(b) When requesting Schedule C exception, agencies must submit to OPM a statement signed by the agency head certifying that the position was not created solely or primarily for the purpose of detailing the incumbent to the White House.

(c) The exception from the competitive service for each position listed in Schedule C by OPM is revoked immediately upon the position becoming vacant. An agency shall notify OPM within 3 working days after a Schedule C position has been vacated.

[60 FR 35120, July 6, 1995]

§ 213.3302 Temporary transitional Schedule C positions.

(a) An agency may establish temporary transitional Schedule C positions necessary to assist a department or agency head during the 1-year period immediately following a change in presidential administration, when a new department or agency head has entered on duty, or when a new department or agency is created. These positions may be established only to meet legitimate needs of the agency in carrying out its mission during the period of transition associated with such changeovers. They must be of a confidential or policy-determining character and are subject to instructions issued by OPM.

(b) The number of temporary transitional Schedule C positions established by an agency cannot exceed either 50 percent of the highest number of permanent Schedule C positions filled by that agency at any time over the previous 5 years, or three positions, whichever is higher. In the event a new department or agency is created, the number of temporary transitional positions should reasonable in light of the size and program responsibility of that department or agency. OPM may approve an increase in an agency's quota to meet a critical need or in unusual circumstances.

(c) Individual appointments under this authority may be made for 120 days, with one extension of an additional 120 days. They may be deemed provisional appointments for purposes of the regulations set out in parts 351, 831, 842, 870, and 890 of this chapter if they meet the criteria set out in §§ 316.401 and 316.403 of this chapter.

(d) An agency shall notify OPM within 5 working days after a temporary transitional Schedule C position has been encumbered and within 3 working days when it has been vacated. The agency must also submit to OPM a statement signed by the agency head certifying that the position was not created solely or primarily for the purpose of detailing the incumbent to the White House.

[60 FR 35120, July 6, 1995]

SCHEDULE D

SOURCE: 77 FR 28213, May 11, 2012, unless otherwise noted.

§ 213.3401 Positions other than those of a confidential or policy determining character for which the competitive service requirements make impracticable the adequate recruitment of sufficient numbers of students attending qualifying educational institutions or individuals who have recently completed qualifying educational programs.

As authorized by OPM, agencies may make appointments under this section to positions other than those of a confidential or policy-determining character for which the competitive service requirements make impracticable the adequate recruitment and selection of sufficient numbers of students attending qualifying educational institutions or individuals who have recently completed qualifying educational programs. These positions, which may be filled in the excepted service to enable more effective recruitment from all segments of society by using means of recruiting and assessing candidates that diverge from the rules generally applicable to the competitive service, constitute Schedule D Pathways Programs. Appointments under this authority are subject to the basic qualification standards established by the Office of Personnel Management for the occupation and grade level unless otherwise stated.

§ 213.3402 Entire executive civil service; Pathways Programs.

(a) *Internship Program; Positions in the Internship Program.* Agencies may make initial appointments of Interns under this authority at any grade level, depending on the candidates' qualifications. Appointments must be made in accordance with the provisions of subpart B of part 362 of this chapter.

(b) *Recent Graduates Program; Positions in the Recent Graduates Program.* (1) Agencies may make initial appointments of Recent Graduates at any grade level, not to exceed GS–09 (or equivalent level under another pay and classification system, including the Federal Wage System (FWS)), depending on the candidates' qualifications, and the position's requirements except that:

(i) Initial appointments to positions for science, technology, engineering, or mathematics (STEM) occupations may be made at the GS–11 level, if the candidate possesses a Ph.D. or equivalent degree directly related to the STEM position the agency is seeking to fill.

(ii) Initial appointments to scientific and professional research positions at the GS–11 level for which the classification and qualification criteria for research positions apply, if the candidate possesses a master's degree or equivalent graduate degree directly related to the position the agency is seeking to fill.

(iii) Initial appointments to scientific and professional research positions at the GS–12 level for which the classification and qualification criteria for research positions apply, if the candidate possesses a Ph.D. or equivalent degree directly related to the position the agency is seeking to fill.

(2) Appointments must be made in accordance with the provisions of subpart C of part 362 of this chapter.

(c) *Presidential Management Fellows Program.* Positions in the Presidential Management Fellows Program. Appointments under this authority may not exceed 2 years except as provided in subpart D of part 362 of this chapter. Agencies may make initial appointments of Fellows at the GS–09, GS–11, or GS–12 level (or equivalent under another pay and classification system such as the FWS), depending on the candidates' qualifications and the positions' requirements. Appointments must be made in accordance with the provisions of subpart D of part 362 of this chapter.

PART 214—SENIOR EXECUTIVE SERVICE

Subpart A [Reserved]

Subpart B—General Provisions

Subpart C—Exclusions

Subpart D—Types of Positions

AUTHORITY: 5 U.S.C. 3132.

SOURCE: 45 FR 62414, Sept. 19, 1980, unless otherwise noted.

Subpart A [Reserved]

Subpart B—General Provisions

§ 214.201 Definitions.

For the purposes of this part:

Agency, Senior Executive Service position, career appointee, limited term appointee, limited emergency appointee, and *noncareer appointee* have the meanings set forth in section 3132(a) of title 5, United States Code.

Equivalent position as used in section 3132(a)(2) of title 5, United States Code, means a position under any pay system where the level of the duties and responsibilities of the position and the rate of pay are comparable to that of a position above GS–15 or at Executive Level IV or V.

Senior Executive Service has the meaning given that term by section 2101a of title 5, United States Code, and includes all positions which meet the definition in section 3132(a)(2) of title 5.

[45 FR 62414, Sept. 19, 1980, as amended at 56 FR 18661, Apr. 23, 1991]

§ 214.202 Authority to make determinations.

(a) Each agency is responsible for determining, in accordance with Office of Personnel Management guidelines, which of its positions should be included in the Senior Executive Service.

(b) Agency determinations may be reviewed by the Office of Personnel Management to ensure adherence with law and regulation.

§ 214.203 Reporting requirements.

Agencies shall report such information as may be requested by OPM relating to positions and employees in the Senior Executive Service.

[60 FR 6385, Feb. 2, 1995]

§ 214.204 Interchange agreements.

(a) In accordance with 5 CFR 6.7, OPM and any agency with an executive personnel system essentially equivalent to the Senior Executive Service (SES) may, pursuant to legislative and regulatory authorities, enter into an agreement providing for the movement of persons between the SES and the other system. The agreement shall define the status and tenure that the persons affected shall acquire upon the movement.

(b) Persons eligible for movement must be serving in permanent, continuing positions with career or career-type appointments. They must meet the qualifications requirements of any position to which moved.

(c) An interchange agreement may be discontinued by either party under such conditions as provided in the agreement.

[60 FR 6385, Feb. 2, 1995]

Subpart C—Exclusions

§214.301 Exclusions.

If not excluded from the Senior Executive Service by section 3132(a) (1) or (2) of title 5, United States Code, an agency, or unit thereof, may be excluded only under the provisions of section 3132 (c) through (f) of title 5.

Subpart D—Types of Positions

§214.401 Types of positions.

There are two types of positions in the Senior Executive Service:

(a) General positions, which may be filled by a career, noncareer, limited emergency, or limited term appointee.

(b) Career reserved positions, which may be filled only by a career appointee.

§214.402 Career reserved positions.

(a) The head of each agency is responsible for designating career reserved positions in accordance with the regulations in this section.

(b) A position shall be designated as a career reserved position if:

(1) The position (except a position in the Executive Office of the President):

(i) Was under the Executive Schedule, or the rate of basic pay was determined by reference to the Executive Schedule, on October 12, 1978;

(ii) Was specifically required under section 2102 of title 5, United States Code, or otherwise required by law to be in the competitive service; and

(iii) Entailed direct responsibility to the public for the management or operation of particular government programs or functions; or

(2) The position must be filled by a career appointee to ensure impartiality, or the public's confidence in the impartiality, of the Government.

(c) The head of an agency shall use the following criteria in determining whether paragraph (b)(2) of this section is applicable to an individual position:

(1) Career reserved positions include positions the principal duties of which involve day-to-day operations, without responsibility for or substantial involvement in the determination or public advocacy of the major controversial policies of the Administration or agency, in the following occupational disciplines:

(i) Adjudication and appeals;

(ii) Audit and inspection;

(iii) Civil or criminal law enforcement and compliance;

(iv) Contract administration and procurement;

(v) Grants administration;

(vi) Investigation and security matters; and

(vii) Tax liability, including the assessment or collection of taxes and the preparation or review of interpretative opinions.

(2) Career reserved positions also include:

(i) Scientific or other highly technical or professional positions where the duties and responsibilities of the specific position are such that it must be filled by a career appointee to insure impartiality, of the Government.

(ii) Other positions requiring impartiality, or the public's confidence in impartiality, as determined by an agency in light of its mission.

(d) The Office of Personnel Management may review agency designations of general and career reserved positions. If the Office finds that an agency has designated any position as general that should be career reserved, it shall direct the agency to make the career reserved designation.

(e) The minimum number of positions in the Senior Executive Service Governmentwide that must be career reserved is 3,571 as determined by the Director of the Office of Personnel Management under section 3133(e) of 5 U.S.C. To assure that this figure is met, the Office may establish a minimum number of career reserved positions for individual agencies. An agency must maintain or exceed this number unless it is adjusted by the Office.

[45 FR 62414, Sept. 19, 1980; 45 FR 83471, Dec. 19, 1980]

§214.403 Change of position type.

An agency may not change the designation of an established position from career reserved to general, or from general to career reserved, without the prior approval of the Office of Personnel Management.

PART 230—ORGANIZATION OF THE GOVERNMENT FOR PERSONNEL MANAGEMENT

AUTHORITY: 5 U.S.C. 1302, 3301, 3302; E.O. 10577; 3 CFR 1954–1958 Comp., p. 218; sec. 230.402 also issued under 5 U.S.C. 1104.

Subparts A–C [Reserved]

Subpart D—Agency Authority To Take Personnel Actions in a National Emergency

§ 230.401 Agency authority to take personnel actions in a national emergency disaster.

(a) Upon an attack on the United States, agencies are authorized to carry out whatever personnel activities may be necessary to the effective functioning of their organizations during a period of disaster without regard to any regulation or instruction of OPM, except those which become effective upon or following an attack on the United States. This authority applies only to actions under OPM jurisdiction.

(b) Actions taken under this section shall be consistent with affected regulations and instructions as far as possible under the circumstances and shall be discontinued as soon as conditions permit the reapplication of the affected regulations and instructions.

(c) An employee may not acquire a competitive civil service status by virtue of any action taken under this section.

(d) Actions taken, and authority to take actions, under this section may be adjusted or terminated in whole or in part by OPM.

(e) Agencies shall maintain records of the actions taken under this section.

[35 FR 5173, Mar. 27, 1970]

§ 230.402 Agency authority to make emergency-indefinite appointments in a national emergency.

(a) *When a national emergency exists*—(1) *Definition.* A national emergency must meet *all* of the following conditions:

(i) It was declared by the President or Congress.

(ii) It involves a danger to the United States' safety, security, or stability that results from specified circumstances or conditions and that is national in scope.

(iii) It requires a national program specifically intended to combat the threat to national safety, security, or stability.

(2) *Termination of a national emergency.* A national emergency no longer exists if it is officially terminated by the President or Congress, or if the *specific* circumstances, conditions, or program cited in the original declaration are terminated or corrected.

(b) *Basic authority.* Agencies may make emergency-indefinite appointments without OPM approval during any national emergency as defined in paragraph (a) of this section. The head of an agency with a defense-related mission may request OPM's approval to make emergency-indefinite appointments without a declared national emergency when the President has authorized the call-up of some portion of the military reserves for some military purpose. The request must demonstrate that normal hiring procedures cannot meet surge employment requirements and that use of emergency-indefinite appointments is necessary for economy and efficiency. Except as provided by paragraphs (c) and (d) of this section, agencies must make emergency-indefinite appointments from appropriate registers of eligibles as long as there are available eligibles.

(c) *Appointment under direct-hire authority.* An agency may make emergency-indefinite appointments under this section using the direct-hire procedures in part 337 of this chapter.

(d) *Appointment noncompetitively.* An agency may give emergency-indefinite appointments under this section to the following classes of persons without regard to registers of eligibles and the provisions in § 332.102 of this chapter:

(1) Persons who were recruited on a standby basis prior to the national emergency;

(2) Members of the National Defense Executive Reserve, designated in accordance with section 710(e) of the Defense Production Act of 1950, Executive Order 11179 of September 22, 1964, and applications issued by the agency authorized to implement the law and Executive Order; and

(3) Former Federal employees eligible for reinstatement.

(e) *Tenure of emergency-indefinite employees.* (1) Emergency-indefinite employees do not acquire a competitive status on the basis of their emergency-indefinite appointments.

(2) An emergency-indefinite appointment may be continued for the duration of the emergency for which it is made.

(f) *Trial period.* (1) The first year of service of an emergency-indefinite employee is a trial period.

(2) The agency may terminate the appointment of an emergency-indefinite employee at any time during the trial period. The employee is entitled to the procedures set forth in §315.804 or §315.805 of this chapter as appropriate.

(g) *Eligibility for within-grade increases.* An emergency-indefinite employee serving in a position subject to the General Schedule is eligible for within-grade increases in accordance with subpart D of part 531 of this chapter.

(h) *Applications of other regulations.* (1) The term *indefinite employee* includes an emergency-indefinite employee or an employee under an emergency appointment as used in the following: parts 351, 353 of this chapter, subpart G of part 550 of this chapter, and part 752 of this chapter.

(2) The selection procedures of part 337 of this chapter apply to emergency-indefinite appointments that use the direct-hire authority under paragraph (c) of this section.

(3) Despite the provisions in §831.201(a)(11) of this chapter, an employee serving under an emergency-indefinite appointment under authority of this section is excluded from retirement coverage, except as provided in paragraph (b) of §831.201 of this chapter.

(i) *Promotion, demotion, or reassignment.* An agency may promote, demote, or reassign an emergency-indefinite employee to any position for which it is making emergency-indefinite appointments.

(5 U.S.C. 1104; Pub. L. 95–454, sec. 3(5))

[44 FR 54691, Sept. 21, 1979, as amended at 60 FR 3057, Jan. 13, 1995; 68 FR 35268, June 13, 2003; 69 FR 33275, June 15, 2004]

PART 250—PERSONNEL MANAGEMENT IN AGENCIES

Subpart A—Authority for Personnel Actions in Agencies

Subpart B—Strategic Human Capital Management

Subpart C—Employee Surveys

AUTHORITY: 5 U.S.C. 1101 note, 1103(a)(5), 1103(c), 1104, 1302, 3301, 3302; E.O. 10577, 12 FR 1259, 3 CFR, 1954–1958 Comp., p. 218; E.O. 13197, 66 FR 7853, 3 CFR 748 (2002).

Subpart B also issued under 5 U.S.C. 1401, 1401 note, 1402.

SOURCE: 58 FR 36119, July 6, 1993, unless otherwise noted.

Subpart A—Authority for Personnel Actions in Agencies

SOURCE: 73 FR 23013, Apr. 28, 2008, unless otherwise noted.

§ 250.101 Standards and requirements for agency personnel actions.

When taking a personnel action authorized by this chapter, an agency must comply with qualification standards and regulations issued by the Office of Personnel Management (OPM), the instructions OPM has published in the Guide to Processing Personnel Actions, and the provisions of any delegation agreement OPM has made with the agency. When taking a personnel action that results from a decision or order of OPM, the Merit Systems Protection Board, Equal Employment Opportunity Commission, or Federal Labor Relations Authority, as authorized by the rules and regulations of those agencies, or as the result of a court order, a judicial or administrative settlement agreement, or an arbitral award under a negotiated agreement, the agency must follow the instructions in the Guide to Processing Personnel Actions and comply with all other relevant substantive and documentary requirements, including those applicable to retirement, life insurance, health benefits, and other benefits provided under this chapter.

§ 250.102 Delegated authorities.

OPM may delegate its authority, including authority for competitive examinations, to agencies, under 5 U.S.C. 1104(a)(2), through a delegation agreement. The delegation agreement developed with the agency must specify the conditions for applying the delegated authorities. The agreement must also set minimum standards of performance and describe the system of oversight by which the agency and OPM will monitor the use of each delegated authority.

§ 250.103 Consequences of improper agency actions.

If OPM finds that an agency has taken an action contrary to a law, rule, regulation, or standard that OPM administers, OPM may require the agency to take corrective action. OPM may suspend or revoke a delegation agreement established under § 250.102 at any time if it determines that the agency is not adhering to the provisions of the agreement. OPM may suspend or withdraw any authority granted under this chapter to an agency, including any authority granted by delegation agreement, when OPM finds that the agency has not complied with qualification standards OPM has issued, instructions OPM has published, or the regulations in this chapter. OPM also may suspend or withdraw these authorities when it determines that doing so is in the interest of the civil service for any other reason.

Subpart B—Strategic Human Capital Management

SOURCE: 81 FR 89364, Dec. 12, 2016, unless otherwise noted.

AUTHORITY: 5 U.S.C. 105; 5 U.S.C. 1103(a)(7), (c)(1), and (c)(2); 5 U.S.C. 1401; 5 U.S.C. 1402(a); 31 U.S.C. 901(b)(1); 31 U.S.C. 1115(a)(3); 31 U.S.C. 1115(f); 31 U.S.C. 1116(c)(5); Public Law 103–62; Public Law 107–296; Public Law 108–136, 1128; Public Law 111–352; 5 CFR 10.2; FR Doc No: 2011—19844; E.O. 13583; E.O. 13583, Sec 2(b)(ii).

§ 250.201 Coverage and purpose.

Pursuant to 5 U.S.C. 1103(c), this subpart defines a set of systems, including standards and metrics, for assessing the management of human capital by Federal agencies. These regulations apply to all Executive agencies as defined in 31 U.S.C. 901(b)(1) and support the performance planning and reporting that is required by sections 1115(a)(3) and (f) and 1116(d)(5) of title 31, United States Code.

§ 250.202 Definitions.

Chief Human Capital Officer (CHCO) is the agency's senior leader whose primary duty is to:

(1) Advise and assist the head of the agency and other agency officials in carrying out the agency's responsibilities for selecting, developing, training, and managing a high-quality, productive workforce in accordance with merit system principles; and

(2) Implement the rules and regulations of the President, the Office of Personnel Management (OPM), and the laws governing the civil service within the agency.

CHCO agency is an Executive agency, as defined by 5 U.S.C. 105, which is required by 5 U.S.C. 1401 and 31 U.S.C. 901(b)(1) to appoint a CHCO.

Director of OPM is, among other things, the President's advisor on actions that may be taken to promote an efficient civil service and a systematic application of the merit system principles, including recommending policies relating to the selection, promotion, transfer, performance, pay, conditions of service, tenure, and separation of employees. The Director of OPM provides governmentwide leadership and direction in the strategic management of the Federal workforce.

Evaluation system is an agency's overarching system for evaluating the results of all human capital planning and implementation of human capital strategies to inform the agency's continuous process improvement efforts. This system is also used for ensuring compliance with all applicable statutes, rules, regulations, and agency policies.

Federal Workforce Priorities Report (FWPR) is a strategic human capital report, published by OPM by the first Monday in February of any year in which the term of the President commences. OPM may extend the date of publication if needed. The report communicates key Governmentwide human capital priorities and suggested strategies. The report also informs agency strategic and human capital planning.

Focus areas are areas that agencies and human capital practitioners must focus on to achieve a system's standard.

HRStat is a strategic human capital performance evaluation process that identifies, measures, and analyzes human capital data to inform the impact of an agency's human capital management on organizational results with the intent to improve human capital outcomes. HRStat, which is a quarterly review process, is a component of an agency's strategic planning and alignment and evaluation systems that are part of the Human Capital Framework.

Human Capital Evaluation Framework underlies the three human capital evaluation mechanisms (*i.e.*, HRStat, Audits, and Human Capital Reviews) to create a central evaluation framework that integrates the outcomes from each to provide OPM and agencies with an understanding of how human capital policies and programs are supporting missions.

Human Capital Framework (HCF) provides comprehensive guidance on the principles of strategic human capital management in the Federal Government. The framework, as described in § 250.203 below, provides direction on human capital planning, implementation, and evaluation in the Federal environment.

Human Capital Operating Plan (HCOP) is an agency's human capital implementation document, which describes how an agency will execute the human capital elements stated within Agency Strategic Plan and Annual Performance Plan (APP). Program specific workforce investments and strategies (e.g., hiring, closing skill gaps, etc.) should be incorporated into the APPs as appropriate. The HCOP should clearly execute each of the four systems of the HCF. The HCOP should align with the Government Performance and Results Act (GPRA) Modernization Act of 2010, annual performance plans and timelines.

Human Capital Review (HCR) is OPM's annual, evidence-based review of an agency's design and implementation of its HCOP, independent audit, and HRStat programs to support mission accomplishment and human capital outcomes.

Independent audit program is a component of an agency's evaluation system designed to review all human capital management systems and select human resources transactions to ensure efficiency, effectiveness, and legal and regulatory compliance.

Skill gap is a variance between the current and projected workforce size and skills needed to ensure an agency has a cadre of talent available to meet its mission and make progress towards achieving its goals and objectives now and into the future.

Standard is a consistent practice within human capital management in which agencies strive towards in each of the four HCF systems. The standards ensure that an agency's human capital management strategies, plans, and practices:

(1) Are integrated with strategic plans, annual performance plans and

goals, and other relevant budget, finance, and acquisition plans;

(2) Contain measurable and observable performance targets;

(3) Are communicated in an open and transparent manner to facilitate cross-agency collaboration to achieve mission objectives; and

(4) Inform the development of human capital management priority goals for the Federal Government.

§ 250.203 Strategic human capital management systems and standards.

Strategic human capital management systems, standards, and focus areas are defined within the Human Capital Framework (HCF). The four systems described below provide definitions and standards for human capital planning, implementation, and evaluation. The HCF systems and standards are:

(a) *Strategic planning and alignment.* A system that ensures agency human capital programs are aligned with agency mission, goals, and objectives through analysis, planning, investment, and measurement. The standards for the strategic planning and alignment system require an agency to ensure their human capital management strategies, plans, and practices—

(1) Integrate strategic plans, annual performance plans and goals, and other relevant budget, finance, and acquisition plans;

(2) Contain measurable and observable performance targets; and

(3) Communicate in an open and transparent manner to facilitate cross-agency collaboration to achieve mission objectives.

(b) *Talent management.* A system that promotes a high-performing workforce, identifies and closes skill gaps, and implements and maintains programs to attract, acquire, develop, promote, and retain quality and diverse talent. The standards for the talent management system require an agency to—

(1) Plan for and manage current and future workforce needs;

(2) Design, develop, and implement proven strategies and techniques and practices to attract, hire, develop, and retain talent; and

(3) Make progress toward closing any knowledge, skill, and competency gaps throughout the agency.

(c) *Performance culture.* A system that engages, develops, and inspires a diverse, high-performing workforce by creating, implementing, and maintaining effective performance management strategies, practices, and activities that support mission objectives. The standards for the performance culture system require an agency to have—

(1) Strategies and processes to foster a culture of engagement and collaboration;

(2) A diverse, results-oriented, high-performing workforce; and

(3) A performance management system that differentiates levels of performance of staff, provides regular feedback, and links individual performance to organizational goals.

(d) *Evaluation.* A system that contributes to agency performance by monitoring and evaluating outcomes of its human capital management strategies, policies, programs, and activities by meeting the following standards—

(1) Ensuring compliance with merit system principles; and

(2) Identifying, implementing, and monitoring process improvements.

§ 250.204 Agency roles and responsibilities.

(a) An agency must use the systems and standards established in this part, and any metrics that OPM subsequently provides in guidance, to plan, implement, evaluate and improve human capital policies and programs. These policies and programs must—

(1) Align with Executive branch policies and priorities, as well as with individual agency missions, goals, and strategic objectives. Agencies must align their human capital management strategies to support the Federal Workforce Priorities Report, agency strategic plan, agency performance plan, and agency budget;

(2) Be based on comprehensive workforce planning and analysis;

(3) Monitor and address skill gaps within governmentwide and agency-specific mission-critical occupations by using comprehensive data analytic methods and gap closure strategies;

(4) Recruit, hire, develop, and retain an effective workforce, especially in the agency's mission-critical occupations;

(5) Ensure leadership continuity by implementing and evaluating recruitment, development, and succession plans for leadership positions;

(6) Implement a knowledge management process to ensure continuity in knowledge sharing among employees at all levels within the organization;

(7) Sustain an agency culture that engages employees by defining, valuing, eliciting, and rewarding high performance; and

(8) Hold the agency head, executives, managers, human capital officers, and human capital staff accountable for efficient and effective strategic human capital management, in accordance with merit system principles.

(b) Each agency must meet the statutory requirements of the Government Performance and Results Act (GPRA) Modernization Act of 2010, by including within the Annual Performance Plan (APP) human capital practices that are aligned to the agency strategic plan. The human capital portion of the APP must include performance goals and indicators.

(c) An agency's Deputy Secretary, equivalent, or designee is responsible for ensuring that the agency's strategic plan includes a description of the operational processes, skills and technology, and human capital information required to achieve the agency's goals and objectives. Specifically, the Deputy Secretary, equivalent, or designee will—

(1) Allocate resources;

(2) Ensure the agency incorporates applicable priorities identified within the Federal Workforce Strategic Priorities Report and is working to close governmentwide and agency-specific skill gaps; and

(3) Remain informed about the progress of their agency's quarterly HRStat reviews, which are led by the CHCO, in collaboration with the PIO.

(d) The Chief Human Capital Officer must design, implement and monitor agency human capital policies and programs that—

(1) Ensure human capital activities support merit system principles;

(2) Use the OPM designated method to identify governmentwide and agency-specific skill gaps;

(3) Demonstrate how the agency is using the principles within the HCF to address strategic human capital priorities and goals;

(4) Establish and maintain an Evaluation System to evaluate human capital outcomes that is—

(i) Formal and documented; and

(ii) Approved by OPM;

(5) Maintain an independent audit program, subject to full OPM participation and evaluation, to review periodically all human capital management systems and the agency's human resources transactions to ensure legal and regulatory compliance. An agency must—

(i) Take corrective action to eliminate deficiencies identified by OPM, or through the independent audit, and to improve its human capital management programs and its human resources processes and practices; and

(ii) Based on OPM or independent audit findings, issue a report to its leadership and OPM containing the analysis, results, and corrective actions taken; and

(6) Improve strategic human capital management by adjusting strategies and practices, as appropriate, after assessing the results of performance goals, indicators, and business analytics.

(7) The agency's human capital policies and programs must support the implementation and monitoring of the Federal Workforce Priorities Report, which is published by OPM every four years, and—

(i) Improve strategic human capital management by using performance goals, indicators, and business analytics to assess results of the human capital management strategies planned and implemented;

(ii) Ensure human capital activities support merit system principles;

(iii) Adjust human capital management strategies and practices in response to outcomes identified during HRStat quarterly data-driven reviews of human capital performance to improve organizational processes; and

(iv) Use the governmentwide and agency-specific human capital strategies to inform resource requests (e.g., staff full-time equivalents, training, analytical software, etc.) into the agency's annual budget process.

§ 250.205 Human Capital Operating Plan (HCOP).

Each agency must develop a Human Capital Operating Plan (HCOP) that aligns with an agency's Strategic Plan and Annual Performance Plan. The HCOP is to be reviewed and approved annually, and updated as needed. The HCOP must demonstrate how an agency's human capital implementation strategies follow the principles and standards of the HCF while including an explanation of how human capital policies, initiatives, objectives, and resources will be used to achieve agencies' human capital goals. The HCOP will be made available to OPM upon request. The HCOP must—

(a) Be established by the CHCO, in collaboration with the agency's senior management team;

(b) Be used to support the execution of an agency's strategic plan, as an agency's human capital can affect whether or not a strategy or strategic goal is achieved;

(c) Explicitly describe the agency-specific skill and competency gaps that must be closed through the use of agency selected human capital strategies;

(d) Include annual human capital performance goals and measures that will support the evaluation of the agency's human capital strategies, through HRStat quarterly reviews, and that are aligned to support mission accomplishment;

(e) Reflect the systems and standards defined in § 250.203 above, consistent with their agency strategic plan and annual performance plan, to address strategic human capital priorities and goals; and

(f) Address the governmentwide priorities identified in the Federal Workforce Strategic Priorities Report.

§ 250.206 Human Capital Reviews.

Each agency must participate with OPM in a Human Capital Review (HCR). The HCR will be conducted during the evaluation phase and OPM will issue guidance about the HCR requirements.

§ 250.207 HRStat.

The Chief Human Capital Officer must design, implement and monitor agency human capital policies and programs that—

(a) Use the HRStat quarterly reviews, in coordination with the agency Performance Improvement Officer (PIO), to assess the agency's progress toward meeting its strategic and performance goals;

(b) Implement the HRStat Maturity guidelines specified by OPM; and

(c) Use HRStat quarterly reviews to evaluate their agency's progress.

§ 250.208 System metrics.

OPM reserves the right to provide additional guidance regarding metrics.

§ 250.209 Consequences of improper agency actions.

If OPM finds that an agency has taken an action contrary to a law, rule, regulation, or standard that OPM administers, OPM may require the agency to take corrective action. OPM may suspend or revoke a delegation agreement established under 5 U.S.C. 1104(a)(2) at any time if it determines that the agency is not adhering to the provisions of the agreement. OPM may suspend or withdraw any authority granted under this chapter to an agency, including any authority granted by delegation agreement, when OPM finds that the agency has not complied with qualification standards OPM has issued, instructions OPM has published, or the regulations in this chapter of the regulation. OPM also may suspend or withdraw these authorities when it determines that doing so is in the interest of the civil service for any other reason.

Subpart C—Employee Surveys

SOURCE: 81 FR 89367, Dec. 12, 2016, unless otherwise noted.

AUTHORITY: 5 U.S.C. 105; 5 U.S.C. 7101 note; Public Law 108–136

§250.301 Definitions.

Agency means an Executive agency, as defined in 5 U.S.C. 105.

§250.302 Survey requirements.

(a) Each executive agency must conduct an annual survey of its employees to assess topics outlined in the National Defense Authorization Act for Fiscal Year 2004, Public Law 108–136, sec. 1128, codified at 5 U.S.C. 7101.

(1) Each executive agency may include additional survey questions unique to the agency in addition to the employee survey questions prescribed by OPM under paragraph (a)(2) of this section.

(2) The 16 prescribed survey questions are listed in the following table:

(i) Leadership and Management practices that contribute to agency performance	
	My work unit has the job-relevant skills necessary to accomplish organizational goals. Managers communicate the goals of the organization. I believe the results of this survey will be used to make my agency a better place to work.
(ii) Employee Satisfaction with—	
(A)	Leadership Policies and Practices: How satisfied are you with your involvement in decisions that affect your work? How satisfied are you with the information you receive from management on what is going on in your organization? Considering everything, how satisfied are you with your organization?
(B)	Work Environment: The people I work with cooperate to get the job done. My workload is reasonable. Considering everything, how satisfied are you with your job? I can disclose a suspected violation of any law, rule or regulation without fear of reprisal.
(C)	Rewards and Recognition: In my work unit, differences in performance are recognized in a meaningful way. How satisfied are you with the recognition you receive for doing a good job?
(D)	Opportunities for professional development and growth: I am given a real opportunity to improve my skills in my organization. My talents are used well in the workplace.
(E)	Opportunity to contribute to achieving organizational mission: I know how my work relates to the agency's goals. I recommend my organization as a good place to work.

§250.303 Availability of results.

(a) Each agency will make the results of its annual survey available to the public and post the results on its Web site unless the agency head determines that doing so would jeopardize or negatively impact national security. The posted survey results will include the following:

(1) The agency's evaluation of its survey results;

(2) How the survey was conducted;

(3) Description of the employee sample, unless all employees are surveyed;

(4) The survey questions and response choices with the prescribed questions identified;

(5) The number of employees surveyed and number of employees who completed the survey; and

(6) The number of respondents for each survey question and each response choice.

(b) Data must be collected by December 31 of each calendar year. Each agency must post the beginning and ending dates of its employee survey and either the survey results described in paragraph (a) of this section, or a statement noting the decision not to post, no later than 120 days after the agency completes survey administration. OPM may extend this date under unusual circumstances.

PART 251—AGENCY RELATIONSHIPS WITH ORGANIZATIONS REPRESENTING FEDERAL EMPLOYEES AND OTHER ORGANIZATIONS

Subpart A—General Provisions

Subpart B—Relationships With Organizations Representing Federal Employees and Other Organizations

Subpart C—Dues Withholding

AUTHORITY: 5 U.S.C. 1104; 5 U.S.C. Chap 7; 5 U.S.C. 7135; 5 U.S.C. 7301; and E.O. 11491.

SOURCE: 61 FR 32915, June 26, 1996, unless otherwise noted.

Subpart A—General Provisions

§ 251.101 Introduction.

(a) The regulations in this part apply to all Federal executive branch departments and agencies and their officers and employees.

(b) This part provides a framework for consulting and communicating with non-labor organizations representing Federal employees and with other organizations on matters related to agency operations and personnel management.

(c) The purposes of consultation and communication are: the improvement of agency operations, personnel management, and employee effectiveness; the exchange of information (e.g., ideas, opinions, and proposals); and the establishment of policies that best serve the public interest in accomplishing the mission of the agency.

(d) An agency's consultation and communication with organizations representing Federal employees and with other organizations under this part may not take on the character of negotiations or consultations regarding conditions of employment of bargaining unit employees, which is reserved exclusively to labor organizations as provided for in Chapter 71 of title 5 of the U.S. Code or comparable provisions of other laws. The regulations in this part do not authorize any actions inconsistent with Chapter 71 of the U.S. Code or comparable provisions of other laws.

(e) The head of a Federal agency may determine that it is in the interest of the agency to consult, from time to time, with organizations other than labor organizations and associations of management officials and/or supervisors to the extent permitted by law. Under section 7(d)(2) and (3) of Executive Order 11491, as amended, recognition of a labor organization does not preclude an agency from consulting or dealing with a veterans organization, or with a religious, social, fraternal, professional, or other lawful association, not qualified as a labor organization, with respect to matters or policies which involve individual members of the organization or association or are of particular applicability to it or its members.

(f) Federal employees, including management officials and supervisors, may communicate with any Federal agency, officer, or other Federal entity on the employee's own behalf. However, Federal employees should be aware that 18 U.S.C. 205, in pertinent part, restricts Federal employees from acting, other than in the proper discharge of their official duties, as agents or attorneys for any person or organization other than a labor organization, before any Federal agency or other Federal entity in connection with any matter in which the United States is a party or has a direct and substantial interest. An exception to the prohibition found in 18 U.S.C. 205 permits Federal employees to represent certain nonprofit organizations before the Government except in connection with specified matters. Agency officials and employees are therefore advised to consult with their designated agency ethics officials for guidance regarding any conflicts of interest that may arise.

[61 FR 32915, June 26, 1996, as amended at 63 FR 2306, Jan. 15, 1998]

§251.102 Coverage.

To be covered by this part, an association or organization:

(a) Must be a lawful, nonprofit organization whose constitution and bylaws indicate that it subscribes to minimum standards of fiscal responsibility and employs democratic principles in the nomination and election of officers;

(b) Must not discriminate in terms of membership or treatment because of race, color, religion, sex, national origin, age, or handicapping condition;

(c) Must not assist or participate in a strike, work stoppage, or slowdown against the Government of the United States or any agency thereof or impose a duty or obligation to conduct, assist, or participate in such strike, work stoppage, or slowdown; and

(d) Must not advocate the overthrow of the constitutional form of Government of the United States.

§251.103 Definitions.

(a) *Organization representing Federal employees and other organizations* means an organization other than a labor organization that can provide information, views, and services which will contribute to improved agency operations, personnel management, and employee effectiveness. Such an organization may be an association of Federal management officials and/or supervisors, a group representing minorities, women or persons with disabilities in connection with the agencies' EEO programs and action plans, a professional association, a civic or consumer group, and organization concerned with special social interests, and the like.

(b) *Association of management officials and/or supervisors* means an association comprised primarily of Federal management officials and/or supervisors, which is not eligible for recognition under Chapter 71 of title 5 of the U.S. Code or comparable provisions of other laws, and which is not affiliated with a labor organization or federation of labor organizations.

(c) *Labor organization* means an organization as defined in 5 U.S.C. 7103(a)(4), which is in compliance with 5 U.S.C. 7120, or as defined in comparable provisions of other laws.

Subpart B—Relationships With Organizations Representing Federal Employees and Other Organizations

§251.201 Associations of management officials and/or supervisors.

(a) As part of agency management, supervisors and managers should be included in the decision-making process and notified of executive-level decisions on a timely basis. Each agency must establish and maintain a system for intra-management communication and consultation with its supervisors and managers. Agencies must also establish consultative relationships with associations whose membership is primarily composed of Federal supervisory and/or managerial personnel, provided that such associations are not affiliated with any labor organization and that they have sufficient agency membership to assure a worthwhile dialogue with executive management. Consultative relationships with other non-labor organizations representing Federal employees are discretionary.

(b) Consultations should have as their objectives the improvement of managerial effectiveness and the working conditions of supervisors and managers, as well as the identification and resolution of problems affecting agency operations and employees, including supervisors and managers.

(c) The system of communication and consultation should be designed so that individual supervisors and managers are able to participate if they are not affiliated with an association of management officials and/or supervisors.

At the same time, the voluntary joining together of supervisory and management personnel in groups of associations shall not be precluded or discouraged.

§ 251.202 Agency support to organizations representing Federal employees and other organizations.

(a) An agency may provide support services to an organization when the agency determines that such action would benefit the agency's programs or would be warranted as a service to employees who are members of the organization and complies with applicable statutes and regulations. Examples of such support services are as follows:

(1) Permitting employees, in appropriate cases, to use agency equipment or administrative support services for preparing papers to be presented at conferences or symposia or published in journals;

(2) Using the authority under 5 U.S.C. 4109 and 4110, as implemented by 5 CFR part 410, to pay expenses of employees to attend professional organization meetings when such attendance is for the purpose of employee development or directly concerned with agency functions or activities and the agency can derive benefits from employee attendance at such meetings; and

(3) Following a liberal policy in authorizing excused absence for other employees who are willing to pay their own expenses to attend a meeting of a professional association or other organization from which an agency could derive some benefits.

(b) Agencies may provide Government resources support to organizations (such as space in Government facilities for meeting purposes and the use of agency bulletin boards, internal agency mail distribution systems, electronic bulletin boards and other means of informing agency employees about meetings and activities) in accordance with appropriate General Services Administration regulations contained in title 41 of the Code of Federal Regulations. The mere provision of such support to any organization is not to be construed as Federal sponsorship, sanction, or endorsement of the organization or its activities.

Subpart C—Dues Withholding

§ 251.301 Associations of management officials and/or supervisors.

Dues withholding for associations of management officials and/or supervisors is covered in 5 CFR 550.331.

§ 251.302 All other organizations.

Under 5 CFR 550.311(b), an agency may permit an employee to make an allotment for any legal purpose deemed appropriate by the head of the agency. Agencies may provide for the allotment of dues for organizations representing Federal employees under that section.

PART 293—PERSONNEL RECORDS

Subpart A—Basic Policies on Maintenance of Personnel Records

Subpart B—Personnel Records Subject to the Privacy Act

Subpart C—Official Personnel Folder

AUTHORITY: 5 U.S.C. 552 and 4315; E.O. 12107 (December 28, 1978), 3 CFR 1954–1958 Comp.; 5 U.S.C. 1103, 1104, and 1302; 5 CFR 7.2; E.O. 9830; 3 CFR 1943–1948 Comp.; 5 U.S.C. 2951(2) and 3301; and E.O. 12107.

SOURCE: 44 FR 65033, Nov. 9, 1979, unless otherwise noted.

Subpart A—Basic Policies on Maintenance of Personnel Records

§293.101 Purpose and scope.

(a) This subpart sets forth basic policies governing the creation, development, maintenance, processing, use, dissemination, and safeguarding of personnel records which the Office of Personnel Management requires agencies to maintain in the personnel management or personnel policy setting process.

(b) Agencies in the Executive Branch of the Federal Government are subject to specific Office of Personnel Management recordkeeping requirements to varying degrees, pursuant to statute, Office regulation, or formal agreements between the Office and agencies. This subpart applies to any department or independent establishment in the Executive Branch of the Federal Government, including a government corporation or Government controlled corporation, except those specifically excluded from Office recordkeeping requirements by statute, Office regulation, or formal agreement between the Office and that agency.

§293.102 Definitions.

In this part:

Agency means any executive department, military department, Government corporation, Government controlled corporation, or other establishment in the Executive Branch of the Government (including the Executive Office of the President), or any independent regulatory agency;

Data subject means the individual about whom the Office or agency is maintaining information in a system of records;

Individual means a citizen of the United States or an alien lawfully admitted for permanent residence;

Information means papers, records, photographs, magnetic storage media, micro storage media, and other documentary materials regardless of physical form or characteristics, containing data about an individual and required by the Office in pursuance of law or in connection with the discharge of official business, as defined by statute, regulation, or administrative procedure;

Maintain includes collect, use, or disseminate;

Office means the Office of Personnel Management;

Personnel record means any record concerning an individual which is maintained an used in the personnel management or personnel policysetting process. (For purposes of this part, this term is not limited just to those personnel records in a system of records and subject to the Privacy Act);

Record means any item, collection, or grouping of information about an individual that is maintained by an agency, including, but not limited to, his or her education, financial transactions, medical history, criminal history, or employment history;

System of records means a group of records under the control of any agency from which information is retrieved by the name of the individual or by some identifying number, symbol, or other identifying particular assigned to the individual.

§ 293.103 Recordkeeping standards.

(a) The head of each agency shall ensure that persons having access to or involved in the creation, development, processing, use, or maintenance of personnel records are informed of pertinent recordkeeping regulations and requirements of the Office of Personnel Management and the agency. Authority to maintain personnel records does not constitute authority to maintain information in the record merely because it may be useful; both Government-wide and internal agency personnel records shall contain only information concerning an individual that is relevant and necessary to accomplish the Federal personnel management purposes required by statute, Executive order, or Office regulation.

(b) The Office is responsible for establishing minimum standards of accuracy, relevancy, necessity, timeliness, and completeness for personnel records it requires agencies to maintain. These standards are discussed in appropriate chapters of the Guide to Personnel Recordkeeping. Before approval of any agency requests for changes in recordkeeping practices governed by the Guide to Personnel Recordkeeping, the Office will examine the proposal or request in the context of such standards set forth by the agency in support of the proposal and in light of the personnel program area that requires these records.

[44 FR 65033, Nov. 9, 1979, as amended at 66 FR 66709, Dec. 27, 2001]

§ 293.104 Collection of information.

(a) Any information in personnel records whether or not those records are in a system of records, used in whole or in part in making a determination about an individual's rights, benefits, or privileges under Federal personnel programs should, to the greatest extent practicable, be collected directly from the individual concerned. Factors to be considered in determining whether to collect the data from the individual concerned or a third party are when:

(1) The nature of the information is such that it can only be obtained from another party;

(2) The cost of collecting the information directly from the individual is unreasonable when compared with the cost of collecting it from another party;

(3) There is virtually no risk that information collected from other parties, if inaccurate, could result in a determination adverse to the individual concerned;

(4) The information supplied by an individual must be verified by another party; or

(5) There are provisions made, to the greatest extent practicable, to vertify information collected from another party with the individual concerned.

§ 293.105 Restrictions on collection and use of information.

(a) First Amendment. Personnel records describing how individuals exercise rights guaranteed by the First Amendment are prohibited unless expressly authorized by statute, or by the individual concerned, or unless pertinent to and within the scope of an authorized law enforcement activity. These rights include, but are not limited to, free exercise of religious and political beliefs, freedom of speech and the press, and freedom to assemble and to petition the government.

(b) Social Security Number.

(1) Agencies may not require individuals to disclose their Social Security Number unless disclosure would be required;

(i) Under Federal statute; or

(ii) Under any statute, Executive order, or regulation that authorizes any Federal, State, or local agency maintaining a system of records that was in existence and operating prior to January 1, 1975, to request the Social Security Number as a necessary means of verifying the identity of an individual.

(2) Individuals asked to voluntarily (circumstances not covered by paragraph (b)(1) of this section) provide

their Social Security Number shall suffer no penalty or denial of benefits for refusing to provide it.

§ 293.106 Safeguarding information about individuals.

(a) To ensure the security and confidentiality of personnel records, in whatever form, each agency shall establish administrative, technical, and physical controls to protect information in personnel records from unauthorized access, use, modification, destruction, or disclosure. As a minimum, these controls shall require that all persons whose official duties require access to and use of personnel records be responsible and accountable for safeguarding those records and for ensuring that the records are secured whenever they are not in use or under the direct control of authorized persons. Generally, personnel records should be held, processed, or stored only where facilities and conditions are adequate to prevent unauthorized access.

(b) Personnel records must be stored in metal filing cabinets which are locked when the records are not in use, or in a secured room. Alternative storage facilities may be employed provided they furnish an equivalent or greater degree of security than these methods. Except for access by the data subject, only employees whose official duties require access shall be allowed to handle and use personnel records, in whatever form or media the records might appear. To the extent feasible, entry into personnel record storage areas shall be similarly limited. Documentation of the removal of records from storage areas must be kept so that adequate control procedures can be established to assure that removed records are returned on a timely basis.

(c) Disposal and destruction of personnel records shall be in accordance with the General Record Schedule issued by the General Services Administration for the records or, alternatively, with Office or agency records control schedules approved by the National Archives and Records Service of the General Services Administration.

§ 293.107 Special safeguards for automated records.

(a) In addition to following the security requirements of § 293.106 of this part, managers of automated personnel records shall establish administrative, technical, physical, and security safeguards for data about individuals in automated records, including input and output documents, reports, punched cards, magnetic tapes, disks, and online computer storage. The safeguards must be in writing to comply with the standards on automated data processing physical security issued by the National Bureau of Standards, U.S. Department of Commerce, and, as a minimum, must be sufficient to:

(1) Prevent careless, accidental, or unintentional disclosure, modification, or destruction of identifiable personal data;

(2) Minimize the risk that skilled technicians or knowledgeable persons could improperly obtain access to, modify, or destroy identifiable personnel data;

(3) Prevent casual entry by unskilled persons who have no official reason for access to such data;

(4) Minimize the risk of an unauthorized disclosure where use is made of identifiable personal data in testing of computer programs;

(5) Control the flow of data into, through, and from agency computer operations;

(6) Adequately protect identifiable data from environmental hazards and unneccessary exposure; and

(7) Assure adequate internal audit procedures to comply with these procedures.

(b) The disposal of identifiable personal data in automated files is to be accomplished in such a manner as to make the data unobtainable to unauthorized personnel. Unneeded personal data stored on reusable media such as magnetic tapes and disks must be erased prior to release of the media for reuse.

§ 293.108 Rules of conduct.

(a) *Scope.* These rules of conduct apply to all Office and agency employees responsible for creation, development, maintenance, processing, use, dissemination, and safeguarding of personnel records. The Office and agencies shall require that such employees are familiar with these and appropriate supplemental agency internal regulations.

(b) *Standards of conduct.* Office and agency employees whose official duties involve personnel records shall be sensitive to individual rights to personal privacy and shall not disclose information from any personnel record unless disclosure is part of their official duties or required by executive order, regulation, or statute (e.g., required by the Freedom of Information Act, 5 U.S.C. 552).

(c) *Improper uses of personnel information.* Any Office or agency employee who makes a disclosure of personnel records knowing that such disclosure is unauthorized, or otherwise knowingly violates these regulations, shall be subject to disciplinary action and may also be subject to criminal penalties where the records are subject to the Privacy Act (5 U.S.C. 552a). Employees are prohibited from using personnel information not available to the public, gained through official duties, for commercial solicitation or sale, or for personal gain.

Subpart B—Personnel Records Subject to the Privacy Act

§ 293.201 Purpose.

The purpose of this subpart is to set forth the criteria to be used to determine when personnel records on individuals are subject both to the regulations contained in this part and to Office or agency regulations implementing the Privacy Act of 1974, 5 U.S.C. 552a. When personnel records are maintained within a system of records, the records are deemed to be within the scope of both the regulations in this part and Office or agency regulations implementing the Privacy Act.

§ 293.202 Records subject to Office or agency Privacy Act regulations.

When the Office of Personnel Management publishes in the FEDERAL REGISTER a notice of system of records for personnel records which are maintained by the agencies or by the Office, that system of records will be subject to the regulations in this part and also to the regulations in part 297 of this chapter. When agencies publish a notice of system of records for personnel records required by the Office that are not included in the Office's notices, those agency systems of records will be subject both to the regulations contained in this part and to agency promulgated regulations that implement the Privacy Act.

§ 293.203 Review of Office or agency practices.

Reviews of agency personnel management policies and practices will be conducted to insure compliance with Office regulations. The Office may direct agencies to take whatever corrective action is necessary. Office or agency officials who have knowledge of violations of these regulations shall take whatever corrective action is necessary. Agencies shall list officials of the Office of Personnel Management as a routine user for personnel records to assist the Office in its oversight responsibilities.

Subpart C—Official Personnel Folder

AUTHORITY: 5 U.S.C. 552; 5 U.S.C. 552a; 5 U.S.C. 1103; 5 U.S.C. 1104; 5 U.S.C. 1302, 5 U.S.C. 2951(2), 5 U.S.C. 3301; 5 U.S.C. 4315; E.O. 12107 (December 28, 1978), 3 CFR 1954–1958 Compilation; E.O. 9830 (February 24, 1947); 3 CFR 1943–1948 Compilation.

SOURCE: 50 FR 3309, Jan. 24, 1985, unless otherwise noted.

§ 293.301 Applicability of regulations.

Except for those agencies specifically excluded from Office of Personnel Management (OPM) recordkeeping requirements by statute, OPM regulation, or formal agreement between OPM and the agency, this subpart applies to—and within this subpart agency means—each executive department and independent establishment of the Federal Government; each corporation wholly owned or controlled by the United States; and, with respect to positions subject to civil service rules and regulations, the legislative and judicial branches of the Federal Government. OPM will list agencies to which this subpart does not apply in the

Guide to Personnel Recordkeeping, and will amend the Guide from time to time to update that list.

[76 FR 52537, Aug. 23, 2011]

§ 293.302 Establishment of Official Personnel Folder.

Each agency shall establish an Official Personnel Folder (OPF) for each employee occupying a position subject to this part, except as provided in § 293.306. Except as provided in the Guide to Personnel Recordkeeping, there will be only one OPF maintained for each employee regardless of service in various agencies.

[50 FR 3309, Jan. 24, 1985, as amended at 66 FR 66709, Dec. 27, 2001]

§ 293.303 The roles and responsibilities of the Office, agencies, and custodians.

(a) The Official Personnel Folder (OPF) of each employee in a position subject to civil service rules and regulations and of each former employee who held such a position is part of the records of the Office of Personnel Management (Office).

(b) The Office has Government-wide responsibility for developing regulations, practices and procedures for the establishment, maintenance, and transfer of OPFs.

(c) Agencies shall be responsible for the following:

(1) The establishment of the OPF for a new appointee or a new employee for whom no OPF has previously been established; and

(2) The maintenance of a previously existing OPF during the period any new appointee or employee remains an agency's employee.

(d)(1) Custodian means the agency in physical possession of an OPF. In the case of an electronic OPF (eOPF), the custodian is the agency that has primary access to an eOPF contained within a document management system approved by the Office.

(2) A custodian shall be responsible for the maintenance and transfer of the OPF or eOPF, and the costs associated with these activities.

(3) An agency is the custodian of an OPF it requests from the National Personnel Records Center (NPRC), for any temporary use, from the date that the OPF is transmitted by the NPRC to the agency until the date that the NPRC receives the OPF back from the agency.

(4) An agency is no longer the custodian of an OPF once the OPF has been transferred to and accepted by the NPRC.

(5) Once NPRC has approved the transfer, the Office is the custodian of the OPF until the destruction date established for the file pursuant to the National Archive and Records Administration's General Records Schedule, unless another agency requests the OPF from the NPRC in the interim.

(e) Agencies and custodians shall carry out their responsibilities with respect to the OPF or eOPF in accordance with this subpart and the Office's Guide to Personnel Recordkeeping.

[76 FR 52537, Aug. 23, 2011]

§ 293.304 Maintenance and content of folder.

The head of each agency shall maintain in the Official Personnel Folder the reports of selection and other personnel actions named in section 2951 of title 5, United States Code. The folder shall contain long-term records affecting the employee's status and service as required by OPM's instructions and as designated in the Guide to Personnel Recordkeeping.

[58 FR 65533, Dec. 15, 1993]

§ 293.305 Type of folder to be used.

Each agency shall use only OPFs from Office of Federal Supply and Services stock (Standard Form 66) for the folders required by this part.

§ 293.306 Use of existing folders upon transfer or reemployment.

When an agency hires a person who has served on or after April 1, 1947, in a position subject to this part, it shall request the transfer of the OPF pertaining to the person's employment. The folder so obtained shall be used in lieu of establishing a new OPF. In the event that the prior service occurred wholly before April 1, 1947, the agency shall request any files or records that may be located in the Federal records storage center. The request shall note that because of the dates of service there will likely be no OPF. Any such file or record found for this individual shall be incorporated into the OPF being established for the employee.

(a) When a person for whom an OPF has been established transfers from one agency to another, the last employing (losing) agency shall, on request, transfer the OPF to the new employing agency.

(b) Before transferring the Official Personnel Folder, the losing agency shall:

(1) Remove those records of a temporary nature filed on the left side of the folder, except for PMRS employees' performance ratings of record including the performance plan on which the most recent rating was based;

(2) Transfer performance ratings of record and the performance plan on which the most recent rating was based from the Employee Performance File of PMRS employees to their Official Personnel Folder, if the ratings and plans are not maintained by the agency in the Official Personnel Folder; and

(3) Ensure that all permanent documents of the folder are complete, correct, and present in the folder in accordance with the Guide to Personnel Recordkeeping.

[50 FR 3309, Jan. 24, 1985, as amended at 50 FR 35494, Aug. 30, 1985; 66 FR 66709, Dec. 27, 2001]

§ 293.307 Disposition of folders of former Federal employees.

(a) Folders of persons separated from Federal employment must be retained by the losing agency for 30 working days after separation, and may be retained for additional 60 days (90 days where administratively necessary, e.g., where an appeal or an allegation of discrimination is made or where an employee retires or dies in service). Thereafter, the OPF must be transferred to the General Services Administration, National Personnel Records Center (Civilian Personnel Records), 111 Winnebago Street, St. Louis, Missouri 63118.

(b) When a former Federal employee is reappointed in the Federal service, the National Personnel Records Center (Civilian Personnel Records) shall, upon request, transfer the OPF to the new employing agency.

(c) Agencies are responsible for all costs associated with the establishment and maintenance of OPFs and the transfer of OPFs to the National Personnel Records Center.

(d) Agencies are responsible for all costs associated with agency-initiated requests for OPFs or services from the National Personnel Records Center.

[50 FR 3309, Jan. 24, 1985; 50 FR 8993, Mar. 6, 1985, as amended at 76 FR 52537, Aug. 23, 2011]

§ 293.308 Removal of temporary records from OPFs.

The employing agency having possession of an OPF shall remove temporary records from the OPF before it is transferred to another agency. For these and also for temporary records of their current employees, maintenance of the records shall be in accordance with General Records Schedule 1, promulgated by the General Services Administration.

§ 293.309 Reconstruction of lost OPFs.

Agencies will take necessary precautions to safeguard all OPFs. In the event of a lost or destroyed OPF, the current (or last, in the case of a former Federal employee) employing agency shall take the necessary action to reconstruct the essential portions of the OPF as specified in the Guide to Personnel Recordkeeping or other Office instructions.

[50 FR 3309, Jan. 24, 1985, as amended at 66 FR 66709, Dec. 27, 2001]

§ 293.310 Response to requests for information.

The Office, or an agency in physical possession of an OPF in response to a third party Freedom of Information Act (FOIA) request may disclose information as provided in this subpart. A current employee's request for access to his/her own OPF (also included are employee performance file system folders and files) that cites the FOIA, as with all stated Privacy Act requests made by current employees, shall be processed in accordance with agency Privacy Act procedures consistent with Office regulations in part 297 of this chapter. All requests for their OPFs from former employees, and FOIA requests for former employee OPFs, shall be referred to the Office's regional or area office nearest to the location of the requester.

§293.311 Availability of information.

(a) The following information from both the OPF and employee performance file system folders, their automated equivalent records, and from other personnel record files that constitute an agency record within the meaning of the FOIA and which are under the control of the Office, about most present and former Federal employees, is available to the public:

(1) Name;

(2) Present and past position titles and occupational series;

(3) Present and past grades;

(4) Present and past annual salary rates (including performance awards or bonuses, incentive awards, merit pay amount, Meritorious or Distinguished Executive Ranks, and allowances and differentials);

(5) Present and past duty stations (includes room numbers, shop designations, or other identifying information regarding buildings or places of employment); and

(6) Position descriptions, identification of job elements, and those performance standards (but not actual performance appraisals) that the release of which would not interfere with law enforcement programs or severely inhibit agency effectiveness. Performance elements and standards (or work expectations) may be withheld when they are so interwined with performance appraisals that their disclosure would reveal an individual's performance appraisal.

(b) The Office or agency will generally not disclose information where the data sought is a list of names, present or past position titles, grades, salaries, performance standards, and/or duty stations of Federal employees which, as determined by the official responsible for custody of the information:

(1) Is selected in such a way that would reveal more about the employee on whom information is sought than the six enumerated items, the disclosure of which would constitute a clearly unwarranted invasion of personal privacy; or

(2) Would otherwise be protected from mandatory disclosure under an exemption of the FOIA.

(c) In addition to the information described in paragraph (a) of this section, a Government official may provide other information from these records (or automated equivalents) of an employee, to others outside of the agency, under a summons, warrant, subpoena, or other legal process; as provided by the Privacy Act (5 U.S.C. 552a(b)(4) through (b)(11)), under those Privacy Act routine uses promulgated by the Office, and as required by the FOIA.

Subpart D—Employee Performance File System Records

AUTHORITY: 5 U.S.C. 552a and 5 U.S.C. 4305 and 4315; E.O. 12107 (December 28, 1978); 5 U.S.C. 1103, 1104, and 1302; 3 CFR 1954–1958 Compilation; 5 CFR 7.2; E.O. 9830, 3 CFR 1943–1948 Compilation.

SOURCE: 47 FR 3080, Jan. 22, 1982, unless otherwise noted.

§293.401 Applicability of regulations.

This subpart applies to Executive agencies as defined in sections 105, 3132(a)(1) and 4301(1) of title 5, U.S. Code, including Military Departments (but not non-appropriated fund employees) as defined in section 102 of title 5, U.S. Code, and independent establishments as defined in section 104 of title 5, U.S. Code. Within those agencies, the requirements of this subpart apply to all employees occupying positions subject to civil service rules and regulations, including Senior Executive Service positions as defined in 5 U.S.C. 3132(a)(2).

§293.402 Establishment of separate employee performance record system.

(a) Copies of employees' performance ratings of record, including the performance plans on which the ratings are based, must be placed in either the employee's Official Personnel Folder (OPF) or in the Employee Performance File (EPF). However, other performance-related documents may be retained in the OPF only when the agency prescribes the use of a separate envelope, temporarily located in the OPF, and removed whenever the OPF (except as required in § 293.404(b)) is transferred to another agency. Performance ratings of record, including the performance plans on which the ratings are based, shall be retained on the left (temporary) side of the OPF. No other performance-related record shall be retained on the left (temporary) or right (long term) side of the OPF or shall be transferred to the National Personnel Records Center (except as required by § 293.404(b)).

(b) Except for performance records maintained in the OPF consistent with paragraph (a) of this section, each agency having employees occupying a position described in § 293.401 shall provide for maintenance of performance-related records for such employees in this EPF system. The agency may elect to retain records in a separate file that is located in the same office with the OPF, or in an envelope kept in the OPF itself. If the agency determines that a separate EPF is cost-effective, such a file may be located in another designated agency office (as specified in the agency's performance appraisal plan) including with supervisors or managers (hereinafter referred to as rating officials) or with Performance Review Boards. Any supporting documents that the agency may prescribe as necessary for agency officials in performance of their duties shall be kept in these files.

(c)(1) Agencies shall provide their employees access to their performance files (automated and manual). Such a request for access shall be processed in accordance with established agency procedures, consistent with Office of Personnel Management regulations regarding access to records contained in part 297 of this chapter. Such access shall be provided to the employee or to the employee's designated representative, and such records may also be disclosed to other officials of the agency who have a need for the documents in the performance of their duties.

(2) All other requests for performance documents made to agency officials (e.g., Freedom of Information Act requests or requests made under the "routine use" provisions of the Privacy Act) shall be processed by the responsible agency official in accordance with agency procedures consistent with Office of Personnel Management regulations regarding disclosures of such records contained in parts 293 and 297 of this chapter.

(3) Privacy Act requests for amendment of records maintained in this system shall be processed by the responsible agency official in accordance with agency procedures consistent with Office of Personnel Management regulations regarding amendment of records contained in part 297 of this chapter.

(d) Agencies maintaining the EPF in an automated or microform system shall issue instructions that contain necessary procedures to ensure that the same requirements as in paragraph (c) of this section, relating to all manual records, are met.

[47 FR 3080, Jan. 22, 1982, as amended at 51 FR 8410, Mar. 11, 1986]

§ 293.403 Contents of employee performance files.

(a) A decision on what constitutes a performance-related document within the meaning of this subpart rests with the agency. Agency implementing instructions, for both incumbents of the Senior Executive Service and other positions, shall provide specific written guidance of the description of what constitutes the agency's official performance-related forms and documents.

(b) Agency implementing instructions describing such records shall indicate where and for how long they are retained and how and when they are to be destroyed. Such instructions shall also describe what records are considered to be performance-related (as specifically as is feasible) and shall include all performance-related records maintained as a system of records within the meaning of the Privacy Act. Such records would generally include:

(1) Any form or other document which records the performance appraisal, including appraisals leading to merit pay determinations.

(2) Any form or other document used by rating officials to recommend a personnel action affecting an employee (including a request for personnel action document, but only when the action is not effected) when the basis for the action (e.g., removal, reassignment, demotion, promotion, or merit

pay or other performance award) is performance-related.

(3) Recommendations for training that are performance-related.

(4) Any form or other document furnished in support of recommended actions such as those listed in paragraph (b)(2) of this section and the agency's final decision on the matter (e.g., a recommendation for merit pay or an agency decision to grant only one-half the comparability pay adjustment).

(5) Any form or other document which the rating official is required by the agency to keep during an appraisal period (e.g., quality control records, production records, or similar records used to track employee performance during the appraisal period.)

(6) Any form or other document regarding Performance Review Board decisions, including supporting documentation and any transcript of hearings or testimony from witnesses.

(7) Any form or other document regarding decisions or recommendations of agency Executive Resources Boards related to performance appraisal or actions resulting from performance appraisals.

(8) Appraisals of potential (e.g., in connection with an agency's merit promotion procedures) if agency implementing instructions specifically require or permit retention of a copy.

(9) Individual development plans.

(10) Copies of licenses, certificates of proficiency, or similar documents required of the position.

(c) General information about the employee, *i.e.*, identification data, information concerning Federal and non-Federal employment experience, and information about any training programs the employee participated in may, if an agency deems it appropriate, be retained in this system.

[47 FR 3080, Jan. 22, 1982, as amended at 63 FR 43867, Aug. 17, 1998]

§ 293.404 Retention schedule.

(a)(1) Except as provided in § 293.405(a), performance ratings or documents supporting them are generally not permanent records and shall, except for appointees to the SES and including incumbents of executive positions not covered by SES, be retained as prescribed below:

(i) Performance ratings of record, including the performance plans on which they are based, shall be retained for 4 years;

(ii) Supporting documents shall be retained for as long as the agency deems appropriate (up to 4 years);

(iii) Performance records superseded (e.g., through an administrative or judicial procedure) and performance-related records pertaining to a former employee (except as prescribed in § 293.405(a)) need not be retained for a minimum of 4 years. Rather, in the former case they are to be destroyed and in the latter case agencies shall determine the retention schedule; and

(iv) Except where prohibited by law, retention of automated records longer than the maximum prescribed here is permitted for purposes of statistical analysis so long as the data are not used in any action affecting the employee when the manual record has been or should have been destroyed.

(2) When an employee is reassigned within the employing agency, disposition of records in this system, including transfer with the employee who changes positions, shall be as agencies prescribe and consistent with § 293.405(a).

(3) Appraisals of unacceptable performance, where a notice of proposed demotion or removal is issued but not effected, and all documents related thereto, manual and automated, pursuant to 5 U.S.C. 4303(d) must be destroyed after the employee completes one year of acceptable performance from the date of the written advance notice of the proposed removal or reduction in grade notice. Under conditions specified by an agency, and earlier destruction date is permitted and destruction must be no later than 30 days after the year is up.

(b) Performance records for Senior Executive Service appointees, including those serving under a Presidential appointment under 5 U.S.C. 3392(c), are to be retained as follows:

(1) Pursuant to 5 U.S.C. 4314(b) (3) and (4), Senior Executive Service appointees shall have their performance-related records maintained for five consecutive years (from the date the appraisal is issued) beginning with the

effective date of appointment, including individuals receiving appointments pursuant to 5 U.S.C. 3593(b).

(2) When an appointee of the Senior Executive Service moves to another position in the Service, either with the same or a different agency, all appropriate performance-related documents five years old or less shall be forwarded in the Employee Performance File along with the individual's OPF.

(3) When an employee in the Senior Executive Service accepts a Presidential appointment pursuant to 5 U.S.C. 3392(c), the employee's performance file shall be retained as long as the employee remains employed under that Presidential appointment. When the appointment ends, and the individual does not return to the Senior Executive Service, the employee's performance file shall be destroyed in accordance with agency procedures.

(c) Where any performance-related document is needed in connection with an ongoing administrative, negotiated, quasi-judicial, or judicial proceeding, and it continues to be retained in this system rather than another system, it may be retained for as long as necessary beyond the retention schedules identified in paragraphs (a) and (b) of this section.

(d) Screening and purging of folders/envelopes and rating official's work files for the purpose of compliance with these retention schedules shall be through any agency process insuring consistency with the requirements.

[47 FR 3080, Jan. 22, 1982, as amended at 51 FR 8411, Mar. 11, 1986; 56 FR 65416, Dec. 17, 1991]

§ 293.405 Disposition of records.

(a) When the OPF of a non-SES employee is sent to another servicing office in the employing agency, to another agency, or to the National Personnel Records Center, the "losing" servicing office shall include in the OPF all performance ratings of record that are 4 years old or less, including the performance plan on which the most recent rating was based, and the summary rating prepared when the employee changes positions, as prescribed in part 430 of this chapter. Also, the "losing" office will purge from the OPF all performance ratings and performance plans that are more than 4 years old, and other performance-related records, according to agency policy established under § 293.404(a)(2) and in accordance with the Guide to Personnel Recordkeeping.

(b) Consistent with transfer instructions pertaining to SES positions contained in this part, employee performance files shall be forwarded to gaining agencies at the same time as the OPF (5 CFR 293.207).

(c) Consistent with retention schedules promulgated in § 293.404, destruction of performance-related records shall be in accordance with agency procedures (e.g., by shredding or burning).

(d) If a former employee returns to an agency, a new employee performance file will be created unless the prior file for this employee is still available. The original file may be reactivated provided that, consistent with the retention schedules and destruction requirements promulgated in this subpart, the contents are properly disposed of.

(e)(1) It is the responsibility of the agency Personnel Director to insure the maintenance of employee performance files in accordance with this subpart and subparts A and B of this part, part 297 of this title, and with Office of Personnel Management guidance.

(2) This responsibility may be delegated in writing to other agency officials as appropriate. Implementing guidelines for agency performance appraisal systems shall provide written instructions for compliance with Office rules and procedures as well as descriptions of the documents and where they are retained, and shall ensure that records are retained in accordance with the provisions of § 293.402.

[47 FR 3080, Jan. 22, 1982, as amended at 51 FR 8411, Mar. 11, 1986; 56 FR 65416, Dec. 17, 1991; 66 FR 66709, Dec. 27, 2001]

§ 293.406 Disclosure of records.

Disclosure as used here means the furnishing of the record to someone other than the individual to whom the record pertains, his/her designated representative, or to an agency official who needs the information in the performance of official duties. Disclosure of information from this file system shall be made only as permitted by the

Privacy Act (5 U.S.C. 552a(b)) and, with regard to the routine use provisions of that section, only under a routine use published by the Office for the system of records covering these records. However, to the extent that this system contains the data identified as being available to the public in § 293.311, for most Federal employees and under the same restrictions listed in that section, that information shall also be made available to the public from this system.

Subpart E—Employee Medical File System Records

SOURCE: 51 FR 33235, Sept. 19, 1986, unless otherwise noted.

§ 293.501 Applicability of regulations.

The applicability of this subpart is identical to that described in § 293.301.

§ 293.502 Definitions.

For the purpose of this Subpart—

Employee is defined at 5 U.S.C. 2105 and excludes student volunteers and contractor employees.

Employee Assistance and Counseling Record means the record created when an employee participates in an agency assistance/counseling program (e.g., drug or alcohol abuse or personal counseling programs under Pub. L. 91–616, 92–255, and 79–658, respectively).

Employee Exposure Record (which is to be interpreted consistent with the term as it is defined at 29 CFR 1910.20(c)(8)) means a record containing any of the following kinds of information concerning employee exposure to toxic substances or harmful physical agents (as defined at 29 CFR 1910.20(c)(11)):

(a) Environmental (workplace) monitoring or measuring, including personal, area, grab, wipe, or other form of sampling, as well as related collection and analytical methodologies, calculations, and other background data relevant to interpretation of the results obtained;

(b) Biological monitoring results which directly assess the absorption of a substance or agent by body systems (e.g., the level of a chemical in the blood, urine, breath, hair, fingernails, etc.) but not including results which assess the biological effect of a substance or agent;

(c) Material safety data sheets; or

(d) Any other record, in the absence of the above, which reveals the identity (e.g., chemical, common, or trade name) of a toxic substance of harmful physical agent.

Employee Medical File System (EMFS) means the agency's complete system (automated, microformed, and paper records) for employee occupational medical records.

Employee Medical Folder (EMF) means a separate file folder (normally SF 66–D) established to contain all of the occupational medical records (both long-tern and short-term records) designated for retention, which will be maintained by the employing agency during the employee's Federal service.

Epidemiological Record means a record maintained by an agency or subelement thereof as a result of an official medical research study conducted under the authority of the agency.

Implementing instructions means any form of internal agency issuance that provides the guidance required in § 293.503 and any other guidance the agency deems appropriate.

Occupational Medical Record means an occupation-related, chronological, cumulative record, regardless of the form or process by which it is maintained (e.g., paper document, microfiche, microfilm, or automatic data processing media), of information about health status developed on an employee, including personal and occupational health histories and the opinions and written evaluations generated in the course of diagnosis and/or employment-related treatment/examination by medical health care professionals and technicians. This definition includes the definition of medical records at 29 CFR 1910.20(c)(6); when the term "Occupational Medical Record" is used in these regulations, it includes "Employee Exposure Records" (as that term is defined in this section) and occupational illness, accident, and injury records.

Non-occupational/Patient Record means a record of treatment or examination, created and maintained by a health care facility, when the person is admitted to or voluntarily seeks treatment at the health care facility for non-job-related reasons. Records maintained by an agency dispensary are patient records for the purposes of these regulations except when such records result as a condition of employment or relate to an on-the-job occurrence. In these cases, the records are "Occupational Medical Records" as defined herein.

Non-personal Record means any agency aggregate or statistical record or report resulting from studies covering employees or resulting from studies or the work-site environment.

§ 293.503 Implementing instructions.

Agencies must issue written internal instructions describing how their EMFS is to be implemented. These instructions must—

(a) Describe overall operation of the system within the agency including the designation of the agency official who will be responsible for overall system management. When the agency has a medical officer, that individual must be named the system manager. The system manager may then designate others within the agency to handle the day-to-day management of the records, e.g., the custodian of the records at the site where they are maintained;

(b) Be prepared with joint participation by agency medical, health, and safety, and personnel officers;

(c) Describe where and under whose custody employee occupational medical records will be physically maintained;

(d) Designate which agency office(s) will be responsible for deciding when and what occupational medical records are to be disclosed either to other agency officials or outside the agency;

(e) Ensure proper records retention and security, and preserve confidentiality of doctor/patient relationships;

(f) Provide that when the agency is requesting an EMF from the National Personnel Records Center (NPRC), the request form will show the name, title, and address of that agency's system manager or designee, who is the only official authorized to receive the EMF;

(g) Be consistent with Office regulations relating to personnel actions when medical evidence is a factor (5 CFR parts 339, 432, 630, 752, and 831);

(h) Provide guidance on how an accounting of any record disclosure, as required by the Privacy Act (5 U.S.C. 552a(c)), will be done in a way that ensures that the accounting will be available for the life of the EMF;

(i) When long-term occupational medical records exist, provide for the creation of an EMF for an employee transferring to another agency or leaving Government service, and whether an EMF is to be established at the time an employee is being reassigned within the agency;

(j) Ensure a right of access (consistent with any special Privacy Act handling procedures invoked) to the records, in whatever format they are maintained, by the employee or a designated representative;

(k) Ensure that a knowledgeable official determines that all appropriate long-term occupational medical records are in an EMF prior to its transfer to another agency, to the NPRC, or to another office within the same employing agency;

(l) Ensure that all long-term occupational medical records an agency receives in an EMF are maintained, whether in that same EMF or by some other agency procedure, and forwarded to a subsequent employing agency or to NPRC;

(m) Ensure that, if occupational medical records are to be physically located in the same office as the Official Personnel Folder (OPF), the records are maintained physically apart from each other;

(n) Sets forth a policy that distinguishes, particularly for purposes of records disclosure, records in the nature of physician treatment records (which are generally not appropriate for disclosure to non-medical officials) from other medical reports properly available to officials making management decisions concerning the employee;

(o) Provide guidance that distinguishes records properly subject to this part from those (e.g., Postal Service or Foreign Service employee medical records) subject to different rules, particularly in Privacy Act and Freedom of Information Act matters;

(p) Ensure that guidance regarding the processing of Privacy Act matters is consistent with Office regulations implementing the Privacy Act at 5 CFR parts 293 and 297; and

(q) Ensure that no security classification is assigned to an EMF by including therein any occupational medical record that has such a classification. In this regard, the agency creating the classified medical record is required to retain it separately from the EMF while placing a notice in the EMF of its existence and describing where requests for this record are to be submitted.

§293.504 Composition of, and access to, the Employee Medical File System.

(a) All employee occupational medical records (which exclude employee assistance/counseling, patient, non-personal, and epidemiological records) whether they are maintained in an automated, microform, or paper mode, and wherever located in the agency, are part of the EMFS. The records maintained in the EMFS are part of a Governmentwide Privacy Act system of records established by the Office. Agencies have the responsibility to ensure that such documents are maintained in accordance with the Office's Privacy Act regulations in part 297 of this chapter, with the agency's instructions implementing those regulations, and with the retention schedule for employee medical records stipulated in §293.511. While non-occupational/patient records pertaining to an employee are not required to be included as a record within the EMFS, under certain conditions to be discussed in subsequent OPM guidance, copies of such records are occupationally-related and, in those cases, may be included in the system.

(b) Agencies must provide employees access to their own EMFS records consistent with Office regulations contained in §297.204(c) of this chapter. When unexcepted access can be provided directly to the employee, such unexcepted access must also be provided to any representative specifically designated in writing by the employee to receive the record. Disclosure of an employee's occupational medical records to agency officials (both medical and non-medical) will be granted only when the specific information sought is needed for the performance of official duties.

(c) Other agencies for employee occupational medical records made to the custodian of the records must be processed in accordance with the disclosure provisions of the Privacy Act (5 U.S.C. 552a(b)) and the Office's regulations at part 297 of this chapter.

(d) Processing of a Privacy Act request for amendment of any EMFS record must be consistent with the Office's regulations contained in part 297 of this chapter regarding amendment of records.

[51 FR 33235, Sept. 19, 1986, as amended at 66 FR 66709, Dec. 27, 2001]

§293.505 Establishment and protection of Employee Medical Folder.

(a) As required by these rules, agencies must establish an EMF when the employee leaves the employing agency and occupational medical records for that employee exist; agencies may also establish an EMF (if none presently exists) for active employees if the agency chooses. An agency must request the transfer of an existing EMF (and maintain that EMF as received) at the same time it requests the transfer of an employee's OPF using the procedures contained in §293.306.

(b) Neither the original occupational medical record nor duplicates are to be retained in the OPF. Prior to the establishment of an EMF for a separating employee, when such records are created, they must be maintained physically apart from the OPF, although they may be kept in the same office.

(c) Records in an EMF, whether or not located in an office other than where the OPF is maintained, must be properly safeguarded using procedures ensuring equal or greater levels of protection as those in §293.106. Disclosures must be made only to those authorized to receive them, as described in §293.504(b), and employees must be able to ascertain from agency implementing instructions the location of all of their medical records. An EMF must be under the control of a specifically designated medical, health, safety, or personnel officer as prescribed in the agency's implementing internal procedures.

§ 293.506 Ownership of the Employee Medical Folder.

The EMF of each employee in a position subject to civil service rules and regulations is part of the records of the Office. When the EMF also contains occupational medical records created during employment in a position not subject to the civil service (e.g., with the Postal Service), the EMF is then part of the records of both the Office and the employing agency.

§ 293.507 Maintenance and content of the Employee Medical Folder.

The agency head must maintain all appropriate employee occupational medical records in the EMFS. When an EMF is established for an employee, as required in § 293.504, the agency's EMFS must be searched to obtain all records designated for retention in the EMF.

§ 293.508 Type of folder to be used.

Each agency must use a folder that (a) has been specifically identified as the EMF and issued through Federal Supply Service contracts (Standard Form 66 D); (b) has been authorized as an exception to this form by the Office for use by a specific agency; or (c) in the case of an EMF containing records under joint control of the Office and another agency, an exception to the use of this form that has been jointly authorized.

§ 293.509 Use of existing Employee Medical Folders upon transfer or reemployment.

The requirements of § 293.306, regarding the use of existing OPFs, apply to the use of existing EMFs upon the employee's transfer to or reemployment in a new employing agency.

§ 293.510 Disposition of Employee Medical Folders.

(a) When an employee transfers to another Federal agency, the EMF must be transferred to the gaining agency at the same time as the employee's OPF. The EMF is to be addressed only to the gaining agency's designated manager (medical, health, safety, or personnel officer, or other designee) of the EMFS.

(b) When an employee is separated from the Federal service, the EMF must be forwarded to the NPRC with the OPF, using the instructions in § 293.307 of this part.

(c) When a former Federal employee is re-employed by an agency, and that agency believes that an EMF exists, either at the last employing agency or at the NPRC, the agency will request the EMF, but no sooner than 30 days after the date of the new appointment. No EMFs will be routinely retrieved during the initial review process (as is done with the OPF) except when authority exists for the agency to require a medical evaluation prior to reaching a decision on employability. EMFs are to be transferred by the NPRC only to the agency-designated manager (medical, health, safety, or personnel, or other designee) shown on the request form.

§ 293.511 Retention schedule.

(a) Temporary EMFS records must not be placed in a newly-created EMF for a separating employee and must be removed from an already existing EMF before its transfer to another agency or to the NPRC. Such records must be disposed of in accordance with General Records Schedule (GRS) 1, item 21, issued by the National Archives and Records Administration (NARA).

(b) Occupational Medical Records considered to be long-term records must be maintained for the duration of employment, plus 30 years or for as long as the OPF is maintained, whichever is longer. Therefore, upon separation, the records must be provided to the employee's new agency, or they must be transferred to the NPRC, which will dispose of them in accordance with GRS 1, item 21, issued by NARA.

PART 294—AVAILABILITY OF OFFICIAL INFORMATION

Subpart A—Procedures for Disclosure of Records Under the Freedom of Information Act

Sec.

Subpart B—The Public Information Function

Subpart C—Office Operations

Subpart D—Cross References

AUTHORITY: 5 U.S.C. 552, Freedom of Information Act, Pub. L. 92–502, as amended by the Freedom of Information Reform Act of 1986, Pub. L. 99–570, and E.O. 12600, 52 FR 23781, 3 CFR, 1987 Comp., p. 235.

Subpart A—Procedures for Disclosure of Records Under the Freedom of Information Act

SOURCE: 54 FR 25094, June 13, 1989, unless otherwise noted.

§294.101 Purpose.

This subpart contains the regulations of the Office of Personnel Management (OPM) implementing the Freedom of Information Act (FOIA), 5 U.S.C. 552. Except as provided by §294.105, OPM will use the provisions of this subpart to process all requests for records.

§294.102 General definitions.

All of the terms defined in the Freedom of Information Act, and the definitions included in the "Uniform Freedom of Information Act Fee Schedule and Guidelines" issued by the Office of Management and Budget apply, regardless of whether they are defined in this subpart.

Direct costs means the expenditures that an agency actually incurs in searching for, duplicating, and reviewing documents to respond to an FOIA request. Overhead expenses (such as the cost of space, and heating or lighting the facility in which the records are stored), are not included in direct costs.

Disclose or disclosure means making records available, on request, for examination and copying, or furnishing a copy of records.

Duplication means the process of making a copy of a document necessary to respond to an FOIA request. Among the forms that such copies can take are paper, microform, audiovisual materials, or machine readable documentation (e.g., magnetic tape or disk).

Records, information, document, and *material* have the same meaning as the term *agency records* in section 552 of title 5, United States Code.

Review means the process of initially examining documents located in response to a request to determine whether any portion of any document located may be withheld. It also includes processing documents for disclosure; e.g., doing all that is necessary to excise them and otherwise prepare them for release. Review does not include time spent resolving general legal and policy issues regarding the application of exemptions.

Search means the time spent looking for material that is responsive to a request, including page-by-page or line-by-line identification of material within documents.

[54 FR 25094, June 13, 1989, as amended at 58 FR 32043, June 8, 1993]

§294.103 Definitions of categories and assignment of requests and requesters to categories.

OPM will apply the definitions and procedures contained in this section to assign requesters to categories. The four categories established by 5 U.S.C. 552(a) are requests for commercial use, requests for non-commercial use made by educational or non-commercial scientific institutions, requests for non-commercial use made by representatives of the news media, and all others.

(a) *Request for commercial use.* A "commercial use request" is from or on behalf of one who seeks information for a use or purpose that furthers the commercial, trade, or profit interests of the requester or the person or institution on whose behalf the request is made. In determining whether a request properly belongs in this category, OPM will look first to the intended use of the documents being requested.

(b) *Request for non-commercial use made by an educational or non-commercial scientific institution.* OPM will include requesters in one of the two categories described in paragraphs (b) (1) and (2) of this section when the request is being made as authorized by, and under the auspices of, a qualifying institution; and the records are sought, not for a commercial use, but in furtherance of scholarly or scientific research.

(1) *Educational institution* refers to any public or private, preschool, elementary, or secondary school, institution of undergraduate or graduate higher education, or institution of professional or vocational education, which operates a program or programs of scholarly or scientific research.

(2) A *non-commercial scientific institution* refers to an institution that is not operated on a *commercial* basis as that term is referenced in paragraph (a) of this section, and which is operated solely to conduct scientific or scholarly research, the results of which are not intended to promote any particular product or industry.

(c) *Request from a representative of the news media.* "Representative of the news media" refers to any person actively gathering news for an entity that is organized and operated to publish, broadcast, or otherwise disseminate news to the public. The term "news" means information that is about current events or that would be of current interest to the public. Examples of news media entities include television or radio stations broadcasting to the public at large, and publishers of periodicals who make their products available for purchase or subscription by the general public. Free-lance journalists may be regarded as representatives of the news media if they demonstrate a solid basis for expecting publication, or some other form of dissemination, through a particular organization even though they are not actually employed by it. OPM will assign news media officials to this category only when a request is not for commercial use. If a person meets the other qualifications for inclusion, OPM will not apply the term "commercial use" to his or her request for records in support of a news dissemination function.

(d) *Requests from others.* The category "all others," consists of any requesters not covered by paragraphs (a), (b), or (c) of this section. However, as provided by § 294.105, OPM will use its Privacy Act regulations, rather than this subpart, when individuals ask for records about themselves that may be filed in OPM systems of records.

§ 294.104 Clarifying a requester's category.

(a) *Seeking clarification of a requester's category.* OPM may seek additional clarification before assigning a person to a specific category if—

(1) There is reasonable cause to doubt the requester's intended use of records; or

(2) The intended use is not clear from the request itself; or

(3) There is any other reasonable doubt about qualifications that may affect the fees applicable or the services rendered under § 294.109.

(b) *Prompt notification to requester.* When OPM seeks clarification as provided by paragraph (a) of this section, it will provide prompt notification either by telephone or in writing of the information or materials needed.

(c) *Effect of seeking clarification on time limits for responding.* When applying the time limits in section 552 of title 5, United States Code, OPM will not officially consider any request for records as being received until the official who is assigned responsibility for making a decision on releasing the records has received any additional clarification sought under paragraphs (a) and (b) of this section; and has determined that the clarifying information is sufficient to correctly place the requester in one of the categories prescribed in this section. If the requested clarifying information is not received within a reasonable time, OPM will, based on the information available, determine a final category for the request and calculate applicable fees.

[54 FR 25094, June 13, 1989, as amended at 58 FR 32043, June 8, 1993]

§294.105 Access to the requester's own records.

When the subject of a record, or a duly authorized representative of the subject, requests his or her own records from a Privacy Act system of records, as defined by 5 U.S.C. 552a (a)(5), and the record is maintained so that it is retrieved by the subject's name or other personal identifier, OPM will process the request under the Privacy Act procedures in part 297 of this chapter.

§294.106 Handbook of Publications, Periodicals, and OPM Issuances.

(a)(1) Annually, OPM publishes OPM-AG-PSD-01, "Handbook of Publications, Periodicals, and Issuances," and accompanying addendum. This handbook and addendum lists material published and offered for sale are available for public inspection or copying. Unless the material is published and offered for sale, OPM makes available for public inspection and copying:

(i) Final opinions made by OPM in the adjudication of cases;

(ii) OPM policy statements and interpretations adopted by OPM but not published in the FEDERAL REGISTER; and

(iii) OPM administrative staff manuals and instructions that affect a member of the public.

(2) To the extent required to prevent a clearly unwarranted invasion of personal privacy, OPM may delete identifying details when it makes available or publishes an opinion, statement of policy, interpretation, or staff manual or instruction.

(b) A copy of this handbook and addendum is available at no cost from the—Publishing Management Branch, Office of Personnel Management, room B464, 1900 E Street, NW., Washington, DC 20415–0001.

(c) OPM indexes material in this handbook and addendum format for the convenience of the public. Indexing does not constitute a determination that all of the material listed is within the category that is required to be indexed by 5 U.S.C. 552(a)(2). Most of OPM's publications may be found in OPM's Library in room 5H27 at the address listed in paragraph (b) of this section.

(d) As provided by 5 U.S.C. 552(a)(2), OPM has determined that it is unnecessary and impractical to publish the "Handbook of Publications, Periodicals, and Issuances" and addendum more frequently than annually because of the small number of revisions that occur.

[57 FR 32150, July 21, 1992, as amended at 66 FR 66710, Dec. 27, 2001]

§294.107 Places to obtain records.

(a) Address requests for OPM records to the officials listed in paragraph (b), (c), or (d) of this section.

(b) The following is a list of key Washington, DC, officials of OPM and their principal areas of responsibility. Address requests for records to the appropriate official using the official's title and the following address: Office of Personnel Management, 1900 E Street, NW., Washington, DC 20415.

Send to—	For subject-matter about—
Associate Director for Administration.	Administrative services; information management, including automated data processing; equal employment opportunity; procurement; and personnel.
Associate Director for Retirement and Insurance.	Retirement; life and health insurance.
Associate Director for Personnel Systems and Oversight.	Personnel management in agencies; pay; position classification; wage grade jobs; performance management; and employee and labor relations.
Assistant Director for Workforce Information.	Governmentwide personnel statistics; official personnel and employee medical folders.
Associate Director for Investigations.	Background investigations and related records on individuals.
Associate Director for Career Entry.	Nationwide examining and testing for employment; promotions; administrative law judges; affirmative employment programs for minorities, women, veterans, and the handicapped; recruiting and employment; and staffing policy.
Chief Financial Officer ...	Financial management.
Director for Human Resources Development.	Training, education, and development; senior executive service.
Director, Washington Area Service Center.	Examining, testing, and training operations in Washington, DC.

(c) Direct requests for records on subjects not specifically referred to in this section or in the handbook or addendum, to Plans and Policies Division (CHP–500), Office of Information Resources Management, Administration Group, Office of Personnel Management, 1900 E Street, NW., Washington, DC 20415.

(d) The following is a list of OPM regional offices. Address requests for regional records to the Regional Director, Office of Personnel Management in the appropriate region:

- Atlanta Region—Richard B. Russell Federal Building, Suite 904, 75 Spring Street, SW., Atlanta, GA 30303–3019.
- Chicago Region—John C. Kluczynski Federal Building, 30th Floor, 230 South Dearborn Street, Chicago, IL 60604.
- Dallas Region—1100 Commerce Street, Dallas, TX 75242.
- Philadelphia Region—William J. Green, Jr., Federal Building, 600 Arch Street, Philadelphia, PA 19106–1596.
- San Francisco Region—211 Main Street, 7th Floor, San Francisco, CA 94105.

(e) *When an organization does not have records in its custody.* When an OPM organization receives a Freedom of Information Act request for OPM records that it does not have in its possession, it will normally either—

(1) Retrieve the records from the organization that has possession of them; or

(2) Promptly forward the request to the appropriate organization. If a person has asked to be kept apprised of anything that will delay the official receipt of a request, OPM will provide notice of this forwarding action. Otherwise, OPM may, at its option, provide such notice.

(f) *Applying the time limits.* When applying the time limits in section 552 of title 5, United States Code, OPM will not officially consider any request to be received until it arrives in the OPM organization that has responsibility for the records sought.

(g) *Records from other Government agencies.* When a person seeks records that originated in another Government agency, OPM may refer the request to the other agency for response. Ordinarily, OPM will provide notice of this type of referral.

(h) *Creating records.* If a person seeks information from OPM in a format that does not currently exist, OPM will not ordinarily compile the information for the purpose of creating a record to respond to the request. OPM will advise the individual that it does not have records in the format sought. If other existing records would reasonably respond to the request or portions of it, OPM may provide these. If fees as provided in § 294.109 apply to any alternative records, OPM will advise the requester before providing the records.

[54 FR 25094, June 13, 1989, as amended at 57 FR 32150, July 21, 1992; 58 FR 32044, June 8, 1993]

§ 294.108 Procedures for obtaining records.

(a) *Mailing or delivering a request.* Any person may ask for records under section 552 of title 5, United States Code, by directing a letter to one of the organizations listed in § 294.107, or by delivering a request in person at the addresses listed in that section during business hours on a regular business day.

(b) *Proper marking.* Each request for records should have a clear and prominent notation on the first page, such as "Freedom of Information Act Request." In addition, if sent by mail or otherwise submitted in an envelope or other cover, mark the outside clearly and prominently with "FOIA Request" or "Freedom of Information Act Request."

(c) *Contents of request letter.* A request must describe the records sought in sufficient detail to enable OPM personnel to locate the records with a reasonable amount of effort.

(1) OPM will regard a request for a specific category of records as fulfilling the requirements of this paragraph, if it enables responsive records to be identified by a technique or process that is not unreasonably burdensome or disruptive to OPM operations.

(2) Whenever possible, a request should include specific information about each record sought, such as the date, number, title or name, author, recipient, and subject matter of the record.

(3) If an OPM organization determines that a request does not reasonably describe the records sought, it will either provide notice of any additional information needed or otherwise state why the request is insufficient. OPM

will also offer the record seeker an opportunity to confer, with the objective of reformulating the request so that it meets the requirements of this section.

(d) *Medical records.* OPM or another Government agency may disclose the medical records of an applicant, employee, or annuitant to the subject of the record, or to a representative designated in writing. However, medical records may contain information about an individual's mental or physical condition that a prudent physician would hesitate to give to the individual. Under such circumstances, OPM may disclose the records, including the exact nature and probable outcome of the condition, only to a licensed physician designated in writing for that purpose by the individual or his or her designated representative.

(e) *Publications.* If the subject matter of a request includes material published and offered for sale (e.g., by the Superintendent of Documents, Government Printing Office), OPM will explain where a person may review and/or purchase the publications.

(f) *Responses within 10 working days.* Except in unusual circumstances (as defined in 5 U.S.C. 552(a)(6)(B)), OPM will determine whether to disclose or deny records within 10 working days after receipt of the request (excluding weekends and holidays) and will provide notice immediately of its determination and the reasons therefor, and of the right to appeal any adverse determination.

[54 FR 25094, June 13, 1989, as amended at 58 FR 32044, June 8, 1993]

§ 294.109 Fees.

(a) *Applicability of fees.* (1) OPM will furnish, without charge, reasonable quantities of material that it has available for free distribution to the public.

(2) OPM may furnish other materials, subject to payment of fees intended to recoup the full allowable direct costs of providing services. Fees for these materials may be waived if the request meets the requirements specified in paragraph (f) of this section.

(3) If a request does not include an acceptable agreement to pay fees and does not otherwise convey a willingness to pay fees, OPM will promptly provide notification of the estimated fees. This notice will offer an opportunity to confer with OPM staff to reformulate the request to meet the requester's needs at a lower cost. Upon agreement to pay the required fees, OPM will further process the request.

(4) As described in § 294.107, OPM ordinarily responds to FOIA requests in a decentralized manner. Because of this, OPM may at times refer a single request to two or more OPM entities to make separate direct responses. In such cases, each responding entity may assess fees as provided by this section, but only for direct costs associated with any response it has prepared.

(5) If fees for document search are authorized as provided in paragraph (c) of this section, OPM may assess charges for employee time spent searching for documents and other direct costs of a search, even if a search fails to locate records or if records located are determined to be exempt from disclosure. Searches should be conducted in the most efficient and least expensive manner so as to minimize the cost for both the agency and the requester, e.g., personnel should not engage in line-by-line search when photocopying an entire document would be a less expensive and quicker way to comply with a request.

(6) Services requested and performed but not required under the FOIA, such as formal certification of records as true copies, will be subject to charges under the Federal User Charge Statute (31 U.S.C. 483a) or other applicable statutes.

(b) *Rates used to compute fees.* The following rates form the basis for assessing reasonable, standard charges for document search, duplication, and review as required by 5 U.S.C. 552(a)(4). The listing of rates below should be used in conjunction with the fee components listed in paragraph (c) of this section:

Service	Rate
Employee time	Salary rate plus 16% to cover benefits.
Photocopies (up to 8½″ × 14″).	$.013 per page.
Printed materials, per 25 pages or fraction thereof.	$.025.
Computer time	Actual direct cost.
Supplies and other materials	Actual direct cost.
Other costs not identified above.	Actual direct cost.

(c) *Assessing fees based on requester's category.* Rates are assessed differently for the different categories of requesters as defined in § 294.103. Requests have three cost components for the purpose of assessing fees: the cost of document search, the cost of duplication, and the cost of review. OPM will apply the rates in paragraph (b) of this section to the cost components that apply to the requester's category as follows:

Requester's category	Search	Review	Duplication
Commercial	Actual direct costs	Actual direct costs	Actual direct costs.
Non-commercial (educational or scientific institution) or news media.	No charge	No charge	Actual direct costs. [1]
All others	Actual direct costs [2]	No charge	Actual direct costs. [1]

[1] First 100 pages of paper copies or reasonable equivalent, such as a microfiche containing the equivalent of 100 pages, are copied free.

[2] First 2 hours of manual search time are free. If requested records are maintained in a computerized data base, OPM will use the following formula, suggested by OMB, to provide the equivalent of 2 hours manual search time free before charging for computer search time: The operator's hourly salary plus 16% will be added to the hourly cost of operating the central processing unit that contains the record information.

(d) *Payment of fees.* Fees are payable by check or money order to the Office of Personnel Management.

(1) If the total charge for fulfilling the request will be less than $25, no fee will be assessed (except as provided in paragraph (d)(3) of this section).

(2) If a request may reasonably result in a fee assessment of more than $25, OPM will not release the records unless the requester agrees in advance to pay the anticipated charges.

(3) OPM may aggregate requests and charge fees accordingly, when there is a reasonable belief that a requester, or a group of requesters acting in concert, is attempting to break down a request into a series of requests to evade the assessment of fees.

(i) If multiple requests of this type occur within a 30-day period, OPM may provide notice that it is aggregating the requests and that it will apply the fee provisions of this section, including any required agreement to pay fees and any advance payment.

(ii) Before aggregating requests of this type made over a period longer than 30 days, OPM will assure that it has a solid basis on which to conclude that the requesters are acting in concert and are acting specifically to avoid payment of fees.

(iii) OPM will not aggregate multiple requests on unrelated subjects from one person.

(e) *Payment of fees in advance.* If OPM estimates or determines that fees are likely to exceed $250, OPM may require the payment of applicable fees in advance.

(1) If an OPM official, who is authorized to make a decision on a particular request, determines that the requester has a history of prompt payment of FOIA fees, OPM will provide notice of the likely cost and obtain satisfactory assurance of full payment.

(2) When a person, or an organization that a person represents, has previously failed to pay assessed fees in a timely manner (*i.e.*, payment was not made within 30 days of the billing date), OPM will require full payment of all fees in advance.

(3) If a person, or an organization that a person represents, has not paid fees previously assessed, OPM will not begin to process any new request for records until the requester has paid the full amount owed plus any applicable interest, and made a full advance payment for the new request.

(f) *Waiver or reduction of fees.* OPM will furnish documents without any charge, or at a reduced charge, if disclosure of the information is in the public interest because it is likely to contribute significantly to public understanding of the operations or activities of the Government, and release of the material is not primarily in the commercial interest of the requester.

(1) In determining whether disclosure is in the public interest because it is likely to contribute significantly to public understanding of the operations or activities of the Government, OPM shall consider the following factors:

(i) The subject of the request: Whether the subject of the requested records concerns "the operations or activities of the Government";

(ii) The information value of the information to be disclosed: Whether the disclosure is "likely to contribute" to an understanding of Government operations or activities;

(iii) The contribution to an understanding of the subject by the general public likely to result from disclosure: Whether disclosure of the requested information will contribute to "public understanding"; and

(iv) The significance of the contribution to public understanding: Whether the disclosure is likely to contribute "significantly" to public understanding of Government operations or activities.

(2) In determining whether disclosure of the information is or is not primarily in the commercial interest of the requester, OPM shall consider the following factors:

(i) *The existence and magnitude of a commercial interest.* Whether the requester has a commercial interest that would be furthered by the requested disclosure; and, if so—

(ii) *The primary interest in disclosure.* Whether the magnitude of the identified commercial interest of the requester is sufficiently large, in comparison with the public interest in disclosure, that disclosure is "primarily in the commercial interest of the requester."

(3) In all cases the burden of proof shall be on the requester to present evidence or information in support of a request for a waiver or reduction of fees.

(g) *Denial of waiver request.* (1) An OPM official may deny a request for a full or partial waiver of fees without further consideration if the request does not include:

(i) A clear statement of the requester's interest in the requested information;

(ii) A clear statement of the use proposed for the information and whether the requester will derive income or other benefit from such use;

(iii) A clear statement of how the public will benefit from OPM's release of the requested information; and

(iv) If specialized use of the documents is contemplated, a clear statement of the requester's qualifications that are relevant to the specialized use.

(2) A requester may appeal the denial of a waiver request as provided by § 294.110 of this part.

(h) *Fees not paid; penalties; debt collection.* (1) If a request, which requires the advance payment of fees under the criteria specified in this section, is not accompanied by the required payment, OPM will promptly notify the requester that the required fee must be paid within 30 days, and that OPM will not further process the request until it receives payment.

(2) OPM may begin assessing interest charges on an unpaid bill starting on the 31st day following the date on which the bill was sent. Interest will be charged at the rate prescribed in 31 U.S.C. 3717, and will accrue from the date of the billing.

(3) To encourage the repayment of debts incurred under this subpart, OPM may use the procedures authorized by Public Law 97–365, the Debt Collection Act of 1982. This may include disclosure to consumer reporting agencies and the use of collection agencies.

[58 FR 32044, June 8, 1993]

§ 294.110 Appeals.

(a) When an OPM official denies records or a waiver of fees under the Freedom of Information Act, the requester may appeal to the—

Office of the General Counsel, Office of Personnel Management, Washington, DC 20415

(b) A person may appeal denial of a Freedom of Information Act request for information maintained by OPM's Office of the General Counsel to the—

Deputy Director, Office of Personnel Management Washington, DC 20415

(c) If an official of another agency denies a Freedom of Information Act request for records in one of OPM's Government-wide systems of records, the requester should consult that agency's regulations for any appeal rights that may apply. An agency may, at its discretion, direct these appeals to OPM's Office of the General Counsel.

(d) An appeal should include a copy of the initial request, a copy of the letter denying the request, and a statement explaining why the appellant believes the denying official erred.

(e) The appeals provided for in this section constitute the final levels of administrative review that are available. If a denial of information or a denial of a fee waiver is affirmed, the requester may seek judicial review in the district court of the United States in the district in which he or she resides, or has his or her principal place of business, or in which the agency records are situated, or in the District of Columbia.

§ 294.111 Custody of records; subpoenas.

(a) The Chief, Plans and Policies Division, Administration Group, OPM, has official custody of OPM records. A subpoena or other judicial order for an official record from OPM should be served on the—

Chief, Plans and Policies Division, Office of Personnel Management, 1900 E Street NW., Washington, DC 20415

(b) See 5 CFR part 297, subpart D—Disclosure of Records, of this title, for the steps other officials should take on receipt of a subpoena or other judicial order for an Office record.

[54 FR 25094, June 13, 1989, as amended at 57 FR 32150, July 21, 1992]

§ 294.112 Confidential commercial information.

(a) In general, OPM will not disclose confidential commercial information in response to a Freedom of Information Act request except in accordance with this section.

(b) The following definitions from Executive Order 12600, apply to this section:

(1) *Confidential commercial information* means records provided to the Government by a submitter that arguably contain material exempt from release under Exemption 4 of the Freedom of Information Act, 5 U.S.C. 552(b)(4), because disclosure could reasonably be expected to cause substantial competitive harm.

(2) *Submitter* means any person or entity who provides confidential commercial information, directly or indirectly, to OPM. The term includes, but is not limited to, corporations, state governments, and foreign governments.

(c) Submitters of information shall designate by appropriate markings, either at the time of submission or at a reasonable time thereafter, any portions of their submissions that they consider to be confidential commercial information. Such designations shall expire 10 years after the date of submission unless the submitter requests, and provides reasonable justification for, a designation period of greater duration.

(d) OPM shall, to the extent permitted by law, provide prompt written notice to an information submitter of Freedom of Information requests or administrative appeals if:

(1) The submitter has made a good faith designation that the requested material is confidential commercial information, or

(2) OPM has reason to believe that the requested material may be confidential commercial information.

(e) The written notice required in paragraph (d) of this section shall either describe the confidential commercial material requested or include as an attachment, copies or pertinent portions of the records.

(f) Whenever OPM provides the notification and opportunity to object required by paragraphs (d) and (h) of this section, it will advise the requester that notice and an opportunity to object are being provided to the submitter.

(g) The notice requirements of paragraph (d) of this section shall not apply if:

(1) OPM determines that the information should not be disclosed;

(2) The information has been lawfully published or officially made available to the public;

(3) Disclosure of the information is required by law (other than 5 U.S.C. 552);

(4) The information was submitted on or after August 20, 1992, and has not been designated by the submitter as exempt from disclosure in accordance

with paragraph (c) of this section, unless OPM has substantial reason to believe that disclosure of the information would result in competitive harm; or

(5) The designation made by the submitter in accordance with paragraph (c) of this section appears obviously frivolous; except that, in such a case, OPM shall, within a reasonable number of days prior to a specified disclosure date, notify the submitter in writing of any final administrative decision to disclose the information.

(h) The notice described in paragraph (d) of this section shall give a submitter a reasonable period from the date of the notice to provide OPM with a detailed written statement of any objection to disclosure. The statement shall specify all grounds for withholding any of the material under any exemption of the Freedom of Information Act. When Exemption 4 of the FOIA is cited as the grounds for withholding, the specification shall demonstrate the basis for any contention that the material is a trade secret or commercial or financial information that is privileged or confidential. It must also include a specification of any claim of competitive harm, including the degree of such harm, that would result from disclosure. Information provided in response to this paragraph may itself be subject to disclosure under the FOIA. Information provided in response to this paragraph shall also be subject to the designation requirements of paragraph (c) of this section. Failure to object in a timely manner shall be considered a statement of no objection by OPM, unless OPM extends the time for objection upon timely request from the submitter and for good cause shown. The provisions of this paragraph concerning opportunity to object shall not apply to notices of administrative appeals, when the submitter has been previously provided an opportunity to object at the time the request was initially considered.

(i) OPM shall consider carefully a submitter's objections and specific grounds for nondisclosure, when received within the period of time described in paragraph (h) of this section, prior to determining whether to disclose the information. Whenever OPM decides to disclose the information over the objection of a submitter, OPM shall forward to the submitter a written notice, which shall include:

(1) A statement of the reasons why the submitter's disclosure objections were not sustained;

(2) A description of the information to be disclosed; and

(3) A specified disclosure date.

(j) OPM will notify both the submitter and the requester of its intent to disclose material a reasonable number of days prior to the specified disclosure date.

(k) Whenever a requester brings suit seeking to compel disclosure of confidential commercial information, OPM shall promptly notify the submitter.

[57 FR 32150, July 21, 1992]

Subpart B—The Public Information Function

§ 294.201 Public information policy.

(a) In addition to the basic policies of the Office relative to the disclosure of information when requested by a member of the public, the Office has an independent public information policy for bringing to the attention of the public through news releases, publications of the Office, or other methods, information concerning the functions of the Office as a Federal agency, and the programs administered by the Office.

(b) The Assistant Director for Public Affairs carries out the public information policy of the Office. In addition, each employee of the Office shall cooperate in carrying out this policy.

[50 FR 3310, Jan. 24, 1985]

Subpart C—Office Operations

§ 294.301 Policy and interpretations.

(a) Statements of Office policy and interpretations of the laws and regulations administered by the Office which the Office has adopted, whether or not published in the FEDERAL REGISTER, are available to the public.

(b) Generally, memoranda, correspondence, opinions, data, staff studies, information received in confidence, and similar documentary material, when prepared for the purpose of internal communication within the Office or between the Office and other agencies, organizations, or persons, are not available to the public.

[50 FR 3310, Jan. 24, 1985, as amended at 66 FR 66710, Dec. 27, 2001]

Subpart D—Cross References

§ 294.401 References.

The table below provides assistance in locating other OPM regulations in title 5 of the Code of Federal Regulations that have provisions on the disclosure of records:

Type of information	Location
Classification appeal records	511.616.
Classification information	175.101.
Employee performance folders	293.311.
Examination and related subjects records.	300.201.
Grade and pay retention records	536.405.
Investigative records	736.104.
Job grading reviews and appeals records.	532.707.
Medical information	297.205 and 293 subpart E.
Official Personnel Folders	293.311.
Privacy and personnel records	297.
Retirement	831.106 and 841.108.

[54 FR 25098, June 13, 1989, as amended at 58 FR 32046, June 8, 1993; 70 FR 31286, May 31, 2005]

PART 295—TESTIMONY BY OPM EMPLOYEES RELATING TO OFFICIAL INFORMATION AND PRODUCTION OF OFFICIAL RECORDS IN LEGAL PROCEEDINGS

Subpart A—General Provisions

Sec.

Subpart B—Requests for Testimony and Production of Documents

Subpart C—Schedule of Fees

Subpart D—Penalties

AUTHORITY: 5 U.S.C. App. (Sec. 1103, Civil Service Reform Act of 1978; 31 U.S.C. 9701).

SOURCE: 73 FR 58020, Oct. 6, 2008, unless otherwise noted.

Subpart A—General Provisions

§ 295.101 Scope and purpose.

(a) This part sets forth policies and procedures you must follow when you submit a demand or request to an employee of the U.S. Office of Personnel Management (OPM) to produce official records and information, or provide testimony relating to official information, in connection with a legal proceeding. You must comply with these requirements when you request the release or disclosure of official records and information.

(b) OPM intends these provisions to:

(1) Promote economy and efficiency in its programs and operations;

(2) Minimize the possibility of involving OPM in controversial issues not related to our functions;

(3) Prevent the misuse of OPM employees as involuntary expert witnesses for private interests or as inappropriate expert witnesses as to the state of the law;

(4) Maintain OPM's impartiality among private litigants where neither OPM nor any other Federal entity is a named party; and

(5) Protect sensitive, confidential information and the deliberative processes of OPM.

(c) In providing for these requirements, OPM does not waive the sovereign immunity of the United States.

(d) This part provides guidance for the internal operations of OPM. It does not create any right or benefits, substantive or procedural, that a party may rely upon in any legal proceeding against the United States.

§ 295.102 Applicability.

This part applies to demands and requests to employees of OPM in legal proceedings in which OPM is not a named party, for factual or expert testimony relating to official information or for production of official records or information. However, it does not apply to:

(a) Demands upon or requests for a current OPM employee to testify as to facts or events that are unrelated to his or her official duties or that are unrelated to the functions of OPM;

(b) Demands upon or requests for a former OPM employee to testify as to matters in which the former employee was not directly or materially involved while at OPM;

(c) Requests for the release of records under the Freedom of Information Act, 5 U.S.C. 552, or the Privacy Act, 5 U.S.C. 552(a); and

(d) Congressional or Government Accountability Office (GAO) demands and requests for testimony or records.

§ 295.103 Definitions.

Demand means a subpoena, or an order or other command of a court or other competent authority, for the production, disclosure, or release of records or for the appearance and testimony of an OPM employee that is issued in a legal proceeding.

General Counsel means the General Counsel of OPM or a person to whom the General Counsel has delegated authority under this part.

Legal proceeding means any matter before a court of law, administrative board or tribunal, commission, administrative law judge, hearing officer, or other body that conducts a legal or administrative proceeding. Legal proceeding includes all phases of litigation.

OPM means the U.S. Office of Personnel Management.

OPM employee or employee means:

(1) Any current or former officer or employee of OPM;

(2) Any other individual hired through contractual agreement by or on behalf of the OPM or who has performed or is performing services under such an agreement for OPM; and

(3) Any individual who served or is serving in any consulting or advisory capacity to OPM, whether formal or informal.

(4) Provided, that this definition does not include persons who are no longer employed by OPM and who are retained or hired as expert witnesses or who agree to testify about general matters available to the public, or matters with which they had no specific involvement or responsibility during their employment with OPM.

Records or official records and information mean:

(1) All documents and materials which are OPM agency records under the Freedom of Information Act, 5 U.S.C. 552;

(2) All other documents and materials contained in OPM files; and

(3) All other information or materials acquired by an OPM employee in the performance of his or her official duties or because of his or her official status.

Request means any informal request, by whatever method, for the production of records and information or for testimony which has not been ordered by a court or other competent authority.

Testimony means any written or oral statements, including depositions, answers to interrogatories, affidavits, declarations, recorded interviews, and statements made by an individual in connection with a legal proceeding.

Subpart B—Requests for Testimony and Production of Documents

§ 295.201 General prohibition.

No employee may produce official records and information or provide any testimony relating to official information in response to a demand or request without the prior, written approval of the General Counsel.

§ 295.202 Factors OPM will consider.

The General Counsel, in his or her sole discretion, may grant an employee permission to testify on matters relating to official information, or produce official records and information, in response to an appropriate demand or request. Among the relevant factors that the General Counsel may consider in making this decision are whether:

(a) The purposes of this part are met;

(b) Allowing such testimony or production of records would be necessary to prevent a miscarriage of justice;

(c) OPM has an interest in the decision that may be rendered in the legal proceeding;

(d) Allowing such testimony or production of records would assist or hinder OPM in performing its statutory duties or use OPM resources in a way that will interfere with the ability of OPM employees to do their regular work;

(e) Allowing such testimony or production of records would be in the best interest of OPM or the United States;

(f) The records or testimony can be obtained from other sources;

(g) The demand or request is unduly burdensome or otherwise inappropriate under the applicable rules of discovery or the rules of procedure governing the case or matter in which the demand or request arose;

(h) Disclosure would violate a statute, Executive order or regulation;

(i) Disclosure would reveal confidential, sensitive, or privileged information, trade secrets or similar, confidential commercial or financial information, otherwise protected information, or would otherwise be inappropriate for release;

(j) Disclosure would impede or interfere with an ongoing law enforcement investigation or proceedings, or compromise constitutional rights;

(k) Disclosure would result in OPM appearing to favor one private litigant over another private litigant;

(l) Disclosure relates to documents that were produced by another agency;

(m) A substantial Government interest is implicated;

(n) The demand or request is within the authority of the party making it;

(o) The demand improperly seeks to compel an OPM employee to serve as an expert witness for a private interest;

(p) The demand improperly seeks to compel an OPM employee to testify as to a matter of law;

(q) The demand or request is sufficiently specific to be answered.

§ 295.203 Filing requirements for demands or requests for documents or testimony.

You must comply with the following requirements whenever you issue demands or requests to an OPM employee for official records and information or testimony.

(a) Your request must be in writing and must be submitted to the General Counsel. If you serve a subpoena on OPM or an OPM employee before submitting a written request and receiving a final determination, OPM will oppose the subpoena on grounds that your request was not submitted in accordance with this subpart.

(b) You written request must contain the following information:

(1) The caption of the legal proceeding, docket number, and name and address of the court or other authority involved.

(2) A copy of the complaint or equivalent document setting forth the assertions in the case and any other pleading or document necessary to show relevance;

(3) A list of categories of records sought, a detailed description of how the information sought is relevant to the issues in the legal proceeding, and a specific description of the substance of the testimony or records sought;

(4) A statement as to how the need for the information outweighs the need to maintain any confidentiality of the information and outweighs the burden on OPM to produce the records or provide testimony;

(5) A statement indicating that the information sought is not available from another source, from other persons or entities, or from the testimony of someone other than an OPM employee, such as a retained expert;

(6) If testimony is requested, the intended use of the testimony, a general summary of the desired testimony, and a showing that no document could be provided and used in lieu of testimony;

(7) A description of all prior decisions, orders, or pending motions in the case that bear upon the relevance of the requested records or testimony;

(8) The name, address, and telephone number of counsel to each party in the case; and

(9) An estimate of the amount of time that the requester and other parties will require with each OPM employee for time spent by the employee to prepare for testimony, in travel, and for attendance in the legal proceeding.

(c) The Office of Personnel Management reserves the right to require additional information to complete your request where appropriate.

(d) Your request should be submitted at least 45 days before the date that records or testimony is required. Requests submitted in less than 45 days before records or testimony is required must be accompanied by a written explanation stating the reasons for the late request and the reasons for expedited processing.

(e) Failure to cooperate in good faith to enable the General Counsel to make an informed decision may serve as the basis for a determination not to comply with your request.

§ 295.204 Service of subpoenas or requests.

Subpoenas or requests for official records or information or testimony must be served on the General Counsel, U.S. Office of Personnel Management, 1900 E Street, NW., Washington, DC 20415.

§ 295.205 Processing demands or requests.

(a) After service of a demand or request to testify, the General Counsel will review the demand or request and, in accordance with the provisions of this subpart, determine whether, or under what conditions, to authorize the employee to testify on matters relating to official information and/or produce official records and information.

(b) OPM will process requests in the order in which they are received. Absent exigent or unusual circumstances, OPM will respond within 45 days from the date that we receive it. The time for response will depend upon the scope of the request.

(c) The General Counsel may grant a waiver of any procedure described by this subpart where a waiver is considered necessary to promote a significant interest of OPM or the United States or for other good cause.

§ 295.206 Final determination.

The General Counsel makes the final determination on demands and requests to employees for production of official records and information or testimony. All final determinations are within the sole discretion of the General Counsel. The General Counsel will notify the requester and the court or other authority of the final determination, the reasons for the grant or denial of the demand or request, and any conditions that the General Counsel may impose on the release of records or information, or on the testimony of an OPM employee.

§ 295.207 Restrictions that apply to testimony.

(a) The General Counsel may impose conditions or restrictions on the testimony of OPM employees including, for example, limiting the areas of testimony or requiring the requester and other parties to the legal proceeding to agree that the transcript of the testimony will be kept under seal or will only be used or made available in the particular legal proceeding for which testimony was requested. The General Counsel may also require a copy of the transcript of testimony at the requester's expense.

(b) OPM may offer the employee's written declaration in lieu of testimony.

(c) If authorized to testify pursuant to this part, an employee may testify as to facts within his or her personal knowledge, but, unless specifically authorized to do so by the General Counsel, the employee shall not:

(1) Disclose confidential or privileged information;

(2) Testify as to facts when the General Counsel determines such testimony would not be in the best interest of OPM or the United States; or

(3) For a current OPM employee, testify as an expert or opinion witness with regard to any matter arising out of the employee's official duties or the functions of OPM unless testimony is being given on behalf of the United States.

§ 295.208 Restrictions that apply to released records.

(a) The General Counsel may impose conditions or restrictions on the release of official records and information, including the requirement that parties to the proceeding obtain a protective order or execute a confidentiality agreement to limit access and any further disclosure. The terms of the protective order or of a confidentiality agreement must be acceptable to the General Counsel. In cases where protective orders or confidentiality agreements have already been executed, OPM may condition the release of official records and information on an amendment to the existing protective order or confidentiality agreement.

(b) If the General Counsel so determines, original OPM records may be presented for examination in response to a demand or request, but they are not to be presented as evidence or otherwise used in a manner by which they could lose their identify as official OPM records, and they are not to be marked or altered. In lieu of the original records, certified copies will be presented for evidentiary purposes (see 28 U.S.C. 1733).

§ 295.209 Procedure when a decision is not made prior to the time a response is required.

If a response to a demand or request is required before the General Counsel can make the determination referred to in Sec.295.206, the General Counsel, when necessary, will provide the court or other competent authority with a copy of this part, inform the court or other competent authority that the demand or request is being reviewed, and seek a stay of the demand or request pending a final determination.

§ 295.210 Procedure in the event of an adverse ruling.

If the court or other competent authority fails to stay the demand, the employee upon whom the demand or request is made, unless otherwise advised by the General Counsel, will appear at the stated time and place, produce a copy of this part, state that the employee has been advised by counsel not to provide the requested testimony or produce documents, and respectfully decline to comply with the demand, citing *United States ex rel. Touhy* v. *Ragen*, 340 U.S. 462 (1951). A written response may be offered to a request, or to a demand, if permitted by the court or other competent authority.

Subpart C—Schedule of Fees

§ 295.301 Fees.

(a) *Generally.* The General Counsel may condition the production of records or appearance for testimony upon advance payment of a reasonable estimate of the costs to OPM.

(b) *Fees for records.* Fees for producing records will include fees for searching, reviewing, and duplicating records, costs of attorney time spent in reviewing the demand or request, and expenses generated by materials and equipment used to search for, produce, and copy the responsive information. Costs for employee time will be calculated on the basis of the hourly pay of the employee (including all pay, allowance, and benefits). Fees for duplication will be the same as those charged by OPM in its Freedom of Information Act regulations at 5 CFR part 294.

(c) *Witness fees.* Fees for attendance by a witness will include fees, expenses, and allowances prescribed by the court's rules. If no such fees are prescribed, witness fees will be determined based upon the rule of the Federal district court closest to the location where the witness will appear. Such fees will include cost of time spent by the witness to prepare for testimony, in travel, and for attendance in the legal proceeding.

(d) *Payment of fees.* You must pay witness fees for current OPM employees and any records certification fees by submitting to the General Counsel a check or money order for the appropriate amount made payable to the Treasury of the United States. In the case of testimony by former OPM employees, you must pay applicable fees directly to the former employee in accordance with 28 U.S.C. 1821 or other applicable statutes.

(e) *Certification (authentication) of copies of records.* The U.S. Office of Personnel Management may certify that records are true copies in order to facilitate their use as evidence. If you seek certification, you must request certified copies from OPM at least 45 days before the date they will be needed. The request should be sent to the General Counsel. You will be charged a certification fee of $15.00 for each document certified.

(f) *Waiver or reduction of fees.* The General Counsel, in his or her sole discretion, may, upon a showing of reasonable cause, waive or reduce any fees in connection with the testimony, production, or certification of records.

(g) *De minimis fees.* Fees will not be assessed if the total charge would be $10.00 or less.

Subpart D—Penalties

§ 295.401 Penalties.

(a) An employee who discloses official records or information or gives testimony relating to official information, except as expressly authorized by OPM or as ordered by a Federal court after OPM has had the opportunity to be heard, may face the penalties provided in 18 U.S.C. 641 and other applicable laws. Additionally, former OPM employees are subject to the restrictions and penalties of 18 U.S.C. 207 and 216.

(b) A current OPM employee who testifies or produces official records and information in violation of this part may be subject to disciplinary action.

PART 297—PRIVACY PROCEDURES FOR PERSONNEL RECORDS

AUTHORITY: Sec. 3, Pub. L. 93–579, 88 Stat. 1896 (5 U.S.C. 552a).

SOURCE: 53 FR 1998, Jan. 26, 1988, unless otherwise noted.

Subpart A—General Provisions

§ 297.101 Purpose and scope.

This part sets forth the regulations of the U.S. Office of Personnel Management (the Office) to govern the maintenance, protection, disclosure, and amendment of records within the systems of records as defned by the Privacy Act of 1974 (5 U.S.C. 552a), Public Law 93–579.

§ 297.102 Definitions.

In this part, the terms *agency, individual, maintain, record, statistical records,* and *systems of records* have the same meanings as defined in the Privacy Act, 5 U.S.C. 552a. In addition:

Access means providing a copy of a record to, or allowing review of the original record by, the data subject or the data subject's authorized representative, parent, or legal guardian;

Act means the Privacy Act of 1974, Public Law 93–579, 5 U.S.C. 552a, as amended;

Agency means any department or independent establishment in the Executive Branch of the Federal Government, including a Government corporation, of Government-controlled corporation, except those specifically excluded from the Office recordkeeping requirements by statute, this title, or formal agreement between the Office and the agency.

Amendment means the correction, addition, deletion, or destruction of a record or specific portions of a record;

Data subject means the individual to whom the information pertains and by whose name or other individual identifier the information is retrieved;

Disclosure means providing personal review of a record, or a copy thereof, to someone other than the data subject or the data subject's authorized representative, parent, or legal guardian;

Office means the U.S. Office of Personnel Management;

Personnel record means any record concerning an individual which is maintained and used in the personnel management or personnel policy-making process; and

System manager means the Office or agency official, designated by the head of the agency, who has the authority to decide Privacy Act matters relative to each system of records maintained by the Office.

§ 297.103 Designations of authority by system manager.

The responsible Office system manager having jurisdiction over a system of records may designate in writing an Office employee to evaluate and issue the Office's decision on Privacy Act matters relating to either internal, central, or Governmentwide systems of records.

§ 297.104 Types of records.

The Office manages three generic types of personnel records systems:

(a) Internal systems of records are under the Office's physical control and are established and maintained by the Office solely on its own employees and, when appropriate, on others in contact with the Office regarding matters within its authority.

(b) Centralized systems of personnel records are physically established and maintained by the Office with regard to most current and former Federal employees and some applicants for Federal employment.

(c) Governmentwide systems of personnel records are maintained by the Office, and through Office delegations of authority, by Federal agencies with regard to their own employees or applicants for employment. Although they are Office records, they are in the physical custody of those agencies. Though in the physical custody of agencies, the Office retains authority under its record management authority and under the Privacy Act to decide appeals of initial agency determinations regarding access to and amendment of material in these systems.

§ 297.105 Agency and Office responsibilities for systems of records and applicability of the regulations.

(a) These regulations apply to processing requests from both current and former Office employees for records contained in internal, central, and Governmentwide systems of records managed by the Office.

(b) Agencies are solely and totally responsible for processing requests regarding records maintained in their internal systems of records. Agency regulations, and not these Office regulations, govern the implementation of the Privacy Act for agency internal systems; there is no right of appeal to the Office from an agency's determination regarding its internal agency records.

(c) For records maintained in the Office's central systems of records, the data subject should contact the appropriate Office system manager concerning Privacy Act matters. These regulations will apply to inquiries regarding records located in the central systems of records.

(d) For records maintained within the Office's Governmentwide systems of records, each agency is responsible, unless specifically excepted by the Office, for responding to initial Privacy

Act access and amendment requests from its own current employees. For records in Office Governmentwide systems, including those in Official Personnel Folders, Employee Performance Folders, and Employee Medical Folders, the Office is responsible for responding to initial Privacy Act access and amendment requests from former Federal employees.

(e) The procedures in this part apply to all such requests. The procedures in this part also apply to appeals from an agency initial determination regarding access to or amendment of records contained in the Office's Governmentwide systems of records.

(f) The Office follows the procedures in this part when—

(1) Processing initial requests regarding access to or amendment of records by its own employees and others that the Office is maintaining information on in its systems of records, including requests from former employees of an agency whose records properly reside in an Office Governmentwide system of records.

(2) Processing Privacy Act appeals regarding access to and amendment of records generated by another Federal agency, but which are contained in the Office's Governmentwide systems of records, after an agency has issued the initial decision.

(3) Processing initial requests and appeals concerning access to and amendment of records contained in the central systems of records.

(g) For requests concerning records and material of another agency that are in the custody of the Office, but not under its control or ownership, the Office reserves the right to either refer the request to the agency primarily responsible for the material or to notify the individual of the proper agency that should be contacted.

§297.106 Contact point for Privacy Act matters.

To determine what records the Office maintains in its system of records, requesters must write to the Assistant Director for Workforce Information, Personnel Systems and Oversight Group, Office of Personnel Management, 1900 E Street, NW., Washington, DC 20415. Using the Office's response, requesters can contact the particular system manager indicated in the Office's notices of its systems published in the FEDERAL REGISTER for further assistance in determining if the Office maintains information pertaining to them.

Subpart B—Request for Access

§297.201 General provisions.

(a) Individual's requesting access to records pertaining to them that are maintained in a system of records should submit a written request to the appropriate system manager and state that the request is being made pursuant to the Privacy Act of 1974.

(b) The Office or agency will require proof of identity from a requester. The Office or agency reserves the right to determine the adequacy of any such proof. The general identifying items the Office will require a requester to provide when a request is made to the Office are—

(1) Full name, signature, and home address;

(2) Social security number (for systems of records that include this identifier);

(3) Current or last place and dates of Federal employment, when appropriate and,

(4) Date and place of birth.

(c) An individual may be represented by another when requesting access to records.

§297.202 Methods of access.

(a) The methods for allowing access to records, when such access has been granted by the Office or agency, are:

(1) Inspection in person in the designated office during the hours specified by the Office or agency; or

(2) Transfer of records at the option of the Office or agency to another more convenient Federal facility.

(b) Generally, Office of Personnel Management offices will not furnish certified copies of records. When copies are to be furnished, they may be provided as determined by the Office and may require payment of any fee levied in accordance with the Office's established fee schedule.

(c) When the requester seeks to obtain original documentation, the Office reserves the right to limit the request to copies of the original records. Original records should be made available for review only in the presence of the system manager or designee. An agency should consult with the Office when it receives a request for original documentation. Section 2701(a) of title 18 of the United States Code makes it a crime to conceal, mutilate, obliterate, or destroy any record filed in a public office, or to attempt to do so.

§ 297.203 Access by the parent of a minor or by the legal guardian of an individual declared to be incompetent.

(a) A parent, legal guardian, or custodian of a minor, upon presentation of suitable personal identification, may access on behalf of a minor any record pertaining to the minor in a system of records maintained by the Office.

(b) A legal guardian, upon presentation of documentation establishing guardianship, may access on behalf of an individual declared to be incompetent by a court of competent jurisdiction, any record pertaining to that individual in a system of records maintained by the Office.

(c) Minors are not precluded from exercising personally those rights provided them by the Privacy Act.

§ 297.204 Access by the representative of the data subject.

A record may be disclosed to a representative of the individual to whom the record pertains after the system manager receives written authorization from the individual who is the subject of the record.

§ 297.205 Access to medical records.

When a request for access involves medical or psychological records that the system manager believes requires special handling, the requester should be advised that the material will be provided only to a physician designated by the data subject. Upon receipt of the designation and upon verification of the physician's identity, the records will be made available to the physician, who will have full authority to disclose those records to the data subject when appropriate.

§ 297.206 Fees charged by the Office.

(a) No fees will be charged for search and review time expended by the Office to produce a record, or for making a photostatic copy of the record, or for having it personally reviewed by the data subject, when a record is retrieved from a system of records pertaining to that data subject. Additional copies provided may be charged under the Office's established fee schedule.

(b) When the fees chargeable under this section will amount to more than $25, the requester will be notified and payment of fees may be required before the records are provided.

(c) Remittance should be made by either a personal check, bank draft, or a money order that is made payable to the U.S. Office of Personnel Management and addressed to the appropriate system manager.

§ 297.207 Denials of access and appeals with respect to such denials.

(a) If an access request is denied, the Office or agency response will be in writing and will include a statement of the reasons for the denial and the procedures available to appeal the denial, including the name, position title, and address of the Office official responsible for the review.

(b) Nothing in this part should be construed to entitle a data subject the right to access any information compiled in reasonable anticipation of a civil action or proceeding.

(c) For denials of access made under this subpart, the following procedures apply:

(1) For initial denials made by an agency, when the record is maintained in an Office Governmentwide system of records, a request for adminstrative review should be made only to the Assistant Director for Workforce Information, Personnel Systems and Oversight Group, U.S. Office of Personnel Management, 1900 E Street NW., Washington, DC 20415.

(2) For denials initially made by an Office official, when a record is maintained in an internal or central system of records, a request for administrative review should be made to the Information and Privacy Appeals Counsel, Office of the General Counsel, U.S. Office

of Personnel Management, 1900 E Street NW., Washington, DC 20415.

(3) Any administrative review decision that either partially or fully supports the initial decision and denies access to the material the individual originally sought should state the requester's right to seek judicial review of the final administrative decision.

§297.208 Judicial review.

Upon receipt of notification that the denial of access has been upheld on administrative review, the requester has the right to judicial review of the decision for up to 2 years from the date on which the cause of action arose. Judicial review may be sought in the district court of the United States in the district in which—

(a) The requester resides;

(b) The requester has his or her principal place of business; or

(c) The agency records are situated; or it may be sought in the district court of the District of Columbia.

Subpart C—Amendment of Records

§297.301 General provisions.

(a) Individuals may request, in writing, the amendment of their records maintained in an Office system of records by contacting the appropriate system manager. The Office or agency will require proof of identity from a requester. The Office or agency reserves the right to determine the adequacy of any such proof. The general identifying items the Office will require a requester to provide when a request is made to the Office are—

(1) Full name, signature, and home address;

(2) Social security number (for systems of records that include this identifier);

(3) Current or last place and dates of Federal employment, when appropriate; and

(4) Date and place of birth.

(b) An individual may be represented by another party when requesting amendment of records.

(c) A request for amendment should include the following:

(1) The precise identification of the records to be amended;

(2) The identification of the specific material to be deleted, added, or changed; and

(3) A statement of the reasons for the request, including all available material substantiating the request.

(d) Requests for amendment of records should include the words "PRIVACY ACT AMENDMENT REQUEST" in capital letters on both the envelope and at the top of the request letter.

(e) A request for administrative review of an agency denial to amend a record in the Office's systems of records should be addressed to the Assistant Director for Workforce Information, Personnel Systems and Oversight Group, U.S. Office of Personnel Management, 1900 E Street NW., Washington, DC 20415.

(f) A request for administrative review of a denial to amend a record by an Office official should be addressed to the Information and Privacy Appeals Counsel, Office of the General Counsel, U.S. Office of Personnel Management, 1900 E Street NW., Washington, DC 20415.

(g) The burden of proof demonstrating the appropriateness of the requested amendment rests with the requester; and, the requester must provide relevant and convincing evidence in support of the request.

§297.302 Time limits.

The system manager should acknowledge receipt of an amendment request within 10 working days and issue a determination as soon as practicable. This timeframe begins when the request is received by the proper Office or agency official.

§297.303 Applicability of amendment provisions.

(a) The amendment procedures are not intended to allow a challenge to material that records an event that actually occurred nor are they designed to permit a collateral attack upon that which has been or could have been the subject of a judicial, quasi-judicial, or administrative proceeding. The amendment procedures are also not designed to change opinions in records pertaining to the individual.

(b) The amendment procedures apply to situations when an occurrence that is documented was challenged through an established judicial, quasi-judicial, or administrative procedure and found to be inaccurately described; when the document is not identical to the individual's copy; or when the document is not created in accordance with the applicable recordkeeping requirements. (For example, the amendment provisions are not designed to allow a challenge to the merits of an agency adverse action that is documented in an individual's Official Personnel Folder.)

§ 297.304 Approval of requests to amend records.

(a) If the system manager determines that amendment of a record is appropriate, the system manager will take the necessary steps to have the necessary changes made and will see that the individual receives a copy of the amended record.

(b) When practicable and appropriate, the system manager will advise all prior recipients of the fact that an amendment of a record has been made.

§ 297.305 Denial of requests to amend records.

(a) If the Office or agency system manager decides not to amend the record in the manner sought, the requester should be notified in writing of the reasons for the denial.

(b) The decision letter should also include the requester's right to appeal the denial and the procedures for appealing the denial to the appropriate official.

§ 297.306 Appeal of a denial of a request to amend a record.

(a) An individual who disagrees with an initial denial to amend a record may file a written appeal of that denial to the appropriate official. In submitting an appeal, the individual should provide a copy of the original request for amendment, a copy of the initial denial decision, and a statement of the specific reasons why the initial denial is believed to be in error. Any appeal should be submitted to the official designated in the initial decision letter. The appeal should include the words "PRIVACY ACT APPEAL" in capital letters on the envelope and at the top of the letter of appeal.

(b) The reviewing official should complete the review and make a final determination in writing no later than 30 working days from the date on which the appeal is received. When circumstances warrant, this timeframe may be extended.

(c) If the Office grants the appeal, it will take the necessary steps either to amend the record itself or to require the originating agency to amend the record. When appropriate and possible, prior recipients of the record should be notified of the Office's action.

(d) The Office reserves the right to hold in abeyance any Privacy Act appeal concerning a record when an individual is involved in challenging an action involving that record in another administrative, judicial, or quasi-judicial forum. At the conclusion of such a challenge, the individual can resubmit the appeal.

(e) If the Office denies the appeal, it will include in the decision letter notification of the appellant's right to judicial review.

§ 297.307 Statement of disagreement.

(a) Upon receipt of a final administrative determination denying a request to amend a record, the requester may file a concise statement of disagreement. Such a statement should be filed with the appropriate system manager and should include the reasons why the requester believes the decision to be incorrect.

(b) The statement of disagreement should be maintained with the record to be amended and any disclosure of the record must include a copy of the statement of disagreement.

(c) When practicable and appropriate, the system manager should provide a copy of the statement of disagreement to any individual or agency to whom the record was previously disclosed as noted by the disclosure accounting.

§ 297.308 Judicial review.

Upon receipt of notification that the denial to amend a record has been upheld on administrative review, the requester has the right to judicial review of the decision for up to 2 years from the date the cause of action arose.

Judicial review may be sought in the district court of the United States in the district in which—

(a) The requester resides;

(b) The requester has his or her principal place of business; or

(c) The agency records are situated; or it may be sought in the district court of the District of Columbia.

Subpart D—Disclosure of Records

§ 297.401 Conditions of disclosure.

An official or employee of the Office or agency should not disclose a record retrieved from a Governmentwide system of records to any person, another agency, or other entity without the express written consent of the subject individual unless disclosure is—

(a) To officers or employees of the Office who have a need for the information in the performance of their duties.

(b) Required by the provisions of the Freedom of Information Act.

(c) For a routine use as published in the FEDERAL REGISTER.

(d) To the Bureau of the Census for uses pursuant to title 13 of the United States Code.

(e)(1) To a recipient who has provided the agency with advance adequate written assurance that the record will be used solely as a statistical research or reporting record. The record will be transferred in a form that is not individually identifiable. The written statement should include as a minimum:

(i) A statement of the purpose for requesting the records; and

(ii) Certification that the records will be used only for statistical purposes.

(2) These written statements should be maintained as records. In addition to deleting personal identifying information from records released for statistical purposes, the system manager will reasonably ensure that the identity of the individual cannot be deduced by combining various statistical records.

(f) To the National Archives of the United States as a record that has sufficient historical or other value to warrant its continued preservation by the United States Government, or for evaluation by the Archivist of the United States or his or her designee to determine whether the record has such value.

(g) To another agency or instrumentality of any governmental jurisdiction within or under the control of the United States for a civil or criminal law enforcement activity if the activity is authorized by law, and if the head of the agency or instrumentality or his designated representative has made a written request to the Office or agency that maintains the record specifying the particular portion desired and the law enforcement activity for which the record is sought.

(h) To a person showing compelling circumstances affecting the health and safety of an individual, not necessarily the individual to whom the record pertains. Upon such disclosure, a notification should be sent to the last known address of the subject individual.

(i) To the Congress or to a Congressional committee, subcommittee, or joint committee to the extent that the subject matter falls within its established jurisdiction.

(j) To the Comptroller General or any authorized representatives of the Comptroller General in the course of the performance of the duties of the General Accounting Office.

(k) Pursuant to the order of a court of competent jurisdiction.

(l) To a consumer reporting agency in accordance with section 3711 (f) of title 31 of the United States Code.

§ 297.402 Disclosure pursuant to a compulsory legal process served on the Office.

For purposes of this section, the Office considers that a subpoena signed by a judge is equivalent to a court order.

(a) The Office may disclose, without prior consent of the data subject, specified information from a system of records whenever such disclosure is pursuant to an order signed by the appropriate official of a court of competent jurisdiction or quasi-judicial agency. In this subpart, a court of competent jurisdiction includes the judicial system of a state, territory, or possession of the United States.

(b) Notice of the order will be provided to the data subject by the Office as soon as practicable after service of the order. The notice should be mailed to the last known address of the individual and state the name and number of the case or proceeding, and the nature of the information sought.

(c) Before complying or refusing to comply with the order, an official with authority to disclose records under this subpart should consult legal counsel to ensure that the response is appropriate.

(d) Before responding to the order or subpoena signed by a judge, an official with authority to disclose records under this subpart in consulting with legal counsel will ensure that—

(1) The requested material is relevant to the subject matter of the related judicial or administrative proceeding;

(2) Motion is made to quash or modify an order that is unreasonable or oppressive:

(3) Motion is made for a protective order when necessary to restrict the use or disclosure of any information furnished for purposes other than those of the involved proceeding; or

(4) Request is made for an extension of time allowed for response, if necessary.

(e) If an order or subpoena signed by a judge for production of documents also requests appearance of an Office employee, the response should be to furnish certified copies of the appropriate records. In those situations where the subpoena is not signed by a judge, the Office will return the document to the sender and indicate that no action will be taken to provide records until the subpoena is signed by a judge.

(f) If oral testimony is requested by the order or subpoena signed by a judge, an explanation that sets forth the testimony desired must be furnished to the Office system manager. The individual who has been ordered or subpoenaed to testify should consult with counsel to determine the matters about which the individual may properly testify.

(g) In all situations concerning an order, subpoena signed by a judge, or other demand for an employee of the Office to produce any material or testimony concerning the records that are subject to the order, that are contained in the Office's systems of records, and that are acquired as part of the employee's official duties, the employee shall not provide the information without the prior approval of the appropriate Office official.

(h) If it is determined that the information should not be provided, the individual ordered or subpoenaed to do so should respectfully decline to comply with the demand based on the instructions from the appropriate Office official.

(i) Notice of the issuance of the ex parte order or subpoena signed by a judge is not required if the system of records has been exempted from the notice requirement of 5 U.S.C. 552a(e)(8) pursuant to 5 U.S.C. 552a(j) by a Notice of Exemption published in the FEDERAL REGISTER.

[53 FR 1998, Jan. 26, 1988, as amended at 57 FR 56732, Nov. 30, 1992]

§ 297.403 Accounting of disclosure.

(a) The Office or agency will maintain a record of disclosures in cases where records about the individual are disclosed from an Office system of records except—

(1) When the disclosure is made pursuant to the Freedom of Information Act, as amended (5 U.S.C. 552); or

(2) When the disclosure is made to those officers and employees of the Office or agency who have a need for the record in the performance of their duties.

(b) This accounting of the disclosures will be retained for at least 5 years or for the life of the record, whichever is longer, and will contain the following information:

(1) A brief description of the record disclosed;

(2) The date, nature, and purpose for the disclosure; and

(3) The name and address of the purpose, agency, or other entity to whom the disclosure is made.

(c) Except for the accounting of disclosure made to agencies, individuals, or entities in law enforcement activities or disclosures made from the Office's exempt systems of records, the accounting of disclosures will be made available to the data subject upon request in accordance with the access procedures of this part.

[53 FR 1998, Jan. 26, 1988. Redesignated at 57 FR 56732, Nov. 30, 1992]

Subpart E—Exempt Records

§297.501 Exemptions.

(a) Several of the Office's internal, central, and Governmentwide systems of records contain information for which exemptions appearing at 5 U.S.C. 552a(k) (1), (2), (3), (5), and (6) may be claimed. The systems of records for which the exemptions are claimed, the specific exemptions determined to be necessary and proper with respect to these systems of records, the records exempted, the provisions of the act from which they are exempted, and the justifications for the exemptions are set forth below.

(b) *Specific exemptions*—(1) *Inspector General Investigations Case File Records (OPM/CENTRAL-4)*. All information in these records that meets the criteria stated in 5 U.S.C. 552a(k) (1), (2), (3), (4), (5), (6), and (7) is exempt from the requirements of 5 U.S.C. 552a(c)(3) and (d). These provisions of the Privacy Act relate to making accountings of disclosures available to the data subject and access to and amendment of records. The specific applicability of the exemptions to this system and the reasons for the exemptions are as follows:

(i) Inspector General investigations may contain properly classified information that pertains to national defense and foreign policy obtained from other systems or another Federal agency. Application of exemption (k)(1) may be necessary to preclude the data subject's access to and amendment of such classified information under 5 U.S.C. 552a(d).

(ii) Inspector General investigations may contain investigatory material compiled for law enforcement purposes other than material within the scope of 5 U.S.C. 552a(j)(2); e.g., investigations into the administration of the merit system. Application of exemption (k)(2) may be necessary to preclude the data subject's access to or amendment of such records under 5 U.S.C. 552(a)(3) and (d).

(iii) Inspector General investigations may contain information obtained from another system or Federal agency that relates to providing protective services to the President of the United States or other individuals pursuant to 18 U.S.C. 3056. Application of exemption (k)(3) may be necessary to preclude the data subject's access to and amendment of such records under 5 U.S.C. 552a(d).

(iv) Inspector General case files may contain information that, by statute, is required to be maintained and used solely as a statistical record. Application of exemption (k)(4) may be necessary to ensure compliance with such a statutory mandate.

(v) All information about individuals in these records that meets the criteria stated in 5 U.S.C. 552a(k)(5) is exempt from the requirements of 5 U.S.C. 552a(c)(3) and (d). This exemption is claimed because this system contains investigatory material that if disclosed may reveal the identity of a source who furnished information to the Government under an express promise that the source's identity would be held in confidence or, prior to September 27, 1975, under an implied promise. The application of exemption (k)(5) will be required to honor promises of confidentiality should the data subject request access to or amendment of the records, or access to the accounting of disclosures of the record.

(vi) All information in these records that meets the criteria stated in 5 U.S.C. 552a(k)(6) is exempt from the requirements of 5 U.S.C. 552a(d) relating to access to and amendment of records by the data subject. This exemption is claimed because portions of a case file record may relate to testing and examining material used solely to determine individual qualifications for appointment or promotion in the Federal service. Access to or amendment of this information by the data subject would compromise the objectivity and fairness of the testing or examining process.

(vii) Inspector General case files may contain evaluation material used to determine potential for promotion in the armed services. Application of exemption (k)(7) may be necessary, but only to the extent that the disclosure of the data would reveal the identity of a source who furnished information to the Government under an express promise that the identity of the source would be held in confidence, or, prior to September 27, 1975, under an implied promise that the identity of the source would be held in confidence.

(2) *Administrative Law Judge Applicant Records (OPM/CENTRAL–6).* (i) All information about individuals in these records that meets the criteria stated in 5 U.S.C. 552a(k)(5) is exempt from the requirement of 5 U.S.C. 552(c)(3) and (d). The exemptions are claimed because this system contains investigatory material compiled solely for determining suitability, eligibility, and qualifications for Federal civilian employment. To the extent that the disclosure of such material would reveal the identity of a source who furnished information to the Government under an express promise that the identity of the source would be held in confidence or, prior to September 27, 1975, under an implied promise that the identity of the source would be held in confidence, the application of exemption (k)(5) will be required to honor promises of confidentialty should the data subject request access to the accounting of disclosures of the record, or access to or amendment of the record.

(ii) All information in these records that meets the criteria stated in 5 U.S.C. 552a(k)(6) is exempt from the requirements of 5 U.S.C. 552a(d), relating to access to and amendment of the records by the data subject. This exemption is claimed because portions of this system relate to testing and examining materials used solely to determine individual qualifications for appointment or promotion in the Federal service. Access to or amendment of this information by the data subject would compromise the objectivity and fairness of the testing or examing process.

(3) *Litigation and Claims Records (OPM/CENTRAL–7).* (i) When litigation or claim cases occur, information from other existing systems of records may be incorporated into the case file. This information may be material for which exemptions have been claimed by the Office in this section. To the extent that such exempt material is incorporated into a litigation or claim case file, the appropriate exemption (5 U.S.C. 552a(k)(1), (2), (3), (4), (5), (6), or (7)) shall also apply to the material as it appears in this system. The exemptions will be only from those provisions of the Act that were claimed for the systems from which the records originated.

(ii) During the course of litigation or claims cases, it may be necessary to conduct investigations to develop information and evidence relevant to the case. These investigative records may include material meeting the criteria stated in 5 U.S.C. 552a(k)(1), (2), (3), (4), (5), (6), and (7). Such material is exempt from the requirement of 5 U.S.C. 552a(c)(3) and (d). These provisions of the Act relate to making accounting of disclosures available to the data subject and access to and amendment of records. The specific applicability of the exemptions to this system and the reasons for the exemptions are:

(A) Such investigations may contain properly classified information that pertains to national defense and foreign policy obtained from another Federal agency. Application of exemption (k)(1) may be necessary to preclude the data subject's access to and amendment of suh classified information under 5 U.S.C 552a(d).

(B) Such investigations may contain investigatory material compiled for law enforcement purposes othe than material within the scope of 5 U.S.C. 552a(j)(2), e.g., administration of the merit system, obtained from another Federal agency. All information about individuals in these records that meets the criteria of 5 U.S.C 552a(k)(2) is exempt from the requirements of 5 U.S.C. 552a(c)(3) and (d). Application of exemption (k)(2) may be necessary to preclude the data subject's access to or amendment of those records.

(C) Such investigations may contain information obtained from another agency that relates to providing protective services to the President of the United States or other individuals pursuant to 18 U.S.C. 3056. All information about individuals in these records that meets the criteria of 5 U.S.C. 552a(k)(3) is exempt from the requirements of 5 U.S.C. 552a(d), relating to access to or amendment of records by the data subject. Application of exemption (k)(3) may be necessary to preclude the data subject's access to and amendment of such records.

(D) Such investigations may contain information that, by statute, is required to be maintained and used solely as a statistical record. Application of exemption (k)(4) may be necessary to ensure compliance with such a statutory mandate.

(E) All information about individuals in these records that meets the criteria stated in 5 U.S.C. 552a(k)(5) is exempt from the requirements of 5 U.S.C. 552a (c)(3) and (d). These exemptions are claimed because this system contains investigatory material compiled solely for determining suitability, eligibility, and qualifications for Federal civilian employment. To the extent that the disclosure of such material would reveal the identity of a source who furnished information to the Government under an express promise that the identity of the source would be held in confidence, or, prior to September 27, 1975, under an implied promise that the identity of the source would be held in confidence, the application of exemption (k)(5) will be required to honor such a promise should the data subject request access to the accounting of disclosure, or access to or amendment of the record, that would reveal the identity of a confidential source.

(F) All information in these records that meets the criteria stated in 5 U.S.C. 552a(k)(6) is exempt from the requirements of 5 U.S.C. 552a(d), relating to access to and amendment of the records by the data subject. This exemption is claimed because portions of this system relate to testing or examining materials used solely to determine individual qualifications for appointment or promotion in the Federal service. Access to or amendment by the data subject of this information would compromise the objectivity and fairness of the testing or examining process.

(G) Such investigations may contain evaluation material used to determine potential for promotion in the armed services. Application of exemption (k)(7) may be necessary, but only to the extent that the disclosure of the data would reveal the identity of a source who furnished information to the Government under an express promise that the identity of the source would be held in confidence, or, prior to September 27, 1975, under an implied promise that the identity of the source would be held in confidence.

(4) *Privacy Act/Freedom of Information Case Records (OPM/CENTRAL–8)*. In this subpart, the Office has claimed exemptions for its other systems of records where it felt such exemptions are appropriate and necessary. These exemptions are claimed under 5 U.S.C. 552a(k) (1), (2), (3), (4), (5), (6) and (7). During the processing of a Privacy Act/Freedom of Information Act request (which may include access requests, amendment requests, and requests for review for initial denials of such requests) exempt materials from those other systems may in turn become part of the case record in this system. To the extent that copies of exempt records from those other systems are entered into this system, the Office hereby claims the same exemptions for the records from those other systems that are entered into this system, as claimed for the original primary system of which they are a part.

(5) *Personnel Investigations Records (OPM/CENTRAL–9)*. All information in these records that meets the criteria stated in 5 U.S.C. 552a(k) (1), (2), (3), (4), (5), (6), and (7) is exempt from the requirements of 5 U.S.C. 552a (c)(3) and (d). These provisions of the Privacy Act relate to making accountings of disclosures available to the data subject and access to and amendment of records. The specific applicability of the exemptions to this system and the reasons for the exemptions are as follows:

(i) Personnel investigations may contain properly classified information which pertains to national defense and foreign policy obtained from another Federal agency. Application of exemption (k)(1) may be necessary to preclude the data subject's access to and amendment of such classified information under 5 U.S.C. 552a(d).

(ii) Personnel investigations may contain investigatory material compiled for law enforcement purposes other than material within the scope of 5 U.S.C. 552a(j)(2); e.g., investigations into the administration of the merit system. Application of exemption (k)(2) may be necessary to preclude the data subject's access to or amended of such records under 5 U.S.C. 552a (c)(3) and (d).

(iii) Personnel investigations may contain information obtained from another Federal agency that relates to providing protective services to the President of the United States or other individuals pursuant to 18 U.S.C. 3056. Application of exemption (k)(3) may be necessary to preclude the data subject's access to and amendment of such records under 5 U.S.C. 552a(d).

(iv) Personnel investigations may contain information that, by statute, is required to be maintained and used solely as a statistical record. Application of exemption (k)(4) may be necessary to ensure compliance with such a statutory mandate.

(v) All information about individuals in these records that meets the criteria stated in 5 U.S.C. 552a(k)(5) is exempt from the requirements of 5 U.S.C. 552a (c)(3) and (d). These exemptions are claimed because this system contains investigatory material compiled solely for determining suitability, eligibility, and qualifications for Federal civilian employment. To the extent that the disclosure of material would reveal the identity of a source who furnished information to the Government under an express promise that the identity of the source would be held in confidence, or, prior to September 27, 1975, under an implied promise that the identity of the source would be held in confidence, the applicability of exemption (k)(5) will be required to honor promises of confidentiality should the data subject request access to or amendment of the record, or access to the accounting of disclosures of the record.

(vi) All information in these records that meets the criteria stated in 5 U.S.C. 552a(k)(6) is exempt from the requirements of 5 U.S.C. 552a(d), relating to access to and amendment of records by the data subject. This exemption is claimed because portions of this system relate to testing or examining materials used solely to determine individual qualifications for appointment or promotion in the Federal service. Access to or amendment of this information by the data subject would compromise the objectivity and fairness of the testing or examining process.

(vii) Personnel Investigations may contain evaluation material used to determine potential for promotion in the armed services. Application of exemption (k)(7) may be necessary, but only to the extent that the disclosure of the data would reveal the identity of a source who furnished information to the Government under an express promise that the identity of the source would be held in confidence, or, prior to September 27, 1975, under an implied promise that the identity of the source would be held in confidence.

(6) *Presidential Management Fellows Program Records (OPM/CENTRAL–11).* All information in these records that meets the criteria stated in 5 U.S.C. 552a(k)(6) is exempt from the requirements of 5 U.S.C. 552a(d), relating to access to and amendment of records by the data subject. This exemption is claimed because portions of this system relate to testing or examining materials used solely to determine individual qualifications for appointment or promotion in the Federal service and access to or amendment of this information by the data subject would compromise the objectivity and fairness of the testing or examining process.

(7) *Recruiting, Examining, and Placement Records (OPM/GOVT–5).* (i) All information about individuals in these records that meets the criteria stated in 5 U.S.C. 552a(k)(5) is exempt from the requirements of 5 U.S.C. 552a(c)(3) and (d). These provisions of the Privacy Act relate to making accountings of disclosures available to the data subject and access to and amendment of records. These exemptions are claimed because this system contains investigative material compiled solely for determining the appropriateness of a request for approval of an objection to an eligible's qualification for employment in the Federal service. To the extent that the disclosure of such material would reveal the identity of a source who furnished information to the Government under an express promise that the identity of the source would be

held in confidence, or prior to September 27, 1975, under an implied promise that the identity of the source would be held in confidence, the application of exemption (k)(5) will be required to honor promises of confidentiality should the data subject request access to the accounting of disclosures of the record, or access to or amendment of the record.

(ii) All information in these records that meets the criteria stated in 5 U.S.C. 552a(K)(6) is exempt from the requirements of 5 U.S.C. 552a(d), relating to access to an amendment of records by the subject. This exemption is claimed because portions of this system relate to testing or examining materials used solely to determine individual qualifications for appointment or promotion in the Federal service and access to or amendment of this information by the data subject would compromise the objectivity and fairness of the testing or examining process.

(8) *Personnel Research and Test Validation Records (OPM/GOVT-6).* (i) All information in these records that meets the criteria stated in 5 U.S.C. 552a(k)(6) is exempt from the requirements of 5 U.S.C. 552a(d), relating to access to and amendment of the records by the data subject. This exemption is claimed because portions of this system relate to testing or examining materials used solely to determine individual qualifications for appointment or promotion in the Federal service. Access to or amendment of this information by the data subject would compromise the objectivity and fairness of the testing or examining process.

(ii) All information in these records that meets the criteria stated in 5 U.S.C. 552a(k)(4) is exempt from the requirements of 5 U.S.C. 552a(d), relating to access to or amendment of the records by the data subject. This exemption is claimed because portions of this system relate to records required by statute to be maintained and used solely for statistical purposes. Access to or amendment of this information by the data subject would compromise the confidentiality of these records and their usefulness for statistical research purposes.

(c) The Office also reserves the right to assert exemptions for records received from another agency that could be properly claimed by that agency in responding to a request. The Office may refuse access to information compiled in reasonable anticipation of a civil action or proceeding.

[53 FR 1998, Jan. 26, 1988, as amended at 57 FR 20956, May 18, 1992; 70 FR 28779, May 19, 2005]

PART 300—EMPLOYMENT (GENERAL)

Subpart G—Statutory Bar to Appointment of Persons Who Fail To Register Under Selective Service Law

AUTHORITY: 5 U.S.C. 552, 2301, 2302, 3301, and 3302; E.O. 10577, 3 CFR 1954–1958 Comp., page 218, unless otherwise noted.

Secs. 300.101 through 300.104 also issued under 5 U.S.C. 7201, 7204, and 7701; E.O. 11478, 3 CFR 1966–1970 Comp., page 803, E.O. 13087; and E.O. 13152.

Secs. 300.401 through 300.408 also issued under 5 U.S.C. 1302(c).

Secs. 300.501 through 300.507 also issued under 5 U.S.C. 1103(a)(5).

Sec. 300.603 also issued under 5 U.S.C. 1104.

Subpart A—Employment Practices

§ 300.101 Purpose.

The purpose of this subpart is to establish principles to govern, as nearly as is administratively feasible and practical, the employment practices of the Federal Government generally, and of individual agencies, that affect the recruitment, measurement, ranking, and selection of individuals for initial appointment and competitive promotion in the competitive service or in positions in the government of the District of Columbia required to be filled in the same manner that positions in the competitive service are filled. For the purpose of this subpart, the term "employment practices" includes the development and use of examinations, qualification standards, tests, and other measurement instruments.

[36 FR 15447, Aug. 14, 1971]

§ 300.102 Policy.

This subpart is directed to implementation of the policy that competitive employment practices:

(a) Be practical in character and as far as possible relate to matters that fairly test the relative capacity and fitness of candidates for the jobs to be filled;

(b) Result in selection from among the best qualified candidates;

(c) Be developed and used without discrimination on the basis of race, color, religion, sex (including pregnancy and gender identity), national origin, age (as defined by the Age Discrimination in Employment Act of 1967, as amended), disability, genetic information (including family medical history), marital status, political affiliation, sexual orientation, labor organization affiliation or nonaffiliation, status as a parent, or any other non-merit-based factor, or retaliation for exercising rights with respect to the categories enumerated above, where retaliation rights are available.

(d) Insure to the candidate opportunity for appeal or administrative review, as appropriate.

[40 FR 15379, Apr. 7, 1975, as amended at 79 FR 43922, July 29, 2014]

§ 300.103 Basic requirements.

(a) *Job analysis.* Each employment practice of the Federal Government generally, and of individual agencies, shall be based on a job analysis to identify:

(1) The basic duties and responsibilities;

(2) The knowledges, skills, and abilities required to perform the duties and responsibilities; and

(3) The factors that are important in evaluating candidates. The job analysis may cover a single position or group of positions, or an occupation or group of occupations, having common characteristics.

(b) *Relevance.* (1) There shall be a rational relationship between performance in the position to be filled (or in the target position in the case of an entry position) and the employment practice used. The demonstration of rational relationship shall include a showing that the employment practice was professionally developed. A minimum educational requirement may not be established except as authorized under section 3308 of title 5, United States Code.

(2) In the case of an entry position the required relevance may be based upon the target position when—

(i) The entry position is a training position or the first of a progressive series of established training and development positions leading to a target position at a higher level; and

(ii) New employees, within a reasonable period of time and in the great majority of cases, can expect to progress to a target position at a higher level.

(c) *Equal employment opportunity and prohibited forms of discrimination.* An employment practice must not discriminate on the basis of race, color, religion, sex (including pregnancy and gender identity), national origin, age (as defined by the Age Discrimination in Employment Act of 1967, as amended), disability, genetic information (including family medical history), marital status, political affiliation, sexual orientation, labor organization affiliation or nonaffiliation, status as a parent, or any other non-merit-based factor, or retaliation for exercising rights with respect to the categories enumerated above, where retaliation rights are available. Employee selection procedures shall meet the standards established by the "Uniform Guidelines on Employee Selection Procedures," where applicable.

[40 FR 15380, Apr. 7, 1975, as amended at 43 FR 38310, Aug. 25, 1978; 79 FR 43922, July 29, 2014]

§300.104 Appeals, grievances and complaints.

(a) *Employment practices.* A candidate who believes that an employment practice which was applied to him or her by the Office of Personnel Management violates a basic requirement in §300.103 is entitled to appeal to the Merit Systems Protection Board under the provisions of its regulations.

(b) *Examination ratings.* A candidate may file an appeal with the Office from his or her examination rating or the rejection of his or her application, except that, where the Office has delegated examining authority to an agency, the candidate should appeal directly to that agency. The appeal and supporting documents shall be filed with the agency office that determined the rating.

(c) *Complaints and grievances to an agency.* (1) A candidate may file a complaint with an agency when he or she believes that an employment practice that was applied to him or her and that is administered by the agency discriminates against him or her on the basis of race, color, religion, sex (including pregnancy and gender identity), national origin, age (as defined by the Age Discrimination in Employment Act of 1967, as amended), disability, genetic information (including family medical history), or retaliation for exercising rights with respect to the categories enumerated above, where retaliation rights are available. The complaint must be filed and processed in accordance with the agency EEO procedures, as appropriate.

(2) Except as provided in paragraph (c)(1) of this section, an employee may file a grievance with an agency when he or she believes that an employment practice which was applied to him or her and which is administered or required by the agency violates a basic requirement in §300.103. The grievance shall be filed and processed under an agency grievance system, if applicable, or a negotiated grievance system as applicable.

[40 FR 15380, Apr. 7, 1975, as amended at 41 FR 51579, Nov. 23, 1976; 44 FR 48951, Aug. 21, 1979; 60 FR 3057, Jan. 13, 1995; 60 FR 47040, Sept. 11, 1995; 79 FR 43922, July 29, 2014]

Subpart B—Examinations and Related Subjects

§300.201 Examinations.

(a) The Office makes available information that will assist members of the public in understanding the purpose of, and preparing for, civil service examinations. This includes the types of questions and the categories of knowledge or skill pertinent to a particular examination. The Office does not release the following: (1) Testing and examination materials used solely to determine individual qualifications, and (2) test material, including test plans, item analysis data, criterion instruments, and other material the disclosure of which would compromise the objectivity of the testing process.

(b) The Office maintains control over the security and release of testing and examination materials which it has developed and made available to agencies for initial competitive appointment or inservice use unless the materials were developed specifically for an agency through a reimbursable contractual agreement. These testing and examination materials include, and are subject to the same controls as, those described in paragraphs (a)(1) and (a)(2) of this section.

(c) Each employee entrusted with test material has a positive duty to protect the confidentiality of that material and to assure release only as required to conduct an examination authorized by the Office.

(d) An applicant may review his or her own answers in a written test, but only in the presence of an employee of the Office or, for the convenience of the Office and requester, in the presence of an employee of another agency designated by OPM. The applicant may not review a test booklet in connection with this review.

(e) The Office will release information concerning the results of examinations only to the individual concerned, or to parties explicitly designated by the individual.

(f) The Office will not reveal the names of applicants for civil service positions or eligibles on civil service registers, certificates, employment lists, or other lists of eligibles, or their ratings or relative standings.

[50 FR 3312, Jan. 24, 1985, as amended at 60 FR 3057, Jan. 13, 1995]

Subpart C—Details of Employees

§ 300.301 Authority.

(a) In accordance with 5 U.S.C. 3341, an agency may detail an employee in the competitive service to a position in either the competitive or excepted service.

(b) In accordance with 5 U.S.C. 3341, an agency may detail an employee in the excepted service to a position in the excepted service and may also detail an excepted service employee serving under Schedule A, Schedule B, or a Veterans Recruitment Appointment, to a position in the competitive service.

(c) Any other detail of an employee in the excepted service to a position in the competitive service may be made only with the prior approval of the Office of Personnel Management or under a delegated agreement between the agency and OPM.

[60 FR 3057, Jan. 13, 1995, as amended at 70 FR 72066, Dec. 1, 2005]

Subpart D—Use of Commercial Recruiting Firms and Nonprofit Employment Services

SOURCE: 53 FR 51222, Dec. 21, 1988, unless otherwise noted.

§ 300.401 Definitions.

For purposes of this subpart:

(a) A *commercial recruiting firm* is a profit-making entity which, by contract, supplies individual candidates for consideration for specific Federal vacancies, in accordance with the requirements set by the Federal agency.

(b) A *nonprofit employment service* is one legally established as nonprofit under State law. It may be operated, for example, by professional societies, organizations of college graduates, social agencies, or a State or local government. Federal agencies may not, however, use a nonprofit employment service sponsored by a partisan political organization. By contract, a nonprofit employment service supplies individual candidates for consideration for specific Federal vacancies, in accordance with the requirements set by the Federal agency.

§ 300.402 Coverage.

This part applies to filling positions in the competitive service; positions in the expected service under Schedules A, B, and C; and positions in the Senior Executive Service.

[57 FR 10124, Mar. 24, 1992]

§ 300.403 When commercial recruiting firms and nonprofit employment services may be used.

An agency may use a commercial recruiting firm and/or a nonprofit employment service in recruiting for vacancies when:

(a) The agency head or designee determines that such use is likely to provide well-qualified candidates who would otherwise not be available or that well-qualified candidates are in short supply;

(b) The agency has provided vacancy notices to appropriate State Employment Service and OPM offices; and

(c) The agency continues its own recruiting efforts.

§300.404 Use of fee-charging firms.

(a) Federal agencies are prohibited from using commercial recruiting firms and nonprofit employment services which charge fees to individuals referred to Federal positions. Federal agencies may not consider a candidate referred by a commercial recruiting firm or nonprofit employment service if the individual has paid or is expected to pay any fee to the firm or service.

(b) The prohibition in paragraph (a) of this section does not apply to registration fees paid by individuals to nonprofit employment services operated by professional organizations when the registration fee is imposed regardless of whether the registrant is referred for employment or placed.

§300.405 Requirement for contract.

(a) A written contract awarded in accordance with procedures stipulated in the Federal Acquisition Regulations is required between the Federal agency and a commercial recruiting firm or nonprofit employment service. The contract will satisfy the "written request" required by 18 U.S.C. 211. That statute prohibits the acceptance of payment for aiding an individual to obtain Federal employment *except* when an employment agency renders services pursuant to the written request of an executive department or agency.

(b) The contract must include the qualifications requirements for the position(s) to be filled and also provide that the firm or service will:

(1) Screen candidates only against the basic qualifications requirements for the position(s) specified by the Federal agency in the contract and refer to the agency all candidates who appear to meet those requirements;

(2) Refer to the Federal agency only those applicants from whom the firm or service has not accepted fees other than those permitted under §300.404(b) of this part;

(3) Not imply that it is the sole or primary avenue for employment with the Federal Government or a specific Federal agency; and

(4) Recruit and refer candidates in accordance with applicable merit principles and equal opportunity laws.

§300.406 Agency responsibilities.

(a) The purpose of a commercial recruiting firm or nonprofit employment service is to serve as an additional source of applicants. Once recruited, applicants must be evaluated and appointed through regular civil service employment procedures.

(1) For a competitive service position, an individual must be appointed in accordance with the terms of applicable competitive service procedures.

(2) For an excepted service position, an individual must be appointed in accordance with the terms of the applicable appointing authority and the requirements set out in part 302 of this chapter.

(3) For a Senior Executive Service position filled by career appointment, an individual must be appointed in accordance with the competitive process described in 5 U.S.C. 3393.

(b) In order to use commercial recruiting firms or nonprofit employment services, agencies are required to:

(1) Make known that applicants may apply directly to the Government and thus need not apply through the commercial recruiting firm or nonprofit employment service;

(2) Give the same consideration to candidates who have applied directly and candidates referred from the commercial recruiting firm or nonprofit employment service; and

(3) Follow all requirements for appointment, including veterans preference, where applicable.

§300.407 Documentation.

(a) Agencies are required to maintain records necessary to determine that using commercial recruiting firms or nonprofit employment services is cost effective and has not resulted in the violation of merit system principles or the commission of any prohibited personnel practice.

(b) When requested by OPM, agencies will provide reports on the use of commercial recruiting firms, based on the records required in paragraph (a) of this section.

[53 FR 51222, Dec. 21, 1988, as amended at 60 FR 3057, Jan. 13, 1995]

§ 300.408 Corrective action.

Upon evidence of failure to comply with these regulations, OPM may, pursuant to its authority, order the agency to take appropriate corrective action.

Subpart E—Use of Private Sector Temporaries

SOURCE: 54 FR 3766, Jan. 25, 1989, unless otherwise noted.

§ 300.501 Definitions.

For purposes of this subpart:

(a) A *temporary help service firm* is a private sector entity which quickly provides other organizations with specific services performed by its pool of employees, possessing the appropriate work skills, for brief or intermittent periods. The firm is the legally responsible employer and maintains that relationship during the time its employees are assigned to a client. The firm, not the client organization, recruits, tests, hires, trains, assigns, pays, provides benefits and leave to, and as necessary, addresses performance problems, disciplines, and terminates its employees. Among other employer obligations, the firm is responsible for payroll deductions and payment of income taxes, social security (FICA), unemployment insurance, and workers' compensation, and shall provide required liability insurance and bonding.

(b) *Private sector temporaries* or *outside temporaries* are those employees of a temporary help service firm who are supervised and paid by that firm and whom that firm assigns to various client organizations who have contracted for the temporary use of their skills when required.

(c) *Parental and family responsibilities* are defined in OPM issuances and include situations such as absence for pregnancy, childbirth, child care, and care for elderly or infirm parents or other dependents.

(d) A *Federal supervisor* of Federal employees is defined in 5 U.S.C. 7103(a)(10) as

an individual employed by an agency having authority in the interest of the agency to hire, direct, assign, promote, reward, transfer, furlough, layoff, recall, suspend, discipline, or remove employees, to adjust their grievances, or to effectively recommend such action, if the exercise of the authority is not merely routine or clerical in nature but requires the consistent exercise of independent judgment * * *

(e) A *critical need* is a sudden or unexpected occurrence; an emergency; a pressing necessity; or an exigency. Such occasions are characterized by additional work or deadlines required by statute, Executive order, court order, regulation, or formal directive from the head of an agency or subordinate official authorized to take final action on behalf of the agency head. A recurring, cyclical peak workload, by itself, is not a critical need.

(f) A *local commuting area* is defined in part 351 of this chapter.

[54 FR 3766, Jan. 25, 1989, as amended at 66 FR 66710, Dec. 27, 2001]

§ 300.502 Coverage.

(a) These regulations apply to the competitive service and to Schedules A and B in the excepted service.

(b) Agencies may not use temporary help services for the Senior Executive Service or for the work of managerial or supervisory positions.

[61 FR 19510, May 2, 1996]

§ 300.503 Conditions for using private sector temporaries.

An agency may enter into a contract or other procurement arrangement with a temporary help service firm for the brief or intermittent use of the skills of private sector temporaries, when required, and may call for those services, subject to these conditions:

(a) One of the following short-term situations exists—

(1) An employee is absent for a temporary period because of a personal need including emergency, accident, illness, parental or family responsibilities, or mandatory jury service, but not including vacations or other circumstances which are not shown to be

compelling in the judgment of the agency, or

(2) An agency must carry out work for a temporary period which cannot be delayed in the judgment of the agency because of a critical need.

(b) The need cannot be met with current employees or through the direct appointment of temporary employees within the time available by the date, and for the duration of time, help is needed. At minimum, this should include an agency determination that there are no qualified candidates on the applicant supply file and on the reemployment priority list (both of which must provide preference for veterans), and no qualified disabled veterans with a compensable service-connected disability of 30 percent or more under 5 U.S.C. 3112, who are immediately available for temporary appointment of the duration required, and that employees cannot be reassigned or detailed without causing undue delay in their regular work. In instances where a need is foreseeable, as when approval of employee absence is requested well in advance, an agency may have sufficient time to follow the temporary appointment recruiting requirements, including veterans' preference found in 5 CFR part 316 to determine whether qualified candidates are available by the date needed and for the length of service required.

(c) These services shall not be used:

(1) In lieu of the regular recruitment and hiring procedures under the civil service laws for permanent appointment in the competitive civil service, or

(2) To displace a Federal employee.

(3) To circumvent controls on employment levels.

(4) In lieu of appointing a surplus or displaced Federal employee as required by 5 CFR part 330, subpart F (Agency Career Transition Assistance Plan for Displaced Employees) and subpart G (Interagency Career Transition Assistance Plan for Displaced Employees.)

[54 FR 3766, Jan. 25, 1989, as amended at 61 FR 19510, May 2, 1996; 66 FR 66710, Dec. 27, 2001]

§ 300.504 Prohibition on employer-employee relationship.

No employer-employee relationship is created by an agency's use of private sector temporaries under these regulations. Services furnished by temporary help firms shall be performed by their employees who shall not be considered or treated as Federal employees for any purpose, shall not be regarded as performing a personal service, and shall not be eligible for civil service employee benefits, including retirement. Further, to avoid creating any appearance of such a relationship, agencies shall observe the following requirements:

(a) *Time limit on use of temporary help service firm.* An agency may use a temporary help service firm(s) in a single situation, as defined in § 300.503, initially for no more than 120 workdays. Provided the situation continues to exist beyond the initial 120 workdays, the agency may extend its use of temporary help services up to the maximum limit of 240 workdays.

(b) *Time limit on use of individual employee of a temporary help service firm.* (1) An individual employee of any temporary help firm may work at a major organizational element (headquarters or field) of an agency for up to 120 workdays in a 24-month period. The 24-month period begins on the first day of assignment.

(2) An agency may make an exception for an individual to work up to a maximum of 240 workdays only when the agency has determined that using the services of the same individual for the same situation will prevent significant delay.

(c) Individual employees of a temporary help firm providing temporary service to a Federal agency may be eligible for competitive civil service employment only if appropriate civil service hiring procedures are applied to them.

(d) Agencies shall train their employees in appropriate procedures for interaction with private sector temporaries to assure that the supervisory responsibilities identified in paragraph (a) of § 300.501 of this subpart are carried out by the temporary help service firm. At the same time, agencies must give technical, task-related instructions to private sector temporaries including orientation, assignment of tasks, and review of work products, in order that the temporaries may properly perform their services under the contract.

[54 FR 3766, Jan. 25, 1989, as amended at 61 FR 19511, May 2, 1996]

§ 300.505 Relationship of civil service procedures.

Agencies continue to have full authority to meet their temporary needs by various means, for example, redistributing work, authorizing overtime, using in-house pools, and making details or time-limited promotions of current employees. In addition, agencies may appoint individuals as civil service employees on various work schedules appropriate for the work to be performed.

[61 FR 19511, May 2, 1996]

§ 300.506 Requirements of procurement.

(a) Agencies must follow the Federal procurement laws and the Federal Acquisition Regulation, as applicable, in procuring services from the private sector.

(b) Agencies should make full use of the provisions of the Federal procurement system to make clear that the firm is the legally responsible employer and to specify the obligations the firm will have to meet to provide effective performance including such matters as the types and levels of skills to be provided, deadlines for providing service, liability insurance, and, when necessary, security requirements. The Federal procurement system also requires contractors to comply with affirmative action requirements to employ and advance in employment qualified disabled and Vietnam era veterans as provided in 41 CFR part 60–250, and with public policy programs including equal employment opportunity, handicapped employment, and small businesses.

§ 300.507 Documentation and oversight.

Agencies are required to maintain records and provide oversight to establish that their use of temporary help service firms is consistent with these regulations. As needed, OPM may require agencies to provide information on their use of temporary help service firms.

[61 FR 19511, May 2, 1996]

Subpart F—Time-In-Grade Restrictions

SOURCE: 56 FR 23002, May 20, 1991, unless otherwise noted.

§ 300.601 Purpose.

The restrictions in this subpart are intended to prevent excessively rapid promotions in competitive service General Schedule positions and to protect competitive principles. They provide a budgetary control on promotion rates and help assure that appointments are made from appropriate registers. These restrictions are in addition to the eligibility requirements for promotion in part 335 of this chapter.

§ 300.602 Definitions.

In this subpart—

Advancement means a promotion (including a temporary promotion) or any type of appointment resulting in a higher grade or higher rate of basic pay.

Competitive appointment means an appointment based on selection from a competitive examination register of eligibles or under a direct hire authority.

Hardship to an agency involves serious difficulty in filling a position, including when:

(a) The situation to be redressed results from circumstances beyond the organization's control and otherwise would require extensive corrective action; or

(b) A position at the next lower grade in the normal line of promotion does not exist and the resulting action is not a career ladder promotion; or

(c) There is a shortage of candidates for the position to be filled.

Inequity to an employee involves situations where a position is upgraded without change in the employee's duties or responsibilities, or where discrimination or administrative error prevented an employee from reaching a higher grade.

Nontemporary appointment means any appointment other than a temporary appointment pending establishment of a register (TAPER) or a temporary or excepted appointment not to exceed 1 year or less.

§ 300.603 Coverage.

(a) *Coverage.* This subpart applies to advancement to a General Schedule position in the competitive service by any individual who within the previous 52 weeks held a General Schedule position under nontemporary appointment in the competitive or excepted service in the executive branch, unless excluded by paragraph (b) of this section.

(b) *Exclusions.* The following actions may be taken without regard to this subpart but must be consistent with all other applicable requirements, such as qualification standards:

(1) Appointment based on selection from a competitive examination register of eligibles or under a direct hire authority.

(2) Noncompetitive appointment based on a special authority in law or Executive order (but not including transfer and reinstatement) made in accordance with all requirements applicable to new appointments under that authority.

(3) Advancement in accordance with part 335 of this chapter up to any General Schedule grade the employee previously held under nontemporary appointment in the competitive or excepted service.

(4) Advancement of an employee from a non-General Schedule position to a General Schedule position unless the employee held a General Schedule position under nontemporary appointment in the executive branch within the previous 52 weeks.

(5) Advancement of an individual whose General Schedule service during the previous 52 weeks has been totally under temporary appointment.

(6) Advancement of an employee under a training agreement established in accordance with OPM's operating manuals. However, an employee may not receive more than two promotions in any 52-week period solely on the basis of one or more training agreements. Also, only OPM may approve a training agreement that provides for consecutive promotions at rates that exceed those permitted by § 300.604 of this part.

(7) Advancement to avoid hardship to an agency or inequity to an employee in an individual meritorious case but only with the prior approval of the agency head or his or her designee. However, an employee may not be promoted more than three grades during any 52-week period on the basis of this paragraph.

(8) Advancement when OPM authorizes it to avoid hardship to an agency or inequity to an employee in individual meritorious situations not defined, but consistent with the definitions, in § 300.602 of this part.

[56 FR 23002, May 20, 1991, as amended at 66 FR 66710, Dec. 27, 2001]

§ 300.604 Restrictions.

The following time-in-grade restrictions must be met unless advancement is permitted by § 300.603(b) of this part:

(a) *Advancement to positions at GS–12 and above.* Candidates for advancement to a position at GS–12 and above must have completed a minimum of 52 weeks in positions no more than one grade lower (or equivalent) than the position to be filled.

(b) *Advancement to positions at GS–6 through GS–11.* Candidates for advancement to a position at GS–6 through GS–11 must have completed a minimum of 52 weeks in positions:

(1) No more than two grades lower (or equivalent) when the position to be filled is in a line of work properly classified at 2-grade intervals; or

(2) No more than one grade lower (or equivalent) when the position to be filled is in a line of work properly classified at 1-grade intervals; or

(3) No more than one or two grades lower (or equivalent), as determined by the agency, when the position to be filled is in a line of work properly classified at 1-grade intervals but has a mixed interval promotion pattern.

(c) *Advancement to positions up to GS–5.* Candidates may be advanced without time restriction to positions up to GS–5 if the position to be filled is no more than two grades above the lowest grade the employee held within the preceding 52 weeks under his or her latest nontemporary competitive appointment.

§ 300.605 Creditable service.

(a) All service at the required or higher grade (or equivalent) in positions to which appointed in the Federal civilian service is creditable towards the time periods required by § 300.604 of this part, except as provided in paragraph (c) of this section. Creditable service includes competitive and excepted service in positions under the General Schedule and other pay systems, including employment with a nonappropriated fund instrumentality. Service while on detail is credited at the grade of the employee's position of record, not the grade of the position to which detailed. Also creditable is service with the District of Columbia Government prior to January 1, 1980 (or prior to September 26, 1980, for those District employees who were converted to the District personnel system on January 1, 1980).

(b) Service in positions not subject to the General Schedule (GS) is credited at the equivalent GS grade by comparing the candidate's rate of basic pay with the representative rate (as defined in § 351.203 of this chapter) of the GS position in effect when the non-GS service was performed. The equivalent GS grade is the GS grade with a representative rate that equals the candidate's rate of basic pay. When the candidate's rate of basic pay falls between the representative rates of two GS grades, the non-GS service is credited at the higher grade.

(c) In applying the restrictions in § 300.604 of this part, prior service under temporary appointment at a level above that of a subsequent nontemporary competitive appointment is credited as if the service had been performed at the level of the nontemporary appointment. This provision applies until the employee has served in pay status for 52 weeks under nontemporary competitive appointment; thereafter, the service is credited at its actual grade level (or equivalent).

§ 300.606 Agency authority.

An agency may expand on these restrictions consistent with the intent of this subpart or may adopt similar policies to control promotion rates of employees not covered by this subpart.

Subpart G—Statutory Bar to Appointment of Persons Who Fail To Register Under Selective Service Law

SOURCE: 52 FR 7400, Mar. 11, 1987, unless otherwise noted.

§ 300.701 Statutory requirement.

Section 3328 of title 5 of the United States Code provides that—

(a) An individual—

(1) Who was born after December 31, 1959, and is or was required to register under section 3 of the Military Selective Service Act (50 U.S.C. App. 453); and

(2) Who is not so registered or knowingly and willfully did not so register before the requirement terminated or became inapplicable to the individual, shall be ineligible for appointment to a position in an executive agency of the Federal Government.

(b) The Office of Personnel Management, in consultation with the Director of the Selective Service System, shall prescribe regulations to carry out this section. Such regulations shall include provisions prescribing procedures for the adjudication within the Office of determinations of whether a failure to register was knowing and willful. Such procedures shall require that such a determination may not be made if the individual concerned shows by a preponderance of the evidence that the failure to register was neither knowing nor willful.

§ 300.702 Coverage.

Appointments in the competitive service, the excepted service, the Senior Executive Service, or any other civil service personnel management system in an executive agency are covered by these regulations.

§ 300.703 Definitions.

In this subpart—

Appointment means any personnel action that brings onto the rolls of an executive agency as a civil service officer or employee as defined in 5 U.S.C. 2104 or 2105, respectively, a person who is not currently employed in that agency. It includes initial employment as well as transfer between agencies and subsequent employment after a break in service. Personnel actions that move an employee within an agency without a break in service are not covered. A break in service is a period of 4 or more calendar days during which an individual is no longer on the rolls of an executive agency.

Covered individual means a male (a) whose application for appointment is under consideration by an executive agency or who is an employee of an executive agency; (b) who was born after December 31, 1959, and is at least 18 years of age or becomes 18 following appointment; (c) who is either a United States citizen or an alien (including parolees and refugees and those who are lawfully admitted to the United States for permanent residence and for asylum) residing in the United States; and (d) is or was required to register under section 3 of the Military Selective Service Act (50 U.S.C. App. 453). Nonimmigrant aliens admitted under section 101(a)(15) of the Immigration and Nationality Act (8 U.S C. 1101), such as those admitted on visitor or student visas, and lawfully remaining in the United States, are exempt from registration.

Executive agency means an agency of the Government of the United States as defined in 5 U.S.C. 105.

Exemptions means those individuals determined by the Selective Service System to be excluded from the requirement to register under sections 3 and 6(a) of the Military Selective Service Act (50 U.S.C. App. 453 and 456(a)) or Presidential proclamation.

Preponderance of the evidence means that degree of relevant evidence that a reasonable person, considering the record as a whole, would accept as sufficient to support a conclusion that the matter asserted is more likely to be true than not true.

Registrant means an individual registered under Selective Service law.

Selective Service law means the Military Selective Service Act, rules and regulations issued thereunder, and proclamations of the President under that Act.

Selective Service System means the agency responsible for administering the registration system and for determining who is required to register and who is exempt.

§ 300.704 Considering individuals for appointment.

(a) An executive agency must request a written statement of Selective Service registration status from each covered individual at an appropriate time during the consideration process prior to appointment, and from each covered employee who becomes 18 after appointment. The individual must complete, sign, and date in ink the statement on a form provided by the agency unless the applicant furnishes other documentation as provided by paragraph (c) of this section.

(b) *Statement of Selective Service registration status.* Agencies should reproduce the following statement, which has been approved by the Office of Management and Budget for use through October 31, 1989, under OMB Control No. 3206–0166:

APPLICANT'S STATEMENT OF SELECTIVE SERVICE REGISTRATION STATUS

If you are a male born after December 31, 1959, and are at least 18 years of age, civil service employment law (5 U.S.C. 3328) requires that you must be registered with the Selective Service System, unless you meet certain exemptions under Selective Service law. If you are required to register but knowingly and willfully fail to do so, you are ineligible for appointment by executive agencies of the Federal Government.

CERTIFICATION OF REGISTRATION STATUS

Check one:

[ ] I certify I am registered with the Selective Service System.

[ ] I certify I have been determined by the Selective Service System to be exempt from the registration provisions of Selective Service law.

[ ] I certify I have not registered with the Selective Service System.

[ ] I certify I have not reached my 18th birthday and understand I am required by law to register at that time.

NON-REGISTRANTS UNDER AGE 26

If you are under age 26 and have not registered as required, you should register promptly at a United States Post Office, or consular office if you are outside the United States.

NON-REGISTRANTS AGE 26 OR OVER

If you were born in 1960 or later, are 26 years of age or older, and were required to register but did not do so, you can no longer register under Selective Service law. Accordingly, you are not eligible for appointment to an executive agency unless you can prove to the Office of Personnel Management (OPM) that your failure to register was neither knowing nor willful. You may request an OPM decision through the agency that was considering you for employment by returning this statement with your written request for an OPM determination together with any explanation and documentation you wish to furnish to prove that your failure to register was neither knowing nor willful.

PRIVACY ACT STATEMENT

Because information on your registration status is essential for determining whether you are in compliance with 5 U.S.C. 3328, failure to provide the information requested by this statement will prevent any further consideration of your application for appointment. This information is subject to verification with the Selective Service System and may be furnished to other Federal agencies for law enforcement or other authorized use in implementing this law.

FALSE STATEMENT NOTIFICATION

A false statement may be grounds for not hiring you, or for firing you if you have already begun work. Also, you may be punished by fine or imprisonment. (Section 1001 of title 18, United States Code.)

____

Legal signature of individual (please use ink)

____

Date signed (please use ink)

(c) At his option, a covered individual may submit, in lieu of the statement described above, a copy of his Acknowledgment Letter or other proof of registration or exemption issued by the Selective Service System. The individual must sign and date the document and add a note stating it is submitted as proof of Selective Service registration or exemption.

(d) An executive agency will give no further consideration for appointment to individuals who fail to provide the information requested above on registration status.

(e) An agency considering employment of a covered individual who is a current or former Federal employee is not required to request a statement when it determines that the individual's Official Personnel Folder contains evidence indicating the individual is registered or currently exempt from registration.

§ 300.705 Agency action following statement.

(a) Agencies must resolve conflicts of information and other questions concerning an individual's registration status prior to appointment. An agency may verify, at its discretion, an individual's registration status by requesting the individual to provide proof of registration or exemption issued by the Selective Service System and/or by contacting the Selective Service System at 888–655–1825.

(b) An agency may continue regular pre-employment consideration of individuals whose statements show they have registered or are exempt.

(c) An agency will take the following actions when a covered individual who is required to register has not done so, and is under age 26:

(1) Advise him to register promptly and, if he wishes further consideration, to submit a new statement immediately to the agency once he has registered. The agency will set a time limit for submitting the statement.

(2) Provide written notice to an individual who still does not register after being informed of the above requirements that he is ineligible for appointment according to 5 U.S.C. 3328 and will be given no further employment consideration.

(d) An agency will take the following actions when a covered individual who is age 26 or over, was required to register, and has not done so:

(1) Provide written notice to the individual that, in accordance with 5 U.S.C. 3328, he is ineligible for appointment unless his failure to register was neither knowing nor willful, and that OPM will decide whether his failure to register was knowing and willful if he submits a written request for such decision and an explanation of his failure to register.

(2) Submit the individual's application, the statement described in § 300.704(b), a copy of the written notice, his request for a decision and explanation of his failure to register, and any other papers pertinent to his registration status for determination to—Registration Review, Staffing Operations Division, Career Entry Group, room 6A12, U.S. Office of Personnel

Management, 1900 E Street, NW., Washington, DC 20415.

(3) An agency is not required to keep a vacancy open for an individual who seeks an OPM determination.

(e) Individuals described in paragraph (c) of this section who do not submit a statement of registration or exemption are not eligible for employment consideration. Individuals described in paragraph (d) of this section are not eligible for employment consideration unless OPM finds that failure to register was neither knowing nor willful. Agencies are not required to follow the objections-to-eligibles procedures described in §332.406 concerning such individuals who were certified or otherwise referred by an OPM examining office or other office delegated examining authority by OPM. Instead, an agency will provide, for information as part of its certification report to that office, a copy of its written notice to the individual.

[52 FR 7400, Mar. 11, 1987, as amended at 64 FR 28713, May 27, 1999]

§300.706 Office of Personnel Management adjudication.

(a) OPM will determine whether failure to register was knowing and willful when an individual has requested a decision and presented a written explanation, as described in §300.705. The Associate Director for Career Entry or his or her designee will make the determination based on the written explanation provided by the individual. The burden of proof will be on the individual to show by a preponderance of the evidence that failure to register was neither knowing nor willful.

(b) OPM may consult with the Selective Service System in making determinations.

(c) The Associate Director for Career Entry or his or her designee will notify the individual and the agency in writing of the determination. The determination is final unless reconsidered at the discretion of the Associate Director. There is no further right to administrative review.

(d) The Director of OPM may reopen and reconsider a determination.

(e) The Director of OPM may, at his or her discretion, delegate to an executive agency the authority to make initial determinations. However, OPM may review any initial determination and make a final adjudication in any case. If a delegation is made under this paragraph, the notice in §300.705(d)(1) will state that the individual may submit a written request that OPM review the agency's initial determination. The agency will forward to OPM copies of all documents relating to the individual's failure to register, including the individual's request for review and his explanation of his failure to register.

§300.707 Termination of employment.

A covered individual who is serving under an appointment made on or after November 8, 1985, and is not exempt from registration, will be terminated by his agency under the authority of the statute and these regulations if he has not registered as required, unless he registers or unless, if no longer eligible to register, OPM determines in response to his explanation that his failure to register was neither knowing nor willful.

PART 301—OVERSEAS EMPLOYMENT

AUTHORITY: 5 U.S.C. 3301, 3302; E.O. 10577, 3 CFR, 1954–1958 Comp., p. 218, as amended by E.O. 10641, 3 CFR, 1954–1958 Comp., p. 274, unless otherwise noted.

SOURCE: 44 FR 54691, Sept. 21, 1979, unless otherwise noted.

Subpart A [Reserved]

Subpart B—Overseas Limited Appointment

§ 301.201 Appointments of United States citizens recruited overseas.

When there is a shortage of eligible applicants, as defined at § 337.202 of this chapter, resulting from a competitive announcement that is open to applicants in the local overseas area, an agency may give an overseas limited appointment to a United States citizen recruited overseas for a position overseas.

[69 FR 33275, June 23, 2004]

§ 301.202 Appointment of citizens recruited outside overseas areas.

When an agency determines that unusual or emergency conditions make it infeasible to appoint from a register, it may give an overseas limited appointment to a United States citizen recruited in an area where an overseas limited appointment is not authorized.

§ 301.203 Duration of appointment.

(a) An appointment under this subpart is of indefinite duration unless otherwise limited.

(b) An agency may make an overseas limited term appointment for a period not in excess of 5 years when a time limitation is imposed as a part of a general program for rotating career and career-conditional employees between overseas areas and the United States after specified periods of overseas service.

(c) An agency may make an overseas limited appointment for 1 year or less to meet administrative needs for temporary employment. An agency may extend such an appointment for up to a maximum of 1 additional year.

(d) Upon request from the headquarters level of a Department or agency, OPM may approve, or delegate to agencies the authority to approve, exceptions to the time limits set out in paragraph (c) of this section.

[44 FR 54691, Sept. 21, 1979, as amended at 60 FR 3057, Jan. 13, 1995]

§ 301.204 Status and trial period.

(a) An overseas limited employee does not acquire a competitive status on the basis of his or her overseas limited appointment. He or she is required to serve a trial period of 1 year when given an overseas limited appointment of indefinite duration or an overseas limited term appointment.

(b) The agency may terminate an overseas limited employee at any time during the trial period. The employee is entitled to the procedures set forth in § 315.804 or § 315.805 of this chapter as appropriate.

§ 301.205 Requirements and restrictions.

The requirements and restrictions in subpart F of part 300 of this chapter apply to appointments under this subpart.

[69 FR 33275, June 15, 2004]

§ 301.206 Within-grade increases.

An employee serving under an overseas limited appointment of indefinite duration or an overseas limited term appointment in a position subject to the General Schedule, is eligible for within-grade increases in accordance with subpart D of part 531 of this chapter.

(5 U.S.C. 3301, 3302, E.O. 10577, 3 CFR, 1954–1958 Comp., p. 218, as amended by E.O. 10641, 3 CFR, 1954–1958 Comp., p. 274)

Subpart C—Overseas Employees Eligible for Noncompetitive Appointment Upon Return to the United States

AUTHORITY: E.O. 12362, 47 FR 21231, 3 CFR, 1982 Comp., p. 182.

SOURCE: 48 FR 52868, Nov. 23, 1983, unless otherwise noted. Correctly designated at 49 FR 5601, Feb. 14, 1984.

§ 301.301 Eligibility under the authority of Executive Order 12362.

Employees who serve under overseas local hire appointments as defined in § 315.608(b) of this chapter and meet the eligibility criteria of § 315.608(a) of this chapter are eligible for noncompetitive career-conditional, term, or temporary limited appointment when they return to the United States.

§ 301.302 Overseas appointing procedures.

Overseas agencies are required to insure that selection of employees for local hire appointments in the overseas area is made on the basis of the ability, knowledge, and skills of eligible candidates, in accordance with applicable law and regulation.

§ 301.303 Performance appraisal.

As soon as practicable, but beginning not later than January 1, 1984, overseas agencies are required to evaluate the performance of employees who serve under overseas local hire appointments as defined in § 315.608(b) of this chapter and who are eligible to meet the criteria established in § 315.608(a), of this chapter in accordance with the agency's performance appraisal plan established under chapter 43 of title 5, U.S. Code, unless the agency is exempt from the provisions of that chapter.

PART 302—EMPLOYMENT IN THE EXCEPTED SERVICE

Subpart A—General Provisions

Subpart B—Eligibility Standards

Subpart C—Accepting, Rating and Arranging Applications

Subpart D—Selection and Appointment; Reappointment; and Qualifications for Promotion

Subpart E—Appeals

AUTHORITY: 5 U.S.C. 1302, 3301, 3302, 8151, E.O. 10577 (3 CFR 1954–1958 Comp., p. 218); § 302.105 also issued under 5 U.S.C. 1104, Pub. L. 95–454, sec. 3(5); § 302.501 also issued under 5 U.S.C. 7701 *et seq.*

SOURCE: 55 FR 9407, Mar. 14, 1990, unless otherwise noted.

Subpart A—General Provisions

§ 302.101 Positions covered by regulations.

(a) *Positions covered.* With respect to the application of veteran preference, this part applies to each position in the Executive Branch of the Federal Government that is not in the competitive service and that is subject to the provisions of title 5, United States Code, or subject to a statutory requirement to follow the veteran preference provisions of title 5. With respect to restoration rights that are due to compensable injury and appeals therefrom, this part applies to those positions covered by 5 U.S.C. 8101(1) that are not in the competitive service.

(b) *Positions not covered.* This part does not apply to a position or appointment that is required by the Congress to be confirmed by, or made with the advice and consent of, the Senate.

(c) *Positions exempt from appointment procedures.* In view of the circumstances and conditions surrounding employment in the following classes of positions, an agency is not required to apply the appointment procedures of this part to them, but each agency shall follow the principle of veteran preference as far as administratively feasible and, on the request of a qualified and available preference eligible, shall furnish him/her with the reasons for his/her nonselection. Also, the exemption from the appointment procedures of this part does not relieve agencies of their obligation to accord persons entitled to priority consideration (see § 302.103) their rights under 5 U.S.C. 8151:

(1) Positions filled by persons appointed without pay or at pay of $1 a year;

(2) Positions outside the continental United States and outside the State of

Hawaii and the Commonwealth of Puerto Rico when filled by persons resident in the locality, and positions in the State of Hawaii and the Commonwealth of Puerto Rico when paid in accordance with prevailing wage rates;

(3) Positions which the exigencies of the national defense program demand be filled immediately before lists of qualified applicants can be established or used, but appointments to these positions shall be temporary appointments not to exceed 1 year which may be renewed for 1 additional year at the discretion of the agency;

(4) Positions filled by appointees serving on an irregular or occasional basis whose hours or days of work are not based on a prearranged schedule and who are paid only for the time when actually employed or for services actually performed;

(5) Positions paid on a fee basis;

(6) Positions included in Schedule A (see subpart C of part 213 of this chapter) and similar types of positions when OPM agrees with the agency that the positions should be included hereunder;

(7) Positions included in Schedule C (see subpart C of part 213 of this chapter) and positions excepted by statute which are of a confidential, policy-making, or policy-advocating nature;

(8) Attorney positions; and

(9) Positions filled by reemployment of an individual in the same agency and commuting area, at the same or lower grade, and under the same appointing authority as the position last held; *Provided That*, there are no candidates eligible for the position on the agency's priority reemployment list established in accordance with § 302.303.

(10) Positions for which a critical hiring need exists when filled under § 213.3102(i)(2) of this chapter.

[55 FR 9407, Mar. 14, 1990, as amended at 58 FR 58260, Nov. 1, 1993; 60 FR 10006, Feb. 23, 1995; 77 FR 28214, May 11, 2012]

§ 302.102 Method of filling positions and status of incumbent.

(a) To the extent permitted by statute and this chapter, each appointment, position change, and removal in the excepted service shall be made in accordance with any regulations or practices that the head of the agency concerned finds necessary.

(b) Except as authorized under paragraph (c) of this section, a person appointed to an excepted position does not acquire a competitive status by reason of the appointment. When an employee serving under a non-temporary appointment in the competitive service is selected for an excepted appointment, the agency must—

(1) Inform the employee that, because the position is in the excepted service, it may not be filled by a competitive appointment, and that acceptance of the proposed appointment will take him/her out of the competitive service while he/she occupies the position; and

(2) Obtain from the employee a written statement that he/she understands he/she is leaving the competitive service voluntarily to accept an appointment in the excepted service.

(c) Upon a finding by OPM that in a particular situation the action will be in the interest of good administration, OPM may authorize an agency to make appointments to specified positions in the excepted service in the same manner as to positions in the competitive service. Persons given career-conditional or career appointments pursuant to a specific authorization by OPM under this paragraph may acquire a competitive status as provided in part 315 of this chapter.

[55 FR 9407, Mar. 14, 1990, as amended at 58 FR 58261, Nov. 1, 1993]

§ 302.103 Definitions.

Person entitled to priority consideration means a person who was furloughed or separated without misconduct, from a position without time limit, because of a compensable injury and whose recovery takes longer than 1 year from the date compensation began. To be eligible under this part the person must apply for reappointment to his or her former agency within 30 days of the date of cessation of compensation.

§ 302.104 Applicability of regulations to applicants and employees.

Each agency shall follow the provisions of this part relating to examination, rating, and selection for appointment of an applicant when a qualified preference eligible or person entitled to priority consideration applies for appointment to a position covered by this part. Each agency, in its discretion, may follow these provisions when no preference eligible or person entitled to priority consideration applies.

§ 302.105 Special agency plans.

An agency having a position subject to this part may establish a system which will result in granting to eligible persons the preference or priority consideration referred to in sections 1302(c) or 8151 of title 5, United States Code, but which does not conform to all the procedural requirements set forth in this part. The agency establishing such a system must ensure that all eligible applicants entitled to veteran preference or priority consideration receive at least as much advantage in referral as they would receive under the procedures set forth in this part.

§ 302.106 Vacancy announcements.

When an agency announces a vacancy in the excepted service, the announcement must contain a reasonable accommodation statement that complies with requirements in part 330, subpart A of this chapter.

[66 FR 63906, Dec. 11, 2001, as amended at 75 FR 67593, Nov. 3, 2010]

Subpart B—Eligibility Standards

§ 302.201 Persons entitled to veteran preference.

In actions subject to this part, each agency shall grant veteran preference as follows:

(a) When numerical scores are used in the evaluation and referral, the agency shall grant 5 additional points to preference eligibles under section 2108(3) (A) and (B) of title 5, United States Code, and 10 additional points to preference eligibles under section 2108(3) (C) through (G) of that title.

(b) When eligible candidates are referred without ranking, the agency shall note preference as "CP" for preference eligibles under 5 U.S.C. 2108(3)(C), as "XP" for preference eligibles under 5 U.S.C. 2108(3) (D) through (G), and as "TP" for all other preference eligibles under that title.

§ 302.202 Qualification requirements.

Before making an appointment to a position covered by this part, each agency shall establish qualification standards such as those relating to experience and training, citizenship, minimum age, physical condition, etc., which shall relate to the duties to be performed. An agency may delegate the establishment of standards relating to a group of positions or a specific position to the appropriate administrative level or subdivision in accordance with the needs of the locality in which the position is located, but the agency shall determine that each standard established is in conformity with this part. Each agency shall make its standards a matter of record in the appropriate office of the agency, and shall furnish information concerning the standards for a position to an applicant on his/her request. Each agency shall apply the standards for a position uniformly to all applicants, except for such waivers as are provided in this part for a preference eligible. An agency shall not include a minimum educational requirement in qualification standards, except for a scientific, technical, or professional position the duties of which the agency decides cannot be performed by a person who does not have a prescribed minimum education. An agency shall not establish a maximum age requirement for any position. Each agency shall make a part of its records the reasons for its decision under this section and shall furnish those reasons to an applicant on his/her request. The qualification standards shall include:

(a) A provision for waiver by the agency of requirements as to age, height, and weight for each preference eligible when the requirements are not essential to the performance of the duties of the position; and

(b) A provision for waiver by the agency of physical requirements for each preference eligible when the agency, after giving due consideration to the recommendation of an accredited physician, finds that the applicant is physically able to discharge the duties of the position.

§ 302.203 Disqualifying factors.

(a) The qualification standards established by an agency or by an administrative level or subdivision of an agency may provide that certain reasons disqualify an applicant for appointment. The following, among others, may be included as disqualifying reasons:

(1) Dismissal from employment for delinquency or misconduct;

(2) Criminal, infamous, dishonest, immoral, or notoriously disgraceful conduct;

(3) Intentional false statement or deception or fraud in examination or appointment;

(4) Habitual use of intoxicating beverages to excess;

(5) Reasonable doubt as to the loyalty of the person involved to the Government of the United States;

(6) Any legal or other disqualification which makes the individual unfit for service; or

(7) Lack of United States citizenship.

(b) An agency may not disqualify an applicant solely because of his/her retired status.

Subpart C—Accepting, Rating, and Arranging Applications

§ 302.301 Receipt of applications.

(a) Each agency shall establish definite rules regarding the acceptance of applications for employment in positions covered by this part and shall make these rules a matter of record.

(b) Each agency shall apply its rules uniformly to all applicants who meet the conditions of the rules and shall furnish information concerning the rules to an applicant on his/her request.

§ 302.302 Examination of applicants.

(a) *Eligibility.* An evaluation of the qualifications of applicants for positions covered by this part may be conducted at any time before an appointment is made. The evaluation may involve only determination of eligibility or ineligibility or may include qualitative rating of candidates. If the evaluation involves only basic eligibility numerical scores will not be assigned and eligible candidates will be referred in accordance with the procedures described in paragraph (b)(5) of § 302.304. If qualitative ranking is desired, numerical scores may be assigned in accordance with paragraph (b) of this section. Each agency shall make a part of the records the reasons for its decision to use ranked or unranked referral and, for ranked actions, the quality ranking factors used. This information shall be made available to an applicant on his/her request.

(b) *Rating.* Numerical scores will be assigned on a scale of 100. Each applicant who meets the qualification requirements for the position established under § 302.202 will be assigned a rating of 70 or more and will be eligible for appointment. Candidates scoring 70 or more will receive additional points for veteran preference as provided in § 302.201. Numerical ratings are not required when all qualified applicants will be offered immediate appointment. When there is an excessive number of applicants, numerical ratings are required only for a sufficient number of the highest qualified applicants to meet the anticipated needs of the agency within a reasonable period of time. The agency must, however, adopt procedures to insure the consideration of preference eligibles in the order in which they would have been considered if all applicants had been assigned numerical ratings. An agency shall furnish a notice of the rating assigned to an applicant on his/her request.

(c) *Nonpreference applicants for certain positions.* An agency may not consider or rate an application for the position of elevator operator, messenger, guard, or custodian submitted by a nonpreference eligible as long as at least three qualified preference eligibles are available for the position.

(d) *Evaluating experience.* When experience is a factor in determining eligibility, an agency shall credit a preference eligible (1) with time spent in the military service of the United States if the position for which he/she is applying is similar to the position which he/she held immediately before his/her entrance into the military service; and (2) with all valuable experience, including experience gained in religious, civic, welfare, service, and organizational activities, regardless of whether pay was received therefor.

§ 302.303 Maintenance of employment lists.

(a) *Establishment*—(1) *Agency's obligation.* An agency must establish a priority reemployment list whenever any applicants rated eligible under § 302.302 meet the conditions set out in paragraphs (b)(1) through (b)(3) of this section and must consider candidates from that list in accordance with § 302.304(a). All applicants not included on the priority reemployment list will be listed on the regular employment list unless the agency elects to establish a reemployment list as provided in paragraph (c) of this section.

(2) *Agency discretion.* In establishing its lists, an agency may, but is not required to: Afford priority consideration to non-preference eligibles who meet the conditions set out in paragraph (b)(4) of this section; afford priority consideration under paragraph (b) of this section for a longer time and/or in a broader geographic area than the minimum requirement; and/or provide reemployment consideration after the priority list is exhausted to additional current and former employees in accordance with paragraph (c) of this section. An agency may limit consideration granted at its discretion to applicants for specific positions or applicants who meet specific conditions, but must make those conditions a matter of record and must apply its policy uniformly to all eligible employees. Generally, full-time employees may be considered only for full-time positions and other-than-full-time employees only for other-than-full-time positions. However, full-time employees may be considered for other-than-full-time positions if there are no other-than-full-time employees on the appropriate priority or reemployment list; and other-than-full time employees may be considered for full-time positions if there are no full-time employees on the appropriate list.

(b) *Priority reemployment list.* Candidates are entered on the priority reemployment list in the geographic areas specified in paragraph (b)(1) of this section and remain on the list for 2 years unless the agency elects to provide a longer period of eligibility. The priority reemployment list includes:

(1) The name of each former employee of the agency who is a preference eligible, has been furloughed or separated from a continuing appointment without delinquency or misconduct, and applies for reemployment. Candidates in this category are considered for positions in the commuting area where they were separated unless the agency elects to provide broader consideration.

(2) The name of each former employee of the agency who is a preference eligible and who, as the result of an appeal under part 752 of this chapter, is found by the Merit Systems Protection Board to have been unjustifiably dismissed from the agency, but who is not entitled to immediate restoration under the Board's decision. Candidates in this category are considered in the commuting area from which separated unless the Board's decision specifies a broader or different area or the agency elects to afford broader geographic consideration.

(3) The name of each former employee of the agency who has been furloughed or separated due to compensable injury sustained under the provisions of 5 U.S.C. chapter 81, subchapter I, who is not entitled to immediate restoration, and who is eligible for priority consideration under this part. Candidates in this category are considered in the commuting area where they last served and, if the agency determines that an appropriate vacancy is unlikely to occur in that area during the candidates' period of reemployment priority, in other locations for which they are available.

(4) At the agency's discretion, the name of each former employee of the agency who is not a preference eligible, has been furloughed or involuntarily separated from a continuing appointment without delinquency or misconduct, and applies for reemployment. Candidates in this category are considered in the geographic area specified by the agency.

(c) *Reemployment list.* A reemployment list may be established at the agency's discretion to include the names of current employees of the agency and of former employees of the agency who are to be considered for future employment and who are not eligible for inclusion on the priority reemployment list. Employees may be entered on the reemployment list only for positions in which tenure and/or work schedule is no greater than that of the position previously held.

(d) *Order of entry.* An agency shall enter the names of all applicants rated eligible under § 302.302 on the appropriate list (priority reemployment, reemployment, or regular employment) in the following order:

(1) *When candidates have been rated only for basic eligibility under § 302.302(a).* (i) Preference eligibles having a compensable, service-connected disability of 10 percent or more (designated as "CP") unless the list will be used to fill professional positions at the GS–9 level or above, or equivalent;

(ii) All other candidates eligible for 10-point veteran preference;

(iii) All candidates eligible for 5-point veteran preference; and

(iv) Qualified candidates not eligible for veteran preference.

(2) *When qualified candidates have been assigned numerical scores under § 302.302(b).* (i) Preference eligibles having a compensable, service-connected disability of 10 percent or more, in the order of their augmented ratings, unless the list will be used to fill professional positions at the GS–9 level or above, or equivalent;

(ii) All other qualified candidates in the order of their augmented ratings. At each score, qualified candidates eligible for 10-point preference will be entered ahead of those eligible for 5-point preference or those not eligible for veteran preference, and those eligible for 5-point preference will be entered ahead of those not eligible for preference.

§ 302.304 Order of consideration.

(a) *Consideration of priority reemployment candidates.* An agency must consider all qualified candidates on its priority reemployment list before it may refer candidates from its reemployment list, if any, or regular employment list. When a qualified candidate is available on the priority list, the agency may appoint an individual who is not on the priority list or who has lower standing than others on that list *only* when necessary to obtain an employee for duties that cannot be taken over without undue interruption to the agency by an individual who is entitled to reemployment priority or has higher standing on the priority reemployment list than the one appointed. The agency must notify each individual on the priority reemployment list who is adversely affected by an appointment under this paragraph of the reasons for the exception and must further notify each such individual who is a preference eligible of his or her right of appeal to the Merit Systems Protection Board.

(b) *Consideration of other candidates.* Except as provided in paragraphs (b)(4) and (b)(5) of this section, an agency shall consider applicants on the reemployment and/or regular employment list who have been assigned eligible ratings for a given position in Order A, Order B, or Order C, as described in paragraphs (b)(1) through (b)(3) of this section. Order A must be used when the agency has not established a reemployment list.

(1) *Order A.* (i) The name of each qualified preference eligible who has a compensable, service-connected disability of 10 percent or more and is entitled to 10-point preference under section 3309 of title 5, United States Code, in the order of his/her numerical ranking.

(ii) The name of each other qualified applicant in the order of his/her numerical ranking.

(2) *Order B.* (i) The name of each qualified preference eligible who has a compensable, service-connected disability of 10 percent or more and is entitled to 10-point preference under section 3309 of title 5, United States Code, and whose name appears on the agency's reemployment list, in the order of his/her numerical ranking.

(ii) The name of each qualified preference eligible who has a compensable, service-connected disability of 10 percent or more and is entitled to 10-point preference under section 3309 of title 5,

United States Code, and whose name appears on the agency's regular employment list, in the order of his/her numerical ranking.

(iii) The name of each other qualified applicant on the agency's reemployment list, in the order of his/her numerical ranking.

(iv) The name of each other qualified applicant on the agency's regular employment list, in the order of his/her numerical ranking.

(3) *Order C*. (i) The name of each qualified preference eligible who has a compensable, service-connected disability of 10 percent or more and is entitled to 10-point preference under section 3309 of title 5, United States Code, and whose name appears on the agency's reemployment list, in the order of his/her numerical ranking.

(ii) The name of each other qualified applicant on the agency's reemployment list, in the order of his/her numerical ranking.

(iii) The name of each qualified preference eligible who has a compensable, service-connected disability of 10 percent or more and is entitled to 10-point preference under section 3309 of title 5, United States Code, and whose name appears on the agency's regular employment list, in the order of his/her numerical ranking.

(iv) The name of each other qualified applicant on the agency's regular employment list, in the order of his/her numerical ranking.

(4) *Professional order*. An agency shall consider applicants who have been assigned eligible ratings for professional and scientific positions at the GS–9 level and above, or equivalent, in the following order:

(i) *Applicants on the agency's reemployment list, if any*. If numerical scores have been assigned, the applicants will be considered in the order of their augmented scores. If numerical scores have not been assigned, all preference eligibles will be considered together regardless of the type of preference, followed by all other priority reemployment candidates.

(ii) *Applicants on the agency's regular employment list*. If numerical scores have been assigned, the applicants will be considered in the order of their augmented scores. If numerical scores have not been assigned, all preference eligibles will be considered together regardless of the type of preference, followed by all other candidates.

(5) *Unranked order*. When numerical scores are not assigned, the agency may consider applicants who have received eligible ratings for positions not covered by paragraph (b)(4) of this section in either of the following orders:

(i) *By preference status*. Under this method, preference eligibles having a compensable service-connected disability of 10 percent or more are considered first, followed, second, by other 10-point preference eligibles, third, by 5-point preference eligibles, and, last, by nonpreference eligibles. Within each category, applicants from the reemployment list will be placed ahead of applicants from the regular employment list.

(ii) *By reemployment/regular list status*. Under this method, all applicants on the reemployment list are considered before applicants on the regular employment list. On each list, preference eligibles having a compensable service-connected disability of 10 percent or more are considered first, followed, second, by other 10-point preference eligibles, third, by 5-point preference eligibles, and, last, by nonpreference eligibles.

Subpart D—Selection and Appointment; Reappointment; and Qualifications for Promotion

§302.401 Selection and appointment.

(a) *Selection*. When making an appointment from a priority reemployment, reemployment, or regular list on which candidates have not received numerical scores, an agency must make its selection from the highest available preference category, as long as at least three candidates remain in that group. When fewer than three candidates remain in the highest category, consideration may be expanded to include the next category. When making an appointment from a list on which candidates have received numerical scores, the agency must make its selection for each vacancy from not more than the highest three names available for appointment in the order provided in

§ 302.304. Under either method, an agency is not required to—

(1) Accord an applicant on its priority reemployment or reemployment list the preference consideration required by § 302.304 if the list on which the applicant's name appears does not contain the names of at least three preference eligibles; or

(2) Consider an applicant who has previously been considered three times or a preference eligible if consideration of his/her name has been discontinued for the position as provided in paragraph (b) of this section.

(b) *Passing over a preference applicant.* When an agency, in making an appointment as provided in paragraph (a) of this section, passes over the name of a preference eligible who is entitled to priority consideration under § 302.304 and selects a nonpreference eligible, it shall record its reasons for so doing, and shall furnish a copy of those reasons to the preference eligible or his/her representative on request. An agency may discontinue consideration of the name of a preference eligible for a position if on three occasions the agency has considered him/her for the position and has passed over his/her name and recorded its reasons for so doing.

§ 302.402 Reappointment.

An agency may reappoint a current or former nontemporary employee of the executive branch of the Federal Government who is a preference eligible to a position covered by this part without regard to the names of qualified applicants on the agency's priority reemployment, reemployment, or regular employment list.

§ 302.403 Qualifications for promotion.

In determining qualifications for promotion with respect to an employee who is a preference eligible, an agency shall waive:

(a) Requirements as to age, height, and weight unless the requirement is essential to the performance of the duties of the position; and

(b) Physical requirements if, in the opinion of the agency, after considering the recommendation of an accredited physician, the preference eligible is physically able to perform efficiently the duties of the position for which the promotion is proposed.

Subpart E—Appeals

§ 302.501 Entitlement.

An individual who is covered by 5 U.S.C. 8101(1) and is entitled to priority consideration under this part (see § 302.103) may appeal a violation of his/her restoration rights to the Merit Systems Protection Board under the provisions of the Board's regulations by presenting factual information that he or she was denied restoration rights because of the employment of another person.

PART 304—EXPERT AND CONSULTANT APPOINTMENTS

Sec.

AUTHORITY: 5 U.S.C. 3109.

SOURCE: 60 FR 45648, Sept. 1, 1995, unless otherwise noted.

§ 304.101 Coverage.

These regulations apply to the appointment of experts and consultants as Federal employees under 5 U.S.C. 3109. They do not apply to the appointments of experts and consultants under other employment authorities or to the procurement of services by contracts under the procurement laws.

§ 304.102 Definitions.

For purposes of this part:

(a) An *agency* is an executive department, a military department, or an independent agency.

(b) A *consultant* is a person who can provide valuable and pertinent advice generally drawn from a high degree of broad administrative, professional, or technical knowledge or experience. When an agency requires public advisory participation, a consultant also may be a person who is affected by a particular program and can provide useful views from personal experience.

(c) A *consultant position* is one that requires providing advice, views, opinions, alternatives, or recommendations on a temporary and/or intermittent basis on issues, problems, or questions presented by a Federal official.

(d) An *expert* is a person who is specially qualified by education and experience to perform difficult and challenging tasks in a particular field beyond the usual range of achievement of competent persons in that field. An expert is regarded by other persons in the field as an authority or practitioner of unusual competence and skill in a professional, scientific, technical or other activity.

(e) An *expert position* is one that requires the services of a specialist with skills superior to those of others in the same profession, occupation, or activity to perform work on a temporary and/or intermittent basis assigned by a Federal official. For example, a microbial contamination specialist may apply new test methods to identify bacteria on products, a computer scientist may adapt advanced methods to develop a complex software system, or a plate maker may engrave a novel design.

(f) *Intemittent employment*, as defined in part 340, subpart D, of this chapter, means employment without a regularly scheduled tour of duty.

(g) *Temporary employment* means employment not to exceed 1 year. An expert or consultant serving under a temporary appointment may have a full-time, part-time, seasonal, or intermittent work schedule.

(h) Employment *without compensation* means unpaid service that is provided at the agency's request and is to perform duties that are unclassified. It is not volunteer service.

§ 304.103 Authority.

(a) *Basic authority*. (1) When authorized by an appropriation or other statute to use 5 U.S.C. 3109, an agency may appoint a qualified expert or consultant to an expert or consultant position that requires only intermittent and/or temporary employment. Such an appointment is excepted from competitive examination, position classification, and the General Schedule pay rates.

(2) An expert or consultant who works on a strictly intermittent basis may be appointed under this authority without time limit or for any period determined by the agency. All other experts and consultants must receive temporary appointments. Temporary experts and consultants may be reappointed in the same agency only as provided in paragraph (c) of this section.

(b) *Inappropriate use*. An agency must not use 5 U.S.C. 3109 to appoint an expert or consultant:

(1) To a position requiring Presidential appointment. However, subject to the conditions of this part, an agency may appoint an individual awaiting final action on a Presidential appointment to an expert or consultant position.

(2) To a Senior Executive Service position (including an FBI or DEA Senior Executive Service position).

(3) To perform managerial or supervisory work (although an expert may act as team leader or director of the specific project for which he/she is hired), to make final decisions on substantive policies, or to otherwise function in the agency chain of command (e.g., to approve financial transactions, personnel actions, etc.).

(4) To do work performed by the agency's regular employees.

(5) To fill in during staff shortages.

(6) Solely in anticipation of giving that individual a career appointment. However, subject to the conditions of this part, an agency may appoint an individual to an expert or consultant position pending Schedule C appointment or noncareer appointment in the Senior Executive Service.

(c) *Reappointment*. An agency may reemploy an expert or consultant to perform demonstrably different duties without regard to the length of that individual's previous expert or consultant service with the agency. Reappointment to perform substantially the same duties is subject to the following limits:

(1) An agency may employ an expert or consultant who works on a full-time basis for a maximum of 2 years—*i.e.*, on an initial appointment not to exceed 1

year and a reappointment not to exceed 1 additional year.

(2) An agency may reappoint an expert or consultant who works on a part-time or intermittent schedule in accordance with one of the following options. The agency must determine which option it will use in advance of any reappointment and must base its determination on objective criteria (e.g., nature of duties, pay level, whether or not work is regularly scheduled). Option 1 must be applied to reappointments of experts and consultants appointed without compensation.

(i) *Option 1—Annual service.* An agency may reappoint an expert or consultant, with no limit on the number of reappointments, as long as the individual is paid for no more than 6 months (130 days or 1,040 hours) of work, or works for no more than that amount of time without compensation, in a service year. (The service year is the calendar year that begins on the date of the individual's initial appointment in the agency.) An expert or consultant who exceeds this limit in his/her first service year may be reappointed for 1 additional year. An expert or consultant who exceeds the limit during any subsequent service year may not be reappointed thereafter.

(ii) *Option 2—Cumulative earnings.* Each expert or consultant will have a lifetime limit of twice the maximum annual rate payable under the annualized basic pay limitations of section 304.105. The agency may adjust this limit to reflect statutory increases in basic pay rates. The agency may reappoint an expert or consultant until his/her total earnings from expert or consultant employment with the agency reach the lifetime maximum, as determined by using the applicable maximum salary rate. At that point, the employment must be terminated.

(3) OPM may authorize reappointment of an expert or consultant as an exception to the limits in the section when necessitated by unforeseen and unusual circumstances.

§ 304.104 Determining rate of pay.

(a) The rate of basic pay for experts and consultants is set by administrative action. The head of an agency, or his or her designee, must determine the appropriate rate of basic pay on an hourly or daily basis, subject to the limitations described in section 304.105.

(b) The head of an agency, or his or her designee, shall consider the following factors in setting the initial rate of basic pay for an expert or consultant:

(1) The level and difficulty of the work to be performed;

(2) The qualifications of the expert or consultant;

(3) The pay rates of comparable individuals performing similar work in Federal or non-Federal sectors; and

(4) The availability of qualified candidates.

(c) An expert or consultant appointed under 5 U.S.C. 3109 may be employed without pay, provided the individual agrees in advance in writing to waive any claim for compensation for those services.

§ 304.105 Daily and biweekly basic pay limitations.

(a) Unless specifically authorized by an appropriation or other statute, agencies subject to chapter 51 and subchapter III of chapter 53 of title 5, United States Code, may not pay for any 1 day an aggregate amount of pay (including basic pay, locality pay under subpart F of part 531 of this chapter, and premium pay under subpart A of part 550 of this chapter) that exceeds the daily equivalent of the highest rate payable under 5 U.S.C. 5332—that is, the daily rate for GS–15, step 10, under the General Schedule (excluding locality pay or any other additional pay). The daily rate is computed by dividing the annual GS–15, step 10, rate by 2,087 hours to find the hourly rate of pay and by multiplying the hourly rate of pay by 8 hours.

(b) Unless specifically authorized by an appropriation or other statute, an expert or consultant shall not be paid for any biweekly pay period an aggregate amount of pay (including basic pay, locality pay under subpart F of part 531 of this chapter, and premium pay under subpart A of part 550 of this chapter) in excess of the biweekly rate of pay for GS–15, step 10, under the General Schedule (excluding locality pay or any other additional pay). The biweekly rate is computed by dividing the annual GS–15, step 10, rate by 2,087 hours to find the hourly rate of pay and by multiplying the hourly rate of pay by 80 hours.

§ 304.106 Pay and leave administration.

(a) The employing agency has the authority to adjust the pay of experts and consultants after initial appointment and to establish appropriate policies governing the amount and timing of any such adjustments, subject to the limitations of § 304.105. In addition to the factors listed in § 304.104(b), the agency may consider factors such as job performance, contributions to agency mission, and the general pay increases granted to other Federal employees. Experts and consultants are not entitled to receive automatic adjustments in their rates of basic pay at the time of general pay increases under 5 U.S.C. 5303 unless specifically provided for in the official appointing document. In the absence of such automatic entitlement, any pay adjustments are at the agency's discretion.

(b) Experts and consultants paid on a daily rate basis are not entitled to overtime pay under section 5542 of title 5, United States Code. Otherwise, experts and consultants qualify for premium pay under subchapter V of chapter 55 of title 5, United States Code, if they meet the applicable eligibility requirements (including the requirement that an employee have a regularly scheduled tour of duty, where applicable).

(c) Experts and consultants may be entitled to overtime pay under the Fair Labor Standards Act if they are nonexempt under OPM regulations implementing that Act for Federal employees. (See 5 CFR part 551).

(d) An expert or consultant may be paid for service on an intermittent basis in more than one expert or consultant position, provided the pay is not received for the same period of time (5 U.S.C. 5533(d)(1)).

(e) Experts and consultants are subject to the provisions of 5 U.S.C. 8344 and 8468 on reduction of basic pay by the amount of annuity received.

(f) Experts and consultants are subject to the provisions of 5 U.S.C. 5532 on reduction of retired military pay.

(g) Experts and consultants with a regularly scheduled tour of duty (*i.e.*, not intermittent) are entitled to sick and annual leave in accordance with chapter 63 of title 5, United States Code, and to pay for any holiday occurring on a workday on which they perform no work, provided that workday is part of the basic workweek. Those employed on an intermittent basis do not earn leave and are not entitled to paid holidays.

§ 304.107 Reports.

As required by 5 U.S.C. 3109(e), each agency shall report to the Office of Personnel Management on an annual basis:

(a) The number of days the agency employed each paid expert or consultant; and

(b) The total amount the agency paid each expert or consultant so employed. (Do not include payments for travel and related expenses.)

§ 304.108 Compliance.

(a) Each agency using 5 U.S.C. 3109 must establish and maintain a system of controls and oversight necessary to assure compliance with 5 U.S.C. 3109 and these regulations. The system must include—

(1) Appropriate training and information procedures to ensure that officials and employees using the authority understand the statutory and regulatory requirements; and

(2) Appropriate provision for review of expert and consultant appointments.

(b) OPM will, as necessary—

(1) Review agency employment of experts and consultants and agency controls and oversight to determine compliance; and

(2) Issue instructions and guidance to agencies on employing experts and consultants and on reporting procedures.

PART 305 [RESERVED]

PART 307—VETERANS RECRUITMENT APPOINTMENTS

Sec.

AUTHORITY: 5 U.S.C. 3301, 3302; E.O. 11521, 3 CFR, 1970 Comp., p. 912; 38 U.S.C. 4214.

SOURCE: 70 FR 72066, Dec. 1, 2005, unless otherwise noted.

§ 307.101 Purpose.

This part implements 38 U.S.C. 4214 and Executive Order 11521, which authorizes agencies to appoint *qualified covered veterans* to positions in the competitive service under Veterans Recruitment Appointments (VRAs) without regard to the competitive examining system.

§ 307.102 Definitions.

For purposes of this part—

Agency, as defined in 38 U.S.C. 4211(5), means any agency of the Federal Government or the District of Columbia, including any Executive agency as defined in section 105 of title 5, and the United States Postal Service and Postal Rate Commission.

Covered veterans, as defined in 38 U.S.C. 4212(a)(3), means any of the following:

(1) Disabled veterans;

(2) Veterans who served on active duty in the Armed Forces during a war or in a campaign or expedition for which a campaign badge has been authorized;

(3) Veterans who, while serving on active duty with the Armed Forces, participated in a United States military operation for which an Armed Forces Service Medal (AFSM) was awarded pursuant to Executive Order 12985 (61 FR 1209); and

(4) Recently separated veterans.

Disabled veteran, as defined in 38 U.S.C. 4211 means:

(1) A veteran who is entitled to compensation (or who, but for the receipt of military retired pay, would be entitled to compensation) under laws administered by the Secretary of Veterans Affairs; or

(2) A person who was discharged or released from active duty because of a service-connected disability.

Qualified, as defined in 38 U.S.C. 4212(a)(3) with respect to employment in a position, means having the ability to perform the essential functions of the position with or without reasonable accommodation for an individual with a disability.

Recently separated veteran, as defined in 38 U.S.C. 4211(6), means any veteran during the three-year period beginning on the date of such veteran's discharge or release from active duty.

Substantially continuous service is defined in 5 CFR 315.201(b)(3).

War means any armed conflict declared by Congress as such.

§ 307.103 Nature of VRAs.

VRAs are excepted appointments, made without competition, to positions otherwise in the competitive service. The veterans' preference procedures of part 302 of this chapter apply when there are preference eligible candidates being considered for a VRA. *Qualified covered veterans* who were separated *under honorable conditions* may be appointed to any position in the competitive service at grade levels up to and including GS–11 or equivalent, provided they meet the qualification standards for the position. To be eligible for a VRA as a *covered veteran* under paragraph (2) or (3) of the definition of that term in § 307.102, the veteran must be in receipt of the appropriate campaign badge, expeditionary medal, or AFSM. For purposes of a VRA, any military service is qualifying at the GS–3 level or equivalent. Upon satisfactory completion of 2 years of substantially continuous service, the incumbent's VRA must be converted to a career or career conditional appointment. An individual may receive more than one VRA appointment as long as the individual meets the definition of a *covered veteran* at the time of appointment.

§ 307.104 Treatment of individuals serving under VRAs.

(a) Because VRAs are made to positions otherwise in the competitive service, the incumbents, like competitive service employees, may be reassigned, promoted, demoted, or transferred in accordance with the provisions of part 335 of this chapter.

(b) A veteran with less than 15 years of education must receive training or education prescribed by the agency.

(c) Appointments are subject to investigation by OPM. A law, Executive order, or regulation that disqualifies a person for appointment in the competitive service also disqualifies a person for a VRA.

(d) The Veterans Recruitment Appointment date for a *recently separated veteran* must occur before the end of the 3-year eligibility period and may not be extended.

§307.105 Appeal rights.

Individuals serving under VRAs have the same appeal rights as excepted service employees under parts 432 and 752 of this chapter. In addition, as established in §315.806 of this chapter, any individual serving under a VRA, whose employment under the appointment is terminated within 1 year after the date of such appointment, has the same right to appeal that termination as a career or career-conditional employee has during the first year of employment.

PART 308—VOLUNTEER SERVICE

AUTHORITY: 5 U.S.C. 3111.

SOURCE: 44 FR 51183, Aug. 31, 1979, unless otherwise noted.

§308.101 Definitions.

In this part: *Student* is an individual who is enrolled not less than half-time in a high school, trade school, technical or vocational institute, junior college, college, university or other accredited educational institution. An individual who is a student is deemed not to have ceased to be a student during an interim between school years if the interim is not more than 5 months and if such individual shows to the satisfaction of the agency that the individual has a bona fide intention of continuing to pursue a course of study or training in the same or different educational institution during the school semester (or other period into which the school year is divided) immediately after the interim.

Volunteer Service under the Act is limited to services performed by a student, with the permission of the institution at which the student is enrolled, as part of an agency program established for the purpose of providing educational experience for the student. Such service is to be uncompensated and will not be used to displace any employee or to staff a position which is a normal part of the agency's work force.

§308.102 Eligibility and status.

(a) *Minimum Age*. The selection of students to participate under the program should be in conformance with either Federal, State, or local laws and standards governing the employment of minors.

(b) *Status*. A student participating under an agency volunteer program is not considered to be a Federal employee for any purposes other than injury compensation or laws related to the Tort Claims Act. Service is not creditable for leave accrual or any other employee benefits.

§308.103 Authority.

Section 301 of the Civil Service Reform Act of 1978, Public Law 95–454, authorized Federal departments and agencies to establish programs designed to provide educationally related work assignments for students in nonpay status.

PART 310—EMPLOYMENT OF RELATIVES

AUTHORITY: 5 U.S.C. 3110.

SOURCE: 70 FR 20457, Apr. 20, 2005, unless otherwise noted.

§310.101 Legal restrictions on public officials in the employment of relatives.

Section 3110 of title 5, United States Code, sets forth the legal restrictions on the employment of relatives.

§ 310.102 Exceptions to the legal restrictions on the employment of relatives.

Subsection (d) of 5 U.S.C. 3110 authorizes the Office of Personnel Management to prescribe regulations authorizing the temporary employment of relatives, in certain conditions, notwithstanding the restrictions. This regulation sets forth exceptions to the restrictions. When necessary to meet urgent needs resulting from an emergency posing an immediate threat to life or property, or a national emergency as defined in § 230.402(a)(1) of this title, a public official may employ relatives to meet those needs without regard to the restrictions on the employment of relatives in 5 U.S.C. 3110. Such appointments are temporary and may not exceed 30 days, but the agency may extend such an appointment for one additional 30-day period if the emergency need still exists at the time of the extension.

PART 315—CAREER AND CAREER-CONDITIONAL EMPLOYMENT

Subpart A [Reserved]

Subpart B—The Career-Conditional Employment System

Sec.

Subpart C—Career or Career-Conditional Employment From Registers

Subpart D—Career or Career-Conditional Employment by Reinstatement

Subpart E—Career or Career-Conditional Employment by Transfer

Subpart F—Career or Career-Conditional Appointment Under Special Authorities

Subpart G—Conversion to Career or Career-Conditional Employment From Other Types of Employment

Subpart H—Probation on Initial Appointment to a Competitive Position

Subpart I—Probation on Initial Appointment to a Supervisory or Managerial Position

AUTHORITY: 5 U.S.C. 1302, 2301, 2302, 3301, and 3302; E.O. 10577, 3 CFR, 1954–1958 Comp. p. 218, unless otherwise noted; and E.O. 13162.

Secs. 315.601 and 315.609 also issued under 22 U.S.C. 3651 and 3652.

Secs. 315.602 and 315.604 also issued under 5 U.S.C. 1104.

Sec. 315.603 also issued under 5 U.S.C. 8151.

Sec. 315.605 also issued under E.O. 12034, 3 CFR, 1978 Comp. p.111.

Sec. 315.606 also issued under E.O. 11219, 3 CFR, 1964–1965 Comp. p. 303.

Sec. 315.607 also issued under 22 U.S.C. 2506.

Sec. 315.608 also issued under E.O. 12721, 3 CFR, 1990 Comp. p. 293.

Sec. 315.610 also issued under 5 U.S.C. 3304(c).

Sec. 315.611 also issued under 5 U.S.C. 3304(f).

Sec. 315.612 also issued under E.O. 13473.

Sec. 315.708 also issued under E.O.13318, 3 CFR, 2004 Comp. p. 265.

Sec. 315.710 also issued under E.O. 12596, 3 CFR, 1987 Comp. p. 229.

Subpart I also issued under 5 U.S. C. 3321, E.O. 12107, 3 CFR, 1978 Comp. p. 264.

SOURCE: 33 FR 12418, Sept. 4, 1968, unless otherwise noted.

EDITORIAL NOTE: Nomenclature changes to part 315 appear at 70 FR 72067, Dec. 1, 2005.

Subpart A [Reserved]

Subpart B—The Career-Conditional Employment System

§315.201 Service requirement for career tenure.

(a) *Service requirement.* A person employed in the competitive service for other than temporary, term, or indefinite employment is appointed as a career or career-conditional employee subject to the probationary period required by subpart H of this part. Except as provided in paragraph (c) of this section, an employee must serve at least 3 years of creditable service as defined in paragraph (b) of this section to become a career employee.

(b) *Creditable service.* Unless otherwise approved by OPM, the service required for career tenure must include service as described in paragraph (b)(1) of this section and total at least 3 years.

(1) *Nontemporary employment.* To be creditable, the 3 years of service must begin with one of the following:

(i) Nontemporary appointment in the competitive service: For this purpose, nontemporary appointment includes a career-conditional appointment. The 3 years may also begin, but not end, with status quo employment under subpart G of part 316 of this chapter, an overseas limited appointment of indefinite duration, or an overseas limited term appointment under part 301 of this chapter. The 3 years also may have begun with permanent employment under now obsolete appointing authorities such as probational, war service indefinite, emergency indefinite, nontemporary appointment from a civil service register to a position in the excepted service before January 23, 1955, temporary appointment pending establishment of a register (also known as TAPER authority), nontemporary appointment to a position in the District of Columbia Government before January 23, 1955, and appointment based on Public Law 83–121. Determinations of whether an obsolete authority provides the basis for creditable service may be obtained from OPM;

(ii) Nontemporary appointment to an excepted position, provided the employee's excepted position was brought into the competitive service and, on that basis, the employee acquired competitive status or was converted to a career-conditional appointment;

(iii) Nontemporary appointment to a nonappropriated fund (NAF) position in or under the Department of Defense or in or under the U.S. Coast Guard, Department of Homeland Security, provided the employee's NAF position was brought into the competitive service and, on that basis, the employee acquired competitive status or was converted to a career or career-conditional appointment;

(iv) Nontemporary excepted or nonappropriated fund appointment, Foreign Service appointment, or appointment in the Canal Zone Merit System, provided the employee is appointed to a competitive service position under the terms of an interchange agreement with another merit system under § 6.7 of this chapter, under Executive Order 11219 as amended by Executive Order 12292, or under Executive Order 11171;

(v) The date of appointment to a position on the White House Staff or in the immediate office of the President or Vice President, provided the service has been continuous and the individual was appointed to a competitive service position under § 315.602 of this chapter;

(vi) The date of nontemporary excepted appointment under § 213.3202(b) of this chapter (the former Student Career Experience Program) as in effect immediately before July 10, 2012, the effective date of the regulations removing that paragraph, provided the student's appointment was converted to a career or career-conditional appointment under Executive Order 12015 or under Executive Order 13562, with or without an intervening term appointment, and without a break in service of one day;

(vii) The date of veterans recruitment appointment (VRA), provided the appointment is converted to a career or career-conditional appointment under § 315.705 of this chapter, or the person is appointed from a civil service register without a break in service while serving under a VRA;

(viii) The date of nontemporary appointment to the Postal Career Service or the Postal Regulatory Commission after July 1, 1971, provided the individual is appointed to a career or career-conditional appointment under 39 U.S.C. 1006;

(ix) The date of nontemporary appointment under Schedule A, § 213.3102(u) of this chapter, of a person with an intellectual disability, severe physical disability, or a psychiatric disability, provided the employee's appointment is converted to a career or career-conditional appointment under § 315.709;

(x) The date of appointment in the Presidential Management Fellows Program under the provisions of Executive Order 13318, provided the employee's appointment was converted without a break in service to a career or career-conditional appointment under § 315.708 as in effect immediately before July 10, 2012, the effective date of the regulations that removed and reserved that section, or under Executive Order 13562;

(xi) The starting date of active service as an administrative enrollee in the United States Merchant Marine Academy;

(xii) Appointment as a career intern under Schedule B, § 213.3202(o) of this chapter, provided the employee's appointment was converted to a career or career-conditional appointment under § 315.712 as in effect immediately before July 10, 2012, the effective date of the regulations that removed and reserved that section;

(xiii) The date of appointment as a Pathways Participant in the Internship Program under Schedule D, § 213.3402(a) of this chapter, provided the employee's appointment is converted to a career or career-conditional appointment under § 315.713(a), with or without an intervening term appointment, and without a break in service of one day;

(xiv) The date of appointment as a Pathways Participant in the Recent Graduates Program under Schedule D, § 213.3402(b) of this chapter, provided the employee's appointment is converted to a career or career-conditional appointment under § 315.713(b), with or without an intervening term appointment, and without a break in service of one day;

(xv) The date of appointment as a Pathways Participant in the Presidential Management Fellows Program under Schedule D, § 213.3402(c) of this chapter, provided the employee's appointment is converted to a career or career-conditional appointment under § 315.713(c), with or without an intervening term appointment, and without a break in service of one day; and

(xvi) Employment with the District of Columbia Government after January 1, 1980 (the date the District implemented an independent merit personnel system not tied to the Federal system), provided the person was a District employee on December 31, 1979, was converted to the District system on January 1, 1980, and is employed by nontemporary appointment in the competitive service.

(2) *Competitive status.* An individual may attain career tenure only when employed (or reemployed) in a permanent appointment in the competitive service that provides or leads to competitive status.

(3) *Crediting service.* An employee's creditable service must total at least 3 years, under the following conditions:

(i) *Work schedule.* (A) Full-time service, and part-time service on or after July 1, 1962, are counted as calendar time from the date of appointment to date of separation.

(B) Intermittent service on or after July 1, 1962, is counted as 1 day for each day an employee is in pay status, regardless of the number of hours for which the employee is actually paid on a given day. Agencies should consult the "260-Day Work Year Chart" in OPM's *Guide to Processing Personnel Actions* to convert intermittent days worked to calendar time. The service requirement may not be satisfied in less than 3 years of calendar time.

(ii) *Nonpay status on the rolls and time off the rolls.* An agency may not credit periods of nonpay status and time off the rolls except as follows:

(A) Credit the first 30 calendar days of each period of nonpay status on the rolls during full-time employment, or during part-time employment on or after July 1, 1962. On this same basis, a seasonal employee receives credit for the first 30 calendar days of each period of nonduty/nonpay status. Nonpay status in excess of 30 days is not creditable.

(B) Credit periods of nonpay status and time off the rolls incident to entry into and return from military service and return from defense transfer, provided the person is reemployed in Federal service during the period of his or her statutory or regulatory restoration or reemployment rights.

(C) Credit periods of nonpay status and time off the rolls incident to transfer to and return from an international organization, provided the person is reemployed in Federal service under subpart C of part 352 of this chapter.

(D) Credit periods of nonpay status during which an employee was eligible to receive continuation of pay or injury compensation from the Office of Workers' Compensation Programs. Also credit periods of time off the rolls during which an employee was eligible to receive injury compensation from the Office of Workers' Compensation Programs, provided the person is reemployed under part 353 of this chapter.

(E) Credit up to 30 calendar days for time off the rolls that follows separation by reduction in force of employees who are eligible for entry on the reemployment priority list under subpart B of part 330 of this chapter, provided the person is reemployed in Federal service during the period of his or her reemployment priority.

(F) Credit up to 30 calendar days for time off the rolls that follow involuntary separation without personal cause of employees who are eligible for a noncompetitive appointment based on an interchange agreement with another merit system under § 6.7 of this chapter, provided the person is employed in the competitive service under the agreement during the period of his or her eligibility.

(G) Credit periods of nonpay status incident to an assignment to a State, local, or Indian tribal government, institution of higher education, or other eligible organization provided the employee returns to a creditable appointment pursuant to an agreement established under subchapter VI of chapter 33, title 5, U.S.C., and part 334 of this chapter.

(iii) *Restoration based on unwarranted or improper actions.* Based on a finding made on or after March 30, 1966, that a furlough, suspension, or separation was unwarranted or improper, an employee restored to duty receives full calendar time credit for the period of furlough, suspension, or separation for which he or she is eligible to receive back pay. If the employee is restored to duty at a date later than the original adverse action, credit for intervening periods of nonpay status is given in accordance with other provisions of this subsection. If the employee had been properly separated from the rolls of the agency before a finding was made that the adverse action was unwarranted or improper, the correction and additional service credit given the employee may not extend beyond the date of the proper separation.

(iv) *Intervening service.* Certain types of service that ordinarily are not creditable are counted when they intervene between two periods of creditable service. Under these conditions, credit each period of service:

(A) In the excepted service of the Federal executive branch, including employment in nonappropriated fund positions in or under any Federal agency;

(B) Under temporary, term, or other nonpermanent employment in the Federal competitive service;

(C) In the Senior Executive Service;

(D) In the Federal legislative branch;

(E) In the Federal judicial branch;

(F) In the armed forces;

(G) In the District of Columbia Government through December 31, 1979. For an employee on the District rolls on December 31, 1979, who converted on January 1, 1980, to the District independent personnel system, credit is also given for service between January 1, 1980, and September 25, 1980. Otherwise, service in the District of Columbia Government on or after January 1, 1980, is not creditable as intervening service; and

(H) Performed overseas by family members, as defined by § 315.608 of this chapter.

(c) *Exceptions from service requirement.* The service requirement for career tenure does not apply to:

(1) An appointment to a position required by law to be filled on a permanent basis, or a conversion under this part while the employee is serving in such a position;

(2) An appointment from a register of a person who once completed the service requirement for career tenure;

(3) An appointment under § 315.601 of a former Canal Zone Merit System employee who completed the service requirement for career tenure under that system; or

(4) The reinstatement of a person who once completed the service requirement for career tenure.

[33 FR 12418, Sept. 4, 1968, as amended at 43 FR 34428, Aug. 4, 1978; 59 FR 68104, Dec. 30, 1994; 60 FR 53504, Oct. 16, 1995; 62 FR 63630, Dec. 2, 1997; 63 FR 57046, Oct. 26, 1998; 65 FR 78078, Dec. 14, 2000; 70 FR 28779, May 19, 2005; 70 FR 44221, Aug. 2, 2005; 71 FR 42245, July 26, 2006; 77 FR 28214, May 11, 2012; 81 FR 78498, Nov. 8, 2016]

§ 315.202 Conversion from career-conditional to career tenure.

A career-conditional employee becomes a career employee automatically on completion of the service requirement for career tenure.

Subpart C—Career or Career-Conditional Employment From Registers

§ 315.301 Tenure on appointment from register.

(a) Except as provided in paragraph (b) of this section, an eligible appointed from a register for other than temporary or term employment becomes a career-conditional employee.

(b) An eligible appointed from a register for other than temporary or term employment becomes a career employee when he is excepted from the service requirement for career tenure by § 315.201(c).

§ 315.302 Acquisition of competitive status.

An employee appointed as provided in § 315.301 acquires a competitive status automatically on completion of probation.

Subpart D—Career or Career-Conditional Employment by Reinstatement

§ 315.401 Reinstatement.

(a) *Agency authority.* Subject to part 335 of this chapter and paragraph (b) of this section, an agency may appoint by reinstatement to a competitive service position a person who previously was employed under career or career-conditional appointment (or equivalent).

(b) *Time limit.* There is no time limit on the reinstatement eligibility of a preference eligible or a person who completed the service requirement for career tenure. Except as provided in paragraph (c) of this section, an agency may reinstate a nonpreference eligible who has not completed the service requirement for career tenure only within 3 years following the date of separation. This time limit begins to run from the date of separation from the last position in which the person served under a career appointment, career-conditioned appointment, indefinite appointment in lieu of reinstatement, or an appointment under which he or she acquired competitive status.

(c) *Extension of time limit.* Intervening service of the following types extends the 3-year limit on reinstatement of eligibility of a nonpreference eligible who has not completed the service requirement for career tenure:

(1) Employment in Federal competitive service positions under temporary, term, indefinite, or other nonpermanent appointment.

(2) Employment in Federal excepted, nonappropriated fund, or Senior Executive Service positions in the executive branch;

(3) Employment in the Federal judicial branch or in the executive or judicial branches of the insular possessions of the United States;

(4) Employment in Federal legislative branch;

(5) Employment in an international governmental organization or a territorial, State, county, municipal, or foreign government in a position in which the agency determines that the proposed appointee acquired valuable training and experience for the position to be filled;

(6) A substantially full-time training course in any educational institution of recognized standing when the agency finds that the proposed appointee acquired valuable training or experience for the position to be filled;

(7) Compulsory service on work of national importance under civilian direction as required by the Military Selective Service Act;

(8) Active military duty terminated under honorable conditions;

(9) Service with the District of Columbia Government prior to January 1, 1980. In addition, for an employee on the District Government rolls on December 31, 1979, who was converted on January 1, 1980, to the District of Columbia merit personnel system, continuous District Government service after that date also extends the 3-year period;

(10) Periods of nonemployment during which a person is eligible for injury compensation under the Office of Workers' Compensation Programs;

(11) Periods of nonemployment during which a person receives disability retirement under the Civil Service or Federal Employees Retirement System;

(12) Employment by a nonfederal organization when the person's function was transferred to the nonfederal organization on a contract basis or by law or executive order;

(13) Volunteer service and training required prior to actual enrollment as a volunteer with Peace Corps, VISTA, and other programs of the Corporation for National and Community Service if it begins within the period the person is eligible for reinstatement; and

(14) Periods of overseas residence during which a spouse or unmarried child, under 21 years of age, of a member of the Armed Forces or of a Federal civilian employee is accompanying that individual on official assignment to an overseas post of duty. Overseas posts of duty are duty locations outside the 50 States of the United States, the District of Columbia, Guam, Puerto Rico, and the Virgin Islands.

[33 FR 12418, Sept. 4, 1968, as amended at 59 FR 68107, Dec. 30, 1994; 60 FR 53504, Oct. 16, 1995]

§315.402 Tenure on reinstatement.

(a) Except as provided in paragraph (b) of this section, a person who is reinstated becomes a career-conditional employee.

(b) A person who is reinstated becomes a career employee when he has completed the service requirement for career tenure or is excepted from it by § 315.201(c).

§ 315.403 Acquisition of competitive status.

A person who was serving probation when he was separated and who is reinstated under § 315.401 acquires a competitive status automatically on completion of probation.

Subpart E—Career or Career-Conditional Employment by Transfer

§ 315.501 Transfer.

Subject to part 335 of this chapter, an agency may appoint by transfer to a competitive service position, without a break in service of a single workday, a current career or career-conditional employee of another agency.

[60 FR 53504, Oct. 16, 1995]

§ 315.502 Tenure on transfer.

(a) *General rule.* Except as provided in paragraph (b) of this section, a career employee who transfers remains a career employee and a career-conditional employee who transfers remains a career-conditional employee.

(b) *Exceptions.* (1) A career-conditional employee who transfers to a position required by law to be filled on a permanent basis becomes a career employee.

(2) A career employee who transfers from a position required by law to be filled on a permanent basis becomes a career-conditional employee unless he or she has completed the service requirement for career tenure.

[60 FR 53504, Oct. 16, 1995]

§ 315.503 Acquisition of competitive status.

An employee who was serving probation when he was appointed under § 315.501 acquires a competitive status automatically on completion of probation.

Subpart F—Career or Career-Conditional Appointment Under Special Authorities

§ 315.601 Appointment of former employees of the Canal Zone Merit System or Panama Canal Employment System.

(a) *Agency authority.* This section may be used by an agency to appoint noncompetitively, for other than temporary or term employment, a United States citizen separated from a career or career-conditional appointment under the Canal Zone Merit System, which was in effect before March 31, 1982, or under the Panama Canal Employment System, which became effective on March 31, 1982. (Appointments of such persons for temporary or term employment are to be made under applicable provisions of part 316 of this chapter.)

(b) *Service requirement.* An agency may appoint such a former employee under this section only when, immediately prior to separation from a qualifying appointment, the employee served continuously for at least one year under a nontemporary appointment in the Canal Zone Merit System, the Panama Canal Employment System, or a combination of the two systems.

(c) *Time limits.* (1) There is no time limit on the appointment under this section of an employee who:

(i) Is a preference eligible; or

(ii) Has completed at least 3 years of service, which did not include any break in service longer than 30 days, under one or more career-conditional or career appointments in the Canal Zone Merit System and/or the Panama Canal Employment System.

(2) An agency may appoint under this section an employee who does not meet the conditions in (c)(1) of this section provided no more than 3 years have elapsed since:

(i) separation from a qualifying Canal Zone Merit System or Panama Canal Employment System appointment; or

(ii) separation from service in Panama in a position excluded from the Canal Zone Merit System or Panama Canal Employment System, when such service immediately followed service under a qualifying appointment in one of those systems.

(d) *Tenure on appointment.* On appointment under paragraph (a) of this section: (1) A former career employee of the Canal Zone Merit System or Panama Canal Employment System becomes a career employee.

(2) A former Canal Zone Merit System and/or Panama Canal Employment System employee whose service from the date of career-conditional appointment in the Canal Zone Merit System or Panama Canal Employment System through the date of noncompetitive appointment under this section, inclusive, does not include any break in service of more than 30 days and totals at least 3 years becomes a career employee.

(3) All other former Canal Zone Merit System and Panama Canal Employment System employees become career-conditional employees.

(e) *Acquisition of competitive status.* A person appointed under paragraph (a) of this section automatically acquires a competitive status:

(1) On appointment, if he or she has satisfactorily completed a 1-year probationary period under the Canal Zone Merit System and/or the Panama Canal Employment System.

(2) On satisfactory completion of probation in accordance with § 315.80 (a)(3) if he or she had not completed a 1-year probationary period under the Canal Zone Merit System or Panama Canal Employment System.

[48 FR 13951, Apr. 1, 1983]

§ 315.602 Appointment based on service in the Office of the President or Vice-President or on the White House Staff.

(a) *Agency authority.* An agency may appoint noncompetitively a person who has served at least 2 years in the immediate Office of the President or Vice-President or on the White House Staff, provided that the appointment is effected without a break in service of 1 full workday.

(b) *Tenure on appointment.* (1) Except as provided in paragraph (b)(2) of this section, a person appointed under paragraph (a) of this section becomes a career-conditional employee.

(2) A person appointed under paragraph (a) of this section becomes a career employee when he or she has completed the service requirement for career tenure or is excepted from it by § 315.201(c).

(c) *Acquisition of competitive status.* A person appointed under paragraph (a) of this section acquires a competitive status automatically on appointment.

[44 FR 54692, Sept. 21, 1979]

§ 315.603 Appointment based on former incumbency of a position brought into the competitive service.

(a) *Agency authority*—(1) *Employee in military service.* An agency may appoint a former incumbent of a permanent excepted position who was serving under an appointment not limited to 1 year or less, or of a position in public or private enterprise when the position was brought into the competitive service on a continuing basis and who left his position after June 30, 1950, to perform active military service when:

(i) The position was brought into the competitive service before or during his military service or during the period in which he had restoration rights thereto, and he left the position to enter military service before the end of the time limits set forth in § 315.701(c);

(ii) He has been released from military service under honorable conditions;

(iii) The agency submits a recommendation for his appointment to OPM within 6 months after release from military service under honorable conditions or after hospitalization continuing after release for not more than 1 year; and

(iv) He performed 6 months of satisfactory service immediately before the date his position was brought into the competitive service in a position or positions brought into the competitive service, or in the civilian executive branch of the Government, unless OPM has excepted his particular type of case from this requirement.

(2) *Employee separated.* An agency may appoint a former incumbent of a permanent excepted position under an appointment not limited to 1 year or less or of a position in public or private enterprise when the position was

brought into the competitive service on a continuing basis, and who was separated thereafter, when:

(i) He is recommended for appointment within the time limits set forth in § 315.701(c); and

(ii) He performed 6 months of satisfactory service immediately before the date his position, was brought into the competitive service, in a position or positions brought into the competitive service or in the civilian executive branch of the Government, unless OPM has excepted his particular type of case from this requirement.

(3) *Employee recovered from compensable injury.* An agency may appoint a former incumbent of a permanent excepted position who was serving under an appointment not limited to 1 year or less, when the position has been brought into the competitive service *and* when:

(i) The employee is entitled to restoration based on recovery from compensable injury in accordance with 5 U.S.C. 8151 and part 353;

(ii) The employee's position was brought into the competitive service either before the employee's separation for compensable injury or during his or her period of statutory restoration rights following such injury, and the employee's separation for compensable injury occurred before the end of the time limits set forth in § 315.701(c);

(iii) The agency initiates the appointment within 6 months after cessation of compensation; and

(iv) The employee performed 6 months of statisfactory service immediately before the date his or her position was brought into the competitive service in the civilian executive branch of the Government, unless OPM has excepted his or her particular type of case from this requirement.

(b) *Review of disapproved recommendations.* Agencies shall establish procedures for reviewing disapprovals of recommendations for appointment under this section when such review is requested within 6 months after the date of disapproval.

(c) *Tenure on appointment.* (1) Except as provided in paragraph (c)(2) of this section, a person appointed under paragraph (a) of this section becomes a career-conditional employee.

(2) A person appointed under paragraph (a) of this section becomes a career employee when he has completed the service requirement for career tenure or is excepted from it by § 315.201(c).

(d) *Acquisition of competitive status.* (1) A person appointed under paragraph (a)(1) of this section acquires a competitive status automatically on appointment.

(2) A person appointed under paragraph (a)(2) or (a)(3) of this section acquires a competitive status automatically on completion of probation.

[33 FR 12418, Sept. 4, 1968, as amended at 43 FR 34428, Aug. 4, 1978; 54 FR 37092, Sept. 7, 1989; 66 FR 66710, Dec. 27, 2001]

§ 315.604 Employment of disabled veterans who have completed a training course under Chapter 31 of title 38, United States Code.

(a) When a disabled veteran satisfactorily completes an approved course of training prescribed by the Veterans Administration under chapter 31, title 38, United States Code, any agency may appoint the veteran noncompetitively to the position of class of positions for which trained.

(b) *Conversion.* An agency may convert to career or career-conditional employment a person appointed under paragraph (a) of this section.

(c) *Disqualifications.* Any law, Executive order, or civil service rule or regulation which would disqualify an applicant for appointment also disqualifies him or her for conversion of his or her employment to career or career-conditional employment under this section.

(d) *Tenure on approval of recommendation.* When an agency converts the employee under paragraph (b) of this section, the employee becomes:

(1) A career-conditional employee, except as provided in paragraph (d)(2) of this section; and

(2) A career employee when he or she has completed the service requirement for career tenure or is excepted from it by § 315.201(c).

(e) *Acquisition of competitive status.* A person whose employment is converted to career or career-conditional employment under this section acquires a competitive status automatically on conversion.

[44 FR 54692, Sept. 21, 1979, as amended at 44 FR 55132, Sept. 25, 1979]

§ 315.605 Appointment of former ACTION volunteers.

(a) *Agency authority.* An agency in the executive branch may appoint noncompetitively, for other than temporary employment, a person whom the Director of ACTION certifies as having served satisfactorily as a volunteer or volunteer leader under the Peace Corps Act (22 U.S.C. 2051 *et seq.*), or as a VISTA volunteer under the Economic Opportunity Act of 1964 (42 U.S.C. 2991 *et seq.*) or the Domestic Volunteer Service Act of 1973 (Pub. L. 93–113), or as a full-time community volunteer (including criminal justice volunteer, volunteer in justice, and VET REACH volunteer) under part C of title I of Pub. L. 93–113. To be qualifying under this section VISTA and community volunteer service must total at least 1 year. In addition, a community volunteer must have served prior to October 1, 1976.

(b) *Time limit.* An agency in the executive branch may make an appointment under this section only within 1 year after the person completes the qualifying service. (For Community volunteers who have completed their service before March 10, 1978, the 1-year period begins on March 10, 1978.) However, an agency may extend the period for 2 more years to a total of 3 years if the person, after the qualifying service, is:

(1) In the military service;

(2) Studying at a recognized institution of higher learning; or

(3) In another activity which, in the agency's view, warrants extension.

(c) *Conditions.* Any law, Executive order, or regulation that disqualifies an applicant for appointment also disqualifies an applicant for appointment under this section.

(d) *Tenure on appointment.* (1) Except as provided in paragraph (d)(2) of this section, a person appointed under paragraph (a) of this section becomes a career-conditional employee.

(2) A person appointed under paragraph (a) or this section becomes a career employee if excepted from the service requirement for career tenure by § 315.201(c).

(e) *Acquisition of competitive status.* A person appointed under paragraph (a) of this section acquires a competitive status automatically on completion of probation.

[39 FR 961, Jan. 4, 1974, as amended at 43 FR 20954, May 16, 1978; 43 FR 34428, Aug. 4, 1978]

§ 315.606 Noncompetitive appointment of certain present and former Foreign Service officers and employees.

Subject to the conditions prescribed by OPM, an agency may appoint noncompetitively a present or former career officer or employee of the Foreign Service who was appointed under authority of the Foreign Service Act of 1946, as amended (22 U.S.C. 801 *et seq.*), or legislation that supplements or replaces that Act, if:

(a) He qualifies under the requirements set forth in Executive Order 11219, and

(b) OPM has concurred in his present or former agency's plan, and substantive changes thereto, for noncompetitive entry of civil service employees into the Foreign Service positions of that agency.

[33 FR 12418, Sept. 4, 1968, as amended at 66 FR 66710, Dec. 27, 2001]

§ 315.607 Noncompetitive appointment of present and former Peace Corps personnel.

(a) An agency in the executive branch may appoint noncompetitively, for other than temporary appointment, an individual:

(1) Who has completed no less than 36 months of continuous service without a break in service of 3 days or more under section 7(a) of the Peace Corps Act (22 U.S.C. 2506) which pertains to the appointment of Peace Corps staff (not volunteers);

(2) Whom the Director of the Peace Corps certifies as having satisfactorily served under such an appointment; and

(3) Who meets OPM qualification standards—including any written test requirements—for the position in question.

(4) Who is not a Peace Corps volunteer as this paragraph does not apply to Peace Corps volunteers.

(b) *Time limitations.* (1) An individual's eligibility under this section extends through September 30, 1982, or until 3 years after separation from qualifying service with the Peace Corps, whichever is later.

(2) An agency may not extend this period.

(c) *Conditions.* Any law, Executive order, or regulation which disqualifies an applicant for appointment in the competitive service also disqualifies an applicant for appointment under this section.

(d) *Acquisition of competitive status.* A person appointed under paragraph (a) of this section acquires competitive status automatically upon completion of probation.

(e) *Tenure on appointment.* (1) Except as provided in paragraph (e)(2) of this section, a person appointed under paragraph (a) of this section becomes a career-conditional employee.

(2) A person appointed under paragraph (a) of this section becomes a career employee if excepted from the service requirement for career tenure by § 315.201(c).

[45 FR 43365, June 27, 1980, as amended at 46 FR 35079, July 7, 1981; 54 FR 37092, Sept. 7, 1989]

§ 315.608 Noncompetitive appointment of certain former overseas employees.

(a) *Authority.* An executive branch agency may noncompetitively appoint, to a competitive service position within the United States (including Guam, Puerto Rico, and the Virgin Islands), an individual who has completed 52 weeks of creditable overseas service as defined in paragraph (b) of this section and is appointed within the time limits in paragraph (d) of this section. Any law, Executive order, or regulation that disqualifies an applicant for appointment in the competitive service, such as the citizenship requirement, also disqualifies the applicant for appointment under this section. An individual may be appointed to any occupation and grade level for which qualified. An agency may waive any requirement for a written test after determining that the duties and responsibilities of the applicant's overseas position were similar enough to make the written test unnecessary.

(1) *Tenure.* A person appointed under this section becomes a career-conditional employee unless he or she has already satisfied the requirements for career tenure or is exempt from the service requirement in 5 CFR 315.201.

(2) *Competitive status.* A person appointed under this section acquires competitive status automatically upon completion of probation.

(b) *Creditable overseas service.* For purposes of this section only, creditable service is service in an appropriated fund position(s) performed by a family member under a local hire appointment(s) overseas during the time the family member was accompanying a sponsor officially assigned to an overseas area and for which the family member received a fully successful or better (or equivalent) performance rating. Creditable overseas service is computed in accordance with the procedures in the OPM Guide to Processing Personnel Actions. Creditable service may have been under more than one appointment and need not be continuous. Leave without pay taken during the time an individual is in the overseas area is credited on the same basis as time worked.

(c) *Service waiver.* Up to 26 weeks of the 52-week service requirement is waived when the head of an agency (or designee) that employed the family member overseas certifies that the family member's expected 52 weeks of employment were cut short because of a nonpersonal situation that necessitated the relocation of the family member from the overseas area. The certification must include the number of weeks waived. For this purpose, a nonpersonal situation includes disaster, conflict, terrorism or the threat of terrorism, and those situations when a family member is forced to return to the United States because of military deployment, drawdowns, or other management-initiated actions. A nonpersonal situation does not include circumstances that specifically relate to a particular individual, for example, ill health or personal interest in relocating.

(d) *Time limit on eligibility.* An individual is eligible for appointment(s) under this authority for a period of 3 years following the date of returning from overseas to the United States to resume residence or until March 31, 1998, whichever date is later. An agency may extend an individual's appointment eligibility beyond 3 years for periods equivalent to—

(1) The time the individual was accompanying a sponsor on official assignment to an area of the United States with no significant opportunities for Federal employment; or

(2) The time an individual was incapacitated for employment.

(e) *Definitions.* In this section terms have the following meaning:

(1) *Family member.* An unmarried child under age 23, a spouse, or a domestic partner. An individual must have been a family member at the time he or she met the overseas service requirement and other conditions but does not need to be a family member at the time of noncompetitive appointment in the United States.

(2) *Sponsor.* A Federal civilian employee, a Federal nonappropriated fund employee, or a member of a uniformed service who is officially assigned to an overseas area.

(i) *Officially assigned.* Under active orders issued by the United States Government.

(ii) *Federal civilian employee.* An employee of the executive, judicial, or legislative branch of the United States Government who serves in an appropriated fund position.

(iii) *Nonappropriated fund employee.* An employee paid from nonappropriated funds of the Army and Air Force Exchange Service, Navy Ship's Stores Ashore, Navy Exchanges, Marine Corps Exchanges, Coast Guard Exchanges, or other instrumentalities of the United States.

(iv) *Member of a uniformed service.* Personnel of the U.S. Armed Forces (including the Coast Guard), the commissioned corps of the Public Health Service, and the commissioned corps of the National Oceanic and Atmospheric Administration.

(3) *Accompanying.* The family member resided in the overseas area while the sponsor was officially assigned to an overseas post of duty. The family member need not have physically resided with the sponsor at all times or have traveled with the sponsor to or from the overseas area.

(4) *Local hire appointment.* An appointment that is not actually or potentially permanent and that is made from among individuals residing in the overseas area. In this section only, a local hire appointment includes nonpermanent employment under:

(i) Overseas limited appointment under 5 CFR 301.203(b) or (c);

(ii) Expected appointment under Schedule A 213.3106(b)(1), 213.3106(b)(6), or 213.3106(d)(1)) when the duration of the appointment is tied to the sponsor's rotation date or when the appointment is made on a not-to-exceed (NTE) basis;

(iii) An "American family member" or "part-time intermittent temporary (PIT)" appointment in U.S. diplomatic establishments;

(iv) 50 U.S.C. 403j; Public Law 86–36 (50 U.S.C. 402, note); the Berlin Tariff Agreement; or as a local national employee paid from appropriated funds; or

(v) Any other nonpermanent appointment in the competitive or excepted service approved by OPM.

(5) *Overseas.* A location outside the 50 States of the United States, the District of Columbia, Guam, Puerto Rico, and the Virgin Islands.

(6) *Domestic partner.* A person in a domestic partnership with a sponsor of the same sex.

(7) *Domestic partnership.* A committed relationship between two adults, of the same sex, in which the partners:

(i) Are each other's sole domestic partner and intend to remain so indefinitely;

(ii) Maintain a common residence, and intend to continue to do so (or would maintain a common residence but for an assignment abroad or other employment-related, financial, or similar obstacle);

(iii) Are at least 18 years of age and mentally competent to consent to contract;

(iv) Share responsibility for a significant measure of each other's financial obligations;

(v) Are not married or joined in a civil union to anyone else;

(vi) Are not the domestic partner of anyone else;

(vii) Are not related in a way that, if they were of opposite sex, would prohibit legal marriage in the U.S. jurisdiction in which the domestic partnership was formed;

(viii) Are willing to certify, if required by the agency, that they understand that willful falsification of any documentation required to establish that an individual is in a domestic partnership may lead to disciplinary action and the recovery of the cost of benefits received related to such falsification, as well as constitute a criminal violation under 18 U.S.C. 1001, and that the method for securing such certification, if required, shall be determined by the agency; and

(ix) Are willing promptly to disclose, if required by the agency, any dissolution or material change in the status of the domestic partnership.

[61 FR 9322, Mar. 8, 1996, as amended at 77 FR 42903, July 20, 2012]

§ 315.609 Appointment based on service in United States positions of the Panama Canal Commission.

(a) *Agency authority.* An agency may appoint noncompetitively, for other than temporary or term employment, a United States citizen who has served under nontemporary appointment in a continuing career position of the Panama Canal Commission located in the United States.

(b) *Service requirement.* An agency may appoint such an individual under this section only when, immediately prior to separation from a qualifying appointment with the Panama Canal Commission in the United States, the individual served continuously for at least 1 year under such qualifying appointment or under a combination of such appointment and nontemporary appointment in the Canal Zone Merit System or the Panama Canal Employment System.

(c) *Time limits.* (1) There is no time limit on the appointment under this section of an employee who:

(i) Is a preference eligible; or

(ii) Has completed at least 3 years of service, which did not include any break in service longer than 30 days, under one or more nontemporary appointments in Panama Canal Commission positions located in the United States or in positions under the Canal Zone Merit System and/or the Panama Canal Employment System.

(2) An agency may appoint under this section an employee who does not meet the conditions in (c)(1) of this section only if no more than 3 years have elapsed since the individual's separation from a qualifying appointment.

(d) *Tenure on appointment.* (1) On appointment under paragraph (a) of this section, an individual whose qualifying service does not include any break in service of more than 30 days and totals at least 3 years becomes a career employee.

(2) All other individuals appointed under this section become career-conditional employees.

(e) *Acquisition of competitive status.* A person appointed under paragraph (a) of this section automatically acquires a competitive status:

(1) On appointment, if he or she has satisfactorily completed a 1-year trial period, which did not include more than 22 workdays in nonpay status, during qualifying employment with the Panama Canal Commission.

(2) On satisfactory completion of probation in accordance with § 315.801(a)(3) if he or she had not completed such a 1-year trial period.

[48 FR 29667, June 28, 1983]

§ 315.610 Noncompetitive appointment of certain National Guard technicians.

(a) An agency may appoint noncompetitively a National Guard technician who—

(1) Was involuntarily separated (other than by removal for cause on charges of misconduct or delinquency);

(2) Has served at least 3 years as a technician;

(3) Meets the qualifications requirements of the job: and

(4) Is appointed within 1 year after separating from service as a Guard Technician.

(b) The noncompetitive appointing authority also applies to National Guard technicians separated before October 29, 1986, provided they are appointed within a year of the date of separation.

[52 FR 5431, Feb. 23, 1987]

§315.611 Appointment of certain veterans who have competed under agency merit promotion announcements.

(a) *Agency authority.* An agency may appoint a preference eligible or a veteran who has substantially completed at least 3 years of continuous active military service provided

(1) The veteran was selected from among the best qualified following competition under a merit promotion announcement open to candidates outside the agency's workforce; and

(2) The veteran's most recent separation from the military was under honorable conditions.

(b) *Definitions.* "Agency" in this context means an executive agency as defined in 5 U.S.C. 105. The agency determines in individual cases whether a candidate was released "shortly before" completing the required 3 years and should therefore be eligible for appointment.

[65 FR 14432, Mar. 17, 2000]

§315.612 Noncompetitive appointment of certain military spouses.

(a) *Agency authority.* In accordance with the provisions of this section, an agency may appoint noncompetitively a spouse of a member of the armed forces serving on active duty who has orders specifying a permanent change of station (not for training), a spouse of a 100 percent disabled service member injured while on active duty, or the unremarried widow or widower of a service member who was killed while performing active duty.

(b) *Definitions.* (1) *Active duty* means full-time duty in the armed forces, including full-time National Guard duty, except that for Reserve Component members the term "active duty" does not include training duties or attendance at service schools.

(2) *Armed forces* has the meaning given that term in 10 U.S.C. 101.

(3) *Duty station* means the permanent location to which a member of the armed forces is assigned for duty as specified on the individual's permanent change of station (PCS) orders.

(4) *Member of the armed forces* or *service member* means an individual who:

(i) Is serving on active duty in the armed forces under orders specifying the individual is called or ordered to active duty for more than 180 consecutive days, has been issued orders for a permanent change of station, and is authorized for dependent travel (*i.e.*, the travel of the service member's family members) as part of the orders specifying the individual's permanent change of station;

(ii) Retired from active duty in the armed forces with a service-connected disability rating of 100 percent as documented by a branch of the armed forces, or retired or was released or discharged from active duty in the armed forces and has a disability rating of 100 percent as documented by the Department of Veterans Affairs; or

(iii) Was killed while serving on active duty in the armed forces.

(5) *Permanent change of station* means the assignment, reassignment, or transfer of a member of the armed forces from his or her present duty station or location without return to the previous duty station or location.

(6) *Spouse* means the husband or wife of a member of the armed forces.

(c) *Eligibility.* (1) A spouse of a member of the armed forces as defined in paragraph (b)(4)(i) of this section must have:

(i) Married the member of the armed forces on, or prior to, the date of the service member's orders authorizing a permanent change of station; and

(ii) Relocated with the member of the armed forces to the new duty station specified in the documentation ordering a permanent change of station.

(2) A spouse of a member of the armed forces as defined in paragraph (b)(4)(iii) of this section must be the un-remarried widow or widower of the member of the armed forces killed on active duty in the armed forces.

(3) For spouses eligible under paragraph (b)(4)(i) of this section, noncompetitive appointment under this section is limited to the geographic area, as specified on the service member's permanent change of station orders. It includes the service member's duty station and the surrounding area from which people reasonably can be expected to travel daily to and from work. The head of an agency, or his or her designee, may waive this limitation (*i.e.*, accept applications from

spouses) if no Federal agency exists in the spouse's geographic area. Spouses of active duty military members who are on retirement or separation PCS orders from active duty are not eligible to be appointed using this authority unless the service member is injured with a 100 percent disability.

(4) Spouses of retired or separated active duty members who have a 100 percent disability are not restricted to a geographical location.

(d) *Conditions.* (1) In accordance with the provisions of this section, spouses are eligible for noncompetitive appointment:

(i) For a maximum of 2 years from the date of the service member's permanent change of station orders;

(ii) From the date of documentation verifying the member of the armed forces is 100 percent disabled; or

(iii) From the date of documentation verifying the member of the armed forces was killed while on active duty.

(2) A spouse may receive only one noncompetitive appointment under this section to a permanent position per the service member's orders authorizing a permanent change of station.

(3) Any law, Executive order, or regulation that disqualifies an applicant for appointment also disqualifies a spouse for appointment under this section.

(e) *Proof of eligibility.* (1) Prior to appointment, the spouse of a member of the armed forces as defined in paragraph (b)(4)(i) of this section must submit to the employing agency:

(i) A copy of the service member's active duty orders which authorize a permanent change of station. This authorization must include:

(A) A statement authorizing the service member's spouse to accompany the member to the new permanent duty station;

(B) The specific location to which the member of the armed forces is to be assigned, reassigned, or transferred pursuant to permanent change of station orders; and

(C) The effective date of the permanent change of station; and

(ii) Documentation verifying marriage to the member of the armed forces (*i.e.*, a marriage license or other legal documentation verifying marriage).

(2) Prior to appointment, the spouse of a member of the armed forces as defined in paragraph (b)(4)(ii) of this section must submit to the employing agency copies of:

(i) Documentation showing the member of the armed forces was released or discharged from active duty due to a service-connected disability;

(ii) Documentation showing the member of the armed forces retired, or was released or discharged from active duty, with a disability rating of 100 percent; and

(iii) Documentation verifying marriage to the member of the armed forces (*i.e.*, a marriage license or other legal documentation verifying marriage).

(3) Prior to appointment, the spouse of a member of the armed forces as defined in paragraph (b)(4)(iii) of this section must submit to the employing agency copies of:

(i) Documentation showing the individual was released or discharged from active duty due to his or her death while on active duty;

(ii) Documentation verifying the member of the armed forces was killed while serving on active duty; and

(iii) Documentation verifying marriage to the member of the armed forces (*i.e.*, a marriage license or other legal documentation verifying marriage); and

(iv) A statement certifying that he or she is the un-remarried widow or widower of the service member.

(f) *Acquisition of competitive status.* A person appointed under paragraph (a) of this section acquires competitive status automatically upon completion of probation.

(g) *Tenure on appointment.* An appointment under paragraph (a) of this section is career-conditional unless the appointee has already satisfied the requirements for career tenure or is exempt from the service requirement pursuant to § 315.201.

[74 FR 40476, Aug. 12, 2009, as amended at 76 FR 54072, Aug. 31, 2011]

Subpart G—Conversion to Career or Career-Conditional Employment From Other Types of Employment

§315.701 Incumbents of positions brought into the competitive service.

(a) *Employee coverage.* This section applies to an employee retained under §§316.701 and 316.702 of this chapter who:

(1) Was serving in a permanent excepted position under an appointment not limited to 1 year or less, or in a public or private enterprise in a position which the agency determines to be a continuing one, at the time his position was brought into the competitive service; and

(2) Performed 6 months of satisfactory service immediately before the date his position was brought into the competitive service, in a position or positions brought into the competitive service, or in the civilian executive branch of the Government, unless OPM has excepted his particular type of case from this requirement.

(b) *Eligibility for conversion.* Within the time limits set forth in paragraph (c) of this section, the employment of an employee covered by paragraph (a) of this section may be converted to career or career-conditional employment.

(c) *Time limits.* Conversion may be initiated under paragraph (b) of this section only within 6 months after the position is brought into the competitive service, except that:

(1) When it is necessary for OPM to determine that §316.701 or §316.702 applies to a group of positions, the recommendation shall be submitted within 6 months after OPM advises the agency of its determination; and

(2) When an employee is absent on an assignment to an organization or agency from which reemployment rights are provided under part 352 of this chapter or by statute, the conversion shall be initiated within 6 months after the employee's return from such assignment, when reemployment occurs within the time limits prescribed in the applicable statute or regulation;

(3) When an employee is absent on approved leave without pay, the conversion shall be initiated within 6 months of the employee's return to duty, when such return occurs within time limits authorized by the agency; and

(4) When an employee who is serving on military duty or who is separated and rehired during the 6-month period after the position is brought into the competitive service is eligible for conversion under the provisions of §315.603, the conversion shall be initiated within the time limits prescribed by that section.

(d) *Tenure on approval of conversion.* Upon conversion under paragraph (b) of this section, the employee becomes:

(1) A career-conditional employee, except as provided in paragraph (b)(2) of this section;

(2) A career employee when he has completed the service requirement for career tenure or is excepted from it by §315.201(c).

(e) *Acquisition of competitive status.* A person whose employment is converted to career or career-conditional employment under this section acquires a competitive status automatically on completion of probation.

(f) *Review of disapproved conversions.* Agencies shall establish procedures for reviewing disapprovals of conversions under this section when such review is requested within 6 months after the date of the disapproval.

[33 FR 12418, Sept. 4, 1968, as amended at 43 FR 34428, Aug. 4, 1978; 66 FR 66710, Dec. 27, 2001]

§315.702 Employees serving without competitive examination in rare cases.

(a) *Recommendation by agency.* An agency may recommend to OPM that the employment of an employee who has completed at least 1 year of satisfactory service under §316.601 be converted to career or career-conditional employment.

(b) *Tenure on approval of recommendation.* When OPM approves the agency's recommendation submitted under paragraph (a) of this section, the employee becomes:

(1) A career-conditional employee, except as provided in paragraph (b)(2) of this section;

(2) A career employee when he has completed the service requirement for

career tenure or is excepted from it by § 315.201(c).

(c) *Acquisition of competitive status.* A person whose employment is converted to career or career-conditional employment under this section acquires a competitive status automatically on conversion.

§ 315.703 Employees formerly reached on a register.

(a) *Employee coverage.* An employee who was serving in a position when his or her name was within reach for career or career-conditional appointment on a register appropriate for that position may be converted to career or career-conditional employment when:

(1) The employee's name was included on an appropriate certificate issued while the employee was serving in the position, or reconstruction of the appropriate register verifies that the employee would have been within reach;

(2) The register was being used for career and career-conditional appointments when he or she was reached;

(3) He or she has been continuously employed since being reached;

(4) Conversion is initiated either before the expiration of the register or during a period of continuous service since the employee was reached; and

(5) When the employee is a nonpreference eligible who was first reached after February 1, 1955, the Office, or the agency, in accordance with an agreement with the Office, determines that satisfactory reasons existed for passing over any preference eligible who preceded the employee on the register when he or she was reached and who is still within reach and available for appointment.

(b) *Tenure on conversion.* An employee whose appointment is converted under paragraph (a) of this section becomes:

(1) A career-conditional employee except as provided in paragraph (b)(2) of this section;

(2) A career employee when he or she has completed the service requirement for career tenure or is excepted from it by § 315.201(c).

(c) *Acquisition of competitive status.* An employee whose employment is converted to career or career-conditional employment under this section acquires a competitive status automatically on completion of probation.

[44 FR 55132, Sept. 25, 1979]

§ 315.704 Conversion to career employment from indefinite or temporary employment.

(a) *General.* Employees serving after February 7, 1968, in competitive positions under indefinite appointments or temporary appointments pending establishment of a register or as status quo employees acquire competitive status and are entitled to have their employment converted to career employment when such employees:

(1) Complete a total of at least 3 years of service in such a position under one or more such appointments without a break in service of more than 30 calendar days or without an interruption by nonqualifying service of more than 30 calendar days;

(2) Have rendered satisfactory service for the 12 months immediately preceding the conversion; and

(3) Meet applicable qualification requirements for the positions and are otherwise eligible for career employment. This paragraph does not apply to employees serving under an overseas limited appointment or in positions above GS–15 or equivalent.

(b) *Creditable service.* (1) In computing creditable service under paragraph (a) of this section for an employee who left a competitive position in which he or she was serving under a qualifying appointment covered in paragraph (a) of this section to enter the armed forces and who is reemployed in such a position within 120 calendar days after separation under honorable conditions, the period from the date he or she left the position to the date of reemployment is creditable.

(2) The Office shall publish in its operating manuals the conditions under which full-time, part-time, and intermittent employment is creditable in meeting the service requirement under paragraph (a) of this section.

(c) *Termination after failure to meet conversion requirements.* An employing agency shall terminate employees covered by paragraph (a) of this section not later than 90 days after they complete the 3-year service requirement referred to in paragraph (a)(1) of this section, if they have not met the requirements and conditions of paragraphs (a)(2) and (3) of this section before the end of the 90-day period. For an employee who is reemployed after intervening service in the armed forces, the 90-day period begins on the date of reemployment if the employee's combined civilian and military service satisfies the 3-year service requirement on that date.

(d) *Administrative error.* When an employee has met the service requirement under paragraph (a)(1) of this section but, because of administrative error or oversight, has not been converted to career employment within the time limits prescribed in this section, the employing agency may effect the employee's conversion as of the date on which he or she met the service requirement, even though the time limit for such conversion has expired.

[44 FR 54692, Sept. 21, 1979. Redesignated at 44 FR 63080, Nov. 2, 1979, as amended at 66 FR 66710, Dec. 27, 2001]

§315.705 Employees serving under transitional or veterans recruitment appointments.

(a) *Agency action.* (1) An agency shall convert the employment of an employee who has served continuously under a transitional appointment for at least 1 year to career or career-conditional employment within 90 calendar days after he completes the program of education or training approved for him.

(2) Within 30 calendar days after an employee completes (i) 2 years of substantially continuous service under a veterans recruitment appointment or under a combination of transitional and veterans recruitment appointments and (ii) his training or educational programs, the employing agency shall convert his appointment to career or career-conditional employment.

(b) *Tenure.* Upon conversion of his employment, the employee becomes:

(1) A career-conditional employee, except as provided in paragraph (b)(2) of this section;

(2) A career employee if he has completed the service requirement for career tenure or is excepted from it by §315.201(c).

(c) *Acquisition of competitive status.* An employee whose employment is converted to career or career-conditional employment under this section, acquires a competitive status automatically on conversion.

[35 FR 5661, Apr. 8, 1970. Redesignated at 44 FR 63080, Nov. 2, 1979]

§315.706 Certain nonpermanent employees of the Department of Energy.

(a) *General.* Employees transferred to the Department of Energy under Public Law 95–91, who are serving in nonpermanent appointments made under competitive procedures of the former Atomic Energy Commission or Energy Research and Development Administration and are determined by the Department to be performing continuing functions, may be converted to career or career-conditional by OPM upon recommendation by the Department.

(b) *Tenure upon conversion.* Employees converted under this section become career-conditional employees unless they have completed the service requirement for career tenure.

(c) *Acquisition of competitive status.* A person whose employment is converted to career or career-conditional employment under this section acquires competitive status automatically.

[43 FR 14002, Apr. 4, 1978. Redesignated at 44 FR 63080, Nov. 2, 1979]

§315.707 Disabled veterans.

(a) *Eligibility.* (1) Subject to requirements concerning qualifications and probationary period published by the Office, an agency may convert the employment of a disabled veteran who meets the conditions below to career or career-conditional employment from a time-limited appointment of more than 60 days.

(2) To be eligible for conversion under this paragraph, the veteran must:

(i) Have been retired from active military service with a disability rating of 30 percent or more;

(ii) Have been rated by the Department of Veterans Affairs since 1991 or later, or by a branch of the Armed

Forces at any time, as having a compensable service-connected disability of 30 percent or more; or

(iii) Have been so rated by the Department of Veterans Affairs, or by a branch of the Armed Forces, at the time of a qualifying temporary appointment effected within the year immediately preceding, or a term appointment effected within four years immediately preceding, the conversion.

(b) *Tenure on conversion.* (1) Except as provided in paragraph (b)(2) of this section, a person converted under paragraph (a) of this section becomes a career-conditional employee.

(2) A person appointed under paragraph (a) of this section becomes a career employee if excepted from the service requirement for career tenure by § 315.201(c).

(c) *Acquisition of competitive status.* A person converted under paragraph (a) of this section acquires a competitive status automatically on completion of probation.

[44 FR 44813, July 31, 1979. Redesignated at 44 FR 63080, Nov. 2, 1979, as amended at 66 FR 66710, Dec. 27, 2001; 73 FR 60611, Oct. 14, 2008]

§ 315.708 [Reserved]

§ 315.709 Appointment for Persons With Disabilities.

(a) *Coverage.* An employee appointed under § 213.3102(u) of this chapter may have his or her appointment converted to a career or career-conditional appointment when he or she:

(1) Completes 2 or more years of satisfactory service, without a break of more than 30 days, under a nontemporary appointment under § 213.3102(u);

(2) Is recommended for such conversion by his or her supervisor;

(3) Meets all requirements and conditions governing career and career-conditional appointment except those requirements concerning competitive selection from a register and medical qualifications; and

(4) Is converted without a break in service of one workday.

(b) *Tenure on conversion.* An employee converted under paragraph (a) of this section becomes:

(1) A career-conditional employee, except as provided in paragraph (b)(2) of this section; or

(2) A career employee if he or she has completed 3 years of substantially continuous service in a temporary appointment under § 213.3102(u) of this chapter, or has otherwise completed the service requirement for career tenure, or is excepted from it by § 315.201(c).

(c) *Acquisition of competitive status.* A person whose employment is converted to career or career-conditional employment under this section acquires a competitive status automatically on conversion.

[71 FR 42245, July 26, 2006]

§ 315.710 Professional and administrative career employees serving under Schedule B appointments.

(a) *Coverage.* This section covers employees serving in occupations that were covered by the Professional and Administrative Career Examination on August 30, 1982, and that were listed in the consent decree entered on November 19, 1981, by the U.S. District Court for the District of Columbia in the civil action known as *Luevano* v. *Devine* and numbered as No. 79–271. Those occupations are designated in these regulations as professional and administrative career (PAC) occupations or positions. OPM will publish a listing of PAC occupations.

(b) *Eligibility.* An agency may, but is not required to, convert appointments of employees occupying PAC positions under nontemporary appointments effected under § 213.3202(1) of this chapter to career or career-conditional appointments at the GS–9 level in any position in a PAC occupation when such employees—

(1) Complete at least 1 year of Schedule B service at the GS–7 level that meets the quality of experience requirement for the GS–9 position in which converted (less than full-time service is credited according to the relation it bears to the full-time workweek);

(2) Demonstrate performance that warrants conversion at GS–9 (a current performance rating of fully successful

or better for the year immediately preceding conversion is necessary for this purpose);

(3) Meet all requirements and conditions governing career and career-conditional appointment except those requirements concerning competitive selection from a register;

(4) Are converted without a break in service of one workday or more; and

(5) Are converted as a result of a deliberate decision by management.

(c) *Tenure on conversion.* An employee converted under paragraph (a) of this section becomes—

(1) A career-conditional employee, except as provided in paragraph (c)(2) of this section;

(2) A career employee if he or she has completed 3 years of substantially continuous service in nontemporary appointments under §213.3202(l) of this chapter, or has otherwise completed the service requirement for career tenure, or is excepted from it by §315.201(c).

(d) *Acquisition of competitive status.* A person whose employment is converted to career or career-conditional employment under this section acquires a competitive status automatically on conversion.

[52 FR 25194, July 6, 1987, as amended at 52 FR 43722, Nov. 15, 1987; 66 FR 66710, Dec. 27, 2001]

§315.711 Readers, interpreters, and personal assistants serving under Schedule A appointments.

(a) *Agency authority.* An agency may convert noncompetitively to career or career-conditional employment, a reader, interpreter, or personal assistant:

(1) Who completed at least 1 year of satisfactory service in such a position under a non-temporary appointment under 5 CFR 213.3102(11); and

(2) Whose employment in such a position is no longer necessary for reasons beyond management control, e.g. resignation or reassignment of the employee being assisted.

(b) *Tenure on appointment.* (1) Except as provided in paragraph (b)(2) of this section, a person appointed under paragraph (a) of this section becomes a career-conditional employee.

(2) A person appointed under paragraph (a) of this section becomes a career employee when he or she has completed the service requirement for career tenure or is excepted from it by §315.201(c).

(c) *Acquisition of competitive status.* A person appointed under paragraph (a) of this section acquires a competitive status automatically on appointment.

[55 FR 12327, Apr. 3, 1990]

§315.712 [Reserved]

§315.713 Conversion based on service in a Pathways Program under part 362 of this chapter.

(a) *Agency authority.* An agency may convert to a career or career-conditional employment in the competitive service, without further competition, the following Pathways Participants:

(1) An Intern who has satisfactorily completed the Internship Program and meets all eligibility requirements for conversion under subpart B of part 362 of this chapter;

(2) A Recent Graduate who has satisfactorily completed the Recent Graduates Program and meets all eligibility requirements for conversion under subpart C of part 362 of this chapter; and

(3) A Presidential Management Fellow who has satisfactorily completed the Fellows Program and meets all eligibility requirements for conversion under subpart D of part 362 of this chapter.

(b) *Tenure on conversion.* An employee whose appointment is converted to career or career-conditional employment under this section becomes:

(1) A career-conditional employee except as provided in paragraph (b)(2) of this section;

(2) A career employee when he or she has completed the service requirement for career tenure or is excepted from it by §315.201(c).

(c) *Acquisition of competitive status.* A Pathways Participant converted to career or career-conditional employment in the competitive service under this section acquires competitive status upon completion of probation.

[77 FR 28215, May 11, 2012]

§315.725 Disqualifications.

Any law, executive order, or civil service rule or regulation which would disqualify an applicant for appointment shall also disqualify an employee for conversion of his employment to career or career-conditional employment under this subpart.

[33 FR 12418, Sept. 4, 1968. Redesignated at 44 FR 63080, Nov. 2, 1979]

Subpart H—Probation on Initial Appoinment to a Competitive Position

§ 315.801 Probationary period; when required.

(a) The first year of service of an employee who is given a career or career-conditional appointment under this part is a probationary period when the employee:

(1) Was appointed from a competitive list of eligibles established under subpart C of this part;

(2) Was reinstated under subpart D of this part unless during any period of service which affords a current basis for reinstatement, the employee completed a probationary period or served with competitive status under an appointment which did not require a probationary period.

(b) A person who is:

(1) Transferred under § 315.501; or

(2) Promoted, demoted, or reassigned; before he completed probation is required to complete the probationary period in the new position.

(c) A person who is reinstated from the Reemployment Priority List to a position in the same agency and the same commuting area does not have to serve a new probationary period, but, if separated during probation, is required to complete the probationary period in the new position.

(d) Upon noncompetitive appointment to the competitive service under the Postal Reorganization Act (39 U.S.C. 101 *et seq.*), an employee of the Postal Career Service (including substitute and part-time flexible) who has not completed 1 year of Postal service, must serve the remainder of a 1-year probationary period in the new agency.

(e) A person who is appointed to the competitive service either by special appointing authority or by conversion under subparts F or G of this part serves a 1-year probationary period unless specifically exempt from probation by the authority itself.

[33 FR 12418, Sept. 4, 1968, as amended at 39 FR 962, Jan. 4, 1974; 45 FR 43365, June 27, 1980; 60 FR 54504, Oct. 16, 1995; 65 FR 14432, Mar. 17, 2000]

§ 315.802 Length of probationary period; crediting service.

(a) The probationary period required by § 315.801 is 1 year and may not be extended.

(b) Prior Federal civilian service (including nonappropriated fund service) counts toward completion of probation when the prior service:

(1) Is in the same agency, e.g., Department of the Army;

(2) Is in the same line of work (determined by the employee's actual duties and responsibilities); and

(3) Contains or is followed by no more than a single break in service that does not exceed 30 calendar days.

(c) Periods of absence while in a pay status count toward completion of probation. Absence in nonpay status while on the rolls (other than for compensable injury or military duty) is creditable up to a total of 22 workdays. Absence (whether on or off the rolls) due to compensable injury or military duty is creditable in full upon restoration to Federal service. Nonpay time in excess of 22 workdays extends the probationary period by an equal amount. An employee serving probation who leaves Federal service to become a volunteer with the Peace Corps or the Corporation for National and Community Service serves the remainder of the probationary period upon reinstatement provided the employee is reinstated within 90 days of termination of service as a volunteer or training for such service.

(d) The probationary period for part-time employees is computed on the basis of calendar time, in the same manner as for full-time employees. For intermittent employees, *i.e.*, those who do not have regularly scheduled tours of duty, each day or part of a day in pay status counts as 1 day of credit toward the 260 days in a pay status required for completion of probation. (However, the probationary period cannot be completed in less than 1 year of calendar time.)

[60 FR 53504, Oct. 16, 1995]

§315.803 Agency action during probationary period (general).

(a) The agency shall utilize the probationary period as fully as possible to determine the fitness of the employee and shall terminate his services during this period if he fails to demonstrate fully his qualifications for continued employment.

(b) Termination of an individual serving a probationary period must be taken in accordance with subpart D of part 752 of this chapter if the individual has completed one year of current continuous service under other than a temporary appointment limited to 1 year or less and is not otherwise excluded by the provisions of that subpart.

[73 FR 7187, Feb. 7, 2008]

§315.804 Termination of probationers for unsatisfactory performance or conduct.

(a) Subject to §315.803(b), when an agency decides to terminate an employee serving a probationary or trial period because his work performance or conduct during this period fails to demonstrate his fitness or his qualifications for continued employment, it shall terminate his services by notifying him in writing as to why he is being separated and the effective date of the action. The information in the notice as to why the employee is being terminated shall, as a minimum, consist of the agency's conclusions as to the inadequacies of his performance or conduct.

(b) Probation ends when the employee completes his or her scheduled tour of duty on the day before the anniversary date of the employee's appointment. For example, when the last workday is a Friday and the anniversary date is the following Monday, the probationer must be separated before the end of the tour of duty on Friday since Friday would be the last day the employee actually has to demonstrate fitness for further employment.

[33 FR 12418, Sept. 4, 1988, as amended at 60 FR 53505, Oct. 16, 1995; 73 FR 7188, Feb. 7, 2008]

§315.805 Termination of probationers for conditions arising before appointment.

Subject to §315.803(b), when an agency proposes to terminate an employee serving a probationary or trial period for reasons based in whole or in part on conditions arising before his appointment, the employee is entitled to the following:

(a) *Notice of proposed adverse action.* The employee is entitled to an advance written notice stating the reasons, specifically and in detail, for the proposed action.

(b) *Employee's answer.* The employee is entitled to a reasonable time for filing a written answer to the notice of proposed adverse action and for furnishing affidavits in support of his answer. If the employee answers, the agency shall consider the answer in reaching its decision.

(c) *Notice of adverse decision.* The employee is entitled to be notified of the agency's decision at the earliest practicable date. The agency shall deliver the decision to the employee at or before the time the action will be made effective. The notice shall be in writing, inform the employee of the reasons for the action, inform the employee of his right of appeal to the Merit Systems Protection Board (MSPB), and inform him of the time limit within which the appeal must be submitted as provided in §315.806(d).

[33 FR 12418, Sept. 4, 1968, as amended at 73 FR 7188, Feb. 7, 2008]

§315.806 Appeal rights to the Merit Systems Protection Board.

(a) *Right of appeal.* An employee may appeal to the Merit Systems Protection Board in writing an agency's decision to terminate him under §315.804 or §315.805 only as provided in paragraphs (b) and (c) of this section. The Merit Systems Protection Board review is confined to the issues stated in paragraphs (b) and (c) of this section.

(b) *On discrimination.* An employee may appeal under this paragraph a termination not required by statute which he or she alleges was based on partisan political reasons or marital status.

(c) *On improper procedure.* A probationer whose termination is subject to §315.805 may appeal on the ground that his termination was not effected in accordance with the procedural requirements of that section.

(d) An employee may appeal to the Board under this section a termination that the employee alleges was based on discrimination because of race, color, religion, sex (including pregnancy and gender identity), national origin, age (as defined by the Age Discrimination in Employment Act of 1967, as amended), or disability. An appeal alleging a discriminatory termination may be filed under this subsection only if such discrimination is raised in addition to one of the issues stated in paragraph (b) or (c) of this section.

[33 FR 12418, Sept. 4, 1968, as amended at 40 FR 15380, Apr. 7, 1975; 44 FR 48951, Aug. 21, 1979; 55 FR 29339, July 19, 1990; 79 FR 43922, July 29, 2014]

Subpart I—Probation on Initial Appointment to a Supervisory or Managerial Position

SOURCE: 44 FR 44811, July 31, 1979, unless otherwise noted.

§ 315.901 Statutory requirement.

5 U.S.C. 3321 provides for "a period of probation . . . before initial appointment as a supervisor or manager becomes final." It also says that a supervisor or manager "who does not satisfactorily complete the probationary period . . . shall be returned to a position of no lower grade and pay than the position from which the individual was transferred, assigned or promoted." This subpart contains OPM regulations implementing those requirements of law.

§ 315.902 Definitions.

In this subpart *supervisory position* and *managerial position* have the meaning given them by the General Schedule Supervisory Guide.

[60 FR 53505, Oct. 16, 1995]

§ 315.903 Coverage.

This subpart applies to appointments and positions without time limitation in the competitive civil service. Agencies may, at their option, apply these provisions to time-limited appointments and positions. This subpart does not apply to appointments or positions in the Senior Executive Service.

§ 315.904 Basic requirement.

(a) An employee is required to serve a probationary period prescribed by the agency upon initial appointment to a supervisory and/or managerial position.

(b) An employee is required to complete a single probationary period in a supervisory position and a single probationary period in a managerial position, regardless of the number of agencies, occupations, or positions in which the employee serves. However, an agency may by regulation provide for exceptions to the probationary period for managers who have satisfactorily completed a probationary period for supervisors when justified on the basis of performance and experience.

(c) Employees who, as of the date this requirement is effective, are serving or have served in Federal civilian supervisory or managerial positions without time limitation, or in time-limited supervisory or managerial positions under an official assignment exceeding 120 days, are exempt from its provisions, except that supervisors who are assigned to managerial positions may, according to agency regulations, be required to serve a probationary period for managers.

§ 315.905 Length of the probationary period.

The authority to determine the length of the probationary period is delegated to the head of each agency, provided that it be of reasonable fixed duration, appropriate to the position, and uniformly applied. An agency may establish different probationary periods for different occupations or a single one for all agency employees.

§ 315.906 Crediting service toward completion of the probationary period.

(a) An employee who is reassigned, transferred, or promoted to another supervisory or managerial position while serving a probationary period under this subpart is subject to the probationary period prescribed for the new position. Service in the former position counts toward completion of the probationary period in the new position. If the former position was supervisory and the new position managerial, service counts in the manner prescribed by agency regulation.

(b) Service on detail, temporary promotion, or reassignment to another supervisory or managerial position while serving probation is creditable toward completion of probation. Service in a nonsupervisory or nonmanagerial position is not creditable.

(c) Absence in nonpay status while on the rolls (other than for compensable injury or military duty) is creditable up to a total of 22 workdays. Absence (whether on or off the rolls) due to compensable injury or military duty is creditable in full upon restoration to Federal service. Nonpay time in excess of 22 workdays extends the probationary period by an equal amount.

(d) Service during a probationary period from which an employee was separated or demoted for performance or conduct reasons does not count toward completion of probation required under a subsequent appointment. In other situations in which an employee does not complete probation, service is creditable as determined by agency policy.

(e) Temporary service in a supervisory or managerial position under temporary appointment, promotion, or reassignment *prior to probation* is creditable as determined by agency policy. Prior service under a detail may be credited only when a detail to a supervisory or managerial position is made permanent without a break in service.

[44 FR 44811, July 31, 1979, as amended at 60 FR 53505, Oct. 16, 1995]

§315.907 Failure to complete the probationary period.

(a) Satisfactory completion of the prescribed probationary period is a prerequisite to continued service in the position. An employee who, for reasons of supervisory or managerial performance, does not satisfactorily complete the probationary period is entitled to be assigned, except as provided in paragraph (b) of this section, to a position in the agency of no lower grade and pay than the one the employee left to accept the supervisory or managerial position.

(b) A nonsupervisory or nonmanagerial employee who is demoted into a position in which probation under §315.904 is required and who, for reasons of supervisory or managerial performance, does not satisfactorily complete the probationary period is entitled to be assigned to a position at the same grade and pay as the position in which he or she was serving probation. The employee is eligible for repromotion in accordance with agency promotion policy.

(c) The agency must notify the employee in writing that he or she is being assigned in accordance with this section.

[49 FR 39287, Oct. 5, 1984, as amended at 60 FR 53505, Oct. 16, 1995]

§315.908 Appeals.

(a) An employee who, in accordance with the provisions of this subpart, is assigned to a nonmanagerial or nonsupervisory position, has no appeal right.

(b) An employee who alleges that an agency action under this subpart was based on partisan political affiliation or marital status, may appeal to the Merit Systems Protection Board.

§315.909 Relationship to other actions.

(a) If an employee is required to concurrently serve both a probationary period under this subpart and a probationary period under subpart H of this part, the latter takes precedence and completion of the probationary period for competitive appointment and fulfills the requirements of this subpart.

(b) An action which demotes an employee to a lower grade than the one the employee left to accept the supervisory or managerial position, and an action against an employee for reasons other than supervisory or managerial performance, is governed by part 432 or part 752 procedures, whichever is applicable. If the employee believes an action under this subpart was based on improper discrimination or other prohibited practices under 5 U.S.C. 2302, he or she may appeal to the Merit Systems Protection Board or the Equal Employment Opportunity Commission, as appropriate.

PART 316—TEMPORARY AND TERM EMPLOYMENT

AUTHORITY: 5 U.S.C. 3301, 3302; E.O. 10577, 3 CFR, 1954–1958 Comp., p. 218.

SOURCE: 33 FR 12423, Sept. 4, 1968, unless otherwise noted.

Subparts A–B [Reserved]

Subpart C—Term Employment

EDITORIAL NOTE: Nomenclature changes to subpart C of part 316 appear at 70 FR 72067, Dec. 1, 2005.

§ 316.301 Purpose and duration.

(a) An agency may make a term appointment for a period of more than 1 year but not more than 4 years to positions where the need for an employee's services is not permanent. Reasons for making a term appointment include, but are not limited to: project work, extraordinary workload, scheduled abolishment, reorganization, contracting out of the function, uncertainty of future funding, or the need to maintain permanent positions for placement of employees who would otherwise be displaced from other parts of the organization. Agencies may extend appointments made for more than 1 year but less than 4 years up to the 4-year limit in increments determined by the agency. The vacancy announcement should state that the agency has the option of extending a term appointment up to the 4-year limit.

(b) OPM may authorize exceptions beyond the 4-year limit when the extension is clearly justified and is consistent with applicable statutory provisions. Requests to make and/or extend appointments beyond the 4-year limit must be initiated by the employing office and sent to the appropriate OPM service center.

[63 FR 63783, Nov. 17, 1998]

§ 316.302 Selection of term employees.

(a) *Competitive term appointment.* An agency may make a term appointment under part 332 of this chapter, by using competitive procedures, or under part 337 of this chapter, by using direct-hire procedures, as appropriate.

(b) *Noncompetitive term appointment.* An agency may give a noncompetitive term appointment, without regard to the requirements of parts 332 and 333 of this chapter, to an individual who is qualified for the position and who is eligible for:

(1) Reinstatement under § 315.401 of this chapter;

(2) Veterans recruitment appointment (VRA) under § 307.103 of this chapter. Term appointments under this section are permitted only at the grade levels authorized for VRA appointments. Such appointments are competitive service appointments not excepted VRA appointments and do not lead to conversion to career-conditional appointment;

(3) Career-conditional appointment under § 315.601, 315.604, 315.605, 315.606, 315.607, 315.608, 315.609, 315.612, or 315.711 of this chapter;

(4) Appointment under 5 U.S.C. 3112 (veterans with compensable service-

connected disability of 30 percent or more). The disability must be documented by a notice of retirement or discharge due to service-connected disability from active military service dated at any time, or by a notice of compensable disability rating from the Department of Veterans Affairs, dated 1991 or later;

(5) Appointment under 31 U.S.C. 732(g) for current and former employees of the General Accounting Office;

(6) Appointment under 28 U.S.C. 602 for current and former employees of the Administrative Office of the U.S. Courts;

(7) Reappointment on the basis of having left a term appointment prior to serving the 4-year maximum amount of time allowed under the appointment. Reappointment must be to a position in the same agency appropriate for filling under term appointment and for which the individual qualifies. Combined service under the original term appointment and reappointment must not exceed the 4-year limit; or

(8) Conversion in the same agency from a current temporary appointment when the employee is or was within reach on a certificate of eligibles for term appointment *at any time during service in the temporary position. Within reach* means that the person could have been selected for the position under competitive hiring procedures, including veterans' preference. The certificate must have been actually used for term appointment. The person must have been continuously employed in the position from the date found within reach to the date converted to a term appointment.

(c) Term employees are eligible for an extension of their appointment in accordance with the time limits in §316.301 even if their eligibility for noncompetitive appointment expires or is lost during the period they are serving under term employment.

[63 FR 63783, Nov. 17, 1998, as amended at 68 FR 35268, June 13, 2003; 69 FR 33275, June 15, 2004; 73 FR 60611, Oct. 14, 2008; 74 FR 40477, Aug. 12, 2009]

§316.303 Tenure of term employees.

(a) A term employee does not acquire a competitive status on the basis of his term appointment.

(b) The employment of a term employee ends automatically on the expiration of his term appointment unless he has been separated earlier in accordance with this chapter.

§316.304 Trial period.

(a) The first year of service of a term employee is a trial period regardless of the method of appointment. Prior Federal civilian service is credited toward completion of the required trial period in the same manner as prescribed by §315.802 of this chapter.

(b) The agency may terminate a term employee at any time during the trial period. The employee is entitled to the procedures set forth in §315.804 or §315.805 of this chapter as appropriate.

[33 FR 12423, Sept. 4, 1968, as amended at 63 FR 63783, Nov. 17, 1998]

Subpart D—Temporary Limited Employment

EDITORIAL NOTE: Nomenclature changes to subpart D of part 316 appear at 70 FR 72067, Dec. 1, 2005.

§316.401 Purpose and duration.

(a) *Appropriate use.* An agency may make a temporary limited appointment—

(1) To fill a short-term position (*i.e.*, one that is not expected to last longer than 1 year);

(2) To meet an employment need that is scheduled to be terminated within the timeframe set out in paragraph (c) of this section for such reasons as abolishment, reorganization, or contracting of the function, anticipated reduction in funding, or completion of a specific project or peak workload; or

(3) To fill positions on a temporary basis when the positions are expected to be needed for placement of permanent employees who would otherwise be displaced from other parts of the organization.

(b) *Certification of appropriate use.* The supervisor of each position filled by temporary appointment must certify that the employment need is truly temporary and that the proposed appointment meets the regulatory time limits. This certification may constitute appropriate documentation of compliance with the limits set out in paragraph (c) of this section. The reason(s) for making a temporary limited appointment must be stated on the form documenting each such appointment.

(c) *Time limits—general.* (1) An agency may make a temporary appointment for a specified period not to exceed 1 year. The appointment may be extended up to a maximum of 1 additional year (24 months of total service). Appointment to a successor position (*i.e.*, to a position that replaces and absorbs the position to which an individual was originally appointed) is considered to be an extension of the original appointment. Appointment to a position involving the same basic duties and in the same major subdivision of the agency and same local commuting area as the original appointment is also considered to be an extension of the original appointment.

(2) An agency may not fill a position by temporary appointment if that position has previously been filled by temporary appointment(s) for an aggregate of 2 years, or 24 months, within the preceding 3-year period.

(d) *Exceptions to general time limits.* (1) Agencies may make and extend temporary appointments to positions involving intermittent or seasonal work without regard to the requirements in paragraph (c) of this section, *provided* that:

(i) Appointments and extensions are made in increments of 1 year or less.

(ii) Employment in the same or a successor position under this and any other appointing authority totals less than 6 months (1,040 hours), excluding overtime, in a service year. The service year is the calendar year that begins on the date of the employee's initial appointment in the agency. Should employment in a position filled under this exception total 6 months or more in any service year, the provisions of paragraph (c) of this section will apply to subsequent extension or reappointment unless OPM approves continued exception under this section. An individual may be employed for training for up to 120 days following initial appointment and up to 2 weeks a year thereafter without regard to the service year limitation.

(2) OPM will authorize exceptions to the limits set out in paragraph (c) of this section only when necessitated by major reorganizations or base closings or other unusual circumstances. Requests based on major reorganization, base closing, restructuring, or other unusual circumstances that apply agencywide must be made by an official at the headquarters level of the Department or agency. Requests involving extension of appointments to a specific position or project based on other unusual circumstances may be submitted by the employing office to the appropriate OPM service center.

[59 FR 46898, Sept. 13, 1994]

§ 316.402 Procedures for making temporary appointments.

(a) *Competitive temporary appointments.* In accordance with the time limits in § 316.401, an agency may make a temporary appointment under part 332 of this chapter, by using competitive procedures, or under part 337 of this chapter, by using direct-hire procedures, as appropriate.

(b) *Noncompetitive temporary appointments.* In accordance with the time limits in § 316.401, an agency may give a noncompetitive temporary appointment, without regard to the requirements of parts 332 and 333 of this chapter, to an individual who is qualified for the position and who is eligible for:

(1) Reinstatement under § 315.401 of this chapter;

(2) Veterans recruitment appointment under § 307.103 of this chapter. Temporary limited appointments under this section are permitted only at the grade levels authorized for VRA appointments. Such appointments are not VRA appointments and do not lead to conversion to career-conditional appointment;

(3) Career-conditional appointment under § 315.601, 315.604, 315.605, 315.606, 315.607, 315.608, 315.609, 315.612, 315.703, or 315.711 of this chapter;

(4) Appointment under 5 U.S.C. 3112 (veterans with compensable service-connected disability of 30 percent of more). The disability must be documented by a notice of retirement or discharge due to service-connected disability from active military service dated at any time, or by a notice of

compensable disability rating from the Department of Veterans Affairs, dated 1991 or later;

(5) Appointment under 31 U.S.C. 732(g) for current and former employees of the General Accounting Office;

(6) Appointment under 28 U.S.C. 602 for current and former employees of the Administrative Office of the U.S. Courts;

(7) Reappointment on the basis of being a former temporary employee of the agency who was originally appointed from a certificate of eligibles or under the provisions of part 333 of this chapter. An agency may not reappoint a former temporary employee if the individual has already served the maximum time allowed in §316.401 or if the position has been filled under temporary appointment for the maximum time allowed in §316.401. Reappointment must be to the same position or another position appropriate for temporary appointment with the same qualification requirements;

(8) Reappointment on the basis of being a former temporary employee who was originally appointed from a certificate of eligibles or under the provisions of part 333 of this chapter and who sustained a compensable injury while serving on the temporary appointment. Reappointment must be to the same position or another position appropriate for temporary appointment with the same qualification requirements. If the compensable injury disqualifies the former individual from performing such a position, reappointment may be to any position for which the individual is qualified. Reappointment must be for a minimum of 120 days.

(c) *Extension of temporary appointments.* An individual who receives a valid temporary appointment will be eligible for an extension in accordance with §316.401 even if his or her eligibility for noncompetitive appointment expires or is lost during the authorized period of temporary employment.

[63 FR 63784, Nov. 17, 1998, as amended at 68 FR 35268, June 13, 2003; 69 FR 33275, June 15, 2004; 73 FR 60611, Oct. 14, 2008; 74 FR 40477, Aug. 12, 2009]

§316.403 Designation of provisional appointments.

(a) *Conditions for designation.* An agency may designate a temporary appointment as a provisional appointment only when all of the following conditions are met:

(1) The appointment is made to fill a continuing position by a provisional appointment leading to permanent appointment when the position must be filled more quickly than would be possible under the procedures required for nontemporary appointment or when such a provisional appointment is a requirement of the applicable authority;

(2) The agency must have current budgetary and appointing authority for the nontemporary appointment (assuming satisfactory completion of the required procedures); and

(3) The agency must have a specific intention to convert the appointee to a nontemporary appointment under appropriate authority before the expiration of the temporary appointment, must state this intention in any written offer of employment and document this intention as part of the permanent record of the initial appointment in accordance with instructions issued by OPM.

(b) *Authority for provisional appointments.* Provisional appointments must be made under an authority established by law, Executive order, or regulation or granted by OPM. Appointments which may be treated as provisional appointments under this paragraph may be made under any appropriate authority, including, but not limited to:

(1) Noncompetitive temporary appointments of disabled veterans under §316.402(b)(5), when the appointments are intended to afford eligibility for conversion in accordance with §315.707 of this chapter and section 3112 of title 5, United States Code;

(2) Temporary appointments of nurses in the Department of Veterans Affairs, when the appointments are made under the provisions of section 4114 of title 38, United States Code, with the intention of converting the appointees to continuing appointments

as soon as the appointees obtain required State certification or registration and/or the agency completes necessary verification of references;

(3) Temporary transitional Schedule C appointments made under § 213.3302 of this chapter, when the appointees are to be converted to nontemporary Schedule C appointments upon OPM approval and completion of necessary clearances.

(4) Senior Executive Service limited term and limited emergency appointments made under § 317.601 of this chapter, when the appointees are to be converted to nontemporary appointments in the Senior Executive Service or to nontemporary Presidential appointments, upon further action, such as OPM approval, White House clearance, and/or confirmation by the Senate; and

(5) Temporary appointments of severely physically handicapped individuals, when such appointments are required to demonstrate qualifications for nontemporary appointment under § 213.3102(u) of this chapter, and when the appointees will be converted to such nontemporary appointment upon successful performance in the trial position.

[56 FR 10142, Mar. 11, 1991, as amended at 60 FR 35120, July 6, 1995; 63 FR 63784, Nov. 17, 1998; 66 FR 66710, Dec. 27, 2001]

Subpart E [Reserved]

Subpart F—Appointment Without Competitive Examination in Rare Cases

§ 316.601 Appointment without competitive examination in rare cases.

(a) An agency may make an appointment without competitive examination when:

(1) The duties and compensation of the position are such, or qualified persons are so rare, that in the interest of good civil service administration the position cannot be filled through open competitive examination;

(2) The person to be appointed meets all applicable qualification requirements for the position; and

(3) The appointment is specifically authorized by the Office or is made under an agreement between the agency and the Office providing for such appointments.

(b) A person appointed under paragraph (a) of this section does not acquire a competitive status on the basis of that appointment.

(c) When a position filled under paragraph (a) of this section becomes vacant, the agency may fill the vacancy by another appointment under paragraph (a) of this section only if the conditions of paragraph (a)(3) of this section are again met.

[44 FR 55132, Sept. 25, 1979]

Subpart G—Retention of Incumbents of Positions Brought Into the Competitive Service

§ 316.701 Public or private enterprise taken over by Government.

(a) When the Office, or an agency acting under an agreement with the Office, finds that the Federal Government has taken over a public or private enterprise, or an identifiable unit thereof, and that a position has thereby been brought into the competitive service, the agency may retain the incumbent of the position.

(b)(1) When an agency retains an employee under paragraph (a) of this section in a position which it determines to be a continuing one, the agency gives the employee a status quo appointment and shall decide on a timely basis whether it will convert that individual's employment to career or career-conditional under § 315.701 of this chapter.

(2) When an agency decides not to effect conversion under § 315.701 of this chapter, or the employee fails to qualify for conversion, the agency, in its discretion, may retain the employee as a status quo employee.

(c) An agency may retain an employee under paragraph (a) of this section in a position that it determines is noncontinuing under a temporary appointment. That appointment may be made for a period not to exceed 1 year and will be subject to the time limits set out in § 316.402.

[44 FR 55133, Sept. 25, 1979, as amended at 60 FR 39101, Aug. 1, 1995; 63 FR 63784, Nov. 17, 1998]

§ 316.702 Excepted positions brought into the competitive service.

(a) When the Office, or an agency acting under an agreement with the Office, finds that an excepted position has been brought into the competitive service by statute, Executive order, or the revocation of an exception under Civil Service Rule VI (§ 6.6 of this chapter), or is otherwise made subject to competitive examination, the agency may retain the incumbent of the position.

(b)(1) When an agency retains an employee under paragraph (a) of this section who was serving in an excepted position under an indefinite appointment or an appointment without time limit, the agency gives the employee a status quo appointment and may convert that employee's appointment to career or career-conditional under § 315.701 of this chapter.

(2) When the agency decides not to effect conversion under § 315.701 of this chapter, or the employee fails to qualify for conversion, the agency, in its discretion, may retain the employee as a status quo employee.

(c) An employee who was serving under an excepted appointment limited to 1 year or less may be retained as a temporary employee under paragraph (a) of this section until the scheduled expiration date of the employee's excepted appointment. Extension of the employee's temporary appointment beyond that date will be subject to the provisions of § 316.402.

(d) An employee who was serving under an excepted appointment with a definite time limit longer than 1 year may be retained under a term appointment. The term appointment is subject to all conditions and time limits applicable to term appointments. Service under excepted appointment does not count against the maximum time limit for term appointment in the competitive service.

[44 FR 55133, Sept. 25, 1979, as amended at 60 FR 39101, Aug. 1, 1995; 63 FR 63784, Nov. 17, 1998]

§ 316.703 Effect on tenure of position change of status quo employees.

(a) A status quo employee who is promoted, demoted, or reassigned becomes:

(1) An indefinite employee when the position change occurs while he is not serving overseas; or

(2) An overseas limited employee when the position change occurs while he is serving overseas.

(b) An employee referred to in paragraph (a) of this section who is changed back to his status quo position becomes a status quo employee.

Subpart H [Reserved]

PART 317—EMPLOYMENT IN THE SENIOR EXECUTIVE SERVICE

Subpart A [Reserved]

Subpart B—General Provisions

Subpart C—Conversion to the Senior Executive Service

Subpart D—Qualifications Standards

Subpart E—Career Appointments

Subpart F—Noncareer and Limited Appointments

Subpart G—SES Career Appointment by Reinstatement

Subpart H—Retention of SES Provisions

Subpart I—Reassignments, Transfers, and Details

Subpart J—Corrective Action

AUTHORITY: 5 U.S.C. 3392, 3393, 3395, 3397,3592, 3593, 3595, 3596, 8414, and 8421.

Subpart A [Reserved]

Subpart B—General Provisions

§ 317.201 Regulatory requirements.

This part contains the regulations of the Office of Personnel Management which implement the following provisions of law:

(a) Section 413 of title IV of the Civil Service Reform Act of 1978;

(b) Subchapter VIII of chapter 33 of title 5, U.S.C. on appointment, reassignment, and transfer in the Senior Executive Service; and

(c) Subchapter V of chapter 35 of title 5, U.S.C. on reinstatement to the Senior Executive Service.

[45 FR 8541, Feb. 8, 1980]

Subpart C—Conversion to the Senior Executive Service

SOURCE: 45 FR 8541, Feb. 8, 1980, unless otherwise noted.

§ 317.301 Conversion coverage.

(a) *When applicable.* These conversion provisions apply in the following circumstances.

(1) The implementation of the Senior Executive Service effective on July 13, 1979, and the initial conversions thereto.

(2) The implementation of the Senior Executive Service in an agency following the revocation of that agency's Presidential exclusion under 5 U.S.C. 3132(e). The Office of Personnel Management shall determine the date on which conversions under this authority shall become effective. Generally, this will be no later than six months following the effective date of the revocation of the Presidential exclusion.

(3) The implementation of the Senior Executive Service in a formerly excluded agency following statutory action extending coverage under 5 U.S.C. 3132(a)(1) to that agency. Except as otherwise provided by law, the Office of Personnel Management shall determine the date on which conversions under this authority shall become effective. Generally, this will be no later than six months following the effective date of the statutory action extending coverage under 5 U.S.C. 3132(a)(1).

(4) The implementation of the SES in a formerly excluded agency when OPM determines that the agency is an "Executive agency" under 5 U.S.C. 3132(a)(1).

(5) The exercise of a reemployment right by an individual who at the time of his/her former agency's implementation of the Senior Executive Service was under a reemployment agreement to a position in that agency which meets the grade level and functional criteria for inclusion under the Senior Executive Service. The effective date of a conversion under this authority is prescribed by § 317.302(d)(5).

(b) *Employees covered.* This subpart covers:

(1) An employee serving in a position at the time it is designated a Senior Executive Service position;

(2) An individual appointed or reinstated to a position after it has been designated a Senior Executive Service position;

(3) An employee transferred, promoted, voluntarily reassigned or voluntarily demoted to a position after it has been designated a Senior Executive Service position;

(4) An employee involuntarily reassigned or involuntarily demoted to a

position after it has been designated a Senior Executive Service position; and

(5) An employee serving in a position which meets the grade level but not the functional criteria for designation as a Senior Executive Service position.

(6) An employee appointed in his/her former agency under a reemployment right provided, however, that the employee was under a reemployment agreement at the time the Senior Executive Service was implemented in his/her former agency and that the reemployment right was to a position which meets the grade level and functional criteria for inclusion under the Senior Executive Service.

(c) *Employees excluded.* The following employees are excluded from coverage of this subpart and are not entitled to conversion to the Senior Executive Service.

(1) An employee in a position designated as Senior Executive Service who is serving under a time limited appointment which will terminate before the operational date of the Senior Executive Service.

(2) An employee serving under a temporary promotion, detail, or temporary assignment in a position designated as Senior Executive Service unless the position which the employee encumbered on a permanent basis just prior to the current temporary action has been designated as Senior Executive Service.

[45 FR 8541, Feb. 8, 1980, as amended at 60 FR 6385, Feb. 2, 1995]

§ 317.302 Conversion procedures.

(a) *Employees appointed prior to designation; employees involuntarily reassigned or demoted after designation*—(1) *Notice.* Each employee covered by this subpart who was appointed prior to the designation of his/her position as a Senior Executive Service position, or who was involuntarily reassigned or involuntarily demoted to a position after it was designated a Senior Executive Service position, shall be given a written notice which includes the following information:

(i) A statement that the employee's position has been designated as either "general" or "career reserved";

(ii) A statement that the employee is being offered an appointment under the Senior Executive Service or that the employee is not being offered an appointment under the Senior Executive Service but will be separated from the civil service pursuant to § 317.305(b)(4) or § 317.306(b)(4); If the employee is offered conversion, the notice shall also include:

(iii) A statement that the employee has 90 calendar days from the date of receipt of the written notice to elect either to join the Senior Executive Service or to remain in his/her current appointment system;

(iv) Identification of the position, SES pay rate, and kind of appointment which the employee will receive if the employee elects to convert to the Senior Executive Service;

(v) For excepted appointees who have reinstatement eligibility to a position in the competitive service, or, as determined by the Office of Personnel Management, have substantial career-oriented service under career-type appointments as defined in § 317.304(a)(2), a statement that the employee may request conversion to career appointment;

(vi) For employees under limited executive assignment who have reinstatement eligibility to a position in the competitive service, or as determined by the Office of Personnel Management, have substantial career-oriented service under career-type appointments as defined in § 317.304(a)(2), and who are covered under § 317.306(b)(3), a statement that the employee may request conversion to career appointment;

(vii) A summary of the features of the Senior Executive Service (this can be accomplished by appending descriptive material prepared by the Office);

(viii) A statement that the employee must submit his/her decision with regard to paragraphs (a)(1)(iii), (v) and (vi) of this section, in writing, on or before the end of the notice period; and

(ix) A statement of the right of an employee who is aggrieved to appeal an action under this subpart to the Merit Systems Protection Board.

An employee whose involuntary reassignment or involuntary demotion to a designated position occurs less than 90 days before the operational date of the Senior Executive Service, shall be given this notice at the time of the personnel action. The employee shall have 90 calendar days from the date of receipt of the notice to make an election on conversion.

(2) *Pay.* Upon conversion to the Senior Executive Service, an employee's SES rate will be determined under 5 CFR part 534, subpart D.

(3) *Freedom of choice.* The employee shall decide whether he/she accepts conversion to the Senior Executive Service. The employing agency shall not attempt to influence the employee's decision through coercion, intimidation or duress.

(4) *Employee's election.* On or before the end of the notice period, the employee shall signify in writing his/her decision to accept or to decline an appointment under the Senior Executive Service. An excepted or limited assignment employee covered under § 317.305(b)(3) or § 317.306(b)(3), respectively, shall also indicate whether he/she requests conversion to career appointment. Failure to respond shall be deemed a declination.

(b) *Employees receiving appointments after designation but before the operational date of the Senior Executive Service*—(1) *Condition of appointment.* Each individual appointed, reinstated, transferred, promoted, voluntarily reassigned or voluntarily demoted to a position after it has been designated a Senior Executive Service position shall be required to accept conversion to the Senior Executive Service. The agency shall advise the individual of this requirement prior to the appointment or other personnel action. The individual shall signify his/her acceptance of conversion in writing at the time of the personnel action.

(2) *Notice.* At the time of the personnel action, or 90 days before the Senior Executive Service becomes operational, whichever is later, the agency shall give the employee a written notice which identifies the position, SES pay rate, and kind of appointment the employee will receive under the Senior Executive Service.

(3) *Pay.* An employee's SES rate will be determined under 5 CFR part 534, subpart D.

(c) *Employees whose positions are not designated Senior Executive Service positions—Notice.* Each employee covered by § 317.301(b)(5) shall be given a written notice advising the employee that his/her position is not designated a Senior Executive Service position; that the employee is not entitled to conversion to the Senior Executive Service; and that the employee has a right to appeal an action under this subpart to the Merit Systems Protection Board.

(d) *Employees appointed under a reemployment right*—(1) *Notice.* At the time the employee exercises his/her reemployment right, the agency shall give the employee a written notice which includes the following information:

(i) A statement that the employee meets the requirements of § 317.301(b)(6) for eligibility for conversion to the Senior Executive Service and that he/she is being offered an appointment under the Senior Executive Service;

(ii) A statement that the employee has 90 calendar days from the date of receipt of the written notice to elect either to join the Senior Executive Service or to remain under the type of appointment upon which the reemployment right was based;

(iii) Identification of the position, SES pay rate, and kind of appointment which the employee will receive if the employee elects to convert to the Senior Executive Service;

(iv) If the reemployment right is to a position in the excepted service and the employee has reinstatement eligibility to a position in the competitive service, or, as determined by the Office of Personnel Management, has substantial career-oriented service under career-type appointments as defined in § 317.304(a)(2), a statement that the employee may request conversion to career appointment;

(v) A summary of the features of the Senior Executive Service (this can be accomplished by appending descriptive material prepared by the Office); and

(vi) A statment that the employee must submit his/her decision with regard to paragraphs (d)(1)(ii) and (iv) of this section, in writing, on or before the end of the notice period.

(2) *Pay.* An employee's SES rate will be determined under 5 CFR part 534, subpart D.

(3) *Freedom of choice.* The employee shall decide whether he/she accepts

conversion to the Senior Executive Service. The employing agency shall not attempt to influence the employee's decision through coercion, intimidation or duress.

(4) *Employee's election.* On or before the end of the notice period, the employee shall signify in writing his/her decision to accept or to decline an appointment under the Senior Executive Service. An excepted service employee shall also indicate whether he/she requests conversion to career appointment. Failure to respond shall be deemed a declination.

(5) *Effective date.* A conversion under this section for an employee who elects to join the SES shall become effective at the end of the notice period.

[45 FR 8541, Feb. 8, 1980, as amended at 45 FR 19213, Mar. 25, 1980; 69 FR 2050, Jan. 13, 2004]

§317.303 Status of employees who decline voluntary conversion to the Senior Executive Service.

(a) An employee who declines conversion pursuant to §317.302(a)(4) or §317.302(d)(4) shall remain in his/her current appointment and pay system, and shall retain the grade, seniority, and other rights and benefits associated with such type of appointment and pay system. The employee may continue in the current SES position or be reassigned to another position within or outside the Senior Executive Service.

(b) The assignment of an employee who declines conversion under this subpart shall not result in the separation or reduction in grade of any other employee in the agency.

(c) Nothing in these regulations affects an agency's right to terminate a limited executive appointment pursuant to Civil Service Rule IX.

[45 FR 8541, Feb. 8, 1980, as amended at 45 FR 19213, Mar. 25, 1980]

§317.304 Conversion of career and career-type appointees.

(a) *Coverage.* This section covers employees serving under:

(1) A career or career-conditional appointment; or

(2) A similar type of appointment ("career-type" appointment) in an excepted service position as determined by the Office. A career-type appointment is an appointment in the excepted service other than an appointment:

(i) To a Schedule C position established under part 213 of this chapter;

(ii) To a position authorized to be filled by noncareer executive assignment under part 305 of this chapter;

(iii) To a position which meets the same criteria as a Schedule C position or a position authorized to be filled by non-career executive assignment; or

(iv) To a position where the incumbent is traditionally changed upon a change in Presidential Administrations.

(b) *Senior Executive Service appointment.* An employee covered by this section shall be converted to a Senior Executive Service career appointment. The employee may be assigned to either a "general" or a "career reserved" position.

§317.305 Conversion of excepted appointees.

(a) *Coverage.* This section covers employees serving under an excepted appointment in a position:

(1) In Schedule C of subpart C of part 213 of title 5, Code of Federal Regulations;

(2) Filled by noncareer executive assignment under subpart F of part 305 of title 5, Code of Federal Regulations;

(3) In the Executive Schedule under subchapter II of chapter 53 of title 5, United States Code, other than a career Executive Schedule position; or,

(4) Filled under an authority equivalent to paragraph (a) (1), (2), or (3) of this section.

(b) *Senior Executive Service appointment.* An employee covered by this section shall be subject to one of the following actions.

(1) If the employee's position is designated a "general" position, the agency may convert the employee to a Senior Executive Service noncareer appointment. The employee may be assigned only to a "general" position.

(2) If the employee's position is designated a "career reserved" position, the agency may convert the employee

to a Senior Executive Service noncareer appointment and assign the employee to a "general" position. The employee cannot remain in a "career reserved" position.

(3) If the employee subject to § 317.302(a) or § 317.302(d) has reinstatement eligibility to a position in the competitive service, or, as determined by the Office of Personnel Management, had substantial career-oriented service under a career-type appointment as defined in § 317.304(a)(2), the employee may request conversion to a career appointment. Such request must be made on or before the end of the notice period.

(i) If the request is approved by the Office, the agency will convert the employee to a Senior Executive Service career appointment. The employee may be assigned to a "general" or a "career reserved" position. The name of the individual and basis for approving the request must be published in the FEDERAL REGISTER.

(ii) If the employee's request for conversion to career is not approved by the Office, or if the employee elects not to make such a request, the agency will convert the employee to a Senior Executive Service noncareer appointment. The employee may be assigned only to a "general" position.

(4) In lieu of action under paragraph (b) (1), (2), or (3) of this section, the agency may separate the employee from the civil service.

§ 317.306 Conversion of employees under time limited appointments.

(a) *Coverage.* This section covers employees serving under:

(1) A limited executive assignment under subpart E of part 305 of title 5, Code of Federal Regulations; or

(2) A similar type of time limited appointment in an excepted service position.

(b) *Senior Executive Service appointment.* An employee covered by this section shall be subject to one of the following actions.

(1) If the position in which the employee is serving under a limited executive assignment or similar type of time limited appointment will terminate within three years from the date of the proposed conversion action, the agency may convert the employee to a Senior Executive Service limited term appointment.

(2) If the position in which the employee is serving under a limited executive assignment or similar type of time limited appointment will not terminate within three years from the date of the proposed conversion action, the agency may convert the employee to a Senior Executive Service noncareer appointment and assign the employee to a "general" position.

(3) If the employee under a limited executive assignment has reinstatement eligibility to a position in the competitive service, or, as determined by the Office of Personnel Management, had substantial career-oriented service under a career-type appointment as defined in § 317.304(a)(2), and if immediately prior to the limited executive assignment and without a break in service the employee served under a career appointment or career-type appointment in a position now being designated a Senior Executive Service position then the employee may request conversion to a career appointment. Such request must be made on or before the end of the notice period.

(i) If the employee requests conversion to career, the agency will convert the employee to a Senior Executive Service career appointment. The employee may be assigned to a "general" or a "career reserved" position. The name of the individual and basis for approving the request must be published in the FEDERAL REGISTER.

(ii) If the employee does not request conversion to career, the agency will convert the employee as provided for in paragraphs (b) (1) and (2) of this section.

(4) In lieu of action under paragraph (b) (1), (2), or (3) of this section, the agency may separate the employee from the civil service.

Subpart D—Qualifications Standards

SOURCE: 54 FR 9758, Mar. 8, 1989, unless otherwise noted.

§ 317.401 General.

(a) The head of each agency is responsible for establishing qualifications standards for Senior Executive Service (SES) positions in accordance with the procedures described in this subpart.

(b) A written qualification standard must be established for a position before any appointment is made to the position. If a position is being filled competitively, the standard must be established before the position is announced.

[54 FR 9758, Mar. 8, 1989, as amended at 60 FR 6385, Feb. 2, 1995]

§ 317.402 Career reserved positions.

(a) The qualifications standard must be in writing and identify the breadth and depth of the professional/technical and executive/managerial knowledges, skills, and abilities, or other qualifications, required for successful performance in the position.

(b) The standard must be specific enough to enable applicants to be rated and ranked according to their degree of qualifications when the position is being filled on a competitive basis.

(c) Each qualifications criterion in the standard must be job related. The standard may not emphasize agency-related experience, however, to the extent that it precludes otherwise well-qualified candidates from outside the agency from appointment consideration.

(d) The standard may not include—

(1) A minimum length of experience requirement beyond that authorized for similar positions in the General Schedule;

(2) A minimum education requirement beyond that authorized for similar positions in the General Schedule; or

(3) Any criterion prohibited by law or regulation.

§ 317.403 General positions.

An agency may apply the criteria in § 317.402 when developing qualifications standards for general positions. If it does not, OPM must be consulted before the agency develops the standard.

§ 317.404 Retention of qualifications standards.

If a qualifications standard is changed, or a position is cancelled, the former standard shall be retained for 2 years.

Subpart E—Career Appointments

SOURCE: 54 FR 9758, Mar. 8, 1989, unless otherwise noted.

§ 317.501 Recruitment and selection for initial SES career appointment be achieved from the brightest and most diverse pool possible.

(a) *Executive Resources Board (ERB).* The head of each agency shall appoint one or more ERBs from among employees of the agency or commissioned officers of the uniformed services serving on active duty in the agency. The ERB shall, in accordance with the requirements of this section, conduct the merit staffing process for initial SES career appointment.

(b) *Recruitment.* (1) As a minimum, the source of recruitment to fill a SES position by career appointment must include all groups of qualified individuals within the civil service (as defined by 5 U.S.C. 2101). It may also include qualified individuals outside the civil service.

(2) Before an agency can fill an SES vacancy by career appointment, it must post a vacancy announcement in USAJOBS for at least 14 calendar days, including the date of publication. Each agency's SES vacancy announcement must comply with criteria in § 330.707 of subpart G of this chapter.

(c) *Merit staffing requirements.* As a minimum, agencies must—

(1) Provide that competition be fair and open, that all candidates compete and be rated and ranked on the same basis, and that selection be based solely on qualifications and not on political or other non-job-related factors. If a candidate is a current SES career appointee or an SES reinstatement eligible, an agency may consider the candidate either competitively or noncompetitively.

(2) Provide that the ERB consider the executive and technical qualifications of each candidate, other than those found ineligible because they do not

meet the requirements of the vacancy announcement. Preliminary qualifications screening, rating, and ranking of candidates may be delegated by the ERB.

(3) Provide that the rating procedures sufficiently differentiate among eligible candidates on the basis of the knowledges, skills, abilities, and other job-related factors in the qualifications standard for the position so as to enable the relative ranking of the candidates. For this purpose, eligible candidates may be grouped into broad categories, such as highly qualified, well qualified, and qualified. Numerical rating and ranking are not required.

(4) Provide that the record be adequately documented to show the basis of qualifications, rating, and ranking determinations.

(5) Provide that the ERB make written recommendations to the appointing authority on the eligible candidates and identify the best qualified candidates. Rating sheets may be used to satisfy the written recommendation requirement for individual candidates, but the ERB must certify in writing the list of candidates to the appointing authority.

(6) Provide that the appointing authority select from among the candidates identified as best qualified by the ERB and certify the candidate's executive and technical qualifications.

(7) Provide that the appointing authority or the ERB certify in writing that appropriate merit staffing procedures were followed.

(d) *Retention of documentation.* Agencies must keep such documentation as OPM prescribes for 2 years to permit reconstruction of merit staffing actions.

(e) *Applicant inquiries and appeals.* Individuals are entitled to obtain information from an agency regarding the process used to recruit and select candidates for career appointment to SES positions. Upon request, applicants must be told whether they were considered qualified for the position and whether they were referred for appointment consideration. Also, they may have access to questionnaires or other written material regarding their own qualifications, except for material that would identify a confidential source. There is no right of appeal by applicants to OPM on SES staffing actions taken by ERBs, Qualifications Review Boards, or appointing authorities.

(f) *OPM review.* OPM may review proposed career appointments to ensure that they comply with all merit staffing requirements and are free of any impropriety. An agency shall take such action as OPM may require to correct an action contrary to any law, rule, or regulation.

[54 FR 9758, Mar. 8, 1989, as amended at 58 FR 58261, Nov. 1, 1993; 60 FR 6385, Feb. 2, 1995; 65 FR 33740, May 25, 2000; 66 FR 63906, Dec. 11, 2001]

§317.502 Qualifications Review Board certification.

(a) A Qualification Review Board (QRB) convened by OPM must certify the executive/managerial qualifications of a candidate before initial career appointment may be made to an SES position. More than one-half of the members of a QRB must be SES career appointees.

(b) Agency requests for certification of a candidate by a QRB must contain such information as prescribed by OPM, including evidence that merit staffing procedures were followed and that the appointing authority has certified the candidate's qualifications for the position.

(c) Qualifications Review Board certification of executive qualifications must be based on demonstrated executive experience; successful completion of an OPM-approved candidate development program; or possession of special or unique qualities that indicate a likelihood of executive success. Any existing time limit on a previously approved certification is removed.

(d) OPM may determine the disposition of agency QRB requests where the QRB has not yet acted if the agency head leaves office or announces an intention to leave office, if the President has nominated a new agency head, or if there is a Presidential transition.

(e) An action to convert a "noncareer-type" employee to a career SES appointment in the employee's current position or a successor to that position will not be forwarded to a QRB. A "noncareer-type" employee includes a noncareer SES appointee, a Schedule C appointee, or equivalent.

(f) A new QRB certification is required for an individual to be reappointed as an SES career appointee following separation of the individual from an SES career appointment if:

(1) The individual was removed during the SES probationary period for performance or disciplinary reasons; or

(2) The individual completed an SES probationary period, or did not have to serve one, and was removed for a reason that made the individual ineligible for reinstatement to the SES under subpart G of this part.

[54 FR 9758, Mar. 8, 1989, as amended at 56 FR 170, Jan. 3, 1991; 60 FR 6385, Feb. 2, 1995; 61 FR 46533, Sept. 4, 1996; 65 FR 33740, May 25, 2000]

§ 317.503 Probationary period.

(a) An individual's initial appointment as an SES career appointee becomes final only after the individual has served a 1-year probationary period as a career appointee; there has been an assessment of the appointee's performance during the probationary period; and the appointing authority, or his or her designee, has certified that the appointee performed at the level of excellence expected of a senior executive during the probationary period.

(b) When a career appointee's executive qualification have been certified by a Qualifications Review Board on the basis of special or unique qualities, as described in § 317.502(c), the probationary assessment must address any executive development activities the agency identified in support of the request for QRB certification.

(c) The probationary period begins on the effective date of the personnel action initially appointing the individual to the SES as a career appointee and ends one calendar year later.

(d) The following conditions apply to crediting service towards completion of the probationary period.

(1) Time on leave with pay while in an SES position is credited. Earned leave for which the employee is compensated by lump-sum payment upon separation is not credited.

(2) Time in a nonpay status while in an SES position is credited up to a total of 30 calendar days (or 22 workdays). After 30 calendar days, the probationary period is extended by adding to it time equal to that served in a nonpay status.

(3) Time absent on military duty or due to compensable injury is credited upon restoration to the SES when no other break in SES service has occurred.

(4) Time following transfer to an SES position in another agency is credited, *i.e.*, the individual does not have to start a new probationary period.

(e) Removal of a career appointee during the probationary period is covered by subpart D of part 359 of this chapter.

(f) A career appointee who resigns or is removed from the SES before completion of the probationary period may not receive another SES career appointment unless selected under SES merit staffing procedures. The individual, however, need not be recertified by a QRB unless the individual was removed for performance or disciplinary reasons.

(g) An individual who separated from the SES during the probationary period and who has been out of the SES more than 30 calendar days must serve a new 1-year probationary period upon reappointment and may not credit previous time in a probationary period. In the following situations, however, there is an exception and the individual is only required to complete the remainder of the previously served probationary period.

(1) The individual left the SES without a break in service for a Presidential appointment and is exercising reinstatement rights under 5 U.S.C. 3593(b).

(2) The individual left the SES without a break in service for other civilian employment that provides a statutory or regulatory reemployment right to the SES when no other break in service occurred.

(3) The break in SES service was the result of military duty or compensable injury, and the time credited under paragraph (c)(3) of this section was not sufficient to complete the probationary period.

[54 FR 9758, Mar. 8, 1989, as amended at 60 FR 6386, Feb. 2, 1995; 65 FR 33740, May 25, 2000]

§ 317.504 [Reserved]

Subpart F—Noncareer and Limited Appointments

SOURCE: 45 FR 62414, Sept. 19, 1980, unless otherwise noted.

§ 317.601 Authorization.

(a) An agency may make a noncareer or limited appointment only to a general position.

(b) Each use of a noncareer appointment authority must be approved individually by the Office of Personnel Management, and the authority reverts to the Office upon departure of the incumbent, unless otherwise provided by the Office.

(c) Use of a limited appointment authority is subject to the conditions in this paragraph.

(1) Agencies are provided a pool of limited appointment authorities equal to 3 percent of their Senior Executive Service (SES) position allocation, or one authority, whichever is greater. An agency may use the pool to make a limited appointment only of an individual who has a career or career-conditional appointment (or an appointment of equivalent tenure) in a permanent civil service position outside the SES. If necessary, the Office of Personnel Management may suspend use of the pool authority.

(2) Each use of a limited appointment authority other than under paragraph (c)(1) of this section must be approved individually by the Office, and the authority reverts to the Office upon departure of the incumbent, unless otherwise provided by the Office.

[60 FR 6386, Feb. 2, 1995, as amended at 65 FR 33741, May 25, 2000]

§ 317.602 Conditions of a limited appointment.

(a) Appointments authorized under this provision may be deemed provisional appointments for purposes of the regulations set out in parts 831, 842, 870, and 890 of this chapter if they meet the criteria set out in §§ 316.401 and 316.403 of this chapter.

(b) A limited appointment is not renewable. If an agency initially made the appointment for less than the maximum period authorized by the Office of Personnel Management, however, the agency may extend the appointment to the maximum period without the approval of the Office. The Office must be notified of the extension.

(c) A limited term or limited emergency appointee may not be appointed to, or continue to hold, a position under such an appointment if, within the preceding 48 months, the individual has served more than 36 months, in the aggregate, under any combination of limited term and limited emergency appointments.

[45 FR 62414, Sept. 19, 1980, as amended at 56 FR 10142, Mar. 11, 1991; 60 FR 6386, Feb. 2, 1995]

§ 317.603 Selection.

An agency may make a noncareer or limited appointment without the use of merit staffing procedures. The appointee, however, must meet the qualifications requirements for the position, as determined in writing by the appointing authority.

[45 FR 62414, Sept. 19, 1980, as amended at 60 FR 6386, Feb. 2, 1995]

§ 317.604 Reassignment.

(a) An agency may reassign a noncareer appointee only with the prior approval of the Office unless otherwise provided by the Office.

(b) An agency may make the following reassignments of limited appointees to positions for which qualified without the prior approval of the Office of Personnel Management. The Office must be notified of the reassignment, however.

(1) An agency may reassign a limited emergency appointee to another general position established to meet a bona fide, unanticipated, urgent need, except that the appointee may not serve in one or more positions in the agency under such appointment in excess of 18 months.

(2) An agency may reassign a limited term appointee to another general position the duties of which will expire at the end of 3 years or less except that the appointee may not serve in one or

more positions in the agency under such appointment in excess of 3 years.

[45 FR 62414, Sept. 19, 1980, as amended at 60 FR 6386, Feb. 2, 1995]

§ 317.605 Tenure of appointees.

(a) A noncareer or limited appointee does not acquire status within the Senior Executive Service on the basis of the appointment.

(b) An agency may terminate a noncareer or limited appointment at any time, unless a limited appointee is covered under 5 CFR 752.601(c)(2). The agency must give the noncareer or limited appointee a written notice at least 1 day prior to the effective date of the removal.

(c) The employment of a limited appointee ends automatically on the expiration of the appointment if the appointment has not been terminated earlier.

(d) An employee: (1) Who received a limited appointment without a break of service in the same agency as the one in which the employee held a career or career conditional appointment (or an appointment of equivalent tenure) in a permanent civil service position outside the Senior Executive Service, and

(2) Whose limited appointment is terminated for reasons other than misconduct, neglect of duty, or malfeasance, shall be entitled to be placed in his/her former position or a position of like status, tenure, and grade.

[45 FR 62414, Sept. 19, 1980, as amended at 60 FR 6386, Feb. 2, 1995]

Subpart G—SES Career Appointment by Reinstatement

SOURCE: 54 FR 9759, Mar. 8, 1989, unless otherwise noted.

§ 317.701 Agency authority.

As provided for in §§ 317.702 and 317.703, an agency may reinstate a former SES career appointee without regard to the merit staffing requirements established by OPM in § 317.501(c).

§ 317.702 General reinstatement: SES career appointees.

(a) *Eligibility for general reinstatement.* A former SES career appointee who meets the following conditions is eligible for reinstatement under this section:

(1) The individual completed an SES probationary period under a previous SES career appointment or was exempted from that requirement; and

(2) The individual's separation from his or her last SES career appointment was not a removal under subpart C of part 359 of this chapter for failure to be recertified as a senior executive; or a removal under subpart E of part 359 of this chapter for less than fully successful executive performance; or under 5 U.S.C. 1207 by order of the Merit Systems Protection Board as a result of a disciplinary action initiated by the Special Counsel under 5 U.S.C. 1206; or under 5 U.S.C. 7532 (National Security); or under subpart F of part 752 of this chapter for misconduct, neglect of duty, or malfeasance; or a resignation after receipt of a notice proposing or directing removal under any of the above conditions. Removal for failure to accept a directed reassignment to another commuting area, or to accompany a position in a transfer of function to another commuting area, does not preclude reinstatement to the SES unless the appointment to the original position included acceptance of a written nationwide mobility agreement or policy.

(b) *Applying for reinstatement; time limit.* Application for reinstatement under this section shall be made directly to the agency in which SES employment is sought. There is no time limit for reinstatement under this section.

(c) *Qualifications.* The individual must meet the qualification requirements of the position to which reinstated. The agency makes this determination.

(d) *Tenure upon reinstatement.* An individual who is reinstated under § 317.702 becomes an SES career appointee.

[54 FR 9759, Mar. 8, 1989, as amended at 56 FR 172, Jan. 3, 1991]

§ 317.703 Guaranteed reinstatement: Presidential appointees.

(a) *Eligibility for reinstatement.* (1) A former SES career appointee who was appointed by the President to a civil service position outside the SES without a break in service, and who left the Presidential appointment for reasons other than misconduct, neglect of duty, or malfeasance, is entitled by law to be reinstated to the SES.

(2) If an individual is serving under a Presidential appointment with reinstatement entitlement and receives another Presidential appointment without a break in service between the two appointments, the individual continues to be entitled to be reinstated to the SES following termination of the second appointment. If there is an interim period between the two Presidential appointments, the individual must be reinstated as an SES career appointee before the effective date of the second appointment to preserve reinstatement entitlement following termination of the second appointment.

(b) *Applying for reinstatement; time limit.* Except as provided in paragraph (d) of this section, an application in writing for reinstatement under this section must be made to OPM within 90 days after separation from the Presidential appointment. An application may be submitted as soon as the Presidential appointee's resignation is requested or submitted.

(c) *Directing reinstatement.* (1) To the extent practicable, OPM will direct reinstatement within 45 days of the date of receipt by OPM of the application for reinstatement or the date of separation from the Presidential appointment, whichever is later.

(2) OPM will use the following order of precedence in directing reinstatement of a former Presidential appointee:

(i) The agency in which the individual last served as an SES career appointee before accepting the Presidential appointment;

(ii) The successor agency to the one in which the individual last served as an SES career appointee;

(iii) The agency or agencies in which the individual served as a Presidential appointee; or

(iv) Any other agency in the Executive branch with positions under the SES.

(3) The agency being directed to take the reinstatement action is responsible for assigning the individual to a position for which he or she meets the qualifications requirements.

(4) When directing the reinstatement of a Presidential appointee, OPM may, as appropriate, allocate an additional SES space authority to the agency.

(5) When a Presidential appointee tenders his or her resignation, voluntarily or upon request, the agency in which the Presidential appointment was held, upon approval by OPM, may place the appointee as an interim measure on an SES limited term or limited emergency appointment as appropriate, pending reinstatement, to preclude a break in service after the Presidential appointment has terminated.

(6) To preserve reinstatement rights under this section, an individual who has been serving in a presidential appointment, if selected by the President for another appointment in the same or a new agency, must be reinstated to an appropriate position as an SES career appointee before the effective date of the new Presidential appointment, unless service as a Presidential appointee would be continuous.

(d) *Reinstatement following direct negotiations with an agency.* (1) A Presidential appointee who qualifies under paragraph (a) of this section may initiate direct negotiations with an agency regarding reinstatement under this section.

(2) An agency may voluntarily reinstate a former Presidential appointee without an order from OPM directing such action.

(3) The agency is responsible for assigning the individual to a position for which he or she meets the qualification requirements.

(4) Direct negotiations with an agency do not extend the time limit stated in paragraph (b) of this section for making application to OPM.

(5) OPM may, when appropriate and upon request by the agency, allocate an additional SES space authority to an agency that voluntarily reinstates a

former Presidential appointee under this paragraph.

(6) An individual who is reinstated under this paragraph because of direct negotiations with an agency is not entitled to further assistance by OPM.

(e) *Tenure upon reinstatement.* (1) An individual reinstated under §317.703 becomes an SES career appointee.

(2) An individual reinstated under §317.703 who was serving an SES probationary period at the time of his or her Presidential appointment is required to complete the 1-year SES probationary period upon reinstatement.

(f) *Compliance.* (1) An agency must comply with an order to reinstate issued by OPM under this section as promptly as possible, but not more than 30 calendar days from the date of the order.

(2) The agency will notify OPM of a reinstatement action taken under this section within 5 workdays of the effective date of the reinstatement.

(3) An individual who declines a reinstatement ordered by OPM is not entitled to further placement assistance by OPM under this section.

[54 FR 9759, Mar. 8, 1989, as amended at 60 FR 6386, Feb. 2, 1995]

Subpart H—Retention of SES Provisions

§317.801 Retention of SES provisions.

(a) *Coverage.* This subpart applies to—

(1) A career appointee in the SES appointed at any time by the President to a civilian position in the executive branch with the advice and consent of the Senate at a rate of basic pay which is equal to or greater than the rate payable for Executive Level V; or

(2) A career appointee in the SES who is not covered under paragraph (a)(1) of this section and who was appointed on or after November 1, 1986, to a civilian position in the executive branch which is covered by the Executive Schedule, or the rate of basic pay for which is fixed by statute at a rate equal to one of the levels of the Executive Schedule.

(b) *Election.* (1) At the time of appointment, an appointee covered by paragraph (a) of this section may elect to retain some, all, or none of the following SES provisions related to basic pay (including the aggregate limitation on pay established by 5 U.S.C. 5307), performance awards, awarding of ranks, severance pay, leave, and retirement. That election will remain in effect for no less than 1 year, unless the appointee leaves the position sooner.

(2) The appointing agency is responsible for advising the appointee of the election opportunity. The election decision must be in writing.

(c) *Change in election.* Except as provided by paragraph (b) of this section, a career appointee is permitted to make an election for purposes of adding or dropping coverage no more than once during any twelve-month period.

[50 FR 6154, Feb. 14, 1985, as amended at 56 FR 15273, Apr. 16, 1991; 57 FR 54677, Nov. 20, 1992; 60 FR 6386, Feb. 2, 1995; 69 FR 2050, Jan. 13, 2004; 72 FR 12035, Mar. 15, 2007]

Subpart I—Reassignments, Transfers, and Details

SOURCE: 54 FR 9760, Mar. 8, 1989, unless otherwise noted.

§317.901 Reassignments.

(a) In this section, *reassignment* means a permanent assignment to another SES position within the employing executive agency or military department. (See 5 U.S.C. 105 for a definition of "executive agency" and 5 U.S.C. 102 for a definition of "military department.")

(b) A career appointee may be reassigned to any SES position for which qualified in accordance with the following conditions:

(1) *Reassignment within a commuting area.* For reassignment within a commuting area, the appointee must receive a written notice at least 15 days before the effective date of the reassignment. This notice requirement may be waived only when the appointee consents in writing.

(2) *Reassignment outside of a commuting area.* For reassignment outside of a commuting area, (i) the agency must consult with the appointee on the reasons for, and the appointee's preferences with respect to, the proposed reassignment; and (ii) following such consultation, the agency must provide

the appointee a written notice, including the reasons for the reassignment, at least 60 days before the effective date of the reassignment. This notice requirement may be waived only when the appointee consents in writing.

(c) A career appointee may not be involuntarily reassigned within 120 days after the appointment of the head of an agency, or within 120 days after the appointment of the career appointee's most immediate supervisor who is a noncareer appointee and who has the authority to make an initial appraisal of the career appointee's performance under subpart C of part 430 of this chapter.

(1) In this paragraph—

(i) *Head of an agency* means the head of an executive or military department or the head of an independent establishment.

(ii) *Noncareer appointee* includes an SES noncareer or limited appointee, an appointee in a position filled by Schedule C, or an appointee in an Executive Schedule or equivalent position that is not required to be filled competitively.

(2) These restrictions do not apply to the involuntary reassignment of a career appointee under 5 U.S.C. 4314(b)(3) based on a final performance rating of "Unsatisfactory" that was issued before the appointment of a new agency head or a new noncareer supervisor as defined in paragraph (c)(1) of this section. If a moratorium is already underway at the time the final rating is issued, then that moratorium must be completed before the reassignment action can be effected.

(3) A voluntary reassignment during the 120-day period is permitted, but the appointee must agree in writing before the reassignment.

(4) For the purpose of calculating the 120-day period, any days, not to exceed a total of 60, during which the career appointee is serving on a detail or other temporary assignment apart from the appointee's regular position shall not be counted. Any days in excess of 60 days on one or more details or other temporary assignments shall be counted.

(5) The prohibition in this paragraph on involuntary reassignments may be applied by an agency, at its discretion, in the case of a detail of an individual as the head of an agency or of a noncareer appointee as a supervisor, or when a noncareer appointee in a deputy position is acting as the agency head or in a vacant supervisory position. If the individual later receives a permanent appointment to the position without a break in service, the 120-day moratorium initiated by the permanent appointment shall include any days spent in the position on an acting basis.

(d) A 15 or 60-day advance notice described in paragraph (b) of this section may be issued during the 120-day moratorium on the involuntary reassignment of a career appointee described in paragraph (c) of this section, but an involuntary reassignment may not be effected until the moratorium has ended.

[54 FR 9760, Mar. 8, 1989, as amended at 57 FR 10124, Mar. 24, 1992; 58 FR 58261, Nov. 1, 1993; 60 FR 6387, Feb. 2, 1995; 63 FR 34258, June 24, 1998]

§ 317.902 Transfers.

(a) *Definition.* In this section, *transfer* means a permanent assignment or appointment to another SES position in a different executive agency or military department.

(b) *Requirements.* Transfers are voluntary and cannot occur without the consent of the appointee and the gaining agency, except transfers connected with a transfer of functions to another agency.

§ 317.903 Details.

(a) *Definition.* In this section, *detail* means the temporary assignment of an SES member to another position (within or outside of the SES) or the temporary assignment of a non-SES member to an SES position, with the expectation that the employee will return to the official position of record upon expiration of the detail. For purposes of pay and benefits, the employee continues to encumber the position from which detailed. The provisions of this section cover details within or outside of the employing agency.

(b) *Time limits.* (1) Details within an executive agency or military department must be made in no more than 120-day increments.

(2) An agency may not detail an SES employee to unclassified duties for more than 240 days.

(3) An agency must use competitive procedures when detailing a non-SES employee to an SES position for more than 240 days unless the employee is eligible for a noncompetitive career SES appointment.

(4) An agency must obtain OPM approval for a detail of more than 240 days if the detail is of:

(i) A non-SES employee to an SES position that supervises other SES positions; or

(ii) An SES employee to a position at the GS–15 or equivalent level or below.

(c) *SES career reserved positions.* Only a career SES appointee or a career-type non-SES appointee may be detailed to a career reserved position.

(d) *SES general positions.* Any SES appointee or non-SES appointee may be detailed to a general position.

[54 FR 9760, Mar. 8, 1989, as amended at 60 FR 6387, Feb. 2, 1995]

§317.904 Change in type of SES appointment.

An agency may not require a career SES appointee to accept a noncareer or limited SES appointment as a condition of appointment to another SES position. If a career appointee elects to accept a noncareer or limited appointment, the voluntary nature of the action must be documented in writing before the effective date of the new appointment. A copy of such documentation must be retained permanently in the appointee's Official Personnel Folder.

Subpart J—Corrective Action

§317.1001 OPM authority for corrective action.

If OPM finds that an agency has taken an action contrary to law or regulation under this part, it may require the agency to take appropriate corrective action.

[54 FR 9761, Mar. 8, 1989]

PART 319—EMPLOYMENT IN SENIOR-LEVEL AND SCIENTIFIC AND PROFESSIONAL POSITIONS

Subpart A—General

Subpart B—Position Allocations and Establishment

Subpart C—Qualifications Requirements

Subpart D—Recruitment and Examination

AUTHORITY: 5 U.S.C. 1104, 3104, 3324, 3325, 5108, and 5376.

SOURCE: 60 FR 6387, Feb. 2, 1995, unless otherwise noted.

Subpart A—General

§319.101 Coverage.

(a) This part covers senior-level (SL) and scientific and professional (ST) positions that are classified above GS–15 and are paid under 5 U.S.C. 5376. See 5 CFR part 534, subpart E, for pay provisions.

(b) Positions that meet the criteria for placement in the Senior Executive Service (SES) under 5 U.S.C. 3132(a) may not be placed in the SL or ST system and are not covered by this part.

§319.102 Senior-level positions.

(a) SL positions are positions classified above GS–15 pursuant to 5 U.S.C. 5108 that are not covered by other pay systems (e.g. the SES and ST systems).

(b) Positions in agencies that are excluded from 5 U.S.C. chapter 51 (Classification) under section 5102(a), or positions that meet one of the exclusions in section 5102(c), are excluded from the SL system.

(c) SL positions in the executive branch are in the competitive service unless the position is excepted by statute, Executive order, or the Office of Personnel Management (OPM).

§ 319.103 Scientific and professional positions.

(a) ST positions are established under 5 U.S.C. 3104 to carry out research and development functions that require the services of specially qualified personnel.

(b) Research and development functions are defined in The Guide to Personnel Data Standards under the data element "Functional Classification." The guide is available for inspection at the Office of Personnel Management library, 1900 E Street, NW., Washington DC 20415.

(c) An ST position must be engaged in research and development in the physical, biological, medical, or engineering sciences, or a closely related field.

(d) ST positions are in the competitive service.

§ 319.104 Applicable instructions.

Provisions in statute, Executive order, or regulations that relate in general to competitive and excepted service positions and employment apply to positions and employment under the SL and ST systems unless there is a specific provision to the contrary.

§ 319.105 Reporting requirements.

Agencies shall report such information as may be requested by OPM relating to SL and ST positions and employees.

Subpart B—Position Allocations and Establishment

§ 319.201 Coverage.

This section applies to SL positions in an executive agency per 5 U.S.C. 5108 and ST positions in any agency per 5 U.S.C. 3104.

§ 319.202 Allocation of positions.

SL and ST positions may be established only under a position allocation approved by OPM.

§ 319.203 Establishment of positions.

(a) Prior approval of OPM is not required to establish individual SL and ST positions within an allocation, but the positions must be established in accordance with the standards and procedures in paragraph (b) of this section. OPM reserves the right to require the prior approval of individual positions if the agency is not in compliance with these standards and procedures.

(b) Before an SL or ST position may be established, an agency must:

(1) Prepare a description of the duties, responsibilities, and supervisory relationships of the position; and

(2) Determine, consistent with published position classification standards and guides and accepted classification principles, that the position is properly classified above GS–15. In addition, for an ST position an agency must determine that the position meets the functional research and development criteria described in § 319.103.

Subpart C—Qualifications Requirements

§ 319.301 Qualifications standards.

(a) *General.* Agency heads are responsible for establishing qualifications standards in accordance with the criteria in this section.

(1) The standard must be in writing and identify the breadth and depth of the knowledges, skills, and abilities, or other qualifications, required for successful performance in the position.

(2) Each criterion in the standard must be job related.

(3) The standard may not include any criterion prohibited by law or regulation.

(b) *Standards for senior-level positions.* (1) The standard must be specific enough to enable applicants to be rated and ranked according to their degree of qualifications when the position is being filled on a competitive basis.

(2) The standard may not include a minimum length of experience or minimum education requirement beyond that authorized for similar positions in the General Schedule.

(c) *Standards for scientific and professional positions.* (1) Unless the agency obtains the approval of OPM, the standard must provide that the candidate have at least 3 years of specialized experience in, or closely related to, the field in which the candidate will work. At least 1 year of this experience must have been in planning and executing difficult programs of national significance or planning and executing specialized programs that show outstanding attainments in the field of research or consultation.

(2) Agencies may require that at least 1 year of the specialized experience must be at least equivalent to experience at GS–15.

(3) Agencies may require applicants to furnish positive evidence that they have performed highly creative or outstanding research where similar abilities are required in the ST position.

§ 319.302 Individual qualifications.

Agency heads are delegated authority to approve the qualifications of individuals appointed to SL and ST positions. The agency head must determine that the individual meets the qualifications standards for the position to which appointed.

Subpart D—Recruitment and Examination

§ 319.401 Senior-level positions.

(a) *General.* SL positions may be in either the competitive or excepted service. This section only applies to appointments in the competitive service from a civil service register. Reassignments, promotions, transfers, and reinstatements to SL positions in the competitive service shall be made in accordance with applicable statutory and regulatory provisions. Employment of SL employees in the excepted service is covered by 5 CFR, part 302.

(1) Agency heads are delegated authority to recruit and examine applicants for SL positions in the competitive service, establish competitor inventories, and issue certificates of eligibility in conformance with the requirements of this section, other applicable regulations, and statute.

(2) Agencies shall take such action as OPM may require to correct an action taken under delegated authority.

(3) Delegated authority may be terminated or suspended at any time by OPM for reasons such as, but not limited to:

(i) Evidence of unequal treatment of candidates; or

(ii) Identifiable merit system abuses.

(b) *Recruitment.* (1) A recruiting plan, with appropriate emphasis on affirmative recruitment, must be developed and followed.

(2) Vacancy announcements must remain open for a minimum of 14 calendar days. The closing date may not be a nonworkday.

(3) State Job Service offices must be notified of the vacancy in accordance with 5 CFR 330.102. Publication in OPM's listing of Senior Executive Service and other executive vacancies, which is provided the offices, will satisfy this requirement.

(c) *Evaluation and selection.* Examination and selection procedures, and rights of applicants, are subject to the same provisions in statute and regulation that govern civil service examinations and appointments in general.

(d) *Records.* (1) Agencies must maintain records sufficient to allow reconstruction of the merit staffing process.

(2) Records must be kept for 2 years after an appointment, or, if no appointment is made, for 2 years after the closing date of the vacancy announcement.

§ 319.402 Scientific and professional positions.

(a) ST positions are filled without competitive examination under 5 U.S.C. 3325.

(b) ST positions are not subject to the citizenship requirements in 5 CFR part 338, subpart A. Agencies, however, must observe any restrictions on the employment of noncitizens in applicable appropriations acts.

(c) ST employees acquire competitive status immediately upon appointment. They are not required to serve a probationary or trial period.

PART 330—RECRUITMENT, SELECTION, AND PLACEMENT (GENERAL)

Subpart A—Filling Vacancies in the Competitive Service

Subpart B—Reemployment Priority List (RPL)

Subpart C [Reserved]

Subpart D—Positions Restricted to Preference Eligibles

Subpart E—Restrictions To Protect Competitive Principles

Subpart F—Agency Career Transition Assistance Plan (CTAP) for Local Surplus and Displaced Employees

Subpart G—Interagency Career Transition Assistance Plan (ICTAP) for Displaced Employees

Subparts H–I [Reserved]

Subpart J—Prohibited Practices

Subparts K–L [Reserved]

Subpart M—Timing of Background Investigations

AUTHORITY: 5 U.S.C. 1104, 1302, 3301, 3302, 3304, and 3330; E.O. 10577, 3 CFR, 1954–58 Comp., p. 218; Section 330.103 also issued under 5 U.S.C. 3327; Section 330.104 also issued under sec. 2(d), Pub. L. 114–137, 130 Stat. 310; Subpart B also issued under 5 U.S.C. 3315 and 8151; Section 330.401 also issued under 5 U.S.C. 3310; Subparts F and G also issued under Presidential Memorandum on Career Transition Assistance for Federal Employees, September 12, 1995; Subpart G also issued under 5 U.S.C. 8337(h) and 8456(b).

SOURCE: 75 FR 67593, Nov. 3, 2010, unless otherwise noted.

Subpart A—Filling Vacancies in the Competitive Service

§330.101 Definitions.

(a) In this part:

Agency means:

(1) An Executive department listed at 5 U.S.C. 101;

(2) A military department listed at 5 U.S.C. 102;

(3) A Government owned corporation in the executive branch;

(4) An independent establishment in the executive branch as described at 5 U.S.C. 104; and

(5) The Government Printing Office.

Component means the first major subdivision of an agency, separately organized, and clearly distinguished in work function and operation from other agency subdivisions (e.g., the Internal Revenue Service under the Department of the Treasury or the National Park Service under the Department of the Interior).

Local commuting area has the meaning given that term in §351.203 of this chapter.

Permanent competitive service workforce and *permanent competitive service employees* mean agency employees serving under career or career-conditional appointments, in tenure group I or II, respectively.

Position change has the meaning given that term in §210.102 of this chapter.

Rating of record has the meaning given that term in §351.203 of this chapter.

Representative rate has the meaning given that term in §351.203 of this chapter.

Tenure groups are described in §351.501 of this chapter.

(b) In this subpart:

Vacancy means a vacant position in the competitive service, regardless of whether the position will be filled by permanent or time-limited appointment, for which an agency is seeking applications from outside its current permanent competitive service workforce.

§330.102 Methods of filling vacancies.

An agency may fill a vacancy in the competitive service by any method authorized in this chapter, including competitive appointment from a list of eligibles, noncompetitive appointment under special authority, reinstatement, transfer, reassignment, change to lower grade, or promotion. The agency must exercise its discretion in each personnel action solely on the basis of merit and fitness, without regard to political or religious affiliation, marital status, or race, and veterans' preference entitlements.

§330.103 Requirement to notify OPM.

An agency must provide the vacancy announcement information to OPM promptly when:

(a) Filling a vacancy for more than 120 days from outside the agency's current permanent competitive service workforce, as required by the Interagency Career Transition Assistance Plan, subpart G of this part, unless the action to be taken is listed in subpart G as an exception to that subpart;

(b) Filling any vacancy under the agency's merit promotion procedures when the agency will accept applications from outside its permanent competitive service workforce; and

(c) Filling a vacancy by open competitive examination, including direct hire procedures under part 337 of this chapter, or in the Senior Executive Service, as required by 5 U.S.C. 3327.

§330.104 Requirements for vacancy announcements.

(a) Each vacancy announcement must contain the following information:

(1) Name of issuing agency;

(2) Announcement number;

(3) Position title, series, pay plan, and grade (or pay rate);

(4) Duty location;

(5) Number of vacancies;

(6) Opening date and application deadline (closing date) and any other information concerning how receipt of applications will be documented, such as by date of receipt or postmark, and

considered, such as by cut-off dates in open continuous announcements;

(7) Qualification requirements, including knowledge, skills, and abilities or competencies;

(8) Starting pay;

(9) Brief description of duties;

(10) Basis of rating;

(11) What to file;

(12) Instructions on how to apply;

(13) Information on how to claim veterans' preference, if applicable;

(14) Definition of "well-qualified," as required by subparts F and G of this part;

(15) Information on how candidates eligible under subparts F and G of this part may apply, including required proof of eligibility;

(16) Contact person or contact point;

(17) Equal employment opportunity statement (Agencies may use the recommended equal employment opportunity statement located on OPM's USAJOBS website.); and

(18) Reasonable accommodation statement.

(b)(1) An agency may use wording of its choice in its statement that conveys the availability of reasonable accommodation required by § 330.104(a)(18). In its reasonable accommodation statement, an agency may not list types of medical conditions or impairments appropriate for accommodation.

(2) Agencies may use the recommended reasonable accommodation statement located on OPM's USAJOBS website.

(c) If an agency is sharing a certificate of eligibles under part 332 of this chapter, the original hiring agency must provide notice in the job opportunity announcement that the resulting list of eligible candidates may be used by one or more hiring agencies, and of how the applicant may opt-in to the disclosure of his or her applicant records to other hiring agencies.

[75 FR 67593, Nov. 3, 2010, as amended at 82 FR 5339, Jan. 18, 2017]

§ 330.105 Instructions on how to add a vacancy announcement to USAJOBS.

An agency can find the instructions to add a vacancy announcement to USAJOBS on OPM's Web site at *http://www.usajobs.gov.* An electronic file of the complete vacancy announcement must be included within USAJOBS.

§ 330.106 Funding.

Each year, OPM will charge a fee for the agency's share of the cost of providing employment information to the public and to Federal employees as authorized by 5 U.S.C. 3330(f).

Subpart B—Reemployment Priority List (RPL)

§ 330.201 Purpose.

(a) The Reemployment Priority List (RPL) is a required component of an agency's placement programs to assist its current and former competitive service employees who will be or were separated by reduction in force (RIF) under part 351 of this chapter, or who have recovered from a compensable work-related injury after more than 1 year, as required by part 353 of this chapter. In filling vacancies, an agency must give its RPL registrants placement priority for most competitive service vacancies before hiring someone from outside its own permanent competitive service workforce. An agency may choose to consider RPL placement priority candidates before other agency permanent competitive service employees under its Career Transition Assistance Plan (CTAP) established under subpart F of this part, after fulfilling agency obligations to its CTAP selection priority candidates.

(b) Agencies must use an RPL to give placement priority to their:

(1) Current competitive service employees with a specific notice of RIF separation or a Certification of Expected Separation issued under part 351 of this chapter;

(2) Former competitive service employees separated by RIF under part 351 of this chapter; and

(3) Former competitive service employees fully recovered from a compensable injury (as defined in part 353 of this chapter) after more than 1 year.

(c) All agency components within the local commuting area use a single RPL and are responsible for giving placement priority to the agency's RPL registrants.

(d) With prior OPM approval, an agency may operate an alternate placement program which satisfies the basic requirements of this subpart, including veterans' preference, as an exception to the RPL regulations under this subpart. This provision is limited to reemployment priority because of RIF separation and allows agencies to adopt different placement strategies that are effective for their programs and satisfy employee entitlements to reemployment priority.

§ 330.202 Definitions.

In this subpart:

Competitive area means a competitive area as described in § 351.402 of this chapter.

Competitive service appointment includes new appointments, reinstatements, reemployment, and transfers as defined in § 210.102 of this chapter, and conversions as defined in OPM's "Guide to Processing Personnel Actions."

Injury, in relation to the RPL, has the meaning given that term in § 353.102 of this chapter.

Overseas has the meaning given that term in § 210.102 of this chapter.

Qualified refers to an RPL registrant who:

(1) Meets OPM-established or -approved qualification standards and requirements for the position, including minimum educational requirements, and agency-established selective factors (as this term is used in OPM's "Operating Manual: Qualification Standards for General Schedule Positions");

(2) Will not cause an undue interruption, as defined in § 351.203 of this chapter, that would prevent the completion of required work by the registrant 90 days after the registrant is placed in the position;

(3) Is physically qualified, with or without reasonable accommodation, to perform the duties of the position;

(4) Meets any special OPM-approved qualifying conditions for the position; and

(5) Meets any other applicable requirements for competitive service appointment.

RPL eligible means a current or former employee of the agency who meets the conditions in either paragraph (a) or (b) of § 330.203. As used in this subpart, "RPL eligible" and "eligible" are synonymous.

RPL placement priority candidate means an RPL registrant who is qualified and available for a specific agency vacancy.

RPL registrant means an RPL eligible who submitted a timely RPL application and who is registered on the agency's RPL. As used in this subpart, "RPL registrant" and "registrant" are synonymous.

Vacancy means any vacant position to be filled by a competitive service permanent or time-limited appointment.

§ 330.203 RPL Eligibility.

An employee must meet the conditions in either paragraph (a) or (b) of this section to be an RPL eligible.

(a) For eligibility based on part 351 of this chapter, the employee:

(1) Must be serving in an appointment in the competitive service in tenure group I or II;

(2) Must have received either a specific notice of separation or a Certification of Expected Separation under part 351 of this chapter that has not been cancelled, rescinded, or modified so that the employee is no longer under notice of separation;

(3) Must have received a rating of record of at least fully successful (Level 3) or equivalent as the most recent performance rating of record; and

(4) Must not have declined an offer under part 351, subpart G, of this chapter of a position with the same type of work schedule and with a representative rate at least as high as that of the position from which the employee will be separated.

(b) For eligibility based on part 353 of this chapter, the employee or former employee:

(1) Must be serving in, or separated from, an appointment in the competitive service in tenure group I or II;

(2) Must either have accepted a position at a lower grade or pay level in lieu of separation or have been separated because of a compensable injury or disability. (For the purposes of this subpart, any reference to the position from which an individual was or will be separated includes the position from

which the RPL eligible accepted the lower graded or pay level position under this paragraph.);

(3) Must have fully recovered more than 1 year after compensation began; and

(4) Must have received notification from the Office of Workers' Compensation Programs, Department of Labor, that injury compensation benefits have ceased or will cease.

§ 330.204 Agency requirements and responsibilities.

(a) An agency must establish policies and maintain an RPL for each local commuting area in which the agency has RPL eligibles.

(b) An agency must give each RPL eligible information about its RPL program, including Merit Systems Protection Board appeal rights under § 330.214, when:

(1) The agency issues a RIF separation notice or a Certification of Expected Separation under part 351 of this chapter; or

(2) The employee accepts a position at a lower grade or pay level or is separated from the agency because of a compensable work-related injury.

(c) An agency must register an RPL eligible on the appropriate RPL no later than 10 calendar days after receiving the eligible's written application.

(d) Agencies must include in their RPL policies established under this subpart how they will assist RPL eligibles who:

(1) Request an RPL application;

(2) Request help in completing the RPL application; and

(3) Request help in identifying and listing on the RPL application those positions within the agency for which they are qualified and interested.

(e) An agency must give RPL registrants placement priority for personnel actions as described in § 330.210.

(f) An agency must not remove an individual from the RPL under § 330.209(a)(1), (b)(1), or (b)(2) without evidence (such as a Postal Service return receipt signed by addressee only) showing that the offer, inquiry, or scheduled interview was made in writing. The written offer, inquiry, or scheduled interview must clearly state that failure to respond will result in removal from the RPL for positions at that grade or pay level and for positions at lower grades and pay levels for which registered.

§ 330.205 Agency RPL applications.

Agencies may develop their own application format which must, at a minimum:

(a) Allow an RPL eligible to register for positions at the same representative rate and work schedule (full-time, part-time, seasonal, or intermittent) as the position from which the RPL eligible was, or will be, separated; and

(b) Allow an RPL eligible to specify the conditions under which he or she will accept a position, including grades or pay levels, appointment type (permanent or time-limited), occupations (e.g., position classification series or career groups), and minimum number of hours of work per week, as applicable.

§ 330.206 RPL registration timeframe and positions.

(a) To register, an RPL eligible must:

(1) Meet the eligibility conditions under § 330.203(a) or (b);

(2) Complete an RPL application prescribed by the current or former agency and keep the agency informed of any significant changes in the information provided; and

(3) Submit the RPL application on or before the RIF separation date or, if an RPL eligible under § 330.203(b), within 30 calendar days after the:

(i) Date injury compensation benefits cease; or

(ii) Date the Department of Labor denies an appeal for continuation of injury compensation benefits.

(b) RPL eligibles may register and receive placement priority for positions for which they are qualified and that:

(1) Have a representative rate no higher than the position from which they were, or will be, separated unless the eligible was demoted as a tenure group I or II employee in a previous RIF. If the eligible was so demoted, the eligible can register for positions with a representative rate up to the representative rate of the position held on a permanent appointment immediately before the RIF demotion was effective;

(2) Have no greater promotion potential than the position from which they were, or will be, separated; and

(3) Have the same type of work schedule as the position from which they were, or will be, separated.

§330.207 Registration area.

(a) Except as provided in paragraphs (b) through (e) of this section, RPL registration is limited to the local commuting area in which the eligible was, or will be, separated.

(b) If the agency has, or will have, no competitive service positions remaining in the local commuting area from which the RPL eligible will be separated under part 351 of this chapter, the agency may designate a different local commuting area where there are continuing positions for the RPL eligible to exercise placement priority. The agency has sole discretion over whether to offer this option and which local commuting area to designate, taking into consideration the size and locations of its workforce, available vacancies, and available funds.

(c) If the RPL eligible agreed to transfer with his or her function under part 351 of this chapter but will be separated by RIF from the gaining competitive area, registration is limited to the RPL covering the gaining competitive area's local commuting area.

(d) For an individual who is eligible under §330.203(b), registration is initially limited to the RPL covering the local commuting area of the position from which the employee was separated. The agency must establish a fair and consistent policy that permits RPL eligibles to expand their registration to available local commuting areas mutually acceptable to the RPL eligible and the agency, up to agency-wide as required by 5 U.S.C. 8151. (For example, an agency could consider the number and location(s) of its positions and funding availability when establishing its policies on expanding consideration.) In lieu of expanded registration, the agency policy may provide for the RPL eligible to elect to receive placement priority for the next best available position in the former local commuting area.

(e) If the RPL eligible was, or will be, separated from an overseas position (*see* part 301 of this chapter), RPL registration is limited to the local commuting area in which the eligible was, or will be, separated, unless:

(1) The agency approves a written request by the RPL eligible for registration in the local commuting area from which employed for overseas service, or in another area within the United States that is mutually acceptable to the eligible and the agency; or

(2) The agency has a formal program for rotating employees between overseas areas and the United States, and the RPL eligible's preceding and prospective overseas service would exceed the maximum duration of an overseas duty tour in the rotation program. In this case, the eligible may register for a local commuting area within the United States that is mutually acceptable to the eligible and the agency.

§330.208 Duration of RPL registration.

(a) RPL registration expires 2 years from the date of reduction in force separation under part 351 of this chapter, or 2 years from the date the agency registers the RPL eligible because of recovery from a compensable work injury under §330.206(a)(3)(i) or (ii). An RPL eligible remains registered for the full 2-year period unless the registrant is removed from the RPL for a reason specified in §330.209.

(b)(1) OPM may extend the registration period when an RPL eligible does not receive a full 2 years of placement priority, for example, because of an agency's administrative or procedural error.

(2) Either the agency or the RPL eligible may request OPM to extend the registration period under paragraph (b)(1) of this section. The request must describe the administrative or procedural error that caused the RPL eligible to be registered for less than the full 2-year period. OPM may request additional information either from the agency or the RPL eligible in connection with any such request. OPM will notify both the agency and the RPL eligible of the decision to approve or deny an extension request. OPM's decision regarding an extension request is not subject to appeal under §330.214.

§ 330.209 Removal from an RPL.

(a) An RPL registrant is removed from the RPL at all registered grades or pay levels if the registrant:

(1) Declines or fails to reply to the agency's inquiry about an RPL offer of a career, career-conditional, or excepted appointment without time limit for a position having the same type of work schedule and a representative rate at least as high as the position from which the registrant was, or will be, separated;

(2) Receives a written cancellation, rescission, or modification to:

(i) The RIF separation notice or Certification of Expected Separation so that the employee no longer meets the conditions for RPL eligibility in § 330.203(a); or

(ii) The notification of cessation of injury compensation benefits so that injury compensation benefits continue;

(3) Separates from the agency for any other reason (such as retirement, resignation, or transfer) before the RIF separation effective date. Registration continues if the RPL registrant retires on or after the RIF separation effective date. This paragraph does not apply to an RPL registrant under § 330.203(b);

(4) Requests the agency to remove his or her name from the RPL;

(5) Is placed in a position without time limit at any grade or pay level within the agency;

(6) Is placed in a position under a career, career-conditional, or excepted appointment without time limit at any grade or pay level in any agency; or

(7) Leaves the area covered by an overseas RPL (see 5 CFR part 301) or is ineligible for continued overseas employment because of previous service or residence.

(b) An RPL registrant is removed from the RPL at registered grades or pay levels with a representative rate at and below the representative rate of a position offered by the agency if the offered position is below the last grade or pay level held and the registrant:

(1) Declines or fails to reply to the agency's inquiry about an RPL offer of a career, career-conditional, or excepted appointment without time limit for a position meeting the acceptable conditions shown on the RPL registrant's application; or

(2) Declines or fails to appear for a scheduled interview.

(c) An RPL registrant removed from the RPL under paragraph (b) of this section at lower grades or pay levels than the last grade or pay level held remains on the RPL for positions with a representative rate higher than the offered position up to the grade or pay level last held, unless registration expires or otherwise terminates.

(d) Declination of time-limited employment does not affect RPL eligibility.

§ 330.210 Applying RPL placement priority.

(a) RPL placement priority applies to:

(1) Permanent and time-limited positions to be filled by competitive service appointment; and

(2) The grade or pay level at which the agency fills the position. If a position is available at multiple grades or pay levels, placement priority applies at the grade or pay level at which the position is ultimately filled.

(b) An agency must not effect a permanent or time-limited competitive service appointment of another individual if there is an RPL placement priority candidate registered for the vacancy, unless the action is listed as an exception in § 330.211.

(c) An agency must document that there are no RPL placement priority candidates for the vacancy when requesting a competitive certificate of eligibles under part 332 of this chapter. Similarly, an agency must offer the vacancy to any RPL placement priority candidate(s) before effecting an appointment under a noncompetitive appointing authority, such as under part 315 of this chapter.

(d) Once an agency has ensured there are no RPL placement priority candidates for a particular vacancy and documents in writing an employment offer that is accepted by another individual, the agency may fulfill that employment offer to that individual.

§ 330.211 Exceptions to RPL placement priority.

An agency may effect the following personnel actions as exceptions to § 330.210:

(a) Fill a vacancy with an employee of the agency's current permanent competitive service workforce through detail or position change, subject to the requirements of subpart F of this part;

(b) Appoint a 10-point preference eligible through an appropriate appointing authority;

(c) Appoint a current or former employee exercising restoration rights under part 353 of this chapter based on return from military service or recovery from a compensable injury or disability within 1 year;

(d) Appoint a current or former employee exercising other statutory or regulatory reemployment rights;

(e) Fill a specific position when all RPL placement priority candidates decline an offer of the position or fail to respond to a written agency inquiry about their availability;

(f) Convert an employee serving under an appointment that provides noncompetitive conversion eligibility to a competitive service appointment, including from:

(1) A Veterans Recruitment Appointment under part 307 of this chapter;

(2) An appointment under 5 U.S.C. 3112 and part 316 of this chapter of a veteran with a compensable service-connected disability of 30 percent or more; and

(3) An excepted service appointment under part 213 of this chapter;

(g) Reappoint without a break in service to the same position currently held by an employee serving under a temporary appointment of 1 year or less (only to another temporary appointment not to exceed 1 year or less);

(h) Extend an employee's temporary or term appointment up to the maximum permitted by the appointment authority or as authorized by OPM; or

(i) Appoint an individual under an excepted service appointing authority.

[75 FR 67593, Nov. 3, 2010, as amended at 77 FR 28215, May 11, 2012]

§330.212 Agency flexibilities.

An agency may provide the following flexibilities within its written RPL policies established under this subpart:

(a) Allow RPL eligibles to register only for certain sub-areas of a local commuting area when the agency has components dispersed throughout a large commuting area. However, an agency cannot deny registration throughout the local commuting area if the RPL eligible requests it.

(b) Suspend an RPL registration for all positions, permanent and time-limited, if the agency is unable, through documented written means, to contact the RPL registrant; however, the agency must reactivate an RPL registration when the registrant submits an updated application or otherwise requests reactivation in writing. Registration suspension and reactivation do not change the expiration date of the original registration period set in §330.208.

(c)(1) Modify the OPM or OPM-approved qualification standard used to determine if an RPL eligible is qualified for a position, provided the:

(i) Exception is applied consistently and equitably in filling a position;

(ii) RPL registrant meets any minimum educational requirements for the position; and

(iii) RPL registrant has the capacity, adaptability, and special skills needed to satisfactorily perform the duties and responsibilities of the position, as determined by the agency.

(2) Any modification to the qualification standard under paragraph (c)(1) of this section does not authorize a waiver of the selection order required under §330.213.

(d) Permit RPL eligibles to register for positions with work schedules different from the work schedule of the position from which they were, or will be, separated.

(e) Permit RPL registrants to update their qualifications or conditions for accepting positions during the RPL registration period. If an agency provides this flexibility in its RPL policies, the agency must update the RPL registrant's registration information within 10 calendar days of receipt of the registrant's written request. The updated registration information would apply only to those vacancies becoming available after the agency updates the RPL registrant's registration.

§ 330.213 Selection from an RPL.

(a) *Methods.* An agency must adopt one of the selection methods in paragraphs (b), (c), or (d) of this section for a single RPL. The agency may adopt the same method for each RPL it establishes or may vary the method by location, but it must adopt a written policy for each RPL it establishes and maintains. While an agency may not vary the method used for an individual vacancy, it may at any time change the selection method for all positions covered by a single RPL.

(b) *Retention standing order.* For each vacancy to be filled, the agency places qualified RPL placement priority candidates in tenure group and subgroup order in accordance with part 351 of this chapter. In making a selection, an agency may not pass over a candidate in tenure group I to select from tenure group II and, within a tenure group, may not pass over a candidate in a higher subgroup to select from a lower subgroup. Within a subgroup, an agency may select any candidate without regard to order of retention standing.

(c) *Numerical scoring.* (1) For each vacancy to be filled, the agency rates RPL placement priority candidates according to their job experience and education. The agency must use job-related evaluation criteria for the position to be filled that can distinguish differences in qualifications measured and must apply the criteria in a fair and consistent manner. The agency assigns the candidates a numerical score of at least 70 on a scale of 100, based on the evaluation criteria developed under this paragraph. The agency must grant 5 additional points to veterans' preference eligibles under 5 U.S.C. 2108(3)(A) and (B), and 10 additional points to veterans' preference eligibles under 5 U.S.C. 2108(3) (C) through (G).

(2) RPL placement priority candidates with an eligible numerical score are ranked in the following order:

(i) Veterans' preference eligibles having a compensable service-connected disability of 10 percent or more in the order of their augmented ratings, unless the position to be filled is a professional or scientific position at or above the GS–9 level, or equivalent; and

(ii) All other candidates in the order of their augmented ratings. At each score, candidates entitled to 10-point veterans' preference will be entered ahead of all other candidates, and those entitled to 5-point veterans' preference will be entered ahead of those candidates not entitled to veterans' preference.

(3) The agency must make its selection from among the highest three candidates available and may not pass over a veterans' preference eligible to select a nonpreference eligible.

(d) *Alternative rating and selection.* (1) For each vacancy to be filled, the agency may use alternative rating and selection procedures (also called category rating) as described in 5 U.S.C. 3319 and part 337 of this chapter. The agency assesses RPL placement priority candidates against job-related evaluation criteria and then places them into two or more pre-defined quality categories.

(2) To use this method, the agency must:

(i) Establish a system for evaluating RPL placement priority candidates that provides for two or more quality categories;

(ii) Define each quality category through job analysis conducted in accordance with the "Uniform Guidelines on Employee Selection Procedures" at 29 CFR part 1607 and part 300 of this chapter. Each quality category must have a clear definition that distinguishes it from other quality categories; and

(iii) Place candidates into the appropriate quality categories based upon their job-related competencies, knowledge, skills, and abilities.

(3) Veterans' preference must be applied as prescribed in 5 U.S.C. 3319(b) and (c)(2). Veterans' preference points as prescribed in paragraph (c)(1) of this section are not applied under this method.

(4) The agency must make its selection from the highest quality category in accordance with its category rating policy established under part 337 of this chapter.

(e) *Application-based procedure.* (1) An agency may adopt an application-based procedure which allows RPL registrants to apply directly for RPL placement priority under an advertised vacancy announcement. Before using this procedure, the agency must establish policies and procedures for:

(i) Informing RPL registrants of available vacancies;

(ii) Informing RPL registrants of acceptable application formats, including how to permanently change initial registration information and how to apply changes only to the specific vacancy announcement for which the application is made;

(iii) Determining the method under which the RPL registrant will be rated and ranked (paragraph (b), (c), or (d) of this section); and

(iv) Informing each RPL registrant who applies under this method whether he or she was determined to be an RPL placement priority candidate and the outcome of the selection process, if the candidate was referred for selection.

(2) RPL registrants may not be removed from the RPL for failure to apply for a vacancy under this paragraph. Registration continues until it expires or the registrant is removed from the RPL under § 330.209.

§ 330.214 Appeal rights.

An RPL registrant who believes the agency violated his or her reemployment rights under this subpart by employing another person who otherwise could not have been appointed properly may appeal to the Merit Systems Protection Board under the Board's regulations in part 1200 of this chapter.

Subpart C [Reserved]

Subpart D—Positions Restricted to Preference Eligibles

§ 330.401 Restricted positions.

Under 5 U.S.C. 3310, competitive examinations for the positions of custodian, elevator operator, guard, and messenger (referred to in this subpart as *restricted positions*) are restricted to preference eligibles as long as a preference eligible is available. For more information on these restricted positions, refer to the OPM Delegated Examining Operations Handbook.

§ 330.402 Exceptions to restriction.

(a) An agency may fill a restricted position with a nonpreference eligible under the following circumstances:

(1) By competitive examination when no preference eligible applies;

(2) By position change (promotion, demotion, or reassignment) to a position in the organizational entity (*i.e.*, the part of an agency from which selections are normally made for promotion or reassignment to the position in question) in which the nonpreference eligible is employed;

(3) By reemployment in the agency where the nonpreference eligible was formerly employed when he or she is being appointed from the Reemployment Priority List under subpart B of this part;

(4) By reinstatement in the agency where the nonpreference eligible was formerly employed when he or she was last separated because of disability retirement; or

(5) By reappointment of certain temporary employees as provided for in part 316 of this chapter.

(b) Except as indicated in paragraph (a) of this section, OPM must authorize any other agency noncompetitive action (e.g., under an authority specified in part 315 of this chapter) to fill a restricted position with a nonpreference eligible.

§ 330.403 Positions brought into the competitive service.

An agency may convert the appointment of a nonpreference eligible whose restricted position was brought into the competitive service under part 316 of this chapter, and who meets the requirements for conversion under part 315 of this chapter, to career or career conditional appointment.

§ 330.404 Displacement of preference eligibles occupying restricted positions in contracting out situations.

An individual agency and OPM both have additional responsibilities when the agency decides, in accordance with the Office of Management and Budget (OMB) Circular A–76, to contract out the work of a preference eligible who holds a restricted position. These additional responsibilities as described in §§ 330.405 and 330.406 are applicable if a preference eligible holds a competitive service position (other than in the Government Printing Office) that is:

(a) A restricted position as designated in 5 U.S.C. 3310 and § 330.401; and

(b) In tenure group I or II, as defined in § 351.501(b)(1) and (2) of this chapter.

§ 330.405 Agency placement assistance.

An agency that separates a preference eligible from a restricted position by reduction in force under part 351 of this chapter because of a contracting out situation covered in § 330.404 must, consistent with § 330.603, advise the employee of the opportunity to participate in available career transition programs. The agency is also responsible for:

(a) Applying OMB's policy directives on the preference eligible's right of first refusal for positions that are contracted out to the private sector; and

(b) Cooperating with State units as designated or created under title I of the Workforce Investment Act of 1998 to retrain displaced preference eligibles for other continuing positions.

§ 330.406 OPM placement assistance.

OPM's responsibilities include:

(a) Assisting agencies in operating positive placement programs, such as the Career Transition Assistance Plan, which is authorized by subpart F of this part;

(b) Providing interagency selection priority through the Interagency Career Transition Assistance Plan, which is authorized by subpart G of this part; and

(c) Encouraging cooperation between local Federal activities to assist these displaced preference eligibles in applying for other Federal positions, including positions with the U.S. Postal Service.

§ 330.407 Eligibility for the Interagency Career Transition Assistance Plan.

(a) A preference eligible who is separated from a restricted position by reduction in force under part 351 of this chapter because of a contracting out situation covered in § 330.404 has interagency selection priority under the Interagency Career Transition Assistance Plan, which is authorized by subpart G of this part.

(b) A preference eligible covered by this subpart is eligible for the Interagency Career Transition Assistance Plan for 2 years following separation by reduction in force from a restricted position.

Subpart E—Restrictions To Protect Competitive Principles

§ 330.501 Purpose.

The restrictions in this subpart are designed to prevent circumvention of the open competitive examination system defined in Civil Service Rule 1.3 (5 CFR 1.3). These restrictions limit an appointee's immediate movement to another position after appointment from a competitive certificate of eligibles.

§ 330.502 General restriction on movement after competitive appointment.

(a) An agency must wait at least 90 days after an employee's latest nontemporary competitive appointment before the agency may take the following actions:

(1) Promote an employee;

(2) Transfer, reinstate, reassign, or detail an employee to a different position; or

(3) Transfer, reinstate, reassign, or detail an employee to a different geographical area.

(b) Upon written request from an agency, OPM may waive the restriction against movement to a different geographical area when moving such an employee is consistent with open competition principles.

§ 330.503 Ensuring agency compliance with the principles of open competition.

OPM will review appointments made from competitive examinations and subsequent position changes to determine if agencies are complying with open competition principles. The fact that an agency waited 90 days to make the changes, as required under this subpart, is not an absolute protection. If OPM finds that an agency has not complied with these principles, either in an individual instance or on a program-wide basis, OPM will order an agency to correct the situation.

§ 330.504 Exception to the general restriction.

The restrictions in this subpart do not apply to a person who is eligible for a competitive appointment from a certificate of eligibles under part 332 of this chapter.

Subpart F—Agency Career Transition Assistance Plan (CTAP) for Local Surplus and Displaced Employees

§ 330.601 Purpose.

(a) An agency's Career Transition Assistance Plan (CTAP) provides intra-agency selection priority for the agency's eligible surplus and displaced employees. This subpart sets forth minimum requirements for agency plans and establishes requirements for CTAP selection priority.

(b) Consistent with these regulations and at their discretion, an agency may supplement these requirements to expand career transition opportunities to its surplus and displaced workers.

(c) With prior OPM approval, an agency may operate an alternate placement program that satisfies the basic requirements of this subpart as an exception to CTAP selection priority under this subpart. This provision allows agencies to adopt different placement strategies that are effective for their programs while satisfying employee entitlements to selection priority.

§ 330.602 Definitions.

For purposes of this subpart:

Agency means an Executive agency as defined in 5 U.S.C. 105.

CTAP eligible means an agency surplus or displaced employee who has a current performance rating of record of at least fully successful (Level 3) or equivalent. As used in this subpart, "CTAP eligible" and "eligible" are synonymous.

CTAP selection priority candidate means a CTAP eligible who applied for and was determined to be well-qualified by the agency and whom the agency must select over any other applicant for the vacancy, unless the action to be taken is listed as an exception under § 330.609.

Displaced describes an agency employee in one of the following two categories:

(1) A current career or career-conditional (tenure group I or II) competitive service employee at grade GS–15 (or equivalent) or below who:

(i) Received a reduction in force (RIF) separation notice under part 351 of this chapter and has not declined an offer under part 351, subpart G, of this chapter of a position with the same type of work schedule and a representative rate at least as high as that of the position from which the employee will be separated; or

(ii) Received a notice of proposed removal under part 752 of this chapter for declining a directed geographic relocation outside of the local commuting area (e.g., a directed reassignment or change in duty station).

(2) A current excepted service employee on an appointment without time limit at grade level GS–15 (or equivalent) or below who:

(i) Is covered by a law providing both noncompetitive appointment eligibility to, and selection priority for, competitive service positions; and

(ii) Received a RIF separation notice under part 351 of this chapter or a notice of proposed removal under part 752 of this chapter for declining a directed geographic relocation outside the local commuting area (e.g., a directed reassignment or a change in duty station).

Surplus describes an agency employee in one of the following three categories:

(1) A current career or career-conditional (tenure group I or II) competitive service employee at grade GS–15 (or equivalent) or below who received a Certification of Expected Separation under part 351 of this chapter or other official agency certification or notification indicating that the employee's position is surplus (for example, a notice of position abolishment or a notice of eligibility for discontinued service retirement).

(2) A current excepted service employee on an appointment without

time limit at grade GS–15 (or equivalent) or below who:

(i) Is covered by a law providing both noncompetitive appointment eligibility to, and selection priority for, competitive service positions; and

(ii) Received a Certification of Expected Separation under part 351 of this chapter or other official agency certification or notification indicating that the employee's position is surplus (for example, a notice of position abolishment or a notice of eligibility for discontinued service retirement).

(3) A current excepted service employee on a Schedule A or B appointment without time limit at grade level GS–15 (or equivalent) or below who is in an agency offering CTAP selection priority to its excepted service employees and who:

(i) Received a Certification of Expected Separation under part 351 of this chapter or other official agency certification indicating that the employee is surplus (for example, a notice of position abolishment, or notice of eligibility for discontinued service retirement); or

(ii) Received a RIF notice of separation under part 351 of this chapter or a notice of proposed removal under part 752 of this chapter for declining a directed geographic relocation outside the local commuting area (e.g., a directed reassignment or a change in duty station).

Vacancy means a vacant competitive service position at grade GS–15 (or equivalent) or below to be filled for a total of 121 days or more, including all extensions, regardless of whether the agency issues a specific vacancy announcement.

§ 330.603 Requirements for agency CTAPs.

(a) Each agency must establish a CTAP for its surplus and displaced employees. Each agency must send its plan, and any modifications, to OPM, Employee Services, after approval by an authorized agency official.

(b) Each agency must uniformly and consistently apply its CTAP and these regulations to all surplus and displaced employees.

(c) In addition to a description of the agency's selection priority policies required by § 330.604, a CTAP must describe the agency's policies with regard to how it will provide career transition services to all its surplus and displaced agency employees, including excepted service and Senior Executive Service employees. The plan must describe:

(1) The types of career transition services the agency will provide;

(2) Policies on employees' and former employees' use of transition services and facilities, including:

(i) Excused absences for transition-related activities;

(ii) Access to services or facilities after separation;

(iii) Orientation sessions on career transition services and information as described in § 330.608(a) and (b), respectively;

(iv) Retraining policies;

(v) Access to agency CTAP services and resources by all employees, including those with disabilities, those in field offices, and those in remote sites;

(vi) Access to other Federal, State, and local resources available to support career transition for employees with disabilities; and

(vii) Availability of employee assistance programs and services.

(d) An agency's CTAP must also describe the agency's policies and procedures for its Reemployment Priority List established under subpart B of this part and the Interagency Career Transition Placement Plan established under subpart G of this part.

§ 330.604 Requirements for agency CTAP selection priority.

In addition to the overall requirements of § 330.603, an agency's CTAP must describe:

(a) How the agency will provide CTAP selection priority to surplus and displaced employees for vacancies in the local commuting area before selecting any other candidate from either within or outside the agency;

(b) Procedures for reviewing CTAP eligibles' qualifications and resolving qualification issues or disputes;

(c) Decisions involving discretionary areas under § 330.607 (such as whether excepted service employees will receive CTAP selection priority, priority of surplus versus displaced employees, designation of agency components, and selection priority beyond the local commuting area); and

(d) When and how the agency will inform its surplus and displaced employees about CTAP eligibility criteria, as required by §330.608(b), how to apply for agency vacancies, and how to request CTAP selection priority.

§330.605 Agency responsibilities for deciding who is well-qualified.

(a) An agency must define what constitutes a well-qualified candidate for its specific vacancies, consistent with this subpart, and uniformly apply that definition to all CTAP eligibles being considered for the vacancy.

(b) An agency must conduct an independent second review and document the specific job-related reasons whenever a CTAP eligible is determined to be not well-qualified under the agency's definition. The agency must give the CTAP eligible the written results of this review as required by §330.608(e).

§330.606 Minimum criteria for agency definition of "well-qualified".

(a) At a minimum, the agency must define "well-qualified" as having knowledge, skills, abilities, and/or competencies clearly exceeding the minimum qualification requirements for the vacancy. The agency definition may or may not equate to the highly or best qualified assessment criteria established for the vacancy; however, the agency definition of "well-qualified" must satisfy the criteria in paragraph (b) of this section.

(b) Under an agency's definition of "well-qualified," the agency must be able to determine whether a CTAP eligible:

(1) Meets the basic eligibility requirements (including employment suitability requirements under part 731 of this chapter and any medical qualifications requirements), qualification standards (including minimum educational and experience requirements), and any applicable selective factors;

(2) Is physically qualified, with or without reasonable accommodation, to perform the essential duties of the position;

(3) Meets any special qualifying conditions of the position;

(4) Is able to satisfactorily perform the duties of the position upon entry; and

(5) At agency discretion, either:

(i) Rates at or above specified level(s) on all quality ranking factors; or

(ii) Rates above minimally qualified in the agency's rating and ranking process.

§330.607 Applying CTAP selection priority.

(a) An agency must not place any other candidate from within or outside the agency into a vacancy if there is an available CTAP selection priority candidate, unless the personnel action to be effected is an exception under §330.609.

(b) In accordance with the conditions of part 300, subpart E, of this chapter, an agency may not procure temporary help services under that subpart until a determination is made that no CTAP eligible is available.

(c) CTAP selection priority applies to a vacancy that:

(1) Is at a grade or pay level with a representative rate no higher than the representative rate of the grade or pay level of the CTAP eligible's permanent position of record;

(2) Has no greater promotion potential than the CTAP eligible's permanent position of record;

(3) Is in the same local commuting area as the CTAP eligible's permanent position of record;

(4) Is filled during the CTAP eligible's eligibility period; and, if applicable,

(5) Is filled under the same excepted appointing authority as the CTAP eligible's permanent position of record if the CTAP eligible is an excepted service employee and the agency CTAP provides selection priority in the excepted service.

(d) An agency may take actions under §335.102 of this chapter to place a permanent competitive service employee into a vacancy if there are no CTAP eligible employees in the local commuting area or if no CTAP eligibles apply for the vacancy.

(e) An agency component may place a component employee within the local commuting area in the vacancy after the component applies CTAP selection priority to its employees.

(f) If there are two or more CTAP selection priority candidates for a vacancy, the agency may place any of them. An agency may decide the specific order of selection among CTAP selection priority candidates. For example, an agency may:

(1) Provide a displaced candidate higher priority than a surplus candidate; or

(2) Provide an internal component candidate higher priority than another component's candidate.

(g) After an agency makes the vacancy available to its CTAP eligibles and meets its obligation to any CTAP selection priority candidates, the agency may place into the vacancy any other permanent competitive service candidate from within its workforce, under appropriate staffing procedures.

(h) An agency may provide CTAP selection priority to eligible employees from another commuting area after fulfilling its obligation to CTAP selection priority candidates in the local commuting area.

(i) An agency may deny a CTAP eligible future selection priority if the eligible:

(1) Declines an offer of a permanent appointment at any grade or pay level in the competitive or excepted service; or

(2) Fails to respond within a reasonable period of time, as defined by the agency, to an offer of a permanent appointment at any grade or pay level in the competitive or excepted service.

(j) Before appointing an individual from outside the agency's permanent competitive service workforce, the agency must follow the requirements of subparts B and G of this part.

§ 330.608 Other agency CTAP responsibilities.

(a) An agency must make a career transition orientation session available to all agency surplus and displaced employees with information on selection priority under this subpart and subparts B and G. Such orientation sessions may be in person or web-based through an agency automated training system or intranet.

(b) An agency must give each agency CTAP eligible written information on selection priority under its plan, explaining how to locate and apply for agency vacancies and request selection priority. The agency may meet this requirement by providing a copy of its CTAP established under § 330.603.

(c) An agency must take reasonable steps to ensure that agency CTAP eligibles have access to information on all vacancies, including how CTAP eligibles can apply, what proof of eligibility is required, and the agency definition of "well-qualified" for the vacancy.

(d) If the agency can document that there are no CTAP eligibles in a local commuting area, the agency need not post the vacancy for CTAP eligibles.

(e) An agency must provide a CTAP eligible who applied for a specific vacancy written notice of the final status of his or her application, including whether the eligible was determined to be well-qualified. The agency notice must include the results of the independent, second review under § 330.605(b), if applicable; whether another CTAP selection priority candidate was hired; whether the position was filled under an exception listed in § 330.609; and whether the recruitment was cancelled.

§ 330.609 Exceptions to CTAP selection priority.

An agency may take the following personnel actions as exceptions to § 330.607:

(a) Reemploy a former agency employee with regulatory or statutory reemployment rights, including the reemployment of an injured worker who either has been restored to earning capacity by the Office of Workers' Compensation Programs, Department of Labor, or has received a notice that his or her compensation benefits will cease because of full recovery from the disabling injury or illness;

(b) Reassign or demote an employee under part 432 or 752 of this chapter;

(c) Appoint an individual for a period limited to 120 or fewer days, including all extensions;

(d) Reassign agency employees between or among positions in the local commuting area (sometimes called job swaps) when there is no change in grade or promotion potential and no actual vacancy results;

(e) Convert an employee currently serving under an appointment providing noncompetitive conversion eligibility to a competitive service appointment, including from:

(1) A Veterans Recruitment Appointment under part 307 of this chapter;

(2) An appointment under 5 U.S.C. 3112 and part 316 of this chapter of a veteran with a compensable service-connected disability of 30 percent or more; and

(3) Make an excepted service appointment under part 213 of this chapter;

(f) Effect a personnel action under, or specifically in lieu of, part 351 of this chapter;

(g) Effect a position change of an employee into a different position as a result of a formal reorganization, as long as the former position ceases to exist and no actual vacancy results;

(h) Assign or exchange an employee under a statutory program, such as subchapter VI of chapter 33 of title 5, United States Code (also called the Intergovernmental Personnel Act), or the Information Technology Exchange Program under chapter 37 of title 5, United States Code;

(i) Appoint an individual under an excepted service appointing authority;

(j) Effect a position change of an employee within the excepted service;

(k) Detail an employee within the agency;

(l) Promote an employee for a period limited to 120 or fewer days, including all extensions;

(m) Effect a position change of a surplus or displaced employee in the local commuting area;

(n) Effect a position change of an employee under 5 U.S.C. 8337 or 8451 to allow continued employment of an employee who is unable to provide useful and efficient service in his or her current position because of a medical condition;

(o) Effect a position change of an employee to a position that constitutes a reasonable offer as defined in 5 U.S.C. 8336(d) and 8414(b);

(p) Effect a position change of an employee resulting from a reclassification action (such as accretion of duties or an action resulting from application of new position classification standards);

(q) Promote an employee to the next higher grade or pay level of a designated career ladder position;

(r) Recall a seasonal or intermittent employee from nonpay status;

(s) Effect a position change of an injured or disabled employee to a position in which he or she can be reasonably accommodated;

(t) Effect a personnel action pursuant to the settlement of a formal complaint, grievance, appeal, or other litigation;

(u) Reassign or demote an employee under § 315.907 of this chapter for failure to complete a supervisory or managerial probationary period;

(v) Retain an individual whose position is brought into the competitive service under part 316 of this chapter and convert that individual, when applicable, under part 315 of this chapter;

(w) Retain an employee covered by an OPM-approved variation under Civil Service Rule 5.1 (5 CFR 5.1);

(x) Reemploy a former agency employee who retired under a formal trial retirement and reemployment program and who requests reemployment under the program's provisions and applicable time limits;

(y) Extend a time-limited promotion or appointment up to the maximum period allowed (including any OPM-approved extensions beyond the regulatory limit on the time-limited promotion or appointment), if the original action was made subject to CTAP selection priority and the original announcement or notice stated that the promotion or appointment could be extended without further announcement;

(z) Transfer an employee between agencies under appropriate authority during an interagency reorganization, interagency transfer of function, or interagency mass transfer;

(aa) Appoint a member of the Senior Executive Service into the competitive service under 5 U.S.C. 3594;

(bb) Transfer an employee voluntarily from one agency to another under a Memorandum of Understanding or similar agreement under appropriate authority resulting from an interagency reorganization, interagency transfer of function, or interagency mass transfer, when both the agencies and the affected employee agree to the transfer;

(cc) Reassign an employee whose position description or other written mobility agreement provides for reassignment outside the commuting area as part of a planned agency rotational program; or

(dd) Transfer or a position change of an employee under part 412 of this chapter.

(ee) Convert an employee's time-limited appointment in the competitive or excepted service to a permanent appointment in the competitive service if the employee accepted the time-limited appointment while a CTAP eligible.

[75 FR 67593, Nov. 3, 2010, as amended at 77 FR 28215, May 11, 2012]

§ 330.610 CTAP eligibility period.

(a) CTAP eligibility begins on the date the employee meets the definition of *surplus* or *displaced* in § 330.602.

(b) CTAP eligibility ends on the date the employee:

(1) Separates from the agency either voluntarily or involuntarily;

(2) Receives a notice rescinding, canceling, or modifying the notice which established CTAP eligibility so that the employee no longer meets the definition of *surplus* or *displaced;*

(3) Is placed in another position within the agency at any grade or pay level, either permanent or time-limited, before the agency separates the employee; or

(4) Is appointed to a career, career-conditional, or excepted appointment without time limit in any agency at any grade or pay level.

§ 330.611 Establishing CTAP selection priority.

(a) CTAP selection priority for a specific agency vacancy begins when:

(1) The CTAP eligible submits all required application materials, including proof of eligibility, within agency-established timeframes; and,

(2) The agency determines the eligible is well-qualified for the vacancy.

(b) An agency may allow CTAP eligible employees to become CTAP selection priority candidates for positions in other local commuting areas only if there are no CTAP selection priority candidates within the local commuting area of the vacancy.

(c) An agency may deny future CTAP selection priority for agency positions if the CTAP eligible declines an offer of permanent appointment at any grade level (whether it is a competitive or excepted appointment).

§ 330.612 Proof of eligibility.

(a) The CTAP eligible must submit a copy of one of the documents listed under the definition of *displaced* or *surplus* in § 330.602 to establish selection priority under § 330.611.

(b) The CTAP eligible may also submit a copy of a RIF notice with an offer of another position, accompanied by the signed declination of the offer. The RIF notice must state that declination of the offer will result in separation under RIF procedures.

§ 330.613 OPM's role in CTAP.

OPM has oversight of CTAP and may conduct reviews of agency compliance and require corrective action at any time.

Subpart G—Interagency Career Transition Assistance Plan (ICTAP) for Displaced Employees

§ 330.701 Purpose.

The Interagency Career Transition Assistance Program (ICTAP) provides eligible displaced Federal employees with interagency selection priority for vacancies in agencies that are filling positions from outside their respective permanent competitive service workforces. The ICTAP selection priority does not apply in the ICTAP eligible's current or former agency and it does not prohibit movement of permanent competitive service employees within an agency, as permitted by subpart F of this part. This subpart establishes requirements for ICTAP selection priority.

§ 330.702 Definitions.

In this subpart:

Agency means an Executive agency as defined in 5 U.S.C. 105.

Displaced describes an individual in one of the following categories:

(1) A current career or career-conditional (tenure group I or II) competitive service employee of any agency at grade GS–15 (or equivalent) or below whose current performance rating of record is at least fully successful (Level 3) or equivalent and who:

(i) Received a reduction in force (RIF) separation notice under part 351 of this chapter and has not declined an offer under part 351, subpart G, of this chapter of a position with the same type of work schedule and a representative rate at least as high as that of the position from which the employee will be separated; or

(ii) Received a notice of proposed removal under part 752 of this chapter for declining a directed geographic relocation outside the local commuting area (e.g., a directed reassignment or a change in duty station).

(2) A former career or career-conditional (tenure group I or II) competitive service employee of any agency at grade GS–15 (or equivalent) or below whose last performance rating of record was at least fully successful (Level 3) or equivalent who was either:

(i) Separated by RIF under part 351 of this chapter and did not decline an offer under part 351, subpart G, of this chapter of a position with the same type of work schedule and a representative rate at least as high as that of the position from which the employee was separated; or

(ii) Removed under part 752 of this chapter for declining a directed geographic relocation outside the local commuting area (e.g., a directed reassignment or a change in duty station).

(3) A former career or career-conditional employee of any agency who was separated because of a compensable work-related injury or illness as provided under 5 U.S.C. chapter 81, subchapter I, whose compensation was terminated and who has received certification from the former employing agency that it is unable to place the employee as required by part 353 of this chapter.

(4) A former career or career-conditional (tenure group I or II) competitive service employee of any agency who retired with a disability annuity under 5 U.S.C. 8337 or 8451 and who has received notification from OPM that the disability annuity has been or will be terminated.

(5) A former Military Reserve Technician or National Guard Technician receiving a special disability retirement annuity under 5 U.S.C. 8337(h) or 8456 and who has certification of such annuity from the military department or National Guard Bureau.

(6) A current or former excepted service employee on an appointment without time limit at grade GS–15 (or equivalent) or below whose current or last performance rating of record is or was at least fully successful (Level 3) or equivalent and who:

(i) Has been provided by law with both noncompetitive appointment eligibility and selection priority for competitive service positions; and

(ii) Has received a RIF separation notice under part 351 of this chapter or notice of proposed removal under part 752 of this chapter for declining a directed geographic relocation outside the local commuting area (e.g., a directed reassignment or a change in duty station) or has been separated by RIF procedures or removed for declining a geographic relocation outside the local commuting area.

ICTAP eligible means an individual who meets the definition of *displaced*. As used in this subpart, "ICTAP eligible" and "eligible" are synonymous.

ICTAP selection priority candidate means an ICTAP eligible who applied for a vacancy, was determined by the agency to be well-qualified for that vacancy, and who the agency must select over any other candidate from outside the agency's current competitive service workforce for the vacancy, unless the action to be taken is listed as an exception under § 330.707.

Vacancy means a vacant competitive service position at grade GS–15 (or equivalent) or below to be filled for 121 days or more, including extensions.

§ 330.703 Agency responsibilities for deciding who is well-qualified.

(a) Agencies must define "well-qualified" for their specific vacancies, consistent with this subpart, and uniformly apply that definition to all

ICTAP eligibles being considered for the vacancy.

(b) Agencies must conduct an independent second review and document the specific job-related reasons whenever an ICTAP eligible is determined to be not well-qualified for the vacancy under the agency's definition. An agency must give the ICTAP eligible the written results of this review as required by § 330.706(d).

§ 330.704 Minimum criteria for agency definition of "well-qualified".

(a) At a minimum, agencies must define "well-qualified" as having knowledge, skills, abilities, and/or competencies clearly exceeding the minimum qualification requirements for the vacancy. The agency definition may or may not equate to the highly or best qualified assessment criteria established for the vacancy; however, the agency definition of "well-qualified" must satisfy the criteria in paragraph (b) of this section.

(b) Under an agency's definition of "well-qualified," the agency must be able to determine whether an ICTAP eligible:

(1) Meets the basic eligibility requirements (including employment suitability requirements under part 731 of this chapter and any medical qualification requirements), qualification standards (including minimum educational and experience requirements), and any applicable selective factors;

(2) Is physically qualified, with or without reasonable accommodation, to perform the essential duties of the position;

(3) Meets any special qualifying conditions of the position;

(4) Is able to satisfactorily perform the duties of the position upon entry; and

(5) At agency discretion, either:

(i) Rates at or above specified level(s) on all quality ranking factors; or

(ii) Rates above minimally qualified in the agency's rating and ranking process.

§ 330.705 Applying ICTAP selection priority.

(a) An agency must not appoint any candidate from outside its permanent competitive service workforce if there is an ICTAP selection priority candidate available for the vacancy, unless the personnel action to be effected is an exception under § 330.707.

(b) ICTAP selection priority applies to a vacancy that:

(1) Is at a grade or pay level with a representative rate no higher than the representative rate of the grade or pay level of the ICTAP eligible's current or last permanent position of record;

(2) Has no greater promotion potential than the ICTAP eligible's current or last permanent position of record;

(3) Is in the same local commuting area as the ICTAP eligible's current or last permanent position of record; and

(4) Is filled during the ICTAP eligible's eligibility period.

(c) An agency may appoint any ICTAP selection priority candidate for a vacancy.

(d)(1) After an agency announces the vacancy and meets its obligation to any ICTAP selection priority candidates, the agency may appoint any other candidate from outside its current permanent competitive service workforce, under appropriate staffing procedures.

(2) An agency may make additional selections or reissue selection certificates in accordance with its merit promotion program without readvertising for ICTAP eligibles only if the additional selections are made from the applicant pool established by the original vacancy announcement, including readvertisements for the same vacancy, under which ICTAP eligibles had an opportunity to apply.

(e) An agency may deny an ICTAP eligible future selection priority for vacancies in that agency if the ICTAP eligible:

(1) Declines an offer of a permanent appointment at any grade or pay level in the competitive or excepted service; or

(2) Fails to respond within a reasonable period of time, as defined by the agency, to an offer or official inquiry of availability for a permanent appointment at any grade or pay level in the competitive or excepted service.

(f) An agency may deny an ICTAP eligible future selection priority for a position previously obtained through ICTAP if the eligible was terminated or removed from that position under part 432 or 752 of this chapter.

§ 330.706 Other agency ICTAP responsibilities.

(a) Before appointing any other candidate from outside the agency's permanent competitive service workforce, the agency must first fulfill its obligation to any employees entitled to selection priority under subparts B and F of this part.

(b) In accordance with the conditions of part 300, subpart E, of this chapter, an agency may not procure temporary help services under that subpart until a determination is made that no ICTAP eligible is available.

(c) An agency must announce all vacancies it intends to fill from outside its permanent competitive service workforce. Vacancy announcements must meet the requirements of subpart A of this part.

(d) An agency must provide an ICTAP eligible who applied for a specific vacancy written notice of the final status of his or her application, including whether the eligible was determined to be well-qualified. The agency notice must include the results of the independent second review under § 330.703(b), if applicable; whether another ICTAP selection priority candidate was hired; whether the position was filled under an exception listed in § 330.707; and whether the recruitment was cancelled.

§ 330.707 Exceptions to ICTAP selection priority.

An agency may take the following personnel actions as exceptions to § 330.705:

(a) Place a current or reinstate a former agency employee with RPL selection priority under subpart B of this part;

(b) Effect a position change of a current permanent competitive service agency employee;

(c) Appoint a 10-point veteran preference eligible through an appropriate appointing authority;

(d) Reemploy a former agency employee with regulatory or statutory reemployment rights, including the reemployment of an injured worker who either has been restored to earning capacity by the Office of Workers' Compensation Programs, Department of Labor, or has received a notice that his or her compensation benefits will cease because of recovery from disabling injury or illness;

(e) Appoint an individual for a period limited to 120 or fewer days, including all extensions;

(f) Effect a personnel action under, or specifically in lieu of, part 351 of this chapter;

(g) Appoint an individual under an excepted service appointing authority;

(h) Convert an employee serving under an appointment that provides noncompetitive conversion eligibility to a competitive service appointment, including from:

(1) A Veterans Recruitment Appointment under part 307 of this chapter;

(2) An appointment under 5 U.S.C. 3112 and part 316 of this chapter of a veteran with a compensable service-connected disability of 30 percent or more; and

(3) An excepted service appointment under part 213 of this chapter;

(i) Transfer an employee between agencies under appropriate authority during an interagency reorganization, interagency transfer of function, or interagency mass transfer;

(j) Reemploy a former agency employee who retired under a formal trial retirement and reemployment program and who requests reemployment under the program's provisions and applicable time limits;

(k) Effect a personnel action pursuant to the settlement of a formal complaint, grievance, appeal, or other litigation;

(l) Extend a time-limited appointment up to the maximum period allowed (including any OPM-approved extension past the regulatory limit on the time-limited appointment), if the original action was made subject to ICTAP selection priority and the original vacancy announcement stated that the appointment could be extended without further announcement;

(m) Reappoint a former agency employee into a hard-to-fill position requiring unique skills and experience to conduct a formal skills-based agency training program;

(n) Retain an individual whose position is brought into the competitive service under part 316 of this chapter and convert that individual, when applicable, under part 315 of this chapter;

(o) Retain an employee covered by an OPM-approved variation under Civil Service Rule 5.1 (5 CFR 5.1);

(p) Appoint an appointee of the Senior Executive Service into the competitive service under 5 U.S.C. 3594;

(q) Assign or exchange an employee under a statutory program, such as subchapter VI of chapter 33 of title 5, United States Code (also called the Intergovernmental Personnel Act), or the Information Technology Exchange Program under chapter 37 of title 5, United States Code;

(r) Detail an employee to another agency;

(s) Transfer employees under an OPM-approved interagency job swap plan designed to facilitate the exchange of employees between agencies to avoid or minimize involuntary separations;

(t) Transfer or reinstate an ICTAP eligible who meets the agency's definition of "well-qualified";

(u) Transfer an employee voluntarily from one agency to another under a Memorandum of Understanding or similar agreement under appropriate authority resulting from an interagency reorganization, interagency transfer of function, or interagency realignment, when both the agencies and the affected employee agree to the transfer; or

(v) Transfer or a position change of an employee under part 412 of this chapter.

[75 FR 67593, Nov. 3, 2010, as amended at 77 FR 28215, May 11, 2012]

§ 330.708 ICTAP eligibility period.

(a) ICTAP eligibility begins on the date the employee or former employee meets the definition of *displaced* in § 330.702.

(b) ICTAP eligibility ends 1 year from the date of:

(1) Separation by RIF under part 351 of this chapter;

(2) Removal by the agency under part 752 of this chapter for declining a directed geographic relocation outside the local commuting area (e.g., a directed reassignment or a change in duty station);

(3) Agency certification that it cannot place the employee under part 353 of this chapter; or

(4) OPM notification that an employee's disability annuity has been, or will be, terminated.

(c) ICTAP eligibility ends 2 years after RIF separation if eligible under subpart D of this part.

(d) ICTAP eligibility also ends on the date the eligible:

(1) Receives a notice rescinding, canceling, or modifying the notice which established ICTAP eligibility so that the employee no longer meets the definition of *displaced* in § 330.702;

(2) Separates from the agency for any reason before the RIF or removal effective date; or

(3) Is appointed to a career, career-conditional, or excepted appointment without time limit in any agency at any grade or pay level.

(e) OPM may extend the eligibility period when an ICTAP eligible does not receive a full 1 year (or 2 years under subpart D of this part) of eligibility, for example, because of administrative or procedural error.

(f) ICTAP eligibility for a former Military Reserve Technician or National Guard Technician described in § 330.702 ends when the Technician no longer receives the special disability retirement annuity under 5 U.S.C. 8337(h) or 8456.

§ 330.709 Establishing ICTAP selection priority.

ICTAP selection priority for a specific vacancy begins when:

(a) The ICTAP eligible submits all required application materials, including proof of eligibility, within agency-established timeframes; and

(b) The agency determines the eligible is well-qualified for the vacancy.

§ 330.710 Proof of eligibility.

(a) The ICTAP eligible must submit a copy of one of the documents listed under paragraphs (1) or (3) through (6) of the definition of *displaced* in § 330.702, as applicable, to establish selection priority under § 330.709. To establish selection priority under the paragraph (2) of the definition of *displaced* in § 330.702, the ICTAP eligible must submit documentation of the separation or removal, as applicable, for example, the Notification of Personnel Action, SF 50.

(b) The ICTAP eligible may also submit a copy of the RIF notice with an offer of another position accompanied by the signed declination of that offer. The RIF notice must state that declination of the offer will result in separation under RIF procedures.

§ 330.711 OPM's role in ICTAP.

OPM has oversight of ICTAP and may conduct reviews of agency compliance and require corrective action at any time.

Subparts H–I [Reserved]

Subpart J—Prohibited Practices

§ 330.1001 Withdrawal from competition.

An applicant for competitive examination, an eligible on a register, and an officer or employee in the executive branch of the Government may not persuade, induce, or coerce, or attempt to persuade, induce, or coerce, directly or indirectly, a prospective applicant to withhold filing application, or an applicant or eligible to withdraw from competition or eligibility, for a position in the competitive service, for the purpose of improving or injuring the prospects of an applicant or eligible for appointment. OPM will cancel the application or eligibility of an applicant or eligible who violates this section, and will impose such other penalty as it considers appropriate.

Subparts K–L [Reserved]

Subpart M—Timing of Background Investigations

SOURCE: 81 FR 86561, Dec. 1, 2016, unless otherwise noted.

§ 330.1300 Timing of suitability inquiries in competitive hiring.

A hiring agency may not make specific inquiries concerning an applicant's criminal or credit background of the sort asked on the OF–306 or other forms used to conduct suitability investigations for Federal employment (*i.e.*, inquiries into an applicant's criminal or adverse credit history) unless the hiring agency has made a conditional offer of employment to the applicant. Agencies may make inquiries into an applicant's Selective Service registration, military service, citizenship status, or previous work history, prior to making a conditional offer of employment to an applicant.

However, in certain situations, agencies may have a business need to obtain information about the background of applicants earlier in the hiring process to determine if they meet the qualifications requirements or are suitable for the position being filled. If so, agencies must request an exception from the Office of Personnel Management in order to determine an applicant's ability to meet qualifications or suitability for Federal employment prior to making a conditional offer of employment to the applicant(s). OPM will grant exceptions only when the agency demonstrates specific job-related reasons why the agency needs to evaluate an applicant's criminal or adverse credit history earlier in the process or consider the disqualification of candidates with criminal backgrounds or other conduct issues from particular types of positions. OPM will consider such factors as, but not limited to, the nature of the position being filled and whether a clean criminal history record would be essential to the ability to perform one of the duties of the position effectively. OPM may also consider positions for which the expense of completing the examination makes it appropriate to adjudicate suitability at the outset of the process (e.g., a position that requires that an applicant complete a rigorous training regimen and pass an examination based upon the training before his or her selection can be finalized). A hiring agency must request and receive an OPM-approved exception prior to issuing public notice for a position for which the agency will collect background information prior to completion of the assessment process and the making of a conditional offer of employment.

PART 332—RECRUITMENT AND SELECTION THROUGH COMPETITIVE EXAMINATION

AUTHORITY: 5 U.S.C. 1103, 1104, 1302, 2108, 3301, 3302, 3304, 3312, 3317, 3318, 3319; sec. 2(d), Pub. L. 114–137, 130 Stat. 310; E.O. 10577, 19 FR 7521, 3 CFR, 1954–1958 Comp., p. 218.

SOURCE: 33 FR 12426, Sept. 4, 1968, unless otherwise noted.

Subpart A—General Provisions

§ 332.101 General policy of competition.

(a) Examinations for entrance into the competitive service shall be open competitive, except that OPM may authorize noncompetitive examinations when sufficient competent persons do not compete.

(b) An examination for promotion, demotion, reassignment, transfer, or reinstatement may be a noncompetitive examination.

§ 332.102 Definitions.

In this part:

Active military duty has the meaning given that term in 5 CFR 211.102(f).

Certificate means a list of eligibles from which an appointing officer selects one or more applicants for appointment.

Objection means an agency's request to remove a candidate from consideration on a particular certificate.

Pass over request means an objection filed against a preference eligible that results in the selection of a non-preference eligible.

[74 FR 30461, June 26, 2009]

Subpart B [Reserved]

Subpart C—Period of Competition and Eligibility

GENERAL

§ 332.301 Termination of eligibility.

(a) Except as provided in paragraph (b) of this section, a person's eligibility on a register is terminated when:

(1) He accepts a career or career-conditional appointment from the register; or

(2) OPM terminates the eligibility of all persons on the register.

(b) OPM may determine that in particular types of cases eligibility may not be terminated in less than 1 year. OPM shall publish the conditions under which eligibility may not be terminated in less than 1 year.

[33 FR 12426, Sept. 4, 1968, as amended at 66 FR 66710, Dec. 27, 2001]

ACCEPTANCE OF APPLICATIONS AFTER CLOSING DATE OF EXAMINATIONS

§ 332.311 Quarterly examinations.

(a) A 10-point preference eligible is entitled to file an application at any time for an examination for any position for which OPM maintains a register, for which a register is about to be established, or for which a nontemporary appointment was made in the preceding three years. For the purposes of this paragraph OPM shall hold an examination not later than the quarterly period succeeding that in which the application is filed.

(b) When there is no appropriate existing register, OPM may establish special registers containing the names of eligibles from the quarterly examinations authorized by paragraph (a) of this section, together with the names of eligibles described in § 332.322, and use these registers for certification to fill appropriate vacancies.

[35 FR 414, Jan. 13, 1970, as amended at 41 FR 22549, June 4, 1976]

§ 332.312 Applicants in military or overseas service.

Subject to the time limits and other conditions published by OPM in its operating manuals, the following persons are entitled to file applications for open competitive examinations after the closing date for receipt of applications when there is an existing register or a register about to be established:

(a) A person who could not file an application during the filing period, or appear for an assembled examination, because of military service, or hospitalization continuing for 1 year or less following discharge from military service;

(b) An employee of the Federal Government who, as a member of a reserve unit of the military service, could not file an application during the filing period, or appear for an assembled examination, because of active duty beyond 15 days with the military service even though the duty is designated for training purposes; and

(c) A United States citizen who could not file an application during the filing period, or appear for an assembled examination, because of overseas service with a Federal agency or with an international organization in which the United States Government participates.

[33 FR 12426, Sept. 4, 1968, as amended at 66 FR 66710, Dec. 27, 2001]

§ 332.313 Preference eligibles separated from competitive positions.

The following persons are entitled to have their names entered on an appropriate existing register in the order prescribed by § 332.401 if they were last employed under career or career-conditional appointments:

(a) A preference eligible who is declared eligible therefor after appeal from furlough or discharge; and

(b) A preference eligible who has been furloughed or separated without delinquency or misconduct and who applies within 90 days after furlough or separation.

§ 332.314 [Reserved]

Restoration of Eligibility

§ 332.321 Preference eligibles who resigned from competitive positions.

A qualified preference eligible who resigned without delinquency or misconduct from career or career-conditional employment is entitled to have his name reentered on each register on which his name formerly appeared (or on a successor register) if he applies within 90 days after separation.

§ 332.322 Persons who lost eligibility because of military service.

(a) A person who lost a period of eligibility on a register because he has served on active military duty since June 30, 1950, is entitled to have his name restored to that register or a successor register when he meets the following conditions:

(1) He has not served more than four years following the date of his entrance on active military duty, exclusive of any additional service imposed pursuant to law. The date of entrance on duty means the first date between June 30, 1950, and July 1, 1971, on which he began a new period of active military duty, whether it was by original entry, reentry or extension.

(2) He is honorably separated from active military duty.

(3) He applies for restoration of eligibility within 90 days after discharge from active military duty or from hospitalization continuing for 1 year or less following separation from active military duty.

(4) He is still qualified to perform the duties of the position for which the register is used.

(b) When a person is entitled to have his name restored to a register under paragraph (a) of this section, OPM shall enter his name at the top of the appropriate group on the register if another eligible standing lower on the register on which his name formerly appeared was given a career or career-conditional appointment from that register. For professional and scientific positions in GS–9 and above and in comparable pay levels under other pay-fixing authorities, all eligibles are in one group. For all other positions, preference eligibles with a compensable service-connected disability of 10 percent or more are in one group and all other eligibles in another.

(c) When there is no appropriate existing register, OPM may establish special registers containing the names of persons entitled to priority of certification under paragraph (b) of this section, together with the names of eligibles described in § 332.311, and use these registers for certification to fill appropriate vacancies.

[33 FR 12426, Sept. 4, 1968, as amended at 35 FR 414, Jan. 13, 1970]

§ 332.323 Employees separated during probation.

An employee who is separated (voluntarily or involuntarily) without delinquency or misconduct during his probationary period is entitled to have his name restored to the register of eligibles from which he was appointed, if he applies for restoration while the register is still in use.

Subpart D—Consideration for Appointment

§ 332.401 Order on registers.

Subject to apportionment, residence, and other requirements of law and this chapter, OPM shall enter the names of eligibles on the appropriate register in accordance with their numerical ratings, except that the names of:

(a) Preference eligibles shall be entered in accordance with their augmented ratings and ahead of others having the same rating; and

(b) Preference eligibles who have a compensable service-connected disability of 10 percent or more shall be entered at the top of the register in the order of their ratings unless the register is for professional or scientific positions in GS–9 and above and in comparable pay levels under other pay-fixing authorities.

§ 332.402 Referring candidates for appointment.

OPM or a Delegated Examining Unit (DEU) will refer candidates for consideration by simultaneously listing a candidate on all certificates for which the candidate is interested, eligible, and within reach, except that, when it is deemed in the interest of good administration and candidates have been so notified, OPM or a DEU may choose to refer candidates for only one vacancy at a time. Selecting officials will receive sufficient names, when available, to allow them to consider at least 3 candidates for each vacancy.

[67 FR 7056, Feb. 15, 2002]

§ 332.403 Selective certification.

When there is no register appropriate as a whole for the certification of eligibles for a particular position, OPM may prepare a certificate from the most nearly appropriate existing register by the selective certification of eligibles qualified for the particular position in the order of their ranking on the register. Special overseas selection factors may also be used as a basis for selective certification from a register used for filling overseas positions. When appropriate, OPM may rerate the eligibles on the register on the basis of the particular requirements of the position.

§ 332.404 Order of selection from certificates.

An appointing officer, with sole regard to merit and fitness, shall select an eligible for:

(a) The first vacancy from the highest three eligibles on the certificate who are available for appointment; and

(b) The second and each succeding vacancy from the highest three eligibles on the certificate who are unselected and available for appointment.

§ 332.405 Three considerations for appointment.

An appointing officer is not required to consider an eligible who has been considered by him for three separate appointments from the same or different certificates for the same position.

§ 332.406 Objections to eligibles.

(a) *Delegated authority.* Except as specified in paragraphs (a)(1) and (a)(2) of this section, OPM has delegated to agencies the authority to adjudicate objections to eligibles, including pass over requests.

(1) OPM retains exclusive authority to approve the sufficiency of an agency's request to pass over preference eligibles who are thirty percent (30%) or more compensably disabled. Such persons have the right, in accordance with 5 U.S.C. 3318, to respond to the pass over request before OPM makes a final decision.

(2) OPM also retains the exclusive authority to approve the sufficiency of an agency's reasons to medically disqualify or medically pass over a preference eligible or disabled veteran in certain circumstances, in accordance with part 339 of this chapter.

(3) An agency must refer any objection (including a pass over request) that is based on material, intentional false statement or deception or fraud in examination or appointment to OPM for a suitability action where warranted, under part 731 of this chapter.

(b) *Standard for objections.* An agency is not required to consider an individual for a position when an objection to (including a request to pass over) the particular individual is sustained or granted. An objection, including a pass over request, may be sustained only if it is based on a proper and adequate reason. The reasons set forth for disqualification by OPM in part 339 of this chapter constitute proper and adequate reasons to sustain an objection. Similarly, the criteria for making suitability determinations in part 731 of this chapter constitute proper and adequate reasons to sustain an objection. In addition, reasons published by OPM in the Delegated Examining Operations Handbook constitute proper and adequate reasons to sustain an objection.

(c) *Sufficiency of the reasons for a pass over.* Subject to the exception set forth in paragraph (e) of this section, an agency may not pass over a preference eligible to select a non-preference eligible unless OPM or an agency with delegated authority also makes a determination that the sufficiency of the reasons is supported by the evidence submitted for the pass over request.

(d) *Agency's obligation while request for objection is pending.* Subject to the exception set forth in paragraph (e) of this section, if an agency makes an objection against an applicant for a position (including seeking to pass over the applicant), and the individual that the agency wishes to select would be within reach of selection only if the objection is sustained, or the pass over granted, that agency may not make a selection for the position until a final ruling is made.

(e) *Applicability of paragraphs (c) and (d).* Paragraphs (c) and (d) of this section do not apply if the agency has more than one position to fill from the same certificate and holds open (in the event the objection is not sustained or the pass over request is denied) a position that could be filled by the individual against whom an objection or a pass over request has been filed.

(f) *Procedures for objections and pass overs.* Agencies must follow the procedures for objecting to or requesting to pass over an eligible that are published by OPM in the *Delegated Examining Operations Handbook.*

(g) *No appeal rights to Merit Systems Protection Board (MSPB).* An individual may not appeal to the MSPB a decision by OPM or an agency with delegated authority to sustain an objection pursuant to this part, including a decision to grant a pass over request, irrespective of the reason for the decision.

[74 FR 30461, June 26, 2009]

§ 332.407 Restriction of consideration to one sex.

An appointing officer may not restrict his consideration of eligibles or employees for competitive appointment or appointment by noncompetitive action to a position in the competitive service to one sex, except in unusual circumstances when OPM finds the action justified.

[34 FR 5367, Mar. 19, 1969. Redesignated at 42 FR 61240, Dec. 2, 1977]

§ 332.408 Shared use of a competitive certificate.

(a) *General authority.* (1) A hiring agency may share a competitive service certificate issued under its delegated examining authority with one or more hiring agencies for a position(s) to be filled on a permanent or term basis. Positions filled on a term basis are subject to the provisions of 5 CFR part 316, subpart C. Positions may be full-time or other than full-time (*i.e.*, part-time, seasonal, on-call, and intermittent).

(2) Another Federal agency may make a selection from a certificate shared with it under paragraph (b) of this section only after it has considered individuals it is required to consider when filling positions from within its own workforce and other internal applicants under paragraph (c) of this section.

(3) All actions taken on a shared certificate must be made within the 240-day period beginning on the date the original hiring agency issued the certificate of eligibles. This period cannot be extended.

(4) The original hiring agency and any receiving agency using a shared certificate must each maintain case file documentation sufficient for each agency to reconstruct its own use of the certificate in accordance with the *Delegated Examining Operations Handbook*, and must safeguard testing and examination materials, examination results, and the names of applicants from disclosure to other persons in accordance with § 300.201 of this chapter.

(5) All actions taken on competitive certificates must be done in accordance with the *Delegated Examining Operations Handbook* and all applicable regulations in this part and part 337 of this chapter.

(6) Agencies sharing certificates must keep records of the instances of sharing certificates and/or using shared certificates.

(b) *Requirements for the original hiring agency.* (1) A hiring agency may share a competitive certificate it has issued under § 332.402 (for traditional rating and ranking) or under 5 CFR 337.303 (for category rating) with one or more hiring agencies for use in filling a position(s) if:

(i) The original hiring agency intends to use the certificate for its own hiring;

(ii) The original hiring agency has provided notice within the job opportunity announcement for the original vacancy that the resulting list of eligible candidates may be used by one or more hiring agencies;

(iii) The original hiring agency has provided an opportunity for applicants to opt-in to have their applications and other personal information shared with one or more hiring agencies;

(iv) The original hiring agency's objections to eligibles or requests to pass over preference eligibles on the certificate under § 332.406 or § 337.304 of this chapter have been resolved by that agency's Delegated Examining Unit;

(v) The original hiring agency has either made a selection from the certificate or has made no selection from the certificate, and has documented its reason for non-selection; and

(vi) The Delegated Examining Unit of the original hiring agency has closed and audited the certificate in accordance with the procedures in the *Delegated Examining Operations Handbook.*

(2) When sharing a certificate of eligibles, the original hiring agency must share all documentation pertaining to the creation of that certificate, including but not limited to the job analysis, testing and examination materials, the job opportunity announcement, and applications, as relevant, and must safeguard any personally identifiable information not needed for effective use of the certificate by the receiving agency. The original hiring agency must share the certificate of eligibles in its original form in order to retain the original ordering of the certificate; must safeguard any personally identifiable information from unauthorized access during the transmission process; and must redact the names of applicants who did not opt-in to the shared certificate, and who therefore may not be considered by the receiving agency.

(3) The original hiring agency may share a certificate of eligibles with one or more agencies.

(4) If the original hiring agency determines that it has made an error that may affect selections by a receiving agency or agencies, it must notify each affected receiving agency.

(c) *Requirements for the receiving agency*—(1) *Vacancies that may be filled.* A receiving agency may use a shared certificate to fill a vacancy in the same occupational series, at the same grade level (or a corresponding rate or level of pay for a position excluded from the General Schedule), with the same full performance level, and in the same duty location as was listed on the original hiring agency's certificate. If the original hiring agency's certificate is for an interdisciplinary position as described in the *Delegated Examining Operations Handbook,* the receiving agency may use it to fill an interdisciplinary position. The receiving agency must verify through its job analysis that the minimum qualification requirements (including use of any selective placement factors) and the competencies, or knowledge, skills, and abilities, that were used for the original position are appropriate for the position to be filled.

(2) *Notification to individuals who applied to the original vacancy.* Before using a shared certificate, a receiving agency must notify the list of candidates of its receipt of their names and application materials and its intention of considering them for a position. The receiving agency must also inform these individuals of its requirement to consider its own employees as well as other individuals the agency is required to consider before consideration of anyone on the shared certificate. At a minimum, the notification must include the agency, position title, series, grade level or equivalent, and duty location.

(3) *Consideration of internal candidates.* Before making a selection from a shared certificate, a receiving agency must provide notice of its intent to fill the available position(s) to its own employees and other individuals the agency is required to consider, to provide these internal candidates the opportunity to apply consistent with the provisions of part 335 of this chapter, and to review the qualifications of the internal candidates.

(i) This notice and opportunity for internal candidates to apply is subject to applicable collective bargaining obligations (to the extent consistent with law). Nothing in this paragraph affects agencies' right to fill a position from any appropriate source under §§ 330.102 and 335.103 of this chapter.

(ii) Agencies are prohibited from providing an application period any longer than 10 days for internal candidates. This time limit cannot be waived or extended.

(iii) Before considering other candidates, a receiving agency must first provide for the consideration for selection required for individuals covered under its Career Transition Assistance Program and its Reemployment Priority List under part 330, subparts B and F, of this chapter.

(4) *Selection from the shared certificate.* After considering internal candidates, a receiving agency may consider candidates referred on the shared certificate.

(i) The receiving agency must consider candidates on a shared certificate independently of the actions of any other agency with which the certificate is simultaneously shared under paragraph (b)(3) of this section.

(ii) The receiving agency may not reassess the applicants for purposes of rating/ranking.

(iii) The receiving agency must provide selection priority to individuals eligible under the Interagency Career Transition Assistance Program under part 330, subpart G, of this chapter who applied to the original job announcement.

(5) *Time limit on selection from a shared certificate.* The receiving agency has 240 days from the date the certificate was issued (in the original hiring agency) to select individuals from the shared certificate.

(6) *Limit on further sharing by the receiving agency.* The receiving agency may not share or distribute the shared certificate to another Federal agency.

[82 FR 5339, Jan. 18, 2017]

PART 333 [RESERVED]

PART 334—TEMPORARY ASSIGNMENTS UNDER THE INTERGOVERNMENTAL PERSONNEL ACT (IPA)

AUTHORITY: 5 U.S.C. 3376; E.O. 11589, 3 CFR 557 (1971–1975)

SOURCE: 71 FR 54565, Sept. 18, 2006, unless otherwise noted.

§ 334.101 Purpose.

The purpose of this part is to implement title IV of the Intergovernmental Personnel Act (IPA) of 1970 and title VI of the Civil Service Reform Act. These statutes authorize the temporary assignment of employees between the Federal Government and State, local, and Indian tribal governments, institutions of higher education and other eligible organizations.

§ 334.102 Definitions.

In this part:

Assignment means a period of service under chapter 33, subchapter VI of title 5, United States Code;

Employee, for purposes of participation in this Program, means an individual serving in a Federal agency under a career or career-conditional appointment, including a career appointee in the Senior Executive Service, an individual under an appointment of equivalent tenure in an excepted service position, or an individual employed for at least 90 days in a career position with a State, local, or Indian tribal government, institution of higher education, or other eligible organization;

Federal agency as defined in 5 U.S.C. 3371(3) means an Executive agency, military department, a court of the United States, the Administrative Office of the United States Courts, the Library of Congress, the Botanic Garden, the Government Printing Office, the Congressional Budget Office, the United States Postal Service, the Postal Rate Commission, the Office of the Architect of the Capitol, the Office of Technology Assessment, and such other similar agencies of the legislative and judicial branches as determined appropriate by the Office of Personnel Management;

Indian tribal government as defined in 5 U.S.C. 3371(2)(c) means any Indian tribe, band, nation, or other organized group or community, including any Alaska Native village as defined in the Alaska Native Claims Settlement Act (85 Stat. 668), which is recognized as eligible for the special programs and services provided by the United States to Indians because of their status as Indians and includes any tribal organization as defined in section 4(c) of the Indian Self-Determination and Education Assistance Act;

Institution of higher education means a domestic, accredited public or private 4-year and/or graduate level college or university, or a technical or junior college;

Local government as defined in 5 U.S.C. 3371(2)(A) and (B) means:

(1) Any political subdivision, instrumentality, or authority of a State or States; and

(2) Any general or special purpose agency of such a political subdivision, instrumentality, or authority;

Other organization as defined in 5 U.S.C. 3371(4) means:

(1) A national, regional, Statewide, area wide, or metropolitan organization representing member State or local governments;

(2) An association of State or local public officials;

(3) A nonprofit organization which offers, as one of its principal functions, professional advisory, research, educational, or development services, or related services, to governments or universities concerned with public management; or

(4) A federally funded research and development center.

State as defined in 5 U.S.C. 3371(1) means a State of the United States, the

District of Columbia, the Commonwealth of Puerto Rico, the Trust Territory of the Pacific Islands, the Northern Mariana Islands, and a territory or possession of the United States; an instrumentality or authority of a State or States; and a Federal-State authority or instrumentality.

[71 FR 54565, Sept. 18, 2006, as amended at 77 FR 28215, May 11, 2012]

§ 334.103 Requirements for approval of instrumentalities or authorities of State and local governments and "other organizations."

(a) Organizations interested in participating in the IPA mobility program as an instrumentality or authority of a State or local government or as an "other organization" as set out in this part must have their eligibility certified by the Federal agency with which they are entering into an assignment.

(b) Written requests for certification must include a copy of the organization's:

(1) Articles of incorporation;

(2) Bylaws;

(3) Internal Revenue Service nonprofit statement; and

(4) Any other information which indicates that the organization has as a principal function the offering of professional advisory, research, educational, or development services, or related services to governments or universities concerned with public management.

(c) Federally funded research and development centers which appear on a master list maintained by the National Science Foundation are eligible to participate in the program.

(d) An organization denied certification by an agency may request reconsideration by the Office of Personnel Management (OPM).

§ 334.104 Length of assignment.

(a) The head of a Federal agency, or his or her designee, may make an assignment for up to 2 years, which may be extended for up to 2 more years if the parties agree.

(b) A Federal agency may not send an employee on an assignment if that person is a Federal employee and has participated in this program for more than a total of 6 years during his or her Federal career. OPM may waive this restriction upon the written request of the agency head, or his or her designee.

(c) A Federal agency may not send or receive an employee on an assignment if the employee has participated in this program for 4 continuous years without at least a 12-month return to duty with the organization from which the employee was originally assigned. Successive assignments with a break of no more than 60 calendar days will be regarded as continuous service under the mobility authority.

§ 334.105 Obligated service requirement.

(a) A Federal employee assigned under this part must agree, as a condition of accepting an assignment, to serve with the Federal Government upon completion of the assignment for a period equal to the length of the assignment.

(b) If the employee fails to carry out this agreement, he or she must reimburse the Federal agency for its share of the costs of the assignment (exclusive of salary and benefits). The head of the Federal agency, or his or her designee, may waive this reimbursement for good and sufficient reason.

§ 334.106 Requirement for written agreement.

(a) Before the assignment begins, the assigned employee and the Federal agency, the State, local, Indian tribal government, institution of higher education, or other eligible organization must enter into a written agreement recording the obligations and responsibilities of the parties, as specified in 5 U.S.C. 3373–3375.

(b) Federal agencies must maintain a copy of each assignment agreement form established under this part, including any modification to the agreement. The agency may determine the appropriate time period for retaining copies of its written agreements.

§ 334.107 Termination of agreement.

(a) An assignment may be terminated at any time at the request of the Federal agency or the State, local, Indian tribal government, institution of higher education, or other organization participating in this program. Where possible, the party terminating the assignment prior to the agreed upon date should provide 30-days advance notice along with a statement of reasons, to the other parties to the agreement.

(b) Federal assignees continue to encumber the positions they occupied prior to assignment, and the position is subject to any personnel actions that might normally occur. At the end of the assignment, the employee must be allowed to resume the duties of the employee's position or must be reassigned to another position of like pay and grade.

(c) An assignment is terminated automatically when the employer-employee relationship ceases to exist between the assignee or original employer.

(d) OPM has the authority to direct Federal agencies to terminate assignments or take other corrective actions when OPM finds assignments have been made in violation of the requirements of the Intergovernmental Personnel Act or this part.

§ 334.108 Reports required.

A Federal agency which assigns an employee to or receives an employee from a State, local, Indian tribal government, institution of higher education, or other eligible organization in accordance with this part must submit to OPM such reports as OPM may request.

PART 335—PROMOTION AND INTERNAL PLACEMENT

Subpart A—General Provisions

Sec.

Subpart B [Reserved]

AUTHORITY: 5 U.S.C. 2301, 2302, 3301, 3302, 3330; E.O. 10577, E.O. 11478, 3 CFR 1966–1970 Comp., page 803, unless otherwise noted, E.O. 13087; and E.O. 13152, 3 CFR 1954–58 Comp., p. 218; 5 U.S.C. 3304(f), and Pub. L. 106–117.

Subpart A—General Provisions

§ 335.101 Effect of position change on status and tenure.

(a) *Status.* A position change authorized by § 335.102 does not change the competitive status of an employee.

(b) *Tenure.* Except as provided in paragraph (c) of this section and § 316.703 of this chapter, a position change authorized by § 335.102 does not change the tenure of an employee.

(c) *Exceptions.* (1) A career-conditional employee who is promoted, demoted, or reassigned to a position paid under chapter 45 of title 39, United States Code, or required by law to be filled on a permanent basis becomes a career employee.

(2) A career employee who is promoted, demoted, or reassigned from a position paid under chapter 45 of title 39, United States Code, or required by law to be filled on a permanent basis to a position under the career-conditional employment system becomes a career-conditional employee unless he has completed the service requirement for career tenure.

[33 FR 12428, Sept. 4, 1968]

§ 335.102 Agency authority to promote, demote, or reassign.

Subject to § 335.103 and, when applicable, to part 319 of this chapter, an agency may:

(a) Promote, demote, or reassign a career or career-conditional employee;

(b) Reassign an employee serving under a temporary appointment pending establishment of a register to a position to which his original assignment could have been made by the same appointing officer from the same recruiting list under the same order of consideration;

(c) Promote, demote, or reassign an employee serving under an overseas limited appointment of indefinite duration or an overseas limited term appointment to another position to which an initial appointment under § 301.201, § 301.202, or § 301.203 of this chapter is authorized;

(d) Promote, demote, or reassign (1) a status quo employee and (2) an employee serving under an indefinite appointment in a competitive position, except that this authority may not be used to move an employee:

(i) From a position in which an initial overseas limited appointment is authorized to another position; or

(ii) To a position in which an initial overseas limited appointment is authorized from another position; and

(e) Promote, demote, or reassign a term employee serving on a given project to another position within the project which the agency has been authorized to fill by term appointment;

(f) Make time-limited promotions to fill temporary positions, accomplish project work, fill positions temporarily pending reorganization or downsizing, or meet other temporary needs for a specified period of not more than 5 years, unless OPM authorizes the agency to make and/or extend time-limited promotions for a longer period.

(1) The agency must give the employee advance written notice of the conditions of the time-limited promotion, including the time limit of the promotion; the reason for a time limit; the requirement for competition for promotion beyond 120 days, where applicable; and that the employee may be returned at any time to the position from which temporarily promoted, or to a different position of equivalent grade and pay, and the return is not subject to the procedures in parts 351, 432, 752, or 771 of this chapter. When an agency effects a promotion under a nondiscretionary provision and is unable to give advance notice to the employee, it must provide the notice as soon as possible after the promotion is made.

(2) This paragraph applies to a career, career-conditional, status quo, indefinite, or term employee and to an employee serving under an overseas limited appointment of indefinite duration, or an overseas limited term appointment.

[33 FR 12428, Sept. 4, 1968, as amended at 35 FR 13075, Aug. 18, 1970; 45 FR 24855, Apr. 11, 1980; 57 FR 10124, Mar. 24, 1992; 58 FR 59347, Nov. 9, 1993]

§335.103 Agency promotion programs.

(a) *Merit promotion plans.* Except as otherwise specifically authorized by OPM, an agency may make promotions under §335.102 of this part only to positions for which the agency has adopted and is administering a program designed to insure a systematic means of selection for promotion according to merit. These programs shall conform to the requirements of this section.

(b) *Merit promotion requirements*—(1) *Requirement 1.* Each agency must establish procedures for promoting employees that are based on merit and are available in writing to candidates. Agencies must list appropriate exceptions, including those required by law or regulation, as specified in paragraph (c) of this section. Actions under a promotion plan—whether identification, qualification, evaluation, or selection of candidates—must be made without regard to race, color, religion, sex (including pregnancy and gender identity), national origin, age (as defined by the Age Discrimination in Employment Act of 1967, as amended), disability, genetic information (including family medical history), marital status, political affiliation, sexual orientation, labor organization affiliation or nonaffiliation, status as a parent, or any other non-merit-based factor, unless specifically designated by statute as a factor that must be taken into consideration when awarding such benefits, or retaliation for exercising rights with respect to the categories enumerated above, where retaliation rights are available, and must be based solely on job-related criteria.

(2) *Requirement 2.* Areas of consideration must be sufficiently broad to ensure the availability of high quality candidates, taking into account the nature and level of the positions covered. Agencies must also ensure that employees within the area of consideration who are absent for legitimate reason, e.g., on detail, on leave, at training courses, in the military service, or serving in public international organizations or on Intergovernmental Personnel Act assignments, receive appropriate consideration for promotion.

(3) *Requirement 3.* To be eligible for promotion or placement, candidates must meet the minimum qualification

standards prescribed by the Office of Personnel Management (OPM). Methods of evaluation for promotion and placement, and selection for training which leads to promotion, must be consistent with instructions in part 300, subpart A, of this chapter. Due weight shall be given to performance appraisals and incentive awards.

(4) *Requirement 4.* Selection procedures will provide for management's right to select or not select from among a group of best qualified candidates. They will also provide for management's right to select from other appropriate sources, such as reemployment priority lists, reinstatement, transfer, handicapped, or Veteran Recruitment Act eligibles or those within reach on an appropriate OPM certificate. In deciding which source or sources to use, agencies have an obligation to determine which is most likely to best meet the agency mission objectives, contribute fresh ideas and new viewpoints, and meet the agency's affirmative action goals.

(5) *Requirement 5.* Administration of the promotion system will include recordkeeping and the provision of necessary information to employees and the public, ensuring that individuals' rights to privacy are protected. Each agency must maintain a temporary record of each promotion sufficient to allow reconstruction of the promotion action, including documentation on how candidates were rated and ranked. These records may be destroyed after 2 years or after the program has been formally evaluated by OPM (whichever comes first) if the time limit for grievance has lapsed before the anniversary date.

(c) *Covered personnel actions*—(1) *Competitive actions.* Except as provided in paragraphs (c)(2) and (3) of this section, competitive procedures in agency promotion plans apply to all promotions under § 335.102 of this part and to the following actions:

(i) Time-limited promotions under § 335.102(f) of this part for more than 120 days to higher graded positions (prior service during the preceding 12 months under noncompetitive time-limited promotions and noncompetitive details to higher graded positions counts toward the 120-day total). A temporary promotion may be made permanent without further competition provided the temporary promotion was originally made under competitive procedures and the fact that might lead to a permanent promotion was made known to all potential candidates;

(ii) Details for more than 120 days to a higher grade position or to a position with higher promotion potential (prior service during the preceding 12 months under noncompetitive details to higher graded positions and noncompetitive time-limited promotions counts toward the 120-day total);

(iii) Selection for training which is part of an authorized training agreement, part of a promotion program, or required before an employee may be considered for a promotion as specified in § 410.302 of this chapter;

(iv) Reassignment or demotion to a position with more promotion potential than a position previously held on a permanent basis in the competitive service (except as permitted by reduction-in-force regulations);

(v) Transfer to a position at a higher grade or with more promotion potential than a position previously held on a permanent basis in the competitive service; and

(vi) Reinstatement to a permanent or temporary position at a higher grade or with more promotion potential than a position previously held on a permanent basis in the competitive service.

(2) *Noncompetitive actions.* Competitive procedures do not apply to:

(i) A promotion resulting from the upgrading of a position without significant change in the duties and responsibilities due to issuance of a new classification standard or the correction of an initial classification error; and

(ii) A position change permitted by reduction-in-force procedures in part 351 of this chapter.

(3) *Discretionary actions.* Agencies may at their discretion except the following actions from competitive procedures of this section:

(i) A promotion without current competition of an employee who was appointed in the competitive from a civil service register, by direct hire, by noncompetitive appointment or noncompetitive conversion, or under competitive promotion procedures for an assignment intended to prepare the employee for the position being filled (the intent must be made a matter of record and career ladders must be documented in the promotion plan);

(ii) A promotion resulting from an employee's position being classified at a higher grade because of additional duties and responsibilies;

(iii) A temporary promotion, or detail to a higher grade position or a position with known promotion potential, of 120 days or less;

(iv) Promotion to a grade previously held on a permanent basis in the competitive service (or in another merit system with which OPM has an interchange agreement approved under § 6.7 of this chapter) from which an employee was separated or demoted for other than performance or conduct reasons;

(v) Promotion, reassignment, demotion, transfer, reinstatement, or detail to a position having promotion potential no greater than the potential of a position an employee currently holds or previously held on a permanent basis in the competitive service (or in another merit system with which OPM has an interchange agreement approved under § 6.7 of this chapter) and did not lose because of performance or conduct reasons; and

(vi) Consideration of a candidate not given proper consideration in a competitive promotion action.

(vii) Appointments of career SES appointees with competitive service reinstatement eligibility to any position for which they qualify in the competitive service at any grade or salary level, including Senior-Level positions established under 5 CFR Part 319—Employment in Senior-Level and Scientific and Professional positions.

(d) *Grievances.* Employees have the right to file a complaint relating to a promotion action. Such complaints shall be resolved under appropriate grievance procedures. The standards for adjudicating complaints are set forth in part 300, subpart A, of this chapter. While the procedures used by an agency to identify and rank qualified candidates may be proper subjects for formal complaints or grievances, nonselection from among a group of properly ranked and certified candidates is not an appropriate basis for a formal complaint or grievance. There is no right of appeal of OPM, but OPM may conduct investigations of substantial violations of OPM requirements.

[59 FR 67121, Dec. 29, 1994, as amended at 63 FR 34258, June 24, 1998; 70 FR 72067, Dec. 1, 2005; 79 FR 43922, July 29, 2014]

§ 335.104 Eligibility for career ladder promotion.

No employee shall receive a career ladder promotion unless his or her current rating of record under part 430 of this chapter is "Fully Successful" (level 3) or higher. In addition, no employee may receive a career ladder promotion who has a rating below "Fully Successful" on a critical element that is also critical to performance at the next higher grade of the career ladder.

[51 FR 8411, Mar. 11, 1986]

§ 335.105 Notice of job announcements to OPM.

Under 5 U.S.C. 3330, agencies are required to report job announcements to OPM for vacancies for which an agency will accept applications from outside the agency's work force. This requirement is implemented through part 330, subpart A of this chapter.

[66 FR 63906, Dec. 11, 2001, as amended at 75 FR 67605, Nov. 3, 2010]

§ 335.106 Special selection procedures for certain veterans under merit promotion.

Preference eligibles or veterans who have been separated under honorable conditions from the armed forces after completing (as determined by the agency) 3 or more years of continuous active military service may compete for vacancies under merit promotion when an agency accepts applications from individuals outside its own workforce. Those veterans selected will be given career or career conditional appointments under § 315.611 of this chapter.

[65 FR 14432, Mar. 17, 2000]

Subpart B [Reserved]

PART 337—EXAMINING SYSTEM

Subpart A—General Provisions

Subpart B—Direct-Hire Authority

Subpart C—Alternative Rating and Selection Procedures

AUTHORITY: 5 U.S.C. 1104(a)(2), 1302, 2302, 3301, 3302, 3304, 3319, 5364; 116 Stat. 2290, sec. 1413, Pub. L. 108–136, 117 Stat. 1392, as amended by sec. 853 of Pub. L. 110–181, 122 Stat. 3; sec. 2(d), Pub. L. 114–137, 130 Stat. 310; E.O. 10577, 19 FR 7521, 3 CFR, 1954–1958 Comp., p. 218.

Subpart A—General Provisions

§ 337.101 Rating applicants.

(a) OPM shall prescribe the relative weights to be given subjects in an examination, and shall assign numerical ratings on a scale of 100. Except as otherwise provided in this chapter, each applicant who meets the minimum requirements for entrance to an examination and is rated 70 or more in the examination is eligible for appointment.

(b) OPM shall add to the earned numerical ratings of applicants who make a passing grade:

(1) Five points for applicants who are preference eligibles under section 2108(3)(A) and (B) of title 5, United States Code; and

(2) Ten points for applicants who are preference eligibles under section 2108(3)(C)–(G) of that title.

(c) When experience is a factor in determining eligibility, OPM shall credit a preference eligible with:

(1) Time spent in the military service (i) as an extension of time spent in the position in which he was employed immediately before his entrance into the military service, or (ii) on the basis of actual duties performed in the military service, or (iii) as a combination of both methods. OPM shall credit time spent in the military service according to the method that will be of most benefit to the preference eligible.

(2) All valuable experience, including experience gained in religious, civic, welfare, service, and organizational activities, regardless of whether pay was received therefor.

[33 FR 12423, Sept. 4, 1968, as amended at 72 FR 12954, Mar. 20, 2007]

§ 337.102 Evaluating qualifications for employees who are in a retained grade.

(a) Employees who are in a retained grade must have the experience they gain subsequent to the downgrading action that placed them in a retained grade considered in the following manner. For placements during the period the employee is in a retained grade, agencies must consider the experience subsequent to the downgrading action to be either:

(1) At the level of the retained grade and in the series of the position which he or she occupied at the time of the downgrading; or

(2) At the grade and in the series of the position to which the employee is downgraded.

(b) Agencies must determine which experience to consider on the basis of which will most likely result in placement. For placements or promotions after the retained grade period, the experience is considered only at the grade level and in the series of the position to which the employee was downgraded.

[45 FR 18365, Mar. 21, 1980]

Subpart B—Direct-Hire Authority

SOURCE: 69 FR 33275, June 15, 2004, unless otherwise noted.

§ 337.201 Coverage and purpose.

OPM will permit an agency with delegated examining authority under 5 U.S.C. 1104(a)(2) to use direct-hire authority under 5 U.S.C. 3304(a)(3) for a permanent or nonpermanent position or group of positions in the competitive service at GS–15 (or equivalent) and below, if OPM determines that there is either a severe shortage of candidates or a critical hiring need for such positions. It is not required that this direct-hire authority be exercised by a delegated examining unit. Requests for direct-hire authority must be submitted by the agency's Chief Human Capital Officer (or equivalent) at the agency headquarters level. OPM will determine the length of the direct-hire authority based on the justification.

§337.202 Definitions.

In this subpart:

(a) A *direct-hire authority* permits hiring without regard to the provisions of 5 U.S.C. 3309 through 3318; part 211 of this chapter; and subpart A of part 337 of this chapter.

(b) A *severe shortage of candidates* for a particular position or group of positions means that an agency is having difficulty identifying candidates possessing the competencies or the knowledge, skills, and abilities required to perform the job requirements despite extensive recruitment, extended announcement periods, and the use, as applicable, of hiring flexibilities such as recruitment or relocation incentives or special salary rates.

(c) A *critical hiring need* for a particular position or group of positions means that an agency has a need to fill the position(s) to meet mission requirements brought about by circumstances such as, but not limited to, a national emergency, threat, potential threat, environmental disaster, or unanticipated or unusual event or mission requirement, or to conform to the requirements of law, a Presidential directive or Administration initiative.

§337.203 Public notice requirements.

Agencies must comply with public notice requirements as prescribed in 5 U.S.C. 3327 and 3330, and subpart A of part 330 of this chapter with respect to any position that an agency seeks to fill using direct-hire authority.

[69 FR 33275, June 15, 2004, as amended at 75 FR 67605, Nov. 3, 2010]

§337.204 Severe shortage of candidates.

(a) OPM will determine when a severe shortage of candidates exists for particular occupations, grades (or equivalent), and/or geographic locations. OPM may decide independently that such a shortage exists, or may make this decision in response to a written request from an agency.

(b) An agency when requesting direct-hire authority under this section, or OPM when deciding independently, must identify the position or positions that are difficult to fill and must provide supporting evidence that demonstrates the existence of a severe shortage of candidates with respect to the position(s). The evidence should include, as applicable, information about:

(1) The results of workforce planning and analysis;

(2) Employment trends including the local or national labor market;

(3) The existence of nationwide or geographic skills shortages;

(4) Agency efforts, including recruitment initiatives, use of other appointing authorities (e.g., schedule A, schedule B) and flexibilities, training and development programs tailored to the position(s), and an explanation of why these recruitment and training efforts have not been sufficient;

(5) The availability and quality of candidates;

(6) The desirability of the geographic location of the position(s);

(7) The desirability of the duties and/or work environment associated with the position(s); and

(8) Other pertinent information such as selective placement factors or other special requirements of the position, as well as agency use of hiring flexibilities such as recruitment or retention allowances or special salary rates.

(c) A department or agency head (other than the Secretary of Defense) may determine, pursuant to section 1413(a) of Public Law 108–136, as amended by section 853 of Public Law 110–181, that a shortage of highly qualified candidates exists for certain Federal acquisition positions (covered under section 433(g)(1)(A) of title 41, United States Code). To make such a determination, the deciding agency official must use the supporting evidence prescribed in 5 CFR 337.204(b)(1)–(8) and must maintain a file of the supporting evidence for documentation and reporting purposes.

[69 FR 33275, June 15, 2004, as amended at 70 FR 44847, Aug. 4, 2005; 74 FR 61263, Nov. 24, 2009]

§ 337.205 Critical hiring needs.

(a) OPM will determine when there is a critical hiring need for particular occupations, grades (or equivalent) and/or geographic locations. OPM may decide independently that such a need exists or may make this decision in response to a written request from an agency.

(b) An agency when requesting direct-hire authority under this section, or OPM when deciding on its own, must:

(1) Identify the position(s) that must be filled;

(2) Describe the event or circumstance that has created the need to fill the position(s);

(3) Specify the duration for which the critical need is expected to exist; and

(4) Include supporting evidence that demonstrates why the use of other hiring authorities is impracticable or ineffective.

§ 337.206 Terminations, modifications, extensions, and reporting.

(a) *Termination and modification.* On a periodic basis, for each direct-hire authority, OPM will review agency use of the authority to ensure proper administration and to determine if continued use of the authority is supportable. OPM will terminate or modify a direct-hire authority if it determines that there is no longer a severe shortage of candidates or a critical hiring need. Likewise, when an agency finds there are adequate numbers of qualified candidates for positions previously filled under direct-hire authorities, based on severe shortage of candidates, the agency is required to report this change of events to OPM. OPM may also terminate an agency's authority when the agency has used an authority improperly.

(b) *Extension.* OPM may extend direct-hire authority if OPM determines, based on relevant, recent, and supportable data, that there is or will continue to be a severe shortage of candidates or a critical hiring need for particular positions as of the date the authority is due to expire. In their requests for extensions of direct-hire authorities, agencies must include an update of the supporting evidence that demonstrated the need for the original authority.

(c) *Reporting requirement.* On a periodic basis, OPM may request information from agencies regarding their use of these direct-hire authorities. The requested information may include numbers of positions, title, series, and grade of positions advertised under the direct-hire authority, the number of qualified applicants, the specific qualification criteria, and the number of applicants appointed under the authority.

(d) No new appointments may be made under the provisions of section 1413 of Public Law 108–136 after September 30, 2012.

[69 FR 33275, June 15, 2004, as amended at 70 FR 44847, Aug. 4, 2005; 74 FR 61263, Nov. 24, 2009]

Subpart C—Alternative Rating and Selection Procedures

SOURCE: 69 FR 33276, June 15, 2004, unless otherwise noted.

§ 337.301 Coverage and purpose.

This subpart implements the category rating and selection procedures at 5 U.S.C. 3319. This law authorizes agencies with delegated examining authority under 5 U.S.C. 1104(a)(2) to develop a category rating method as an alternative process to assess applicants for jobs filled through competitive examining.

§ 337.302 Definitions.

In this subpart:

(a) *Category rating* is synonymous with alternative rating as described at 5 U.S.C. 3319, and is a process of evaluating qualified eligibles by quality categories rather than by assigning individual numeric scores. The agency assesses candidates against job-related criteria and then places them into two or more pre-defined categories.

(b) *Quality categories* are groupings of individuals with similar levels of job-related competencies or similar levels of knowledge, skills, and abilities.

§337.303 Agency responsibilities.

To use a category rating procedure, agencies must:

(a) Establish a system for evaluating applicants that provides for two or more quality categories;

(b) Define each quality category through job analysis conducted in accordance with the *"Uniform Guidelines on Employee Selection Procedures"* at 29 CFR part 1607 and part 300 of this chapter. Each category must have a clear definition that distinguishes it from other categories;

(c) Describe each quality category in the job announcement and apply the provisions of part 330, subparts B, F, and G of this chapter;

(d) Place applicants into categories based upon their job-related competencies or their knowledge, skills, and abilities; and

(e) Establish documentation and record keeping procedures for reconstruction purposes.

§337.304 Veterans' preference.

In this subpart:

(a) Veterans' preference must be applied as prescribed in 5 U.S.C. 3319(b) and (c)(7);

(b) Veterans' preference points as prescribed in §337.101 are not applied in category rating; and

(c) Sections 3319(b) and 3319(c)(7) of title 5 U.S.C. constitute veterans' preference requirements for purposes of 5 U.S.C. 2302(b)(11)(A) and (B).

[82 FR 5340, Jan. 18, 2017]

PART 338—QUALIFICATION REQUIREMENTS (GENERAL)

AUTHORITY: 5 U.S.C. 3301, 3302, 3304; E.O. 10577, 3 CFR, 1954–1958 comp., p. 218.

Subpart A—Citizenship Requirements

§338.101 Citizenship.

(a) A person may be admitted to competitive examination only if he is a citizen of or owes permanent allegiance to the United States.

(b) A person may be given an appointment in the competitive service only if he or she is a citizen of or owes permanent allegiance to the United States. However, a noncitizen may be given an appointment in rare cases under §316.601 of this chapter, unless the appointment is prohibited by statute.

(c) Paragraph (b) of this section applies to reinstatement and transfer as well as to other noncompetitive appointments, and to conversion to career or career-conditional employment.

[33 FR 12429, Sept. 4, 1968, as amended at 57 FR 10124, Mar. 24, 1992]

Subpart B [Reserved]

Subpart C—Consideration for Appointment

§338.301 Competitive service appointment.

Agencies must ensure that employees who are given competitive service appointments meet the requirements included in the Office of Personnel Management's Operating Manual: Qualification Standards for General Schedule Positions. The Operating Manual is available to the public for review at agency personnel offices and Federal depository libraries, and for purchase from the Government Printing Office.

[62 FR 44535, Aug. 22, 1997]

Subparts D–E [Reserved]

Subpart F—Age Requirements

§ 338.601 Prohibition of maximum-age requirements.

A maximum-age requirement may not be applied in either competitive or noncompetitive examinations for positions in the competitive service except as provided by:

(a) Section 3307 of title 5, United States Code; or

(b) Public Law 93–259 which authorizes OPM to establish a maximum-age requirement after determining that age is an occupational qualification necessary to the performance of the duties of the position.

[40 FR 42734, Sept. 16, 1975]

PART 339—MEDICAL QUALIFICATION DETERMINATIONS

AUTHORITY: 5 U.S.C. 1104(a), 1302(a), 3301, 3302, 3304, 3312, 3318, 3320, 3504, 5112; 39 U.S.C. 1005, Executive Order 10577, Rule II, codified as amended in 5 CFR 2.1(a).

SOURCE: 82 FR 5350, Jan. 18, 2017, unless otherwise noted.

Subpart A—General

§ 339.101 Coverage.

This part applies to—

(a) Applicants for and employees in competitive service positions; and

(b) Applicants for and employees in positions excepted from the competitive service when medical issues arise in connection with an OPM regulation that governs a particular personnel action, such as removal of a preference eligible employee in the excepted service under part 752.

§ 339.102 Purpose and effect.

(a) This part defines the circumstances under which OPM permits medical documentation to be required and examinations and/or evaluations conducted to determine the nature of a medical condition that affects safe and efficient performance.

(b) Personnel decisions based wholly or in part on the review of medical documentation, as defined below, and the results of medical examinations and evaluations must be made in accordance with appropriate sections of this part.

(c) Failure to meet medical (which may include psychological) standards and/or physical requirements established under this part means that the applicant or employee is not qualified for the position, unless reasonable accommodation or a waiver is appropriate, in accordance with §§ 339.103 and 339.204. An employee's refusal to be examined or provide medical documentation, as defined below, in accordance with a proper agency order authorized under this part, constitutes a basis for appropriate disciplinary or adverse action. After a tentative job offer of employment conditioned on completion of a medical examination, an applicant's refusal to be examined or provide medical documentation, as defined below, may result in the applicant's removal from further consideration for the position.

§ 339.103 Compliance with disability laws.

(a) The Americans with Disabilities Act (ADA) of 1990, as amended by the Amendments Act of 2008 (collectively the ADA), establishes prohibitions against discrimination and the requirements for reasonable accommodation that apply to the Federal Government through the Rehabilitation Act of 1973, as amended, 29 U.S.C. 791(f). Consequently, actions under this part must comply with the non-discrimination provisions of the Rehabilitation Act, the non-discrimination provisions of the ADA, and their implementing regulations.

(b) Use of the term "qualified" in this part must comply with the Rehabilitation Act, as amended, and the ADA, as amended. Specifically, a "qualified individual with a disability" means that the individual possess the requisite skill, experience, education, and other job-related requirements of an employment position that the individual holds or seeks, and can perform the essential functions of the position with or without reasonable accommodation.

§ 339.104 Definitions.

For purposes of this part—

Accommodation means *reasonable accommodation* as described in the ADA.

Arduous or hazardous positions means positions that are dangerous or physically demanding to such a degree that an employee's medical and/or physical condition is necessarily an important consideration in determining ability to perform safely and efficiently.

Medical condition means a health impairment which results from birth, injury or disease, including mental disorder.

Medical documentation or *documentation of a medical condition* means a copy of a dated, written and signed statement, or a dated copy of actual medical office or hospital records, from a licensed physician or other licensed health practitioner, as these terms are defined below, that contains necessary and relevant information to enable the agency to make an employment decision. To be acceptable, the diagnosis or clinical impression must be justified according to established diagnostic criteria and the conclusions and recommendations must be consistent with generally accepted professional standards. The determination that the diagnosis meets these criteria is made by or in coordination with a licensed physician or, if appropriate, a practitioner of the same discipline as the one who issued the documentation. An acceptable diagnosis must include the information identified by the agency as necessary and relevant to its employment decision. This information may include, but is not limited to, the following:

(1) The history of the medical condition(s), including references to findings from previous examinations, treatment, and responses to treatment;

(2) Clinical findings from the most recent medical evaluation, including any of the following: Findings of physical examination; results of laboratory tests; X-rays; EKGs and/or other special evaluations or diagnostic procedures; and, in the case of psychiatric examination or psychological assessment, the findings of a mental status examination and/or the results of psychological tests, if appropriate;

(3) Diagnosis, including the current clinical status;

(4) Prognosis, including plans for future treatment and an estimate of the expected date of full or partial recovery;

(5) An explanation of the impact of the medical condition(s) on overall health and activities, including the basis for any conclusion as to whether restrictions or accommodations are necessary and, if determined to be necessary, an explanation supporting that determination; and, either of the following:

(6) An explanation of the medical basis for any conclusion that indicates the likelihood that the applicant or employee will suffer sudden incapacitation or subtle incapacitation by carrying out, with or without accommodation, the tasks or duties of a specific position; or

(7) Narrative explanation of the medical basis for any conclusion that the medical condition has or has not become static or well-stabilized and the likelihood that the applicant or employee may experience sudden incapacitation or subtle incapacitation as a result of the medical condition. In this context, "static or well-stabilized" medical condition means a medical condition which is not likely to change

as a consequence of the natural progression of the condition, such as a result of the normal aging process, or in response to the work environment or the work itself.

Medical evaluation program means a program of recurring medical examinations or tests established by written agency policy or directive, to safeguard the health of employees whose work may subject them or others to significant health or safety risks due to occupational or environmental exposure or demands. For example, an agency policy or directive may include medical clearances and medical surveillance to test for occupational exposure to biological, chemical, and/or radiological hazardous agents, occupational diseases, and occupational risk.

Medical restriction is a medical determination that an applicant or employee is limited, or prevented from performing a certain type or duration of work or activity (e.g., standing and/or ability to concentrate) or motion (e.g., bending, lifting, pulling), because of a particular medical condition or physical limitation. The purpose of a medical restriction is to try to prevent aggravation, acceleration, exacerbation, or permanent worsening of the medical condition or physical limitation.

Medical standard is a written description of the minimum medical requirements necessary for an applicant or employee to perform essential job duties as a condition of employment.

Medical surveillance is the on-going systematic collection and analysis of health data to improve and protect the health and safety of employees in the workplace, and to monitor for health trends both in individual workers and in population of workers. Medical surveillance can include the tracking of occupational injuries, illnesses, hazards, and exposures, as well as laboratory and examination-based medical data, in order to identify findings that could provide an early warning of, or indicate the risk for, an occupational disease. Medical surveillance also is part of compliance with those Federal and state regulations that require medical monitoring when employees use or are exposed to certain hazardous materials.

Physical requirement is a written description of job-related physical abilities that are essential for performance of the duties of a specific position.

Physician means a licensed Doctor of Medicine or Doctor of Osteopathy, or a physician who is serving on active duty in the uniformed services and is designated by the uniformed service to conduct examinations under this part.

Practitioner means a person providing health services who is not a medical doctor, but who is certified by a national organization, licensed by a State, and/or registered as a health professional to provide the health service in question.

Subtle incapacitation means gradual, initially imperceptible impairment of physical or mental function, whether reversible or not, which is likely to result in safety, performance and/or conduct issues that may undermine the agency's commitment to maintaining a safe working environment for all employees and others.

Sudden incapacitation means abrupt onset of loss of control of physical or mental function(s), whether reversible or not, which is likely to result in safety, performance or conduct issues that may undermine the agency's commitment to maintaining a safe working environment for all employees and others.

Subpart B—Medical Standards, Physical Requirements, and Medical Evaluation Programs

§ 339.201 Disqualification by OPM.

OPM must review and decide upon an agency's request to pass over a candidate, who is a preference eligible, on medical grounds pursuant to § 339.306. OPM may deny an applicant employment by reason of physical or mental unfitness for the position for which he or she has applied. An OPM decision under this section or § 339.306 is separate and distinct from a determination of disability pursuant to statutory provisions for disability retirement under the Civil Service Retirement System and the Federal Employees' Retirement System.

§339.202 Medical standards.

OPM may establish and/or approve medical standards for a Government-wide occupation (*i.e.*, an occupation common to more than one agency) or approve revisions to its established medical standards. An individual agency may establish medical standards for positions that predominate in that agency (*i.e.*, where the agency has 50 percent or more of the positions in a particular occupation). Such standards must be justified on the basis that the duties of the positions are arduous or hazardous, or require a certain level of health status for successful performance when the nature of the positions involves a high degree of responsibility toward the public or sensitive national security concerns. The rationale for establishing the standard must be documented and supported by a study(ies) or evaluation(s) establishing the medical standard is job-related to the occupation(s). Medical standards established by agencies must be approved by OPM prior to implementation. Standards established by OPM or an agency must be:

(a) Established by written directive and uniformly applied, and

(b) Directly related to the actual performance and requirements necessary for the performance of the duties of the position.

§339.203 Physical requirements.

(a) An agency may establish physical requirements for individual positions without OPM approval when such requirements are considered essential for performance of the duties of a specific position. Physical requirements must be clearly supported by the actual duties of the position, documented in the position description, and supported by a study(ies) or evaluation(s) establishing physical requirement(s) is job-related to the occupation(s).

(b) An applicant or employee may not be disqualified arbitrarily on the basis of physical requirements or other criteria that do not relate specifically to performance of the duties of a specific position.

§339.204 Waiver of standards and requirements and medical review boards.

(a) An agency must waive a medical standard or physical requirement established under this part when an applicant or employee, unable to meet that standard or requirement, presents sufficient evidence that the applicant or employee, with or without reasonable accommodation, can perform the essential duties of the position without endangering the health and safety of the applicant or employee or others. Additional information obtained by the agency may be considered in determining whether a waiver is appropriate. An agency may establish timeframes, in writing, for submission of initial or additional information for consideration, with allowance for reasonable extensions.

(b) Agencies may, but are not required to, establish medical review boards to help the agency provide a case-by-case, fact-based, individualized assessment whenever an individual is found to not meet agency medical standards or physical requirements. An agency may also use a medical review board as a forum for a higher level of review within the agency when medical questions or issues arise. If established, the Board is expected to recommend administrative actions that are consistent with applicable law, as well as applicable and current medical practice standards of care, through the combined expertise of its members.

(c) The use and composition of a medical review board will be determined by the agency. Upon request, an agency will provide to OPM information regarding the composition and use of medical review boards. OPM may issue guidance from time to time as to best practices with respect to the composition and use of such boards.

§339.205 Medical evaluation programs.

Agencies may establish periodic medical examinations, medical surveillance, or immunization programs by written policies or directives to safeguard the health of employees whose work may expose them or others to significant health or safety risks due to occupational or environmental exposure or demands. This may include the requirement to undergo vaccination with products approved by the Food and Drug Administration (e.g., for national security reasons or in order to fulfill the duties of a position designated as national security sensitive). The need for a medical evaluation program must be clearly supported by the nature of the work. The specific positions covered must be identified and the applicants or employees notified in writing of the reasons for including the positions in the program.

§ 339.206 Disqualification on the basis of medical history.

An employee or applicant may not be disqualified for any position solely on the basis of medical history. For positions subject to medical standards and/or physical requirements, and for positions under medical evaluation programs, a history of a particular medical condition may result in medical disqualification only if the condition at issue is itself disqualifying, recurrence of the condition is based on reasonable medical judgment, and the duties of the position are such that a recurrence of the condition would pose a significant risk of substantial harm to the health and safety of the applicant or employee or others that cannot be eliminated or reduced by reasonable accommodation or any other agency efforts to mitigate risk.

Subpart C—Medical Examinations

§ 339.301 Authority to require an examination.

(a) A routine pre-employment medical examination is appropriate only for a position with specific medical standards and/or physical requirements, or that is covered by a medical evaluation program established under this part.

(b) Subject to § 339.103, an agency may require an applicant or employee who has applied for or occupies a position that has medical standards and/or physical requirements, or is covered by a medical evaluation program established under this part, to report for a medical examination:

(1) Subsequent to a tentative offer of employment or reemployment (including return to work from medically based absence on the basis of a medical condition);

(2) On a regularly recurring, periodic basis after appointment in accordance with § 339.205; or

(3) Whenever the agency has a reasonable belief, based on objective evidence, that there is a question about an employee's continued capacity to meet the medical standards or physical requirements of a position.

(c) An agency may require an employee who has applied for or is receiving continuation of pay or compensation as a result of an injury or disease covered under the provisions of the Federal Employees' Compensation Act to report for an examination to determine medical limitations that may affect job placement decisions.

(d) An agency may require an employee who is released from his or her competitive level in a reduction in force under part 351 of this chapter to undergo a relevant medical evaluation if the position to which the employee has assignment rights has medical standards and/or physical requirements, that are different from those required in the employee's current position.

(e)(1) An agency may order a psychiatric examination (including a psychological assessment) only when:

(i) The result of a current general medical examination that the agency has the authority to order under this section indicates no physical explanation for behavior or actions that may affect the safe and efficient performance of the applicant or employee, the safety of others, and/or the vulnerability of business operation and information systems to potential threats, or

(ii) A psychiatric examination or psychological assessment is part of the medical standards for a position having medical standards or required under a medical evaluation program established under this part.

(2) A psychiatric examination or psychological assessment authorized under paragraphs (e)(1) of this section must be conducted in accordance with accepted professional standards by a licensed physician certified in psychiatry by the American Board of Psychiatry and Neurology or the American Osteopathic Board of Psychiatry and

Neurology, or by a licensed psychologist or clinical neuropsychologist, and may only be used to make inquiry into a person's mental fitness as it directly relates to successfully performing the duties of the position without significant risk to the applicant or employee or others, and/or to the vulnerability of business operation and information systems to potential threats.

§339.302 Authority to offer examinations.

An agency may, at its option, offer a medical examination (including a psychiatric examination or psychological assessment) in situations where the agency needs additional medical documentation to make an informed management decision. This may include situations where an employee requests, for medical reasons, a change in duty status, assignment, working conditions, or any other different treatment (including reasonable accommodation or return to work on the basis of full or partial recovery from a medical condition) or where the employee has a performance or conduct problem that may require agency action. Reasons for offering an examination must be documented. When an offer of an examination has been made by an agency and the offer has been accepted by the applicant or employee, the examination must be carried out in accordance with the authorities cited in §339.103. The results of the examination must also be used in accordance with the authorities cited in §339.103.

§339.303 Medical examination procedures.

(a) When an agency requires or offers a medical or psychiatric examination or psychological assessment under this subpart, it must inform the applicant or employee in writing of its reasons for doing so, the consequences of failure to cooperate, and the right to submit medical information from his or her private physician or practitioner. A single written notification is sufficient to cover a series of regularly recurring or periodic examinations ordered under this subpart. An agency may establish timeframes, in writing, for submission of medical documentation, with allowances for reasonable extensions.

(1) Refusal or failure to report for a medical examination ordered by the agency may be a basis for a determination that the applicant or employee is not qualified for the position. In addition, an employee may be subject to adverse action.

(2) Refusal or failure on the part of an applicant or the employee to authorize release of any results from an agency ordered or offered medical examination issued in accordance with §§339.301 or 339.302, or the results of any previous medical treatments or evaluations relative to the identified medical issue, to authorized agency representatives, including the agency physician or medical review officer and/or independent medical specialists, may be a basis for disqualification for the position by the hiring agency. In addition, an employee may be subject to adverse action.

(b) The agency designates the examining physician or other appropriate practitioner, but must offer the applicant or employee an opportunity to submit medical documentation from his or her private physician or practitioner for consideration in the medical examination process. The agency must review and consider all such documentation supplied by the private physician or practitioner. The applicant or employee must authorize release of this documentation to all authorized agency representatives. In situations where the medical documentation of the applicant or employee's private physician or practitioner is contradictory and cannot be resolved by the examining physician or the agency physician or medical review officer, the agency may, at its option, pursue another opinion from an appropriate specialist at agency expense. An applicant or employee also may, at his or her option, pursue another opinion from an appropriate specialist at his or her expense in the event of conflicting or contradictory medical documentation.

§339.304 Payment for examination.

(a) An agency must pay for all medical and/or psychological and/or psychiatric examinations required or offered by the agency under this subpart, whether conducted by the agency's physician or medical review officer, an independent medical evaluation specialist (e.g., occupational audiologist) identified by the agency, or a licensed physician or practitioner chosen by the applicant or employee. This includes special evaluations or diagnostic procedures required by an agency.

(b) Following conclusion of the initial medical, psychological, and/or psychiatric examination, the agency physician or medical review officer will render a final medical determination. In certain final medical ineligibility determinations, the agency physician or medical review officer may reference supplemental medical examination, testing or documentation, which the applicant or employee may submit to the agency for consideration and further review relative to potential medical eligibility. Under these circumstances, the applicant or employee is responsible for payment of this further examination, testing and documentation.

(c) An applicant or employee must pay to obtain all relevant medical documentation from his or her private licensed physician or required practitioners in instances where no medical examination is required or offered by the agency, but where the agency requests the applicant or employee to provide medical documentation relative to an identified medical or physical condition in question or where the agency needs medical documentation to render an informed management decision.

(d) An applicant or employee must pay for a medical examination conducted by his or her private licensed physician or practitioner where the purpose of the examination is to secure a change sought by an applicant (e.g., new employment) or by an employee (e.g., a request for change in duty status, reasonable accommodation, and/or job modification).

§ 339.305 Records and reports.

(a) Agencies will receive and maintain all medical documentation and records of examinations obtained under this part in accordance with part 293, subpart E, of this chapter.

(b) The report of an examination conducted under this subpart must be made available to the applicant or employee under the provisions of part 297 of this chapter.

(c) Agencies must forward to the Office of Workers' Compensation Programs (OWCP), Employment Standards Administration, Department of Labor, a copy of all medical documentation and reports of examinations of employees who are receiving or have applied for injury compensation benefits under 5 U.S.C. chapter 81, including continuation of pay. The agency must also report to OWCP the failure of such employees to report for examinations that the agency orders under this subpart. When the employee has applied for disability retirement, this information and any medical documentation or reports of examination must be forwarded to OPM.

§ 339.306 Processing medical eligibility determinations.

(a) In accordance with the provisions of this part, agencies are authorized to medically disqualify a nonpreference eligible. A nonpreference eligible so disqualified has a right to a higher level review of the determination within the agency.

(b) OPM must approve the sufficiency of the agency's reasons to:

(1) Medically disqualify or pass over a preference eligible in order to select a nonpreference eligible for:

(i) A competitive service position under part 332 of this chapter; or

(ii) An excepted service position in the executive branch subject to title 5, U.S. Code;

(2) Medically disqualify or pass over a 30 percent or more compensably disabled veteran for a position in the U.S. Postal Service in favor of a nonpreference eligible;

(3) Medically disqualify a 30 percent or more compensably disabled veteran for assignment to another position in a reduction in force under § 351.702(d) of this chapter; or

(4) Medically disqualify a 30 percent or more disabled veteran for noncompetitive appointment, for example, under § 316.302(b)(4) of this chapter.

PART 340—OTHER THAN FULL-TIME CAREER EMPLOYMENT (PART-TIME, SEASONAL, ON-CALL, AND INTERMITTENT)

AUTHORITY: 5 U.S.C. 3401 *et seq.*, unless otherwise noted.

SOURCE: 44 FR 57380, Oct. 5, 1979, unless otherwise noted.

Subpart A—Principal Statutory Requirements—Part-Time Employment

§ 340.101 Principal statutory requirements.

This subpart incorporates for the benefit of the user of the principal statutory requirements governing part-time career employment, as contained in 5 U.S.C. 3401–3408, and related provisions of Public Law 95–437.

SHORT TITLE

SEC. 1. This Act may be cited as the "Federal Employees Part-Time Career Employment Act of 1978".

CONGRESSIONAL FINDINGS AND PURPOSE

SEC. 2. (a) The Congress finds that—

(1) many individuals in our society possess great productive potential which goes unused because they cannot meet the requirements of a standard workweek; and

(2) part-time permanent employment—

(A) provides older individuals with a gradual transition into retirement;

(B) provides employment opportunities to handicapped individuals or others who require a reduced workweek;

(C) provides parents opportunities to balance family responsibilities with the need for additional income;

(D) benefits students who must finance their own education or vocational training;

(E) benefits the Government, as an employer, by increasing productivity and job satisfaction, while lowering turnover rates and absenteeism, offering management more flexibility in meeting work requirements, and filling shortages in various occupations; and

(F) benefits society by offering a needed alternative for those individuals who require or prefer shorter hours (despite the reduced income), thus increasing jobs available to reduce unemployment while retaining the skills of individuals who have training and experience.

(b) The purpose of this Act is to provide increased part-time career employment opportunities throughout the Federal Government.

"§ 3401. Definitions

"For the purpose of this subchapter—

"(1) 'agency' means—

"(A) an Executive agency;

"(B) a military department;

"(C) an agency in the judicial branch;

"(D) the Library of Congress;

"(E) the Botanic Garden; and

"(F) the Office of the Architect of the Capitol; but does not include—

"(i) a Government controlled corporation;

"(ii) the Tennessee Valley Authority;

"(iii) the Alaska Railroad;

"(iv) the Virgin Island Corporation;

"(v) the Panama Canal Company;

"(vi) the Federal Bureau of Investigation, Department of Justice;

"(vii) the Central Intelligence Agency; and

"(viii) the National Security Agency, Department of Defense; and

"(2) 'part-time career employment' means part-time employment of 16 to 32 hours a week under a schedule consisting of an equal or varied number of hours per day, whether in a position which would be part-time without regard to this section or one established to allow job-sharing or comparable arrangements, but does not include employment on a temporary or intermittent basis.

"§ 3402. Establishment of part-time career employment programs

"(a) (1) In order to promote part-time career employment opportunities in all grade levels, the head of each agency, by regulation, shall establish and maintain a program for part-time career employment within such agency. Such regulations shall provide for—

"(A) the review of positions which, after such positions become vacant, may be filled on a part-time career employment basis (including the establishment of criteria to be used in identifying such positions);

"(B) procedures and criteria to be used in connection with establishing or converting positions for part-time career employment, subject to the limitations of section 3393 of this title;

"(C) annual goals for establishing or converting positions for part-time career employment, and a timetable setting forth interim and final deadlines for achieving such goals;

"(D) a continuing review and evaluation of the part-time career employment program established under such regulations; and

"(E) procedures for notifying the public of vacant part-time positions in such agency, utilizing facilities and funds otherwise available to such agency for the dissemination of information.

"(2) The head of each agency shall provide for communication between, and coordination of the activities of, the individuals within such agency whose responsibilities relate to the part-time career employment program established within that agency.

"(3) Regulations established under paragraph (1) of this subsection may provide for such exceptions as may be necessary to carry out the mission of the agency.

"(b) (1) The Civil Service Commission, by regulation, shall establish and maintain a program under which it shall, on the request of an agency, advise and assist such agency in the establishment and maintenance of its part-time career employment program under this subchapter.

"(2) The Commission shall conduct a research and demonstration program with respect to part-time career employment within the Federal Government. In particular, such program shall be directed to—

"(A) determining the extent to which part-time career employment may be used in filling positions which have not traditionally been open for such employment on any extensive basis, such as supervisory, managerial, and professional positions;

"(B) determining the extent to which job-sharing arrangements may be established for various occupations and positions; and

"(C) evaluating attitudes, benefits, costs, efficiency, and productivity associated with part-time career employment, as well as its various sociological effects as a mode of employment.

"§ 3403. Limitations

"(a) An agency shall not abolish any position occupied by an employee in order to make the duties of such position available to be performed on a part-time career employment basis.

"(b) Any person who is employed on a full-time basis in an agency shall not be required to accept part-time employment as a condition of continued employment.

"§ 3404. Personnel ceilings

"In administering any personnel ceiling applicable to an agency (or unit therein), an employee employed by such agency on a part-time career employment basis shall be counted as a fraction which is determined by dividing 40 hours into the average number of hours of such employee's regularly scheduled workweek. This section shall become effective on October 1, 1980.

"§ 340.101 Nonapplicability

"(a) If, on the date of enactment of this subchapter, there is in effect with respect to positions within an agency a collective-bargaining agreement which establishes the number of hours of employment a week, then this subchapter shall not apply to those positions.

"(b) This subchapter shall not require part-time career employment in positions the rate of basic pay for which is fixed at a rate equal to or greater than the minimum rate fixed for GS–16 of the General Schedule.

"§ 340.101 Regulations

"Before any regulation is prescribed under this subchapter, a copy of the proposed regulation shall be published in the FEDERAL REGISTER and an opportunity provided to interested parties to present written comment and, where practicable, oral comment. Initial regulations shall be prescribed not later than 180 days after the date of the enactment of this subchapter.

"§ 3407. Reports

"(a) Each agency shall prepare and transmit on a biannual basis a report to the Office of Personnel Management on its activities under this subchapter, including—

"(1) details on such agency's progress in meeting part-time career employment goals established under section 3392 of this title; and

"(2) an explanation of any impediments experienced by such agency in meeting such goals or in otherwise carrying out the provisions of this subchapter, together with a statement of the measures taken to overcome such impediments.

"(b) The Commission shall include in its annual report under section 1308 of this title a statement of its activities under this subchapter, and a description and evaluation of the activities of agencies in carrying out the provisions of this subchapter.

"§ 3408. Employee organization representation

"If an employee organization has been accorded exclusive recognition with respect to a unit within an agency, then the employee organization shall be entitled to represent all employees within that unit employed on a part-time career employment basis.".

(b) Subpart B of the table of chapters of part III of the analysis of chapter 33 of title

5, United States Code, is amended by inserting after the item relating to section 3385 the following:

"SUBCHAPTER VII—PART-TIME CAREER EMPLOYMENT OPPORTUNITIES

"Sec.
"3401. Definitions.
"3402. Establishment of part-time career employment programs.
"3403. Limitations.
"3404. Personnel ceilings.
"3405. Nonapplicability.
"3406. Regulations.
"3407. Reports.
"3408. Employee organization representation.

SEC. 4. (a) Section 8347(g) of title 5, United States Code, is amended by adding at the end thereof the following: "However, the Commission may not exclude any employee who occupies a position on a part-time career employment basis (as defined in section 3391(2) of this title).".

(b) Section 8716(b) of such title 5 is amended—

(1) by striking out of the second sentence "or part-time";

(2) by striking out "or" at the end of clause (1);

(3) by striking out the period at the end of clause (2) and inserting in lieu thereof "; or"; and

(4) by adding at the end thereof the following:

"(3) an employee who is occupying a position on a part-time career employment basis (as defined in section 3391(2) of this title).".

(c) (1) Section 8913(b) of such title 5 is amended—

(A) by striking out "or" at the end of clause (1);

(B) by striking out the period at the end of clause (2) and inserting in lieu thereof "; or"; and

(C) by adding at the end thereof the following:

"(3) an employee who is occupying a position on a part-time career employment basis (as defined in section 3391(2) of this title).".

(2) (A) Section 8906(b) of such title 5 is amended—

(i) by striking out "paragraph (2)" in paragraph (1) and inserting in lieu thereof "paragraphs (2) and (3)"; and

(ii) by adding at the end thereof the following new paragraph:

"(3) In the case of an employee who is occupying a position on a part-time career employment basis (as defined in section 3391 (2) of this title), the biweekly Government contribution shall be equal to the percentage which bears the same ratio to the percentage determined under this subsection (without regard to this paragraph) as the average number of hours of such employee's regularly scheduled workweek bears to the average number of hours in the regularly scheduled workweek of an employee serving in a comparable position on a full-time career basis (as determined under regulations prescribed by the Commission)".

(B) The amendments made by subparagraph (A) shall not apply with respect to any employee serving in a position on a part-time career employment basis on the date of the enactment of this Act for such period as the employee continues to serve without a break in service in that or any other position on such part-time basis.

SEC. 5. Each report prepared by an agency under section 3397(a) of title 5, United States Code (as added by this Act), shall, to the extent to which part-time career employment opportunities have been extended by such agency during the period covered by such report to each group referred to in subparagraphs (A), (B), (C), and (D), of section 2(a)(2) of this Act.

[44 FR 57380, Oct. 5, 1979, as amended at 49 FR 17722, Apr. 25, 1984]

Subpart B—Regulatory Requirements—Part-Time Employment

SOURCE: 44 FR 57380, Oct. 5, 1979; 49 FR 17722, Apr. 25, 1984, unless otherwise noted.

§ 340.201 Regulatory requirements.

This subpart contains the regulations of the Office of Personnel Management which implement the above sections of chapter 34 (as set out in § 340.101).

§ 340.202 General.

(a) *Definitions. Part-time career employment* means regularly scheduled work of from 16 to 32 hours per week performed by an employee of an agency as defined in 5 U.S.C. 3401 (a) through (f), who has an appointment in tenure group I or II and who becomes employed on such part-time basis on or after April 8, 1979.

Tenure group I applies to employees in the competitive service under career appointments who are not serving probation and permanent employees in the excepted service whose appointments carry no restrictions or conditions.

Tenure group II applies to employees in the competitive service serving probation, career-conditional employees, and career employees in obligated positions. It also includes employees in the excepted service serving trial periods, whose tenure is indefinite solely because they occupy obligated positions; or whose tenure is equivalent to career-conditional in the competitive service.

(b) *Agency Exceptions.* As an exception to the general definition of part-time employment in § 340.202(a) and under the authority provided in 5 U.S.C. 3402(a)(3), an agency may permit an employee who has an appointment in tenure group I or II to perform regularly scheduled work of from 1 to 15 hours per week.

(c) *Mixed Tours of Duty.* The provisions of this subpart and the term "part-time career employment" do not apply to employees with appointments in tenure groups I or II who work under mixed tours of duty. For this purpose, a mixed tour of duty consists of annually recurring periods of full-time, part-time, or intermittent service as long as the employee does not work part-time more than 6 pay periods per calendar year.

[44 FR 57380, Oct. 5, 1979, as amended at 49 FR 17722, Apr. 25, 1984; 60 FR 3061, Jan. 13, 1995]

§ 340.203 Technical assistance.

(a) The Office of Personnel Management shall provide, within available resources, consultation and technical advice and assistance to agencies to aid them in expanding career part-time employment opportunities. This assistance shall include but not be limited to:

(1) Help in developing part-time career employment programs;

(2) Information on public and private sector part-time employment practices;

(3) Development of special recruitment and selection techniques for filling part-time positions;

(4) Interpretations of part-time employment law, regulations and policy;

(5) Guidance on job sharing and position restructuring.

(b) Request for information and assistance should be directed to the Associate Director for Staffing Services, Office of Personnel Management, 1900 E Street, NW., Washington, DC 20415, or the nearest OPM regional office.

§ 340.204 Agency reporting.

(a) Agency reports required under 5 U.S.C. 3407 shall be based on data as of March 31 and September 30 each year and shall be provided to the Office of Personnel Management no later than May 15 and November 15 respectively.

(b) Each agency shall include with such reports a copy of any agencywide part-time career employment program regulations and instructions issued during the 6-month period preceding the report date.

(c) Reports should be sent to the Associate Director for Staffing Services, Office of Personnel Management, 1900 E Street, NW., Washington, DC 20415.

Subpart C [Reserved]

Subpart D—Seasonal and intermittent Employment

SOURCE: 60 FR 3061, Jan. 13, 1995, unless otherwise noted.

§ 340.401 Definitions.

(a) *Seasonal employment* means annually recurring periods of work of less than 12 months each year. Seasonal employees are permanent employees who are placed in nonduty/nonpay status and recalled to duty in accordance with preestablished conditions of employment.

(b) *Intermittent employment* means employment without a regularly scheduled tour of duty.

§ 340.402 Seasonal employment.

(a) *Appropriate use.* Seasonal employment allows an agency to develop an experienced cadre of employees under career appointment to perform work which recurs predictably year-to-year. Consistent with the career nature of the appointments, seasonal employees receive the full benefits authorized to attract and retain a stable workforce. As a result, seasonal employment is appropriate when the work is expected to last at least 6 months during a calendar year. Recurring work that lasts less than 6 months each year is normally best performed by temporary employees. Seasonal employment may not be used as a substitute for full-time employment or as a buffer for the full-time workforce.

(b) *Length of the season.* Agencies determine the length of the season, subject to the condition that it be clearly tied to nature of the work. The season must be defined as closely as practicable so that an employee will have a reasonably clear idea of how much work he or she can expect during the year. To minimize the adverse impact of seasonal layoffs, an agency may assign seasonal employees to other work during the projected layoff period. While in nonpay status, a seasonal employee may accept other employment, Federal or non-Federal, subject to the regulations on political activity (part 733 of this title) and on employee responsibilities and conduct (part 735), as well as applicable agency policies. Subject to the limitation on pay from more than one position (5 U.S.C. 5533), a seasonal employee may hold more than one appointment.

(c) *Employment agreement.* An employment agreement must be executed between the agency and the seasonal employee prior to the employee's entering on duty. At a minimum, the agreement must inform the employee:

(1) That he or she is subject to periodic release and recall as a condition of employment,

(2) The minimum and maximum period the employee can expect to work,

(3) The basis on which release and recall procedures will be effected, and

(4) The benefits to which the employee will be entitled while in a nonpay status.

(d) *Release and recall procedures.* A seasonal employee is released to nonpay status at the end of a season and recalled to duty the next season. Release and recall procedures must be established in advance and uniformly applied. They may be based on performance, seniority, veterans' preference, other appropriate indices, or a combination of factors. A seasonal layoff is not subject to the procedures for furlough prescribed in parts 351 and 752 of this title. Reduction in force or adverse action procedures, as applicable, are required for a seasonal layoff that is not in accordance with the employment agreement, for example, if an agency intends to have an employee work less than the minimum amount of time specified in the employment agreement. However, an agency may develop a new employment agreement to reflect changing circumstances.

(e) *Noncompetitive movement.* Seasonal employees serving under career appointment may move to other positions in the same way as other regular career employees.

§ 340.403 Intermittent employment.

(a) *Appropriate use.* An intermittent work schedule is appropriate only when the nature of the work is sporadic and unpredictable so that a tour of duty cannot be regularly scheduled in advance. When an agency is able to schedule work in advance on a regular basis, it has an obligation to document the change in work schedule from intermittent to part-time or full-time to ensure proper service credit.

(b) *Noncompetitive movement.* Intermittent employees serving under career appointment may move to other positions in the same way as other regular career employees.

PART 351—REDUCTION IN FORCE

Subpart A [Reserved]

Subpart B—General Provisions

Subpart C—Transfer of Function

Subpart D—Scope of Competition

Subpart E—Retention Standing

Subpart F—Release From Competitive Level

Subpart G—Assignment Rights (Bump and Retreat)

Subpart H—Notice to Employee

Subpart I—Appeals and Corrective Action

Subpart J [Reserved]

AUTHORITY: 5 U.S.C. 1302, 3502, 3503; sec. 351.801 also issued under E.O. 12828, 58 FR 2965.

SOURCE: 51 FR 319, Jan. 3, 1986, unless otherwise noted.

Subpart A [Reserved]

Subpart B—General Provisions

§ 351.201 Use of regulations.

(a)(1) Each agency is responsible for determining the categories within which positions are required, where they are to be located, and when they are to be filled, abolished, or vacated. This includes determining when there is a surplus of employees at a particular location in a particular line of work.

(2) Each agency shall follow this part when it releases a competing employee from his or her competitive level by furlough for more than 30 days, separation, demotion, or reassignment requiring displacement, when the release is required because of lack of work; shortage of funds; insufficient personnel ceiling; reorganization; the exercise of reemployment rights or restoration rights; or reclassification of an employee's position die to erosion of duties when such action will take effect after an agency has formally announced a reduction in force in the employee's competitive area and when the reduction in force will take effect within 180 days.

(b) This part does not require an agency to fill a vacant position. However, when an agency, at its discretion, chooses to fill a vacancy by an employee who has been reached for release from a competitive level for one of the reasons in paragraph (a)(2) of this section, this part shall be followed.

(c) Each agency is responsible for assuring that the provisions in this part are uniformly and consistently applied in any one reduction in force.

(d) An agency authorized to administer foreign national employee programs under section 408 of the Foreign Service Act of 1980 (22 U.S.C. 3968) may include special plans for reduction in force in its foreign national employee programs. In these special plans an agency may give effect to the labor laws and practices of the locality of employment by supplementing the selection factors in subparts D and E of this part to the extent consistent with the public interest. Subpart I of this part does not apply to actions taken under the special plans authorized by this paragraph.

§ 351.202 Coverage.

(a) *Employees covered.* Except as provided in paragraph (b) of this section, this part applies to each civilian employee in:

(1) The executive branch of the Federal Government; and

(2) Those parts of the Federal Government outside the executive branch

which are subject by statute to competitive service requirements or are determined by the appropriate legislative or judicial administrative body to be covered hereunder. Coverage includes administrative law judges except as modified by part 930 of this chapter.

(b) *Employees excluded.* This part does not apply to an employee:

(1) In a position in the Senior Executive Service; or

(2) Whose appointment is required by Congress to be confirmed by, or made with the advice and consent of, the United States Senate, except a postmaster.

(c) *Actions excluded.* This part does not apply to:

(1) The termination of a temporary or term promotion or the return of an employee to the position held before the temporary or term promotion or to one of equivalent grade and pay.

(2) A change to lower grade based on the reclassification of an employee's position due to the application of new classification standards or the correction of a classification error.

(3) A change to lower grade based on reclassification of an employee's position due to erosion of duties, except that this exclusion does not apply to such reclassification actions that will take effect after an agency has formally announced a reduction in force in the employee's competitive area and when the reduction in force will take effect within 180 days. This exception ends at the completion of the reduction in force.

(4) The change of an employee from regular to substitute in the same pay level in the U.S. Postal Service field service.

(5) The release from a competitive level of a National Guard technician under section 709 of title 32, United States Code.

(6) Placement of an employee serving on an intermittent, part-time, on-call, or seasonal basis in a nonpay and nonduty status in accordance with conditions established at time of appointment.

(7) A change in an employee's work schedule from other-than-full-time to full-time. (A change from full-time to other than full-time for a reason covered in §351.201(A)(2) is covered by this part.)

[51 FR 319, Jan. 3, 1986, as amended at 60 FR 3062, Jan. 13, 1995]

§351.203 Definitions.

In this part:

Competing employee means an employee in tenure group I, II, or III.

Current rating of record is the rating of record for the most recently completed appraisal period as provided in §351.504(b)(3).

Days means calendar days.

Function means all or a clearly identifiable segment of an agency's mission (including all integral parts of that mission), regardless of how it is performed.

Furlough under this part means the placement of an employee in a temporary nonduty and nonpay status for more than 30 consecutive calendar days, or more than 22 workdays if done on a discontinuous basis, but not more than 1 year.

Local commuting area means the geographic area that usually constitutes one area for employment purposes. It includes any population center (or two or more neighboring ones) and the surrounding localities in which people live and can reasonably be expected to travel back and forth daily to their usual employment.

Modal rating is the summary rating level assigned most frequently among the actual ratings of record that are:

(1) Assigned under the summary level pattern that applies to the employee's position of record on the date of the reduction in force;

(2) Given within the same competitive area, or at the agency's option within a larger subdivision of the agency or agencywide; and

(3) On record for the most recently completed appraisal period prior to the date of issuance of reduction in force notices or the cutoff date the agency specifies prior to the issuance of reduction in force notices after which no new ratings will be put on record.

Rating of record has the meaning given that term in §430.203 of this chapter. For an employee not subject to 5 U.S.C. Chapter 43, or part 430 of this chapter, it means the officially designated performance rating, as provided for in the agency's appraisal system, that is considered to be an equivalent rating of record under the provisions of § 430.201(c) of this chapter.

Reorganization means the planned elimination, addition, or redistribution of functions or duties in an organization.

Representative rate means:

(1) The fourth step of the grade for a position covered by the General Schedule, using the locality rate authorized by 5 U.S.C. 5304 and subpart F of part 531 of this chapter for General Schedule positions;

(2) The prevailing rate for a position covered by a wage-board or similar wage-determining procedure, such as provided in the definition of representative rate for Federal Wage System positions in 5 CFR 532.401 of this chapter;

(3) For positions in a pay band, the rate (or rates) the agency designates as representative of that pay band or competitive levels within the pay band, including (as appropriate) any applicable locality payment authorized by 5 U.S.C. 5304 and subpart F of part 531 of this chapter (or equivalent payment under other legal authority); and

(4) For other positions (e.g., positions in an unclassified pay system), the rate the agency designates as representative of the position, including (as appropriate) any applicable locality payment authorized by subpart F of part 531 (or equivalent payment under other legal authority).

Transfer of function means the transfer of the performance of a continuing function from one competitive area and its addition to one or more other competitive areas, except when the function involved is virtually identical to functions already being performed in the other competitive area(s) affected; or the movement of the competitive area in which the function is performed to another commuting area.

Undue interruption means a degree of interruption that would prevent the completion of required work by the employee 90 days after the employee has been placed in a different position under this part. The 90-day standard should be considered within the allowable limits of time and quality, taking into account the pressures of priorities, deadlines, and other demands. However, a work program would generally not be unduly interrupted even if an employee needed more than 90 days after the reduction in force to perform the optimum quality or quantity of work. The 90-day standard may be extended if placement is made under this part to a low priority program or to a vacant position.

[51 FR 319, Jan. 3, 1986, as amended at 58 FR 65533, Dec. 15, 1993; 60 FR 3062, Jan. 13, 1995; 62 FR 62500, Nov. 24, 1997; 73 FR 29388, May 21, 2008]

§ 351.204 Responsibility of agency.

Each agency covered by this part is responsible for following and applying the regulations in this part when the agency determines that a reduction force is necessary.

§ 351.205 Authority of OPM.

The Office of Personnel Management may establish further guidance and instructions for the planning, preparation, conduct, and review of reductions in force. OPM may examine an agency's preparations for reduction in force at any stage. When OPM finds that an agency's preparations are contrary to the express provisions or to the spirit and intent of these regulations or that they would result in violation of employee rights or equities, OPM may require appropriate corrective action.

[51 FR 319, Jan. 3, 1986, as amended at 66 FR 66710, Dec. 27, 2001]

Subpart C—Transfer of Function

SOURCE: 52 FR 10024, Mar. 30, 1987, unless otherwise noted.

§ 351.301 Applicability.

(a) This subpart is applicable when the work of one or more employees is moved from one competitive area to another as a transfer of function regardless of whether or not the movement is made under authority of a statute, Executive order, reorganization plan, or other authority.

(b) In a transfer of function, the function must cease in the losing competitive area and continue in an identical form in the gaining competitive area (*i.e.*, in the gaining competitive area, the function continues to be carried out by competing employees rather than by noncompeting employees).

[52 FR 10024, Mar. 30, 1987, as amended at 60 FR 3062, Jan. 13, 1995]

§ 351.302 Transfer of employees.

(a) Before a reduction in force is made in connection with the transfer of any or all of the functions of a competitive area to another continuing competitive area, each competing employee in a position identified with the transferring function or functions shall be transferred to the continuing competitive area without any change in the tenure of his or her employment.

(b) An employee whose position is transferred under this subpart solely for liquidation, and who is not identified with an operating function specifically authorized at the time of transfer to continue in operation more than 60 days, is not a competing employee for other positions in the competitive area gaining the function.

(c) Regardless of an employee's personal preference, an employee has no right to transfer with his or her function, unless the alternative in the competitive area losing the function is separation or demotion.

(d) Except as permitted in paragraph (e) of this section, the losing competitive area must use the adverse action procedures found in 5 CFR part 752 if it chooses to separate an employee who declines to transfer with his or her function.

(e) The losing competitive area may, at its discretion, include employees who decline to transfer with their function as part of a concurrent reduction in force.

(f) An agency may not separate an employee who declines to transfer with the function any sooner than it transfers employees who chose to transfer with the function to the gaining competitive area.

(g) Agencies may ask employees in a canvass letter whether the employee wishes to transfer with the function when the function transfers to a different local commuting area. The canvass letter must give the employee information concerning entitlements available to the employee if the employee accepts the offer to transfer, and if the employee declines the offer to transfer. An employee may later change and initial acceptance offer without penalty. However, an employee may not later change an initial declination of the offer to transfer.

[52 FR 10024, Mar. 30, 1987, as amended at 60 FR 3062, Jan. 13, 1995]

§ 351.303 Identification of positions with a transferring function.

(a) The competitive area losing the function is responsible for identifying the positions of competing employees with the transferring function. A competing employee is identified with the transferring function on the basis of the employee's official position. Two methods are provided to identify employees with the transferring function:

(1) Identification Method One; and

(2) Identification Method Two.

(b) Identification Method One must be used to identify each position to which it is applicable. Identification Method Two is used only to identify positions to which Identification Method One is not applicable.

(c) Under Identification Method One, a competing employee is identified with a transferring function if—

(1) The employee performs the function during at least half of his or her work time; or

(2) Regardless of the amount of time the employee performs the function during his or her work time, the function performed by the employee includes the duties controlling his or her grade or rate of pay.

(3) In determining what percentage of time an employee performs a function in the employee's official position, the agency may supplement the employee's official position description by the use of appropriate records (e.g., work reports, organizational time logs, work schedules, etc.).

(d) Identification Method Two is applicable to employees who perform the function during less than half of their work time and are not otherwise covered by Identification Method One. Under Identification Method Two, the losing competitive area must identify the number of positions it needed to perform the transferring function. To determine which employees are identified for transfer, the losing competitive area must establish a retention register in accordance with this part that includes the name of each competing employee who performed the function. Competing employees listed on the retention register are identified for transfer in the inverse order of their retention standing. If for any retention register this procedure would result in the separation or demotion by reduction in force at the losing competitive area of any employee with higher retention standing, the losing competitive area must identify competing employees on that register for transfer in the order of their retention standing.

(e)(1) The competitive area losing the function may permit other employees to volunteer for transfer with the function in place of employees identified under Identification Method One or Identification Method Two. However, the competitive area may permit these other employees to volunteer for transfer only if no competing employee who is identified for transfer under Identification Method One or Identification Method Two is separated or demoted solely because a volunteer transferred in place of him or her to the competitive area that is gaining the function.

(2) If the total number of employees who volunteer for transfer exceeds the total number of employees required to perform the function in the competitive area that is gaining the function, the losing competitive area may give preference to the volunteers with the highest retention standing, or make selections based on other appropriate criteria.

[52 FR 10024, Mar. 30, 1987, as amended at 60 FR 3062, Jan. 13, 1995]

Subpart D—Scope of Competition

§ 351.401 Determining retention standing.

Each agency shall determine the retention standing of each competing employee on the basis of the factors in this subpart and in subpart E of this part.

§ 351.402 Competitive area.

(a) Each agency shall establish competitive areas in which employees compete for retention under this part.

(b) A competitive area must be defined solely in terms of the agency's organizational unit(s) and geographical location and, except as provided in paragraph (e) of this section, it must include all employees within the competitive area so defined. A competitive area may consist of all or part of an agency. The minimum competitive area is a subdivision of the agency under separate administration within the local commuting area.

(c) When a competitive area will be in effect less than 90 days prior to the effective date of a reduction in force, a description of the competitive area shall be submitted to the OPM for approval in advance of the reduction in force. Descriptions of all competitive areas must be made readily available for review.

(d) Each agency shall establish a separate competitive area for each Inspector General activity established under authority of the Inspector General Act of 1978, Public Law 95–452, as amended, in which only employees of that office shall compete for retention under this part.

(e) When an agency finds that a competitive area defined under paragraph (b) of this section includes pay band positions and positions not covered by a pay band, the agency may, at its discretion, define a separate (and additional) competitive area, otherwise consistent with paragraph (b) of this section, to include only pay band positions. The original competitive area would then include only the remaining positions (*i.e.*, those positions not covered by a pay band).

[51 FR 319 Jan. 3, 1986, as amended at 56 FR 65416, Dec. 17, 1991; 62 FR 62500, Nov. 24, 1997; 73 FR 46532, Aug. 11, 2008]

§ 351.403 Competitive level.

(a)(1) Each agency shall establish competitive levels consisting of all positions in a competitive area which are in the same grade (or occupational level) and classification series, and which are similar enough in duties, qualification requirements, pay schedules, and working conditions so that an agency may reassign the incumbent of one position to any of the other positions in the level without undue interruption.

(2)(i) Except as provided in paragraph (a)(2)(ii) of this section for pay band positions, competitive level determinations are based on each employee's official position of record (including the official position description), not the employee's personal qualifications.

(ii) To establish a competitive level comprised of pay band positions, an agency may supplement an employee's official position of record with other applicable records that document the employee's actual duties and responsibilities.

(3) Sex may not be the basis for a competitive level determination, except for a position OPM designates that certification of eligibles by sex is justified.

(4) A probationary period required by subpart I of part 315 of this chapter for initial appointment to a supervisory or managerial position is not a basis for establishing a separate competitive level.

(5) If a competitive area includes positions in one or more pay bands, each set of interchangeable positions in the pay band under paragraphs (a)(1) through (4) of this section is a separate competitive level (e.g., with interchangeable positions under paragraphs (a)(1) through (4) of this section, each pay band is one competitive level; if the positions are not interchangeable under paragraphs (a)(1) through (4) of this section, the pay band may include multiple competitive levels).

(b) Each agency shall establish separate competitive levels according to the following categories:

(1) *By service.* Separate levels shall be established for positions in the competitive service and in the excepted service.

(2) *By appointment authority.* Separate levels shall be established for excepted service positions filled under different appointment authorities.

(3) *By pay schedule.* Separate levels shall be established for positions under different pay schedules.

(4) *By work schedule.* Separate levels shall be established for positions filled on a full-time, part-time, intermittent, seasonal, or on-call basis. No distinction may be made among employees in the competitive level on the basis of the number of hours or weeks scheduled to be worked.

(5) *By trainee status.* Separate levels shall be established for positions filled by an employee in a formally designated trainee or developmental program having all of the characteristics covered in § 351.702(e)(1) through (e)(4) of this part.

(c) An agency may not establish a competitive level based solely upon:

(1) A difference in the number of hours or weeks scheduled to be worked by other-than-full-time employees who would otherwise be in the same competitive level;

(2) A requirement to work changing shifts;

(3) The grade promotion potential of the position; or

(4) A difference in the local wage areas when a competitive area includes positions covered by more than one wage-board or similar wage-determining procedure;

(5) A difference in locality payments under 5 U.S.C. 5304 and subpart F of part 531 of this chapter when a competitive level includes more than one locality pay area listed in § 531.603 of this chapter; or

(6) Representative rates in different local commuting areas when a competitive area includes General Schedule (GS) and Federal Wage System (FWS) positions in multiple GS locality pay areas, and/or FWS local wage areas.

[51 FR 319, Jan. 3, 1986, as amended at 60 FR 3062, Jan. 13, 1995; 62 FR 62500, Nov. 24, 1997; 73 FR 29388, May 21, 2008; 73 FR 46532, Aug. 11, 2008]

§ 351.404 Retention register.

(a) When a competing employee is to be released from a competitive level under this part, the agency shall establish a separate retention register for that competitive level. The retention register is prepared from the current retention records of employees. Upon displacing another employee under this part, an employee retains the same status and tenure in the new position. Except for an employee on military duty with a restoration right, the agency shall enter on the retention register, in the order of retention standing, the name of each competing employee who is:

(1) In the competitive level;

(2) Temporarily promoted from the competitive level by temporary or term promotion; or

(3) Detailed from the competitive level under 5 U.S.C. 3341 or other appropriate authority.

(b)(1) The name of each employee serving under a time limited appointment or promotion to a position in a competitive level shall be entered on a list apart from the retention register for that competitive level, along with the expiration date of the action.

(2) The agency shall list, at the bottom of the list prepared under paragraph (b)(1) of this section, the name of each employee in the competitive level with a written decision of removal under part 432 or 752 of this chapter.

[51 FR 319, Jan. 3, 1986, as amended at 62 FR 62500, Nov. 24, 1997]

§ 351.405 Demoted employees.

An employee who has received a written decision under part 432 or 752 of this chapter to demote him or her competes under this part from the position to which he or she will be or has been demoted.

[62 FR 62500, Nov. 24, 1997]

Subpart E—Retention Standing

§ 351.501 Order of retention—competitive service.

(a) Competing employees shall be classified on a retention register on the basis of their tenure of employment, veteran preference, length of service, and performance in descending order as follows:

(1) By tenure group I, group II, group III; and

(2) Within each group by veteran preference subgroup AD, subgroup A, subgroup B; and

(3) Within each subgroup by years of service as augmented by credit for performance under § 351.504, beginning with the earliest service date.

(b) Groups are defined as follows:

(1) Group I includes each career employee who is not serving a probationary period. (A supervisory or managerial employee serving a probationary period required by subpart I of part 315 of this title is in group I if the employee is otherwise eligible to be included in this group.) The following employees are in group I as soon as the employee completes any required probationary period for initial appointment:

(i) An employee for whom substantial evidence exists of eligibility to immediately acquire status and career tenure, and whose case is pending final resolution by OPM (including cases under Executive Order 10826 to correct certain administrative errors);

(ii) An employee who acquires competitive status and satisfies the service requirement for career tenure when the employee's position is brought into the competitive service;

(iii) An administrative law judge;

(iv) An employee appointed under 5 U.S.C. 3104, which provides for the employment of specially qualified scientific or professional personnel, or a similar authority; and

(v) An employee who acquires status under 5 U.S.C. 3304(c) on transfer to the competitive service from the legislative or judicial branches of the Federal Government.

(2) Group II includes each career-conditional employee, and each employee serving a probationary period under subpart H of part 315 of this chapter. (A supervisory or managerial employee serving a probationary period required by subpart I of part 315 of this title is in group II if the employee has not completed a probationary period under subpart H of part 315 of this title.) Group II also includes an employee when substantial evidence exists of the employee's eligibility to immediately acquire status and career-conditional tenure, and the employee's case is pending final resolution by OPM (including cases under Executive Order 10826 to correct certain administrative errors).

(3) Group III includes all employees serving under indefinite appointments,

temporary appointments pending establishment of a register, status quo appointments, term appointments, and any other nonstatus nontemporary appointments which meet the definition of provisional appointments contained in §§316.401 and 316.403 of this chapter.

(c) Subgroups are defined as follows:

(1) Subgroup AD includes each preference eligible employee who has a compensable service-connected disability of 30 percent or more.

(2) Subgroup A includes each preference eligible employee not included in subgroup AD.

(3) Subgroup B includes each nonpreference eligible employee.

(d) A retired member of a uniformed service is considered a preference eligible under this part only if the member meets at least one of the conditions of the following paragraphs (d)(1), (2), or (3) of this section, except as limited by paragraph (d)(4) or (d)(5):

(1) The employee's military retirement is based on disability that either:

(i) Resulted from injury or disease received in the line of duty as a direct result of armed conflict; or

(ii) Was caused by an instrumentality of war incurred in the line of duty during a period of war as defined by sections 101 and 301 of title 38, United States Code.

(2) The employee's retired pay from a uniformed service is not based upon 20 or more years of full-time active service, regardless of when performed but not including periods of active duty for training.

(3) The employee has been continuously employed in a position covered by this part since November 30, 1964, without a break in service of more than 30 days.

(4) An employee retired at the rank of major or above (or equivalent) is considered a preference eligible under this part if such employee is a disabled veteran as defined in section 2108(2) of title 5, United States Code, and meets one of the conditions covered in paragraph (d)(1), (2), or (3) of this section.

(5) An employee who is eligible for retired pay under chapter 67 of title 10, United States Code, and who retired at the rank of major or above (or equivalent) is considered a preference eligible under this part at age 60, only if such employee is a disabled veteran as defined in section 2108(2) of title 5, United States Code.

[51 FR 319, Jan. 3, 1986, as amended at 56 FR 10142, Mar. 11, 1991; 60 FR 3062, Jan. 13, 1995; 62 FR 62500, Nov. 24, 1997]

§ 351.502 Order of retention—excepted service.

(a) Competing employees shall be classified on a retention register in tenure groups on the basis of their tenure of employment, veteran preference, length of service, and performance in descending order as set forth under §351.501(a) for competing employees in the competitive service.

(b) Groups are defined as follows:

(1) Group I includes each permanent employee whose appointment carries no restriction or condition such as conditional, indefinite, specific time limit, or trial period.

(2) Group II includes each employee:

(i) Serving a trial period; or

(ii) Whose tenure is equivalent to a career-conditional appointment in the competitive service in agencies having such excepted appointments.

(3) Group III includes each employee:

(i) Whose tenure is indefinite (*i.e.*, without specific time limit), but not actually or potentially permanent;

(ii) Whose appointment has a specific time limitation of more than 1 year; or

(iii) Who is currently employed under a temporary appointment limited to 1 year or less, but who has completed 1 year of current continuous service under a temporary appointment with no break in service of 1 workday or more.

[60 FR 3063, Jan. 13, 1995]

§ 351.503 Length of service.

(a) All civilian service as a Federal employee, as defined in 5 U.S.C. 2105(a), is creditable for purposes of this part. Civilian service performed in employment that does not meet the definition of *Federal employee* set forth in 5 U.S.C. 2105(a) is creditable for purposes of this part only if specifically authorized by statute as creditable for retention purposes.

(b)(1) As authorized by 5 U.S.C. 3502(a)(A), all active duty in a uniformed service, as defined in 5 U.S.C. 2101(3), is creditable for purposes of this part, except as provided in paragraphs (b)(2) and (b)(3) of this section.

(2) As authorized by 5 U.S.C. 3502(a)(B), a retired member of a uniformed service who is covered by §351.501(d) is entitled to credit under this part only for:

(i) The length of time in active service in the Armed Forces during a war, or in a campaign or expedition for which a campaign or expedition badge has been authorized; or

(ii) The total length of time in active service in the Armed Forces if the employee is considered a preference eligible under 5 U.S.C. 2108 and 5 U.S.C. 3501(a), as implemented in §351.501(d).

(3) An employee may not receive dual service credit for purposes of this part for service performed on active duty in the Armed Forces that was performed during concurrent civilian employment as a Federal employee, as defined in 5 U.S.C. 2105(a).

(c)(1) The agency is responsible for establishing both the service computation date, and the adjusted service computation date, applicable to each employee competing for retention under this part. If applicable, the agency is also responsible for adjusting the service computation date and the adjusted service computation date to withhold retention service credit for noncreditable service.

(2) The service computation date includes all actual creditable service under paragraph (a) and paragraph (b) of this section.

(3) The adjusted service computation date includes all actual creditable service under paragraph (a) and paragraph (b) of this section, and additional retention service credit for performance authorized by §351.504 (d) and (e).

(d) The service computation date is computed on the following basis:

(1) The effective date of appointment as a Federal employee under 5 U.S.C. 2105(a) when the employee has no previous creditable service under paragraph (a) or (b) of this section; or if applicable,

(2) The date calculated by subtracting the employee's total previous creditable service under paragraph (a) or (b) of this section from the most recent effective date of appointment as a Federal employee under 5 U.S.C. 2105(a).

(e) The adjusted service computation date is calculated by subtracting from the date in paragraph (d)(1) or (d)(2) of this section the additional service credit for retention authorized by §351.504(d) and (e).

[64 FR 16800, Apr. 7, 1999; 64 FR 23531, May 3, 1999]

§351.504 Credit for performance.

NOTE TO §351.504: Compliance dates: Subject to the requirements of 5 U.S.C. Section 7116(a)(7), agencies may implement revised §351.504 at any time between December 24, 1997 and October 1, 1998. For reduction in force actions effective between December 24, 1997 and September 30, 1998, agencies may use either §351.504 effective December 24, 1997, or the prior §351.504 in 5 CFR part 351 (January 1, 1997 edition).

(a) *Ratings used.* (1) Only ratings of record as defined in §351.203 shall be used as the basis for granting additional retention service credit in a reduction in force.

(2) For employees who received ratings of record while covered by part 430, subpart B, of this chapter, those ratings of record shall be used to grant additional retention service credit in a reduction in force.

(3) For employees who received performance ratings while not covered by the provisions of 5 U.S.C. Chapter 43 and part 430, subpart B, of this chapter, those performance ratings shall be considered ratings of record for granting additional retention service credit in a reduction in force only when it is determined that those performance ratings are equivalent ratings of record under the provisions of §430.201(c) of this chapter. The agency conducting the reduction in force shall make that determination.

(b)(1) An employee's entitlement to additional retention service credit for performance under this subpart shall be based on the employee's three most recent ratings of record received during the 4-year period prior to the date of issuance of reduction in force notices, except as otherwise provided in paragraphs (b)(2) and (c) of this section.

(2) To provide adequate time to determine employee retention standing, an agency may provide for a cutoff

date, a specified number of days prior to the issuance of reduction in force notices after which no new ratings of record will be put on record and used for purposes of this subpart. When a cutoff date is used, an employee will receive performance credit for the three most recent ratings of record received during the 4-year period prior to the cutoff date.

(3) To be creditable for purposes of this subpart, a rating of record must have been issued to the employee, with all appropriate reviews and signatures, and must also be on record (*i.e.*, the rating of record is available for use by the office responsible for establishing retention registers).

(4) The awarding of additional retention service credit based on performance for purposes of this subpart must be uniformly and consistently applied within a competitive area, and must be consistent with the agency's appropriate issuance(s) that implement these policies. Each agency must specify in its appropriate issuance(s):

(i) The conditions under which a rating of record is considered to have been received for purposes of determining whether it is within the 4-year period prior to either the date the agency issues reduction in force notices or the agency-established cutoff date for ratings of record, as appropriate; and

(ii) If the agency elects to use a cutoff date, the number of days prior to the issuance of reduction in force notices after which no new ratings of record will be put on record and used for purposes of this subpart.

(c) *Missing ratings.* Additional retention service credit for employees who do not have three actual ratings of record during the 4-year period prior to the date of issuance of reduction in force notices or the 4-year period prior to the agency-established cutoff date for ratings of record permitted in paragraph (b)(2) of this section shall be determined under paragraphs (d) or (e) of this section, as appropriate, and as follows:

(1) An employee who has not received any rating of record during the 4-year period shall receive credit for performance based on the modal rating for the summary level pattern that applies to the employee's official position of record at the time of the reduction in force.

(2) An employee who has received at least one but fewer than three previous ratings of record during the 4-year period shall receive credit for performance on the basis of the value of the actual rating(s) of record divided by the number of actual ratings received. If an employee has received only two actual ratings of record during the period, the value of the ratings is added together and divided by two (and rounded in the case of a fraction to the next higher whole number) to determine the amount of additional retention service credit. If an employee has received only one actual rating of record during the period, its value is the amount of additional retention service credit provided.

(d) *Single rating pattern.* If all employees in a reduction in force competitive area have received ratings of record under a single pattern of summary levels as set forth in § 430.208(d) of this chapter, the additional retention service credit provided to employees shall be expressed in additional years of service and shall consist of the mathematical average (rounded in the case of a fraction to the next higher whole number) of the employee's applicable ratings of record, under paragraphs (b)(1) and (c) of this section computed on the following basis:

(1) Twenty additional years of service for each rating of record with a Level 5 (Outstanding or equivalent) summary;

(2) Sixteen additional years of service for each rating of record with a Level 4 summary; and

(3) Twelve additional years of service for each rating of record with a Level 3 (Fully Successful or equivalent) summary.

(e) *Multiple rating patterns.* If an agency has employees in a competitive area who have ratings of record under more than one pattern of summary levels, as set forth in § 430.208(d) of this chapter, it shall consider the mix of patterns and provide additional retention service credit for performance to employees expressed in additional years of service in accordance with the following:

(1) Additional years of service shall consist of the mathematical average

(rounded in the case of a fraction to the next higher whole number) of the additional retention service credit that the agency established for the summary levels of the employee's applicable rating(s) of record.

(2) The agency shall establish the amount of additional retention service credit provided for summary levels only in full years; the agency shall not establish additional retention service credit for summary levels below Level 3 (Fully Successful or equivalent).

(3) When establishing additional retention service credit for the summary levels at Level 3 (Fully Successful or equivalent) and above, the agency shall establish at least 12 years, and no more than 20 years, additional retention service credit for a summary level.

(4) The agency may establish the same number of years additional retention service credit for more than one summary level.

(5) The agency shall establish the same number of years additional retention service credit for all ratings of record with the same summary level in the same pattern of summary levels as set forth in § 430.208(d) of this chapter.

(6) The agency may establish a different number of years additional retention service credit for the same summary level in different patterns.

(7) In implementing paragraph (e) of this section, the agency shall specify the number(s) of years additional retention service credit that it will establish for summary levels. This information shall be made readily available for review.

(8) The agency may apply paragraph (e) of this section only to ratings of record put on record on or after October 1, 1997. The agency shall establish the additional retention service credit for ratings of record put on record prior to that date in accordance with paragraph (d) of this section.

[62 FR 62501, Nov. 24, 1997]

§ 351.505 Records.

(a) The agency is responsible for maintaining correct personnel records that are used to determine the retention standing of its employees competing for retention under this part.

(b) The agency must allow its retention registers and related records to be inspected by:

(1) An employee of the agency who has received a specific reduction in force notice, and/or the employee's representative if the representative is acting on behalf of the individual employee; and

(2) An authorized representative of OPM.

(c) An employee who has received a specific notice of reduction in force under authority of subpart H of this part has the right to review any completed records used by the agency in a reduction in force action that was taken, or will be taken, against the employee, including:

(1) The complete retention register with the released employee's name and other relevant retention information (including the names of all other employees listed on that register, their individual service computation dates calculated under § 351.503(d), and their adjusted service computation dates calculated under § 351.503(e)) so that the employee may consider how the agency constructed the competitive level, and how the agency determined the relative retention standing of the competing employees; and

(2) The complete retention registers for other positions that could affect the composition of the employee's competitive level, and/or the determination of the employee's assignment rights (e.g., registers to which the released employee may have potential assignment rights under § 351.701(b) and (c)).

(d) An employee who has not received a specific reduction in force notice has no right to review the agency's retention registers and related records.

(e) The agency is responsible for ensuring that each employee's access to retention records is consistent with both the Freedom of Information Act (5 U.S.C. 552), and the Privacy Act (5 U.S.C. 552a).

(f) The agency must preserve all registers and records relating to a reduction in force for at least 1 year after the date it issues a specific reduction in force notice.

[64 FR 16800, Apr. 7, 1999]

§ 351.506 Effective date of retention standing.

Except for applying the performance factor as provided in § 351.504:

(a) The retention standing of each employee released from a competitive level in the order prescribed in § 351.601 is determined as of the date the employee is so released.

(b) The retention standing of each employee retained in a competitive level as an exception under § 351.606(b), § 351.607, or § 351.608, is determined as of the date the employee would have been released had the exception not been used. The retention standing of each employee retained under any of these provisions remains fixed until completion of the reduction in force action which resulted in the temporary retention.

(c) When an agency discovers an error in the determination of an employee's retention standing, it shall correct the error and adjust any erroneous reduction-in-force action to accord with the employee's proper retention standing as of the effective date established by this section.

[51 FR 319, Jan. 3, 1986, as amended at 60 FR 3063, Jan. 13, 1995; 62 FR 10682, Mar. 10, 1997]

Subpart F—Release From Competitive Level

§ 351.601 Order of release from competitive level.

(a) Each agency must select competing employees for release from a competitive level (including release from a competitive level involving a pay band) under this part in the inverse order of retention standing, beginning with the employee with the lowest retention standing on the retention register. An agency may not release a competing employee from a competitive level while retaining in that level an employee with lower retention standing except:

(1) As required under § 351.606 when an employee is retained under a mandatory exception or under § 351.806 when an employee is entitled to a new written notice of reduction in force; or

(2) As permitted under § 351.607 when an employee is retained under a permissive continuing exception or under § 351.608 when an employee is retained under a permissive temporary exception.

(b) At its option an agency may provide for intervening displacement within the competitive level before final release of the employee with the lowest-retention standing from the competitive level.

(c) When employees in the same retention subgroup have identical service dates and are tied for release from a competitive level, the agency may select any tied employee for release.

[73 FR 29388, May 21, 2008]

§ 351.602 Prohibitions.

An agency may not release a competing employee from a competitive level while retaining in that level an employee with:

(a) A specifically limited temporary appointment;

(b) A specifically limited temporary or term promotion;

(c) A written decision under part 432 or 752 of this chapter of removal or demotion from the competitive level.

[51 FR 319, Jan. 3, 1986, as amended at 62 FR 62502, Nov. 24, 1997]

§ 351.603 Actions subsequent to release from competitive level.

An employee reached for release from a competitive level shall be offered assignment to another position in accordance with subpart G of this part. If the employee accepts, the employee shall be assigned to the position offered. If the employee has no assignment right or does not accept an offer under subpart G, the employee shall be furloughed or separated.

§ 351.604 Use of furlough.

(a) An agency may furlough a competing employee only when it intends within 1 year to recall the employee to duty in the position from which furloughed.

(b) An agency may not separate a competing employee under this part while an employee with lower retention standing in the same competitive level is on furlough.

(c) An agency may not furlough a competing employee for more than 1 year.

(d) When an agency recalls employees to duty in the competitive level from which furloughed, it shall recall them in the order of their retention standing, beginning with highest standing employee.

§ 351.605 Liquidation provisions.

When an agency will abolish all positions in a competitive area within 180 days, it must release employees in group and subgroup order consistent with § 351.601(a). At its discretion, the agency may release the employees in group order without regard to retention standing within a subgroup, except as provided in § 351.606. When an agency releases an employee under this section, the notice to the employee must cite this authority and give the date the liquidation will be completed. An agency may also apply §§ 351.607 and 351.608 in a liquidation.

[60 FR 2678, Jan. 11, 1995]

§ 351.606 Mandatory exceptions.

(a) *Armed Forces restoration rights.* When an agency applies § 351.601 or § 351.605, it shall give retention priorities over other employees in the same subgroup to each group I or II employee entitled under 38 U.S.C. 2021 or 2024 to retention for, as applicable, 6 months or 1 year after restoration, as provided in part 353 of this chapter.

(b) *Use of annual leave to reach initial eligibility for retirement or continuance of health benefits.* (1) An agency shall make a temporary exception under this section to retain an employee who is being involuntarily separated under this part, and who elects to use annual leave to remain on the agency's rolls after the effective date the employee would otherwise have been separated by reduction in force, in order to establish initial eligibility for immediate retirement under 5 U.S.C. 8336, 8412, or 8414, and/or to establish initial eligibility under 5 U.S.C. 8905 to continue health benefits coverage into retirement.

(2) An agency shall make a temporary exception under this section to retain an employee who is being involuntarily separated under authority of part 752 of this chapter because of the employee's decision to decline relocation (including transfer of function), and who elects to use annual leave to remain on the agency's rolls after the effective date the employee would otherwise have been separated by adverse action, in order to establish initial eligibility for immediate retirement under 5 U.S.C. 8336, 8412, or 8414, and/or to establish initial eligibility under 5 U.S.C. 8905 to continue health benefits coverage into retirement.

(3) An employee retained under paragraph (b) by this section must be covered by chapter 63 of title 5, United States Code.

(4) An agency may not retain an employee under paragraph (b) of this section past the date that the employee first becomes eligible for immediate retirement, or for continuation of health benefits into retirement, except that an employee may be retained long enough to satisfy both retirement and health benefits requirements.

(5) Except as permitted by 5 CFR 351.608(d), an agency may not approve an employee's use of any other type of leave after the employee has been retained under a temporary exception authorized by paragraph (b) of this section.

(6) Annual leave for purposes of paragraph (b) of this section is described in § 630.212 of this chapter.

(c) *Documentation.* Each agency shall record on the retention register, for inspection by each employee, the reasons for any deviation from the order of release required by § 351.601 or § 351.605.

[62 FR 10682, Mar. 10, 1997]

§ 351.607 Permissive continuing exceptions.

An agency may make exception to the order of release in § 351.601 and to the action provisions of § 351.603 when needed to retain an employee on duties that cannot be taken over within 90 days and without undue interruption to the activity by an employee with higher retention standing. The agency shall notify in writing each higher-standing employee reached for release from the same competitive level of the reasons for the exception.

§ 351.608 Permissive temporary exceptions.

(a) *General.* (1) In accordance with this section, an agency may make a temporary exception to the order of release in § 351.601, and to the action provisions of § 351.603, when needed to retain an employee after the effective date of a reduction in force. Except as otherwise provided in paragraphs (c) and (e) of this section, an agency may not make a temporary exception for more than 90 days.

(2) After the effective date of a reduction in force action, an agency may not amend or cancel the reduction in force notice of an employee retained under a temporary exception so as to avoid completion of the reduction in force action. This does not preclude the employee from receiving or accepting a job offer in the same competitive area in accordance with a Reemployment Priority List established under part 330, subpart B, of this chapter, or under a Career Transition Assistance Plan established under part 330, subpart E, of this chapter, or equivalent programs.

(b) *Undue interruption.* An agency may make a temporary exception for not more than 90 days when needed to continue an activity without undue interruption.

(c) *Government obligation.* An agency may make a temporary exception to satisfy a Government obligation to the retained employee without regard to the 90-day limit set forth under paragraph (a)(1) of this section.

(d) *Sick leave.* An agency may make a temporary exception to retain on sick leave a lower standing employee covered by chapter 63 of title 5, United States Code (or other applicable leave system for Federal employees), who is on approved sick leave on the effective date of the reduction in force, for a period not to exceed the date the employee's sick leave is exhausted. Use of sick leave for this purpose must be in accordance with the requirements in part 630, subpart D, of this chapter (or other applicable leave system for Federal employees). Except as authorized by § 351.606(b), an agency may not approve an employee's use of any other type of leave after the employee has been retained under this paragraph (d).

(e)(1) An agency may make a temporary exception to retain on accrued annual leave a lower standing employee who:

(i) Is being involuntarily separated under this part;

(ii) Is covered by a Federal leave system under authority other than chapter 63 of title 5, United States Code; and,

(iii) Will attain first eligibility for an immediate retirement benefit under 5 U.S.C. 8336, 8412, or 8414 (or other authority), and/or establish eligibility under 5 U.S.C. 8905 (or other authority) to carry health benefits coverage into retirement during the period represented by the amount of the employee's accrued annual leave.

(2) An agency may not approve an employee's use of any other type of leave after the employee has been retained under this paragraph (e).

(3) This exception may not exceed the date the employee first becomes eligible for immediate retirement or for continuation of health benefits into retirement, except that an employee may be retained long enough to satisfy both retirement and health benefits requirements.

(4) Accrued annual leave includes all accumulated, accrued, and restored annual leave, as applicable, in addition to annual leave earned and available to the employee after the effective date of the reduction in force. When approving a temporary exception under this provision, an agency may not advance annual leave or consider any annual leave that might be credited to an employee's account after the effective date of the reduction in force other than annual leave earned while in an annual leave status.

(f) *Other exceptions.* An agency may make a temporary exception under this section to extend an employee's separation date beyond the effective date of the reduction in force when the temporary retention of a lower standing employee does not adversely affect the right of any higher standing employee who is released ahead of the lower standing employee. The agency may establish a maximum number of days, up to 90 days, for which an exception may be approved.

(g) *Notice to employees.* When an agency approves an exception for more than 30 days, it must:

(1) Notify in writing each higher standing employee in the same competitive level reached for release of the reasons for the exception and the date the lower standing employee's retention will end; and

(2) List opposite the employee's name on the retention register the reasons for the exception and the date the employee's retention will end.

[62 FR 10682, Mar. 10, 1997]

Subpart G—Assignment Rights (Bump and Retreat)

§ 351.701 Assignment involving displacement.

(a) *General.* When a group I or II competitive service employee with a current annual performance rating of record of minimally successful (Level 2) or equivalent, or higher, is released from a competitive level, an agency shall offer assignment, rather than furlough or separate, in accordance with paragraphs (b), (c), and (d) of this section to another competitive position which requires no reduction, or the lease possible reduction, in representative rate. The employee must be qualified for the offered position. The offered position shall be in the same competitive area, last at least 3 months, and have the same type of work schedule (e.g., full-time, part-time, intermittent, or seasonal) as the position from which the employee is released. Upon accepting an offer of assignment, or displacing another employee under this part, an employee retains the same status and tenure in the new position. The promotion potential of the offered position is not a consideration in determining an employee's right of assignment.

(b) *Lower subgroup—bumping.* A released employee shall be assigned in accordance with paragraph (a) of this section and bump to a position that:

(1) Is held by another employee in a lower tenure group or in a lower subgroup within the same tenure group; and

(2) Is no more than three grades (or appropriate grade intervals or equivalent) below the position from which the employee was released.

(c) *Same subgroup-retreating.* A released employee shall be assigned in accordance with paragraphs (a) and (d) of this section and retreat to a position that:

(1) Is held by another employee with lower retention standing in the same tenure group and subgroup; and

(2) Is not more than three grades (or appropriate grade intervals or equivalent) below the position from which the employee was released, except that for a preference eligible employee with a compensable service-connected disability of 30 percent or more the limit is five grades (or appropriate grade intervals or equivalent). (The agency uses the grade progression of only the released employee's position of record to determine the applicable grades (or appropriate grade intervals or equivalent) of the employee's retreat right. The agency does not consider the grade progression of the position to which the employee has a retreat right.); and

(3) Is the same position, or an essentially identical position, formerly held by the released employee on a permanent basis as a competing employee in a Federal agency (*i.e.*, when held by the released employee in an executive, legislative, or judicial branch agency, the position would have been placed in tenure groups I, II, or III, or equivalent). In determining whether a position is essentially identical, the determination is based on the competitive level criteria found in § 351.403, but not necessarily in regard to the respective grade, classification series, type of work schedule, or type of service, of the two positions.

(d) *Limitation.* An employee with a current annual performance rating of record of minimally successful (Level 2) or equivalent may be assigned under paragraph (c) of this section only to a position held by another employee with a current annual performance rating of record no higher than minimally successful (Level 2) or equivalent.

(e) *Pay rates.* (1) The determination of equivalent grade intervals shall be based on a comparison of representative rates.

(2) Each employee's assignment rights shall be determined on the basis of the pay rates in effect on the date of issuance of specific reduction-in-force

notices, except that when it is officially known on the date of issuance of notices that new pay rates have been approved and will become effective by the effective date of the reduction in force, assignment rights shall be determined on the basis of the new pay rates.

(f)(1) In determining applicable grades (or grade intervals) under §§351.701(b)(2) and 351.701(c)(2), the agency uses the grade progression of the released employee's position of record to determine the grade (or interval) limits of the employee's assignment rights.

(2) For positions covered by the General Schedule, the agency must determine whether a one-grade, two-grade, or mixed grade interval progression is applicable to the position of the released employee.

(3) For positions not covered by the General Schedule, the agency must determine the normal line of progression for each occupational series and grade level to determine the grade (or interval) limits of the released employee's assignment rights. If the agency determines that there is no normal line of progression for an occupational series and grade level, the agency provides the released employee with assignment rights to positions within three actual grades lower on a one-grade basis. The normal line of progression may include positions in different pay systems.

(4) For positions where no grade structure exists, the agency determines a line of progression for each occupation and pay rate, and provides assignment rights to positions within three grades (or intervals) lower on that basis.

(5) If the released employee holds a position that is less than three grades above the lowest grade in the applicable classification system (e.g., the employee holds a GS–2 position), the agency provides the released employee with assignment rights up to three actual grades lower on a one-grade basis in other pay systems.

(g) If a competitive area includes more than one local commuting area, the agency determines assignment rights under this part on the basis of the representative rates for one local commuting area within the competitive area (*i.e.*, the same local commuting area used to establish competitive levels under §351.403(c)(4), (5), and (6)).

(h) If a competitive area includes positions under one or more pay bands, a released employee shall be assigned in accordance with paragraphs (a) through (d) of this section to a position in an equivalent pay band or one pay band lower, as determined by the agency, than the pay band from which released. A preference eligible with a service-connected disability of 30 percent or more must be assigned in accordance with paragraphs (a) through (d) of this section to a position in an equivalent pay band or up to two pay bands lower, as determined by the agency, than the pay band from which released.

(i) If a competitive area includes positions under one or more pay bands, and other positions not covered by a pay band (e.g., GS and/or FWS positions), the agency provides assignment rights under this part by:

(1) Determining the representative rate of positions not covered by a pay band, consistent with §351.203;

(2) Determining the representative rate of each pay band, or competitive level within the pay band(s), consistent with §351.203;

(3) As determined by the agency, providing assignment rights under paragraph (b) of this section (bumping), or paragraphs (c) and (d) of this section (retreating), consistent with the grade intervals covered in paragraphs (b)(2) and (c)(2) of this section, and the pay band intervals in paragraph (h) of this section.

[51 FR 319, Jan. 3, 1986, as amended at 56 FR 65417, Dec. 17, 1991; 60 FR 3063, Jan. 13, 1995; 60 FR 44254, Aug. 25, 1995; 62 FR 62502, Nov. 24, 1997; 63 FR 32594, June 15, 1998; 65 FR 62991, Oct. 20, 2000; 73 FR 29389, May 21, 2008]

§351.702 Qualifications for assignment.

(a) Except as provided in §351.703, an employee is qualified for assignment under §351.701 if the employee:

(1) Meets the OPM standards and requirements for the position, including any minimum educational requirement, and any selective placement factors established by the agency;

(2) Is physically qualified, with reasonable accommodation where appropriate, to perform the duties of the position;

(3) Meets any special qualifying condition which the OPM has approved for the position; and

(4) Has the capacity, adaptability, and special skills needed to satisfactorily perform the duties of the position without undue interruption. This determination includes recency of experience, when appropriate.

(b) The sex of an employee may not be considered in determining whether an employee is qualified for a position, except for positions which OPM has determined certification of eligibles by sex is justified.

(c) An employee who is released from a competitive level during a leave of absence because of a corpensable injury may not be denied an assignment right solely because the employee is not physically qualified for the duties of the position if the physical disqualification resulted from the compensable injury. Such an employee must be afforded appropriate assignment rights subject to recovery as provided by 5 U.S.C. 8151 and part 353 of this chapter.

(d) If an agency determines, on the basis of evidence before it, that a preference eligible employee who has a compensable service-connected disability of 30 percent or more is not able to fulfill the physical requirements of a position to which the employee would otherwise have been assigned under this part, the agency must notify the OPM of this determination. At the same time, the agency must notify the employee of the reasons for the determination and of the right to respond, within 15 days of the notification, to the OPM which will require the agency to demonstrate that the notification was timely sent to the employee's last known address. The OPM shall make a final determination concerning the physical ability of the employee to perform the duties of the position. This determination must be made before the agency may select any other person for the position. When the OPM has completed its review of the proposed disqualification on the basis of physical disability, it must sent its finding to both the agency and the employee. The agency must comply with the findings of the OPM. The functions of the OPM under this paragraph may not be delegated to an agency.

(e) An agency may formally designate as a trainee or developmental position a position in a program with all of the following characteristics:

(1) The program must have been designed to meet the agency's needs and requirements for the development of skilled personnel;

(2) The program must have been formally designated, with its provisions made known to employees and supervisors;

(3) The program must be developmental by design, offering planned growth in duties and responsibilities, and providing advancement in recognized lines of career progression; and

(4) The program must be fully implemented, with the participants chosen through standard selection procedures. To be considered qualified for assignment under § 351.701 to a formally designated trainee or developmental position in a program having all of the characteristics covered in paragraphs (e)(1), (2), (3), and (4) of this section, an employee must meet all of the conditions required for selection and entry into the program.

[51 FR 319, Jan. 3, 1986, as amended at 60 FR 3063, Jan. 13, 1995]

§ 351.703 Exception to qualifications.

An agency may assign an employee to a vacant position under § 351.201(b) or § 351.701 of this part without regard to OPM's standards and requirements for the position if:

(a) The employee meets any minimum education requirement for the position; and

(b) The agency determines that the employee has the capacity, adaptability, and special skills needed to satisfactorily perform the duties and responsibilities of the position.

[56 FR 65417, Dec. 17, 1991]

§ 351.704 Rights and prohibitions.

(a)(1) An agency may satisfy an employee's right to assignment under

§ 351.701 by assignment to a vacant position under § 351.201(b), or by assignment under any applicable administrative assignment provisions of § 351.705, to a position having a representative rate equal to that the employee would be entitled under § 351.701. An agency may also offer an employee assignment under § 351.201(b) to a vacant position in lieu of separation by reduction in force under 5 CFR part 351. Any offer of assignment under § 351.201(b) to a vacant position must meet the requirements set forth under § 351.701.

(2) An agency may, at its discretion, choose to offer a vacant other-than-full-time position to a full-time employee or to offer a vacant full-time position to an other-than-full-time employee in lieu of separation by reduction in force.

(b) Section 351.701 does not:

(1) Authorize or permit an agency to assign an employee to a position having a higher representative rate;

(2) Authorize or permit an agency to displace a full-time employee by an other-than-full-time employee, or to satisfy an other-than-full-time employee's right to assignment by assigning the employee to a vacant full-time position.

(3) Authorize or permit an agency to displace an other-than-full-time employee by a full-time employee, or to satisfy a full-time employee's right to assignment by assigning the employee to a vacant other-than-full-time position.

(4) Authorize or permit an agency to assign a competing employee to a temporary position (*i.e.*, a position under an appointment not to exceed 1 year), except as an offer of assignment in lieu of separation by reduction in force under this part when the employee has no right to a position under § 351.701 or § 351.704(a)(1) of this part. This option does not preclude an agency from, as an alternative, also using a temporary position to reemploy a competing employee following separation by reduction in force under this part.

(5) Authorize or permit an agency to displace an employee or to satisfy a competing employee's right to assignment by assigning the employee to a position with a different type of work schedule (e.g., full-time, part-time, intermittent, or seasonal) than the position from which the employee is released.

[51 FR 319, Jan. 3, 1986, as amended at 56 FR 65417, Dec. 17, 1991; 60 FR 3063, Jan. 13, 1995; 63 FR 63591, Nov. 16, 1998]

§ 351.705 Administrative assignment.

(a) An agency may, at its discretion, adopt provisions which:

(1) Permit a competing employee to displace an employee with lower retention standing in the same subgroup consistent with § 351.701 when the agency cannot make an equally reasonable assignment by displacing an employee in a lower subgroup;

(2) Permit an employee in subgroup III-AD to displace an employee in subgroup III-A or III-B, or permit an employee in subgroup III-A to displace an employee is subgroup III-B consistent with § 351.701; or

(3) Provide competing employees in the excepted service with assignment rights to other positions under the same appointing authority on the same basis as assignment rights provided to competitive service employees under § 351.701 and in paragraphs (a) (1) and (2) of this section.

(b) Provisions adopted by an agency under paragraph (a) of this section:

(1) Shall be consistent with this part;

(2) Shall be uniformly and consistently applied in any one reduction in force;

(3) May not provide for the assignment of an other-than-full-time employee to a full-time position;

(4) May not provide for the assignment of a full-time employee to an other-than-full-time position;

(5) May not provide for the assignment of an employee in a competitive service position to a position in the excepted service; and

(6) May not provide for the assignment of an employee in an excepted position to a position in the competitive service.

[51 FR 319, Jan. 3, 1986, as amended at 62 FR 62502, Nov. 24, 1997]

Subpart H—Notice to Employee

SOURCE: 60 FR 2679, Jan. 11, 1995, unless otherwise noted.

§ 351.801 Notice period.

(a)(1) Each competing employee selected for release from a competitive level under this part is entitled to a specific written notice at least 60 full days before the effective date of release.

(2) At the same time an agency issues a notice to an employee, it must give a written notice to the exclusive representative(s), as defined in 5 U.S.C. 7103(a)(16), of each affected employee at the time of the notice. When a significant number of employees will be separated, an agency must also satisfy the notice requirements of §§ 351.803 (b) and (c).

(b) When a reduction in force is caused by circumstances not reasonably foreseeable, the Director of OPM, at the request of an agency head or designee, may approve a notice period of less than 60 days. The shortened notice period must cover at least 30 full days before the effective date of release. An agency request to OPM shall specify:

(1) The reduction in force to which the request pertains;

(2) The number of days by which the agency requests that the period be shortened;

(3) The reasons for the request; and

(4) Any other additional information that OPM may specify.

(c) The notice period begins the day after the employee receives the notice.

(d) When an agency retains an employee under § 351.607 or § 351.608, the notice to the employee shall cite the date on which the retention period ends as the effective date of the employee's release from the competitive level.

[60 FR 2678, Jan. 11, 1995, as amended at 60 FR 44254, Aug. 25, 1995; 63 FR 32594, June 15, 1998; 65 FR 25623, May 3, 2000]

§ 351.802 Content of notice.

(a)(1) The action to be taken, the reasons for the action, and its effective date;

(2) The employee's competitive area, competitive level, subgroup, service date, and three most recent ratings of record received during the last 4 years;

(3) The place where the employee may inspect the regulations and record pertinent to this case;

(4) The reasons for retaining a lower-standing employee in the same competitive level under § 351.607 or § 351.608;

(5) Information on reemployment rights, except as permitted by § 351.803(a); and

(6) The employee's right, as applicable, to appeal to the Merit Systems Protection Board under the provisions of the Board's regulations or to grieve under a negotiated grievance procedure. The agency shall also comply with § 1201.21 of this title.

(b) When an agency issues an employee a notice, the agency must, upon the employee's request, provide the employee with a copy of OPM's retention regulations found in part 351 of this chapter.

[60 FR 2678, Jan. 11, 1995, as amended at 60 FR 44254, Aug. 25, 1995; 62 FR 62502, Nov. 24, 1997; 63 FR 32595, June 15, 1998]

§ 351.803 Notice of eligibility for reemployment and other placement assistance.

(a) An employee who receives a specific notice of separation under this part must be given information concerning the right to reemployment consideration and career transition assistance under subparts B (Reemployment Priority List), F, and G (Career Transition Assistance Programs) of part 330 of this chapter. The employee must also be given a release to authorize, at his or her option, the release of his or her resume and other relevant employment information for employment referral to the State unit or entity established under title I of the Workforce Investment Act of 1998 and potential public or private sector employers. The employee must also be given information concerning how to apply both for unemployment insurance through the appropriate State program and benefits available under the State's Workforce Investment Act of 1998 programs, and an estimate of severance pay (if eligible).

(b) When 50 or more employees in a competitive area receive separation notices under this part, the agency must provide written notification of the action, at the same time it issues specific notices of separation to employees, to:

(1) The State or the entity designated by the State to carry out rapid response activities under title I of the Workforce Investment Act of 1998;

(2) The chief elected official of local government(s) within which these separations will occur; and

(3) OPM.

(c) The notice required by paragraph (b) of this section must include:

(1) The number of employees to be separated from the agency by reduction in force (broken down by geographic area or other basis specified by OPM);

(2) The effective date of the separations; and

(3) Any other information specified by OPM, including information needs identified from consultation between OPM and the Department of Labor to facilitate delivery of placement and related services.

[60 FR 2679, Jan. 11, 1995, as amended at 62 FR 62502, Nov. 24, 1997; 65 FR 64133, Oct. 26, 2000]

§351.804 Expiration of notice.

(a) A notice expires when followed by the action specified, or by an action less severe than specified, in the notice or in an amendment made to the notice before the agency takes the action.

(b) An agency may not take the action before the effective date in the notice; instead, the agency may cancel the reduction in force notice and issue a new notice subject to this subpart.

[62 FR 62502, Nov. 24, 1997]

§351.805 New notice required.

(a) An employee is entitled to a written notice of at least 60 full days if the agency decides to take an action more severe than first specified.

(b) An agency must give an employee an amended written notice if the reduction in force is changed to a later date. A reduction in force action taken after the date specified in the notice given to the employee is not invalid for that reason, except when it is challenged by a higher-standing employee in the competitive level who is reached out of order for a reduction in force action as a result of the change in dates.

(c) An agency must give an employee an amended written notice and allow the employee to decide whether to accept a better offer of assignment under subpart G of this part that becomes available before or on the effective date of the reduction in force. The agency must give the employee the amended notice regardless of whether the employee has accepted or rejected a previous offer of assignment, provided that the employee has not voluntarily separated from his or her official position.

[62 FR 62502, Nov. 24, 1997, as amended at 65 FR 25623, May 3, 2000]

§351.806 Status during notice period.

When possible, the agency shall retain the employee on active duty status during the notice period. When in an emergency the agency lacks work or funds for all or part of the notice period, it may place the employee on annual leave with or without his or her consent, or leave without pay with his or her consent, or in a nonpay status without his or her consent.

§351.807 Certification of Expected Separation.

(a) For the purpose of enabling otherwise eligible employees to be considered for eligibility to participate in dislocated worker programs under the Workforce Investment Act of 1998 administered by the U.S. Department of Labor, an agency may issue a Certificate of Expected Separation to a competing employee who the agency believes, with a reasonable degree of certainty, will be separated from Federal employment by reduction in force procedures under this part. A certification may be issued up to 6 months prior to the effective date of the reduction in force.

(b) This certification may be issued to a competing employee only when the agency determines:

(1) There is a good likelihood the employee will be separated under this part;

(2) Employment opportunities in the same or similar position in the local commuting area are limited or nonexistent;

(3) Placement opportunities within the employee's own or other Federal agencies in the local commuting area are limited or nonexistent; and

(4) If eligible for optional retirement, the employee has not filed a retirement application or otherwise indicated in writing an intent to retire.

(c) A certification is to be addressed to each individual eligible employee and must be signed by an appropriate agency official. A certification must contain the expected date of reduction in force, a statement that each factor in paragraph (b) of this section has been satisfied, and a description of Workforce Investment Act of 1998, title I, programs, the Interagency Placement Program, and the Reemployment Priority List.

(d) A certification may not be used to satisfy any of the notice requirements elsewhere in this subpart.

(e) An agency determination of eligibility for certification may not be appealed to OPM or the Merit Systems Protection Board.

(f) An agency may also enroll eligible employees on the agency's Reemployment Priority List up to 6 months in advance of a reduction in force. For requirements and criteria, see subpart B of part 330 of this chapter.

[60 FR 2678, Jan. 11, 1995, as amended at 60 FR 44254, Aug. 25, 1995; 65 FR 64134, Oct. 26, 2000; 66 FR 29896, June 4, 2001]

Subpart I—Appeals and Corrective Action

§ 351.901 Appeals.

An employee who has been furloughed for more than 30 days, separated, or demoted by a reduction in force action may appeal to the Merit Systems Protection Board.

[52 FR 46051, Dec. 4, 1987]

§ 351.902 Correction by agency.

When an agency decides that an action under this part was unjustified or unwarranted and restores an individual to the former grade or rate of pay held or to an intermediate grade or rate of pay, it shall make the restoration retroactively effective to the date of the improper action.

Subpart J [Reserved]

PART 352—REEMPLOYMENT RIGHTS

Subpart A [Reserved]

Subpart B—Reemployment Rights Based on Movement Between Executive Agencies During Emergencies

Subpart C—Detail and Transfer of Federal Employees to International Organizations

Subpart D—Employment of Presidential Appointees and Elected Officers by the International Atomic Energy Agency

Subpart E—Reinstatement Rights After Service Under Section 233(d) and 625(b) of the Foreign Assistance Act of 1961

Subpart F [Reserved]

Subpart G—Reemployment Rights of Former Bureau of Indian Affairs and Indian Health Service Employees After Service Under the Indian Self-Determination Act in Tribal Organizations

Subpart H—Reemployment Rights Under the Taiwan Relations Act

Subpart I—Reemployment Rights After Service With the Panama Canal Commission

SOURCE: 33 FR 12433, Sept. 4, 1968, unless otherwise noted.

EDITORIAL NOTE: Nomenclature changes to part 352 appear at 69 FR 2050, Jan. 13, 2004.

Subpart A [Reserved]

Subpart B—Reemployment Rights Based on Movement Between Executive Agencies During Emergencies

AUTHORITY: 5 U.S.C. 3101 note, 3301, 3131 *et seq*. 3302; E.O. 10577, 3 CFR 1954–1958 Com., p. 218; sec. 352. 209 also issued under 5 U.S.C. 7701, *et seq*.

§ 352.201 Letter of Authority.

(a) *Definition*. A Letter of Authority is an authorization from OPM to an agency appointing officer to grant reemployment rights.

(b) *Scope of authority*. A Letter of Authority shall specify the conditions under which it may be used, including the types of positions covered and the organizational and geographic areas to which it is restricted.

(c) *Time limit of authority*. A Letter of Authority shall remain in force for one year from date of issuance unless earlier revoked by OPM. Renewals or extensions will not be issued unless justified by exceptional circumstances.

§ 352.202 Request for Letter of Authority.

When an agency believes that an emergency situation is so critical as to justify offers of reemployment rights, it may request OPM to issue a Letter of Authority. In submitting the request the agency shall present its justification in terms of the standards provided in § 352.203.

§ 352.203 Standards for issuing Letters of Authority.

OPM will determine the standards to be used in issuing Letters of Authority, which shall include the following:

(a) The positions to be filled must be related to emergency situations for which the usual recruiting methods are inadequate.

(b) The positions must be a part of a specific program immediately essential to the national interest.

(c) The positions must be essential to the functioning of the program.

(d) There must be substantial basis for the belief that reemployment rights will be a significant and reasonable aid in meeting the emergency situation.

§ 352.204 Basic eligibility for reemployment rights.

(a) *Employees eligible.* The following employees in the executive branch of the Government are eligible to be granted reemployment rights when they are hired by another executive agency without break in service of a full workday by transfer or reinstatement, or by excepted appointment, in a position which the agency is currently authorized to fill with reemployment rights:

(1) An employee serving in a competitive position under a career or career-conditional appointment;

(2) An employee serving under a career appointment in the Senior Executive Service (SES); or

(3) A nontemporary excepted employee.

(b) *Employees not eligible.* The following employees are not eligible to be granted reemployment rights:

(1) An employee who is serving a probationary or trial period under an appointment to a position in the excepted or competitive service or the SES.

(2) An employee serving in an obligated position;

(3) An employee serving with reemployment rights granted under this subpart;

(4) An employee who has received a notice of involuntary separation because of reduction in force or otherwise; or

(5) An employee who has already submitted a resignation.

[33 FR 12433, Sept. 4, 1968, as amended at 51 FR 25187, July 11, 1986]

§ 352.205 Appeal of losing agency.

An appointing officer who intends to employ with reemployment rights an employee of another executive agency shall give the losing agency written notice at least 15 calendar days before the effective date of the proposed action. If the losing agency believes the grant of reemployment rights would be detrimental to the public interest, it may appeal the proposed grant to OPM within 15 calendar days after receipt of the notice. The losing agency, at the same time, shall furnish a copy of the appeal to the prospective appointing officer, who shall withhold the proposed grant pending decision on the appeal. OPM shall determine whether the employee will be given reemployment rights and notify both agencies accordingly. If the losing agency does not appeal within 15 calendar days, the employee shall be granted reemployment rights.

§ 352.205a Authority to return employee to his or her former or successor agency.

The transfer of an employee with a grant of reemployment rights under this subpart authorizes the return of the employee to his or her former or successor agency without regard to part 351, 752, or 771 of this chapter when the employee is reemployed in his or her former or successor agency—

(a) Without a break in service of 1 workday or more in a position at the same or higher grade in the same occupational field and geographical area as the position he or she last held in the former or successor agency; and

(b) At not less than the rate of pay he or she would have been receiving in the position last held in the former or successor agency if he or she had not been transferred.

[51 FR 25187, July 11, 1986]

§ 352.205b Authority to return an SES employee to his or her former or successor agency.

The transfer of a career SES appointee with a grant of reemployment rights under this subpart authorizes the return of the employee to his or her former or successor agency when the employee is reemployed in his or her former or successor agency—

(a) Without a break in service of 1 workday or more in any position in the SES for which the employee is qualified; and

(b) At not less than the SES rate of basic pay as determined under 5 CFR part 534, subpart D at which the employee was being paid immediately before his or her transfer.

[51 FR 25187, July 11, 1986]

§ 352.206 Expiration of reemployment rights.

Reemployment rights granted under a Letter of Authority expire at the end of 2 years following the date of the personnel action, unless exercised or otherwise terminated before that time, except that the reemployment rights of an employee serving outside the continental United States extend for an additional period of 3 months.

§352.207 Exercise or termination of reemployment rights.

(a) *Exercise.* The time limits for application for reemployment under this subpart are:

(1) Within 30 calendar days before the expiration of the term of reemployment rights;

(2) Within 30 calendar days after receipt of notice of involuntary separation;

(3) At least 30 calendar days in advance of the person's scheduled entry into active military duty. In this case he shall be reemployed and separated, furloughed, or granted leave of absence for military service by the reemploying agency; or

(4) At any time before the expiration of the term of reemployment rights with the written consent of the current employing agency if application for reemployment is made within 30 days after date of separation, or after receipt of advance notice of proposed demotion by the current employing agency.

(b) *Termination.* An employee's reemployment rights terminate if:

(1) He fails to apply within the time limits stated in paragraph (a) of this section;

(2) He resigns without the written consent of the current employing agency; or

(3) Within 10 calendar days, he fails to accept an offer of reemployment made under §352.208 which is determined to be a proper offer of reemployment by the reemploying agency or by the Merit Systems Protection Board on appeal.

§352.208 Agency's obligation to reemploy.

(a) *Employee's right to reemployment.* An employee is entitled to be reemployed by the reemploying agency as promptly as possible but not more than 30 calendar days after receipt of his application. Except as provided in paragraph (c) of this section, the employee is entitled to reemployment in the occupational field and at the same grade or level and in the same geographical area as the position which the employee last held in that agency. If the reemployment would cause the separation or demotion of another employee, the applicant shall then be considered an employee for the purpose of applying the reduction-in-force regulations (5 CFR part 351) to determine to what, if any, position, he or she is entitled.

(b) *Reemployment in a higher grade.* The reemploying agency may reemploy the employee in a position of higher grade than that to which he is entitled, but not if this reemployment would cause the displacement of another employee.

(c) *Reemployment in SES.* When the employee's right is to a position in the SES, reemployment or return may be to any position in the SES for which the employee is qualified.

(d) *Seniority in postal service.* On reemployment in the postal service, the employee is entitled to the seniority he would have attained had he remained in the postal service.

(e) *Basis for agency refusal to reemploy.* An agency may refuse to reemploy under this section only when the employee was last separated for serious cause evidencing his unsuitability for reemployment.

[33 FR 12433, Sept. 4, 1968, as amended at 51 FR 25187, July 11, 1986]

§352.209 Employee appeals to the Merit Systems Protection Board.

When an agency denies reemployment to a person claiming reemployment rights under this subpart, the agency shall inform him or her of that denial by a written notice. In the same notice, the agency shall inform him/her of his/her right to appeal to the Merit Systems Protection Board under the provisions of the Board's regulations. The agency shall comply with the provisions of §1201.21 of this title.

[44 FR 48952, Aug. 21, 1979]

Subpart C—Detail and Transfer of Federal Employees to International Organizations

AUTHORITY: 5 U.S.C. 3584, E.O. 11552, 3 CFR 1966–1970 Comp., p. 954; Section 352.313 also issued under 5 U.S.C. 7701, *et seq.*

SOURCE: 35 FR 16525, Oct. 23, 1970, unless otherwise noted.

§ 352.301 Purpose.

The purpose of this subpart is to encourage details and transfers of employees for service with international organizations as authorized by sections 3343 and 3581–3584 of title 5, United States Code, and to provide procedures for participation in the program.

§ 352.302 Definitions.

In this subpart:

(a) *Agency, employee, international organization*, and *transfer* have the meaning given them by section 3581 of title 5, United States Code;

(b) *Detail* has the meaning given it by section 3343 of title 5, United States Code; and

(c) *Term of employment* means not more than (1) 5 consecutive years of employment, except that when the Secretary of State determines it to be in the national interest, the detail or transfer may be extended up to an additional 3 years, or (2) the period of less than 5 years specified at the time of consent to transfer or detail, beginning with entrance on duty in the international organization.

§ 352.303 [Reserved]

§ 352.304 International organizations covered.

(a) An agency may detail or transfer an employee under this subpart, without prior approval, to an organization which the Department of State has designated as an international organization.

(b) An agency may detail or transfer an employee under this subpart to any other public international organization or international organization preparatory commission only when the Department of State agrees that the organization concerned could be designated as an international organization covered by sections 3343 and 3581 of title 5, United States Code.

[73 FR 64860, Oct. 31, 2008]

§ 352.305 Eligibility for detail.

An employee is eligible for detail to an international organization with the rights provided for in, and in accordance with, section 3343 of title 5, United States Code, and this subpart, except the following:

(a) A Presidential appointee (other than a postmaster, Foreign Service officer or a Foreign Service information officer), regardless of whether the appointment was made by and with the advice and consent of the Senate.

(b) A person serving in the executive branch in a confidential or policy-determining position excepted from the competitive service under Schedule C of part 213 of this chapter.

(c) A person serving under a non-career, limited emergency, or limited term appointment in the Senior Executive Service (SES).

(d) A person serving under a temporary appointment.

[73 FR 64860, Oct. 31, 2008]

§ 352.306 Length of details.

The total length of a detail or several details combined must not exceed 5 consecutive years, except that when the Secretary of State, on the recommendation of the head of the agency, determines it to be in the national interest, the 5 years allowed for details may be extended for up to an additional 3 years. A detail or combination of details and transfers must not exceed 8 years in the aggregate throughout an employee's Federal career.

[73 FR 64860, Oct. 31, 2008]

§ 352.307 Eligibility for transfer.

An employee is eligible for transfer to an international organization with the rights provided for in, and in accordance with, sections 3581–3584 of title 5, United States Code, and this subpart, except the following:

(a) A Presidential appointee (other than a postmaster, a Foreign Service officer or a Foreign Service information officer), regardless of whether his appointment was made by and with the advice and consent of the Senate.

(b) A person serving in the executive branch in a confidential or policy-determining position excepted from the competitive service under Schedule C of part 213 of this chapter.

(c) A person serving under a noncareer, limited emergency, or limited term appointment in the SES.

(d) A person serving under a temporary appointment pending establishment of a register.

(e) A person serving under an appointment specifically limited to 1 year or less.

(f) A person serving on a seasonal, intermittent, or part-time basis.

[35 FR 16525, Oct. 23, 1970, as amended at 51 FR 25188, July 11, 1986; 57 FR 10124, Mar. 24, 1992]

§ 352.308 Effecting employment by transfer.

(a) *Authority to approve transfers.* On written request by an international organization for the services of an employee, the agency may authorize the transfer of the employee to the organization for any period not to exceed 5 years, except that when the Secretary of State determines it to be in the national interest, a period of employment by transfer may be extended, subject to the approval of the head of the agency, for up to an additional 3 years. A transfer or series of transfers or combination of details and transfers shall not exceed 8 years in the aggregate. Refusal by the head of the agency to authorize the transfer or the extension of the transfer is not reviewable by or appealable to OPM.

(b) *Letter of consent.* When an agency consents to the transfer of an employee, the agency shall give its consent in writing to the international organization and shall furnish the employee with a copy of the consent.

(c) *Effective date.* The agency and the international organization shall establish the effective date of transfer by mutual agreement.

(d) *Recording requirement.* The agency must furnish the employee with a leave statement, showing his or her annual and sick leave balances at the time of transfer. In addition, the notification of personnel action effecting the employee's separation for transfer must include:

(1) Identification of the international organization to which the employee is transferring,

(2) A clear statement of the period during which the employee has reemployment rights in the agency under section 3582 of title 5, United States Code, and this subpart, and

(3) The legal and regulatory conditions for reemployment.

[35 FR 16525, Oct. 23, 1970, as amended at 73 FR 64860, Oct. 31, 2008]

§ 352.309 Retirement, health benefits, and group life insurance.

(a) *Agency action.* An employee who is transferred to an international organization with the consent of the employing agency is entitled to retain coverage for retirement, health benefits, and group life insurance purposes if he or she so chooses. The period during which coverage, rights, and benefits are retained under this paragraph, during employment with the international organization, is deemed employment by the United States. At the time an employing Federal agency consents to the transfer of an employee, the agency must advise the employee in writing of the employee's right to continue retirement, health benefits, and group life insurance coverage, as applicable, for the duration of the assignment or transfer. The notice must explain the conditions for continued coverage and the employee's obligations and responsibilities with regard to continued coverage. The notice must also explain that, if the employee elects to retain coverage, the agency will continue to make the agency contributions to the funds, and the employee's coverage will continue as long as employee payments are currently deposited in the respective funds.

(b) *Employee action.* The employee must acknowledge, in writing, receipt of the notice and state whether or not he or she wishes to retain coverage under the retirement, health benefits, and group life insurance systems or any of them by continuing the required employee payments. The employee must make a written election to retain benefits, as applicable, and make arrangements for the required employee payments. An employee who transfers to an international organization is not eligible to participate in the Thrift Savings Plan (TSP) while employed by the international organization even if he or she elects to retain Federal retirement coverage. However, upon reemployment, an employee who elected to retain Federal retirement coverage while employed by the international organization and has made all deposits required for such coverage may make contributions to the TSP which he or she missed as a result of the service with an international organization, and receive make-up agency contributions and lost earnings on the agency contributions, as provided under § 352.311(e).

(c) *Agency responsibility*. For retirement and group life insurance purposes, the employing agency is responsible for determining the applicable rate of pay in accordance with the provisions of section 3583 of title 5, United States Code. The agency is also responsible for collecting, accounting for, and depositing in the respective funds all retirement, health benefits, and group life insurance employee payments required to be made for the purpose of protecting the rights of the employee so transferred; and for accounting for and depositing in the respective funds all agency contributions. The agency must furnish the employee with specific information as to how, when, and where the payments are to be submitted.

(d) *Coverage*. Employee payments are considered to be currently deposited if received by the agency before, during, or within 3 months after the end of the pay period covered by the deposit. If the contributions are not currently deposited, coverage terminates on the last day of the pay period for which the required contributions were currently deposited, subject to a 31-day extension of group life insurance and health benefits coverage as provided in parts 870 and 890 of this chapter and to the conversion benefits provided in parts 870 and 890 of this chapter. Coverage so terminated may not be re-established before the employee actually enters on duty, on the first day in a pay status in an agency. However, terminated retirement, health benefits, and group life insurance coverage must be reinstated retroactively when, in the judgment of OPM, the failure to make the required current deposit was due to circumstances beyond the employee's control and the required payments were deposited at the first opportunity. Coverage under a system other than the Civil Service Retirement System must be reinstated retroactively if the agency which administers the retirement system determines that the failure to make the required current deposit was due to circumstances beyond the control of the employee and the required payments were deposited at the first opportunity.

[73 FR 64860, Oct. 31, 2008]

§ 352.310 [Reserved]

§ 352.311 Reemployment.

(a) An employee who transferred to an international organization with the consent of the employing agency is entitled to be reemployed in his or her former position, or one of like seniority, status, and pay, within 30 days of applying for reemployment if the employee:

(1) Is separated, either voluntarily or involuntarily, without cause, within the term of employment with an international organization; and

(2) Applies for reemployment with the employing agency or its successor no later than 90 days after separation from the international organization.

(b) Pay upon reemployment will be set at that to which the employee would have been entitled had the employee remained with the employing agency.

(c) When an employee's reemployment right is to a position in the SES, reemployment may be to any position in the SES for which the employee is qualified. The employee must be returned at not less than the SES rate of basic pay as determined under 5 CFR part 534, subpart D, at which the employee was being paid immediately before transfer to the international organization, or if pay has been adjusted under § 352.314(c), at not less than the adjusted pay level.

(d) The period of separation caused by the employment of the employee with the international organization and the period necessary to effect reemployment are creditable service for all appropriate civil service employment purposes (e.g., tenure, service computation date, retirement, time in grade). Employees, upon return, are also entitled to restoration of any sick leave.

(e) An employee who elected to retain Federal retirement coverage while employed by the international organization and has made all deposits required for such coverage may make contributions to the TSP which he or she missed as a result of the service with the international organization, and receive make-up agency contributions and lost earnings on the agency contributions, consistent with applicable TSP requirements.

[73 FR 64861, Oct. 31, 2008]

§ 352.312 When to apply.

An employee may apply for reemployment, in writing, either before or after separation from the international organization. If the employee applies before separation, the 30-day period prescribed in § 352.311 begins either with the date of the application or 30 days before the employee's date of separation from the international organization, whichever is later. If the employee applies for reemployment after separation, the application must be received by the employing agency no later than 90 days after separation from the international organization.

[73 FR 64861, Oct. 31, 2008]

§ 352.313 Failure to reemploy and right of appeal.

(a) When an agency fails to reemploy an employee within 30 days of receiving the employee's application, it must notify the employee, in writing, of the reasons and of the employee's right to appeal to the Merit Systems Protection Board under the provisions of the Board's regulations. The agency must comply with the provisions of § 1201.21 of this title.

(b) If the agency fails to reach and issue a decision to the employee within 30 days from the date of the application for reemployment, the employee is entitled to appeal the agency's failure to issue a decision to the Merit Systems Protection Board under the provisions of the Board's regulations.

(c) An employee may submit an appeal, alleging that the agency has failed to comply with any of the other provisions of sections 3343 and 3581–3584 of title 5, United States Code, or of this part, to the Merit Systems Protection Board under the provisions of the Board's regulations.

[73 FR 64861, Oct. 31, 2008]

§ 352.314 Consideration for promotion and pay increases.

(a) The employing agency must consider an employee who is detailed or transferred to an international organization for all promotions for which the employee would be considered if not absent. A promotion based on this consideration is effective on the date it would have been effective if the employee were not absent.

(b) When the position of an employee who is absent on detail or transfer to an international organization is upgraded during the employee's absence, the employing agency must place the employee in the upgraded position upon return.

(c) The employing agency must consider an employee who is detailed or transferred to an international organization from an ungraded pay system for all pay increases for which the employee would have been considered if not absent. An increase is effective on the date it would have been effective if the employee were not absent.

[73 FR 64861, Oct. 31, 2008]

Subpart D—Employment of Presidential Appointees and Elected Officers by the International Atomic Energy Agency

AUTHORITY: Sec. 6(c), 71 Stat. 455; 22 U.S.C. 2025(c); E.O. 10774, 3 CFR, 1954–1958 Comp., p. 418, as amended by E.O. 10804, 3 CFR, 1959–1963 Comp., p. 328.

§ 352.401 Purpose.

The purpose of this subpart is to implement section 6(b) of the International Atomic Energy Agency Participation Act of 1957 and Executive Order 10774 as amended by Executive Order 10804 to protect the civil service rights and privileges, wherever appropriate, of Presidential appointees and elected officers who leave their positions and within 90 days enter employment with the International Atomic Energy Agency.

§ 352.402 Coverage.

This subpart applies to all officers, as defined in § 352.403(b), of any branch of the Federal Government.

§ 352.403 Definitions.

In this subpart:

(a) *Agency* means the International Atomic Energy Agency;

(b) *Officer* means any Presidential appointee or elected officer who leaves his position after August 27, 1957, and within 90 days enters employment with the agency; and

(c) *Term of employment* means not more than 3 consecutive years of employment beginning with entrance on duty in the agency.

§ 352.404 Retirement and insurance.

(a) *Coverage.* (1) To obtain retirement benefits for a term of employment with the agency, an officer covered by subchapter III of chapter 83 of title 5 United States Code, within 90 days after the date he is separated from the agency, shall pay to OPM all necessary employee deductions and agency contributions for coverage under that subchapter for his term of employment with the agency. Interest shall not be charged an officer on any payment of necessary employee deductions and agency contributions. The amount of the employee deductions so paid shall be added to the officer's lump-sum credit in the Civil Service Retirement and Disability Fund.

(2) To retain coverage under chapter 87 of title 5, United States Code, during his term of employment with the agency, an officer covered by that chapter shall currently pay employee deductions and agency contributions necessary for coverage under that chapter for his term of employment with the agency. Collections may be made under procedures which may be determined in accordance with written agreements reached between accounting representatives of OPM and the agency.

(3) All retirement and insurance benefits and obligations shall be computed in the same manner as if the rate of basic pay the officer was receiving on the last day he was in his Federal position before employment with the agency had continued without change.

(4) An officer not covered by either subchapter III of chapter 83, or chapter 87, of title 5, United States Code, in the Federal position which he last held or from which he separates to enter employment with the agency does not acquire coverage or benefits under these statutes based on employment with the agency.

(b) *Death coverage.* An officer who dies during his term of employment or within 90 days of his separation therefrom is deemed to have died in the Federal Service.

§ 352.405 Resumption of Federal service.

(a) *Pay increase.* Except for an employee whose right is to a position in the Senior Executive Service (SES), an officer who is reemployed in the Federal position which he or she left or one of like seniority, status, and pay within 90 days of his or her separation from the agency following a term of employment, is entitled to the rate of basic pay to which he/she would have been entitled had he or she remained in the Federal service. When the employee's right is to a position in the SES, this subpart authorizes reemployment to any position in the SES for which the employee is qualified at not less than the SES rate of basic pay as determined under 5 CFR part 534, subpart D at which the employee was being paid immediately before his or her transfer.

(b) *Sick leave account.* An officer shall have any sick leave account which he may have had in his last Federal position reestablished for credit or charge, if he returns to an appropriate leave system within 52 calendar weeks after the date he is separated from his term of employment with the agency.

(c) *Service credit for agency employment.* An officer who is reemployed in the Federal service within 90 days after completion of his term of employment with the agency is entitled to credit as

Federal service for his term of employment with the agency. However, OPM shall give service credit for subchapter III of chapter 83 of title 5, United States Code, purposes only if the officer complies with the requirements of § 352.404(a)(1).

[33 FR 12433, Sept. 4, 1968, as amended at 51 FR 25188, July 11, 1986]

Subpart E—Reinstatement Rights After Service Under Section 233(d) and 625(b) of the Foreign Assistance Act of 1961

AUTHORITY: Sec. 625, 75 Stat. 449; 22 U.S.C. 2385; E.O. 10973; 3 CFR 1959–1963 Comp., p. 493; Section 352.508 also issued under 5 U.S.C. 7701 *et seq.*

§ 352.501 Purpose.

This subpart governs reinstatement authorized by sections 233(d) and 625(b) of the Foreign Assistance Act of 1961, as amended (22 U.S.C. 2193(d) and 22 U.S.C. 235(b)).

[36 FR 13897, July 28, 1971]

§ 352.502 Coverage.

This subpart applies to any of the following serving in a position in the Federal Government:

(a) A person serving in the competitive service under a career or career-conditional appointment.

(b) A person serving under a career appointment in the Senior Executive Service (SES).

(c) A person serving in the excepted service under an appointment without a specific time limitation.

(d) A person appointed or assigned under authority of the Foreign Service Act of 1946, as amended (22 U.S.C. 801 *et seq.*).

[33 FR 12433, Sept. 4, 1968, as amended at 51 FR 25188, July 11, 1986]

§ 352.503 Definitions.

In this subpart:

(a) *Act* means the Foreign Assistance Act of 1961, as amended (22 U.S.C. 2151 *et seq.*); and

(b) *Former position* means the position that an employee was occupying at the time of his appointment to a position under authority of section 233(d) or section 625(b) of the Act.

[36 FR 13897, July 28, 1971]

§ 352.504 Basic entitlement.

Subject to the conditions specified in this subpart, an employee who is appointed to a position under authority of section 233(d) or section 625(b) of the Act is entitled, on termination of that appointment for any reason other than his or her own misconduct or delinquency, to be reinstated in his or her former position or in one of like seniority, status, and pay in the same agency. When the employee's right is to a position in the SES, reinstatement may be to any position in the SES for which the employee is qualified. The employee shall be returned at not less than the SES rate of basic pay as determined under 5 CFR part 534, subpart D at which the employee was being paid immediately before his or her transfer. If the functions with which the employee's former position was identified have been transferred to another agency, the employee's right to reinstatement is in the gaining agency.

[51 FR 25188, July 11, 1986]

§ 352.505 Proposed termination.

At least 45 days before termination of the appointment of an employee entitled to reinstatement, the agency terminating the employee shall notify the employee and his former agency in writing of the proposed termination. However, notification under this section is not required when:

(a) The termination is at the employee's own request; or

(b) The employee is reinstated without a break in service under an arrangement made between the agencies concerned.

§ 352.506 Application for reinstatement.

An employee who desires reinstatement shall apply for reinstatement, in writing, no later than 30 days after his appointment under authority of section 233(d) or section 625(b) of the Act is terminated, unless arrangement has been made for his reinstatement without a break in service under § 352.505(b).

[36 FR 13897, July 28, 1971]

§ 352.507 Reinstatement.

An employee eligible for reinstatement is entitled to be reinstated as soon as possible after his application for reinstatement, filed in accordance with § 352.506, is received. In any event, he is entitled to be reinstated (a) within 30 days after his application for reinstatement is received, or (b) on termination of the appointment made under authority of section 233(d) or section 625(b) of the act, whichever is later.

[36 FR 13897, July 28, 1971]

§ 352.508 Appeals to the Merit Systems Protection Board.

(a) If an agency determines that an employee who has applied for reinstatement is not eligible for reinstatement, it shall notify the employee as promptly as possible of its decision, of the basis therefor, and of the employee's appeal rights under this subpart. The employee is entitled to appeal the decision to the Merit Systems Protection Board under the provisions of the Board's regulations. The agency shall comply with the provisions of § 1201.21 of this title.

(b) If an agency fails to reinstate an employee within the time limits specified in § 352.507, the employee is entitled to appeal to the Merit Systems Protection Board under the provisions of the Board's regulations.

(c) If an employee considers that his reinstatement is not in accordance with the act and this subpart, he or she is entitled to appeal to the Merit Systems Protection Board under the provisions of the Board's regulations.

[44 FR 48952, Aug. 21, 1979]

Subpart F [Reserved]

Subpart G—Reemployment Rights of Former Bureau of Indian Affairs and Indian Health Service Employees After Service Under the Indian Self-Determination Act in Tribal Organizations

AUTHORITY: Sec. 105(i), Pub. L. 93–638, 88 Stat. 2210 (25 U.S.C. 450); E.O. 11899; 41 FR 3459; Section 352.707 also issued under 5 U.S.C. 7701, *et seq.*

SOURCE: 41 FR 27713, July 6, 1976, unless otherwise noted.

§ 352.701 Purpose.

This subpart governs reemployment rights authorized by section 105(i) of the Indian Self-Determination Act (88 Stat. 2210; Pub. L. 93–638, the Act) and E.O. 11899 after service in an Indian tribal organization under the Act.

§ 352.702 Definitions.

In this subpart:

(a) *Agency* means the Bureau of Indian Affairs and the Indian Health Service. For reemployment purposes, the Public Health Service shall be considered the agency to which Indian Health Service employees may return.

(b) *Competitive area* is the same as defined in § 351.402 of this title.

(c) *Tribal organization* is defined in section 4(c) of the Indian Self-Determination Act (88 Stat. 2204).

§ 352.703 Basic entitlement to reemployment rights on leaving Federal employment.

(a) *Employees entitled.* The following employees of the Bureau of Indian Affairs, Department of the Interior, and the Indian Health Service and the Public Health Service of the Department of Health and Human Services, are granted reemployment rights subject to the conditions of this subpart, to the Bureau of Indian Affairs, the Indian Health Service, or the Public Health Service, as appropriate, if they leave their Federal employment to be employed, with no break in service following separation from their agency, by an Indian tribal organization to work in a function of their respective agency contracted under the Indian Self-Determination Act to be performed by that tribal organization:

(1) An employee serving in a competitive position under a career or career-conditional appointment and who has satisfactorily completed at least 6 months of a probationary period; or

(2) A non-temporary excepted service employee who has satisfactorily completed at least 6 months of a trial period if one is required by the agency.

(3) An employee serving under a career appointment in the Senior Executive Service (SES) who is not serving a probationary period.

(b) *Employees not entitled.* The following employees are not entitled to reemployment rights under this subpart:

(1) An employee who has received a notice of involuntary separation because of reduction in force, or other cause, not directly related to contracting under the Act to a tribal organization;

(2) An employee whose resignation has been accepted for reasons other than to accept tribal employment under this subpart; or

(3) An employee serving under a Schedule C excepted appointment.

(c) *Not related to other benefits.* Entitlement to reemployment rights does not depend on continuation of Federal employee benefits coverage during service with a tribal organization.

[41 FR 27713, July 6, 1976, as amended at 51 FR 25188, July 11, 1986; 57 FR 10124, Mar. 24, 1992]

§352.704 Duration of reemployment rights.

(a) *Termination of authority.* Rights are not granted to persons who leave Federal employment for employment with a tribal organization after the date (December 31, 1985, at present) specified in section 105(e) of the Indian Self-Determination Act (88 Stat. 2209).

(b) *Maximum period of entitlement.* Entitlement to reemployment terminates at the end of 6 years following the date employment commences in the tribal organization unless exercised or otherwise terminated before that time as provided in this subpart.

§352.705 Return to Federal employment.

(a) *Conditions.* Reemployment rights may be exercised only under the following conditions. The individual must apply in writing to the former employing agency for reemployment not later than 30 calendar days after:

(1) Receipt of notice of involuntary separation from tribal employment. For this purpose, involuntary separation means any separation against the will and without consent of the individual.

(2) Reversion of the function to Federal operation, whether reversion is through tribal or Federal action; or

(3) Separation with the joint consent of the tribal organization and the Federal agency for reasons of personal hardship or other special circumstances.

(b) *Termination.* A former employee's entitlement to reemployment terminates for:

(1) Failure to apply for reemployment within the time limit stated in paragraph (a) of this section;

(2) Resignation from tribal service without the joint consent, described in paragraph (a)(3) of this section, of the tribal organization and the Federal employer; or

(3) Failure to accept, within 10 calendar days of receipt thereof, an offer of reemployment made under §352.706 which is determined by the employing agency or by the Merit Systems Protection Board on appeal to be a proper offer of reemployment.

§352.706 Agency response to reemployment application.

(a) *Employee's right to reemployment.* An employee is entitled to be reemployed by the reemploying agency as promptly as possible, and, in any event, within 45 calendar days after agency receipt of application.

(1) Within the competitive area the employee is entitled to reemployment in:

(i) The position held immediately before leaving the agency;

(ii) One in the same competitive level; or

(iii) Another position for which qualified and eligible at the same grade or level and in the same competitive area as the position the employee last held in the agency. The employing agency determines the position under paragraph (a)(1) (i), (ii), or (iii) of this section to which the employee is entitled. Reduction-in-force procedures shall be applied where necessary in determining the position to which the employee has a right. In applying the reduction-in-force regulations, the applicant shall be considered an employee of the agency.

(2) *Extending the area.* Responsibility for reemploying an applicant is nationwide within the agency. If the applicant is not placed under paragraph (a)(1) of this section, the agency must extend reemployment rights, based on the employee's availability, for assignment outside the competitive area. The employee is entitled to a position, for which qualified and eligible, at the same grade or level as the position last held in the agency. Where necessary, reduction-in-force procedures shall be applied in determining the position to which the employee has a right. The applicant shall be considered an employee for the purpose of applying the reduction-in-force regulations.

(b) *Employee option.* Before the competitive area is extended under paragraph (a)(2) of this section, an employee who cannot be placed under paragraph (a)(1) of this section, in the competitive area at the same grade or level as the position last held is entitled, if the employee elects, to reemployment in a position at a lower grade or level identified under the same conditions and procedures as paragraph (a)(1) of this section.

(c) *Agency option.* At any stage in the process, the agency has the option to satisfy the employee's right to reemployment by offering a vacant position which, under reduction-in-force regulations, is in accord with the employee's rights. Also, with the employee's consent, right to reemployment can be met by placement in a vacant position, for which the employee is qualified according to agency determination, and available, outside the organizational or geographic area of entitlement, either at the appropriate grade or at a grade other than the one to which entitled.

(d) *Reemployment to an SES position.* When the employee's right is to a position in the SES, reemployment or return may be to any position in the SES for which the employee is qualified. The employee shall be returned at not less than the SES rate of basic pay as determined under 5 CFR part 534, subpart D at which the employee was being paid immediately before his or her transfer.

(e) *Basis for agency refusal to reemploy.* An agency may refuse to reemploy when the employee was last separated from tribal employment for serious cause establishing unsuitability for reemployment.

(f) *Basis for agency inability to reemploy.* An agency may find it is unable to reemploy in the event no position can be found under procedures in this section.

[41 FR 27713, July 6, 1976, as amended at 51 FR 25188, July 11, 1986]

§ 352.707 Employee appeals to the Merit Systems Protection Board.

(a) If an agency denies reemployment to a person claiming reemployment rights under this subpart, the agency shall inform the individual of that denial and of the reasons therefor by a written notice. In the same notice, the agency shall inform the employee of the right to appeal to the Merit Systems Protection Board under the provisions of the Board's regulations. The agency shall comply with the provisions of § 1201.21 of this title.

(b) If an employee considers reemployment to be not in accordance with this subpart, the employee is entitled to appeal to the Merit Systems Protection Board under the provisions of the Board's regulations.

(c) Refusal of a tribe to hire a Federal employee is not appealable to the Merit Systems Protection Board.

[44 FR 48953, Aug. 21, 1979]

Subpart H—Reemployment Rights Under the Taiwan Relations Act

AUTHORITY: 22 U.S.C. 3310; E.O. 12143, 44 FR 37191; Section 352.807 also issued under 22 U.S.C. 3310; E.O. 12143, 45 FR 37452.

SOURCE: 46 FR 8433, Jan. 27, 1981, unless otherwise noted.

§ 352.801 Purpose.

This subpart governs reemployment rights authorized by section 11(a) (1) and (2) of the Taiwan Relations Act (Pub. L. 96–8) after service in the American Institute in Taiwan (AIT) under the Act.

§ 352.802 Definitions.

For the purposes of this subpart:

Act refers to Taiwan Relations Act (Pub. L. 96–8).

Competitive area is the same as defined in §351.402 of this title;

Institute means the American Institute in Taiwan.

Specified period of service shall be a period of not more than 6 years.

§352.803 Basic entitlement to reemployment rights on leaving Federal employment.

(a) This subpart applies to all executive agencies as defined in section 105 of title 5, United States Code, the U.S. Postal Service, the Postal Rate Commission, and to the employees thereof, and to those positions in the competitive civil service and the employees occupying those positions.

(b) The agency must give employees entitled to reemployment rights under this subpart written notice of these rights at the time of their separation.

(c) *Employees entitled.* The following employees or former employees are granted reemployment rights subject to the conditions of this subpart, if they leave their Federal employment to be employed (on the date of incorporation of AIT or within 30 calendar days following separation from their agency) by the Institute for a specified period of service.

(1) An employee serving in a competitive position under a career or career-conditional appointment;

(2) A non-temporary excepted service employee; or

(3) An employee serving under a career appointment in the Senior Executive Service.

(d) *Employees not entitled.* The following employees are not entitled to reemployment rights under this subpart:

(1) An employee who has received a notice of involuntary separation because of reduction in force, or other cause, not directly related to employment with the Institute under the Act;

(2) An employee whose resignation has been accepted for reasons other than to accept employment with the Institute under this subpart;

(3) An employee serving under a Schedule C excepted appointment; or

(4) An employee serving under a noncareer, limited emergency, or limited term appointment in the Senior Executive Service.

[46 FR 8433, Jan. 27, 1981, as amended at 57 FR 10124, Mar. 24, 1992]

§352.804 Maximum period of entitlement to reemployment.

Entitlement to reemployment terminates at the end of 6 years and 30 days, following the date employment commences in the Institute unless exercised or otherwise terminated before that time as provided in this subpart.

§352.805 Position to which entitled on reemployment.

(a) *Basic position entitlement.* (1) On reemployment, an employee is entitled to be appointed to a position in the employee's former or successor agency in the following order:

(i) To the position last held in the former agency:

(A) If that position has been identified for transfer to a different agency, reemployment rights must be exercised with the gaining agency.

(B) If that position has been reclassified, the employee should be placed in the reclassified position;

(ii) A position in the same competitive level; or

(iii) Another position for which otherwise qualified at the same grade or level and in the same competitive area.

(2) *The employing agency determines under paragraph (a)(1) of this section the position to which the employee is entitled.* Reduction-in-force procedures shall be applied when necessary in determining the position to which the employee has a right. In applying reduction-in-force procedures, the applicant shall be considered an employee of the agency.

(3) *Extending the area.* Responsibility for reemploying an applicant is agencywide. If the applicant is not placed under paragraph (a)(1) of this section, the agency must extend reemployment rights, based on the agency's need, for assignment outside the competitive area. The employee is entitled to a position, for which qualified and eligible, at the same grade or level as the position last held in the agency. Where necessary, reduction-in-force procedures shall be applied in determining the position to which the employee has

a right. The applicant shall be considered an employee for the purpose of applying the reduction-in-force procedures.

(b) *Employee option.* Before the competitive area is extended under paragraph (a)(3) of this section, an employee who cannot be placed under paragraph (a)(1) of this section in the same competitive area at the grade or level as the position last held, is entitled, if the employee elects, to reemployment in a position at a lower grade or level identified under the same conditions and procedures as paragraph (a)(1) of this section.

(c) *Agency option.* At any stage in the process, the agency has the option to satisfy the employee's right to reemployment by offering a vacant position which, under reduction-in-force regulations, is in accord with the employee's rights. Also, with the employee's consent, right to reemployment can be met by placement in a vacant position, for which the employee is qualified according to agency determination and need, outside the organizational or geographic area of entitlement, either at the appropriate grade or at a grade other than the one to which entitled.

(d) *Basic position entitlement in the Senior Executive Service.* (1) On reemployment, an employee (who meets the requirements to § 352.803(c)(3)) is entitled to be given a career appointment in the Senior Executive Service the employee's former or successor agency.

(2) The employee may be assigned to any position in the Senior Executive Service for which he/she meets the qualifications requirements.

(3) The employee may elect to accept reemployment in a position outside the Senior Executive Service. Such placement would be subject to the provisions of paragraphs (b) and (c) of this section.

§ 352.806 Return to Federal employment.

(a) *Conditions:* Reemployment rights may be exercised only under the following conditions. The employees must apply in writing to their former or successor agency:

(1) No less that 30 calendar days before completion of the specified period of service with the Institute; or

(2) No more than 30 calendar days after involuntary separation from the Institute; or

(3) No more than 30 calendar days after separation based on personal hardship or other special circumstances with the consent of Institute and former employing agency.

(b) An agency must act on the former employee's request for reemployment within 30 calendar days of receipt thereof, *i.e.*, the agency must provide the employee with a written notice stating the agency's decision whether to reemploy and the position being offered, if the employee is to be reemployed.

(c) *Termination of reemployment rights.* A former employee's entitlement to reemployment terminates for:

(1) Failure to apply, except for good cause shown, for reemployment within the time limits stated in paragraph (a) of this section;

(2) Resignation from the Institute without the consent of the Institute or the former employing agency; or

(3) Failure to accept, within 15 workdays of receipt thereof, an offer of reemployment under § 352.803 which is determined to be a proper offer of reemployment by the employing agency and by Merit Systems Protection Board (MSPB), if appealed.

§ 352.807 Appeals.

An employee may appeal to MSPB, under the provisions of the Board's regulations, an agency's decision on his or her request for reemployment which he or she believes is in violation of this subpart.

Subpart I—Reemployment Rights After Service With the Panama Canal Commission

AUTHORITY: Pub. L. 96–70, 22 U.S.C. 3643.

SOURCE: 50 FR 13963, Apr. 9, 1985, unless otherwise noted.

§ 352.901 Purpose.

This subpart implements section 1203 of the Panama Canal Act of 1979, which provides for the detail or transfer of Federal employees to the Panama Canal Commission with reemployment rights in the former agency.

§ 352.902 Definitions.

In this subpart—

Act means the Panama Canal Act of 1979 (22 U.S.C. 3601 *et seq.*).

Agency means an Executive agency, the United States Postal Service, and the Smithsonian Institution.

Commission means the Panama Canal Commission as established by section 1101 of the Act.

Competitive area is defined in § 351.402 of part 351 of this chapter.

Competitive level is defined in § 351.403(a) of part 351 of this chapter.

Detail is the assignment of loan of an employee to the Commission without the employee's transfer. The employee remains an employee of the agency in which employed and continues to be the incumbent of the position from which detailed.

Term of employment means the period of employment specified in the written agreement between the Commission and the agency for the transfer of an employee or extension of transfer.

Transfer means the change in appointment of an employee from an agency to a new appointment with the Commission.

§ 352.903 Effecting a detail or transfer.

(a) *Authority to approve.* The head of an agency may enter into written agreements with the Commission for the detail or voluntary transfer, for set periods of time, of agency employees to the Commission in accordance with section 3643 of title 22, United States Code, and this subpart. Refusal by the head of the agency to agree to a detail or transfer, or extension of detail or transfer, is not reviewable by the Office of Personnel Management or appealable.

(b) *Employee notice.* The agency will furnish the employee with a copy of the written agreement which must contain a statement of the time limits for exercising reemployment rights and the conditions of reemployment.

§ 352.904 Eligibility.

This subpart covers only eligible employees transferred or detailed to Commission positions with duty stations in the Republic of Panama.

(a) *Employees eligible.* Except as provided in paragraph (b) of this section, an employee serving in a position in an agency under any of the following appointments may be granted rights under this subpart:

(1) Career or career-conditional appointment in the competitive service;

(2) An appointment without a specific time limit in the excepted service; or

(3) A career appointment in the Senior Executive Service.

(b) *Employee not eligible.* The following employees are not eligible under this subpart:

(1) An employee who is serving a trial period or probationary period under an initial appointment;

(2) An employee who has received a proposed notice of involuntary separation (e.g., separation based on reduction in force, adverse action, or performance);

(3) An employee who is serving in a position excepted from the competitive service under Schedule C of part 213 of this chapter, or under Presedential appointment; or

(4) An employee whose resignation has been accepted for reasons other than to accept employment with the Commission.

[50 FR 13963, Apr. 9, 1985, as amended at 57 FR 10125, Mar. 24, 1992]

§ 352.905 Employees on detail.

(a) An employee detailed to the Commission is subject to the same conditions of employment at his or her employing agency as if the employee has not been detailed.

(b) The Commission and the employing agency will arrange for the termination of a detail and the agency will return the employee to his or her former position or an equivalent one as provided in § 352.908 (b) and (c).

§ 352.906 Termination of transfer.

At the conclusion of a term of employment agreed upon as provided in § 352.903, employment with the Commission may be terminated without regard to parts 351, 359, 432, 752, or 771 of this chapter.

§ 352.907 Exercise or termination of reemployment rights.

(a) *Exercise.* An individual who has been transferred under this subpart to the Commission and wishes to be reemployed must apply in writing to the former employing agency. The time limits for application for reemployment are—

(1) No later than 30 calendar days after the expiration of the term of employment with the Commission;

(2) No later than 30 calendar days after receipt of notice of involuntary separation during the term of employment with the Commission; or

(3) No later than 30 calendar days after resignation with the consent of the Commission.

(b) *Termination.* Reemployment rights terminate if the individual—

(1) Fails to apply within the time limits stated in paragraph (a) of this section;

(2) Resigns without the written consent of the Commission; or

(3) Within 10 calendar days, fails to accept an offer of reemployment made under § 352.908 that is determined to be a proper offer of reemployment by the reemploying agency or by the Merit Systems Protection Board on appeal.

§ 352.908 Agency obligation.

(a) *Time limits.* An employee is to be reemployed by the reemploying agency as promptly as possible, but not later than 30 calendar days after receipt of the reemployment application or on termination of the term of employment with the Commission, whichever is later.

(b) *Conditions.* An employee will be reemployed or returned from detail without loss of pay, seniority, or other rights or benefits to which the employee would have been entitled had he or she not been transferred or detailed. An employee in the Senior Executive Service will be reemployed or returned at not less than the rate at which paid immediately before the transfer or detail. An employee who is reemployed is not eligible for grade or pay retention under part 536 of this chapter based on a grade or rate of pay attained while employed by the Commission.

(c) *Position to which entitled.* (1) If the function with which the employee's former position was identified has been transferred, the employee's right is to a position in the gaining agency or activity.

(2) An employee whose right is to a position in the Senior Executive Service may be reemployed in or returned to any Senior Executive Service position in the former agency for which qualified.

(3) All other employees are entitled to be reemployed in or returned to a position at the same grade or level and in the same competitive area as the position last held in the former agency. If the reemployment would cause the separation or demotion of another employee, the applicant should be considered an employee for the purpose of applying the reduction-in-force regulations to determine to what, if any, position the employee is entitled. If the employee is not placed at the former grade or level, the agency must extend consideration beyond the competitive area. Responsibility for reemployment is agencywide.

(4) Reemployment may be at a higher grade than that to which the employee is entitled if all appropriate standards and requirements are satisfied and if this will not cause the displacement of another employee.

(5) The reemployment obligation may be satisfied by placement in any position within the agency that is acceptable to the employee.

(d) *Agency refusal to reemploy.* An agency may refuse to reemploy under this section only when the employee was separated from the Commission for serious cause showing unsuitability for reemployment.

§ 352.909 Appeals.

(a) If an agency denies reemployment to an applicant who claims reemployment rights under this subpart, the agency must notify the applicant in writing of that denial and its reasons. In the same notice, the agency will inform the applicant of the right to appeal to the Merit Systems Protection Board under the provisions of the Board's regulations. The agency must comply with the provisions of § 1201.21 of this title.

(b)(1) When an agency has reemployed or returned an employee, it will advise the employee of the right of appeal if he or she considers the reemployment or return not to be in accordance with the Act and this subpart.

(2) An employee in a bargaining unit covered by a negotiated grievance procedure that does not exclude this matter must use the negotiated grievance procedure.

(3) An employee to whom paragraph (b)(2) of this section does not apply is entitled to appeal to the Merit Systems Protection Board under the provisions of the Board's regulations. The agency must comply with the provisions of §1201.21 of this title.

PART 353—RESTORATION TO DUTY FROM UNIFORMED SERVICE OR COMPENSABLE INJURY

AUTHORITY: 38 U.S.C. 4301 et. seq., and 5 U.S.C. 8151.

SOURCE: 60 FR 45652, Sept. 1, 1995, unless otherwise noted.

Subpart A—General Provisions

§ 353.101 Scope.

The rights and obligations of employees and agencies in connection with leaves of absence or restoration to duty following uniformed service under 38 U.S.C. 4301 et. seq., and restoration under 5 U.S.C. 8151 for employees who sustain compensable injuries, are subject to the provisions of this part. Subpart A covers those provisions that are common to both of the above groups of employees. Subpart B deals with provisions that apply just to uniformed service and subpart C covers provisions that pertain just to injured employees.

§ 353.102 Definitions.

In this part:

Agency means.

(1) With respect to restoration following a compensable injury, any department, independent establishment, agency, or corporation in the executive branch, including the U.S. Postal Service and the Postal Rate Commission, and any agency in the legislative or judicial branch; and

(2) With respect to uniformed service, an executive agency as defined in 5 U.S.C. 105 (other than an intelligence agency referred to in 5 U.S.C. 2302(a)(2)(C)(ii), including the U.S. Postal Service and Postal Rate Commission, a nonappropriated fund instrumentality of the United States, or a military department as defined in 5 U.S.C. 102. In the case of a National Guard technician employed under 32 U.S.C. 709, the employing agency is the adjutant general of the State in which the technician is employed.

Fully recovered means compensation payments have been terminated on the basis that the employee is able to perform all the duties of the position he or she left or an equivalent one.

Injury means a compensable injury sustained under the provisions of 5 U.S.C. chapter 81, subchapter 1, and includes, in addition to accidental injury, a disease proximately caused by the employment.

Leave of absence means military leave, annual leave, without pay

(LWOP), furlough, continuation of pay, or any combination of these.

Military leave means paid leave provided to Reservists and members of the National Guard under 5 U.S.C. 6323.

Notice means any written or verbal notification of an obligation or intention to perform service in the uniformed services provided to an agency by the employee performing the service or by the uniformed service in which the service is to be performed.

Partially recovered means an injured employee, though not ready to resume the full range of his or her regular duties, has recovered sufficiently to return to part-time or light duty or to another position with less demanding physical requirements. Ordinarily, it is expected that a partially recovered employee will fully recover eventually.

Physically disqualified means that:

(1)(i) For medical reasons the employee is unable to perform the duties of the position formerly held or an equivalent one, or

(ii) There is a medical reason to restrict the individual from some or all essential duties because of possible incapacitation (for example, a seizure) or because of risk of health impairment (such as further exposure to a toxic substance for an individual who has already shown the effects of such exposure).

(2) The condition is considered permanent with little likelihood for improvement or recovery.

Reasonable efforts in the case of actions required by an agency for a person returning from uniformed service means actions, including training, that do not place an undue hardship on the agency.

Service in the uniformed services means the performance of duty on a voluntary or involuntary basis in a uniformed service under competent authority and includes active duty, active duty for training, initial active duty for training, inactive duty training, full-time National Guard duty, and a period for which a person is absent from employment for the purpose of examination to determine fitness to perform such duty.

Status means the particular attributes of a specific position. This includes the rank or responsibility of the position, its duties, working conditions, pay, tenure, and seniority.

Undue hardship means actions taken by an agency requiring significant difficulty or expense, when considered in light of—

(1) The nature and cost of actions needed under this part;

(2) The overall financial resources of the facility involved in taking the action; the number of persons employed at the facility; the effect on expenses and resources, or the impact otherwise of the action on the operation of the facility; and

(3) The overall size of the agency with respect to the number of employees, the number, type, and location of its facilities and type of operations, including composition, structure, and functions of the work force.

Uniformed services means the Armed Forces, the Army National Guard and the Air National Guard when engaged in active duty for training, inactive duty training, or full-time National Guard duty, the Commissioned Corps of the Public Health Service, and any other category of persons designated by the President in time of war or emergency.

§ 353.103 Persons covered.

(a) The provisions of this part pertaining to the uniformed services cover each agency employee who enters into such service regardless of whether the employee is located in the United States or overseas. However, an employee serving under a time-limited appointment completes any unexpired portion of his or her appointment upon return from uniformed service.

(b) The provisions of this part concerning employee injury cover a civil officer or employee in any branch of the Government of the United States, including an officer or employee of an instrumentally wholly owned by the United States, who was separated or furloughed from an appointment without time limitation, or from a temporary appointment pending establishment of a register (TAPER) as a result of a compensable injury; but do not include—

(1) A commissioned officer of the Regular Corps of the Public Health Service;

(2) A commissioned officer of the Reserve Corps of the Public Health Service on active duty; or

(3) A commissioned officer of the National Oceanic and Atmospheric Administration.

[60 FR 45652, Sept. 1, 1995, as amended at 64 FR 31487, June 11, 1999]

§ 353.104 Notification of rights and obligations.

When an agency separates, grants a leave of absence, restores or fails to restore an employee because of uniformed service or compensable injury, it shall notify the employee of his or her rights, obligations, and benefits relating to Government employment, including any appeal and grievance rights. However, regardless of notification, an employee is still required to exercise due diligence in ascertaining his or her rights, and to seek reemployment within the time limits provided by chapter 43 of title 38, United States Code, for restoration after uniformed service, or as soon as he or she is able after a compensable injury.

§ 353.105 Maintenance of records.

Each agency shall identify the position vacated by an employee who is injured or leaves to enter uniformed service. It shall also maintain the necessary records to ensure that all such employees are preserved the rights and benefits granted by law and this part.

§ 353.106 Personnel actions during employee's absence.

(a) An employee absent because of service in the uniformed services is to be carried on leave without pay unless the employee elects to use other leave or freely and knowingly provides written notice of intent not to return to a position of employment with the agency, in which case the employee can be separated. (NOTE: A separation under this provision affects only the employee's seniority while gone; it does not affect his or her restoration rights.)

(b) An employee absent because of compensable injury may be carried on leave without pay or separated unless the employee elects to use sick or annual leave.

(c) Agency promotion plans must provide a mechanism by which employees who are absent because of compensable injury or uniformed service can be considered for promotion. In addition, agencies have an obligation to consider employees absent on military duty for any incident or advantage of employment that they may have been entitled to had they not been absent. This is determined by:

(1) Considering whether the "incident or advantage" is one generally granted to all employees in that workplace and whether it was denied solely because of absence for military service;

(2) Considering whether the person absent on military duty was treated the same as if the person had remained at work; and

(3) Considering whether it was reasonably certain that the benefit would have accrued to the employee but for the absence for military service.

[60 FR 45652, Sept. 1, 1995, as amended at 64 FR 31487, June 11, 1999]

§ 353.107 Service credit upon reemployment.

Upon reemployment, an employee absent because of uniformed service or compensable injury is generally entitled to be treated as though he or she had never left. This means that a person who is reemployed following uniformed service or full recovery from compensable injury receives credit for the entire period of the absence for purposes of rights and benefits based upon seniority and length of service, including within-grade increases, career tenure, completion of probation, leave rate accrual, and severance pay.

§ 353.108 Effect of performance and conduct on restoration rights.

The laws covered by this part do not permit an agency to circumvent the protections afforded by other laws to employees who face the involuntary loss of their positions. Thus, an employee may not be denied restoration rights because of poor performance or conduct that occurred prior to the employee's departure for compensable injury or uniformed service. However, separation for cause that is substantially unrelated to the injury or to the performance of uniformed service negates restoration rights. Additionally, if during the period of injury or uniformed service the employee's conduct is such that it would disqualify him or her for employment under OPM or agency regulations, restoration rights may be denied.

§ 353.109 Transfer of function to another agency.

If the function of an employee absent because of uniformed service or compensable injury is transferred to another agency, and if the employee would have been transferred with the function under part 351 of this chapter had he or she not been absent, the employee is entitled to be placed in a position in the gaining agency that is equivalent to the one he or she left. It shall also assume the obligation to restore the employee in accordance with law and this part.

§ 353.110 OPM placement assistance.

(a) *Employee returning from uniformed service.* (1) OPM will offer placement in the executive branch to the following categories of employees upon notification by the agency and application by the employee: (Such notification should be sent to the Associate Director for Employment, OPM, 1900 E Street, NW., Washington, DC 20415.)

(i) Executive branch employees (other than an employee of an intelligence agency) when *OPM determines* that:

(A) their agencies no longer exist and the functions have not been transferred, or;

(B) it is otherwise impossible or unreasonable for their former agencies to place them;

(ii) Legislative and judicial branch employees when *their employers* determine that it is impossible or unreasonable to reemploy them;

(iii) National Guard technicians when the Adjutant General of a State determines that it is impossible or unreasonable to reemploy a technician otherwise eligible for restoration under 38 U.S.C. 4304 and 4312 (pertaining to character and length of service), and the technician is a noncareer military member who was separated invountarily from the Guard for reasons beyond his or her control; and

(iv) Employees of the intelligence agencies (defined in 5 U.S.C. 2302(a)(2)(C)(ii)) when *their agencies* determine that it is impossible or unreasonable to reemploy them.

(2) OPM will determine if a vacant position equivalent (in terms of pay, grade, and status) to the one the individual left exists, for which the individual is qualified, in the commuting area in which he or she was employed immediately before entering the uniformed services. If such a vacancy exists, OPM will order the agency to place the individual. If no such position is available, the individual may elect to be placed in a lesser position in the commuting area, or OPM will attempt to place the individual in an equivalent position in another geographic location determined by OPM. If the individual declines an offer of equivalent employment, he or she has no further restoration rights.

(b) Employee returning from compensable injury. OPM will provide placement assistance to an employee with restoration rights in the executive, legislative, or judicial branches who cannot be placed in his or her former agency and who either has competitive status or is eligible to acquire it under 5 U.S.C. 3304(C). If the employee's agency is abolished and its functions are not transferred, or it is not possible for the employee to be restored in his or her former agency, the employee is eligible for placement assistance under the Interagency Career Transition Assistance Plan (ICTAP) under part 330, subpart G, of this chapter. This paragraph does not apply to an employee serving under a temporary appointment pending establishment of a register (TAPER).

[60 FR 45652, Sept. 1, 1995, as amended at 64 FR 31487, June 11, 1999; 66 FR 29897, June 4, 2001]

Subpart B—Uniformed Service

§ 353.201 Introduction.

The Uniformed Services Employment and Reemployment Rights Act of 1994 revised and strengthened the existing Veterans' Reemployment Rights law, made the Department of Labor responsible for investigating employee complaints, required OPM to place certain returning employees in other agencies, established a separate restoration rights program for employees of the intelligence agencies, and altered the appeals rights process. The new law applies to persons exercising restoration rights on or after December 12, 1994.

§ 353.202 Discrimination and acts of reprisal prohibited.

A person who seeks or holds a position in the Executive branch may not be denied hiring, retention in employment, or any other incident or advantage of employment because of any application, membership, or service in the uniformed services. Furthermore, an agency may not take any reprisal against an employee for taking any action to enforce a protection, assist or participate in an investigation, or exercise any right provided for under chapter 43 of title 38, United States Code.

§ 353.203 Length of service.

(a) *Counting service after the effective date of USERRA (12/12/94).* To be entitled to restoration rights under this part, cumulative service in the uniformed services while employed by the Federal Government may not exceed 5 years. However, the 5-year period does not include any service—

(1) That is required beyond 5 years to complete an initial period of obligated service;

(2) During which the individual was unable to obtain orders releasing him or her from service in the uniformed services before expiration of the 5-year period, and such inability was through no fault of the individual;

(3) Performed as required pursuant to 10 U.S.C. 10147, under 32 U.S.C. 502(a) or 503, or to fulfill additional training requirements determined and certified in writing by the Secretary of the military department concerned to be necessary for professional development or for completion of skill training or retraining;

(4) Performed by a member of a uniformed service who is:

(i) Ordered to or retained on active duty under sections 12301(a), 12301(g), 12302, 12304, 12305, or 688 of title 10, United States Code, or under 14 U.S.C. 331, 332, 359, 360, 367, or 712;

(ii) Ordered to or retained on active duty (other than for training) under any provision of law during a war or during a national emergency declared by the President or the Congress, as determined by the Secretary concerned.

(iii) Ordered to active duty (other than for training) in support, as determined by the Secretary of the military department concerned, of an operational mission for which personnel have been ordered to active duty under 10 U.S.C. 12304;

(iv) Ordered to active duty in support, as determined by the Secretary of the military department concerned, of a critical mission or requirement of the uniformed services, or

(v) Called into Federal service as a member of the National Guard under chapter 15 or under section 12406 of title 10, United States Code.

(b) *Counting service prior to the effective date of USERRA.* In determining the 5-year total that may not be exceeded for purposes of exercising restoration rights, service performed prior to December 12, 1994, is considered only to the extent that it would have counted under the previous law (the Veterans' Reemployment Rights statute). For example, the service of a National Guard technician who entered on an Active Guard Reserve (AGR) tour under section 502(f) of title 32, United States Code, was not counted toward the 4-year time limit under the previous statute because it was specifically considered active duty for training. However, title 32, section 502(f) AGR service is not exempt from the cumulative time limits allowed under USERRA and service after the effective date counts under USERRA rules. Thus, if a technician was on a 32 U.S.C. 502(f) AGR tour on October 13, 1994, (the date USERRA was signed into law), but exercised restoration rights after December 11, 1994, (the date USERRA became fully effective), AGR service prior to December 12 would not count in computing the 5-year total, but all service beginning with that date would count.

(c) *Nature of Reserve service and resolving conflicts.* An employee who is a member of the Reserve or National Guard has a dual obligation—to the military and to his or her employer.

Given the nature of the employee's service obligation, some conflict with job demands is often unavoidable and a good-faith effort on the part of both the employee and the agency is needed to minimize conflict and resolve differences. Some accommodation may be necessary by both parties. Most Reserve component members are required, as a minimum, to participate in drills for 2 days each month and in 2 weeks of active duty for training per year. But some members are required to participate in longer or more frequent training tours. USERRA makes it clear that the timing, frequency, duration, and nature of the duty performed is not an issue so long as the employee gave proper notice, and did not exceed the time limits specified. However, to the extent that the employee has influence upon the timing, frequency, or duration of such training or duty, he or she is expected to use that influence to minimize the burden upon the agency. The employee is expected to provide the agency with as much advance notice as possible whenever military duty or training will interfere with civilian work. When a conflict arises between the Reserve duty and the legitimate needs of the employer, the agency may contact appropriate military authorities to express concern. Where the request would require the employee to be absent from work for an extended period, during times of acute need, or when, in light of previous leaves, the requested leave is cumulatively burdensome, the agency may contact the military commander of the employee's military unit to determine if the military duty could be rescheduled or performed by another member. If the military authorities determine that the military duty cannot be rescheduled or cancelled, the agency is required to permit the employee to perform his or her military duty.

(d) *Mobilization authority*. By law, members of the Selected Reserve (a component of the Ready Reserve), can be called up under a presidential order for purposes other than training for as long as 270 days. If the President declares a national emergency, the remainder of the Ready Reserve—the Individual Ready Reserve and the Inactive National Guard—may be called up. The Ready Reserve as a whole is subject to as much as 24 consecutive months of active duty in a national emergency declared by the President.

[60 FR 45652, Sept. 1, 1995, as amended at 64 FR 31487, June 11, 1999]

§ 353.204 Notice to employer.

To be entitled to restoration rights under this part, an employee (or an appropriate officer of the uniformed service in which service is to be performed) must give the employer advance written or verbal notice of the service except that no notice is required if it is precluded by military necessity or, under all relevant circumstances, the giving of notice is otherwise impossible or unreasonable.

§ 353.205 Return to duty and application for reemployment.

Periods allowed for return to duty are based on the length of time the person was performing service in the uniformed services, as follows:

(a) An employee whose uniformed service was for *less than 31 days*, or who was absent for the purpose of an examination to determine fitness for the uniformed services, is required to report back to work not later than the beginning of the first regularly scheduled work day on the first full calendar day following completion of the period of service and the expiration of 8 hours after a period allowing for the safe transportation of the employee from the place of service to the employee's residence, or as soon as possible after the expiration of the 8-hour period if reporting within the above period is impossible or unreasonable through no fault of the employee.

(b) If the service was for *more than 30 but less than 181 days*, the employee must submit an application for reemployment with the agency not later than 14 days after completing the period of service. (If submitting the application is impossible or unreasonable through no fault of the individual, it must be submitted the next full calendar day when it becomes possible to do so.)

(c) If the period of service was for *more than 180 days*, the employee must submit an application for reemployment not later than 90 days after completing the period of service.

(d) An employee who is hospitalized or convalescing from an injury or illness incurred in, or aggravated during uniformed service is required to report for duty at the end of the period that is necessary for the person to recover, based on the length of service as discussed in paragraphs (a), (b), and (c) of this section, except that the period of recovery may not exceed 2 years (extended by the minimum time required to accommodate circumstances beyond the employee's control which make reporting within the period specified impossible or unreasonable).

(e) A person who does not report within the time limits specified does not automatically forfeit restoration rights, but, rather, is subject to whatever policy and disciplinary action the agency would normally apply for a similar absence without authorization.

§ 353.206 Documentation upon return.

Upon request, a returning employee who was absent for more than 30 days, or was hospitalized or convalescing from an injury or illness incurred in or aggravated during the performance of service in the uniformed services, must provide the agency with documentation that establishes the timeliness of the application for reemployment, and length and character of service. If documentation is unavailable, the agency must restore the employee until documentation becomes available.

§ 353.207 Position to which restored.

(a) *Timing.* An employee returning from the uniformed services following an absence of more than 30 days is entitled to be restored as soon as possible after making application, but in no event later than 30 days after receipt of the application by the agency.

(b) *Nondisabled.* If the employee's uniformed service was for less than 91 days, he or she must be employed in the position for which qualified that he or she would have attained if continuously employed. If not qualified for this position after reasonable efforts by the agency to qualify the employee, he or she is entitled to be placed in the position he or she left. For service of 91 days or more, the agency has the option of placing the employee in a position of like seniority, status, and pay. (NOTE: Upon reemployment, a term employee completes the unexpired portion of his or her original appointment.) If unqualified (for any reason other than disability incurred in or aggravated during service in the uniformed services) after reasonable efforts by the agency to qualify the employee for such position or the position the employee left, he or she must be restored to any other position of lesser status and pay for which qualified, with full seniority.

(c) *Disabled.* An employee with a disability incurred in or aggravated during uniformed service and who, after reasonable efforts by the agency to accommodate the disability, is entitled to be placed in another position for which qualified that will provide the employee with the same seniority, status, and pay, or the nearest approximation consistent with the circumstances in each case. The agency is not required to reemploy a disabled employee if, after making due efforts to accommodate the disability, such reemployment would impose an undue hardship on the agency.

(d) *Two or more persons entitled to restoration in the same position.* If two or more persons are entitled to restoration in the same position, the one who left the position first has the prior right to restoration in that position. The other employee(s) is entitled to be placed in a position as described in paragraphs (b) and (c) of this section.

(e) *Relationship to an entitlement based on veterans' preference.* An employee's right to restoration under this part does not entitle the person to retention, preference, or displacement rights over any person with a superior claim based on veterans' preference.

§ 353.208 Use of paid time off during uniformed service.

An employee performing service with the uniformed services must be permitted, upon request, to use any accrued annual leave under 5 U.S.C. 6304, military leave under 5 U.S.C. 6323, earned compensatory time off for travel under 5 U.S.C. 5550b, or sick leave under 5 U.S.C. 6307, if appropriate, during such service.

[72 FR 62767, Nov. 7, 2007]

§ 353.209 Retention protections.

(a) *During uniformed service.* An employee may not be demoted or separated (other than military separation) while performing duty with the uniformed services except for cause. (Reduction in force is not considered "for cause" under this subpart.) He or she is not a "competing employee" under § 351.404 of this chapter. If the employee's position is abolished during such absence, the agency must reassign the employee to another position of like status, and pay.

(b) *Upon reemployment.* Except in the case of an employee under time-limited appointment who finishes out the unexpired portion of his or her appointment upon reemployment, an employee reemployed under this subpart may not be discharged, except for cause—

(1) If the period of uniformed service was more than 180 days, within 1 year; and

(2) If the period of uniformed service was more than 30 days, but less than 181 days, within 6 months.

§ 353.210 Department of Labor assistance to applicants and employees.

USERRA requires the Department of Labor's Veterans' Employment and Training Service [VETS] to provide employment and reemployment assistance to any Federal employee or applicant who requests it. VETS staff will attempt to resolve employment disputes brought to investigate. If dispute resolution proves unsuccessful, VETS will, at the request of the employee, refer the matter to the Office of the Special Counsel for representation before the Merit Systems Protection Board (MSPB).

[64 FR 31487, June 11, 1999]

§ 353.211 Appeal rights.

An individual who believes an agency has not complied with the provisions of law and this part relating to the employment or reemployment of the person by the agency may—

(a) File a complaint with the Department of Labor, as noted in § 353.210, or

(b) Appeal directly to MSPB if the individual chooses not to file a complaint with the Department of Labor, or is informed by either Labor or the Office of the Special Counsel that they will not pursue to the case. However, National Guard technicians do not have the right to appeal to MSPB a denial of reemployment rights by the Adjutant General. Technicians may file complaints with the appropriate district court in accordance with 38 U.S.C. 4323 (USERRA).

[60 FR 45652, Sept. 1, 1995, as amended at 64 FR 31487, June 11, 1999]

Subpart C—Compensable Injury

§ 353.301 Restoration rights.

(a) *Fully recovered within 1 year.* An employee who fully recovers from a compensable injury within 1 year from the date eligibility for compensation began (or from the time compensable disability recurs if the recurrence begins after the employee resumes regular full-time employment with the United States), is entitled to be restored immediately and unconditionally to his or her former position or an equivalent one. Although these restoration rights are agencywide, the employee's basic entitlement is to the former position or equivalent in the local commuting area the employee left. If a suitable vacancy does not exist, the employee is entitled to displace an employee occupying a continuing position under temporary appointment or tenure group III. If there is no such position in the local commuting area, the agency must offer the employee a position (as described above) in another location. This paragraph also applies when an injured employee accepts a lower-grade position in lieu of separation and subsequently fully recovers. A fully recovered employee is expected to return to work immediately upon the cessation of compensation.

(b) *Fully recovered after 1 year.* An employee who separated because of a compensable injury and whose full recovery takes longer than 1 year from the date eligibility for compensation began (or from the time compensable disability recurs if the recurrence begins after the injured employee resumes regular full-time employment with the United States), is entitled to priority consideration, agencywide, for restoration to the position he or she left or an equivalent one provided he or she applies for reappointment within 30 days of the cessation of compensation. Priority consideration is accorded by entering the individual on the agency's reemployment priority list for the competitive service or reemployment list for the excepted service. If the individual cannot be placed in the former commuting area, he or she is entitled to priority consideration for an equivalent position elsewhere in the agency. (See parts 302 and 330 of this chapter for more information on how this may be accomplished for the excepted and competitive services, respectively.) This subpart also applies when an injured employee accepts a lower-graded position in lieu of separation and subsequently fully recovers.

(c) *Physically disqualified.* An individual who is physically disqualified for the former position or equivalent because of a compensable injury, is entitled to be placed in another position for which qualified that will provide the employee with the same status, and pay, or the nearest approximation thereof, consistent with the circumstances in each case. This right is agencywide and applies for a period of 1 year from the date eligibility for compensation begins. After 1 year, the individual is entitled to the rights accorded individuals who fully or partially recover, as applicable.

(d) *Partially recovered.* Agencies must make every effort to restore in the local commuting area, according to the circumstances in each case, an individual who has partially recovered from a compensable injury and who is able to return to limited duty. At a minimum, this would mean treating these employees substantially the same as other handicapped individuals under the Rehabilitation Act of 1973, as amended. (See 29 U.S.C. 791(b) and 794.) If the individual fully recovers, he or she is entitled to be considered for the position held at the time of injury, or an equivalent one. A partially recovered employee is expected to seek reemployment as soon as he or she is able.

§353.302 Retention protections.

An injured employee enjoys no special protection in a reduction in force. Separation by reduction in force or for cause while on compensation means the individual has no restoration rights.

§353.303 Restoration rights of TAPER employees.

An employee serving in the competitive service under a temporary appointment pending establishment of a register (TAPER) under §316.201 of this chapter (other than an employee serving in a position classified above GS–15), is entitled to be restored to the position he or she left or an equivalent one in the same commuting area.

§353.304 Appeals to the Merit Systems Protection Board.

(a) Except as provided in paragraphs (b) and (c) of this section, an injured employee or former employee of an agency in the executive branch (including the U.S. Postal Service and the Postal Rate Commission) may appeal to the MSPB an agency's failure to restore, improper restoration, or failure to return an employee following a leave of absence. All appeals must be submitted in accordance with MSPB's regulations.

(b) An individual who fully recovers from a compensable injury more than 1 year after compensation begins may appeal to MSPB as provided for in parts 302 and 330 of this chapter for excepted and competitive service employees, respectively.

(c) An individual who is partially recovered from a compensable injury may appeal to MSPB for a determination of whether the agency is acting arbitrarily and capriciously in denying restoration. Upon reemployment, a partially recovered employee may also appeal the agency's failure to credit time spent on compensation for purposes of rights and benefits based upon length of service.

PART 359—REMOVAL FROM THE SENIOR EXECUTIVE SERVICE; GUARANTEED PLACEMENT IN OTHER PERSONNEL SYSTEMS

AUTHORITY: 5 U.S.C. 1302, 3302, and 3596, unless otherwise noted.

SOURCE: 54 FR 18876, May 3, 1989, unless otherwise noted.

Subpart A [Reserved]

Subpart B—General Provisions

§ 359.201 Regulatory requirements.

This part contains the regulations of the Office of Personnel Management (OPM) that implement subchapter V of chapter 35 of title 5, United States Code, on the Senior Executive Service (SES).

§ 359.202 Definitions.

Agency, Senior Executive Service position, senior executive, career appointee, limited emergency appointee, limited term appointee, and *noncareer appointee,* are defined in 5 U.S.C. 3132(a).

Probation and *probationary period* mean the 1-year probation required by 5 U.S.C. 3393(d) upon initial career appointment to the SES.

Reemployed annitant means an individual who is receiving an annuity under the Civil Service Retirement System or the Federal Employees' Retirement System on the basis of his or her former Federal service. A reemployed annuitant serves at the pleasure of the appointing authority.

Subpart C [Reserved]

Subpart D—Removal of Career Appointees During Probation

§ 359.401 General exclusions.

This subpart does not apply to the removal of a career appointee during probation when—

(a) The action is initiated under 5 U.S.C. 1206(g) or 5 U.S.C. 7542;

(b) The removal is effected under subpart C of this part for failure to be recertified; or

(c) The appointee is a reemployed annuitant. See subpart I of this part for removal of a reemployed annuitant.

[56 FR 172, Jan. 3, 1991]

§ 359.402 Removal: Unacceptable performance.

(a) *Coverage.* This section covers the removal of a career appointee from the SES during the probationary period for unacceptable performance.

(b) *Basis for action.* A removal under this section need not be based upon a final rating under the agency's SES performance appraisal system established under subpart C of part 430 of this chapter. Even if a removal is based on such a rating, the removal action is taken under this section.

(c) *Procedures.* The agency shall notify the appointee in writing before the effective date of the action. The notice shall, as a minimum—

(1) State the agency's conclusions as to the inadequacies of the appointee's performance;

(2) State whether the appointee has placement rights under § 359.701 and, if so, identify the position to which the appointee will be assigned; and

(3) Show the effective date of the action.

§ 359.403 Removal: Conduct.

(a) *Coverage.* (1) This section covers the removal of a career appointee from the SES during the probationary period for misconduct, neglect of duty, malfeasance, or failure to accept a directed reassignment or to accompany a position in a transfer of function.

(2) This section does not apply, however, when the appointee was covered under 5 U.S.C. 7511 immediately before appointment to the SES. In that case, the removal is subject to the provisions of part 752, subpart F, of this chapter.

(b) *Procedures.* The agency shall notify the appointee in writing before the effective date of the action. The notice shall, as a minimum—

(1) State the basis for the removal action (including the act(s) of misconduct, neglect of duty, or malfeasance if those factors are involved); and

(2) Show the effective date of the action.

§ 359.404 Removal: Conditions arising before appointment.

(a) *Coverage.* (1) This section covers the removal of a career appointee from the SES during the probationary period when the action is based in whole or in part on conditions arising before the appointment.

(2) This section does not apply, however, when the career appointee was covered under 5 U.S.C. 7511 immediately before appointment to the SES. In that case, the removal is subject to the provisions of part 752, subpart F, of this chapter.

(b) *Procedures.* (1) The agency shall give the appointee an advance written notice stating the specific reasons for the proposed removal.

(2) The appointee shall be given a reasonable time to reply.

(3) The agency shall give the appointee a written decision showing the reasons for the action and the effective date. The decision shall be given to the appointee at or before the time the action will be made effective.

§ 359.405 Removal: Reduction in force.

(a) *Coverage.* This section covers the removal of a career appointee from the SES during the probationary period under a reduction in force.

(b) *Basis for action.* The appointee must have been identified for removal from the SES under competitive procedures established by the agency in accordance with the requirements of 5 U.S.C. 3595(a). Removal action shall be taken under 5 U.S.C. 3592(a).

(c) *Procedures.* The agency shall notify the appointee in writing before the effective date of the action. The notice shall state, as a minimum—

(1) Whether the appointee has placement rights under § 359.701 to a position outside the SES and, if so, the position to which the appointee will be assigned;

(2) The effective date of the action;

(3) The appointee's appeal rights, including the time limit for appeal and the location of the Merit System Protection Board office to which an appeal should be sent; and

(4) Such other information as may be required by OPM.

§ 359.406 Restrictions.

(a) Removal from the SES under §§ 359.402 through 359.404 may not be made effective within 120 days after—

(1) The appointment of a new agency head; or

(2) The appointment in the agency of the career appointee's most immediate supervisor who—

(i) Is a noncareer appointee; and

(ii) Has the authority to remove the career appointee.

(b) For purposes of this section, a noncareer appointee includes an SES noncareer or limited appointee, an appointee in a position filled by Schedule C, or an appointee in an Executive Schedule or equivalent position other than a career Executive Schedule or equivalent position.

(c) The restrictions in paragraph (a) of this section do not apply—

(1) When the career appointee has received a final rating of unsatisfactory under the performance appraisal system established by the agency under subchapter II of chapter 43 of title 5, United States Code, before the appointment of a new agency head or the appointment of the career appointee's most immediate noncareer supervisor who has the authority to remove the career appointee;

(2) To a disciplinary action initiated before the appointment of a new agency head or the appointment of the career appointee's most immediate noncareer supervisor who has the authority to remove the career appointee;

(3) To a disciplinary action when there is a reasonable cause to believe that the career appointee has committed a crime for which a sentence of imprisonment can be imposed; or

(4) To a disciplinary action when the circumstances are such that retention of the career appointee—

(i) May pose a threat to the appointee or others;

(ii) May result in loss of or damage to Government property; or

(iii) May otherwise jeopardize legitimate Government interests.

(d) The following procedures must be observed when an agency invokes an exception to the 120-day restriction under paragraphs (c)(3) or (c)(4) of this section:

(1) The agency shall include in the notice the reasons for invoking the exception.

(2) The appointee shall be given a reasonable time, but no less than 7 days, to respond regarding the propriety of the use of the exception.

(3) The agency shall give the appointee a notice of decision on the propriety of the use of the exception at or before the time the action will be effective.

(4) When circumstances require immediate action, the agency may place the appointee in a nonduty status with pay for such time as necessary to effect the action.

(e) The imposition of the 120-day moratorium does not extend the probationary period.

[54 FR 18876, May 3, 1989, as amended at 57 FR 10125, Mar. 24, 1992]

§ 359.407 Appeals.

(a) Removal under § 359.402, 359.403, or 359.404 is not appealable to the Merit Systems Protection Board under 5 U.S.C. 7701.

(b) Removal under § 359.405 is appealable to the Merit Systems Protection Board under 5 U.S.C. 7701 as to whether the reduction in force complies with the competitive procedures required under 5 U.S.C. 3595(a).

Subpart E—Removal of Career Appointees for Less Than Fully Successful Executive Performance

§ 359.501 General.

(a) *Coverage.* (1) This subpart covers—

(i) A career appointee who has completed the probationary period in the SES; and

(ii) A career appointee who is not required to serve a probationary period in the SES.

(2) This subpart does not cover, however, a career appointee who is serving as a reemployed annuitant. See subpart I of this part for removal of a reemployed annuitant.

(b) *Definitions*—(1) *Final rating* means the rating of record made by an appointing authority under the SES performance appraisal system in accordance with the requirements of 5 U.S.C. 4314(c)(3) and part 430, subpart C, of this chapter.

(2) A *less than fully successful* final rating means a rating of unsatisfactory or minimally satisfactory.

(c) *Optional removal from the SES*. The agency may remove a career appointee from the SES after the appointee has been given one final rating of unsatisfactory.

(d) *Mandatory removal from the SES*. The agency must remove a career appointee from the SES after—

(1) The appointee has been given two final ratings of unsatisfactory within 5 consecutive years; or

(2) The appointee has been given two final ratings of less than fully successful within 3 consecutive years.

§ 359.502 Procedures.

(a) *Notice*. The agency shall notify the career appointee in writing at least 30 calendar days before the effective date of the action. The notice shall advise the appointee of—

(1) The basis for the action;

(2) The appointee's placement rights under subpart G of this part—the position to which the appointee will be assigned shall be identified either in this advance notice or in a supplementary notice issued no later than 10 calendar days before the effective date of the action;

(3) The appointee's right to request an informal hearing from the Merit Systems Protection Board;

(4) The effective date of the removal action; and

(5) When applicable, the appointee's eligibility for immediate retirement under 5 U.S.C. 8336(h) or 8414(a).

(b) *Informal hearing*. (1) A career appointee being removed from the SES under this section shall, at least 15 days before the effective date of the removal, be entitled, upon request, to an informal hearing before an official designated by the Merit Systems Protection Board. The appointee shall submit the request for an informal hearing to the Board. This request may be made at any time after the appointee has received the notice described in paragraph (a) of this section, but no later than 15 days before the effective date of action. The informal hearing shall be conducted in accordance with the regulations and procedures established by the Board. See 5 CFR 1201.141, Right to hearing, and 5 CFR 1201.142, Hearing procedures; referral of the record.

(2) Neither the granting nor the conduct of an informal hearing shall provide a basis for appeal to the Merit Systems Protection Board under 5 U.S.C. 7701. The removal action need not be delayed because of the granting of an informal hearing.

§ 359.503 Restrictions.

(a) Removal from the SES under this subpart may not be made effective within 120 days after—

(1) The appointment of a new agency head; or

(2) The appointment in the agency of the career appointee's most immediate supervisor who—

(i) Is a noncareer appointee; and

(ii) Has the authority to remove the career appointee.

(b) For purposes of this section, a noncareer appointee includes an SES noncareer or limited appointee, an appointee in a position filled by Schedule C, or an appointee in an Executive Schedule or equivalent position other than a career Executive Schedule or equivalent position.

(c) This restriction does not apply when the career appointee has received a final rating of unsatisfactory under the performance appraisal system established by the agency under subchapter II of chapter 43 of title 5, United States Code, before the appointment of a new agency head or the appointment of the career appointee's most immediate noncareer supervisor who has the authority to remove the career appointee.

[54 FR 18876, May 3, 1989, as amended at 57 FR 10125, Mar. 24, 1992]

§ 359.504 Appeals.

An action taken under § 359.501 is not appealable to the Merit Systems Protection Board under 5 U.S.C. 7701.

Subpart F—Removal of Career Appointees as a Result of Reduction in Force

§ 359.601 General.

(a) *Coverage.* (1) This subpart covers the removal of a career appointee from the SES as a result of a reduction in force.

(2) This subpart does not cover, however, a career appointee who is serving as a reemployed annuitant. See subpart I of this part for removal of a reemployed annuitant.

(b) *Definitions*—(1) *Probationary period* is defined in § 359.202 of this part.

(2) *Reduction in force* is defined in 5 U.S.C. 3595(d) as including "the elimination or modification of a position due to a reorganization, due to a lack of funds or curtailment of work, or due to any other factor."

(3) *Agency* in this subpart means an executive department or an independent establishment.

(c) *Agency procedures.* An agency must have issued written procedures before conducting a reduction in force. A copy of the procedures shall be provided OPM upon issuance.

[54 FR 18876, May 3, 1989, as amended at 60 FR 6388, Feb. 2, 1995]

§ 359.602 Agency reductions in force.

(a) *Competitive procedures.* (1) This paragraph applies to all SES career appointees in the agency, including appointees serving a probationary period.

(2) An agency shall establish competitive procedures in writing to determine who will be removed from the SES in any reduction in force of career appointees within the agency. Such competitive procedures shall be based primarily on performance. When performance ratings are used, they shall be the final ratings under 5 CFR part 430, subpart C.

(3) An appointee who has completed the probationary period must be retained over an appointee who has not completed the probationary period if they both have the same retention standing.

(4) Competitive procedures are not required if an agency is being abolished, without a transfer of functions, and all SES appointees will be separated at the same time or within 3 months of abolishment.

(b) *Placement within the agency.* (1) This paragraph applies to any SES career appointee who has completed the probationary period, or was not required to serve a probationary period, and who has been identified for reduction in force under paragraph (a) of this section.

(2) The appointee is entitled to be offered any vacant SES position in the agency for which the appointee meets the qualifications requirements. If there is more than one vacancy, the agency has the option of which position to offer the appointee.

(3) An appointee covered by this paragraph is entitled to be placed in a vacant SES position over an appointee who is still serving a probationary period.

[54 FR 18876, May 3, 1989, as amended at 60 FR 6388, Feb. 2, 1995]

§ 359.603 OPM priority placement.

(a) *Agency certification.* (1) If there is no vacant SES position within the agency for which an appointee covered by § 359.602(b) is qualified, the agency head, or the acting agency head in the absence of the agency head, shall certify to OPM in writing that no such position is available. This certification may not be delegated below the Assistant Secretary level in a department, or an equivalent level above the director of personnel in other agencies.

(2) The 45-day period during which OPM will attempt to place the appointee begins on the day the certification is akcnowledged by OPM.

(3) It is the continuing responsibility of an agency that has a surplus career appointee to place the appointee in any vacant SES position in the agency for which the appointee is qualified, even after the appointee is certified to OPM.

(4) An individual remains a career SES appointee in his or her agency during the OPM placement period.

(b) *OPM authority.* As provided by § U.S.C. 3595(b)(3), OPM may require an agency to take any action that OPM considers necessary to carry out a placement.

(c) *OPM referrals.* (1) OPM may formally refer a career appointee to an agency for a specific SES vacancy or general priority consideration. Such a referral may not become a part of the regular competitive staffing process. The appointee must be considered by the agency for a noncompetitive SES appointment.

(2) Any objection by the agency to the qualifications of the appointee must be based on the professional/technical qualifications in the standard for the position. An agency may not rely solely on lack of agency-specific experience for an objection based on lack of professional/technical qualifications if the appointee is otherwise qualified.

(d) *Agency response.* (1) In order to expedite placement of surplus career appointees, an agency shall respond to an OPM referral within the time period prescribed by OPM.

(2) If an agency fails to place a referred career appointee in an SES position because of objection to the appointee's qualifications or because of any other reason, the agency response must be in writing and must be signed by the agency head, or the acting agency head in the absence of the agency head. The response may not be delegated below the Assistant Secretary level in a department, or an equivalent level above the director of personnel in other agencies.

(3) If an agency cancels a position while a referral to the position is pending, the appointee will be entitled to priority consideration for the position if it or a successor position is reestablished in the SES within 1 year of the cancellation date and the appointee has not been placed in another SES position.

(e) *Corrective action.* If an agency fails to provide bona fide priority consideration, OPM may order appropriate corrective action.

(f) *Declination by employee.* If a career appointee declines a reasonable offer of placement, OPM's placement efforts will cease. The appointee may be removed from the SES at the expiration of the agency notice period.

[54 FR 18876, May 3, 1989, as amended at 60 FR 6388, Feb. 2, 1995]

§ 359.604 Removal from the SES and placement rights outside the SES.

(a) If a probationary appointee is identified for reduction in force under § 359.602(a), removal action is taken under § 359.405. Placement rights outside the SES are covered under subpart G of this part.

(b) If a career appointee who has completed the probationary period, or who did not have to serve one, is identified for reduction in force under § 359.602(a) and is not placed elsewhere in the SES under § 359.602(b) or § 359.603, or declines a placement offer under § 359.603, removal action is taken under § 359.604(b). Placement rights outside the SES are covered under subpart G of this part.

§ 359.605 Notice requirements.

(a) Each career appointee subject to removal under § 359.604(b) is entitled to a specific, written notice at least 45 calendar days before the effective date of the removal. The notice shall state, as a minimum—

(1) The action to be taken and its prospective effective date;

(2) The nature of the competition, including the appointee's competitive area, if less than the agency, and standing on the retention register;

(3) The place where the appointee may inspect the regulations and records pertinent to the action;

(4) Placement rights within the agency and through OPM, including how the employee can apply for OPM placement assistance; and

(5) The appointee's appeal rights, including the time limit for appeal and the location of the Merit Systems Protection Board office to which an appeal should be sent.

(b) A career appointee who has received a notice under paragraph (a) of this section is entitled to a second notice in writing at least 1 day before removal from the SES. The notice shall state, as a minimum—

(1) The basis for the removal, *i.e.*, 5 U.S.C. 3595(b)(5) if the basis is expiration of the 45-day OPM placement period, or 5 U.S.C. 3595(b)(4) if the basis is declination of a reasonable offer of placement, in which case identify the position offered and the date on which it was declined;

(2) The effective date of the removal;

(3) Placement rights outside the SES and, when applicable, the appointee's

eligibility for discontinued service retirement in lieu of placement; and

(4) Reminder of the appointee's appeal rights.

[60 FR 6389, Feb. 2, 1995]

§ 359.606 Appeals.

A career appointee may appeal to the Merit Systems Protection Board whether the reduction in force complies with the competitive procedures in § 359.602(a).

§ 359.607 Records.

Each agency shall maintain current records needed to determine the retention standing of its competing appointees. The agency shall allow the inspection of its retention registers and related records by an appointee to the extent that they have a bearing on the appointee's situation. The agency shall preserve intact all registers and records relating to a reduction-in-force action for at least 2 years from the effective date of the action.

§ 359.608 Transfer of function.

(a) *Transfer of function* means the transfer of the performance of a continuing function from one agency to one or more other agencies.

(b) A career appointee is entitled to accompany his or her function to the new agency without any change in tenure if the alternative is removal from the SES in the current agency under reduction in force.

Subpart G—Guaranteed Placement

§ 359.701 Coverage.

This subpart covers career appointees, other than reemployed annuitants, who are removed from the SES under any of the following conditions:

(a) Removal during the probationary period under subpart C of this part or under subpart D of this part for other than misconduct, neglect of duty, malfeasance, or other disciplinary reasons under § 359.403, § 359.404, or part 752, subpart F, of this chapter, if at the time of appointment to the SES the individual held a career or career-conditional appointment or an appointment of equivalent tenure, as determined by OPM. An appointment of equivalent tenure is considered to be an appointment in the excepted service other than an appointment—

(1) To a Schedule C position established under part 213 of this chapter;

(2) To a position that meets the same criteria as a Schedule C position; or

(3) To a position where the incumbent is traditionally changed upon a change in Presidential Administrations.

(b) Removal as the result of:

(1) Failure to be recertified under subpart C of this part;

(2) Less than fully successful executive performance under subpart E of this part; or

(3) A reduction in force under subpart F of this part. The appointee must have completed the required probationary period under the SES or was not required to serve a probationary period.

[54 FR 18876, May 3, 1989, as amended at 56 FR 172, Jan. 3, 1991; 57 FR 10125, Mar. 24, 1992]

§ 359.702 Placement rights.

(a) An appointee covered by this subpart is entitled to be placed in a vacant civil service position (other than an SES position) in any agency that is—

(1) A continuing position at GS–15 or above, or equivalent, that will last at least three months; and

(2) A position for which the appointee meets the qualifications requirements.

(b) A probationary appointee, or a nonprobationary appointee who at the time of appointment to the SES held a career or career-conditional appointment (or an appointment of equivalent tenure, as defined in § 359.701(a)), is entitled to be placed in a position of tenure equivalent to that of the appointment held at the time of appointment to the SES. This tenure requirement does not apply—

(1) If the agency taking the removal action does not have a position of equivalent tenure for which the appointee meets the qualifications requirements; or

(2) If the appointee is willing to accept a position having a different tenure.

§359.703 Responsibility for placement.

The agency taking the removal action is responsible for placing the appointee in an appropriate position within the agency, or for arranging a transfer to an appropriate position in another agency. Any transfer must be mutually acceptable to the appointee and the gaining agency.

§359.704 Restrictions.

Placement of an appointee under this subpart shall not cause the separation or reduction in grade of any other employee.

§359.705 Pay.

(a) An appointee placed under this subpart in a position outside the SES (in the same or different agency) is entitled to receive basic pay at the highest of—

(1) The rate of basic pay in effect for the position in which the appointee is being placed (*i.e.*, a rate of basic pay within the normal rate range of the position in which placed, consistent with the rules of the pay system covering such position);

(2) The rate of basic pay currently in effect for the position the appointee held immediately before being appointed to the SES; or

(3) The rate of basic pay in effect for the appointee immediately before removal from the SES.

(b)(1) The rate of basic pay under paragraph (a)(1) and (2) of this section includes any applicable locality payment under 5 U.S.C. 5304, special rate supplement under 5 U.S.C. 5305, or similar payment under other legal authority.

(2) When an employee is entitled to a payable rate of basic pay under paragraph (a)(2) or (3) of this section which exceeds the maximum payable rate of basic pay for the grade or level of the employee's position after placement, the resulting saved rate is subject to the adjustment and termination rules in paragraphs (d) through (f) of this section.

(c)(1) For an employee placed in a General Schedule position, a saved rate established under this section may not be supplemented by a locality payment under 5 U.S.C. 5304, a special rate supplement under 5 U.S.C. 5305, or a similar payment under other legal authority.

(2) A saved rate established under this section is subject to the limitation on Senior Executive Service pay in 5 U.S.C. 5382 of the rate for level II of the Executive Schedule.

(3) A saved rate established under this section is considered an employee's rate of basic pay for the same purposes as a retained rate under 5 CFR part 536, as described in 5 CFR 536.307.

(d) A saved rate established under this section must be adjusted in connection with a pay schedule adjustment according to the following rules:

(1) When the maximum payable rate of basic pay for the grade or level of an employee's position is increased while the employee is receiving a saved rate, the employee is entitled to a pay adjustment equal to 50 percent of the amount of the increase in that maximum payable rate, except as otherwise provided in this section.

(2) If an employee's official worksite is changed while the employee is receiving a saved rate, a change in the applicable range maximum because of a change in an employee's official worksite is not considered in applying paragraph (d)(1) of this section. Instead, any adjustment of the employee's saved rate in conjunction with a change in official worksite must be determined under paragraph (e) of this section. If an employee's range maximum is increased because of a pay schedule adjustment on the same effective date as a change in the employee's official worksite, the saved rate must be adjusted under paragraph (d)(1) of this section before applying paragraph (e) of this section.

(3) A change in an employee's rate range maximum resulting from a change in the employee's position (e.g., change in occupational series) that causes the employee to be covered by a different pay schedule does not result in application of paragraph (d)(1) of this section.

(4) When an employee's saved rate becomes equal to or lower than the maximum payable rate of basic pay for the grade or level of the employee's position, the employee is entitled to the maximum payable rate, and saved pay under this section ceases to apply.

(e) When an employee receiving a saved rate established under this section is covered by a pay system that provides different basic pay schedules based on geographic location (such as the General Schedule pay system), the saved rate must be adjusted in conjunction with a change in the employee's official worksite consistent with the geographic conversion rule for retained rates under 5 CFR 536.303(b).

(f) A saved rate established under this section must be terminated if—

(1) The employee has a break in service of 1 workday or more;

(2) The employee is demoted based on unacceptable performance or conduct or at the employee's request; or

(3) The employee becomes entitled to a rate of basic pay that is equal to or higher than the saved rate.

(g) If an employee is receiving a saved rate established under this section on May 1, 2005 (when section 301 of Pub. L. 108–411 took effect), any locality payment under 5 U.S.C. 5304 formerly paid in addition to the employee's saved rate no longer applies as of that date. Any locality-adjusted saved rate in effect and payable on April 30, 2005, must be converted to an equal saved rate effective on May 1, 2005. If the employee received no locality payment because of a pay limitation, no conversion under this paragraph is required.

[70 FR 31286, May 31, 2005, as amended at 73 FR 66151, Nov. 7, 2008]

Subpart H—Furloughs in the Senior Executive Service

AUTHORITY: 5 U.S.C. 3133 and 3136.

SOURCE: 48 FR 11925, Mar. 2, 1983, unless otherwise noted.

§ 359.801 Agency authority.

This subpart sets the conditions under which an agency may furlough career appointees in the Senior Executive Service. The furlough of a noncareer, limited term, or limited emergency appointee is not subject to this subpart. The furlough of a reemployed annuitant holding a career appointment also is not subject to the subpart.

§ 359.802 Definitions.

For the purpose of this subpart, *furlough* means the placing of an appointee in a temporary status without duties and pay because of lack of work or funds or other nondisciplinary reasons.

§ 359.803 Competition.

Any furlough for more than 30 calendar days, or for more than 22 workdays if the furlough does not cover consecutive calendar days, shall be made under competitive procedures established by the agency. The procedures shall be made known to the SES members in the agency.

[48 FR 11925, Mar. 2, 1983, as amended at 60 FR 6389, Feb. 2, 1995]

§ 359.804 Length of furlough.

A furlough may not extend more than one year. It may be made only when the agency intends to recall the appointee within one year.

§ 359.805 Appeals.

A career appointee who has been furloughed and who believes this subpart or the agency's procedures have not been correctly applied may appeal to the Merit Systems Protection Board under provisions of the Board's regulations.

§ 359.806 Notice.

(a) An appointee is entitled to a 30 days' advance written notice of a furlough. The full notice period may be shortened, or waived, only in the event of unforseeable circumstances, such as sudden emergencies requiring immediate curtailment of activities.

(b) The written notice shall advise the appointee of:

(1) The reason for the agency decision to take the furlough action.

(2) The expected duration of the furlough and the effective dates;

(3) The basis for selecting the appointee for furlough when some but not all Senior Executive Service appointees in a given organizational unit are being furloughed;

(4) The reason if the notice period is less than 30 days;

(5) The place where the appointee may inspect the regulations and records pertinent to the action; and

(6) The appointee's appeal rights, including the time limit for the appeal and the location of the Merit Systems Protection Board office to which the appeal should be sent.

§ 359.807 Records.

The agency shall preserve all records relating to an action under this subpart for at least one year from the effective date of the action.

Subpart I—Removal of Noncareer and Limited Appointees and Reemployed Annuitants

§ 359.901 Coverage.

(a) This subpart covers the removal from the SES of—

(1) A noncareer appointee;

(2) A limited emergency or a limited term appointee; and

(3) A reemployed annuitant holding any type of appointment under the SES.

(b) Coverage does not include, however, a limited emergency or a limited term appointee who is being removed for disciplinary reasons and who is covered by 5 CFR 752.601(c)(2).

§ 359.902 Conditions of removal.

(a) *Authority.* The agency may remove an appointee subject to this subpart at any time.

(b) *Notice.* The agency shall notify the appointee in writing before the effective date of the removal.

(c) *Placement rights.* An appointee covered by this subpart is not entitled to the placement rights provided for career appointees under subpart G of this part.

(d) *Appeals.* Actions taken under this subpart are not appealable to the Merit Systems Protection Board under 5 U.S.C. 7701.

PART 362—PATHWAYS PROGRAMS

Subpart A—General Provisions

Sec.

Subpart B—Internship Program

Subpart C—Recent Graduates Program

Subpart D—Presidential Management Fellows Program

AUTHORITY: E.O. 13562, 75 FR 82585. 3 CFR, 2010 Comp., p. 291

SOURCE: 77 FR 28215, May 11, 2012, unless otherwise noted.

Subpart A—General Provisions

§ 362.101 Program administration.

(a) The Pathways Programs authorized under Executive Order 13562 consist of the following three Programs:

(1) The Internship Program;

(2) The Recent Graduates Program; and

(3) The Presidential Management Fellows (PMF) Program.

(b) An agency may rename the Programs specified in paragraphs (a)(1) through (3) of this section, provided that the agency-specific name includes the Pathways Program name identified in paragraph (a) of this section, e.g., Treasury Internship Program.

(c) Agencies must provide for equal employment opportunity in the Pathways Programs without regard to race, ethnicity, color, religion, sex (including pregnancy and gender identity), national origin, age, disability, sexual orientation, genetic information, or any other non-merit-based factor.

§ 362.102 Definitions.

For the purposes of this part:

Advanced degree means a professional or graduate degree, e.g., master's, Ph.D., J.D.

Agency means an agency as defined in 5 U.S.C. 105, and the Government Printing Office.

Certificate program means post-secondary education, in a qualifying educational institution, equivalent to at least one academic year of full-time study that is part of an accredited college-level, technical, trade, vocational, or business school curriculum.

Director means the Director of OPM or his or her designee.

OPM means the Office of Personnel Management.

Participant Agreement means a written agreement between the agency and each Pathways Participant.

Program Participant or Pathways Participant means any individual appointed under a Pathways Program.

Qualifying educational institution means—

(1) A public high school whose curriculum has been approved by a State or local governing body, a private school that provides secondary education as determined under State law, or a homeschool that is allowed to operate in a State; and

(2) Any of the following educational institutions or curricula that have been accredited by an accrediting body recognized by the Secretary of the U.S. Department of Education:

(i) A technical or vocational school;

(ii) A 2-year or 4-year college or university;

(iii) A graduate or professional school (e.g., law school, medical school); or

(iv) A post-secondary homeschool curriculum.

§ 362.103 Authority.

An agency may make an appointment under this part to a position defined in § 213.3402 of this chapter, provided a Memorandum of Understanding between the head of the agency or his or her designee and OPM is in effect.

§ 362.104 Agency requirements.

(a) *Memorandum of Understanding.* In order to make any appointment under a Pathways authority, a Memorandum of Understanding (Pathways MOU) must be in effect between the head of an agency, or his or her designee, and OPM for the administration and use of Pathways Programs, to be re-executed no less frequently than every 2 years.

(b) The Director may revoke an agency's Pathways MOU when agency use of these Programs is inconsistent with Executive Order 13562, this part, or the Pathways MOU.

(c) The Pathways MOU must:

(1) Include information about any agency-specific program labels that will be used, subject to the Federal naming conventions identified in § 362.101 (e.g., OPM Internship Program);

(2) State the delegations of authority for the agency's use of the Pathways Programs (e.g., department-wide vs. bureaus or components);

(3) Include any implementing policy or guidance that the agency determines would facilitate successful implementation and administration for each Pathways Program;

(4) Prescribe criteria and procedures for agency-approved extensions for Recent Graduates and PMFs, not to exceed 120 days. Extension criteria should be limited to circumstances that would render the agency's compliance with the regulations impracticable or impossible;

(5) Describe how the agency will design, implement, and document formal training and/or development, as well as the type and duration of assignments, and necessary exceptions for short term temporary work, such as summer jobs;

(6) Include a commitment from the agency to:

(i) Provide to OPM any information it requests on the agency's Pathways Programs;

(ii) Adhere to any caps on the Pathways Programs imposed by the Director;

(iii) Provide information to OPM about opportunities for individuals interested in participating in the Pathways Programs, as required by this part;

(iv) Ensure adherence to the requirements for accepting applications, assessing applicants, rating and ranking qualified candidates, and affording veterans' preference in accordance with the provisions of part 302; and

(v) Provide a meaningful on-boarding process for each Pathways Program;

(7) Identify the agency's Pathways Programs Officer (PPO), who:

(i) Must be in a position at the agency's headquarters level, or at the headquarters level of a departmental component, in a position at or higher than grade 12 of the General Schedule (GS) (or the equivalent under the Federal Wage System (FWS) or another pay and classification system);

(ii) Is responsible for administering the agency's Pathways Programs, including coordinating the recruitment and on-boarding process for Pathways Programs Participants, and coordinating the agency's Pathways Programs plan with agency stakeholders and other hiring plans (e.g., merit promotion plans, plans for hiring people with disabilities);

(iii) Serves as a liaison with OPM by providing updates on the agency's implementation of its Pathways Programs, clarifying technical or programmatic issues, sharing agency best practices, and other similar duties; and

(iv) Reports to OPM on the agency's implementation of its Pathways Programs and individuals hired under these Programs, in conjunction with the agency's Pathways MOU; and

(8) Identify the agency's PMF coordinator responsible for administering the agency PMF Program and serving as a liaison with OPM.

§362.105 Filling positions.

(a) *Workforce Planning.* Before filling any positions under these Programs, agencies should include measures in their workforce planning to ensure that an adequate number of permanent positions will be available to convert Pathways Participants who successfully complete their Programs.

(b) *Announcements.* When an agency accepts applications from individuals outside its own workforce, it must provide OPM information concerning Pathways Programs job opportunities as provided in each Pathways Program. For the purposes of this paragraph, "agency" means an Executive agency as defined in 5 U.S.C. 105 and the Government Printing Office. An Executive department may treat each of its bureaus or components (first major subdivision that is separately organized and clearly distinguished from other bureaus or components in work function and operation) as a separate agency or as part of one agency, but must do so consistent with its Delegated Examining Agreement.

(c) *Appointments.* (1) Agencies must fill positions under the Pathways Programs using the excepted service appointing authority provided by §213.3402 (a), (b), or (c) of this chapter, as applicable.

(2) Agencies must follow the procedures of part 302 of this chapter when filling a position under a Pathways Program.

(3) Appointments are subject to all the requirements and conditions governing term, career, or career-conditional employment, including investigation to establish an appointee's qualifications and suitability.

(d) *Eligibility.* Except as set forth in this section, eligibility requirements for appointment under a Pathways Program are specified in each Pathways Program.

(e) *Citizenship.* (1) An agency may appoint a non-citizen provided that:

(i) The Pathways Participant is lawfully admitted to the United States as a permanent resident or is otherwise authorized to be employed; and

(ii) The agency is authorized to pay aliens under the annual Appropriations Act ban and any agency-specific enabling and appropriation statutes.

(2) A Pathways Participant must be a United States citizen to be eligible for noncompetitive conversion to the competitive service.

(f) *Employment of relatives.* In accordance with part 310 of this chapter, a Pathways Participant may work in the same agency with a relative when there is no direct reporting relationship and the relative is not in a position to influence or control the Participant's appointment, employment, promotion or advancement within the agency.

(g) *Length of Appointments.* Except as provided in subpart B, Recent Graduate and PMF appointments under this authority may not exceed 2 years plus any agency-approved extension of up to 120 days.

(h) *Terminations.* An agency may terminate a Pathways Participant for reasons including misconduct, poor performance, or suitability under the provisions of this chapter.

(i) *Performance and progress evaluation.* Each Participant must be placed on a performance plan, as prescribed by part 430 of this chapter or other applicable law or regulation, establishing performance elements and standards that are directly related to acquiring and demonstrating the various leadership, technical, and/or general competencies expected of the Participant, as well as the elements and standards established for the duties assigned.

(j) *Compensation.* The rules for setting pay upon the initial appointment of a Participant are governed by the pay administration rules of the pay system or pay plan of the Participant's position under the Pathways program. In determining the Participant's compensation, agencies may also use any applicable pay flexibilities available under that pay system or pay plan (e.g., recruitment, relocation, and retention incentives under part 575 of this chapter; student loan repayments under part 537; and, for General Schedule positions, special rates under part 530, subpart C, and the superior qualifications and special needs pay setting authority and the maximum payable rate rule under part 531, subpart B).

§ 362.106 Participant Agreement.

Agencies must execute a written Participant Agreement with each Pathways Participant that clearly identifies expectations, including but not limited to:

(a) A general description of duties;

(b) Work schedules;

(c) The length of the appointment and termination date;

(d) Mentorship opportunities;

(e) Training requirements as applicable;

(f) Evaluation procedures that will be used for the Participant;

(g) Requirements for continuation and successful completion of the Program; and

(h) Minimum eligibility requirements for noncompetitive conversion to term or permanent competitive service employment according to the requirements of the applicable Pathways Program.

§ 362.107 Conversion to the competitive service.

(a) Subject to any limits on conversion imposed by the Director, and in accordance with the provisions of each Pathways Program, an agency may noncompetitively convert an eligible Pathways Participant to a term or permanent competitive service position.

(b) A Pathways Participant who is noncompetitively converted to a competitive service term appointment may be subsequently converted noncompetitively to a permanent competitive service position.

(c) *Noncompetitive conversion.* (1) An Intern may be converted to a position within the employing agency or any other agency within the Federal Government.

(2) A Recent Graduate or Presidential Management Fellow may be converted within the employing agency. Agencies may not convert Recent Graduates or Presidential Management Fellows from other agencies.

(d) The provisions of the career transition assistance programs in subparts B, F and G of part 330 of this chapter do not apply to conversions made under this part.

(e) Time spent serving as a Pathways Participant counts towards career tenure when the individual is noncompetitively converted to a permanent position in the competitive service upon completion of the Program, with or without an intervening term appointment, and without a break in service of one day.

(f) Though Pathways Participants are eligible for noncompetitive conversion to the competitive service upon successful completion of their Program and any other applicable conversion requirements, service in a Pathways Program confers no right to further employment in either the competitive or excepted service. An agency wishing to convert a Pathways Participant must therefore execute the required actions to do so.

§ 362.108 Program oversight.

(a) The Director may establish caps on the number of Pathways Participants who may be appointed or converted in any Pathways Program within a specific agency or throughout the Federal Government.

(b) The Director may establish such caps based on agency or Governmentwide use of the Pathways Programs, input from the Executive agencies, and consideration of the following:

(1) Agency MOU compliance;

(2) Agency approach to entry-level hiring;

(3) Agency engagement in sound workforce planning to ensure that an adequate number of permanent positions will be available to which Pathways Participants who successfully complete their Programs can be converted;

(4) Agency record in using the Pathways Programs as a supplement to competitive examining, rather than as a substitute for it;

(5) Agency record of publicizing their positions in the Pathways Programs and recruiting and selecting from a broad array of sources; and

(6) Any other information the Director deems relevant.

(c) In the event the Director determines that any caps would be appropriate, OPM will publish notice of such caps in a manner chosen by the Director.

§ 362.109 Reporting requirements.

Agencies must provide information requested by OPM regarding workforce planning strategies that includes:

(a) Information on the entry-level occupations targeted for filling positions under this part in the coming year;

(b) The percentage of overall hiring expected in the coming year under the Internship, Recent Graduates, and Presidential Management Fellows Programs; and

(c) For the previous year:

(1) The number of individuals initially appointed under each Pathways Program;

(2) The percentage of the agency's overall hires made from each Pathways Program;

(3) The number of Pathways Participants, per Program, converted to the competitive service; and

(4) The number of Pathways Participants, per Program, who were separated.

§ 362.110 Transition.

OPM will provide written guidance for the orderly transition of employees currently appointed as students under the Student Educational Employment Program and current PMFs to the applicable Pathways Program and may revise that guidance as necessary.

Subpart B—Internship Program

§ 362.201 Agency authority.

The Internship Program provides students in high schools, colleges, trades schools and other qualifying educational institutions, as defined in § 362.102 of this part, the opportunity to explore Federal careers as paid employees while completing their education. Students appointed under this authority are referred to as Interns.

§ 362.202 Definitions.

In this subpart:

Student means an individual accepted for enrollment or enrolled and seeking a degree (diploma, certificate, etc.) in a qualifying educational institution, on a full or half-time basis (as defined by the institution in which the student is enrolled), including awardees of the Harry S. Truman Foundation Scholarship Program under Public Law 93–842. Students need not be in actual physical attendance, so long as all other requirements are met. An individual who needs to complete less than the equivalent of half an academic/vocational or technical course-load immediately prior to graduating is still considered a student for purposes of this Program.

§ 362.203 Filling positions.

(a) *Announcement.* (1) When an agency accepts applications from individuals outside its own workforce, it must provide OPM information concerning opportunities to participate in the agency's Internship Program. For the purposes of this paragraph (a), "agency" means an Executive agency as defined in 5 U.S.C. 105 and the Government Printing Office. An Executive department may treat each of its bureaus or components (first major subdivision that is separately organized and clearly distinguished from other bureaus or components in work function and operation) as a separate agency or as part of one agency, but must do so consistent with its Delegated Examining Agreement. The information must include:

(i) Position title, series and grade;

(ii) Geographic location of the position, and

(iii) How to apply. A public source (e.g., a link to the agency's Web site with information on how to apply) for interested individuals to seek further information about how to apply for Internship opportunities; and

(iv) Any other information OPM considers appropriate.

(2) OPM will publish information on Internship opportunities in such form as the Director may determine.

(b) *Eligibility.* Except as provided in paragraph (h) of this section, Interns must meet the definition of *student* in § 362.202 throughout the duration of their appointment.

(c) *Qualifications.* Individuals may be evaluated against either agency-developed standards or the OPM Qualification Standard for the position being filled.

(d) *Appointments.* (1) An agency may make Intern appointments, pursuant to its Pathways MOU, using the Schedule D excepted service appointing authority provided in § 213.3402(a) of this chapter.

(2) Appointments may be made to any position for which the individual is qualified. The duties of the position to which the individual is appointed should be related to either the Intern's academic or career goals.

(3) An agency may:

(i) Appoint an Intern for an initial period expected to last more than 1 year. Intern appointments are not required to have an end date. However, agencies are required to specify an end date of the appointment in the Participant Agreement with the Intern; or

(ii) Appoint an Intern on a temporary basis, not to exceed 1 year, to complete temporary projects, to perform labor-intensive tasks not requiring subject-matter expertise, or to fill traditional summer jobs. The agency may extend these temporary appointments as provided in part 213 of this chapter.

(e) *Promotion.* An agency may promote any Intern who meets the qualification requirements for the position. This provision does not confer entitlement to promotion.

(f) *Classification.* (1) Intern positions under the General Schedule or appropriate pay plan must be classified to the –99 series of the appropriate occupational group.

(2) Intern positions under the Federal Wage System must be classified to the –01 series of the appropriate occupational group.

(g) *Schedules.* There are no limitations on the number of hours an Intern can work per week (so long as any applicable laws and regulations governing overtime and hours of work are adhered to). Agencies and students should agree on a formally-arranged schedule of school and work so that:

(1) Work responsibilities do not interfere with academic schedule;

(2) Completion of the educational program (awarding of diploma/certificate/degree) and the Internship Program is accomplished in a reasonable and appropriate timeframe;

(3) The agency is informed of and prepared for the student's periods of employment; and

(4) Requirements for noncompetitive conversion to a term or permanent position in the competitive service are understood by all parties.

(h) *Breaks in program.* A break in program is defined as a period of time when an Intern is working but is unable to go to school, or is neither attending classes nor working at the agency. An agency may use its discretion in either approving or denying a request for a break in program.

§362.204 Conversion to the competitive service.

(a) An agency may noncompetitively convert an Intern who is a U.S. citizen, to a term or permanent appointment in the competitive service.

(b) To be eligible for conversion, the Intern must have:

(1) Completed at least 640 hours of work experience acquired through the Internship Program, except as provided in paragraphs (c) and (d) of this section, while enrolled as a full-time or part-time, degree- or certificate-seeking student;

(2) Completed a course of academic study, within the 120-day period preceding the appointment, at a qualifying educational institution conferring a diploma, certificate, or degree;

(3) Received a favorable recommendation for appointment by an official of the agency or agencies in which the Intern served;

(4) Met the qualification standards for the position to which the Intern will be converted; and

(5) Met agency-specific requirements as specified in the agency's Participant Agreement with the Intern.

(c)(1) An agency may evaluate, consider, and grant credit for up to one-half (320 hours) of the 640-hour service requirement in paragraph (b)(1) of this section for comparable non-Federal internship experience in a field or functional area related to the student's target position and acquired while the student:

(i) Worked in, but not for, a Federal agency, pursuant to a formal internship agreement, comparable to the Internship Program under this subpart, between the agency and an accredited academic institution;

(ii) Worked in, but not for, a Federal agency, pursuant to a written contract with a third-party internship provider officially established to provide internship experiences to students that are comparable to the Internship Program under this subpart; or

(iii) Served as an active duty member of the armed forces (including the National Guard and Reserves), as defined in 5 U.S.C. 2101, provided the veteran's discharge or release is under honorable conditions.

(2) Student volunteer service under part 308 of this chapter and other Federal programs designed to give internship experience to students (e.g., fellowships and similar programs), may be evaluated, considered, and credited under this section when the agency determines the experience is comparable to experience gained in the Internship Program.

(d) An agency may waive up to one-half (*i.e.*, 320 hours) of the 640-hour minimum service requirement in paragraph (b)(1) of this section when an Intern completes 320 hours of career-related work experience under an Internship Program appointment and demonstrates high potential by outstanding academic achievement and exceptional job performance. For purposes of this paragraph:

(1) *Outstanding academic achievement* means an overall grade point average of 3.5 or better, on a 4.0 scale; standing in the top 10 percent of the student's graduating class; and/or induction into a nationally-recognized scholastic honor society.

(2) *Exceptional job performance* means a formal evaluation conducted by the student's Internship supervisor(s), consistent with the applicable performance appraisal program that results in a rating of record (or summary rating) of higher than Fully Successful or equivalent.

(e) An agency may not grant a credit or waiver (or a combination of a credit and waiver) totaling more than 320 hours of the 640-hour service requirement in paragraph (b)(1) of this section.

§362.205 Reduction in force (RIF) and termination.

(a) *Reduction in force.* Interns are covered by part 351 of this chapter for purposes of RIF.

(1) *Tenure Groups.* (i) An Intern serving under an appointment for an initial period expected to last more than 1 year is in excepted service Tenure Group II.

(ii) A temporary Intern, serving under an appointment not to exceed 1 year, who has not completed 1 year of service, is in excepted service Tenure Group 0.

(iii) A temporary Intern serving under an appointment not to exceed 1 year, who has completed 1 year of current, continuous service, is in excepted service Tenure Group III.

(2) [Reserved]

(b) *Termination.* As a condition of employment, an Intern appointment expires:

(1) 120 days after completion of the designated academic course of study, unless the Participant is selected for noncompetitive conversion under §362.204, or

(2) Upon expiration of the temporary Internship appointment.

Subpart C—Recent Graduates Program

§362.301 Program administration.

The Recent Graduates Program provides an entry-level developmental experience designed to lead to a civil service career in the Federal Government after successfully completing 1 year under the Program, unless the training requirements of the position warrant a longer and more structured training program. Employment under the Recent Graduates Program may not exceed 2 years plus any agency approved extension of up to an additional 120 days. Individuals appointed under this authority are referred to as Recent Graduates. An agency wishing to participate in the Recent Graduates Program must:

(a) Identify in the MOU the duration of its Recent Graduates Program, including any criteria used to determine the need for a longer and more structured training program that exceeds 1 year;

(b) Ensure, within 90 days of appointment, that each Recent Graduate is assigned a mentor who is an employee outside the Recent Graduates' chain of command;

(c) Ensure, within 45 days of appointment, that each Recent Graduate has an Individual Development Plan (IDP) that is approved by his or her supervisor; and

(d) Provide at least 40 hours of formal interactive training per year that advances the goals and competencies outlined in each Recent Graduate's IDP. Mandatory annual training, such as information security and ethics training, does not count towards the 40-hour requirement.

§362.302 Eligibility.

(a) A Recent Graduate is an individual who obtained a qualifying associates, bachelors, master's, professional, doctorate, vocational or technical degree or certificate from a qualifying educational institution, within the previous 2 years or other applicable period provided below.

(b)(1) Except as provided in paragraph (b)(2) of this section, an individual may apply for a position in the Recent Graduates Program only if the individual's application is received not later than 2 years after the date the individual completed all requirements of an academic course of study leading to a qualifying associates, bachelor's, master's, professional, doctorate, vocational or technical degree or certificate from a qualifying educational institution.

(2) A veteran, as defined in 5 U.S.C. 2108, who, due to a military service obligation, was precluded from applying to the Recent Graduates Program during any portion of the 2-year eligibility period described in paragraph (b)(1) of this section shall have a full 2-year period of eligibility upon his or her release or discharge from active duty. In no event, however, may the individual's eligibility period extend beyond 6 years from the date on which the individual completed the requirements of an academic course of study.

§362.303 Filling positions.

(a) *Announcement.* (1) When an agency accepts applications from individuals outside its own workforce, it must provide OPM information concerning opportunities to participate in the agency's Recent Graduates Program. For the purposes of this paragraph, "agency" means an Executive agency as defined in 5 U.S.C. 105 and the Government Printing Office. An Executive department may treat each of its bureaus or components (first major subdivision that is separately organized and clearly distinguished from other bureaus or components in work function and operation) as a separate agency or as part of one agency, but must do so consistent with its Delegated Examining Agreement. The information must include:

(i) Position title, series and grade;

(ii) Geographic location of the position;

(iii) How to apply. A public source (e.g., a link to the agency's Web site with information on how to apply for interested individuals to seek further information about how to apply); and

(iv) Any other information OPM considers appropriate.

(2) OPM will publish information on Recent Graduate opportunities in such form as the Director may determine.

(b) *Appointments.* (1) An agency may make appointments to the Recent Graduates Program, pursuant to a Pathways MOU executed with the OPM, under Schedule D of the excepted service in accordance with part 302 of this chapter.

(2) An agency must appoint a Recent Graduate using the excepted service appointing authority provided by § 213.3402(b) of this chapter.

(3)(i) An agency may make an initial appointment of a Recent Graduate to any position filled under this authority for which the Recent Graduate qualifies, up to the GS–09 level (or equivalent under another pay and classification system, such as the Federal Wage System), except as provided in paragraphs (b)(3)(ii) through (iv) of this section.

(ii) Initial appointments to positions for science, technology, engineering, or mathematics (STEM) occupations may be made at the GS–11 level, if the candidate possesses a Ph.D. or equivalent degree directly related to the STEM position the agency is seeking to fill.

(iii) Initial appointments to scientific and professional research positions at the GS–11 level for which the classification and qualification criteria for research positions apply, if the candidate possesses a master's degree or equivalent graduate degree directly related to the position the agency is seeking to fill.

(iv) Initial appointments to scientific and professional research positions at the GS–12 level for which the classification and qualification criteria for research positions apply, if the candidate possesses a Ph.D. or equivalent degree directly related to the position the agency is seeking to fill.

(v) Positions must have progressively more responsible duties that provide career advancement opportunities (*i.e.*, positions must provide for career ladder advancement).

(c) *Extensions.* An agency may extend the Program period for up to an additional 120 days to cover rare or unusual circumstances or situations. The agency's Pathways MOU must identify criteria for approving extensions.

(d) *Qualifications.* An agency must evaluate candidates using OPM Qualification Standards for the occupation and grade level of the position being filled.

(e) *Promotions.* An agency may promote any Recent Graduate who meets the qualification requirements for the position. This provision does not confer entitlement to promotion.

(f) *Trial period.* The duration of the Recent Graduates appointment in the excepted service is a trial period.

§ 362.304 Movement between agencies.

(a) A Recent Graduate may apply for and accept a new Recent Graduates appointment with another agency covered by this part, as long as the agency meets all the requirements for participating in the Recent Graduates Program.

(b) To move to the new agency, the Recent Graduate must separate from the current employing agency.

(c) The new employing agency must appoint the Recent Graduate without a break in service.

(d) Time served under the previous agency's Recent Graduates Program is credited toward the Program requirements for noncompetitive conversion eligibility to the competitive service. Because there is no break in service, the Recent Graduate does not begin a new period in the Program upon moving to the new agency.

(e) The new employing agency's plan must identify requirements for Program completion and eligibility for noncompetitive conversion.

§ 362.305 Conversion to the competitive service.

(a) An agency may noncompetitively convert a Recent Graduate who is a U.S. citizen to a competitive service term or permanent position when the Recent Graduate has:

(1) Successfully completed at least 1-year of continuous service in addition to all the requirements of the Recent Graduates Program;

(2) Demonstrated successful job performance consistent with the applicable performance appraisal program established under the agency's approved performance appraisal system that results in a rating of record (or summary rating) of at least Fully Successful or equivalent and a recommendation for conversion by the first-level supervisor; and

(3) Met the OPM Qualification Standard for the competitive service position to which the Recent Graduate will be converted.

(b) An agency must make the noncompetitive conversion effective on the date the service requirement is met, or at the end of an agency-approved extension, if applicable.

§ 362.306 Reduction in force and termination.

(a) *Reduction in force.* Recent Graduates are in excepted service Tenure Group II for purposes of § 351.502 of this chapter. Expiration of the Recent Graduates appointment is not otherwise subject to part 351 of this chapter.

(b) *Terminations.* (1) Except as provided in paragraph (b)(2) of this section, as a condition of employment, a Recent Graduate appointment expires at the end of the agency prescribed Program period, plus any agency-approved extension, unless the Participant is selected for noncompetitive conversion under § 362.306.

(2) A Recent Graduate who held a career-conditional or career appointment in an agency immediately before entering the Program, and fails to complete the Program for reasons that are not related to misconduct, poor performance, or suitability, may, at the agency's discretion, be placed in a permanent competitive service position, as appropriate, in the employing agency.

Subpart D—Presidential Management Fellows Program

§ 362.401 Definitions.

For purposes of this subpart:

Agency PMF Coordinator is an individual, at the appropriate agency component level, who coordinates the placement, development, and other Program-related activities of PMFs appointed in his or her agency. The agency Pathways Programs Officer may also serve as the PMF Coordinator.

Executive Resources Board (ERB) has the same meaning as specified in § 317.501(a) of this section; in those agencies that are not required to have an ERB pursuant to that section, it means the senior agency official or officials who have been given responsibility for executive resources management and oversight by the agency head.

Presidential Management Fellow (PMF) or *Fellow* is an individual appointed, at the GS–9, GS–11, or GS–12 level (or equivalent under a non-GS pay and classification system such as the Federal Wage System), in the excepted service under § 213.3402(c) of this chapter.

§ 362.402 Program administration.

(a) The Director may determine the number of Fellows who may be appointed during any given year. This determination will be based on input from the Chief Human Capital Officers Council, as well as input from agencies not represented on the Council.

(b) Thereafter, subject to the provisions and requirements of this chapter, an agency may appoint individuals selected by the Director as Fellows finalists according to its short-, medium-, and long-term senior leadership and related (senior policy, professional, technical, and equivalent) recruitment, development, and succession requirements.

(c) The Director will establish the qualification requirements for evaluating applicants for the PMF Program.

(d) An agency that hires Fellows in field locations outside the Washington, DC, Metropolitan Area may:

(1) In advance of making the appointment, discuss whether the finalist wants to do a developmental rotation

to agency headquarters and, if so, make a commitment to allow and fund such a rotation, to the maximum extent practicable, in accordance with §362.405(b) of this part; and

(2) Promote interaction among regional Fellows with the agency Federal Executive Board (FEB) and permit Fellows to attend FEB-sanctioned activities in that region.

§362.403 Announcement, eligibility, and selection.

(a) OPM will announce the opportunity to apply for the PMF Program and conduct a competition for the selection of finalists as set forth in this section.

(b) A Presidential Management Fellow is an individual who, within the previous 2 years, completed an advanced degree from a qualifying educational institution.

(c) An individual may apply for the PMF Program if:

(1) The individual has obtained an advanced degree within the 2-year period preceding the Program announcement described in paragraph (a) of this section, or

(2) The individual is still a student attending a qualifying educational institution, as defined in paragraph (2)(iii) of the definition of *Qualifying educational institution in* §362.102, and he or she expects to complete a qualifying advanced degree by August 31 of the academic year in which the competition is held.

(d) An individual may apply for the PMF Program more than once as long as he or she meets the eligibility criteria. However, if an individual becomes a finalist and subsequently applies for the Program during the next open announcement, the individual will forfeit his or her status as a finalist.

(e) OPM will select Fellow finalists based on an OPM evaluation of each candidate's experience and accomplishments according to his or her application and the results of a rigorous structured assessment process.

(f) OPM will publish and provide participating agencies the Fellow finalists list for appointment consideration.

§362.404 Appointment and extension.

(a) *Appointments.* (1) An agency may make 2-year appointments to the PMF Program, pursuant to a Pathways MOU executed with the OPM, under Schedule D of the excepted service in accordance with part 302 of this chapter.

(2) An agency must appoint a PMF using the excepted service appointing authority provided by §213.3402(c) of this chapter.

(3) OPM will establish an eligibility period during which agencies may appoint Fellow finalists.

(b) *Extension.* An agency may extend a Fellow's appointment for up to 120 days to cover rare or unusual circumstances or situations. The agency's Pathways MOU must identify the criteria for approving extensions.

(c) *Grade.* An agency may appoint a Fellow at the GS–09, GS–11, or GS–12 level or equivalent depending on his or her qualifications.

(d) *Trial period.* The duration of the PMF appointment in the excepted service is a trial period.

§362.405 Development, evaluation, promotion, and certification.

(a) *Individual Development Plans.* An agency must approve, within 45 days, an Individual Development Plan (IDP) for each of its Fellows that sets forth the specific developmental activities that are mutually agreed upon by each Fellow and his or her supervisor. The IDP must be developed in consultation with the Agency PMF Coordinator and/or the mentor assigned to the Fellow under paragraph (b)(3) of this section.

(b) *Required developmental activities.* (1) OPM will provide an orientation program for each class or cohort of Fellows and will provide information on available training opportunities known to it.

(2) The agency must provide each Fellow a minimum of 80 hours of formal interactive training per year that addresses the competencies outlined in the IDP. Mandatory annual training, such as information security and ethics training, does not count towards the 80-hour requirement.

(3) Within the first 90 days of a Fellow's appointment, the agency must assign the Fellow a mentor, who is a

managerial employee outside the Fellow's chain of command.

(4) The agency must provide each Fellow with at least one rotational or developmental assignment with full-time management and/or technical responsibilities consistent with the Fellow's IDP. With respect to this requirement:

(i) Each Fellow must receive at least one developmental assignment of 4 to 6 months in duration, with management and/or technical responsibilities consistent with the Fellow's IDP. As an alternative, a Fellow may choose to participate in an agency-wide initiative or other Presidential or Administration initiative that will provide the Fellow with the experience he or she would have gained through the 4-to-6-month developmental assignment; and

(ii) The developmental assignment may be within the Fellow's organization, in another component of the agency, or in another Federal agency.

(5) The Fellow may receive other short-term rotational assignments of 1 to 6 months in duration, at the agency's discretion.

(6) Upon the request of OPM, the appointing agency must make Fellows available to assist in the assessment process for subsequent PMF classes. Any interactive training provided to a Fellow in connection with assisting OPM in the assessment process may be counted toward the minimum 80-hour training requirement in paragraph (b)(2) of this section.

(c) *Promotion.* An agency may promote any Fellow who meets the qualification requirements for the position. This provision does not confer entitlement to promotion.

(d) *Certification of completion.* (1) Upon completion of the Program, the agency's ERB must evaluate each Fellow and determine whether it can certify in writing that the Fellow met all of the requirements of the Program, including the performance and developmental expectations set forth in the individual's performance plan and IDP. The ERB may consult the Fellow's mentor in reaching its determination.

(2) The ERB must notify the Fellow of its decision regarding certification of successful completion.

(3) ERB certifications must be forwarded to OPM.

(4)(i) If the ERB decides not to certify a Fellow, the Fellow may request reconsideration of that determination by the Director. Such reconsideration must be requested in writing, with appropriate documentation and justification, within 15 calendar days of the date of the agency's decision. The Director's decision on reconsideration is not subject to appeal.

(ii) The Fellow may continue in the Program pending the outcome of his or her request for reconsideration. The agency must continue to provide appropriate developmental activities during this period.

§ 362.406 Movement between agencies.

(a) At any time during his or her appointment in the Program, a Fellow may move to another agency covered by this part, as long as the agency meets all the requirements for participating in the PMF Program. To move from one agency to another during the Program, the Fellow must separate from the current agency. The new employing agency must appoint the Participant without a break in service.

(b) The Fellow does not begin a new Program period upon appointment by the new employing agency. Because there is no break in service, time served under the previous Program appointment will apply towards the completion of the Program with the new employing agency.

(c) An agency must notify OPM when appointing a Fellow currently appointed in another agency.

(d) If the move occurs within the first 6 months of the Fellow's appointment, the original appointing agency may request reimbursement of one-quarter of the placement fee from the new appointing agency.

§ 362.407 Withdrawal and readmission.

(a) *Withdrawal.* (1) A Fellow may withdraw from the Program at any time. Such withdrawal will be treated as a resignation from the Federal service; however, any obligations established upon admission and appointment (for example, as a result of accepting a recruitment incentive under part 575 of this chapter) still apply.

(2) A Fellow who held a permanent appointment in the competitive service in an agency immediately before entering the Program, and who withdraws from the Program for reasons that are not related to misconduct, poor performance, or suitability, may, at the employing agency's discretion, be placed in a permanent competitive service position, as appropriate, in that agency. The employing agency's determination in this regard is not subject to appeal.

(3) An agency must notify OPM when a Fellow withdraws from the Program.

(b) *Readmission.* (1) If a Fellow withdraws from the Program for reasons that are related to misconduct, poor performance, or suitability, as determined by the agency, he or she will not be readmitted to the Program at any time.

(2) If a Fellow withdraws from the Program for reasons that are not related to misconduct, poor performance, or suitability, he or she may petition the employing original agency for readmission and reappointment to the Program. Such a petition must be in writing and include appropriate justification. The agency may approve or deny the request for readmission. An agency must submit written notification of approved readmission requests to OPM. The individual's status in the Program upon readmission and reappointment must be addressed as part of the agency's submission. The Director may overrule the agency's decision to readmit and reappoint, and the Director's decision is not subject to appeal.

§362.408 Termination and reduction in force.

(a) *Termination.* (1) An agency may terminate a Fellow for reasons related to misconduct, poor performance, or suitability.

(2) As a condition of employment, a Fellow's appointment expires at the end of the 2-year Program period, plus any agency-approved extension, unless the Participant is selected for noncompetitive conversion. If an agency does not convert a Fellow at the end of the Program, as provided in §362.409 of this part, or extend the individual's initial appointment under §362.404, the appointment expires when certification for Program completion is denied or when the Director denies the agency's request for an extension.

(3) The agency must provide written notification to OPM when a Fellow is terminated for any reason.

(b) *Reduction in force.* Fellows are in the excepted service Tenure Group II for purposes of §351.502 of this chapter.

§362.409 Conversion to the competitive service.

(a) A Fellow must complete the Program within the time limits prescribed in §362.404 of this part, including any agency-approved extension. At the conclusion of that period, the Fellow may be converted, as provided in paragraph (b) of this section.

(b) An agency may convert, without a break in service, an ERB-certified Fellow to a competitive service term or permanent appointment.

PART 370—INFORMATION TECHNOLOGY EXCHANGE PROGRAM

Sec.

AUTHORITY: Pub. L. 107–347, 116 Stat. 2923–2931 (5 U.S.C. 3707).

SOURCE: 70 FR 47714, Aug. 15, 2005, unless otherwise noted.

§370.101 Purpose.

(a) The purpose of this part is to implement sections 209(b)(6) and (c) of the E-Government Act of 2002 (Pub. L. 107–347), which authorize the Office of Personnel Management to establish an Information Technology Exchange Program. This statute authorizes the temporary detail of information technology employees between the Federal Government and private sector organizations. The statute also gives Federal agencies the authority to accept private sector information technology employees detailed under the Information Technology Exchange Program.

(b) Agency heads, or their designees, may approve details as a mechanism for improving the Federal workforce's competency in using information technology to deliver Government information and services. Details under this part allow Federal employees to serve with private sector organizations for a limited time period without loss of employee rights and benefits. Agencies may not make details under this part to circumvent personnel ceilings, or as a substitute for other more appropriate personnel decisions or actions. Approved details must meet the strategic program goals of the agency. The benefits to the Federal agency and the private sector organization are the primary considerations in initiating details; not the desires or personal needs of an individual employee.

§ 370.102 Definitions.

In this part: *Agency* means an Executive agency as defined in 5 U.S.C. 105, with the exception of the Government Accountability Office.

Core Competencies are those IT competencies identified by the Federal Chief Information Officer (CIO) Council as a baseline for use by Federal agencies in complying with the Clinger-Cohen Act, Public Law 104–106, to determine the training and development needs of the Federal IT workforce.

Detail means: (1) The assignment or loan of an employee of an agency to a private sector organization without a change of position from the agency that employs the individual (5 U.S.C. 3701(2)(A)), or

(2) The assignment or loan of a private sector organization employee to an agency without a change of position from the private sector organization that employs the individual (5 U.S.C. 3701(2)(B)).

Exceptional employee means an employee who is rated at the highest levels of the applicable performance appraisal system or, in the case of an employee under an appraisal system that does not have a summary rating level above "fully successful" or equivalent, is rated at the highest summary level used by the performance appraisal system and demonstrates sustained quality performance significantly above that expected in the type of position involved, as determined under performance-related criteria established by the agency.

Information technology (IT) management means the planning, organizing, staffing, directing, integrating, or controlling of information technology as defined by Office of Management and Budget Circular A–130 which states, the term "information technology" means any equipment or interconnected system or subsystem of equipment, that is used in the automatic acquisition, storage, manipulation, management, movement, control, display, switching, interchange, transmission, or reception of data or information by an executive agency. For purposes of the preceding sentence, equipment is used by an executive agency if the equipment is used by the executive agency directly or is used by a contractor under a contract with the executive agency which requires the use of such equipment, or requires the use, to a significant extent, of such equipment in the performance of a service or the furnishing of a product. The term "information technology" includes computers, ancillary equipment, software, firmware and similar procedures, services (including support services), and related resources. The term "information technology" does not include any equipment that is acquired by a Federal contractor incidental to a Federal contract. The term "information technology" does not include national security systems as defined in the Clinger-Cohen Act of 1996 (40 U.S.C. 1452).

OPM means the Office of Personnel Management.

Private sector organization means a profit-making business entity that is registered in the Central Contractor Registration Database (*http://www.ccr.gov*) as required for the conduct of business with the Government.

Small business concern means a business concern that satisfies the definitions and standards specified by the Administrator of the Small Business Administration (SBA), under section 3(a)(2) of the Small Business Act, codified at 13 CFR 121. Federal agencies can find more information through the "Frequently Asked Questions" page on the SBA's Web site at *http://www.sba.gov*, which addresses small business size standards.

§370.103 Eligibility.

(a) To be eligible for a detail under this part, an individual must:

(1) Work in the field of information technology management;

(2) Be considered an exceptional employee by the individual's current employer; and

(3) Be expected by the individual's current employer to assume increased information technology management responsibilities in the future.

(b) To be eligible for a detail under this part, a Federal employee, in addition to meeting the requirements of paragraph (a) of this section, must be serving in a position at the GS–11 level or above (or equivalent), under a career or career-conditional appointment or an appointment of equivalent tenure in the excepted service. For purposes of this part, positions of equivalent tenure in the excepted service are limited to permanent appointments. In addition, only career members of the Senior Executive Service are eligible to be detailed under this part.

(c) To be eligible to participate in the Information Technology Exchange Program, a private sector organization must be registered in the Central Contractor Registration Database located at *http://www.ccr.gov*, except as permitted by the Federal Acquisition Regulation (48 CFR 4.1102).

(d) To be eligible for a detail to a Federal agency under this part, a private sector employee, in addition to meeting the requirements of paragraph (a) of this section, must meet citizenship requirements for Federal employment in accordance with 5 CFR 7.3 and 338.101, as well as any other statutory limitation.

§370.104 Length of details.

(a) Details may be for a period of between 3 months and 1 year, and may be extended in 3-month increments for a total of not more than 1 additional year, in accordance with 5 U.S.C. 3702(d).

(b) Agencies may not approve or extend details after December 17, 2007. An individual serving on a detail prior to this date may continue to do so as long as the detail began or was extended on or before December 17, 2007.

(c) For the life of the ITEP, a Federal agency may not send on assignment an employee who has served on a detail under this part for more than 6 years during his or her Federal career. OPM may waive this provision upon request of the agency head, or his or her designee.

§370.105 Written agreements.

Before the detail begins, the agency and private sector organization must enter into a written agreement with the individual(s) detailed. The written agreement must be a three-party agreement between the Federal agency (agency head or designee), the individual (private sector or Federal), and the private sector organization. The written agreement must include, but is not limited to, the following elements:

(a) The duties to be performed, duration, and terms under which extensions to the detail may be granted;

(b) An individual development plan describing the core IT competencies and technical skills that the detailee will be expected to enhance or acquire;

(c) Whether the individual will be supervised by a Federal or private sector employee; and a description of the supervision;

(d) The requirement for Federal employees to return to their employing agency upon completion of the detail for a period equal to the length of the detail including any extensions; and

(e) The obligations and responsibilities of all parties as described in 5 U.S.C. 3702 through 3704.

§370.106 Terms and conditions.

(a) A Federal employee detailed under this part:

(1) Remains a Federal employee without loss of employee rights and benefits attached to that status. These include, but are not limited to:

(i) Consideration for promotion;

(ii) Leave accrual;

(iii) Continuation of retirement benefits and health, life, and long-term care insurance benefits; and

(iv) Pay increases the employee otherwise would have received if he or she had not been detailed;

(2) Remains covered for purposes of the Federal Tort Claims Act, and for purposes of injury compensation as described in 5 U.S.C. chapter 81; and

(3) Is subject to any action that may impact the employee's position while he or she is detailed.

(b) An individual detailed from a private sector organization under this part:

(1) Is deemed to be an employee of the Federal agency for purposes of:

(i) Title 5, United States Code, chapter 73 (Suitability, Security, and Conduct);

(ii) Title 18, United States Code, section 201 (Bribery of Public Officials and Witnesses), section 203 (Compensation to Members of Congress, Officers, and Others in Matters Affecting the Government), section 205 (Activities of Officers and Employees in Claims Against and Other Matters Affecting the Government), section 207 (Restrictions on Former Officers, Employees, and Elected Officials of the Executive and Legislative Branches), section 208 (Acts Affecting a Personal Financial Interest), section 209 (Salary of Government Officials and Employees Payable Only by the United States), section 603 (Making Political Contributions), section 606 (Intimidation to Secure Political Contributions), section 607 (Place of Solicitation), section 643 (Accounting Generally for Public Money), section 654 (Officer or Employee of United States Converting Property of Another), section 1905 (Disclosure of Confidential Information Generally), and section 1913 (Lobbying with Appropriated Moneys);

(iii) Title 31, United States Code, section 1343 (Buying and Leasing Passenger Motor Vehicles and Aircraft), section 1344 (Passenger Carrier Use), and section 1349(b), (Adverse Personnel Actions);

(iv) The Federal Tort Claims Act and any other Federal tort liability statute;

(v) The Ethics in Government Act of 1978;

(vi) Internal Revenue Code of 1986, section 1043 (Sale of Property to Comply with Conflict-of-Interest Requirements); and

(vii) Title 41, United States Code, section 423 (Prohibition on Former Official's Acceptance of Compensation From Contractor).

(2) Does not have any right or expectation for Federal employment solely on the basis of his or her detail;

(3) May not have access to any trade secrets or to any other nonpublic information which is of commercial value to the private sector organization from which he or she is detailed;

(4) Is subject to such regulations as the President may prescribe; and

(5) Is covered by 5 U.S.C. chapter 81, Compensation for Work Injuries, as provided in 5 U.S.C. 3704(c).

(c) Individuals detailed under this part may be supervised either by Federal or private sector managers. For example, a Federal employee on detail to a private sector organization may be supervised by a private sector manager. Likewise, a private sector employee on detail to an agency may be supervised by a Federal manager.

(d) As provided in 5 U.S.C. 3704(d), a private sector organization may not charge the Federal Government, as direct or indirect costs under a Federal contract, for the costs of pay or benefits paid by that private sector organization to an employee detailed to an agency under this part.

(e) Details may be terminated by the agency (agency head or designee) or private sector organization concerned for any reason at any time.

§ 370.107 Details to small business concerns.

(a) The head of each agency must take such actions as may be necessary to ensure that, of the details made to private sector organizations in each calendar year, at least 20 percent are to small business concerns, in accordance with 5 U.S.C. 3703(e)(1).

(b) Agencies must round up to the nearest whole number when calculating the percentage of details to small business concerns needed to meet the requirements of this section. For example, if an agency detailed 11 individuals to private sector organizations during a given year, to meet the 20 percent requirement, that agency must have made at least 3 (rounded up from 2.2) of these details to small business concerns.

(c) For purposes of this section, "year" refers to the 12-month period beginning on date of the enactment of the Act, December 17, 2002, and each succeeding 12-month period in which any assignments are made. Assignments "made" in a year are those commencing in such year, in accordance with 5 U.S.C. 3703(e)(2).

(d) Agencies that do not meet the requirements of this section are subject to the reporting requirements in 5 U.S.C. 3703(e)(3).

(e) An agency that makes fewer than five details to private sector organizations in any year is not subject to this section.

§ 370.108 Reporting requirements.

(a) Agencies using this part must prepare and submit to OPM semiannual reports in accordance with 5 U.S.C. 3706 which must include:

(1) The total number of individuals detailed to, and the total number of individuals detailed from, the agency during the report period;

(2) A brief description of each detail reported under paragraph (a)(1) of this section including:

(i) The name of the detailed individual, and the private sector organization and the agency (including the specific bureau or other agency component) to or from which such individual was detailed;

(ii) The respective positions to and from which the individual was detailed, including the duties and responsibilities and the pay grade or level associated with each; and

(iii) The duration and objectives of the individual's detail; and

(3) Such other information as OPM considers appropriate.

(b) Reports are due to OPM no later than April 7 and October 7 of each year for the immediately preceding 6-month periods ending March 31 and September 30, respectively.

(c) Agencies that do not meet the requirements of § 370.107 must prepare and submit annual reports to Congress in accordance with 5 U.S.C. 3703(e)(3), as appropriate.

§ 370.109 Agency plans.

Before detailing agency employees or receiving private sector employees under this part, an agency must establish an Information Technology Exchange Program Plan. The plan must include, but is not limited to, the following elements:

(a) Designation of the agency officials with authority to review and approve details;

(b) Estimated number of candidates needed, both private sector and Federal employees, to address IT workforce needs within the agency;

(c) Criteria for the selection of agency employees for a detail under this part. At a minimum, each agency must:

(1) Announce the detail, including eligibility requirements, to all eligible employees;

(2) Provide for employee nomination by their organization or self-nomination, to include endorsement by their respective supervisor;

(3) Forward nominations to designated agency reviewing and approving official for final selection.

(4) Consider:

(i) The extent to which the employee's current competencies and skills are being utilized in the agency;

(ii) The employee's capability to improve, enhance, or learn skills and acquire competencies needed in the agency; and

(iii) The benefits to the agency which would result from selecting the employee for detail.

(d) Return rights and continuing service requirements for Federal employees returning from a detail; and

(e) Documentation and recordkeeping requirements sufficient to allow reconstruction of each action taken under this part to meet agency reporting requirements under § 370.108(a) and (b).

PART 410—TRAINING

Subpart A—General Provisions

Subpart B—Planning and Evaluating Training

Subpart C—Establishing and Implementing Training Programs

Subpart D—Paying for Training Expenses

Subpart E—Accepting Contributions, Awards, and Payments From Non-Government Organizations

Subpart F—Reporting

AUTHORITY: 5 U.S.C. 1103(c), 2301, 2302, 4101, *et seq.;* E.O. 11348, 3 CFR, 1967 Comp., p. 275, E.O. 11478, 3 CFR 1966–1970 Comp., page 803, unless otherwise noted, E.O. 13087; and E.O. 13152.

SOURCE: 61 FR 66193, Dec. 17, 1996, unless otherwise noted.

Subpart A—General Provisions

§ 410.101 Definitions.

In this part:

(a) *Agency, employee, Government, Government facility,* and *non-Government facility* have the meanings given these terms in section 4101 of title 5, United States Code.

(b) Exceptions to organizations and employees covered by this subpart include:

(1) Those named in section 4102 of title 5, United States Code, and

(2) The U.S. Postal Service and Postal Rate Commission and their employees, as provided in Pub. L. 91–375, enacted August 12, 1970.

(c) *Training* has the meaning given to the term in section 4101 of title 5, United States Code.

(d) *Mission-related training* is training that supports agency goals by improving organizational performance at any appropriate level in the agency, as determined by the head of the agency. This includes training that:

(1) Supports the agency's strategic plan and performance objectives;

(2) Improves an employee's current job performance;

(3) Allows for expansion or enhancement of an employee's current job;

(4) Enables an employee to perform needed or potentially needed duties outside the current job at the same level of responsibility; or

(5) Meets organizational needs in response to human resource plans and re-engineering, downsizing, restructuring, and/or program changes.

(e) *Retraining* means training and development provided to address an individual's skills obsolescence in the current position and/or training and development to prepare an individual for a different occupation, in the same agency, in another Government agency, or in the private sector.

(f) *Continued service agreement* has the meaning given to service agreements in section 4108 of title 5, United States Code.

(g) *Interagency training* means training provided by one agency for other agencies or shared by two or more agencies.

(h) *State and local government* have the meanings given to these terms by section 4762 of title 42, United States Code.

(i) *Established contact hours* are the number of academic credit hours assigned to a course(s) times the number of weeks in a term times the number of terms required to complete the degree.

[61 FR 66193, Dec. 17, 1996, as amended at 69 FR 33276, June 15, 2004]

Subpart B—Planning and Evaluating Training

§410.201 Responsibilities of the head of an agency.

Agency employee development plans and programs should be designed to build or support an agency workforce capable of achieving agency mission and performance goals and facilitating continuous improvement of employee and organizational performance. In developing strategies to train employees, heads of agencies or their designee(s), under section 4103 of title 5, United States Code, and Executive Order 11348, are required to:

(a) Establish, budget for, operate, maintain, and evaluate plans and programs for training agency employees by, in, and through Government or non-Government facilities, as appropriate;

(b) Establish policies governing employee training, including a statement of the alignment of employee training and development with agency strategic plans, the assignment of responsibility to ensure the training goals are achieved, and the delegation of training approval authority to the lowest appropriate level;

(c) Establish priorities for training employees and allocate resources according to those priorities; and

(d) Develop and maintain plans and programs that:

(1) Identify mission-critical occupations and competencies;

(2) Identify workforce competency gaps;

(3) Include strategies for closing competency gaps; and

(4) Assess periodically, but not less often than annually, the overall agency talent management program to identify training needs within the agency as required by section 303 of Executive Order 11348.

[74 FR 65387, Dec. 10, 2009]

§410.202 Responsibilities for evaluating training.

Agencies must evaluate their training programs annually to determine how well such plans and programs contribute to mission accomplishment and meet organizational performance goals.

[74 FR 65387, Dec. 10, 2009]

§410.203 Options for developing employees.

Agencies may use a full range of options to meet their mission-related organizational and employee development needs, such as classroom training, on-the-job training, technology-based training, satellite training, employees' self-development activities, coaching, mentoring, career development counseling, details, rotational assignments, cross training, and developmental activities at retreats and conferences.

[61 FR 66193, Dec. 17, 1996. Redesignated at 74 FR 65388, Dec. 10, 2009]

Subpart C—Establishing and Implementing Training Programs

§410.301 Scope and general conduct of training programs.

(a) *Authority.* The requirements for establishing training programs and plans are found in section 4103(a) of title 5, United States Code, and Executive Order 11348.

(b) *Alignment with other human resource functions.* Training programs established by agencies under chapter 41 of title 5, United States Code, should be integrated with other personnel management and operating activities, under administrative agreements as appropriate, to the maximum possible extent.

§410.302 Responsibilities of the head of an agency.

(a) *Specific responsibilities.* (1) The head of each agency must prescribe procedures as are necessary to ensure that the selection of employees for training is made without regard to race, color, religion, sex (including pregnancy and gender identity), national origin, age (as defined by the Age Discrimination in Employment Act of 1967, as amended), disability, genetic information (including family medical history), marital status, political affiliation, sexual orientation, labor organization affiliation or nonaffiliation, status as parent, or any other non-merit-based factor, unless specifically designated by statute as a factor that must be taken into consideration when awarding such benefits, or retaliation for exercising rights with respect to the categories enumerated above, where retaliation rights are available, and with proper regard for their privacy and constitutional rights as provided by merit system principles set forth in 5 U.S.C. 2301(b)(2).

(2) The head of each agency shall prescribe procedures as are necessary to ensure that the training facility and curriculum are accessible to employees with disabilities.

(3) The head of each agency shall not allow training in a facility that discriminates in the admission or treatment of students.

(b)(1) *Training of Presidential appointees*. The Office of Personnel Management delegates to the head of each agency authority to authorize training for officials appointed by the President. In exercising this authority, the head of an agency must ensure that the training is in compliance with chapter 41 of title 5, United States Code, and with this part. This authority may not be delegated to a subordinate.

(2) *Records*. When exercising this delegation of authority, the head of an agency must maintain records that include:

(i) The name and position title of the official;

(ii) A description of the training, its location, vendor, cost, and duration; and

(iii) A statement justifying the training and describing how the official will apply it during his or her term of office.

(3) *Review of delegation*. Exercise of this authority is subject to U.S. Office of Personnel Management review.

(c) *Training for the head of an agency*. Since self-review constitutes a conflict of interest, heads of agencies must submit their own requests for training to the U.S. Office of Personnel Management for approval.

(d) The head of the agency shall establish the form and manner of maintaining agency records related to training plans, expenditures, and activities.

(e) The head of the agency shall establish written procedures which cover the minimum requirements for continued service agreements. (See also 5 CFR 410.310.)

(f) The head of each agency shall prescribe procedures, as authorized by section 402 of Executive Order No. 11348, for obtaining U.S. Department of State advice before assigning an employee who is stationed within the continental limits of the United States to training outside the continental United States that is provided by a foreign government, international organization, or instrumentality of either.

[61 FR 66193, Dec. 17, 1996, as amended at 63 FR 43867, Aug. 17, 1998; 79 FR 43923, July 29, 2014]

§410.303 Employee responsibilities.

Employees are responsible for self-development, for successfully completing and applying authorized training, and for fulfilling continued service agreements. In addition, they share with their agencies the responsibility to identify training needed to improve individual and organizational performance and identify methods to meet those needs, effectively and efficiently.

§410.304 Funding training programs.

Section 4112 of title 5, United States Code, provides for agencies paying the costs of their training programs and plans from applicable appropriations or from other funds available. Training costs associated with program accomplishment may be funded by appropriations applicable to that program area. In addition, section 4109(a)(2) of title 5, United States Code, provides authority for agencies and employees to share the expenses of training.

§410.305 Establishing and using interagency training.

Executive departments, independent establishments, Government corporations subject to chapter 91 of title 31, the Library of Congress, and the Government Printing office may provide or share training programs developed for its employees of other agencies under section 4120 of title 5, United States Code, when this would result in better training, improved service, or savings to the Government. Section 302(d) of Executive Order 11348 allows agencies excluded from section 4102 of title 5,

United States Code, to also receive interagency training when this would result in better training, improved service, or savings to the Government. Section 201(e) of Executive Order 11348 provides for the Office of Personnel Management to coordinate interagency training conducted by and for agencies (including agencies and portions of agencies excepted by section 4102(a) of Title 5, United States Code).

§410.306 Selecting and assigning employees to training.

(a) Each agency shall establish criteria for the fair and equitable selection and assignment of employees to training consistent with merit system principles specified in 5 U.S.C. 2301(b)(1) and (2).

(b) Persons on Intergovernmental Personnel Act mobility assignments may be assigned to training if that training is in the interest of the Government.

(1) A State or local government employee given an appointment in a Federal agency under the authority of section 3374(b) of title 5 of the United States Code, is deemed an employee of the Federal agency. The agency may provide training for the State or local government employee as it does for other agency employees.

(2) A State or local government employee on detail to a Federal agency under the authority of section 3374(c) of title 5 of the United States Code, is not deemed an employee of the Federal agency. However, the detailed State or local government employee may be admitted to training programs the agency has established for Federal personnel and may be trained in the rules, practices, procedures and/or systems pertaining to the Federal government.

(c) Subject to the prohibitions of §410.308(a) of this part, an agency may pay all or part of the training expenses of students hired under the Student Career Experience Program (see 5 CFR 213.3202(d)(10)).

[61 FR 66193, Dec. 17, 1996; 61 FR 68119, Dec. 27, 1996]

§410.307 Training for promotion or placement in other positions.

(a) *General.* In determining whether to provide training under this section, agencies should take into account:

(1) Agency authority to modify qualification requirements in certain situations as provided in the OPM Operating Manual for Qualification Standards for General Schedule Positions;

(2) Agency authority to establish training programs that provide intensive and directly job-related training to substitute for all or part of the experience (but not education, licensing, certification, or other specific credentials), required by OPM qualification standards. Such training programs may be established to provide employees with the opportunity to acquire the experience and knowledge, skills, and abilities necessary to qualify for another position (including at a higher grade) at an accelerated rate; and

(3) Time-in-grade restrictions on advancement (see 5 CFR 300.603(b)(6)).

(b) *Training for promotion.* Under the authority of 5 U.S.C. 4103, and consistent with merit system principles set forth in 5 U.S.C. 2301(b)(1) and (2), an agency may provide training to non-temporary employees that in certain instances may lead to promotion. An agency must follow its competitive procedures under part 335 of this chapter when selecting a non-temporary employee for training that permits noncompetitive promotion after successful completion of the training.

(c) *Training for placement in other agency positions, in other agencies, or outside Government*—(1) *Grade or pay retention.* Under the authority of 5 U.S.C. 4103 and 5 U.S.C. 5364, an agency may train an employee to meet the qualification requirements of another position in the agency if the new position is at or below the retained grade or the grade of the position the employee held before pay retention.

(2) *Training for placement in another agency.* Under the authority of 5 U.S.C. 4103(b), and consistent with merit system principles set forth in 5 U.S.C. 2301, an agency may train an employee to meet the qualification requirements of a position in another agency if the head of the agency determines that

such training would be in the interest of the Government.

(i) Before undertaking any training under this section, the head of the agency shall determine that there exists a reasonable expectation of placement in another agency.

(ii) When selecting an employee for training under this section, the head of the agency shall consider:

(A) The extent to which the employee's current skills, knowledge, and abilities may be utilized in the new position;

(B) The employee's capability to learn skills and acquire knowledge and abilities needed in the new position; and

(C) The benefits to the Government which would result from retaining the employee in the Federal service.

(3) *Training displaced or surplus employees.* Displaced or surplus employees as defined in 5 CFR 330.602 may be eligible for training or retraining for positions outside Government through programs provided under 29 U.S.C. 1651, or similar authorities. An agency may use its appropriated funds for training displaced or surplus employees for positions outside Government only when specifically authorized by legislation to do so.

(4) *Career transition assistance plans.* Under 5 CFR part 330, subpart F, agencies are required to establish career transition assistance plans (CTAP) to provide career transition services to displaced and surplus employees.

(i) Under the authority of 5 U.S.C. 4109, an agency may:

(A) Train employees in the use of the CTAP services;

(B) Provide vocational and career assessment and counseling services;

(C) Train employees in job search skills, techniques, and strategies; and

(D) Pay for training related expenses as provided in 5 U.S.C. 4109(a)(2).

(ii) Agency CTAP's will include plans for retraining displaced or surplus employees covered by this part.

[61 FR 66193, Dec. 17, 1996, as amended at 75 FR 67605, Nov. 3, 2010]

§ 410.308 Training to obtain an academic degree.

(a) An agency may authorize training for an employee to obtain an academic degree under conditions prescribed at 5 U.S.C. 4107(a).

(b) Colleges and universities participating in an academic degree training program must be accredited by a nationally recognized body. A "nationally recognized body" is a regional, national, or international accrediting organization recognized by the U.S. Department of Education. The listing of accrediting bodies is available through the Department.

(c) The selection of employees for an academic degree training program must follow the requirements of § 335.103(b)(3), § 335.103(c)(1)(iii), and subpart A of part 300 of this chapter. The selection and assignment must be accomplished to meet one or more of the criteria identified in 5 U.S.C. 4107(a). Therefore, an agency may competitively select and assign an employee to an academic degree training program that qualifies the employee for promotion to a higher graded position or to a position that requires an academic degree.

(d) Agency heads must assess and maintain records on the effectiveness of training assignments under this section.

(e) On a periodic basis, OPM may request agency information on the use and effectiveness of training assignments under this section.

[69 FR 33277, June 15, 2004]

§ 410.309 Agreements to continue in service.

(a) *Authority.* Continued service agreements are provided for in section 4108 of title 5, United States Code. Agencies have the authority to determine when such agreements will be required.

(b) *Requirements.* (1) The head of the agency shall establish written procedures which include the minimum requirements for continued service agreements. These requirements shall include procedures the agency considers necessary to protect the Government's interest should the employee fail to successfully complete training.

(2) An employee selected for training subject to an agency continued service agreement must sign an agreement to continue in service after training prior to starting the training. The period of

service will equal at least three times the length of the training.

(3) The head of an agency shall establish procedures to compute length of training period for academic degree training programs in accordance with §410.310(d).

(c) *Failure to fulfill agreements.* With a signed agreement, the agency has a right to recover training costs, except pay or other compensation, if the employee voluntarily separates from Government service. The agency shall provide procedures to enable the employee to obtain a reconsideration of the recovery amount or to appeal for a waiver of the agency's right to recover.

[61 FR 66193, Dec. 17, 1996; 63 FR 72097, Dec. 31, 1998, as amended at 69 FR 33277, June 15, 2004]

§410.310 Computing time in training.

For the purpose of computing time in training for continued service agreements under section 4108 of title 5, United States Code:

(a) An employee on an 8-hour day work schedule assigned to training is counted as being in training for the same number of hours he or she is in pay status during the training assignment. If the employee is not in pay status during the training, the employee is counted as being in training for the number of hours he or she is granted leave without pay for the purpose of the training.

(b) For an employee on an alternative work schedule, the agency is responsible for determining the number of hours the employee is in pay status during the training assignment. If the employee is not in pay status during the training, the employee is counted as being in training for the number of hours he or she is granted leave without pay for the purpose of the training.

(c) An employee on an 8-hour or an alternative work schedule assigned to training on less than a full-time basis is counted as being in training for the number of hours he or she spends in class, in formal computer-based training, in satellite training, in formal self-study programs, or with the training instructor, unless a different method is determined by the agency.

(d) When an employee is pursuing an academic degree through an agency academic degree training program, an agency may compute the length of the academic degree training period based on the academic institution's established contact hours.

[61 FR 66193, Dec. 17, 1996, as amended at 69 FR 33277, June 15, 2004]

Subpart D—Paying for Training Expenses

§410.401 Determining necessary training expenses.

(a) The head of an agency determines which expenses constitute necessary training expenses under section 4109 of title 5, United States Code.

(b) An agency may pay, or reimburse an employee, for necessary expenses incurred in connection with approved training as provided in section 4109(a)(2) of title 5, United States Code. Necessary training expenses do not include an employee's pay or other compensation.

§410.402 Paying premium pay.

(a) *Prohibitions.* Except as provided by paragraph (b) of this section, an agency may not use its funds, appropriated or otherwise available, to pay premium pay to an employee engaged in training by, in, or through Government or nongovernment facilities.

(b) *Exceptions.* The following are excepted form the provision in paragraph (a) of this section prohibiting the payment of premium pay:

(1) *Continuation of premium pay.* An employee given training during a period of duty for which he or she is already receiving premium pay for overtime, night, holiday, or Sunday work shall continue to receive that premium pay. This exception does not apply to an employee assigned to full-time training at institutions of higher learning.

(2) *Training at night.* An employee given training at night because situations that he or she must learn to handle occur only at night shall be paid by the applicable premium pay.

(3) *Cost savings.* An employee given training on overtime, on a holiday, or on a Sunday because the costs of the training, premium pay included, are less than the costs of the same training

confined to regular work hours shall be paid the applicable premium pay.

(4) *Availability pay.* An agency shall continue to pay availability pay during agency-sanctioned training to a criminal investigator who is eligible for it under 5 U.S.C. 5545a and implementing regulations. Agencies may, at their discretion, provide availability pay to investigators during periods of initial, basic training. (See 5 CFR 550.185 (b) and (c).)

(5) *Standby and administratively uncontrollable duty.* An agency may continue to pay annual premium pay for regularly scheduled standby duty or administratively uncontrollable overtime work, during periods of temporary assignment for training as provided by 5 CFR 550.162(c).

(6) *Firefighter overtime pay.* (i) A firefighter compensated under part 550, subpart M, of this chapter shall receive basic pay and overtime pay for the firefighter's regular tour of duty (as defined in § 550.1302 of this chapter) in any week in which attendance at agency-sanctioned training reduces the hours in the firefighter's regular tour of duty.

(ii) The special pay protection provided by paragraph (b)(6)(i) of this section does not apply to firefighters who voluntarily participate in training during non-duty hours, leave hours, or periods of excused absence. It also does not apply if the firefighter is entitled to a greater amount of pay based on actual work hours during the week in which training occurs.

(7) *Agency exemption.* An employee given training during a period not otherwise covered by a provision of this paragraph may be paid premium pay when the employing agency has been granted an exception to paragraph (a) of this section by the U.S. Office of Personnel Management.

(8) *Border Patrol agent overtime supplement.* A Border Patrol agent may receive an overtime supplement under 5 U.S.C. 5550 and 5 CFR part 550, subpart P, during training, subject to the limitation in 5 U.S.C. 5550(b)(2)(G) and (b)(3)(G) and 5 CFR 550.1622(b).

(c) An employee who is excepted under paragraph (b) of this section is eligible to receive premium pay in accordance with the applicable pay authorities.

(d) Regulations governing overtime pay for employees covered by Fair Labor Standards Act (FLSA) during training, education, lectures, or conferences are found in § 551.423 of this chapter. The prohibitions on paying premium pay found in paragraph (a) of this section are not applicable for the purpose of paying FLSA overtime pay.

(e) Compensation for time spent traveling to and from training. (1) Compensation provisions are contained in 5 CFR 550.112(g) for time spent traveling for employees subject to title 5 of the United States Code.

(2) Compensation provisions are contained in 5 CFR 551.422 for time spent traveling for employees covered by the Fair Labor Standards Act. (See also 29 CFR 785.33 through § 785.41.)

[61 FR 66193, Dec. 17, 1996, as amended at 63 FR 64592, Nov. 23, 1998; 64 FR 69172, Dec. 10, 1999; 67 FR 15466, Apr. 2, 2002; 80 FR 58111, Sept. 25, 2015]

§ 410.403 Payments for temporary duty training assignments.

Section 4109(a)(2) of title 5, United States Code, provides that an agency may pay, or reimburse an employee for, all or a part of the necessary expenses of training, including the necessary costs of travel; per diem expenses; or limited relocation expenses including transportation of the immediate family, household goods and personal effects:

(a) If an agency chooses to pay per diem, or in unusual circumstances the actual subsistence, expenses for an employee on a temporary duty training assignment, payment must be in accordance with 41 CFR part 301–7 or 41 CFR part 301–8 (or, for commissioned officers of the National Oceanic and Atmospheric Administration, in accordance with sections 404 and 405 of title 37, United States Code, and the Joint Federal travel Regulations for the Uniformed Services).

(b) An agency may pay a reduced per diem rate, such as a standardized payment less than the maximum per diem rate for a geographical area. If a reduced or standardized per diem rate was not authorized in advance of the travel and the fees paid to a training institution include lodging or meal costs, an appropriate deduction shall be made from the total per diem rate payable on the travel voucher (see 41 CFR 301–7.12).

(c) An agency may pay limited relocation expenses for the transportation of the employee's immediate family, household goods and personal effects, including packing, crating, temporarily storing, draying, and unpacking the household goods in accordance with section 5724 of title 5, United States Code (or, for commissioned officers of the National Oceanic and Atmospheric Administration, in accordance with sections 406 and 409 of title 37, United States Code, and the Joint federal travel Regulations for the uniformed Services). Limited relocation expenses are payable only when the estimated costs of transportation and related services are less than the estimated aggregate per diem or actual subsistence expense payments for the period of training. An employee selected for temporary duty training may receive travel and per diem (or actual subsistence expenses) for the period of the assignment or payment of limited relocation expenses, but not both.

[61 FR 66193, Dec. 17, 1996; 61 FR 66821, Dec. 30, 1996]

§410.404 Determining if a conference is a training activity.

Agencies may sponsor an employee's attendance at a conference as a developmental assignment under section 4110 of title 5, United States Code, when—

(a) The announced purpose of the conference is educational or instructional;

(b) More than half of the time is scheduled for a planned, organized exchange of information between presenters and audience which meets the definition of training in section 4101 of title 5, United States Code;

(c) The content of the conference is germane to improving individual and/or organizational performance, and

(d) Development benefits will be derived through the employee's attendance.

§410.405 Protection of Government interest.

The head of an agency shall establish such procedures as he or she considers necessary to protect the Government's interest when employees fail to complete, or to successfully complete, training for which the agency pays the expenses.

Subpart E—Accepting Contributions, Awards, and Payments From Non-Government Organizations

§410.501 Scope.

(a) Section 4111 of title 5, United States Code, describes conditions for employee acceptance of contributions, awards, and payments made in connection with non-Government sponsored training or meetings which an employee attends while on duty or when the agency pays the training or meeting attendance expenses, in whole or in part.

(b) This subpart does not limit the authority of an agency head to establish procedures on the acceptance of contributions, awards, and payments in connection with any training and meetings that are outside the scope of this subpart in accordance with laws and regulations governing Government ethics and governing acceptance of travel reimbursements from non-Federal sources.

[61 FR 66193, Dec. 17, 1996, as amended at 63 FR 16877, Apr. 7, 1998]

§410.502 Authority of the head of an agency.

(a) In writing, the head of an agency may authorize an agency employee to accept a contribution or award (in cash or in kind) incident to training or to accept payment (in cash or in kind) of travel, subsistence, and other expenses incident to attendance at meetings if

(1) The conditions specified in section 4111 of title 5, United States Code, are met; and

(2) In the judgment of the agency head, the following two conditions are met:

(i) The contribution, award, or payment is not a reward for services to the organization prior to the training or meeting; and

(ii) Acceptance of the contribution, award, or payment:

(A) Would not reflect unfavorably on the employee's ability to carry out official duties in a fair and objective manner;

(B) Would not compromise the honesty and integrity of Government programs or of Government employees and their official actions or decisions;

(C) Would be compatible with the Ethics in Government Act of 1978, as amended; and

(D) Would otherwise be proper and ethical for the employee concerned given the circumstances of the particular case.

(b) Delegation of authority. An agency head may delegate authority to authorize the acceptance of contributions, awards, and payments under this section. The designated official must ensure that—

(1) The policies of the agency head are reflected in each decision; and

(2) The circumstances of each case are fully evaluated under conditions set forth in § 410.502(a).

(c) Acceptance of contributions, awards, and payments. An employee may accept a contribution, award, or payment (whether made in cash or in kind) that falls within the scope of this section only when he or she has specific written authorization.

(d) When more than one non-Government organization participates in making a single contribution, award, or payment, the "organization" referred to in this subsection is the one that:

(1) Selects the recipient; and

(2) Administers the funds from which the contribution, award, or payment is made.

§ 410.503 Records.

An agency shall maintain, in such form and manner as the agency head considers appropriate, the following records in connection with each contribution, awards, or payment made and accepted under authority of this section: The recipient's name; the organization's name; the amount and nature of the contribution, award, or payment and the purpose for which it is to be used; and a copy of the written authorization required by § 410.502(a).

Subpart F—Reporting

§ 410.601 Reporting.

(a) Each agency shall maintain records of training plans, expenditures, and activities in such form and manner as necessary to submit the recorded data to the Office of Personnel Management (OPM) through the OPM Governmentwide Electronic Data Collection System.

(b) Beginning December 31, 2006, each agency shall report the training data for its employees' training and development at such times and in such form as required for the OPM Governmentwide Electronic Data Collection System, which is explained in the *Guide to Personnel Recordkeeping* and the *Guide to Human Resources Reporting.*

(c) Each agency shall establish a Schedule of Records for information required to be maintained by this chapter in accordance with regulations promulgated by the National Archives and Records Administration (NARA).

[71 FR 28547, May 17, 2006. Redesignated and amended at 74 FR 65388, Dec. 10, 2009]

PART 412—SUPERVISORY, MANAGEMENT, AND EXECUTIVE DEVELOPMENT

Subpart A—General Provisions

Subpart B—Succession Planning

Subpart C—Senior Executive Service Candidate Development Programs

Subpart D—Executive Development

AUTHORITY: 5 U.S.C. 1103 (c)(2)(C), 3396, 3397, 4101 *et seq.*

SOURCE: 74 FR 65388, Dec. 10, 2009, unless otherwise noted.

Subpart A—General Provisions

§ 412.101 Coverage.

This part applies to all incumbents of, and candidates for, supervisory, managerial, and executive positions in the General Schedule, the Senior Executive Service (SES), or equivalent pay systems also covered by part 410 of this chapter.

§ 412.102 Purpose.

(a) This part implements for supervisors, managers, and executives the provisions of 5 U.S.C. chapter 41, related to training, and 5 U.S.C. 3396, related to the criteria for programs of systematic development of candidates for the SES and the continuing development of SES members.

(b) This part identifies a continuum of leadership development, starting with supervisory positions and proceeding through management and executive positions Governmentwide. For this reason, this part provides requirements by which agencies:

(1) Develop the competencies needed by supervisors, managers, and executives;

(2) Provide learning through continuing development and training in the context of succession planning; and

(3) Foster a broad agency and Governmentwide perspective to prepare individuals for advancement, thus supplying the agency and the Government with an adequate number of well-prepared and qualified candidates to fill leadership positions.

Subpart B—Succession Planning

§ 412.201 Management succession.

The head of each agency, in consultation with OPM, must develop a comprehensive management succession program, based on the agency's workforce succession plans, to fill agency supervisory and managerial positions. These programs must be supported by employee training and development programs. The focus of the program should be to develop managers as well as strengthen organizational capability, and to ensure an adequate number of well-prepared and qualified candidates for leadership positions. These programs must:

(a) Implement developmental training consistent with agency succession management plans;

(b) Provide continuing learning experiences throughout an employee's career, such as details, mentoring, coaching, learning groups, and projects. These experiences should provide broad knowledge and practical experience linked to OPM's Federal leadership competencies, as well as agency-identified, mission-related competencies, and should be consistent with the agency's succession management plan; and

(c) Include program evaluations pursuant to 5 CFR 410.202.

§ 412.202 Systematic training and development of supervisors, managers, and executives.

All agencies must provide for the development of individuals in supervisory, managerial and executive positions, as well as individuals whom the agency identifies as potential candidates for those positions, based on the agencies' succession plans. Agencies also must issue written policies to ensure they:

(a) Design and implement leadership development programs integrated with the employee development plans, programs, and strategies required by 5 CFR 410.201, and that foster a broad agency and Governmentwide perspective;

(b) Provide training within one year of an employee's initial appointment to a supervisory position and follow up periodically, but at least once every three years, by providing each supervisor and manager additional training on the use of appropriate actions, options, and strategies to:

(1) Mentor employees;

(2) Improve employee performance and productivity;

(3) Conduct employee performance appraisals in accordance with agency appraisal systems; and

(4) Identify and assist employees with unacceptable performance.

(c) Provide training when individuals make critical career transitions, for instance from non-supervisory to manager or from manager to executive. This training should be consistent with assessments of the agency's and the individual's needs.

Subpart C—Senior Executive Service Candidate Development Programs

§412.301 Obtaining approval to conduct a Senior Executive Service candidate development program (SESCDP).

(a) An SESCDP is an OPM-approved training program designed to develop the executive qualifications of employees with strong executive potential to qualify them for and authorize their initial career appointment in the SES. An agency conducting an SESCDP may submit program graduates for Qualifications Review Board (QRB) review of their executive qualifications under 5 CFR 317.502. A program graduate certified by a QRB may receive an initial career appointment without further competition to any SES position for which he or she meets the professional and technical qualifications requirements.

(b) An agency covered by subchapter II of chapter 31 of title 5, United States Code, may apply to OPM to conduct an SESCDP alone or on behalf of a group of agencies. (In this subpart, the term "agency" refers to either a single agency or a group of agencies acting in partnership under this subpart.) Any agency developing an SESCDP must submit a policy document describing its program methodologies to OPM for formal approval before implementing the SESCDP. An agency must seek OPM approval every five years thereafter, and must also consult OPM before implementing a change substantially altering how the SESCDP complies with the requirements of this regulation. An agency implementing an SESCDP without first obtaining formal approval may not submit graduates of the program for QRB review.

(c) An agency that obtained OPM approval under previous regulations must apply for re-approval in accordance with requirements in paragraph (b) and this subpart before initiating a new SESCDP. All existing SESCDP approvals expire within 2 years after publication of this regulation.

(d) An agency covered by subchapter II of chapter 31 of title 5, United States Code, may authorize a major agency component employing senior executives to apply directly to OPM for approval to conduct an SESCDP. Such an application from a component must be accompanied by the agency's written endorsement. To obtain approval, the component must meet the SESCDP requirements of this subpart independent of agency involvement.

(e) As always, agencies should be mindful of merit principles in carrying out their functions under this subpart.

§412.302 Criteria for a Senior Executive Service candidate development program (SESCDP).

(a) *Executive Resources Board requirements.* An agency's Executive Resources Board (ERB) must oversee the SESCDP. The ERB ensures the development program lasts a minimum of 12 months and includes substantive developmental experiences that should equip a successful candidate to accomplish Federal Government missions as a senior executive. The agency ERB must oversee and be accountable for SESCDP recruitment, merit staffing, and assessment. The agency ERB must ensure the program follows SES merit staffing provisions in 5 CFR 317.501, subject to the condition explained in §412.302(d)(1) of this part. The ERB also must oversee development, evaluation, progress in the program, and graduation of candidates, and submit for QRB review within 90 workdays of graduation those candidates determined by the ERB to possess the executive core qualifications. The ERB must also oversee the writing and implementation of a removal policy for program candidates who do not make adequate progress.

(b) *Recruitment.* In recruiting, the agency, consistent with the merit system principles in 5 U.S.C. 2301 (b)(1) and (2), takes into consideration the goal of achieving a diversified workforce. Recruitment for the program is from all groups of qualified individuals within the civil service, or all groups of qualified individuals whether or not within the civil service. The number of expected SES vacancies must be considered as one factor in determining the number of selected candidates.

(c) *Senior Executive Service candidate development program requirements.* An SESCDP lasts a minimum of 12 months. To graduate, a candidate must accomplish the requirements of the program established by his or her agency. Each individual participating in an SESCDP must have:

(1) A documented development plan based upon a competency-based needs determination and approved by the agency ERB. The components of the development plan must:

(i) Address the executive core qualifications (ECQs);

(ii) Address Federal Government leadership challenges crucial to the senior executive;

(iii) Provide increased knowledge and understanding of the overall functioning of the agency, so the participant is prepared for a range of positions and responsibilities;

(iv) Include interaction with senior employees outside the candidate's department or agency to foster a broader perspective; and

(v) Have Governmentwide or multi-agency applicability in the nature and scope of the training;

(2) A formal interagency and/or multi-sector training experience lasting at least 80 hours that addresses the ECQs and their application to SES positions Governmentwide. The training experience must include interaction with senior employees outside the candidate's department or agency;

(3) A developmental assignment of at least 4 months of full-time service to include at least one assignment of 90 continuous days in a position other than, and substantially different from, the candidate's position of record. The assignment must include executive-level responsibility and differ from the candidate's current and past assignments in ways that broaden the candidate's experience, as well as challenge the candidate with respect to leadership competencies and the ECQs. Assignments need not be restricted to the agency, the Executive Branch, or the Federal Government, so long as they can be accomplished in compliance with applicable law and Federal and agency specific ethics regulations. The candidate is held accountable for organizational or agency results achieved during the assignment. If the assignment is in a non-Federal organization, the ERB must provide for adequate documentation of the individual's actions and accomplishments and must determine the assignment will contribute to development of the candidate's executive qualifications; and

(4) A mentor who is a member of the SES or is otherwise determined by the ERB to have the knowledge and capacity to advise the candidate, consistent with goals of the SESCDP. The mentor and the candidate are jointly responsible for a productive mentoring relationship; however, the agency must establish methods to assess these relationships and, if necessary, facilitate them or make appropriate changes in the interest of the candidate.

(d) An SESCDP is a training opportunity for which agencies must recruit consistent with merit system principles and paragraph (d)(1) of this section. An agency must provide procedures under which selections are made from among either all qualified persons or all qualified persons in the civil service. If selected, the individual participates in the agency's SESCDP.

(1) An individual who does not currently hold a career or career-type civil service appointment may only participate in an SESCDP by means of a Schedule B appointment authorized by 5 CFR 213.3202(j) to a full-time position created for developmental purposes connected with the SESCDP. Exercising its authority under §302.101(c)(6) of this chapter, OPM hereby exempts these full-time positions created for developmental purposes connected with the SESCDP from the appointment procedures of part 302 of this chapter. Competition for these appointments must be conducted pursuant to SES merit staffing procedures at §317.501 of this chapter, except agencies must follow the principle of veterans' preference as far as administratively feasible, in accordance with §302.101(c) of this chapter. Candidates serving under this Schedule B appointment

may not be used to fill an agency's regular positions on a continuing basis.

(2) An individual who currently holds a career or career-type appointment in the civil service must be selected through SES merit staffing procedures at §317.501 of this chapter. Subject to the approval of the agency in which the selectee is employed, such an individual may be selected for and participate in an SESCDP in any agency while serving in his or her position of record. The individual may continue to participate in the SESCDP upon moving to other civil service positions under career or career-type appointment, assuming the employing agency approves. An SESCDP competition does not satisfy the requirements of part 335 of this chapter and therefore does not provide an independent basis to appoint or promote a career or career-type appointee.

(3) A career or career-type appointee may participate in an SESCDP conducted by an agency other than his or her employing agency under such terms as are mutually agreeable and outlined in a Memorandum of Understanding (MOU) signed by both agencies involved. The MOU should be submitted to OPM after the candidate is selected and before the program begins. Terms of the MOU must be consistent with applicable provisions of 5 U.S.C. chapter 41, and a copy must be provided to OPM. Either agency may decline or discontinue a candidate's participation if such terms cannot be negotiated or are not fulfilled.

(4) Any candidate's participation in an SESCDP is at the discretion of the employing agency and subject to provisions established under 5 CFR 412.302(a) for removing a participant who does not make adequate progress in the program.

(5) For purposes of this paragraph (d), a "career-type" appointment means a career or career-conditional appointment or an appointment of equivalent tenure. An appointment of equivalent tenure is considered to be an appointment in the excepted service that is placed in Group I or Group II under section 351.502(b).

Subpart D—Executive Development

§412.401 Continuing executive development.

(a) Each agency must establish a program or programs for the continuing development of its senior executives in accordance with 5 U.S.C 3396(a). Such agency programs must include preparation, implementation, and regular updating of an Executive Development Plan (EDP) for each senior executive. The EDPs will:

(1) Function as a detailed guide of developmental experiences to help SES members, through participation in short-term and longer-term experiences, meet organizational needs for leadership, managerial improvement, and organizational results;

(2) Address enhancement of existing executive competencies and such other competencies as will strengthen the executive's performance;

(3) Outline developmental opportunities and assignments to allow the individual to develop a broader perspective in the agency as well as Government-wide; and

(4) Be reviewed annually and revised as appropriate by an ERB or similar body designated by the agency to oversee executive development, using input from the performance evaluation cycle.

(b) Consistent with 5 U.S.C. 3396(d) and other applicable statutes, EDPs may provide for executive sabbaticals and other long-term assignments outside the Federal sector.

PART 430—PERFORMANCE MANAGEMENT

Subpart A—Performance Management

Subpart B—Performance Appraisal for General Schedule, Prevailing Rate, and Certain Other Employees

Subpart C—Managing Senior Executive Performance

Subpart D—Performance Appraisal Certification for Pay Purposes

AUTHORITY: 5 U.S.C. chapter 43 and 5307(d).

Subpart A—Performance Management

SOURCE: 60 FR 43943, Aug. 23, 1995, unless otherwise noted.

§ 430.101 Authority.

Chapter 43 of title 5, United States Code, provides for the performance appraisal of Federal employees. This subpart supplements and implements this portion of the law.

§ 430.102 Performance management.

(a) Performance management is the systematic process by which an agency involves its employees, as individuals and members of a group, in improving organizational effectiveness in the accomplishment of agency mission and goals.

(b) Performance management integrates the processes an agency uses to—

(1) Communicate and clarify organizational goals to employees;

(2) Identify individual and, where applicable, team accountability for accomplishing organizational goals;

(3) Identify and address developmental needs for individuals and, where applicable, teams;

(4) Assess and improve individual, team, and organizational performance;

(5) Use appropriate measures of performance as the basis for recognizing and rewarding accomplishments; and

(6) Use the results of performance appraisal as a basis for appropriate personnel actions.

Subpart B—Performance Appraisal for General Schedule, Prevailing Rate, and Certain Other Employees

SOURCE: 60 FR 43943, Aug. 23, 1995, unless otherwise noted.

§ 430.201 General.

(a) *Statutory authority.* Chapter 43 of title 5, United States Code, provides for the establishment of agency performance appraisal systems and requires the Office of Personnel Management (OPM) to prescribe regulations governing such systems. The regulations in this subpart in combination with statute set forth the requirements for agency performance appraisal system(s) and program(s) for employees covered by subchapter I of chapter 43.

(b) *Savings provision.* The performance appraisal system portion of an agency's Performance Management Plan approved by OPM as of September 22, 1995 shall constitute an approved performance appraisal system under the regulations in this subpart until such time changes to the system are approved. No provision of the regulations in this subpart shall be applied in such a way as to affect any administrative proceeding related to any action taken under regulations in this chapter pending on September 22, 1995.

(c) *Equivalent ratings of record.* (1) If an agency has administratively adopted and applied the procedures of this subpart to evaluate the performance of its employees, the ratings of record resulting from that evaluation are considered ratings of record for reduction in force purposes.

(2) Other performance evaluations given while an employee is not covered by the provisions of this subpart are considered ratings of record for reduction in force purposes when the performance evaluation—

(i) Was issued as an officially designated evaluation under the employing agency's performance evaluation system,

(ii) Was derived from the appraisal of performance against expectations that are established and communicated in advance and are work related, and

(iii) Identified whether the employee performed acceptably.

(3) When the performance evaluation does not include a summary level designator and pattern comparable to those established at § 430.208(d), the agency may identify a level and pattern based on information related to the appraisal process.

[60 FR 43943, Aug. 23, 1995; 60 FR 47646, Sept. 13, 1995, as amended at 62 FR 62502, Nov. 24, 1997]

§ 430.202 Coverage.

(a) *Employees and agencies covered by statute.* (1) Section 4301(1) of title 5, United States Code, defines agencies covered by this subpart.

(2) Section 4301(2) of title 5, United States Code, defines employees covered by statute by this subpart. Besides General Schedule (GS/GM) and prevailing rate employees, coverage includes, but is not limited to, senior-level and scientific and professional employees paid under 5 U.S.C. 5376.

(b) *Statutory exclusions.* This subpart does not apply to agencies or employees excluded by 5 U.S.C. 4301(1) and (2), the United States Postal Service, or the Postal Rate Commission.

(c) *Administrative exclusions.* OPM may exclude any position or group of positions in the excepted service under the authority of 5 U.S.C. 4301(2)(G). The regulations in this subpart exclude excepted service positions for which employment is not reasonably expected to exceed the minimum period established under § 430.207(a) in a consecutive 12-month period.

(d) *Agency requests for exclusions.* Heads of agencies or their designees may request the Director of OPM to exclude positions in the excepted service. The request must be in writing, explaining why the exclusion would be in the interest of good administration.

§ 430.203 Definitions.

In this subpart, terms are defined as follows:

Additional performance element means a dimension or aspect of individual, team, or organizational performance that is not a critical or non-critical element. Such elements are not used in assigning a summary level but, like critical and non-critical elements, are useful for purposes such as communicating performance expectations and serving as the basis for granting awards. Such elements may include, but are not limited to, objectives, goals, program plans, work plans, and other means of expressing expected performance.

Appraisal means the process under which performance is reviewed and evaluated.

Appraisal period means the established period of time for which performance will be reviewed and a rating of record will be prepared.

Appraisal program means the specific procedures and requirements established under the policies and parameters of an agency appraisal system.

Appraisal system means a framework of policies and parameters established by an agency as defined at 5 U.S.C. 4301(1) for the administration of performance appraisal programs under subchapter I of chapter 43 of title 5, United States Code, and this subpart.

Critical element means a work assignment or responsibility of such importance that unacceptable performance on the element would result in a determination that an employee's overall performance is unacceptable. Such elements shall be used to measure performance only at the individual level.

Non-critical element means a dimension or aspect of individual, team, or organizational performance, exclusive of a critical element, that is used in assigning a summary level. Such elements may include, but are not limited to, objectives, goals, program plans, work plans, and other means of expressing expected performance.

Performance means accomplishment of work assignments or responsibilities.

Performance appraisal system: See *Appraisal system.*

Performance plan means all of the written, or otherwise recorded, performance elements that set forth expected performance. A plan must include all critical and non-critical elements and their performance standards.

Performance rating means the written, or otherwise recorded, appraisal of performance compared to the performance standard(s) for each critical and non-critical element on which there has been an opportunity to perform for the minimum period. A performance rating may include the assignment of a summary level within a pattern (as specified in § 430.208(d)).

Performance standard means the management-approved expression of the performance threshold(s), requirement(s), or expectation(s) that must be met to be appraised at a particular level of performance. A performance standard may include, but is not limited to, quality, quantity, timeliness, and manner of performance.

Progress review means communicating with the employee about performance compared to the performance standards of critical and non-critical elements.

Rating of record means the performance rating prepared at the end of an appraisal period for performance of agency-assigned duties over the entire period and the assignment of a summary level within a pattern (as specified in § 430.208(d)), or (2) in accordance with § 531.404(a)(1) of this chapter. These constitute official ratings of record referenced in this chapter.

[60 FR 43943, Aug. 23, 1995, as amended at 62 FR 62503, Nov. 24, 1997]

§ 430.204 Agency performance appraisal system(s).

(a) Each agency as defined at section 4301(1) of title 5, United States Code, shall develop one or more performance appraisal systems for employees covered by this subpart.

(b) An agency appraisal system shall establish agencywide policies and parameters for the application and operation of performance appraisal within the agency for the employees covered by the system. At a minimum, an agency system shall—

(1) Provide for—

(i) Establishing employee performance plans, including, but not limited to, critical elements and performance standards;

(ii) Communicating performance plans to employees at the beginning of an appraisal period;

(iii) Evaluating each employee during the appraisal period on the employee's elements and standards;

(iv) Recognizing and rewarding employees whose performance so warrants;

(v) Assisting employees in improving unacceptable performance; and

(vi) Reassigning, reducing in grade, or removing employees who continue to have unacceptable performance, but only after an opportunity to demonstrate acceptable performance.

(2) Identify employees covered by the system;

(3) Specify the flexibilities an agency program established under the system has for setting—

(i) The length of the appraisal period (as specified in § 430.206(a));

(ii) The length of the minimum period (as specified in § 430.207(a));

(iii) The number(s) of performance levels at which critical and non-critical elements may be appraised (as specified in § 430.206(b)(7) (i)(A) and (ii)(A)); and

(iv) The pattern of summary levels that may be assigned in a rating of record (as specified in § 430.208(d));

(4) Include, where applicable, criteria and procedures for establishing separate appraisal programs under an appraisal system; and

(5) Require that an appraisal program shall conform to statute, the regulations of this chapter, and the requirements established by the appraisal system.

(c) Agencies are encouraged to involve employees in developing and implementing their system(s). When agencies involve employees, the method of involvement shall be in accordance with the law.

[60 FR 43943, Aug. 23, 1995; 60 FR 47646, Sept. 13, 1995]

§ 430.205 Agency performance appraisal program(s).

(a) Each agency shall establish at least one appraisal program of specific procedures and requirements to be implemented in accordance with the applicable agency appraisal system. At a minimum, each appraisal program shall specify the employees covered by the program and include the procedures and requirements for planning performance (as specified in § 430.206), monitoring performance (as specified in § 430.207), and rating performance (as specified in § 430.208).

(b) An agency program shall establish criteria and procedures to address employee performance for employees who are on detail, who are transferred, and for other special circumstances as established by the agency.

(c) An agency may permit the development of separate appraisal programs under an appraisal system.

(d) Agencies are encouraged to involve employees in developing and implementing their program(s). When agencies involve employees, the method of involvement shall be in accordance with law.

§ 430.206 Planning performance.

(a) *Appraisal period.* (1) An appraisal program shall designate an official appraisal period for which a performance plan shall be prepared, during which performance shall be monitored, and for which a rating of record shall be prepared.

(2) Each program shall specify a single length of time as its appraisal period. The appraisal period generally shall be 12 months so that employees are provided a rating of record on an annual basis. A program's appraisal period may be longer when work assignments and responsibilities so warrant or performance management objectives can be achieved more effectively.

(b) *Performance plan.* (1) Agencies shall encourage employee participation in establishing performance plans.

(2) Performance plans shall be provided to employees at the beginning of each appraisal period (normally within 30 days).

(3) An appraisal program shall require that each employee be covered by an appropriate written, or otherwise recorded, performance plan based on work assignments and responsibilities.

(4) Each performance plan shall include all elements which are used in deriving and assigning a summary level, including at least one critical element and any non-critical element(s).

(5) Each performance plan may include one or more additional performance elements, which—

(i) Are not used in deriving and assigning a summary level, and

(ii) Are used to support performance management processes as described at § 430.102(b).

(6) A performance plan established under an appraisal program that uses only two summary levels (pattern A as specified in § 430.208(d)(1)) shall not include non-critical elements.

(7) An appraisal program shall establish how many and which performance levels may be used to appraise critical and non-critical elements.

(8) Elements and standards shall be established as follows—

(i) For a critical element—

(A) At least two levels for appraisal shall be used with one level being "Fully Successful" or its equivalent and another level being "Unacceptable," and

(B) A performance standard shall be established at the "Fully Successful" level and may be established at other levels.

(ii) For non-critical elements, when established,—

(A) At least two levels for appraisal shall be used, and

(B) A performance standard(s) shall be established at whatever level(s) is appropriate.

(iii) The absence of an established performance standard at a level specified in the program shall not preclude a determination that performance is at that level.

[60 FR 43943, Aug. 23, 1995, as amended at 62 FR 62503, Nov. 24, 1997]

§430.207 Monitoring performance.

(a) *Minimum period.* An appraisal program shall establish a minimum period of performance that must be completed before a performance rating may be prepared.

(b) *Ongoing appraisal.* An appraisal program shall include methods for appraising each critical and non-critical element during the appraisal period. Performance on each critical and non-critical element shall be appraised against its performance standard(s). Ongoing appraisal methods shall include, but not be limited to, conducting one or more progress reviews during each appraisal period.

(c) *Marginal performance.* Appraisal programs should provide assistance whenever performance is determined to be below "Fully Successful" or equivalent but above "Unacceptable."

(d) *Unacceptable performance.* An appraisal program shall provide for—

(1) Assisting employees in improving unacceptable performance at any time during the appraisal period that performance is determined to be unacceptable in one or more critical elements; and

(2) Taking action based on unacceptable performance.

§430.208 Rating performance.

(a) As soon as practicable after the end of the appraisal period, a written, or otherwise recorded, rating of record shall be given to each employee.

(1) A rating of record shall be based only on the evaluation of actual job performance for the designated appraisal period.

(2) An agency shall not issue a rating of record that assumes a level of performance by an employee without an actual evaluation of that employee's performance.

(3) Except as provided in §430.208(i), a rating of record is final when it is issued to an employee with all appropriate reviews and signatures.

(b) Rating of record procedures for each appraisal program shall include a method for deriving and assigning a summary level as specified in paragraph (d) of this section based on appraisal of performance on critical elements and, as applicable, non-critical elements.

(1) A Level 1 summary ("Unacceptable") shall be assigned if and only if performance on one or more critical elements is appraised as "Unacceptable."

(2) Consideration of non-critical elements shall not result in assigning a Level 1 summary (" Unacceptable").

(c) The method for deriving and assigning a summary level may not limit or require the use of particular summary levels (*i.e.*, establish a forced distribution of summary levels). However, methods used to make distinctions among employees or groups of employees such as comparing, categorizing, and ranking employees or groups on the basis of their performance may be used for purposes other than assigning a summary level including, but not limited to, award determinations and promotion decisions.

(d) *Summary levels.* (1) An appraisal program shall use one of the following patterns of summary levels:

Pattern	Summary level				
	1	2	3	4	5
A	X	....	X		
B	X	....	X	....	X
C	X	....	X	X	
D	X	X	X		
E	X	....	X	X	X
F	X	X	X	....	X
G	X	X	X	X	
H	X	X	X	X	X

(2) Within any of the patterns shown in paragraph (d)(1) of this section, summary levels shall comply with the following requirements:

(i) Level 1 through Level 5 are ordered categories, with Level 1 as the lowest and Level 5 as the highest;

(ii) Level 1 is "Unacceptable";

(iii) Level 3 is "Fully Successful" or equivalent; and

(iv) Level 5 is "Outstanding" or equivalent.

(3) The term "Outstanding" shall be used only to describe a Level 5 summary.

(4) The designation of a summary level and its pattern shall be used to provide consistency in describing ratings of record and as a reference point for applying other related regulations, including, but not limited to, assigning additional retention service credit under §351.504 of this chapter.

(5) Under the provisions of § 351.504(e) of this chapter, the number of years of additional retention service credit established for a summary level of a rating of record shall be applied in a uniform and consistent manner within a competitive area in any given reduction in force, but the number of years may vary:

(i) In different reductions in force;

(ii) In different competitive areas; and

(iii) In different summary level patterns within the same competitive area.

(e) A rating of record of "Unacceptable" (Level 1) shall be reviewed and approved by a higher level management official.

(f) The rating of record or performance rating for a disabled veteran shall not be lowered because the veteran has been absent from work to seek medical treatment as provided in Executive Order 5396.

(g) When a rating of record cannot be prepared at the time specified, the appraisal period shall be extended. Once the conditions necessary to complete a rating of record have been met, a rating of record shall be prepared as soon as practicable.

(h) Each rating of record shall cover a specified appraisal period. Agencies shall not carry over a rating of record prepared for a previous appraisal period as the rating of record for a subsequent appraisal period(s) without an actual evaluation of the employee's performance during the subsequent appraisal period.

(i) When either a regular appraisal period or an extended appraisal period ends and any agency-established deadline for providing ratings of record passes or a subsequent rating of record is issued, an agency shall not produce or change retroactively a rating of record that covers that earlier appraisal period except that a rating of record may be changed—

(1) Within 60 days of issuance based upon an informal request by the employee;

(2) As a result of a grievance, complaint, or other formal proceeding permitted by law or regulation that results in a final determination by appropriate authority that the rating of record must be changed or as part of a *bona fide* settlement of a formal proceeding; or

(3) Where the agency determines that a rating of record was incorrectly recorded or calculated.

(j) A performance rating may be prepared at such other times as an appraisal program may specify for special circumstances including, but not limited to, transfers and performance on details.

[60 FR 43943, Aug. 23, 1995, as amended at 62 FR 62503, Nov. 24, 1997; 63 FR 53276, Oct. 5, 1998]

§ 430.209 Agency responsibilities.

An agency shall—

(a) Submit to OPM for approval a description of its appraisal system(s) as specified in § 430.204(b) of this subpart, and any subsequent changes that modify any element of the agency's system(s) that is subject to a regulatory requirement in this part;

(b) Transfer the employee's most recent ratings of record, and any subsequent performance ratings, when an employee transfers to another agency or is assigned to another organization within the agency in compliance with part 293 of this chapter and instructions in the OPM Operating Manual, THE GUIDE TO PERSONNEL RECORDKEEPING, for sale by the U.S. Government Printing Office, Superintendent of Documents;

(c) Communicate with supervisors and employees (e.g., through formal training) about relevant parts of its performance appraisal system(s) and program(s);

(d) Evaluate the performance appraisal system(s) and performance appraisal program(s) in operation in the agency;

(e) Report ratings of record data to the Central Personnel Data File in compliance with instructions in the OPM Operating Manual, FEDERAL WORKFORCE REPORTING SYSTEMS, for sale by the U.S. Government Printing Office, Superintendent of Documents;

(f) Maintain and submit such records as OPM may require; and

(g) Take any action required by OPM to ensure conformance with applicable law, regulation, and OPM policy.

§430.210 OPM responsibilities.

(a) OPM shall review and approve an agency's performance appraisal system(s).

(b) OPM may evaluate the operation and application of an agency's performance appraisal system(s) and program(s).

(c) If OPM determines that an appraisal system or program does not meet the requirements of applicable law, regulation, or OPM policy, it shall direct the agency to implement an appropriate system or program or to take other corrective action.

Subpart C—Managing Senior Executive Performance

SOURCE: 80 FR 57694, Sept. 25, 2015, unless otherwise noted.

§430.301 General.

(a) *Statutory authority.* Chapter 43 of title 5, United States Code, provides for the establishment of Senior Executive Service (SES) performance appraisal systems and appraisal of senior executive performance. This subpart prescribes regulations for managing SES performance to implement the statutory provisions at 5 U.S.C. 4311–4315.

(b) *Purpose.* In order to improve the overall performance of Government, agencies must establish performance management systems that hold senior executives accountable (within their assigned areas of responsibility and control) for their individual performance and for organizational performance by—

(1) Encouraging excellence in senior executive performance;

(2) Aligning executive performance plans with the results-oriented goals required by the Government Performance and Results Act Modernization Act of 2010 (GPRAMA) or other strategic planning initiatives;

(3) Setting and communicating individual and organizational goals and expectations that clearly fall within the executive's area of responsibility and control;

(4) Reporting on the success of meeting organizational goals (including any factors that may have impacted success);

(5) Systematically appraising senior executive performance using measures that balance organizational results with customer and employee perspectives, and other perspectives as appropriate; and

(6) Using performance appraisals as a basis for pay, awards, development, retention, removal, and other personnel decisions.

(c) *Savings provision.* Agencies without OPM approval to use the basic SES appraisal system issued by U.S. Office of Personnel Management (OPM) and the Office of Management and Budget on January 4, 2012, must design, obtain OPM approval for, and implement systems conforming to the requirements of this subpart no later than one year after October 26, 2015. No provision of this subpart will affect any administrative proceedings related to any action initiated under a provision of this chapter before October 26, 2015.

§430.302 Coverage.

This subpart applies to—

(a) All senior executives covered by subchapter II of chapter 31 of title 5, United States Code; and

(b) Agencies as defined in §430.303.

§430.303 Definitions.

In this subpart—

Agency means an agency as that term is defined in 5 U.S.C. 3132(a)(1) and an Office of Inspector General, which is a separate agency for all provisions of the Senior Executive Service under the Inspector General Act of 1978 (5 U.S.C. App 6(d)).

Annual summary rating means the overall rating level that an appointing authority assigns at the end of the appraisal period after considering (1) the initial summary rating, (2) any input from the executive or a higher level review, and (3) the applicable Performance Review Board's recommendations. This is the official final rating for the appraisal period.

Appointing authority means the department or agency head, or other official with authority to make appointments in the Senior Executive Service (SES).

Appraisal period means the established period of time for which a senior executive's performance will be appraised and rated.

Critical element means a key component of an executive's work that contributes to organizational goals and results and is so important that unsatisfactory performance of the element would make the executive's overall job performance unsatisfactory.

Initial summary rating means an overall rating level the supervisor derives, from appraising the senior executive's performance during the appraisal period in relation to the critical elements and performance standards and requirements, and forwards to the Performance Review Board.

Oversight official means the agency head or the individual specifically designated by the agency head who provides oversight of the performance management system and issues performance appraisal guidelines.

Performance means the accomplishment of the work described in the senior executive's performance plan.

Performance appraisal means the review and evaluation of a senior executive's performance against critical elements and performance standards and requirements.

Performance management system means the framework of policies and practices that an agency establishes under subchapter II of chapter 43 of title 5, United States Code, subpart A, and this subpart for planning, monitoring, developing, evaluating, and rewarding both individual and organizational performance and for using resulting performance information in making personnel decisions.

Performance requirement means a description of what a senior executive must accomplish, or the competencies demonstrated, for a critical element. A performance requirement establishes the criteria to be met to be rated at a specific level of performance and generally includes quality, quantity, timeliness, cost savings, manner of performance, or other factors.

Performance standard means a normative description of a single level of performance within five such described levels of performance ranging from unsatisfactory performance to outstanding performance. Performance standards provide the benchmarks for developing performance requirements against which actual performance will be assessed.

Progress review means a review of the senior executive's progress in meeting the performance requirements. A progress review is not a performance rating.

Senior executive performance plan means the written critical elements and performance requirements against which performance will be evaluated during the appraisal period by applying the established performance standards. The plan includes all critical elements, performance standards, and performance requirements, including any specific goals, targets, or other measures established for the senior executive.

Strategic planning initiatives means agency strategic plans as required by the GPRA Modernization Act of 2010, annual performance plans, organizational work plans, and other related initiatives.

System standards means the OPM-established requirements for performance management systems.

§ 430.304 SES performance management systems.

(a) To encourage excellence in senior executive performance, each agency must develop and administer one or more performance management systems for its senior executives in accordance with the system standards established in § 430.305.

(b) Performance management systems must provide for—

(1) Identifying executives covered by the system;

(2) Monitoring progress in accomplishing critical elements and performance requirements and conducting progress reviews at least once during the appraisal period, including informing executives on how well they are performing;

(3) Establishing an official performance appraisal period for which an annual summary rating must be prepared;

(4) Establishing a minimum appraisal period of at least 90 days;

(5) Ending the appraisal period at any time after the minimum appraisal period is completed, but only if the agency determines there is an adequate

basis on which to appraise and rate the senior executive's performance and the shortened appraisal period promotes effectiveness; and

(6) Establishing criteria and procedures to address performance of senior executives who are on detail, temporarily reassigned, or transferred as described at § 430.312(c)(1), and for other special circumstances established by the agency.

§ 430.305 System standards for SES performance management systems.

(a) Each agency performance management system must incorporate the following system standards:

(1) Use critical elements based on OPM-validated executive competencies to evaluate executive leadership and results, including the quality of the executive's performance;

(2) Align performance requirements with agency mission and strategic planning initiatives;

(3) Define performance standards for each of the summary rating performance levels, which also may be used for the individual elements or performance requirements being appraised;

(4) Appraise each senior executive's performance at least annually against performance requirements based on established performance standards and other measures;

(5) Derive an annual summary rating through a mathematical method that ensures executives' performance aligns with level descriptors contained in performance standards that clearly differentiate levels above fully successful, while prohibiting a forced distribution of rating levels for senior executives;

(6) Establish five summary performance levels as follows:

(i) An outstanding level;

(ii) An exceeds fully successful level;

(iii) A fully successful level;

(iv) A minimally satisfactory level; and

(v) An unsatisfactory level;

(7) Include equivalency statements in the system description for agency-specific terms for the five summary performance levels aligning them with the five performance levels required in § 430.305(a)(6); and

(8) Use performance appraisals as a basis to adjust pay, reward, retain, and develop senior executives or make other personnel decisions, including removals as specified in § 430.312.

(b) An agency may develop its own performance management system for senior executives in accordance with the requirements of this section.

(c) OPM may establish, and refine as needed, a basic performance management system incorporating all requirements of this section, which agencies may adopt, with limited adaptation, for performance management of its senior executives.

§ 430.306 Planning and communicating performance.

(a) Each senior executive must have a performance plan that describes the individual and organizational expectations for the appraisal period that clearly fall within the senior executive's area of responsibility and control.

(b) Supervisors must develop performance plans in consultation with senior executives and communicate the plans to them in writing, including through the use of automated systems, on or before the beginning of the appraisal period.

(c) A senior executive performance plan must include—

(1) *Critical elements.* Critical elements must reflect individual performance results or competencies as well as organizational performance priorities within each executive's respective area of responsibility and control, and be based on OPM-validated executive competencies.

(2) *Performance standards.* Performance plans must include the performance standards describing each level of performance at which a senior executive's performance can be appraised. Performance standards describe the general expectations that must be met to be rated at each level of performance and provide the benchmarks for developing performance requirements.

(3) *Performance requirements.* At a minimum, performance requirements must describe expected accomplishments or demonstrated competencies for fully successful performance by the executive. An agency may establish performance requirements associated with other levels of performance as

well. These performance requirements must align with agency mission and strategic planning initiatives. Performance requirements must contain measures of the quality, quantity, timeliness, cost savings, or manner of performance, as appropriate, expected for the applicable level of performance.

(d) Agencies may require a review of senior executive performance plans at the beginning of the appraisal period to ensure consistency of agency-specific performance requirements. Such reviews may be performed by the Performance Review Board (PRB) or another body of the agency's choosing.

§430.307 Monitoring performance.

Supervisors must monitor each senior executive's performance throughout the appraisal period and hold at least one progress review. At a minimum, supervisors must inform senior executives during the progress review about how well they are performing with regard to their performance plan. Supervisors must provide advice and assistance to senior executives on how to improve their performance. Supervisors and senior executives may also discuss available development opportunities for the senior executive.

§430.308 Appraising performance.

(a) Agencies must establish appropriate timelines for communicating performance plans, conducting appraisals, and assigning and communicating annual summary ratings.

(b) At least annually, agencies must appraise each senior executive's performance in writing, including through the use of automated systems, and assign an annual summary rating at the end of the appraisal period.

(c) Agencies must appraise a senior executive's performance on the critical elements and performance requirements in the senior executive's performance plan.

(d) Agencies must base appraisals of senior executive performance on both individual and organizational performance as it applies to the senior executive's area of responsibility and control, taking into account factors such as—

(1) Results achieved in accordance with agency mission and strategic planning initiatives;

(2) Overall quality of performance rendered by the executive,

(3) Performance appraisal guidelines that must be based upon assessments of the agency's performance and are provided by the oversight official to senior executives, rating and reviewing officials, PRB members, and appointing authorities at the conclusion of the appraisal period and before completion of the initial summary ratings;

(4) Customer perspectives;

(5) Employee perspectives;

(6) The effectiveness, productivity, and performance results of the employees for whom the senior executive is responsible;

(7) Leadership effectiveness in promoting diversity, inclusion and engagement as set forth, in part, under section 7201 of title 5, United States Code; and

(8) Compliance with the merit system principles set forth under section 2301 of title 5, United States Code.

§430.309 Rating performance.

(a) When rating senior executive performance, each agency must—

(1) Comply with the requirements of this section, and

(2) Establish a PRB as described at §430.311.

(b) Each performance management system must provide that an appraisal and rating for a career appointee's performance may not be made within 120 days after the beginning of a new President's term.

(c) When an agency cannot prepare an annual summary rating at the end of the appraisal period because the senior executive has not completed the minimum appraisal period or for other reasons, the agency must extend the executive's appraisal period. Once the appropriate conditions are met, the agency will then prepare the annual summary rating.

(d) Senior executive performance appraisals and ratings are not appealable.

(e) Procedures for rating senior executives must provide for the following:

(1) *Initial summary rating.* The supervisor must develop an initial summary

rating of the senior executive's performance, in writing, including through the use of automated systems, and share that rating with the senior executive. The senior executive may respond in writing.

(2) *Higher-level review (HLR).* A senior executive may ask for a higher-level official to review the initial summary rating before the rating is given to the PRB. The agency must provide each senior executive an opportunity for review of the initial summary rating by an employee, or (with the consent of the senior executive) a commissioned officer in the uniformed services on active duty in the agency, in a higher level in the agency.

(i) A single review by an official at a higher level who did not participate in determining the executive's initial summary rating will satisfy this requirement. An official providing HLR may not change the initial summary rating but may recommend a different rating to the PRB. HLR may be provided by an official who is at a higher level in the agency than the appointing authority who will approve the final rating under paragraph (e)(4) of this section.

(ii) When an agency cannot provide review by a higher-level official for an executive who receives an initial summary rating from the agency head because no such official exists in the agency, the agency must offer an alternative review as it determines appropriate, except that the review may not be provided by a member of the PRB or an official who participated in determining the initial summary rating.

(iii) If a senior executive declines review by agency-designated higher-level officials, the agency may offer an alternative review but it not obligated to do so. The agency must document the executive's declination of the HLR opportunity provided by the agency before offering an alternative review.

(iv) Copies of findings and recommendations of the HLR official or the official performing an alternative review under paragraph (e)(2)(ii) through (iii) of this section must be given to the senior executive, the supervisor, and the PRB.

(3) *PRB review.* The PRB must receive and review the initial summary rating, the senior executive's response to the initial rating if made, and findings and recommendations of any HLR or any alternative review under paragraph (e)(2) of this section before making recommendations to the appointing authority, as provided in §430.311.

(4) *Annual summary rating.* The appointing authority must assign the annual summary rating of the senior executive's performance after considering the applicable PRB's recommendations. This rating is the official final rating for the appraisal period and must be communicated to the executive in writing, including through the use of automated systems, in accordance with the timelines developed under §430.308(a).

(5) *Shortened appraisal periods.* The procedures of this section apply whenever an agency terminates an appraisal period under §430.304(b)(5).

§430.310 Details and job changes.

(a) When a senior executive is detailed or temporarily reassigned for 120 days or longer, the gaining organization must set performance goals and requirements for the detail or temporary assignment. The gaining organization must appraise the senior executive's performance in writing, including through the use of automated systems, and this appraisal must be considered when deriving the initial summary rating.

(b) When a senior executive is reassigned or transferred to another agency after completing the minimum appraisal period, the supervisor must appraise the executive's performance in writing, including through the use of automated systems, before the executive leaves and provide this information to the executive.

(c) The most recent annual summary rating and any subsequent appraisals must be transferred to the gaining agency or organization. The gaining supervisor must consider the rating and appraisals when deriving the initial summary rating at the end of the appraisal period.

§430.311 Performance Review Boards (PRBs).

Each agency must establish one or more PRBs to make recommendations to the appointing authority on the performance of its senior executives.

(a) *Membership.* (1) Each PRB must have three or more members who are appointed by the agency head, or by another official or group acting on behalf of the agency head. Agency heads are encouraged to consider diversity and inclusion in establishing their PRBs.

(2) PRB members must be appointed in a way that assures consistency, stability, and objectivity in SES performance appraisal.

(3) When appraising a career appointee's performance or recommending a career appointee for a performance-based pay adjustment or performance award, more than one-half of the PRB's members must be SES career appointees.

(4) The agency must publish notice of PRB appointments in the FEDERAL REGISTER before service begins.

(b) *Functions.* (1) Each PRB must consider agency performance as communicated by the oversight official through the performance appraisal guidelines when reviewing and evaluating the initial summary rating, any senior executive's response, and any higher-level official's findings and recommendations on the initial summary rating or the results of an alternative review. The PRB may conduct any further review needed to make its recommendations. The PRB may not review an initial summary rating to which the executive has not been given the opportunity to respond in writing, including through the use of automated systems.

(2) The PRB must make a written recommendation, including through the use of automated systems, to the appointing authority about each senior executive's annual summary rating, performance-based pay adjustment, and performance award.

(3) PRB members may not take part in any PRB deliberations involving their own appraisals, performance-based pay adjustments, and performance awards.

§ 430.312 Using performance results.

(a) Agencies must use performance appraisals as a basis for adjusting pay, granting awards, retaining senior executives, and making other personnel decisions. Performance appraisals also will be a factor in assessing a senior executive's continuing development needs.

(b) Agencies are required to provide appropriate incentives and recognition (including pay adjustments and performance awards under part 534, subpart D) for excellence in performance.

(c) A career executive may be removed from the SES for performance reasons, subject to the provisions of part 359, subpart E, as follows:

(1) An executive who receives an unsatisfactory annual summary rating must be reassigned or transferred within the SES, or removed from the SES;

(2) An executive who receives two unsatisfactory annual summary ratings in any 5-year period must be removed from the SES; and

(3) An executive who receives less than a fully successful annual summary rating twice in any 3-year period must be removed from the SES.

§ 430.313 Training and evaluation.

(a) To assure effective implementation of agency performance management systems, agencies must provide appropriate information and training to agency leadership, supervisors, and senior executives on performance management, including planning and appraising performance.

(b) Agencies must periodically evaluate the effectiveness of their performance management system(s) and implement improvements as needed. Evaluations must provide for both assessment of effectiveness and compliance with relevant laws, OPM regulations, and OPM performance management policy.

(c) Agencies must maintain all performance-related records for no fewer than 5 years from the date the annual summary rating is issued, as required in 5 CFR 293.404(b)(1).

§ 430.314 OPM review of agency systems.

(a) Agencies must submit proposed SES performance management systems to OPM for approval. Agency systems must address the system standards and requirements specified in this subpart.

(b) OPM will review agency systems for compliance with the requirements of law, OPM regulations, and OPM performance management policy, including the system standards specified at §430.305.

(c) If OPM finds that an agency system does not meet the requirements and intent of subchapter II of chapter 43 of title 5, United States Code, or of this subpart, OPM will identify the requirements that were not met and direct the agency to take corrective action, and the agency must comply.

Subpart D—Performance Appraisal Certification for Pay Purposes

SOURCE: 69 FR 45550, 45551, July 29, 2004, unless otherwise noted.

NOTE TO SUBPART D: Regulations identical to this subpart appear at 5 CFR part 1330, subpart D.

§430.401 Purpose.

(a) This subpart implements 5 U.S.C. 5307(d), as added by section 1322 of the Chief Human Capital Officers Act of 2002 (Title XIII of Public Law 107–296, the Homeland Security Act of 2002; November 25, 2002), which provides a higher aggregate limitation on pay for certain members of the Senior Executive Service (SES) under 5 U.S.C. 5382 and 5383 and employees in senior-level (SL) and scientific or professional (ST) positions paid under 5 U.S.C. 5376. In addition, this subpart is necessary to administer rates of basic pay for members of the SES under 5 U.S.C. 5382, as amended by section 1125 of the National Defense Authorization Act for Fiscal Year 2004. The regulations in this subpart strengthen the application of pay-for-performance principles to senior executives and senior professionals. Specifically, the statutory provisions authorize an agency to apply a higher maximum rate of basic pay for senior executives (consistent with 5 CFR part 534, subpart D, when effective) and apply a higher aggregate limitation on pay (consistent with 5 CFR part 530, subpart B) to its senior employees, but only after OPM, with OMB concurrence, has certified that the design and application of the agency's appraisal systems for these employees make meaningful distinctions based on relative performance. This subpart establishes the certification criteria and procedures that OPM will apply in considering agency requests for such certification.

(b) Senior executives generally may receive an annual rate of basic pay up to the rate for level III of the Executive Schedule under 5 U.S.C. 5382 and 5 CFR part 534, subpart D, when effective. Senior employees generally may receive total compensation in a calendar year up to the rate for level I of the Executive Schedule under 5 U.S.C. 5307(a) and 5 CFR 530.203(a). Only employees covered by an appraisal system that OPM, with OMB concurrence, certifies under this subpart are eligible for a maximum annual rate of basic pay for senior executives up to the rate for level II of the Executive Schedule (consistent with 5 U.S.C. 5382 and 5 CFR part 534, subpart D, when effective) and a higher aggregate pay limitation equivalent to the total annual compensation payable to the Vice President (consistent with 5 U.S.C. 5307(d) and 5 CFR 530.203(b)).

§430.402 Definitions.

In this subpart—

Appraisal system means the policies, practices, and procedures an agency establishes under 5 U.S.C. chapter 43 and 5 CFR part 430, subparts B and C, or other applicable legal authority, for planning, monitoring, developing, evaluating, and rewarding employee performance. This includes appraisal systems and appraisal programs as defined at §430.203 and performance management systems as defined at §430.303.

GPRA means the Government Performance and Results Act of 1993.

OMB means the Office of Management and Budget.

OPM means the Office of Personnel Management.

Outstanding performance means performance that substantially exceeds the normally high performance expected of any senior employee, as evidenced by exceptional accomplishments or contributions to the agency's performance.

Performance evaluation means the comparison of the actual performance of senior employees against their performance expectations and may take into account their contribution to agency performance, where appropriate.

Performance expectations means critical and other performance elements and performance requirements that constitute the senior executive performance plans (as defined in § 430.303) established for senior executives, the performance elements and standards that constitute the performance plans (as defined in § 430.203) established for senior professionals, or other appropriate means authorized under performance appraisal systems not covered by 5 U.S.C. chapter 43 for communicating what a senior employee is expected to do and the manner in which he/she is expected to do it, and may include contribution to agency performance, where appropriate.

Program performance measures means results-oriented measures of performance, whether at the agency, component, or function level, which include, for example, measures under the Government Performance and Results Act.

PRB means Performance Review Board, as described at § 430.310.

Relative performance means the performance of a senior employee with respect to the performance of other senior employees, including their contribution to agency performance, where appropriate, as determined by the application of a certified appraisal system.

Senior employee means a senior executive or a senior professional.

Senior executive means a member of the Senior Executive Service (SES) paid under 5 U.S.C. 5383.

Senior professional means an employee in a senior-level (SL) or scientific or professional position (ST) paid under 5 U.S.C. 5376.

§ 430.403 System certification.

(a) The performance appraisal system(s) covering senior employees must be certified by OPM, with OMB concurrence, as making meaningful distinctions based on relative performance before an agency may apply a maximum annual rate of basic pay for senior executives equal to the rate for level II of the Executive Schedule or apply an annual aggregate limitation on payments to senior employees equal to the salary of the Vice President under 5 U.S.C. 5307(d)). OPM, with OMB concurrence, will certify an agency's appraisal system(s) only when a review of that system's design, application, and administration reveals that the agency meets the certification criteria established in § 430.404 and has followed the procedures for certifying agency appraisal systems in § 430.405.

(b) Except as provided in paragraph (c) of this section, agencies subject to 5 U.S.C. chapter 43 and 5 CFR part 430 seeking certification of their appraisal systems must submit systems that have been approved by OPM under § 430.312 or § 430.210, as applicable. In some agencies, the performance appraisal system(s) covers employees in many organizations and/or components, and their ability to meet the certification criteria in § 430.404 may vary significantly. In such cases, an agency may establish and/or submit separate performance appraisal systems for each of these distinct organizations and/or components to ensure timely certification of those performance appraisal system(s) that meet the criteria. New appraisal systems established under 5 CFR part 430, subpart B or C, as applicable based on the employees covered, must be approved by OPM.

(c) When an agency establishes a new appraisal system for the purpose of seeking certification under this subpart, the agency may submit that system for certification even if it has not yet been approved by OPM under § 430.312 or § 430.210, as applicable. OPM will certify, with OMB concurrence, only those systems that OPM determines meet the approval requirements of 5 CFR part 430, subpart B or C, as applicable.

(d) An agency must establish an appraisal system(s), as defined in § 430.402, for its senior professionals that meets the requirements of 5 CFR part 430, subpart B, and is separate from the system(s) established to cover its SES members under 5 CFR part 430, subpart C. For the purpose of certification under this subpart, such senior professional appraisal system(s) must meet the certification criteria set forth in § 430.404. At its discretion, an agency may include system features in its senior professional appraisal system(s) that are the same as, or similar to, the features of its SES appraisal system(s), as appropriate, including procedures that correspond to the higher level review procedures under § 430.308(b) and PRB reviews of summary ratings under § 430.308(c).

(e) For agencies subject to 5 U.S.C. chapter 43 and 5 CFR part 430, OPM approval of the agency performance appraisal system(s) is a prerequisite to certification. Agencies not subject to the appraisal provisions of 5 U.S.C. chapter 43 and 5 CFR part 430 and which are seeking certification of their appraisal system(s) under this subpart must submit appropriate documentation to demonstrate that each system complies with the appropriate legal authority that governs the establishment, application, and administration of that system.

§ 430.404 Certification criteria.

(a) To be certified, an agency's applicable appraisal system(s) for senior executives or senior professionals must make meaningful distinctions based on relative performance and meet the other requirements of 5 U.S.C. chapter 43, as applicable, in addition to the particular criterion cited here (*i.e.*, consultation). Such system(s) must provide for the following:

(1) Alignment, so that the performance expectations for individual senior employees derive from, and clearly link to, the agency's mission, GPRA strategic goals, program and policy objectives, and/or annual performance plans and budget priorities;

(2) Consultation, so that the performance expectations for senior employees meet the requirements of 5 CFR part 430, subparts B and C, as applicable, and/or other applicable legal authority; are developed with the input and involvement of the individual senior employees who are covered thereby; and are communicated to them at the beginning of the applicable appraisal period, and/or at appropriate times thereafter;

(3) Results, so that the performance expectations for individual senior employees apply to their respective areas of responsibility; reflect expected agency and/or organizational outcomes and outputs, performance targets or metrics, policy/program objectives, and/or milestones; identify specific programmatic crosscutting, external, and partnership-oriented goals or objectives, as applicable; and are stated in terms of observable, measurable, and/or demonstrable performance;

(4) Balance, so that in addition to expected results, the performance expectations for individual senior employees include appropriate measures or indicators of employee and/or customer/stakeholder feedback; quality, quantity, timeliness, and cost effectiveness, as applicable; and those technical, leadership and/or managerial competencies or behaviors that contribute to and are necessary to distinguish outstanding performance;

(5) Appropriate assessments of the agency's performance—overall and with respect to each of its particular missions, components, programs, policy areas, and support functions—such as reports of the agency's GPRA goals, annual performance plans and targets, program performance measures, and other appropriate indicators, as well as evaluation guidelines based, in part, upon those assessments, that are communicated by the agency head, or an individual specifically designated by the agency head for such purpose, to senior employees, appropriate senior employee rating and reviewing officials, and PRB members. These assessments and guidelines are to be provided at the conclusion of the appraisal period but before individual senior employee performance ratings are recommended, so that they may serve as a basis for individual performance evaluations, as appropriate. The guidance provided may not take the form of quantitative limitations on the number of ratings at any given rating level, and must conform to 5 CFR part 430, subpart B or C, as applicable;

(6) Oversight by the agency head or the individual specifically designated under paragraph (a)(5) of this section, who certifies, for a particular senior employee appraisal system, that—

(i) The senior employee appraisal process makes meaningful distinctions based on relative performance;

(ii) The results of the senior employee appraisal process take into account, as appropriate, the agency's assessment of its performance against program performance measures, as well as other relevant considerations; and

(iii) Pay adjustments, cash awards, and levels of pay based on the results of the appraisal process accurately reflect and recognize individual performance and/or contribution to the agency's performance;

(7) Accountability, so that final agency head decisions and any PRB recommendations regarding senior employee ratings consistent with 5 CFR part 430, subparts B and C, individually and overall, appropriately reflect the employee's performance expectations, relevant program performance measures, and such other relevant factors as the PRB may find appropriate; in the case of supervisory senior employees, ratings must reflect the degree to which performance standards, requirements, or expectations for individual subordinate employees clearly link to organizational mission, GPRA strategic goals, or other program or policy objectives and take into account the degree of rigor in the appraisal of their subordinate employees;

(8) Performance differentiation, so that the system(s) includes at least one summary level of performance above fully successful, including a summary level that reflects outstanding performance, as defined in § 430.402, and so that its annual administration results in meaningful distinctions based on relative performance that take into account the assessment of the agency's performance against relevant program performance measures, as described in paragraph (a)(6) of this section, employee performance expectations, and such other relevant factors as may be appropriate. Relative performance does not require ranking senior employees against each other; such ranking is prohibited for the purpose of determining performance ratings. For equivalent systems that do not use summary ratings, the appraisal system must provide for clear differentiation of performance at the outstanding level; and

(9) Pay differentiation, so that those senior employees who have demonstrated the highest levels of individual performance and/or contribution to the agency's performance receive the highest annual summary ratings or ratings of record, as applicable, as well as the largest corresponding pay adjustments, cash awards, and levels of pay, particularly above the rate for level III of the Executive Schedule. Agencies must provide for transparency in the processes for making pay decisions, while assuring confidentiality.

(b) Consistent with the requirements in section 3(a) of the Inspector General Act of 1978, an agency's Inspector General or an official he or she designates must perform the functions listed in paragraphs (a)(5) and (6) of this section for senior employees in the Office of the Inspector General.

§ 430.405 Procedures for certifying agency appraisal systems.

(a) *General.* To receive system certification, an agency must provide documentation demonstrating that its appraisal system(s), in design, application, and administration, meets the certification criteria in § 430.404 as well as the procedural requirements set forth in this section.

(b) *Certification requests.* In order for an agency's appraisal system to be certified, the head of the agency or designee must submit a written request for full or provisional certification of its appraisal system(s) to OPM. Certification requests may cover an agency-wide system or a system that applies to one or more agency organizations or components and must include—

(1) A full description of the appraisal system(s) to be certified, including—

(i) Organizational and employee coverage information;

(ii) Applicable administrative instructions and implementing guidance; and

(iii) The system's use of rating levels that are capable of clearly differentiating among senior employees based on appraisals of their relative performance against performance expectations in any given appraisal period reflecting performance evaluation results that make meaningful distinctions based on relative performance, and which include—

(A) For the agency's senior executives covered by 5 CFR part 430, subpart C, at least four, but not more than five, summary rating levels—an outstanding level, a fully successful level, an optional level between outstanding and fully successful, a minimally satisfactory level, and an unsatisfactory level;

(B) For the agency's senior professionals covered by 5 CFR part 430, subpart B, at least three, but not more than five, summary levels—an outstanding level, a fully successful level, an optional level between outstanding and fully successful, an unacceptable level, and an optional level between fully successful and unacceptable; and

(C) For agencies not subject to 5 CFR part 430, subparts B and C, a summary rating level that reflects outstanding performance or a methodology that clearly differentiates outstanding performance, as defined in § 430.402;

(2) A clearly defined process for reviewing—

(i) The initial summary ratings and ratings of record, as applicable, of senior employees to ensure that annual summary ratings or ratings of record are not distributed arbitrarily or on a rotational basis, and

(ii) In the case of senior employees with supervisory responsibilities—

(A) The performance standards, requirements, or expectations for the employees they supervise to ensure that they clearly link to organizational mission, GPRA strategic goals, or other program and policy objectives, as appropriate, and

(B) The performance standards, requirements, or expectations and the performance ratings of the employees they supervise to ensure that they reflect distinctions in individual and organizational performance, as appropriate;

(3) Documentation showing that the appraisal system(s) meets the applicable certification criteria, as follows:

(i) For provisional certification, the requirements in § 430.404(a)(1)–(4); and

(ii) For full certification, all of the requirements in § 430.404.

(4) For full certification, data on senior executive annual summary ratings and senior professional ratings of record, as applicable (or other documentation for agencies that do not use summary ratings), for the two appraisal periods preceding the request, as well as corresponding pay adjustments, cash awards, and levels of pay provided to those senior employees; and

(5) Any additional information that OPM and OMB may require to make a determination regarding certification.

(c) *Certification actions.* At the request of an agency, the Director of OPM, at his or her discretion and in accordance with the requirements of this subpart and with OMB concurrence, may grant full or provisional certification of the agency's appraisal system(s). OPM, with OMB concurrence, may—

(1) Grant full certification of an agency's senior employee appraisal system(s) for 2 calendar years when an agency has demonstrated that it has designed and fully implemented and applied an appraisal system(s) for its senior executives or senior professionals, as applicable, that meets the certification criteria in § 430.404 and the documentation requirements of this section.

(2) Grant provisional certification of an agency's senior employee appraisal system(s) for 1 calendar year when an agency has designed, but not yet fully implemented or applied, an appraisal system(s) for its senior executives or senior professionals, as applicable, that meets the certification criteria in § 430.404. OPM may extend provisional certification into the following calendar year in order to permit an agency to take any actions needed to adjust pay based on annual summary ratings, ratings of record, or other performance appraisal results determined during the calendar year for which the system was certified; or

(3) Suspend certification under paragraph (h) of this section if, at any time during the certification period, OPM, with OMB concurrence, determines that the agency appraisal system is not in compliance with certification criteria.

(d) *Pay limitations.* Absent full or provisional certification of its appraisal system(s), an agency must—

(1) Set a senior executive's rate of basic pay at a rate that does not exceed

the rate for level III of the Executive Schedule, consistent with 5 CFR part 534, subpart D, when effective; and

(2) Limit aggregate compensation paid to senior employees in a calendar year to the rate for level I of the Executive Schedule, consistent with 5 CFR 530.203(b).

(e) *Full certification.* (1) OPM, with OMB concurrence, may grant full certification when a review of the agency's request and accompanying documentation demonstrates that the design, application, and administration of the agency's appraisal system(s) meet the criteria in §430.404 and the documentation requirements of this section.

(2) An agency with a fully-certified appraisal system(s) may set the rate of basic pay under 5 CFR part 534, subpart D, when effective, for a senior executive covered by a certified system at a rate that does not exceed the rate for level II of the Executive Schedule and pay senior employees covered by certified system(s) aggregate compensation in a certified calendar year in an amount up to the Vice President's salary under 3 U.S.C. 104.

(3) Full certification of an agency's appraisal system will be renewed automatically for an additional 2 calendar years, if—

(i) The agency meets the annual reporting requirements in paragraph (g) of this section; and

(ii) Based on those annual reports, OPM determines, and OMB concurs, that the appraisal system(s) continues to meet the certification criteria and procedural requirements set forth in this subpart.

(f) *Provisional certification.* (1) OPM, with OMB concurrence, may grant provisional certification when the design of an agency's appraisal system(s) for senior executives or senior professionals, as applicable, meets the requirements set forth in this subpart, but insufficient documentation exists to determine whether the actual application and administration of the appraisal system(s) meet the requirements for full certification. OPM, with OMB concurrence, may grant provisional certification to an agency more than once.

(2) During the 1-year period of provisional certification, an agency may set the rate of basic pay for a senior executive covered by the provisionally certified system at a rate that does not exceed the rate for level II of the Executive Schedule (consistent with 5 CFR part 534, subpart D, when effective) and pay senior employees covered by provisionally certified systems aggregate compensation in the certified calendar year in an amount up to the Vice President's salary under 3 U.S.C. 104 (consistent with 5 CFR part 530, subpart B).

(3) An agency must resubmit an application requesting provisional certification for every calendar year for which it intends to maintain provisional certification. An agency with a provisionally certified appraisal system(s) may request that OPM, with OMB concurrence, grant full certification upon a showing that its performance appraisal systems for senior executives and senior professionals, as applicable, meet the certification criteria in §430.404 and the documentation requirements in this section, particularly with respect to the implementation and administration of the system(s) over at least two consecutive performance appraisal periods.

(g) *Annual reporting requirement.* Agencies with certified appraisal systems must provide OPM with a general summary of the annual summary ratings and ratings of record, as applicable, and rates of basic pay, pay adjustments, cash awards, and aggregate total compensation (including any lump-sum payments in excess of the applicable aggregate limitation on pay that were paid in the current calendar year as required by §530.204) for their senior employees covered by a certified appraisal system at the conclusion of each appraisal period that ends during a calendar year for which the certification is in effect, in accordance with OPM instructions.

(h) *Suspension of certification.* (1) When OPM determines that an agency's certified appraisal system is no longer in compliance with certification criteria, OPM, with OMB concurrence, may suspend such certification, as provided in paragraph (c)(3) of this section.

(2) An agency's system certification is automatically suspended when OPM withdraws performance appraisal system approval or mandates corrective action because of misapplication of the system as authorized under §§430.210(c), 430.312(c), and 430.403(e).

(3) OPM will notify the head of the agency at least 30 calendar days in advance of the suspension and the reason(s) for the suspension, as well as any expected corrective action. Upon such notice, and until its system certification is reinstated, the agency must set a senior executive's rate of basic pay under 5 CFR part 534, subpart D, when effective, at a rate that does not exceed the rate for level III of the Executive Schedule. While certification is suspended, an agency must limit aggregate compensation received in a calendar year by a senior employee to the rate for level I of the Executive Schedule. Pay adjustments, cash awards, and levels of pay in effect prior to that notice will remain in effect unless OPM finds that any such decision and subsequent action was in violation of law, rule, or regulation.

(4) OPM, with OMB concurrence, may reinstate an agency's suspended certification only after the agency has taken appropriate corrective action.

(5) OPM may reinstate the certification of an appraisal system that has been automatically suspended under paragraph (h)(2) of this section upon the agency's compliance with the applicable OPM-mandated corrective action(s).

PART 432—PERFORMANCE BASED REDUCTION IN GRADE AND REMOVAL ACTIONS

Sec.

AUTHORITY: 5 U.S.C. 4303, 4305.

SOURCE: 54 FR 26179, June 21, 1989, unless otherwise noted.

§432.101 Statutory authority.

This part applies to reduction in grade and removal of employees covered by the provisions of this part based solely on performance at the unacceptable level. 5 U.S.C. 4305 authorizes the Office of Personnel Management to prescribe regulations to carry out the purposes of title 5, chapter 43, United States Code, including 5 U.S.C. 4303, which covers agency actions to reduce in grade or remove employees for unacceptable performance. (The provisions of 5 U.S.C. 7501 *et seq.*, may also be used to reduce in grade or remove employees. See part 752 of this chapter.)

[58 FR 65533, Dec. 15, 1993]

§432.102 Coverage.

(a) *Actions covered.* This part covers reduction in grade and removal of employees based on unacceptable performance.

(b) *Actions excluded.* This part does not apply to:

(1) The reduction in grade of a supervisor or manager who has not completed the probationary period under 5 U.S.C. 3321(a)(2) if such a reduction is based on supervisory or managerial performance and the reduction is to the grade held immediately before becoming a supervisor or manager in accordance with 5 U.S.C. 3321(b);

(2) The reduction in grade or removal of an employee in the competitive service who is serving a probationary or trial period under an initial appointment;

(3) The reduction in grade or removal of an employee in the competitive service serving in an appointment that requires no probationary or trial period who has not completed 1 year of current continuous employment in the same or similar position under other than a temporary appointment limited to 1 year or less;

(4) The reduction in grade or removal of an employee in the excepted service who has not completed 1 year of current continuous employment in the same or similar positions;

(5) An action imposed by the Merit Systems Protection Board under the authority of 5 U.S.C. 1206;

(6) An action taken under 5 U.S.C. 7521 against an administrative law judge;

(7) An action taken under 5 U.S.C. 7532 in the interest of national security;

(8) An action taken under a provision of statute, other than one codified in title 5 of the U.S. Code, which excepts the action from the provisions of title 5 of the U.S. Code;

(9) A removal from the Senior Executive Service to a civil service position outside the Senior Executive Service under part 359 of this chapter;

(10) A reduction-in-force governed by part 351 of this chapter;

(11) A voluntary action by the employee;

(12) A performance-based action taken under part 752 of this chapter;

(13) An action that terminates a temporary or term promotion and returns the employee to the position from which temporarily promoted, or to a different position of equivalent grade and pay if the agency informed the employee that it was to be of limited duration;

(14) A termination in accordance with terms specified as conditions of employment at the time the appointment was made; and

(15) An involuntary retirement because of disability under part 831 of this chapter.

(c) *Agencies covered.* This part applies to:

(1) The executive departments listed at 5 U.S.C. 101;

(2) The military departments listed at 5 U.S.C. 102;

(3) Independent establishments in the executive branch as described at 5 U.S.C. 104, except for a Government corporation; and

(4) The Government Printing Office.

(d) *Agencies excluded.* This part does not apply to:

(1) A Government corporation;

(2) The Central Intelligence Agency;

(3) The Defense Intelligence Agency;

(4) The National Security Agency;

(5) Any executive agency or unit thereof which is designated by the President and the principal function of which is the conduct of foreign intelligence or counterintelligence activities;

(6) The General Accounting Office;

(7) The U.S. Postal Service; and

(8) The Postal Rate Commission.

(e) *Employees covered.* This part applies to individuals employed in or under a covered agency as specified at § 432.102(c) except as listed in § 432.102(f).

(f) *Employees excluded.* This part does not apply to:

(1) An employee in the competitive service who is serving a probationary or trial period under an initial appointment;

(2) An employee in the competitive service serving in an appointment that requires no probationary or trial period, who has not completed 1 year of current continuous employment in the same or similar positions under other than a temporary appointment limited to 1 year or less;

(3) An employee in the excepted service who has not completed 1 year of current continuous employment in the same or similar positions;

(4) An employee outside the United States who is paid in accordance with local native prevailing wage rates for the area in which employed;

(5) An individual in the Foreign Service of the United States;

(6) An employee who holds a position with the Veterans Health Administration which has been excluded from the competitive service by or under a provision of title 38, United States Code, unless such employee was appointed to such a position under section 7401(3) of title 38;

(7) An administrative law judge appointed under 5 U.S.C. 3105;

(8) An individual in the Senior Executive Service;

(9) An individual appointed by the President;

(10) An employee occupying a position in Schedule C as authorized under part 213 of this chapter;

(11) A reemployed annuitant;

(12) A technician in the National Guard described in 5 U.S.C. 8337(h)(1), employed under section 709(b) of title 32;

(13) An individual occupying a position in the excepted service for which employment is not reasonably expected to exceed 120 calendar days in a consecutive 12 month period; and

(14) A manager or supervisor returned to his or her previously held grade pursuant to 5 U.S.C. 3321 (a)(2) and (b).

[54 FR 26179, June 21, 1989, as amended at 57 FR 10125, Mar. 24, 1992; 57 FR 20042, May 11, 1992; 58 FR 13192, Mar. 10, 1993; 58 FR 65533, Dec. 15, 1993]

§ 432.103 Definitions.

For the purpose of this part—

(a) *Acceptable performance* means performance that meets an employee's performance requirement(s) or standard(s) at a level of performance above "unacceptable" in the critical element(s) at issue.

(b) *Critical element* means a work assignment or responsibility of such importance that unacceptable performance on the element would result in a determination that an employee's overall performance is unacceptable.

(c) *Current continuous employment* means a period of employment or service immediately preceding an action under this part in the same or similar positions without a break in Federal civilian employment of a workday.

(d) *Opportunity to demonstrate acceptable performance* means a reasonable chance for the employee whose performance has been determined to be unacceptable in one or more critical elements to demonstrate acceptable performance in the critical element(s) at issue.

(e) *Reduction in grade* means the involuntary assignment of an employee to a position at a lower classification or job grading level.

(f) *Removal* means the involuntary separation of an employee from employment with an agency.

(g) *Similar positions* mean positions in which the duties performed are similar in nature and character and require substantially the same or similar qualifications, so that the imcumbents could be interchanged without significant training or undue interruption to the work.

(h) *Unacceptable performance* means performance of an employee that fails to meet established performance standards in one or more critical elements of such employee's position.

[54 FR 26179, June 21, 1989, as amended at 54 FR 49076, Nov. 29, 1989; 55 FR 25950, June 26, 1990; 57 FR 23045, June 1, 1992; 57 FR 60717, Dec. 22, 1992; 58 FR 65534, Dec. 15, 1993; 60 FR 43946, Aug. 23, 1995]

§ 432.104 Addressing unacceptable performance.

At any time during the performance appraisal cycle that an employee's performance is determined to be unacceptable in one or more critical elements, the agency shall notify the employee of the critical element(s) for which performance is unacceptable and inform the employee of the performance requirement(s) or standard(s) that must be attained in order to demonstrate acceptable performance in his or her position. The agency should also inform the employee that unless his or her performance in the critical element(s) improves to and is sustained at an acceptable level, the employee may be reduced in grade or removed. For each critical element in which the employee's performance is unacceptable, the agency shall afford the employee a reasonable opportunity to demonstrate acceptable performance, commensurate with the duties and responsibilities of the employee's position. As part of the employee's opportunity to demonstrate acceptable performance, the agency shall offer assistance to the employee in improving unacceptable performance.

[55 FR 25950, June 26, 1990, as amended at 58 FR 65534, Dec. 15, 1993]

§ 432.105 Proposing and taking action based on unacceptable performance.

(a) *Proposing action based on unacceptable performance.* (1) Once an employee has been afforded a reasonable opportunity to demonstrate acceptable performance pursuant to § 432.104, an agency may propose a reduction-in-grade or removal action if the employee's performance during or following the opportunity to demonstrate acceptable performance is unacceptable in 1 or more of the critical elements for which the employee was afforded an opportunity to demonstrate acceptable performance.

(2) If an employee has performed acceptably for 1 year from the beginning of an opportunity to demonstrate acceptable performance (in the critical element(s) for which the employee was afforded an opportunity to demonstrate acceptable performance), and the employee's performance again becomes unacceptable, the agency shall afford the employee an additional opportunity to demonstrate acceptable performance before determining whether to propose a reduction in grade or removal under this part.

(3) A proposed action may be based on instances of unacceptable performance which occur within a 1 year period ending on the date of the notice of proposed action.

(4) An employee whose reduction in grade or removal is proposed under this part is entitled to:

(i) *Advance notice.* (A) The agency shall afford the employee a 30 day advance notice of the proposed action that identifies both the specific instances of unacceptable performance by the employee on which the proposed action is based and the critical element(s) of the employee's position involved in each instance of unacceptable performance.

(B) An agency may extend this advance notice period for a period not to exceed 30 days under regulations prescribed by the head of the agency. An agency may extend this notice period further without prior OPM approval for the following reasons:

(*1*) To obtain and/or evaluate medical information when the employee has raised a medical issue in the answer to a proposed reduction in grade or removal;

(*2*) To arrange for the employee's travel to make an oral reply to an appropriate agency official, or the travel of an agency official to hear the employee's oral reply;

(*3*) To consider the employee's answer if an extention to the period for an answer has been granted (e.g., because of the employee's illness or incapacitation);

(*4*) To consider reasonable accommodation of a handicapping condition;

(*5*) If agency procedures so require, to consider positions to which the employee might be reassigned or reduced in grade; or

(*6*) To comply with a stay ordered by a member of the Merit Systems Protection Board under 5 U.S.C. 1208(b).

(C) If an agency believes that an extension of the advance notice period is necessary for another reason, it may request prior approval for such extension from the Chief, Family Programs and Employee Relations Division, Office of Labor Relations and Workforce Performance, Personnel Systems and Oversight Group, Office of Personnel Management, 1900 E Street NW., Washington, DC 20415.

(ii) *Opportunity to answer.* The agency shall afford the employee a reasonable time to answer the agency's notice of proposed action orally and in writing.

(iii) *Representation.* The agency shall allow the employee to be represented by an attorney or other representative. An agency may disallow as an employee's representative an individual whose activities as a representative would cause a conflict of interest or position or an employee whose release from his or her official position would give rise to unreasonable costs to the Government or whose priority work assignment precludes his or her release from official duties.

(iv) *Consideration of medical conditions.* The agency shall allow an employee who wishes to raise a medical condition which may have contributed to his or her unacceptable performance to furnish medical documentation (as defined in §339.102 of this chapter of the condition for the agency's consideration. Whenever possible, the employee shall supply this documentation following the agency's notification of unacceptable performance under §432.104. If the employee offers such documentation after the agency has proposed a reduction in grade or removal, he or she shall supply this information in accordance with §432.105(a)(4)(ii). In considering documentation submitted in connection with the employee's claim of a medical condition, the agency may require or offer a medical examination in accordance with the criteria and procedures of part 339 of this chapter, and shall be aware of the affirmative obligations of 29 CFR 1613.704. If the employee who raises a medical condition has the requisite years of service under the Civil Service Retirement System or the Federal Employees Retirement System, the agency shall provide information concerning application for disability retirement. As provided at § 831.501(d) of this chapter, an employee's application for disability retirement shall not preclude or delay any other appropriate agency decision or personnel action.

(b) *Final written decision.* The agency shall make its final decision within 30 days after expiration of the advance notice period. Unless proposed by the head of the agency, such written decision shall be concurred in by an employee who is in a higher position than the person who proposed the action. In arriving at its decision, the agency shall consider any answer of the employee and/or his or her representative furnished in response to the agency's proposal. A decision to reduce in grade or remove an employee for unacceptable performance may be based only on those instances of unacceptable performance that occurred during the 1 year period ending on the date of issuance of the advance notice of proposed action under § 432.105(a)(4)(i). The agency shall issue written notice of its decision to the employee at or before the time the action will be effective. Such notice shall specify the instances of unacceptable performance by the employee on which the action is based and shall inform the employee of any applicable appeal and/or grievance rights.

[54 FR 26179, June 21, 1989. Redesignated and amended at 54 FR 49076, Nov. 29, 1989. Redesignated and amended at 58 FR 65534, Dec. 15, 1993]

§ 432.106 Appeal and grievance rights.

(a) *Appeal rights.* An employee covered under § 432.102(e) who has been removed or reduced in grade under this part may appeal to the Merit Systems Protection Board if the employee is:

(1) In the competitive service and has completed a probationary or trial period;

(2) In the competitive service serving in an appointment which is not subject to a probationary or trial period, and has completed 1 year of current continuous employment in the same or similar position(s) under other than a temporary appointment limited to 1 year or less;

(3) A preference eligible in the excepted service who has completed 1 year of current continuous employment in the same or similar position(s); or

(4) A nonpreference eligible in the excepted service who is covered by subparts C and D of part 752 of this chapter.

(b) *Grievance rights.* (1) A bargaining unit employee covered under § 432.102(e) who has been removed or reduced in grade under this part may file a grievance under an applicable negotiated grievance procedure if the removal or reduction in grade action falls within its coverage (*i.g.*, is not excluded by the parties to the collective bargaining agreement) and the employee is:

(i) In the competitive service and has completed a probationary or trial period.

(ii) In the competitive service, serving in an appointment which is not subject to a probationary or trial period, and has completed 1 year of current continuous employment in the same or similar position(s) under other than a temporary appointment limited to 1 year or less;

(iii) A preference eligible in the excepted service who has completed 1 year of current continuous employment in the same or similar position(s); or

(iv) A nonpreference eligible in the excepted service who is covered by subparts C and D of part 752 of the chapter.

(2) 5 U.S.C. 7114(a)(5) and 7121(b)(3), and the terms of an applicable collective bargaining agreement govern representation for employees in an exclusive bargaining unit who grieve a matter under this section through the negotiated grievance process.

(c) *Election of forum.* As provided at 5 U.S.C. 7121(e)(1), a bargaining unit employee who by law may file an appeal or a grievance, and who has exercised his or her option to appeal an action taken under this part to the Merit Systems Protection Board, may not also file a grievance on the matter under a negotiated grievance procedure. Likewise, a bargaining unit employee who has exercised his or her option to grieve an action taken under this part may not also file an appeal on the matter with the Merit Systems Protection Board.

[54 FR 26179, June 21, 1989. Redesignated at 54 FR 49076, Nov. 29, 1989; 57 FR 20043, May 11, 1992; 58 FR 13192, Mar. 10, 1993. Redesignated at 58 FR 65534, Dec. 15, 1993]

§ 432.107 Agency records.

(a) *When the action is effected.* The agency shall preserve all relevant documentation concerning a reduction in grade or removal which is based on unacceptable performance and make it available for review by the affected employee or his or her representative. At a minimum, the agency's records shall consist of a copy of the notice of proposed action, the answer of the employee when it is in writing, a summary thereof when the employee makes an oral reply, the written notice of decision and the reasons therefor, and any supporting material including documentation regarding the opportunity afforded the employee to demonstrate acceptable performance.

(b) *When the action is not affected.* As provided at 5 U.S.C. 4303(d), if, because of performance improvement by the employee during the notice period, the employee is not reduced in grade or removed, and the employee's performance continues to be acceptable for 1 year from the date of the advanced written notice provided in accordance with § 432.105(a)(4)(i), any entry or other notation of the unacceptable performance for which the action was proposed shall be removed from any agency record relating to the employee.

[55 FR 25950, June 26, 1990, as amended at 58 FR 65534, Dec. 15, 1993]

PART 451—AWARDS

Subpart A—Agency Awards

Subpart B—Presidential Awards

Subpart C—Presidential Rank Awards

AUTHORITY: 5 U.S.C. 4302, 4501–4509; E.O. 11438, 33 FR 18085, 3 CFR, 1966–1970 Comp., p. 755; E.O. 12828, 58 FR 2965, 3 CFR, 1993 Comp., p. 569.

Subpart A—Agency Awards

SOURCE: 60 FR 43946, Aug. 23, 1995, unless otherwise noted.

§ 451.101 Authority and coverage.

(a) Chapter 45 of title 5, United States Code authorizes agencies to pay a cash award to, grant time-off to, and incur necessary expense for the honorary recognition of, an employee (individually or as a member of a group) and requires the Office of Personnel Management to prescribe regulations governing such authority. Chapter 43 of title 5, United States Code, provides for recognizing and rewarding employees whose performance so warrants. The regulations in this subpart, in combination with chapters 43 and 45 of title 5, United States Code, and any other applicable law, establish the requirements for agency award programs.

(b) Section 4 of E.O. 11438 (Prescribing Procedures Governing Interdepartmental Cash Awards to the Members of the Armed Forces, December 3, 1968) requires the Office of Personnel Management to prescribe procedures for covering the cost of a cash award recommended by more than one agency for a member of the armed forces for the adoption or use of a suggestion, invention, or scientific achievement. Section 1 of E.O. 12828 (Delegation of Certain Personnel Management Authorities, January 5, 1993) delegates to the Office of Personnel Management the authority of the President to permit performance-based cash awards under 5 U.S.C. 4505a to be paid to categories of employees who would not be eligible otherwise.

(c) This subpart applies to employees as defined by section 2105 and agencies as defined by section 4501 of title 5, United States Code, except as provided in §§451.105 and 451.201(b).

(d) For the regulatory requirements for granting performance awards to Senior Executive Service (SES) employees under 5 U.S.C. 5384, refer to §534.405 of this chapter.

(e) An agency may grant performance-based cash awards on the basis of a rating of record at the fully successful level (or equivalent) or above under the authority of 5 U.S.C. 4505a and the provisions of this part to eligible non-GS employees who are covered by 5 U.S.C. chapter 45 and this part and who are not otherwise covered by an explicit statutory authority for the payment of such awards, including 5 U.S.C. 5384 (SES performance awards).

[60 FR 43946, Aug. 23, 1995; 60 FR 47646, Sept. 13, 1995, as amended at 69 FR 70359, Dec. 6, 2004; 72 FR 1270, Jan. 11, 2007]

§451.102 Definitions.

Award means something bestowed or an action taken to recognize and reward individual or team achievement that contributes to meeting organizational goals or improving the efficiency, effectiveness, and economy of the Government or is otherwise in the public interest. Such awards include, but are not limited to, employee incentives which are based on predetermined criteria such as productivity standards, performance goals, measurement systems, award formulas, or payout schedules.

Award program means the specific procedures and requirements established by an agency or a component of an agency for granting awards under subchapter I of chapter 43 and subchapter I of chapter 45 of title 5, United States Code, and this subpart.

§451.103 Agency award program(s).

(a) Agencies shall develop one or more award programs for employees covered by this subpart.

(b) Agencies are encouraged to involve employees in developing such programs. When agencies involve employees, the method of involvement shall be in accordance with law.

(c) An agency award program shall provide for—

(1) Obligating funds consistent with applicable agency financial management controls and delegations of authority; and

(2) Documenting justification for awards that are not based on a rating of record (as defined in §430.203 of this chapter).

[60 FR 43946, Aug. 23, 1995; 60 FR 47646, Sept. 13, 1995]

§451.104 Awards.

(a) An agency may grant a cash, honorary, or informal recognition award, or grant time-off without charge to leave or loss of pay consistent with chapter 45 of title 5, United States Code, and this part to an employee, as an individual or member of a group, on the basis of—

(1) A suggestion, invention, superior accomplishment, productivity gain, or other personal effort that contributes to the efficiency, economy, or other improvement of Government operations or achieves a significant reduction in paperwork;

(2) A special act or service in the public interest in connection with or related to official employment; or

(3) Performance as reflected in the employee's most recent rating of record (as defined in §430.203 of this chapter), provided that the rating of record is at the fully successful level (or equivalent) or above, except that performance awards may be paid to SES members only under §534.405 of this chapter and not on the basis of this subpart.

(b) A cash award under this subpart is a lump sum payment and is not basic pay for any purpose.

(c) An award is subject to applicable tax rules, such as withholding.

(d) When an award is approved for—

(1) An employee of another agency, the benefiting agency shall make arrangements to transfer funds to the employing agency to cover the award. If the administrative costs of transferring funds would exceed the amount of the award, the employing agency shall absorb the award costs and pay the award; and

(2) A member of the armed forces for a suggestion, invention, or scientific achievement, arrangements shall be made to transfer funds to the agency having jurisdiction over the member in accordance with E.O. 11438, "Prescribing Procedures Governing Interdepartmental Cash Awards to the Members of the Armed Forces".

(e) An award may be granted to a separated employee or the legal heir(s) or estate of a deceased employee.

(f) A time-off award granted under this subpart shall not be converted to a cash payment under any circumstances.

(g) When granting an award paid as a percentage of basic pay under 5 U.S.C. 4505a(a)(2), the rate of basic pay used must include any applicable locality payment under 5 CFR part 531, subpart F; special rate supplement under 5 CFR part 530, subpart C; or similar payment or supplement under other legal authority. For an employee receiving a retained rate under 5 CFR part 536, subpart C (or similar authority, such as 5 CFR 359.705), the rate of basic pay is the maximum payable rate for the employee's grade or level, rather than the retained rate.

(h) Programs for granting performance-based cash awards on the basis of a rating of record at the fully successful level (or equivalent) or above, as designed and applied, must make meaningful distinctions based on levels of performance.

[60 FR 43946, Aug. 23, 1995, as amended at 69 FR 70359, Dec. 6, 2004; 70 FR 31287, May 31, 2005; 70 FR 74995, Dec. 19, 2005; 72 FR 1270, Jan. 11, 2007]

§ 451.105 Award restrictions.

(a) In accordance with 5 U.S.C. 4508, agencies shall not grant awards under this subpart during a Presidential election period to employees who are—

(1) In a Senior Executive Service position and not a career appointee as defined under 5 U.S.C. 3132(a)(4); or

(2) In an excepted service position of a confidential or policy-determining character (schedule C).

(b) In accordance with 5 U.S.C. 4509, agencies shall not grant cash awards under this subpart to employees appointed by the President with Senate confirmation who serve in—

(1) An Executive Schedule position, or

(2) A position for which pay is set in statute by reference to a section or level of the Executive Schedule.

§ 451.106 Agency responsibilities.

(a) In establishing and operating its award program(s), an agency shall assure that a program does not conflict with or violate any other law or Governmentwide regulation.

(b) When a recommended award would grant more than $10,000 to an individual employee, the agency shall submit the recommendation to OPM for approval.

(c) Agencies shall provide for communicating with employees and supervisors (e.g., through formal training) about the relevant parts of their award program(s).

(d) Agencies shall evaluate their award program(s).

(e) Agencies shall document all cash and time off awards in compliance with instructions in the OPM Operating Manual, THE GUIDE TO PROCESSING PERSONNEL ACTIONS, for sale by the U.S. Government Printing Office, Superintendent of Documents.

(f) Agencies shall file award documents in the Official Personnel Folder in compliance with instructions in the OPM Operating Manual, THE GUIDE TO PERSONNEL RECORDKEEPING, for sale by the U.S. Government Printing Office, Superintendent of Documents.

(g) Agencies shall report award data to the Central Personnel Data File in Compliance with instructions in the OPM Operating Manual, FEDERAL WORKFORCE REPORTING SYSTEMS, for sale by the U.S. Government Printing Office, Superintendent of Documents.

(h) Agencies shall maintain and submit to OPM such records as OPM may require.

(i) Agencies shall give due weight to an award granted under this part in qualifying and selecting an employee for promotion as provided in 5 U.S.C. 3362.

(j) Agencies shall take any corrective action required by OPM to ensure conformance with applicable law, regulation, and OPM policy.

§451.107 OPM responsibilities.

(a) OPM shall review and approve or disapprove each agency recommendation for an award that would grant more than $10,000 to an individual employee.

(b) When a recommended award would grant more than $25,000 to an individual employee, OPM shall review the recommendation and submit it (if approved) to the President for final approval.

(c) OPM shall review and approve or disapprove a request from the head of an Executive agency to extend the provisions of 5 U.S.C. 4505a to any category of employees within that agency that would not be covered otherwise.

(d) OPM may evaluate the operation and application of an agency's award program(s).

Subpart B—Presidential Awards

SOURCE: 51 FR 8419, Mar. 11, 1986, unless otherwise noted.

§451.201 Authority and coverage.

(a) Under chapter 45 of title 5, United States Code, the President may pay a cash award to and incur necessary expenses for the honorary recognition of an employee who:

(b) Awards granted under paragraph (a) of this section are subject to the restrictions as specified in §451.105.

(1) By his/her suggestion, invention or other personal effort contributes to the efficiency, economy, or other improvement of Government operations, or achieves a significant reduction in paperwork; or

(2) Performs an exceptionally meritorious special act or service in the public interest in connection with or related to official employment.

(c) Except as provided in paragraph (b) of this section, this subpart applies to employees as defined by section 2105 of title 5, United States Code.

(d) This subpart applies to agencies as defined in section 4501 of title 5, United States Code.

[51 FR 8419, Mar. 11, 1986, as amended at 58 FR 65534, Dec. 15, 1993; 60 FR 43947, Aug. 23, 1995; 67 FR 52596, Aug. 13, 2002]

§451.202 Payment.

(a) A Presidential award is paid by the agency(ies) primarily benefiting from the employee contribution.

(b) A Presidential award may be in addition to an agency award under subpart A of this part.

§451.203 Responsibilities of the Office of Personnel Management.

(a) The Office of Personnel Management, in accordance with Executive Order 10717, as amended, shall review agency recommendations for the President's Award for Distinguished Federal Civilian Service and recommend to the President which career employees should receive this award.

(b) Under Executive Order 11228, section 2, the Office of Personnel Management has the authority to determine the activity or activities primarily benefiting from any suggestion, invention, or other contribution which forms the basis for a Presidential award under 5 U.S.C. 4504.

[51 FR 8419, Mar. 11, 1986, as amended at 58 FR 65534, Dec. 15, 1993; 67 FR 52596, Aug. 13, 2002]

Subpart C—Presidential Rank Awards

SOURCE: 67 FR 52596, Aug. 13, 2002, unless otherwise noted.

§451.301 Ranks for the Senior Executive Service.

(a) The circumstances under which the President may award the rank of Distinguished Executive and Meritorious Executive to a Senior Executive Service (SES) career appointee are set forth in 5 U.S.C. 4507.

(b) To be eligible for a rank award, a senior executive must:

(1) Hold a career appointment in the SES, as defined at 5 U.S.C. 3132(a)(4), on the nomination deadline set by OPM;

(2) Be an employee of the agency, as defined at 5 U.S.C. 3132(a)(1), on the nomination deadline set by OPM; and

(3) Have at least 3 years of career or career-type Federal civilian service at the SES level. Service need not be continuous.

(i) Qualifying service includes appointments in the SES, the Senior Foreign Service, the Defense Intelligence Senior Executive Service, and similar senior executive systems.

(ii) Qualifying service does not include noncareer, limited term, or limited emergency appointments in the SES or their equivalent, Scientific and Professional (ST) appointments, and Senior-Level (SL) appointments.

(c) Each agency may nominate up to 9 percent of its SES career appointees for rank awards.

§ 451.302 Ranks for senior career employees.

(a) The circumstances under which the President may award the rank of Distinguished Senior Professional and Meritorious Senior Professional to a senior career employee are set forth in 5 U.S.C. 4507a.

(b) To be eligible for a rank award, a senior career employee must:

(1) Hold a career appointment in a Senior-Level (SL) or Scientific-Professional (ST) position that is subject to OPM position allocations under part 319 of this chapter and paid under 5 U.S.C. 5376 on the nomination deadline set by OPM;

(2) Be an employee of the agency on the nomination deadline set by OPM; and

(3) Have at least 3 years of career or career-type Federal civilian service above GS–15. Service need not be continuous. Qualifying service includes appointments that are not—

(i) Time-limited; or

(ii) To positions that are excepted from the competitive service because of their confidential or policy-making character.

(c) Each agency may nominate up to 9 percent of its senior career employees for rank awards.

[67 FR 52596, Aug. 13, 2002, as amended at 72 FR 44367, Aug. 8, 2007]

§ 451.303 Restrictions.

(a) *Governmentwide limitations*—SES. During any fiscal year—

(1) The number of career SES appointees awarded the rank of Meritorious Executive may not exceed 5 percent of the career SES; and

(2) The number of career SES appointees awarded the rank of Distinguished Executive may not exceed 1 percent of the career SES.

(b) *Governmentwide limitations*—Senior career employees. During any fiscal year—

(1) The number of senior career employees awarded the rank of Meritorious Senior Professional may not exceed 5 percent of the total number of career appointees to OPM-allocated Senior-Level (SL) and Scientific-Professional (ST) positions; and

(2) The number of senior career employees awarded the rank of Distinguished Senior Professional may not exceed 1 percent of the total number of career appointees to OPM-allocated Senior-Level (SL) and Scientific-Professional (ST) positions.

(c) *Frequency of awards.* Individuals awarded a Distinguished or Meritorious rank under this subpart shall not be entitled to be awarded that rank during the following 4 fiscal years.

[67 FR 52596, Aug. 13, 2002, as amended at 72 FR 44367, Aug. 8, 2007]

§ 451.304 Payment of Rank Awards.

(a) Receipt of the Distinguished rank by an SES career appointee or a senior career employee entitles the individual to a lump-sum payment of an amount equal to 35 percent of annual basic pay, which shall be in addition to the basic pay paid under 5 U.S.C. 5376 or 5382, or any award paid under 5 U.S.C. 5384.

(b) Receipt of the Meritorious rank by an SES career appointee or a senior career employee entitles such individual to a lump-sum payment of an amount equal to 20 percent of annual basic pay, which shall be in addition to the basic pay paid under 5 U.S.C. 5376 or 5382, or any award paid under 5 U.S.C. 5384.

(c) Payment of rank awards must comply with the restrictions on annual aggregate compensation at 5 U.S.C. 5307.

[67 FR 52596, Aug. 13, 2002, as amended at 72 FR 44367, Aug. 8, 2007]

§ 451.305 Responsibilities of the Office of Personnel Management.

(a) Annually, OPM shall establish criteria, including terms, conditions, and evaluation factors, for rank award nominations, in consultation with agencies and other stakeholders. Agencies shall nominate individuals for rank awards in accordance with OPM criteria and any other instructions.

(b) Annually, OPM shall review agency recommendations for Presidential Rank Awards for SES career appointees and senior career employees under 5 U.S.C. 4507 and 4507a, and recommend to the President which of those individuals should receive rank awards.

PART 470—PERSONNEL MANAGEMENT RESEARCH PROGRAMS AND DEMONSTRATIONS PROJECTS

AUTHORITY: 5 U.S.C. 4706.

SOURCE: 48 FR 2726, Jan. 21, 1983, unless otherwise noted.

Subpart A—General Provisions

§ 470.101 Statutory authority.

(a) Section 4702, title 5, United States Code, provides the Office of Personnel Management (OPM) with the authority to:

(1) Establish and maintain, and assist in the establishment and maintenance of, research programs to study improved methods and technologies in Federal personnel management;

(2) Evaluate the research programs established under paragraph (a)(1) of this section;

(3) Establish and maintain a program for the collection and public dissemination of information relating to personnel management research, and for encouraging and facilitating the exchange of information among interested persons and entities; and

(4) Carry out the preceding functions directly or through agreement or contract.

(b) Section 4703, title 5, United States Code, provides OPM with the authority to conduct and evaluate demonstration projects to determine whether a specified change in personnel management policies or procedures would result in improved Federal personnel management.

(c) This part supplements and implements the provisions of chapter 47 of title 5, United States Code, relating to the conduct of personnel research programs and demonstration projects, and must be read together with those provisions of law.

§ 470.103 Definitions.

In this part:

Demonstration Project means a project conducted by the Office of Personnel Management, or under its supervision, to determine whether a specified change in personnel management policies or procedures would result in improved Federal personnel management (5 U.S.C. 4701). The project must require the waiver of a provision of law, rule, or regulation which is eligible for waiver under the demonstration authority contained in 5 U.S.C. 4703. A project which can be undertaken under an agency's own authority and does not require the waiver of a provision of law, rule, or regulation is not considered a "demonstration project" for purposes of this part.

Research means systematic, intensive study directed toward fuller scientific knowledge or understanding of the subject studied. Activities classified as research are structured experimental or descriptive investigations conducted according to sound methodological principles.

Research Program means a planned study of the manner in which public management policies and systems are operating or have operated, the effects of those policies and systems, the possibilities for change, and comparisons among policies and systems.

Subpart B—Regulatory Requirements Pertaining to Research Programs

§ 470.201 Purposes of research programs.

The purposes of research programs undertaken under this subpart are to stimulate and conduct personnel management research which:

(a) Develops new knowledge, techniques, and materials about personnel management;

(b) Seeks solutions to personnel management problems;

(c) Provides a factual base to support existing or proposed changes in personnel management policies, techniques, and materials;

(d) Modifies or develops personnel management systems which improve the management of the Federal Government's human resources;

(e) Gathers, makes explicit, systematizes, and transmits the knowledge and techniques of practicing managers for the guidance of others and as a factual basis for research needs determination;

(f) Develops new methods or provides new standards for conducting personnel management research; or

(g) Designs systems for the assessment and transmittal of relevant personnel management strategies.

§ 470.203 Eligible parties.

Research may be conducted by the Office of Personnel Management, or under contract or agreement, as appropriate, by:

(a) Federal agencies;

(b) State and local governments;

(c) Institutions of higher education; or

(d) Other public or private institutions or organizations, profit or nonprofit.

§ 470.205 Initiation of research programs.

OPM will announce opportunities for research contracts by issuing Requests for Proposals (RFP's) in accordance with Federal procurement regulations. Unsolicited proposals may be accepted; however the relevance of the proposed research to OPM research needs will determine the acceptability of the proposal.

Subpart C—Regulatory Requirements Pertaining to Demonstration Projects

§ 470.301 Program expectations.

(a) Demonstration projects permit the Office of Personnel Management and Federal agencies to test alternative personnel management concepts in controlled situations to determine the likely effects and ramifications of proposed changes before putting them into general effect. OPM will assist agencies, within available resources, in developing projects which demonstrate new or improved personnel methods.

(b) The demonstration project must be proposed in a research context. The project plan must include a research design which contains:

(1) Measurable goals or objectives;

(2) Acceptable expected results or outcomes;

(3) A description of the procedures, methods and techniques to be demonstrated in achieving the desired goals or objectives;

(4) An evaluation section describing the data collection and analysis procedures to be used to assess the success or failure of the project from a qualitative and quantitative standpoint; and

(5) An itemization of all costs and benefits associated with the project, to the agency, the Government, and the community.

(c) OPM may establish and maintain activities which publish, exchange and apply the results of demonstration projects.

(d) OPM may seek legislation, or to the extent already authorized by law, make changes in regulation to implement permanently successful procedures, techniques, new management knowledge, and materials which improve personnel management programs or techniques.

§470.303 Eligible parties.

(a) Any Federal agency, or groups of two or more Federal agencies, eligible to propose demonstration projects under 5 U.S.C. 4701(a)(1) and 4701(b) may conduct demonstration projects after approval by the Office of Personnel Management and required Congressional and public review.

(b) While only a Federal agency may propose and conduct a demonstration project, the agency may be assisted in the development and evaluation of the project under contract or agreement with public or private institutions and organizations.

§470.305 Submission of proposals for demonstration projects.

(a) OPM will accept project proposals at any time. However, OPM may delay action for a reasonable amount of time on submitted proposals until comparisons can be made with other existing projects or with project proposals of a similar nature not yet received by OPM but known to be under development.

(b) Agencies must submit the project proposal in the form of a project plan to OPM for approval. OPM will prescribe the content of a project plan in its guidance and instructions, which at a minimum will contain the items identified in 5 U.S.C. 4703(b)(1) and 5 CFR 470.301(b).

(c) Agencies will outline, at the time proposed demonstration projects are submitted to OPM for approval, what discussions of the project have been held with labor organizations which have been accorded exclusive recognition for bargaining units containing employees involved in or affected by the proposed demonstration project.

(d) OPM may combine and evaluate similar project proposals received from different agencies as a single project, with the approval of the agencies involved.

§470.307 Notification responsibilities.

(a) 5 U.S.C. 4703 requires notification of tentatively approved demonstration project plans to Congress, employees, labor organizations, and the public.

(b) OPM shall:

(1) Notify each House of the Congress 180 days in advance of the beginning of each project; and

(2) Publish each tentatively approved project plan as a notice in the FEDERAL REGISTER.

(c) Each agency having a tentatively approved project plan shall:

(1) Notify and make available copies of the project plan to:

(i) All employees who may be interested in or affected by the activities of the demonstration project; and

(ii) All labor organizations accorded exclusive recognition for bargaining units which include employees in or affected by the project plan.

(2) Certify to OPM in writing when and how the requirements of §470.307(c)(1) were carried out and document the manner in which it insured that all affected employees were notified.

(3) Observe the consultation and negotiation requirements of 5 U.S.C. 4703 (f) and (g).

§470.309 Public hearing.

(a) *Notice of public hearing.* OPM shall hold a public hearing no less than 30 days after the date of its notice in the FEDERAL REGISTER during which interested persons or organizations may present their written or oral views concerning the proposed demonstration project. The notice of public hearing shall be published in the FEDERAL REGISTER and shall:

(1) State the date, time, place and purpose of the hearing;

(2) Describe briefly the project;

(3) Indicate where more information and a copy of the project plan may be obtained;

(4) State the name and address of the person who will receive written comments from those unable to attend the hearing; and

(5) Indicate the date by which written comments must be received to be considered.

(b) *Nature of public hearing.* The hearing will be informal to encourage effective oral presentations by interested individuals and organizations. The presiding officer, designated by the Director, OPM, shall in his or her reasonable discretion regulate the course of the proceedings and the conduct of those present at the hearing by appropriate means.

(c) A written summary shall be made of the oral evidence.

(d) The record shall be left open for 2 weeks after the conclusion of the hearing to receive additional written data, views, and arguments from the parties participating in the hearing.

§ 470.311 Final project approval.

(a) The Office of Personnel Management will consider all timely relevant oral and written views, arguments, and data before final approval or disapproval of a project plan. OPM may request that the agency modify the tentatively approved project plan before final approval because of comments and data received from the Congress, the public, labor organizations, and affected employees. OPM will not permit the agency to implement the project until all required consultation or negotiation has been completed, including the conclusion of impasse resolution and negotiability disputes.

(b) The Office of Personnel Management shall provide a copy of the final version of the project plan to each House of the Congress at least 90 days in advance of the date the project is to take effect.

(c) Agencies involved in the project shall communicate the content of the final project plan to:

(1) Labor organizations and affected employees; and

(2) Individuals and groups known to be interested in the project's activities.

§ 470.313 Project implementation regulations.

Agencies will prepare demonstration project implementing regulations, as appropriate, to replace Government-wide statutes and regulations waived for the project. Demonstration project implementing regulations issued pursuant to an OPM-approved demonstration project must be approved by OPM and shall have full force and authority pursuant to Title VI of the Civil Service Reform Act of 1978.

§ 470.315 Project modification and extension.

OPM-approved projects permit the testing of alternative personnel systems and procedures in accordance with the provisions of the project plan. The provisions of approved project plans will not be modified, duplicated in organizations not listed in the project plan, or extended by agencies to individuals or groups of employees not included in the project plan without the approval of the Office of Personnel Management. OPM will inform the agency of notification responsibilities under § 470.307. The extent of notification requirements will depend on the nature and extent of the requested project modification.

§ 470.317 Project evaluation.

(a) *Compliance evaluation.* OPM will review the operation of the project periodically to determine its compliance with the requirements of this part and the approved project plan. If OPM determines that an agency is not meeting legal, regulatory, or project plan requirements, it may, as appropriate, direct the agency to take corrective action or terminate the project.

(b) *Results evaluation.* All approved project plans will contain an evaluation section to measure the impact of the project results in relation to its objectives and to determine whether or not permanent changes in law and/or regulation should be considered or proposed. Where the project plan provides for agency evaluation of project results, OPM will review those project evaluation efforts, may conduct evaluations of its own, on a sample basis, to verify results, and may report its own conclusions. If OPM or the agency determines that an experiment is creating a substantial hardship on, or is not in the best interest of, the public, the Federal Government, employees, or eligibles, even though the experiment is being conducted properly, OPM or the agency may jointly or unilaterally terminate the project.

PART 511—CLASSIFICATION UNDER THE GENERAL SCHEDULE

Subpart A—General Provisions

Subpart B—Coverage of the General Schedule

Subparts C–E [Reserved]

Subpart F—Classification Appeals

Subpart G—Effective Dates of Position Classification Actions or Decisions

AUTHORITY: 5 U.S.C. 5115, 5338, 5351.

SOURCE: 33 FR 12445, Sept. 4, 1968, unless otherwise noted.

Subpart A—General Provisions

§511.101 Definitions.

In this part:

(a) *Agency* and *employee* have the meanings given them by section 5102 of title 5, United States Code.

(b) *Class* means all positions which are sufficiently similar as to (1) kind or subject-matter of work, (2) level of difficulty and responsibility, and (3) the qualification requirements of the work, to warrant similar treatment in personnel and pay administration.

(c) *Classification* means the analysis and identification of a position and placing it in a class under the position-classification plan established by OPM under chapter 51 of title 5, United States Code.

(d) *Grade* means all classes of positions which (although different with respect to kind or subject-matter of work) are sufficiently equivalent as to (1) level of difficulty and responsibility, and (2) level of qualification requirements of the work, to warrant their inclusion within one range of rates of basic pay.

(e) *Position* means the work, consisting of the duties and responsibilities, assigned by competent authority for performance by an employee.

Subpart B—Coverage of the General Schedule

§511.201 Coverage of and exclusions from the General Schedule.

This part and chapter 51 of the title 5, United States Code, apply to all positions in the agencies except those specifically excluded by section 5102 of title 5, United States Code. (5 U.S.C. 5102)

(5 U.S.C. 1104; Pub. L. 95–454, sec. 3(5))

[44 FR 54693, Sept. 21, 1979]

§511.202 Authority of agency.

Subject to the provisions of subpart F of this part and §511.203, an agency may determine whether a position is subject to, or is excluded from, chapter 51 of title 5, United States Code, by section 5102(c) (7) and (8) thereof.

§511.203 Exercise of authority.

An agency may exercise the authority under §511.202 only in accordance with guidelines and standards issued by OPM.

Subparts C–E [Reserved]

Subpart F—Classification Appeals

SOURCE: 46 FR 9913, Jan. 30, 1981, unless otherwise noted.

§511.601 Applicability of regulations.

This subpart applies to a request from an employee or an agency for the Office to review the classification of a position subject to chapter 51 of title 5, United States Code, or for the Office to determine whether a position is subject to that chapter.

§511.602 Notification of classification decision.

An employee whose position is reclassified to a lower grade which is based in whole or in part on a classification decision is entitled to a prompt written notice from the agency. This includes employees who are eligible for retained grade or pay. If the reclassification is due to an Office classification certificate issued under the authority of 5 U.S.C. 5110, the agency will also explain the reasons for the reclassification action to the employee. This notice shall inform the employee:

(a) Of his or her right to appeal the classification decision to the agency (if the agency has an established appeal system and it has the authority to review the classification decision), or to the Office as provided in this subpart if such an appeal has not already been made;

(b) Of the time limits within which the employee's appeal must be filed in order to preserve any retroactive benefits under §511.703; and

(c) Any other appeal or grievance rights available under applicable law, rule, regulation or negotiated agreement.

§511.603 Right to appeal.

(a) *Employee appeal.* An employee, or the employee's designated representative acting on behalf of an employee, may request an Office decision as to:

(1) The appropriate occupational series or grade of the employee's official position.

(2) The inclusion under or exclusion from chapter 51 of title 5, United States Code, of the official position by the employee's agency or the Office, except in the case of a position located in the Office of the Architect of the Capitol.

(b) *Agency appeal.* The head of an agency, or an authorized representative, may appeal any classification certificate issued by the Office under sections 5103 or 5110 of title 5, U.S.C., with respect to any position in the agency.

§511.604 Filing an appeal.

(a) *Employee.* An employee may appeal by writing to the Office directly, or by forwarding the appeal through the employing agency.

(b) Referral of an employee appeal to the Office. An agency shall forward, within 60 calendar days of its receipt in the agency, and employee's appeal filed through the agency to the Office when:

(1) The employee has directed the appeal to the Office and the agency's written decision is not favorable; or

(2) The agency is not authorized to act on the employee's appeal; or

(3) The agency has not decided the appeal within the established time period.

§511.605 Time limits.

(a) *Employees.* (1) An employee may submit an appeal of his or her official position at any time. If the employee has suffered a loss in grade or pay, is not entitled to retained grade or pay, and desires retroactive adjustments, the time limits in §511.703 must be observed.

(2) If the employee is appealing an agency decision or an Office classification certificate issued under 5 U.S.C. 5103 or 5110, the employee shall promptly appeal if he or she disagrees with the classification certificate. Employees must meet the time limits provided in §511.703 in order to preserve the right to retroactive adjustment.

(b) *Agency.* An agency may appeal an Office classification certificate issued under authority of section 5103 or 5110 of title 5, United States Code, at any time. Heads of agencies should appeal prior to the implementation date of the certificate if they disagree with the classification rationale.

(c) *Reconsideration.* An employee or agency may request reconsideration of an Office appellate decision. The request must be in writing, and filed not later than 45 calendar days after the decision is issued. This time limit may be waived under exceptional circumstances by either the Director or the Director's designee.

[46 FR 9913, Jan. 30, 1981, as amended at 71 FR 37489, June 30, 2006]

§511.606 Form and content of an appeal.

(a) *Employee appeal.* An employee's appeal shall be in writing, and shall contain the reasons why the employee believes his or her position is erroneously classified, or should be brought under or excluded from chapter 51 of title 5, United States Code. The agency, when forwarding the employee's appeal or when requested by the Office, shall furnish all relevant facts concerning the position and the agency's justification for its classification decision. The agency shall also comment on the information submitted by the employee if requested to do so by the Office. Either the employee or agency may submit relevant information to the Office at any time following the initial filing of an appeal.

(b) *Agency appeal.* An agency's appeal shall be in writing, and shall contain its reasons and justification for requesting a review of the Office's certificate.

(c) *Inspection of the Office's appellate record.* The employee, an employee's representative and the agency will be permitted to inspect the Office's appellate record on request. Agencies will make available to appellants copies of any and all information submitted by the agency to the Office with respect to the appellant's individual appeal.

§511.607 Nonappealable issues.

(a) The following issues are not appealable to the Office under this subpart. Such issues may be reviewed under administrative or negotiated grievance procedures if applicable:

(1) The accuracy of the official position description including the inclusion or exclusion of a major duty in the official position description. When the accuracy of the official position description is questioned by the employee, the employee will be directed to review this matter with his or her supervisor. If management and the employee cannot resolve their differences informally, the accuracy of the position description should be reviewed in accordance with administrative or negotiated grievance procedures. If the accuracy of the position description cannot be resolved in this manner, the Office will decide the appeal on the basis of the actual duties and responsibilities assigned by management and performed by the employee;

(2) An assignment or detail out of the scope of normally performed duties as outlined in the official position description;

(3) The accuracy, consistency or use of agency supplemental classification guides; or,

(4) The title of the position unless a specific title is authorized in a published Office classification standard or guide, or the title reflects a qualification requirement or authorized area of specialization.

(b) The following issues are neither appealable nor reviewable:

(1) The class, grade, or pay system of a position to which the employee is not officially assigned by an official personnel action;

(2) An agency's proposed classification decision;

(3) The class, grade, or pay system of a position to which the employee is detailed or promoted on a time-limited basis, except that employees serving under time-limited promotion for 2 years or more may appeal the classification of their positions to the Office under these procedures.

(4) The classification of the employee's position based on position-to-position comparisons and not standards;

(5) The accuracy of grade level criteria contained in an Office classification guide or standard; or

(6) A classification decision that has been issued by the Office under this subpart when there has been no change in the governing classification standard(s) or the major duties of the position.

[46 FR 9913, Jan. 30, 1981, as amended at 58 FR 59348, Nov. 9, 1993]

§511.608 Employee representatives.

An employee may select a representative of his or her choice to assist in the preparation and presentation of an appeal. An agency may disallow an employee's representative when the individual's activities as a representative would cause a conflict of interest or position; an employee who cannot be released from his or her official duties because of the priority needs of the Government; or an employee whose release would give rise to unreasonable costs to the Government.

§ 511.609 Ascertainment of facts.

The employee, a designated representative, and the agency shall furnish such facts as may be requested by the Office within the time frames specified. The facts shall be in writing when so requested. The Office, in its discretion, may investigate or audit the position. A representative may not participate in OPM on-site audits unless specifically requested to do so by the Office.

§ 511.610 Notification.

The Office shall notify the employee, or a representative if one is designated, and the agency in writing of its decision.

§ 511.611 Cancellation of an employee appeal.

An employee's appeal shall be cancelled and the employee so notified in writing in the following circumstances:

(a) On receipt of the employee's written request for cancellation.

(b) On failure to prosecute, when the employee or the designated representative does not furnish requested information, or proceed with the advancement of the appeal.

The Office may at its discretion reopen a cancelled appeal on a showing that circumstances beyond the control of the employee prevented pursuing the appeal.

§ 511.612 Finality of decision.

An appellate decision made by the Office is final unless reconsidered by the Office. There is no further right of appeal. The Office may reconsider a decision at its discretion. The decision shall constitute a certificate which is mandatory and binding on all administrative, certifying, payroll, disbursing, and accounting officials of the Government. Agencies shall review their own classification decisions for identical, similar or related positions to insure consistency with the Office's certificate.

§ 511.613 Appeals reconsideration by the Office.

The Office may, at its discretion, reopen and reconsider a certificate issued under this subpart.

(a) Requests which contain new and material information, or disagreements over the significance of information, will be remanded to the Director's designee for a decision.

(b) The Office may reopen and reconsider a decision only when written argument or evidence is presented which establishes a reasonable doubt concerning the technical accuracy of the decision.

[71 FR 37489, June 30, 2006]

§ 511.614 Review by the Director.

The Director may, at his or her discretion, reopen and reconsider any decision when written argument or evidence is submitted which tends to establish that:

(a) The previous decision involves an erroneous interpretation of law or regulation, or a misapplication of established policy:

(b) The previous decision is of a precedential nature involving a new or unreviewed policy consideration that may have effects beyond the actual case at hand, or is otherwise of such an exceptional nature as to merit the personal attention of the Director.

§ 511.615 Temporary compliance authority.

Agencies may use temporary or conditional compliance action, e.g., a temporary promotion or a temporary reassignment when available, if:

(a) A position has been certified by the Office under either section 5110 or 5112 of title 5, United States Code;

(b) The certificate has not been suspended; and,

(c) The agency or employee has requested reconsideration.

This authority will not be used if the position has been downgraded and the employee is entitled to retained grade under section 5362 of title 5, United States Code.

§511.616 Availability of information.

(a) The Office, upon a request which identifies the individual from whose file the information is sought, shall disclose the following information from an appeal file to a member of the public, except when the disclosure would constitute a clearly unwarranted invasion of personal privacy:

(1) Confirmation of the name of the individual from whose file the information is sought and the names of the other parties concerned;

(2) The status of the appeal;

(3) The results of the appeal (*i.e.*, proper title, pay plan, series, and grade);

(4) the classification requested (*i.e.*, title, pay plan, series, and grade); and

(5) With the consent of the parties concerned, other reasonably identified information from the file.

(b) The Office will disclose to the parties concerned the information contained in an appeal file in proceedings under this part. For the purposes of this section, *the parties concerned* means the Government employee or former Government employee involved in the proceedings, his or her representative designated in writing, and the representative of the agency or the Office involved in the proceeding.

(5 U.S.C. 552, Freedom of Information Act, Pub. L. 92–502)

[50 FR 3313, Jan. 24, 1985]

Subpart G—Effective Dates of Position Classification Actions or Decisions

SOURCE: 46 FR 9915, Jan. 30, 1981, unless otherwise noted.

§511.701 Effective dates generally.

(a) *Agency classification actions.* (1) A classification action is a determination to establish or change the title, series, grade or pay system of a position based on application of published position classification standards or guides. This is a position action.

(i) The effective date of a position action taken by an agency shall be the date an official with properly delegated authority approves (certifies) the proposed classification. This is accomplished when the authorized official(s) signs the allocation of the position.

(ii) The effective date of a position action may be extended to correspond with the effective date of the personnel action when:

(A) The position is being changed to lower grade or pay; and

(B) The employee occupying the position is eligible for retained grade or pay under 5 U.S.C. 5362–5363.

(2) A position action is implemented by a personnel action. The personnel action must occur within a reasonable period of time following the date of the position action.

(3) If the position action requires a personnel action which will result in a loss of grade or pay to the occupant of the position, the agency must advise the employee, in writing, of the position action and the proposed date of the personnel action. This notice shall be issued prior to taking a personnel action.

(4) Except as provided in §511.703, classification actions may not be made retroactive.

(b) *Office of Personnel Management's classification decision.* (1) The effective date of a classification decision made by means of a certificate issued under the authority of section 5110, title 5, United States Code is not earlier than the date of the certificate, and not later than the beginning of the fourth pay period following the date of the certificate, unless a subsequent date is specifically stated in the certificate. Except as otherwise provided by this paragraph the filing of an appeal of such a certificate does not delay its effective date.

(2) The implementation of the certificate may be suspended when it is determined before its effective date that a review of the classification decision is warranted and suspension is desirable. The determination to suspend implementation may be made by the Director or the Director's designee. Suspending the implementation of a certificate does not automatically change the effective date except when the certificate requires that the grade or pay of the position be reduced and the employee is not entitled to retained grade or pay.

(3) When the original decision requires that the grade or pay of the position be reduced and the employee is not entitled to retained grade or pay the reviewing authority shall issue a new certificate if it sustains the original decision. Since demotions cannot be made retroactive, the effective date of the new certificate shall be not earlier than the date of the certificate, and not later than the beginning of the fourth pay period after the date of the certificate unless a subsequent date is specifically stated in the certificate.

[46 FR 9915, Jan. 30, 1981, as amended at 58 FR 65534, Dec. 15, 1993; 71 FR 37489, June 30, 2006]

§ 511.702 Agency or Office classification appeal decisions.

(a) Subject to § 511.703, the effective date of a change in the classification of a position resulting from a classification appeal decision by either an agency or the Office is not earlier than the date of the decision and not later than the beginning of the fourth pay period following the date of the decision, except when a subsequent date is specifically provided in the decision.

(b) The implementation of the decision may be suspended by the Office when it determines before the effective date that a review of the decision is warranted. The determination to suspend implementation may be made by the Director or the Director's designee. Suspending the implementation does not change the effective date of the decision except when the original decision requires that the grade or pay of the position be reduced and the employee is not entitled to grade or pay retention.

(c) When the original decision requires that the grade or pay of the position be reduced and the employee is not entitled to grade or pay retention, the reviewing authority, if sustaining the original decision, shall issue a new certificate and the effective date of the new certificate shall be not earlier than the date of the new decision and not later than the beginning of the fourth pay period following the date of the new decision, unless a subsequent date is specifically stated in the new decision.

[46 FR 9915, Jan. 30, 1981, as amended at 71 FR 37489, June 30, 2006]

§ 511.703 Retroactive effective date.

(a) *Applicability.* A retroactive effective date may be required only if the employee is wrongfully demoted.

(b) *Downgrading.* (1) The effective date of a classification appellate certificate or agency appellate decision can be retroactive only if it corrects a classification action which resulted in a loss of grade or pay. In order for the decision to be made retroactive, the employee must file the initial request for review with either the agency or the Office not later than 15 calendar days after the effective date of the reclassification action.

(2) However, if the appellate decision raises the grade of the position above the original grade, retroactivity will apply only to the extent of restoration to the original grade.

(3) The right to a retroactive effective date provided by this section is preserved on subsequent appeals from an agency or Office classification decision when the subsequent appeal is filed not later than 15 calendar days following receipt of written notification of a final agency administrative decision or 15 calendar days after the effective date of the action taken as a result of the classification decision, whichever is later.

(c) *Grade change based on new duties and responsibilities.* Retroactivity may be based only on duties and responsibilities existing at the time of demotion and cannot be based on duties and responsibilities assigned later.

(d) *Retroactivity when time limits are extended.* The right to a retroactive effective date provided by this section may be preserved at the discretion of the Office, on a showing by the employee that he or she was not notified of the applicable time limit and was not otherwise aware of it, or that circumstances beyond his or her control prevented filing an appeal within the prescribed time limit.

PART 530—PAY RATES AND SYSTEMS (GENERAL)

AUTHORITY: 5 U.S.C. 5305 and 5307; subpart C also issued under 5 U.S.C. 5338, sec. 4 of the Performance Management and Recognition System Termination Act of 1993 (Pub. L. 103–89), 107 Stat. 981, and sec. 1918 of Public Law 111–84, 123 Stat. 2619.

Subpart A [Reserved]

Subpart B—Aggregate Limitation on Pay

SOURCE: 69 FR 70360, Dec. 6, 2004, unless otherwise noted.

§ 530.201 Purpose.

This subpart establishes regulations for limiting an employee's aggregate annual compensation. An employee's aggregate compensation received in any given calendar year may not exceed the rate of pay for level I of the Executive Schedule or the rate payable to the Vice President at the end of the calendar year, whichever is applicable to the employee based on the certification status under 5 CFR part 430, subpart D, of the performance appraisal system covering that employee. These regulations must be applied in conjunction with 5 U.S.C. 5307.

§ 530.202 Definitions.

In this subpart:

Agency means an executive agency as defined at 5 U.S.C. 105.

Aggregate compensation means the total of—

(1) Basic pay received as an employee of the executive branch or as an employee outside the executive branch to whom the General Schedule applies;

(2) Premium pay under 5 U.S.C. chapter 53, subchapter IV;

(3) Premium pay under 5 U.S.C. chapter 55, subchapter V;

(4) Incentive awards and performance-based cash awards under 5 U.S.C. chapters 45 and 53;

(5) Recruitment and relocation incentives under 5 U.S.C. 5753 and retention incentives under 5 U.S.C. 5754;

(6) Extended assignment incentives under 5 U.S.C. 5757;

(7) Supervisory differentials under 5 U.S.C. 5755;

(8) Post differentials under 5 U.S.C. 5925;

(9) Danger pay allowances under 5 U.S.C. 5928;

(10) Post differentials based on environmental conditions for employees stationed in nonforeign areas under 5 U.S.C. 5941(a)(2);

(11) Physicians' comparability allowances under 5 U.S.C. 5948;

(12) Continuation of pay under 5 U.S.C. 8118;

(13) Lump-sum payments in excess of the aggregate limitation on pay as required by § 530.204; and

(14) Other similar payments authorized under title 5, United States Code, excluding—

(i) Overtime pay under the Fair Labor Standards Act of 1938, as amended, and 5 CFR part 551;

(ii) Severance pay under 5 U.S.C. 5595;

(iii) Lump-sum payments for accumulated and accrued annual leave upon separation under 5 U.S.C. 5551 or 5552;

(iv) Back pay awarded to an employee under 5 U.S.C. 5596 because of an unjustified personnel action;

(v) Student loan repayments under 5 U.S.C. 5379; and

(vi) Nonforeign area cost-of-living allowances under 5 U.S.C. 5941(a)(1).

Aggregate limitation means the limitation on aggregate compensation received in any given calendar year as established by 5 U.S.C. 5307. For an executive branch employee (including employees in Senior Executive Service positions paid under 5 U.S.C. 5383 and employees in senior-level or scientific or professional positions paid under 5 U.S.C. 5376), a General Schedule employee in the legislative branch, or General Schedule employee in the judicial branch (excluding those paid under 28 U.S.C. 332(f), 603, and 604), the limitation on aggregate compensation is equal to the rate for level I of the Executive Schedule in effect at the end of the applicable calendar year. For an employee in a Senior Executive Service position paid under 5 U.S.C. 5383 and an employee in a senior-level or scientific or professional position paid under 5 U.S.C. 5376 covered by an applicable performance appraisal system that has been certified under 5 CFR part 430, subpart D, the limitation on aggregate compensation is equal to the total annual compensation payable to the Vice President under 3 U.S.C. 104 at the end of a calendar year.

Basic pay means the total amount of pay received at a rate fixed by law or administrative action for the position held by an employee, including any special rate under 5 CFR part 530, subpart C, or any locality-based comparability payment under 5 CFR part 531, subpart F, or other similar payment under other legal authority, before any deductions. *Basic pay* includes night and environmental differentials for prevailing rate employees under 5 U.S.C. 5343(f) and 5 CFR 532.511. *Basic pay* excludes additional pay of any other kind.

Discretionary payment means a payment an agency has discretion to make to an employee. Payments that are authorized to be made to an employee under the terms of a service agreement or preauthorized to be made to an employee at a regular fixed rate each pay period are not *discretionary payments.*

Employee has the meaning given that term in 5 U.S.C. 2105.

Estimated aggregate compensation means the agency's projection of the aggregate compensation an employee actually would receive during a calendar year but for application of the aggregate limitation to future payments. This projection must be based upon known factors. Estimated aggregate compensation includes—

(1) The total amount of basic pay the employee will receive during the calendar year;

(2) Any lump-sum payment of excess amounts from a previous calendar year, as described in § 530.204;

(3) The total amount of nondiscretionary payments the employee would be entitled to receive during the calendar year; and

(4) The total amount of discretionary payments the employee would be authorized to receive during the calendar year.

[69 FR 70360, Dec. 6, 2004, as amended at 70 FR 25739, May 13, 2005; 72 FR 67837, Dec. 3, 2007]

§ 530.203 Administration of aggregate limitation on pay.

(a) Except as provided in paragraph (b) of this section, no executive branch employee or General Schedule employee in the legislative branch (or General Schedule employee in the judicial branch, excluding those paid under 28 U.S.C. 332(f), 603, and 604), may receive any allowance, differential, bonus, award, or other similar cash payment under title 5, United States Code, in any calendar year which, in combination with the employee's basic pay (whether received under title 5, United States Code, or otherwise), would cause the employee's aggregate compensation to exceed the rate for level I of the Executive Schedule on the last day of that calendar year (*i.e.,* the aggregate limitation).

(b)(1) Subject to paragraph (b)(2) of this section, an employee in a Senior Executive Service position paid under 5 U.S.C. 5383 and an employee in a senior-level or scientific or professional position paid under 5 U.S.C. 5376 may not receive any allowance, differential, bonus, award, or other similar cash payment under title 5, United States Code, in any calendar year which, in combination with the employee's basic pay, would cause the employee's aggregate compensation to exceed the rate of pay for level I of the Executive Schedule.

(2) An employee covered by a performance appraisal system that has been certified under 5 CFR part 430, subpart D, may not receive any allowance, differential, bonus, award, or other similar cash payment under title 5, United States Code, in any calendar year which, in combination with the employee's basic pay, would cause the employee's aggregate compensation to exceed the total annual compensation payable to the Vice President under 3 U.S.C. 104 on the last day of that calendar year (*i.e.*, the aggregate limitation).

(3) An agency must make corrective actions as provided in paragraphs (g) and (h) of this section if the agency underestimated or overestimated an employee's aggregate compensation in a calendar year as a result of receiving or losing certification of its applicable performance appraisal system under 5 CFR part 430, subpart D.

(c) The aggregate limitations described in paragraphs (a) and (b) of this section apply to the aggregate compensation an employee actually received during the calendar year without regard to when the compensation was earned.

(d) When an agency authorizes a discretionary payment for an employee, the agency must defer any portion of such payment that, when added to the estimated aggregate compensation the employee is projected to receive, would cause the employee's aggregate compensation during the calendar year to exceed the applicable aggregate limitation. Any portion of a discretionary payment deferred under this paragraph must be available for payment as provided in § 530.204. When a discretionary payment is authorized but not required to be paid in the current calendar year, an agency official's decision to set the payment date in the next calendar year is not considered a deferral under this paragraph.

(e) An agency may not defer or discontinue nondiscretionary payments for any period of time to make a discretionary payment that would otherwise cause an employee's pay to exceed the applicable aggregate limitation. An agency may not defer or discontinue basic pay under any circumstance.

(f) If, after an agency defers discretionary payments as required by paragraph (d) of this section, the estimated aggregate compensation to which an employee is entitled exceeds the applicable aggregate limitation, the agency must defer all nondiscretionary payments (other than basic pay) as necessary to avoid payments in excess of that limitation. An agency must defer all nondiscretionary payments at the time when otherwise continuing to pay such payments would cause an employee's estimated aggregate compensation for that calendar year to exceed the applicable aggregate limitation. An agency must pay any portion of a nondiscretionary payment deferred under this paragraph at a later date, as provided in § 530.204.

(g)(1) If an agency determines that it underestimated an employee's aggregate compensation at an earlier date in the calendar year, or the aggregate limitation applicable to the employee is reduced during the calendar year, the sum of the employee's remaining payments of basic pay may exceed the difference between the aggregate compensation the employee has actually received to date in that calendar year and the applicable aggregate limitation. In such cases, the employee will become indebted to the Federal Government for any amount paid in excess of the applicable aggregate limitation. The head of the agency may waive the debt under 5 U.S.C. 5584, if warranted.

(2) To the extent that any excess amount is attributable to amounts that should have been deferred and would have been payable at the beginning of the next calendar year, an agency must extinguish the excess amount on January 1 of the next calendar year. As part of the correction of the error, the agency must deem the excess amount to have been paid on January 1 of the next calendar year (when the debt was extinguished) as if it were a deferred excess payment, as

described in § 530.204, and must consider this deemed deferred excess payment to be part of the employee's aggregate compensation for the new calendar year.

(h) If an agency determines that it overestimated an employee's aggregate compensation at an earlier date in the calendar year, which caused the agency to defer payments unnecessarily under this section, or the aggregate limitation applicable to the employee is increased during the calendar year, the agency may make appropriate corrective payments to the employee during the calendar year, notwithstanding § 530.204.

[69 FR 70360, Dec. 6, 2004, as amended at 70 FR 25740, May 13, 2005]

§ 530.204 Payment of excess amounts.

(a) An agency must pay the amounts that were deferred because they were in excess of the aggregate limitation (as described in § 530.203) as a lump-sum payment at the beginning of the following calendar year, except as otherwise provided in this section. This payment is part of the employee's aggregate compensation for the new calendar year.

(b) If a lump-sum payment under paragraph (a) of this section causes an employee's estimated aggregate compensation to exceed the aggregate limitation in the current calendar year, an agency must consider only the employee's basic pay that is expected to be paid in the current year in determining the extent to which the lump-sum payment may be paid. An agency must defer all other payments, as provided in § 530.203, in order to pay as much of the lump-sum excess amount as possible. Any payments deferred under this paragraph, including any portion of the lump-sum excess amount that was not payable, are payable at the beginning of the next calendar year, as provided in paragraph (a) of this section.

(c) If an employee transfers to another agency, the gaining agency is responsible for making any lump-sum payment required by paragraph (a) of this section. The previous employing agency must provide the gaining agency with documentation regarding the employee's excess amount, as provided in § 530.205. The previous employing agency must provide a fund transfer equal to the total cost of the lump-sum payment to the gaining agency through the Department of the Treasury's Intra-Governmental Payment and Collection System. If an employee leaves Federal service, the employing agency is responsible for making the lump-sum payment to the employee as provided in paragraph (d) of this section.

(d) An agency must pay any excess amount regardless of the calendar year limitation under the following conditions:

(1) If an employee dies, the employing agency must pay the entire excess amount as part of the settlement of accounts, in accordance with 5 U.S.C. 5582.

(2) If an employee separates from Federal service, the employing agency must pay the entire excess amount following a 30-day break in service. If the individual is reemployed in the Federal service within the same calendar year as the separation, any previous payment of an excess amount must be considered part of that year's aggregate compensation for the purpose of applying the aggregate limitation for the remainder of the calendar year.

§ 530.205 Records.

An agency must maintain appropriate records to administer this subpart and must transfer such records to any agency to which an employee may transfer. An agency must make such records available to any agency that may employ the employee later during the same calendar year. An agency's records must document the source of any deferred excess amount remaining to the employee's credit at the time of separation from the agency. In the case of an employee who separates from Federal service for at least 30 days, the agency records also must document any payment of a deferred excess amount made by the agency after separation.

Subpart C—Special Rate Schedules for Recruitment and Retention

SOURCE: 70 FR 31287, May 31, 2005, unless otherwise noted.

GENERAL PROVISIONS

§530.301 Purpose and applicability.

(a) *Purpose.* This subpart contains OPM regulations implementing 5 U.S.C. 5305, which authorizes the establishment of special rates of pay for Federal employees in executive agencies to address significant recruitment or retention problems. This subpart also contains rules for determining an employee's rate of pay when a special rate schedule is established, increased, decreased, or discontinued, or when conditions for coverage under a special rate schedule are changed. All other pay actions for special rate employees are governed by the pay-setting rules in 5 CFR parts 531 and 536.

(b) *Applicability.* Except as explained in §530.303(a), this subpart applies only to GS employees.

§530.302 Definitions.

In this subpart:

Agency means an executive agency as defined in 5 U.S.C. 105.

Authorized agency official means the head of the agency or an official who is authorized to act for the head of the agency in the matter concerned.

Employee has the meaning given that term in 5 U.S.C. 2105.

General Schedule or *GS* means the classification and pay system established under 5 U.S.C. chapter 51 and subchapter III of chapter 53. It also refers to the pay schedule of GS rates established under 5 U.S.C. 5332, as adjusted under 5 U.S.C. 5303 or other law (including GS rates payable to GM employees). Law enforcement officers (LEOs) receiving LEO special base rates are covered by the GS classification and pay system, but receive higher base rates of pay in lieu of GS rates at grades GS–3 through GS–10.

GM employee has the meaning given that term in 5 CFR 531.203.

GS rate means a rate of basic pay within the General Schedule, excluding any LEO special base rate and additional pay of any kind such as locality payments or special rate supplements. A rate payable to a GM employee is considered a GS rate.

Highest applicable rate range means the rate range applicable to an employee's position that provides the highest rates of basic pay, excluding any retained rates. For example, a rate range of special rates may exceed an applicable locality rate range. In certain circumstances, the *highest applicable rate range* may consist of two types of pay rates from different pay schedules—e.g., a range where special rates (based on a fixed dollar supplement) are higher in the lower portion of the range and locality rates are higher in the higher portion of the range.

Law enforcement officer or *LEO* has the meaning given that term in 5 CFR 550.103.

LEO special base rate means a special base rate established for GS law enforcement officers at grades GS–3 through GS–10 under section 403 of the Federal Employees Pay Comparability Act of 1990 (section 529 of Pub. L. 101–509, November 5, 1990, as amended) which is used in lieu of a GS rate.

Locality payment has the meaning given that term in 5 CFR 531.602.

Locality rate means a GS rate or an LEO special base rate, if applicable, plus any applicable locality payment.

Official worksite means the official location of an employee's position of record as determined under 5 CFR 531.605. *Official worksite* is synonymous with the term "official duty station" as used in 5 U.S.C. 5305(i).

OPM means the Office of Personnel Management.

Pay schedule means a set of rate ranges established for GS employees under a single authority—*i.e.*, the General Schedule, an LEO special base rate schedule (for grades GS–3 through 10), a locality rate schedule based on GS rates, a locality rate schedule based on LEO special base rates (for grades GS–3 through 10), a special rate schedule under this subpart, or a similar schedule under 38 U.S.C. 7455. A pay schedule applies to or covers a defined category of employees based on established coverage conditions (e.g., official worksite, occupation). A pay schedule is considered to apply to or cover an employee who meets the established coverage conditions even when a rate under that schedule is not currently payable to the employee because of a higher pay entitlement under another pay schedule.

Position of record means an employee's official position (defined by grade, occupational series, employing agency, LEO status, and any other condition that determines coverage under a pay schedule (other than official worksite)), as documented on the employee's most recent Notification of Personnel Action (Standard Form 50 or equivalent) and current position description. A position to which an employee is temporarily detailed is not documented as a position of record. For an employee whose change in official position is followed within 3 workdays by a reduction in force resulting in the employee's separation before he or she is required to report for duty in the new position, the position of record in effect immediately before the position change is deemed to remain the position of record through the date of separation.

Rate of basic pay means the rate of pay fixed by law or administrative action for the position held by an employee before any deductions, including a GS rate, an LEO special base rate, a locality rate, a special rate under this subpart or a similar rate under 38 U.S.C. 7455, or a retained rate, but excluding additional pay of any other kind.

Rate range or *range* means the range of rates of basic pay for a grade within an established pay schedule, excluding any retained rate. A rate range may consist of GS rates, LEO special base rates, locality rates, special rates, or similar rates under other legal authority.

Retained rate means a rate above the maximum rate of the rate range applicable to the employee which is payable under 5 CFR part 536 or, for a former member of the Senior Executive Service, under 5 CFR 359.705.

Special rate means a rate of pay within a special rate schedule established under this subpart.

Special rate schedule means a pay schedule established under this subpart to provide higher rates of pay for specified categories of GS positions or employees at one or more grades. An increased or decreased special rate schedule refers to an increase or decrease in one or more rate ranges within that schedule.

Special rate supplement means the portion of a special rate paid above an employee's GS rate. However, for a law enforcement officer receiving an LEO special base rate who is also entitled to a special rate, the special rate supplement equals the portion of the special rate paid above the officer's LEO special base rate. When a special rate schedule covers both LEO positions and other positions, the value of the special rate supplement will be less for law enforcement officers receiving an LEO special base rate (since that rate is higher than the corresponding GS rate). The payable amount of a special rate supplement is subject to the Executive Schedule level IV limitation on special rates, as provided in § 530.304(a).

[70 FR 31287, May 31, 2005, as amended at 73 FR 66151, Nov. 7, 2008]

§ 530.303 Coverage.

(a) Under 5 U.S.C. 5305, OPM may establish special rates for employees paid under a statutory pay system (as defined in 5 U.S.C. 5302(1)) or any other pay system established by or under Federal statute for civilian positions in the executive branch. Special rates apply only to GS employees unless the approved schedule coverage criteria specifically state otherwise. OPM will establish special rate schedules covering employees under a non-GS pay system only at the request of the agency responsible for administering that system. For employees covered by a non-GS pay system, the responsible agency is subject to the requirements in 5 U.S.C. 5305. To the extent the statutory or regulatory provisions governing the non-GS pay system differ from the regulatory provisions of this subpart, the responsible agency must follow policies that are consistent as possible with this subpart.

(b) An employee's coverage under a special rate schedule is subject to the coverage conditions established by OPM for that schedule, except as provided in paragraph (c) of this section.

The coverage conditions for a special rate schedule may be based on occupation, grade, employing agency, geographic location of official worksite, or other factors OPM may determine to be appropriate. An agency determination as to whether an employee meets the coverage conditions for a special rate schedule must be based on the employee's position of record and official worksite. An agency also may be required to consider other employee-specific factors established by OPM to determine special rate coverage, such as special qualifications or certifications.

(c) An agency must pay the applicable special rate to any employee who meets the coverage conditions established by OPM with respect to a special rate schedule unless an authorized agency official determines that a category of employees of the agency will not be covered by a proposed or existing special rate schedule, subject to the following requirements:

(1) An authorized agency official may determine that a category of employees of the agency will not be covered by a special rate request or a proposed new special rate schedule. The official must provide written notice to OPM that identifies the specific category or categories of employees who will not be covered by the special rate schedule. The notice must be received by OPM before the effective date of the new special rate schedule.

(2) An authorized agency official may remove a category of employees of the agency from coverage under an existing special rate schedule. The official must provide written notice to OPM that identifies the specific category or categories of employees who will not be covered by the special rate schedule. The loss of coverage under a special rate schedule will become effective on the first day of the first pay period beginning on or after the date of the notice to OPM.

(d) An employee covered by a special rate schedule is not entitled to a special rate for any purpose with respect to any period during which the employee is entitled to a higher rate of basic pay under any other legal authority. For example, an employee is not entitled to a special rate if he or she is entitled to a higher locality rate or a retained rate.

§ 530.304 Establishing or increasing special rates.

(a) OPM may increase the minimum rates of pay otherwise payable to a category of employees in one or more areas or locations, grades or levels, occupational groups, series, classes, or subdivisions thereof, when it is necessary to address existing or likely significant recruitment or retention difficulties. OPM will consider the circumstances listed in paragraph (b) of this section and the factors listed in § 530.306 when evaluating the need for special rates. When OPM establishes a minimum special rate under this authority, corresponding increases also may be made in one or more of the remaining rates of the affected grade or level. For any given grade, a minimum special rate may not exceed the maximum rate of basic pay for the rate range (excluding any locality rate, other special rate, or similar payment under other legal authority) by more than 30 percent. A special rate may not exceed the rate for level IV of the Executive Schedule.

(b) The circumstances considered by OPM in evaluating the need for special rates are the following:

(1) Rates of pay offered by non-Federal employers which are significantly higher than those payable by the Government within the area, location, occupational group, or other category of positions under GS pay system;

(2) The remoteness of the area or location involved;

(3) The undesirability of the working conditions or the nature of the work involved (including exposure to toxic substances or other occupational hazards);

(4) Locality pay authorized under 5 U.S.C. 5304 for the area involved;

(5) A nonforeign area cost-of-living allowance authorized under 5 U.S.C. 5941(a)(1) for the area involved; or

(6) Any other circumstances OPM considers appropriate.

(c) In setting the level of special rates within a rate range for a category of employees, OPM will compute the special rate supplement by adding a fixed dollar amount or a fixed percentage to all GS rates within that range, except that an alternate method may be used—

(1) For grades GS–1 and GS–2, where within-grade increases vary throughout the range; and

(2) In the nonforeign areas listed in 5 CFR 591.205 for special rate schedules established before January 1, 2012.

(d) If OPM establishes a special rate schedule that covers only law enforcement officers, OPM may compute the special rate supplement for grades GS–3 through 10 as a fixed percentage of LEO special base rates instead of GS rates. With respect to such a schedule, references to GS rates in § 530.307 are deemed to be references to LEO special base rates.

(e) Using its authority in section 1918(a)(1) of the Non-Foreign Area Retirement Equity Assurance Act of 2009 in combination with its authority under 5 U.S.C. 5305, OPM may establish a separate special rate schedule for a category of employees who are in GS positions covered by a nonforeign area special rate schedule in effect on January 1, 2012, and who are employed in a nonforeign area before an OPM-specified effective date. Such a separate schedule may be established if the existing special rate schedule is being reduced. An employee's coverage under the separate special rate schedule is contingent on the employee being continuously employed in a covered GS position in the nonforeign area after the OPM-specified effective date. Such a separate special rate schedule must be designed to provide temporary pay protection and be phased out over time until all affected employees are covered under the pay schedule that would otherwise apply to the category of employees in question.

[70 FR 31287, May 31, 2005, as amended at 73 FR 66151, Nov. 7, 2008; 76 FR 68633, Nov. 7, 2011]

§ 530.305 Agency requests for new or increased special rates.

(a) An agency may request that a special rate schedule be established or increased or that its employees be covered by an existing special rate schedule at any time. An authorized agency official in the agency headquarters office must submit to OPM any request to establish or increase special rates for a category of agency employees. The request must include a certification by the authorized agency official that the requested special rates are necessary to ensure adequate staffing levels to accomplish the agency's mission.

(b) The authorized agency official is responsible for submitting complete supporting data for any request for new or higher special rates. OPM may require that the supporting data include a survey of prevailing non-Federal pay rates in the relevant labor market.

(c) OPM may coordinate an agency special rate request with other agencies that have similar categories of employees. OPM may designate a lead agency to assist in coordinating the collection of relevant data. Each affected agency is responsible for submitting complete supporting data upon request to OPM or the lead agency, as appropriate, unless the agency determines that a category of its employees will not be covered by the proposed special rate schedule, as provided in § 530.303(c).

§ 530.306 Evaluating agency requests for new or increased special rates.

(a) In evaluating agency requests for new or increased special rates, OPM may consider the following factors:

(1) The number of existing vacant positions and the length of time they have been vacant;

(2) The number of employees who have quit (*i.e.*, voluntarily left Federal service), including, when available, a subcount of the number of employees who quit to take a comparable position offering higher pay;

(3) Evidence to support a conclusion that recruitment or retention problems likely will develop (if such problems do not already exist) or will worsen;

(4) The number of vacancies an agency tried to fill, compared to the number of hires and offers made;

(5) The nature of the existing labor market;

(6) The degree to which an agency has considered and used other available pay flexibilities to alleviate staffing problems, including the superior qualifications and special needs pay-setting

authority in 5 CFR 531.212 and recruitment, relocation, and retention incentives under 5 CFR part 575;

(7) The degree to which an agency has considered relevant non-pay solutions to staffing problems, such as conducting an aggressive recruiting program, using appropriate appointment authorities, redesigning jobs, establishing training programs, and improving working conditions;

(8) The effect of the staffing problem on the agency's mission;

(9) The level of non-Federal rates paid for comparable positions. Data on non-Federal salary rates may be supplemented, if appropriate, by data on Federal salary rates for comparable positions established under a non-GS pay system; and

(10) The level of any locality pay authorized under 5 U.S.C. 5304 and any nonforeign area cost-of-living allowance authorized under 5 U.S.C. 5941(a)(1) for the area involved.

(b) In determining the level at which to set special rates, OPM may consider the following factors:

(1) The pay levels that, in OPM's judgment, are necessary to recruit or retain an adequate number of qualified employees based on OPM's findings with respect to the factors set forth in paragraph (a) of this section;

(2) The dollar costs that will be incurred if special rates are not authorized;

(3) The level of pay for comparable positions; and

(4) The need to provide for a reasonable progression in pay from lower grade levels to higher grade levels to avoid pay alignment problems (e.g., such as might result from applying the two-step promotion rule in 5 U.S.C. 5334(b)).

(c) No one factor or combination of factors specified in paragraph (a) or (b) of this section requires OPM to establish or increase special rates or to set special rates at any given level.

[70 FR 31287, May 31, 2005, as amended at 76 FR 68634, Nov. 7, 2011]

§ 530.307 OPM review and adjustment of special rate schedules.

(a) OPM may review an established special rate schedule at any time to determine whether that schedule should be increased, decreased, or discontinued, taking into account the circumstances listed in § 530.304(b) and the factors listed in § 530.306 that led to establishing the schedule. An authorized agency official may request that OPM conduct such a review of one or more special rate schedules.

(b) OPM may designate lead agencies to assist in the review of designated special rate schedules and to coordinate the collection of relevant data. Each affected agency is responsible for submitting complete supporting data upon request to OPM or the lead agency, as appropriate.

(c) OPM will adjust a special rate schedule by determining the amount of the special rate supplement to be paid on top of the current GS rate for each rate range within the schedule. OPM will determine the extent to which special rate supplements are to be adjusted (increased or decreased), if at all, and when the special rate supplements are to be adjusted. As provided in 5 U.S.C. 5305(d), special rate schedule adjustments made by OPM have the force and effect of statute.

(d)(1) For special rate schedules computed by applying a fixed-percentage supplement on top of each GS rate within a rate range, OPM may require that a change in the underlying GS rate automatically results in an adjusted special rate schedule, unless OPM determines that an adjustment in the supplement percentage is appropriate for one or more special rate schedules.

(2) For special rate schedules computed by applying a fixed-dollar supplement on top of each GS rate within a rate range, OPM may require that special rate supplements generally be adjusted to reflect the increase in GS rates, unless OPM determines that a different adjustment is appropriate for one or more special rate schedules.

(e) If OPM determines that a special rate schedule, or a rate range within a special rate schedule, is no longer needed to ensure satisfactory recruitment or retention of qualified employees, OPM may discontinue the schedule or rate range. Consistent with § 530.303(d), if all employees and positions covered by a special rate schedule or rate range are entitled to a higher rate of basic pay, the schedule or rate range (as applicable) will be automatically discontinued.

(f) OPM may change the established conditions for coverage under a special rate schedule at any time based on a reevaluation of the circumstances and factors that led to establishing the schedule. Expansion of coverage is equivalent to establishing a special rate schedule for a category of affected employees. Reduction of coverage is the equivalent of discontinuing a special rate schedule for a category of affected employees.

(g) When a special rate schedule is adjusted or discontinued, or when there is a change in a schedule's coverage criteria, the rate of pay for affected employees must be set as provided in §§ 530.321 through 530.323.

§ 530.308 Treatment of special rate as basic pay.

Except as otherwise specifically provided under other legal authority, a special rate is considered a rate of basic pay only for the following purposes:

(a) The purposes for which a locality rate is considered to be a rate of basic pay in computing other payments or benefits to the extent provided by 5 CFR 531.610, except as otherwise provided in paragraphs (b) and (c) of this section;

(b) Computation of foreign area post differentials under 5 U.S.C. 5925(a) and danger pay allowances under 5 U.S.C. 5928; and

(c) Application of pay administration provisions for prevailing rate employees which consider rates of basic pay under the GS pay system in setting pay (except as otherwise provided in 5 CFR part 532), subject to the requirement that, if the employee's actual special rate would not apply at the official worksite for the prevailing rate position, a special rate may be used only if it is a corresponding special rate on a special rate schedule that would cover the employee if his or her GS position of record were located at the same official worksite as the prevailing rate position, consistent with the geographic conversion rule in 5 CFR 531.205.

[70 FR 31287, May 31, 2005, as amended at 76 FR 68634, Nov. 7, 2011]

§ 530.309 Miscellaneous provisions.

(a) A special rate may be paid only for those hours for which an employee is in a pay status.

(b) A pay increase caused by an employee becoming entitled to a new or higher special rate supplement is not an equivalent increase in pay within the meaning of 5 U.S.C. 5335. (See 5 CFR 531.407(c).)

(c) A special rate is included in an employee's *total remuneration,* as defined in 5 CFR 551.511(b), and *straight time rate of pay,* as defined in 5 CFR 551.512(b), for the purpose of overtime pay computations under the Fair Labor Standards Act of 1938, as amended.

(d) Consistent with § 530.308, the reduction or termination of an employee's special rate supplement in accordance with the requirements of this subpart is not an adverse action under 5 CFR part 752, subpart D, or an action under 5 CFR 930.211.

[70 FR 31287, May 31, 2005, as amended at 73 FR 66151, Nov. 7, 2008]

SETTING AN EMPLOYEE'S RATE OF PAY

§ 530.321 General.

(a) This section and §§ 530.322 and 530.323 provide conversion rules for setting an employee's pay when a special rate schedule is established, increased, decreased, or discontinued, or when an employee's coverage under an existing special rate schedule is affected by a change in coverage criteria. These conversion rules do not apply to changes in an employee's special rate entitlements based on a change in the employee's position of record or official worksite. Pay-setting rules for other personnel actions affecting special rate employees are provided in 5 CFR parts 531 and 536. For example, if an employee becomes covered by a special rate schedule as a result of a change in the employee's official worksite, the geographic conversion rule in 5 CFR 531.205 must be used to set the employee's rate(s) of basic pay in the new location before considering any other simultaneous pay action (other than a general pay adjustment).

(b) The conversion rules in §§ 530.322 and 530.323 are considered general pay adjustments for the purpose of applying 5 CFR 531.206 (dealing with the order of precedence for processing simultaneous pay actions). The rate(s) of pay resulting from these conversion rules are considered the employee's existing rate(s) of pay before processing the next simultaneous pay action in the order of precedence.

§530.322 Setting pay when a special rate schedule is newly established or increased.

(a) *General rule.* When an employee holds a position that becomes covered by a newly established special rate schedule (including a schedule for which coverage is expanded) or increased special rate schedule (including an increased special rate range within a schedule), the agency must set the employee's special rate at the step (or relative position in range for a GM employee) of the grade on the new special rate schedule that corresponds to the employee's existing numerical step (or relative position in range for a GM employee) as in effect immediately before the new special rate schedule takes effect, except as otherwise provided in this section. The corresponding special rate is determined by adding the applicable special rate supplement on top of the employee's GS rate, subject to the limitation that no special rate may exceed the rate for level IV of the Executive Schedule. For an employee receiving an LEO special base rate, add the applicable special rate supplement to the GS rate for the employee's grade and step, except as otherwise provided under §530.304(d).

(b) *Employee entitled to a higher rate of basic pay.* As provided in §530.303(d), if an employee meeting the coverage conditions for a newly established or increased special rate schedule is entitled to a higher rate of basic pay under other legal authority, the employee must be paid at that higher rate.

(c) *Employee receiving a retained rate.* When an employee is receiving a retained rate immediately before the employee's position is covered by a newly established or increased special rate schedule, the agency must determine the employee's rate of pay consistent with the requirements in 5 CFR part 536, subpart C (or 5 CFR 359.705 for a former member of the Senior Executive Service receiving a retained rate under that section).

[70 FR 31287, May 31, 2005, as amended at 73 FR 66151, Nov. 7, 2008]

§530.323 Setting pay when a special rate is discontinued or decreased.

(a) *General.* This section applies when a special rate applicable to a position is discontinued or decreased because of—

(1) A reduction or termination of the rates of the special rate schedule (or of rates of a rate range within a schedule); or

(2) The reduction in the scope of coverage of the special rate schedule.

(b) *Employee entitled to pay retention.* When a special rate applicable to a position is discontinued or decreased, and an employee holding the position is entitled to pay retention under 5 CFR part 536 as a result, the employee's rate of pay must be set consistent with the requirements in 5 CFR part 536, subpart C.

(c) *Employee not entitled to pay retention.* When a special rate applicable to a position is discontinued or decreased, and an employee holding the position is not entitled to pay retention under 5 CFR part 536, the employee's rate of pay is set in the highest applicable rate range at the grade and step (or relative position in range for a GM employee) that corresponds to the grade and step (or relative position in range for a GM employee) for the employee's existing special rate (as in effect immediately before the schedule change).

(d) *Employee receiving a retained rate.* When a special rate applicable to a position is discontinued or decreased, and the employee holding the position is receiving a retained rate immediately before the schedule change, the employee's rate of pay must be set consistent with the requirements in 5 CFR part 536, subpart C (or 5 CFR 359.705 for a former member of the Senior Executive Service receiving a retained rate under that section).

[70 FR 31287, May 31, 2005, as amended at 73 FR 66152, Nov. 7, 2008]

PART 531—PAY UNDER THE GENERAL SCHEDULE

Subpart A [Reserved]

Subpart B—Determining Rate of Basic Pay

GENERAL PROVISIONS

SETTING PAY WHEN APPOINTMENT OR POSITION CHANGES

USING A HIGHEST PREVIOUS RATE UNDER THE MAXIMUM PAYABLE RATE RULE

SPECIAL RULES FOR GM EMPLOYEES

Subpart C [Reserved]

Subpart D—Within-Grade Increases

Subpart E—Quality Step Increases

Subpart F—Locality-Based Comparability Payments

Subpart G [Reserved]

AUTHORITY: 5 U.S.C. 5115, 5307, and 5338; sec. 4 of Public Law 103–89, 107 Stat. 981; and E.O. 12748, 56 FR 4521, 3 CFR, 1991 Comp., p. 316; Subpart B also issued under 5 U.S.C. 5303(g), 5305, 5333, 5334(a) and (b), and 7701(b)(2); Subpart D also issued under 5 U.S.C. 5335 and 7701(b)(2); Subpart E also issued under 5 U.S.C. 5336; Subpart F also issued under 5 U.S.C. 5304, 5305, and 5941(a); E.O. 12883, 58 FR 63281, 3 CFR, 1993 Comp., p. 682; and E.O. 13106, 63 FR 68151, 3 CFR, 1998 Comp., p. 224.

Subpart A [Reserved]

Subpart B—Determining Rate of Basic Pay

SOURCE: 70 FR 31291, May 31, 2005, unless otherwise noted.

GENERAL PROVISIONS

§ 531.201 Purpose.

This subpart contains regulations of the Office of Personnel Management (OPM) implementing 5 U.S.C 5332, 5333, and 5334, which deal with setting and adjusting rates of basic pay for General Schedule (GS) employees. These regulations are supplemented by regulations on GS within-grade increases in subpart D of this part; GS quality step increases in subpart E of this part; locality rates in subpart F of this part; special rates in 5 CFR part 530, subpart C; and grade and pay retention in 5 CFR part 536.

§ 531.202 Coverage.

This subpart covers employees who occupy positions classified and paid under the GS classification and pay system, as provided in 5 U.S.C. 5102 and 5331 or other applicable laws. Law enforcement officers (LEOs) receiving LEO special base rates are covered by the GS classification and pay system, but receive higher base rates of pay in lieu of GS rates at grades GS–3 through GS–10. This subpart also covers GS employees who receive special rates under 5 U.S.C. 5305 and 5 CFR part 530, subpart C.

§ 531.203 Definitions.

In this subpart:

Agency means an Executive agency as defined in 5 U.S.C. 105 or an agency in the legislative branch with employees covered by this subpart. To the extent that the regulations in this subpart relate to non-GS service in the Federal Government, *agency* includes any other agency in the Federal Government.

Demotion means a change of an employee, while continuously employed, from one GS grade to a lower GS grade, with or without a reduction in pay.

Employee means an employee as defined in 5 U.S.C. 2105 who is covered by this subpart. For the purpose of determining eligibility under the superior qualifications and special needs pay-setting authority in § 531.212 and applying the maximum payable rate provisions in §§ 531.216 and 531.221 (which consider rates of pay received during non-GS service in the Federal Government), *employee* also includes any employee as defined in 5 U.S.C. 2105 and—

(1) An individual employed by the U.S. Postal Service or the Postal Rate Commission who would be considered an employee under 5 U.S.C. 2105 but for the exclusion in section 2105(e); and

(2) An individual employed by a Department of Defense or Coast Guard nonappropriated fund instrumentality (as described in 5 U.S.C. 2105(c)) for service covered by § 531.216 (for the purpose of applying that section and §§ 531.211 and 531.212).

Existing rate means the rate received immediately before a pay action takes effect, after processing a general pay adjustment and any other simultaneous pay action that is higher in the order of precedence under § 531.206. For example, the *existing rate* immediately before a promotion action must reflect any geographic conversion under § 531.205 and any simultaneous within-grade increase or quality step increase.

Federal Government means all entities of the Government of the United States, including the U.S. Postal Service and the Postal Rate Commission. The District of Columbia is deemed to be part of the Federal Government with respect to employees of the government of the District of Columbia (DC) who were first employed by that government before October 1, 1987. A Department of Defense or Coast Guard nonappropriated fund instrumentality (as described in 5 U.S.C. 2105(c)) is not considered part of the Federal Government except for the purpose of applying §§ 531.211 and 531.212 to employees covered by § 531.216 upon employment in a GS position.

General Schedule or *GS* means the classification and pay system established under 5 U.S.C. chapter 51 and subchapter III of chapter 53. It also refers to the pay schedule of GS rates established under 5 U.S.C. 5332, as adjusted under 5 U.S.C. 5303 or other law (including GS rates payable to GM employees). Law enforcement officers (LEOs) receiving LEO special base rates are covered by the GS classification and pay system but receive higher base rates of pay in lieu of GS rates at grades GS–3 through GS–10.

GM employee means a GS employee who was formerly covered by the Performance Management and Recognition System under 5 U.S.C. chapter 54 on October 31, 1993 (and therefore became covered on November 1, 1993, by section 4 of Pub. L. 103–89, the Performance Management and Recognition System Termination Act of 1993), and who continues thereafter to occupy a position as a supervisor or management official (as defined in 5 U.S.C. 7103(a)(10) and (11)) in the same grade of the General Schedule (GS–13, 14, or 15) and in the same agency without a break in service of more than 3 days. (See § 531.241.) Any reference to employees, grades, positions, or rates of basic pay under the General Schedule includes GM employees.

GS rate means a rate of basic pay within the General Schedule, excluding any LEO special base rate and additional pay of any kind such as locality payments or special rate supplements. A rate payable to a GM employee is considered a GS rate even though the rate may fall between GS step rates.

Highest applicable rate range means the rate range applicable to a GS employee based on a given position of record and official worksite that provides the highest rates of basic pay, excluding any retained rates. For example, a rate range of special rates may exceed an applicable locality rate range. In certain circumstances, the *highest applicable rate range* may consist of two types of pay rates from different pay schedules—e.g., a range where special rates (based on a fixed dollar supplement) are higher in the lower portion of the range and locality rates are higher in the higher portion of the range.

Law enforcement officer or *LEO* has the meaning given that term in 5 CFR 550.103.

LEO special base rate means a special base rate established for GS law enforcement officers at grades GS–3 through GS–10 under section 403 of the Federal Employees Pay Comparability Act of 1990 (section 529 of Pub. L. 101–509, November 5, 1990, as amended) which is used in lieu of a GS rate.

Locality payment means a locality-based comparability payment payable to GS employees under 5 U.S.C. 5304 and 5 CFR part 531, subpart F.

Locality rate means a GS rate or an LEO special base rate, if applicable, plus any applicable locality payment.

Official worksite means the official location of the employee's position of record, as determined under 5 CFR 531.605.

OPM means the Office of Personnel Management.

Payable rate means the highest rate of basic pay to which an employee is entitled based on the employee's position of record, official worksite, and step (or relative position in range for a GM employee) or, if applicable, a retained rate.

Pay schedule means a set of rate ranges established for GS employees under a single authority—*i.e.*, the General Schedule, an LEO special base rate schedule (for grades GS–3 through 10), a locality rate schedule based on GS rates, a locality rate schedule based on LEO special base rates (for grades GS–3 through 10), or a special rate schedule. A pay schedule applies to or covers a defined category of employees based on established coverage conditions (e.g., official worksite, occupation). A pay schedule is considered to apply to or cover an employee who meets the established coverage conditions even when a rate under that schedule is not currently payable to the employee because of a higher pay entitlement under another pay schedule.

Position of record means an employee's official position (defined by grade, occupational series, employing agency, LEO status, and any other condition that determines coverage under a pay schedule (other than official worksite)), as documented on the employee's most recent Notification of Personnel Action (Standard Form 50 or equivalent) and current position description. A position to which an employee is temporarily detailed is not documented as a position of record. For an employee whose change in official position is followed within 3 workdays by a reduction in force resulting in the employee's separation before he or she is required to report for duty in the new position, the position of record in effect immediately before the position change is deemed to remain the position of record through the date of separation.

Promotion means a GS employee's movement from one GS grade to a higher GS grade while continuously employed (including such a movement in conjunction with a transfer).

Rate of basic pay means the rate of pay fixed by law or administrative action for the position held by a GS employee before any deductions, including a GS rate, an LEO special base rate, a special rate, a locality rate, and a retained rate, but exclusive of additional pay of any other kind. For the purpose of applying the maximum payable rate rules in §§ 531.216 and 531.221 using a rate under a non-GS pay system as an employee's highest previous rate, *rate of basic pay* means a rate of pay under other legal authority which is equivalent to a rate of basic pay for GS employees, as described in this definition, excluding a rate under § 531.223. (See also 5 CFR 530.308, 531.610, and 536.307.)

Rate range or *range* means a range of rates of basic pay for a grade within an established pay schedule, excluding any retained rate. A rate range may consist of GS rates, LEO special base rates, locality rates, special rates, or, for non-GS employees, similar rates under other legal authority.

Reassignment means a change of an employee, while serving continuously in the same agency, from one position to another without promotion or demotion.

Reemployment means employment, including reinstatement or another type of appointment, after a break in service of at least 1 full workday.

Retained rate means a rate above the maximum rate of the rate range applicable to a GS employee which is payable under 5 CFR part 536 or, for a former member of the Senior Executive Service, under 5 CFR 359.705.

Special rate means a rate of pay within a special rate schedule established under 5 CFR part 530, subpart C, or a similar rate for GS employees established under other legal authority (e.g., 38 U.S.C. 7455). The term *special rate* does not include an LEO special base rate or an adjusted rate including market pay under 38 U.S.C. 7431(c).

Special rate schedule means a pay schedule established under 5 CFR part 530, subpart C, to provide higher rates of pay for specified categories of GS positions or employees at one or more grades or levels or a similar schedule established for GS employees under other legal authority (e.g., 38 U.S.C. 7455).

Special rate supplement means the portion of a special rate paid above an employee's GS rate. However, for a law enforcement officer receiving an LEO special base rate who is also entitled to a special rate, the special rate supplement equals the portion of the special rate paid above the officer's LEO special base rate. When a special rate schedule covers both LEO positions and other positions, the value of the special rate supplement will be less for law enforcement officers receiving an LEO special base rate (since that rate is higher than the corresponding GS rate). The payable amount of a special rate supplement is subject to the Executive Schedule level IV limitation on special rates, as provided in 5 CFR 530.304(a).

Temporary promotion means a time-limited promotion with a not-to-exceed date or a specified term.

Transfer means a change of an employee, without a break in service of 1 full workday, from one branch of the Federal Government (executive, legislative, or judicial) to another or from one agency to another.

Where different pay schedules apply means, in the context of applying the geographic conversion rule, that an employee's official worksite is changed to a new location that would cause the employee to lose or gain coverage under a location-based pay schedule (*i.e.*, locality rate schedule or special rate schedule) if the employee were to remain in the same position of record.

Within-grade increase has the meaning given that term in § 531.403.

[70 FR 31291, May 31, 2005, as amended at 73 FR 66152, Nov. 7, 2008; 73 FR 76847, Dec. 18, 2008]

§ 531.204 Entitlement to other rates of pay.

(a) A law enforcement officer is entitled to LEO special base rates in lieu of GS rates at grades GS–3 through GS–10. A law enforcement officer is entitled to the LEO special base rate that corresponds to his or her grade and step. If an employee loses LEO status, the employee is entitled to the GS rate for his or her grade and step unless a higher rate is set under the maximum payable rate rule in § 531.221 or under the pay retention rules in 5 CFR part 536, as applicable. LEO special base rates are used in computing locality rates, as provided in subpart F of this part. A law enforcement officer may be entitled to a special rate that is computed using the underlying GS rate for the LEO's grade and step.

(b) When an employee's GS rate or LEO special base rate is determined under the rules of this subpart, the agency must determine any other rate of basic pay to which the employee is entitled, including a locality rate under subpart F of this part and a special rate under 5 CFR part 530, subpart C, or other legal authority (e.g., 38 U.S.C. 7455). The employee is entitled to the highest applicable rate of basic pay as his or her payable rate. When an employee's special rate is surpassed by a higher locality rate, his or her entitlement to a special rate is terminated, as provided in § 530.303(d).

(c) When application of the rules in this subpart results in setting an employee's payable rate in the highest applicable pay schedule (e.g., a locality rate schedule or a special rate schedule), the agency must determine the employee's underlying GS rate or LEO special base rate, as applicable, based on that payable rate (*i.e.*, by finding the corresponding underlying rate with the same grade and step (or relative position in range for a GM employee) as the payable rate).

[70 FR 31291, May 31, 2005, as amended at 73 FR 66152, Nov. 7, 2008]

§ 531.205 Converting pay upon change in location of employee's official worksite.

When an employee's official worksite is changed to a new location where different pay schedules apply, the agency must convert the employee's rate(s) of basic pay to the applicable pay schedule(s) in the new location before processing any simultaneous pay action (other than a general pay adjustment, as provided in § 531.206). The agency must first set the employee's rate(s) of basic pay in the applicable pay schedule(s) in the new location based on his or her position of record (including grade) and step (or a GM employee's GS rate) immediately before the change in the employee's official worksite. The resulting rate must be used as the existing rate in processing the next simultaneous pay action in the order of precedence, using the applicable pay schedules in the new location. In conjunction with any simultaneous pay actions, the employee's rate(s) of basic pay will then be set based on the employee's new position of record and new official worksite.

[70 FR 31291, May 31, 2005, as amended at 73 FR 66152, Nov. 7, 2008]

§ 531.206 Order of processing simultaneous pay actions.

When multiple pay actions with the same effective date affect an employee's rate of basic pay, the actions will be processed in the following order:

(a) Process general pay adjustments before any individual pay action that takes effect at the same time. General pay adjustments include an annual adjustment in the General Schedule under 5 U.S.C. 5303; an adjustment in LEO special base rates; an adjustment of a locality pay percentage under subpart F of this part; the establishment or adjustment of a special rate schedule under 5 CFR part 530, subpart C, or similar legal authority (e.g., 38 U.S.C. 7455); and an adjustment of a retained rate under 5 CFR 359.705(d)(1) and 536.305(a)(1) based on the establishment or adjustment of a pay schedule.

(b) Convert the employee's rate(s) of pay to reflect any change in the location of the employee's official worksite, as prescribed in § 531.205 (or similar geographic conversion provision).

(c) Process any within-grade increase or quality step increase to which the employee is entitled.

(d) Process any promotion action using the rates of pay and rate ranges in the sequence prescribed in § 531.214.

(e) Except as otherwise provided in paragraphs (a) through (d) of this section or other regulation, process individual pay actions that take effect at the same time in the order that gives the employee the maximum benefit.

§531.207 Applying annual pay adjustments.

(a) Except as otherwise provided in this section, on the effective date of a GS pay adjustment under 5 U.S.C. 5303 or similar authority, an agency initially must set the GS rate of a GS employee at the new rate of the adjusted General Schedule corresponding to the employee's grade and step in effect immediately before the effective date of the pay adjustment. Any simultaneous pay actions must be processed after the pay adjustment, as provided in §531.206.

(b) For employees receiving a retained rate immediately before the effective date of a GS annual pay adjustment, the agency must adjust the employee's rate of basic pay under the rules in 5 CFR 536.305 (or under 5 CFR 359.705 for former members of the Senior Executive Service receiving a retained rate under that section).

(c) For GM employees, the agency must follow the rules in §531.244.

SETTING PAY WHEN APPOINTMENT OR POSITION CHANGES

§531.211 Setting pay for a newly appointed employee.

(a) *First appointment.* An agency must set the payable rate of basic pay for an employee receiving his or her first appointment (regardless of tenure) as a civilian employee of the Federal Government at the minimum rate of the highest applicable rate range for the employee's position of record, except as provided in §531.212.

(b) *Reemployment.* For an employee who has previous civilian service in the Federal Government, an agency must set the payable rate of basic pay upon reemployment at the minimum rate of the highest applicable rate range for the employee's position of record unless—

(1) The employee meets the conditions in §531.212 and an agency determines it is appropriate to set pay under that section; or

(2) The employee is eligible for a higher payable rate under the maximum payable rate rule in §531.221 and the agency chooses to apply that rule.

§531.212 Superior qualifications and special needs pay-setting authority.

(a) *Agency authority.* (1) An agency may use the superior qualifications or special needs pay-setting authority in 5 U.S.C. 5333 to set the payable rate of basic pay for an employee above the minimum rate of the highest applicable rate range for the employee's position of record. The superior qualifications or special needs pay-setting authority may be used for—

(i) A first appointment (regardless of tenure) as a civilian employee of the Federal Government; or

(ii) A reappointment that is considered a new appointment under 5 U.S.C. 5333 because it meets the conditions prescribed in paragraph (a)(2) and (3) of this section.

(2) An agency may use the superior qualifications and special needs pay-setting authority for a reappointment only when the employee has had a break in service of at least 90 days from the last period of civilian employment with the Federal Government, except as provided in paragraph (a)(3) of this section.

(3) Except as provided in paragraph (a)(5) of this section, an agency may use the superior qualifications and special needs pay-setting authority for a reappointment without requiring a 90-day break in service if the candidate's civilian employment with the Federal Government during the 90-day period immediately preceding the appointment was limited to one or more of the following:

(i) A time-limited appointment in the competitive or excepted service;

(ii) A non-permanent appointment in the competitive or excepted service;

(iii) Employment with the government of the District of Columbia (DC) when the candidate was first appointed by the DC government on or after October 1, 1987;

(iv) An appointment as an expert or consultant under 5 U.S.C. 3109 and 5 CFR part 304;

(v) Employment under a provisional appointment designated under 5 CFR 316.403;

(vi) Employment under an Internship Program appointment under § 213.3402(a) of this chapter ; or

(vii) Employment as a Senior Executive Service limited term appointee or limited emergency appointee (as defined in 5 U.S.C. 3132(a)(5) and (a)(6), respectively).

(4) Service as an employee of a non-appropriated fund instrumentality (NAFI) of the Department of Defense or Coast Guard is not considered employment by the Federal Government under this section except for employees covered by § 531.216 upon appointment or reappointment (*i.e.*, employees who move from NAFI position to GS position with a break in service of 3 days or less and without a change in agency). Employees covered by § 531.216 upon appointment or reappointment to a GS position are not eligible to have pay set under the superior qualifications or special needs authority, since their NAFI employment is considered employment by the Federal Government. Otherwise, NAFI employment does not block application of this section.

(5) An agency may not apply an exception in paragraph (a)(3) of this section if the candidate's civilian employment with the Federal Government during the 90-day period immediately preceding the appointment was in one or more of the following types of positions:

(i) A position to which an individual is appointed by the President, by and with the advice and consent of the Senate;

(ii) A position in the Senior Executive Service as a noncareer appointee (as defined in 5 U.S.C. 3132(a)(7));

(iii) A position excepted from the competitive service by reason of its confidential, policy-determining, policy-making, or policy-advocating character;

(iv) A position to which an individual is appointed by the President without the advice and consent of the Senate;

(v) A position designated as the head of an agency, including an agency headed by a collegial body composed of two or more individual members;

(vi) A position in which the employee is expected to receive an appointment as the head of an agency; or

(vii) A position to which an individual is appointed as a Senior Executive Service limited term appointee or limited emergency appointee (as defined in 5 U.S.C. 3132(a)(5) and (a)(6), respectively) when the appointment must be cleared through the White House Office of Presidential Personnel.

(b) *Superior qualifications or special needs determination.* An agency may set the payable rate of basic pay of a newly appointed employee above the minimum rate of the grade under this section if the candidate meets one of the following criteria:

(1) The candidate has superior qualifications. An agency may determine that a candidate has superior qualifications based on the level, type, or quality of the candidate's skills or competencies demonstrated or obtained through experience and/or education, the quality of the candidate's accomplishments compared to others in the field, or other factors that support a superior qualifications determination. The candidate's skills, competencies, experience, education, and/or accomplishments must be relevant to the requirements of the position to be filled. These qualities must be significantly higher than that needed to be minimally required for the position and/or be of a more specialized quality compared to other candidates; or

(2) The candidate fills a special agency need. An agency may determine that a candidate fills a special agency need if the type, level, or quality of skills and competencies or other qualities and experiences possessed by the candidate are relevant to the requirements of the position and are essential to accomplishing an important agency mission, goal, or program activity. A candidate also may meet the special needs criteria by meeting agency workforce needs, as documented in the agency's strategic human capital plan.

(c) *Pay rate determination.* An agency may consider one or more of the following factors, as applicable in the case at hand, to determine the step at which to set an employee's payable rate of basic pay using the superior qualifications and special needs pay-setting authority:

(1) The level, type, or quality of the candidate's skills or competencies;

(2) The candidate's existing salary, recent salary history, or salary documented in a competing job offer (taking into account the location where the salary was or would be earned and comparing the salary to payable rates of basic pay in the same location);

(3) Significant disparities between Federal and non-Federal salaries for the skills and competencies required in the position to be filled;

(4) Existing labor market conditions and employment trends, including the availability and quality of candidates for the same or similar positions;

(5) The success of recent efforts to recruit candidates for the same or similar positions;

(6) Recent turnover in the same or similar positions;

(7) The importance/criticality of the position to be filled and the effect on the agency if it is not filled or if there is a delay in filling it;

(8) The desirability of the geographic location, duties, and/or work environment associated with the position;

(9) Agency workforce needs, as documented in the agency's strategic human capital plan; or

(10) Other relevant factors.

(d) *Consideration of recruitment incentive.* In determining whether to use the superior qualifications and special needs pay-setting authority and the level at which the employee's payable rate of basic pay should be set, an agency must consider the possibility of authorizing a recruitment incentive under 5 CFR part 575, subpart A.

(e) *Approval and documentation requirements.* (1) An agency must approve each determination to use the superior qualifications and special needs pay-setting authority prior to the candidate entering on duty. Each determination must be made in writing and reviewed and approved by an official of the agency who is at least one level higher than the employee's supervisor, unless there is no official at a higher level in the agency.

(2) An agency must document all of the following for each determination to use the superior qualifications and special needs pay-setting authority sufficient to allow reconstruction of the action taken in each case:

(i) The superior qualifications of the candidate under paragraph (b)(1) of this section or the special agency need for the candidate's services under paragraph (b)(2) of this section which justifies a higher than minimum rate;

(ii) An explanation of the factor(s) and supporting documentation under paragraph (c) of this section which were used to justify the rate at which the employee's pay is set. The written documentation must explain how the factors directly relate to the rate approved; and

(iii) The reasons for authorizing a higher than minimum rate instead of or in addition to a recruitment incentive under 5 CFR part 575, subpart A.

(f) *Ensuring compliance.* An agency must establish appropriate internal guidelines and evaluation procedures to ensure compliance with the law, this section of OPM regulations, and agency policies.

[70 FR 31291, May 31, 2005, as amended at 73 FR 66152, Nov. 7, 2008; 77 FR 28222, May 11, 2012; 78 FR 49362, Aug. 14, 2013]

§531.213 Setting pay upon change in position without a change in grade.

For an employee who is moved laterally (by transfer, reassignment, change in type of appointment, change in official worksite, or other change in position) from one GS position to a different GS position without a change in grade or a break in service, the agency must determine the employee's payable rate of basic pay and any underlying rate(s)s of basic pay based on the employee's new position of record, new official worksite, and the step (or relative position in range for a GM employee) in effect before the position change. If an employee is eligible to receive a higher rate under the maximum payable rate rule in §531.221, the agency may choose to apply that rule. If an employee is entitled to pay retention, the agency must apply the rules in 5 CFR part 536.

[70 FR 31291, May 31, 2005, as amended at 73 FR 66152, Nov. 7, 2008]

§ 531.214 Setting pay upon promotion.

(a) *General.* An agency must set an employee's payable rate of basic pay upon promotion following the rules in this section, consistent with 5 U.S.C. 5334(b). The promotion rule in 5 U.S.C. 5334(b) and the implementing rules in this section apply only to a GS employee who is promoted from one GS grade to a higher GS grade. Consistent with § 531.206, any general pay adjustment that takes effect on the same day as a promotion action must be processed before applying the rules in this section.

(b) *Geographic conversion.* When an employee's official worksite is changed to a new location where different pay schedules apply, the agency must convert the employee to the applicable pay schedule(s) and rate(s) of basic pay for the new official worksite based on the employee's position of record before promotion as provided in § 531.205 before processing a simultaneous promotion action.

(c) *Simultaneous within-grade increase.* When an employee is entitled to a within-grade increase or a quality step increase that is effective at the same time as a promotion, the agency must process that increase before processing the promotion action.

(d) *Promotion rule*—(1) *General.* An agency must determine an employee's payable rate of basic pay upon promotion using the standard method in paragraph (d)(3) of this section or the alternate method in paragraph (d)(4) of this section, subject to the special rule in paragraph (d)(5) of this section for employees receiving a retained rate before promotion. A determination regarding whether the alternate method is used in place of the standard method depends on the pay schedules that apply to an employee before and after promotion, as provided in paragraph (d)(2) of this section. In this paragraph (d), references to an employee's rate or range "before promotion" mean the rate or range before promotion but after any geographic conversion required by paragraph (b) of this section.

(2) *Determining applicable method.* The following rules govern determinations regarding which promotion method to use:

(i) Apply the standard method exclusively if the employee is covered by the same pay schedules before and after promotion. For example, an employee may be covered by the General Schedule and the same locality rate schedule before and after promotion.

(ii) Apply the alternate method if the employee is covered by different pay schedules before and after promotion and if the alternate method will produce a higher payable rate upon promotion than the standard method. For example, an employee may be covered after promotion by a special rate schedule that did not apply to him or her before promotion, and the alternate method will produce a higher rate.

(iii) Apply the standard method in all other circumstances, except that an agency may, at its sole and exclusive discretion, apply the alternate method for an employee covered by different pay schedules before and after promotion even though the method produces a lesser payable rate than the standard method, but only under the following conditions:

(A) The agency determines it would be inappropriate to use the standard method based on a finding that the higher pay for the position before promotion is not sufficiently related to the knowledge and skills required for the position after promotion; and

(B) The agency informs the employee of the determination to use the alternate method before the effective date of the promotion.

(3) *Standard method.* (i) The standard method of applying the promotion rule is presented in the following table:

Promotion Rule—Standard Method

Step A	If applicable, apply the geographic conversion rule in § 531.205 to determine the employee's rate(s) and range(s) of basic pay based on the employee's position of record before promotion and the new official worksite, as required by paragraph (b) of this section. Also, if applicable, provide any simultaneous within-grade increase or quality step increase, as required by paragraph (c) of this section. Use the resulting rate(s) of basic pay as the existing rate(s) in effect immediately before promotion in applying steps B and C.
Step B	Identify the employee's existing GS rate (or LEO special base rate) in the grade before promotion, and increase that rate by two GS within-grade increases for that grade.

Step C	Determine the payable (highest) rate of basic pay for the step or rate determined in step B by applying any locality payment or special rate supplement applicable to the given grade, based on the employee's position of record before promotion and official worksite after promotion. (If the rate determined in step B is above the range maximum, use the same locality payment or special rate supplement that applies to rates within the rate range.)
Step D	Identify the highest applicable rate range for the employee's position of record after promotion and find the lowest step rate in that range that equals or exceeds the rate determined in step C. This is the employee's payable rate of basic pay upon promotion. (If the rate identified in step C exceeds the maximum of the rate range identified in this step, the employee's payable rate is that maximum rate, or, if the employee's existing rate is higher than that maximum rate, a retained rate under 5 CFR part 536 equal to that existing rate.)

(ii) Example of standard method: A GS–11, step 5, employee in Los Angeles is promoted to a GS–12 position in Kansas City. In Kansas City, a special rate schedule would apply to the employee's GS–11 position, but at GS–12 no special rate range applies; instead, just a locality rate range applies. Thus, different pay schedules apply to the employee in Kansas City before and after promotion. The agency determines that the standard method produces a higher rate than the alternate method because the employee is covered by a special rate schedule before promotion but not after promotion, The agency also determines it will not invoke the exception provision under paragraph (d)(2)(iii). The agency applies the standard method as follows:

Step A	Apply the geographic conversion rule to determine the rates of basic pay for the GS–11, step 5, position in Kansas City. The pay schedules applicable to the employee in Kansas City are the General Schedule, the locality rate schedule applicable in Kansas City, and the special rate schedule applicable to the employee's position in Kansas City.
Step B	Using the underlying General Schedule, increase the GS–11, step 5, rate by two within-grade increases, which produces the GS–11, step 7, rate.
Step C	The payable (highest) rate of basic pay for GS–11, step 7, is the corresponding GS–11, step 7, special rate that would be applicable to the GS–11 position in Kansas City.
Step D	The highest applicable rate range for the GS–12 position after promotion is the GS–12 locality rate range under the Kansas City locality rate schedule. Find the lowest step rate in that range that equals or exceeds the GS–11, step 7, special rate from step C. That step rate is the payable rate of basic pay upon promotion.

(4) *Alternate method.* (i) The alternate method of applying the promotion rule, which involves using pay schedules applicable before promotion and then converting pay to a different schedule applicable after promotion, is presented in the following table:

Promotion Rule—Alternate Method

Steps A, B, C	Same as standard method in paragraph (d)(3) of this section.
Step D	Identify the highest applicable rate range for the employee's grade after promotion based on consideration of any pay schedule that applied to the employee's position of record *before* promotion (after any geographic conversion). (Do not consider pay schedules that apply only to the employee's new position of record after promotion. For example, if a particular special rate schedule applies only to an employee's position of record after promotion, disregard that schedule in applying this step.) Find the lowest step in the highest applicable rate range that equals or exceeds the rate identified in step C. (If the rate identified in step C exceeds the maximum of the rate range identified in this step, the employee's payable rate is that maximum rate, or, if the employee's existing rate is higher than that maximum rate, a retained rate under 5 CFR part 536 equal to that existing rate.)
Step E	Convert the lowest step rate identified in step D to a corresponding step rate (same step) in the highest applicable rate range for the employee's new position of record after promotion. This is the employee's alternate payable rate of basic pay upon promotion. (If the rate derived under step D was a retained rate, determine the alternate payable rate of basic pay as provided in paragraph (d)(4)(ii) of this section.)
Step F	If the alternate payable rate identified in step E exceeds the payable rate resulting from the standard method in paragraph (d)(3) of this section, the employee is entitled to the alternate rate upon promotion. Otherwise, the employee is entitled to the payable rate derived under the standard method, except as provided in paragraph (d)(2)(iii) of this section.

(ii) In applying step E of the table in paragraph (d)(4)(i) of this section, if the rate derived under step D was a retained rate, compare the retained rate to the highest applicable rate range identified in step E. If the retained rate exceeds the maximum of that rate range, the retained rate continues and is the employee's alternate payable rate upon promotion. If the retained rate is below the rate range maximum, the employee's alternate payable rate upon promotion is the maximum rate of the range (step 10).

(iii) Example of alternate method: A GS–7, step 7, employee in Atlanta is promoted to a GS–9 position in Washington, DC. The promotion involves not only a change in grade but also a change in the employee's occupational series. In Washington, DC, no special rate schedule would apply to a GS–7 or GS–9 position in the old occupational series, but a special rate schedule does apply to the GS–9 position in the new occupational series. Thus, different pay schedules apply before and after promotion, and the alternate method would result in a higher rate than the standard method. As provided in paragraph (d)(2)(ii) of this section, the agency must apply the alternate method and compare the result to the result derived under the standard method, as follows:

Step A	Apply the geographic conversion rule in § 531.205 to determine the rates of basic pay for the GS–7, step 7, position in Washington, DC. Based on the GS–7 position before promotion (including the old occupational series), the pay schedules applicable to the employee in Washington, DC, would be the General Schedule and the locality rate schedule applicable in Washington, DC.
Step B	Using the underlying General Schedule, increase the GS–7, step 7, rate by two within-grade increases, which produces the GS–7, step 9, rate.
Step C	The payable (highest) rate of basic pay for GS–7, step 9, is the corresponding GS–7, step 9, locality rate in Washington, DC.
Step D	If the employee were promoted to a GS–9 position in the old occupational series, the highest applicable rate range for that GS–9 position after promotion would be the GS–9 locality rate range in Washington, DC. The GS–9, step 3, locality rate is the lowest step rate in that range that equals or exceeds the GS–7, step 9, locality rate from step C.
Step E	Convert the GS–9, step 3, locality rate to the higher GS–9, step 3, special rate that applies to the employee's position after promotion (including the new occupational series). That GS–9, step 3, special rate is the payable rate of basic pay upon promotion.
Step F	Assume that the standard method would have compared the GS–7, step 9, locality rate directly to the higher GS–9 range of special rates and produced a rate of GS–9, step 1. Since the rate produced by the alternate method (GS–9, step 3) is greater than the rate produced by the standard method, the result of the alternate method is used.

(5) *If employee was receiving a retained rate before promotion.* (i) If an employee's existing payable rate of basic pay before promotion is a retained rate, apply the applicable promotion methods in paragraphs (d)(3) or (d)(4) of this section as if the employee were receiving the maximum rate of the employee's grade before promotion.

(ii) If the payable rate of basic pay after promotion determined under paragraph (d)(5)(i) of this section is greater than the employee's existing retained rate, the employee is entitled to that payable rate.

(iii) If the existing retained rate is greater than the rate determined under paragraph (d)(5)(i) of this section, the retained rate must be compared to the highest applicable rate range for the position after promotion, as provided in 5 CFR 536.304. The employee is entitled to the lowest step rate in the range that equals or exceeds the retained rate or, if the retained rate exceeds the range maximum, to the retained rate.

(6) *If employee is promoted from GS–1 or GS–2.* In applying the promotion rule to an employee who is promoted from step 9 or 10 of grade GS–1 or GS–2, the value of two within-grade increases is determined by doubling the within-grade increase between step 9 and 10 for the applicable grade.

(e) *Temporary promotions.* Pay is set for an employee receiving a temporary promotion on the same basis as a permanent promotion. Upon expiration or termination of the temporary promotion, pay is set as provided in § 531.215(c). If a temporary promotion is made permanent immediately after the temporary promotion ends, the agency may not return the employee to the lower grade; instead, the agency must convert the employee's temporary promotion to a permanent promotion without a change in pay.

(f) *Corrections of demotions.* The promotion rule in this section may not be used in correcting an erroneous demotion. (See §531.215(e).)

[70 FR 31291, May 31, 2005, as amended at 70 FR 74995, Dec. 19, 2005]

§531.215 Setting pay upon demotion.

(a) *General.* Except as otherwise provided in this section, an employee who is demoted is entitled to the minimum payable rate of basic pay for the lower grade unless the agency sets the employee's pay at a higher rate under—

(1) The grade and pay retention rules in 5 CFR part 536, as applicable; or

(2) The maximum payable rate rule in §531.221, as applicable.

(b) *Geographic conversion.* If the employee's official worksite after demotion is in a different geographic location where different pay schedules apply, the agency must first convert the employee's payable rate of pay as required by §531.205 before setting the demoted employee's pay using the grade and pay retention rules in 5 CFR part 536 or the maximum payable rate rule in §531.221.

(c) *Expiration or termination of a temporary promotion.* (1) When an employee is returned to the lower grade from which promoted on expiration or termination of a temporary promotion, the agency must set the employee's payable rate of basic pay in the lower grade as if he or she had not been temporarily promoted, unless the agency sets pay at a higher rate under the maximum payable rate rule in §531.221. As provided in subpart D of this part, time during the temporary promotion may be creditable service towards GS within-grade increases in the lower grade.

(2) If a temporary promotion is made permanent immediately after the temporary promotion ends, the agency may not return the employee to the lower grade. (See §531.214(e).)

(d) *Demotion upon failure to complete a supervisory probationary period.* When an employee promoted to a supervisory or managerial position does not satisfactorily complete a probationary period established under 5 U.S.C. 3321(a)(2) and is returned to a position at the lower grade held before the promotion, the agency must set the employee's payable rate of basic pay upon return to the lower grade as if the employee had not been promoted to the supervisory or managerial position, unless the agency sets pay at a higher rate under the maximum payable rate rule in §531.221. As provided in subpart D of this part, time served following the promotion may be creditable service towards GS within-grade increases in the lower grade. However, nothing in this paragraph prohibits an agency from taking action against an employee serving under a probationary period under 5 U.S.C. 3321(a)(2) for cause unrelated to supervisory or managerial performance and setting pay in accordance with such action.

(e) *Correcting an erroneous demotion.* When a demotion is determined to be erroneous and is canceled, the agency must set the employee's rate of basic pay as if the employee had not been demoted. The action is a correction of the original demotion action and may not be treated as a promotion under §531.214. For example, when a demotion based on a reclassification of the employee's position is found to be erroneous and is corrected retroactively under 5 CFR 511.703, the corrective action is cancellation of the original demotion.

[70 FR 31291, May 31, 2005, as amended at 73 FR 66152, Nov. 7, 2008]

§531.216 Setting pay when an employee moves from a Department of Defense or Coast Guard nonappropriated fund instrumentality.

(a) *General.* This section governs the setting of pay for an employee who moves to a GS position in the Department of Defense or the Coast Guard from a position in a nonappropriated fund instrumentality (NAFI) (as described in 5 U.S.C. 2105(c)) of the Department of Defense or the Coast Guard, respectively, without a break in service of more than 3 days. If an employee moves from a NAFI position to a GS position with a break of more than 3 days or moves from a NAFI position in the Department of Defense or the Coast Guard to a GS position outside of the Department of Defense or the Coast Guard, respectively, the employee has no special conversion rights and this section does not apply.

(b) *NAFI highest previous rate.* For the purpose of this section, the term

"NAFI highest previous rate" means the highest rate of basic pay received by an employee during service in a NAFI position, as described in 5 U.S.C. 2105(c).

(c) *Voluntary move.* (1) For a Department of Defense or Coast Guard employee who moves voluntarily, without a break in service of more than 3 days, from a NAFI position in the Department of Defense or the Coast Guard to a GS position in the Department of Defense or the Coast Guard, respectively, the agency may set the employee's initial payable rate of basic pay at the lowest step rate in the highest applicable rate range currently in effect for the employee's GS position of record and official worksite which equals or exceeds the employee's NAFI highest previous rate of pay, or any lower step rate, except as provided in paragraph (c)(2) or (3) of this section. The employee's initial payable rate of basic pay may not exceed the maximum step rate (step 10).

(2) If the highest applicable rate range would be different if the official worksite for the employee's position of record were located at the place where the employee was stationed while earning the NAFI highest previous rate, the agency must determine the employee's maximum payable rate of basic pay as follows:

(i) Compare the NAFI highest previous rate to the highest applicable rate range currently in effect in the location where the employee was stationed while earning that rate. The highest applicable rate range is determined based on the pay schedules that would be applicable to the employee's current GS position of record if the employee were stationed in that location. Identify the lowest step rate in the highest applicable rate range that was equal to or exceeded the NAFI highest previous rate. If the NAFI highest previous rate is less than the range minimum, identify the minimum step rate (step 1). If the NAFI highest previous rate exceeds the range maximum, identify the maximum step rate (step 10).

(ii) Identify the step rate in the highest applicable rate range for the employee's current official worksite and position of record that corresponds to the step rate derived under paragraph (c)(2)(i) of this section. That corresponding rate is the maximum payable rate at which the agency may set the employee's pay under this section, except as provided by paragraph (c)(3) of this section. The agency may set the employee's rate of basic pay at any step rate that does not exceed that maximum payable rate.

(3) An agency may choose to apply the maximum payable rate rule in § 531.221 based on a non-NAFI rate of basic pay if that rule provides a higher rate than provided by paragraph (c)(1) or (2) of this section.

(d) *Involuntary move.* (1) For a Department of Defense or Coast Guard employee who is moved involuntarily (as defined in paragraph (d)(3) of this section), without a break in service of more than 3 days, from a NAFI position in the Department of Defense or the Coast Guard to a GS position with substantially the same duties in the Department of Defense or the Coast Guard, respectively, the employee is entitled to an initial payable rate of basic pay at the lowest step rate of the grade that is equal to or greater than the employee's rate of basic pay in the NAFI position immediately before the move. If the employee's former NAFI rate exceeds the range maximum, identify the maximum step rate (step 10).

(2) For an employee covered by paragraph (d)(1) of this section, the agency may set the initial payable rate of basic pay at any of the following rates, unless the employee is entitled to receive a higher rate of basic pay under paragraph (d)(1) of this section:

(i) The lowest step rate within the highest applicable rate range for the employee's GS position of record and official worksite that equals or exceeds the employee's NAFI highest previous rate, or any lower step rate (consistent with the method prescribed in paragraphs (c)(1) and (2) of this section);

(ii) A rate determined under the maximum payable rate rule in § 531.221 (using non-NAFI rates of basic pay); or

(iii) A rate determined under the authority to grant pay retention in 5 CFR 536.302(a).

(3) For the purpose of this paragraph (d), "moved involuntarily" means the movement of the incumbent of an NAFI position in the Department of

Defense or the Coast Guard with the position when it is moved to the civil service employment system of the Department of Defense or the Coast Guard, respectively.

[70 FR 31291, May 31, 2005, as amended at 74 FR 23938, May 22, 2009]

§531.217 Special conversion rules for certain non-GS employees.

When an employee moves (without a break in service) to a GS position from a non-GS system under an authority in 5 U.S.C. chapters 47, 95, or similar provision of law, and that authority provides that an employee will be converted to GS-equivalent rates immediately before leaving the non-GS system, the employee is considered a GS employee in applying the provisions of this subpart.

USING A HIGHEST PREVIOUS RATE UNDER THE MAXIMUM PAYABLE RATE RULE

§531.221 Maximum payable rate rule.

(a) *General.* (1) An agency may apply the maximum payable rate rule as described in this section to determine an employee's payable rate of basic pay under the GS pay system at a rate higher than the otherwise applicable rate upon reemployment, transfer, reassignment, promotion, demotion, change in type of appointment, termination of a critical position pay authority under 5 CFR part 535, movement from a non-GS pay system, or termination of grade or pay retention under 5 CFR part 536. (NOTE: Special rules for GM employees are provided in §531.247.) A payable rate set under this section must take effect on the effective date of the action involved. This section may not be used to set an employee's rate of basic pay retroactively unless a retroactive action is required to comply with a nondiscretionary agency policy.

(2) At its discretion, an agency may set an employee's rate(s) of basic pay at the maximum rate identified under this section or at a lower rate. However, the employee's rate may not be lower than the rate to which he or she is entitled under any other applicable pay-setting rule.

(3) In applying this section, an agency must use applicable annual rates of pay or, if a rate under a non-GS system is an hourly rate, convert the hourly rate to an annual rate.

(4) In applying this section, an agency must treat a critical position pay rate under 5 CFR part 535 as if it were a rate under a non-GS pay system, as described in paragraph (d) of this section.

(5) In applying this section, an agency must treat an adjusted GS rate that includes market pay under 38 U.S.C. 7431(c) as if it were a rate under a non-GS pay system, as described in paragraph (d) of this section.

(b) *When highest previous rate is based on a GS rate or LEO special base rate.* When an employee's highest previous rate (as determined under §531.222) is based on a GS rate or an LEO special base rate paid under the GS pay system, an agency must determine the maximum payable rate of basic pay that may be paid to the employee as follows:

(1) Compare the employee's highest previous rate with the GS rates for the grade in which pay is currently being set. For this comparison, use the schedule of GS rates in effect at the time the highest previous rate was earned. In applying this paragraph to an employee who was a law enforcement officer receiving an LEO special base rate when the highest previous rate was earned, compare the highest previous rate to the applicable LEO special base rates in lieu of GS rates if the grade in which pay is currently being set is one of the grades from GS–3 through GS–10.

(2) Identify the lowest step in the grade at which the GS rate (or LEO special base rate, if applicable) was equal to or greater than the employee's highest previous rate. If the employee's highest previous rate was greater than the maximum GS rate (or LEO special base rate, if applicable) for the grade, identify the step 10 rate (*i.e.*, maximum rate of the grade).

(3) Identify the rate on the currently applicable range of GS rates or LEO special base rates for the employee's current position of record and grade that corresponds to the step identified in paragraph (b)(2) of this section. This rate is the maximum payable GS rate or LEO special base rate the agency

may pay the employee under this section.

(4) After setting the employee's GS or LEO special base rate within the rate range for the grade (not to exceed the maximum payable rate identified in paragraph (b)(3) of this section), the agency must determine the employee's payable rate of basic pay based on the employee's GS or LEO special base rate.

(c) *When highest previous rate is based on a GS employee's special rate.* When a GS employee is reassigned under the conditions described in § 531.222(c), the employee's former special rate in effect immediately before the reassignment may be used as the employee's highest previous rate. If the employee's former special rate schedule is being adjusted on the effective date of the employee's reassignment, the agency must determine what the employee's special rate would have been on that adjusted schedule (before any other simultaneous action) and treat the resulting special rate as the employee's former special rate in applying paragraph (c)(1) and (2) of this section. The agency must apply the maximum payable rate rule as follows:

(1) When the employee is assigned to an official worksite within the geographic boundaries of a formerly applicable special rate schedule, compare the former special rate to the rates of basic pay in the highest applicable rate range for the employee's current position of record and current official worksite. Identify the lowest step rate in that range that equals or exceeds the former special rate (or the maximum step rate, if the former special rate exceeds the range maximum). That step rate is the employee's maximum payable rate of basic pay.

(2) When the employee is assigned to an official worksite outside the geographic boundaries of the formerly applicable special rate schedule, determine the maximum payable rate as follows:

(i) Convert the former special rate to a corresponding rate (same step) in the current highest applicable rate range for the new official worksite based on the employee's position of record immediately before the reassignment.

(ii) If the rate resulting from the geographic conversion under paragraph (c)(2)(i) of this section is a special rate, that converted special rate is deemed to be the employee's former special rate and highest previous rate in applying paragraph (c)(2)(iii) of this section. If the resulting rate is not a special rate, this paragraph (c) may not be used to determine the employee's maximum payable rate. Instead, paragraph (b) of this section must be used.

(iii) Compare the employee's highest previous rate (*i.e.*, the former special rate after the geographic conversion) with the rates on the current highest applicable rate range for the new official worksite based on the employee's position of record after the reassignment. Identify the lowest step rate in that range that equals or exceeds the highest previous rate (or the maximum step rate, if the highest previous rate exceeds the range maximum). That step rate is the employee's maximum payable rate of basic pay.

(3) After setting the employee's rate of basic pay in the highest applicable rate range (not to exceed the maximum payable rate), the agency must determine any underlying rate of basic pay to which the employee is entitled based on the employee's step rate.

(d) *When highest previous rate is based on a rate under a non-GS pay system.* When an employee's highest previous rate (as provided in § 531.222) is based on a rate of basic pay in a non-GS pay system, the agency must determine the maximum payable rate of basic pay that may be paid to the employee in his or her current GS position of record as follows:

(1) Compare the highest previous rate to the highest applicable rate range in effect at the time and place where the highest previous rate was earned. The highest applicable rate range is determined as if the employee held the current GS position of record (including grade in which pay is being set) at that time and place. Identify the lowest step rate in that range that was equal to or higher than the highest previous rate (or the maximum step rate if the highest previous rate exceeded the range maximum).

(2) Convert the step rate identified in paragraph (d)(1) of this section to a

corresponding rate (same step) in the current highest applicable rate range for the employee's current GS position of record and official worksite. That step rate is the employee's maximum payable rate of basic pay.

(3) After setting the employee's rate of basic pay in the current highest applicable rate range (not to exceed the maximum payable rate), the agency must determine any underlying rate of basic pay to which the employee is entitled at the determined step rate.

[70 FR 31291, May 31, 2005, as amended at 73 FR 66152, Nov. 7, 2008]

§531.222 Rates of basic pay that may be used as the highest previous rate.

(a)(1) Subject to the conditions in this section and §531.223, the highest previous rate used in applying §531.221 is—

(i) The highest rate of basic pay previously received by an individual while employed in a civilian position in any part of the Federal Government (including service with the government of the District of Columbia for employees first employed by that government before October 1, 1987), without regard to whether the position was in the GS pay system; or

(ii) The highest rate of basic pay in effect when a GS employee held his or her highest GS grade and highest step within that grade.

(2) The highest previous rate must be a rate of basic pay received by an employee while serving on a regular tour of duty—

(i) Under an appointment not limited to 90 days or less; or

(ii) For a continuous period of not less than 90 days under one or more appointments without a break in service.

(b) For periods of service as a GS employee, the highest previous rate may not be a special rate, except as provided in paragraph (c) of this section. If the highest previous rate is a locality rate, the underlying GS rate or an LEO special base rate associated with that locality rate must be used as the highest previous rate in applying §531.221(b).

(c) An agency may use a GS employee's special rate established under 5 U.S.C. 5305 and 5 CFR part 530, subpart C, or 38 U.S.C. 7455 as the highest previous rate when all of the following conditions apply:

(1) The employee is reassigned to another position in the same agency at the same grade level;

(2) The special rate is the employee's rate of basic pay immediately before the reassignment; and

(3) An authorized agency official finds that the need for the services of the employee, and the employee's contribution to the program of the agency, will be greater in the position to which reassigned. An agency must make such determinations on a case-by-case basis. In each case, the agency must document the determination to use the special rate as an employee's highest previous rate in writing.

(d) When an agency is barred from using a special rate established under 5 U.S.C. 5305 and 5 CFR part 530, subpart C, or 38 U.S.C. 7455 as an employee's highest previous rate under §531.223(g), the agency must consider a special rate employee's underlying GS rate (or LEO special base rate, if applicable) in determining the employee's highest previous rate for the purpose of applying paragraph (b) of this section.

[70 FR 31291, May 31, 2005, as amended at 70 FR 74995, Dec. 19, 2005]

§531.223 Rates of basic pay that may not be used as the highest previous rate.

The highest previous rate may not be based on the following:

(a) A rate received under an appointment as an expert or consultant under 5 U.S.C. 3109;

(b) A rate received in a position to which the employee was temporarily promoted for less than 1 year, except upon permanent placement in a position at the same or higher grade;

(c) A rate received in a position from which the employee was reassigned or reduced in grade for failure to satisfactorily complete a probationary period as a supervisor or manager;

(d) A rate received by an individual while employed by the government of the District of Columbia who was first employed by that government on or after October 1, 1987;

(e) A rate received by an individual while employed by a Department of Defense or Coast Guard nonappropriated fund instrumentality;

(f) A rate received solely during a period of interim relief under 5 U.S.C. 7701(b)(2)(A);

(g) A special rate established under 5 U.S.C. 5305 and 5 CFR part 530, subpart C, or 38 U.S.C. 7455 (except as provided in § 531.222(c));

(h) A rate received under a void appointment or a rate otherwise contrary to applicable law or regulation;

(i) A rate received as a member of the uniformed services; or

(j) A retained rate under 5 U.S.C. 5363 or a similar rate under another legal authority.

[70 FR 31291, May 31, 2005, as amended at 73 FR 66153, Nov. 7, 2008]

SPECIAL RULES FOR GM EMPLOYEES

§ 531.241 Retaining and losing GM status.

(a) An employee retains status as a GM employee (as defined in § 531.203) when detailed to any position or when reassigned to another GS position in which the employee continues to be a supervisor or management official (as defined in 5 U.S.C. 7103(a)(10) and (11)).

(b) An employee permanently loses status as a GM employee if he or she is promoted (including a temporary promotion), transferred, demoted, reassigned to a position in which the employee will no longer be a supervisor or management official, has a break in service of more than 3 days, or becomes entitled to a retained rate under 5 CFR part 536. (A retained grade is not considered in determining whether a GM employee has been reduced in grade. See 5 CFR 536.205.)

§ 531.242 Setting pay upon loss of GM status.

(a) On loss of status as a GM employee under § 531.241 (except as provided in paragraph (b) of this section), an employee must receive his or her existing payable rate of basic pay, plus any of the following adjustments that may be applicable on the effective date of the loss of status, in the order specified:

(1) The amount of any annual adjustment in GS rates under 5 U.S.C. 5303, and the amount of any adjustment in locality payments or special rate supplements, to which the employee otherwise would be entitled on that date;

(2) The amount of any within-grade increase to which the employee otherwise would be entitled on that date under 5 U.S.C. 5335 and subpart D of this part;

(3) The amount resulting from a promotion effective on that date (consistent with § 531.243(c));

(4) In the case of an employee who loses GM status without a change of grade and whose GS rate falls between two steps of a GS grade, the amount of any increase needed to pay the employee the rate for the next higher step of that grade; and

(5) In the case of an employee whose resulting GS rate is below the minimum rate of a GS grade, the amount of any increase needed to pay the employee the minimum rate for that grade.

(b) For an employee who loses status as a GM employee as a result of a demotion, pay must be set as provided in § 531.215. A GM employee's off-step GS rate at the grade before demotion is not converted to a GS step rate before the demotion, but the employee must be placed on a GS step rate when pay is set in the lower grade.

§ 531.243 Promotion of a GM employee.

(a) Upon promotion, an employee's status as a GM employee ends, as provided in § 531.241(b).

(b) When an employee loses status as a GM employee because of a temporary promotion and is returned to the lower grade upon expiration or termination of the temporary promotion under § 531.215(c)(1), he or she will be deemed to have been placed at the lowest step rate that equals or exceeds the employee's former GS rate (as a GM employee) on the effective date of the temporary promotion, before applying any other step increases based on his or her service during the temporary promotion.

(c) A GM employee's GS rate is used as the existing rate of pay in applying the promotion rule in § 531.214. A GM employee's off-step GS rate in the grade before promotion is not converted to a GS step rate in applying the promotion rule, but the employee must be placed on a GS step rate in the post-promotion grade.

§ 531.244 Adjusting a GM employee's rate at the time of an annual pay adjustment.

(a) On the effective date of an annual pay adjustment under 5 U.S.C. 5303 or similar authority, an agency must set the new GS rate for a GM employee as follows:

(1) For a GM employee whose GS rate equals a regular GS step rate, set the employee's rate at the new step rate in the adjusted General Schedule that corresponds to the employee's grade and step as in effect immediately before the effective date of the pay adjustment.

(2) For a GM employee whose GS rate is below the minimum rate of the GS rate range for the employee's grade, increase the existing GS rate by the same percentage as the annual pay adjustment for the GS rate range applicable to the employee's grade, with the result rounded to the nearest dollar (not to exceed the minimum rate of the range).

(3) For a GM employee whose GS rate is between GS step rates, apply the following method:

Step A	Using the rates and ranges in effect immediately *before* the annual pay adjustment, find the difference between the GM employee's GS rate and the minimum rate of the GS rate range for the employee's grade.
Step B	Find the difference between the maximum rate and minimum rate of the GS rate range in effect immediately before the annual pay adjustment. (If the GS maximum rate was not payable because of the EX level V pay limitation in 5 U.S.C. 5303(f), use the uncapped maximum rate.)
Step C	Divide the result from step A by the result from step B. Carry this result to the seventh decimal place and truncate, rather than round, the result. This decimal factor represents the employee's relative position in the rate range.
Step D	Using rates and ranges in effect *after* the annual pay adjustment, find the difference between the maximum rate and minimum rate of the new GS rate range for the employee's grade. (If the GS maximum rate was not payable because of the EX level V pay limitation, use the uncapped maximum rate.)
Step E	Multiply the result from step D by the factor derived from step C.
Step F	Add the result from step E to the minimum rate of the employee's current GS rate range and round to the next higher whole dollar. The resulting rate is the GM employee's new GS rate (subject to the EX level V pay limitation).

(b) [Reserved]

[70 FR 31291, May 31, 2005, as amended at 73 FR 66153, Nov. 7, 2008]

§ 531.245 Computing locality rates and special rates for GM employees.

Locality rates and special rates are computed for GM employees in the same manner as locality rates and special rates for other GS employees. The applicable locality payment or special rate supplement is added on top of the GM employee's GS rate.

§ 531.246 Within-grade increases for GM employees.

GM employees are entitled to within-grade increases as provided under subpart D of this part. A within-grade increase may not cause a GM employee's GS rate to exceed the maximum GS rate of his or her grade. GM employees may receive quality step increases as provided in subpart E of this part.

[73 FR 66153, Nov. 7, 2008]

§ 531.247 Maximum payable rate rule for GM employees.

(a) A rate received by a GM employee may qualify as a highest previous rate under § 531.222.

(b) As provided in §§ 531.221(a) and 531.241(b), if an employee loses status as a GM employee because of a transfer, promotion, demotion, or reassignment to a position in which the employee will no longer be a supervisor or management official, and if the employing agency after the action chooses to apply the maximum payable rate rule, the agency must follow the rules in § 531.221.

(c) If an employee retains GM status after an action that allows application of the maximum payable rate rule in § 531.221 to set the employee's pay, the rules in § 531.221 must be applied in accordance with the following special provisions:

(1) In comparing the employee's highest previous rate to an applicable rate

range for the grade in which pay is being set, do not identify the lowest step rate that equals or exceeds the highest previous rate. Instead, identify the rate in the rate range that equals the highest previous rate unless that highest previous rate is below the range minimum or above the range maximum. If the highest previous rate is below the range minimum, identify the minimum rate (step 1) of the grade. If the highest previous rate is above the range maximum, identify the maximum rate (step 10) of the grade.

(2) In applying §531.221(b) for an employee whose highest previous rate is a GS rate, the highest previous rate must be compared to the GS rate range for the grade in which pay is currently being set, but which was in effect at the time the highest previous rate was earned. If the highest previous rate was earned while the current GS rate range was in effect, the rate identified under paragraph (c)(1) of this section is the maximum payable GS rate. Otherwise, based on the rate identified in paragraph (c)(1) of this section, the agency must determine the corresponding rate in the current GS rate range for the grade in which pay is currently being set. That corresponding rate is the maximum payable GS rate. If the highest previous rate was above the range minimum and below the range maximum, the corresponding rate in the current GS rate range must be derived as follows:

Step A	Find the difference between the employee's highest previous rate and the minimum rate for the GS rate range (for the employee's current grade) in effect at the time the highest previous rate was earned.
Step B	Find the difference between the maximum rate and the minimum GS rate for the rate range identified in step A. (If the GS maximum rate was not payable because of the EX level V pay limitation, use the uncapped maximum rate.)
Step C	Divide the result from step A by the result from step B. Carry this result to the seventh decimal place and truncate, rather than round, the result. This decimal factor represents the employee's relative position in the rate range.
Step D	Using the current GS rate range (for the employee's current grade), find the difference between the maximum rate and the minimum rate. (If the maximum GS rate was not payable because of the EX level V pay limitation, use the uncapped maximum GS rate.)
Step E	Multiply the result from step D by the factor derived under step C.
Step F	Add the result from step E to the minimum rate for the employee's current GS rate range and round to the next higher whole dollar. This rate is the maximum payable GS rate the agency may pay the employee (subject to the EX level V pay limitation).

(3) In applying §531.221(c) for an employee whose highest previous rate is a special rate, the highest previous rate (after any geographic conversion) must be compared directly to the current highest applicable rate range for the employee's position of record and official worksite after reassignment. Thus, the rate identified under paragraph (c)(1) of this section is the maximum payable rate of basic pay.

[70 FR 31291, May 31, 2005, as amended at 73 FR 66153, Nov. 7, 2008]

Subpart C [Reserved]

Subpart D—Within-Grade Increases

SOURCE: 46 FR 2319, Jan. 9, 1981, unless otherwise noted.

§531.401 Principal authorities.

The following are the principal authorities for the regulations in this subpart:

(a) Section 2301(b)(3) of title 5, United States Code, provides in part that "appropriate incentives and recognition should be provided for excellence in performance."

(b) Section 5301(a)(2) of title 5, United States Code, provides that "pay distinctions be maintained in keeping with work and performance distinctions."

(c) Section 5338 of title 5, United States Code, provides that "The Office of Personnel Management may prescribe regulations necessary for the administration" of General Schedule pay rates, including within-grade increases.

(d) Section 4 of the Performance Management and Recognition System Termination Act of 1993 (Pub. L. 103–89) provides that "the Office of Personnel Management shall prescribe regulations necessary for the administration of this section."

[51 FR 8419, Mar. 11, 1986, as amended at 59 FR 40793, Aug. 10, 1994; 60 FR 33098, June 27, 1995]

§531.402 Employee coverage.

(a) Except as provided in paragraph (b) of this section, this subpart applies to employees who—

(1) Are classified and paid under the General Schedule;

(2) Occupy permanent positions; and

(3) Are paid less than the maximum rate of their grade.

(b) This subpart does not apply to any employee who is appointed by the President, by and with the advice and consent of the Senate.

[70 FR 31301, May 31, 2005]

§531.403 Definitions.

In this subpart:

Acceptable level of competence means performance by an employee that warrants advancement of the employee's rate of basic pay to the next higher step of the grade or the next higher rate within the grade (as defined in this section) of his or her position, subject to the requirements of §531.404 of this subpart, as determined by the head of the agency (or designee).

Agency means an agency with employees covered by this subpart, as provided in §531.402.

Calendar week means a period of any seven consecutive calendar days.

Critical element has the meaning given that term in §430.203 of this chapter.

Employee has the meaning given that term in 5 U.S.C. 2105, except that for the purpose of applying the provisions regarding equivalent increases and creditable service with respect to non-GS service, *employee* also includes—

(1) An individual employed by the U.S. Postal Service or the Postal Rate Commission who would be considered an employee under 5 U.S.C. 2105 but for the exclusion in section 2105(e); and

(2) An individual employed by a non-appropriated fund instrumentality for service that is creditable under §531.406(b)(4).

Equivalent increase means an increase in an employee's rate of basic pay, or an opportunity for such an increase under a non-GS pay system, as described in §531.407.

General Schedule or *GS* means the classification and pay system established under 5 U.S.C. chapter 51 and subchapter III of chapter 53. The term also refers to the pay schedule of GS rates established under 5 U.S.C. 5332, as adjusted under 5 U.S.C. 5303 or other law (including GS rates payable to GM employees). Law enforcement officers receiving LEO special base rates are covered by the GS classification and pay system, but receive higher base rates of pay in lieu of GS rates at grades GS–3 through GS–10.

GM employee has the meaning given that term in 5 CFR 531.203.

GS rate means a rate of basic pay within the General Schedule, excluding additional pay of any kind such as locality payments under subpart F of this part and special rate supplements under 5 CFR part 530, subpart C, or 38 U.S.C. 7455. A rate payable to a GM employee is considered a GS rate.

Law enforcement officer or *LEO* has the meaning given that term in 5 CFR 550.103.

LEO special base rate means a special base rate established for GS law enforcement officers at grades GS–3 through GS–10 under section 403 of the Federal Employees Pay Comparability

Act of 1990 (section 529 of Pub. L. 101–509, November 5, 1990, as amended) which is used in lieu of a GS rate.

Next higher rate within the grade for a GM employee means the rate of basic pay that exceeds the employee's existing rate of basic pay by one within-grade increase, not to exceed the maximum rate of the grade. For the purpose of this definition, a within-grade increase equals the dollar value of the GS within-grade increase for the applicable grade (excluding any locality payment, special rate supplement, or any other additional payment).

Permanent position means a position filled by an employee whose appointment is not designated as temporary by law and does not have a definite time limitation of one year or less. "Permanent position" includes a position to which an employee is promoted on a temporary or term basis for at least one year.

Promotion means an employee's movement from one grade or level to a higher grade or level while continuously employed (including such a movement in conjunction with a transfer).

Rate of basic pay means the rate of pay fixed by law or administrative action for the position held by an employee before any deductions and exclusive of additional pay of any kind. For an employee covered by the General Schedule, that *rate of basic pay* is the GS rate or, if applicable, an LEO special base rate.

Scheduled tour of duty means any work schedule established for an employee in accordance with the regular procedures for the establishment of workweeks in § 610.111 of this chapter. For a full-time employee this includes the basic 40-hour workweek. For a part-time employee this is any regularly scheduled work of less than 40-hours during the administrative workweek.

Temporary promotion means a time-limited promotion with a not-to-exceed date or a specified term.

Waiting period means the minimum time requirement of creditable service to become eligible for consideration for a within-grade increase.

Within-grade increase is synonymous with the term "step increase" used in 5 U.S.C. 5335 and means—* *

(1) A periodic increase in an employee's rate of basic pay from one step of the grade of his or her position to the next higher step of that grade in accordance with section 5335 of title 5, United States Code, and this subpart; or

(2) For a GM employee whose rate does not equal a regular GS step rate (*i.e.*, an off-step rate), a periodic increase in an employee's rate of basic pay from the employee's current rate to the next higher rate within the grade (as defined in this section) consistent with section 4 of Public Law 103–89.

[46 FR 2319, Jan. 9, 1981, as amended at 46 FR 41019, Aug. 14, 1981; 48 FR 49486, Oct. 25, 1983; 51 FR 8420, Mar. 11, 1986; 58 FR 65536, Dec. 15, 1993; 59 FR 40793, Aug. 10, 1994; 60 FR 33098, June 27, 1995; 60 FR 43947, Aug. 23, 1995; 70 FR 31301, May 31, 2005]

§ 531.404 Earning within-grade increase.

An employee paid at less than the maximum rate of the grade of his or her position shall earn advancement in pay to the next higher step of the grade or the next higher rate within the grade (as defined in § 531.403) upon meeting the following three requirements established by law:

(a) The employee's performance must be at an acceptable level of competence, as defined in this subpart. To be determined at an acceptable level of competence, the employee's most recent rating of record (as defined in § 430.203 of this chapter) shall be at least Level 3 ("Fully Successful" or equivalent).

(1) When a within-grade increase decision is not consistent with the employee's most recent rating of record a more current rating of record must be prepared.

(2) The rating of record used as the basis for an acceptable level of competence determination for a within-grade increase must have been assigned no earlier than the most recently completed appraisal period.

(b) The employee must have completed the required waiting period for advancement to the next higher step of the grade of his or her position.

(c) The employee must not have received an equivalent increase during the waiting period.

[51 FR 8420, Mar. 11, 1986, as amended at 58 FR 65536, Dec. 15, 1993; 60 FR 43948, Aug. 23, 1995]

§531.405 Waiting periods for within-grade increase.

(a) *Length of waiting period.* (1) For an employee with a scheduled tour of duty, the waiting periods for advancement to the next higher step in all General Schedule grades (or the next higher rate within the grade, as defined in §531.403) are:

(i) Rate of basic pay less than the rate of basic pay at step 4–52 calendar weeks of creditable service;

(ii) Rate of basic pay equal to or greater than the rate of basic pay at step 4 and less than the rate of basic pay at step 7–104 calendar weeks of creditable service; and

(iii) Rate of basic pay equal to or greater than the rate of basic pay at step 7–156 calendar weeks of creditable service.

(2) For an employee without a scheduled tour of duty, the waiting periods for advancement to the next higher step of all General Schedule grades (or the next higher rate within the grade, as defined in §531.403) are:

(i) Rate of basic pay less than the rate of basic pay at step 4–260 days of creditable service in a pay status over a period of not less than 52 calendar weeks;

(ii) Rate of basic pay equal to or greater than the rate of basic pay at step 4 and less than the rate of basic pay at step 7–520 days of creditable service in a pay status over a period of not less than 104 calendar weeks; and

(iii) Rate of basic pay equal to or greater than the rate of basic pay at step 7–780 days of creditable service in a pay status over a period of not less than 156 calendar weeks.

(b) *Commencement of a waiting period.* A waiting period begins;

(1) On the first appointment as an employee of the Federal Government, regardless of tenure;

(2) On receiving an equivalent increase; or

(3) After a period of nonpay status or a break in service (alone or in combination) in excess of 52 calendar weeks, unless the nonpay status or break in service is creditable service under §531.406 of this subpart.

(c) A waiting period is not interrupted by non-workdays intervening between an employee's last scheduled workday in one position and his or her first scheduled workday in a new position.

[46 FR 2319, Jan. 9, 1981, as amended at 58 FR 65536, Dec. 15, 1993; 59 FR 40794, Aug. 10, 1994]

§531.406 Creditable service.

(a) *General.* Civilian employment in any branch of the Federal Government (executive, legislative, or judicial) or with a Government corporation as defined in section 103 of title 5, United States Code, is creditable service in the computation of a waiting period. Service credit is given during this employment for periods of annual, sick, and other leave with pay; advanced annual and sick leave; service under a temporary or term appointment; and service under an interim appointment made under §772.102 of this chapter. Depending on the specific provision of law or regulation, service may be creditable for the completion of one waiting period or for the completion of successive waiting periods. Paragraph (b) of this section identifies service which is creditable in the computation of a single waiting period. Paragraph (c) identifies service which is creditable in the computation of successive waiting periods.

(b) *Service creditable for one within-grade increase.* (1) Military service as defined in section 8331(13) of title 5, United States Code, is creditable service in the computation of a waiting period when an employee is reemployed with the Federal Government not later than 52 calendar weeks after separation from such service or hospitalization continuing thereafter for a period of not more than one year.

(2) Time in a nonpay status (based upon the tour of duty from which the time was charged) is creditable service in the computation of a waiting period for an employee with a scheduled tour of duty when it does not exceed an aggregate of:

(i) Two workweeks in the waiting period for an employee whose rate of basic pay is less than the rate of basic pay for step 4 of the applicable grade;

(ii) Four workweeks in the waiting period for an employee whose rate of basic pay is equal to or greater than the rate of basic pay for step 4 of the applicable grade and less than the rate of basic pay for step 7 of the applicable grade; and

(iii) Six workweeks in the waiting period for an employee whose rate of basic pay is equal to or greater than the rate of basic pay for step 7 of the applicable grade.

(3) Except as provided in paragraph (c) of this section, time in a nonpay status (based upon the tour of duty from which the time was charged) that is in excess of the allowable amount shall extend a waiting period by the excess amount.

(4) Service by an employee of a nonappropriated fund instrumentality of the Department of Defense or the Coast Guard, as defined in 5 U.S.C. 2105(c), who moves, within the civil service employment system of the Department of Defense or the Coast Guard, respectively, and without a break in service of more than 3 days, to a position classified and paid under the General Schedule, is creditable service in the computation of a waiting period.

(c) *Service creditable for succesive within-grade increases.* (1) A leave of absence from a position in which an employee is covered by this subpart, whether the employee is on leave without pay or is considered to be on furlough, is creditable service in the computation of waiting periods for successive within-grade increases when:

(i) The employee is absent for the purpose of engaging in military service as defined in section 8331(13) of title 5, United States Code, and returns to a pay status through the exercise of a restoration right provided by law, Executive order, or regulation;

(ii) The employee is receiving injury compensation under subchapter I of chapter 81 of title 5, United States Code;

(iii) The employee is performing service that is creditable under section 8332(b) (5) or (7) of title 5, United States Code;

(iv) The employee is temporarily employed by another agency in a position covered by this subpart; or

(v) The employee is assigned to a State or local government or institution of higher education under sections 3371–3376 of title 5, United States Code.

(2) The period from the date of an employee's separation from Federal service with a restoration or reemployment right granted by law, Executive order, or regulation to the date of restoration or reemployment with the Federal Government through the exercise of that right is creditable service in the computation of waiting periods for successive within-grade increases.

(3) The period during which a separated employee is in receipt of injury compensation under subchapter I of chapter 81 of title 5, United States Code, as a result of an injury incurred by the employee in the performance of duty is creditable service in the computation of waiting periods for successive within-grade increases when the employee is reemployed with the Federal Government.

[46 FR 2319, Jan. 9, 1981, as amended at 46 FR 41019, Aug. 14, 1981; 46 FR 43371, Aug. 28, 1981; 46 FR 45747, Sept. 15, 1981; 57 FR 3712, Jan. 31, 1992; 57 FR 12404, Apr. 10, 1992; 59 FR 40794, Aug. 10, 1994; 59 FR 66332, Dec. 28, 1994; 73 FR 66153, Nov. 7, 2008]

§ 531.407 Equivalent increase determinations.

(a) *GS employees.* For a GS employee, an equivalent increase is considered to occur at the time of any of the following personnel actions:

(1) A within-grade increase, excluding a quality step increase granted under subpart E of this part or an interim within-grade increase if that increase is later terminated under § 531.414;

(2) A promotion (permanent or temporary) to a higher grade, including the promotion of an employee receiving a retained rate under 5 CFR 359.705 or 5 CFR part 536 that does not result in a pay increase, but excluding—

(i) A temporary promotion if, at the end of the that temporary promotion, the employee is returned to the grade from which promoted; or

(ii) A promotion to a higher-graded supervisory or managerial position when the employee does not satisfactorily complete a probationary period established under 5 U.S.C. 3321(a)(2) and is returned to a position at the lower grade held before promotion;

(3) Application of the maximum payable rate rule in §531.221 that results in a higher step rate within the employee's GS grade (or an increase for a GM employee to the next higher rate within the grade), except for application of that rule in a demotion to the extent that the employee's rate of basic pay after demotion does not exceed the lowest step rate that equals or exceeds the employee's rate of basic pay immediately before the demotion;

(4) Application of the superior qualifications and special needs pay-setting authority in §531.212 that results in a higher step rate within the employee's GS grade (or an increase for a GM employee to the next higher rate within the grade); or

(5) Application of the qualifications pay authority in 5 U.S.C. 9814 to an employee of the National Aeronautics and Space Administration, when the employee fulfills the 1-year service requirement in the position for which qualifications pay was paid or in a successor position.

(b) *Non-GS employees who move to the GS pay system.* When an employee performs service under a non-GS pay system for Federal employees and that service is potentially creditable towards a GS within-grade increase waiting period, an equivalent increase is considered to occur at the time of any of the following personnel actions in the non-GS pay system:

(1) A promotion to a higher grade or work level within the non-GS pay system (unless the promotion is cancelled and the employee's rate of basic pay is redetermined as if the promotion had not occurred); or

(2) An opportunity to receive a within-level or within-range increase that results in forward movement in the applicable range of rates of basic pay (including an increase granted immediately upon movement to the non-GS pay system from another pay system—e.g., to account for the value of accrued within-grade increases under the former pay system or to provide a promotion-equivalent increase), where "forward movement in the applicable range" means any kind of increase in the employee's rate of basic pay other than an increase that is directly and exclusively linked to—

(i) A general structural increase in the employee's basic pay schedule or rate range (including the adjustment of a range minimum or maximum); or

(ii) The employee's placement under a new basic pay schedule within the same pay system, when such placement results in a nondiscretionary basic pay increase to account for occupational pay differences.

(c) *Locality rates and special rates.* Since locality rates under subpart F of this part and special rates under 5 CFR part 530, subpart C, and similar rates under other legal authority (e.g., 38 U.S.C. 7455) are not rates of basic pay for the purpose of this subpart, increases in pay resulting from an adjustment in an employee's locality payment or special rate supplement or from placement on a new locality rate or special rate schedule are not considered in making equivalent increase determinations.

[70 FR 31301, May 31, 2005, as amended at 70 FR 74995, Dec. 19, 2005; 73 FR 66153, Nov. 7, 2008]

§531.408 [Reserved]

§531.409 Acceptable level of competence determinations.

(a) *Responsibility.* The head of the agency or other agency official to whom such authority is delegated shall determine which employees are performing at an acceptable level of competence.

(b) *Basis for determination.* When applicable, an acceptable level of competence determination shall be based on a current rating of record made under part 430, subpart B, of this chapter. For those agencies not covered by chapter 43 of title 5, United States Code, and for employees in positions excluded from 5 U.S.C. 4301, an acceptable level of competence determination shall be based on performance appraisal requirements established by the agency. If an employee has been reduced in grade because of unacceptable performance and has served in one position at the lower grade for at least the minimum period established by the agency, a rating of record at the lower grade shall be used as the basis for an acceptable level of competence determination.

(c) *Delay in determination.* (1) An acceptable level of competence determination shall be delayed when, and only when, either of the following applies:

(i) An employee has not had the minimum period of time established at § 430.207(a) of this chapter to demonstrate acceptable performance because he or she has not been informed of the specific requirements for performance at an acceptable level of competence in his or her current position, and the employee has not been given a performance rating in any position within the minimum period of time (as established at § 430.207(a) of this chapter) before the end of the waiting period; or

(ii) An employee is reduced in grade because of unacceptable performance to a position in which he or she is eligible for a within-grade increase or will become eligible within the minimum period as established at § 430.207(a) of this chapter.

(2) When an acceptable level of competence determination has been delayed under this subpart:

(i) The employee shall be informed that his or her determination is postponed and the appraisal period extended and shall be told of the specific requirements for performance at an acceptable level of competence.

(ii) An acceptable level of competence determination shall then be made based on the employee's rating of record completed at the end of the extended appraisal period.

(iii) If, following the delay, the employee's performance is determined to be at an acceptable level of competence, the within-grade increase will be granted retroactively to the beginning of the pay period following completion of the applicable waiting period.

(d) *Waiver of requirement for determination.* (1) An acceptable level of competence determination shall be waived and a within-grade increase granted when an employee has not served in any position for the minimum period under an applicable agency performance appraisal program during the final 52 calendar weeks of the waiting period for one or more of the following reasons:

(i) Because of absences that are creditable service in the computation of a waiting period or periods under § 531.406 of this subpart;

(ii) Because of paid leave;

(iii) Because the employee received service credit under the back pay provisions of subpart H of part 550 of this chapter;

(iv) Because of details to another agency or employer for which no rating has been prepared;

(v) Because the employee has had insufficient time to demonstrate an acceptable level of competence due to authorized activities of official interest to the agency not subject to appraisal under part 430 of this chapter (including, but not limited to, labor-management partnership activities under section 2 of Executive Order 12871 and serving as a representative of a labor organization under chapter 71 of title 5, United States Code); or

(vi) Because of long-term training.

(2) When an acceptable level of competence determination has been waived and a within-grade increase granted under paragraph (d)(1) of this section, there shall be a presumption that the employee would have performed at an acceptable level of competence had the employee performed the duties of his or her position of record for the minimum period under the applicable agency performance appraisal program.

(e) *Notice of determination.* (1) A level of competence determination shall be communicated to an employee in writing as soon as possible after completion of the waiting period or other period upon which it was based.

(2) When the head of an agency or his or her designee determines that an employee's performance is not at an acceptable level of competence, the negative determination shall be communicated to the employee in writing and shall:

(i) Set forth the reasons for any negative determination and the respects in which the employee must improve his or her performance in order to be granted a within-grade increase under §531.411 of this subpart.

(ii) Inform the employee of his or her right to request that the appropriately designated agency official reconsider the determination.

[46 FR 2319, Jan. 9, 1981, as amended at 51 FR 8420, Mar. 11, 1986; 60 FR 43948, Aug. 23, 1995; 62 FR 62503, Nov. 24, 1997]

§531.410 Reconsideration of a negative determination.

(a) When an agency head, or his or her designee, issues a negative determination the following procedures are established in accordance with section 5335(c) of title 5, United States Code for reconsideration of the negative determination:

(1) An employee or an employee's personal representative may request reconsideration of a negative determination by filing, not more than 15 days after receiving notice of determination, a written response to the negative determination setting forth the reasons the agency shall reconsider the determination;

(2) When an employee files a request for reconsideration, the agency shall establish an employee reconsideration file which shall contain all pertinent documents relating to the negative determination and the request for reconsideration, including copies of the following:

(i) The written negative determination and the basis therefore;

(ii) The employee's written request for reconsideration;

(iii) The report of investigation when an investigation is made;

(iv) The written summary or transcript of any personal presentation made; and

(v) The agency's decision on the request for reconsideration.

The file shall not contain any document that has not been made available to the employee or his or her personal representative with an opportunity to submit a written exception to any summary of the employee's personal presentation;

(3) An employee in a duty status shall be granted a reasonable amount of official time to review the material relied upon to support the negative determination and to prepare a response to the determination; and

(4) The agency shall provide the employee with a prompt written final decision.

(b) The time limit to request a reconsideration may be extended when the employee shows he or she was not notified of the time limit and was not otherwise aware of it, or that the employee was prevented by circumstances beyond his or her control from requesting reconsideration within the time limit.

(c) An agency may disallow as an employee's personal representative an individual whose activities as a representative would cause a conflict of interest of position, an employee whose release from his or her official duties and responsibilities would give rise to unreasonable costs to the Government, or an employee whose priority work assignment precludes his or her release from official duties and responsibilities. Section 7114 of title 5, United States Code, and the terms of any applicable collective bargaining agreement govern representation for employees in an exclusive bargaining unit.

(d) When a negative determination is sustained after reconsideration, an employee shall be informed in writing of the reasons for the decision and of his or her right to appeal the decision to the Merit Systems Protection Board. However, for an employee covered by a collective bargaining agreement a reconsideration decision that sustains a negative determination is only reviewable in accordance with the terms of the agreement.

[46 FR 2319, Jan. 9, 1981, as amended at 50 FR 45389, Oct. 31, 1985]

§531.411 Continuing evaluation after withholding a within-grade increase.

When a within-grade increase has been withheld, an agency may, at any time thereafter, prepare a new rating of record for the employee and grant the within-grade increase when it determines that he or she has demonstrated sustained performance at an acceptable level of competence. However, the agency shall determine whether the employee's performance is at an acceptable level of competence after no more than 52 calendar weeks following the original eligibility date for the within-grade increase and, for as long as the within-grade increase continues to be denied, determinations will be made after no longer than each 52 calendar weeks.

[51 FR 8421, Mar. 11, 1986]

§ 531.412 Effective date of a within-grade increase.

(a) Except as provided in paragraph (b) of this section, a within-grade increase shall be effective on the first day of the first pay period following completion of the required waiting period and in compliance with the conditions of eligibility. Interim within-grade increases shall become effective as provided in § 541.414(b).

(b) When an acceptable level of competence is achieved at some time after a negative determination, the effective date is the first day of the first pay period after the acceptable determination has been made.

[46 FR 2319, Jan. 9, 1981, as amended at 46 FR 41020, Aug. 14, 1981; 59 FR 24029, May 10, 1994]

§ 531.413 Reports and evaluation of within-grade increase authority.

(a) *Reports.* The Office of Personnel Management may require agencies to maintain records and report on the use of the authority to grant or withhold within-grade increases.

(b) *Evaluation.* The Office of Personnel Management may evaluate an agency's use of the authority to grant or withhold within-grade increases. An agency shall take any corrective action required by the Office.

§ 531.414 Interim within-grade increase.

(a) An interim within-grade increase shall be granted to an employee who has:

(1) Appealed a negative within-grade increase determination to the Merit Systems Protection Board under 5 U.S.C 5335(c); and

(2) Been granted a favorable within-grade increase determination under the interim relief provisions of 5 U.S.C. 7701(b)(2).

(b) An interim within-grade increase granted under paragraph (a) of this section shall become effective on the date of the appellate decision ordering interim relief under 5 U.S.C. 7701(b)(2)(A).

(c) If the final decision of the Merit Systems Protection Board upholds the negative within-grade increase determination, an interim within-grade increase granted under this section shall be terminated on the date of the Board's final decision.

(d) If the final decision of the Merit Systems Protection Board overturns the negative within-grade increase determination, an interim within-grade increase granted under this section shall be made permanent and shall be granted retroactively to the first day of the first pay period beginning on or after completion of the applicable waiting period.

(e) An employee may not appeal the termination of an interim within-grade increase under paragraph (c) of this section.

[57 FR 3712, Jan. 31, 1992, as amended at 59 FR 24030, May 10, 1994; 59 FR 65703, Dec. 21, 1994]

Subpart E—Quality Step Increases

SOURCE: 33 FR 12448, Sept. 4, 1968, unless otherwise noted.

§ 531.501 Applicability.

This subpart contains regulations of the Office of Personnel Management to carry out section 5336 of title 5, United States Code, which authorizes the head of an agency, or another official to whom such authority is delegated, to grant quality step increases.

[60 FR 43948, Aug. 23, 1995]

§ 531.502 Definitions.

Agency means an agency defined in section 5102 of title 5, United States Code.

Employee means an employee of an agency.

Quality step increase is synonymous with the term "step increase" used in section 5336 of title 5, United States Code, and means an increase in an employee's rate of basic pay from one step or rate of the grade of his or her position to the next higher step of that grade or next higher rate within the grade (as defined in §531.403) in accordance with section 5336 of title 5, United States Code, section 4 of the Performance Management and Recognition System Termination Act of 1993 (Pub. L. 103–89), and this subpart.

[46 FR 2322, Jan. 9, 1981, as amended at 46 FR 41020, Aug. 14, 1981; 58 FR 65537, Dec. 15, 1993; 59 FR 40794, Aug. 10, 1994]

§531.503 Purpose of quality step increases.

The purpose of quality step increases is to provide appropriate incentives and recognition for excellence in performance by granting faster than normal step increases.

[60 FR 43948, Aug. 23, 1995]

§531.504 Level of performance required for quality step increase.

A quality step increase shall not be required but may be granted only to—

(a) An employee who receives a rating of record at Level 5 ("Outstanding" or equivalent), as defined in part 430, subpart B, of this chapter; or

(b) An employee who, when covered by a performance appraisal program that does not use a Level 5 summary—

(1) Receives a rating of record at the highest summary level used by the program; and

(2) Demonstrates sustained performance of high quality significantly above that expected at the "Fully Successful" level in the type of position concerned, as determined under performance-related criteria established by the agency.

[60 FR 43948, Aug. 23, 1995]

§531.505 Restrictions on granting quality step increases.

As provided by 5 U.S.C. 5336, a quality step increase may not be granted to an employee who has received a quality step increase within the preceding 52 consecutive calendar weeks.

[51 FR 8421, Mar. 11, 1986]

§531.506 Effective date of a quality step increase.

The quality step increase should be made effective as soon as practicable after it is approved.

[60 FR 43948, Aug. 23, 1995]

§531.507 Agency responsibilities.

(a) Agencies shall maintain and submit to OPM such records as OPM may require.

(b) Agencies shall report quality step increases to the Central Personnel Data File in compliance with instructions in the OPM Operating Manual, FEDERAL WORKFORCE REPORTING SYSTEMS, for sale by the U.S. Government Printing Office, Superintendent of Documents.

[60 FR 43948, Aug. 23, 1995]

§531.508 Evaluation of quality step increase authority.

The Office of Personnel Management may evaluate an agency's use of the authority to grant quality step increases. The agency shall take any corrective action required by the Office.

[60 FR 43948, Aug. 23, 1995]

Subpart F—Locality-Based Comparability Payments

SOURCE: 58 FR 69174, Dec. 30, 1993, unless otherwise noted.

EDITORIAL NOTE: Nomenclature changes to subpart F of part 531 appear at 70 FR 31305, May 31, 2005.

§531.601 Purpose.

This subpart contains Office of Personnel Management (OPM) regulations implementing 5 U.S.C. 5304, which authorizes locality payments in defined geographic areas for GS employees and other categories of employees to whom locality payments are extended. These regulations must be read together with 5 U.S.C. 5304.

[70 FR 31302, May 31, 2005]

§531.602 Definitions.

In this subpart:

CSA means the geographic scope of a Combined Statistical Area, as defined by the Office of Management and Budget (OMB) in OMB Bulletin No. 13–01, plus any areas subsequently added to the CSA by OMB.

Employee means—

(1) An employee in a position to which 5 U.S.C. chapter 53, subchapter III, applies, including a GM employee, and whose official worksite is located in a locality pay area; and

(2) An employee in a category of positions described in 5 U.S.C. 5304(h)(1)(A)–(D) for which the President (or designee) has authorized locality-based comparability payments under 5 U.S.C. 5304(h)(2) and whose official worksite is located in a locality pay area.

General Schedule or *GS* means the classification and pay system established under 5 U.S.C. chapter 51 and subchapter III of chapter 53. It also refers to the pay schedule of GS rates established under 5 U.S.C. 5332, as adjusted under 5 U.S.C. 5303 or other law (including GS rates payable to GM employees). Law enforcement officers (LEOs) receiving LEO special base rates are covered by the GS classification and pay system, but receive higher base rates of pay in lieu of GS rates at grades GS–3 through GS–10.

GM employee has the meaning given that term in 5 CFR 531.203.

GS rate means a rate of basic pay within the General Schedule, excluding any LEO special base rate and additional pay of any kind such as locality payments or special rate supplements. A rate payable to a GM employee is considered a GS rate.

Law enforcement officer or *LEO* has the meaning given that term in 5 CFR 550.103.

LEO special base rate means a special base rate established for GS law enforcement officers at grades GS–3 through GS–10 under section 403 of the Federal Employees Pay Comparability Act of 1990 (section 529 of Pub. L. 101–509, November 5, 1990, as amended) which is used in lieu of a GS rate.

Locality pay area means an area listed in §531.603 of this part, as established and modified under 5 U.S.C. 5304 by the Pay Agent designated by the President under 5 U.S.C. 5304(d)(1).

Locality payment means a locality-based comparability payment payable under 5 U.S.C. 5304 and this subpart. An employee's locality payment is the difference between the employee's locality rate and the employee's scheduled annual rate of pay.

Locality pay percentage means the percentage authorized for a locality pay area under 5 U.S.C. 5304 or 5304a which is used to compute a locality payment (before applying any maximum pay limitations under §531.606).

Locality rate means a scheduled annual rate of pay plus an applicable locality payment. An employee's locality rate is computed under §531.604.

MSA means the geographic scope of a Metropolitan Statistical Area, as defined by the Office of Management and Budget (OMB) in OMB Bulletin No. 13–01, plus any areas subsequently added to the MSA by OMB.

Official worksite means the official location of an employee's position of record as determined under §531.605.

Position of record means an employee's official position (defined by grade, occupational series, employing agency, LEO status, and any other condition that determines coverage under a pay schedule (other than official worksite)), as documented on the employee's most recent Notification of Personnel Action (Standard Form 50 or equivalent) and current position description. A position to which an employee is temporarily detailed is not documented as a position of record. For an employee whose change in official position is followed within 3 workdays by a reduction in force resulting in the employee's separation before he or she is required to report for duty in the new position, the position of record in effect immediately before the position change is deemed to remain the position of record through the date of separation.

Rate range or *range* means a range of rates of basic pay for a grade within an established pay schedule, excluding any retained rate. A rate range may consist of GS rates, LEO special base rates, locality rates, special rates, or, for non-GS employees, similar rates under other legal authority.

Retained rate means a rate above the maximum rate of the rate range applicable to the employee which is payable under 5 CFR part 536 or similar legal authority.

Scheduled annual rate of pay means, as applicable—

(1) The annual GS rate payable to an employee;

(2) An annual LEO special base rate; or

(3) For an employee in a category of positions described in 5 U.S.C. 5304(h)(1)(A)–(D) for which the President (or designee) has authorized locality payments under 5 U.S.C. 5304(h)(2), the annual rate of pay fixed by law or administrative action, exclusive of any locality-based adjustments (including adjustments equivalent to local special rate supplements under 5 CFR part 530, subpart C) or additional pay of any other kind.

Special rate means a rate of pay within a special rate schedule established under 5 CFR part 530, subpart C, or a similar rate established under other legal authority (e.g., 38 U.S.C. 7455). The term *special rate* does not include an LEO special base rate.

Special rate schedule means a pay schedule established under 5 CFR part 530, subpart C, to provide higher rates of pay for specified categories of positions or employees at one or more grades or levels or a similar schedule established under other legal authority (e.g., 38 U.S.C. 7455).

Special rate supplement means the portion of a special rate paid above an employee's scheduled annual rate of pay. However, for a law enforcement officer receiving an LEO special base rate who is also entitled to a special rate, the special rate supplement equals the portion of the special rate paid above the officer's LEO special base rate. When a special rate schedule covers both LEO positions and other positions, the value of the special rate supplement will be less for law enforcement officers receiving an LEO special base rate (since that rate is higher than the corresponding GS rate). The payable amount of a special rate supplement is subject to the Executive Schedule level IV limitation on special rates, as provided in 5 CFR 530.304(a).

Telework agreement means a formal oral or written agreement between a supervisor and an employee to permit the employee to work at an alternative worksite (*i.e.*, telework) instead of the location of the employee's assigned organization.

[58 FR 69174, Dec. 30, 1993, as amended at 59 FR 67605, Dec. 30, 1994; 61 FR 3540, Feb. 1, 1996; 62 FR 25425, May 9, 1997; 64 FR 69173, Dec. 10, 1999; 66 FR 67070, Dec. 28, 2001; 68 FR 19708, Apr. 22, 2003; 69 FR 2050, Jan. 13, 2004; 69 FR 75453, Dec. 17, 2004; 70 FR 31302, May 31, 2005; 70 FR 74995, Dec. 19, 2005; 73 FR 66153, Nov. 7, 2008; 76 FR 32862, June 7, 2011; 78 FR 5115, Jan. 24, 2013; 80 FR 65610, Oct. 27, 2015]

§531.603 Locality pay areas.

(a) Locality rates of pay under this subpart shall be payable to employees whose official worksites are located in the locality pay areas listed in paragraph (b) of this section.

(b) The following are locality pay areas for the purposes of this subpart:

(1) Alaska—consisting of the State of Alaska;

(2) Albany-Schenectady, NY—consisting of the Albany-Schenectady, NY CSA and also including Berkshire County, MA;

(3) Albuquerque-Santa Fe-Las Vegas, NM—consisting of the Albuquerque-Santa Fe-Las Vegas, NM CSA;

(4) Atlanta—Athens-Clarke County—Sandy Springs, GA-AL—consisting of the Atlanta—Athens-Clarke County—Sandy Springs, GA CSA and also including Chambers County, AL;

(5) Austin-Round Rock, TX—consisting of the Austin-Round Rock, TX MSA;

(6) Boston-Worcester-Providence, MA-RI-NH-CT-ME—consisting of the Boston-Worcester-Providence, MA-RI-NH-CT CSA, except for Windham County, CT, and also including Androscoggin County, ME, Cumberland County, ME, Sagadahoc County, ME, and York County, ME;

(7) Buffalo-Cheektowaga, NY—consisting of the Buffalo-Cheektowaga, NY CSA;

(8) Charlotte-Concord, NC-SC—consisting of the Charlotte-Concord, NC-SC CSA;

(9) Chicago-Naperville, IL-IN-WI—consisting of the Chicago-Naperville, IL-IN-WI CSA;

(10) Cincinnati-Wilmington-Maysville, OH-KY-IN—consisting of the Cincinnati-Wilmington-Maysville, OH-KY-IN CSA and also including Franklin County, IN;

(11) Cleveland-Akron-Canton, OH—consisting of the Cleveland-Akron-Canton, OH CSA and also including Harrison County, OH;

(12) Colorado Springs, CO—consisting of the Colorado Springs, CO MSA and also including Fremont County, CO, and Pueblo County, CO;

(13) Columbus-Marion-Zanesville, OH—consisting of the Columbus-Marion-Zanesville, OH CSA;

(14) Dallas-Fort Worth, TX–OK—consisting of the Dallas-Fort Worth, TX–OK CSA and also including Delta County, TX, and Fannin County, TX;

(15) Davenport-Moline, IA–IL—consisting of the Davenport-Moline, IA–IL CSA;

(16) Dayton-Springfield-Sidney, OH—consisting of the Dayton-Springfield-Sidney, OH CSA and also including Preble County, OH;

(17) Denver-Aurora, CO—consisting of the Denver-Aurora, CO CSA and also including Larimer County, CO;

(18) Detroit-Warren-Ann Arbor, MI—consisting of the Detroit-Warren-Ann Arbor, MI CSA;

(19) Harrisburg-Lebanon, PA—consisting of the Harrisburg-York-Lebanon, PA CSA, except for Adams County, PA, and York County, PA, and also including Lancaster County, PA;

(20) Hartford-West Hartford, CT–MA—consisting of the Hartford-West Hartford, CT CSA and also including Windham County, CT, Franklin County, MA, Hampden County, MA, and Hampshire County, MA;

(21) Hawaii—consisting of the State of Hawaii;

(22) Houston-The Woodlands, TX—consisting of the Houston-The Woodlands, TX CSA and also including San Jacinto County, TX;

(23) Huntsville-Decatur-Albertville, AL—consisting of the Huntsville-Decatur-Albertville, AL CSA;

(24) Indianapolis-Carmel-Muncie, IN—consisting of the Indianapolis-Carmel-Muncie, IN CSA and also including Grant County, IN;

(25) Kansas City-Overland Park-Kansas City, MO–KS—consisting of the Kansas City-Overland Park-Kansas City, MO–KS CSA and also including Jackson County, KS, Jefferson County, KS, Osage County, KS, Shawnee County, KS, and Wabaunsee County, KS;

(26) Laredo, TX—consisting of the Laredo, TX MSA;

(27) Las Vegas-Henderson, NV–AZ—consisting of the Las Vegas-Henderson, NV–AZ CSA;

(28) Los Angeles-Long Beach, CA—consisting of the Los Angeles-Long Beach, CA CSA and also including Kern County, CA, and Santa Barbara County, CA;

(29) Miami-Fort Lauderdale-Port St. Lucie, FL—consisting of the Miami-Fort Lauderdale-Port St. Lucie, FL CSA and also including Monroe County, FL;

(30) Milwaukee-Racine-Waukesha, WI—consisting of the Milwaukee-Racine-Waukesha, WI CSA;

(31) Minneapolis-St. Paul, MN–WI—consisting of the Minneapolis-St. Paul, MN–WI CSA;

(32) New York-Newark, NY–NJ–CT–PA—consisting of the New York-Newark, NY–NJ–CT–PA CSA and also including all of Joint Base McGuire-Dix-Lakehurst;

(33) Palm Bay-Melbourne-Titusville, FL—consisting of the Palm Bay-Melbourne-Titusville, FL MSA;

(34) Philadelphia-Reading-Camden, PA–NJ–DE–MD—consisting of the Philadelphia-Reading-Camden, PA–NJ–DE–MD CSA, except for Joint Base McGuire-Dix-Lakehurst;

(35) Phoenix-Mesa-Scottsdale, AZ—consisting of the Phoenix-Mesa-Scottsdale, AZ MSA;

(36) Pittsburgh-New Castle-Weirton, PA–OH–WV—consisting of the Pittsburgh-New Castle-Weirton, PA–OH–WV CSA;

(37) Portland-Vancouver-Salem, OR–WA—consisting of the Portland-Vancouver-Salem, OR–WA CSA;

(38) Raleigh-Durham-Chapel Hill, NC—consisting of the Raleigh-Durham-Chapel Hill, NC CSA and also including Cumberland County, NC, Hoke County, NC, Robeson County, NC, Scotland County, NC, and Wayne County, NC;

(39) Richmond, VA—consisting of the Richmond, VA MSA and also including Cumberland County, VA, King and Queen County, VA, and Louisa County, VA;

(40) Sacramento-Roseville, CA–NV—consisting of the Sacramento-Roseville, CA CSA and also including Carson City, NV, and Douglas County, NV;

(41) San Diego-Carlsbad, CA—consisting of the San Diego-Carlsbad, CA MSA;

(42) San Jose-San Francisco-Oakland, CA—consisting of the San Jose-San Francisco-Oakland, CA CSA and also including Monterey County, CA;

(43) Seattle-Tacoma, WA—consisting of the Seattle-Tacoma, WA CSA and also including Whatcom County, WA;

(44) St. Louis-St. Charles-Farmington, MO–IL—consisting of the St. Louis-St. Charles-Farmington, MO–IL CSA;

(45) Tucson-Nogales, AZ—consisting of the Tucson-Nogales, AZ CSA and also including Cochise County, AZ;

(46) Washington-Baltimore-Arlington, DC–MD–VA–WV–PA—consisting of the Washington-Baltimore-Arlington, DC–MD–VA–WV–PA CSA and also including Kent County, MD, Adams County, PA, York County, PA, King George County, VA, and Morgan County, WV; and

(47) Rest of U.S.—consisting of those portions of the United States and its territories and possessions as listed in 5 CFR 591.205 not located within another locality pay area.

[58 FR 69174, Dec. 30, 1993, as amended at 61 FR 42939, Aug. 19, 1996; 65 FR 75154, Dec. 1, 2000; 70 FR 31302, May 31, 2005; 72 FR 34362, June 22, 2007; 74 FR 49308, Sept. 28, 2009; 75 FR 60286, Sept. 30, 2010; 76 FR 32862, June 7, 2011; 80 FR 65611, Oct. 27, 2015]

§531.604 Determining an employee's locality rate.

(a) An annual locality rate consists of a scheduled annual rate of pay plus an applicable locality payment (representing an annual dollar amount), as determined under paragraph (b) of this section.

(b) An agency determines an employee's locality rate by—

(1) Determining the employee's official worksite consistent with the rules in §531.605;

(2) Determining the locality pay area in which the employee's official worksite is located, consistent with the locality pay areas established in §531.603;

(3) Identifying the locality pay percentage in effect in the applicable locality pay area;

(4) Increasing the employee's scheduled annual rate of pay by the applicable locality pay percentage and rounding the result to the nearest whole dollar (counting 50 cents and over as the next higher dollar); and

(5) Applying any applicable limitation as described in §531.606.

(c) A locality rate may be expressed as an hourly, daily, weekly, or biweekly rate, as provided in §531.607.

[70 FR 31303, May 31, 2005]

§531.605 Determining an employee's official worksite.

(a)(1) Except as otherwise provided in this section, the official worksite is the location of an employee's position of record where the employee regularly performs his or her duties.

(2) If the employee's work involves recurring travel or the employee's work location varies on a recurring basis, the official worksite is the location where the work activities of the employee's position of record are based, as determined by the employing agency, subject to the requirement that the official worksite must be in a locality pay area in which the employee regularly performs work.

(3) An agency must document an employee's official worksite on an employee's Notification of Personnel Action (Standard Form 50 or equivalent).

(b) For an employee who is relocated and authorized to receive relocation expenses under 5 U.S.C. chapter 57, subchapter II (or similar authority), the official worksite is the established worksite for the position in the area to which the employee has been relocated. For an employee authorized to receive relocation expenses under 5 U.S.C. 5737 in connection with an extended assignment resulting in a temporary change of station, the worksite associated with the extended assignment is the official worksite. (See 41 CFR 302–1.1.)

(c) For an employee whose assignment to a new worksite is followed within 3 workdays by a reduction in force resulting in the employee's separation before he or she is required to report for duty at the new location, the official worksite in effect immediately before the assignment remains the official worksite through the date of separation.

(d) For an employee covered by a telework agreement, the following rules apply:

(1) If the employee is scheduled to work at least twice each biweekly pay period on a regular and recurring basis at the regular worksite for the employee's position of record, the regular worksite (where the employee's work activities are based) is the employee's official worksite. However, in the case of such an employee whose work location varies on a recurring basis, the employee need not work at least twice each biweekly pay period at the regular official worksite (where the employee's work activities are based) as long as the employee is regularly performing work within the locality pay area for that worksite.

(2) An authorized agency official may make an exception to the twice-in-a-pay-period standard in paragraph (d)(1) of this section in appropriate situations of a temporary nature, such as the following:

(i) An employee is recovering from an injury or medical condition;

(ii) An employee is affected by an emergency situation, which temporarily prevents the employee from commuting to his or her regular official worksite;

(iii) An employee has an extended approved absence from work (e.g., paid leave);

(iv) An employee is in temporary duty travel status away from the official worksite; or

(v) An employee is temporarily detailed to work at a location other than a location covered by a telework agreement.

(3) If an employee covered by a telework agreement does not meet the requirements of paragraphs (d)(1) or (d)(2) of this section, the employee's official worksite is the location of the employee's telework site.

(4) An agency must determine a telework employee's official worksite on a case-by-case basis. A determination made under this paragraph (d) is within the sole and exclusive discretion of the authorized agency official, subject only to OPM review and oversight.

(e) In applying paragraph (d) of this section for the purpose of other location-based pay entitlements under other regulations that refer to this section, the reference to a *locality pay area* is deemed to be a reference to the applicable geographic area associated with the given pay entitlement. For example, for the purpose of special rates under 5 CFR part 530, subpart C, the reference to a *locality pay area* is deemed to be a reference to the geographic area covered by a special rate schedule.

[73 FR 66154, Nov. 7, 2008]

§ 531.606 Maximum limits on locality rates.

(a) Except as provided by paragraph (b) of this section, a locality rate may not exceed the rate of basic pay payable for level IV of the Executive Schedule.

(b)(1) A locality rate for an employee in a category of positions described in 5 U.S.C. 5304(h)(1)(A) and 5304(h)(1)(B) may not exceed the rate for level III of the Executive Schedule.

(2) A locality rate for an employee in a category of positions described in 5 U.S.C. 5304(h)(1)(C) may not exceed—

(i) The rate for level III of the Executive Schedule, when the positions are not covered by an appraisal system certified under 5 U.S.C. 5307(d); or

(ii) The rate for level II of the Executive Schedule, when the positions are covered by an appraisal system certified under 5 U.S.C. 5307(d).

(3) A locality rate for an employee in a category of positions described in 5 U.S.C. 5304(h)(1)(D) may not exceed—

(i) The rate for level IV of the Executive Schedule, when the maximum scheduled annual rate of pay (excluding any retained rate) for such positions is less than or equal to the maximum payable scheduled annual rate of pay for GS–15; or

(ii) The rate for level III of the Executive Schedule, when the maximum scheduled annual rate of pay (excluding any retained rate) for such positions exceeds the maximum payable scheduled annual rate of pay for GS–15, but is not more than the rate for level IV of the Executive Schedule.

(4) If initial application of paragraph (b)(3) of this section otherwise would reduce an employee's existing locality rate, the employee's locality rate is capped at the higher of—

(i) The amount of the employee's locality rate on the day before paragraph (b)(3) of this section was initially applied; or

(ii) The rate for level IV of the Executive Schedule.

(c) Paragraph (b) of this section does not apply to experts and consultants appointed under 5 U.S.C. 3109 if the pay for those experts and consultants is limited to the highest rate payable under 5 U.S.C. 5332 (*i.e.*, the unadjusted maximum GS-15 rate). Such experts and consultants are subject to the pay limitations established in 5 CFR 304.105.

(d) A portion of a locality payment that is not payable because of an applicable limitation is not considered in applying any other provision of law or regulation.

[70 FR 31304, May 31, 2005, as amended at 76 FR 32863, June 7, 2011]

§531.607 Computing hourly, daily, weekly, and biweekly locality rates.

(a) Apply the following methods to convert an annual locality rate to an hourly, daily, weekly, or biweekly rate:

(1) To derive an hourly rate, divide the annual locality rate by 2,087 and round to the nearest cent, counting one-half cent and over as the next higher cent.

Example:
Annual locality rate = $50,000
Computation of hourly rate: $50,000 ÷ 2,087 = 23.957 or $23.96.

(2) To derive a daily rate, multiply the hourly rate by the number of daily hours of service required by the employee's basic daily tour of duty.

Example:
Hourly rate = $23.96
Daily hours = 8
Computation of daily rate: $23.96 × 8 = $191.68

(3) To derive a weekly or biweekly rate, multiply the hourly rate by 40 or 80, as applicable.

Example:
Hourly rate = $23.96
Biweekly hours = 80
Computation of biweekly rate: $23.96 × 80 = $1,916.80

(b) Notwithstanding paragraph (a) of this section, for a firefighter whose pay is computed under 5 U.S.C. 5545b, a firefighter hourly locality rate is computed using a divisor of 2,756 hours instead of 2,087, as prescribed in 5 CFR part 550, subpart M. Also, such a firefighter's weekly and biweekly locality rates must be based on the firefighter's extended tour of duty as prescribed in that subpart.

[70 FR 31304, May 31, 2005]

§531.608 Relationship of locality rates to other pay rates.

(a) An employee must receive the greatest of the following rates of pay, as applicable—

(1) The scheduled annual rate of pay payable to the employee;

(2) A locality rate under this subpart;

(3) A special rate under 5 CFR part 530, subpart C, or a similar rate under other legal authority (e.g., 38 U.S.C. 7455); or

(4) A retained rate under 5 CFR part 536 or a similar rate under other legal authority.

(b) A GS employee receiving a special rate is entitled to any applicable locality payment on the same basis as any other GS employee. The locality payment is computed based on the employee's scheduled annual rate of pay, which excludes any special rate. The employee is entitled to the higher of the locality rate or the corresponding special rate. As provided in 5 U.S.C. 5305(h) and 5 CFR 530.303(d), when an employee's locality rate exceeds a corresponding special rate, the employee's entitlement to the special rate is terminated.

[70 FR 31304, May 31, 2005]

§531.609 Adjusting or terminating locality rates.

(a) When an employee's official worksite is changed to a different locality pay area, the employee's entitlement to the locality rate for the new locality pay area begins on the effective date of the change in official worksite.

(b) A locality rate must be adjusted as of the effective date of any change in the applicable scheduled annual rate of pay or any change in the applicable locality percentage.

(c) Except as provided in paragraph (d) of this section, entitlement to a locality rate associated with a particular locality pay area under this subpart terminates on the date—

(1) An employee's official worksite is no longer in the locality pay area;

(2) An employee is no longer in a position covered by this subpart; or

(3) An employee separates from Federal service.

(d) In the event of a change in the geographic coverage of a locality pay area, the effective date of any change in an employee's entitlement to a locality rate of pay under this subpart is the first day of the first pay period beginning on or after the effective date indicated in the applicable final rule published in the FEDERAL REGISTER.

(e) As provided in § 531.205, when an employee becomes covered by one or more different pay schedule(s) because the employee is stationed at a new official worksite in a different geographic location, the employee's pay (including a locality rate) must first be converted to the applicable pay schedule(s) in the new location before applying any other pay action (other than a general pay adjustment).

[70 FR 31304, May 31, 2005, as amended at 72 FR 34363, June 22, 2007; 78 FR 5115, Jan. 24, 2013]

§ 531.610 Treatment of locality rate as basic pay.

A locality rate is considered to be an employee's rate of basic pay only for the purpose of computing or applying—

(a) Retirement deductions, contributions, and benefits under 5 U.S.C. chapters 83 and 84;

(b) Life insurance premiums and benefits under 5 U.S.C. chapter 87;

(c) Premium pay under 5 U.S.C. chapter 55, subchapter V, and 5 CFR part 550, subparts A and I (including the computation of limitations on premium pay);

(d) Severance pay under 5 U.S.C. 5595 and 5 CFR part 550, subpart G;

(e) Advances in pay under 5 U.S.C. 5524a and 5 CFR part 550, subpart B;

(f) Post differentials under 5 U.S.C. 5925(a) and danger pay allowances under 5 U.S.C. 5928 for an employee temporarily working in a foreign area when the employee's official worksite is located in a locality pay area;

(g) Nonforeign area cost-of-living allowances and post differentials under 5 U.S.C. 5941 and 5 CFR part 591, subpart B;

(h) Recruitment, relocation, and retention incentives, supervisory differentials, and extended assignment incentives under 5 U.S.C. chapter 57, subchapter IV, and 5 CFR part 575;

(i) Performance-based cash awards under 5 U.S.C. 4505a and 5 CFR part 451, subpart A, when such awards are computed as a percentage of an employee's rate of basic pay;

(j) GS pay administration provisions (e.g., GS promotion provisions) to the extent provided in subpart B of this part;

(k) Pay administration provisions for prevailing rate employees which consider rates of basic pay under the GS pay system in setting pay (except as otherwise provided in 5 CFR part 532), subject to the requirement that, if the employee's actual locality rate would not apply at the official worksite for the prevailing rate position, that locality rate must be converted to a corresponding rate on the locality rate schedule for that official worksite;

(l) Lump-sum payments under 5 CFR part 550, subpart L, for accumulated and accrued annual leave;

(m) Grade and pay retention under 5 U.S.C. chapter 53, subchapter VI, to the extent provided by 5 CFR part 536;

(n) Other provisions as specified in other statute or OPM regulations; and

(o) Payments or benefits equivalent to those listed in this section under other legal authority, as determined by the head of the agency or other authorized official responsible for administering such payments or benefits.

[70 FR 31304, May 31, 2005, as amended at 70 FR 74996, Dec. 19, 2005; 73 FR 66154, Nov. 7, 2008; 76 FR 68634, Nov. 7, 2011]

§ 531.611 Miscellaneous provisions.

(a) A locality rate may be paid only for those hours for which an employee is in a pay status.

(b) Payment of, or an increase in, a locality rate is not an equivalent increase in pay within the meaning of 5 U.S.C. 5335. (*See* § 531.407(c).)

(c) A locality rate is included in an employee's *total remuneration*, as defined in 5 CFR 551.511(b), and *straight time rate of pay*, as defined in 5 CFR 551.512(b), for the purpose of overtime pay computations under the Fair Labor Standards Act of 1938, as amended.

(d) Consistent with § 531.610, a reduction or termination of a locality rate under § 531.609 is not an adverse action for the purpose of 5 CFR part 752, subpart D, or an action under 5 CFR 930.211.

[70 FR 31305, May 31, 2005, as amended at 73 FR 66154, Nov. 7, 2008]

Subpart G [Reserved]

PART 532—PREVAILING RATE SYSTEMS

Subpart A—General Provisions

Sec.

Subpart B—Prevailing Rate Determinations

Subpart C—Determining Rates for Principal Types of Federal Positions

Subpart D—Pay Administration

Subpart E—Premium Pay and Differentials

Subpart F—Job Grading System

Subpart G—Job Grading Reviews and Appeals

Subpart H—Payment of Unrestricted Rates for Recruitment or Retention Purposes

AUTHORITY: 5 U.S.C. 5343, 5346; § 532.707 also issued under 5 U.S.C. 552.

SOURCE: 46 FR 21344, Apr. 10, 1981, unless otherwise noted.

Subpart A—General Provisions

§ 532.101 Scope.

This part provides common policies, systems, and practices for uniform application by all agencies subject to section 5342 of title 5, United States Code, in fixing pay for prevailing rate employees as nearly as is consistent with the public interest in accordance with prevailing rates.

§ 532.103 Coverage.

The provisions of this part shall apply to prevailing rate employees and agencies covered by section 5342 of title 5, United States Code.

§ 532.105 Pay-fixing authority.

The head of each agency shall authorize application of the rates established by the lead agency or the Office of Personnel Management (OPM) to prevailing rate employees within the appropriate wage area, in accordance with the provisions of this part.

Subpart B—Prevailing Rate Determinations

§ 532.201 Definitions.

For the purposes of this part:

Full-scale survey means a survey conducted at least every 2 years in which data are collected from a current sampling of establishments in the private sector by personal visit of data collectors.

Host activity is the local Federal activity designated by the lead agency to obtain employment statistics from other Federal activities in the wage area and to provide support facilities and clerical assistance for the wage survey.

Lead agency means the agency designated by the Office of Personnel Management to plan and conduct wage surveys, analyze wage survey data, and determine and issue required wage schedules for a wage area.

Survey area means that part of the wage area where the private enterprise establishments included in the wage survey are located.

Wage area means that geographic area within which a single set of regular wage schedules is applied uniformly by Federal installations to covered occupations.

Wage change survey means a survey in which rate change data are collected from the same establishments and for the same establishment occupations represented in the full-scale survey. These data may be collected by telephone, mail, or personal visit.

§532.203 Structure of regular wage schedules.

(a) Each nonsupervisory and leader regular wage schedule shall have 15 grades, which shall be designated as follows:

(1) *WG* means an appropriated fund nonsupervisory grade;

(2) *WL* means an appropriated fund leader grade;

(3) *NA* means a nonappropriated fund nonsupervisory grade; and

(4) *NL* means a nonappropriated fund leader grade.

(b) Each supervisory regular wage schedule shall have 19 grades, which shall be designated as follows:

(1) *WS* means an appropriated fund supervisory grade; and

(2) *NS* means a nonappropriated fund supervisory grade.

(c) The step 2 or payline rate for each grade of a leader regular wage schedule shall be equal to 110 percent of the rate for step 2 of the corresponding grade of the nonsupervisory regular wage schedule for the area.

(d) The step 2 or payline rate for each grade of an appropriated fund supervisory regular wage schedule shall be:

(1) For grades WS–1 through WS–10, equal to the rate for step 2 of the corresponding grade of the nonsupervisory regular wage schedule for the area, plus 30 percent of the rate for step 2 of WG–10;

(2) For grades WS–11 through WS–18, the second rate of WS–10, plus 5, 11.5, 19.6, 29.2, 40.3, 52.9, 67.1, and 82.8 percent, respectively, of the difference between the step 2 rates of WS–10 and WS–19; and

(3) For grade WS–19, the third rate in effect for General Schedule grade GS–14 at the time of the area wage schedule adjustment. The WS–19 rate shall include any cost of living allowance payable for the area under 5 U.S.C. 5941.

(e) The step 2 or payline rate for each grade of a nonappropriated fund supervisory regular wage schedule shall be:

(1) For grades NS–1 through NS–8, equal to the rate for step 2 of the corresponding grade of the nonsupervisory regular wage schedule for the area, plus 20 percent of the rate for step 2 of NA–8;

(2) For grades NS–9 through NS–15, equal to 120 percent of the rate for step 2 of the corresponding grade of the nonsupervisory regular wage schedule for the area;

(3) For grades NS–16 through NS–19, the rates will be 25, 30, 35 and 40 percent, respectively, above the step 2 rate of NA–15;

(f) The number of within-grade steps and the differentials between steps for each nonsupervisory grade on a regular wage schedule shall be established in accordance with 5 U.S.C. 5343(e)(1). Each grade on a leader and supervisory regular wage schedule shall have 5 within-grade steps with step 2 set according to paragraphs (c), (d), or (e) of this section, as appropriate, and—

(1) Step 1 set at 96 percent of the step 2 rate;

(2) Step 3 set at 104 percent of the step 2 rate;

(3) Step 4 set at 108 percent of the step 2 rate; and

(4) Step 5 set at 112 percent of the step 2 rate.

[46 FR 21344, Apr. 10, 1981, as amended at 48 FR 13385, Mar. 30, 1983; 49 FR 28347, July 11, 1984; 55 FR 46140, Nov. 1, 1990]

§532.205 The use of Federal, State, and local minimum wage requirements in determining prevailing rates.

(a) Wage schedules, including special schedules, shall not include any rates of pay less than the higher of:

(1) The minimum rate prescribed by section 6(a)(1) of the Fair Labor Standards Act of 1938, as amended, or

(2) The highest State or local minimum wage rate in the local wage area which is applicable to the private industry counterparts of the single largest Federal industry/occupation in the wage area.

(b) Wage data below the minimum wage rates prescribed by section 6(a)(1) of the Fair Labor Standards Act of 1938, as amended, shall not be used in determining prevailing rates.

(c) Adjustments to regular wage schedules to comply with the minimum wage rate determined to be applicable under paragraph (a) of this section shall be computed as follows:

(1) The step 2 rate of grade 1 of the nonsupervisory wage schedule shall be set at a rate which, upon application of the 4 percent step-rate differential, provides a step 1 rate which is equal to the applicable minimum wage rate.

(2) An intergrade differential shall be determined as 5 percent of the rate established as the step 2 rate of grade 1, rounded to the nearest whole cent. This intergrade differential shall be added to the step 2 rate of each grade, beginning with grade 1, to determine the step 2 rate for the succeeding grade until the grade is reached at which the step 2 rate established through the wage survey process equals or exceeds the rate determined under this procedure. Rates of all grades above that point shall be computed in accordance with § 532.221(b) of this subpart.

(3) Steps 1, 3, 4, and 5 of each grade adjusted under paragraph (c) of this section shall be set at 96, 104, 108, and 112 percent of the step 2 rate, respectively.

(4) The leader and supervisory wage schedule grades corresponding to each nonsupervisory grade adjusted under paragraph (c) of this section shall be constructed in accordance with the procedures of § 532.203 of this subpart, on the basis of the step 2 rates established under this paragraph for the nonsupervisory wage schedule grades.

(d) All wage schedule adjustments made under this section shall be effective on the effective date of the applicable minimum wage rate.

§ 532.207 Time schedule for wage surveys.

(a) Wage surveys shall be conducted on a 2-year cycle at annual intervals.

(b) A full-scale survey shall be made in the first year of the 2-year cycle and shall include development of a current sample of establishments and the collection of wage data by visits to establishments.

(c) A wage-change survey shall be made every other year using only the same employers, occupations, survey jobs, and establishment weights used in the preceding full-scale survey. Data may be collected by telephone, mail, or personal contact.

(d) Scheduling of surveys shall take into consideration the following criteria:

(1) The best timing in relation to wage adjustments in the principal local private enterprise establishments;

(2) Reasonable distribution of workload of the lead agency;

(3) The timing of surveys for nearby or selected wage areas; and

(4) Scheduling relationships with other pay surveys.

(e) The Office of Personnel Management may authorize adjustments in the normal cycle as requested by the lead agency and based on the criteria in paragraph (d) of this section or to accommodate special studies or adjustments consistent with determining local prevailing rates.

(f) The beginning month of appropriated and nonappropriated fund wage surveys and the fiscal year during which full-scale surveys will be conducted are set out as appendices A and B to this subpart and are incorporated in and made part of this section.

[55 FR 46141, Nov. 1, 1990]

§ 532.209 Lead agency.

(a) The Office of Personnel Management shall select a lead agency for each appropriated and nonappropriated fund wage area based on the number of agency employees covered by the regular wage schedule for that area and the capability of the agency in providing administrative and clerical support at the local level necessary to conduct a wage survey.

(b) OPM may authorize exceptions to these criteria where this will improve the administration of the local wage survey.

(c) The listing in appendix A to this subpart shows the lead agency for each appropriated fund wage area. The Department of Defense is the lead agency for each nonappropriated fund wage area.

[55 FR 46141, Nov. 1, 1990]

§532.211 Criteria for establishing appropriated fund wage areas.

(a) Each wage area shall consist of one or more survey areas along with nonsurvey areas, if any.

(1) *Survey area:* A survey area is composed of the counties, parishes, cities, or townships in which survey data are collected. Except in very unusual circumstances, a wage area that includes a Metropolitan Statistical Area shall have the Metropolitan Statistical Area as the survey area or part of the survey area.

(2) *Nonsurvey area:* Nonsurvey counties, parishes, cities, or townships may be combined with the survey area(s) to form the wage area through consideration of the criteria in paragraph (d)(1) of this section.

(b) Wage areas shall include wherever possible a recognized economic community such as a Metropolitan Statistical Area or a political unit such as a county. Two or more economic communities or political units, or both, may be combined to constitute a single wage area; however, except in unusual circumstances and as an exception to the criteria, an individually defined Metropolitan Statistical Area or county shall not be subdivided for the purpose of defining a wage area.

(c) Except as provided in paragraph (a) of this section, wage areas shall be established when:

(1) There is a minimum of 100 wage employees of one agency subject to the regular schedule and the agency involved indicates that its local installation has the capacity to do the survey; and

(2) There is, within a reasonable commuting distance of the concentration of Federal employment;

(i) A minimum of either 20 establishments within survey specifications having at least 50 employees each; or 10 establishments having at least 50 employees each, with a combined total of 1,500 employees; and

(ii) The total private enterprise employment in the industries surveyed in the survey area is at least twice the Federal wage employment in the survey area.

(d)(1) Adjacent economic communities or political units meeting the separate wage area criteria in paragraphs (b) and (c) of this section may be combined through consideration of:

(i) Distance, transportation facilities, and geographic features;

(ii) Commuting patterns; and

(iii) Similarities in overall population, employment, and the kinds and sizes of private industrial establishments.

(2) Generally, the criteria listed in paragraph (d)(1) of this section are considered in the order listed.

(3) When two wage areas are combined, the survey area of either or both may be used, depending on the concentrations of Federal and private employment and locations of establishments, the proximity of the survey areas to each other, and the extent of economic similarites or differences as indicated by relative levels of wage rates in each of the potential survey areas.

(e) Appropriated fund wage and survey area definitions are set out as appendix C to this subpart and are incorporated in and made part of this section.

(f) A single contiguous military installation defined as a Joint Base that would otherwise overlap two separate wage areas shall be included in only a single wage area. The wage area of such a Joint Base shall be defined to be the wage area with the most favorable payline based on an analysis of the simple average of the 15 nonsupervisory second step rates on each one of the regular wage schedules applicable in the otherwise overlapped wage areas.

[55 FR 46142, Nov. 1, 1990, as amended at 57 FR 29783, July 7, 1992; 81 FR 86249, Nov. 30, 2016]

§532.213 Industries included in regular appropriated fund wage surveys.

(a) The lead agency must include the industries in the following North American Industry Classification System (NAICS) codes in all regular appropriated fund wage surveys:

2012 NAICS codes	2012 NAICS industry titles
311 through 339 (except 323).	All manufacturing classes except printing and related support activities (NAICS 323).
221	Utilities.
481	Air transportation.
482	Rail transportation.
484	Truck transportation.
485 (except 4853)	Transit and ground passenger transportation except taxi and limousine service (NAICS 4853).
487 (except 4872)	Scenic and sightseeing transportation except scenic and sightseeing transportation, water (NAICS 4872).
488 (except 4883 and 4884).	Support activities for transportation except support activities for water transportation (NAICS 4883) and support activities for road transportation (NAICS 4884).
492	Couriers and messengers.
493	Warehousing and storage.
515	Broadcasting (except Internet).
517	Telecommunications.
5621	Waste collection.
5622	Waste Treatment and Disposal.
423	Merchant wholesalers, durable goods.
424	Merchant wholesalers, nondurable goods.

(b) A lead agency may add other industry classes to a regular survey in an area where these industries account for significant proportions of local private employment of the kinds and levels found in local Federal employment.

(c) Specifically excluded from all wage surveys for regular wage schedules are food service and laundry establishments and industries having peculiar employment conditions that directly affect the wage rates paid and that are the basis for special wage surveys.

[55 FR 46142, Nov. 1, 1990, as amended at 71 FR 35373, June 20, 2006; 73 FR 45853, Aug. 7, 2008; 78 FR 58153, Sept. 23, 2013]

§ 532.215 Establishments included in regular appropriated fund surveys.

(a) All establishments having a total employment of 50 or more employees in the prescribed industries within a survey area shall be included within the survey universe. On rare occasions and as an exception to the rule, OPM may authorize lower minimum size levels based on a recommendation of the lead agency for the wage area.

(b) Establishments to be covered in surveys shall be selected under standard probability sample selection procedures. In areas with relatively few establishments, surveys shall cover all establishments within the prescribed industry and size groups.

(c) A lead agency may not delete from a survey an establishment properly included in an establishment list drawn under statistical sampling procedures.

[55 FR 46142, Nov. 1, 1990]

§ 532.217 Appropriated fund survey jobs.

(a) A lead agency shall survey the following required jobs:

Job title	Job grade
Janitor (Light)	1
Janitor (Heavy)	2
Material Handler	2
Maintenance Laborer	3
Packer	4
Warehouse Worker	5
Forklift Operator	5
Material Handling Equipment Operator	5
Truckdriver (Medium)	6
Truckdriver (Heavy)	7
Machine Tool Operator II	8
Machine Tool Operator I	9
Carpenter	9
Electrician	10
Automotive Mechanic	10
Sheet Metal Mechanic	10
Pipefitter	10
Welder	10
Machinist	10
Electronics Mechanic	11
Toolmaker	13

(b) A lead agency may not omit a required survey job from a regular schedule wage survey.

(c) A lead agency may survey the following jobs on an optional basis:

Job title	Job grade
Aircraft Structures Assembler B	7
Aircraft Structures Assembler A	9
Aircraft Mechanic	10
Electrician, Ship	10
Pipefitter, Ship	10

Job title	Job grade
Shipfitter	10
Shipwright	10
Machinist, Marine	10
Cable Splicer (Electric)	10
Electrical Lineman	10
Electrician (Powerplant)	10
Telephone Installer-Repairer	9
Central Office Repairer	11
Heavy Mobile Equipment Mechanic	10
Heavy Mobile Equipment Operator	10
Air Conditioning Mechanic	10
Rigger	10
Trailer Truck Driver	8
Tool Crib Attendant	6
Painter (Finish)	9
Light Vehicle Operator	5
Helper (Trades)	5
Boiler Plant Operator	10
Meat Cutter	8
Equipment Mechanic	10
Boom Crane Operator	9
Boom Crane Operator (Precision)	11
Tool and Parts Attendant	4
Painter (Rough)	7
Electronic Industrial Controls Mechanic	11
Electronic Test Equipment Repairer	11
Electronic Computer Mechanic	11
Television Station Mechanic	11
Maintenance Mechanic	10

(d) A lead agency may add the following survey jobs to the survey when the Hospital industry is included in the survey:

Job title	Job grade
Laundry Worker	1
Food Service Worker	2
Cook	8

(e) A lead agency must obtain prior approval of OPM to add a job not authorized under paragraph (a), (c), or (d) of this section.

[55 FR 46142, Nov. 1, 1990, as amended at 64 FR 69183, Dec. 10, 1999; 68 FR 460, Jan. 6, 2003; 69 FR 26475, May 13, 2004]

§532.219 Criteria for establishing nonappropriated fund wage areas.

(a) Each wage area shall consist of one or more survey areas along with nonsurvey areas, if any, having nonappropriated fund employees.

(1) *Survey area:* A survey area is composed of the counties, parishes, cities, or townships in which survey data are collected.

(2) *Nonsurvey area:* Nonsurvey counties, parishes, or townships may be combined with the survey area to form the wage area through consideration of the criteria in paragraph (c) of this section.

(b) Wage areas shall be established when:

(1) There is a minimum of 26 NAF wage employees in the survey area and local activities have the capability to do the survey; and

(2) There is within the survey area a minimum of 1,800 private enterprise employees in establishments within survey specifications.

(c)(1) Two or more counties may be combined to constitute a single wage area through consideration of:

(i) Proximity of largest activity in each county;

(ii) Transportation facilities and commuting patterns; and

(iii) Similarities of the counties in:

(A) Overall population;

(B) Private employment in major industry categories; and

(C) Kinds and sizes of private industrial establishments.

(2) Generally, the criteria listed in paragraph (c)(1) of this section are considered in the order listed.

(d) The nonappropriated fund wage and survey area definitions are set out as appendix D to this subpart and are incorporated in and made part of this section.

[55 FR 46143, Nov. 1, 1990, as amended at 57 FR 29783, July 7, 1992]

§532.221 Industries included in regular nonappropriated fund surveys.

(a) The lead agency must include the following North American Industry Classification System (NAICS) codes in all regular nonappropriated fund wage surveys:

2012 NAICS codes	2012 NAICS industry titles
42312	Motor vehicle supplies and new parts merchant wholesalers.
4232	Furniture and home furnishing merchant wholesalers.
42362	Electrical and electronic appliance, television, and radio set merchant wholesalers.
42369	Other electronic parts and equipment merchant wholesalers.
42371	Hardware merchant wholesalers.
42391	Sporting and recreational goods and supplies merchant wholesalers.
42399	Other miscellaneous durable goods merchant wholesalers.

2012 NAICS codes	2012 NAICS industry titles
4241	Paper and paper product merchant wholesalers.
42421	Drugs and druggists' sundries merchant wholesalers.
4243	Apparel, piece goods, and notions merchant wholesalers.
42445	Confectionery merchant wholesalers.
4247	Petroleum and petroleum products merchant wholesalers.
4249	Miscellaneous nondurable goods merchant wholesalers.
44132	Tire dealers.
443	Electronics and appliance stores.
44411	Home centers.
44611	Pharmacies and drug stores.
4471	Gasoline stations.
44814	Family clothing stores.
4521	Department stores.
45299	All other general merchandise stores.
45321	Office supplies and stationery stores.
4542	Vending machine operators.
71391	Golf courses and country clubs.
71395	Bowling centers.
72111	Hotels (except casino hotels) and motels.
7224	Drinking places (alcoholic beverages).
7225	Restaurants and other eating places.

(b) A lead agency may add other industry classes from within the wholesale, retail, and service industry divisions in an area where these industries account for significant proportions of local private employment of the kinds and levels found in local NAF employment.

(c) Additional industries shall be defined in terms of entire industry classes (fourth digit breakdown).

[55 FR 46143, Nov. 1, 1990, as amended at 71 FR 35374, June 20, 2006; 73 FR 45853, Aug. 7, 2008; 78 FR 58153, Sept. 23, 2013]

§ 532.223 Establishments included in regular nonappropriated fund surveys.

(a) All establishments having 20 or more employees in the prescribed industries within a survey area must be included in the survey universe. Establishments in NAICS codes 4471, 4542, 71391, and 71395 must be included in the survey universe if they have eight or more employees.

(b) Establishment selection procedures are the same as those prescribed for appropriated fund surveys in paragraphs (b) and (c) of § 532.213 of this subpart.

[55 FR 46143, Nov. 1, 1990, as amended at 71 FR 35374, June 20, 2006]

§ 532.225 Nonappropriated fund survey jobs.

(a) A lead agency shall survey the following required jobs:

Job title	Job grade
Janitor (Light)	1
Food Service Worker	1
Food Service Worker	2
Fast Food Worker	2
Janitor	2
Laborer (Light)	2
Laborer (Heavy)	3
Service Station Attendant	3
Stock Handler	4
Short Order Cook	5
Materials Handling Equipment Operator	5
Warehouseman	5
Service Station Attendant	5
Truck Driver (Light)	5
Truck Driver (Medium)	6
Truck Driver (Heavy)	7
Cook	8
Carpenter	9
Painter	9
Automotive Mechanic	10
Electrician	10

(b) A lead agency may not omit a required survey job from a regular schedule wage survey.

(c) A lead agency may survey the following jobs on an optional basis:

Job title	Job grade
Service Station Attendant	1
Groundskeeper	4
Grill Attendant	4
Tractor Operator	6
Bowling Equipment Mechanic	7
Building Maintenance Worker	7
Vending Machine Mechanic	8
Building Maintenance Worker	8
Air Conditioning Equipment Mechanic	8
Truck Driver (Trailer)	8
Air Conditioning Equipment Mechanic	10

(d) A lead agency must obtain prior approval of OPM to add a job not listed under paragraph (a) or (c) of this section.

[55 FR 46143, Nov. 1, 1990]

§532.227 Agency wage committee.

(a) Each lead agency shall establish an agency wage committee for the purpose of considering matters relating to the conduct of wage surveys, the establishment of wage schedules and making recommendations thereon to the lead agency.

(b) The Agency Wage Committee shall consist of five members, with the chairperson and two members designated by the head of the lead agency, and the remaining two members designated as follows:

(1) For the Department of Defense Wage Committee, one member shall be designated by each of the two labor organizations having the largest number of wage employees covered by exclusive recognition in the Department of Defense; and

(2) For other lead agencies, two members shall be designated by the labor organization having the largest number of wage employees by exclusive recognition in the agency.

(c) Recommendations of agency wage committees shall be developed by majority vote. Any member of an agency wage committee may submit a minority report to the lead agency along with the recommendations of the committee.

[46 FR 21344, Apr. 10, 1981. Redesignated at 55 FR 46141, Nov. 1, 1990]

§532.229 Local wage survey committee.

(a)(1) A lead agency shall establish a local wage survey committee in each wage area for which it has lead agency responsibility and in which a labor organization represents, by exclusive recognition, wage employees subject to the wage schedules for which the survey is conducted.

(2) The local wage survey committee shall assist the lead agency in the conduct of wage surveys and make recommendations to the lead agency thereon.

(b)(1) Local wage survey committees shall consist of three members, with the chairperson and one member recommended by Federal agencies and designated by the lead agency, and one member recommended by the labor organization having the largest number of wage employees under the regular wage schedule who are under exclusive recognition in the wage area.

(2) All members of local wage survey committees for appropriated fund surveys shall be Federal employees appointed by their employing agencies.

(3) Members for nonappropriated fund surveys shall be nonappropriated fund employees appointed by their employing agencies.

(4) The member recommended by the labor organization must be an employee of a Federal activity for appropriated fund surveys or nonappropriated fund activity for nonappropriated fund surveys who is covered by one of the regular wage schedules in the wage area in which the activity is located.

(5) In selecting and appointing employees recommended by labor organizations and by Federal agencies to serve as committee members, consideration shall be given to the requirement in the prevailing rate law for labor and agency representatives to participate in the wage survey process, the qualifications of the recommended employees, the need of the employees' work units for their presence on the job, and the prudent management of available financial and human resources. Employing agencies and activities shall cooperate and appoint the recommended employees unless exceptional circumstances prohibit their consideration. When the recommended employees cannot be appointed to serve as local wage survey committee members, the responsible lead agency or labor organization shall provide additional recommendations expeditiously to avoid any delay in the survey process.

(6) Employers shall cooperate and release appointed employees for committee proceedings unless the employers can demonstrate that exceptional circumstances directly related to the accomplishment of the work units' missions require their presence on their regular jobs. Employees serving as committee members are considered to be on official assignment to an

interagency function, rather than on leave.

(c) A local wage survey committee shall be established before each full-scale wage survey. Responsibility for providing members shall remain with the same agency and the same labor organization until the next full-scale survey.

(d) Recommendations of local wage survey committees shall be developed by majority vote. Any member of a local wage survey committee may submit a minority report to the lead agency relating to any local wage survey committee majority recommendation.

(e) The lead agency shall establish the type of local wage survey organization it considers appropriate in a wage area which does not qualify for a local wage survey committee under paragraph (a) of this section.

[46 FR 21344, Apr. 10, 1981, as amended at 55 FR 46140, Nov. 1, 1990. Redesignated at 55 FR 46141, Nov. 1, 1990; 58 FR 15415, Mar. 23, 1993]

§ 532.231 Responsibilities of participating organizations.

(a) The Office of Personnel Management:

(1) Defines the boundaries of wage and survey areas;

(2) Prescribes the required industries to be surveyed;

(3) Prescribes the required job coverage for surveys;

(4) Designates a lead agency for each wage area;

(5) Establishes, jointly with lead agencies, a nationwide schedule of wage surveys;

(6) Arranges for technical services with other Government agencies;

(7) Considers recommendations of the national headquarters of any agency or labor organization relating to the Office of Personnel Management's responsibilities for the Federal Wage System; and

(8) Establishes wage schedules and rates for prevailing rate employees who are United States citizens outside of the United States, District of Columbia, the Commonwealth of Puerto Rico, the Canal Zone, the Territories and Possessions of the United States, and the Trust Territory of the Pacific Islands.

(b) *Federal Prevailing Rate Advisory Committee.* This committee functions in accordance with the requirements set forth under section 5347 of title 5, United States Code.

(c) *Employing agencies*—(1) *Heads of agencies.* The head of an agency is responsible, within the policies and procedures of the Federal Wage System, for authorizing application of wage schedules developed by a lead agency and fixing and administering rates of pay for wage employees of his/her organization.

(2) *Heads of local activities.* The head of each activity in a wage area is responsible for providing employment information, wage survey committee members, the prescribed number of data collectors, and any other assistance needed to conduct local wage survey committee functions.

(d) Lead agencies are responsible for:

(1) Planning and conducting the wage survey for that area;

(2) Developing survey specifications and providing or arranging for the identification of establishments to be surveyed;

(3) Officially ordering wage surveys;

(4) Establishing wage schedules, applying wage schedules authorized by the head of the agency; and

(5) Referring pertinent matters to the agency wage committee and the Office of Personnel Management.

(e) *Agency wage committees.* As appropriate, agency wage committees consider and make recommendations to the lead agency on wage schedules and any matters involving survey specifications for full-scale surveys if the lead agency chooses not to accept recommendations of the local wage survey committee or those in a minority report filed by a local wage survey committee member.

(f) *Local wage survey committees.* The local wage survey committee plans and conducts the wage survey in the designated wage area.

[46 FR 21344, Apr. 10, 1981, as amended at 55 FR 46140, Nov. 1, 1990. Redesignated at 55 FR 46141, Nov. 1, 1990; 58 FR 15415, Mar. 23, 1993]

§ 532.233 Preparation for full-scale wage surveys.

(a) The local wage survey committee, prior to each full-scale survey:

(1) Shall hold a public hearing to receive recommendations from interested parties concerning the area, industries, establishments and jobs to be covered in the wage survey.

(2) Shall prepare a summary of the hearings and submit it to the lead agency together with the committees' recommendations concerning the survey specifications prescribed in paragraph (c) of this section.

(3) May make any other recommendations concerning the local wage survey which it considers appropriate.

(b) The lead agency shall consider the local wage survey committee's report if:

(1) The lead agency proposes not to accept the recommendations of the local wage survey committee concerning the specifications of the local wage survey; or

(2) The local wage survey committee's report is accompanied by a minority report.

(c) The lead agency shall develop survey specifications after taking into consideration the reports and recommendations received from the local wage survey committee and, if applicable, the agency wage committee. The survey specifications shall include:

(1) The counties to be surveyed;

(2) The industries to be surveyed;

(3) The standard minimum size of establishments to be surveyed;

(4) Establishments to be surveyed with certainty; and

(5) The survey jobs.

(d) A list of establishments to be surveyed shall be prepared through use of statistical sampling techniques in accordance with the specifications developed by the lead agency. A copy of this list shall be forwarded to the local wage survey committee.

(e) *Selection and appointment of data collectors.* (1) The local wage survey committee, after consultation with the lead agency, shall determine the number of regular and alternate data collectors needed for the survey based upon the estimated number and location of establishments to be surveyed.

(2) Wage data for appropriated fund surveys shall be collected by teams consisting of one local Federal Wage System employee recommended by the committee member representing the qualifying labor organization and one Federal employee recommended by Federal agencies. The data collectors shall be selected and appointed by their employing agency.

(3) Wage data for nonappropriated fund surveys shall be collected by teams, each consisting of one local nonappropriated fund employee recommended by the committee member representing the qualifying labor organization and one nonappropriated fund employee recommended by nonappropriated fund activities. The data collectors shall be selected and appointed by their employing agency.

(4) The local wage survey committee shall provide employers with the names of employees recommended by labor organizations and by Federal agencies to serve as data collectors and shall indicate the number of regular and alternate data collectors to be selected and appointed by the employers.

(5) In selecting and appointing employees recommended by labor organizations and by Federal agencies to serve as data collectors, consideration shall be given to the requirement in the prevailing rate law for labor and agency representatives to participate in the wage survey process, the qualifications of the recommended employees, the need of the employees' work units for their presence on the job, and the prudent management of available financial and human resources. Employing agencies and activities shall cooperate and appoint the recommended employees unless exceptional circumstances prohibit their consideration. When the required number of employees cannot be appointed to serve as data collectors from among those recommended, the local wage survey committee shall obtain additional recommendations expeditiously to avoid any delay in the survey process.

(6) Employers shall cooperate and release appointed employees to serve as data collectors throughout the duration of the data collection period unless the employers can demonstrate that exceptional circumstances directly related to the accomplishment of the work units' missions require their presence on their regular jobs.

Employees serving as data collectors are considered to be on official assignment to an interagency function, rather than on leave.

(f)(1) Each member of a local wage survey committee, each data collector, and any other person having access to data collected must retain this information in confidence, and is subject to disciplinary action by the employing agency or activity if the employee violates the confidence of data secured from private employers.

(2) Any violation of the above provision by a Federal employee must be reported to the employing agency and, in the case of a participant designated by a labor organization, to the recognized labor organization and its headquarters, and shall be cause for the lead agency immediately to remove the offending person from participation in the wage survey function.

[46 FR 21344, Apr. 10, 1981, as amended at 55 FR 46140, Nov. 1, 1990. Redesignated at 55 FR 46141, Nov. 1, 1990; 58 FR 15415, Mar. 23, 1993]

§ 532.235 Conduct of full-scale wage survey.

(a) Wage survey data shall not be collected before the date the survey is ordered by the lead agency.

(b) Data collection for a full-scale wage survey shall be accomplished by personal visit to the establishment. The following required data shall be collected:

(1) General information about the size, location, and type of product or service of the establishment sufficient to determine whether the establishment is within the scope of the survey and properly weighted, if the survey is a sample survey;

(2) Specific information about each job within the establishment that is similar to one of the jobs covered by the survey, including a brief description of the establishment job, the number of employees in the job, and their rate(s) of pay to the nearest mill (including any cost-of-living adjustments required by contract or that are regular and customary and monetary bonuses that are regular and customary); and

(3) Any other information the lead agency believes is appropriate and useful in determining local prevailing rates.

(c) The data collectors shall submit the data they collect to the local wage survey committee together with their recommendations about the use of the data.

[46 FR 21344, Apr. 10, 1981, as amended at 55 FR 46140, Nov. 1, 1990. Redesignated at 55 FR 46141, Nov. 1, 1990]

§ 532.237 Review by the local wage survey committee.

(a) The local wage survey committee shall review all establishment information and survey job data collected in the wage survey for completeness and accuracy and forward all of the data collected to the lead agency together with a report of its recommendations concerning the use of the data. The local wage survey committee may make any other recommendations concerning the wage survey which it considers appropriate.

[46 FR 21344, Apr. 10, 1981. Redesignated at 55 FR 46141, Nov. 1, 1990]

§ 532.239 Review by the lead agency.

(a) The lead agency shall review all material and wage survey data forwarded by the local wage survey committee to:

(1) Assure that the survey was conducted within the prescribed procedures and specifications;

(2) Consider matters included in the local wage survey committee report and recommendations;

(3) Exclude unusable data;

(4) Resolve questionable job matching and wage rate data; and

(5) Verify all computations reported on wage data collection forms.

(b) The lead agency shall determine whether the usable data collected in the wage survey are adequate for computing paylines, according to the following criteria:

(1) The wage survey data collected in an appropriated fund wage survey are adequate if the unweighted job matches include at least one survey job in the WG–01 through 04 range, one survey job in the WG–05 through 08 range, and two survey jobs in the WG–09 and above range, each providing at least 20 samples; and at least six other survey

jobs, each providing at least 10 samples.

(2) The wage survey data collected in a nonappropriated fund wage survey are adequate if the unweighted job matches include at least two survey jobs in the NA–01 through 04 range providing 10 samples each, one survey job in the NA–01 through 04 range and three survey jobs in the NA–05 through 15 range providing five samples each; two other survey jobs, each providing at least five samples, and at least 100 unweighted samples for all survey jobs combined are used in the computation of the final payline.

(c)(1) If the wage survey data do not meet the adequacy criteria in paragraph (b) of this section, the lead agency shall analyze the data, construct lines and wage schedules, submit them to the agency wage committee for its review and recommendations and issue wage schedules, in accordance with the requirements of this subpart, as if the adequacy criteria were met.

(2) The lead agency may determine such a wage area to be adequate if the quantity of data obtained is large enough to construct paylines even though it was obtained for fewer than the prescribed number of jobs, or at different grade levels, or in different combinations than prescribed in paragraph (b) of this section.

(3) The lead agency may not determine a nonappropriated fund wage area to be adequate if fewer than 100 usable unweighted job matches were used in the final payline computation.

(d) If the lead agency determines a wage area to be inadequate under paragraph (c) of this section, it shall promptly refer the problem to OPM for resolution. OPM shall:

(1) Authorize the lead agency to continue to survey the area if the lead agency believes the survey is likely to be adequate in the next full-scale survey;

(2) Authorize the lead agency to expand the scope of the survey; or

(3) Abolish the wage area and establish it as part of one or more other wage areas.

[46 FR 21344, Apr. 10, 1981, as amended at 55 FR 46140, Nov. 1, 1990. Redesignated at 55 FR 46141, Nov. 1, 1990]

§532.241 Analysis of usable wage survey data.

(a)(1) The lead agency shall compute a weighted average rate for each appropriated fund survey job having at least 10 unweighed matches and for each nonappropriated fund job having at least 5 unweighed matches. The weighted average rates shall be computed using the survey job data collected in accordance with §§532.235 and 532.247 and the establishment weight.

(2)(i) Incentive and piece-work rates shall be excluded when computing weighted average rates if, after establishment weights have been applied, 90 percent or more of the total usable wage survey data reflect rates paid on a straight-time basis only.

(ii) When sufficient incentive and piece-work rate data are obtained, the full incentive rate shall be used in computing the job weighted average rate when it is equal to or less than the average nonincentive rate. If the full incentive rate is greater than the average nonincentive rate, the incentive rate shall be discounted by 15 percent. The discounted incentive rate shall be compared with the guaranteed minimum rate and the average nonincentive rate, and the highest rate shall be used in computing the job weighted average rate.

(b) The lead agency shall compute paylines using the weighted average rates computed under paragraph (a) of this section.

(1) The lead agency shall compute unit and frequency paylines using the straight-line, least squares regression formula: $Y = a + bx$, where Y is the hourly rate, x is grade, a is the intercept of the payline with the Y-axis, and b is the slope of the payline.

(i) The unit payline shall be computed using a weight of one for each of the usable survey jobs and the weighted average rates identified and computed under paragraph (a) of this section.

(ii) The frequency payline shall be computed using a weight equal to the number of weighted matches for each of the usable survey jobs and the weighted average rates identified and computed under paragraph (a) of this section.

(2) Either or both of the lines computed according to paragraph (b)(1) of this section may be recomputed after eliminating survey job data that cause distortion in the lines.

(3) The lead agency may compute midpoint paylines using the following formula: $Y = (a_u + a_f)/2 + ((b_u + b_f)/2)x$, where Y is the hourly rate, x is the grade, a_u is the intercept of the unit payline, a_f is the intercept of the frequency payline, b_u is the slope of the unit payline, and b_f is the slope of the frequency payline. A midpoint line may be computed using the paylines based on all of the usable survey job data as described in paragraph (b)(1) of this section, and a second midpoint line may be computed using the paylines based on limited survey job data authorized in paragraph (b)(2) of this section.

(4) The lead agency may compute other paylines for the purpose of instituting changes in the scope of the survey.

(c) Usable data obtained from a particular establishment may not be modified or deleted in order to reduce the effect of an establishment's rates on survey findings, *i.e.*, data will not be deleted or modified to avoid establishment domination.

[46 FR 21344, Apr. 10, 1981, as amended at 55 FR 46141, Nov. 1, 1990. Redesignated at 55 FR 46141, Nov. 1, 1990; 58 FR 32273, June 9, 1993; 60 FR 62701, Dec. 7, 1995]

§ 532.243 Consultation with the agency wage committee.

(a) The lead agency shall submit to the agency wage committee:

(1) The data collected in the wage survey;

(2) The report and recommendations of the local wage survey committee concerning the use of data;

(3) The lead agency's analysis of the data; and

(4) The lines computed from the data.

(b) After considering the information available to it, the agency wage committee shall report to the lead agency its recommendation for a proposed wage schedule derived from the data.

[46 FR 21344, Apr. 10, 1981. Redesignated at 55 FR 46141, Nov. 1, 1990]

§ 532.245 Selection of payline and issuance of wage schedules.

(a) The lead agency shall select a payline and construct wage schedules therefrom for issuance as the regular wage schedules for the wage area, after considering all of the information, analysis, and recommendations made available to it pursuant to this subpart.

(b)(1) The lead agency shall prepare and maintain a record of all of the analysis and deliberations made under this subpart, documenting fully the basis for its determination under paragraph (a) of this section.

(2) The lead agency shall include in the record all of the wage survey data obtained and the recommendations and reports received from the local wage survey committee and the agency wage committee.

(c)(1) The lead agency shall issue the nonsupervisory, leader, and supervisory regular wage schedules for the local wage area, showing the rates of pay for all grades and steps.

(2) The wage schedules shall have a single effective date for all employees in the wage area, determined by the lead agency in accordance with 5 U.S.C. 5344.

(d) The head of each agency having employees in the local wage area to whom the regular wage schedules apply shall authorize the application of the wage schedules issued under paragraph (c) of this section to those employees, effective on the date specified by the lead agency.

[46 FR 21344, Apr. 10, 1981. Redesignated at 55 FR 46141, Nov. 1, 1990]

§ 532.247 Wage change surveys.

(a) Wage change surveys shall be conducted in each wage area in years during which full-scale wage surveys are not conducted.

(b) Data shall be collected in wage change surveys only from establishments which participated in the preceding full-scale survey. Information concerning pay adjustments of general application in effect for jobs matched in each establishment which participated in the preceding full-scale survey shall be obtained.

(c) Data may be obtained in wage change surveys by telephone, mail, or personal visit. The chairperson of the local wage survey committee shall determine the manner in which establishments will be contacted for collection of data. Data may be collected by the local wage survey committee members or by data collectors appointed and assigned to two member teams in accordance with § 532.233(e) of this subpart.

(d) Wage change survey data may not be collected before the date ordered by the lead agency.

(e) The local wage survey committee shall review all wage change survey data collected and forward the data to the lead agency. Where appropriate, the committee shall also forward to the lead agency a report of unusual circumstances surrounding the survey.

(f) The lead agency shall review the wage change survey data and, if applicable, the report filed by the local wage survey committee.

(g)(1) The lead agency shall recompute the line selected under § 532.245(a) of this subpart in the preceding full-scale survey using the wage change survey data and shall construct wage schedules therefrom in accordance with § 532.203 and, if appropriate, § 532.205 of this subpart.

(2) The lead agency shall consult with the agency wage committee in accordance with § 532.243 of this subpart.

(3) Records of this process shall be maintained in accordance with § 532.245(b) of this subpart.

(h) The wage schedules shall be issued and authorized in accordance with § 532.245 (c) and (d) of this subpart.

[46 FR 21344, Apr. 10, 1981. Redesignated at 55 FR 46141, Nov. 1, 1990; 58 FR 32274, June 9, 1993]

§ 532.249 Minimum rates for hard-to-fill positions.

(a) The lead agency for a wage area may establish the rate of the second, third, fourth, or fifth step of one or more grades of an occupation as the mandatory minimum rate or rates payable by any agency for the occupation at one or more locations within a wage area based on findings that:

(1) The hiring rates prevailing for an occupation in private sector establishments in the wage area are higher than the rate of the first step of the grade or grades of the occupation; and

(2) Federal installations and activities in the wage area are unable to recruit qualified employees at the rate of the first step of the grade or grades of the occupation.

(b) Any authorizations made under paragraph (a) of this section shall be indicated on the regular wage schedule for the wage area.

(c) Any authorizations made under paragraph (a) of this section shall be terminated with the issuance of a new regular wage schedule unless the conditions that warrant the authorizations continue and the new regular wage schedule continues that authorization.

(d) The lead agency, prior to terminating any authorization made under paragraph (a) of this section, shall require the appropriate official or officials at all installations or activities to which the authorization applies to discuss the termination with the appropriate official or officials of exclusively recognized employee organizations representing employees in the affected occupation. The agency officials shall report the results of these discussions to the lead agency.

(e) No employee shall have his/her pay reduced because of cancellation of an authorization made under paragraph (a) of this section.

[46 FR 21344, Apr. 10, 1981. Redesignated at 55 FR 46141, Nov. 1, 1990]

§ 532.251 Special rates.

(a) A lead agency, with the approval of OPM, may establish special rates for use within all or part of a wage area for a designated occupation or occupational specialization and grade, in lieu of rates on the regular schedule. OPM may authorize special rates to the extent it considers necessary to overcome existing or likely significant handicaps in the recruitment or retention of well-qualified personnel when these handicaps are due to any of the following circumstances:

(1) Rates of pay offered by private sector employers for an occupation or occupational specialization and grade are significantly higher than those paid by the Federal Government within the competitive labor market;

(2) The remoteness of the area or location involved; or

(3) Any other circumstances that OPM considers appropriate.

(b) In authorizing special rates, OPM shall consider—

(1) The number of existing or likely vacant positions and the length of time they have been vacant, including evidence to support the likelihood that a recruitment problem will develop if one does not already exist;

(2) The number of employees who have or are likely to quit, including the number quitting for higher pay positions and evidence to support the likelihood that employees will quit;

(3) The number of vacancies employing agencies tried to fill and the number of hires and offers made;

(4) The nature of the existing labor market;

(5) The degree to which employing agencies have considered or used increased minimum rates for hard-to-fill positions;

(6) The degree to which employing agencies have considered relevant non-pay solutions to the staffing problem, such as conducting an aggressive recruiting program, using appropriate appointment authorities, redesigning jobs, establishing training programs, and improving working conditions;

(7) The impact of the staffing problem on employers' missions;

(8) The level of private sector rates paid for comparable positions; and

(9) As appropriate, the extent to which the use of unrestricted rates authorized under § 532.801 of this part was considered.

(c) In determining at what level to set special rates, OPM shall consider—

(1) The level of rates it believes necessary to recruit or retain an adequate number of well-qualified persons;

(2) The offsetting costs that will be incurred if special rates are not authorized; and

(3) The level of private sector rates paid for comparable positions.

(d) No one factor or combination of factors specified in paragraphs (b) or (c) of this section requires special rates to be established or to be adjusted to any given level. Each request to establish special rates shall be judged on its own merits, based on the extent to which it meets these factors. Increased minimum rates are not a prerequisite to the establishment of special rates under this section.

(e) Special rates shall be based on private sector wage data, or a percentage thereof, as specified by OPM at the time the special rates are authorized. The private sector data shall be calculated as a weighted average or payline, as appropriate. A single rate shall be used when this represents private sector practice, and five rates shall be used when rate ranges are used by the private sector. When a five-step rate range is used, the differentials between steps shall be set in accordance with § 532.203(f) of this subpart.

(f) Once approved by OPM, special rates may be adjusted by the lead agency on the same cycle as the applicable regular schedule to the extent deemed necessary to ensure the continued recruitment or retention of well-qualified personnel. The amount of the special rate adjustment may be up to the percentage (rounded to the nearest one-tenth of 1 percent) by which the market rate has changed since the last adjustment. Special rates may not exceed the percentage of market rates initially approved by OPM unless a request for higher special rates is made and approved under paragraphs (a) through (e) of this section.

(g) Any special rates established under paragraph (a) of this section shall be shown on the regular schedule or published as an amendment to the regular schedule and shall indicate the wage area (or part thereof) and each occupation or occupational specialization and grade for which the rates are authorized. These rates shall be paid by all agencies having such positions in the wage area (or part thereof) specified.

(h) The scheduled special rate payable under this section may not, at any time, be less than the unrestricted (uncapped) rate otherwise payable for such positions under the applicable regular wage schedule.

(i) If a special rate is terminated under paragraph (f) of this section, the lead agency shall provide written notice of such termination to OPM.

(j) Employers using special rates shall maintain current recruitment and retention data for all authorized special rates. Such data shall be made available to the lead agency prior to the wage area regular schedule adjustment date for the purpose of determining whether there is a continuing need for special rates and the amount of special rate adjustment necessary to recruit or retain well-qualified employees.

[57 FR 57875, Dec. 8, 1992]

§532.253 Special rates or rate ranges for leader, supervisory, and production facilitating positions.

(a) When special rates or rate ranges are established for nonsupervisory positions, a lead agency also shall establish special rates for leader, supervisory, and production facilitating positions, classified to the same occupational series and title, that lead, supervise, or perform production facilitating work directly relating to the nonsupervisory jobs covered by the special rates.

(b) The step rate structure shall be the same as that of the related nonsupervisory special rate or rate range.

(c) The following formulas shall be used to establish a special rate or rate range:

(1) A single rate shall equal the top step of the appropriate leader, supervisory, or production facilitating grade on the regular schedule, plus the cents per hour difference between the top step of the appropriate nonsupervisory grade on the regular schedule and the special nonsupervisory rate.

(2) For a multiple rate range, the step 2 rate shall equal the step 2 rate of the appropriate leader, supervisory, or production facilitating grade on the regular schedule, plus the cents per hour difference between the prevailing rate of the appropriate nonsupervisory grade on the regular schedule and the prevailing rate of the special rate position. Other required step rates shall be computed in accordance with the formula established in §532.203 of this subpart.

[55 FR 46144, Nov. 1, 1990]

§532.254 Special schedules.

(a) A lead agency, with the approval of OPM, may establish special schedules for use within an area for specific occupations that are critical to the mission of a Federal activity based on findings that—

(1) Unusual prevailing pay practices exist in the private sector that are incompatible with regular schedule practices, and serious recruitment or retention problems exist or will likely develop if employees are paid from the authorized regular schedule; or

(2) Administrative considerations require the establishment of special schedules to address unique agency missions or other unusual circumstances that OPM considers appropriate.

(b) An OPM authorization for a special schedule shall include instructions for its construction, application, and administration.

(c) Unless otherwise specified, positions covered by special schedules shall be subject to the general provisions of this part and to other applicable rules and regulations of OPM.

[57 FR 57876, Dec. 8, 1992]

§532.255 Regular appropriated fund wage schedules in foreign areas.

(a) The Department of Defense shall establish and issue regular appropriated fund wage schedules for U.S. citizens who are employees in foreign areas. These wage schedules shall provide rates of pay for nonsupervisory, leader, supervisory, and production facilitating employees.

(b) Schedules shall be—

(1) Computed on the basis of a simple average of all regular appropriated fund wage area schedules in effect on December 31; and

(2) Effective on the first day of the first pay period that begins on or after January 1 of the succeeding year.

(c) Step 2 rates for each nonsupervisory grade shall be derived by computing a simple average of each step 2 rate for each of the 15 grades of all nonsupervisory wage rate schedules designated in paragraph (b) of this section.

(d) Through the use of the step 2 rates derived under the schedule averaging process, the step rates for each of the 15 grades of the nonsupervisory schedule and all scheduled pay rates for leaders and supervisors shall be developed by using the standard formulas established in 5 CFR 532.203, Structure of regular wage schedules.

(e) Pay schedules for production facilitating positions shall be established in accordance with the table in § 532.263(c) of this subpart.

[50 FR 38634, Sept. 24, 1985, as amended at 51 FR 28799, Aug. 12, 1986; 51 FR 39853, Nov. 3, 1986; 54 FR 52011, Dec. 20, 1989. Redesignated and amended at 55 FR 46141, Nov. 1, 1990; 58 FR 13194, Mar. 10, 1993]

§ 532.257 Regular nonappropriated fund wage schedules in foreign areas.

(a) The Department of Defense shall establish and issue regular nonappropriated fund wage schedules for U.S. citizens who are wage employees in foreign areas. These schedules will provide rates of pay for nonsupervisory, leader, and supervisory employees.

(b) Schedules will be—

(1) Computed on the basis of a simple average of all regular nonappropriated fund wage area schedules defined for the 48 contiguous states and the District of Columbia in effect on the first Sunday in January; and

(2) Effective on the first Sunday in January of each year.

(c) Step 2 rates for each nonsupervisory grade will be derived by computing a simple average of each step 2 rate for each of the 15 grades of all nonsupervisory wage rate schedules designated in paragraph (b) of this section.

(d) Through the use of the step 2 rates derived under the schedule averaging process, the step rates for each of the 15 grades of the nonsupervisory schedule and all scheduled pay rates for leaders and supervisors will be developed by using the standard formulas established in 5 CFR 532.203, Structure of regular wage schedules.

[50 FR 38634, Sept. 24, 1985, as amended at 51 FR 28799, Aug. 12, 1986; 54 FR 52011, Dec. 20, 1989. Redesignated and amended at 55 FR 46141, Nov. 1, 1990]

§ 532.259 Special appropriated fund wage schedules for U.S. insular areas.

(a) Lead agencies shall establish and issue special wage schedules for U.S. civil service wage employees in certain U.S. insular areas. The Department of Defense is the lead agency for Guam, Midway, and the U.S. Virgin Islands. The Department of Transportation is the lead agency for American Samoa. The Department of the Interior is the lead agency for the Commonwealth of the Northern Mariana Islands. These schedules shall provide rates of pay for nonsupervisory, leader, supervisory, and production facilitating employees.

(b) Special schedules shall be established at the same time and with rates identical to the foreign area appropriated fund wage schedules established under § 532.255 of this subpart.

(c) Wage employees recruited from outside the insular area where employed, who meet the same eligibility requirements as those specified for General Schedule employees in § 591.209 of subpart B of part 591, are also paid as a part of basic pay a differential for recruitment and retention purposes. The differential rate shall be that established for General Schedule employees in appendix B of subpart B of part 591 and shall be adjusted effective concurrently with the special schedules.

[58 FR 13194, Mar. 10, 1993]

§ 532.261 Special wage schedules for leader and supervisory schedules for leader and supervisory wage employees in the Puerto Rico wage area.

(a) The Department of Defense shall establish special wage schedules for leader and supervisory wage employees in the Puerto Rico wage area.

(b) The step 2 rate for each grade of the leader wage schedule shall be equal to 120 percent of the rate for step 2 of the corresponding grade of the nonsupervisory regular wage schedule for the Puerto Rico wage area.

(c) The step 2 rate for the supervisory wage schedule shall be:

(1) For grades WS–1 through WS–10, equal to the rate for step 2 of the corresponding grade of the nonsupervisory regular wage schedule for the Puerto

Rico wage area, plus 60 percent of the rate for step 2 of WG–10;

(2) For grades WS–11 through WS–18, the second rate of WS–10 plus 5, 11.5, 19.6, 29.2, 40.3, 52.9, 67.1, and 82.8 percent, respectively, of the difference between the step 2 rates of WS–10 and WS–19; and

(3) For grade WS–19, the third rate in effect for General Schedule grade GS–14 at the time of the area wage schedule adjustment. The WS–19 rate shall include any cost of living allowance payable for the area under 5 U.S.C. 5941.

(d) Step rates shall be developed by using the formula established in §532.203 of this subpart.

[55 FR 46144, Nov. 1, 1990]

§532.263 Special wage schedules for production facilitating positions.

(a) The lead agency in each FWS wage area shall establish special nonsupervisory and supervisory production facilitating wage schedules for employees properly allocable to production facilitating positions under applicable Federal Wage System job grading standards.

(b) Nonsupervisory schedules shall have 11 pay levels, and supervisory schedules shall have 9 pay levels.

(c) Pay levels and rates of pay for nonsupervisory (WD) schedules and supervisory (WN) schedules shall be identical to the pay levels and rates of pay for the corresponding grades on the local FWS regular supervisory wage schedule. Pay levels shall be determined in accordance with the following table:

	WN supervisory level	WS grade
WD nonsupervisory Level:		
1	....	3
2	....	4
3	....	5
4	....	6
5	1	7
6	2	8
7	3	9
8	4	10
9	5	11
10	6	12
11	7	13
	8	14
	9	15

(d) Special production facilitating wage schedules shall be effective on the same date as the regular wage schedules in the FWS wage area.

[55 FR 46144, Nov. 1, 1990]

§532.265 Special wage schedules for apprentices and shop trainees.

(a) Agencies may establish special wage schedules for apprentices and shop trainees who are included in:

(1) Formal apprenticeship programs involving training for journeyman level duties in occupations that are recognized as apprenticeable by the Bureau of Apprenticeship and Training, U.S. Department of Labor; or

(2) Formal shop trainee programs involving training for journeyman level duties in nonapprenticeable occupations that require specialized trade or craft skill and knowledge.

(b) Special schedules shall consist of a single wage rate for each training period. Wage rates shall be determined as follows:

(1) Rates shall be based on the current second step rate of the target journeyman grade level on the regular nonsupervisory wage schedule for the area where the apprentice or trainee is employed.

(2) The entrance rate shall be computed at 65 percent of the journeyman level, step 2, rate, or the WG–1, step 1, rate, whichever is greater.

(3) When the WG–1, step 1, rate is used, the apprentice rate shall be increased by a minimum of 5 cents per hour for each succeeding increment interval until the rate obtained by this method equals the rate computed under the formula. No increase shall be less then 5 cents per hour.

(c) Advancement to higher increments shall be at 26-week intervals, regardless of the total length of the training period. Intermediate rates shall be established by subtracting the entrance rate from the journeyman level, step 2 rate, and dividing the difference by the number of 26-week periods of the particular training term. The resulting quotient equals the increment for each succeeding rate.

(d) Agencies may hire at advanced rates or accelerate progression through scheduled wage rates if prescribed by approved agency training standards or programs.

(e) If the employee is promoted to the target job or to a job at the same grade level, the promotion shall be to the second step rate. If the employee is assigned to a job at a grade level that is less than the grade level of the target job, existing pay fixing rules shall be followed.

[55 FR 46144, Nov. 1, 1990]

§ 532.267 Special wage schedules for aircraft, electronic, and optical instrument overhaul and repair positions in Puerto Rico.

(a) The Department of Defense shall conduct special industry surveys and establish special wage schedules for wage employees in Puerto Rico whose primary duties involve the performance of work related to aircraft, electronic equipment, and optical instrument overhaul and repair.

(b) Except as provided in this section, regular appropriated fund wage survey and wage-setting procedures are applicable.

(c) Special survey specifications are as follows:

(1) Surveys must, at a minimum, include the air transportation and electronics industries in the following North American Industry Classification System (NAICS) codes:

2012 NAICS codes	2012 NAICS industry titles
333316	Photographic and photocopying equipment manufacturing.
3341	Computer and peripheral equipment manufacturing.
33422	Radio and television broadcasting and wireless communications equipment manufacturing.
33429	Other communications equipment manufacturing.
3343	Audio and video equipment manufacturing.
334412	Bare printed circuit board manufacturing.
334413	Semiconductor and related device manufacturing.
334418	Printed circuit assembly (electronic assembly) manufacturing.
334419	Other electronic component manufacturing.
334511	Search, detection, navigation, guidance, aeronautical, and nautical system and instrument manufacturing.
334515	Instrument manufacturing for measuring and testing electricity and electrical signals.
334613	Blank magnetic and optical recording media manufacturing.
42342	Office equipment merchant wholesalers.
42343	Computer and computer peripheral equipment and software merchant wholesalers.
4811	Scheduled air transportation.
4812	Nonscheduled air transportation.
4879	Scenic and sightseeing transportation, other.
4881	Support activities for air transportation.
4921	Couriers and express delivery services.
56172	Janitorial services.
62191	Ambulance services.
81142	Reupholstery and furniture repair.

(2) Surveys shall cover all establishments in the surveyed industries.

(3) Surveys shall, as a minimum, include all the following jobs:

Job titles	Job grades
Aircraft Cleaner	3
Fleet Service Worker	5
Aircraft Mechanic	10
Industrial Electronic Controls Repairer	10
Aircraft Instrument Mechanic	11
Electronic Test Equipment Repairer	11
Electronics Mechanic	11
Electronic Computer Mechanic	11
Television Station Mechanic	11

(d) The data collected in a special wage survey shall be considered adequate if there are as many weighted matches used in computing the nonsupervisory payline as there are employees covered by the special wage rate schedules.

(e) Each survey job used in computing the nonsupervisory payline must include a minimum of three unweighted matches.

(f) Special schedules shall have three step rates with the payline fixed at step 2. Step 1 shall be set at 96 percent of the payline rate, and step 3 shall be set at 104 percent of the payline rate.

(g) The waiting period for within-grade increases shall be 26 weeks between steps 1 and 2 and 78 weeks between steps 2 and 3.

(h) Special wage schedules shall be effective on the same date as the regular wage schedules for the Puerto Rico wage area.

[55 FR 46145, Nov. 1, 1990, as amended at 60 FR 62701, Dec. 7, 1995; 71 FR 35374, June 20, 2006; 73 FR 45853, Aug. 7, 2008; 78 FR 58154, Sept. 23, 2013]

§532.269 Special wage schedules for Corps of Engineers, U.S. Army navigation lock and dam employees.

(a) The Department of Defense shall establish special wage schedules for nonsupervisory, leader, and supervisory wage employees of the Corps of Engineers, U.S. Army, who are engaged in operating lock and dam equipment or who repair and maintain navigation lock and dam operating machinery and equipment.

(b) Employees shall be subject to one of the following pay provisions:

(1) If all navigation lock and dam installations under a District headquarters office are located within a single wage area, the employees shall be paid from special wage schedules having rates identical to the regular wage schedule applicable to that wage area.

(2) If navigation lock and dam installations under a District headquarters office are located in more than one wage area, employees shall be paid from a special wage schedule having rates identical to the regular wage schedule authorized for the headquarters office.

(c) Each special wage schedule shall be effective on the same date as the regular schedule on which it is based.

[55 FR 46145, Nov. 1, 1990]

§532.271 Special wage schedules for National Park Service positions in overlap areas.

(a)(1) The Department of the Interior shall establish special schedules for wage employees of the National Park Service whose duty station is located in one of the following NPS jurisdictions:

(i) Blue Ridge Parkway;

(ii) Natchez Trace Parkway; and

(iii) Great Smoky Mountains National Park.

(2) Each of these NPS jurisdictions is located in (*i.e.*, overlaps) more than one FWS wage area.

(b) The special overlap wage schedules in each of the NPS jurisdictions shall be based on a determination concerning which regular nonsupervisory wage schedule in the overlapped FWS wage areas provides the most favorable payline for the employees.

(c) The most favorable payline shall be determined by computing a simple average of the 15 nonsupervisory second step rates on each one of the regular schedules authorized for each wage area overlapped. The highest average obtained by this method will identify the regular schedule that produces the most favorable payline.

(d) Each special schedule shall be effective on the same date as the regular schedule on which it is based.

(e) If there is a change in the identification of the most favorable payline, the special scheule for the current year shall be issued on its normal effective date. The next special scheule shall be issued on the effective date of the next regular schedule that produced the most favorable payline for the NPS jurisdiction in the previous year.

[55 FR 46145, Nov. 1, 1990]

§532.273 Special wage schedules for United States Information Agency Radio Antenna Rigger positions.

(a) The United States Information Agency shall establish special wage schedules for Radio Antenna Riggers employed at transmitting and relay stations in the United States.

(b) The wage rate shall be the regular wage rate for the appropriate grade for Radio Antenna Rigger for the wage area in which the station is located, plus 25 percent of that rate.

(c) The 25 percent differential shall be in lieu of any environmental differential that would otherwise be payable.

(d) The special schedules shall be effective on the same date as the regular wage schedules for the wage area in which the positions are located.

[55 FR 46145, Nov. 1, 1990]

§532.275 Special wage schedules for ship surveyors in Puerto Rico.

(a) The Department of Defense shall establish special wage schedules for nonsupervisory ship surveyors and supervisory ship surveyors in Puerto Rico.

(b) Rates shall be computed as follows:

(1) The step 2 rate for nonsupervisory ship surveyors shall be set at 149.5 percent of the WG–10, step 2, rate on the overseas schedule.

(2) The step 2 rate of supervisory ship surveyors shall be set at 166.75 percent of the WG–10, step 2, rate on the overseas schedule.

(3) Step rates shall be developed by using the standard formulas established in § 532.203 of this part.

(c) The special wage schedules shall be effective on the same date as the regular wage schedules applicable to the Puerto Rico wage area.

[55 FR 46145, Nov. 1, 1990]

§ 532.277 Special wage schedules for U.S. Navy positions in Bridgeport, California.

(a) The Department of Defense shall establish special wage schedules for prevailing rate employees at the United States Marine Corps Mountain Warfare Training Center in Bridgeport, California.

(b) Schedules shall be established by increasing the step 2 rates on the Reno, Nevada, regular wage schedule by 10 percent.

(c) Step rates shall be developed by using the standard formulas established in § 532.203 of this subpart.

(d) The special wage schedules shall be effective on the same date as the regular wage schedules applicable to the Reno, Nevada, wage area.

[55 FR 46146, Nov. 1, 1990]

§ 532.281 Special wage schedules for divers and tenders.

(a) Agencies are authorized to establish special schedule payments for prevailing rate employees who perform diving and tending duties.

(b) Employees who perform diving duties shall be paid 175 percent of the locality WG–10, step 2, rate for all payable hours of the shift.

(c) Employees who perform tending duties shall be paid at the locality WG–10, step 2, rate for all payable hours of the shift.

(d) Employees whose regular scheduled rate exceeds the diving/tending rate on the day they perform such duties shall retain their regular scheduled rate on that day.

(e) An employee's diving/tending rate shall be used as the basic rate of pay for computing all premium payments for a shift.

(f) Employees who both dive and tend on the same shift shall receive the higher diving rate as the basic rate for all hours of the shift.

[55 FR 46146, Nov. 1, 1990]

§ 532.283 Special wage schedules for nonappropriated fund tipped employees classified as waiter/waitress.

(a) Tipped employees shall be paid from the regular nonappropriated fund (NAF) schedule applicable to the employee's duty station.

(b) A tip offset may be authorized for employees classified as Waiter/Waitress. For purposes of this section, a tipped employee is one who is engaged in an occupation in which he or she customarily and regularly receives more than $30 a month in tips, and a tip offset is the amount of money by which an employer, in meeting legal minimum wage standards, may reduce a tipped employee's cash wage in consideration of the receipt of tips.

(c) A tip offset may be established, abolished, or adjusted by NAF instrumentalities on an annual basis and at such additional times as new or revised minimum wage statutes require. The amount of any tip offset may vary within a single instrumentality based on location, type of service, or time of service.

(d) If tipped employees are represented by a labor organization holding exclusive recognition, the employing NAF instrumentality shall negotiate with such organization to arrive at a determination as to whether, when, and how much tip offset shall be applied. Changes in tip offset practices may be made more frequently than annually as a result of collective bargaining agreement.

(e) Tip offset practices shall be governed by the Fair Labor Standards Act, as amended, or the applicable statutes of the State, possession or territory where an employee works, whichever provides the greater benefit to the employee. In locations where tip offset is prohibited by law, the requirements of paragraphs (c) and (d) of this section do not apply.

[55 FR 46146, Nov. 1, 1990]

§532.285 Special wage schedules for supervisors of negotiated rate Bureau of Reclamation employees.

(a) The Department of the Interior shall establish and issue special wage schedules for wage supervisors of negotiated rate wage employees in the Bureau of Reclamation. These schedules shall be based on annual special wage surveys conducted by the Bureau of Reclamation in each special wage area. Survey jobs representing Bureau of Reclamation positions at up to four levels will be matched to private industry jobs in each special wage area. Special schedule rates for each position will be based on prevailing rates for that particular job in private industry.

(b) Each supervisory job shall be described at one of four levels corresponding to the four supervisory situations described in Factor I and four levels of Subfactor IIIA of the FWS Job Grading Standard for Supervisors. They shall be titled in accordance with regular FWS practices, with the added designation of level I, II, III, or IV. The special survey and wage schedule for a given special wage area includes only those occupations and levels having employees in that area. For each position on the special schedule, there shall be three step rates. Step 2 is the prevailing rate as determined by the survey; step 1 is 96 percent of the prevailing rate; and step 3 is 104 percent of the prevailing rate.

(c) For each special wage area, the Bureau of Reclamation shall designate and appoint a special wage survey committee, including a chairperson and two other members (at least one of whom shall be a supervisor paid from the special wage schedule), and one or more two-person data collection teams (each of which shall include at least one supervisor paid from the special wage schedule). The local wage survey committee shall determine the prevailing rate for each survey job as a weighted average. Survey specifications are as follows for all surveys:

(1) Based on Bureau of Reclamation activities and types of supervisory positions in the special wage area, the Bureau of Reclamation must survey private industry companies, with no minimum employment size requirement for establishments, in the following North American Industry Classification System code subsectors:

2012 NAICS codes	2012 NAICS industry titles
211	Oil and gas extraction.
212	Mining (except oil and gas).
213	Support activities for mining.
221	Utilities.
333	Machinery manufacturing.
334	Computer and electronic product manufacturing.
335	Electrical equipment, appliance, and component manufacturing.
484	Truck transportation.
492	Couriers and messengers.
493	Warehousing and storage.
515	Broadcasting (except Internet).
517	Telecommunications.
562	Waste management and remediation services.
811	Repair and maintenance.

(2) Each local wage survey committee shall compile lists of all companies in the survey area known to have potential job matches. For the first survey, all companies on the list will be surveyed. Subsequently, companies shall be removed from the survey list if they prove not to have job matches, and new companies will be added if they are expected to have job matches. Survey data will be shared with other local wage survey committees when the data from any one company is applicable to more than one special wage area.

(3) For each area, survey job descriptions shall be tailored to correspond to the position of each covered supervisor in that area. They will be described at one of four levels (I, II, III, or IV) corresponding to the definitions of the four supervisory situations described in Factor I and four levels of Subfactor IIIA of the FWS Job Grading Standard for Supervisors. A description of the craft, trade, or labor work supervised will be included in each supervisory survey job description.

(d) Special wage area boundaries shall be identical to the survey areas covered by the special wage surveys. The areas of application in which the special schedules will be paid are generally smaller than the survey areas, reflecting actual Bureau of Reclamation worksites and the often scattered location of surveyable private sector jobs. Special wage schedules shall be established in the following areas:

THE GREAT PLAINS REGION

Special Wage Survey Area (Counties)

Montana: All counties except Lincoln, Sanders,Lake, Flathead, Mineral, Missoula, Powell, Granite, and Ravalli
Wyoming: All counties except Lincoln, Teton, sublette, Uinta, and Sweetwater
Colorado: All counties except Moffat, Rio Blanco, Garfield, Mesa, Delta, Montrose, San Miguel, Ouray, Delores, San Juan, Montezuma, La Plata, and Archuleta
North Dakota: All counties
South Dakota: All counties

Special Wage Area of Application (Counties)

Montana: Broadwater, Jefferson,Lewis and Clark, Yellowstone, and Bighorn Counties
Wyoming: All counties except Lincoln, Teton, Sublette, Uinta, and Sweetwater
Colorado: Boulder, Chaffee, Clear Creek, Eagle, Fremont, Gilpin, Grand, Lake, Larimer, Park, Pitkin, Pueblo, and Summitt
Beginning month of survey: August

THE MID-PACIFIC REGION

Special Wage Survey Area (Counties)

California: Shasta, Sacramento, Butte, San Francisco, Merced, Stanislaus

Special Wage Area of Application (Counties)

California: Shasta, Sacramento, Fresno, Alameda, Tehoma, Tuolumne, Merced
Beginning month of survey: February

GREEN SPRINGS POWER FIELD STATION

Special Wage Survey Area (Counties)

Oregon: Jackson

Special Wage Area of Application (Counties)

Oregon: Jackson
Beginning month of survey: April

PACIFIC NW. REGION DRILL CREW

Special Wage Survey Area (Counties)

Montana: Flathead, Missoula
Oregon: Lane, Bend, Medford, Umatilla, Multnomah
Utah: Salt Lake
Idaho: Ada, Canyon, Adams
Washington: Spokane, Grant, Lincoln, Okanogan

Special Wage Area of Application (Counties)

Oregon: Deschutes, Jackson, Umatilla
Montana: Missoula
Idaho: Ada
Washington: Grant, Lincoln, Douglas, Okanogan, Yakima
Beginning month of survey: April

SNAKE RIVER AREA OFFICE (CENTRAL SNAKE/ MINIDOKA)

Special Wage Survey Area (Counties)

Idaho: Ada, Caribou, Bingham, Bannock

Special Wage Area of Application (Counties)

Idaho: Gem, Elmore, Bonneville, Minidoka, Boise, Valley, Power
Beginning month of survey: April

HUNGRY HORSE PROJECT OFFICE

Special Wage Survey Area (Counties)

Montana: Flathead, Missoula, Cascade, Sanders, Lake
Idaho: Bonner
Washington: Pend Oreille

Special Wage Area of Application (Counties)

Montana: Flathead
Beginning month of survey: March

GRAND COULEE POWER OFFICE (GRAND COULEE PROJECT OFFICE)

Special Wage Survey Area (Counties)

Oregon: Multnomah
Washington: Spokane, King

Special Wage Area of Application (Counties)

Washington: Grant, Douglas, Lincoln, Okanogan
Beginning month of survey: April

UPPER COLUMBIA AREA OFFICE (YAKIMA)

Special Wage Survey Area (Counties)

Washington: King, Yakima
Oregon: Multnomah

Special Wage Area of Application (Counties)

Washington: Yakima
Oregon: Umatilla
Beginning Month of Survey: September

COLORADO RIVER STORAGE PROJECT AREA

Special Wage Survey Area (Counties)

Arizona: Apache, Coconino, Navajo
Colorado: Moffat, Montrose, Routt, Gunnison, Rio Blanco, Mesa, Garfield, Eagle, Delta, Pitkin, San Miguel, Delores, Montezuma, La Plata, San Juan, Ouray, Archuleta, Hindale, Mineral
Wyoming: Unita, Sweetwater, Carbon, Albany, Laramie, Goshen, Platte, Niobrara, Converse, Natrona, Fremont, Sublette, Lincoln
Utah: Beaver, Box Elder, Cache, Carbon, Daggett, Davis, Duchesne, Emery, Garfield, Grand, Iron, Juab, Kane, Millard, Morgan, Piute, Rich, Salt Lake, San Juan, Sanpete, Sevier, Summit, Tooele, Uintah, Utah, Wasatch, Washington, Wayne, Weber

Special Survey Area of Application (Counties)

Arizona: Coconino
Colorado: Montrose, Gunnison, Mesa
Wyoming: Lincoln
Utah: Daggett
Beginning month of survey: March

ELEPHANT BUTTE AREA

Special Wage Survey Area (Counties)

New Mexico: Grant, Hidalgo, Luna, Donña Ana, Otero, Eddy, Lea, Roosevelt, Chaves, Lincoln, Sierra, Socorro, Catron, Cibola, Valencia, Bernalillo, Torrance, Guadalupe, De Baca, Curry, Quay
Texas: El Paso, Hudspeth, Culberson, Jeff Davis, Presido, Brewster, Pecos, Reeves, Loving, Ward, Winkler
Arizona: Apache, Greenlee, Graham, Cochise

Special Wage Area of Application (Counties)

New Mexico: Sierra
Beginning month of survey: June

LOWER COLORADO DAMS AREA

Special Wage Survey Area (Counties)

Nevada: Clark
California: Los Angeles
Arizona: Maricopa

Special Wage Area of Application (Counties)

Nevada: Clark
California: San Bernardino
Arizona: Mohave
Beginning month of survey: August

YUMA PROJECTS AREA

Special Wage Survey Area (Counties)

California: San Diego
Arizona: Maricopa, Yuma

NOTE: Bureau of Reclamation may add other survey counties for dredge operator supervisors because of the uniqueness of the occupation and difficulty in finding job matches.)

Special Wage Area of Application (Counties)

Arizona: Yuma
Beginning month of survey: November (Maintenance) and April (Dredging)

BUREAU OF RECLAMATION, DENVER, CO, AREA

Special Wage Survey Area (Counties)

Colorado: Jefferson, Denver, Adams, Arapahoe, Boulder, Larimer

Special Wage Survey Area of Application (Counties)

Colorado: Jefferson
Beginning month of survey: February

(e) These special schedule positions will be identified by pay plan code XE, grade 00, and the Federal Wage System occupational codes will be used. New employees shall be hired at step 1 of the position. With satisfactory or higher performance, advancement between steps shall be automatic after 52 weeks of service.

(f)(1) In the first year of implementation, all special areas will have full-scale surveys.

(2) Current employees shall be placed in step 2 of the new special schedule, or, if their current rate of pay exceeds the rate for step 2, they shall be placed in step 3. Pay retention shall apply to any employee whose rate of basic pay would otherwise be reduced as a result of placement in these new special wage schedules.

(3) The waiting period for within-grade increases shall begin on the employee's first day under the new special schedule.

[60 FR 5310, Jan. 27, 1995, as amended at 69 FR 7105, Feb. 13, 2004; 71 FR 35375, June 20, 2006; 73 FR 45853, Aug. 7, 2008; 78 FR 58154, Sept. 23, 2013]

§ 532.287 Special wage schedules for nonappropriated fund automotive mechanics.

(a) The Department of Defense (DOD) will establish a flat rate pay system for nonappropriated fund (NAF) automotive mechanics. This flat rate pay system will take into account local prevailing rates, the mechanic's skill level, and the standard number of hours required to complete a particular job.

(b) DOD will issue special wage schedules for NAF automotive mechanics who are covered by the flat rate pay system. These special schedules will provide rates of pay for nonsupervisory, leader, and supervisory employees. These special schedule positions will be identified by pay plan codes XW (nonsupervisory), XY (leader), and XZ (supervisory), grades 8–10, and will use the Federal Wage System occupational code 5823.

(c) DOD will issue special wage schedules for NAF automotive mechanics based on annual special flat rate surveys of similar jobs conducted in each special schedule wage area.

(1) The survey area for these special surveys will include the same counties as the regular NAF survey area.

(2) The survey jobs used will be Automotive Worker and Automotive Mechanic.

(3) The special surveys will include data on automotive mechanics that are paid under private industry flat rate pay plans as well as those paid by commission.

(4) In addition to all standard North American Industry Classification System (NAICS) codes currently used on the regular surveys, the industries surveyed will include—

2012 NAICS Codes	2012 NAICS Industry titles
441110	New car dealers.
441310	Automotive parts and accessory stores.
811111	General automotive repair.
811191	Automotive oil change and lubrication shops.

(5) The surveys will cover establishments with a total employment of eight or more.

(6) The special schedules for NAF automotive mechanics will be effective on the same dates as the regular wage schedules in the NAF FWS wage area.

(d) New employees will be hired at step 1 of the position under the flat rate pay system. Current employees will be moved to these special wage schedules on a step-by-step basis. Pay retention will apply to any employee whose rate of basic pay would otherwise be reduced as a result of placement in these new special schedules.

[79 FR 22765, Apr. 24, 2014]

§ 532.289 Special wage schedules for U.S. Army Corps of Engineers flood control employees of the Vicksburg District in Mississippi.

(a)(1) The Department of Defense will establish special wage schedules for wage employees of the U.S. Army Corps of Engineers who work at flood control dams (also known as reservoir projects) and whose duty station is located in one of the lakes that comprise the Vicksburg District of the Mississippi Valley Division.

(2) These special wage schedules will provide rates of pay for nonsupervisory, leader, and supervisory employees. These special schedule positions will be identified by pay plan codes XR (nonsupervisory), XT (leader), and XU (supervisory).

(b) The Vicksburg District of the Mississippi Valley Division is comprised of the following four lakes:

(1) Grenada Lake in Grenada County, MS

(2) Enid Lake in Yalobusha County, MS

(3) Sardis Lake in Panola County, MS

(4) Arkabutla Lake in Tate County, MS

(c) Special wage schedules shall be established at the same time and with rates identical to the Memphis, TN, appropriated fund wage schedule.

[80 FR 61277, Oct. 13, 2015]

Appendix A to Subpart B of Part 532—Nationwide Schedule of Appropriated Fund Regular Wage Surveys

This appendix shows the annual schedule of wage surveys. It lists all States alphabetically, each State being followed by an alphabetical listing of all wage areas in the State. Information given for each wage area includes—

(1) The lead agency responsible for conducting the survey;

(2) The month in which the survey will begin; and

(3) Whether full-scale surveys will be done in odd or even numbered fiscal years.

State	Wage area	Lead agency	Beginning month of survey	Fiscal year of full-scale survey odd or even
Alabama	Anniston-Gadsden	DoD	April	Even.
	Birmingham	DoD	January	Even.
	Dothan	DoD	July	Odd.
	Huntsville	DoD	April	Even.
Alaska	Alaska	DoD	July	Even.
Arizona	Northeastern Arizona	DoD	March	Odd.
	Phoenix	DoD	March	Odd.
	Tucson	DoD	March	Odd.
Arkansas	Little Rock	DoD	August	Even.
California	Fresno	DoD	February	Odd.
	Los Angeles	DoD	September	Even.
	Sacramento	DoD	February	Odd.
	Salinas-Monterey	DoD	February	Even.
	San Bernardino-Riverside-Ontario	DoD	September	Even.
	San Diego	DoD	September	Odd.
	San Francisco	DoD	September	Odd.
	Santa Barbara	DoD	September	Even.
	Stockton	DoD	February	Odd.
Colorado	Denver	DoD	January	Odd.
	Southern Colorado	DoD	January	Even.
Connecticut	New Haven-Hartford	DoD	April	Odd.
	New London	DoD	September	Even.
Delaware	Wilmington	DoD	November	Even.
District of Columbia	Washington, D.C	DoD	August	Odd.
Florida	Cocoa Beach-Melbourne	DoD	October	Even.
	Jacksonville	DoD	January	Odd.
	Miami	DoD	January	Odd.
	Panama City	DoD	September	Even.
	Pensacola	DoD	September	Odd.
	Tampa-St. Petersburg	DoD	April	Even.
Georgia	Albany	DoD	August	Odd.
	Atlanta	DoD	May	Odd.
	Augusta	DoD	June	Odd.
	Columbus	DoD	August	Odd.
	Macon	DoD	June	Odd.
	Savannah	DoD	May	Odd.
Hawaii	Hawaii	DoD	June	Even.
Idaho	Boise	DoD	July	Odd.
Illinois	Central Illinois	DoD	September	Odd.
	Chicago	DoD	September	Even.
Indiana	Bloomington-Bedford-Washington	DoD	October	Odd.
	Fort Wayne-Marion	DoD	October	Odd.
	Indianapolis	DoD	October	Odd.
Iowa	Cedar Rapids-Iowa City	DoD	July	Even.
	Davenport-Rock Island-Moline	DoD	October	Even.
	Des Moines	DoD	September	Odd.
Kansas	Topeka	DoD	November	Even.
	Wichita	DoD	November	Even.
Kentucky	Lexington	DoD	February	Even.
	Louisville	DoD	February	Odd.
Louisiana	Lake Charles-Alexandria	DoD	April	Even.
	New Orleans	DoD	November	Odd.
	Shreveport	DoD	May	Even.
Maine	Augusta [1]	DoD	May	Even.
	Central and Northern Maine	DoD	June	Even.
Maryland	Baltimore	DoD	September	Odd.
	Hagerstown-Martinsburg-Chambersburg	DoD	January	Even.
Massachusetts	Boston	DoD	August	Even.
	Central and Western Massachusetts	DoD	June	Even.
Michigan	Detroit	DoD	January	Odd.
	Northwestern Michigan	DoD	August	Odd.
	Southwestern Michigan [1]	DoD	October	Even.
Minnesota	Duluth	DoD	June	Odd.
	Minneapolis-St. Paul	DoD	March	Odd.
Mississippi	Biloxi	DoD	November	Even.
	Northern Mississippi	DoD	February	Even.
	Jackson	DoD	February	Odd.
	Meridian	DoD	February	Odd.
Missouri	Kansas City	DoD	October	Odd.

State	Wage area	Lead agency	Beginning month of survey	Fiscal year of full-scale survey odd or even
	St. Louis	DoD	October	Odd.
	Southern Missouri	DoD	October	Odd.
Montana	Montana	DoD	July	Even.
Nebraska	Omaha	DoD	October	Odd.
Nevada	Las Vegas	DoD	September	Even.
	Reno	DoD	March	Even.
New Hampshire	Portsmouth	DoD	September	Even.
New Mexico	Albuquerque	DoD	April	Odd.
New York	Albany-Schenectady-Troy	DoD	March	Odd.
	Buffalo [1]	DoD	September	Odd.
	New York	DoD	January	Even.
	Northern New York	DoD	March	Odd.
	Rochester	DoD	February	Even.
	Syracuse-Utica-Rome	DoD	March	Even.
North Carolina	Asheville	DoD	June	Even.
	Central North Carolina	DoD	May	Even.
	Charlotte	DoD	August	Odd.
	Southeastern North Carolina	DoD	January	Odd.
North Dakota	North Dakota	DoD	March	Even.
Ohio	Cincinnati	DoD	January	Odd.
	Cleveland	DoD	April	Odd.
	Columbus	DoD	January	Odd.
	Dayton	DoD	January	Even.
Oklahoma	Oklahoma City	DoD	August	Odd.
	Tulsa	DoD	August	Odd.
Oregon	Portland	DoD	August	Even.
	Southwestern Oregon	DoD	June	Even.
Pennsylvania	Harrisburg	DoD	January	Even.
	Philadelphia	DoD	October	Even.
	Pittsburgh	DoD	July	Odd.
	Scranton-Wilkes-Barre	DoD	August	Odd.
Puerto Rico	Puerto Rico	DoD	July	Odd.
Rhode Island	Narragansett Bay	DoD	January	Odd.
South Carolina	Charleston	DoD	July	Even.
	Columbia	DoD	May	Even.
South Dakota	Eastern South Dakota [1]	DoD	October	Even.
Tennessee	Eastern Tennessee	DoD	February	Odd.
	Memphis	DoD	February	Even.
	Nashville	DoD	February	Even.
Texas	Austin	DoD	June	Even.
	Corpus Christi	DoD	June	Even.
	Dallas-Fort Worth	DoD	October	Odd.
	El Paso	DoD	April	Even.
	Houston-Galveston-Texas City	DoD	March	Even.
	San Antonio	DoD	June	Odd.
	Texarkana	DoD	April	Odd.
	Waco	DoD	May	Odd.
	Western Texas	DoD	May	Odd.
	Wichita Falls-Southwestern Oklahoma	DoD	August	Even.
Utah	Utah	DoD	July	Odd.
Virginia	Norfolk-Portsmouth-Newport News-Hampton.	DoD	May	Even.
	Richmond	DoD	November	Odd.
	Roanoke	DoD	November	Even.
Washington	Seattle-Everett-Tacoma	DoD	September	Even.
	Southeastern Washington-Eastern Oregon.	DoD	June	Odd.
	Spokane	DoD	July	Odd.
West Virginia	West Virginia	DoD	March	Odd.
Wisconsin	Madison	DoD	July	Even.
	Milwaukee	DoD	June	Odd.
	Southwestern Wisconsin	DoD	June	Even.
Wyoming	Wyoming	DoD	January	Even.

[1] The revised fiscal year entries are scheduled to begin for Augusta, Maine, in fiscal year 1996; for Buffalo, New York, and Southwestern Michigan in fiscal year 1997; and for Eastern South Dakota in fiscal year 1998.

[46 FR 21344, Apr. 10, 1981]

EDITORIAL NOTE: For FEDERAL REGISTER citations affecting appendix A, see the List of CFR Sections Affected, which appears in the Finding Aids section of the printed volume and at *www.fdsys.gov*.

APPENDIX B TO SUBPART B OF PART 532—NATIONWIDE SCHEDULE OF NON-APPROPRIATED FUND REGULAR WAGE SURVEYS

This appendix shows the annual schedule of NAF wage surveys. It lists all States alphabetically, each State being followed by an alphabetical listing of all wage areas in the State. Information given for each wage area includes—

(1) The lead agency responsible for conducting the survey;

(2) The month in which the survey will begin; and

(3) Whether full-scale surveys will be conducted in odd or even numbered calendar years.

State	Wage area	Beginning month of survey	Calendar year of full-scale survey odd or even
Alabama	Calhoun	April	Even.
	Madison	April	Even.
	Montgomery	April	Odd.
Alaska	Anchorage	June	Even.
Arizona	Maricopa	October	Even.
	Pima	October	Even.
	Yuma	October	Even.
Arkansas	Pulaski	April	Odd.
California	Kern	September	Odd.
	Los Angeles	September	Even.
	Monterey	September	Odd.
	Orange	September	Even.
	Riverside	September	Even.
	Sacramento	February	Odd.
	San Bernardino	September	Even.
	San Diego	September	Odd.
	San Joaquin	February	Odd.
	Santa Barbara	September	Even.
	Solano	September	Odd.
	Ventura	September	Even.
Colorado	Arapahoe-Denver	July	Even.
	El Paso	July	Even.
Connecticut	New London	July	Even.
Delaware	Kent	August	Odd.
District of Columbia	Washington, DC	August	Even.
Florida	Bay	January	Even.
	Brevard	January	Odd.
	Miami-Dade	January	Odd.
	Duval	January	Odd.
	Escambia	January	Even.
	Hillsborough	January	Odd.
	Monroe	January	Odd.
	Okaloosa	January	Even.
	Orange	January	Even.
Georgia	Chatham	March	Odd.
	Cobb	June	Odd.
	Columbus	June	Odd.
	Dougherty	March	Odd.
	Houston	April	Odd.
	Lowndes	March	Odd.
	Richmond	April	Odd.
Guam	Guam	September	Even.
Hawaii	Honolulu	May	Even.
Idaho	Ada-Elmore	July	Odd.
Illinois	Lake	April	Even.
	St. Clair	April	Even.
Kansas	Leavenworth-Jackson-Johnson	April	Even.
	Sedgwick	April	Odd.
Kentucky	Christian-Montgomery	February	Even.
	Hardin-Jefferson	March	Even.
Louisiana	Bossier-Caddo	March	Odd.
	Orleans	June	Odd.
	Rapides	March	Odd.
Maine	York	October	Odd.
Maryland	Anne Arundel	August	Even.
	Charles-St. Mary's	August	Even.
	Frederick	August	Even.
	Harford	May	Even.
	Montgomery-Prince George's	August	Even.
Massachusetts	Hampden	October	Odd.
	Middlesex	October	Odd.
Michigan	Macomb	May	Odd.

State	Wage area	Beginning month of survey	Calendar year of full-scale survey odd or even
Minnesota	Hennepin	July	Odd.
Mississippi	Harrison	March	Even.
	Lauderdale	March	Odd.
	Lowndes	March	Odd.
Montana	Cascade	July	Odd.
Nebraska	Douglas-Sarpy	April	Even.
Nevada	Churchill-Washoe	January	Even.
	Clark	January	Even.
New Jersey	Burlington	August	Odd.
	Morris	August	Odd.
New Mexico	Bernalillo	February	Odd.
	Curry	June	Odd.
	Dona Ana	February	Odd.
New York	Jefferson	May	Odd.
	Kings-Queens	October	Even.
	Niagara	May	Odd.
	Orange	May	Odd.
North Carolina	Craven	March	Even.
	Cumberland	March	Even.
	Onslow	February	Even.
	Wayne	March	Even.
North Dakota	Grand Forks	July	Odd.
	Ward	July	Odd.
Ohio	Greene-Montgomery	April	Odd.
Oklahoma	Comanche	March	Even.
	Oklahoma	March	Even.
Pennsylvania	Allegheny	May	Odd.
	Cumberland	May	Even.
	York	May	Even.
Puerto Rico	Guaynabo-San Juan	February	Even.
Rhode Island	Newport	July	Even.
South Carolina	Charleston	February	Even.
	Richland	March	Even.
South Dakota	Pennington	June	Even.
Tennessee	Shelby	February	Even.
Texas	Bell	June	Odd.
	Bexar	June	Even.
	Dallas	June	Even.
	El Paso	February	Odd.
	McLennan	May	Odd.
	Nueces	June	Even.
	Tarrant	June	Even.
	Taylor	June	Odd.
	Tom Green	June	Odd.
	Wichita	March	Even.
Utah	Davis-Salt Lake-Weber	July	Odd.
Virginia	Alexandria-Arlington-Fairfax	August	Even.
	Chesterfield-Richmond	August	Odd.
	Hampton-Newport News	May	Even.
	Norfolk-Portsmouth-Virginia Beach	May	Even.
	Prince William	August	Even.
Washington	Kitsap	June	Even.
	Pierce	July	Even.
	Snohomish	July	Even.
	Spokane	July	Odd.
Wyoming	Laramie	July	Even.

[46 FR 21344, Apr. 10, 1981]

EDITORIAL NOTE: For FEDERAL REGISTER citations affecting appendix B, see the List of CFR Sections Affected, which appears in the Finding Aids section of the printed volume and at *www.fdsys.gov*.

APPENDIX C TO SUBPART B OF PART 532—APPROPRIATED FUND WAGE AND SURVEY AREAS

This appendix lists the wage area definitions for appropriated fund employees. With a few exceptions, each area is defined in terms of county units, independent cities, or, in the New England States, of entire township or city units. Each wage area definition consists of:

(1) *Wage area title.* Wage areas usually carry the title of the principal city in the area. Sometimes, however, the area title reflects a broader geographic area, such as Wyoming or Eastern Tennessee.

(2) *Survey area definition.* Lists each county, independent city, or township in the survey area.

(3) *Area of application definition.* Lists each county, independent city, or township which, in addition to the survey area, is in the area of application.

DEFINITIONS OF WAGE AND WAGE SURVEY AREAS

ALABAMA

ANNISTON-GADSDEN

Survey Area

Alabama:
- Calhoun
- Etowah
- Talladega

Area of Application. Survey area plus:

Alabama:
- Cherokee
- Clay
- Cleburne
- De Kalb
- Randolph

BIRMINGHAM

Survey Area

Alabama:
- Jefferson
- St. Clair
- Shelby
- Tuscaloosa
- Walker

Area of Application. Survey area plus:

Alabama:
- Bibb
- Blount
- Chilton
- Cullman
- Fayette
- Greene
- Hale
- Lamar
- Marengo
- Perry
- Pickens

DOTHAN

Survey Area

Alabama:
- Dale
- Houston

Georgia:
- Early

Area of Application. Survey area plus:

Alabama:
- Barbour
- Coffee
- Geneva
- Henry

Georgia:
- Clay
- Miller
- Seminole

HUNTSVILLE

Survey Area

Alabama:
- Limestone
- Madison
- Marshall
- Morgan

Area of Application. Survey area plus:

Alabama:
- Colbert
- Franklin
- Jackson
- Lauderdale
- Lawrence
- Marion
- Winston

Tennessee:
- Franklin
- Giles
- Lawrence
- Lincoln
- Moore
- Wayne

ALASKA

Survey Area

Alaska:
- Anchorage
- Fairbanks
- Juneau (and the areas within a 24-kilometer (15-mile) radius of their corporate city limits)

Area of Application.

State of Alaska (except special area schedules)

ARIZONA

NORTHEASTERN ARIZONA

Survey Area

Arizona:
- Apache
- Coconino
- Navajo

New Mexico:

McKinley
San Juan

Area of Application. Survey area plus:

Colorado:
Dolores
Gunnison (Only includes the Curecanti National Recreation Area portion)
La Plata
Montezuma
Montrose
Ouray
San Juan
San Miguel
Utah:
Kane
San Juan (Does not include the Canyonlands National Park portion.)

PHOENIX

Survey Area

Arizona:
Gila
Maricopa

Area of Application. Survey area plus:

Arizona:
Pinal
Yavapai

TUCSON

Survey Area

Arizona:
Pima

Area of Application. Survey area plus:

Arizona:
Cochise
Graham
Greenlee
Santa Cruz

ARKANSAS

LITTLE ROCK

Survey Area

Arkansas:
Jefferson
Pulaski
Saline

Area of Application. Survey area plus:

Arkansas:
Arkansas
Ashley
Baxter
Boone
Bradley
Calhoun
Chicot
Clay
Clark
Cleburne
Cleveland
Conway
Dallas
Desha
Drew
Faulkner
Franklin
Fulton
Garland
Grant
Greene
Hot Spring
Independence
Izard
Jackson
Johnson
Lawrence
Lincoln
Logan
Lonoke
Marion
Monroe
Montgomery
Newton
Ouachita
Perry
Phillips
Pike
Polk
Pope
Prairie
Randolph
Scott
Searcy
Sharp
Stone
Union
Van Buren
White
Woodruff
Yell

CALIFORNIA

FRESNO

Survey Area

California:
Fresno
Kings
Tulare

Area of Application. Survey area plus:

California:
Kern (Does not include China Lake Naval Weapons Center, Edwards Air Force Base, and portions occupied by Federal activities in Boron (City))
Madera (Does not include Devils Postpile National Monument and Yosemite National Park portions)

LOS ANGELES

Survey Area

California:
Los Angeles

Area of Application. Survey area plus:

California:
- Inyo (Includes the China Lake Naval Weapons Center portion only)
- Kern (Includes the China Lake Naval Weapons Center, Edwards Air Force Base, and portions occupied by Federal activities at Boron (City) only)
- Orange
- Riverside (Includes the Joshua Tree National Monument portion only)
- San Bernardino (All of San Bernardino County except that portion occupied by, and south and west of, the Angeles and San Bernardino National Forests)
- Ventura

SACRAMENTO

Survey Area

California:
- Placer
- Sacramento
- Sutter
- Yolo
- Yuba

Area of Application. Survey area plus:

California:
- Alpine
- Amador
- Butte
- Colusa
- Del Norte
- El Dorado
- Glenn
- Humboldt
- Lake
- Modoc
- Nevada
- Plumas
- Shasta
- Sierra
- Siskiyou
- Tehama
- Trinity

SALINAS-MONTEREY

Survey Area

California:
- Monterey

Area of Application. Survey area.

SAN BERNARDINO-RIVERSIDE-ONTARIO

Survey Area

California:
- Riverside (Does not include the Joshua Tree National Monument portion)
- San Bernardino (Only that portion occupied by, and south and west of the Angeles and San Bernardino National Forests)

Area of Application. Survey area.

SAN DIEGO

Survey Area

California:
- San Diego

Area of Application. Survey area plus:

California:
- Imperial

Arizona:
- La Paz
- Yuma

SAN FRANCISCO

California:
- Alameda
- Contra Costa
- Marin
- Napa
- San Francisco
- San Mateo
- Santa Clara
- Solano

Area of Application. Survey area plus:

California:
- Mendocino
- San Benito
- Santa Cruz
- Sonoma

SANTA BARBARA

Survey Area

California:
- Santa Barbara

Area of Application. Survey area plus:

California:
- San Luis Obispo

STOCKTON

Survey Area

Calfornia:
- San Joaquin

Area of Application. Survey area plus:

California:
- Calaveras
- Madera (Only includes Yosemite National Park portion)
- Mariposa
- Merced
- Stanislaus
- Tuolumne

COLORADO

DENVER

Survey Area

Colorado:
- Adams

Arapahoe
Boulder
Broomfield
Denver
Douglas
Gilpin
Jefferson

Area of Application. Survey area plus:

Colorado:
Clear Creek
Eagle
Elbert
Garfield
Grand
Jackson
Lake
Larimer
Logan
Morgan
Park
Phillips
Pitkin
Rio Blanco
Routt
Sedgwick
Summit
Washington
Weld
Yuma

SOUTHERN COLORADO

Survey Area

Colorado:
El Paso
Pueblo
Teller

Area of Application. Survey area plus:

Colorado:
Alamosa
Archuleta
Baca
Bent
Chaffee
Cheyenne
Conejos
Costilla
Crowley
Custer
Delta
Fremont
Gunnison (Does not include the Curecanti National Recreation Area portion)
Hinsdale
Huerfano
Kiowa
Kit Carson
Las Animas
Lincoln
Mineral
Otero
Prowers
Rio Grande
Saguache

CONNECTICUT

NEW HAVEN—HARTFORD

Survey Area

Connecticut:
Hartford
New Haven

Area of application. Survey area plus:

Connecticut:
Fairfield
Litchfield
Middlesex
Tolland

NEW LONDON

Survey Area

Connecticut:
New London

Area of application. Survey area.

DELAWARE

WILMINGTON

Survey Area

Delaware:
Kent
New Castle
Maryland:
Cecil
New Jersey:
Salem

Area of Application. Survey area plus:

Delaware:
Sussex
Maryland:
Caroline
Dorchester
Kent
Somerset
Talbot
Wicomico
Worcester (Does not include the Assateague Island portion)

DISTRICT OF COLUMBIA, WASHINGTON, DC

Survey Area

District of Columbia:
Washington, DC
Maryland:
Charles
Frederick
Montgomery
Prince George's
Virginia (cities):
Alexandria
Fairfax
Falls Church
Manassas
Manassas Park
Virginia (counties):

Arlington
Fairfax
Loudoun
Prince William

Area of Application. Survey area plus:

Maryland:
Calvert
St. Mary's
Virginia (city):
Fredericksburg
Virginia (counties):
Clarke
Culpeper
Fauquier
King George
Rappahannock
Spotsylvania
Stafford
Warren
West Virginia:
Jefferson

FLORIDA

COCOA BEACH-MELBOURNE

Survey Area

Florida:
Brevard

Area of Application. Survey area plus:

Florida:
Indian River

JACKSONVILLE

Survey Area

Florida:
Alachua
Baker
Clay
Duval
Nassau
St. Johns

Area of Application. Survey area plus:

Florida:
Bradford
Citrus
Columbia
Dixie
Flagler
Gilchrist
Hamilton
Lafayette
Lake
Levy
Madison
Marion
Orange
Osceola
Putnam
Seminole
Sumter
Suwannee
Taylor
Union
Volusia
Georgia:
Camden
Charlton

MIAMI

Survey Area

Florida:
Miami-Dade

Area of Application. Survey area plus:

Florida:
Broward
Collier
Glades
Hendry
Highlands
Martin
Monroe
Okeechobee
Palm Beach
St. Lucie

PANAMA CITY

Survey Area

Florida:
Bay
Gulf

Area of Application. Survey area plus:

Florida:
Calhoun
Franklin
Gadsden
Holmes
Jackson
Jefferson
Leon
Liberty
Wakulla
Washington

PENSACOLA

Survey Area

Florida:
Escambia
Santa Rosa

Area of Application. Survey area plus:

Florida
Okaloosa
Walton
Alabama:
Baldwin
Clarke
Conecuh
Covington
Escambia
Mobile
Monroe
Washington

TAMPA-ST. PETERSBURG

Survey Area

Florida:
Hillsborough
Pasco
Pinellas

Area of Application. Survey area plus:

Florida:
Charlotte
De Soto
Hardee
Hernando
Lee
Manatee
Polk
Sarasota

GEORGIA

ALBANY

Survey Area

Georgia:
Colquitt
Dougherty
Lee
Mitchell
Worth

Area of Application. Survey area plus:

Georgia:
Atkinson
Baker
Ben Hill
Berrien
Brooks
Calhoun
Clinch
Coffee
Cook
Decatur
Echols
Grady
Irwin
Lanier
Lowndes
Randolph
Sumter
Terrell
Thomas
Tift
Turner
Ware

ATLANTA

Survey Area

Georgia:
Butts
Cherokee
Clayton
Cobb
De Kalb
Douglas
Fayette
Forsyth
Fulton
Gwinnett
Henry
Newton
Paulding
Rockdale
Walton

Area of Application. Survey area plus:

Georgia:
Banks
Barrow
Bartow
Carroll
Chattooga
Clarke
Coweta
Dawson
Fannin
Floyd
Franklin
Gilmer
Gordon
Greene
Habersham
Hall
Haralson
Heard
Jackson
Jasper
Lamar
Lumpkin
Madison
Meriwether
Morgan
Murray
Oconee
Oglethorpe
Pickens
Pike
Polk
Rabun
Spalding
Stephens
Towns
Union
White
Whitfield

AUGUSTA

Survey Area

Georgia:
Columbia
McDuffie
Richmond
South Carolina:
Aiken

Area of Application. Survey area plus:

Georgia:
Burke
Elbert
Emanuel

Glascock
Hart
Jefferson
Jenkins
Lincoln
Taliaferro
Warren
Wilkes
South Carolina:
Allendale
Bamberg
Barnwell
Edgefield
McCormick

COLUMBUS

Survey Area

Alabama:
Autauga
Elmore
Lee
Macon
Montgomery
Russell
Georgia
Chattahoochee
Columbus

Area of Application. Survey area plus:

Alabama:
Bullock
Butler
Chambers
Coosa
Crenshaw
Dallas
Lowndes
Pike
Tallapoosa
Wilcox
Georgia:
Harris
Marion
Quitman
Schley
Stewart
Talbot
Taylor
Troup
Webster

MACON

Survey Area

Georgia:
Bibb
Houston
Jones
Laurens
Twiggs
Wilkinson

Area of Application. Survey area plus:

Georgia:
Baldwin
Bleckley
Crawford
Crisp
Dodge
Dooly
Hancock
Johnson
Macon
Monroe
Montgomery
Peach
Pulaski
Putnam
Telfair
Treutlen
Upson
Washington
Wheeler
Wilcox

SAVANNAH

Survey Area

Georgia:
Bryan
Chatham
Effingham
Liberty

Area of Application. Survey area plus:

Georgia:
Appling
Bacon
Brantley
Bulloch
Candler
Evans
Glynn
Jeff Davis
Long
McIntosh
Pierce
Screven
Tattnall
Toombs
Wayne
South Carolina:
Beaufort (The portion south of Broad River)
Hampton
Jasper

HAWAII

Survey Area

Hawaii:
Honolulu

Area of Application. Survey area plus:

Hawaii:
Hawaii
Kauai (Kauai county includes the islands of Kauai and Niihau.)
Maui (Maui county includes the islands of Maui, Molokai, Lanai and Kohoolawe.)

IDAHO

BOISE

Survey Area

Idaho:
- Ada
- Boise
- Canyon
- Elmore
- Gem

Area of Application. Survey area plus:

Idaho:
- Adams
- Bannock
- Bear Lake
- Bingham
- Blaine
- Bonneville
- Butte
- Camas
- Caribou
- Cassia
- Clark
- Custer
- Fremont
- Gooding
- Jefferson
- Jerome
- Lemhi
- Lincoln
- Madison
- Minidoka
- Oneida
- Owyhee
- Payette
- Power
- Teton
- Twin Falls
- Valley
- Washington

ILLINOIS

CENTRAL ILLINOIS

Survey Area

Illinois:
- Champaign
- Menard
- Sangamon
- Vermilion

Area of Application. Survey area plus:

Illinois:
- Christian
- Clark
- Coles
- Crawford
- Cumberland
- De Witt
- Douglas
- Edgar
- Ford
- Jasper
- Logan
- McLean
- Macon
- Moultrie
- Piatt
- Shelby

CHICAGO

Survey Area

Illinois:
- Cook
- Du Page
- Kane
- Lake
- McHenry
- Will

Area of Application. Survey area plus:

Illinois:
- Boone
- De Kalb
- Grundy
- Iroquois
- Kankakee
- Kendall
- La Salle
- Lee
- Livingston
- Ogle
- Stephenson
- Winnebago

Indiana:
- Jasper
- Lake
- La Porte
- Newton
- Porter
- Pulaski
- Starke

Wisconsin:
- Kenosha

INDIANA

BLOOMINGTON-BEDFORD-WASHINGTON

Survey Area

Indiana:
- Daviess
- Greene
- Knox
- Lawrence
- Martin
- Monroe
- Orange

Area of Application. Survey area plus:

Indiana:
- Crawford
- Dubois
- Gibson
- Jackson
- Owen
- Perry
- Pike
- Posey
- Spencer

Vanderburgh
Warrick
Illinois:
Edwards
Gallatin
Hardin
Lawrence
Richland
Wabash
White
Kentucky:
Crittenden
Daviess
Hancock
Henderson
Livingston
McLean
Ohio
Union
Webster

FORT WAYNE-MARION

Survey Area

Indiana:
Adams
Allen
DeKalb
Grant
Huntington
Wells

Area of Application. Survey area plus:

Indiana:
Blackford
Case
Elkhart
Fulton
Jay
Kosciusko
Lagrange
Marshall
Miami
Noble
St. Joseph
Steuben
Wabash
White
Whitley
Ohio:
Allen
Defiance
Henry
Mercer
Paulding
Putnam
Van Wert
Williams

INDIANAPOLIS

Survey Area

Indiana:
Boone
Hamilton
Hancock
Hendricks
Johnson
Marion
Morgan
Shelby

Area of Application. Survey area plus:

Indiana:
Bartholomew
Benton
Brown
Carroll
Clay
Clinton
Decatur
Delaware
Fayette
Fountain
Henry
Howard
Madison
Montgomery
Parke
Putnam
Rush
Sullivan
Tippecanoe
Tipton
Vermillion
Vigo
Warren

IOWA

CEDAR RAPIDS-IOWA CITY

Survey Area

Iowa:
Benton
Black Hawk
Johnson
Linn

Area of Application. Survey area plus:

Iowa:
Allamakee
Bremer
Buchanan
Butler
Cedar
Chickasaw
Clayton
Davis
Delaware
Fayette
Floyd
Grundy
Henry
Howard
Iowa
Jefferson
Jones
Keokuk
Mitchell
Tama
Van Buren
Wapello
Washington

Winneshiek

DAVENPORT-ROCK ISLAND-MOLINE

Survey Area

Iowa:
- Scott

Illinois:
- Henry
- Rock Island

Area of Application. Survey area plus

Iowa:
- Clinton
- Des Moines
- Dubuque
- Jackson
- Lee
- Louisa
- Muscatine

Illinois:
- Adams
- Brown
- Bureau
- Carroll
- Cass
- Fulton
- Hancock
- Henderson
- Jo Daviess
- Knox
- McDonough
- Marshall
- Mason
- Mercer
- Peoria
- Putnam
- Schuyler
- Stark
- Tazewell
- Warren
- Whiteside
- Woodford

DES MOINES

Survey Area

Iowa:
- Polk
- Story
- Warren

Area of Application. Survey area plus:

Iowa:
- Adair
- Appanoose
- Boone
- Calhoun
- Carroll
- Cerro Gordo
- Clarke
- Dallas
- Decatur
- Franklin
- Greene
- Guthrie
- Hamilton
- Hancock
- Hardin
- Humboldt
- Jasper
- Kossuth
- Lucas
- Madison
- Mahaska
- Marion
- Marshall
- Monroe
- Poweshiek
- Ringgold
- Union
- Wayne
- Webster
- Winnebago
- Worth
- Wright

KANSAS

TOPEKA

Survey Area

Kansas:
- Geary
- Jefferson
- Osage
- Shawnee

Area of Application. Survey area plus:

Kansas:
- Brown
- Clay
- Cloud
- Coffey
- Dickinson
- Jackson
- Lyon
- Marshall
- Morris
- Nemaha
- Ottawa
- Pottawatomie
- Republic
- Riley
- Saline
- Webaunsee
- Washington

WICHITA

Survey Area

Kansas:
- Butler
- Sedgwick

Area of Application. Survey area plus:

Kansas:
- Barber
- Barton
- Chase
- Chautauqua
- Cheyenne
- Clark

Comanche
Cowley
Decatur
Edwards
Elk
Ellis
Ellsworth
Finney
Ford
Gove
Graham
Grant
Gray
Greeley
Greenwood
Hamilton
Harper
Harvey
Haskell
Hodgeman
Jewell
Kearny
Kingman
Kiowa
Labette
Lane
Lincoln
Logan
McPherson
Marion
Meade
Mitchell
Montgomery
Morton
Neosho
Ness
Norton
Osborne
Pawnee
Phillips
Pratt
Rawlins
Reno
Rice
Rooks
Rush
Russell
Scott
Seward
Sheridan
Sherman
Smith
Stafford
Stanton
Stevens
Sumner
Thomas
Trego
Wallace
Wichita
Wilson
Woodson

KENTUCKY

LEXINGTON

Survey Area

Kentucky:
Bourbon
Clark
Fayette
Jessamine
Madison
Scott
Woodford

Area of Application. Survey area plus:

Kentucky:
Anderson
Bath
Bell
Boyle
Breathitt
Casey
Clay
Estill
Fleming
Franklin
Garrard
Green
Harrison
Jackson
Knott
Knox
Laurel
Lee
Leslie
Lincoln
McCreary
Marion
Menifee
Mercer
Montgomery
Morgan
Nicholas
Owen
Owsley
Perry
Powell
Pulaski
Robertson
Rockcastle
Rowan
Taylor
Washington
Wayne
Whitley
Wolfe

LOUISVILLE

Survey Area

Kentucky:
Bullitt
Hardin
Jefferson
Oldham
Indiana:
Clark

Floyd
Jefferson

Area of Application. Survey area plus:

Kentucky:
Breckinridge
Grayson
Hart
Henry
Larue
Meade
Nelson
Shelby
Spencer
Trimble
Indiana:
Harrison
Jennings
Scott
Washington

LOUISIANA

LAKE CHARLES-ALEXANDRIA

Survey Area

Louisiana:
Allen
Beauregard
Calcasieu
Grant
Rapides
Sabine
Vernon

Area of Application. Survey area plus:

Louisiana:
Acadia
Avoyelles
Caldwell
Cameron
Catahoula
Concordia
Evangeline
Franklin
Iberia
Jefferson Davis
Lafayette
La Salle
Madison
Natchitoches
St. Landry
St. Martin
Tensas
Vermilion
Winn

NEW ORLEANS

Survey Area

Louisiana:
Jefferson
Orleans
Plaquemines
St. Bernard
St. Charles
St. John the Baptist
St. Tammany

Area of Application. Survey area plus:

Louisiana:
Ascension
Assumption
East Baton Rouge
East Feliciana
Iberville
Lafourche
Livingston
Pointe Coupee
St. Helena
St. James
St. Mary
Tangipahoa
Terrebonne
Washington
West Baton Rouge
West Feliciana

SHREVEPORT

Survey Area

Louisiana: (parishes)
Bossier
Caddo
Webster

Area of Application. Survey area plus:

Louisiana: (parishes)
Bienville
Claiborne
De Soto
East Carroll
Jackson
Lincoln
Morehouse
Ouachita
Red River
Richland
Union
West Carroll
Texas:
Cherokee
Gregg
Harrison
Panola
Rusk
Upshur

MAINE

AUGUSTA

Survey Area

Maine:
Kennebec
Knox
Lincoln

Area of Application. Survey area.

CENTRAL AND NORTHERN MAINE

Survey Area

Maine:

Aroostook
Penobscot

Area of Application. Survey area plus:

Maine:
Hancock
Piscataquis
Somerset
Waldo
Washington

MARYLAND

BALTIMORE

Survey Area

Maryland:
Baltimore City
Anne Arundel
Baltimore
Carroll
Harford
Howard

Area of Application. Survey area plus:

Maryland:
Queen Anne's

HAGERSTOWN-MARTINSBURG-CHAMBERSBURG

Survey Area

Maryland:
Washington
Pennsylvania:
Franklin
West Virginia:
Berkeley

Area of Application. Survey area plus:

Maryland:
Allegany
Garrett
Pennsylvania:
Fulton
Virginia (cities):
Harrisonburg
Winchester
Virginia (counties):
Frederick
Madison
Page
Rockingham
Shenandoah
West Virginia:
Hampshire
Hardy
Mineral
Morgan

MASSACHUSETTS

BOSTON

Survey Area

Massachusetts:
The following cities and towns in:
Essex County
Beverly
Boxford
Danvers
Hamilton
Lynn
Lynnfield
Manchester
Marblehead
Middleton
Nahant
Peabody
Salem
Saugus
South Hamilton
Swampscott
Topsfield
Wenham
Middlesex County
Acton
Arlington
Ashland
Bedford
Belmont
Boxborough
Burlington
Cambridge
Carlisle
Concord
Everett
Framingham
Holliston
Lexington
Lincoln
Malden
Medford
Melrose
Natick
Newton
North Reading
North Wilmington
Reading
Sherborn
Somerville
Stoneham
Sudbury
Wakefield
Waltham
Watertown
Wayland
West Concord
Weston
Wilmington
Winchester
Woburn
Norfolk County
Bellingham
Braintree
Brookline
Canton
Cohasset
Dedham
Dover
East Walpole
Foxborough
Franklin
Harding
Holbrook

Islington
Medfield
Medway
Millis
Milton
Needham
Norfolk
North Cohasset
Norwood
Quincy
Randolph
Sharon
South Walpole
Stoughton
Walpole
Wellesley
Westwood
Weymouth
Wrentham
Plymouth County
Abington
Duxbury
Hanover
Hanson
Hingham
Hull
Kingston
Marshfield
Marshfield Hills
North Scituate
Norwell
Oceanbluff
Pembroke
Rockland
Scituate
Shore Acres
South Duxbury
South Hingham
West Hanover
Suffolk County

Area of Application. Survey area plus:

Massachusetts:
Barnstable
Dukes
Nantucket
Plymouth (non-survey area part)
The following cities and towns in:
Bristol County
Easton
Essex County
Andover
Essex
Gloucester
Ipswich
Lawrence
Methuen
Rockport
Rowley
Middlesex County
Ayer
Billerica
Chelmsford
Dracut
Dunstable
Groton
Hopkinton
Hudson
Littleton
Lowell
Marlborough
Maynard
Pepperell
Stow
Tewksbury
Tyngsborough
Westford
Norfolk County
Avon

CENTRAL AND WESTERN MASSACHUSETTS

Survey Area

Massachusetts:
The following cities and towns in:
Hampden County
Agawam
Chicopee
East Longmeadow
Feeding Hills
Hampden
Holyoke
Longmeadow
Ludlow
Monson
Palmer
Southwick
Springfield
Three Rivers
Westfield
West Springfield
Wilbraham
Hampshire County
Easthampton
Granby
Hadley
Northampton
South Hadley
Worcester County
Warren
West Warren

Area of Application. Survey area plus:

Connecticut
Windham
Massachusetts:
Berkshire
Franklin
Worcester (except Blackstone and Millville)
The following cities and towns in:
Hampden County
Blandford
Brimfield
Chester
Granville
Holland
Montgomery
Russell
Tolland
Wales
Hampshire County
Amherst
Belchertown

Chesterfield
Cummington
Goshen
Hatfield
Huntington
Middlefield
Pelham
Plainfield
Southampton
Ware
Westhampton
Williamsburg
Worthington
Middlesex County
Ashby
Shirley
Townsend
New Hampshire:
Belknap
Carroll
Cheshire
Grafton
Hillsborough
Merrimack
Sullivan
Vermont:
Addison
Bennington
Caledonia
Essex
Lamoille
Orange
Orleans
Rutland
Washington
Windham
Windsor

MICHIGAN

DETROIT

Survey Area

Michigan:
Lapeer
Livingston
Macomb
Oakland
St. Clair
Wayne

Area of Application. Survey area plus:

Michigan:
Arenac
Bay
Clare
Clinton
Eaton
Genesee
Gladwin
Gratiot
Huron
Ingham
Isabella
Lenawee
Midland
Monroe
Saginaw
Sanilac
Shiawassee
Tuscola
Washtenaw
Ohio:
Fulton
Lucas
Wood

NORTHWESTERN MICHIGAN

Survey Area

Michigan:
Delta
Dickinson
Marquette

Area of Application. Survey area plus:

Michigan:
Alcona (Effective date January 1, 1994.)
Alger
Alpena (Effective date January 1, 1994.)
Antrim (Effective date January 1, 1994.)
Baraga
Benzie (Effective date January 1, 1994.)
Charlevoix (Effective date January 1, 1994.)
Cheboygan (Effective date January 1, 1994.)
Chippewa
Crawford (Effective date January 1, 1994.)
Emmet (Effective date January 1, 1994.)
Gogebic
Grand Traverse (Effective date January 1, 1994.)
Houghton
Iosco (Effective date January 1, 1994.)
Iron
Kalkaska (Effective date January 1, 1994.)
Keweenaw
Leelanau (Effective date January 1, 1994.)
Luce
Mackinac
Manistee (Effective date January 1, 1994.)
Menominee
Missaukee (Effective date January 1, 1994.)
Montmorency (Effective date January 1, 1994.)
Ogemaw (Effective date January 1, 1994.)
Ontonagon
Oscoda (Effective date January 1, 1994.)
Otsego (Effective date January 1, 1994.)
Presque Isle (Effective date January 1, 1994.)
Roscommon (Effective date January 1, 1994.)
Schoolcraft
Wexford (Effective date January 1, 1994.)

SOUTHWESTERN MICHIGAN

Survey Area

Michigan:
Barry
Calhoun
Kalamazoo
Van Buren

Area of Application. Survey area plus:

Michigan:
- Allegan
- Berrien
- Branch
- Cass
- Hillsdale
- Ionia
- Jackson
- Kent
- Lake
- Mason
- Mecosta
- Montcalm
- Muskegon
- Newaygo
- Oceana
- Osceola
- Ottawa
- St. Joseph

MINNESOTA

DULUTH

Survey Area

Minnesota:
- Carlton
- St. Louis

Wisconsin:
- Douglas

Area of Application. Survey area plus:

Minnesota:
- Aitkin
- Becker (Including the White Earth Indian Reservation portion only)
- Beltrami
- Cass
- Clearwater
- Cook
- Crow Wing
- Hubbard
- Itasca
- Koochiching
- Lake
- Lake of the Woods
- Mahnomen
- Pine

Wisconsin:
- Ashland
- Bayfield
- Burnett
- Iron
- Sawyer
- Washburn

MINNEAPOLIS-ST. PAUL

Survey Area

Minnesota:
- Anoka
- Carver
- Chisago
- Dakota
- Hennepin
- Ramsey
- Scott
- Washington
- Wright

Wisconsin:
- St. Croix

Area of Application. Survey area plus:

Minnesota:
- Benton
- Big Stone
- Blue Earth
- Brown
- Chippewa
- Cottonwood
- Dodge
- Douglas
- Faribault
- Fillmore
- Freeborn
- Goodhue
- Grant
- Isanti
- Kanabec
- Kandiyohi
- Lac Qui Parle
- Le Sueur
- McLeod
- Martin
- Meeker
- Mille Lacs
- Morrison
- Mower
- Nicollet
- Olmsted
- Pope
- Redwood
- Renville
- Rice
- Sherburne
- Sibley
- Stearns
- Steele
- Stevens
- Swift
- Todd
- Traverse
- Wabasha
- Wadena
- Waseca
- Watonwan
- Yellow Medicine

Wisconsin:
- Pierce
- Polk

MISSISSIPPI

BILOXI

Survey Area

Mississippi:
- Hancock
- Harrison
- Jackson

Area of Application. Survey area plus:

Mississippi:
- George
- Pearl River
- Stone (Effective as of November 1, 1997.)

JACKSON

Survey Area

Mississippi:
- Hinds
- Rankin
- Warren

Area of Application. Survey area plus:

Mississippi:
- Adams (Effective as of February 1, 1997.)
- Amite
- Attala
- Claiborne (Effective as of February 1, 1997.)
- Copiah
- Covington
- Franklin
- Holmes
- Humphreys
- Issaquena
- Jefferson (Effective as of February 1, 1997.)
- Jefferson Davis
- Lawrence
- Lincoln
- Madison
- Marion
- Pike
- Scott
- Sharkey
- Simpson
- Smith
- Walthall
- Wilkinson
- Yazoo

MERIDIAN

Survey Area

Mississippi:
- Forest
- Lamar (Effective as of February 1, 1997.)
- Lauderdale

Alabama:
- Choctaw

Area of Application. Survey area plus:

Mississippi:
- Clarke
- Greene
- Jasper
- Jones
- Kemper
- Leake
- Neshoba
- Newton
- Perry
- Wayne

Alabama:
- Sumter

NORTHERN MISSISSIPPI

Survey Area

Mississippi:
- Clay
- Grenada
- Lee
- Leflore
- Lowndes
- Monroe
- Oktibbeha

Area of Application. Survey area plus:

Mississippi:
- Alcorn
- Bolivar
- Calhoun
- Carroll
- Chickasaw
- Choctaw
- Coahoma
- Itawamba
- Lafayette (Does not include the Holly Springs National Forest portion)
- Montgomery
- Noxubee
- Pontotoc (Does not include the Holly Springs National Forest portion)
- Prentiss
- Quitman
- Sunflower
- Tallahatchie
- Tishomingo
- Union (Does not include the Holly Springs National Forest portion)
- Washington
- Webster
- Winston
- Yalobusha

MISSOURI

KANSAS CITY

Survey Area

Kansas:
- Johnson
- Leavenworth
- Wyandotte

Missouri:
- Cass
- Clay
- Jackson
- Platte
- Ray

Area of Application. Survey area plus:

Kansas:
- Allen
- Anderson
- Atchison
- Bourbon
- Doniphan
- Douglas
- Franklin
- Linn

Miami
Missouri:
Adair
Andrew
Atchison
Bates
Buchanan
Caldwell
Carroll
Chariton
Clinton
Cooper
Daviess
De Kalb
Gentry
Grundy
Harrison
Henry
Holt
Howard
Johnson
Lafayette
Linn
Livingston
Macon
Mercer
Nodaway
Pettis
Putnam
Saline
Schuyler
Sullivan
Worth

ST. LOUIS

Survey Area

Illinois:
Clinton
Madison
Monroe
St. Clair
Missouri: (city)
St. Louis
Missouri: (counties)
Franklin
Jefferson
St. Charles
St. Louis

Area of Application. Survey area plus:

Illinois:
Alexander
Bond
Calhoun
Clay
Effingham
Fayette
Franklin
Greene
Hamilton
Jackson
Jefferson
Jersey
Johnson
Macoupin
Marion
Massac
Montgomery
Morgan
Perry
Pike
Pope
Pulaski
Randolph
Saline
Scott
Union
Washington
Wayne
Williamson
Missouri:
Audrain
Bollinger
Boone
Callaway
Cape Girardeau
Clark
Cole
Crawford
Gasconade
Knox
Lewis
Lincoln
Marion
Moniteau
Monroe
Montgomery
Osage
Perry
Pike
Ralls
Randolph
St. Francois
Ste. Genevieve
Scotland
Shelby
Warren
Washington

SOUTHERN MISSOURI

Survey Area

Missouri:
Christian
Greene
Laclede
Phelps
Pulaski
Webster

Area of Application. Survey area plus:

Kansas:
Cherokee
Crawford
Missouri:
Barry
Barton
Benton
Butler
Camden
Carter
Cedar
Dade

Dallas
Dent
Douglas
Hickory
Howell
Iron
Jasper
Lawrence
Madison
Maries
Miller
Mississippi
Morgan
New Madrid
Newton
Oregon
Ozark
Polk
Reynolds
Ripley
St. Clair
Scott
Shannon
Stoddard
Stone
Taney
Texas
Vernon
Wayne
Wright

MONTANA

Survey Area

Montana:
Cascade
Lewis and Clark
Yellowstone

Area of Application. Survey area plus:

Montana:
Beaverhead
Big Horn
Blaine
Broadwater
Carbon
Carter
Chouteau
Custer
Daniels
Dawson
Deer Lodge
Fallon
Fergus
Flathead
Gallatin
Garfield
Glacier
Golden Valley
Granite
Hill
Jefferson
Judith Basin
Lake
Liberty
Lincoln
McCone
Madison
Meagher
Mineral
Missoula
Musselshell
Park
Petroleum
Phillips
Pondera
Powder River
Powell
Prairie
Ravalli
Richland
Roosevelt
Rosebud
Sanders
Sheridan
Silver Bow
Stillwater
Sweet Grass
Teton
Toole
Treasure
Valley
Wheatland
Wibaux
Wyoming:
Big Horn
Park
Teton

NEBRASKA

OMAHA

Survey Area

Nebraska:
Douglas
Lancaster
Sarpy
Iowa:
Pottawattamie

Area of Application. Survey area plus:

Nebraska:
Adams
Antelope
Arthur
Blaine
Boone
Boyd
Brown
Buffalo
Burt
Butler
Cass
Cedar
Chase
Cherry
Clay
Colfax
Cuming
Custer
Dakota
Dawson
Dixon

Dodge
Dundy
Fillmore
Franklin
Frontier
Furnas
Gage
Garfield
Gosper
Grant
Greeley
Hall
Hamilton
Harlan
Hayes
Hitchcock
Holt
Hooker
Howard
Jefferson
Johnson
Kearney
Keith
Keya Paha
Knox
Lincoln
Logan
Loup
McPherson
Madison
Merrick
Nance
Nemaha
Nuckolls
Otoe
Pawnee
Perkins
Phelps
Pierce
Platte
Polk
Red Willow
Richardson
Rock
Saline
Saunders
Seward
Sherman
Stanton
Thayer
Thomas
Thurston
Valley
Washington
Wayne
Webster
Wheeler
York

Iowa:
Adams
Audubon
Buena Vista
Cass
Cherokee
Clay
Crawford
Fremont
Harrison
Ida
Mills
Monona
Montgomery
O'Brien
Page
Palo Alto
Plymouth
Pocahontas
Sac
Shelby
Sioux
Taylor
Woodbury

South Dakota
Union

NEVADA

LAS VEGAS

Survey Area

Nevada:
Clark
Nye

Area of Application. Survey area plus:

Nevada:
Esmeralda
Lincoln

Arizona:
Mohave

California:
Inyo (Excludes the China Lake Naval Weapons Center portion only)

RENO

Survey Area

Nevada:
Lyon
Mineral
Storey
Washoe

Area of Application. Survey area plus:

Nevada (cities):
Carson City

Nevada (counties):
Churchill
Douglas
Elko
Eureka
Humboldt
Lander
Pershing
White Pine

California:
Lassen
Madera (Includes only the Devils Postpile National Monument portion)
Mono (Does not cover locations to which Bridgeport, Calif, special schedule applies)

NEW HAMPSHIRE

PORTSMOUTH

Survey Area

Maine:
Androscoggin
Cumberland
Sagadahoc
York
Massachusetts:
The following cities and towns in:
Essex County
Amesbury
Georgetown
Groveland
Haverhill
Merrimac
Newbury
Newburyport
North Andover
Salisbury
South Byfield
West Newbury
New Hampshire:
Rockingham (except the following cities and towns: Newton, Plaistow, Salem, and Westville)
Strafford

Area of Application. Survey area plus:

Maine
Franklin
Oxford
New Hampshire
Coos
The following cities and towns in:
Rockingham County
Newton
Plaistow
Salem
Westville

NEW MEXICO

ALBUQUERQUE

Survey Area

New Mexico:
Bernalillo
Sandoval

Area of Application. Survey area plus:

New Mexico:
Catron
Cibola
Colfax
Curry
De Baca
Guadalupe
Harding
Lincoln (Does not include White Sands Missile Range portion)
Los Alamos
Mora
Quay
Rio Arriba
Roosevelt
San Miguel
Santa Fe
Socorro (Does not include White Sands Missile Range portion)
Taos
Torrance
Union
Valencia

NEW YORK:

ALBANY-SCHENECTADY-TROY

Survey Area

New York:
Albany
Montgomery
Rensselaer
Saratoga
Schenectady

Area of Application. Survey area plus:

New York:
Columbia
Delaware
Fulton
Greene
Schoharie
Ulster
Warren
Washington

BUFFALO

Survey Area

New York:
Erie
Niagara

Area of Application. Survey area plus:

New York:
Cattaraugus
Chautauqua
Pennsylvania:
Elk (Only includes the Allegheny National Forest portion)
Forest (Only includes the Allegheny National Forest portion)
McKean
Warren

NEW YORK

Survey Area

New Jersey:
Bergen
Essex
Hudson
Middlesex
Morris
Passaic
Somerset
Union
New York:
Bronx
Kings

Nassau
New York
Orange
Queens
Suffolk
Westchester

Area of Application. Survey area plus:

New Jersey:
Burlington (Joint Base McGuire-Dix-Lakehurst portion only)
Hunterdon
Monmouth
Ocean
Sussex
New York:
Dutchess
Putnam
Richmond
Rockland
Pennsylvania
Pike

NORTHERN NEW YORK

Survey Area

New York:
Clinton
Franklin
Jefferson
St. Lawrence
Vermont:
Chittenden
Franklin
Grand Isle

Area of Application. Survey area plus:

New York:
Essex
Lewis

ROCHESTER

Survey Area

New York:
Livingston
Monroe
Ontario
Orleans
Steuben
Wayne

Area of Application. Survey area plus:

New York:
Allegany
Chemung
Genesee
Schuyler
Seneca
Wyoming
Yates
Pennsylvania:
Tioga

SYRACUSE-UTICA-ROME

Survey Area

New York:
Herkimer
Madison
Oneida
Onondaga
Oswego

Area of Application. Survey area plus:

New York:
Broome
Cayuga
Chenango
Cortland
Hamilton
Otsego
Tioga
Tompkins

NORTH CAROLINA

ASHEVILLE

Survey Area

North Carolina:
Buncombe
Haywood
Henderson
Madison
Transylvania

Area of Application. Survey area plus:

North Carolina:
Alexander
Avery
Burke
Caldwell
Catawba
Cherokee
Clay
Graham
Jackson
McDowell
Macon
Mitchell
Polk
Rutherford
Swain
Yancey

CENTRAL NORTH CAROLINA

Survey Area

North Carolina:
Cumberland
Durham
Harnett
Hoke
Johnston
Orange
Wake
Wayne

Area of Application. Survey area plus:

North Carolina:

Alamance
Bladen
Caswell
Chatham
Davidson
Davie
Edgecombe
Franklin
Forsyth
Granville
Guilford
Halifax
Lee
Montgomery
Moore
Nash
Northampton
Person
Randolph
Richmond
Robeson
Rockingham
Sampson
Scotland
Stokes
Surry
Vance
Warren
Wilson
Yadkin

South Carolina:
Dillon
Marion
Marlboro

CHARLOTTE

Survey Area

North Carolina:
Cabarrus
Gaston
Mecklenburg
Rowan
Union

Area of Application. Survey area plus:

North Carolina:
Anson
Cleveland
Iredell
Lincoln
Stanly
Wilkes

South Carolina:
Chester
Chesterfield
Lancaster
York

SOUTHEASTERN NORTH CAROLINA

Survey Area

North Carolina:
Brunswick
Carteret
Columbus
Craven
Jones
Lenoir
New Hanover
Onslow
Pamlico
Pender

Area of Application. Survey area plus:

North Carolina:
Beaufort
Bertie
Dare
Duplin
Greene
Hertford
Hyde
Martin
Pitt
Tyrrell
Washington

South Carolina:
Horry

NORTH DAKOTA

Survey Area

North Dakota:
Burleigh
Cass
Grand Forks
McLean
Mercer
Morton
Oliver
Traill
Ward

Minnesota:
Clay
Polk

Area of Application. Survey area plus:

North Dakota:
Adams
Barnes
Benson
Billings
Bottineau
Bowman
Burke
Cavalier
Dickey
Divide
Dunn
Eddy
Emmons
Foster
Golden Valley
Grant
Griggs
Hettinger
Kidder
La Moure
Logan
McHenry
McIntosh
McKenzie

Mountrail
Nelson
Pembina
Pierce
Ramsey
Ransom
Renville
Richland
Rolette
Sargent
Sheridan
Sioux
Slope
Stark
Steele
Stutsman
Towner
Walsh
Wells
Williams

Minnesota:
Becker (Excluding the White Earth Indian Reservation portion)
Kittson
Marshall
Norman
Otter Tail
Pennington
Red Lake
Roseau
Wilkin

OHIO

CINCINNATI

Survey Area

Indiana:
Dearborn

Kentucky:
Boone
Campbell
Kenton

Ohio:
Clermont
Hamilton
Warren

Area of Application: Survey area plus:

Indiana:
Franklin
Ohio
Ripley
Switzerland
Union

Kentucky:
Bracken
Carroll
Gallatin
Grant
Mason
Pendleton

Ohio:
Adams
Brown
Butler
Highland

CLEVELAND

Survey Area

Ohio:
Cuyahoga
Geauga
Lake
Medina

Area of Application. Survey area plus:

Ohio:
Ashland
Ashtabula
Carroll
Columbiana
Erie
Huron
Lorain
Mahoning
Ottawa
Portage
Sandusky
Seneca
Stark
Summit
Trumbull
Wayne

Pennsylvania
Mercer

COLUMBUS

Survey Area

Ohio:
Delaware
Fairfield
Franklin
Licking
Madison
Pickaway

Area of Application. Survey area plus:

Ohio:
Coshocton
Crawford
Fayette
Guernsey
Hancock
Hardin
Hocking
Holmes
Knox
Marion
Morrow
Muskingum
Perry
Richland
Ross
Union
Wyandot

DAYTON

Ohio:
Champaign
Clark
Greene

Miami
Montgomery
Preble

Area of Application. Survey area plus:

Indiana:
Randolph
Wayne
Ohio:
Auglaize
Clinton
Darke
Logan
Shelby

OKLAHOMA

OKLAHOMA CITY

Survey Area

Oklahoma:
Canadian
Cleveland
McCain
Oklahoma
Pottawatomie

Area of Application. Survey area plus:

Oklahoma:
Alfalfa
Atoka
Beckham
Blaine
Bryan
Caddo
Carter
Coal
Custer
Dewey
Ellis
Garfield
Garvin
Grady
Grant
Harper
Hughes
Johnston
Kingfisher
Lincoln
Logan
Love
Major
Marshall
Murray
Noble
Payne
Pontotoc
Roger Mills
Seminole
Washita
Woods
Woodward

TULSA

Survey Area

Oklahoma:
Creek
Mayes
Muskogee
Osage
Pittsburg
Rogers
Tulsa
Wagoner

Area of Application. Survey area plus:

Oklahoma:
Adair
Cherokee
Choctaw
Craig
Delaware
Haskell
Kay
Latimer
LeFlore
McCurtain
McIntosh
Nowata
Okfuskee
Okmulgee
Ottawa
Pawnee
Pushmataha
Sequoyah
Washington
Arkansas:
Benton
Carroll
Crawford
Madison
Sebastian
Washington
Missouri:
McDonald

OREGON

PORTLAND

Survey Area

Oregon:
Clackamas
Marion
Multnomah
Polk
Washington
Washington:
Clark

Area of Application. Survey area plus:

Oregon:
Clatsop
Columbia
Gilliam
Hood River
Sherman
Tillamook
Wasco
Yamhill
Washington:
Cowlitz
Klickitat

Pacific
Skamania
Wahkiakum

SOUTHWESTERN OREGON

Survey Area

Oregon:
Douglas
Jackson
Lane

Area of Application. Survey area plus:

Oregon:
Benton
Coos
Crook
Curry
Deschutes
Jefferson
Josephine
Klamath
Lake
Lincoln
Linn

PENNSYLVANIA

HARRISBURG

Survey Area

Pennsylvania:
Cumberland
Dauphin
Lebanon
York

Area of Application. Survey area plus:

Pennsylvania:
Adams
Berks
Juniata
Lancaster
Lycoming (Allenwood Federal Prison Camp portion only)
Mifflin
Northumberland
Perry
Schuylkill
Snyder
Union

PHILADELPHIA

Survey Area

New Jersey:
Burlington (Excluding the Joint Base McGuire-Dix-Lakehurst portion)
Camden
Gloucester
Pennsylvania:
Bucks
Chester
Delaware
Montgomery
Philadelphia

Area of Application. Survey area plus:

New Jersey:
Atlantic
Cape May
Cumberland
Mercer
Warren
Pennsylvania:
Carbon
Lehigh
Northampton

PITTSBURGH

Survey Area

Pennsylvania:
Allegheny
Beaver
Butler
Washington
Westmoreland

Area of Application. Survey area plus:

Ohio:
Belmont
Harrison
Jefferson
Tuscarawas
Pennsylvania:
Armstrong
Bedford
Blair
Cambria
Cameron
Centre
Clarion
Clearfield
Clinton
Crawford
Elk (Does not include the Allegheny National Forest portion)
Erie
Fayette
Forest (Does not include the Allegheny National Forest portion)
Greene
Huntingdon
Indiana
Jefferson
Lawrence
Potter
Somerset
Venango
West Virginia:
Brooke
Hancock
Marshall
Ohio

SCRANTON-WILKES-BARRE

Survey Area

Pennsylvania:
Lackawanna
Luzerne
Monroe

Area of Application. Survey area plus:

New York
Sullivan
Pennsylvania:
Bradford
Columbia
Lycoming (Excluding Allenwood Federal Prison Camp)
Montour
Sullivan
Susquehanna
Wayne
Wyoming

PUERTO RICO

Survey Area

Puerto Rico (Municipios):
San Juan
Bayamon
Canovanas
Carolina
Catano
Guaynabo
Humacao
Loiza
Toa Baja
Trujillo Alto

Area of Application: Puerto Rico

RHODE ISLAND

NARRAGANSETT BAY

Survey Area

Rhode Island:
Bristol
Newport
The following cities and towns:
Kent County
Anthony
Coventry
East Greenwich
Greene
Warwick
West Warwick
Providence County
Ashton
Burrillville
Central Falls
Cranston
Cumberland
Cumberland Hill
East Providence
Esmond
Forestdale
Greenville
Harrisville
Johnston
Lincoln
Manville
Mapleville
North Providence
North Smithfield
Oakland
Pascoag
Pawtucket
Providence
Saylesville
Slatersville
Smithfield
Valley Falls
Wallum Lake
Woonsocket
Washington County
Davisville
Galilee
Lafayette
Narragansett
North Kingstown
Point Judith
Quonset Point
Saunderstown
Slocum
Massachusetts:
The following cities and towns:
Bristol County
Attleboro
Fall River
North Attleboro
Rehoboth
Seekonk
Somerset
Swansea
Westport
Norfolk County
Caryville
Plainville
South Bellingham
Worcester County
Blackstone
Millville

Area of Application. Survey area plus:

Rhode Island:
The following cities and towns in:
Kent County
West Greenwich
Providence County
Foster
Glocester
Scituate
Washington County
Charlestown
Exeter
Hopkinton
New Shoreham
Richmond
South Kingstown
Westerly
Massachusetts:
The following cities and towns in:
Bristol County
Acushnet
Berkley
Dartmouth
Dighton
Fairhaven
Freetown
Mansfield
New Bedford
Norton
Raynham

Taunton

SOUTH CAROLINA

CHARLESTON

Survey Area

South Carolina:
- Berkeley
- Charleston
- Dorchester

Area of Application. Survey area plus:

South Carolina:
- Beaufort (The portion north of Broad River.)
- Colleton
- Georgetown
- Williamsburg

COLUMBIA

Survey Area

South Carolina:
- Darlington
- Florence
- Kershaw
- Lee
- Lexington
- Richland
- Sumter

Area of Application. Survey area plus:

South Carolina:
- Abbeville
- Anderson
- Calhoun
- Cherokee
- Clarendon
- Fairfield
- Greenville
- Greenwood
- Laurens
- Newberry
- Oconee
- Orangeburg
- Pickens
- Saluda
- Spartanburg
- Union

SOUTH DAKOTA

EASTERN SOUTH DAKOTA

Survey Area

South Dakota:
- Minnehaha

Area of Application. Survey area plus:

South Dakota:
- Aurora
- Beadle
- Bennett
- Bon Homme
- Brookings
- Brown
- Brule
- Buffalo
- Campbell
- Charles Mix
- Clark
- Clay
- Codington
- Corson
- Davison
- Day
- Deuel
- Dewey
- Douglas
- Edmunds
- Faulk
- Grant
- Gregory
- Haakon
- Hamlin
- Hand
- Hanson
- Hughes
- Hutchinson
- Hyde
- Jerauld
- Jones
- Kingsbury
- Lake
- Lincoln
- Lyman
- McCook
- McPherson
- Marshall
- Mellette
- Miner
- Moody
- Potter
- Roberts
- Sanborn
- Spink
- Stanley
- Sully
- Todd
- Tripp
- Turner
- Walworth
- Yankton
- Ziebach

Iowa:
- Dickinson
- Emmet
- Lyon
- Osceola

Minnesota:
- Jackson
- Lincoln
- Lyon
- Murray
- Nobles
- Pipestone
- Rock

TENNESSEE

EASTERN TENNESSEE

Survey Area

Tennessee:

Carter
Hawkins
Sullivan
Unicoi
Washington
Virginia (city):
Bristol
Virginia (counties):
Scott
Washington

Area of Application. Survey area plus:

Tennessee:
Cocke
Greene
Hancock
Johnson
Virginia:
Buchanan
Grayson
Lee
Russell
Smyth
Tazewell
North Carolina:
Alleghany
Ashe
Watauga
Kentucky:
Harlan
Letcher

MEMPHIS

Survey Area

Arkansas:
Crittenden
Mississippi
Mississippi:
De Soto
Tennessee:
Shelby
Tipton

Area of Application. Survey area plus:

Arkansas:
Craighead
Cross
Lee
Poinsett
St. Francis
Mississippi:
Benton
Lafayette (Holly Springs National Forest portion only)
Marshall
Panola
Pontotoc (Holly Springs National Forest portion only)
Tate
Tippah
Tunica
Union (Holly Springs National Forest portion only)
Missouri:
Dunklin
Pemiscot
Tennessee:
Carroll
Chester
Crockett
Dyer
Fayette
Gibson
Hardeman
Hardin
Haywood
Lake
Lauderdale
Madison
McNairy
Obion

NASHVILLE

Survey Area

Tennessee:
Cheatham
Davidson
Dickson
Montgomery
Robertson
Rutherford
Sumner
Williamson
Wilson
Kentucky:
Christian

Area of Application. Survey area plus:

Tennessee:
Anderson
Bedford
Benton
Bledsoe
Blount
Bradley
Campbell
Cannon
Claiborne
Clay
Coffee
Cumberland
Decatur
DeKalb
Fentress
Grainger
Grundy
Hamblen
Hamilton
Henderson
Henry
Hickman
Houston
Humphreys
Jackson
Jefferson
Knox
Lewis
Loudon
McMinn
Macon
Marion

Marshall
Maury
Meigs
Monroe
Morgan
Overton
Perry
Pickett
Polk
Putnam
Rhea
Roane
Scott
Sequatchie
Sevier
Smith
Stewart
Trousdale
Union
Van Buren
Warren
Weakley
White

Kentucky:
Adair
Allen
Ballard
Barren
Butler
Caldwell
Calloway
Carlisle
Clinton
Cumberland
Edmonson
Fulton
Graves
Hickman
Hopkins
Logan
Lyon
McCracken
Marshall
Metcalfe
Monroe
Muhlenberg
Russell
Simpson
Todd
Trigg
Warren

Georgia:
Catossa
Dade
Walker

TEXAS

AUSTIN

Survey Area

Texas:
Hays
Milam
Travis
Williamson

Area of Application. Survey area plus:

Texas:
Bastrop
Blanco
Burnet
Caldwell
Fayette
Lee
Llano
Mason
San Saba

CORPUS CHRISTI

Survey Area

Texas:
Nueces
San Patricio

Area of Application. Survey area plus:

Texas:
Aransas
Bee
Brooks (Effective as of the first day of the first applicable pay period beginning on or after April 17, 1996.)
Calhoun
Cameron (Effective as of the first day of the first applicable pay period beginning on or after April 17, 1996.)
Goliad
Hidalgo (Effective as of the first day of the first applicable pay period beginning on or after April 17, 1996.)
Jim Wells
Kenedy (Effective as of the first day of the first applicable pay period beginning on or after April 17, 1996.)
Kleberg
Live Oak
Refugio
Starr (Effective as of the first day of the first applicable pay period beginning on or after April 17, 1996.)
Victoria
Willacy (Effective as of the first day of the first applicable pay period beginning on or after April 17, 1996.)

DALLAS-FORT WORTH

Survey Area

Texas:
Collin
Dallas
Denton
Ellis
Grayson
Hood
Johnson
Kaufman
Parker
Rockwall
Tarrant
Wise

Area of Application. Survey area plus:

Texas:
- Cooke
- Delta
- Erath
- Fannin
- Henderson
- Hopkins
- Hunt
- Jack
- Lamar
- Montague
- Navarro
- Palo Pinto
- Rains
- Smith
- Somervell
- Van Zandt
- Wood

EL PASO

Survey Area

New Mexico:
- Dona Ana
- Otero

Texas:
- El Paso

Area of Application. Survey area plus:

New Mexico:
- Chaves
- Eddy
- Grant
- Hidalgo
- Lincoln (Only White Sands Missile Range portion)
- Luna
- Sierra
- Socorro (Only White Sands Missile Range portion)

Texas:
- Culberson
- Hudspeth

HOUSTON-GALVESTON-TEXAS CITY

Survey Area

Texas:
- Brazoria
- Fort Bend
- Galveston
- Harris
- Liberty
- Montgomery
- Waller

Area of Application. Survey area plus:

Texas:
- Angelina
- Austin
- Chambers
- Colorado
- Grimes
- Hardin
- Houston
- Jackson
- Jasper
- Jefferson
- Lavaca
- Madison
- Matagorda
- Nacogdoches
- Newton
- Orange
- Polk
- Sabine
- San Augustine
- San Jacinto
- Shelby
- Trinity
- Tyler
- Walker
- Washington
- Wharton

SAN ANTONIO

Survey Area

Texas:
- Bexar
- Comal
- Guadalupe

Area of Application. Survey area plus:

Texas:
- Atascosa
- Bandera
- De Witt
- Dimmit
- Duval
- Edwards
- Frio
- Gillespie
- Gonzales
- Jim Hogg
- Karnes
- Kendall
- Kerr
- Kinney
- La Salle
- McMullen
- Maverick
- Medina
- Real
- Uvalde
- Val Verde
- Webb
- Wilson
- Zapata
- Zavala

TEXARKANA

Survey Area

Texas:
- Bowie

Arkansas:
- Little River
- Miller

Area of Application. Survey area plus:

Texas:

Camp
Cass
Franklin
Marion
Morris
Red River
Titus
Arkansas:
Columbia
Hempstead
Howard
Lafayette
Nevada
Sevier

WACO

Survey Area

Texas:
Bell
Coryell
McLennan

Area of Application. Survey area plus:

Texas:
Anderson
Bosque
Brazos
Burleson
Falls
Freestone
Hamilton
Hill
Lampasas
Leon
Limestone
Mills
Robertson

WESTERN TEXAS

Survey Area

Texas:
Callahan
Ector
Howard
Jones
Lubbock
Midland
Nolan
Taylor
Tom Green

Area of Application. Survey area plus:

Texas:
Andrews
Armstrong
Bailey
Borden
Brewster
Briscoe
Brown
Carson
Castro
Childress
Cochran
Coke
Coleman
Collingsworth
Comanche
Concho
Cottle
Crane
Crockett
Crosby
Dallam
Dawson
Deaf Smith
Dickens
Donley
Eastland
Fisher
Floyd
Gaines
Garza
Glasscock
Gray
Hale
Hall
Hansford
Hartley
Haskell
Hemphill
Hockley
Hutchinson
Irion
Jeff Davis
Kent
Kimble
King
Lamb
Lipscomb
Loving
Lynn
McCulloch
Martin
Menard
Mitchell
Moore
Motley
Ochiltree
Oldham
Parmer
Pecos
Potter
Presidio
Randall
Reagan
Reeves
Roberts
Runnels
Schleicher
Scurry
Shackelford
Sherman
Stephens
Sterling
Stonewall
Sutton
Swisher
Terrell
Terry
Throckmorton

Upton
Ward
Wheeler
Winkler
Yoakum
Oklahoma:
Beaver
Cimarron
Texas
New Mexico:
Lea

WICHITA FALLS, TEXAS—SOUTHWESTERN OKLAHOMA

Survey Area

Texas:
Archer
Clay
Wichita
Oklahoma:
Comanche
Cotton
Stephens
Tillman

Area of Application. Survey area plus:

Texas:
Baylor
Foard
Hardeman
Knox
Wilbarger
Young
Oklahoma:
Greer
Harmon
Jackson
Jefferson
Kiowa

UTAH

Survey Area

Utah:
Box Elder
Davis
Salt Lake
Tooele
Utah
Weber

Area of Application. Survey area plus:

Utah:
Beaver
Cache
Carbon
Daggett
Duchesne
Emery
Garfield
Grand
Iron
Juab
Millard
Morgan
Piute
Rich
San Juan (Only includes the Canyonlands National Park portion)
Sanpete
Sevier
Summit
Uintah
Wasatch
Washington
Wayne
Colorado:
Mesa
Moffat
Idaho:
Franklin

VIRGINIA

NORFOLK-PORTSMOUTH-NEWPORT NEWS-HAMPTON

Survey Area

Virginia (cities):
Chesapeake
Hampton
Newport News
Norfolk
Poquoson
Portsmouth
Suffolk
Virginia Beach
Williamsburg
Virginia (counties):
Gloucester
James City
York
North Carolina:
Currituck

Area of Application. Survey area plus:

Virginia (cities):
Franklin
Virginia (counties):
Accomack
Isle of Wight
Mathews
Northampton
Southampton
Surry
North Carolina:
Camden
Chowan
Gates
Pasquotank
Perquimans
Maryland:
Assateague Island part of Worcester

RICHMOND

Survey Area

Virginia (cities):
Colonial Heights
Hopewell
Petersburg
Richmond

Virginia (counties):
- Charles City
- Chesterfield
- Dinwiddie
- Goochland
- Hanover
- Henrico
- New Kent
- Powhatan
- Prince George

Area of Application. Survey area plus:

Virginia (cities):
- Charlottesville
- Emporia

Virginia (counties):
- Albemarle
- Amelia
- Brunswick
- Buckingham
- Caroline
- Charlotte
- Cumberland
- Essex
- Fluvanna
- Greene
- Greensville
- King and Queen
- King William
- Lancaster
- Louisa
- Lunenberg
- Mecklenburg
- Middlesex
- Nelson
- Northumberland
- Nottoway
- Orange
- Prince Edward
- Richmond
- Sussex
- Westmoreland

ROANOKE

Survey Area

Virginia (cities):
- Radford
- Roanoke
- Salem

Virginia (counties):
- Botetourt
- Craig
- Montgomery
- Roanoke

Area of Application. Survey area plus:

Virginia (cities):
- Bedford
- Buena Vista
- Clifton Forge
- Covington
- Danville
- Galax
- Lexington
- Lynchburg
- Martinsville
- South Boston
- Staunton
- Waynesboro

Virginia (counties):
- Alleghany
- Amherst
- Appomattox
- Augusta
- Bath
- Bedford
- Bland
- Campbell
- Carroll
- Floyd
- Franklin
- Giles
- Halifax
- Henry
- Highland
- Patrick
- Pittsylvania
- Pulaski
- Rockbridge
- Wythe

WASHINGTON

SEATTLE-EVERETT-TACOMA

Survey Area

Washington:
- King
- Kitsap
- Pierce
- Snohomish

Area of Application. Survey area plus:

Washington:
- Chelan (North Cascades Park section only.)
- Clallam
- Grays Harbor
- Island
- Jefferson
- Lewis
- Mason
- San Juan
- Skagit
- Thurston
- Whatcom

SOUTHEASTERN WASHINGTON-EASTERN OREGON

Survey Area

Oregon:
- Umatilla

Washington:
- Benton
- Franklin
- Walla Walla
- Yakima

Area of Application. Survey area plus:

Oregon:
- Baker
- Grant
- Harney

Malheur
Morrow
Union
Wallowa
Wheeler
Washington:
Columbia
Kittitas (Only includes the Yakima Firing Range portion)

SPOKANE

Survey Area

Washington:
Spokane

Area of Application. Survey area plus:

Idaho:
Benewah
Bonner
Boundary
Clearwater
Idaho
Kootenai
Latah
Lewis
Nez Perce
Shoshone
Washington:
Adams
Asotin
Chelan (Does not include the North Cascades National Park portion)
Douglas
Ferry
Garfield
Grant
Kittitas (Does not include the Yakima Firing Range portion)
Lincoln
Okanogan
Pend Oreille
Stevens
Whitman

WEST VIRGINIA

Survey Area

West Virginia:
Cabell
Harrison
Kanawha
Marion
Monongalia
Putnam
Wayne
Ohio:
Lawrence
Kentucky:
Boyd
Greenup

Area of Application. Survey area plus:

West Virginia:
Barbour
Boone
Braxton
Calhoun
Clay
Doddridge
Fayette
Gilmer
Grant
Greenbrier
Jackson
Lewis
Lincoln
Logan
McDowell
Mason
Mercer
Mingo
Monroe
Nicholas
Pendleton
Pleasants
Pocahontas
Preston
Raleigh
Randolph
Ritchie
Roane
Summers
Taylor
Tucker
Tyler
Upshur
Webster
Wetzel
Wirt
Wood
Wyoming
Ohio:
Athens
Gallia
Jackson
Meigs
Monroe
Morgan
Noble
Pike
Scioto
Vinton
Washington
Kentucky:
Carter
Elliott
Floyd
Johnson
Lawrence
Lewis
Magoffin
Martin
Pike
Virginia (city):
Norton (Effective as of April 17, 1996.)
Virginia (counties):
Dickenson
Wise

WISCONSIN

MADISON

Survey Area

Wisconsin:
Dane

Area of Application. Survey area plus:

Wisconsin:
Adams
Columbia
Dodge
Grant
Green
Green Lake
Iowa
Jefferson
Lafayette
Marquette
Rock
Sauk
Waushara

MILWAUKEE

Survey Area

Wisconsin:
Milwaukee
Ozaukee
Washington
Waukesha

Area of Application. Survey area plus:

Wisconsin:
Brown
Calumet
Door
Fond du Lac
Kewaunee
Manitowoc
Oconto
Outagamie
Racine
Sheboygan
Walworth
Winnebago

SOUTHWESTERN WISCONSIN

Survey Area

Wisconsin:
Chippewa
Eau Claire
La Crosse
Monroe
Trempealeau

Area of Application. Survey area plus:

Minnesota:
Houston
Winona
Wisconsin:
Barron
Buffalo
Clark
Crawford
Dunn
Florence
Forest
Jackson
Juneau
Langlade
Lincoln
Marathon
Marinette
Menominee
Oneida
Pepin
Portage
Price
Richland
Rusk
Shawano
Taylor
Vernon
Vilas
Waupaca
Wood

WYOMING

Survey Area

Wyoming:
Albany
Laramie
Natrona
South Dakota:
Pennington

Area of application. Survey area plus:

Wyoming:
Campbell
Carbon
Converse
Crook
Fremont
Goshen
Hot Springs
Johnson
Lincoln
Niobrara
Platte
Sheridan
Sublette
Sweetwater
Uinta
Washakie
Weston
Nebraska:
Banner
Box Butte
Cheyenne
Dawes
Deuel
Garden
Kimball
Morrill
Scotts Bluff
Sheridan
Sioux
South Dakota:
Butte

Custer
Fall River
Harding
Jackson
Lawrence
Meade
Perkins
Shannon

[46 FR 21344, Apr. 10, 1981]

EDITORIAL NOTE: For FEDERAL REGISTER citations affecting appendix C, see the List of CFR Sections Affected, which appears in the Finding Aids section of the printed volume and at *www.fdsys.gov*.

APPENDIX D TO SUBPART B OF PART 532—NONAPPROPRIATED FUND WAGE AND SURVEY AREAS

This appendix lists the wage area definitions for NAF employees. With a few exceptions, each area is defined in terms of county units or independent cities. Each wage area definition consists of:

(1) *Wage area title.* Wage areas usually carry the title of the county or counties surveyed.

(2) *Survey area definition.* Lists each county or independent city in the survey area.

(3) *Area of application definition.* Lists each county or independent city which, in addition to the survey area, is in the area of application.

DEFINITIONS OF WAGE AREAS AND WAGE AREA SURVEY AREAS

ALABAMA

CALHOUN

Survey Area

Alabama:
Calhoun

Area of Application. Survey area plus:

Alabama:
Jefferson

MADISON

Survey Area

Alabama:
Madison

Area of Application. Survey area plus:

Tennessee:
Coffee
Davidson
Hamilton
Rutherford

MONTGOMERY

Survey Area

Alabama:
Montgomery

Area of Application. Survey area plus:

Alabama:
Dale
Dallas
Macon

ALASKA

ANCHORAGE

Survey Area

Alaska: (borough)
Anchorage

Area of Application. Survey area plus:

Alaska: (boroughs and census areas)
Fairbanks North Star
Juneau
Kenai Peninsula
Ketchikan Gateway
Kodiak Island
Sitka
Southeast Fairbanks
Valdez-Cordova
Yukon-Koyukuk

ARIZONA

MARICOPA

Survey Area

Arizona:
Maricopa

Area of Application. Survey area plus:

Arizona:
Coconino
Yavapai

PIMA

Survey Area

Arizona:
Pima

Area of Application. Survey area plus:

Arizona:
Cochise

YUMA

Survey Area

Arizona:
Yuma

Area of Application. Survey area plus:

California:
Imperial

ARKANSAS

PULASKI

Survey Area

Arkansas:
Pulaski

Area of Application. Survey area plus:

Arkansas:
Jefferson
Sebastian
Washington

CALIFORNIA

KERN

Survey Area

California:
Kern

Area of Application. Survey area plus:

California:
Fresno
Kings

LOS ANGELES

Survey Area

California:
Los Angeles

Area of Application. Survey area.

MONTEREY

Survey Area

California:
Monterey

Area of Application. Survey area plus:

California:
Santa Clara

ORANGE

Survey Area

California:
Orange

Area of Application. Survey area.

RIVERSIDE

Survey Area

California:
Riverside

Area of Application. Survey area.

SACRAMENTO

Survey Area

California:
Sacramento

Area of Application. Survey area plus:

California:
Yuba

Oregon:
Jackson
Klamath

SAN BERNARDINO

Survey Area

California:
San Bernardino

Area of Application. Survey area.

SAN DIEGO

Survey Area

California:
San Diego

Area of Application. Survey area.

SAN JOAQUIN

Survey Area

California:
San Joaquin

Area of Application. Survey area.

SANTA BARBARA

Survey Area

California:
Santa Barbara

Area of Application. Survey area plus:

California:
San Luis Obispo

SOLANO

Survey Area

California:
Solano

Area of Application. Survey area plus:

California:
Alameda
Contra Costa
Marin
Napa
San Francisco
Sonoma

VENTURA

Survey Area

California:
Ventura

Area of Application. Survey area.

COLORADO

ARAPAHOE-DENVER

Survey Area

Colorado:
Arapahoe
Denver

Area of Application. Survey area plus:

Colorado:
Mesa

EL PASO

Survey Area

Colorado:
El Paso

Area of Application. Survey area plus:

Colorado:
Bent
Otero
Pueblo

CONNECTICUT

NEW LONDON

Survey Area

Connecticut:
New London

Area of Application. Survey area plus:

Connecticut:
New Haven

DELAWARE

KENT

Survey Area

Delaware:
Kent

Area of Application. Survey area plus:

Delaware:
Sussex

Maryland:
Kent

DISTRICT OF COLUMBIA

WASHINGTON, DC

Survey Area

District of Columbia:
Washington, DC

Area of Application. Survey area.

FLORIDA

BAY

Survey Area

Florida:
Bay

Area of Application. Survey area.

BREVARD

Survey Area

Florida:
Brevard

Area of Application. Survey area.

DUVAL

Survey Area

Florida:
Duval

Area of Application. Survey area plus:

Florida:
Alachua
Clay
Columbia

Georgia:
Camden

ESCAMBIA

Survey Area

Florida:
Escambia

Area of Application. Survey area plus:

Florida:
Santa Rosa

HILLSBOROUGH

Survey Area

Florida:
Hillsborough

Area of Application. Survey area plus:

Florida:
Lee
Pinellas
Polk

MIAMI-DADE

Survey Area

Florida:
Miami-Dade

Area of Application. Survey area plus:

Florida:
Broward
Palm Beach

MONROE

Survey Area

Florida:
Monroe

Area of Application. Survey area.

OKALOOSA

Survey Area

Florida:
Okaloosa

Area of Application. Survey area plus:

Florida:
Walton

ORANGE

Survey Area

Florida:
Orange

Area of Application. Survey area.

GEORGIA

CHATHAM

Survey Area

Georgia:
Chatham

Area of Application. Survey area plus:

Georgia:
Glynn
Liberty

South Carolina:
Beaufort

COBB

Survey Area

Georgia:
Cobb

Area of Application. Survey area plus:

Georgia:
Bartow
De Kalb
Fulton

COLUMBUS

Survey Area

Georgia:
Columbus

Area of Application. Survey area plus:

Georgia:
- Chattahoochee

DOUGHERTY

Survey Area

Georgia:
- Dougherty

Area of Application. Survey area.

HOUSTON

Survey Area

Georgia:
- Houston

Area of Application. Survey area plus:

Georgia:
- Laurens

LOWNDES

Survey Area

Georgia:
- Lowndes

Area of Application. Survey area plus.

Florida:
- Leon

RICHMOND

Survey Area

Georgia:
- Richmond

Area of Application. Survey area plus:

South Carolina:
- Aiken

GUAM

GUAM

Survey Area

Guam

Area of Application. Survey area.

HAWAII

HONOLULU

Survey Area

Hawaii:
- Honolulu

Area of Application. Survey area plus:

Hawaii (counties):
- Hawaii
- Kauai
- Maui

Pacific Islands:
- Midway Islands
- Johnston Atoll
- American Samoa

IDAHO

ADA-ELMORE

Survey Area

Idaho:
- Ada
- Elmore

Area of Application. Survey area.

ILLINOIS

LAKE

Survey Area

Illinois:
- Lake

Area of Application. Survey area plus:

Illinois:
- Cook
- Rock Island
- Vermilion

Iowa:
- Johnson

Michigan:
- Dickinson
- Marquette

Wisconsin:
- Brown
- Dane
- Milwaukee

ST. CLAIR

Survey Area

Illinois:
- St. Clair

Area of Application. Survey area plus:

Illinois:
- Madison
- Williamson

Indiana:
- Vanderburgh

Missouri: (city)
- St. Louis

Missouri: (counties)
- Jefferson
- Pulaski

KANSAS

LEAVENWORTH/JACKSON-JOHNSON

Survey Area

Kansas:
- Leavenworth

Missouri:
- Jackson
- Johnson

Area of Application. Survey area plus:

Kansas:
- Shawnee

Missouri:
- Boone
- Camden
- Cass

SEDGWICK

Survey Area

Kansas:
- Sedgwick

Area of Application. Survey area plus:

Kansas:
Geary
Saline

KENTUCKY

CHRISTIAN-MONTGOMERY

Survey Area

Kentucky:
Christian

Tennessee:
Montgomery

Area of Application. Survey area.

HARDIN-JEFFERSON

Survey Area

Kentucky:
Hardin
Jefferson

Area of Application. Survey area plus:

Indiana:
Jefferson
Martin

Kentucky:
Fayette
Madison
Warren

LOUISIANA

BOSSIER-CADDO

Survey Area

Louisiana: (parishes)
Bossier
Caddo

Area of Application. Survey area plus:

Texas:
Bowie

ORLEANS

Survey Area

Louisiana: (parish)
Orleans

Area of Application. Survey area plus:

Louisiana: (parish)
Plaquemines

RAPIDES

Survey Area

Louisiana: (parish)
Rapides

Area of Application. Survey area plus:

Louisiana: (parish)
Vernon

MAINE

YORK

Survey Area

Maine:
York

Area of Application. Survey area plus:

Maine:
Cumberland
Kennebec
Penobscot

New Hampshire:
Rockingham

Vermont:
Windsor

MARYLAND

ANNE ARUNDEL

Survey Area

Maryland:
Anne Arundel

Area of Application. Survey area plus:

Maryland: (city)
Baltimore

Maryland: (county)
Baltimore

CHARLES-ST. MARY'S

Survey Area

Maryland:
Charles
St. Mary's

Area of Application. Survey area plus:

Maryland:
Calvert

Virginia:
King George

FREDERICK

Survey Area

Maryland:
Frederick

Area of Application. Survey area plus:

West Virginia:
Berkeley

HARFORD

Survey Area

Maryland:
Harford

Area of Application. Survey area plus:

Maryland:
Cecil

MONTGOMERY-PRINCE GEORGE'S

Survey Area

Maryland:
Montgomery
Prince George's

Area of Application. Survey area.

MASSACHUSETTS

HAMPDEN

Survey Area

Massachusetts:
Hampden

Area of Application. Survey area plus:

Connecticut:
  Hartford

Massachusetts:
  Hampshire

MIDDLESEX

Survey Area

Massachusetts:
  Middlesex

Area of Application. Survey area plus:

Massachusetts:
  Norfolk
  Plymouth
  Suffolk

New Hampshire:
  Hillsborough

MICHIGAN

MACOMB

Survey Area

Michigan:
  Macomb

Area of Application. Survey area plus:

Michigan:
  Alpena
  Calhoun
  Crawford
  Grand Traverse
  Huron
  Iosco
  Kent
  Leelanau
  Ottawa
  Saginaw
  Washtenaw
  Wayne

Ohio:
  Ottawa

MINNESOTA

HENNEPIN

Survey Area

Minnesota:
  Hennepin

Area of Application. Survey area plus:

Minnesota:
  Morrison
  Murray
  Ramsey
  Stearns
  St. Louis

Wisconsin:
  Juneau
  Monroe
  Polk

MISSISSIPPI

HARRISON

Survey Area

Mississippi:
  Harrison

Area of Application. Survey area plus:

Alabama:
  Mobile

Mississippi:
  Forest
  Hancock
  Jackson

LAUDERDALE

Survey Area

Mississippi:
  Lauderdale

Area of Application. Survey area plus:

Mississippi:
  Hinds
  Rankin
  Warren

LOWNDES

Survey Area

Mississippi:
  Lowndes

Area of Application. Survey area plus:

Alabama:
  Tuscaloosa

MONTANA

CASCADE

Survey Area

Montana:
  Cascade

Area of Application. Survey area plus:

Montana:
  Fergus
  Flathead
  Hill
  Lewis and Clark
  Valley
  Yellowstone

NEBRASKA

DOUGLAS-SARPY

Survey Area

Nebraska:
  Douglas
  Sarpy

Area of Application. Survey area plus:

Iowa:
  Marion
  Polk
  Woodbury

Nebraska:
  Hall
  Lancaster

Saunders
South Dakota:
Minnehaha

NEVADA

CHURCHILL-WASHOE

Survey Area

Nevada:
Churchill
Washoe

Area of Application. Survey area plus:

California:
Lassen
Mono
Nevada:
Mineral

CLARK

Survey Area

Nevada:
Clark

Area of Application. Survey area.

NEW JERSEY

BURLINGTON

Survey Area

New Jersey:
Burlington

Area of Application. Survey area plus:

Delaware:
New Castle
New Jersey:
Atlantic
Cape May
Monmouth
Ocean
Salem
Pennsylvania:
Chester
Montgomery
Philadelphia

MORRIS

Survey Area

New Jersey:
Morris

Area of Application. Survey area plus:

New Jersey:
Somerset
Pennsylvania:
Luzerne
Monroe

NEW MEXICO

BERNALILLO

Survey Area

New Mexico:
Bernalillo

Area of Application. Survey area plus:

New Mexico:
McKinley

CURRY

Survey Area

New Mexico:
Curry

Area of Application. Survey area plus:

Texas:
Lubbock
Potter

DONA ANA

Survey Area

New Mexico:
Dona Ana

Area of Application. Survey area plus:

New Mexico:
Chaves
Otero

NEW YORK

JEFFERSON

Survey Area

New York:
Jefferson

Area of Application. Survey area plus:

New York:
Albany
Oneida
Onondaga
Ontario
Schenectady
Steuben

KINGS-QUEENS

Survey Area

New York:
Kings
Queens

Area of Application. Survey area plus:

New Jersey:
Essex
Hudson
New York:
Bronx
Nassau
New York
Richmond
Suffolk

NIAGARA

Survey Area

New York:
Niagara

Area of Application. Survey area plus:

New York:
Erie
Genesee
Pennsylvania:
Erie

ORANGE

Survey Area

New York:
 Orange

Area of Application. Survey area plus:

New York:
 Dutchess
 Westchester

NORTH CAROLINA

CRAVEN

Survey Area

North Carolina:
 Craven

Area of Application. Survey area plus:

North Carolina:
 Carteret
 Dare

CUMBERLAND

Survey Area

North Carolina:
 Cumberland

Area of Application. Survey area plus:

North Carolina:
 Durham
 Forsyth
 Rowan

ONSLOW

Survey Area

North Carolina:
 Onslow

Area of Application. Survey area plus:

North Carolina:
 New Hanover

WAYNE

Survey Area

North Carolina:
 Wayne

Area of Application. Survey area plus:

North Carolina:
 Halifax

NORTH DAKOTA

GRAND FORKS

Survey Area

North Dakota:
 Grand Forks

Area of Application. Survey area plus:

North Dakota:
 Cass
 Cavalier
 Pembina
 Steele

WARD

Survey Area

North Dakota:
 Ward

Area of Application. Survey area plus:

North Dakota:
 Divide

OHIO

GREENE-MONTGOMERY

Survey Area

Ohio:
 Greene
 Montgomery

Area of Application. Survey area plus:

Indiana:
 Allen
 Grant
 Marion
 Miami

Ohio:
 Clinton
 Franklin
 Hamilton
 Licking
 Ross

West Virginia:
 Raleigh
 Wayne

OKLAHOMA

COMANCHE

Survey Area

Oklahoma:
 Comanche

Area of Application. Survey area plus:

Oklahoma:
 Cotton
 Jackson

OKLAHOMA

Survey Area

Oklahoma:
 Oklahoma

Area of Application. Survey area plus:

Oklahoma:
 Garfield
 Muskogee
 Pittsburg
 Tulsa

PENNSYLVANIA

ALLEGHENY

Survey Area

Pennsylvania:
 Allegheny

Area of Application. Survey area plus:

Ohio:
 Cuyahoga
 Trumball

Pennsylvania:
 Butler

Westmoreland
West Virginia:
Harrison

CUMBERLAND

Survey Area

Pennsylvania:
Cumberland

Area of Application. Survey area plus:

Pennsylvania:
Blair
Franklin

YORK

Survey Area

Pennsylvania:
York

Area of Application. Survey area plus:

Pennsylvania:
Lebanon

PUERTO RICO

GUAYNABO-SAN JUAN

Survey Area

Puerto Rico: (municipalities)
Guaynabo
San Juan

Area of Application. Survey area plus:

Puerto Rico: (municipalities)
Aguadilla
Bayamon
Ceiba
Isabela
Ponce
Salinas
Toa Baja
Vieques
U.S. Virgin Islands:
St. Croix
St. Thomas

RHODE ISLAND

NEWPORT

Survey Area

Rhode Island:
Newport

Area of Application. Survey area plus:

Massachusetts:
Barnstable
Nantucket
Rhode Island:
Providence
Washington

SOUTH CAROLINA

CHARLESTON

Survey Area

South Carolina:
Charleston

Area of Application. Survey area plus:

South Carolina:
Berkeley
Horry

RICHLAND

Survey Area

South Carolina:
Richland

Area of Application. Survey area plus:

North Carolina:
Buncombe
Mecklenburg
South Carolina:
Sumpter
Tennessee:
Washington

SOUTH DAKOTA

PENNINGTON

Survey Area

South Dakota:
Pennington

Area of Application. Survey area plus:

Montana:
Custer
South Dakota:
Fall River
Meade
Wyoming:
Sheridan

TENNESSEE

SHELBY

Survey Area

Tennessee:
Shelby

Area of Application. Survey area plus:

Missouri:
Butler

TEXAS

BELL

Survey Area

Texas:
Bell

Area of Application. Survey area plus:

Texas:
Burnet
Coryell
Falls

BEXAR

Survey Area

Texas:
Bexar

Area of Application. Survey area plus:

Texas:
Comal

Kerr
Travis
Val Verde

DALLAS

Survey Area

Texas:
Dallas

Area of Application. Survey area plus:

Texas:
Angelina
Fannin
Galveston
Harris

EL PASO

Survey Area

Texas:
El Paso

Area of Application. Survey area.

MCLENNAN

Survey Area

Texas:
McLennan

Area of Application. Survey area.

NUECES

Survey Area

Texas:
Nueces

Area of Application. Survey area plus:

Texas:
Bee
Calhoun
Cameron
Kleberg
San Patricio
Webb

TARRANT

Survey Area

Texas:
Tarrant

Area of Application. Survey area plus:

Texas:
Cooke
Palo Pinto

TAYLOR

Survey Area

Texas:
Taylor

Area of Application. Survey area.

TOM GREEN

Survey Area

Texas:
Tom Green

Area of Application. Survey area plus:

Texas:
Howard

WICHITA

Survey Area

Texas:
Wichita

Area of Application. Survey area.

UTAH

DAVIS-SALT LAKE-WEBER

Survey Area

Utah:
Davis
Salt Lake
Weber

Area of Application. Survey area plus:

Utah:
Box Elder
Tooele
Uintah

VIRGINIA

ALEXANDRIA-ARLINGTON-FAIRFAX

Survey Area

Virginia: (city)
Alexandria

Virginia: (counties)
Arlington
Fairfax

Area of Application. Survey area.

CHESTERFIELD-RICHMOND

Survey Area

Virginia: (city)
Richmond

Virginia: (county)
Chesterfield

Area of Application. Survey area plus:

Virginia: (cities)
Bedford
Charlottesville
Salem

Virginia: (counties)
Caroline
Nottoway
Prince George

West Virginia:
Pendleton

HAMPTON-NEWPORT NEWS

Survey Area

Virginia: (cities)
Hampton
Newport News

Area of Application. Survey area plus:

Virginia: (city)
Williamsburg

Virginia: (county)
York

NORFOLK-PORTSMOUTH-VIRGINIA BEACH

Survey Area

Virginia: (cities)
  Norfolk
  Portsmouth
  Virginia Beach

Area of Application. Survey area plus:

North Carolina:
  Pasquotank
Virginia: (cities)
  Chesapeake
  Suffolk
Virginia: (counties)
  Accomack
  Northampton

PRINCE WILLIAM

Survey Area

Virginia:
  Prince William

Area of Application. Survey area plus:

Virginia:
  Fauquier

WASHINGTON

KITSAP

Survey Area

Washington:
  Kitsap

Area of Application. Survey area plus:

Washington:
  Clallam
  Jefferson

PIERCE

Survey Area

Washington:
  Pierce

Area of Application. Survey area plus:

Oregon:
  Clatsop
  Coos
  Douglas
  Lane
  Multnomah
  Tillamook
Washington:
  Clark
  Grays Harbor

SNOHOMISH

Survey Area

Washington:
  Snohomish

Area of Application. Survey area plus:

Washington:
  Island
  King
  Yakima

SPOKANE

Survey Area

Washington:
  Spokane

Area of Application. Survey area plus:

Washington:
  Adams
  Walla Walla

WYOMING

LARAMIE

Survey Area

Wyoming:
  Laramie

Area of Application. Survey area.

[75 FR 49351, Aug. 13, 2010, as amended at 76 FR 9640, Feb. 22, 2011; 76 FR 31786, June 2, 2011; 76 FR 53046, Aug. 25, 2011; 77 FR 28472, May 15, 2012; 78 FR 29612, May 21, 2013; 78 FR 60181, 60182, Oct. 1, 2013; 82 FR 40669, Aug. 28, 2017; 82 FR 41321, Aug. 31, 2017]

Subpart C—Determining Rates for Principal Types of Positions

§532.301 Definitions.

For purposes of this subpart:

Nearest similar wage area means the nearest wage area which is most similar to the local wage area in terms of private employment, population, relative numbers of private employers in major industry categories, and kinds and sizes of industry establishments and in which adequate private establishments exist in the survey area whose activities are similar to those in the dominant industry.

Principal types of appropriated or nonappropriated fund positions means those groups of occupations which require work of a specialized nature and which are peculiar to a specific Government industry which is the dominant industry among the total wage employment in the wage area.

Specialized private industry means private industry establishments in those industry groups, comparable to the specialized Government industries listed in §532.303 of this section, which must be included in a wage survey in order to obtain data comparable to a dominant industry.

§532.303 Specialized industry.

(a)(1) Under the appropriated fund wage system, a "specialized industry" is a Federal activity engaged in the production or repair of aircraft, ammunition, artillery and combat vehicles, communication equipment, electronic equipment, guided missiles, heavy duty equipment, shipbuilding, sighting and fire control equipment, or small arms.

(2) Under the nonappropriated fund wage system a "specialized industry" includes only nonappropriated fund operated eating and drinking places. Additional industries may be considered as specialized industries upon approval of the Office of Personnel Management.

§532.305 Dominant industry.

(a)(1) A specialized industry is a "dominant industry" if the number of wage employees in the wage area who are subject to the wage schedule for which the survey is made and employed in occupations which comprise the principal types of appropriated or nonappropriated fund positions in the specialized industry comprise:

(i) For appropriated fund activities,

(A) At least 25 percent of the total wage employment or

(B) 1,000 or more employees in a wage area having more than 4,000 wage employees; and

(ii) For nonappropriated fund activities

(A) At least 25 percent of the total wage employment or

(B) 100 or more wage employees in a wage area having 400 or more wage employees.

(2) If two or more specialized industries in a wage area qualify as dominant industries, the two specialized industries having the largest number of wage employees shall be the dominant industries for purposes of applying the requirements of this subpart.

§532.307 Determinating whether a dominant industry exists in a wage area.

(a) The chairperson of the local wage survey committee shall, before a full-scale wage survey is scheduled to begin, notify all appropriated or nonappropriated fund activities having employees subject to the wage schedules for which the survey is conducted so that organizations and individuals may submit written recommendations and supporting evidence to the local wage survey committee concerning principal types of appropriated or nonappropriated fund positions in the area. Each appropriated or nonappropriated fund activity shall publicize the opportunity to make such recommendations.

(b)(1) Before conducting a full-scale wage survey an occupational inventory of employees subject to the wage schedules for which the survey is conducted shall be obtained from each appropriated or nonappropriated fund activity in the area having such employees.

(2) After reviewing the occupational inventory and considering the recommendations received pursuant to paragraph (a) of this section, the local wage survey committee shall formulate its recommendations and prepare a written report concerning the existence of specialized industries within the wage area.

(3) The report of the recommendations, the occupational inventory, and the recommendations and supporting evidence received pursuant to paragraph (a) of this section shall be forwarded to the lead agency.

(c) The lead agency shall refer the occupational inventory and the reports received pursuant to paragraph (b) of this section to the agency wage committee for its consideration and recommendation if:

(1) The lead agency proposes not to accept the recommendation of the local wage survey committee concerning the specifications of the local wage survey; or

(2) The local wage survey committee's report is accompanied by a minority report.

(d) The lead agency shall determine, in writing, after taking into consideration the reports and recommendations received under paragraphs (b) and (c) of this section, and prior to ordering a full-scale wage survey to begin, whether the principal types of appropriated or nonappropriated fund positions in a local wage area comprise a dominant industry. The determination shall remain in effect until the next full-scale wage survey in the area.

[46 FR 21344, Apr. 10, 1981, as amended at 55 FR 46179, Nov. 1, 1990]

§532.309 Determining adequacy of specialized private industry.

(a) Specialized private industry comparable to an appropriated fund dominant industry is adequate when:

(1) The survey area is one of the 25 largest Standard Metropolitan Statistical Areas, or the total number of employees of private industry establishments in the specialized private industry located in the survey area is at least equal to the total number of appropriated fund wage employees in occupations which comprise the principal types of appropriated positions in the dominant industry who are subject to the wage schedules for which the survey is made; or

(2) For any dominant industry except "ammunition," the job matches obtained from the specialized private industry include one regular survey job in the WG–01 through 04 range, one regular survey job in the WG–05 through 08 range, one regular survey job in the WG–09 and above range, and one special survey job in the WG–09 and above range all providing at least 20 unweighted samples each; and three other regular or special survey jobs, each providing at least 10 unweighted samples.

(3) For the dominant industry "ammunition," the job matches obtained from the specialized survey industries include one regular survey job in the WG–01 through 04 range, one special survey job in the WG–05 through 08 range, and one regular survey job in the WG–09 through 15 range, all providing at least 20 unweighted samples each; and three other regular or special survey jobs, each providing at least 10 unweighted samples.

(b) Specialized private industry comparable to a nonappropriated fund dominant industry is adequate when:

(1) The total number of employees of private industry establishments similar to the dominant industry located in the survey are at least equal to the number of nonappropriated fund wage employees in positions which comprise the principal types of nonappropriated fund positions in the dominant industry who are subject to the wage schedules for which the survey is made; and

(2) The job matches obtained from all industries surveyed for regular survey jobs related to the dominant industry include one regular survey job in the NA–01 through 04 range providing at least 10 samples; and one regular survey job in the NA–05 through 15 range and one other regular survey job, each providing at least five samples.

§532.311 Survey of specialized private industry related to a dominant industry.

If it is determined that there are one or more dominant industries within a wage area, the lead agency shall insure that the survey includes the industries and survey jobs related to the dominant industries. When the related industry within the local wage survey area fails to meet the criteria in §532.309 of this subpart, the lead agency shall obtain data related to the dominant industry from the survey area of the wage area which is determined to be the nearest similar area which will provide adequate data under the criteria in §532.309 of this subpart.

[46 FR 21344, Apr. 10, 1981, as amended at 55 FR 46179, Nov. 1, 1990]

§532.313 Private sector industries.

(a) For appropriated fund surveys, the lead agency must use the private sector industries in the following North American Industry Classification System (NAICS) codes when it makes its wage schedule determinations for each specialized Federal industry:

2012 NAICS codes	2012 NAICS industry titles
	Aircraft Specialized Industry
332912	Fluid power valve and hose fitting manufacturing.
336411	Aircraft manufacturing.
336412	Aircraft engine and engine parts manufacturing.
336413	Other aircraft part and auxiliary equipment manufacturing.
336415	Guided missile and space vehicle propulsion unit and propulsion unit parts manufacturing.
336419	Other guided missile and space vehicle parts and auxiliary equipment manufacturing.
4811	Scheduled air transportation.
4812	Nonscheduled air transportation.

2012 NAICS codes	2012 NAICS industry titles
4879	Scenic and sightseeing transportation, other.
4881	Support activities for air transportation.
4921	Couriers.
541712	Research and development in the physical, engineering, and life sciences (except biotechnology).
56172	Janitorial services.
62191	Ambulance services.
81142	Reupholstery and furniture repair.
	Ammunition Specialized Industry
32592	Explosives manufacturing.
332992	Small arms ammunition manufacturing.
332993	Ammunition (except small arms) manufacturing.
	Artillery and Combat Vehicles Specialized Industry
2211	Electric power generation, transmission, and distribution.
2212	Natural gas distribution.
32732	Ready-mix concrete manufacturing.
332216	Saw blade and hand tool manufacturing.
332323	Ornamental and architectural metal work manufacturing.
332439	Other metal container manufacturing.
332994	Small arms, ordnance, and ordnance accessories manufacturing.
332999	All other miscellaneous fabricated metal product manufacturing.
33311	Agricultural implement manufacturing.
33312	Construction machinery manufacturing.
333611	Turbine and turbine generator set units manufacturing.
333618	Other engine equipment manufacturing.
333922	Conveyor and conveying equipment manufacturing.
333923	Overhead traveling crane, hoist, and monorail system manufacturing.
333924	Industrial truck, tractor, trailer, and stacker machinery manufacturing.
3361	Motor vehicle manufacturing.
336211	Motor vehicle body manufacturing.
336212	Truck trailer manufacturing.
33631	Motor vehicle gasoline engine and engine parts manufacturing.
33632	Motor vehicle electrical and electronic equipment manufacturing.
33633	Motor vehicle steering and suspension components (except spring) manufacturing.
33634	Motor vehicle brake system manufacturing.
33635	Motor vehicle transmission and power train parts manufacturing.
33639	Other motor vehicle parts manufacturing.
33651	Railroad rolling stock manufacturing.
336992	Military armored vehicle, tank, and tank component manufacturing.
4231	Motor vehicle and motor vehicle parts and supplies merchant wholesalers.
42381	Construction and mining (except oil well) machinery and equipment merchant wholesalers.
42382	Farm and garden machinery and equipment merchant wholesalers.
4413	Automotive parts, accessories, and tire stores.
44421	Outdoor power equipment stores.
484	Truck transportation.
4862	Pipeline transportation of natural gas.
492	Couriers and messengers.
5171	Wired telecommunications carriers.
5172	Wireless telecommunications carriers (except satellite).
517911	Telecommunications resellers.
5621	Waste collection.
	Communications Specialized Industry
33422	Radio and television broadcasting and wireless communications equipment manufacturing.
33429	Other communications equipment manufacturing.
334511	Search, detection, navigation, guidance, aeronautical and nautical system and instrument manufacturing.
334514	Totalizing fluid meter and counting device manufacturing.
334515	Instrument manufacturing for measuring and testing electricity and electrical signals.
335311	Power, distribution, and specialty transformer manufacturing.
48531	Taxi service.
5151	Radio and television broadcasting.
5152	Cable and other subscription programming.
5171	Wired telecommunications carriers.
5172	Wireless telecommunications carriers (except satellite).
5174	Satellite telecommunications.
517911	Telecommunications resellers.
	Electronics Specialized Industry
333316	Photographic and photocopying equipment manufacturing.

2012 NAICS codes	2012 NAICS industry titles
3341	Computer and peripheral equipment manufacturing.
33422	Radio and television broadcasting and wireless communications equipment manufacturing.
33429	Other communications equipment manufacturing.
33431	Audio and video equipment manufacturing.
334412	Bare printed circuit board manufacturing.
334413	Semiconductor and related device manufacturing.
334416	Electronic coil, transformer, and other inductor manufacturing.
334417	Electronic connector manufacturing.
334418	Printed circuit assembly (electronic assembly) manufacturing.
334419	Other electronic component manufacturing.
334511	Search, detection, navigation, guidance, aeronautical and nautical system and instrument manufacturing.
334515	Instrument manufacturing for measuring and testing electricity and electrical signals.
334613	Magnetic and optical recording media manufacturing.
42342	Office equipment merchant wholesalers.
42343	Computer and computer peripheral equipment and software merchant wholesalers.
	Guided Missiles Specialized Industry
332912	Fluid power valve and hose fitting manufacturing.
333316	Photographic and photocopying equipment manufacturing.
3341	Computer and peripheral equipment manufacturing.
33422	Radio and television broadcasting and wireless communications equipment manufacturing.
33429	Other communications equipment manufacturing.
334418	Printed circuit assembly (electronic assembly) manufacturing.
334511	Search, detection, navigation, guidance, aeronautical and nautical system and instrument manufacturing.
334515	Instrument manufacturing for measuring and testing electricity and electrical signals.
334613	Magnetic and optical recording media manufacturing.
3364	Aerospace product and parts manufacturing.
54131	Architectural services.
54133	Engineering services.
54136	Geophysical surveying and mapping services.
54137	Surveying and mapping (except geophysical) services.
541712	Research and development in the physical, engineering, and life sciences (except biotechnology).
	Heavy Duty Equipment Specialized Industry
332439	Other metal container manufacturing.
332999	All other miscellaneous fabricated metal product manufacturing.
33312	Construction machinery manufacturing.
333923	Overhead traveling crane, hoist, and monorail system manufacturing.
333924	Industrial truck, tractor, trailer, and stacker machinery manufacturing.
33651	Railroad rolling stock manufacturing.
42381	Construction and mining (except oil well) machinery and equipment merchant wholesalers.
	Shipbuilding Specialized Industry
336611	Ship building and repairing.
48839	Other support activities for water transportation.
	Sighting and Fire Control Equipment Specialized Industry
333314	Optical instrument and lens manufacturing.
333316	Photographic and photocopying equipment manufacturing.
3341	Computer and peripheral equipment manufacturing.
33422	Radio and television broadcasting and wireless communications equipment manufacturing.
33429	Other communications equipment manufacturing.
334418	Printed circuit assembly (electronic assembly) manufacturing.
334511	Search, detection, navigation, guidance, aeronautical and nautical system and instrument manufacturing.
334515	Instrument manufacturing for measuring and testing electricity and electrical signals.
334613	Magnetic and optical recording media manufacturing.
	Small Arms Specialized Industry
332994	Small arms manufacturing.

(b) For wage surveys involving the specialized Federal industry "Artillery and Combat Vehicles" in paragraph (a) of this section, the lead agency must limit special job coverage for industries in NAICS codes 2211, 2212, 32732,

484, 4862, 5621, 492, 5171, 5172, and 5173 to automotive mechanic, diesel engine mechanic, and heavy mobile equipment mechanic.

(c) For nonappropriated fund wage surveys, the lead agency must use NAICS codes 71111, 7221, 7222, 72231, 72232, and 7224 (eating and drinking places) when it determines a wage schedule for a specialized industry.

[71 FR 35375, June 20, 2006, as amended at 73 FR 45853, Aug. 7, 2008; 78 FR 58154, Sept. 23, 2013; 79 FR 21121, Apr. 15, 2014]

§ 532.315 Additional survey jobs.

(a) For appropriated fund surveys, when the lead agency adds to the industries to be surveyed, it shall add to the required survey jobs the specialized survey jobs listed below opposite the industry added:

Specialized industry	Specialized survey jobs	Grade
Aircraft	Electronics Mechanic	WG–11
	Aircraft Structures Assembler B	WG–7
	Aircraft Structures Assembler A	WG–9
	Aircraft Mechanic	WG–10
	Aircraft Mechanic includes.	
	Aircraft Electrician	WG–10
	Aircraft Welder	WG–10
	Aircraft Sheetmetal Worker	WG–10
	Hydromechanical Fuel Control Repairer.	WG–10
	Aircraft Engine Mechanic	WG–10
	Aircraft Jet Engine Mechanic	WG–10
	Flight Line Mechanic	WG–10
	Aircraft Attendant (ground services).	WG–7
Ammunition	Munitions Handler	WG–4
	Munitions Operator	WG–4
	Munitions Operator	WG–6
	Munitions Operator	WG–8
	Munitions Operator	WG–9
	Explosives Operator	WG–9
Artillery and combat vehicles.	Automotive Mechanic (limited to data obtained in special industries).	WG–10
	Heavy Mobile Equipment Mechanic.	WG–10
	Artillery Repairer	WG–9
	Combat Vehicle Mechanic	WG–8
	Combat Vehicle Mechanic (Engine).	WG–10
	Combat Vehicle Mechanic	WG–11
	Diesel Engine Mechanic (limited to data obtained in special industries.	WG–10
Communications.	Telephone Installer-Repairer	WG–9
	Central Office Repairer	WG–11
	Electronic Test Equipment Repairer.	WG–11
	Television Station Mechanic	WG–11
Electronics	Electronics Mechanic	WG–11
	Industrial Electronic Controls Repairer.	WG–10
	Electronic Test Equipment Repairer.	WG–11
	Electronic Computer Mechanic	WG–11
	Television Station Mechanic	WG–11
Guided missiles.	Electronic Computer Mechanic	WG–11
	Guided Missile Mechanical Repairer.	WG–11
Heavy duty equipment.	Heavy Mobile Equipment Mechanic.	WG–10
Shipbuilding	Electronics Mechanic	WG–11
	Electrician, Ship	WG–10
	Pipefitter, Ship	WG–10
	Shipfitter	WG–10
	Shipwright	WG–10
	Machinist (Marine)	WG–10
Sighting and fire control.	Electronic Computer Mechanic	WG–11
	Fire Control Instrument Repairman.	WG–11
	Electronic Fire Control Systems Repairer.	WG–11
	Electronic Fire Control Systems Repairer.	WG–12
	Electronic Fire Control Systems Repairer.	WG–13
Small arms	Small Arms Repairer	WG–8

(b) For nonappropriated fund surveys, a lead agency must obtain prior approval of OPM to add a job not listed in § 532.223 of this subpart.

[55 FR 46180, Nov. 1, 1990]

§ 532.317 Use of data from the nearest similar area.

(a)(1) For prevailing rate employees other than those in the Department of Defense, the lead agency shall, in establishing the regular schedule under the provisions of this subpart, analyze and use the acceptable data from the nearest similar wage area together with the data obtained from inside the local wage survey area. The regular schedule for Department of Defense prevailing rate employees shall be based on local wage data only.

(2) The total number of job matches obtained from the nearest similar wage area shall be equal to the number required for adequacy in § 532.309(a) (2) and (3) of this subpart for appropriated fund surveys and § 532.309(b)(2) of this subpart for nonappropriated fund surveys.

(3) Data shall be selected for inclusion on the basis of the most populous survey jobs as determined by the weighted job matches found in the dominant industry in the selected reference area. In identifying survey jobs for which reference area samples will

be included, the jobs required at limited grade ranges shall be selected before jobs in the unlimited grade range. When there is a tie in the selection procedure, the highest graded job shall be selected first.

(4) If there are two dominant industries for which data are obtained from nearest similar areas, the procedure described in paragraph (a)(2) of this section shall be applied independently for each of the specialized industries.

(b)(1) The wage rates established for a grade by using data from the nearest similar area may not exceed the wage rates for the same grade in the nearest similar area.

(2) If data are obtained from two nearest similar areas for two dominant industries, the wage rates established for a grade by using these data may not exceed the higher of the wage rates for the same grade in the two nearest similar areas.

(c) The wage data obtained from the nearest similar area or areas may not be used to reduce the wage rates for any grade in the local area below the rates that would be established for that grade without the use of the data from the nearest similar area or areas.

[46 FR 21344, Apr. 10, 1981, as amended at 54 FR 38197, Sept. 15, 1989. Redesignated and amended at 55 FR 46179, Nov. 1, 1990]

Subpart D—Pay Administration

§532.401 Definitions.

In this subpart:

Change to lower grade means a change in the position of an employee who, while continuously employed—

(1) Moves from a position in one grade of a prevailing rate schedule established under this part to a position in a lower grade of the same type prevailing rate schedule, whether in the same or different wage area;

(2) Moves from a position under a prevailing rate schedule established under this part to a position under a different prevailing rate schedule (e.g., WL to WG) with a lower representative rate; or

(3) Moves from a position not under a prevailing rate schedule to a position with a lower representative rate under a prevailing rate schedule.

Equivalent increase means an increase or increases in an employee's rate of basic pay equal to or greater than the difference between the rate of pay for the grade and step occupied by the employee and the rate of pay for the next higher step of that grade, except in the situations specified in §532.417 of this subpart. In the case of a promotion, the grade and step occupied means the grade and step to which promoted.

Existing scheduled rate of pay means the scheduled rate of pay received immediately before the effective date of a transfer, reassignment, promotion, change to a lower grade, within-grade increase, or revision of a wage schedule.

Highest previous rate means the highest scheduled rate of pay previously paid to a person while employed in a job in any branch of the Federal Government, a mixed-ownership corporation, or the government of the District of Columbia. It is based on a regular tour of duty under an appointment not limited to 90 days or less, or for a continuous period of no less than 90 days under one or more appointments without a break in service.

Promotion means a change in the position of an employee who, while continuously employed—

(1) Moves from a position in one grade of a prevailing rate schedule established under this part to a position in a higher grade of the same type prevailing rate schedule, whether in the same or different wage area;

(2) Moves from a position under a prevailing rate schedule established under this part to a position under a different prevailing rate schedule (e.g., WG to WL) with a higher representative rate; or

(3) Moves from a position not under a prevailing rate schedule to a position with a higher representative rate under a prevailing rate schedule.

Rate of basic pay means the scheduled rate of pay plus any night or environmental differential.

Reassignment means a change of an employee, while serving continuously in the same agency, from one job to another without promotion or change to a lower grade.

Representative rate means the going rate, *i.e.*, the rate or step keyed to the prevailing rate determination. For example:

(1) The established rate on a single rate schedule;

(2) The second rate on a five-rate regular wage schedule;

(3) The fourth rate on the General Schedule; or

(4) The fourth rate of a class under the Foreign Service Officer and Foreign Service Staff schedule.

Retained rate means the rate of pay an employee is receiving which is higher than the maximum scheduled rate of pay of the Federal Wage System grade or pay level to which the employee is assigned.

Scheduled rate of pay means the rate of pay fixed by law or administrative action, including a retained rate of pay, for the job held by an employee before any deductions and exclusive of additional pay of any kind.

[46 FR 21344, Apr. 10, 1981, as amended at 55 FR 46180, Nov. 1, 1990; 60 FR 62701, Dec. 7, 1995]

§ 532.403 New appointments.

(a) Except as provided in paragraphs (b) and (c) of this section, a new appointment to a position shall be made at the minimum rate of the appropriate grade.

(b) An agency may make a new appointment at a rate above the minimum rate of the appropriate grade in recognition of an appointees' special qualifications.

(c) An agency shall make a new appointment at a step-rate above the minimum rate of a grade if the lead agency for the wage area has designated, in accordance with § 532.249, a step-rate above the first step-rate of a grade as the minimum step-rate at which a position may be filled.

[46 FR 21344, Apr. 10, 1981, as amended at 58 FR 32274, June 9, 1993]

§ 532.405 Use of highest previous rate.

(a)(1) Subject to the provisions of § 532.407 of this subpart and part 536 of this chapter, when an employee is reemployed, reassigned, transferred, promoted, or changed to a lower grade, the agency may fix the pay at any rate of the new grade which does not exceed the employee's highest previous rate.

(2) However, if the employee's highest previous rate falls between two step-rates of the new grade, the agency may fix the pay at the higher of the two.

(b)(1) When an employee's type of appointment is changed in the same job, an agency may continue to pay the existing scheduled rate or may pay any higher rate of the grade which does not exceed the employee's highest previous rate.

(2) However, if the highest previous rate falls between two step rates of the grade, the agency may pay the higher rate.

(c)(1) The highest previous rate, if earned in a wage job, is the current rate of the grade and step-rate of the former job on the same type of wage schedule in the wage area in which the employee is being employed, or the actual earned rate, whichever is higher.

(2) If earned on a General Schedule or another pay system other than the Federal Wage System, it is the current rate for the same grade and rate of that schedule.

(d) The highest previous rate may be based upon a rate of pay received during a temporary promotion, so long as the temporary promotion is for a period of not less than 1 year. This limitation does not apply upon permanent placement in a position at the same or higher grade.

[46 FR 21344, Apr. 10, 1981, as amended at 60 FR 62701, Dec. 7, 1995]

§ 532.407 Promotion.

(a) An employee who is promoted is entitled to be paid at the lowest scheduled rate of the grade to which promoted which exceeds the employee's existing scheduled rate of pay by at least four percent of the representative rate of the grade from which promoted.

(b) If there is no rate in the grade to which an employee is promoted which meets the requirement of paragraph (a) of this section the employee shall be entitled to the higher of: (1) the existing scheduled rate of pay in accordance with part 536 of this chapter; or (2) the maximum scheduled rate of the grade to which promoted.

(c) If the promotion is to a position in a different wage area, the agency shall determine the employee's pay entitlement as if there were two pay actions—a promotion and a reassignment—and shall process them in the order which gives the employee the maximum benefit.

§532.409 Grading or regrading of positions.

Except as provided in §532.703(b)(10), a change in an employee's rate of basic pay as a result of the grading or regrading of the employee's position shall be effective on the date the grading or regrading action is finally approved by the agency or on a subsequent specifically stated date.

§532.411 Details.

An appropriated fund employee detailed to a position other than the position to which appointed shall be paid at the rate of the position to which appointed.

§532.413 Simultaneous action.

(a) If an employee becomes entitled to more than one pay change at the same time, the employing agency shall process the pay changes in the order which will provide the maximum benefit, except as required by paragraph (b) of this section.

(b) If an employee becomes entitled to an increase in pay and subject to a personnel or appointment change at the same time, the increased rate of pay is deemed to be the employee's existing scheduled rate of pay when the personnel or appointment change is processed.

§532.415 Application of new or revised wage schedules.

(a) The head of each installation or activity in a wage area shall place new or revised wage schedules into effect at the beginning of the first full shift on the date specified on the schedule by the lead agency.

(b) No agency may retroactively change any personnel or pay actions taken between the effective date of a new or revised wage schedule and the date it is actually put into effect if the personnel or pay actions taken during this period of time are more advantageous to an employee than the same personnel or pay action would have been had the new or revised wage schedule been placed into effect on the date specified by the lead agency.

(c) In applying a new or revised wage schedule, the scheduled rate of pay of an employee paid at one of the steps of the employee's grade on an old wage schedule shall be adjusted upward to the newly adjusted rate for the same numerical step of the grade whenever there is an increase in rates. Except when there is a decrease in wage rates because of a statutory reduction in scheduled rates, the employee is entitled to pay retention as provided in 5 CFR 536.301(a)(8).

[46 FR 21344, Apr. 10, 1981, as amended at 60 FR 62701, Dec. 7, 1995; 70 FR 31305, May 31, 2005]

§532.417 Within-grade increases.

(a) An employee paid under a regular Federal Wage System schedule with a work performance rating of satisfactory or better shall advance automatically to the next higher step within the grade in accordance with section 5343(e)(2) of title 5, United States Code.

(b) Waiting periods for within-grade increases shall begin:

(1) On the first day of a new appointment as an employee subject to this part;

(2) On the first day of a period of service after a break in service or time in a nonppay status in excess of 52 weeks; or

(3) On receipt of an equivalent increase.

(c) Creditable service. The following periods of time shall be considered creditable service for purposes of waiting periods for within-grade increases:

(1) Time during which an employee is in receipt of pay, including periods of leave with pay;

(2) Time during which an employee with a prearranged regular scheduled tour of duty is in a nonpay status to the extent that the time in a nonpay status does not exceed, in the aggregate:

(i) One workweek in the waiting period for step 2;

(ii) Three workweeks in the waiting period for step 3; or

(iii) Four workweeks in the waiting period for steps 4 and 5;

(3) Time during which an employee or former employee is on leave of absence or is separated from Federal service and is entitled to continuation of pay or compensation under subchapter I of chapter 81 of title 5, United States Code. This does not apply to prevailing rate employees within a Department of Defense or Coast Guard nonappropriated fund instrumentality;

(4) A period of military service when:

(i) An employee is on leave of absence to perform such service and returns to pay status through the exercise of a restoration right provided by law, Executive order, or regulation; or

(ii) A former employee is reemployed with the Federal Service not later than 52 calendar weeks after separation from such service or hospitalization continuing thereafter for a period of not more than one year. Military service means honorable active service in the Armed Forces, in the Regular or Reserve Corps of the Public Health Service after June 30, 1960, or as a commissioned officer of the Environmental Science Services Administration after June 30, 1961, but does not include service in the National Guard, except when ordered to active duty in the service of the United States.

(5) The time between an employee's separation from an earlier position and the date of the employee's return to a civilian position through the exercise of a reemployment right granted by law, Executive Order, or regulation;

(6) Time during which an employee is performing service, which is creditable under section 8332(b) (5) or (7) of title 5, United States Code;

(7) The time during which an employee is detailed to a non-Federal position under subchapter VI of chapter 33 of title 5, United States Code; and

(8) Nonworkdays intervening between an employee's last regularly scheduled workday in one position and the first regularly scheduled workday in a new position.

(9) Time during which an employee is temporarily employed by another agency in a position covered by this subpart.

(d) Effective date. A within-grade increase shall be effective at the beginning of the first applicable pay period following the day an employee becomes eligible for the increase.

(e) *Equivalent increase.* The following shall not be counted as equivalent increases:

(1) Application of a new or revised wage schedule or application of a new pay or evaluation plan;

(2) Payment of additional compensation in the form of nonforeign or foreign post differentials or nonforeign cost-of-living allowances;

(3) Adjustment of the General Schedule;

(4) Premium payment for overtime and holiday duty;

(5) Payment of night shift differential;

(6) Hazard pay differentials;

(7) Payment of rates above the minimum rate of the grade in recognition of specific qualifications, or in jobs in specific hard-to-fill occupations;

(8) Correction of an error in a previous demotion or reduction in pay;

(9) Temporary limited promotion followed by change to lower grade to the former or a different lower grade;

(10) A transfer or reassignment in the same grade and step to another local wage area with a higher wage schedule;

(11) Repromotion to a former or intervening grade of any employee whose earlier change to lower grade was not for cause and was not at the employee's request; and

(12) An increase resulting from the grant of a quality step increase under the General Schedule.

[46 FR 21344, Apr. 10, 1981, as amended at 49 FR 37055, Sept. 21, 1984; 55 FR 46180, Nov. 1, 1990]

§532.419 Grade and pay retention.

(a) In accordance with section 9(a)(1) of Public Law 92–392 (86 Stat. 564, 573), an employee's initial rate of pay on conversion to a wage schedule established under the provisions of subchapter IV of chapter 53, title 5, United States Code, shall be determined under conversion rules prescribed by the Office of Personnel Management.

(b) Except as provided in paragraph (a) of this section, an employee's eligibility for grade and/or pay retention shall be determined in accordance with the provisions of part 536 of this title.

Subpart E—Premium Pay and Differentials

§ 532.501 Definitions.

In this subpart:

Administrative workweek means a period of seven consecutive calendar days.

Basic workweek for full time employees means the days and hours within an administrative workweek which make up the employee's regularly scheduled 40-hour workweek.

Environmental differential means a differential paid for a duty involving unusually severe hazards or working conditions.

Irregular or occasional overtime work means overtime work which is not part of the regularly scheduled administrative workweek.

Night shift differential means the differential paid the employee when the majority of regularly scheduled nonovertime hours worked fall between 3 p.m. and 8 a.m.

Overtime work means authorized and approved hours of work performed by an employee in excess of eight hours in a day or in excess of 40 hours in an administrative workweek, and includes irregular or occasional overtime work and regular overtime work.

Premium pay means additional compensation for overtime, or Sunday work, and standby duty.

Sunday work means work performed during a regularly scheduled tour of duty within a basic workweek when any part of that work which is not overtime work is performed on Sunday.

Regular overtime work means overtime work which is a part of the regularly scheduled administrative workweek.

Regularly scheduled administrative workweek means:

(1) For full-time employees, the period within an administrative workweek within which employees are scheduled to be on duty regularly.

(2) For part-time employees, it means the days and hours within an administrative workweek during which these employees are scheduled to be on duty regularly.

Tour of duty means the hours of a day, *i.e.*, a daily tour of duty, and the days of an administrative workweek, *i.e.*, a weekly tour of duty, that are scheduled in advance and during which an employee is required to perform on a regularly recurring basis.

§ 532.503 Overtime pay.

(a)(1) Employees who are exempt from the overtime pay provisions of the Fair Labor Standards Act of 1938, as amended, shall be paid overtime pay in accordance with 5 U.S.C. 5544 and this section. Employees who are nonexempt shall be paid overtime pay in accordance with part 551 of this chapter.

(2) Hours of work in excess of eight in a day are not included in computing hours of work in excess of 40 hours in an administrative workweek.

(b) *Effect of leave on overtime pay.* (1) Hours during which an employee is absent from duty on paid leave during time when the employee otherwise would have been required to be on duty shall be considered hours of work in determining whether the employee is entitled to overtime pay for work performed in excess of eight hours a day or 40 hours a week.

(2) For the purposes of paragraph (b)(1) of this section paid leave includes but is not limited to:

(i) Annual or sick leave;

(ii) Authorized absence on a day off from duty granted by Executive or administrative order; or

(iii) Authorized absence on a legal holiday;

(3) Hours during which an employee is absent from duty on leave without pay during a time when he/she otherwise would have been required to be on duty shall not be considered hours of work in determining whether he/she is entitled to overtime pay for work performed in excess of eight hours in a day or 40 hours in a week.

(c) *Callback overtime work.* Irregular or occasional overtime work performed by an employee on a day when work was not regularly scheduled for the employee or for which the employee has been required to return to the place of employment shall be considered to be at least two hours in duration for the purpose of overtime pay, regardless of whether the employee performs work for two hours.

(d)(1) An employee regularly assigned to a night shift, who performs overtime work which extends into or falls entirely within a day shift, shall be entitled to overtime pay computed on the night rate.

(2) When the overtime is performed on a nonworkday the employee shall be entitled to overtime pay computed on the rate of the employee's last previous regularly scheduled shift.

(e)(1) An employee regularly assigned to a rotating schedule involving work on both day and night shifts who performs overtime work which extends or falls entirely within the succeeding shift shall be entitled to overtime pay computed on the rate of the employee's regularly scheduled shift in effect for that calendar day.

(2) When the overtime is performed on a nonworkday, the employee shall be entitled to overtime pay computed on the average rate of basic pay for all regularly scheduled shifts worked by the employee during the basic workweek.

(f) For an employee covered by 5 U.S.C. 5544, hours in a standby or on-call status or while sleeping or eating shall not be credited for the purpose of determining hours of work in excess of 8 hours in a day.

[46 FR 21344, Apr. 10, 1981, as amended at 56 FR 20341, May 3, 1991; 57 FR 59279, Dec. 15, 1992]

§ 532.504 Compensatory time off.

(a) At the request of an employee, the head of an agency may grant compensatory time off from an employee's tour of duty instead of payment under § 532.503 or the Fair Labor Standards Act of 1938, as amended, for an equal amount of irregular or occasional overtime work.

(b) At the request of an employee, the head of an agency may grant compensatory time off from an employee's basic work requirement under a flexible work schedule under 5 U.S.C. 6122 instead of payment under § 532.503 or the Fair Labor Standards Act of 1938, as amended, for an equal amount of overtime work, whether or not irregular or occasional in nature.

(c) An agency may not require that an employee be compensated for overtime work with an equal amount of compensatory time off from the employee's tour of duty. An employee may not directly or indirectly intimidate, threaten, or coerce, or attempt to intimidate, threaten, or coerce any other employee for the purpose of interfering with such employee's rights to request or not to request compensatory time off in lieu of payment for overtime hours.

(d) The head of a department may fix a time limit for an employee to request or take compensatory time off and may provide that an employee who fails to take compensatory time earned under paragraph (a) or (b) of this section before the time limit fixed shall lose the right to compensatory time off and to overtime pay unless the failure is due to an exigency of the service beyond the employee's control.

[62 FR 28307, May 23, 1997]

§ 532.505 Night shift differentials.

(a) Employees shall be entitled to receive night shift differentials in accordance with section 5343 of title 5, United States Code.

(b) *Absence on holidays.* An employee regularly assigned to a shift for which a night shift differential is payable shall be paid the night shift differential for a period of excused absence on a legal holiday or other day off from duty granted by Executive or administrative order.

(c) *Travel status.* An employee regularly assigned to a shift for which a night shift differential is payable shall be paid the night shift differential for hours of the employee's tour of duty while in official travel status, regardless of whether the employee is performing work.

(d) *Temporary tour of duty.* (1) An employee regularly assigned to a night shift who is temporarily assigned to a day shift or to a night shift having a lower night shift differential shall continue to receive the regular night shift differential, a temporary detail for training purposes is also included—see 5 CFR 410.602.

(2) An employee regularly assigned to a night shift, who is temporarily assigned to another night shift having a higher differential, shall be paid the higher differential if a majority of the

employee's regularly scheduled non-overtime hours of work on the temporary shift fall within hours having the higher differential.

(3) An employee regularly assigned to a day shift who is temporarily assigned to a night shift shall be paid a night shift differential.

(e) *Leave with pay.* (1) An employee regularly assigned to a night shift shall be paid a night shift differential during a period of leave with pay.

(2) An employee regularly assigned to a day shift who is temporarily assigned to a night shift shall be paid a night shift differential for any leave with pay taken when scheduled to work night shifts.

(3) An employee assigned to a regular rotating schedule involving work on both day and night shifts shall be paid a night shift differential only for any leave with pay taken when scheduled to work night shifts.

(4) An employee who is not regularly assigned to a day shift or a night shift but whose shift is changed at irregular intervals shall be paid a night shift differential during leave with pay if the employee received a night shift differential for the last shift worked preceding leave with pay.

§532.507 Pay for holiday work.

(a) An employee who is entitled to holiday premium pay and who performs work on a holiday which is not overtime work shall be paid the employee's rate of basic pay plus premium pay at a rate equal to the rate of basic pay.

(b) An employee shall be paid for overtime work performed on a holiday at the same rate as for overtime on other workdays.

(c) An employee who is entitled to holiday premium pay and who is required to report for work on a holiday shall be paid at least two hours of holiday pay whether or not work is actually performed.

§532.509 Pay for Sunday work.

A wage employee whose regular work schedule includes a period of service of up to 8 hours which is not overtime work, a part of which is on Sunday, is entitled to additional pay under the provisions of section 5544 of title 5, United States Code.

[76 FR 52539, Aug. 23, 2011]

§532.511 Environmental differentials.

(a) *Entitlements to environmental differential pay.* (1) In accordance with section 5343(c)(4) of title 5, United States Code, an employee shall be paid an environmental differential when exposed to a working condition or hazard that falls within one of the categories approved by the Office of Personnel Management.

(2) Each installation or activity must evaluate its situations against the guidelines issued by the Office of Personnel Management to determine whether the local situation is covered by one or more of the defined categories.

(b) *Amount of environmental differential payable.* (1) An employee entitled to an environmental differential shall be paid an amount equal to the percentage rate authorized by the Office of Personnel Management for the category in which the working condition or hazard falls, multiplied by the rate for the second step of WG–10 for the appropriated fund employees and NA–10 for the nonappropriated fund employees on the current regular non-supervisory wage schedule for the wage area for which the differential is payable, counting one-half cent and over as a whole cent.

(2) An employee entitled to an environmental differential on an actual exposure basis shall be paid a minimum of one hour's differential pay for the exposure. For exposure beyond one hour, the employee shall be paid in increments of one quarter hour for each 15 minutes or portion thereof in excess of 15 minutes. Entitlement begins with the first instance of exposure and ends one hour later, except that when exposure continues beyond the hour, it shall be considered ended at the end of the quarter hour in which exposure actually terminated.

(3) An employee entitled to an environmental differential on the basis of hours in a pay status shall be paid for all hours in a pay status on the day on which he/she is exposed to the situation.

(4) An employee may not be paid more than one environmental differential for a particular period of work.

(5) The payment of environmental differential pay is computed on the basis of the highest environmental differential rate authorized during the period of entitlement.

(6) The number of hours an employee is paid environmental differential shall not exceed the number of hours of duty performed by the employee on the day of exposure except as required by paragraph (b)(3) of this section.

(c) *Basic pay.* Environmental differential pay is part of basic pay and shall be used to compute premium pay (pay for overtime, holiday, or Sunday work), the amount from which retirement deductions are made, and the amount on which group life insurance is based. It is not part of basic pay for purposes of lump-sum annual leave payments and severance pay nor is its loss an adverse action.

(d) The schedule of environmental differentials is set out as appendix A to this subpart and is incorporated in and made a part of this section.

[46 FR 21344, Apr. 10, 1981, as amended at 49 FR 49841, Dec. 24, 1984; 55 FR 46180, Nov. 1, 1990]

§ 532.513 Flexible and compressed work schedules.

Federal Wage System employees who are authorized to work flexible and compressed work schedules under sections 6122 and 6127 of title 5, United States Code, shall be paid premium pay in accordance with subchapter II of chapter 61 of title 5, United States Code. Subpart D of part 610 of this chapter supplements subchapter II and must be read together with it.

[62 FR 28307, May 23, 1997]

Appendix A to Subpart E of Part 532—Schedule of Environmental Differentials Paid for Exposure to Various Degrees of Hazards, Physical Hardships, and Working Conditions of an Unusual Nature

This appendix lists the environmental differentials authorized for exposure to various degrees of hazards, physical hardships, and working conditions of an unusual nature.

Part I—Payment for Actual Exposure

Differential rate (percent)	Category for which payable	Effective date
100	1. *Flying.* Participating in flights under one or more types of the following conditions a. Test flights of a new or repaired plane or modified plane when the repair or modification may affect the flight characteristics of the plane; b. Flights for test performance of plane under adverse conditions such as in low altitude or severe weather conditions, maximum load limits, or overload; c. Test missions for the collection of measurement data where two or more aircraft are involved and flight procedures require formation flying and/or rendezvous at various altitudes and aspect angles; d. Flights deliberately undertaken in extreme weather conditions such as flying into a hurricane to secure weather data; e. Flights to deliver aircraft which have been prepared for one-time flight without being test flown prior to delivery flight; f. Flights for pilot proficiency training in aircraft new to the pilot under simulated emergency conditions which parallel conditions encountered in performing flight tests; g. Low-level flights in small aircraft including helicopters at altitude of 150 meters (500 feet) and under in daylight and 300 meters (1,000 feet) and under at night when the flights are over mountainous terrain, or in fixed-wing aircraft involving maneuvering at the heights and times specified above, or in helicopters maneuvering and hovering over water at altitudes of less than 150 meters (500 feet); h. Low-level flights in an aircraft flying at altitudes of 60 meters (200 feet) and under while conducting wildlife surveys and law enforcement activities, animal depredation abatement and making agricultural applications, and conducting or facilitating search and rescue operations; flights in helicopters at low levels involving line inspection, maintenance, erection, or salvage operations; i. Flights involving launch or recovery aboard an aircraft carrier; j. Reduced gravity light testing in an aircraft flying a parabolic flight path and providing a testing environment ranging from weightlessness up through 20 meters per second^2 (2 gravity) conditions;	Nov. 1, 1970.
25	2. *High work*	Nov. 1, 1970.

PART I—PAYMENT FOR ACTUAL EXPOSURE—Continued

Differential rate (percent)	Category for which payable	Effective date
	a. Working on any structure of at least 30 meters (100 feet) above the ground, deck, floor or roof, or from the bottom of a tank or pit;	
	b. Working at a lesser height:	
	(1) If the footing is unsure or the structure is unstable; or	
	(2) If safe scaffolding, enclosed ladders or other similar protective facilities are not adequate (for example, working from a swinging stage, boatswain chair, a similar support); or	
	(3) If adverse conditions such as darkness, steady rain, high wind, icing, lightning or similar environmental factors render working at such height(s) hazardous.	
15	3. *Floating targets.* Servicing equipment on board a target ship or barge in which the employee is required to board or leave the target vessel by small boat or helicopter.	Nov. 1, 1970.
4	4. *Dirty work.* Performing work which subjects the employee to soil of body or clothing:	Nov. 1, 1970.
	a. Beyond that normally to be expected in performing the duties of the classification; and	
	b. Where the condition is not adequately alleviated by the mechanical equipment or protective devices being used, or which are readily available, or when such devices are not feasible for use due to health considerations (excessive temperature, asthmatic conditions, etc); or	
	c. When the use of mechanical equipment, or protective devices, or protective clothing results in an unusual degree of discomfort.	
4	5. *Cold work.* a. Working in cold storage or other climate-controlled areas where the employee is subjected to temperatures at or below freezing (0 degrees Celsius (32 degrees Fahrenheit)).	Nov. 1, 1970.
	b. Working in cold storage or other climate-controlled areas where the employee is subjected to temperatures at or below freezing (0 degrees Celsius (32 degrees Fahrenheit)) where such exposure is not practically eliminated by the mechanical equipment or protective devices being used.	Mar. 13, 1977.
4	6. *Hot work.* a. Working in confined spaces wherein the employee is subjected to temperatures in excess of 43 degrees Selsius (110 degrees Fahrenheit).	Nov. 1, 1970.
	b. Working in confined spaces wherein the employee is subjected to temperatures in excess of 43 degrees Selsius (110 degrees Fahrenheit) where such exposure is not practically eliminated by the mechanical equipment or protective devices being used.	Mar. 13, 1977.
4	7. *Welding preheated metals.* Welding various metals or performing an integral part of the welding process when the employee must work in confined spaces in which large sections of metal have been preheated to 66 degrees Celsius (150 degrees Fahrenheit) or more, and the discomfort is not alleviated by protective devices or other means, or discomforting protective equipment must be worn.	Nov. 1, 1970.
4	8. *Micro-soldering or wire welding and assembly.* Working with binocular-type microscopes under conditions which severely restrict the movement of the employee and impose a strain on the eyes, in the soldering or wire welding and assembly of miniature electronic components..	Nov. 1, 1970.
25	9. *Exposure to hazardous weather or terrain.* Exposure to dangerous conditions of terrain, temperature and/or wind velocity, while working or traveling when such exposure introduces risk of significant injury or death to employees; such as the following:	July 1, 1972.
	Examples:	
	—Working on cliffs, narrow ledges, or steep mountainous slopes, with or without mechanical work equipment, where a loss of footing would result in serious injury or death.	
	—Working in areas where there is a danger of rockfalls or avalanches.	
	—Traveling in the secondary or unimproved roads to isolated mountaintop installations at night, or under adverse weather conditions (snow, rain, or fog) which limits visibility to less than 30 meters (100 feet), when there is danger of rock, mud, or snowslides	
	—Traveling in the wintertime, either on foot or by vehicle, over secondary or unimproved roads or snowtrails, in sparsely settled or isolated areas to isolated installations when there is danger of avalanches, or during "whiteout" phenomenon which limits visibility to less than 3 meters (10 feet)	
	—Working or traveling in sparsely settled or isolated areas with exposure to temperatures and/or wind velocity shown to be of considerable or very great danger on the windchill chart (Exhibit 1 of this appendix), and shelter (other than temporary shelter) or assistance is not readily available	
	—Snowplowing or snow and ice removal on primary, secondary or other class of roads, when (a) there is danger of avalanche or (b) there is danger of missing the road and falling down steep mountainous slopes, because of lack of snow-stakes, "whiteout" conditions, or sloping icepack covering the snow	
25	10. *Unshored work.* Working in excavation areas before the installation of proper shoring or other securing barriers, or in catastrophe areas, where there is a possibility of cave-in, building collapse or falling debris when such exposures introduce risk of significant injury or death to employees, such as the following:	July 1, 1972.
	Examples:	
	—Working adjacent to the walls of an unshored excavation at depths greater than 1.8 meters (6 feet) (except when the full depth of the excavation is in stable solid rock, hard slag, or hard shale, or the walls have been graded to the angle of repose; that is, where the danger of slides is practically eliminated), when work is performed at a distance from the wall which is less than the height of the wall	

PART I—PAYMENT FOR ACTUAL EXPOSURE—Continued

Differential rate (percent)	Category for which payable	Effective date
	—Working within or immediately adjacent to a building or structure which has been severely damaged by earthquake, fire, tornado or similar cause —Working underground in the construction and/or inspection of tunnels and shafts before the necessary lining of the passageway have been installed —Duty underground in abandoned mines where lining of tunnels or shafts is in a deteriorated condition	
15	11. *Ground work beneath hovering helicopter.* Participating in operation to attach or detach external load to helicopter hovering just overhead.	July 1, 1972.
15	12. *Hazardous boarding or leaving of surface craft.* Boarding or leaving vessels or transferring equipment to or from a surface craft under adverse conditions of foul weather, ice, or night when sea state is high (0.9 meter (3 feet) and above), and deck conditions and/or wind velocity in relation to the size of the craft introduce unusual risks to employees. *Examples:* —Boarding or leaving vessels at sea. —Boarding or leaving, or transferring equipment between small boats or rafts and steep, rocky, or coral-surrounded shorelines —Transferring equipment between a small boat and a rudimentary dock by improvised or temporary facility such as an unfastened plank leading from boat to dock —Boarding or leaving, or transferring equipment from or to ice covered floats, rafts, or similar structures when there is danger of capsizing due to the added weight of the ice	July 1, 1972.
8	13. *Cargo handling during lightering operations.* Off-lading of cargo and supplies from surface ships to Landing Craft-Medium (LCM) boats when swells or wave action are sufficiently severe as to cause sudden listing or pitching of the deck surface or shifting or falling of equipment, cargo, or supplies which could subject the employee to falls, crushing, ejection into the water or injury by swinging cargo hooks.	July 1, 1972.
15	14. *Duty aboard surface craft.* Duty aboard a surface craft when the deck conditions or sea state and wind velocity in relation to the size of the craft introduces the risk of significant injury or death to employees, such as the following:. Participating as a member of a water search and rescue team in adverse weather conditions when winds are blowing at 56 km/h (35 m.p.h.) (classified as gale winds) or in water search and rescue operations at night —Participating as a member of a weather projects team when work is performed under adverse weather conditions, when winds are blowing at 56 km/h (35 m.p.h.), and/ or when seas are in excess of 4.3 meters (14 feet), or when working on outside decks when decks are slick and icy when swells are in excess of 0.9 meter (3 feet) —When embarking, disembarking or traveling in small craft (boat) on Lake Ponchartrain when wind direction is from north northeast or northwest, and wind velocity is over 7.7 meters per second (15 knots); or when travel on Lake Ponchartrain is necessary in small craft, without radar equipment, due to emergency or unavoidable conditions and the trip is made in dense fog run procedures —Participating in deep research vessel sea duty wherein the team member is engaged in handling equipment on or over the side of the vessel when the sea state is high (6.2-meter-per-second (12-knot) winds and 0.9 meter (3-foot) waves) and the work is done on relatively unprotected deck areas —Transferring from a ship to another ship via a chair harness hanging from a highline between the ships when both vessels are under way —Duty performed on floating platforms, camels, or rafts, using tools equipment or materials associated with ship repair or construction activities, where swells or wave action are sufficiently severe to cause sudden listing or pitching of the deck surface or dislodgement of equipment which could subject the employee to falls, crushing, or ejection into the water	July 30, 1972.
50	15. *Work at extreme heights.* Working at heights 30 meters (100 feet) or more above the ground, deck, floor or roof, or from the bottom of a tank or pit on such open structures as towers, girders, smokestacks and similar structures: (1) If the footing is unsure or the structure is unstable; or (2) If safe scaffolding, enclosed ladders or other similar protective facilities are not adequate (for example, working from a swinging stage, boatswain chair, or a similar support); or (3) If adverse conditions such as darkness, steady rain, high wind, icing, lightning, or similar environmental factors render working at such height(s) hazardous	Oct. 22, 1972.
6	16. *Fibrous Glass Work.* Working with or in close proximity to fibrous glass material which results in exposure of the skin, eyes or respiratory system to irritating fibrous glass particles or slivers where exposure is not practically eliminated by the mechnical equipment or protective devices being used.	Feb. 28, 1975.
50	17. *High Voltage Electrical Energy.* Working on energized electrical lines rated at 4,160 volts or more which are suspended from utility poles or towers, when adverse weather conditions such as steady rain, high winds, icing, lightning, or similar environmental factors make the work unusually hazardous.	Apr. 11, 1977.

PART I—PAYMENT FOR ACTUAL EXPOSURE—Continued

Differential rate (percent)	Category for which payable	Effective date
6	18. *Welding, Cutting or Burning in Confined Spaces.* Welding, cutting, or burning within a confined space which necessitates working in a horizontal or nearly horizontal position, under conditions requiring egress of at least 4.3 meters (14 feet) over and through obstructions including: (1) access openings and baffles having dimensions which greatly restrict movements, and (2) irregular inner surfaces of the structure or structure components.	Jan. 18, 1978.

PART II—PAYMENT ON BASIS OF HOURS IN PAY STATUS

Differential rate (percent)	Category for which payable	Effective date
50	1. *Duty aboard submerged vessel.* Duty aboard a submarine or other vessel such as a deep-research vehicle while submerged..	Nov. 1, 1970.
8	2. *Explosives and incendiary material—high degree hazard.* Working with or in close proximity to explosives and incendiary material which involves potential personal injury such as permanent or temporary, partial or complete loss of sight or hearing, partial or complete loss of any or all extremities; other partial or total disabilities of equal severity; and/or loss of life resulting from work situations wherein protective devices and/or safety measures either do not exist or have been developed but have not practically eliminated the potential for such personal injury. Normally, such work situations would result in extensive property damage requiring complete replacement of equipment and rebuilding of the damaged area; and could result in personal injury to adjacent employees. *Examples* —Working with, or in close proximity to operations involved in research, in testing, manufacturing, inspection, renovation, maintenance and disposal, such as: —Screening, blending, drying, mixing, and pressing of sensitive explosives and pyrotechnic compositions such as lead azide, black powder and photoflash powder —Manufacture and distribution of raw nitroglycerine —Nitration, neutralization, crystallization, purification, screening and drying of high explosives —Manufacture of propellants, high explosives and incendiary materials —Melting, cast loading, pellet loading, drilling, and thread cleaning of high explosives —Manufacture of primary or initiating explosives such as lead azide —Manufacture of primer or detonator mix —Loading and assembling high-energy output flare pellets —All dry-house activities involving propellants or explosives —Demilitarization, modification, renovation, demolition, and maintenance operations on sensitive explosives and incendiary materials —All operations involving fire fighting on an artillery range or at an ammunition manufacturing plant or storage area, including heavy duty equipment operators, truck drivers, etc. —All operations involving regrading and cleaning of artillery ranges —At-sea shock and vibration tests. Arming explosive charges and/or working with, or in close proximity to, explosive-armed charges in connection with at-sea shock and vibration tests of naval vessels, machinery, equipment and supplies —Handling or engaging in destruction operations on an armed (or potentially armed) warhead	Nov. 1, 1970.
4	3. *Explosives and incendiary material—low degree hazard.* a. Working with or in close proximity to explosives and incendiary material which involves potential injury such as laceration of hands, face, or arms of the employee engaged in the operation and possible adjacent employees; minor irritation of the skin; minor burns and the like; minimal damage to immediate or adjacent work area or equipment being used.	Nov. 1, 1970.
	b. Working with or in close proximity to explosives and incendiary material which involves potential injury such as laceration of hands, face, or arms of the employee engaged in the operation and possible adjacent employees; minor irritation of the skin; minor burns and the like; minimal damage to immediate or adjacent work area or equipment being used and wherein protective device and/or safety measures have not practically eliminated the potential for such injury *Examples* —All operations involving loading, unloading, storage and hauling of explosive and incendiary ordnance material other than small arms ammunition. (Distribution of raw nitroglycerine is covered under high degree hazard—see category 2 above.) —Duties such as weighing, scooping, consolidating and crimping operations incident to the manufacture of stab, percussion, and low energy electric detonators (initiators) utilizing sensitive primary explosives compositions where initiation would be kept to a low order of propagation due to the limited amounts permitted to be present or handled during the operations —Load, assembly and packing of primers, fuses, propellant charges, lead cups, boosters, and time-train rings —Weighing, scooping, loading in bags and sewing of ignitor charges and propellant zone charges —Loading, assembly, and packing of hand-held signals, smoke signals, and colored marker signals	Mar. 13, 1977.

PART II—PAYMENT ON BASIS OF HOURS IN PAY STATUS—Continued

Differential rate (percent)	Category for which payable	Effective date
	—Proof-testing weapons with a known overload of powder or charges	
	—Arming/disarming or the installation/removal of any squib, explosive device, or component thereof, connected to or part of a solid propulsion system, including work situations involving removal, inspection, test and installation of aerospace vehicle egress and jettison systems and other cartridge actuated devices and rocket assisted systems or components thereof, when accidental or inadvertent operation of the system or a component might occur	
8	4. *Poisons (toxic chemicals)—high degree hazard.* Working with or in close proximity to poisons (toxic chemicals), other than tear gas or similar irritants, which involves potential serious personal injury such as permanent or temporary, partial or complete loss of faculties and/or loss of life including exposure of an unusual degree to toxic chemicals, dust, or fumes of equal toxicity generated in work situations by processes required to perform work assignments wherein protective devices and/or safety measures have been developed but have not practically eliminated the potential for such personal injury.	Nov. 1, 1970.
	Examples	
	—Handling and storing toxic chemical agents including monitoring of areas to detect presence of vapor or liquid chemical agents; examining of material for signs of leakage or deteriorated material; decontaminating equipment and work sites; work relating to disposal of deteriorated material (exposure to conjunctivitis, pulmonary edema, blood infection, impairment of the nervous system, possible death)	
	—Renovation, maintenance, and modification of toxic chemicals, guided missiles, and selected munitions	
	—Operating various types of chemical engineering equipment in a restricted area such as reactors, filters, stripping units, fractioning columns, blenders, mixers, pumps, and the like utilized in the development, manufacturing, and processing of toxic or experimental chemical warfare agents	
	—Demilitarizing and neutralizing toxic chemical munitions and chemical agents	
	—Handling or working with toxic chemicals in restricted areas during production operations	
	—Preparing analytical reagents, carrying out colorimetric and photometric techniques, injecting laboratory animals with compounds having toxic, incapacitating or other effects	
	—Recording analytical and biological tests results where subject to above types of exposure	
	—Visually examining chemical agents to determine conditions or detect leaks in storage containers	
	—Transferring chemical agents between containers	
	—Salvaging and disposing of chemical agents	
4	5. *Poisons (toxic chemicals)—low egress hazard.* a. Working with or in close proximity to poisons (toxic chemicals other than tear gas or similar irritating substances) in situations for which the nature of the work does not require the individual to be in as direct contact with, or exposure to, the more toxic agents as in the case with the work described under high hazard for this class of hazardous agents.	Nov. 1, 1970.
	b. Working with or in close proximity to poisons (toxic chemicals other than tear gas or similar irritating substances) in situations for which the nature of the work does not require the individual to be in as direct contact with, or exposure to, the more toxic agents as in the case with the work described under high hazard for this class of hazardous agents and wherein protective devices and/or safety measures have not practically eliminated the potential for personal injury	Mar. 13, 1977.
	Example	
	—Handling for shipping, marking, labeling, hauling and storing loaded containers of toxic chemical agents that have been monitored	
8	6. *Micro-organisms—high degree hazard.* Working with or in close proximity to micro-organisms which involves potential personal injury such as death, or temporary, partial, or complete loss of faculties or ability to work due to acute, prolonged, or chronic disease. These are work situations wherein the use of safety devices and equipment, medical prophylactic procedures such as vaccines and antiserims and other safety measures do not exist or have been developed but have not practically eliminated the potential for such personal injury.	Nov. 1, 1970.
	Examples	
	—Direct contact with primary containers of organisms pathogenic for man such as culture flasks, culture test tubes, hypodermic syringes and similar instruments, and biopsy and autopsy material. Operating or maintaining equipment in biological experimentation or production	
	—Cultivating virulent organisms on artificial media, including embryonated hen's eggs and tissue cultures where inoculation or harvesting of living organisms is involved for production of vaccines, toxides, etc., or for sources of material for research investigations such as antigenic analysis and chemical analysis	
4	7. *Micro-organisms—low degree hazard.* a. Working with or in close proximity to micro-organisms in situations for which the nature of the work does not require the individual to be in direct contact with primary containers of organisms pathogenic for man, such as culture flasks, culture test tubes, hypodermic syringes and similar instruments, and biopsy and autopsy material	Nov. 1, 1970.

PART II—PAYMENT ON BASIS OF HOURS IN PAY STATUS—Continued

Differential rate (percent)	Category for which payable	Effective date
	b. Working with or in close proximity to micro-organisms in situations for which the nature of the work does not require the individual to be in direct contact with primary containers of organisms pathogenic for man, such as culture flasks, culture test tubes, hypodermic syringes and similar instruments, and biopsy and autopsy material and wherein the use of safety devices and equipment and other safety measures have not practically eliminated the potential for personal injury	Mar. 13, 1977.
8	8. *Pressure chamber and centrifugal stress.* Exposure in pressure chamber which subjects employee to physical stresses or where there is potential danger to participants by reason of equipment failure or reaction to the test conditions; or exposure which subjects an employee to a high degree of centrifugal force which causes an unusual degree of discomfort	July 1, 1972.
	Examples	
	—Participating as a subject in diving research tests which seek to establish limits for safe pressure profiles by working in a pressure chamber simulating diving or, as an observer to the test or as a technician assembling underwater mock-up components for the test, when the observer or technician is exposed to high pressure gas piping systems, gas cylinders, and pumping devices which are susceptible to explosive ruptures	
	—Participating in altitude chamber studies ranging from 5500 to 45,700 meters (18,000 to 150,000 feet) either as subject or as observer exposed to the same conditions as the subject	
	—Participating as subject in centrifuge studies involving elevated G forces above the level of 49 meters per second^2 (5 G's) whether or not at reduced atmospheric pressure	
	—Participating as a subject in a rotational flight simulator in studies involving continuous rotation in one axis through 360° at rotation rates greater than 15 r.p.m. for periods exceeding three minutes	
8	9. *Work in fuel storage tanks.* When inspecting, cleaning or repairing fuel storage tanks where there is no ready access to an exit, under conditions requiring a breathing apparatus because all or part of the oxygen in the atmosphere has been displaced by toxic vapors or gas, and failure of the breathing apparatus would result in serious injury or death within the time required to leave the tank	July 1, 1972.
	10. *Firefighting.* Participating or assisting in firefighting operations on the immediate fire scene and in direct exposure to the hazards inherent in containing or extinguishing fires	July 1, 1972.
25	*High degree*	
	—Fighting forest and range fires on the fireline	
8	*Low degree*	
	—All other firefighting	
8	11. *Experimental landing/recovery equipment tests*	July 1, 1972.
	—Participating in tests of experimental or prototype landing and recovery equipment where personnel are required to serve as test subjects in spacecraft being dropped into the sea or laboratory tanks	
8	12. *Land impact or pad abort of space vehicle.* Actual participation in dearming and safing explosive ordnance, toxic propellant, and high-pressure vessels on vehicles that have land impacted or on vehicles on the launch pad that have reached a point in the countdown where no remote means are available for returning the vehicle to a safe condition	July 1, 1972.
4	13. *Mass explosives and/or incendiary material.* Working within a controlled danger area in, on, or around wharves, transfer areas, or temporary holding areas in a transshipment facility when explosives are in the process of being shifted to or from a conveyance	July 1, 1972.
	Such an area shall include land and sea areas within which it has been determined that personnel are subject to an unusual degree of exposure or liability to serious injury or death from potential explosive effect	
	A transshipment facility for this purpose is a port or sea terminal established for the marshalling or temporary assembly of explosives prior to shipment where amounts in excess of 113,400 kilograms (250,000 pounds) net explosive weight (NEW) are present on a regular or recurring basis	
4	14. *Duty aboard aircraft carrier.* Duty aboard an aircraft carrier when exposed to hazards connected with aircraft launch and recovery:	July 1, 1972.
	Examples	
	—Participating in carrier suitability trials aboard aircraft carriers when work is performed on the flight deck during launch, recovery and refueling operations	
	—Operating or monitoring camera equipment adjacent to flight deck in the area of maximum hazard during landing sequence while conducting photographic surveys aboard aircraft carriers during periods of heavy aircraft operations	Mar. 4, 1974.
8	15. *Participating in missile liquid propulsion or solid propulsion situations.* Participating in research and development, or preoperational test and evaluation situation involving missile liquid or solid propulsion systems where mechanical, or other equipment malfunction, or accidental combination of certain fuels and/or chemicals, or transient voltage and current buildup on or within the system when the system is in a "go" condition on the test stand, or sled, can result in explosion, fire, premature ignition or firing	
	Examples	
	—Test stand or track tests, when adequate protective devices and/or safety measures either do not exist or have been developed but have not practically eliminated the potential for personal injury, under any of the following conditions:	

PART II—PAYMENT ON BASIS OF HOURS IN PAY STATUS—Continued

Differential rate (percent)	Category for which payable	Effective date
	a. Tanks are being pressurized above normal servicing pressure b. Assembly, disassembly, or repair of contaminated plumbing containing inhibited red fuming nitric acid and unsymmetrical dimethylhydrazine or other hypergolic fuels is required c. Fueling and defeuling —Hoisting hypergolic liquid fueled systems into, or out of, a test stand, where the working area is confined, and external plumbing is present resulting in a situation where the plumbing may be damaged causing a leak —Tests on foreign missiles where technical data is questionable or not available —Manned test firings of small, close support missiles for which safety performance data are not yet available —Removal of a missile, propulsion system or component thereof from a test stand, fixture, or environmental chamber where there is reason to believe that the item may be unusually hazardous due to damage resulting from the test	
8	16. *Asbestos.* Working in an area where airborne concentrations of asbestos fibers may expose employees to potential illness or injury. This differential will be determined by applying occupational safety and health standards consistent with the permissible exposure limit promulgated by the Secretary of Labor under the Occupational Safety and Health Act of 1970 as published in title 29, Code of Federal Regulations, §§ 1910.1001 or 1926.1101. Regulatory changes in §§ 1910.1001 or 1926.1101 are hereby incorporated in and made a part of this category, effective on the first day of the first pay period beginning on or after the effective date of the changes.	Nov. 24, 2003.
8	17. *Working at high altitudes.* Performing work at a land-based work site more than 3900 meters (12,795 feet) in altitude, provided the employee is required to commute to the work site on the same day from a substantially lower altitude under circumstances in which the rapid change in altitude may result in acclimation problems	April 2, 1999.

EXHIBIT 1

WINDCHILL CHART IN METRIC UNITS

Wind Speed (KPH)	Local Temperature (OC)										
	0	-5	-10	-15	-20	-25	-30	-35	-40	-45	-50
Calm	0 C	-5	-10	-15	-20	-25	-30	-35	-40	-45	-50
8	-2	-7	-12	-17	-23	-28	-33	-38	-44	-49	-54
16	-8	-14	-20	-26	-32	-38	-44	-51	-57	-63	-69
24	-11	-18	-25	-32	-38	-45	-51	-58	-65	-72	-78
32	-14	-21	-28	-36	-42	-49	-57	-64	-71	-78	-85
40	-16	-23	-31	-39	-46	-53	-61	-68	-76	-83	-90
48	-17	-24	-33	-41	-48	-56	-63	-72	-78	-86	-94
56	-18	-26	-34	-42	-49	-57	-65	-73	-81	-88	-97
64	-19	-27	-35	-43	-51	-59	-66	-74	-82	-91	-98
72	-19	-28	-36	-43	-52	-59	-67	-76	-83	-91	-99
80	-20	-28	-36	-44	-52	-60	-68	-76	-84	-92	-100
	Little danger		Considerable danger			Very great danger					
	For properly clothed persons					Danger of freezing of exposed flesh					

WINDCHILL CHART IN NON-METRIC UNITS

Exhibit 1

WINDCHILL CHART

	Local temperature (°F)										
Wind Speed (MPH)	32	23	14	5	−4	−13	−22	−31	−40	−49	−58
Calm	32	23	14	5	−4	−13	−22	−31	−40	−49	−58
5	29	20	10	1	−9	−18	−28	−37	−47	−56	−65
10	18	7	−4	−15	−26	−37	−48	−59	−70	−81	−92
15	13	−1	−13	−25	−37	−49	−61	−73	−85	−97	−109
20	7	−6	−19	−32	−44	−57	−70	−83	−96	−109	−121
25	3	−10	−24	−37	−50	−64	−77	−90	−104	−117	−130
30	1	−13	−27	−41	−54	−68	−82	−97	−109	−123	−137
35	−1	−15	−29	−43	−57	−71	−85	−99	−113	−127	−142
40	−3	−17	−31	−45	−59	−74	−87	−102	−116	−131	−145
45	−3	−18	−32	−46	−61	−75	−89	−104	−118	−132	−147
50	−4	−18	−33	−47	−62	−76	−91	−105	−120	−134	−148
For properly clothed persons	Little danger		Considerable danger			Very great danger					
	Danger from freezing of exposed flesh										

[55 FR 46180, Nov. 1, 1990; 55 FR 52267, Dec. 21, 1990; 55 FR 53608, Dec. 31, 1990, as amended at 58 FR 32274, June 9, 1993; 64 FR 15916, Apr. 2, 1999; 70 FR 21613, Apr. 27, 2005; 71 FR 8922, Feb. 22, 2006]

Subpart F—Job Grading System

§ 532.601 General.

The Office of Personnel Management shall establish a job grading system in accordance with section 5346 of title 5, United States Code. Appropriate instructions to agencies on the application of the job grading system shall be published by the Office of Personnel Management. Agencies are required to grade all jobs subject to this part in accordance with such instructions.

Subpart G—Job Grading Reviews and Appeals

§ 532.701 General.

A prevailing rate employee may at any time appeal the occupational series, grade, or title to which the employee's job is assigned, but may not appeal under this subpart the standards established for the job, nor other matters such as the accuracy of the job description, the rate of pay, or the propriety of a wage schedule rate. The filing of a job-grading appeal does not negate any other appeal or grievance rights which may be available under applicable law, rule, regulation, or negotiated agreement.

[51 FR 18561, May 21, 1986]

§ 532.703 Agency review.

(a) Each agency shall establish a system processing an employee's application for review of the correctness of the series, grade or title of the employee's job.

NOTE: Application for review will be hereafter referred to as an "application".

(b) In establishing the system required by this subpart, an agency, as a minimum, shall provide that the following requisites be met.

(1) The provisions of the system shall be published and the agency's employees shall be informed where a published copy is available for review.

(2) An application shall be in writing and contain the reasons the employee believes the position is erroneously graded.

(3) An application may be filed at any time. However, when the application involves a downgrading or other job-grading action which resulted in a reduction in grade or loss or pay, in order to be entitled to retroactive corrective action, an employee must request a review under the provisions of this subpart within 15 calendar days of the effective date of the change to lower grade.

(4) An employee may select a representative, and the employee and the representative, when the representative is also employed by the same agency, shall be granted a reasonable time in presenting the application and shall be assured freedom from restraint, interference, coercion, or reprisal in presenting the application.

(5) An employee shall promptly furnish such facts as may be requested by the agency.

(6) An application shall be canceled and the employee so notified in the following circumstances:

(i) On receipt of a written request by the employee;

(ii) Failure of the employee to furnish required information or otherwise fail to proceed with the advancement of his application in a timely manner; however, instead of cancellation for failure by the employee to prosecute, the application may be adjudicated by the agency if the information is sufficient for that purpose; or

(iii) On notice that the employee has left the job, except when the employee would be entitled to the retroactive benefits including benefits allowable after the death of an employee appellant.

(7) The application shall be processed and decided promptly. No more than one level of review may be established within an agency before a final decision is issued, and that level of review, when possible, must be above the level of classification authority which classified the position.

(8) When an employee applies for a review of a downgrading or other job-grading action that resulted in a reduction of pay, and the decision of an agency reverses in whole or in part the downgrading or other job-grading action, the effective date of that decision shall be retroactive to the effective date of the action being reviewed when the initial application to the agency was submitted in accordance with paragraph (b)(3) of this section. However, when the agency decision raises the grade or level of the job above its grade or level immediately preceding the downgrading, retroactivity shall apply only to the extent of restoration to the grade or level immediately preceding the downgrading.

(9) The right to a retroactive effective date is preserved when an agency finds that an employee was not notified of the applicable time limit for review and was not otherwise aware of the limit or that circumstances beyond the employee's control prevented filing the application within the prescribed time limit.

(10) The effective date of a change in the series, title or grade of a job shall be specified in the agency decision and, unless otherwise required by this subpart, may not be earlier than the date of the decision. However, in no case may it be later than the beginning of the first pay period which begins after the 60th calendar day from the date the application was filed. However, when the agency decision will result in a downgrading or other job-grading action that will reduce the pay of the incumbent of the job, the effective date may not be set earlier than the date on which the decision can be effected in accordance with procedures required by applicable law and regulation. The retroactive reclassification may be based only on duties and responsibilities existing at the time of downgrading or loss of pay and not on duties and responsibilities later assigned.

(11) When an application has been properly filed and the employee dies before the application has been processed, if a favorable decision would entitle the employee to retroactive corrective action, the application will be

processed to completion after the employee's death and any appropriate corrective action made by amending the records of the agency.

(12) The decision on an application shall:

(i) Be based on the record,

(ii) Be in writing,

(iii) Inform the employee either in the decision or as an attachment to the decision of the reasons for the decision, including an analysis of the employee's job, *i.e.*, comparing the job with the appropriate standard, and

(iv) Inform the employee of the right to appeal the decision to the Office of Personnel Management and of the time limits within which the application must be filed.

(c) The agency is responsible for compiling and maintaining a job-grading review file which will constitute the record and which will not contain any document or information which the employee has not been given an opportunity to review.

[46 FR 21344, Apr. 10, 1981, as amended at 51 FR 18561, May 21, 1986]

§ 532.705 Appeal to the Office of Personnel Management.

(a)(1) An employee may appeal the occupation series, grade or title of the job to the appropriate office of the Office of Personnel Management only (i) after the agency has issued a decision under the system established under § 532.703; and (ii) if the employee files the appeal with the Office of Personnel Management within 15 calendar days after receipt of the decision of the agency.

(2) The Office of Personnel Management may extend this time limit if it is shown that the employee was not notified of the applicable time limit and was not otherwise aware of the limit, or that circumstances beyond the employee's control prevented filing an appeal within the prescribed time limit.

(b) An employee shall make the appeal in writing and shall identify specifically the portions of the decision or job analysis of the agency with which the employee disagrees.

(c) The Office of Personnel Management shall base its decision on the record established in the agency, except that when the Office of Personnel Management investigates or audits the job it may take the results of the investigation or audit into consideration. In the event the Office of Personnel Management audits the job, the employee's representative may not be present.

(d) The Office of Personnel Management shall notify the employee and the agency in writing of its decision. The effective date of a change in the series, title and grade of a job directed by the Office of Personnel Management shall be specified in the decision of the Office of Personnel Management, computed from the date the employee filed the application with the agency, and determined under § 532.703(b)(10). However, when the decision will result in a downgrading or other job-grading action that will reduce the pay of the incumbent of the job, the effective date may not be set earlier than the date on which the decision can be effected in accordance with procedures required by applicable law and regulation.

(e) The appeal of an employee shall be canceled and the employee so notified in the following circumstances:

(1) On receipt of the employee's written request;

(2) On failure to prosecute, when the employee does not furnish requested information and duly proceed with the advancement of the appeal; however, instead of cancellation for failure to prosecute, an appeal may be adjudicated if the information is sufficient for that purpose. The Office of Personnel Management may reopen a canceled appeal on a showing that circumstances beyond the control of the employee prevented the employee from prosecuting the appeal; or

(3) On notice that the employee has left the job, except when entitled to retroactive benefits, including benefits allowable after the death of an appellant.

(f) The Office of Personnel Management may, at its discretion, reopen and reconsider any job-grading decision made by the Office when requested by an employee or an agency. This authority may be used under circumstances such as the following:

(1) An employee or an agency presents material facts not previously considered by the Office;

(2) There is room for reasonable doubt as to the appropriateness of the decision; or

(3) The potential impact of a decision on similar jobs is sufficiently significant to make further review of the decision desirable.

(g) The Director of the Office of Personnel Management may, at his or her discretion, reopen and reconsider any previous decision when the party requesting reopening submits written argument or evidence which tends to establish that:

(1) New and material evidence is available that was not readily available when the previous decision was issued;

(2) The previous decision involves an erroneous interpretation of law or regulation or a misapplication of established policy; or

(3) The previous decision is of a precedential nature involving a new or unreviewed policy consideration that may have effects beyond the actual case at hand, or is otherwise of such an exceptional nature as to merit the personal attention of the Director of the Office of Personnel Management.

(h) A final decision by the Office of Personnel Management constitutes a certificate which is mandatory and binding on all administrative, certifying, payroll, disbursing, and accounting officials of the Government.

[46 FR 21344, Apr. 10, 1981, as amended at 51 FR 18561, May 21, 1986; 71 FR 37490, June 30, 2006]

§532.707 Availability of information.

(a) The Office, upon a request which identifies the individual from whose file the information is sought, shall disclose the following information from an appeal file to a member of the public, except when the disclosure would constitute a clearly unwarranted invasion of personal privacy:

(1) Confirmation of the name of the individual from whose file the information is sought and the names of the other parties concerned;

(2) The status of the appeal;

(3) The results of the appeal (*i.e.*, proper title, pay plan, series, and grade);

(4) The classification requested (*i.e.*, title, pay plan, series, and grade); and

(5) With the consent of the parties concerned, other reasonably identified information from the file.

(b) The Office will disclose to the parties concerned the information contained in an appeal file in proceedings under this part. For the purposes of this section, *the parties concerned* means the Government employee or former Government employee involved in the proceedings, his or her representative designated in writing, and the representative of the agency or the Office involved in the proceeding.

[50 FR 3313, Jan. 24, 1985]

Subpart H—Payment of Unrestricted Rates for Recruitment or Retention Purposes

§532.801 Payment of unrestricted rates for recruitment or retention purposes.

(a) When authorized by specific statutory authority providing for exceptions to pay limitations imposed by statute, the Office of Personnel Management (OPM) may approve exceptions to the pay limitations if OPM determines that such exceptions are necessary to ensure the recruitment or retention of qualified employees.

(b) Requests for payment of unrestricted rates under this subpart shall be submitted by employing agencies' headquarters to the appropriate lead agency. The lead agency shall coordinate each request with other agencies, as necessary, and submit a consolidated request to OPM. The consolidated request shall include any available supporting wage survey data and a formal recommendation by the lead agency to approve or disapprove the request.

(c) Rates authorized under paragraph (a) of this section shall be equal to the regular or special schedule unrestricted (uncapped) rates and may be authorized for use within all or part of a wage area for a designated occupation or occupational specialization and grade.

(d) In approving rates under this subpart, OPM shall consider the factors specified in §532.251(b) of this part.

(e) The unrestricted rates authorized under this subpart shall be shown on the appropriate regular or special schedule or as an amendment to the schedule and shall indicate the wage area (or part thereof) and each occupation or occupational specialization and grade for which the rates are authorized. These rates shall be paid by all agencies having such positions in the wage area (or part thereof) specified.

[57 FR 57876, Dec. 8, 1992]

PART 534—PAY UNDER OTHER SYSTEMS

AUTHORITY: 5 U.S.C. 1104, 3161(d), 5307, 5351, 5352, 5353, 5376, 5382, 5383, 5384, 5385, 5541, 5550a, sec. 1125 of the National Defense Authorization Act for FY 2004, Pub. L. 108–136, 117 Stat. 1638 (5 U.S.C. 5304, 5382, 5383, 7302; 18 U.S.C. 207); and sec. 2 of Pub. L. 110–372, 122 Stat. 4043 (5 U.S.C. 5304, 5307, 5376).

Subpart A [Reserved]

Subpart B—Student-Employees in Government Hospitals

SOURCE: 44 FR 54693, Sept. 21, 1979, unless otherwise noted.

§ 534.201 General.

Under subchapter V of chapter 53 of title 5, United States Code (U.S.C. 5351–5356), agencies may pay stipends and provide certain services to certain student-employees assigned or attached to hospitals, clinics, or medical or dental laboratories operated by agencies. Student-employees covered under the program are excluded from certain provisions of law relating to classification, General Schedule pay, premium pay, leave, and hours of duty. This subpart authorizes the coverage of certain positions under this program and establishes maximum stipends for student-employees in the program.

§ 534.202 Coverage.

In addition to the student-employees specified in 5 U.S.C. 5351(2)(A), the following student-employees are covered under this program, provided they are assigned or attached principally for training purposes to a hospital, clinic, or medical or dental laboratory operated by an agency:

(1) Any student-employee whom an agency finds is properly covered under this program, provided that the student-employee is a registered student at an accredited academic institution and that the assignment or attachment

for training purposes to the hospital, clinic, or medical or dental laboratory is a part of a medical or dental training program accredited by an appropriate accrediting body;

(2) Any student-employee whom an agency finds is properly covered under this program, provided that the student-employee, during the period of assignment or attachment to the hospital, clinic, or medical or dental laboratory, will receive experience or training that is required to obtain a certificate or license in a medical or dental field; or

(3) Any student-employee not otherwise covered under this program whom the Office of Personnel Management approves for coverage as a student-employee under this program.

[44 FR 54693, Sept. 21, 1979, as amended at 64 FR 68931, Dec. 9, 1999]

§ 534.203 Maximum stipends.

(a) Except as authorized under paragraph (b) or (c) of this section, stipends are to be set by the agency, subject to the maximum stipends prescribed in the following table:

MAXIMUM STIPENDS PRESCRIBED

Code symbol	Academic level of approved training program	Maximums by grade and step [1]
L-A	Below high school graduation	GS–1–1 (minus 3 steps).
L-1	First year college undergraduate	GS–2–1 (minus 3 steps).
L-2	Second year college undergraduate	GS–3–1 (minus 3 steps).
L-3	Third year college undergraduate	GS–3–3 (minus 3 steps).
L-4	Fourth year college undergraduate	GS–4–2 (minus 3 steps).
L-5	First year postgraduate predoctoral	GS–5–1 (minus 3 steps).
L-6	Second year postgraduate predoctoral	GS–7–1 (minus 3 steps).
L-6	Third year medical school	GS–7–1 (minus 3 steps).
L-7	Third year postgraduate predoctoral	GS–9–1 (minus 3 steps).
L-7	Fourth year medical school	GS–9–1 (minus 3 steps).
L-8	Fourth year postgraduate predoctoral	GS–10–1 (minus 3 steps).
L-8	Medical or dental internship	GS–10–1 (minus 3 steps).
L-9	Fifth year postgraduate w/o doctorate	GS–11–1 (minus 3 steps).
L-9	First year postgraduate (Ph. D.)	GS–11–1 (minus 3 steps).
L-9	First year medical or dental residency	GS–11–1 (minus 3 steps).
L-10	Second year postdoctoral (Ph. D.)	GS–12–1 (minus 3 steps).
L-10	Second year medical or dental residency	GS–12–1 (minus 3 steps).
L-11	Third year medical or dental residency	GS–12–4 (minus 3 steps).
L-12	Fourth year medical or dental residency	GS–13–1 (minus 3 steps).
L-13	Fifth year medical residency	GS–14–1 (minus 3 steps).

[1] The maximum money amount in each case is derived by subtracting from the statutory salary for the appropriate grade a sum equivalent to three step increments of that grade. This amount includes overtime pay, maintenance allowances, and other payments in money or kind.

(b) An agency may pay a student-employee a stipend in excess of the amount prescribed under paragraph (a) of this section only if the Office of Personnel Management has determined that a higher maximum stipend is warranted for the student-employee.

(c) Maximum stipends for positions in the Public Health Service in which duty requires intimate contact with persons afflicted with leprosy are increased above the rates prescribed in paragraph (a) of this section to the same extent that additional pay is provided by Public Health Service Regulations (42 CFR 22.1) for employees subject to the General Schedule (part 531 of this chapter).

(d) Overtime pay, maintenance allowances, and other payments in money or kind for a student-employee must be considered as part of the student-employee's stipend for the purposes of this section, and therefore, may not be used to cause the stipend to exceed the maximum stipend established under this section.

(e) A trainee at a non-Federal hospital, clinic, or medical or dental laboratory who is assigned to a Federal hospital, clinic, or medical or dental laboratory as an affiliate for a part of his or her training may not receive a stipend from the Federal agency other than any maintenance allowance that is provided.

§ 534.204 Previous authorizations.

The provisions of this subpart do not terminate any authorization approved by the Civil Service Commission or the Office of Personnel Management before February 15, 1979, and such authorizations remain in effect until modified or terminated by an agency or the Office of Personnel Management in accordance with the provisions of this subpart.

Subpart C—Basic Pay for Employees of Temporary Organizations

SOURCE: 67 FR 3582, Jan. 25, 2002, unless otherwise noted.

§ 534.301 Purpose.

This subpart provides rules for determining the rate of basic pay and locality-adjusted rate of basic pay for employees who are appointed to positions in temporary organizations and compensated under 5 U.S.C. 3161. Such temporary organizations are established by law or Executive order. This subpart does not provide authority to establish other forms of compensation and benefits not authorized by title 5, United States Code, or another specific statutory authority.

[67 FR 63049, Oct. 10, 2002]

§ 534.302 Coverage.

This subpart applies to employees in executive level and staff positions in temporary organizations. Such employees are not subject to the provisions applicable to General Schedule employees covered by chapter 51 and subchapter III of chapter 53 of title 5, United States Code.

[67 FR 63049, Oct. 10, 2002]

§ 534.303 Basic pay for executive level positions.

Rates of basic pay for executive level positions of temporary organizations may not exceed the rate for level III of the Executive Schedule.

[69 FR 70362, Dec. 6, 2004]

§ 534.304 Basic pay for staff positions.

(a)(1) Rates of basic pay for staff or other non-executive level positions of temporary organizations may not exceed the maximum rate of basic pay for grade GS–15 of the General Schedule under 5 U.S.C. 5332, excluding any locality-based comparability payment under 5 U.S.C. 5304.

(2) In establishing rates of basic pay for staff and other non-executive level positions of temporary organizations, the head of a temporary organization must give consideration to the significance, scope, and technical complexity of the position and the qualifications required for the work involved. The head of a temporary organization must also take into account the rates of pay applicable to Federal employees who have duties that are similar in terms of difficulty and responsibility.

(b) Employees in staff and other non-executive level positions of temporary organizations must be paid locality payments in addition to basic pay in the same manner as employees covered by 5 U.S.C. 5304. Locality-adjusted rates of basic pay may not exceed the locality-adjusted rate of basic pay for grade GS–15 of the General Schedule under 5 U.S.C. 5304, for the locality pay area involved (not to exceed the rate for level IV of the Executive Schedule).

(c) Notwithstanding the limitations in paragraphs (a) and (b) of this section, the rate of basic pay and locality-adjusted rate of basic pay for a senior staff position of a temporary organization may, in a case determined by the head of a temporary organization to be exceptional, exceed the maximum rates established under those paragraphs. However, the higher payable rates may not exceed the rate for level III of the Executive Schedule.

[67 FR 3582, Jan. 25, 2002, as amended at 67 FR 63050, Oct. 10, 2002; 69 FR 70362, Dec. 6, 2004]

§ 534.305 Pay periods and computation of pay.

(a) The requirements of 5 U.S.C. 5504, must be applied to employees of temporary organizations. This includes requirements for biweekly pay periods and requirements for converting an annual rate of basic pay to a basic hourly, daily, weekly, or biweekly rate.

(b) Employees of temporary organizations must receive basic pay on an hourly basis.

Subpart D—Pay and Performance Awards Under the Senior Executive Service

SOURCE: 54 FR 2987, Jan. 23, 1989, unless otherwise noted.

§ 534.401 Purpose.

This subpart contains the rules for setting and adjusting rates of basic pay and granting performance awards for members of the Senior Executive Service (SES), as provided by 5 U.S.C. 5382, 5383, and 5384. An agency must set and adjust the rate of basic pay for an SES member on the basis of the employee's performance and/or contribution to the agency's performance, as determined by the agency through the administration of its performance management system(s) for senior executives. These regulations must be read in combination with applicable statutes and with the regulations for the approval of an SES performance management system under 5 CFR part 430, subpart C, and certification of an SES performance appraisal system under 5 CFR part 430, subpart D.

[69 FR 70362, Dec. 6, 2004]

§ 534.402 Definitions.

In this subpart—

Agency means an executive agency or military department, as defined by 5 U.S.C. 105 and 102.

Authorized agency official means the head of an agency or an official who is authorized to act for the head of the agency in the matter concerned. The agency's Inspector General is the *authorized agency official* for senior executive positions in the Office of the Inspector General, consistent with the requirements in section 3(a) of the Inspector General Act of 1978.

Outstanding performance means performance that substantially exceeds the normally high performance expected of any senior executive, as evidenced by exceptional accomplishments or contributions to the agency's performance.

Performance expectations means the critical and other performance elements and performance requirements that constitute the senior executive performance plans (as defined in § 430.303).

PRB means Performance Review Board, as described in § 430.310.

Rate of basic pay means the rate of pay fixed by law or administrative action for the senior executive, within the established SES rate range or, in the case of a senior executive entitled to pay retention, the employee's retained rate of pay, excluding any applicable locality-based comparability payments under 5 U.S.C. 5304, but before any deductions and exclusive of additional pay of any other kind.

Relative performance means the performance of a senior executive with respect to the performance of other senior executives, including their contribution to agency performance, where appropriate, as determined by the application of a certified performance appraisal system under 5 CFR part 430, subpart D.

Senior executive means a member of the Senior Executive Service (SES) paid under 5 U.S.C. 5383.

SES rate means a rate of basic pay within the SES rate range assigned to a member of the SES under § 534.403(a).

SES rate range means the range of rates of basic pay established for the SES under 5 U.S.C. 5382 and § 534.403(a).

[69 FR 70362, Dec. 6, 2004]

§ 534.403 SES rate range.

(a) *SES rate range.* (1) On the first day of the first applicable pay period beginning on or after January 1, 2004, the minimum rate of basic pay of the SES rate range is set at an amount equal to the minimum rate of basic pay under 5 U.S.C. 5376 for senior-level positions (excluding any locality-based comparability payment under 5 U.S.C. 5304). The minimum rate of basic pay for the SES rate range will increase consistent with any increase in the minimum rate of basic pay for senior-level positions under 5 U.S.C. 5376. An SES member may not receive less than the minimum rate of the SES rate range. Except as provided in paragraph (a)(2) of this section, the maximum rate of basic pay of the SES rate range is set at the rate for level III of the Executive Schedule. An SES member's rate of basic pay must be set at one of the rates within the SES rate range based on the senior executive's performance and/or contribution to the agency's performance.

(2) The maximum rate of basic pay of the SES rate range is set at the rate for level II of the Executive Schedule for senior executives in an agency who are covered by a performance appraisal system that makes meaningful distinctions based on relative performance, as certified by the Office of Personnel Management (OPM), with concurrence by the Office of Management and Budget (OMB), under 5 U.S.C. 5307(d) and 5 CFR part 430, subpart D. A senior executive's rate of basic pay may not exceed the maximum rate of the applicable SES rate range, except as provided in § 534.404(h)(2). The applicable maximum rate of basic pay for the SES rate range will increase with any increase in the rate for levels II or III of the Executive Schedule under 5 U.S.C. 5318.

(3) Rates of basic pay higher than the rate for level III of the Executive Schedule but less than or equal to the rate for level II of the Executive Schedule generally are reserved for those senior executives who have demonstrated the highest levels of individual performance and/or made the greatest contributions to the agency's performance, as determined by the agency through the administration of its performance appraisal system for senior executives, or, in the case of newly-appointed senior executives, those who possess superior leadership or other competencies, consistent with the agency's strategic human capital plan.

(b) *Suspension of certification of performance appraisal system.* A senior executive whose rate of basic pay is higher than the rate for level III of the Executive Schedule may not suffer a reduction in pay because his or her agency's applicable performance appraisal system certification is suspended under 5 CFR 430.405(h). The senior executive will continue to receive his or her current SES rate and is not eligible for a pay adjustment until the senior executive is assigned to a position that would allow the employee to receive a pay adjustment or until certification of the employing agency's applicable performance appraisal system is reinstated under 5 CFR part 430, subpart D. The SES rate of pay is not considered a retained rate of pay for the purpose of applying 5 U.S.C. 3594 and 5 CFR part 359, subpart G, or 5 U.S.C. 5363 and 5 CFR part 536, subpart C.

[69 FR 70362, Dec. 6, 2004, as amended at 70 FR 31305, May 31, 2005]

§ 534.404 Setting and adjusting pay for senior executives.

(a) *Setting pay upon initial appointment to the SES.* An authorized agency official may set the rate of basic pay of an individual at any rate within the SES rate range upon initial appointment to the SES, subject to the limitation on the maximum rate of basic pay in § 534.403(a). Rates of basic pay above the rate for level III of the Executive Schedule but less than or equal to the rate for level II of the Executive Schedule generally are reserved for those newly appointed senior executives who possess superior leadership or other competencies, as determined by the agency as part of its strategic human capital plan. In setting a new senior executive's rate of basic pay, an agency must consider the nature and quality of the individual's experience, qualifications, and accomplishments as they relate to the requirements of the SES position, as well as the individual's current responsibilities.

(b) *Adjusting the pay of SES members.* (1) An authorized agency official may adjust (increase or reduce) the rate of basic pay of a senior executive consistent with the agency's plan for setting and adjusting SES rates of basic pay under paragraph (g) of this section.

(2) A senior executive who receives an annual summary rating of outstanding performance must be considered for an annual pay increase, subject to the limitation on the maximum rate of basic pay in § 534.403(a).

(3) An agency may provide a pay increase to allow a senior executive to advance his or her relative position within the SES rate range only upon a determination by the authorized agency official that the senior executive's individual performance and/or contributions to agency performance so warrant. In assessing a senior executive's performance and/or contribution

to the agency's performance, the authorized agency official may consider such things as unique skills, qualifications, or competencies that the individual possesses, and their significance to the agency's performance, as well as the senior executive's current responsibilities. Senior executives who demonstrate the highest levels of individual performance and/or make the greatest contributions to the agency's performance, as determined by the agency through the administration of its performance appraisal system, or, in the case of newly-appointed senior executives, those who possess superior leadership or other competencies, as determined by the agency as part of its strategic human capital plan, must receive the highest rates of basic pay or pay adjustments.

(4)(i) On the effective date of an increase in the minimum or maximum rate of basic pay of the SES rate range under § 534.403(a)(1) or (2), an authorized agency official may increase the rate of basic pay of a senior executive who meets or exceeds his or her performance expectations by an amount that does not exceed the amount necessary to maintain the senior executive's relative position in the SES rate range, except as provided in paragraph (b)(4)(ii) and (b)(4)(iii) of this section. A pay increase made under this paragraph is not considered a pay adjustment for the purpose of applying § 534.404(c).

(ii) A pay increase under paragraph (b)(4)(i) of this section may not be provided to a senior executive whose rate of basic pay is at or below the rate for level III of the Executive Schedule if such an increase would cause the senior executive's rate of basic pay to exceed the rate for level III of the Executive Schedule unless the senior executive has received an annual summary rating of outstanding for the most recently completed appraisal period and the agency head or designee who performs the functions described in 5 CFR 430.404(a)(5) or (6) (including the Inspector General, where applicable) has approved the increase in pay.

(iii) A pay increase under paragraph (b)(4)(i) of this section may not be provided to a senior executive whose rate of basic pay is above the rate for level III of the Executive Schedule unless the senior executive has received an annual summary rating of outstanding for the most recently completed appraisal period and the agency head or designee who performs the functions described in 5 CFR 430.404(a)(5) or (6) (including the Inspector General, where applicable) has approved the increase in pay. However, in the case of a senior executive whose rate of basic pay is above the rate for level III of the Executive Schedule and who has been rated below outstanding, but above fully successful, for the most recently completed appraisal period, the agency head or designee who performs the functions described in 5 CFR 430.404(a)(5) or (6) (including the Inspector General, where applicable) may approve such a pay increase in limited circumstances, such as for an exceptionally meritorious accomplishment.

(5) A senior executive who receives a summary rating of less than fully successful may not receive an increase in pay for the current appraisal period.

(6) An authorized agency official may reduce the rate of basic pay of a senior executive for performance and/or disciplinary reasons, consistent with the restrictions on reducing the rate of basic pay of a career senior executive in paragraph (j) of this section and in § 534.406(b).

(c) *12-month rule.* (1) An authorized agency official may adjust (*i.e.*, increase or reduce) the rate of basic pay of a senior executive not more than once during any 12-month period. However, an agency may make a determination to provide an additional pay increase under certain conditions as prescribed in paragraph (c)(3) and (4) of this section without regard to whether the senior executive has received a pay adjustment during the previous 12-month period.

(2) The following pay actions are considered pay adjustments for the purpose of applying this paragraph:

(i) The setting of an individual's rate of basic pay upon initial appointment or reappointment to the SES under paragraphs (a) and (i)(1) of this section and upon reinstatement to the SES under paragraph (i)(2)(ii) of this section; and

(ii) Any adjustment (increase or reduction) in an SES rate of basic pay granted to a senior executive, except as provided in paragraph (c)(3) of this section.

(3) The following pay actions are not considered pay adjustments for the purpose of applying this paragraph:

(i) The conversion of senior executives to the new SES pay system under § 534.406 and the conversion of other employees to equivalent senior executive positions;

(ii) A determination by an authorized agency official to make a zero adjustment in pay after reviewing a senior executive's annual summary rating;

(iii) A zero adjustment in pay made during the 12-month period preceding the first day of the first applicable pay period beginning on or after January 1, 2004, caused by the former limitation on basic pay plus locality-based comparability payments under 5 U.S.C. 5304(g)(2) for a senior executive who was granted an increase in his or her rate of basic pay that did not result in an actual increase in pay;

(iv) A determination to provide an additional pay increase under paragraph (f) of this section when there is an increase in Executive Schedule rates of pay;

(v) [Reserved]

(vi) A determination to provide a pay increase under paragraph (b)(4) of this section to allow a senior executive to maintain his or her relative position in the SES rate range; and

(vii) An increase in pay equivalent to the minimum amount necessary to ensure that a senior executive's rate of basic pay does not fall below the minimum rate of the SES rate range.

(4) An authorized agency official may approve increases in a senior executive's rate of basic pay more than once during a 12-month period if the agency head or designee who performs the functions described in 5 CFR 430.404(a)(5) or (6) (including the Inspector General, where applicable) determines that—

(i) The senior executive's exceptionally meritorious accomplishment significantly contributes to the agency's performance;

(ii) A pay increase is necessary to reassign a senior executive to a position with substantially greater scope and responsibility or to recruit a senior executive with superior leadership or other competencies from a position in another agency;

(iii) The retention of the senior executive is critical to the mission of the agency and the senior executive would be likely to leave the agency in the absence of a pay increase; or

(iv) Such action conforms to an otherwise applicable executive appraisal and pay adjustment cycle (e.g., in the case of a senior executive who was appointed to an SES position within the past 12 months or a senior executive who was transferred to an SES position from an agency with a different senior executive appraisal and pay adjustment cycle within the past 12 months).

(5) An authorized agency official must provide written documentation approving an exception under paragraph (c)(4) of this section. Any pay adjustment made as a result of a determination under paragraph (c)(4) of this section is considered a pay adjustment for the purpose of applying § 534.404(c) and begins a new 12-month period.

(d) *Adjustments in pay prior to certification of applicable performance appraisal system.* An authorized agency official may adjust a senior executive's rate of basic pay converted under § 534.406 on the first day of the first applicable pay period beginning on or after January 1, 2004, or on any date thereafter prior to obtaining certification under 5 CFR part 430, subpart D, but only up to the rate for level III of the Executive Schedule. The authorized agency official may provide an increase in pay if warranted under the conditions prescribed in paragraph (b) of this section and the senior executive is otherwise eligible for such an increase (*i.e.*, he or she did not receive a pay adjustment under § 534.404(c) during the previous 12-month period). An adjustment in pay made under this paragraph is considered a pay adjustment for the purpose of applying § 534.404(c).

(e) *Adjustments in pay after certification of applicable performance appraisal system.* (1) In the case of an agency that obtains certification of a performance appraisal system for senior executives under 5 CFR part 430, subpart D, an authorized agency official may increase a covered senior executive's rate of basic pay up to the rate for level II of the Executive Schedule, consistent with the limitations in § 534.403(a)(3). The authorized agency official may provide an increase in pay if warranted under the conditions prescribed in paragraph (b) of this section and if the senior executive is otherwise eligible for such an increase (*i.e.*, he or she did not receive a pay adjustment under § 534.404(c) during the previous 12-month period). An adjustment in pay made under this paragraph is considered a pay adjustment for the purpose of applying § 534.404(c).

(2) [Reserved]

(f) *Effect of increase in Executive Schedule rates of pay.* (1) If there is an additional increase in the rates for the Executive Schedule in a calendar year, and if that increase becomes effective on the first day of the first pay period beginning on or after January 1 (*i.e.*, the date prescribed in 5 U.S.C. 5318), an agency may review any previous determination to adjust the pay of a senior executive that was made effective on or after the effective date of the first increase in the rates for the Executive Schedule to determine whether, and to what extent, an additional pay increase may be warranted for senior executives based on the same criteria used for the previous determination. If the agency determines that an additional pay increase is warranted, that increase must be made effective as of the effective date of the previous pay increase and is not considered a pay adjustment for the purpose of applying § 534.404(c).

(2) If there is an increase in the rates of pay for the Executive Schedule under 5 U.S.C. 5318 after an agency has already granted pay increases to its senior executives following the applicable performance appraisal period, an agency may review any previous determination to increase the pay of a senior executive whose rate of basic pay is equivalent to the rate for level II (if covered under a performance appraisal system that is certified) or level III (if covered under a performance appraisal system that is not certified) when the applicable maximum rate is increased to determine whether, and to what extent, an additional pay increase may be warranted for the senior executive based on the same criteria used for the previous determination. The determination to provide an additional pay increase must be approved and made effective as of the effective date of increases in the Executive Schedule under 5 U.S.C. 5318 (*i.e.*, the first day of the first pay period beginning on or after January 1). An additional pay increase under this paragraph is not considered a pay adjustment for the purpose of applying § 534.404(c).

(g) *Agency plan for setting and adjusting SES rate of basic pay.* Each agency must establish a plan for setting and adjusting the rates of basic pay for SES members. Agencies must provide for transparency in the processes for making pay decisions, while assuring confidentiality. In developing its plan for setting and adjusting SES rates, an agency may consider the senior executive's broad scope of authority and level of responsibility and his or her personal accountability for the success (or failure) of an agency's programs. The agency's plan must require that any decisions to adjust pay must reflect meaningful distinctions among senior executives based on individual performance and/or contribution to agency performance and must include—

(1) The criteria that will be used to set and adjust a senior executive's rate of basic pay to ensure that individual pay rates or pay adjustments, as well as their overall distribution within the SES rate range, reflect meaningful distinctions within a single performance rating level (e.g., the higher the employee's relative performance within a rating level, the higher the pay adjustment) and/or between performance rating levels (e.g., the higher the rating level, the higher the pay adjustment);

(2) The criteria that will be used to set and adjust a senior executive's rate of basic pay at a rate that exceeds the rate for level III of the Executive Schedule if the applicable agency performance appraisal system has been certified under 5 CFR part 430, subpart D;

(3) The designation of the authorized agency official who has authority to set and adjust SES rates of pay for individual senior executives, subject to

the requirement that the agency head or designee who performs the functions described in 5 CFR 430.404(a)(5) and (6) (including the Inspector General, where applicable) must approve any determination to set a senior executive's rate of basic pay higher than the rate for level III of the Executive Schedule and must approve any determination to increase a senior executive's rate of basic pay more than once in any 12-month period; and

(4) The administrative and management controls that will be applied to ensure compliance with applicable statutes, OPM's regulations, the agency's plan, and, where applicable, the certification requirements set forth in 5 CFR 430, subpart D, and the limitation on the maximum rate of basic pay in § 534.403(a).

(h) *Setting pay upon transfer.* (1) An authorized agency official may set the pay of a senior executive transferring from another agency at any rate within the SES rate range, subject to the limitation on the maximum rate of basic pay in § 534.403(a) and the restrictions on reducing the pay of career senior executives in paragraph (h)(2) of this section (upon transfer to an agency whose applicable performance appraisal system is not certified) and in § 534.406(b) (for 12 months following the effective date of the new SES pay system). If pay is set at the same SES rate the senior executive received in his or her former agency, the action is not considered a pay adjustment for the purpose of applying § 534.404(c).

(2) A senior executive whose rate of basic pay is higher than the rate for level III of the Executive Schedule may not suffer a reduction in pay as a result of transferring to an agency where the maximum rate of basic pay for the applicable SES rate range is equal to the rate for level III of the Executive Schedule. The senior executive will continue to receive his or her current SES rate and is not eligible for a pay adjustment until the senior executive is assigned to a position that would allow the employee to receive a pay adjustment or the employing agency's applicable performance appraisal system is certified under 5 CFR part 430, subpart D. The SES rate of pay is not considered a retained rate of pay for the purpose of applying 5 U.S.C. 3594 and 5 CFR part 359, subpart G, or 5 U.S.C. 5363 and 5 CFR part 536, subpart C.

(i) *Setting pay following a break in SES service*—(1) *General.* Upon reappointment to the SES, an authorized agency official may set the rate of basic pay of a former senior executive at any rate within the SES rate range, subject to the limitations in § 534.403(a), if there has been a break in SES service of more than 30 days. If there has been a break in SES service of 30 days or less, the senior executive's rate of basic pay may be set at any rate within the SES rate range (without regard to whether the employee received a pay adjustment during the previous 12-month period), but not higher than the senior executive's former SES rate of basic pay. Where there has been a break in service of 30 days or less, the agency head or designee who performs the functions described in 5 CFR 430.404(a)(5) and (6) (including the Inspector General, where applicable) may approve a higher rate than the senior executive's former rate of basic pay, if warranted. Setting a rate of basic pay upon reappointment to the SES is considered a pay adjustment under § 534.404(c).

(2) *Reinstatement from a Presidential appointment requiring Senate confirmation.* The following provisions apply to a former career senior executive who is reinstated under 5 CFR 317.703:

(i) If the individual elected to remain subject to the SES pay provisions while serving under a Presidential appointment, his or her SES rate may be adjusted upon reinstatement to the SES, whether in the agency where the individual held the Presidential appointment or in another agency, if at least 12 months have elapsed since the employee's last SES pay adjustment. If fewer than 12 months have elapsed since the employee's last SES pay adjustment, an authorized agency official may approve an additional pay increase under § 534.404(c)(4) if the additional pay increase is warranted. Any pay adjustment must be made in accordance with paragraphs (b), (d), and (e) of this section and the agency's plan for adjusting SES rates of pay in paragraph (g) of this section.

(ii) If the individual did not elect to remain subject to the SES pay provisions while serving under a Presidential appointment, his or her SES rate may be set upon reinstatement to the SES at any rate within the SES rate range, subject to the limitations in § 534.403(a).

(iii) Setting a rate of basic pay upon reinstatement to the SES under paragraphs (i)(2)(i) and (ii) of this section is considered a pay adjustment for the purpose of applying § 534.404(c).

(j) *Restrictions on reducing the pay of career senior executives.* (1) An authorized agency official may reduce a career senior executive's SES rate of basic pay by not more than 10 percent for performance or disciplinary reasons, subject to the restriction on reducing the pay of career senior executives in § 534.406(b) or setting pay below the minimum rate of the SES rate range in § 534.403(a).

(2) The SES rate of basic pay of a career senior executive may be reduced without the employee's consent by the senior executive's agency or upon transfer of function to another agency only—

(i) If the senior executive has received a less than fully successful annual summary rating under 5 CFR part 430, subpart C, or has otherwise failed to meet the performance requirements for a critical element as defined in 5 CFR 430.303; or

(ii) As a disciplinary or adverse action resulting from conduct-related activity, including, but not limited to, misconduct, neglect of duty, or malfeasance.

(3) Prior to reducing a career senior executive's rate of basic pay, the agency must provide the senior executive with the following:

(i) Written notice of such reduction at least 15 days in advance of its effective date;

(ii) A reasonable period of time, but not less than 7 days, for the senior executive to respond to such notice orally and/or in writing and to furnish affidavits and other documentary evidence in support of that response;

(iii) An opportunity to be represented in the matter by an attorney or other representative;

(iv) A written decision and specific reasons for the pay reduction at the earliest practicable date after the senior executive's response, if any; and

(v) An opportunity to request, within 7 days after the date of that decision, reconsideration by the head of the agency, whose determination with respect to that request will be final and not subject to further review.

(4) Reductions in pay under paragraph (j) of this section are not appealable under 5 U.S.C. 7543.

[69 FR 70363, Dec. 6, 2004, as amended at 70 FR 31305, May 31, 2005; 71 FR 38754, July 10, 2006; 79 FR 12357, Mar. 5, 2014]

§ 534.405 Performance awards.

(a) This section covers the payment of performance awards to career appointees in the Senior Executive Service (SES).

(1) To be eligible for an award, the individual must have been an SES career appointee as of the end of the performance appraisal period; and the individual's most recent performance rating of record under part 430, subpart C, of this chapter for the appraisal period must have been "Fully Successful" or higher.

(2) Individuals eligible for a performance award include:

(i) A former SES career appointee who elected to retain award eligibility under 5 CFR part 317, subpart H. If the rate of basic pay of the individual is higher than the maximum rate of basic pay for the applicable SES rate range, the maximum rate of that SES rate range is used for crediting the agency award pool under paragraph (b) of this section and the amount the individual may receive under paragraph (c) of this section.

(ii) A reemployed annuitant with an SES career appointment.

(iii) An SES career appointee who is on detail. If the detail is to another agency, eligibility is in the individual's official employing agency, *i.e.*, the agency from which detailed. If the appointee is on a reimbursable detail, the agency to which the appointee is detailed may reimburse the employing agency for some or all of any award, as agreed upon by the two agencies; but the reimbursement does not affect the award pool for either agency as calculated under paragraph (b) or this section.

(3) When making recommendations on performance awards, more than one-half of the membership of a Performance Review Board must be career SES appointees. The only exception is if OPM has determined under § 430.307(d) of this chapter that the Board does not have to have a majority of career members when making recommendations on performance appraisals of career appointees because there exists an insufficient number of career appointees.

(4) The agency head must consider the recommendations of the Performance Review Board (PRB), but the agency head has the final authority as to who is to receive a performance award and the amount of the award.

(b)(1) The total amount of performance awards paid during a fiscal year by an agency may not exceed the greater of—

(i) Ten percent of the aggregate career SES rates of basic pay for the agency as of the end of the fiscal year prior to the fiscal year in which the award payments are made; or

(ii) Twenty percent of the average annual rates of basic pay for career SES appointees of the agency as of the end of the fiscal year prior to the fiscal year in which the award payments are made.

(2) In determining the aggregate career SES rates of basic pay and the average annual rate of basic pay as of the end of FY 2003 for the purpose of applying paragraph (b) of this section, agencies must use the annual rate of basic pay, plus any applicable locality-based comparability payment under 5 U.S.C. 5304 or special geographic pay adjustment established for law enforcement officers under section 404(a) of the Federal Employees Pay Comparability Act of 1990 (Pub. L. 101–509), which the SES appointees were receiving at the end of FY 2003.

(c) The amount of a performance award paid to an individual career appointee may not be less than 5 percent nor more than 20 percent of the appointee's SES rate of basic pay as of the end of the performance appraisal period.

(d) OPM shall issue guidance concerning the distribution of performance awards within an agency.

(e) Agencies shall submit their distribution of performance awards, the total amount of awards, and the aggregate payroll or average rate of basic pay as computed under paragraph (b) of this section to OPM no later than 14 days after the date the performance awards are approved by the agency. If OPM determines that an agency's payments do not meet the requirements of law or regulations, the agency shall take any corrective action directed by OPM.

(f) Performance awards must be paid in a lump sum except in those instances when it is not possible to pay the full amount because of the applicable aggregate limitation on pay during a calendar year under 5 CFR part 530, subpart B. In that case, any amount in excess of the applicable aggregate limitation must be paid at the beginning of the following calendar year in accordance with 5 CFR part 530, subpart B. The full performance award, however, is charged against the agency bonus pool under § 534.405(b) for the fiscal year in which the initial payment was made.

[52 FR 2, Jan. 2, 1987, as amended at 55 FR 1353, Jan. 16, 1990; 57 FR 10125, Mar. 24, 1992; 60 FR 6389, Feb. 2, 1995; 64 FR 72889, Dec. 29, 1999; 69 FR 2051, Jan. 13, 2004. Redesignated and amended at 69 FR 70362, 70366, Dec. 6, 2004]

§ 534.406 Conversion to the SES pay system.

(a) On the first day of the first applicable pay period beginning on or after January 1, 2004, agencies must convert an existing SES rate of basic pay for a senior executive to an SES rate of basic pay that is equal to the employee's rate of basic pay, plus any applicable locality-based comparability payment under 5 U.S.C. 5304 which the senior executive was receiving immediately before that date, except as provided in paragraph (b) of this section. The newly converted rate is the senior executive's SES rate of basic pay. An agency's establishment of an SES rate of basic pay for a senior executive under this paragraph is not considered a pay adjustment for the purpose of applying §534.404(c).

(b) An SES member's rate of basic pay, plus any applicable locality-based comparability payment under 5 U.S.C. 5304 to which the employee was entitled on November 24, 2003, may not be reduced for 1 year after the first day of the first applicable pay period beginning on or after January 1, 2004. If an SES member's rate of basic pay, plus any applicable locality-based comparability payment under 5 U.S.C. 5304 to which the employee was entitled on November 23, 2003, is higher than the rate in effect immediately prior to the first day of the first applicable pay period beginning on or after January 1, 2004, the agency must use the higher rate for the purpose of converting SES members to the SES pay system.

(c) An SES member who is assigned to a position outside the 48 contiguous States and the District of Columbia to a position overseas or in Alaska, Hawaii, Guam or the Commonwealth of the Northern Mariana Islands, Puerto Rico, the U.S. Virgin Islands, or other U.S. territories and possessions as of the first day of the first applicable pay period beginning on or after January 1, 2004, will be converted to a new rate of basic pay that equals the senior executive's current rate of basic pay, plus the amount of locality pay authorized under 5 U.S.C. 5304 for the applicable locality pay area upon the employee's initial reassignment to a position in the 48 contiguous States or the District of Columbia. The adjustment will be prospective, not retroactive, and it will not be considered a pay adjustment for the purpose of applying §534.404(c). If the senior executive's rate of basic pay did not exceed the rate for level III of the Executive Schedule while assigned to a position outside the 48 contiguous States or the District of Columbia, upon initial reassignment to a locality pay area the senior executive's converted rate of basic pay may not exceed the rate for level III of the Executive Schedule. The newly converted rate is the senior executive's SES rate of basic pay.

(d) On the first day of the first applicable pay period beginning on or after January 1, 2004, a law enforcement officer (LEO), as defined in 5 CFR 531.301, who is a member of the SES will have his or her rate of basic pay, plus any applicable special geographic pay adjustment established for LEOs under section 404(a) of the Federal Employees Pay Comparability Act of 1990 (Pub. L. 101–509) to which he or she was entitled immediately before that date, converted to a new SES rate of basic pay. The newly converted rate is the senior executive's SES rate of basic pay, and any pay adjustments approved on or after January 11, 2004, must be computed based on the senior executive's converted rate of basic pay. Conversion to a new SES rate of basic pay is not considered a pay adjustment for the purpose of applying §534.404(c).

[69 FR 70366, Dec. 6, 2004]

§534.407 Pay computation and aggregate compensation.

(a) Except as provided in paragraph (b) of this section, pay for members of the SES must be computed in accordance with 5 U.S.C. 5504(b).

(b) To determine the hourly rate of pay for members of the SES, divide the annual SES rate of basic pay by 2,087 and round to the nearest cent, counting one-half cent and over as a whole cent. To derive the biweekly rate, multiply the hourly rate by 80.

(c) Senior executives are subject to the applicable aggregate limitation on pay in 5 CFR part 530, subpart B.

[69 FR 70367, Dec. 6, 2004]

§534.408 Restrictions on premium pay and compensatory time.

(a) Under 5 U.S.C. 5541(2)(xvi) and 5 CFR 550.101(b)(18), members of the Senior Executive Service (SES) are excluded from premium pay, including overtime pay.

(b) Since SES members are not eligible for overtime pay, they also are not eligible for compensatory time in lieu of overtime pay for work performed as an SES member. SES members are eligible, however, for compensatory time off for religious purposes under 5 U.S.C. 5550a and 5 CFR part 550, subpart J.

[60 FR 6390, Feb. 2, 1995. Redesignated and amended at 69 FR 70362, 70367, Dec. 6, 2004]

Subpart E—Pay for Senior-Level and Scientific or Professional Positions

SOURCE: 79 FR 12357, Mar. 5, 2014, unless otherwise noted.

§ 534.501 Purpose.

This subpart provides rules for setting and adjusting rates of basic pay for senior-level (SL) and scientific or professional (ST) employees under 5 U.S.C. 5376. Section 5376, as amended by section 2 of the Senior Professional Performance Act of 2008 (Pub. L. 110–372, October 8, 2008), promotes performance-based pay by enabling an agency that attains certification of a performance appraisal system covering senior professionals to fix rates of basic pay for those employees up to the rate payable for level II of the Executive Schedule. Under 5 U.S.C. 5307(d) and subpart D of part 430 of this chapter, the Office of Personnel Management (OPM), with Office of Management and Budget (OMB) concurrence, grants certification only to a performance appraisal system that, in its design and application, makes meaningful distinctions based upon relative performance. This subpart implements the purpose of the law by providing for pay determinations for SL and ST employees to be based on individual performance, contributions to the agency's performance, or both, as determined through administration of the agency's performance management system(s) for SL and ST employees.

§ 534.502 Coverage.

(a) This subpart implements 5 U.S.C. 5376 and applies to—

(1) Senior-level (SL) positions classified above GS–15 pursuant to 5 U.S.C. 5108; and

(2) Scientific or professional (ST) positions established under 5 U.S.C. 3104.

(b) This subpart does not apply to—

(1) Senior Executive Service positions established under 5 U.S.C. 3132, unless the incumbent of the position declined to convert to the SES and, under § 317.303 of this chapter, remained at grade GS–16, 17, or 18 (now the SL pay system) or under the ST pay system;

(2) Positions in the Federal Bureau of Investigation and Drug Enforcement Administration Senior Executive Service, Defense Intelligence Executive Service, or Senior Cryptologic Executive Service; or

(3) Positions for which pay is fixed by administrative action and is limited to level IV of the Executive Schedule under 5 U.S.C. 5373.

§ 534.503 Definitions.

In this subpart—

Agency means—

(1) An Executive agency as defined in 5 U.S.C. 105;

(2) The Library of Congress; and

(3) Any other entity that is not part of an Executive agency, for which OPM has approved establishment of one or more scientific or professional positions under 5 U.S.C. 3104.

Authorized agency official means the head of an agency or an official who is authorized to act for the head of the agency in the matter concerned.

Certified means having the certification that OPM, with OMB concurrence, grants under 5 U.S.C. 5307(d) and part 430, subpart D of this chapter only to a performance appraisal system that makes, in its design and application, meaningful distinctions based on relative performance. In this subpart, the term "certified" refers to a performance appraisal system that has this certification, including a performance appraisal system for which certification has been reinstated after suspension under § 430.405(h) of this chapter.

Movement means a change of an SL or ST employee from one SL or ST position to a different SL or ST position without a break in service under procedures that meet applicable requirements for staffing positions in the competitive service and excepted service. As used in this subpart, the term "movement" applies only to an appointment, not a detail, and is used without reference to the pay consequences of an action. Unless otherwise specified, the term refers to position changes both within and between agencies.

Not certified means lacking the certification that OPM, with OMB concurrence, grants under 5 U.S.C. 5307(d) and part 430, subpart D of this chapter only to a performance appraisal system that makes, in its design and application, meaningful distinctions based on relative performance. In this subpart, the term "not certified" refers to a performance appraisal system that does not have this certification, or for which a previously granted certification has expired or is suspended under §430.405(h) of this chapter.

Off-cycle pay increase means any increase in a senior professional's rate of basic pay that becomes effective on a date other than the date specified in §534.507(a)(1).

OMB means the Office of Management and Budget.

OPM means the Office of Personnel Management.

Performance appraisal system means the policies, practices, and procedures an agency establishes under 5 U.S.C. chapter 43 and 5 CFR part 430, subpart B, or other applicable legal authority, for planning, monitoring, developing, evaluating, and rewarding employee performance. For a senior professional employee, this term refers to appraisal programs or appraisal systems as defined in §430.203 of this chapter.

Performance management system means the framework of policies and practices that an agency uses to implement performance management, as described in §430.102 of this chapter. As used in this subpart, the term includes, but is not limited to, those disciplines and activities by which an agency addresses the criteria identified in §430.404(a)(1) through (9) of this chapter.

Performance rating means the written, or otherwise recorded, appraisal of performance compared to the SL or ST employee's performance standard(s) for each critical and non-critical element on which there has been an opportunity to perform for a minimum of 90 days. A performance rating may include the assignment of a summary level within a pattern as specified in §430.208(d) of this chapter.

Rate of basic pay means the rate of pay fixed by law or administrative action for an SL or ST employee under the provisions of 5 U.S.C. 5376 and this subpart before any deductions and exclusive of additional pay of any other kind.

Rating of record means the performance rating prepared at the end of an appraisal period for performance of agency-assigned duties over the entire period and the assignment of a summary level within a pattern as specified in §430.208(d) of this chapter that has been reviewed and approved in accordance with §534.505(a).

Scientific or professional (ST) employee means an individual appointed to a position described in §319.103 and authorized by OPM under §319.202 of this chapter or otherwise established under 5 U.S.C. 3104.

Senior-level (SL) employee means an individual appointed to a position described in §319.102 and authorized by OPM under §319.202 of this chapter.

Senior professional means an SL or ST employee.

Transfer means any movement, as defined in this section, that is a change of a senior professional from an SL or ST position in one agency to an SL or ST position in another agency without a break in service of at least 1 full workday.

§534.504 Pay range.

(a) A rate of basic pay under this subpart must be—

(1) Not less than 120 percent of the minimum rate of basic pay payable for GS–15 of the General Schedule, and

(2) Not greater than—

(i) The rate of basic pay payable for level III of the Executive Schedule (EX–III), or

(ii) In the case of an SL or ST employee who is covered by a certified performance appraisal system or whose established rate of basic pay is preserved under §534.509, the rate of basic pay payable for level II of the Executive Schedule (EX–II).

(b) An agency may not set or adjust the rate of basic pay for an SL or ST employee higher than the maximum in—

(1) Paragraph (a)(2)(i) of this section (*i.e.*, EX–III) when the SL or ST employee is covered by a performance appraisal system that is not certified or when the SL or ST employee is not subject to a performance appraisal system, except as provided in §534.509; or

(2) Paragraph (a)(2)(ii) of this section (*i.e.*, EX–II) when the SL or ST employee is covered by a certified performance appraisal system.

§ 534.505 Written procedures.

(a) Each agency with positions subject to this subpart must establish written procedures for setting the rate of basic pay and increasing the rate of basic pay of incumbents of the positions in accordance with law and this subpart. Agencies must provide for transparency in the processes for making pay decisions, while assuring confidentiality. The agency's plan for setting and increasing rates of basic pay must reflect meaningful distinctions among SL and ST employees based on individual performance, contribution to agency performance, or both, and must include—

(1) The criteria that will be used to set and increase a senior professional's rate of basic pay to ensure that individual pay rates or pay increases, as well as their overall distribution within the senior professional pay range, reflect meaningful distinctions within a single performance level (e.g., the higher the employee's relative performance within a rating level, the higher the pay increase), between performance rating levels (e.g., the higher the rating level, the higher the pay increase), or both;

(2) The criteria that will be used to set and increase a senior professional's rate of basic pay at a rate that exceeds the rate for level III of the Executive Schedule if the applicable agency performance appraisal system has been certified under part 430, subpart D of this chapter;

(3) Any system, methods, or criteria the agency uses to establish pay ranges applicable to various SL or ST positions within the pay range that applies under § 534.504(a), consistent with the requirement that pay be determined based upon individual performance, contributions to the agency's performance, or both;

(4) The designation of the authorized agency official(s) who will have the authority to set and adjust rates of basic pay for SL and ST employees, subject to the requirements of paragraph (c) of this section; and

(5) The administrative and management controls that will be applied to assure compliance with applicable statutes, OPM regulations, the agency's written procedures established under this section, the applicable maximum rate of basic pay in § 534.504(a), and, where applicable, the certification requirements set forth in part 430, subpart D of this chapter. In an agency that employs ten or more senior professionals, these controls must include centralized review of ratings proposed under § 430.208 of this chapter and pay actions proposed under § 534.507 by a panel of individuals designated by the agency head to provide advice from an agency-wide perspective for authorized agency officials to consider before approving pay adjustments on whether—

(i) Ratings of record and performance ratings proposed for senior professionals accurately reflect their individual performance, contributions to agency performance, or both, and take into account, as appropriate, assessment of the agency's performance against program performance measures and other relevant considerations; and

(ii) Proposed pay adjustments for senior professionals conform to the requirements of § 534.507 and appropriately correspond to proposed ratings of record and performance ratings.

(b) Each agency's written procedure must provide that, effective at the beginning of the first applicable pay period commencing on or after the first day of the month in which an adjustment takes effect under 5 U.S.C. 5303 in the rates of basic pay under the General Schedule, the head of an agency will adjust a senior professional's rate of basic pay under the provisions of § 534.507.

(c) The following actions must be approved by the agency head or by a designee who provides the certifications described in § 430.404(a)(6)(i), (ii) and (iii) of this chapter for all senior professionals in the agency, and this approval authority may not be further delegated:

(1) Any pay-setting action under § 534.506 or any pay increase under § 534.507 that results in a rate of basic pay that is within the highest 10 percent of the applicable rate range under § 534.504. A rate of basic pay equal to or

above the amount derived using the following rules is considered to be within the highest 10 percent of the applicable pay range (in 2015, $177,166 or above if the applicable system is certified, or $164,026 or above if the applicable system is not certified or performance appraisal does not apply):

(i) Subtract the minimum rate of basic pay from the maximum rate of basic pay for the applicable rate range under § 534.504 (in 2015, $183,300 − $121,956 = $61,344 if the applicable system is certified, or $168,700 − $121,956 = $46,744 if the applicable system is not certified or performance appraisal does not apply);

(ii) Multiply the amount derived in paragraph (c)(1)(i) of this section by 0.10 (in 2015, $61,344 − 0.10 = $6,134 if the applicable system is certified, or $46,744 − 0.10 = $4,674 if the applicable system is not certified or performance appraisal does not apply); and

(iii) Subtract the amount derived in paragraph (c)(1)(ii) of this section from the maximum rate of basic pay applicable under § 534.504 (in 2015, $183,300 − $6,134 = $177,166 if the applicable system is certified, or $168,700 − $4,674 = $164,026 if the applicable system is not certified or performance appraisal does not apply);

(2) Any pay increase under § 534.507 that results in a rate of basic pay more than 10 percent above the SL or ST employee's rate of basic pay as in effect on the last day of the preceding fiscal year or, if the individual was first appointed as an SL or ST employee in the agency after the last day of the preceding fiscal year, more than 10 percent above the rate of basic pay set at the time of that appointment. A rate of basic pay more than 10 percent above the applicable rate of basic pay is considered to be any rate of basic pay that exceeds the amount derived by multiplying the applicable rate of basic pay by a factor of 1.1;

(3) Any pay-setting action under § 534.506(c)(2) that results in a higher rate of basic pay than the senior professional had upon leaving the agency; and

(4) Any off-cycle pay increase under § 534.510.

(d) An agency must keep its written procedures for setting and increasing rates of basic pay up to date, make them available to affected SL and ST employees, periodically provide training or supplemental guidance to clarify how they are applied, and provide a copy to OPM upon request.

(e)(1) The head of an agency may delegate to an Inspector General the authority to set and adjust pay for senior professionals in the Office of the Inspector General, including authority for pay actions described in paragraph (c) of this section.

(2) An agency head who delegates to an Inspector General the authority to set and adjust pay for all senior professionals in the Office of the Inspector General, including all pay actions described in paragraph (c) of this section, may exclude those senior professionals from the count of agency senior professionals for the purpose of determining whether centralized review under paragraph (a)(5) of this section is required.

(3) An Inspector General to whom an agency head delegates authority to set and adjust pay for 10 or more senior professionals in the Office of the Inspector General must provide the centralized review required by paragraph (a)(5) of this section and may use Federal employees from outside the agency for that purpose or from the Inspector General community, whether or not in the same agency.

(f)(1) A panel performing centralized review under paragraphs (a)(5) or (e)(3) of this section for a senior professional who holds a career or career-conditional appointment or an appointment of equivalent tenure in the excepted service must have a majority of career appointees.

(2) For the purpose of paragraph (f)(1) of this section, a career appointee is considered to be a career SES member or a senior professional who holds a career or career-conditional appointment or an appointment of equivalent tenure in the excepted service.

(3) An agency head may include Federal employees from outside the agency on a panel performing centralized review.

(4) An agency using the discretion provided in § 430.403(d) of this chapter

must do so in accordance with paragraphs (a)(5), (e) and (f) of this section, as applicable.

[79 FR 12357, Mar. 5, 2014, as amended at 80 FR 57698, Sept. 25, 2015]

§ 534.506 Setting a rate of basic pay upon appointment.

(a) An authorized agency official may set the rate of basic pay of an individual who is not currently an SL or ST appointee of the agency at any rate within the applicable rate range under § 534.504(a) upon appointment to an SL or ST position in the agency, subject to the requirements of this section. In setting a new senior professional's rate of basic pay, an agency must consider the nature and quality of the individual's experience, accomplishments, and any unique skills, qualifications, or competencies the individual possesses as they relate to requirements of the senior professional position and its impact on the agency's performance. Rates of basic pay above the rate for level III of the Executive Schedule, but less than or equal to the rate for level II of the Executive Schedule, generally are reserved for those newly appointed senior professionals who possess superior leadership, scientific, professional or other competencies necessary to address key program and mission requirements, as determined by the agency through its strategic human capital planning process.

(b) Consistent with the agency's written procedures and paragraph (a) of this section, an authorized agency official may set the rate of basic pay for an SL or ST employee upon transfer from another agency at any rate of basic pay within the pay range that applies to the SL or ST position under § 534.504(a), except as provided in § 534.509(a).

(c)(1) Consistent with the agency's written procedures and paragraph (a) of this section, except as provided in paragraph (c)(2) of this section, an authorized agency official may set pay upon reappointment of a former SL or ST employee at any rate of basic pay within the pay range that applies to the SL or ST position under § 534.504(a).

(2) If a former agency SL or ST employee is reappointed within 30 days to the same position or a successor position in the same agency, the agency may not give the individual a higher rate of basic pay upon reappointment unless the agency head or a designee who provides the certifications described in § 430.404(a)(6)(i), (ii) and (iii) of this chapter for all senior professionals in the agency determines that a higher rate of basic pay is warranted.

§ 534.507 Annual increases in basic pay.

(a)(1) Effective at the beginning of the first applicable pay period commencing on or after the first day of the month in which an adjustment takes effect under 5 U.S.C. 5303 in the rates of basic pay under the General Schedule, the head of an agency must adjust a senior professional's rate of basic pay under paragraph (b) of this section by an amount he or she considers appropriate, subject to the applicable maximum rate under § 534.504(a), the agency's written procedures under § 534.505, and the provisions of this section.

(2) A determination by an authorized agency official to make a zero adjustment in pay after reviewing a senior professional's current rating of record or performance rating meets the requirement of paragraph (a)(1) of this section only if the notice required by paragraph (h) of this section is provided to the senior professional.

(3) A pay adjustment under paragraph (a)(1) or a determination under paragraph (a)(2) of this section does not restrict the authority of an agency head to increase pay at other times under § 534.510, if warranted.

(b)(1) An agency may provide a pay increase to a senior professional only upon a determination by the authorized agency official that the senior professional's performance and/or contributions to agency performance so warrant.

(2) Increases resulting in a rate of basic pay that exceeds the rate for level III of the Executive Schedule, but is less than or equal to the rate for level II of the Executive Schedule, are reserved for those senior professionals who demonstrate the highest levels of individual performance, make the greatest contributions to the agency's performance, or both, as determined by the agency through the administration

of its performance management system.

(3) A pay increase must reflect the agency's judgment concerning the value of the employee's characteristic and continuing service to the agency in the SL or ST position. A single noteworthy contribution that is not characteristic of the employee's continuing performance requirements, individual performance or contributions to the agency's performance should be recognized by an appropriate award under part 451, subpart A of this chapter or other appropriate authority, rather than by a permanent increase in the rate of basic pay.

(c) An agency must document the basis for each pay increase granted under paragraph (b) by means of—

(1) A current rating of record; or

(2) A performance rating that covers a period of at least 90 days and is assigned in accordance with subpart B of part 430 of this chapter and the centralized review required by § 534.505(a)(5), but only if a rating of record is not available or does not reflect current performance.

(d) Any increase under this section that results in a rate of basic pay above the rate for level III of the Executive Schedule may not be made effective unless—

(1) The rating of record or performance rating used to justify the increase covers a period of at least 90 days of performance during which the applicable performance appraisal system has continuously been certified under 5 U.S.C. 5307(d) and part 430, subpart D of this chapter;

(2) The rating of record or performance rating used to justify the increase becomes final while the applicable performance appraisal system is certified;

(3) The rating and pay increase are reviewed and approved in accordance with § 534.505(a);

(4) The pay increase is approved in accordance with § 534.505(c), as applicable, and the agency's written procedures; and

(5) The pay increase becomes effective while the applicable performance appraisal system is certified.

(e) Upon the initial certification under 5 U.S.C. 5307(d) and part 430, subpart D of this chapter by OPM, with OMB concurrence, of an agency performance appraisal system covering SL or ST employees, OPM may waive the requirement of paragraph (d)(1) of this section. The requirement may be waived only if OPM determines that the agency has, for a period of no less than 90 days prior to certification, consistently applied the same performance appraisal system to covered SL or ST employees in a manner consistent with certification. If OPM waives this requirement, OPM will notify the agency in writing.

(f) Except as required by paragraph (g) of this section, a pay increase under this section may not be provided to an employee—

(1) Who has a current rating of record below Level 3 (Fully Successful or equivalent), as described in § 430.208 of this chapter; or

(2) Who, after receiving a rating of record at Level 3 or above, receives a more recent performance rating that rates performance in a critical element at a level below Fully Successful, as described in § 430.206(b)(8)(i) of this chapter.

(g) An SL or ST employee whose rate of basic pay would otherwise fall below the minimum rate of the SL and ST pay range under § 534.504(a)(1) must be provided a pay adjustment sufficient to maintain the minimum rate of basic pay.

(h)(1) If the rates of basic pay under the General Schedule are increased under 5 U.S.C. 5303 on the date specified in paragraph (a)(1) of this section and the agency head decides upon a zero adjustment for an SL or ST employee who has a current rating of record or applicable performance rating at Level 3 or above, as described in § 430.208 of this chapter, the agency must communicate the reasons for that decision to the employee in writing.

(2) Paragraph (h)(1) of this section does not apply to a senior professional with a rate of basic pay described in § 534.505(c)(1) unless—

(i) The rates of basic pay for the Executive Schedule are also increased on the date specified in paragraph (a)(1) of this section; and

(ii) The senior professional has a current rating of record or applicable performance rating at Level 4 in an appraisal program that uses summary level pattern C or G, or at Level 5 in an appraisal program that uses summary level pattern B, E, F, or H, as described in § 430.208 of this chapter.

(3) Paragraphs (h)(1) and (h)(2) of this section may not be construed to require a pay increase for any senior professional employee.

§ 534.508 Reductions in a rate of basic pay.

(a) Any reduction in a rate of basic pay for an SL or ST employee is subject to part 752, subpart D of this chapter except as otherwise provided in this section.

(b) If an employee is removed from an SL or ST position and placed in a General Schedule position under procedures in part 752, subpart D of this chapter or part 432 of this chapter providing for reduction in grade, or otherwise moves voluntarily or involuntarily to a General Schedule position, the employee is entitled to the minimum rate of basic pay, as defined in § 531.203 of this chapter, for the General Schedule grade unless the agency sets the employee's pay at a higher rate under—

(1) The maximum payable rate rule in § 531.221 of this chapter, if applicable;

(2) The superior qualifications and special needs pay-setting authority in § 531.212 of this chapter, if applicable; or

(3) The pay retention rules in part 536, subpart C of this chapter, if applicable.

(c) An agency may reduce an SL or ST employee's rate of basic pay, subject to part 752, subpart D of this chapter, upon movement to a different SL or ST position within the agency. If an SL or ST employee elects to accept a reduction in pay to facilitate a reassignment and the agency documents the voluntary nature of the action, the resulting pay reduction is not subject to part 752, subpart D of this chapter.

(d) If an agency justifies an increase in an SL or ST employee's rate of basic pay under § 534.510 upon the employee's movement to another SL or ST position having a substantially greater impact on agency performance with the understanding that the employee will be reduced to his or her former rate of basic pay upon movement out of the position, and the agency documents the voluntary nature of the action, the resulting reduction to the former rate of basic pay (or to a higher rate of basic pay determined under this subpart that is within the pay range applicable to the SL or ST position under § 534.504(a)) is not subject to part 752, subpart D of this chapter.

(e) A reduction in the rate of basic pay of an SL or ST employee under § 534.506(b) upon transfer is considered voluntary upon the employee's acceptance of the appointment and is not subject to part 752, subpart D of this chapter, except that an SL or ST employee's rate of basic pay may not be reduced upon transfer under circumstances described in § 534.509(a). A reduction in the rate of basic pay of an SL or ST employee upon a transfer of function under part 351, subpart C of this chapter from another agency is subject to part 752, subpart D of this chapter unless otherwise provided by statute.

§ 534.509 Preservation of an established rate of basic pay.

(a) An SL or ST employee whose rate of basic pay is higher than the rate for level III of the Executive Schedule may not suffer a reduction in pay as a result of transfer to an SL or ST position in another agency where the maximum rate of basic pay for the applicable SL or ST rate range is equal to the rate for level III of the Executive Schedule.

(b) An SL or ST employee whose rate of basic pay is higher than the rate for level III of the Executive Schedule may not suffer a reduction in pay because his or her agency's applicable performance appraisal system certification expires or is suspended under § 430.405(h) of this chapter. See § 530.203(g) and (h) of this chapter for treatment of the aggregate pay limit when certification status changes during the calendar year.

(c) An agency may continue an SL or ST employee's rate of basic pay above the rate for level III of the Executive Schedule upon that employee's movement within the agency to an SL or ST position that is not under a certified performance appraisal system. Pay may be reduced upon the movement only as provided in §534.508.

(d) If an agency grants a temporary pay increase under conditions described in §534.508(d) to an SL or ST employee subject to a certified performance appraisal system who, prior to the temporary pay increase, has a rate of basic pay above the rate for level III of the Executive Schedule, the agency may return the employee to an SL or ST position that is not subject to a certified performance appraisal system when the temporary assignment ends and set the SL or ST employee's rate of basic pay at the rate in effect immediately before the temporary pay increase.

(e) When a rate of basic pay that is higher than the rate for level III of the Executive Schedule is preserved under a provision of this section, the SL or ST employee will continue to receive his or her current rate of basic pay and is not eligible for a pay increase until he or she is assigned to an SL or ST position covered by a certified performance appraisal system or his or her rate of basic pay is less than the rate for level III of the Executive Schedule.

(f) An agency that is otherwise subject to the limitation in §534.504(a)(2)(i) with respect to an SL or ST position occupied by an SL or ST employee whose rate of basic pay is authorized to be preserved under paragraph (a), (b), (c), or (d) of this section may set that employee's rate of basic pay above EX–III only at the level required to preserve the applicable rate.

(g) Preservation of a rate of basic pay under this section does not preclude a subsequent reduction in pay as provided in §534.508.

(h) The provisions of this section do not apply upon the appointment of a senior professional employee to a position in the Senior Executive Service or upon the appointment of a member of the Senior Executive Service to a senior professional position.

§534.510 Off-cycle pay increases.

(a) An authorized agency official may provide an off-cycle pay increase to a senior professional if, and only if, the agency head or a designee who provides the certifications described in §430.404(a)(6)(i), (ii) and (iii) of this chapter for all senior professionals in the agency determines an off-cycle pay increase is warranted and approves the amount of the increase, subject to the requirements of this section and the agency's written procedures established under §534.505. The authority to approve an off-cycle pay increase under this section may not be further delegated.

(b) Except as provided in paragraph (d) of this section, an off-cycle pay increase must be supported by factors that distinguish the level of the senior professional's performance and/or contributions to agency performance from that of his or her peers, as applicable, and from that sufficiently rewarded through the annual pay adjustment. In assessing the warrant for an off-cycle pay increase, the approving official may consider such factors as—

(1) A senior professional's exceptionally meritorious accomplishments that contribute significantly to the agency's performance;

(2) The need to offer a pay increase to reassign a senior professional to a position that has a substantially greater impact on agency performance; and

(3) The need to retain a senior professional whose contributions are critical to the agency and who is likely to leave the agency in the absence of a pay increase.

(c) Each off-cycle pay increase that is based upon such factors as are described in paragraphs (b)(1) through (3) of this section must be documented in accordance with §534.507(b) through (e), except that the agency must also provide information to explain how each applicable factor was considered in determining the pay increase. This information may be derived from the agency's written pay procedures established under §534.505, agency performance management system activities, or other sources the agency deems useful for this purpose.

(d) If the maximum rate of basic pay applicable to an agency's senior professionals increases during the 1 year period following the annual pay adjustment under §534.507(a)(1) for reasons other than a change in the certification status of an applicable performance appraisal system, the agency head or a designee who provides the certifications described in § 430.404(a)(6)(i), (ii) and (iii) of this chapter for all senior professionals in the agency may consider whether, and to what extent, an additional pay increase may be warranted for a senior professional based on the same criteria used in determining his or her annual pay increase. However, if the increase in maximum rate of basic pay is due to a change in the certification status of an applicable performance appraisal system, the requirements of paragraphs (a), (b), and (c) of this section apply.

(e) An off-cycle pay increase granted under this section will be effective prospectively, not retroactively.

§ 534.511 Exemption from performance appraisal requirements.

(a) An agency responsible for setting and adjusting rates of basic pay for SL or ST employees or positions excluded from performance appraisal by or under statute is, with respect to those employees or positions, exempt from any provision of this subpart to the extent that it makes a pay determination contingent upon performance appraisal, including—

(1) Section 534.505(a)(1), (2) and (3) to the extent these paragraphs require that an agency's plan for setting and increasing rates of basic pay reflect meaningful distinctions among SL and ST employees based upon individual performance and include criteria that ensure individuals with the highest levels of individual performance, or the greatest contributions to agency performance, or both, receive the highest pay increases. The agency must still provide written procedures for setting and adjusting rates of pay for covered SL and ST employees that specify criteria that will be applied consistent with applicable law. The remaining provisions of § 534.505 apply, except for references in § 534.505(a)(5) to compliance with certification requirements and centralized review of ratings and pay actions;

(2) Section 534.507(b), (c), (d), (e), and (f). The agency must still document in writing the basis for each pay increase under § 534.507 in accordance with criteria specified in the agency's written procedures under § 534.505(a); and

(3) Section 534.510(b) and (c). The agency must still document in writing the basis for each off-cycle pay increase under § 534.510 in accordance with criteria specified in the agency's written procedures under § 534.505(a).

(b) Except as specified in paragraph (a) of this section, an agency responsible for setting and adjusting rates of basic pay for SL or ST employees excluded from performance appraisal by or under statute is subject to the requirements of this subpart with respect to those employees.

(c) The maximum rate of basic pay for an SL or ST employee or position not subject to performance appraisal is the maximum rate described in § 534.504(a)(2)(i). An agency head who uses the exemption in paragraph (a) of this section to set the rate of basic pay for SL or ST employees who are not subject to performance appraisal may not certify that those employees are covered by a performance appraisal system meeting the certification criteria established in part 430, subpart D of this chapter for purposes of authorizing rates of basic pay above the rate for level III of the Executive Schedule.

(d) Notwithstanding paragraph (c) of this section, an agency responsible for setting and adjusting rates of basic pay for SL or ST employees or positions excluded from performance appraisal by or under statute is subject to § 534.509(a) when setting a rate of basic pay for an SL or ST employee upon transfer to such a position. The agency may also apply § 534.509(c) upon movement of an SL or ST employee whose rate of basic pay was initially set under § 534.509(a) or (c) to another SL or ST position that is excluded from performance appraisal. Pay may be reduced upon the movement only as provided in § 534.508. In either case, the employee will not be eligible for a pay increase until he or she is appointed to an SL or ST position that is subject to a certified performance appraisal system or until his or her rate of basic pay is less than the rate for level III of the Executive Schedule.

Subpart F—Pay for Administrative Appeals Judge Positions

SOURCE: 66 FR 63908, Dec. 11, 2001, unless otherwise noted.

§534.601 Coverage.

(a) This subpart implements 5 U.S.C. 5372b and applies to administrative appeals judge positions, the duties of which are not classifiable above GS–15 under 5 U.S.C. 5108 and which primarily involve reviewing decisions of administrative law judges appointed under 5 U.S.C. 3105 and rendering final administrative decisions.

(b) This subpart does not apply to—

(1) Senior-level positions classified above GS–15 pursuant to 5 U.S.C. 5108;

(2) Scientific or professional positions established under 5 U.S.C. 3104;

(3) Senior Executive Service positions established under 5 U.S.C. 3132 or 3151;

(4) Positions for which pay is fixed by administrative action and limited to level IV of the Executive Schedule under 5 U.S.C. 5373;

(5) Administrative law judge positions appointed under 5 U.S.C. 3105; or

(6) Positions in agencies that are excluded from chapter 51 of title 5, United States Code, by section 5102(a) or 5102(c) or other provision of law.

§534.602 Definitions.

Administrative appeals judge position means a position not classified above GS–15 under 5 U.S.C. 5108 and for which the duties primarily involve reviewing decisions of administrative law judges appointed under 5 U.S.C. 3105 and rendering final administrative decisions.

Administrative law judge means an individual in an *administrative law judge* position as that term is defined in section 930.202 of this chapter.

Agency means an *Executive agency*, as defined in 5 U.S.C. 105, excluding the U.S. General Accounting Office.

Head of an agency means the head of an Executive agency or an official who has been delegated the authority to act for the head of the agency in the matter concerned.

§534.603 Rates of basic pay.

(a) The administrative appeals judge pay system (AA) has six rates of basic pay—AA–1, 2, 3, 4, 5, and 6. These rates correspond to the rates of basic pay for AL-3/A, B, C, D, E, and F, respectively, of the administrative law judge pay system established under 5 U.S.C. 5372 and part 930, subpart B, of this chapter.

(b) The rates of basic pay of the administrative appeals judge pay system will be adjusted at the same time and in the same manner as adjustments are made in the corresponding rates of basic pay for the administrative law judge pay system under 5 U.S.C. 5372.

§534.604 Pay administration.

(a) The head of each agency must fix the rate of basic pay for each administrative appeals judge position within the agency.

(b) Upon initial appointment, an agency must set the rate of basic pay of an administrative appeals judge at the minimum rate AA–1 of the administrative appeals judge pay system, except as provided in paragraphs (b)(1), (b)(2), and (b)(3) of this section.

(1) An agency must set the pay of an employee under the General Schedule pay system who is appointed to an administrative appeals judge position without a break in service at the lowest rate of basic pay of the administrative appeals judge pay system that equals or exceeds the rate of basic pay the employee received immediately prior to such appointment, not to exceed the rate of basic pay for AA–6. If the resulting basic pay increase is less than one-half of the dollar value of the employee's next within-grade increase, the agency must set the employee's rate of basic pay at the next higher rate of basic pay in the basic rate range of the administrative appeals judge pay system.

(2) An agency may offer an administrative appeals judge applicant with prior Federal service a rate up to the lowest rate of basic pay of the administrative appeals judge pay system that equals or exceeds the employee's highest previous rate of basic pay in a Federal civil service position, not to exceed the rate of basic pay for AA–6.

(3) An agency may offer an administrative appeals judge applicant with superior qualifications who is not a current Federal employee a higher than minimum rate when such a rate is

clearly necessary to meet the needs of the Government. An agency may pay a higher than minimum rate of pay that is next above the applicant's existing pay or earnings, up to the maximum rate AA–6. Superior qualifications for applicants include, but are not limited to, having legal practice before the hiring agency, having practice in another forum with legal issues of concern to the hiring agency, or having an outstanding reputation among others in the field.

(c) Administrative appeals judges will advance successively to rates AA–2, 3, and 4 upon completion of 52 weeks of service in the next lower rate, and to rates 5 and 6 upon completion of 104 weeks of service in the next lower rate. Advancement to a higher rate takes effect on the first day of the first pay period beginning on or after completion of the required period of service. Time in a nonpay status is creditable service in the computation of a waiting period in so far as it does not exceed 2 weeks for each 52 weeks of service. Time in a nonpay status is fully creditable if the absence is due to military service, as defined in 5 U.S.C. 8331(13), or receipt of injury compensation under chapter 81 of title 5, United States Code. Time under pay systems outside the administrative appeals judge pay system is not creditable service in computing the required waiting period, except that time under the administrative law judge pay system established under 5 U.S.C. 5372 is creditable when an individual moves from that system to the administrative appeals judge pay system without a break in service.

(d) An agency must use the following procedures to convert an administrative appeals judge's annual rate of basic pay to an hourly, daily, weekly, or biweekly rate:

(1) To derive an hourly rate, divide the annual rate of pay by 2,087 and round to the nearest cent, counting one-half cent and over as the next higher cent.

(2) To derive a daily rate, multiply the hourly rate by the number of daily hours of service required by the administrative appeals judge's basic daily tour of duty.

(3) To derive a weekly or biweekly rate, multiply the hourly rate by 40 or 80, as the case may be.

§ 534.605 Conversion.

On the first day of the first pay period beginning on or after December 11, 2001, agencies must convert the rate of basic pay of an administrative appeals judge to the lowest rate of basic pay provided by § 534.603(a) of this subpart that equals or exceeds the rate of basic pay the administrative appeals judge received immediately before that date.

PART 535—CRITICAL POSITION PAY AUTHORITY

Sec.

AUTHORITY: 5 U.S.C. 5377; E.O. 13415, 71 FR 70641.

SOURCE: 73 FR 50181, Aug. 26, 2008, unless otherwise noted.

§ 535.101 Purpose.

The purpose of this part is to provide a regulatory framework for the critical position pay authority authorized by 5 U.S.C. 5377. The Office of Personnel Management (OPM), in consultation with the Office of Management and Budget (OMB), may grant authority to the head of an agency to fix the rate of basic pay for one or more positions under this part.

§ 535.102 Definitions.

Agency has the meaning given that term in 5 U.S.C. 5102.

Critical position means a position for which OPM has granted authority to the head of an agency to exercise the pay-setting authority provided in 5 U.S.C. 5377.

Critical position pay authority means the authority that may be granted to the head of an agency by OPM under 5 U.S.C. 5377 to set the rate of basic pay for a given critical position under the provisions of that section.

Critical position pay rate means the specific rate of pay established by the head of an agency for an employee in a critical position based upon the exercise of the critical position pay authority. A critical position pay rate is a rate of basic pay to the extent provided in §535.106.

Employee means an employee (as defined in 5 U.S.C. 2105) in or under an agency.

Head of an agency means the agency head or an official who has been delegated the authority to act for the agency head in the matter concerned.

§535.103 Authority.

(a) Subject to a grant of authority from OPM in consultation with OMB and all other requirements in this part, the head of an agency may fix the rate of basic pay for a critical position at a rate not less than the rate of basic pay that would otherwise be payable for the position, but not greater than—

(1) The rate payable for level II of the Executive Schedule (unless paragraph (a)(2) or (a)(3) of this section applies);

(2) The rate payable for level I of the Executive Schedule in exceptional circumstances based on information and data that justify a rate higher than the rate payable for level II of the Executive Schedule; or

(3) A rate in excess of the rate for level I of the Executive Schedule that is established in rare circumstances with the written approval of the President.

(b) The head of an agency may exercise his or her critical position pay authority only—

(1) When such a position requires expertise of an extremely high level in a scientific, technical, professional, or administrative field and is critical to the agency's successful accomplishment of an important mission; and

(2) To the extent necessary to recruit or retain an individual exceptionally well-qualified for the critical position.

(c) If critical position pay authority is granted for a position, the head of an agency may determine whether it is appropriate to exercise the authority with respect to any proposed appointee or incumbent of the position.

(d) An agency granted critical position pay authority may continue to use the authority for an authorized position as long as needed. OPM will monitor the use of critical position pay authorities annually, through the agency's required reports under §535.107, and will terminate the authority associated with a given position after notifying the agency if, in OPM's judgment in consultation with OMB, the authority is no longer needed.

§535.104 Requests for and granting critical position pay authority.

(a) An agency may request critical position pay authority only after determining that the position in question cannot be filled with an exceptionally well-qualified individual through the use of other available human resources flexibilities and pay authorities. Agency requests must include the information in paragraph (d) of this section. OPM, in consultation with OMB, will review agency requests. OPM will advise the requesting agency as to whether the request is approved and when the agency's critical position pay authority becomes effective.

(b) A request for critical position pay authority (or authorities) must be signed by the head of an agency and submitted to OPM. Requests covering multiple positions must include a list of the positions in priority order. The head of an agency may request coverage of positions of a type not listed in 5 U.S.C. 5377(a)(2), as authorized by 5 U.S.C. 5377(i)(2) and Executive Order 13415.

(c) Requests for critical position pay authority to set pay above the rate for level II of the Executive Schedule and up to the rate for level I of the Executive Schedule because of exceptional circumstances require information and data that justify the higher pay. Requests for critical position pay authority to set pay above the rate for level I of the Executive Schedule due to rare circumstances require approval by the President. The head of an agency must submit such requests to OPM with the information required in paragraph (d) of this section. If OPM, in consultation with OMB, concurs with a request to set pay above the rate for level I of the Executive Schedule, OPM will seek the President's approval. The President may establish a maximum limitation on the critical pay rate.

(d) At a minimum, all requests for critical position pay authority must include:

(1) Position title;

(2) Position appointment authority (for Senior Executive Service positions, appointment authority for any incumbent);

(3) Pay plan and grade/level;

(4) Occupational series of the position;

(5) Geographic location of the position;

(6) Current salary of the position or incumbent;

(7) Name of incumbent (or "Vacant");

(8) Length of time the incumbent has been in the position or length of time the position has been vacant;

(9) A written evaluation of the need to designate the position as critical. Such an evaluation must include—

(i) The kinds of work required by the position and the context within which it operates;

(ii) The range of positions and qualification requirements that characterize the occupational field, including those that require extremely high levels of expertise;

(iii) The rates of pay reasonably and generally required in the public and private sectors for similar positions; and

(iv) The availability of individuals who possess the qualifications to do the work required by the position;

(10) Documentation, with appropriate supporting data, of the agency's experience and, as appropriate, the experience of other organizations, in efforts to recruit or retain exceptionally well-qualified individuals for the position or for a position sufficiently similar with respect to the occupational field, required qualifications, and other pertinent factors, to provide a reliable comparison;

(11) Assessment of why the agency could not, through diligent and comprehensive recruitment efforts and without using the critical position pay authority, fill the position within a reasonable period with an individual who could perform the duties and responsibilities in a manner sufficient to fulfill the agency's mission. This assessment must include a justification as to why the agency could not, as an effective alternative, use other human resources flexibilities and pay authorities, such as recruitment, relocation, and retention incentives under 5 CFR part 575;

(12) An explanation regarding why the position should be designated a critical position and made eligible for a higher rate of pay under this part within its organizational context (*i.e.*, relative to other positions in the organization) and, when applicable, how it compares with other critical positions in the agency. The agency must include an explanation of how it will deal with perceived inequities among agency employees (e.g., situations in which employees in positions designated as critical would receive higher rates of pay than their peers, supervisors, or other employees in positions with higher-level duties and responsibilities);

(13) Documentation of the effect on the successful accomplishment of important agency missions if the position is not designated as a critical position, including an explanation and justification for OPM and OMB to expedite processing in cases where the agency believes that urgency warrants expedited processing;

(14) Any additional information the agency may deem appropriate to demonstrate that higher pay is needed to recruit or retain an employee for a critical position;

(15) Unless the position is an Executive Schedule position, a copy of the position description and qualification standard for the critical position; and

(16) The desired rate of basic pay for requests to set pay above the rate for level II of the Executive Schedule and justification to show that such a rate is necessary to recruit and retain an individual exceptionally well-qualified for the critical position.

§ 535.105 Setting and adjusting rates of basic pay.

(a) The rate of basic pay for a critical position may not be less than the rate of basic pay, including any locality-based comparability payments established under 5 U.S.C. 5304 or special rate supplement under 5 U.S.C. 5305 (or other similar payment or supplement under other legal authority) that would otherwise be payable for the position.

(b) If critical position pay authority is granted for a position, the head of an agency may set pay initially at any amount up to the rate of pay for level II or level I of the Executive Schedule, as applicable, without further approval unless a higher maximum rate is approved by the President under § 535.104(c).

(c) The head of an agency may make subsequent adjustments in the rate of basic pay for a critical position each January at the same time general pay adjustments are authorized for Executive Schedule employees under section 5318 of title 5, United States Code. Such adjusted rates may not exceed the new rate for Executive Schedule level II or other applicable maximum established for the critical position. However, the employee must have at least a rating of Fully Successful or equivalent, and subsequent adjustments must be based on labor market factors, recruitment and retention needs, and individual accomplishments and contributions to an agency's mission.

(d) Employees receiving critical position pay are not entitled to locality-based comparability payments established under 5 U.S.C. 5304, special rate supplements under 5 U.S.C. 5305, or other similar payments or supplements under other legal authority.

(e) If an agency discontinues critical position pay for a given position (on its own initiative or because OPM, in consultation with OMB, terminates the authority under § 535.103(d)), the employee's rate of basic pay will be set at the rate to which the employee would be entitled had he or she not received critical pay, as determined by the head of the agency, unless the employee is eligible for a higher payable rate under the General Schedule maximum payable rate rule in § 531.221 and the agency chooses to apply that rule.

§ 535.106 Treatment as rate of basic pay.

A critical position pay rate is considered a rate of basic pay for all purposes, including any applicable premium pay, except—

(a) Application of any saved pay or pay retention provisions (e.g., 5 U.S.C. 5363); or

(b) Application of any adverse action provisions (e.g., 5 U.S.C. 7512).

§ 535.107 Annual reporting requirements.

(a) OPM must submit an annual report to Congress on the use of the critical position pay authority. Agencies must submit the following information to OPM by January 31 of each year on their use of critical position pay authority for the previous calendar year:

(1) The name, title, pay plan, and grade/level of each employee receiving a higher rate of basic pay under this subpart;

(2) The annual rate or rates of basic pay paid in the preceding calendar year to each employee in a critical position;

(3) The beginning and ending dates of such rate(s) of basic pay, as applicable;

(4) The rate or rates of basic pay that would have been paid but for the grant of critical position pay. This includes what the rate or rates of basic pay were, or would have been, without critical position pay at the time critical position pay is initially exercised and any subsequent adjustments to basic pay that would have been made if critical position pay authority had not been exercised; and

(5) Whether the authority is still needed for the critical position(s).

PART 536—GRADE AND PAY RETENTION

Subpart A—General Provisions

Sec.

Subpart B—Grade Retention

Subpart C—Pay Retention

Subpart D—Appeals and Miscellaneous Provisions

AUTHORITY: 5 U.S.C. 5361–5366; sec. 4 of the Performance Management and Recognition System Termination Act of 1993 (Pub. L. 103–89), 107 Stat. 981; § 536.301(b) also issued under 5 U.S.C. 5334(b); § 536.308 also issued under sec. 301(d)(2) of the Federal Workforce Flexibility Act of 2004 (Pub. L. 108–411), 118 Stat. 2305; § 536.310 also issued under sections 1913 and 1918 of the Non-Foreign Area Retirement Equity Assurance Act of 2009 (subtitle B of title XIX of Pub. L.111–84), 123 Stat. 2619; § 536.405 also issued under 5 U.S.C. 552, Freedom of Information Act, Public Law 92–502.

SOURCE: 45 FR 85656, Dec. 30, 1980, unless otherwise noted.

Subpart A—General Provisions

SOURCE: 70 FR 31305, May 31, 2005, unless otherwise noted.

§ 536.101 Purpose.

This part contains OPM regulations for the administration of grade and pay retention. This part supplements and implements the provisions of 5 U.S.C. 5361–5366 and must be read together with those sections of law. Under 5 U.S.C. 5362, an employee under a covered pay system who is placed in a lower grade (e.g., as a result of a reduction in force or when his or her position is reduced in grade as a result of a reclassification) is entitled to retain the grade held immediately before the reduction for a period of 2 years under the circumstances prescribed in this part. Under 5 U.S.C. 5363, an employee whose rate of basic pay otherwise would be reduced as a result of a management action is entitled to retain his or her rate of basic pay under the circumstances prescribed in this part.

§ 536.102 Coverage.

(a) Subject to the exclusions in paragraphs (b) through (e) of this section, this part covers any employee who, at the time this part is applied—

(1) Is in a covered pay system; or

(2) Is moving to a position under a covered pay system from a position not under a covered pay system, as long as the individual was an *employee* as defined in 5 CFR 536.103 while serving in the position in a noncovered pay system.

(b) An agency may not provide grade or pay retention under this part to an employee who—

(1) Is reduced in grade or pay for personal cause or at the employee's request;

(2) Was employed on a temporary or term basis immediately before the action causing the reduction in grade or pay;

(3) Does not satisfactorily complete the probationary period prescribed by 5 U.S.C. 3321(a)(2), and, as a result, is removed from a supervisory or managerial position;

(4) Is entitled to receive a saved rate of basic pay under 5 U.S.C. 3594(c) and 5 CFR 359.705 because of removal from the Senior Executive Service and placement in a civil service position (other than a Senior Executive Service position) under 5 U.S.C. 3594(b)(2);

(5) Moves from an Executive Schedule position paid under 5 U.S.C. chapter 53, subchapter II, or a position whose rate of pay is fixed by law at a rate equal to a rate for the Executive Schedule;

(6) Moves between positions not under a covered pay system or from a position under a covered pay system to a position not under a covered pay system;

(7) Moves to a nonappropriated fund position as described in 5 U.S.C. 2105(c) (except a position occupied by a prevailing rate employee);

(8) Moves from a nonappropriated fund position as described in 5 U.S.C. 2105(c) (except a position occupied by a prevailing rate employee) to a position in a covered pay system, unless covered by §536.302(a); or

(9) Is reduced in pay upon termination of a critical position pay authority under 5 CFR part 535.

(c) An agency may not provide grade or pay retention under this part based on the grade or rate of basic pay held by the employee during a temporary promotion or temporary reassignment. However, a temporary promotion or temporary reassignment does not affect an employee's preexisting entitlement to grade or pay retention.

(d) An agency may not provide grade retention under subpart B of this part to an employee who moves from a position not under a covered pay system to a position under a covered pay system.

(e) An employee loses eligibility for or entitlement to grade or pay retention under the conditions specified in §§536.207, 536.208, and 536.308.

[70 FR 31305, May 31, 2005, as amended at 73 FR 50183, Aug. 26, 2008]

§536.103 Definitions.

For the purpose of this part:

Authorized agency official means the head of the agency or an official who is authorized to act for the head of the agency in the matter concerned.

Comparison rate means—

(1) For the purpose of comparing grades that are under different covered pay systems under §536.105 and after applying any applicable geographic conversion under §536.105(b) for positions with different official worksites—

(i) The highest rate of basic pay that applies to the fourth step of the grade for a position covered by the General Schedule; and

(ii) The highest rate of basic pay that applies to the second step of the grade of a position under a regular prevailing rate system established under 5 U.S.C. chapter 53, subchapter IV, or, in the case of a prevailing rate position with a single rate, the single rate of basic pay for that position; and

(2) For the purpose of comparing grades or levels of work in making reasonable offer determinations when one of the grades or levels of work is not under a covered pay system and after applying any applicable geographic conversion rules under §536.105(b) for positions with different official worksites—

(i) The maximum payable rate of basic pay that applies to the grade of a position covered by the General Schedule;

(ii) The maximum payable rate of basic pay that applies to the grade of a position under a regular prevailing rate system established under 5 U.S.C. chapter 53, subchapter IV, or in the case of a prevailing rate position with a single rate, the single rate of basic pay for that position; and

(iii) The maximum payable rate of basic pay that applies to the grade or level of work in the case of a position not covered by paragraph (2)(i) or (ii) of this definition. In the case of a position with a single rate under such a schedule, the single rate of basic pay for that position is the comparison rate.

Covered pay system means a covered pay schedule as defined in 5 U.S.C. 5361(5)—*i.e.*, the General Schedule pay system established under 5 U.S.C. chapter 53, subchapter III; a prevailing rate system established under 5 U.S.C. chapter 53, subchapter IV; or a special occupational pay system established under 5 U.S.C. chapter 53, subchapter IX. The various prevailing rate systems under 5 U.S.C. chapter 53, subchapter IV, are considered separate systems if they have separate job grading structures.

Employed on a temporary or term basis means employment under an appointment having a definite time limitation or designated as temporary or term.

Employee has the meaning given that term in 5 U.S.C. 2105, except that *employee* also includes—

(1) An individual employed by the U.S. Postal Service or the Postal Rate Commission who would be considered an employee under 5 U.S.C. 2105 but for the exclusion in section 2105(e); and

(2) An individual employed by a Department of Defense or Coast Guard nonappropriated fund instrumentality (as described in 5 U.S.C. 2105(c)) who is moved without a break in service of

more than 3 days from employment in such an instrumentality to a position under a covered pay system in the same agency.

FEPCA means the Federal Employees Pay Comparability Act of 1990 (section 529 of Pub. L. 101–509, November 5, 1990, as amended).

General Schedule or *GS* means the classification and pay system established under 5 U.S.C. chapter 51 and subchapter III of chapter 53. This term also refers to the pay schedule established under 5 U.S.C. 5332.

Highest applicable rate range means the rate range applicable to an employee based on a given position of record and official worksite that provides the highest rates of basic pay, excluding any retained rates. For example, a rate range of special rates under 5 U.S.C. 5305 may exceed an applicable locality rate range under 5 U.S.C. 5304 for General Schedule employees. In certain circumstances, the *highest applicable rate range* may consist of two types of pay rates from different pay schedules—e.g., a range where special rates are higher in the lower portion of the range and locality rates are higher in the higher portion of the range.

Management action means an action (not for personal cause) by an agency official not initiated or requested by an employee which may adversely affect the employee's grade or rate of basic pay. However, an employee's placement in or transfer to a position under a formal employee development program established by an agency for recruitment and employee advancement purposes (e.g., Recent Graduates Program) is considered a management action even though the employee initiates or requests such placement or transfer.

Official worksite means the official location of the employee's position of record as determined under the rules of the applicable pay system (e.g., 5 CFR 531.605 for General Schedule employees). *Official worksite* is synonymous with the term "official duty station" as used in 5 U.S.C. 5363(c).

OPM means the Office of Personnel Management.

Payable rate means the highest rate of basic pay to which an employee is entitled based on the employee's position of record, official worksite, and step (or relative position in range for a GM employee) or, if applicable, a retained rate.

Pay schedule means a set of rate ranges established under a single authority—*i.e.*, the General Schedule, a law enforcement officer special base rate schedule (for grades GS–3 through 10) under section 403 of FEPCA; a prevailing rate schedule (including a special schedule or special rate schedule) under 5 U.S.C. chapter 53, subchapter IV; a locality rate schedule under 5 U.S.C. 5304 based on GS rates; a locality rate schedule under 5 U.S.C. 5304 based on law enforcement officer special base rates (for grades GS–3 through 10); or a special rate schedule under 5 U.S.C. 5305 or similar authority. A pay schedule applies to or covers a defined category of employees based on established coverage conditions (e.g., official worksite, occupation). A pay schedule is considered to apply to or cover an employee who meets the established coverage conditions even when a rate under that schedule is not currently payable to the employee because of a higher pay entitlement under another pay schedule.

Position of record means an employee's official position (defined by grade, occupational series, employing agency, LEO status, and any other condition that determines coverage under a pay schedule (other than official worksite)), as documented on the employee's most recent Notification of Personnel Action (Standard Form 50 or equivalent) and current position description. A position to which an employee is temporarily detailed is not documented as a position of record. For an employee whose change in official position is followed within 3 workdays by a reduction in force resulting in the employee's separation before he or she is required to report for duty in the new position, the position of record in effect immediately before the position change is deemed to remain the position of record through the date of separation.

Prevailing rate employee has the meaning given that term in 5 U.S.C. 5342(a)(2) and refers to an employee in a position covered by a prevailing rate system or schedule established under 5 U.S.C. chapter 53, subchapter IV.

Rate of basic pay means the rate of pay fixed by law or administrative action for the position held by an employee before any deductions, including a General Schedule rate under 5 U.S.C. 5332; a law enforcement officer special base rate under section 403 of FEPCA; a special rate under 5 CFR part 530, subpart C, or similar payment under other legal authority; a locality rate under 5 CFR part 531, subpart F, or similar payment under other legal authority; a prevailing rate under 5 U.S.C. 5343; or a retained rate under this part, but excluding additional pay of any other kind (such as premium payments, differentials, and allowances).

Rate range or *range* means the range of rates of basic pay for a grade within an established pay schedule, excluding any retained rate.

Reasonable offer means an offer that meets the conditions in §536.104.

Reduced in grade or pay at the employee's request means a reduction in grade or rate of basic pay that is initiated by the employee for his or her benefit, convenience, or personal advantage. A reduction in grade or pay that is caused or influenced by a management action is not considered to be at an employee's request, except that the voluntary reduction in grade or pay of an employee in response to a management action directly related to personal cause is considered to be at the employee's request.

Reduced in grade or pay for personal cause means a reduction in grade or rate of basic pay based on the conduct, character, or unacceptable performance of an employee. In situations in which an employee is reduced in grade or pay for inability to perform the duties of his or her position because of a medical or physical condition beyond the employee's control, the reduction in grade or pay is not considered to be for personal cause.

Reorganization means the planned elimination, addition, redistribution, or restructuring of functions or duties either wholly within an agency or between agencies.

Retained rate means a rate above the maximum rate of the employee's highest applicable rate range that is payable under subpart C of this part.

Temporary promotion means a promotion that has a definite time limitation or is otherwise designated as temporary when the affected employee is informed in advance.

Temporary reassignment means a reassignment that has a definite time limitation or is otherwise designated as temporary when the affected employee is informed in advance.

Where different pay schedules apply means, in the context of applying the geographic conversion rule, that an employee's official worksite is changed to a new location that would cause the employee to lose or gain coverage under a location-based pay schedule if the employee were to remain in the same position of record.

[70 FR 31305, May 31, 2005, as amended at 73 FR 66154, Nov. 7, 2008; 77 FR 28222, May 11, 2012]

§536.104 Reasonable offer.

(a) For the purpose of determining whether grade retention eligibility or entitlement must be terminated under §536.207 or 536.208, the offer of a position is a reasonable offer if the position's grade is equal to or higher than the retained grade and if all the conditions in paragraph (c) of this section are met. If the offered position is in a different pay system, §536.105 must be applied to determine whether the grade of the offered position is equal to or greater than the retained grade.

(b) For the purpose of determining whether pay retention eligibility or entitlement must be terminated under §536.308, the offer of a position is a reasonable offer if the employee's rate of basic pay in the position would be equal to or greater than the rate to which the employee is or would be entitled under the pay retention provisions and if all the conditions in paragraph (c) of this section are met.

(c) An offer of a position must meet the following additional conditions to qualify as a reasonable offer:

(1) The offer must be in writing and must include an official position description of the offered position;

(2) The offer must inform the employee that entitlement to grade or pay retention will terminate if the offer is declined and that the employee

may appeal the reasonableness of the offer as provided in § 536.402;

(3) The offered position must be of equal or greater tenure than the employee's position before the action resulting in the grade or pay retention entitlement;

(4) The offered position must be full-time, unless the employee's position immediately before the action resulting in entitlement to grade or pay retention was less than full-time, in which case the offered position must have a work schedule providing for no fewer hours of work per week or per pay period than the position held before the action; and

(5) The offered position must be in the same commuting area as the employee's position immediately before the offer, unless the employee is subject to a mobility agreement or a published agency policy that requires employee mobility.

§ 536.105 Comparing grades under different pay systems.

(a) *General.* An agency must compare the comparison rates (as defined in § 536.103) of the applicable grades to determine whether a grade of a position is equal to, higher than, or lower than the grade of another position when—

(1) Determining eligibility for grade retention upon movement from a position under a covered pay system to a lower-graded position under a different covered pay system (including determinations under § 536.203 that involve different covered pay systems);

(2) Determining whether grade retention eligibility is lost or grade retention is terminated when an employee is placed in a lower-graded position under a different covered pay system and the action is taken for personal cause or at the employee's request;

(3) Determining whether grade retention eligibility is lost or grade retention is terminated based on movement to a position under a different covered pay system with an equal or higher grade;

(4) Determining whether grade retention eligibility is lost or grade retention is terminated based on declination of a reasonable offer of a position under a different pay system with an equal or higher grade; and

(5) Determining whether pay retention eligibility is lost or a retained rate is terminated when an employee is placed in a lower-graded position under a different covered pay system and the action is taken for personal cause or at the employee's request.

(b) *Geographic conversion.* When comparing positions under paragraph (a) of this section which are stationed in different geographic locations where different pay schedules apply, the comparison rate of the employee's existing position of record (as in effect before the movement to a position in a different pay system) must be determined as if the official worksite of that position of record were the same as the official worksite of the new or offered position of record. Geographic conversion is not necessary for the purpose of comparing grades if an employee is being moved to (or given a reasonable offer of) a position under the same covered pay system (*i.e.*, same grading structure).

[70 FR 31305, May 31, 2005, as amended at 73 FR 66155, Nov. 7, 2008]

Subpart B—Grade Retention

SOURCE: 70 FR 31305, May 31, 2005, unless otherwise noted.

§ 536.201 Mandatory grade retention.

(a) Subject to the requirements in this section and in §§ 536.102 and 536.203, an agency must provide grade retention to an employee who moves from a position under a covered pay system to a lower-graded position under a covered pay system as a result of—

(1) Reduction in force procedures, or

(2) A reclassification process.

(b) An agency must apply § 536.105 in determining whether a position under a different covered pay system is a lower-graded position.

(c) An employee's movement to a lower-graded position is considered to be the result of reduction in force procedures when the employee has received a specific reduction in force notice and—

(1) The employee is placed in the position offered in the notice; or

(2) The employee is placed in a position other than that offered in the notice but in the same agency, if the position was offered in writing and at the initiative of management.

(d) An employee's movement to a lower-graded position is considered to be the result of a reclassification process when—

(1) The employee remains in his or her position after it is reclassified; or

(2) The employee is placed in a different position in the same agency before the effective date of the reclassification action, if the position was offered in writing and at the initiative of management after the employee received a specific written notice that the position would be reclassified to a lower grade.

[70 FR 31305, May 31, 2005, as amended at 73 FR 66155, Nov. 7, 2008]

§536.202 Optional grade retention.

(a) Subject to the requirements in §§536.102 and 536.203, an authorized agency official may provide grade retention to an employee moving from a position under a covered pay system to a lower-graded position under a covered pay system when—

(1) Management announces a reorganization or reclassification decision in writing (including a general notice or a specific notice) that may or would affect the employee; and

(2) The employee moves to a lower-graded position (either at the employee's initiative or in response to a management-initiated offer) on or before the date the announced reorganization or reclassification is effected.

(b) An agency must apply §536.105 in determining whether a position under a different covered pay system is a lower-graded position.

(c) When an employee is offered a position with grade retention under this section in anticipation of a reduction in grade, the agency must inform the employee in writing that acceptance of the position is not required and that declination of the offer will not affect the employee's entitlement to grade retention under §536.201 if the agency actually moves the employee to the lower-graded position.

[70 FR 31305, May 31, 2005, as amended at 73 FR 66155, Nov. 7, 2008]

§536.203 Additional eligibility requirements for grade retention.

(a) An employee is eligible for grade retention under §536.201(a)(1) only if the employee has served for at least 52 consecutive weeks in one or more positions under a covered pay system at one or more grades higher than the grade of the position in which the employee is being placed. Such service is deemed to include service performed by an employee of a nonappropriated fund instrumentality of the Department of Defense or the Coast Guard (as defined in 5 U.S.C. 2105(c)) who is moved to a position in the civil service employment system of the Department of Defense or the Coast Guard, respectively, without a break in service of more than 3 days.

(b) An employee is eligible for grade retention under §536.201(a)(2) based on a reclassification of his or her position only if, immediately before the reduction in grade, that position was classified at the existing grade or a higher grade for a continuous period of at least 1 year.

(c) An employee is eligible for grade retention under §536.202 only if, immediately before being placed in the lower grade, the employee has served for at least 52 consecutive weeks in one or more positions under a covered pay system at one or more grades higher than that lower grade. Such service is deemed to include service performed by an employee of a nonappropriated fund instrumentality of the Department of Defense or the Coast Guard (as defined in 5 U.S.C. 2105(c)) who is moved to a position in the civil service employment system of the Department of Defense or the Coast Guard, respectively, without a break in service of more than 3 days.

(d) Eligibility for grade retention under §536.201 or §536.202 ceases under the conditions specified in §536.207.

§536.204 Period of grade retention.

(a) Unless grade retention is terminated under §536.208, an employee is entitled to retain the grade held immediately before the action that provides entitlement to grade retention for 2 years beginning on the date the employee is placed in the lower-graded position.

(b) During the 2-year period of grade retention, if an agency further reduces an employee in grade under circumstances also entitling the employee to grade retention, the employee must continue to retain the previous retained grade for the remainder of the first 2-year period. At the end of the first 2-year period, the employee is entitled to retain the grade of the position from which the second reduction in grade was made for 2 years following the effective date of the second reduction in grade.

(c) Notwithstanding § 536.207(a)(1), grade retention continues to apply to an employee serving under an interim appointment made under 5 CFR 772.102 for the duration of the original 2-year grade retention period if the employee's grade was retained under this part in the appointment immediately preceding the interim appointment.

§ 536.205 Applicability of retained grade.

(a) Except as provided in paragraph (b) of this section, an agency must treat an employee's retained grade as the employee's grade for all purposes, including pay and pay administration, premium pay, retirement, life insurance, and eligibility for training. If the employee's actual position of record is under a different covered pay system than the covered pay system associated with the retained grade, the agency also must treat the employee as being under the covered pay system associated with the retained grade for the same purposes.

(b) An agency may not use an employee's retained grade—

(1) In any reduction in force procedure;

(2) To determine whether an employee has been reduced in grade for the purpose of terminating grade or pay retention (*i.e.*, based on personal cause or at the employee's request);

(3) To determine whether an employee retains status as a GM employee (as defined in 5 CFR 531.203); or

(4) To determine whether an employee is exempt or nonexempt from the Fair Labor Standards Act of 1938, as amended.

§ 536.206 Determining an employee's rate of basic pay under grade retention.

(a) *General.* (1) When an employee becomes entitled to grade retention or becomes covered by one or more different pay schedules (because of a change in the employee's position of record, a change in the employee's official worksite, or the establishment of a new pay schedule) during a period of grade retention, the agency must apply the rules in this section to determine the employee's rate of basic pay.

(2) This section does not apply to an employee whose entitlement to grade retention is terminated under one of the conditions in § 536.208. (See § 536.208(d).)

(b) *Preexisting rate within a range.* If an employee is entitled to a rate of basic pay within the applicable rate range before the action resulting in application of this section, the employee is entitled to the rate(s) of basic pay in the applicable pay schedule(s) for the employee's position of record after the action (including the retained grade) which correspond to the employee's grade and step (or relative position in range for a GM employee) immediately before the action. The employee's payable rate is the corresponding rate in the highest applicable rate range for the employee's position of record after the action (including the retained grade). If an employee's rate of basic pay otherwise would be reduced because of placement under a lower-paying pay schedule (excluding any reduction that results from a geographic conversion), the employee would be eligible for pay retention under subpart C of this part to the same extent as other employees holding the same position of record whose actual grade is the same as the employee's retained grade.

(c) *Preexisting retained or saved rate.* (1) If an employee is entitled to a retained rate immediately before the action resulting in application of this section, the agency must determine the employee's payable rate of basic pay under §§ 536.303 and 536.304.

(2) If an employee is entitled to a saved rate under 5 CFR 359.705, the agency must determine the employee's payable rate of basic pay under that section.

(d) *Order of processing pay actions.* When an action resulting in application of this section takes effect on the same effective date as other pay actions that affect an employee's rate of basic pay (e.g., within-grade increase), the actions will be processed in the order prescribed in the rules governing the covered pay system of the employee's position of record (e.g., 5 CFR 531.206 for GS positions and 5 CFR 532.413 for Federal Wage System positions).

[70 FR 31305, May 31, 2005, as amended at 73 FR 66155, Nov. 7, 2008]

§ 536.207 Loss of eligibility for grade retention.

(a) Eligibility for grade retention as a result of an entitlement under § 536.201 ceases if any of the following conditions occurs at any time after the employee receives written notice of the reduction in grade, but before the commencement of the 2-year period of grade retention:

(1) The employee has a break in service of 1 workday or more;

(2) The employee is reduced in grade for personal cause or at the employee's request (based on the actual grade of the employee's position rather than the employee's retained grade and, when a movement to a different covered pay system is involved, a comparison of comparison rates under § 536.105);

(3) The employee moves to a position under a covered pay system with a grade that is equal to or higher than the retained grade (as determined under § 536.105), excluding a temporary promotion;

(4) The employee declines a reasonable offer of a position with a grade equal to or higher than the retained grade (as determined under §§ 536.104 and 536.105);

(5) The employee elects in writing to terminate the benefits of grade retention; or

(6) The employee moves to a position not under a covered pay system.

(b) Eligibility for grade retention as a result of entitlement under § 536.202 ceases if any of the following conditions occurs at any time after management informs the employee of an impending reorganization or reclassification that will or could result in a reduction in grade, but before the commencement of the 2-year period of grade retention:

(1) Any of the conditions listed in paragraph (a) of this section except that an employee's request for placement in a lower-graded position, in lieu of displacing another employee at his or her grade under reduction in force procedures, is not a declination of a reasonable offer for grade retention purposes; or

(2) The employee fails to enroll in, or to comply with reasonable written requirements established to assure full consideration under, a program providing priority consideration for placement.

(c) If an employee loses eligibility for grade retention under this section, the employee's rate of basic pay must be set in accordance with the pay-setting rules and pay rates applicable to the employee's position of record (e.g., 5 CFR part 531, subpart B, for GS positions). An employee is not eligible for pay retention under subpart C of this part based on an action that provided eligibility for grade retention if the employee elects to terminate eligibility for grade retention under paragraph (a)(5) or (b) of this section.

[70 FR 31305, May 31, 2005, as amended at 73 FR 66155, Nov. 7, 2008]

§ 536.208 Termination of grade retention.

(a) Grade retention under § 536.201 terminates if any of the conditions listed in § 536.207(a) occurs after commencement of the 2-year period of grade retention.

(b) Grade retention under § 536.202 terminates if any of the conditions listed in § 536.207(b) occurs after the commencement of the 2-year period of grade retention.

(c) Termination of grade retention benefits takes effect—

(1) At the end of the day before separation from service if termination is the result of a break in service;

(2) At the end of the day before placement if the termination is the result of

the employee's placement in another position; or

(3) At the end of the last day of the pay period in which the employee—

(i) Declines a reasonable offer;

(ii) Elects to terminate grade retention benefits (except that, if an employee's election specifically provides that the termination will take effect at the end of a later pay period, the election is considered to be made effective on the last day of that later pay period for the purpose of applying this paragraph); or

(iii) Fails to enroll in, or comply with reasonable written requirements established to assure full consideration under, a program providing priority consideration for placement.

(d) If an employee's entitlement to grade retention terminates under this section, the employee's rate of basic pay must be set in accordance with the pay-setting rules and pay rates applicable to the employee's position of record (e.g., 5 CFR part 531, subpart B, for GS positions). An employee is not entitled to pay retention under subpart C of this part based on a reduction in basic pay resulting from waiver of the employee's grade retention entitlement under paragraph (a)(5) or (b) of § 536.207.

[70 FR 31305, May 31, 2005, as amended at 73 FR 66155, Nov. 7, 2008]

Subpart C—Pay Retention

SOURCE: 70 FR 31310, May 31, 2005, unless otherwise noted.

§ 536.301 Mandatory pay retention.

(a) Subject to the requirements in § 536.102 and this section, an agency must provide pay retention to an employee who moves between positions under a covered pay system or from a position not under a covered pay system to a position under a covered pay system and whose payable rate of basic pay otherwise would be reduced (after application of any applicable geographic conversion under § 536.303(a)) as a result of—

(1) The expiration of the 2-year period of grade retention under subpart B of this part;

(2) A reduction in force or reclassification action that places an employee in a lower-graded position when the employee does not meet the eligibility requirements for grade retention under subpart B of this part;

(3) A management action that places an employee in a non-special rate position or in a lower-paid special rate position from a special rate position;

(4) A management action that places an employee under a different pay schedule;

(5) A management action that places an employee in a formal employee development program generally utilized Governmentwide (e.g., Recent Graduates Program); or

(6) A reduction or elimination of scheduled rates, special schedules, or special rate schedules, excluding—

(i) A statutory reduction in scheduled rates of pay under the General Schedule, including a reduction authorized under 5 U.S.C. 5303(b); or

(ii) A statutory reduction in a prevailing rate schedule established under 5 U.S.C. chapter 53, subchapter IV, and 5 CFR part 532.

(b) An agency must establish a retained rate when application of a promotion increase rule for General Schedule or prevailing rate employees results in a payable rate of basic pay that exceeds the maximum rate of the highest applicable rate range for the employee's new position. (See the promotion increase rules in 5 U.S.C. 5334(b) and 5 CFR 531.214 for GS employees and in 5 CFR 532.407 for prevailing rate employees—in particular, the special provisions in these promotion increase rules on establishing a retained rate equal to an employee's existing rate when that existing rate exceeds the applicable range maximum.) Once established, such a retained rate is governed by the provisions of this subpart.

(c) If an employee's official worksite changes in conjunction with an action that may entitle the employee to pay retention under paragraph (a) of this section, the agency must apply the geographic conversion rule in § 536.303(a) before determining whether an employee's rate of basic pay otherwise would be reduced.

(d) An employee is considered "placed" under paragraph (a)(2), (3), (4), and (5) of this section only when the employee remains in a position in the same agency. Optional pay retention under §536.302 may apply when an employee transfers to a different agency as a result of a reduction in force or reclassification action or is selected by a different agency to fill a position under a formal employee development program, if all other qualifying conditions are met.

(e) Eligibility for pay retention under this section ceases under the conditions specified in §536.308.

[70 FR 31310, May 31, 2005, as amended at 73 FR 66155, Nov. 7, 2008; 77 FR 28223, May 11, 2012]

§536.302 Optional pay retention.

(a) Subject to the requirements in §536.102 and this section, an authorized agency official may provide pay retention to an employee not entitled to pay retention under §536.301, but whose payable rate of basic pay otherwise would be reduced (after application of any applicable geographic conversion under §536.303(a)) as the result of a management action. This includes a management action to move an employee's position, without a break in service of more than 3 days, from a Department of Defense or Coast Guard nonappropriated fund instrumentality (as defined in 5 U.S.C. 2105(c)) to a position under a covered pay system in the same agency.

(b) If an employee's official worksite changes in conjunction with an action that may entitle the employee to pay retention under paragraph (a) of this section, the agency must apply the geographic conversion rule in §536.303(a) before determining whether an employee's rate of basic pay otherwise would be reduced.

(c) Eligibility for pay retention under this section ceases under the conditions specified in §536.308.

§536.303 Geographic conversion.

(a) *Geographic conversion at time of action that may provide initial entitlement to pay retention.* If, in conjunction with a pay action that may entitle the employee to pay retention under §§536.301 or 536.302, an employee's official worksite is changed to a new location where different pay schedules apply, the agency must convert the employee's rate(s) of basic pay to the applicable pay schedule(s) in the new location before applying the pay retention rules in this subpart or any other simultaneous pay action (other than a general pay adjustment). The agency must identify the highest applicable rate range that would apply to the employee's position of record before the pay action as if that position were stationed at the new official worksite and determine the employee's converted payable rate of basic pay based on the step (or relative position in range for a GM employee) in that range that corresponds to the employee's step (or relative position in range for a GM employee) before the pay action. A reduction in an employee's payable rate of basic pay resulting from this geographic conversion is not a basis for entitlement to pay retention. The pay retention rules in this subpart must be applied as if the employee's payable rate of basic pay after geographic conversion is the employee's existing payable rate of basic pay in effect immediately before the action.

(b) *Geographic conversion when a retained rate employee's official worksite is changed.* When an employee is receiving a retained rate and the employee's official worksite is changed to a new location where different pay schedules apply, the agency must apply the following rules (after applying any simultaneous general pay adjustment under §536.305) to derive the converted retained rate that will be used as the existing retained rate in determining the employee's pay retention entitlement in the new position of record and at the new official worksite:

(1) Identify the maximum rate for the highest applicable rate range that applies to the employee's former position of record based on the former official worksite;

(2) Identify the maximum rate for the highest applicable rate range that would apply to the employee's former position of record if the employee were stationed at the official worksite for the new position of record;

(3) Divide the maximum rate identified in paragraph (b)(2) of this section by the maximum rate identified in paragraph (b)(1) of this section and

round the result to the fourth decimal place; and

(4) Multiply the factor resulting from paragraph (b)(3) of this section by the employee's former retained rate and round to the nearest whole dollar (for an annual rate) or the nearest whole cent (for an hourly rate) to derive the employee's converted retained rate at the new official worksite.

[70 FR 31310, May 31, 2005, as amended at 73 FR 66155, Nov. 7, 2008]

§ 536.304 Determining an employee's pay retention entitlement.

(a) *General.* (1) When an employee becomes entitled to pay retention under § 536.301 or 536.302 or undergoes a change in his or her position of record or pay schedule while receiving a retained rate (when the terminating conditions for pay retention under § 536.308 do not apply), the agency must determine the employee's pay retention entitlement following the rules in this section.

(2) Any general pay adjustment (including a retained rate adjustment under § 536.305) that takes effect on the same date as an action described in paragraph (a)(1) of this section must be processed first, before any other pay action and before applying the rules in paragraphs (a)(3), (a)(4), (b), or (c) of this section, as applicable.

(3) If the location of an employee's official worksite changes in conjunction with an action that may provide initial entitlement to pay retention, the agency must apply the geographic conversion rule under § 536.303(a) before applying the rules in paragraph (b) of this section. The converted rate of basic pay must be treated as the employee's existing payable rate of basic pay in applying those rules.

(4) If the location of an employee's official worksite changes while he or she is receiving a retained rate, the agency must apply the geographic conversion rule under § 536.303(b) before applying the rules in paragraph (c) of this section. The converted retained rate must be treated as the employee's existing retained rate in applying those rules.

(5) When an employee's pay retention entitlement is established or redetermined under this section on the same effective date as other pay actions that affect an employee's rate of basic pay, the actions must be processed in the order prescribed under the rules governing the covered pay system of the employee's position of record (e.g., 5 CFR 531.206 for GS positions and 5 CFR 532.413 for Federal Wage System positions).

(6) In applying this section, an agency must convert an employee's existing annual rate of pay to an hourly rate of pay if the employee's new position is under a pay system that uses only hourly rates. An agency must convert an employee's existing hourly rate of pay to an annual rate of pay if the employee's new position is under a pay system that uses annual rates of pay.

(b) *Determining initial pay retention entitlement.* When an employee becomes entitled to pay retention under § 536.301 or 536.302, the agency must determine the employee's pay retention entitlement under the following rules (subject to the requirements in paragraph (a) of this section):

(1) If an employee's existing payable rate of basic pay is less than or equal to the maximum rate of the highest applicable rate range for the grade of the employee's position of record immediately after the event causing the pay retention entitlement, the employee is entitled to the lowest rate of basic pay in such rate range that equals or exceeds the employee's existing payable rate of basic pay. If an employee's payable rate of basic pay is set at or below the maximum rate of the highest applicable rate range, pay retention under this subpart ceases to apply to the employee.

(2) If the employee's existing payable rate of basic pay is greater than the maximum rate of the highest applicable rate range for the grade of the employee's position immediately after the event causing the pay retention entitlement, the employee is entitled to a retained rate equal to the employee's existing payable rate of basic pay, subject to the limitations in paragraph (b)(3) of this section.

(3) A newly established retained rate may not exceed—

(i) 150 percent of the maximum payable rate of basic pay of the highest applicable rate range for the grade of the employee's position of record; or

(ii) The Executive Level IV maximum rate limitation established under §536.306.

(4) In applying this section for an employee who becomes eligible for pay retention while serving on a temporary promotion or temporary reassignment, the agency must use the rate of basic pay the employee would have received if the temporary promotion or temporary reassignment had not occurred.

(c) *Redetermining pay retention entitlement at time of change in position or pay schedule.* When an employee receiving a retained rate undergoes a change in position or pay schedule that results in a new highest applicable rate range (and when the terminating conditions for pay retention under §536.308(a)(1), (3), (4), and (5) do not apply), the agency must determine the employee's pay retention entitlement under the following rules (subject to the requirements in paragraph (a) of this section):

(1) If the employee's grade and pay system are not changing and if the employee's existing retained rate is less than or equal to the maximum rate of the highest applicable rate range for the employee's position of record immediately after the position or schedule change, the employee is entitled to the maximum rate of the highest applicable rate range, and pay retention ceases to apply.

(2) If the employee's grade and pay system are not changing and if the employee's existing retained rate is greater than the maximum rate on the highest applicable rate range for the employee's position of record immediately after the position or schedule change, the employee continues to be entitled to the existing retained rate.

(3) If the employee's pay system is not changing but the employee is being promoted to a higher-graded position, the agency must apply the applicable promotion rules to determine the employee's payable rate of basic pay (e.g., the rules in 5 CFR 531.214(d)(5) for GS positions and 5 CFR 532.407 for Federal Wage System positions). If the promotion action results in a terminating condition as described in §536.308 (e.g., the resulting rate is equal to or greater than the existing retained rate), pay retention ceases to apply. Otherwise, the employee's existing retained rate continues.

(4) If the employee is moving to a position under a different covered pay system whose grade has a higher comparison rate, the agency must apply the applicable pay administration rules to determine the employee's payable rate of basic pay (e.g., part 531, subpart B, for GS positions and part 532 for Federal Wage System provisions). If the promotion action results in a terminating condition as described in §536.308 (e.g., the resulting rate is equal to or greater than the existing retained rate), pay retention ceases to apply. Otherwise, the employee's existing retained rate continues.

(5) In applying this section to a retained rate employee who receives a temporary promotion or temporary reassignment, the temporary promotion or temporary reassignment is not a basis for permanently terminating an employee's pay retention entitlement. When the temporary promotion or temporary reassignment ends, the employee's pay retention entitlement will be determined as if the employee had not received the temporary promotion or temporary reassignment.

(6) Notwithstanding §536.308(a)(1), an agency must continue a retained rate entitlement for an employee serving under an interim appointment made under 5 CFR 772.102 if the employee's pay was retained under this subpart under the appointment immediately preceding the interim appointment.

[70 FR 31310, May 31, 2005, as amended at 73 FR 66156, Nov. 7, 2008]

§536.305 Adjusting an employee's retained rate when a pay schedule is adjusted.

(a)(1) Except as otherwise provided in this section, when the maximum rate of the highest applicable rate range for an employee's position of record is increased while the employee is receiving a retained rate, the employee is entitled to 50 percent of the amount of the increase in that maximum rate, subject to the maximum rate limitation in §536.306. This 50-percent adjustment rule applies only when the maximum rate increases are attributable to the adjustment of the employee's existing pay schedule or the establishment of a new pay schedule that covers the employee's existing position of record.

(2) As provided in 5 CFR 531.206, a retained rate adjustment under paragraph (a)(1) of this section is a general pay adjustment that must be applied before any geographic conversion under § 536.303(b) or any other simultaneous pay action. The retained rate adjustment under paragraph (a)(1) of this section must be determined based on the employee's position of record and official worksite as in effect immediately before the effective date of the adjustment.

(3) Consistent with 5 U.S.C. 5363(c), a change in the maximum rate of the highest applicable rate range based on a change in the employee's official worksite is not considered in applying paragraph (a)(1) of this section. The employee's new retained rate must be determined under the geographic conversion rule in § 536.303(b).

(4) Paragraph (a)(1) of this section does not apply to an increase in an employee's highest applicable rate range that results from a change in the employee's position of record. Such an increase is not attributable to an adjustment in the pay schedule applicable to the employee's position and thus is not an increase as described in 5 U.S.C. 5363(b)(2)(B).

(b) When a pay schedule adjustment causes an employee's retained rate (after any adjustment under this section) to become equal to or lower than the maximum rate of the highest applicable rate range for the grade of the employee's position, the employee is entitled to the maximum rate of the highest applicable rate range, and pay retention ceases to apply.

§ 536.306 Limitation on retained rates.

(a) A retained rate may not at any time exceed the rate payable for level IV of the Executive Schedule.

(b) When an employee's retained rate is limited under this section, an agency may not apply this subpart or the provisions of any other law or regulation to the rate of basic pay the employee would have received but for this limitation.

§ 536.307 Treatment of a retained rate as basic pay for other purposes.

(a) A retained rate is considered to be an employee's rate of basic pay for the purpose of computing or applying—

(1) Retirement deductions, contributions, and benefits under 5 U.S.C. chapters 83 and 84;

(2) Life insurance premiums and benefits under 5 U.S.C. chapter 87;

(3) Premium pay under 5 U.S.C. chapter 55, subchapter V, and 5 CFR part 532 and part 550, subparts A and I;

(4) Severance pay under 5 U.S.C. 5595 and 5 CFR part 550, subpart G;

(5) Post differentials under 5 U.S.C. 5925 and danger pay allowances under 5 U.S.C. 5928;

(6) Nonforeign area cost-of-living allowances and post differentials under 5 U.S.C. 5941(a) and 5 CFR part 591, subpart B;

(7) Lump-sum payments for accumulated and annual leave under 5 CFR part 550, subpart L;

(8) General Schedule pay administration provisions (e.g., promotion increases) to the extent provided in 5 CFR part 531, subpart B;

(9) Pay administration provisions for prevailing rate employees to the extent provided in 5 CFR part 532;

(10) Adverse action provisions in 5 CFR part 752;

(11) Other provisions as specified in other statutes or regulations; and

(12) Payments and benefits equivalent to those listed in this section under other legal authorities, as determined by the head of the agency or other authorized official responsible for administering such payments or benefits.

(b) For the purpose of applying other laws and regulations not listed in paragraph (a) of this section to an employee receiving a retained rate, the employee's rate of basic pay is deemed to be the applicable maximum rate of basic pay for the employee's position of record (e.g., the maximum rate of basic pay for a locality rate range or special rate range, as applicable, for the purpose of computing a percentage-based award under 5 CFR 451.104(g)).

[70 FR 31310, May 31, 2005, as amended at 73 FR 66156, Nov. 7, 2008]

§ 536.308 Loss of eligibility for or termination of pay retention.

(a) Eligibility for pay retention ceases if any of the following conditions occurs at any time after the employee has received written notification that the employee's pay will be reduced, and entitlement to pay retention terminates if any of the following conditions occurs after the commencement of pay retention:

(1) The employee has a break in service of 1 workday or more;

(2) The employee is entitled to a rate of basic pay under a covered pay system which is equal to or greater than the employee's retained rate (after applying any applicable geographic conversion under paragraph (b) of this section), except that entitlement to a retained rate will not be terminated based on entitlement to an equal or higher rate of basic pay during a temporary promotion or temporary reassignment but will be held in abeyance during that temporary period.

(3) The employee declines a reasonable offer (as determined under § 536.104) of a position in which the employee's rate of basic pay would be equal to or greater than the employee's retained rate (after applying any applicable geographic conversion under paragraph (b) of this section);

(4) The employee is reduced in grade for personal cause or at the employee's request (based on the actual grade of the employee's position rather than the employee's retained grade and, when a movement to a different covered pay system is involved, a comparison of comparison rates under § 536.105); or

(5) The employee moves to a position not under a covered pay system.

(b) When the rate comparison required by paragraph (a)(2) or (3) of this section involves a new or offered position that is located in a different geographic area where different pay schedules would apply to the employee's existing position of record, the agency must convert the employee's existing retained rate using the geographic conversion rules in § 536.303(b) before making the rate comparison. The converted retained rate must be compared to the payable rate of basic pay for the new or offered position in determining whether the rate of basic pay for an offered position is equal to or higher than the employee's retained rate.

(c) Termination of pay retention benefits takes effect—

(1) At the end of the day before separation from service if termination is the result of a break in service;

(2) At the end of the day before the employee becomes entitled to an equal or greater rate as described in paragraph (a)(2) of this section;

(3) At the end of the day before placement or movement if the termination is the result of the employee's placement in or movement to another position; or

(4) At the end of the last day of the pay period in which the employee declines a reasonable offer.

(d) If an employee's eligibility for pay retention ceases or entitlement to pay retention terminates under this section, the employee's rate of basic pay must be set using the pay-setting rules applicable to the employee's position of record (e.g., 5 CFR part 531, subpart B, for GS positions). However, when an employee's retained rate is terminated under paragraph (a)(2) or (3) of this section and the employee's grade is unchanged, the employee's payable rate of basic pay may not be set below the maximum rate of the highest applicable rate range.

[70 FR 31310, May 31, 2005, as amended at 73 FR 66156, Nov. 7, 2008]

§ 536.309 Converting retained rates on May 1, 2005.

(a) Consistent with section 301(d)(2) of Public Law 108–411, an agency must convert an employee's retained rate or similar rate, as described in paragraph (b) of this section, to a retained rate under this subpart on May 1, 2005. The new retained rate must equal the retained rate in effect on April 30, 2005, as adjusted to include any applicable locality payment under 5 U.S.C. 5304 or similar provision of law.

(b) This section applies to an employee under a covered pay system who, on April 30, 2005, was receiving—

(1) A retained rate under 5 U.S.C. 5363;

(2) A rate paid under the authority of 5 U.S.C. 5334(b) or 5 U.S.C. 5362 which was greater than the maximum rate of

basic pay payable for the grade of the employee's position of record; or

(3) A continued rate of pay under 5 CFR part 531, subpart C or G (as contained in the January 1, 2005, edition of title 5, Code of Federal Regulations, parts 1 to 699) which was greater than the maximum rate of basic pay payable for the grade of the employee's position.

(c) The conversion rules in this section must be applied before any simultaneous pay action that takes effect on May 1, 2005.

§ 536.310 Exceptions for certain employees in nonforeign areas.

(a) Notwithstanding §§ 536.304(b)(3) and 536.306(a), an employee who is receiving a retained rate in excess of Executive Schedule level IV on January 1, 2012, consistent with the Non-Foreign Retirement Equity Assurance Act of 2009 (subtitle B of title XIX of Pub. L. 111–84), may continue to receive a retained rate higher than Executive Schedule level IV until—

(1) The retained rate becomes equal to or falls below Executive Schedule level IV; or

(2) The employee ceases to be entitled to pay retention under § 536.308.

(b) Notwithstanding 5 U.S.C. 5361(1) and § 536.102(b)(2), an employee who is employed on a temporary or term basis is not barred from receiving a retained rate if such employee—

(1) Is receiving a special rate above Executive Schedule level IV on January 1, 2012, and is covered by paragraph (a) of this section; or

(2) Is receiving a special rate incorporating an additional adjustment under section 1915(b)(1) of the Non-Foreign Retirement Equity Assurance Act (subtitle B of title XIX of Pub. L. 111–84) at the time the employee's special rate schedule is reduced or terminated.

[76 FR 68634, Nov. 7, 2011]

Subpart D—Appeals and Miscellaneous Provisions

SOURCE: 45 FR 85656, Dec. 30, 1980, unless otherwise noted. Redesignated at 70 FR 31310, May 31, 2005.

§ 536.401 Placement and classification plans.

(a) Agencies which employ individuals subject to this part are required to establish in writing placement and classification plans.

(b) The placement and classification plans must commit the agency to:

(1) Identify and correct classification errors; and

(2) Correct position management problems; and

(3) Carry out specific planned efforts to place employees subject to this part; and

(4) Pursue placement efforts that do not adversely affect affirmative action goals.

[45 FR 85656, Dec. 30, 1980. Redesignated at 70 FR 31310, May 31, 2005.]

§ 536.402 Appeal of termination of benefits because of reasonable offer.

(a) Except as provided for in paragraph (e) of this section, an employee whose grade or pay retention benefits are terminated on the grounds the employee declined a reasonable offer of a position the grade or pay of which is equal to or greater than his or her retained grade or pay may appeal the termination to the Office of Personnel Management.

(b) An employee who appeals under this section shall file the appeal in writing with the Office of Personnel Management not later than 20 calendar days after being notified that his or her grade of pay retention benefits have been terminated, and shall state in the appeal the reasons why the employee believes the offer of a position was not a reasonable offer.

(c) The Office of Personnel Management may conduct any investigation or hearing it determines necessary to ascertain the facts of the case.

(d) If a decision by the Office of Personnel Management on an appeal under this section requires corrective action by an agency, including the retroactive or prospective restoration of grade or pay retention benefits, the agency shall take that corrective action.

(e) Termination of benefits based on a declination of a reasonable offer by an employee in an exclusively recognized bargaining unit may be reviewed under the negotiated grievance and arbitration procedures in accordance with chapter 71 of title 5, United States Code, and the terms of any applicable collective bargaining agreement. An employee in an exclusively recognized bargaining unit may not appeal a termination of benefits to the Office of Personnel Management if the grievance procedure of the agreement by which he or she is covered provides for this review.

(f) Decisions issued by the Office of Personnel Management shall be considered final decisions. OPM may, at its discretion, reconsider an original appellate decision when new and material information is presented, in writing, by the employee or the agency, which establishes a reasonable doubt as to the appropriateness of the original decision. The request must show that the information was not readily available when the decision was issued. A request for reconsideration of an original appeal decision must be submitted to OPM within 30 calendar days of the date of the original decision.

[45 FR 85656, Dec. 30, 1980, as amended at 50 FR 428, Jan. 4, 1985; 50 FR 45389, Oct. 31, 1985. Redesignated at 70 FR 31310, May 31, 2005]

§ 536.403 Documentation.

The application of the provisions of this part shall be documented in writing as a permanent part of the employee's Official Personnel Folder. As a minimum this documentation will include a copy of the letter described in § 536.404.

[45 FR 85656, Dec. 30, 1980. Redesignated and amended at 70 FR 31310, May 31, 2005]

§ 536.404 Issuance of employee letters.

When an employee is entitled to grade and/or pay retention, the employing agency shall give to the employee, with a copy of the Notification of Personnel Action (SF–50) documenting entitlement to grade and/or pay retention, a letter describing the circumstances warranting grade and/or pay retention, and the nature of that entitlement.

[45 FR 85656, Dec. 30, 1980. Redesignated at 70 FR 31310, May 31, 2005]

§ 536.405 Availability of information.

(a) The Office, upon a request which identifies the individual from whose file the information is sought, shall disclose the following information from an appeal file to a member of the public, except when the disclosure would constitute a clearly unwarranted invasion of personal privacy:

(1) Confirmation of the name of the individual from whose file the information is sought and the names of the other parties concerned;

(2) The status of the appeal;

(3) The results of the appeal (*i.e.*, proper title, pay plan, series, and grade);

(4) The classification requested (*i.e.*, title, pay plan, series, and grade); and

(5) With the consent of the parties concerned, other reasonably identified information from the file.

(b) The Office will disclose to the parties concerned, the information contained in an appeal file in proceedings under this part, except when the disclosure would violate the proscription against the disclosure of medical information in § 297.205 of this chapter. For the purposes of this section, "the parties concerned" means the Government employee or former Government employee involved in the proceedings, his or her representative designated in writing, and the representative of the agency or the Office involved in the proceeding.

[50 FR 3313, Jan. 24, 1985, as amended at 54 FR 18879, May 3, 1989. Redesignated and amended at 70 FR 31310, May 31, 2005]

PART 537—REPAYMENT OF STUDENT LOANS

Sec.

AUTHORITY: 5 U.S.C. 2301, 2302, and 5379(g); E.O. 11478, 3 CFR 1966–1970 Comp., page 803, unless otherwise noted, E.O. 13087; and E.O. 13152.

SOURCE: 73 FR 64865, Oct. 31, 2008, unless otherwise noted.

§ 537.101 Purpose.

This part implements 5 U.S.C. 5379, which authorizes agencies to establish a student loan repayment program for the purpose of recruiting or retaining highly qualified personnel. Under such a program, an agency may agree to repay (by direct payment to the loan holder on behalf of the employee) all or part of any outstanding qualifying student loan or loans previously taken out by a job candidate to whom an offer of employment has been made, or by a current employee of the agency.

§ 537.102 Definitions.

The definitions in this section apply only to part 537. In this part:

Agency has the meaning given that term in subparagraphs (A) through (E) of 5 U.S.C. 4101(1).

Authorized agency official means the head of an Executive agency or an official who is authorized to act for the head of the agency in the matter concerned.

Employee means an employee of an agency who satisfies the definition of the term in 5 U.S.C. 2105.

Loan payment means the net payment made by an agency to the holder of a student loan (after deducting any tax withholdings that may be made from the gross student loan repayment benefit credited to the employee).

Service agreement means a written agreement between an agency and an employee (or job candidate) under which the employee (or job candidate) agrees to a specified period of service in exchange for student loan repayment benefits, subject to the conditions set forth under this part.

Student loan means—

(1) A loan made, insured, or guaranteed under parts B, D or E of title IV of the Higher Education Act of 1965; or

(2) A health education assistance loan made or insured under part A of title VII of the Public Health Service Act or under part E of title VIII of that Act.

Student loan repayment benefit means the benefit provided to an employee under this part in which an agency repays (by a direct payment on behalf of the employee) a qualifying student loan as described in § 537.106(b) previously taken out by such employee. The dollar value of this benefit is the gross amount credited to the employee at the time of a loan payment to the holder of the student loan, before deducting any employee tax withholdings from that gross amount as described in § 537.106(a)(6)(iii). A student loan repayment benefit is not considered basic pay for any purpose.

Time-limited appointment means a nonpermanent appointment including—

(1) A temporary appointment under 5 CFR part 316, subpart D, or similar authority;

(2) A term appointment under 5 CFR part 316, subpart C, or similar authority;

(3) An overseas limited appointment with a time limitation under 5 CFR part 301, subpart B;

(4) A limited term or limited emergency appointment in the Senior Executive Service, as defined in 5 U.S.C. 3132(a), or an equivalent appointment made for similar purposes;

(5) A Veterans Recruitment Appointment under 5 CFR part 307;

(6) A Presidential Management Fellows Program appointment under § 213.3402(c) of this chapter;

(7) A Recent Graduates Program appointment under § 213.3402(b) of this chapter; and

(8) An appointment under the fellowship and similar programs authority at 5 CFR 213.3102(r).

[73 FR 64865, Oct. 31, 2008, as amended at 77 FR 28223, May 11, 2012]

§ 537.103 Agency student loan repayment plans.

Before providing student loan repayment benefits under this part, an agency must establish a student loan repayment plan. This plan must include the following elements:

(a) The designation of officials with authority to review and approve offering student loan repayment benefits (which may parallel the approval delegations used for other recruitment, relocation, and retention incentives);

(b) The situations in which the student loan repayment authority may be used;

(c) The criteria to meet or consider in authorizing student loan repayment benefits, including criteria for determining the size and timing of the loan payment(s);

(d) A system for selecting employees (or job candidates) to receive student loan repayment benefits that ensures fair and equitable treatment;

(e) The requirements associated with service agreements (including a basis for determining the length of service to be required if it is greater than the statutory minimum);

(f) The procedures for making loan payments;

(g) The provisions for recovering any amount outstanding from an employee who fails to satisfy a service agreement and conditions for waiving an employee's obligation to reimburse the agency for payments made under this part; and

(h) Documentation and recordkeeping requirements sufficient to allow reconstruction of each action to approve a student loan repayment benefit.

§537.104 Employee eligibility.

(a) Subject to the conditions in 5 U.S.C. 5379 and this part, an authorized agency official may approve student loan repayment benefits to recruit a highly qualified job candidate or retain a highly qualified employee who, during the service period established under a service agreement (consistent with §537.107), will be serving under—

(1) An appointment other than a time-limited appointment; or

(2) A time-limited appointment if—

(i) The employee (or job candidate) will have at least 3 years remaining under the appointment after the beginning of the service period established under a service agreement; or

(ii) The time-limited appointment authority leads to conversion to another appointment of sufficient duration so that his or her employment with the agency is projected to last for at least 3 additional years after the beginning of the service period established under a service agreement.

(b) An employee occupying a position that is excepted from the competitive service because of its confidential, policy-determining, policy-making, or policy-advocating character is ineligible for student loan repayment benefits.

(c) An employee becomes ineligible for student loan repayment benefits under the conditions described in §537.108.

§537.105 Criteria for payment.

(a) *General criteria.* Before authorizing student loan repayment benefits for an employee (or job candidate), an agency must make a written determination that—

(1) The employee (or job candidate) is highly qualified and otherwise eligible (as described in §537.104); and

(2)(i) In a case where the authorization is granted to recruit a job candidate to fill an agency position, the agency otherwise would encounter difficulty in filling a position with a highly qualified individual; or

(ii) In a case where the authorization is granted to retain a current employee of the agency, the employee otherwise is likely to leave the agency for employment outside the Federal service and it is essential to retain the employee based on the employee's high or unique qualifications or a special need of the agency.

(b) *Retention considerations.* In making a determination under paragraph (a)(2)(ii) of this section, an agency must consider the extent to which the employee's departure would affect the agency's ability to carry out an activity or perform a function that is deemed essential to its mission.

(c) *Current Federal employees.* An agency may not authorize student loan repayment benefits to recruit an individual from outside the agency who is currently employed in the Federal service.

(d) *Selection.* When selecting employees (or job candidates) to receive student loan repayment benefits, agencies must ensure that benefits are awarded without regard to race, color, religion, sex (including pregnancy and gender identity), national origin, age (as defined by the Age Discrimination in Employment Act of 1967, as amended), disability, genetic information (including family medical history), marital status, political affiliation, sexual orientation, labor affiliation or nonaffiliation, status as a parent, or any other non-merit-based factor, unless specifically designated by statute as a factor that must be taken into consideration when awarding such benefits, or retaliation for exercising rights with respect to the categories enumerated above, where retaliation rights are available.

[73 FR 64865, Oct. 31, 2008, as amended at 79 FR 43923, July 29, 2014]

§ 537.106 Conditions and procedures for providing student loan repayment benefits.

(a) *General conditions.* (1) Student loan repayment benefits may be provided at the discretion of the agency and are subject to such terms, limitations, or conditions as may be mutually agreed to in writing by the agency and the employee (or job candidate) as part of a service agreement under § 537.107.

(2) The student loan to be repaid must be a qualifying student loan as set forth in paragraph (b) of this section.

(3) The agency must document in writing each approval of student loan repayment benefits. An authorized agency official must review and approve each written determination. The written determination must show the employee (or job candidate) meets the criteria specified in § 537.105.

(4) An authorized agency official must approve student loan repayment benefits in connection with a recruitment action before the job candidate actually enters on duty in the position for which he or she was recruited. The agency and the job candidate may sign the service agreement consistent with § 537.107 before the job candidate begins serving in the position, but the agency may not begin making loan payments until the job candidate begins serving in the position.

(5) Student loan repayment benefits are in addition to basic pay and any other form of compensation otherwise payable to the employee involved.

(6) Appropriate tax withholdings must be deducted or applied at the time any payment is made. Since these tax implications could create a financial hardship for the recipient of the student loan repayment benefit, agencies may lessen the impact of tax withholdings on an employee's paycheck in one of the following ways:

(i) Make smaller payments at periodic intervals throughout the year, rather than issue payments under this part in one lump sum;

(ii) Allow the employee to write a check to the agency to cover his or her tax liability, rather than have the tax liability withheld from the employee's paycheck;

(iii) Deduct the amount of taxes to be withheld from the student loan repayment benefit before the balance is issued as a loan payment to the holder of the loan.

NOTE TO § 537.106(a)(6): Contact the Internal Revenue Service for further details concerning these options, as well as the tax withholding implications of payments under this part.

(b) *Qualifying student loans.* (1) The agency may make loan payments only for student loan debts that are outstanding at the time the agency and the employee (or job candidate) enter into a service agreement. Before authorizing loan payments, an agency must verify with the holder of the loan that the employee (or job candidate) has an outstanding student loan that qualifies for repayment under this part. The agency must verify remaining balances to ensure that loans are not overpaid.

(2) The agency may repay more than one loan if the employee's student loan repayment benefit does not exceed the limits set forth in paragraph (c) of this section.

(3) These regulations do not impose a limit on the age of a student loan for qualification purposes. The agency may, however, specify in its agency plan that only student loans made within a certain timeframe are eligible for repayment.

(c) *Benefit amount.* (1) In determining the amount of student loan repayment benefits to approve, an agency must consider the employee's (or job candidate's) value to the agency and how far in advance the agency is permitted to commit funds. If an agency decides to make additional student loan repayment benefits contingent on budget levels or other factors, it must address these contingent benefits in the written service agreement as described in §537.107(a).

(2) The amount of student loan repayment benefits provided by an agency is subject to both of the following limits:

(i) $10,000 per employee per calendar year; and

(ii) A total of $60,000 per employee.

(3) In applying the limits in paragraph (c)(2) of this section, the agency must count the full student loan repayment benefit (*i.e.*, before deducting any tax withholdings as described in paragraph (a)(6)(iii) of this section).

(d) *Employee responsibility.* Loan payments made by an agency under this part do not exempt an employee from his or her responsibility and/or liability for any loan(s) the individual has taken out. The employee also is responsible for any income tax obligations resulting from the student loan repayment benefit.

§537.107 Service agreements.

(a) Before an employing agency makes any loan payments for an employee, the employee (or job candidate) must sign a written service agreement to complete a specified period of service with the agency and to reimburse the agency for the student loan repayment benefit when required by §537.109. The service agreement also may specify any other employment conditions the agency considers to be appropriate, including the employee's (or job candidate's) position and the duties he or she is expected to perform, his or her work schedule, his or her level of performance, and the geographic location of his or her position. (See §§537.108 and 537.109.) The service agreement may address the possibility that, during the period the agreement is in effect, the agency may modify the agreement to provide student loan repayment benefits in addition to those fixed in the agreement based on contingencies or conditions specified in the agreement.

(b) The minimum period of service to be established under a service agreement is 3 years, regardless of the amount of student loan repayment benefits authorized. The agency and the employee may mutually agree to modify an existing service agreement, subject to the limitations at §537.106(c)(2), to provide additional student loan repayment benefits for additional service without the need for an entirely new service agreement (which would require a new 3-year minimum service period). Periods of leave without pay, or other periods during which the employee is not in a pay status, do not count toward completion of the required service period. Thus, the service completion date must be extended by the total amount of time spent in nonpay status. However, as provided by 5 CFR 353.107, absence because of uniformed service or compensable injury is considered creditable toward the required service period upon reemployment.

(c) A service agreement made under this part in no way constitutes a promise of, or right or entitlement to, appointment, continued employment, or noncompetitive conversion to the competitive service. This condition should be stated in the service agreement.

(d) The service period begins on the date specified in the service agreement. That beginning date may not be—

(1) Earlier than the date the service agreement is signed; or

(2) Earlier than the date the individual begins serving in the position for which he or she was recruited (when student loan repayment benefits are approved to recruit a job candidate to fill an agency position).

(e) The service agreement must contain a provision addressing whether the individual would be required to reimburse the paying agency for student loan repayment benefits if he or she voluntarily separates from the paying agency to work for another agency before the end of the service period. (See §537.109(b)(2).)

(f) The agency may include in a service agreement specific conditions (in addition to those required by law) that trigger the loss of eligibility for student loan repayment benefits and/or a requirement that the employee reimburse the agency for student loan repayment benefits already received. (See §§537.108(a)(3) and 537.109(a)(2).)

However, a service agreement may not require reimbursement based on—

(1) An employee's failure to maintain performance at a particular level (unless the employee is separated based on unacceptable performance); or

(2) An involuntary separation for reasons other than misconduct, unacceptable performance, or a negative suitability determination under 5 CFR part 731 (e.g., an involuntary separation resulting from a reduction in force or medical reasons).

§ 537.108 Loss of eligibility for student loan repayment benefits.

(a) An employee receiving student loan repayment benefits from an agency is ineligible for continued benefits from that agency if the employee—

(1) Separates from the agency;

(2) Does not maintain an acceptable level of performance, as determined under standards and procedures prescribed by the agency; or

(3) Violates a condition in the service agreement, if the agreement specifically provides that eligibility is lost when the condition is violated.

(b) For the purpose of applying paragraph (a)(2) of this section, an acceptable level of performance is one that is equivalent to level 3 ("Fully Successful" or equivalent) or higher, as described in 5 CFR 430.208(d). An employee loses eligibility for student loan repayment benefits if his or her most recent official performance evaluation does not meet this requirement.

§ 537.109 Employee reimbursements to the Government.

(a) An employee is indebted to the Federal Government and must reimburse the paying agency for the amount of any student loan repayment benefits received under a service agreement if he or she—

(1) Fails to complete the period of service required in the applicable service agreement (except as provided by paragraph (b) of this section); or

(2) Violates any other condition that specifically triggers a reimbursement requirement under the agreement.

(b) An agency may not apply paragraph (a) of this section based on an employee's failure to complete the required period of service established under a service agreement if—

(1) The employee is involuntarily separated for reasons other than misconduct, unacceptable performance, or a negative suitability determination under 5 CFR part 731; or

(2) The employee leaves the paying agency voluntarily to enter into the service of any other agency, unless reimbursement to the agency is otherwise required in the service agreement, as provided by § 537.107(e).

(c) If an agency and an employee mutually agree to modify an existing service agreement to provide additional student loan repayment benefits for additional service (as provided by § 537.107(b)), the modified service agreement may stipulate that, if the employee completes the initial service period but fails to complete the additional service period, he or she is required to reimburse the paying agency only for the amount of any student loan repayment benefits received during the additional service period.

(d) If an employee fails to reimburse the paying agency for the amount owed under paragraph (a) of this section, a sum equal to the amount outstanding is recoverable from the employee under the agency's regulations for collection by offset from an indebted Government employee under 5 U.S.C. 5514 and 5 CFR part 550, subpart K, or through the appropriate provisions governing Federal debt collection if the individual is no longer a Federal employee.

(e) An authorized agency official may waive, in whole or in part, a right of recovery of an employee's debt if he or she determines that recovery would be against equity and good conscience or against the public interest. (See 5 U.S.C. 5379(c)(3).)

(f) Any amount reimbursed by, or recovered from, an employee under this section must be credited to the appropriation account from which the amount involved was originally paid. Any amount so credited must be merged with other sums in such account and must be available for the same purposes and time period, and subject to the same limitations (if any), as the sums with which merged. (See 5 U.S.C. 5379(c)(4).)

§ 537.110 Records and reports.

(a) Each agency must keep a record of each determination to provide student loan repayment benefits under this part and make such records available for review upon request by OPM. Such a record may be destroyed when 3 years have elapsed since the end of the service period specified in the employee's service agreement unless any dispute has arisen regarding the agreement. If the service agreement has not been fulfilled, there are other disputes regarding the agreement or the loan payouts, or the agreement has become the subject of litigation, the records should be kept until the agency is notified by agency counsel that all pending claims have been resolved, all litigation concluded, and any applicable periods for seeking further review has elapsed and, in any event, for a minimum of 6 years from the date the facts giving rise to the dispute occurred. If debt collection is pursued against the employee for repayments made by the agency, the agency must keep the records until the agency is notified by agency counsel that the debt is fully collected, compromised, or settled finally and that any applicable period for seeking further review has elapsed.

(b) By March 31st of each year, each agency must submit a written report to OPM containing information about student loan repayment benefits it provided to employees during the previous calendar year. Each report must include the following information:

(1) The number of employees who received student loan repayment benefits;

(2) The job classifications of the employees who received student loan repayment benefits; and

(3) The cost to the Federal Government of providing student loan repayment benefits.

PART 550—PAY ADMINISTRATION (GENERAL)

Subpart A—Premium Pay

GENERAL PROVISIONS

Sec.

Subpart B—Advances in Pay

Subpart C—Allotments From Federal Employees

DEFINITIONS

GENERAL PROVISIONS

LABOR ORGANIZATION

ASSOCIATION OF MANAGEMENT OFFICIALS AND/OR SUPERVISORS

COMBINED FEDERAL CAMPAIGN

INCOME TAX WITHHOLDING

ALIMONY AND/OR CHILD SUPPORT

FOREIGN AFFAIRS AGENCY ORGANIZATIONS

Subpart D—Payments During Evacuation

Subpart E—Pay From More Than One Position

Subpart F—Computation of Pay for Biweekly Pay Periods

Subpart G—Severance Pay

Subpart H—Back Pay

Subpart I—Pay for Duty Involving Physical Hardship or Hazard

Subpart J—Adjustment of Work Schedules for Religious Observances

Subpart K—Collection by Offset From Indebted Government Employees

Subpart L—Lump-Sum Payment for Accumulated and Accrued Annual Leave

Subpart M—Firefighter Pay

Subpart N—Compensatory Time Off for Travel

Subpart O—Flag Recognition Benefit for Fallen Federal Civilian Employees

Subpart P—Overtime Pay for Border Patrol Agents

GENERAL PROVISIONS

ASSIGNMENT OF REGULAR TOUR OF DUTY AND OVERTIME SUPPLEMENT

TREATMENT OF OVERTIME WORK

RELATIONSHIP TO OTHER PROVISIONS

SOURCE: 33 FR 12458, Sept. 4, 1968, unless otherwise noted.

Subpart A—Premium Pay

AUTHORITY: 5 U.S.C. 5304 note, 5305 note, 5504(d), 5541(2)(iv), 5545a(h)(2)(B) and (i), 5547(b) and (c), 5548, and 6101(c); sections 407 and 2316, Pub. L. 105–277, 112 Stat. 2681–101 and 2681–828 (5 U.S.C. 5545a); section 2(h), Pub. L. 113–277, 128 Stat. 3005; E.O. 12748, 3 CFR, 1992 Comp., p. 316.

GENERAL PROVISIONS

§ 550.101 Coverage and exemptions.

(a) *Employees to whom this subpart applies.* (1) This subpart applies to each employee in or under an Executive agency, as defined in 5 U.S.C. 105, except those named in paragraphs (b) and (c) of this section.

(2) The sections in this subpart incorporating special provisions for certain types of work (§§ 550.141 through 550.164, inclusive) apply also to each employee of the judicial branch or the legislative branch who is subject to subchapter V of chapter 55 of title 5, United States Code.

(b) *Employees to whom this subpart does not apply.* This subpart does not apply to:

(1) An elected official;

(2) The head of a department;

(3) [Reserved]

(4) An employee whose pay is fixed and adjusted from time to time in accordance with prevailing rates under subchapter IV of chapter 53 of title 5, United States Code, or by a wage board or similar administrative authority serving the same purpose, except that § 550.113(d) is applicable to such an employee whose rate of basic pay is fixed on an annual or monthly basis;

(5) An employee outside the continental United States or in Alaska who is paid in accordance with local prevailing wage rates for the area in which employed;

(6) An employee of the Tennessee Valley Authority;

(7) An employee of the Central Intelligence Agency (sec. 10, 63 Stat. 212, as amended; 50 U.S.C. 403j);

(8) A seaman to whom section 1(a) of the act of March 24, 1943 (57 Stat. 45; 50 U.S.C. App. 1291(a)) applies;

(9) A member of the United States Park Police or the United States Secret Service Uniformed Division, except for the purpose of night pay under §§ 550.121 and 550.122, pay for holiday work under §§ 550.131 and 550.132, and pay for Sunday work under §§ 550.171 and 550.172 of this subpart;

(10) An officer or member of the crew of a vessel, whose pay is fixed and adjusted from time to time as nearly as is consistent with the public interest in accordance with prevailing rates and practices in the maritime industry (30 Comp. Gen. 158);

(11) A civilian keeper of a lighthouse, or a civilian employed on a lightship or another vessel of the Coast Guard (14 U.S.C. 432(f));

(12) A physician, dentist, nurse, or any other employee in the Department of Medicine and Surgery, Veterans Administration, whose pay is fixed under chapter 73 of title 38, United States Code;

(13) A student-employee as defined by section 5351 of title 5, United States Code;

(14) An employee of the Environmental Science Services Administration engaged in the conduct of meteorological investigations in the Arctic region (62 Stat. 286; 15 U.S.C. 327);

(15) An employee of a Federal land bank, a Federal intermediate credit bank, or a bank for cooperatives;

(16) A "teacher" or an individual holding a "teaching position" as defined by section 901 of title 20, United States Code;

(17) A Foreign Service officer or a member of the Senior Foreign Service; or

(18) A member of the Senior Executive Service.

(c) *Employees to whom §§ 550.111, 550.113, and 550.114 of this subpart do not apply.* Except for the purpose of determining hours of work in excess of 8 hours in a day, §§ 550.111, 550.113, and 550.114 of this subpart do not apply to an employee who is subject to the overtime pay provisions of section 7 of the

Fair Labor Standards Act of 1938 and part 551 of this chapter.

(d) *Services to which this subpart does not apply.* This subpart does not apply to overtime, night, Sunday, or holiday services for which additional pay is provided by the act of:

(1) February 13, 1911, as amended (36 Stat. 899, as amended; 19 U.S.C. 261, 267), involving customs inspectors and canine enforcement officers;

(2) July 24, 1919 (41 Stat. 241; 7 U.S.C. 394), involving employees engaged in enforcement of the Meat Inspection Act;

(3) March 2, 1931 (46 Stat. 1467; 8 U.S.C. 1353*a*), involving inspectors and employees, Immigration and Naturalization Service;

(4) May 27, 1936, as amended (49 Stat. 1380, as amended; 46 U.S.C. 382b), involving local inspectors of steam vessels and assistants, U.S. shipping commissioners, deputies, and assistants, and customs officers and employees;

(5) March 23, 1941 (55 Stat. 46; 47 U.S.C. 154(f)(3)), involving certain engineers of the Federal Communications OPM;

(6) August 4, 1949 (63 Stat. 495; 7 U.S.C. 349a), involving employees of the Bureau of Animal Industry who work at establishments which prepare virus, serum, toxin, and analogous products for use in the treatment of domestic animals; or

(7) August 28, 1950 (64 Stat. 561; 7 U.S.C. 2260), involving employees of the Department of Agriculture performing inspection or quarantine services relating to imports into and exports from the United States.

[33 FR 12458, Sept. 4, 1968, as amended at 48 FR 3933, Jan. 28, 1983; 56 FR 20341, May 3, 1991; 57 FR 2432, Jan. 22, 1992; 64 FR 69174, Dec. 10, 1999]

§550.102 Entitlement.

A department (and for the purpose of §§550.141 through 550.164, inclusive, a legislative or judicial branch agency) must determine an employee's entitlement to premium pay consistent with subchapter V of chapter 55 of title 5, United States Code.

[64 FR 69174, Dec. 10, 1999]

§550.103 Definitions.

In this subpart:

Administrative workweek means any period of 7 consecutive days (as defined in this section) designated in advance by the head of the agency under section 6101 of title 5, United States Code.

Agency means—

(1) A *department* as defined in this section; and

(2) A legislative or judicial branch agency which has positions that are subject to subchapter V of chapter 55 of title 5, United States Code.

Basic workweek, for full-time employees, means the 40-hour workweek established in accordance with §610.111 of this chapter.

Criminal investigator means a law enforcement officer as defined in 5 U.S.C. 5541(3) and this section—

(1) Whose position is properly classified under the GS–1811 or GS–1812 series in the General Schedule classification system based on OPM classification standards (or would be so classified if covered under that system);

(2) Who is a pilot employed by the United States Customs Service;

(3) Who is a special agent in the Diplomatic Security Service in a position which has been properly determined by the Department of State to have a Foreign Service primary skill code of 2501;

(4) Who is a special agent in the Diplomatic Security Service who has been placed by the Department of State in a non-covered position on a long-term training assignment that will be career-enhancing for a current or future assignment as a Diplomatic Security Service special agent, provided the employee is expected to return to duties as a special agent in a Foreign Service position with a 2501 primary skill code or to a position properly classified in the GS–1811 series immediately following such training;

(5) Who occupies a position in the Department of State in which he or she performs duties and responsibilities of a special agent requiring Foreign Service primary skill code 2501, pending the opening of a position with primary skill code 2501 and placement in that position as a special agent; or

(6) Who is a special agent in the Diplomatic Security Service with a Foreign Service personal primary skill code of 2501 (or whose position immediately prior to the detail was properly

classified in the GS–1811 series) and who meets all of the following three conditions:

(i) The individual is assigned outside the Department of State;

(ii) The assigned position would have a primary skill code of 2501 (or would be properly classified in the GS–1811 series under the General Schedule classification system based on OPM classification standards) if the position were under the Foreign Service (or General Schedule) in the Department of State; and

(iii) The individual is expected to return to a position as a special agent in the Diplomatic Security Service with a 2501 primary skill code (or to a position that is properly classified in the GS–1811 series) immediately following such outside assignment.

Day (for overtime pay purposes) means any 24-hour period designated by an agency within the administrative workweek applicable to the employee. A day need not correspond to the 24-hour period of a calendar day. If the agency has not designated another period of time, a day is a calendar day.

Department means an executive agency and a military department as defined by sections 105 and 102 of title 5, United States Code.

Emergency means a temporary condition posing a direct threat to human life or property, including a forest wildfire emergency.

Employee means an employee to whom this subpart applies.

Head of a department means the head of a department and, except for the purpose of § 550.101(b)(2), an official who has been delegated authority to act for the head of a department in the matter concerned.

Holiday work means nonovertime work performed by an employee during a regularly scheduled daily tour of duty on a holiday designated in accordance with § 610.202 of this chapter.

Irregular or occasional overtime work means overtime work that is not part of an employee's regularly scheduled administrative workweek.

Law enforcement officer means an employee who—

(1) Is a law enforcement officer within the meaning of 5 U.S.C. 8331(20) (as further defined in § 831.902 of this chapter) or 5 U.S.C. 8401(17) (as further defined in § 842.802 of this chapter), as applicable;

(2) In the case of an employee who holds a secondary position, as defined in § 831.902 of this chapter, and is subject to the Civil Service Retirement System, but who does not qualify to be considered a law enforcement officer within the meaning of 5 U.S.C. 8331(20), would so qualify if such employee had transferred directly to such position after serving as a law enforcement officer within the meaning of such section;

(3) In the case of an employee who holds a secondary position, as defined in § 842.802 of this chapter, and is subject to the Federal Employees Retirement System, but who does not qualify to be considered a law enforcement officer within the meaning of 5 U.S.C. 8401(17), would so qualify if such employee had transferred directly to such position after performing duties described in 5 U.S.C. 8401(17)(A) and (B) for at least 3 years; and

(4) In the case of an employee who is not subject to either the Civil Service Retirement System or the Federal Employees Retirement System—

(i) Holds a position that the agency head (as defined in §§ 831.902 and 842.802 of this chapter) determines would satisfy paragraph (1), (2), or (3) of this definition if the employee were subject to the Civil Service Retirement System or the Federal Employees Retirement System (subject to OPM oversight as described in §§ 831.911 and 842.808 of this chapter); or

(ii) Is a special agent in the Diplomatic Security Service.

Nightwork has the meaning given that term in § 550.121, and includes any nightwork preformed by an employee as part of his or her regularly scheduled administrative workweek.

Overtime work has the meaning given that term in § 550.111 and includes irregular or occasional overtime work and regular overtime work.

Performing work in connection with an emergency means performing work that is directly related to resolving or coping with an emergency or its immediate aftermath.

Premium pay means the dollar value of earned hours of compensatory time off and additional pay authorized by subchapter V of chapter 55 of title 5, United States Code, and this subpart for overtime, night, Sunday, or holiday work; or for standby duty, administratively uncontrollable overtime work, or availability duty. This excludes overtime pay paid to employees under the Fair Labor Standards Act and compensatory time off earned in lieu of such overtime pay. This includes an overtime supplement received by a Border Patrol agent under 5 U.S.C. 5550 and subpart P of this part for regularly scheduled overtime hours within the agent's regular tour of duty and the dollar value of hours of compensatory time off earned by such an agent.

Protective duties means duties authorized by section 3056(a) of title 18, United States Code, or by section 2709(a)(3) of title 22, United States Code.

Rate of basic pay means the rate of pay fixed by law or administrative action for the position held by an employee, including any applicable locality payment under 5 CFR part 531, subpart F; special rate supplement under 5 CFR part 530, subpart C; or similar payment or supplement under other legal authority, before any deductions and exclusive of additional pay of any other kind.

Regular overtime work means overtime work that is part of an employee's regularly scheduled administrative workweek.

Regular tour of duty, with respect to a Border Patrol agent covered by 5 U.S.C. 5550 and subpart P of this part, means the basic 40-hour workweek plus any regularly scheduled overtime work hours that the agent is assigned to work as part of an officially established 5-day weekly work schedule generally consisting of—

(1) 10-hour workdays (including 2 overtime hours each workday) in exchange for a 25-percent overtime supplement (Level 1); or

(2) 9-hour workdays (including 1 overtime hour each workday) in exchange for a 12.5-percent overtime supplement (Level 2).

Regularly scheduled administrative workweek, for a full-time employee, means the period within an administrative workweek, established in accordance with §610.111 of this chapter, within which the employee is regularly scheduled to work. For a part-time employee, it means the officially prescribed days and hours within an administrative workweek during which the employee is regularly scheduled to work.

Regularly scheduled work means work that is scheduled in advance of an administrative workweek under an agency's procedures for establishing workweeks in accordance with §610.111, excluding any such work to which availability pay under §550.181 applies.

Sunday work means nonovertime work performed by an employee during a regularly scheduled daily tour of duty when any part of that daily tour of duty is on a Sunday. For any such tour of duty, not more than 8 hours of work are Sunday work, unless the employee is on a compressed work schedule, in which case the entire regularly scheduled daily tour of duty constitutes Sunday work.

Tour of duty means the hours of a day (a daily tour of duty) and the days of an administrative workweek (a weekly tour of duty) that constitute an employee's regularly scheduled administrative workweek.

[33 FR 12458, Sept. 4, 1968]

EDITORIAL NOTE: For FEDERAL REGISTER citations affecting §550.103, see the List of CFR Sections Affected, which appears in the Finding Aids section of the printed volume and at *www.fdsys.gov*.

MAXIMUM EARNINGS LIMITATIONS

§550.105 Biweekly maximum earnings limitation.

(a) Except as provided in paragraph (c) of this section, an employee may receive premium pay under this subpart only to the extent that the payment does not cause the total of his or her basic pay and premium pay for any biweekly pay period to exceed the greater of—

(1) The maximum biweekly rate of basic pay payable for GS–15 (including any applicable locality-based comparability payment under section 5304 or similar provision of law and any applicable special rate of pay under 5 U.S.C. 5305 or similar provision of law); or

(2) The biweekly rate payable for level V of the Executive Schedule.

(b) In applying the biweekly limitation under this section, premium pay of the types listed in § 550.107(a) must be paid before paying any other type of premium pay.

(c) This section does not apply to—

(1) Any pay period during which an employee is subject to an annual limitation as provided in § 550.106;

(2) An employee of the Federal Aviation Administration or the Department of Defense who receives premium pay under 5 U.S.C. 5546a.

(d) The biweekly rates of pay for the GS–15 maximum rate and for level V of the Executive Schedule are computed as follows:

(1) Compute an hourly rate by dividing the applicable published annual rate of basic pay by 2,087 hours and rounding the result to the nearest cent.

(2) Compute the biweekly rate by multiplying the hourly rate from paragraph (d)(1) of this section by 80 hours.

(e) Notwithstanding any other provision in this section, premium pay for protective services authorized by 18 U.S.C. 3056(a) is subject to the requirements in section 118 of the Treasury and General Government Appropriations Act of 2001 (as enacted into law by section 1(3) of Public Law 106–554).

[67 FR 19320, Apr. 19, 2002, as amended at 69 FR 55942, Sept. 17, 2004]

§ 550.106 Annual maximum earnings limitation.

(a)(1) For any pay period in which the head of an agency (or designee), or the Office of Personnel Management on its own motion, determines that an emergency exists, the agency must pay an affected employee premium pay under the limitations described in paragraph (c) of this section and § 550.107 instead of under the biweekly limitation described in § 550.105(a). An employee is affected if he or she has been determined by the head of the agency (or designee) to be performing work in connection with the emergency or its aftermath. (See definition of "emergency" in § 550.103.)

(2) The head of an agency (or designee) must make the determination under paragraph (a)(1) of this section as soon as practicable after the work in connection with the emergency or its aftermath begins. Entitlement to premium pay under this annual limitation becomes effective on the first day of the pay period in which such work began.

(b)(1) For any pay period in which the head of an agency (or designee), in his or her sole discretion, determines that an employee is needed to perform work that is critical to the mission of the agency, the agency may pay premium pay under the limitations described in paragraph (c) of this section and § 550.107 instead of under the biweekly limitation described in § 550.105(a).

(2) Entitlement to premium pay under this annual limitation becomes effective on the first day of the pay period designated by the head of the agency (or designee).

(c) In any calendar year during which an employee has been determined to be performing emergency or mission-critical work as provided in paragraphs (a) or (b) of this section, the employee may receive premium pay under this subpart (excluding the types of premium pay identified in § 550.107) only to the extent that the payment does not cause the total of his or her basic pay and premium pay for the calendar year to exceed the greater of—

(1) The maximum annual rate of basic pay payable for GS–15 (including any applicable locality-based comparability payment under section 5304 or similar provision of law and any applicable special rate of pay under 5 U.S.C. 5305 or similar provision of law) in effect on the last day of the calendar year; or

(2) The annual rate payable for level V of the Executive Schedule in effect on the last day of the calendar year.

(d) The annual rates under paragraphs (c)(1) and (2) of this section must be computed as follows:

(1) Compute an hourly rate by dividing the published annual rate of basic pay by 2,087 hours and rounding the result to the nearest cent;

(2) Compute a biweekly rate by multiplying the hourly rate from paragraph (d)(1) of this section by 80 hours;

(3) Compute an annual rate of pay by multiplying the biweekly rate from paragraph (d)(2) of this section by the

number of pay periods for which a salary payment is issued in the given calendar year under the agency's payroll cycle (*i.e.*, either 26 or 27 pay periods).

(e) An agency may defer payment of some or all of the additional premium pay owed an employee as a result of the annual limitation until the end of the calendar year.

(f) Any payment made in the current calendar year that corrects an underpayment of premium pay in a previous calendar year must be treated as being made in the previous calendar year for the purpose of applying the annual cap under this section.

(g) If an agency determines that the emergency or mission-critical work conditions are no longer in effect for an employee, it must resume application of the biweekly limitation. However, any premium pay the employee receives during the remainder of the calendar year is also subject to the annual limitation (as applied to any given pay period as described in paragraph (c) of this section).

[67 FR 19321, Apr. 19, 2002, as amended at 69 FR 55943, Sept. 17, 2004]

§550.107 Premium payments capped on a biweekly basis when an annual limitation otherwise applies.

(a) The following types of premium pay remain subject to a biweekly limitation when other premium payments are subject to an annual limitation under §550.106:

(1) Standby duty pay under 5 U.S.C. 5545(c)(1);

(2) Administratively uncontrollable overtime pay under 5 U.S.C. 5545(c)(2);

(3) Availability pay for criminal investigators under 5 U.S.C. 5545a;

(4) Overtime pay for hours in the regular tour of duty of a firefighter covered by 5 U.S.C. 5545b; and

(5) An overtime supplement for regularly scheduled overtime hours within a Border Patrol agent's regular tour of duty under 5 U.S.C. 5550.

(b) An employee must receive premium pay of the types identified in paragraph (a) of this section before receiving any other type of premium pay.

(c) In any pay period during which an employee is subject to an annual limitation under §550.106, the employee may receive the types of premium pay identified in paragraph (a) of this section only to the extent that the payment does not cause the total of his or her basic pay and such premium pay for the pay period to exceed the greater of—

(1) The maximum biweekly rate of basic pay payable for GS–15 (including any applicable locality-based comparability payment under section 5304 or similar provision of law and any applicable special rate of pay under 5 U.S.C. 5305 or similar provision of law); or

(2) The biweekly rate payable for level V of the Executive Schedule.

(d) The biweekly rates under paragraph (c) of this section are computed as provided in §550.105(d).

(e) Premium pay paid, or projected to be paid, under this section is included in determining whether the sum of the employee's basic pay and premium pay would exceed the annual limitation under §550.106.

[67 FR 19321, Apr. 19, 2002, as amended at 69 FR 55943, Sept. 17, 2004; 80 FR 58111, Sept. 25, 2015]

Overtime Pay

§550.111 Authorization of overtime pay.

(a) Except as provided in paragraphs (d), (f), and (g) of this section, overtime work means work in excess of 8 hours in a day or in excess of 40 hours in an administrative workweek that is—

(1) Officially ordered or approved; and

(2) Performed by an employee. Hours of work in excess of 8 in a day are not included in computing hours of work in excess of 40 hours in an administrative workweek.

(b) Except as otherwise provided in this subpart, a department shall pay for overtime work at the rates provided in §550.113.

(c) Overtime work in excess of any included in a regularly scheduled administrative workweek may be ordered or approved only in writing by an officer or employee to whom this authority has been specifically delegated.

(d) For an employee for whom the first 40 hours of duty in an administrative workweek is his basic workweek under § 610.111(b) of this chapter, overtime work means work in excess of 40 hours in an administrative workweek that is:

(1) Officially ordered or approved, and

(2) Performed by an employee, when the employee's basic pay exceeds the minimum rate for GS–10 (including any applicable special rate of pay for law enforcement officers or special pay adjustment for law enforcement officers under section 403 or 404 of the Federal Employees Pay Comparability Act of 1990 (Pub. L. 101–509), respectively; a locality-based comparability payment under 5 U.S.C. 5304; and any applicable special rate of pay under 5 U.S.C. 5305 or similar provision of law) or when the employee is engaged in professional or technical, engineering or scientific activities. For purposes of this section and section 5542(a) of title 5. United States Code, an employee is engaged in professional or technical engineering or scientfic activities when he or she is assigned to perform the duties of a profeesional or support technician position in the physical, mathematical, natural, medical, or social sciences or engineering or architecture.

(e) Notwithstanding paragraphs (a) and (d) of this section, when an employee's basic workweek includes a daily tour of duty of more than 8 hours and his hourly rate of basic pay exceeds the hourly rate of overtime pay provided by § 550.113, the department shall pay him at his basic rate of pay for each hour of his daily tour of duty within his basic workweek.

(f)(1) Except as provided in paragraph (f)(2) of this section, for any criminal investigator receiving availability pay under § 550.181, overtime work means actual work that is scheduled in advance of the administrative workweek—

(i) In excess of 10 hours on a day containing hours that are part of such investigator's basic 40-hour workweek; or

(ii) On a day not containing hours that are part of such investigator's basic 40-hour workweek.

(2) Notwithstanding paragraph (f)(1) of this section, all overtime work scheduled in advance of the administrative workweek on a day containing part of a criminal investigator's basic 40-hour workweek must be compensated under this section if both of the following conditions are met:

(i) The overtime work involves protective duties authorized by section 3056(a) of title 18, United States Code, or section 2709(a)(3) of title 22, United States Code; and

(ii) The investigator performs on that same day at least 2 consecutive hours of overtime work that are not scheduled in advance of the administrative workweek and are compensated by availability pay.

(3) Any work that would be overtime work under this section but for paragraphs (f)(1) and (f)(2) of this section will be compensated by availability pay under § 550.181.

(g) For firefighters compensated under subpart M of this part, overtime work means officially ordered or approved work in excess of 106 hours in a biweekly pay period, or, if the agency establishes a weekly basis for overtime pay computations, in excess of 53 hours in an administrative workweek.

(h) Availability hours, as described in § 550.182(c), are not hours of work for the purpose of determining overtime pay under this section.

(i) An employee is not entitled to overtime pay under this subpart for time spent in training, except as provided in § 410.402 of this chapter.

(j) For Border Patrol agents covered by 5 U.S.C. 5550 and subpart P of this part, overtime work means hours of work in excess of applicable thresholds, as specified in § 550.1623, excluding hours that are—

(1) Compensated by payment of an overtime supplement for regularly scheduled overtime within the agent's regular tour of duty under § 550.1621;

(2) Compensated by the earning of compensatory time off under § 550.1625; or

(3) Used in substitution or application under § 550.1626.

[33 FR 12458, Sept. 4, 1968, as amended at 34 FR 19495, Dec. 10, 1969; 48 FR 36805, Aug. 15, 1983; 56 FR 20341, May 3, 1991; 57 FR 2434, Jan. 22, 1992; 59 FR 66151, Dec. 23, 1994; 61 FR 3542, Feb. 1, 1996; 63 FR 64592, Nov. 23, 1998; 64 FR 4520, Jan. 29, 1999; 64 FR 69175, Dec. 10, 1999; 80 FR 58111, Sept. 25, 2015]

§ 550.112 Computation of overtime work.

The computation of the amount of overtime work of an employee is subject to the following conditions:

(a) *Time spent in principal activities.* Principal activities are the activities that an employee is employed to perform. They are the activities that an employee performs during his or her regularly scheduled administrative workweek (including regular overtime work) and activities performed by an employee during periods of irregular or occasional overtime work authorized under § 550.111. Overtime work in principal activities shall be credited as follows:

(1) An employee shall be compensated for every minute of regular overtime work.

(2) A quarter of an hour shall be the largest fraction of an hour used for crediting irregular or occasional overtime work under this subpart. When irregular or occasional overtime work is performed in other than the full fraction, odd minutes shall be rounded up or rounded down to the nearest full fraction of an hour used to credit overtime work.

(b) *Time spent in preshift or postshift activities.* A preshift activity is a preparatory activity that an employee performs prior to the commencement of his or her principal activities, and a postshift activity is a concluding activity that an employee performs after the completion of his or her principal activities. Such activities are not principal activities as defined in paragraph (a) of this section.

(1) (i) If the head of a department reasonably determines that a preshift or postshift activity is closely related to an employee's principal activities, and is indispensable to the performance of the principal activities, and that the total time spent in that activity is more than 10 minutes per daily tour of duty, he or she shall credit all of the time spent in that activity, including the 10 minutes, as hours of work.

(ii) If the time spent in a preshift or postshift activity is compensable as hours of work, the head of the department shall schedule the time period for the employee to perform that activity. An employee shall be credited with the actual time spent in that activity during the time period scheduled by the head of the department. In no case shall the time credited for the performance of an activity exceed the time scheduled by the head of the department. If the time period scheduled by the head of the department for the performance of a pereshift or postshift activity is outside the employee's daily tour of duty, the employee shall be credited with the time spent performing that activity in accordance with paragraph (a)(2) of this section.

(2) A preshift or postshift activity that is not closely related to the performance of the principal activities is considered a preliminary or postliminary activity. Time spent in preliminary or postliminary activities is excluded from hours of work and is not compensable, even if it occurs between periods of activity that are compensable as hours of work.

(c) *Leave with pay.* An employee's absence from duty on authorized leave with pay under subchapter I of chapter 61 of title 5, United States Code, during the time when he would otherwise have been required to be on duty during a basic workweek (including authorized absence on a legal holiday, on a nonworkday established by Executive or administrative order, and on compensatory time off as provided in § 550.114) is deemed employment and does not reduce the amount of overtime pay to which the employee is entitled during an administrative workweek. Leave of absence with pay under subchapter I of chapter 61 of title 5, United States Code, is charged only for an absence that occurs during a basic workweek.

(d) *Leave without pay.* (1) For a period of leave without pay in an employee's basic workweek, an equal period of service performed outside the basic workweek, but in the same administrative workweek, shall be substituted and paid for at the rate applicable to his basic workweek before any remaining period of service may be paid for at the overtime rate on the basis of exceeding 40 hours in a workweek.

(2) For a period of leave without pay in an employee's daily tour of duty, an equal period of service performed outside the daily tour, but in the same workday, shall be substituted and paid

for at the rate applicable to his daily tour of duty before any remaining period of service may be paid for at the overtime rate on the basis of exceeding 8 hours in a workday.

(e) *Absence during overtime periods.* Except as provided by paragraph (a) of this section, as expressly authorized by statute, or to the extent authorized while the employee is in a travel status, a period is counted as overtime work only when the employee actually performs work during the period or is taking compensatory time off as provided in § 550.114.

(f) *Night, Sunday, or holiday work.* Hours of night, Sunday, or holiday work are included in determining for overtime pay purposes the total number of hours of work in an administrative workweek.

(g) *Time in travel status.* Time in travel status away from the official duty-station of an employee is deemed employment only when:

(1) It is within his regularly scheduled administrative workweek, including regular overtime work; or

(2) The travel—

(i) Involves the performance of actual work while traveling;

(ii) Is incident to travel that involves the performance of work while traveling;

(iii) Is carried out under such arduous and unusual conditions that the travel is inseparable from work; or

(iv) Results from an event which could not be scheduled or controlled administratively, including travel by an employee to such an event and the return of the employee to his or her official-duty station.

(h) *Call-back overtime work.* Irregular or occasional overtime work performed by an employee on a day when work was not scheduled for him, or for which he is required to return to his place of employment, is deemed at least 2 hours in duration for the purpose of premium pay, either in money or compensatory time off.

(i) Periods of duty that are compensated by annual premium pay under 5 U.S.C. 5545(c) (1) or (2) shall not be credited for the purpose of determining hours of work in excess of 8 hours in a day.

(j) *Official duty station.* An agency may prescribe a mileage radius of not greater than 50 miles to determine whether an employee's travel is within or outside the limits of the employee's official duty station for determining entitlement to overtime pay for travel under paragraph (g) of this section except that—

(1) An agency's definition of an employee's official duty station for determining overtime pay for travel may not be smaller than the definition of "official station and post of duty" under the Federal Travel Regulation issued by the General Services Administration (41 CFR 300–3.1); and

(2) Travel from home to work and vice versa is not hours of work. When an employee travels directly from home to a temporary duty location outside the limits of his or her official duty station, the time the employee would have spent in normal home to work travel shall be deducted from hours of work.

(k) *Standby duty.* (1) An employee is on duty, and time spent on standby duty is hours of work if, for work-related reasons, the employee is restricted by official order to a designated post of duty and is assigned to be in a state of readiness to perform work with limitations on the employee's activities so substantial that the employee cannot use the time effectively for his or her own purposes. A finding that an employee's activities are substantially limited may not be based on the fact that an employee is subject to restrictions necessary to ensure that the employee will be able to perform his or her duties and responsibilities, such as restrictions on alcohol consumption or use of certain medications.

(2) An employee is not considered restricted for "work-related reasons" if, for example, the employee remains at the post of duty voluntarily, or if the restriction is a natural result of geographic isolation or the fact that the employee resides on the agency's premises. For example, in the case of an employee assigned to work in a remote wildland area or on a ship, the fact that the employee has limited mobility when relieved from duty would not be a

basis for finding that the employee is restricted for work-related reasons.

(l) *On-call status.* An employee is off duty, and time spent in an on-call status is not hours of work if—

(1) The employee is allowed to leave a telephone number or carry an electronic device for the purpose of being contacted, even though the employee is required to remain within a reasonable call-back radius; or

(2) The employee is allowed to make arrangements for another person to perform any work that may arise during the on-call period.

(m) *Sleep and meal time.* (1) Bona fide sleep and meal periods may not be considered hours of work, except as provided in paragraphs (m)(2), (m)(3), and (m)(4) of this section. If a sleep or meal period is interrupted by a call to duty, the time spent on duty is hours of work.

(2) Sleep and meal periods during regularly scheduled tours of duty are hours of work for employees who receive annual premium pay for regularly scheduled standby duty under 5 U.S.C. 5545(c)(1).

(3) When employees are assigned to work shifts of 24 hours or more during which they must remain within the confines of their duty station in a standby status, and for which they do not receive annual premium pay for regularly scheduled standby duty under 5 U.S.C. 5545(c)(1), the amount of bona fide sleep and meal time excluded from hours of work may not exceed 8 hours in any 24-hour period. No sleep time may be excluded unless the employee had the opportunity to have an uninterrupted period of at least 5 hours of sleep during the applicable sleep period. For work shifts of less than 24 hours, agencies may not exclude on-duty sleep periods from hours of work, but must exclude bona fide meal periods during which the employee is completely relieved from duty.

(4) For firefighters compensated under 5 U.S.C. 5545b, on-duty sleep and meal time may not be excluded from hours of work.

[33 FR 12458, Sept. 4, 1968, as amended at 33 FR 18669, Dec. 18, 1968; 48 FR 3934, Jan. 28, 1983; 48 FR 36805, Aug. 15, 1983; 56 FR 20342, May 3, 1991; 57 FR 59279, Dec. 15, 1992; 59 FR 66632, Dec. 28, 1994; 64 FR 69175, Dec. 10, 1999; 72 FR 12035, Mar. 15, 2007]

§ 550.113 Computation of overtime pay.

(a) For each employee whose rate of basic pay does not exceed the minimum rate for GS–10 (including any applicable special rate of pay for law enforcement officers or special pay adjustment for law enforcement officers under section 403 or 404 of the Federal Employees Pay Comparability Act of 1990 (Pub. L. 101–509), respectively; a locality-based comparability payment under 5 U.S.C. 5304; and any applicable special rate of pay under 5 U.S.C. 5305 or similar provision of law), the overtime hourly rate is 1½ times his or her hourly rate of basic pay.

(b) For each employee whose rate of basic pay exceeds the minimum rate for GS–10 (as determined under paragraph (a) of this section), the overtime hourly rate is equal to the greater of— (i) one and one-half times the applicable minimum hourly rate of basic pay for GS–10 (as determined under paragraph (a) of this section); or (ii) the employee's hourly rate of basic pay, except as provided in 5 U.S.C. 5542(a)(3) and (5).

(c) An employee is paid for overtime work performed on a Sunday or a holiday at the same rate as for overtime work performed on another day.

(d) An employee whose rate of basic pay is fixed on an annual or monthly basis and adjusted from time to time in accordance with prevailing rates by a wage board or similar administrative authority serving the same purpose is entitled to overtime pay in accordance with the provisions of section 5544 of title 5, United States Code. The rate of pay for each hour of overtime work of such an employee is computed as follows:

(1) If the rate of basic pay of the employee is fixed on an annual basis, divide the rate of basic pay by 2,087 and multiply the quotient by one and one-half; and

(2) If the rate of basic pay of the employee is fixed on a monthly basis, multiply the rate of basic pay by 12 to derive an annual rate of basic pay, divide the annual rate of basic pay by 2,087, and multiply the quotient by one and one-half.

Rates are computed in full cents, counting a fraction of a cent as the next higher cent.

(e)(1) For firefighters compensated under subpart M of this part, the overtime hourly rate for all overtime hours is 1½ times the firefighter's hourly rate of basic pay under § 550.1303(a) or (b)(2), as applicable, except as provided in paragraph (e)(2) of this section.

(2) For firefighters compensated under subpart M of this part who areexempt from the overtime provisions of the Fair Labor Standards Act and whose hourly rate of basic pay under § 550.1303(a) or (b)(2), as applicable, exceeds the applicable minimum hourly rate of basic pay for GS–10 (as computed under paragraph (a) of this section by dividing the annual rate of basic pay by 2087 hours), the overtime hourly rate is equal to the greater of—

(i) One and one-half times the applicable minimum hourly rate of basic pay for GS–10 (as computed under paragraph (a) of this section by dividing the annual rate of basic pay by 2087 hours); or

(ii) The individual's own firefighter hourly rate of basic pay under § 550.1303(a) and (b)(2), as applicable.

[33 FR 12458, Sept. 4, 1968, as amended at 56 FR 20342, May 3, 1991; 57 FR 2434, Jan. 22, 1992; 59 FR 11701, Mar. 14, 1994; 61 FR 3542, Feb. 1, 1996; 63 FR 64592, Nov. 23, 1998; 69 FR 26476, May 13, 2004]

§ 550.114 Compensatory time off.

(a) At the request of an employee, the head of an agency (or designee) may grant compensatory time off from an employee's tour of duty instead of payment under § 550.113 for an equal amount of irregular or occasional overtime work.

(b) At the request of an employee, as defined in 5 U.S.C. 2105, the head of an agency (or designee) may grant compensatory time off from an employee's basic work requirement under a flexible work schedule under 5 U.S.C. 6122 instead of payment under § 550.113 for an equal amount of overtime work, whether or not irregular or occasional in nature.

(c) The head of an agency may provide that an employee whose rate of basic pay exceeds the maximum rate for GS–10 (including any applicable special rate of pay for law enforcement officers or special pay adjustment for law enforcement officers under section 403 or 404 of the Federal Employees Pay Comparability Act of 1990 (Pub. L. 101–509), respectively; a locality-based comparability payment under 5 U.S.C. 5304; and any applicable special rate of pay under 5 U.S.C. 5305 or similar provision of law) shall be compensated for irregular or occasional overtime work with an equivalent amount of compensatory time off from the employee's tour of duty instead of payment under § 550.113 of this part.

(d) Except as provided in paragraph (f)(2) of this section, an employee must use accrued compensatory time off to which he or she is entitled under paragraph (a) or (b) of this section by the end of the 26th pay period after the pay period during which it was earned. The head of an agency, at his or her sole and exclusive discretion, may provide that an employee who fails to take compensatory time off to which he or she is entitled within 26 pay periods after the pay period during which it was earned must—

(1) Receive payment for such unused compensatory time off at the dollar value prescribed in paragraph (g) of this section; or

(2) Forfeit the unused compensatory time off, unless the failure to take the compensatory time off is due to an exigency of the service beyond the employee's control, in which case the agency head must provide payment for the unused compensatory time off at the dollar value prescribed in paragraph (g) of this section.

(e) Except as provided in paragraph (f)(2) of this section, compensatory time off to an employee's credit as of May 14, 2007 must be used by the end of the pay period ending 3 years after May 14, 2007. The head of an agency, at his or her sole and exclusive discretion, may provide that an employee who fails to take compensatory time off to which he or she is entitled by the end of the pay period ending 3 years after May 14, 2007 must—

(1) Receive payment for such unused compensatory time off at the dollar value prescribed in paragraph (g) of this section; or

(2) Forfeit the unused compensatory time off, unless the failure to take the compensatory time off is due to an exigency of the service beyond the employee's control, in which case the agency head must provide payment for the unused compensatory time off at the dollar value prescribed in paragraph (g) of this section.

(f)(1) Except as provided in paragraph (f)(2) of this section, an employee with unused compensatory time off under paragraph (a) or (b) of this section who transfers to another agency or separates from Federal service before the expiration of the time limit established under paragraphs (d) or (e) of this section may receive overtime pay or forfeit the unused compensatory time off, consistent with the employing agency's policy established under paragraphs (d) and (e) of this section.

(2) If an employee with unused compensatory time off under paragraph (a) or (b) of this section separates from Federal service or is placed in a leave without pay status under the following circumstances, the employee must be paid for unused compensatory time off at the dollar value prescribed in paragraph (g) of this section:

(i) The employee separates or is placed in a leave without pay status to perform service in the uniformed services (as defined in 38 U.S.C. 4303 and §353.102); or

(ii) The employee separates or is placed in a leave without pay status because of an on-the-job injury with entitlement to injury compensation under 5 U.S.C. chapter 81.

(g) The dollar value of compensatory time off when it is liquidated, or for the purpose of applying pay limitations, is the amount of overtime pay the employee otherwise would have received for the hours of the pay period during which compensatory time off was earned by performing overtime work.

[33 FR 12458, Sept. 4, 1968, as amended at 56 FR 20342, May 3, 1991; 57 FR 2434, Jan. 22, 1992; 61 FR 3542, Feb. 1, 1996; 62 FR 28307, May 23, 1997; 64 FR 69175, Dec. 10, 1999; 72 FR 12035, Mar. 15, 2007]

NIGHT PAY

§550.121 Authorization of night pay differential.

(a) Except as provided by paragraph (b) of this section, nightwork is regularly scheduled work performed by an employee between the hours of 6 p.m. and 6 a.m. Subject to §550.122, and except as otherwise provided in this subpart, an employee who performs nightwork is entitled to pay for that work at his or her rate of basic pay plus a night pay differential amounting to 10 percent of his or her rate of basic pay.

(b) The head of a department may designate a time after 6 p.m. and a time before 6 a.m. as the beginning and end, respectively, of nightwork for the purpose of paragraph (a) of this section, at a post outside the United States where the customary hours of business extend into the hours of nightwork provided by paragraph (a) of this section. Times so designated as the beginning or end of nightwork shall correspond reasonably with the end or beginning, respectively, of the customary hours of business in the locality.

(c) An employee is not entitled to night pay differential while engaged in training, except as provided in §410.402 of this chapter.

[33 FR 12458, Sept. 4, 1968, as amended at 48 FR 3934, Jan. 28, 1983; 64 FR 69175, Dec. 10, 1999]

§550.122 Computation of night pay differential.

(a) *Absence on holidays or in travel status.* An employee is entitled to a night pay differential for a period when he is excused from nightwork on a holiday or other nonworkday and for night hours of his tour of duty while he is in an official travel status, whether performing actual duty or not.

(b) *Absence on leave.* An employee is entitled to a night pay differential for a period of paid leave only when the total amount of that leave in a pay period, including both night and day hours, is less than 8 hours.

(c) *Relation to overtime, Sunday, and holiday pay.* Night pay differential is in addition to overtime, Sunday, or holiday pay payable under this subpart and it is not included in the rate of basic pay used to compute the overtime, Sunday, or holiday pay.

(d) *Temporary assignment to a different daily tour of duty.* An employee is entitled to a night pay differential when he or she is temporarily assigned during the administrative workweek to a daily tour of duty that includes nightwork. This temporary change in a daily tour of duty within the employee's regularly scheduled administrative workweek is distinguished from a period of irregular or occasional overtime work in addition to the employee's regularly scheduled administrative workweek.

(e) *Border Patrol agents.* For a Border Patrol agent covered by 5 U.S.C. 5550 and subpart P of this part, no night pay differential is payable for regularly scheduled overtime hours within the agent's regular tour of duty, as required by 5 U.S.C. 5550(b)(2)(C), (b)(3)(C), and (c)(1)(A). The overtime supplement payable for such scheduled overtime hours is not part of the agent's rate of basic pay used in computing the night pay differential for other hours that qualify for such a differential.

[33 FR 12458, Sept. 4, 1968, as amended at 48 FR 3934, Jan. 28, 1983; 80 FR 58111, Sept. 25, 2015]

PAY FOR HOLIDAY WORK

§550.131 Authorization of pay for holiday work.

(a) Except as otherwise provided in this subpart, an employee who performs holiday work is entitled to pay at his or her rate of basic pay plus premium pay at a rate equal to his or her rate of basic pay for that holiday work that is not in excess of 8 hours.

(b) An employee is entitled to pay for overtime work on a holiday at the same rate as for overtime work on other days.

(c) An employee who is assigned to duty on a holiday is entitled to pay for at least 2 hours of holiday work.

(d) An employee is not entitled to holiday premium pay while engaged in training, except as provided in §410.402 of this chapter.

[33 FR 12458, Sept. 4, 1968, as amended at 48 FR 3934, Jan. 28, 1983; 64 FR 69175, Dec. 10, 1999]

§550.132 Relation to overtime, night, and Sunday pay.

(a) Premium pay for holiday work is in addition to overtime pay or night pay differential, or premium pay for Sunday work payable under this subpart and is not included in the rate of basic pay used to compute the overtime pay or night pay differential or premium pay for Sunday work.

(b) Notwithstanding premium pay for holiday work, the number of hours of holiday work are included in determining for overtime pay purposes the total number of hours of work performed in the administrative workweek in which the holiday occurs.

(c) The number of regularly scheduled hours of duty on a holiday that fall within an employee's basic workweek on which the employee is excused from duty are part of the basic workweek for overtime pay computation purposes.

(d) For a Border Patrol agent covered by 5 U.S.C. 5550 and subpart P of this part, no holiday premium pay is payable for regularly scheduled overtime hours within the agent's regular tour of duty, as required by 5 U.S.C. 5550(b)(2)(C), (b)(3)(C), and (c)(1)(A). The overtime supplement payable for such scheduled overtime hours is not part of the agent's rate of basic pay used in computing the holiday premium pay for other hours that qualify for such premium pay.

[33 FR 12458, Sept. 4, 1968, as amended at 80 FR 58111, Sept. 25, 2015]

REGULARLY SCHEDULED STANDBY DUTY PAY

§550.141 Authorization of premium pay on an annual basis.

An agency may pay premium pay on an annual basis, instead of the premium pay prescribed in this subpart for regularly scheduled overtime, night, holiday, and Sunday work, to an employee in a position requiring him or her regularly to remain at, or within the confines of, his or her station during longer than ordinary periods of duty, a substantial part of which consists of remaining in a standby status rather than performing work. Premium pay under this section is determined as an appropriate percentage, not in excess of 25 percent, of that part of the employee's rate of basic pay which does not exceed the minimum rate of basic pay for GS–10 (including any applicable locality-based comparability payment under 5 U.S.C. 5304 or special rate of pay under 5 U.S.C. 5305 or similar provision of law).

[56 FR 20342, May 3, 1991, as amended at 61 FR 3542, Feb. 1, 1996]

§550.142 General restrictions.

An agency may pay premium pay under §550.141 only if that premium pay, over a period appropriate to reflect the full cycle of the employee's duties and the full range of conditions in his position, would be:

(a) More than the premium pay which would otherwise be payable under this subpart for the hours of actual work customarily required in his position, excluding standby time during which he performs no work; and

(b) Less than the premium pay which would otherwise be payable under this subpart for the hours of duty required in his position, including standby time during which he performs no work.

§550.143 Bases for determining positions for which premium pay under §550.141 is authorized.

(a) The requirement for the type of position referred to in §550.141 that an employee regularly remain at, or within the confines of, his station must meet all the following conditions:

(1) The requirement must be definite and the employee must be officially ordered to remain at his station. The employee's remaining at his station must not be merely voluntary, desirable, or a result of geographic isolation, or solely because the employee lives on the grounds.

(2) The hours during which the requirement is operative must be included in the employee's tour of duty. This tour of duty must be established on a regularly recurring basis over a substantial period of time, generally at least a few months. The requirement must not be occasional, irregular, or for a brief period.

(3) The requirement must be associated with the regularly assigned duties of the employee's job, either as a continuation of his regular work which includes standby time, or as a requirement to stand by at his post to perform his regularly assigned duties if the necessity arises.

(b) The words "at, or within the confines, of his station", in §550.141 mean one of the following:

(1) At an employee's regular duty station.

(2) In quarters provided by an agency, which are not the employee's ordinary living quarters, and which are specifically provided for use of personnel required to stand by in readiness to perform actual work when the need arises or when called.

(3) In an employee's living quarters, when designated by the agency as his duty station and when his whereabouts is narrowly limited and his activities are substantially restricted. This condition exists only during periods when an employee is required to remain at his quarters and is required to hold himself in a state of readiness to answer calls for his services. This limitation on an employee's whereabouts and activities is distinguished from the limitation placed on an employee who is subject to call outside his tour of duty but may leave his quarters provided he arranges for someone else to respond to calls or leaves a telephone number by which he can be reached should his services be required.

(c) The words "longer than ordinary periods of duty" in §550.141 mean more than 40 hours a week.

(d) The words "a substantial part of which consists of remaining in a standby status rather than performing work" in §550.141 refer to the entire tour of duty. This requirement is met:

(1) When a substantial part of the entire tour of duty, at least 25 percent, is spent in a standby status which occurs throughout the entire tour;

(2) If certain hours of the tour of duty are regularly devoted to actual work

and others are spent in a standby status, that part of the tour of duty devoted to standing by is at least 25 percent of the entire tour of duty; or

(3) When an employee has a basic workweek requiring full-time performance of actual work and is required, in addition, to perform standby duty on certain nights, or to perform standby duty on certain days not included in his basic workweek.

(e) An employee is in a standby status, as referred to in § 550.141, only at times when he is not required to perform actual work and is free to eat, sleep, read, listen to the radio, or engage in other similar pursuits. An employee is performing actual work, rather than being in a standby status, when his full attention is devoted to his work, even though the nature of his work does not require constant activity (for example, a guard on duty at his post and a technician continuously observing instruments are engaged in the actual work of their positions). Actual work includes both work performed during regular work periods and work performed when called out during periods ordinarily spent in a standby status.

§ 550.144 Rates of premium pay payable under § 550.141.

(a) An agency may pay the premium pay on an annual basis referred to in § 550.141 to an employee who meets the requirements of that section, at one of the following percentages of that part of the employee's rate of basic pay which does not exceed the minimum rate of basic pay for GS–10 (including any applicable locality-based comparability payment under 5 U.S.C. 5304 or special rate of pay under 5 U.S.C. 5305 or similar provision of law):

(1) A position with a tour of duty of the 24 hours on duty, 24 hours off duty type and with a schedule of: 60 hours a week—5 percent, unless 25 or more hours of actual work is customarily required, in which event—10 percent; 72 hours a week—15 percent, unless 24 or more hours of actual work is customarily required, in which event—20 percent; 84 hours or more a week—25 percent.

(2) A position with a tour of duty requiring the employee to remain on duty during all daylight hours each day, or for 12 hours each day, or for 24 hours each day, with the employee living at his station during the period of his assignment to his tour, and with a schedule of: 5 days a week—5 percent, unless 25 or more hours of actual work is customarily required, in which event—10 percent; 6 days a week—15 percent, unless 30 or more hours of actual work is customarily required, in which event 20 percent; 7 days a week—25 percent.

(3) A position in which the employee has a basic workweek requiring fulltime performance of actual work, and is required, in addition, to remain on standby duty: 14 to 18 hours a week on regular workdays, or extending into a nonworkday in continuation of a period of duty within the basic workweek—15 percent; 19 to 27 hours a week on regular workdays, or extending into a nonworkday in continuation of a period of duty within the basic workweek—20 percent; 28 or more hours a week on regular workdays, or extending into a nonworkday in continuation of a period of duty within the basic workweek—25 percent; 7 to 9 hours on one or more of his regular weekly nonworkdays—15 percent; 10 to 13 hours on one or more of his regular weekly nonworkdays—20 percent; 14 or more hours on one or more of his regular weekly nonworkdays—25 percent.

(4) When an agency pays an employee one of the rates authorized by paragraph (a)(1), (2), or (3) of this section, the agency shall increase this rate by adding (i) 2½ percent to the rate when the employee is required to perform Sunday work on an average of 20 to 40 Sundays over a year's period or (ii) 5 percent to the rate when the employee is required to perform Sunday work on an average of 41 or more Sundays over a year's period but the rate thus increased may not exceed 25 percent.

(b) If an employee is eligible for premium pay on an annual basis under § 550.141, but none of the percentages in paragraph (a) of this section is applicable, or unusual conditions are present which seem to make the applicable rate unsuitable, the agency may propose a rate of premium pay on an annual basis for OPM approval. The proposal shall include full information bearing on the employee's tour of duty; the number of hours of actual work required; and how it is distributed over the tour of duty; the number of hours in a standby status required and the extent to which the employee's whereabouts and activities are restricted during standby periods; the extent to which the assignment is made more onerous by night, holiday, or Sunday duty or by hours of duty beyond 8 in a day or 40 in a week; and any other pertinent conditions.

[33 FR 12458, Sept. 4, 1968, as amended at 56 FR 20342, May 3, 1991; 61 FR 3543, Feb. 1, 1996]

ADMINISTRATIVELY UNCONTROLLABLE WORK

§550.151 Authorization of premium pay on an annual basis.

An agency may pay premium pay on an annual basis, instead of other premium pay prescribed in this subpart (except premium pay for regular overtime work, and work at night, on Sundays, and on holidays), to an employee in a position in which the hours of duty cannot be controlled administratively and which requires substantial amounts of irregular or occasional overtime work, with the employee generally being responsible for recognizing, without supervision, circumstances which require the employee to remain on duty. Premium pay under this section is determined as an appropriate percentage, not less than 10 percent nor more than 25 percent, of the employee's rate of basic pay (as defined in §550.103).

[57 FR 2435, Jan. 22, 1992, as amended at 61 FR 3543, Feb. 1, 1996]

§550.152 [Reserved]

§550.153 Bases for determining positions for which premium pay under §550.151 is authorized.

(a) The requirement in §550.151 that a position be one in which the hours of duty cannot be controlled administratively is inherent in the nature of such a position. A typical example of a position which meets this requirement is that of an investigator of criminal activities whose hours of duty are governed by what criminals do and when they do it. He is often required to perform such duties as shadowing suspects, working incognito among those under suspicion, searching for evidence, meeting informers, making arrests, and interviewing persons having knowledge of criminal or alleged criminal activities. His hours on duty and place of work depend on the behavior of the criminals or suspected criminals and cannot be controlled administratively. In such a situation, the hours of duty cannot be controlled by such administrative devices as hiring additional personnel; rescheduling the hours of duty (which can be done when, for example, a type of work occurs primarily at certain times of the day); or granting compensatory time off duty to offset overtime hours required.

(b) In order to satisfactorily discharge the duties of a position referred to in §550.151, an employee is required to perform substantial amounts of irregular or occasional overtime work. In regard to this requirement:

(1) A substantial amount of irregular or occasional overtime work means an average of at least 3 hours a week of that overtime work.

(2) The irregular or occasional overtime work is a continual requirement, generally averaging more than once a week.

(3) There must be a definite basis for anticipating that the irregular or occasional overtime work will continue over an appropriate period with a duration and frequency sufficient to meet the minimum requirements under paragraphs (b)(1) and (2) of this section.

(c) The words in §550.151 that an employee is generally "responsible for recognizing, without supervision, circumstances which require him to remain on duty" mean that:

(1) The responsibility for an employee remaining on duty when required by circumstances must be a definite, official, and special requirement of his position.

(2) The employee must remain on duty not merely because it is desirable, but because of compelling reasons inherently related to continuance of his duties, and of such a nature that failure to carry on would constitute negligence.

(3) The requirement that the employee is responsible for recognizing

circumstances does not include such clear-cut instances as, for example, when an employee must continue working because a relief fails to report as scheduled.

(d) The words "circumstances which require him to remain on duty" as used in § 550.151 mean that:

(1) The employee is required to continue on duty in continuation of a full daily tour of duty or that after the end of his regular workday, the employee resumes duty in accordance with a prearranged plan or an awaited event. Performance of only call-back overtime work referred to in § 550.112(h) does not meet this requirement.

(2) The employee has no choice as to when or where he may perform the work when he remains on duty in continuation of a full daily tour of duty. This differs from a situation in which an employee has the option of taking work home or doing it at the office; or doing it in continuation of his regular hours of duty or later in the evening. It also differs from a situation in which an employee has such latitude in his working hours, as when in a travel status, that he may decide to begin work later in the morning and continue working later at night to better accomplish a given objective.

[33 FR 12458, Sept. 4, 1968, as amended at 35 FR 6311, Apr. 18, 1970; 64 FR 69175, Dec. 10, 1999]

§ 550.154 Rates of premium pay payable under § 550.151.

(a) An agency may pay the premium pay on an annual basis referred to in § 550.151 to an employee who meets the requirements of that section, at one of the following percentages of the employee's rate of basic pay (as defined in § 550.103):

(1) A position which requires an average of at least 3 but not more than 5 hours a week of irregular or occasional overtime work—10 percent;

(2) A position which requires an average of over five but not more than 7 hours a week of irregular or occasional overtime work—15 percent;

(3) A position which requires an average of over seven but not more than 9 hours a week or irregular or occasional overtime work—20 percent;

(4) A position which requires an average of over 9 hours a week of irregular or occasional overtime work—25 percent.

(b) If an agency proposes to pay an employee premium pay on an annual basis under § 550.151 but unusual conditions seem to make the applicable rate in paragraph (a) of this section unsuitable, the agency may propose a rate of premium pay on an annual basis for OPM approval. The proposal shall include full information bearing on the frequency and duration of the irregular or occasional overtime work required; the nature of the work which prevents hours of duty from being controlled administratively; the necessity for the employee being generally responsible for recognizing, without supervision, circumstances which require him to remain on duty; and any other pertinent conditions.

(c) The period of time during which an employee continues to receive premium pay on an annual basis under § 550.151 under the authority of paragraphs (c) or (g) of § 550.162 is not considered in computing the average hours of irregular and occasional overtime work under this section.

[33 FR 12458, Sept. 4, 1968, as amended at 35 FR 6311, Apr. 18, 1970; 55 FR 41178, Oct. 10, 1990; 57 FR 2435, Jan. 22, 1992; 61 FR 3543, Feb. 1, 1996; 67 FR 6641, Feb. 13, 2002]

General Rules Governing Payments of Premium Pay on an Annual Basis

§ 550.161 Responsibilities of the agencies.

The head of each agency, or an official who has been delegated authority to act for the head of an agency in the matter concerned, is responsible for:

(a) Fixing tours of duty; ordering employees to remain at their stations in a standby status; and placing responsibility on employees for remaining on duty when required by circumstances.

(b) Determining, in accordance with section 5545(c) of title 5, United States Code, and this subpart, which employees shall receive premium pay on an annual basis under § 550.141 or § 550.151. These determinations may not be retroactive.

(c) Determining the number of hours of actual work to be customarily required in positions involving longer than ordinary periods of duty, a substantial part of which consists of standby duty. This determination shall be based on consideration of the time required by regular, repetitive operations, available records of the time required in the past by other activities, and any other information bearing on the number of hours of actual work which may reasonably be expected to be required in the future.

(d) Determining the number of hours of irregular or occasional overtime work to be customarily required in positions which require substantial amounts of irregular or occasional overtime work with the employee generally being responsible for recognizing, without supervision, circumstances which require him to remain on duty. This determination shall be based on consideration of available records of the hours of irregular or occasional overtime work required in the past, and any other information bearing on the number of hours of duty which may reasonably be expected to be required in the future.

(e) Determining the rate of premium pay fixed by OPM under §550.144 or §550.154 which is applicable to each employee paid under §550.141 or §550.151; or, if no rate fixed under §550.144 or §550.154 is considered applicable, proposing a rate of premium pay on an annual basis to OPM.

(f) Reviewing determinations under paragraphs (b), (c), (d) and (e) of this section at appropriate intervals, and discontinuing payments or revising rates of premium pay on an annual basis in each instance when that action is necessary to meet the requirements of section 5545(c) of title 5, United States Code, and this subpart.

[33 FR 12458, Sept. 4, 1968, as amended at 35 FR 6311, Apr. 18, 1970]

§550.162 Payment provisions.

(a) Except as otherwise provided in this section, an employee's premium pay on an annual basis under §550.141 or §550.151 begins on the date that he enters on duty in the position concerned for purposes of basic pay, and ceases on the date that he ceases to be paid basic pay in the position.

(b) When an employee is in a position in which conditions warranting premium pay on an annual basis under §550.141 or §550.151 exist only during a certain period of the year, such as during a given season, an agency may pay the employee premium pay on an annual basis only during the period he is subject to these conditions.

(c) An agency may continue to pay an employee premium pay on an annual basis under §550.141 or §550.151:

(1) For a period of not more than 10 consecutive prescribed workdays on temporary assignment to other duties in which conditions do not warrant payment of premium pay on an annual basis, and for a total of not more than 30 workdays in a calendar year while on such a temporary assignment.

(2) For an aggregate period of not more than 60 prescribed workdays on temporary assignment to a formally approved program for advanced training duty directly related to duties for which premium pay on an annual basis is payable.

An agency may not continue to pay an employee premium pay on an annual basis under this paragraph for more than 60 workdays in a calendar year.

(d) When an employee is not entitled to premium pay on an annual basis under §550.141, he is entitled to be paid for overtime, night, holiday, and Sunday work in accordance with other sections of this subpart.

(e) An agency shall continue to pay an employee premium pay on an annual basis under §550.141 or §550.151 while he is on leave with pay during a period in which premium pay on an annual basis is payable under paragraphs (a), (b), and (c) of this section.

(f) Unless an agency discontinues authorization of premium pay under §550.141 or §550.151 for all similar positions, it may not discontinue authorization of such premium pay for an individual employee's position—

(1) During a period of paid leave elected by the employee and approved by the agency in lieu of benefits under the Federal Employees' Compensation Act, as amended (5 U.S.C. 8101 *et seq.*), following a job-related injury;

(2) During a period of continuation of pay under the Federal Employees' Compensation Act, as amended (5 U.S.C. 8101 *et seq.*);

(3) During a period of leave without pay, if the employee is in receipt of benefits under the Federal Employees' Compensation Act, as amended (5 U.S.C. 8101 *et seq.*). (Note: No premium pay is payable during leave without pay; however, the continued authorization may prevent a reduction in an employee's retirement benefits if the leave without pay period occurs during the employee's high-3 average salary period.)

(g) Notwithstanding paragraph (c)(1) of this section, an agency may continue to pay premium pay under § 550.151 to an employee during a temporary assignment that would not otherwise warrant the payment of AUO pay, if the temporary assignment is directly related to a national emergency declared by the President. An agency may continue to pay premium pay under § 550.151 for not more than 30 consecutive workdays for such a temporary assignment and for a total of not more than 90 workdays in a calendar year while on such a temporary assignment.

[33 FR 12458, Sept. 4, 1968, as amended at 35 FR 6312, Apr. 18, 1970; 64 FR 69175, Dec. 10, 1999; 67 FR 6641, Feb. 13, 2002; 68 FR 4681, Jan. 30, 2003]

§ 550.163 Relationship to other payments.

(a) An employee receiving premium pay on an annual basis under § 550.141 may not receive premium pay for regular overtime work or work at night or on a holiday or on Sunday under any other section of this subpart. An agency shall pay the employee in accordance with §§ 550.113 and 550.114 for irregular or occasional overtime work.

(b) An employee receiving premium pay on an annual basis under § 550.151 may not receive premium pay for irregular or occasional overtime work under any other section of this subpart. An agency shall pay the employee in accordance with other sections of this subpart for regular overtime work, and work at night, on Sundays, and on holidays.

(c) Overtime, night, holiday, or Sunday work paid under any statute other than subchapter V of chapter 55 of title 5, United States Code, is not a basis for payment of premium pay on an annual basis under § 550.141 or § 550.151.

(d) (1) Except as provided in paragraph (d)(2) of this section, premium pay on an annual basis under § 550.141 or § 550.151 is not base pay and is not included in the base used in computing foreign and nonforeign allowances and differentials, or any other benefits or deductions that are computed on base pay alone.

(2) Premium pay on an annual basis under § 550.141 is base pay for the purpose of section 5595(c), section 8114(e), section 8331(3), and section 8704(c) of title 5, United States Code.

(e) Premium pay on an annual basis under § 550.141 or § 550.151 may not be paid to a criminal investigator receiving availability pay under § 550.181.

[33 FR 12458, Sept. 4, 1968, as amended at 33 FR 19897, Dec. 28, 1968; 35 FR 6312, Apr. 18, 1970; 59 FR 66151, Dec. 23, 1994]

§ 550.164 Construction and computation of existing aggregate rates.

(a) Pursuant to section 208(b) of the act of September 1, 1954 (68 Stat. 1111), nothing in this subpart relating to the payment of premium pay on an annual basis may be construed to decrease the existing aggregate rate of pay of an employee on the rolls of an agency immediately before the date section 5545(c) of title 5, United States Code, is made applicable to him by administrative action.

(b) When it is necessary to determine an employee's existing aggregate rate of pay (referred to in this section as existing aggregate rate), an agency shall determine it on the basis of the earnings the employee would have received over an appropriate period (generally 1 year) if his tour of duty immediately before the date section 5545(c) of title 5, United States Code, is made applicable to him had remained the same. In making this determination, basic pay and premium pay for overtime, night, holiday, and Sunday work are included in the earnings the employee would have received. Premium pay for irregular or occasional overtime work may be included only if it was of a significant amount in the past and the conditions which required it are expected to continue.

(c) An agency shall recompute an employee's rate of pay based on premium pay on an annual basis when he received subsequent increases in his rate of basic pay in order to determine whether or not the employee should continue to receive an existing aggregate rate or be paid premium pay on an annual basis.

(d) Except as otherwise provided by statute, an agency may not use subsequent increases in an employee's rate of basic pay to redetermine or increase the employee's existing aggregate rate. However, these increases shall be used for other pay purposes, such as the computation of retirement deductions and annuities, payment of overseas allowances and post differentials, and determination of the highest previous rate under part 531 of this chapter.

(e) When an agency elects to pay an employee premium pay on an annual basis, he is entitled to continue to receive hourly premium pay properly payable under sections 5542, 5543, 5545 (a) and (b), and 5546 of title 5, United States Code, until his base pay plus premium pay on an annual basis equals or exceeds his existing aggregate rate. When this occurs, the agency shall pay the employee his base pay plus premium pay on an annual basis.

(f) Except when terminated under paragraph (e) of this section, an agency shall continue to pay an employee an existing aggregate rate so long as:

(1) He remains in a position to which §550.141, §550.151, or §550.162(c) is applicable;

(2) His tour of duty does not decrease in length; and

(3) He continues to perform equivalent night, holiday, and irregular or occasional overtime work.

(g) If an employee who is entitled to an existing aggregate rate moves from one position to another in the same agency, both of which are within the scope of section 5545(c) of title 5, United States Code, he is entitled to be paid an existing aggregate rate in the new position such as he would have received had he occupied that position when the agency elected to make section 5545(c) applicable to it.

PAY FOR SUNDAY WORK

§550.171 Authorization of pay for Sunday work.

(a) An employee is entitled to pay at his or her rate of basic pay plus premium pay at a rate equal to 25 percent of his or her rate of basic pay for each hour of Sunday work (as defined in §550.103).

(b) An employee is not entitled to Sunday premium pay while engaged in training, except as provided in §410.402 of this chapter.

[60 FR 33098, June 27, 1995, as amended at 60 FR 67287, Dec. 29, 1995; 64 FR 69175, Dec. 10, 1999; 72 FR 12036, Mar. 15, 2007; 76 FR 52539, Aug. 23, 2011]

§550.172 Relation to overtime, night, and holiday pay.

(a) Premium pay for Sunday work is in addition to premium pay for holiday work, overtime pay, or night pay differential payable under this subpart and is not included in the rate of basic pay used to compute the pay for holiday work, overtime pay, or night pay differential.

(b) For a Border Patrol agent covered by 5 U.S.C. 5550 and subpart P of this part, no Sunday premium pay is payable for regularly scheduled overtime hours within the agent's regular tour of duty, as required by 5 U.S.C. 5550(b)(2)(C), (b)(3)(C), and (c)(1)(A). The overtime supplement payable for such scheduled overtime hours is not part of the agent's rate of basic pay used in computing the Sunday premium pay for other hours that qualify for such premium pay.

[33 FR 12458, Sept. 4, 1968, as amended at 80 FR 58111, Sept. 25, 2015]

LAW ENFORCEMENT AVAILABILITY PAY

§550.181 Coverage.

(a) Each employee meeting the definition of *criminal investigator* in §550.103, and fulfilling the conditions and requirements of 5 U.S.C. 5545a and §§550.181 through 550.186, must receive availability pay to compensate the criminal investigator for unscheduled duty in excess of the 40-hour workweek based on the needs of the employing agency, except as provided in paragraph (b) of this section.

(b) Any Office of Inspector General that employs fewer than five criminal investigators may elect not to cover such criminal investigators under the availability pay provisions of 5 U.S.C. 5545a.

[64 FR 4520, Jan. 29, 1999]

§550.182 Unscheduled duty.

(a) *Unscheduled Duty Hours.* For the purpose of availability pay, unscheduled duty hours are those hours during which a criminal investigator performs work, or (except for a special agent in the Diplomatic Security Service) is determined by the employing agency to be available for work, that are not—

(1) Part of the 40-hour basic workweek of the investigator; or

(2) Regularly scheduled overtime hours compensated under 5 U.S.C. 5542 and §550.111.

(b) *Regularly Scheduled Overtime Hours.* For criminal investigators receiving availability pay, regularly scheduled overtime hours compensated under 5 U.S.C. 5542 and §550.111 are those overtime hours scheduled in advance of the investigator's administrative workweek, excluding—

(1) The first 2 hours of overtime work on any day containing a part of the investigator's basic 40-hour workweek, as required by §550.111(f)(1)); or

(2) The first 2 hours of overtime work performing protective duties authorized by section 3056(a) of title 18, United States Code, or section 2709(a)(3) of title 22, United States Code, on any day containing a part of the investigator's basic 40-hour workweek, unless the investigator performs 2 or more consecutive hours of unscheduled overtime work on that same day.

(c) *Actual work hours.* To be considered to be performing work under paragraph (a) of this section, a criminal investigator must be performing work as officially ordered or approved, including work performed without specific supervisory preapproval, if circumstances require the criminal investigator to perform the duty to meet the needs of the employing agency, subject to agency policies and procedures (including any requirements for after-the-fact validation or approval).

(d) *Availability Hours.* To be considered available for work under paragraph (a) of this section, a criminal investigator must be determined by the employing agency to be generally and reasonably accessible to perform unscheduled duty based on the needs of the agency. Generally, the agency will place the investigator in availability status by directing the investigator to be available during designated periods to meet agency needs, as provided by agency policies and procedures. Placing the investigator in availability status is not considered scheduling the investigator for overtime hours compensated under 5 U.S.C. 5542 and §550.111. Availability hours may include hours during which an investigator places himself or herself in availability status to meet the needs of the agency, subject to agency policies and procedures (including any requirements for after-the-fact validation or approval). A special agent in the Diplomatic Security Service may not be credited with availability hours and will be credited with only hours actually worked.

(e) *Ensuring availability.* Except as provided in paragraphs (e) and (f) of this section, an employing agency shall ensure that each criminal investigator's hours of unscheduled duty are sufficient to enable the investigator to meet the substantial hours requirement in §550.183 and make the certification required under §550.184.

(f) *Voluntary opt-out.* Notwithstanding paragraph (d) of this section, an employing agency may, at its discretion, approve a criminal investigator's voluntary request that the investigator generally be assigned no overtime work (including unscheduled duty) for a designated period of time because of a personal or family hardship situation. The investigator must sign a written statement documenting this request and his or her understanding that availability pay will not be payable during the designated period.

(g) *When availability pay is suspended.* The employing agency is not subject to the requirement of paragraph (d) of this section in the case of a criminal investigator for whom availability pay is suspended in accordance with

§550.184(d) due to denial or cancellation of the required certification based on—

(1) Failure to perform unscheduled duty as assigned or reported; or

(2) Inability to perform unscheduled duty for an extended period because of a physical or health condition.

[59 FR 66151, Dec. 23, 1994, as amended at 64 FR 4520, Jan. 29, 1999]

§550.183 Substantial hours requirement.

(a) A criminal investigator shall be eligible for availability pay only if the annual average number of hours of unscheduled duty per regular workday is 2 hours or more, as certified in accordance with §550.184. This average is computed by dividing the total unscheduled duty hours for the annual period (numerator) by the number of regular workdays (denominator).

(b) For the purpose of this section, *regular workday* means each day in the criminal investigator's basic workweek during which the investigator works at least 4 hours, excluding—

(1) Overtime hours compensated under 5 U.S.C. 5542 and §550.111;

(2) Unscheduled duty hours compensated by availability pay under 5 U.S.C. 5545a and this subpart; and

(3) Hours during which an investigator is engaged in agency-approved training, is traveling under official travel orders, is on approved leave, or is on excused absence with pay (including paid holidays).

(c) In computing average hours under paragraph (a) of this section, the total unscheduled duty hours in the numerator shall include—

(1) Any unscheduled duty hours on a regular workday; and

(2) Any unscheduled duty hours actually worked by an investigator on days that are not regular workdays.

[59 FR 66151, Dec. 23, 1994]

§550.184 Annual certification.

(a) Each newly hired criminal investigator who will receive availability pay and the appropriate supervisory officer (as designated by the head of the agency or authorized designee) shall make an initial certification to the head of the agency attesting that the investigator is expected to meet the substantial hours requirement in §550.183 during the upcoming 1-year period. A similar certification shall be made for a criminal investigator who will begin receiving availability pay after a period of nonreceipt (e.g., a designated voluntary opt-out period under §550.182(e)).

(b) Each criminal investigator who is receiving availability pay and the appropriate supervisory officer (as designated by the head of the agency or authorized designee) shall make an annual certification to the head of the agency attesting that the investigator currently meets, and is expected to continue to meet during the upcoming 1-year period, the substantial hours requirement in §550.183.

(c) A certification shall no longer apply when the employee separates from Federal service, is employed by another agency, moves to a position that does not qualify as a criminal investigator position, or begins a voluntary opt-out period under §550.182(e).

(d) The employing agency shall ensure that criminal investigators receiving availability pay comply with the substantial hours requirement in §550.183, as certified in accordance with this section. The employing agency may deny or cancel a certification based on a finding that an investigator has failed to perform unscheduled duty (availability or work) as assigned or reported, or is unable to perform unscheduled duty for an extended period due to physical or health reasons. If a certification is denied or canceled, the investigator's entitlement to availability pay shall be suspended for an appropriate period, consistent with agency policies. If the investigator's certification was valid when made, the suspension of availability pay shall be effected prospectively.

(e) An involuntary suspension of availability pay resulting from a denial or cancellation of certification under paragraph (d) of this section is a reduction in pay for the purpose of applying the adverse action procedures of 5 U.S.C. 7512 and part 752 of this chapter, except for special agents in the Foreign Service. For special agents in the Foreign Service, an involuntary suspension of availability pay resulting from a denial or cancellation of certification under paragraph (d) of this section will be administered under procedures established by regulations of the Department of State.

(f) The head of an agency (or authorized designee) may prescribe any additional regulations necessary to administer the certification requirement, including procedures for retroactive correction in cases in which a certification is issued belatedly or lapses due to administrative error.

[59 FR 66151, Dec. 23, 1994, as amended at 64 FR 4520, Jan. 29, 1999]

§550.185 Payment of availability pay.

(a) Availability pay is paid only for periods of time during which a criminal investigator receives basic pay. Availability pay is an amount equal to the lesser of—(1) 25 percent of a criminal investigator's rate of basic pay, as defined in §550.103, including amounts designated as "salary" for special agents in the Diplomatic Security Service; or

(2) The maximum amount that may be paid to avoid exceeding the maximum earnings limitation on premium pay for law enforcement officers in 5 U.S.C. 5547(c).

(b) Except as provided in paragraph (c) of this section, a criminal investigator who is eligible for availability pay shall continue to receive such pay during any period such investigator is attending agency-sanctioned training, on agency-ordered travel status, on agency-approved leave with pay, or on excused absence with pay for relocation purposes.

(c) Agencies may, at their discretion, provide availability pay to criminal investigators during training that is considered initial, basic training usually provided in the first year of service.

(d) Agencies may, at their discretion, provide for the continuation of availability pay when a criminal investigator is on excused absence with pay, except where payment is mandatory under paragraph (b) of this section.

(e) The amount of availability pay payable to a criminal investigator for a pay period is not affected by the occurrence of a paid holiday during that period.

[59 FR 66151, Dec. 23, 1994, as amended at 60 FR 67287, Dec. 29, 1995; 64 FR 4521, Jan. 29, 1999]

§550.186 Relationship to other payments.

(a) Standby duty pay under §550.141 and administratively uncontrollable overtime pay under §550.151 may not be paid to a criminal investigator receiving availability pay. Receipt of availability pay does not affect an investigator's entitlement to other types of premium pay (including overtime pay under §550.111) based on hours other than unscheduled duty hours. However, a criminal investigator receiving availability pay may not be paid any other premium pay based on unscheduled duty hours.

(b) Availability pay is treated as part of basic pay or basic salary only for the following purposes:

(1) 5 U.S.C. 5524a, pertaining to advances in pay;

(2) 5 U.S.C. 5595(c), pertaining to severance pay;

(3) 5 U.S.C. 8114(e), pertaining to workers' compensation;

(4) 5 U.S.C. 8331(3) and 5 U.S.C. 8401(4), pertaining to retirement benefits;

(5) Subchapter III of chapter 84 of title 5, United States Code, pertaining to the Thrift Savings Plan;

(6) 5 U.S.C. 8704(c), pertaining to life insurance;

(7) Sections 609(b)(1), 805, 806, and 856 of the Foreign Service Act of 1980, as amended (Pub. L. 96–465), pertaining to Foreign Service retirement benefits; and

(8) For any other purposes explicitly provided for by law or as the Office of Personnel Management or the Secretary of State (for matters exclusively within the jurisdiction of the Secretary) may prescribe by regulation.

(c) The minimum wage and the hours of work and overtime pay provisions of the Fair Labor Standards Act do not apply to criminal investigators receiving availability pay.

[59 FR 66151, Dec. 23, 1994, as amended at 64 FR 4521, Jan. 29, 1999; 64 FR 36771, July 8, 1999]

§ 550.187 Transitional provisions.

(a) Except as provided in paragraph (b) of this section, not later than the first day of the first pay period beginning on or after October 30, 1994, each criminal investigator qualified to receive availability pay and the appropriate supervisory officer (as designated by the agency head or authorized designee) shall make an initial certification to the head of the agency that the investigator is expected to meet the substantial hours requirement in § 550.183. The head of an agency may prescribe procedures necessary to administer this paragraph.

(b)(1) In the case of criminal investigators who are employed in offices of Inspectors General and who, immediately prior to September 30, 1994, were not receiving administratively uncontrollable overtime pay, or were receiving such pay at a rate of less than 25 percent, the employing office may delay implementation of availability pay; however, availability pay shall be implemented (in accordance with §§ 550.181 through 550.186) no later than—

(i) September 30, 1995, for investigators who are not receiving administratively uncontrollable overtime pay; or

(ii) The first day of the last pay period ending on or before September 30, 1995, for investigators who were receiving administratively uncontrollable overtime pay at a rate of less than 25 percent immediately prior to September 30, 1994.

(2) A criminal investigator who is employed in an Inspector General office and was receiving administratively uncontrollable overtime pay at a rate of less than 25 percent immediately prior to September 30, 1994, shall continue to receive at least that rate or a higher rate, if increased by the employing agency, until the availability pay provision is implemented for the position (no later than as provided in paragraph (b)(1)(ii) of this section).

(3) Implementation of availability pay for criminal investigators under paragraph (b)(1) of this section shall be in accordance with the requirements and conditions set forth in §§ 550.181 through 550.186. For qualified investigators, an initial certification shall be made, consistent with paragraph (a) of this section.

[59 FR 66151, Dec. 23, 1994]

Subpart B—Advances in Pay

AUTHORITY: 5 U.S.C. 5524a, 5527, 5545a(h)(2)(B), 5550(d)(1)(B); E.O. 12748, 3 CFR, 1992 comp., p. 316.

SOURCE: 56 FR 12837, Mar. 28, 1991, unless otherwise noted.

§ 550.201 Purpose.

This subpart provides regulations to implement 5 U.S.C. 5524a which provides that the head of each agency may make advance payments of basic pay, covering not more than 2 pay periods, to any individual who is newly appointed to a position in the agency.

§ 550.202 Definitions.

In this subpart: *Agency* means an Executive agency, as defined in 5 U.S.C. 105.

Employee means an individual employed in or under an agency who is appointed to a position with a scheduled tour of duty.

Head of agency means the head of an agency or an official who has been delegated the authority to act for the head of the agency in the matter concerned.

Newly appointed means—

(a) The first appointment, regardless of tenure, as an employee of the Federal Government;

(b) A new appointment following a break in service of at least 90 days; or

(c) A permanent appointment in the competitive service following termination of employment in an Internship Program (as described in 5 CFR part 362, subpart B), provided such employee—

(1) Was separated from the service, in a nonpay status, or a combination of both during the entire 90-day period immediately before the permanent appointment; and

(2) Has fully repaid any former advance in pay under § 550.205.

Offset or *setoff* means repayment in installments of an advance in pay by payroll deductions or an administrative offset under subpart K of this part to collect a debt under 5 U.S.C. 5514 from an indebted Government employee.

Pay period means the pay period established by an agency for an employee under 5 U.S.C. 5504.

Rate of basic pay means the rate of pay fixed by law or administrative action for the position held by an employee, excluding additional pay of any kind except the following, as applicable:

(1) Any locality payment under 5 CFR part 531, subpart F; special rate supplement under 5 CFR part 530, subpart C; or similar payment or supplement under other legal authority;

(2) Annual premium pay under 5 U.S.C. 5545(c) or availability pay under 5 U.S.C. 5545a;

(3) Straight-time pay for regular overtime hours for firefighters under 5 U.S.C. 5545b (as provided in § 550.1305(b));

(4) Night differential for prevailing rate employees under 5 U.S.C. 5343(f); and

(5) An overtime supplement for regularly scheduled overtime within a Border Patrol agent's regular tour of duty under 5 U.S.C. 5550 (as allowed under 5 U.S.C. 5550(d)(1)(B)).

[56 FR 12837, Mar. 28, 1991, as amended at 57 FR 2435, Jan. 22, 1992; 58 FR 41625, Aug. 5, 1993; 59 FR 66153, Dec. 23, 1994; 61 FR 3543, Feb. 1, 1996; 63 FR 64592, Nov. 23, 1998; 64 FR 69176, Dec. 10, 1999; 70 FR 31313, May 31, 2005; 73 FR 66156, Nov. 7, 2008; 77 FR 28223, May 11, 2012; 80 FR 58111, Sept. 25, 2015]

§ 550.203 Advances in pay.

(a) The head of an agency may provide for the advance payment of basic pay, in one or more installments covering not more than 2 pay periods, to an employee who is newly appointed to a position in the agency.

(b) The maximum amount of pay that may be advanced to an employee shall be based on the rate of basic pay to which the employee is entitled on the date of his or her new appointment with the agency, reduced by the amount of any allotments or deductions that would normally be deducted from the employee's first regular paycheck.

(c) An advance in pay may be made to an employee no earlier than the date of appointment with the agency and no later than 60 days after the date of appointment.

(d) An advance in pay under this subpart may not be made to any employee when an agency expects to make an advance in pay to the same employee under 5 U.S.C. 5927 within 2 pay periods after the employee's appointment.

(e) An advance in pay may not be made to the head of an agency or to an employee appointed to a position in the expectation of receiving an appointment as the head of an agency.

[56 FR 12837, Mar. 28, 1991; 56 FR 40360, Aug. 14, 1991; 58 FR 41625, Aug. 5, 1993]

§ 550.204 Agency procedures.

(a) Each agency shall establish written procedures governing advance payments. These procedures shall include—

(1) Criteria to be considered before approval or denial of employee requests for advance payments;

(2) Criteria to be considered before waiving all or part of advance payments; and

(3) Processing and accounting procedures governing advance payments.

(b) Before making an advance payment, an agency shall require that the employee sign an agreement to repay to the Federal Government any amount for which repayment has not been waived by the agency head under § 550.206 of this part.

(c) Before making an advance payment, an agency shall provide the following information to the employee in writing:

(1) A statement indicating how the advance in pay will be recovered from the employee by the Federal Government, either in installments under agency procedures for payroll deductions or by salary offset procedures under subpart K of this part;

(2) The total amount of the advance in pay, the total number of pay periods for repayment of the advance in pay, and the amount that will be deducted from the pay of the employee by payroll deductions or salary offset for each pay period;

(3) A statement indicating that the employee may prepay all or part of the balance of the advance payment at any time before the money is due, including

instructions as to where and how such prepayments may be made.

(4) A statement indicating that the amount of the advance in pay not yet repaid by an employee or waived by the agency head is due and must be repaid by the employee if the employee transfers to another agency or the individual's employment with the agency is terminated for any reason; and

(5) A statement indicating that any amount of the remaining balance of the advance in pay that has not been waived or repaid by the employee on transfer or termination for any reason must be recovered by salary offset under subpart K of this part and/or by such other method as is provided by law.

(d) The head of an agency may establish procedures under which an employee is permitted to make allotments out of an advance in pay for such purposes as the head of the agency considers appropriate.

[56 FR 12837, Mar. 28, 1991, as amended at 58 FR 41625, Aug. 5, 1993]

§ 550.205 Recovery of advances in pay.

(a) Unless repayment is waived in whole or in part under § 550.206 of this part, an agency shall recover an advance in pay by installments under agency procedures for payroll deductions or by salary offset procedures established under subpart K of this part. An employee may prepay all or part of the remaining balance of an advance in pay at any time before payments are due.

(b) An agency shall establish a recovery period for each employee to repay an advance in pay, but no agency may establish a recovery period of longer than 14 pay periods beginning on the date the advance in pay is made to the employee under § 550.203 of this part. If a longer period for recovery is necessary to avoid exceeding the limitation on deductions described in § 550.1104(i) of this part, recovery may be accomplished under salary offset procedures established under subpart K of this part. Upon written request, an employee may elect a recovery period of less than 14 pay periods.

(c) If an employee transfers to another agency or employment with an agency is terminated for any reason, the remaining balance of an advance in pay not yet repaid is due and must be repaid to the Federal Government unless repayment is waived in whole or in part under § 550.206 of this part.

(d) Any remaining balance of an advance in pay that has not been waived under § 550.206 of this part or repaid by an employee upon transfer or termination of employment must be recovered by an agency using procedures for salary offset under subpart K of this part and/or by such other method as is provided by law.

[56 FR 12837, Mar. 28, 1991, as amended at 58 FR 41625, Aug. 5, 1993; 64 FR 69176, Dec. 10, 1999]

§ 550.206 Waiver of repayment.

The head of an agency may waive in whole or in part a right of recovery of an advance payment under 5 U.S.C. 5524a and this subpart if he or she determines that recovery would be against equity and good conscience or against the public interest under criteria established by the agency.

Subpart C—Allotments From Federal Employees

AUTHORITY: 5 U.S.C. 5527, E.O. 10982, 3 CFR 1959–1963 Comp., p. 502.

SOURCE: 46 FR 2325, Jan. 9, 1981, unless otherwise noted.

DEFINITIONS

§ 550.301 Definitions.

In this subpart:

Agency means an Executive agency as defined by section 105 of Title 5, United States Code.

Allotment means a recurring specified deduction for a legal purpose from pay authorized by an employee to be paid to an allottee.

Allottee means the person or institution to whom an allotment is made payable.

Allotter means the employee from whose pay an allotment is made.

Association of management officials and/or supervisors means an association composed of either management officials and/or supervisors with which the agency has established official relationships.

Combined Federal Campaign means an organization of voluntary health and welfare agencies authorized to solicit charitable contributions in a local area in accordance with arrangements prescribed by the Director of the Office of Personnel Management under Executive Order 10927.

Continental United States means the several States and the District of Columbia, but excluding Alaska and Hawaii.

Dues means the regular periodic amount specified by an allotter to be withheld from his or her pay which is required to maintain the allotter as a member in good standing in a labor organization or association of management officials and/or supervisors or other organization.

Employee means an employee of an agency who satisfies the definition of that term in 5 U.S.C. 2105.

Foreign affairs agency means the Department of State, the International Communications Agency, the Agency for International Development and its successor agency or agencies.

Labor organization means a labor organization as defined by section 7103(a)(4) of title 5, United States Code, unless specified otherwise.

[46 FR 2325, Jan. 9, 1981, as amended at 65 FR 44644, July 19, 2000; 71 FR 66828, Nov. 17, 2006]

GENERAL PROVISIONS

§ 550.311 Authority of agency.

(a) *Mandatory allotments.* An agency must permit an employee to make—

(1) An allotment for dues to a labor organization under section 7115 of Title 5, United States Code;

(2) An allotment for dues to an association of management officials and/or supervisors under § 550.331;

(3) An allotment for charitable contributions to a Combined Federal Campaign under § 550.341;

(4) An allotment for income tax withholding under § 550.351;

(5) Two or more allotments to an employee's personal account(s) at a financial organization;

(6) An allotment for child support and/or alimony payments under § 550.361; and

(7) Any allotment effecting a salary reduction as part of a flexible benefits plan established by the Office of Personnel Management in conformance with section 125 of title 26, United States Code.

(b) *Discretionary allotments.* In addition to those allotments provided for in paragraph (a) of this section, an agency may permit an employee to make an allotment for any legal purpose deemed appropriate by the head of the agency (or designee). This paragraph does not constitute an independent authority for an agency to permit pretax allotments in addition to those authorized by the Office of Personnel Management as described in paragraph (a)(7) of this section.

(c) The head of an agency may prescribe such additional regulations governing allotments as appropriate which are consistent with subchapter III of chapter 55 of title 5, United States Code, and this subpart. Discretionary allotments under this subpart may be limited in number as determined appropriate by the head of the agency.

[46 FR 2325, Jan. 9, 1981, as amended at 64 FR 69176, Dec. 10, 1999; 65 FR 44644, July 19, 2000; 66 FR 49086, Sept. 26, 2001; 66 FR 67477, Dec. 31, 2001; 71 FR 66828, Nov. 17, 1006]

§ 550.312 General limitations.

(a) The allotter must specifically designate the allottee and the amount of the allotment.

(b) The total amount of allotments may not exceed the pay due the allotter for a particular period.

(c) The allotter must personally authorize a change or cancellation of an allotment.

(d) The agency has no liability in connection with any authorized allotment disbursed by the agency in accordance with the allotter's request.

(e) Any disputes regarding any authorized allotment are a matter between the allotter and the allottee.

(f) Notwithstanding the requirements in paragraphs (a) and (c) of this section, an agency may make an allotment for an employee's share of Federal Employees Health Benefits premiums under § 550.311(a)(7) and part 892 of this chapter without specific authorization from the employee, unless the employee specifically waives such allotment. Agency procedures for processing employee waivers must be consistent with procedures established by the Office of Personnel Management. (See part 892 of this chapter.)

[46 FR 2325, Jan. 9, 1981, as amended at 64 FR 69176, Dec. 10, 1999; 65 FR 44644, July 19, 2000; 71 FR 66828, Nov. 17, 2006]

LABOR ORGANIZATION

§550.321 Authority.

Section 7115, title 5, United States Code, authorizes an employee to make an allotment for dues to a labor organization as defined in subchapter 1 of chapter 71 of title 5, United States Code. Such an allotment shall be effected in accordance with such rules and regulations as may be prescribed by the Federal Labor Relations Authority.

§550.322 Saving provision.

An agency shall permit a supervisor who so desires, to continue an allotment of dues to a labor organization as defined by section 2(e) of Executive Order 11491, as amended, which was permissible when the supervisor was excluded from a formal or exclusive unit by reason of the requirements of former section 24(d) of this Order.

ASSOCIATION OF MANAGEMENT OFFICIALS AND/OR SUPERVISORS

§550.331 Scope.

An agency shall permit an employee to make an allotment for dues to an association of management officials and/or supervisors when the employee is a supervisor or management official, and the employee is a member of an association of management officials and/or supervisors with which the agency has agreed in writing to deduct allotments for the payment of dues to the association.

COMBINED FEDERAL CAMPAIGN

§550.341 Scope.

An agency must permit an employee to make an allotment for charitable contributions to a Combined Federal Campaign in accordance with §950.901 of this chapter.

[64 FR 69176, Dec. 10, 1999]

INCOME TAX WITHHOLDING

§550.351 Scope.

When an employee has a legal obligation to pay, but the agency has no legal obligation to withhold, State, District of Columbia, or local income or employment taxes, an agency shall permit an employee to make an allotment for payment of the taxes.

ALIMONY AND/OR CHILD SUPPORT

§550.361 Scope.

An agency shall permit an employee to make an allotment for alimony and/or child support when he or she voluntarily elects to do so. However, this provision does not apply to garnishment orders issued to enforce child support and/or alimony obligations which are codified at part 581 of this title.

[46 FR 2325, Jan. 9, 1981. Redesignated at 71 FR 66828, Nov. 17, 2006]

FOREIGN AFFAIRS AGENCY ORGANIZATIONS

§550.371 Scope.

If an agency permits an employee to make an allotment for dues to a foreign affairs agency organization, the agency must also provide, in accordance with section 15 of Executive Order 11636:

(a) that the employee be allowed to revoke the authorization at least every six months; and

(b) that the allotment terminates when the dues withholding agreement between a foreign affairs agency and the organization is terminated or ceases to be applicable to the employee.

[46 FR 2325, Jan. 9, 1981. Redesignated at 71 FR 66828, Nov. 17, 2006]

Subpart D—Payments During Evacuation

AUTHORITY: 5 U.S.C. 5527; E.O. 10982, 3 CFR 1959–1963, p. 502.

SOURCE: 59 FR 66632, Dec. 28, 1994, unless otherwise noted.

§ 550.401 Purpose, applicability, authority, and administration.

(a) *Purpose.* This subpart provides regulations to administer subchapter III (except sections 5524a and 5525) of chapter 55 of title 5, United States Code. The regulations provide for Governmentwide uniformity in making payments during an evacuation to employees or their dependents, or both, who are evacuated in the United States because of natural disasters or for military or other reasons that create imminent danger to their lives.

(b) *Applicability.* This subpart applies to—

(1) Executive agencies, as defined in section 105 of title 5, United States Code.

(2) Employees of an agency who are U.S. citizens or who are U.S. nationals;

(3) Employees of an agency who are not citizens or nationals of the United States, but who were recruited with a transportation agreement that provides return transportation to the area from which recruited; and

(4) Alien employees of an agency hired within the United States.

(c) *Authority.* The head of an agency may make advance payments and evacuation payments and pay special allowances as provided by this subpart. If the head of an agency proposes to issue regulations that deviate from the provisions of this subpart, prior approval of the agency regulations, as required by section 4(b) of Executive Order 10982 of December 25, 1961, must be secured from the Office of Personnel Management.

(d) *Administration.* The head of an agency having employees subject to this subpart is responsible for the proper administration of this subpart. Payment of advance payments and evacuation payments and any required adjustments shall be made in accordance with procedures established by the agency.

[59 FR 66632, Dec. 28, 1994, as amended at 65 FR 41869, July 7, 2000]

§ 550.402 Definitions.

Agency means an Executive agency, as defined in section 105 of title 5, United States Code.

Day means a calendar day, except when otherwise specified by the head of an agency.

Dependent means a family member of the employee residing with the employee and dependent on the employee for support.

Designated representative means a person 16 years of age or over who is named by an employee for the purpose of caring for a dependent.

Domestic partner means a person in a domestic partnership with an employee or annuitant of the same sex.

Domestic partnership means a committed relationship between two adults of the same sex in which the partners—

(1) Are each other's sole domestic partner and intend to remain so indefinitely;

(2) Maintain a common residence, and intend to continue to do so (or would maintain a common residence but for an assignment abroad or other employment-related, financial, or similar obstacle);

(3) Are at least 18 years of age and mentally competent to consent to contract;

(4) Share responsibility for a significant measure of each other's financial obligations;

(5) Are not married or joined in a civil union to anyone else;

(6) Are not the domestic partner of anyone else;

(7) Are not related in a way that, if they were of opposite sex, would prohibit legal marriage in the U.S. jurisdiction in which the domestic partnership was formed;

(8) Are willing to certify, if required by the agency, that they understand that willful falsification of any documentation required to establish that an individual is in a domestic partnership may lead to disciplinary action and the recovery of the cost of benefits received related to such falsification, as well as constitute a criminal violation under 18 U.S.C. 1001, and that the method for securing such certification, if required, will be determined by the agency; and

(9) Are willing promptly to disclose, if required by the agency, any dissolution or material change in the status of the domestic partnership.

Evacuated employee means an employee of an agency who has received an order to evacuate.

Family member means an individual with any of the following relationships to the employee:

(1) Spouse, and parents thereof;

(2) Sons and daughters, and spouses thereof;

(3) Parents, and spouses thereof;

(4) Brothers and sisters, and spouses thereof;

(5) Grandparents and grandchildren, and spouses thereof;

(6) Domestic partner, and children and parents thereof, including a domestic partner of any individual in paragraphs (2)–(5) of this definition; and

(7) Any individual related by blood or affinity whose close association with the employee is the equivalent of a family relationship.

Order to evacuate means an oral or written order to evacuate an employee from an assigned area.

Safe haven means a designated area to which an employee or dependent will be or has been evacuated.

United States means the 50 States, the District of Columbia, the Commonwealths of Puerto Rico and the Northern Mariana Islands, and any territory or possession of the United States.

[59 FR 66632, Dec. 28, 1994, as amended at 65 FR 41869, July 7, 2000; 77 FR 42904, July 20, 2012]

§ 550.403 Advance payments; evacuation payments; special allowances.

(a) An advance payment of pay, allowances, and differentials may be made to an employee who has received an order to evacuate, provided that, in the opinion of the agency head or designated official, payment in advance of the date on which an employee otherwise would be entitled to be paid is required to help the employee defray immediate expenses incidental to the evacuation.

(b) Evacuation payments of pay, allowances, and differentials may be made to an employee during an evacuation and shall be paid on the employee's regular pay days when feasible.

(c) Special allowances, including travel expenses and per diem, may be paid to evacuated employees to offset any direct added expenses that are incurred by the employee as a result of his or her evacuation or the evacuation of his or her dependents.

(d) An advance payment or an evacuation payment may be paid to the employee, a dependent 16 years of age or over, or a designated representative. When payment is made to someone other than the employee, prior written authorization by the employee must have been provided to the authorizing agency official.

(e) Any agency may make payments in an evacuation situation to an employee of another Federal agency (or his or her dependent(s) or personal representative) who has received an order to evacuate. When a payment is made under this subpart by an agency other than the employee's agency, the agency making the payment shall immediately report the amount and date of the payment to the employee's agency in order that prompt reimbursement may be made.

§ 550.404 Computation of advance payments and evacuation payments; time periods.

(a) Payments shall be based on the rate of pay (including allowances, differentials, or other authorized payments) to which the employee was entitled immediately before the issuance of the order of evacuation. All deductions authorized by law, such as retirement or social security deductions, authorized allotments, Federal withholding taxes, and others, when applicable, shall be made before advance payments or evacuation payments are made.

(b)(1) The amount of advance payments shall cover a time period not to exceed 30 days or a lesser number of days, as determined by the authorizing agency official.

(2) Evacuation payments shall cover the period of time during which the order to evacuate remains in effect, unless terminated earlier, but shall not exceed 180 days. When feasible, evacuation payments shall be paid on the employee's regular pay days.

(c) When an advance payment has been made to or for the account of an employee, the amount of the advance payment shall not diminish the amount of the evacuation payments that would otherwise be due the employee.

(d)(1) For full-time and part-time employees, the amount of an advance payment or an evacuation payment shall be computed on the basis of the number of regularly scheduled workdays for the time period covered.

(2) For intermittent employees, the amount of an advance payment or evacuation payment shall be computed on the basis of the number of days on which the employee would be expected to work during the time period covered. The number of days shall be determined, whenever possible, by approximating the number of days per week normally worked by the employee during an average 6-week period, as determined by the agency.

[59 FR 66633, Dec. 28, 1994; 60 FR 3303, Jan. 13, 1995]

§ 550.405 Determination of special allowances.

In determining the direct added expenses that may be payable as special allowances, the following shall be considered:

(a) An agency must determine the travel expenses and per diem for an evacuated employee and the travel expenses for his or her dependents in accordance with the Federal Travel Regulation (FTR) and any applicable implementing agency regulations, whether or not the employee or dependents are actually covered by or subject to the FTR. In addition, an agency may authorize per diem for dependents of an evacuated employee at a rate equal to the rate payable to the employee, as determined in accordance with the FTR (except that the rate for dependents under 12 years of age is one-half this rate), whether or not the employee or dependents are actually covered by or subject to the FTR. Per diem for an employee and his or her dependents is payable from the date of departure from the evacuated area through the date of arrival at the safe haven, including any period of delay en route that is beyond an evacuee's control or that may result from evacuation travel arrangements.

(b) Subsistence expenses for an evacuated employee or his or her dependents shall be determined at applicable per diem rates for the safe haven or for a station other than the safe haven that has been approved by appropriate authority. Such subsistence expenses shall begin to be paid on the date following arrival and may continue until terminated. The subsistence expenses shall be computed on a daily rate basis, as follows:

(1) An agency must compute the applicable maximum per diem rate by using the "lodgings-plus per diem system," as defined in the FTR, for the employee and each dependent who is 12 years of age or over. For each dependent under 12 years of age, the per diem rate is one-half of the applicable maximum per diem rate for employees and dependents who are 12 years of age or over. An agency may pay these maximum rates for a period not to exceed the first 30 days of evacuation.

(2) If, after expiration of the 30-day period, the evacuation has not been terminated, the per diem rate shall be computed at 60 percent of the rates prescribed in paragraph (b)(1) of this section until a determination is made by the agency that subsistence expenses are no longer authorized. This rate may be paid for a period not to exceed 180 days after the effective date of the order to evacuate.

(3) The daily rate of the subsistence expense allowance actually paid an employee shall be either a rate determined in accordance with paragraphs (b) (1) and (2) of this section or a lower rate determined by the agency to be appropriate for necessary living expenses.

(c) Payment of subsistence expenses shall be decreased by the applicable per-person amount for any period during which the employee is authorized regular travel per diem in accordance with the FTR.

[59 FR 66632, Dec. 28, 1994, as amended at 65 FR 41869, July 7, 2000]

§ 550.406 Work assignments during evacuation; return to duty.

(a) Evacuated employees at safe havens may be assigned to perform any work considered necessary or required to be performed during the period of the evacuation without regard to the grades or titles of the employees. Failure or refusal to perform assigned work may be a basis for terminating further evacuation payments.

(b) When part-time employees are given assigned work at the safe haven, records of the number of hours worked shall be maintained so that payment may be made for any hours of work that are greater than the number of hours on which evacuation payments are computed.

(c) Not later than 180 days after the effective date of the order to evacuate, or when the emergency or evacuation situation is terminated, whichever is earlier, an employee must be returned to his or her regular duty station, or appropriate action must be taken to reassign him or her to another duty station.

§ 550.407 Termination of payments during evacuation.

Advance payments or evacuation payments terminate when the agency determines that—

(a) The employee is assigned to another duty station outside the evacuation area;

(b) The employee abandons or is otherwise separated from his or her position;

(c) The employee's employment is terminated by his or her transfer to retirement rolls or other type of annuity based on cessation of civilian employment;

(d) The employee resumes his or her duties at the duty station from which he or she was evacuated;

(e) The agency determines that payments are no longer warranted; or

(f) The date the employee is determined to be covered by the Missing Persons Act (50 App. U.S.C. 1001 *et seq.*), unless payment is earlier terminated under these regulations.

§ 550.408 Review of accounts; service credit.

(a) The payroll office having jurisdiction over the employee's account shall review each employee's account for the purpose of making adjustments at the earliest possible date after the evacuation is terminated (or earlier if the circumstances justify), after the employee returns to his or her assigned duty station, or when the employee is reassigned officially.

(b) The employee's pay shall be adjusted on the basis of the rates of pay, allowances, or differentials, if any, to which he or she would otherwise have been entitled under all applicable statutes other than section 5527 of title 5, United States Code. Any adjustments in the employee's account shall also reflect advance payments made to the employee under § 550.403(a) of this subpart.

(c)(1) After an employee's account is reviewed as required by paragraph (a) of this section, if it is found that the employee is indebted for any part of the advance payment made to him or her or his or her dependent(s) or designated representative, recovery of the indebtedness shall be effected by the payroll office having jurisdiction over the employee's account, unless a waiver of recovery has been approved. Repayment of the indebtedness may be made either in full or in partial payments, as determined by the head of the agency or designated official.

(2) Recovery of indebtedness for advance payment shall not be required when it is determined by the head of the agency or designated official that the recovery would be against equity or good conscience or against the public interest. Findings that formed the basis for waiver of recovery shall be filed in the employee's personnel folder on the permanent side.

(d) For the period or periods covered by any payments made under this subpart, the employee shall be considered as performing active Federal service in his or her position without a break in service.

§ 550.409 Evacuation payments during a pandemic health crisis.

(a) An agency may order one or more employees to evacuate from their worksite and perform work from their home (or an alternative location mutually agreeable to the agency and the employee) during a pandemic health crisis without regard to whether the agency and the employee have a telework agreement in place at the time the order to evacuate is issued. Under these circumstances, an agency may designate the employee's home (or an alternative location mutually agreeable to the agency and the employee) as a safe haven and provide evacuation payments to the employee. An agency must compute the evacuation payments and determine the time period during which such payments will be made in accordance with § 550.404. An evacuated employee at a safe haven may be assigned to perform any work considered necessary or required to be performed during the period of evacuation without regard to his or her grade, level, or title. The employee must have the necessary knowledge and skills to perform the assigned work. Failure or refusal to perform assigned work may be a basis for terminating evacuation payments, as well as disciplinary action.

(b) The head of an agency, in his or her sole and exclusive discretion, may grant special allowance payments, based upon a case-by-case analysis, to offset the direct added expenses incidental to performing work from home (or an alternative location mutually agreeable to the agency and the employee) during a pandemic health crisis.

(c) An agency may terminate evacuation payments under the conditions listed in § 550.407. An agency must make any necessary adjustments in pay consistent with § 550.408 after the evacuation is terminated.

[71 FR 47693, Aug. 17, 2006, as amended at 72 FR 33148, June 15, 2007]

Subpart E—Pay From More Than One Position

AUTHORITY: 5 U.S.C. 5533.

§ 550.501 Scope.

(a) *Applicability.* (1) This subpart and section 5533 of title 5, United States Code, apply in determining an employee's entitlement to receive pay from more than one position.

(2) This subpart and section 5533(a) of title 5, United States Code, apply only to an employee holding more than one position when the aggregate number of hours worked during a week exceeds 40.

(b) *Coverage.* This subpart and section 5533(a) of title 5, United States Code, apply to each department and agency (including each corporation owned or controlled by the Government of the United States and including nonappropriated fund instrumentalities under the jurisdiction of the armed forces) in the legislative (except as provided in section 5533(c) of that title), judicial, and executive branches of the Government of the United States and to the government of the District of Columbia.

§ 550.502 Definitions.

In this subpart:

Employee means a person holding a position.

Pay means pay paid for services in a position but excludes fees paid on other than a time basis.

Position has the meaning given that term by section 5531 of title 5, United States Code.

Week means the period of 7 calendar days from Sunday through Saturday.

[33 FR 12458, Sept. 4, 1968, as amended at 60 FR 67287, Dec. 29, 1995]

§ 550.503 Exceptions in emergencies.

Section 5533(a) of title 5, United States Code, does not apply to pay from a position for services performed under emergency conditions relating to health, safety, protection of life or property, or national emergency.

§ 550.504 Other exceptions.

(a) When a department, agency, or the government of the District of Columbia encounters difficulty in obtaining employees to perform required personal services because of section 5533(a) of title 5, United States Code, it may make an exception from that section upon determining that the required services cannot be readily obtained otherwise. The exception shall specify the position(s) to which it applies.

(b) The Office of Personnel Management will publish exceptions of general application.

(5 U.S.C. 1104; Pub. L. 95–454, sec. 3(5))

[44 FR 54694, Sept. 21, 1979, as amended at 66 FR 66711, Dec. 27, 2001]

§550.505 Report to OPM.

OPM may require a department, agency, or the government of the District of Columbia to submit a periodic report on its use of the exceptions from section 5533(a) of title 5, United States Code.

[33 FR 12458, Sept. 4, 1968. Redesignated at 37 FR 22717, Oct. 21, 1972]

Subpart F—Computation of Pay for Biweekly Pay Periods

AUTHORITY: 5 U.S.C. 5504; Public Law 108–136, 117 Stat. 1637.

SOURCE: 70 FR 24477, May 10, 2005, unless otherwise noted.

§550.601 Purpose.

This subpart provides regulations to implement 5 U.S.C. 5504 to compute pay on a biweekly pay period basis for employees in an agency, as defined in §550.603.

§550.602 Coverage.

(a) This subpart applies to—

(1) An employee in or under an agency, except an employee excluded by paragraph (b) of this section;

(2) The head of an agency;

(3) The head of a military department, as defined in 5 U.S.C. 102;

(4) A Foreign Service officer;

(5) A member of the Senior Foreign Service;

(6) A member of the Senior Executive Service; or

(7) A member of the Federal Bureau of Investigation and Drug Enforcement Administration Senior Executive Service.

(b) This subpart does not apply to—

(1) An employee on the Isthmus of Panama in the service of the Panama Canal Commission; or

(2) An employee or individual excluded from the definition of employee in 5 U.S.C. 5541(2), except employees excluded by 5 U.S.C. 5541(2)(ii), (iii), and (xiv) through (xvii) are covered by this subpart.

§550.603 Definitions.

In this subpart—

Agency means an executive agency, as defined in 5 U.S.C. 105.

Employee has the meaning given that term in 5 U.S.C. 2105.

§550.604 Biweekly pay periods and computation of pay.

Agencies must apply the biweekly pay period and computation of pay provisions of 5 U.S.C. 5504 for employees covered by §550.602(a).

§550.605 Exceptions.

An agency head or designee may deem that an employee excluded from coverage under §550.602(b)(2) is covered by 5 U.S.C. 5504 in situations where he or she determines that continuing to calculate the pay of such employees on a monthly or other basis would diminish the level of services provided to the public by the agency. An agency head or designee also may deem that otherwise excluded employees are covered by 5 U.S.C. 5504 when he or she determines that computing the pay of such employees under that provision of law would provide cost savings in agency operations.

§550.606 Reporting exceptions to OPM.

Each agency must notify OPM in writing of any exceptions made under §550.605.

Subpart G—Severance Pay

AUTHORITY: 5 U.S.C. 5595; E.O. 11257, 3 CFR, 1964–1965 Comp., p. 357.

SOURCE: 55 FR 6593, Feb. 26, 1990, unless otherwise noted.

§550.701 Introduction.

This subpart contains regulations of the Office of Personnel Management to implement the provisions of 5 U.S.C. 5595. These regulations authorize severance pay for employees who are involuntarily separated from Federal service and who meet other conditions of eligibility.

§550.702 Coverage.

Except as provided in 5 U.S.C. 5595(a)(2) (i) through (viii), this subpart applies to each full-time or part-time employee; that is, an employee with a regularly scheduled tour of duty who is serving under a qualifying appointment, as defined in § 550.703.

§ 550.703 Definitions.

In this subpart:

Agency means an agency as defined in 5 U.S.C. 5595(a)(1), except the government of the District of Columbia.

Commuting area means the geographic area surrounding a work site that encompasses the localities where people live and reasonably can be expected to travel back and forth daily to work, as established by the employing agency based on the generally held expectations of the local community. When an employee's residence is within the standard commuting area for a work site, the work site is within the employee's commuting area. When an employee's residence is outside the standard commuting area for a proposed new work site, the employee's commuting area is deemed to include the expanded area surrounding the employee's residence and including all destinations that can be reached via a commuting trip that is not significantly more burdensome than the current commuting trip. This excludes a commuting trip from a residence where the employee planned to stay only temporarily until he or she could find a more permanent residence closer to his or her work site. For this purpose, a commuting trip to a new work site is considered significantly more burdensome if it would compel the employee to change his or her place of residence in order to continue employment, taking into account commuting time and distance, availability of public transportation, cost, and any other relevant factors.

Comparison rate has the meaning given that term in § 536.103 of this chapter, except paragraph (2) of that definition should be used for the purpose of comparing grades or levels of work for all situations not covered by paragraph (1) of that definition.

Employed by the Government of the United States refers to employment by any part of the Government of the United States, including the United States Postal Service and similar independent entities, but excluding enlistment or activation in the armed forces (as defined in 5 U.S.C. 2101).

Employee (for the purpose of establishing initial entitlement to severance pay upon separation) means an employee as defined in 5 U.S.C. 5595(a)(2), excluding an individual employed by the government of the District of Columbia.

NOTE TO DEFINITION OF "EMPLOYEE": The term "individual employed" in 5 U.S.C. 5595(a)(2)(A) refers to an "employee" as defined in 5 U.S.C. 2105.

Immediate annuity means—

(a) A recurring benefit payable under a retirement system applicable to Federal civilian employees or members of the uniformed services that the individual is eligible to receive (disregarding any offset described in § 550.704(b)(5)) at the time of the involuntary separation from civilian service or that begins to accrue within 1 month after such separation, excluding any Social Security retirement benefit; or

(b) A benefit that meets the conditions in paragraph (a) of this definition, except that the benefit begins to accrue more than 1 month after separation solely because the employee elected a later commencing date (such as allowed under § 842.204 of this chapter).

Inefficiency means unacceptable performance or conduct that leads to a separation under part 432 or 752 of this chapter or an equivalent procedure.

Involuntary separation means a separation initiated by an agency against the employee's will and without his or her consent for reasons other than inefficiency, including a separation resulting from the expiration of a time-limited appointment effected within 3 calendar days after separation from a qualifying appointment. In addition, when an employee is separated because he or she declines to accept reassignment outside his or her commuting area, the separation is "involuntary" if the employee's position description or other written agreement does not provide for such a reassignment. However, an employee's separation is not "involuntary" if, after such a written mobility agreement is added, the employee accepts one reassignment outside his or her commuting area, but subsequently declines another such reassignment.

Nonqualifying appointment means an appointment that does not convey eligibility for severance pay under this subpart, including—

(a) An appointment at a noncovered agency;

(b) An appointment in which the employee has an intermittent work schedule;

(c) A Presidential appointment;

(d) An emergency appointment;

(e) An excepted appointment under Schedule C; a noncareer appointment in the Senior Executive Service, as defined in 5 U.S.C. 3132(a); or an equivalent appointment made for similar purposes; and

(f) A time-limited appointment (except for a time-limited appointment that is qualifying because it is made effective within 3 calendar days after separation from a qualifying appointment), including—

(1) A term appointment;

(2) An overseas limited appointment with a time limitation;

(3) A limited term or limited emergency appointment in the Senior Executive Service, as defined in 5 U.S.C. 3132(a), or an equivalent appointment made for similar purposes;

(4) A Veterans Recruitment Appointment under part 307 of this chapter; and

(5) A Presidential Management Fellows Program appointment under § 213.3402(c) of this chapter.

Qualifying appointment means—

(a) A career or career-conditional appointment in the competitive service or the equivalent in the excepted service;

(b) A career appointment in the Senior Executive Service;

(c) An excepted appointment without time limitation, except under Schedule C or an equivalent appointment made for similar purposes;

(d) An overseas limited appointment without time limitation;

(e) A status quo appointment, including one that becomes indefinite when the employee is promoted, demoted, or reassigned;

(f) A time-limited appointment in the Foreign Service, when the employee was assigned under a statutory authority that carried entitlement to reemployment in the same agency, but this right of reemployment has expired; and

(g) A time-limited appointment (including a series of time-limited appointments by the same agency without any intervening break in service) for full-time employment that takes effect within 3 calendar days after the end of one of the qualifying appointments listed in paragraphs (a) through (f) of this definition, provided the time-limited appointment is not nonqualifying on grounds other than the time-limited nature of the appointment.

Rate of basic pay means the rate of pay fixed by law or administrative action for the position held by an employee, excluding additional pay of any kind except the following, as applicable:

(1) Any locality payment under 5 CFR part 531, subpart F; special rate supplement under 5 CFR part 530, subpart C; or similar payment or supplement under other legal authority;

(2) Annual premium pay under 5 U.S.C. 5545(c) or availability pay under 5 U.S.C. 5545a;

(3) Straight-time pay for regular overtime hours for firefighters under 5 U.S.C. 5545b (as provided in § 550.1305(b));

(4) Night differential for prevailing rate employees under 5 U.S.C. 5343(f); and

(5) An overtime supplement for regularly scheduled overtime within a Border Patrol agent's regular tour of duty under 5 U.S.C. 5550 (as required by 5 U.S.C. 5550(d)(1)(A)).

Reasonable offer means the offer of a position that meets all the following conditions:

(a) The offer is in writing;

(b) The employee meets established qualification requirements; and

(c) The offered position is—

(1) In the employee's agency, including an agency to which the employee is transferred with his or her function in a transfer of functions between agencies;

(2) Within the employee's commuting area, unless geographic mobility is a condition of employment;

(3) Of equal or greater tenure and with the same work schedule (part-time or full-time); and

(4) Not lower than two grade or pay levels below the employee's current grade or pay level, without consideration of grade or pay retention under part 536 of this chapter or other authority. In movements between pay schedules or pay systems, the comparison rate of the offered position must not be lower than the comparison rate of the grade or pay level that is two grades below the grade of the current position on the same pay schedule as the current position.

Severance pay fund means the total severance pay to which an employee is entitled during a single entitlement under 5 U.S.C. 5595. It includes a basic severance pay allowance and, where applicable, an age adjustment allowance, as computed under § 550.707.

[55 FR 6593, Feb. 26, 1990, as amended at 56 FR 20342, May 3, 1991; 56 FR 23736, May 23, 1991; 57 FR 59279, Dec. 15, 1992; 58 FR 58262, Nov. 1, 1993; 59 FR 66153, Dec. 23, 1994; 61 FR 3543, Feb. 1, 1996; 63 FR 64593, Nov. 23, 1998; 64 FR 69176, Dec. 10, 1999; 70 FR 31313, May 31, 2005; 70 FR 28783, May 19, 2005; 70 FR 72068, Dec. 1, 2005; 73 FR 66156, Nov. 7, 2008; 77 FR 28223, May 11, 2012; 80 FR 58112, Sept. 25, 2015]

§ 550.704 Eligibility for severance pay.

(a) To be eligible for severance pay, an employee must:

(1) Be serving under a qualifying appointment;

(2) Have completed at least 12 months of continuous service, as described in § 550.705; and

(3) Be removed from Federal service by involuntary separation.

(b) An employee is not eligible for severance pay if he or she:

(1) Is serving under a nonqualifying appointment;

(2) Declines a reasonable offer;

(3) Is serving under a qualifying appointment in an agency scheduled by law or Executive order to be terminated within 1 year after the date of the appointment, unless on the date of separation, the agency's termination has been postponed to a date more than 1 year after the date of the appointment, or the appointment is effected within 3 calendar days after separation from a qualifying appointment;

(4) Is receiving injury compensation under subchapter I of chapter 81 of title 5, United States Code, unless the compensation is being received concurrently with pay or is the result of someone else's death; or

(5) Is eligible upon separation for an immediate annuity from a Federal civilian retirement system or from the uniformed services. Such an employee is ineligible even if all or part of the annuity is offset by payments from a non-Federal retirement system the employee elected instead of Federal civilian retirement benefits or disability benefits received from the Department of Veterans Affairs.

§ 550.705 Criteria for meeting the requirement for 12 months of continuous employment.

(a) The requirement for 12 months of continuous employment is met if, on the date of separation, an employee has held one or more civilian Federal positions over a period of 12 months without a single break in service of more than 3 calendar days. The positions held must have been under:

(1) One or more qualifying appointments;

(2) One or more nonqualifying temporary appointments that precede the current qualifying appointment; or

(3) An appointment to a position in a nonappropriated fund instrumentality of the Department of Defense or the Coast Guard that precedes the current qualifying appointment in the Department of Defense or the Coast Guard, respectively.

(b) When a break in service that is covered by severance pay interrupts otherwise continuous Federal employment, the entire period is considered continuous service.

(c) The period during which an employee receives continuation of pay or compensation for an injury on the job under chapter 81 of title 5, United States Code, is considered continuous Federal service.

[55 FR 6593, Feb. 26, 1990, as amended at 57 FR 12405, Apr. 10, 1992]

§ 550.706 Criteria for meeting the requirement for involuntary separation.

(a) An employee who resigns because he or she expects to be involuntarily separated is considered to have been involuntarily separated if the employee resigns after receiving—

(1) Specific written notice that he or she will be involuntarily separated by a particular action effective on a particular date; or

(2) A general written notice of reduction in force or transfer of functions which—

(i) Is issued by a properly authorized agency official;

(ii) Announces that the agency has decided to abolish, or transfer to another commuting area, all positions in the competitive area (as defined in § 351.402 of this chapter) by a particular date (no more than 1 year after the date of the notice); and

(iii) States that, for all employees in that competitive area, a resignation following receipt of the notice constitutes an involuntary separation for severance pay purposes.

(b) Except for resignations under the conditions described in paragraph (a) of this section, all resignations are voluntary separations and do not carry entitlement to severance pay.

(c) A resignation is not considered an involuntary separation if the specific or general written notice is canceled before the separation (based on that resignation) takes effect.

[55 FR 6593, Feb. 26, 1990, as amended at 64 FR 69177, Dec. 10, 1999]

§ 550.707 Computation of severance pay fund.

(a) *Basic severance pay allowance.* Except as provided in paragraph (b) of this section, the basic severance pay allowance consists of the following:

(1) One week of pay at the rate of basic pay for the position held by the employee at the time of separation for each full year of creditable service through 10 years;

(2) Two weeks of pay at the rate of basic pay for the position held by the employee at the time of separation for each full year of creditable service beyond 10 years; and

(3) Twenty-five percent of the otherwise applicable amount for each full 3 months of creditable service beyond the final full year.

(b) *Basic severance pay allowance for employees with variable work schedules or rates of basic pay.* In the following circumstances, the weekly rate of basic pay used in computing the basic severance pay allowance must be determined based on the weekly average for the last position held by the employee during the 26 biweekly pay periods immediately preceding separation, as follows:

(1) For positions in which the number of hours in the employee's basic work schedule (excluding overtime hours) varies during the year because of part-time work requirements, compute the weekly average of those hours and multiply that average by the hourly rate of basic pay in effect at separation.

(2) For positions in which the rate of annual premium pay for standby duty regularly varies throughout the year, compute the average standby duty premium pay percentage and multiply that percentage by the weekly rate of basic pay (as defined in § 550.103) in effect at separation.

(3) For prevailing rate positions in which the amount of night shift differential pay under 5 U.S.C. 5343(f) varies from week to week under a regularly recurring cycle of work schedules, determine for each week in the averaging period the value of night shift differential pay expressed as a percentage of each week's scheduled rate of pay (as defined in § 532.401 of this chapter), compute the weekly average percentage, and multiply that percentage by the weekly scheduled rate of pay in effect at separation.

(4) For positions with seasonal work requirements, compute the weekly average of hours in a pay status (excluding overtime hours) and multiply that average by the hourly rate of basic pay in effect at separation.

(5) For positions held by firefighters compensated under subpart M of this part, where the firefighter has a recurring cycle of variable workweeks within his or her regular tour of duty (as defined in § 550.1302), compute the weekly average of hours in the regular tour of duty and determine the weekly rate of basic pay based on the average workweek and the rate of basic pay in effect at separation.

(c) *Age adjustment allowance.* The basic severance pay allowance is augmented by an age adjustment allowance consisting of 2.5 percent of the basic severance pay allowance for each full 3 months of age over 40 years.

(d) *Lifetime limitation.* The severance pay fund is limited to that amount which would provide 52 weeks of severance pay (taking into account weeks of severance pay previously received, as provided in § 550.712).

[55 FR 6593, Feb. 26, 1990, as amended at 63 FR 64593, Nov. 23, 1998; 64 FR 69177, Dec. 10, 1999]

§ 550.708 Creditable service.

The following types of service are creditable for computing an employee's severance pay under § 550.707:

(a) Civilian service as an employee (as defined in 5 U.S.C. 2105), excluding time during a period of nonpay status that is not creditable for annual leave accrual purposes under 5 U.S.C. 6303(a);

(b) Service performed with the United States Postal Service or the Postal Rate Commission;

(c) Military service, including active or inactive training with the National Guard, when performed by an employee who returns to civilian service through the exercise of a restoration right provided by law, Executive order, or regulation;

(d) Service performed by an employee of a nonappropriated fund instrumentality of the Department of Defense or the Coast Guard, as defined in 5 U.S.C. 2105(c), who moves to a position within the civil service employment system of the Department of Defense or the Coast Guard, respectively, without a break in service of more than 3 days; and

(e) Service performed with the government of the District of Columbia by an individual first employed by that government before October 1, 1987, excluding service as a teacher or librarian of the public schools of the District of Columbia.

[55 FR 6593, Feb. 26, 1990, as amended at 57 FR 12405, Apr. 10, 1992; 58 FR 33499, June 18, 1993; 64 FR 69177, Dec. 10, 1999]

§ 550.709 Accrual and payment of severance pay.

(a) Severance pay accrues on a day-to-day basis following the recipient's separation from Federal employment. If severance pay begins in the middle of a pay period, 1 day of severance pay accrues for each workday or applicable holiday left in the pay period at the same rate at which basic pay would have accrued if the recipient were still employed. Thereafter, accrual is based on days from Monday through Friday, with each day worth one-fifth of 1 week's severance pay. Accrual ceases when the severance pay entitlement is suspended or terminated, as provided in §§ 550.710 and 550.711. If severance pay is suspended during a nonqualifying time-limited appointment as provided in § 550.710, accrual will resume following separation from that appointment.

(b) Severance payments must be made at the same pay period intervals that salary payments would be made if the recipient were still employed. The amount of the severance payment is computed using the recipient's rate of basic pay in effect immediately before separation, with credit for each day of severance pay accrual during the pay period corresponding to the payment date. A severance payment is subject to appropriate deductions for income and Social Security taxes. Severance payments are the responsibility of the agency employing the recipient at the time of the involuntary separation that triggered the current entitlement to severance pay.

(c) When an individual receives severance pay as the result of an involuntary separation from a qualifying time-limited appointment, the severance payment is based on the rate of basic pay received at the time of that separation. Severance payments are the responsibility of the agency that employed the individual under the qualifying time-limited appointment.

(d) When an individual is in a nonpay status immediately before separation, the amount of the severance payment is determined using the basic pay that he or she would have received if he or she had been in a pay status at the time of separation.

(e) When an individual's severance pay fund is computed under § 550.707(b) using an average rate of basic pay, that average rate is used to determine the amount of the severance payment. Exception: In the case of a seasonal employee, the agency may choose instead to use the employee's rate of basic pay at separation (as computed based on the employee's work schedule during the established seasonal work period) and then authorize severance payments only during that seasonal work period.

(f) In the case of individuals who become employed by a nonappropriated fund instrumentality of the Department of Defense or the Coast Guard under the conditions described in 5 U.S.C. 5595(h)(4), payment of severance pay may be suspended consistent with the rules in 5 U.S.C. 5595(h) and any supplemental regulations issued by the Department of Defense.

(g) Notwithstanding paragraph (b) of this section, an agency may pay severance pay in a single lump sum if expressly authorized by law.

[64 FR 69177, Dec. 10, 1999]

§550.710 Suspension of severance pay.

When an individual entitled to severance pay is employed by the Government of the United States or the government of the District of Columbia under a nonqualifying time-limited appointment, severance pay must be suspended during the life of the appointment. Severance pay resumes, without any recomputation, when the employee separates from the nonqualifying time-limited appointment. The resumed severance payments are the responsibility of the agency that originally triggered the individual's severance pay entitlement by separating the individual while he or she was serving under a qualifying appointment.

[64 FR 69178, Dec. 10, 1999]

§550.711 Termination of severance pay entitlement.

Entitlement to severance pay ends when—

(a) The individual entitled to severance pay is employed by the Government of the United States or the government of the District of Columbia, unless employed under a nonqualifying time-limited appointment as described in §550.710; or

(b) The severance pay fund is exhausted.

[64 FR 69178, Dec. 10, 1999]

§550.712 Reemployment; recredit of service.

(a) When a former employee is reemployed, the employing agency shall record on the appointment document the number of weeks of severance pay received (including partial weeks).

(b) If an employee again becomes entitled to severance pay, the agency in which entitlement arises shall recompute the severance pay allowance on the basis of all creditable service and current age and deduct from the number of weeks it would take to exhaust the allowance the number of weeks for which severance pay previously was received.

§550.713 Records.

Agencies shall maintain records, by fiscal year, of the number of employees who receive severance pay and the total amount of severance pay paid. The Office of Personnel Management may require agencies to report such information to the Office.

[55 FR 6593, Feb. 26, 1990, as amended at 64 FR 69178, Dec. 10, 1999]

§550.714 Panama Canal Commission employees.

(a) Notwithstanding any other provisions of this subpart, an employee separated from employment with the Panama Canal Commission as a result of the implementation of any provision of the Panama Canal Treaty of 1977 and related agreements shall not be entitled to severance pay if he or she—

(1) Receives a written offer of reasonably comparable employment when such offer is made before separation from Commission employment;

(2) Accepts reasonably comparable employment within 30 days after separation from Commission employment; or

(3) Was hired by the Commission on or after December 18, 1997.

(b) The term *reasonably comparable employment* means a position that meets all the following conditions:

(1) The position is with the Panamanian public entity that assumes the functions of managing, operating, and maintaining the Panama Canal as a result of the Panama Canal Treaty of 1977;

(2) The rate of basic pay of the position is not more than 10 percent below the employee's rate of basic pay as a Panama Canal Commission employee;

(3) The position is within the employee's commuting area;

(4) The position carries no fixed time limitation as to length of appointment; and

(5) The work schedule (that is, part-time or full-time) of the position is the same as that of the position held by the employee at the Panama Canal Commission.

(c) A Panama Canal Commission employee who resigns prior to receiving an official written notice that he or she will not be offered reasonably comparable employment shall be considered to be voluntarily separated. Section 550.706(a) shall be applied, as appropriate, to any employee who resigns after receiving such notice.

(d) Except as otherwise provided by paragraphs (a) through (c) of this section, the provisions of this subpart remain applicable to Panama Canal Commission employees.

[62 FR 49127, Sept. 19, 1997]

Subpart H—Back Pay

AUTHORITY: 5 U.S.C. 5596(c); Pub. L. 100–202, 101 Stat. 1329.

§ 550.801 Applicability.

(a) This subpart contains regulations of the Office of Personnel Management to carry out section 5596 of title 5, United States Code, which authorizes the payment of back pay, interest, and reasonable attorney fees for the purpose of making an employee financially whole (to the extent possible) when, on the basis of a timely appeal or an administrative determination (including a decision relating to an unfair labor practice or a grievance), the employee is found by an appropriate authority to have been affected by an unjustified or unwarranted personnel action that resulted in the withdrawal, reduction, or denial of all or part of the pay, allowances, and differentials otherwise due to the employee. This subpart should be read together with this section of law.

(b) This subpart does not apply to any reclassification action.

[46 FR 58275, Dec. 1, 1981, as amended at 53 FR 18072, May 20, 1988]

§ 550.802 Coverage.

(a) Except as provided in paragraph (b) of this section, this subpart applies to employees, as defined in § 550.803 of this subpart.

(b) This subpart does not apply to—

(1) Employees of the government of the District of Columbia; and

(2) Employees of the Tennessee Valley Authority.

[46 FR 58275, Dec. 1, 1981]

§ 550.803 Definitions.

In this subpart:

Agency has the meaning given that term in section 5596(a) of title 5, United States Code.

Appropriate authority means an entity having authority in the case at hand to correct or direct the correction of an unjustified or unwarranted personnel action, including (a) a court, (b) the Comptroller General of the United States, (c) the Office of Personnel Management, (d) the Merit Systems Protection Board, (e) the Equal Employment Opportunity Commission, (f) the Federal Labor Relations Authority and its General Counsel, (g) the Foreign Service Labor Relations Board, (h) the Foreign Service Grievance Board, (i) an arbitrator in a binding arbitration case, and (j) the head of the employing agency or another official of the employing agency to whom such authority is delegated.

Collective bargaining agreement has the meaning given that term in section 7103(a)(8) of title 5, United States Code, and (with respect to members of the Foreign Service) in section 1002 of the Foreign Service Act of 1980 (22 U.S.C. 4102(4)).

Employee means an employee of an agency. When the term *employee* is used to describe an individual who is making a back pay claim, it also may mean a former employee.

Grievance has the meaning given that term in section 7103(a)(9) of title 5, United States Code, and (with respect to members of the Foreign Service) in section 1101 of the Foreign Service Act of 1980 (22 U.S.C. 4131). Such a grievance includes a grievance processed under an agency administrative grievance system, if applicable.

Pay, allowances, and differentials means pay, leave, and other monetary employment benefits to which an employee is entitled by statute or regulation and which are payable by the employing agency to an employee during periods of Federal employment. Agency and employee contributions to a retirement investment fund, such as the Thrift Savings Plan, are not covered. Monetary benefits payable to separated or retired employees based upon a separation from service, such as retirement benefits, severance payments, and lump-sum payments for annual leave, are not covered.

Unfair labor practice means an unfair labor practice described in section 7116 of title 5, United States Code, and (with respect to members of the Foreign Service) in section 1015 of the Foreign Service Act of 1980 (22 U.S.C. 4115).

Unjustified or unwarranted personnel action means an act of commission or an act of omission (*i.e.*, failure to take an action or confer a benefit) that an appropriate authority subsequently determines, on the basis of substantive or procedural defects, to have been unjustified or unwarranted under applicable law, Executive order, rule, regulation, or mandatory personnel policy established by an agency or through a collective bargaining agreement. Such actions include personnel actions and pay actions (alone or in combination).

[46 FR 58275, Dec. 1, 1981, as amended at 60 FR 47040, Sept. 11, 1995; 64 FR 69178, Dec. 10, 1999]

§ 550.804 Determining entitlement to back pay.

(a) When an appropriate authority has determined that an employee was affected by an unjustified or unwarranted personnel action, the employee shall be entitled to back pay under section 5596 of title 5, United States Code, and this subpart only if the appropriate authority finds that the unjustified or unwarranted personnel action resulted in the withdrawal, reduction, or denial of all or part of the pay, allowances, and differentials otherwise due the employee.

(b) The requirement for a "timely appeal" is met when—

(1) An employee or an employee's personal representative initiates an appeal or grievance under an appeal or grievance system, including appeal or grievance procedures included in a collective bargaining agreement; a claim against the Government of the United States; a discrimination complaint; or an unfair labor practice charge; and

(2) An appropriate authority accepts that appeal, grievance, claim, complaint, or charge as timely filed.

(c) The requirement for an "administrative determination" is met when an appropriate authority determines, in writing, that an employee has been affected by an unjustified or unwarranted personnel action that resulted in the withdrawal, reduction, or denial of all or part of the pay, allowances, and differentials otherwise due the employee.

(d) The requirement for "correction of the personnel action" is met when an appropriate authority, consistent with law, Executive order, rule, regulation, or mandatory personnel policy established by an agency or through a collective bargaining agreement, after a review, corrects or directs the correction of an unjustified or unwarranted personnel action that resulted in the withdrawal, reduction, or denial of all or part of the pay, allowances, and differentials otherwise due the employee.

(e)(1) The pay, allowances, and differentials paid as back pay under this subpart (including payments made under any grievance or arbitration decision or any settlement agreement) may not exceed that authorized by any applicable law, rule, regulation, or collective bargaining agreement, including any applicable statute of limitations.

(2) An agency may not authorize pay, allowances, and differentials under this subpart in any case for a period beginning more than 6 years before the date of the filing of a timely appeal, or, absent such filing, the date of the administrative determination that the employee is entitled to back pay, consistent with 31 U.S.C. 3702(b). (See also § 178.104 of this chapter.)

(3) For back pay claims dealing with payments under the Fair Labor Standards Act of 1938, as amended (29 U.S.C. 207, *et seq.*), an agency must apply the 2-year statute of limitations (3 years

for willful violations) in 29 U.S.C. 255a. (See also § 551.702 of this chapter.)

[46 FR 58275, Dec. 1, 1981, as amended at 64 FR 72458, Dec. 28, 1999]

§ 550.805 Back pay computations.

(a) When an appropriate authority corrects or directs the correction of an unjustified or unwarranted personnel action that resulted in the withdrawal, reduction, or denial of all or part of the pay, allowances, and differentials otherwise due an employee—

(1) The employee shall be deemed to have performed service for the agency during the period covered by the corrective action; and

(2) The agency shall compute for the period covered by the corrective action the pay, allowances, and differentials the employee would have received if the unjustified or unwarranted personnel action had not occurred.

(b) No employee shall be granted more pay, allowances, and differentials under section 5596 of title 5, United States Code, and this subpart than he or she would have been entitled to receive if the unjustified or unwarranted personnel action had not occurred.

(c) Except as provided in paragraph (d) of this section, in computing the amount of back pay under section 5596 of title 5, United States Code, and this subpart, an agency may not include—

(1) Any period during which an employee was not ready, willing, and able to perform his or her duties because of an incapacitating illness or injury; or

(2) Any period during which an employee was unavailable for the performance of his or her duties for reasons other than those related to, or caused by, the unjustified or unwarranted personnel action.

(d) In computing the amount of back pay under section 5596 of title 5, United States Code, and this subpart, an agency shall grant, upon request of an employee, any sick or annual leave available to the employee for a period of incapacitation if the employee can establish that the period of incapacitation was the result of illness or injury.

(e) In computing the net amount of back pay payable under section 5596 of title 5, United States Code, and this subpart, an agency must make the following offsets and deductions (in the order shown) from the gross back pay award:

(1) Any outside earnings (gross earnings less any associated business losses and ordinary and necessary business expenses) received by an employee for other employment (including a business enterprise) undertaken to replace the employment from which the employee was separated by the unjustified or unwarranted personnel action during the interim period covered by the corrective action. Do not count earnings from additional or "moonlight" employment the employee may have engaged in while Federally employed (before separation) and while erroneously separated.

(2) Any erroneous payments received from the Government as a result of the unjustified or unwarranted personnel action, which, in the case of erroneous payments received from a Federal employee retirement system, must be returned to the appropriate system. Such payments must be recovered from the back pay award in the following order:

(i) Retirement annuity payments (*i.e.*, gross annuity less deductions for life insurance and health benefits premiums, if those premiums can be recovered by the affected retirement system from the insurance carrier);

(ii) Refunds of retirement contributions (*i.e.*, gross refund before any deductions);

(iii) Severance pay (*i.e.*, gross payments before any deductions); and

(iv) A lump-sum payment for annual leave (*i.e.*, gross payment before any deductions).

(3) Authorized deductions of the type that would have been made from the employee's pay (if paid when properly due) in accordance with the normal order of precedence for deductions from pay established by the agency, subject to any applicable law or regulation, including, but not limited to, the following types of deductions, as applicable:

(i) Mandatory employee retirement contributions toward a defined benefit plan, such as the Civil Service Retirement System or the defined benefit component of the Federal Employees Retirement System;

(ii) Social Security taxes and Medicare taxes;

(iii) Health benefits premiums, if coverage continued during a period of erroneous retirement (with paid premiums recoverable by the retirement system) or is retroactively reinstated at the employee's election under 5 U.S.C. 8908(a);

(iv) Life insurance premiums if—

(A) Coverage continued during a period of erroneous retirement;

(B) Coverage was stopped during an erroneous suspension or separation and the employee suffered death or accidental dismemberment during that period (consistent with 5 U.S.C. 8706(d)); or

(C) Additional premiums are owed because of a retroactive increase in basic pay; and

(v) Federal income tax withholdings.

NOTE TO PARAGRAPH (e)(3): See appendix A to this subpart for additional information on computing certain deductions.

(4) Administrative offsets under 31 U.S.C. 3716 to recover any other outstanding debt(s) owed to the Federal Government by the employee, as appropriate.

(f) For the purpose of computing the amount of back pay under paragraph (e) of this section, interest shall be included in the amount from which deductions for erroneous payments are made, as required by § 550.805(e)(2) of this part.

(g) An agency shall credit annual leave restored to an employee as a result of the correction of an unjustified or unwarranted personnel action in excess of the maximum leave accumulation authorized by law to a separate leave account for use by the employee. The employee shall schedule and use annual leave in such a separate leave account as follows:

(1) A full-time employee shall schedule and use excess annual leave of 416 hours or less by the end of the leave year in progress 2 years after the date on which the annual leave is credited to the separate account. The agency shall extend this period by 1 leave year for each additional 208 hours of excess annual leave or any portion thereof.

(2) A part-time employee shall schedule and use excess annual leave in an amount equal to or less than 20 percent of the employee's scheduled tour of duty over a period of 52 calendar weeks by the end of the leave year in progress 2 years after the date on which the annual leave is credited to the separate account. The agency shall extend this period by 1 leave year for each additional number of hours of excess annual leave, or any portion thereof, equal to 10 percent of the employee's scheduled tour of duty over a period of 52 calendar weeks.

(h) Agencies must correct errors that affect an employee's Thrift Savings Plan account consistent with regulations prescribed by the Federal Retirement Thrift Investment Board. (See parts 1605 and 1606 of this title.)

[46 FR 58275, Dec. 1, 1981, as amended at 53 FR 18072, May 20, 1988, and 53 FR 45886, Nov. 15, 1988; 59 FR 66634, Dec. 28, 1994; 64 FR 69178, Dec. 10, 1999]

§ 550.806 Interest computations.

(a)(1) Interest begins to accrue on the date or dates (usually one or more pay dates) on which the employee would have received the pay, allowances, and differentials if the unjustified or unwarranted personnel action had not occurred.

(2) Interest accrual ends at a time selected by the agency that is no more than 30 days before the date of the back pay interest payment. No interest is payable if a complete back pay payment is made within 30 days after any erroneous withdrawal, reduction, or denial of a payment, and the interest accrual ending date is set to coincide with the interest accrual starting date.

(b) In computing the amount of interest due under section 5596 of title 5, United States Code, the agency shall reduce the amount of pay, allowances, and differentials due for each date described in paragraph (a) of this section by an amount determined as follows:

(1) Divide the employee's earnings from other employment during the period covered by the corrective action, as described in § 550.805(e)(1) of this part, by the total amount of back pay prior to any deductions;

(2) Multiply the ratio obtained in paragraph (b)(1) of this section by the amount of pay, allowances, and differentials due for each date described in paragraph (a) of this section.

(c) The agency shall compute interest on the amount of back pay computed under section 5596 of title 5, United States Code, and this subpart before making deductions for erroneous payments, as required by § 550.805(e)(2) of this part.

(d) The rate or rates used to compute the interest payment shall be the annual percentage rate or rates established by the Secretary of the Treasury as the overpayment rate under section 6621(a)(1) of title 26, United States Code (or its predecessor statute), for the period or periods of time for which interest is payable.

(e) On each day for which interest accrues, the agency shall compound interest by dividing the applicable interest rate (expressed as a decimal) by 365 (366 in a leap year).

(f) The agency shall compute the amount of interest due, and shall issue the interest payment within 30 days of the date on which accrual of interest ends.

(g) To the extent administratively feasible, the agency shall issue payments of back pay and interest simultaneously. If all or part of the payment of back pay is issued on or before the date on which accrual of interest ends and the interest payment is issued after the payment of back pay is issued, the amount of the payment of back pay shall be subtracted from the accrued amount of back pay and interest, effective with the date the payment of back pay was issued. Interest shall continue to accrue on the remaining unpaid amount of back pay (if any) and interest until the date on which accrual of interest ends.

[53 FR 18072, May 20, 1988, and 53 FR 45886, Nov. 15, 1988; 64 FR 69179, Dec. 10, 1999]

§ 550.807 Payment of reasonable attorney fees.

(a) An employee or an employee's personal representative may request payment of reasonable attorney fees related to an unjustified or unwarranted personnel action that resulted in the withdrawal, reduction, or denial of all or part of the pay, allowances, and differentials otherwise due the employee. Such a request may be presented only to the appropriate authority that corrected or directed the correction of the unjustified or unwarranted personnel action. However, if the finding that provides the basis for a request for payment of reasonable attorney fees is made on appeal from a decision by an appropriate authority other than the employing agency, the employee or the employee's personal representative shall present the request to the appropriate authority from which the appeal was taken.

(b) The appropriate authority to which such a request is presented shall provide an opportunity for the employing agency to respond to a request for payment of reasonable attorney fees.

(c) Except as provided in paragraph (e) of this section, when an appropriate authority corrects or directs the correction of an unjustified or unwarranted personnel action that resulted in the withdrawal, reduction, or denial of all or part of the pay, allowances, and differentials otherwise due an employee, the payment of reasonable attorney fees shall be deemed to be warranted only if—

(1) Such payment is in the interest of justice, as determined by the appropriate authority in accordance with standards established by the Merit Systems Protection Board under section 7701(g) of title 5, United States Code; and

(2) There is a specific finding by the appropriate authority setting forth the reasons such payment is in the interest of justice.

(d) When an appropriate authority determines that such payment is warranted, it shall require payment of attorney fees in an amount determined to be reasonable by the appropriate authority. When an appropriate authority determines that such payment is not warranted, no such payment shall be required.

(e) When a determination by an appropriate authority that an employee has been affected by an unjustified or unwarranted personnel action that resulted in the withdrawal, reduction, or denial of all or part of the pay, allowances, and differentials otherwise due the employee is based on a finding of discrimination prohibited under section 2302(b)(1) of title 5, United States Code, the payment of attorney fees shall be in accordance with the standards prescribed under section 706(k) of the Civil Rights Act of 1964, as amended (42 U.S.C. 2000e–5(k)).

(f) The payment of reasonable attorney fees shall be allowed only for the services of members of the Bar and for the services of law clerks, paralegals, or law students, when assisting members of the Bar. However, no payment may be allowed under section 5596 of title 5, United States Code, and this subpart for the services of any employee of the Federal Government, except as provided in section 205 of title 18, United States Code, relating to the activities of officers and employees in matters affecting the Government.

(g) A determination concerning whether the payment of reasonable attorney fees is in the interest of justice and concerning the amount of any such payment shall be subject to review or appeal only if provided for by statute or regulation.

(h) This section does not apply to any administrative proceeding that was pending on January 11, 1979.

[46 FR 58275, Dec. 1, 1981. Redesignated at 53 FR 18072, May 20, 1988, and 53 FR 45886, Nov. 15, 1988]

§ 550.808 Prohibition against setting aside proper promotions.

Nothing in section 5596 of title 5, United States Code, or this subpart shall be construed as authorizing the setting aside of an otherwise proper promotion by a selecting official from a group of properly ranked and certified candidates.

[46 FR 58275, Dec. 1, 1981, as amended at 53 FR 18072, May 20, 1988, and 53 FR 45886, Nov. 15, 1988]

Appendix A to Subpart H of Part 550—Information on Computing Certain Common Deductions From Back Pay Awards

To determine the net back payment owed an employee, an agency must make certain required deductions. (See § 550.805(e)(3).) To compute these deductions, an agency must determine the appropriate base or follow other rules, consistent with applicable law. Some deductions, such as tax deductions, are not subject to OPM regulation. To assist agencies, this appendix summarizes the rules for certain common deductions. For further information on Federal tax deductions from back pay awards, please contact the Internal Revenue Service directly or review relevant IRS publications.

Type of deduction	How to Compute the deduction
(a) Mandatory employee retirement contributions	Compute the deduction based on the basic pay portion of gross back pay before adding interest or applying any offset or deduction.
(b) Life insurance premiums	Compute the deduction based on the basic pay portion of gross back pay before adding interest or applying any offset or deduction.
(c) Social Security (OASDI) and Medicare taxes	Compute the deduction based on adjusted gross back pay (gross back pay less the offset for outside earnings under § 550.805(e)(1), but before adding interest). The deduction may be reduced dollar-for-dollar by the amount of any Social Security or Medicare taxes that were withheld from erroneous payments made in the same calendar year as the back pay award, but only if— (1) Those erroneous payments were actually recovered by the Government by offsetting the back pay award as provided in § 550.805(e)(2); and (2) Those withheld taxes have not already been repaid to the employee. Note: Social Security taxes are subject to the applicable Social Security tax wage base limit. In addition, see IRS guidance regarding possible correction and refunding of Social Security and Medicare taxes withheld from erroneous payments in a prior calendar year.
(d) Federal income tax withholdings	Compute the deduction based on adjusted gross back pay (gross back pay less the offset for outside earnings under § 550.805(e)(1), but before adding interest) less any part of back pay not subject to income tax deductions, such as nonforeign area cost-of-living allowances and contributions to the Thrift Savings Plan that are deducted from the pay of the employee. The deduction may be reduced dollar-for-dollar by the amount of any Federal income taxes withheld from erroneous payments made in the same calendar year as the back pay award, but only if—

Type of deduction	How to Compute the deduction
	(1) Those erroneous payments were actually recovered by the Government by offsetting the back pay award as provided in § 550.805(e)(2); and (2) Those withheld taxes have not already been repaid to the employee. Note: Additional Federal income tax withholdings from the interest portion of the back pay award may be required by the Internal Revenue Service in certain specific circumstances.

[64 FR 69179, Dec. 10, 1999]

Subpart I—Pay for Duty Involving Physical Hardship or Hazard

AUTHORITY: 5 U.S.C. 5545(d), 5548(b).

§ 550.901 Purpose.

This subpart prescribes the regulations required by sections 5545(d) and 5548(b) of title 5, United States Code, for the payment of differentials for duty involving unusual physical hardship or hazard to employees.

[56 FR 20344, May 3, 1991]

§ 550.902 Definitions.

In this subpart: *Agency* has the meaning given that term in 5 U.S.C. 5102(a)(1).

Duty involving physical hardship means duty that may not in itself be hazardous, but causes extreme physical discomfort or distress and is not adequately alleviated by protective or mechanical devices, such as duty involving exposure to extreme temperatures for a long period of time, arduous physical exertion, or exposure to fumes, dust, or noise that causes nausea, skin, eye, ear, or nose irritation.

Employee means an employee covered by the General Schedule (*i.e.*, covered by chapter 51 and subchapter III of chapter 53 of title 5, United States Code).

Hazardous duty means duty performed under circumstances in which an accident could result in serious injury or death, such as duty performed on a high structure where protective facilities are not used or on an open structure where adverse conditions such as darkness, lightning, steady rain, or high wind velocity exist.

Hazard pay differential means additional pay for the performance of hazardous duty or duty involving physical hardship.

Head of an agency means the head of an agency or an official who has been delegated the authority to act for the head of the agency in the matter concerned.

[56 FR 20344, May 3, 1991, as amended at 59 FR 33416, June 29, 1994; 64 FR 69179, Dec. 10, 1999]

§ 550.903 Establishment of hazard pay differentials.

(a) A schedule of hazard pay differentials, the hazardous duties or duties involving physical hardship for which they are payable, and the period during which they are payable is set out as appendix A to this subpart and incorporated in and made a part of this section.

(b) Amendments to appendix A of this subpart may be made by OPM on its own motion or at the request of the head of an agency (or authorized designee). The head of an agency (or authorized designee) may recommend the rate of hazard pay differential to be established and must submit, with its request for an amendment, information about the hazardous duty or duty involving physical hardship showing—

(1) The nature of the duty;

(2) The degree to which the employee is exposed to hazard or physical hardship;

(3) The length of time during which the duty will continue to exist;

(4) The degree to which control may be exercised over the physical hardship or hazard; and

(5) The estimated annual cost to the agency if the request is approved.

[56 FR 20344, May 3, 1991, as amended at 64 FR 69179, Dec. 10, 1999]

§550.904 Authorization of hazard pay differential.

(a) An agency shall pay the hazard pay differential listed in appendix A of this subpart to an employee who is assigned to and performs any duty specified in appendix A of this subpart. However, hazard pay differential may not be paid to an employee when the hazardous duty or physical hardship has been taken into account in the classification of his or her position, without regard to whether the hazardous duty or physical hardship is grade controlling, unless payment of a differential has been approved under paragraph (b) of this section.

(b) The head of an agency may approve payment of a hazard pay differential when—

(1) The actual circumstances of the specific hazard or physical hardship have changed from that taken into account and described in the position description; and

(2) Using the knowledge, skills, and abilities that are described in the position description, the employee cannot control the hazard or physical hardship; thus, the risk is not reduced to a less than significant level.

(c) For the purpose of this section, the phrase "has been taken into account in the classification of his or her position" means that the duty constitutes an element considered in establishing the grade of the position—*i.e.*, the knowledge, skills, and abilities required to perform that duty are considered in the classification of the position.

(d) The head of the agency shall maintain records on the use of the authority described in paragraph (b) of this section, including the specific hazardous duty or duty involving physical hardship; the authorized position description(s); the number of employees paid the differential; documentation of the conditions described in paragraph (b) of this section; and the annual cost to the agency.

(e) So that OPM can evaluate agencies' use of this authority and provide the Congress and others with information regarding its use, each agency shall maintain such other records and submit to OPM such other reports and data as OPM shall require.

[59 FR 33416, June 29, 1994]

§550.905 Payment of hazard pay differential.

(a) When an employee performs duty for which a hazard pay differential is authorized, the agency must pay the hazard pay differential for the hours in a pay status on the day (a calendar day or a 24-hour period, when designated by the agency) on which the duty is performed, except as provided in paragraph (b) of this section. Hours in a pay status for work performed during a continuous period extending over 2 days must be considered to have been performed on the day on which the work began, and the allowable differential must be charged to that day.

(b) Employees may not be paid a hazardous duty differential for hours for which they receive annual premium pay for regularly scheduled standby duty under §550.141, annual premium pay for administratively uncontrollable overtime work under §550.151, or availability pay for criminal investigators under §550.181.

[64 FR 69180, Dec. 10, 1999]

§550.906 Termination of hazard pay differential.

An agency shall discontinue payment of hazard pay differential to an employee when—

(a) One or more of the conditions requisite for such payment ceases to exist;

(b) Safety precautions have reduced the element of hazard to a less than significant level of risk, consistent with generally accepted standards that may be applicable, such as those published by the Occupational Safety and Health Administration, Department of Labor; or

(c) Protective or mechanical devices have adequately alleviated physical discomfort or distress.

[56 FR 20345, May 3, 1991, as amended at 59 FR 33417, June 29, 1994]

§550.907 Relationship to additional pay payable under other statutes.

Hazard pay differential is in addition to any additional pay or allowances payable under other statutes. It shall not be considered part of the employee's rate of basic pay in computing additional pay or allowances payable under other statutes.

[56 FR 20345, May 3, 1991]

Appendix A to Subpart I of Part 550—Schedule of Pay Differentials Authorized for Hazardous Duty Under Subpart I

HAZARD PAY DIFFERENTIAL, OF PART 550 PAY ADMINISTRATION (GENERAL)

Duty	Rate of hazard pay differential (percent)	Effective date
Exposure to Hazardous Weather or Terrain:		
(1) *Work in rough and remote terrain.* When working on cliffs, narrow ledges, or near vertical mountainous slopes where a loss of footing would result in serious injury or death, or when working in areas where there is danger of rock falls or avalanches.	25	First pay period beginning after July 1, 1969.
(2) *Traveling under hazardous conditions.* (a) When travel over secondary or unimproved roads to isolated mountain top installations is required at night, or under adverse weather conditions (such as snow, rain, or fog) which limits visibility to less than 30 meters (100 feet), when there is danger of rock, mud, or snow slides.	25	Do.
(b) When travel in the wintertime, either on foot or by means of vehicle, over secondary or unimproved roads or snow trails, in sparsely settled or isolated areas to isolated installations is required when there is danger of avalanches, or during "whiteout" phenomenon which limits visibility to less than 3 meters (10 feet).	25	Do.
(c) When work or travel in sparsely settled or isolated areas results in exposure to temperatures and/or wind velocity shown to be of considerable danger, or very great danger, on the windchill chart (appendix A–1), and shelter (other than temporary shelter) or assistance is not readily available.	25	Do.
(3) *Snow or ice removal operations.* When participating in snowplowing or snow or ice removal operations, regardless of whether on primary, secondary or other class of roads, when (a) there is danger of avalanche, or (b) there is danger of missing the road and falling down steep mountainous slopes because of lack of snow stakes, "white-out" conditions, or sloping ice-pack covering the snow.	25	Do.
(4) *Water search and rescue operations.* Participating as a member of a water search and rescue team in adverse weather conditions when winds are blowing at 56 km/h (35 m.p.h.) (classified as gale winds) or in water search and rescue operations conducted at night.	25	Do.
(5) *Travel on Lake Pontchartrain.* (a) When embarking, disembarking or traveling in small craft (boat) on Lake Pontchartrain when wind direction is from north, northeast, or northwest, and wind velocity is over 7.7 meters per second (15 knots); or.	25	Do.
(b) When travelling in small crafts, where craft is not radar equipped, on Lake Pontchartrain is necessary due to emergency or unavoidable conditions and the trip is made in a dense fog under fog run procedures.	25	Do.
(6) *Hazardous boarding or leaving of vessels.* When duties (a), (b), or (c) are performed under adverse conditions of foul weather, ice, or night and when the sea state is high (0.9 meter (3 feet) and above):		
(a) Boarding or leaving vessels at sea or standing offshore during lightering or personnel transfer operations.	25	First pay period beginning after May 7, 1970.
(b) Boarding, leaving, or transferring equipment between small boats or rafts and steep, rocky, or coral surrounded shorelines.		
(c) Transferring equipment between a small boat and rudimentary dock by improvised or temporary facility such as an unfastened plank leading from boat to dock.		
(7) *Small craft tests under unsafe sea conditions.* Conducting craft tests to determine the seakeeping characteristics of small craft in a seaway when U.S. storm warnings normally indicate unsafe seas for a particular size craft.	25	First pay period beginning on or after Sept. 28, 1972.
(8) *Working on a drifting sea ice floe.* When the job requires that the work be performed out on sea ice, e.g., installing scientific instruments and making observations for research purposes.	25	First pay period beginning after March 16, 1973.
Exposure to Physiological Hazards:		
(1) *Pressurechamber subject.* (a) Participating as a subject in diving research tests which seek to establish limits for safe pressure profiles by working in a pressure chamber simulating diving or, as an observer to the test or as a technician assembling underwater mock-up components for the test, when the observer or technician is exposed to high pressure gas piping systems, gas cylinders, and pumping devices which are susceptible to explosive ruptures.	25	Do.
(b) *Working in pressurized sonar domes.* Performing checkout of sonar system after sonar dome has been pressurized. This may include such duties as changing transducer elements, setting of transducer turntables, checking of cables, piping, valves, circuits, underwater telephone, and pressurization plugs.	8	First pay period beginning after Feb. 16, 1975.

HAZARD PAY DIFFERENTIAL, OF PART 550 PAY ADMINISTRATION (GENERAL)

Duty	Rate of hazard pay differential (percent)	Effective date
(c) Working in nonpressurized sonar domes that are a part of an underwater system. Performing certification pretrial inspections, involving such duties as calibrating, adjusting, and photographing equipment, in limited space and with limited egress.	4	First pay period beginning after Feb. 16, 1975.
(2) *Simulated altitude chamber subjects. Observers.* Participating in simulated altitude studies ranging from 5500 to 45,700 meters (18,000 to 150,000 feet) either as subject or as observer exposed to the same conditions as the subject.	25	Do.
(3) *Centrifuge subjects.* Participating as subject in centrifuge studies involving elevated G forces above the level of 49 meters per second^2 (5 G's) whether or not at reduced atmospheric pressure.	25	Do.
(4) *Rotational flight simulator subject.* Participating as a subject in a Rotational Flight Simulator in studies involving continuous rotation in one axis through 360° or in a combination of any axes through 360° at rotation rates greater than 15 r.p.m. for periods exceeding three minutes.	25	First pay period beginning after July 1, 1969.
Hot Work—Working in confined spaces wherein the employee is subject to temperatures in excess of 43 °C (110 °F).	4	First pay period beginning after Feb. 16, 1975.
(5) *Environmental thermal-chamber tests:* Subjects and observers exposed to the hazards and physical hardships of an environmental chamber-thermal test which simulates adverse weather or sea conditions such as the exposure to subzero temperatures; high heat and humidiity; and cold water, spray, wind, and wave action.	25	May 4, 1988.
(6) *Working at high altitudes.* Performing work at a land-based worksite more than 3900 meters (12,795 feet) in altitude, provided the employee is required to commute to the worksite on the same day from a substantially lower altitude under circumstances in which the rapid change in altitude may result in acclimation problems..	8	January 11, 1999.
Exposure to Hazardous Agents, work with or in close proximity to:		
(1) *Explosive or incendiary materials.* Explosive or incendiary materials which are unstable and highly sensitive.	25	First pay period beginning after July 1, 1969.
(2) *At-sea shock and vibration tests.* Arming explosive charges and/or working with, or in close proximity to, explosive armed charges in connection with at-sea shock and vibration tests of naval vessels, machinery, equipment and supplies.	25	Do.
(3) *Toxic chemical materials.* Toxic chemical materials when there is a possibility of leakage or spillage.	25	Do.
(4) *Fire retardant materials tests.* Conducting tests on fire retardant materials when the tests are performed in ventilation restricted rooms where the atmosphere is continuously contaminated by obnoxious odors and smoke which causes irritation to the eyes and respiratory tract.	25	Do.
(5) *Virulent biologicals.* Materials of micro-organic nature which when introduced into the body are likely to cause serious disease or fatality and for which protective devices do not afford complete protection.	25	Do.
(6) Asbestos. Significant risk of exposure to airborne concentrations of asbestos fibers in excess of the permissible exposure limits (PELS) in the standard for asbestos provided in title 29, Code of Federal Regulations, §§ 1910.1001 or 1926.58, when the risk of exposure is directly connected with the performance of assigned duties. Regulatory changes in § 1910.1001 or 1926.58 are hereby incorporated in and made a part of this category, effective on the first day of the first pay period beginning on or after the effective date of the changes.	8	June 8, 1993
Participating in Liquid Missile Propulsion Tests and Certain Solid Propulsion Operations:		
(1) *Tanking and detanking.* Tanking or detanking operations of a missile or the test stand "run" bottles with liquid propellants.	25	First pay period beginning after July 1, 1969.
(2) *Hoisting a tanked missile.* Hoisting a tanked missile or a solid propellant propulsion system into and/or over the test stand.	25	Do.
(3) *Pressure tests.* Pressure tests on loaded missiles, missile tanks, or run bottles during prefire preparations.	25	Do.
(4) *Test stand tests.* Test stand operations on loaded missiles under environmental conditions where the high or low temperatures could cause a failure of a critical component.	25	Do.
(5) *Disassembly and breakdown.* Disassembly and breakdown of a contaminated missile system or test stand plumbing after test.	25	Do.
(6) *"Go" condition test stand work.* Working on any test stand above the 15-meter (50-foot) level or any stand work while the system is in a "go" condition.	25	Do.
(7) *Arming and dearming propulsion systems.* Arming, dearming or the installation and/or removal of any squib, explosive device, or a component thereof connected to, or part of, any live or potentially expended liquid or solid propulsion system.	25	Do.
(8) *Demolition and destruct tests.* Demolition, hazards classification, or destruct type tests where the specimen is nonstandard and/or unproven and the test techniques do not conform to standard or proven procedures.	25	Do.

HAZARD PAY DIFFERENTIAL, OF PART 550 PAY ADMINISTRATION (GENERAL)

Duty	Rate of hazard pay differential (percent)	Effective date
Work in Fuel Storage Tanks:		
When inspecting, cleaning or repairing fuel storage tanks where there is no ready access to an exit, under conditions requiring a breathing apparatus because all or part of the oxygen in the atmosphere has been displaced by toxic vapors or gas, and failure of the breathing apparatus would result in serious injury or death within the time required to leave the tank.	25	Do.
Firefighting:		
(1) *Forest and range fires.* Participating as a member of a firefighting crew in fighting forest and range fires on the fireline.	25	Do.
(2) *Equipment, installation, or building fires.* Participating as an emergency member of a firefighting crew in fighting fires of equipment, installations, or buildings.	25	Do.
(3) *In-water under-pier firefighting operations.* Participating in in-water under-pier firefighting operations (involving hazards beyond those normally encountered in firefighting on land, e.g., strong currents, cold water temperature, etc.).	25	Do.
Work in Open Trenches:		
Work in an open trench 4.6 meters (15 feet) or more deep until proper shoring has been installed.	25	Do.
Underground Work:		
Work underground performed in the construction of tunnels and shafts, and the inspection of such underground construction, until the necessary lining of the shaft or tunnel has eliminated the hazard.	25	Do.
Underwater Duty:		
(1) *Submerged submarine or deep research vehicle.* Duty aboard a submarine or deep research vehicle when it submerges.	25	Do.
(2) *Diving.* Diving, including SCUBA (self-contained underwater breathing apparatus) diving, required in scientific and engineering pursuits, or search and rescue operations, when:	25	Do.
(a) at a depth of 6 meters (20 feet) or more below the surface; or,		
(b) visibility is restricted; or,		
(c) in rapidly flowing or cold water; or,		
(d) vertical access to the surface is restricted by ice, rock, or other structure; or,		
(e) testing or working with hardware which presents special hazards (such as work with high voltage equipment or work with underwater mockup components in an underwater space simulation study).		
Sea Duty Aboard Deep Research Vessels:		
Participating in sea duty wherein the team member is engaged in handling equipment on or over the side of the vessel when the sea-state is high (6.2 meter-per-second winds (12-knot winds) and 0.9-meter waves (3-foot waves) and the work is done on deck in relatively unprotected areas.	25	Do.
Collection of Aircraft Approach and Landing Environmental Data:		
When operating or monitoring camera equipment adjacent to flight deck in the area of maximum hazard during landing sequence while conducting photographic surveys aboard aircraft carriers during periods of heavy aircraft operations.	25	First pay period beginning after July 1, 1969.
Experimental Landing/Recovery Equipment Tests:		
Participating in tests of experimental or prototype landing and recovery equipment where personnel are required to serve as test subjects in spacecraft being dropped into the sea or laboratory tanks.	25	Do.
Land Impact or Pad Abort of Space Vehicle:		
Actual participating in dearming and safing explosive ordinance, toxic propellant and high pressure vessels on vehicles that have land impacted or on vehicles on the launch pad that have reached a point in the countdown where no remote means are available for returning the vehicle to a safe condition.	25	Do.
Height Work:		
Working on any structure of at least 15 meters (50 feet) above the base level, ground, deck, floor, roof, etc., under open conditions, if the structure is unstable or if scaffolding guards or other suitable protective facilities are not used, or if performed under adverse conditions such as snow, sleet, ice on walking surfaces, darkness, lightning, steady rain, or high wind velocity.	25	Do.
Flying, participating in:		
(1) *Pilot proficiency training.* Flights for pilot proficiency training in aircraft new to the pilot under simulated emergency conditions which parallel conditions encountered in performing flight tests.	25	Do.

HAZARD PAY DIFFERENTIAL, OF PART 550 PAY ADMINISTRATION (GENERAL)

Duty	Rate of hazard pay differential (percent)	Effective date
(2) *Delivery of new aircraft for flight testing.* Flights to deliver aircraft which has been prepared for one-time flight without being test flown prior to delivery flight.	25	Do.
(3) *Test flights of new modified, or repaired aircraft.* Test flights of a new or repaired aircraft or modified aircraft when the modification may affect the flight characteristics of the aircraft.	25	Do.
(4) *Reduced gravity—parabolic arc flights—subjects/observers.* Reduced gravity flight testing in an aircraft flying a parabolic flight path and providing a testing environment ranging from weightlessness up through + 20 meters per second^2 (+ 2 gravity conditions).	25	Do.
(5) *Launch and recovery.* Test flights involving launch and recovery aboard an aircraft carrier.	25	Do.
(6) *Limited control flights.* Flights undertaken under unusual and adverse conditions (such as extreme weather, maximum load or overload, limited visibility, extreme turbulence, or low level flights involving fixed or tactical patterns) which threaten or severely limit control of the aircraft.	25	Do.
(7) *Flight tests of expandable aircraft tires.* Landing to test aircraft tires designed to deflate upon retraction, undertaken to appraise the normal deflate-reinflate cycle and also to evaluate the capability to make a satisfactory landing with the tires deflated.	25	Do.
(8) *Landing and taking-off in polar areas.* Landing in polar areas on unprepared snow or ice surfaces and/or taking-off under the same conditions.	25	Do.
Experimental Parachute Jumps:		
Participating as a jumper in field exercises to test and evaluate new types of jumping equipment and/or jumping techniques.	25	Do.
Ground Work Beneath Hovering Helicopter:		
Participating in ground operations to attach external load to helicopter hovering just overhead.	25	Do.
Sling-suspended transfers. When performance of duties requires transfer from a helicopter to a ship via a sling on the end of a steel cable or from a ship to another ship via a chair harness hanging from a highline between the ships when both vessels are underway.	25	First pay period beginning after Oct. 11, 1969.
Carrier suitability trials aboard aircraft carriers. Participating in carrier suitability trials aboard aircraft carriers when work is performed on the flight deck during launch, recovery, and refueling operations.	25	Do.
Cargo handling during lightering operations. Off-loading of cargo and supplies from surface ships to Landing Craft—Medium (LCM) boats involving exposure not only to falling cargo but such other hazards as shifting cargo within the LCM, swinging cargo hooks, and possibility of falling between the LCM and cargo vessel.	25	Do.
Work in unsafe structures: Working within or immediately adjacent to a building or structure which has been severely damaged by earthquake, fire, tornado, flood, or similar cause, when the structure has been declared unsafe by competent technical authority, and when such work is considered necessary for the safety of personnel or recovery of valuable materials or equipment, and the work is authorized by competent authority.	25	First pay period beginning on or after Apr. 11, 1976.
Tropical Jungle Duty: Work outdoors in undeveloped jungle regions outside the continental United States. Work must involve both of the following: (1) An unusual degree of physical hardship caused by high heat, humidity, or other inclement conditions; and (2) An unusual danger of serious injury or illness due to: (a) Travel on unimproved roads or rudimentary trails in rugged terrain (e.g., walking on narrow trails in steep mountainous areas, fording deep, fast-moving rivers, and crossing deep crevasses via log or other unsafe means); (b) Immediate presence of dangerous wildlife (e.g., venomous snakes, poisonous insects, and large carnivores); or (c) Known exposure to serious disease for which adequate protection cannot be provided.	25	June 14, 1989.

(5 U.S.C. 5595; E.O. 11257, 3 CFR 1964–1965 Comp., p. 357)

[34 FR 11083, July 1, 1969; 34 FR 12623, Aug. 2, 1969, as amended at 34 FR 15747, Oct. 11, 1969; 35 FR 7172, May 7, 1970; 37 FR 20248, Sept. 28, 1972; 39 FR 7115, Mar. 16, 1973; 40 FR 7437, Feb. 20, 1975; 41 FR 12635, Mar. 26, 1976; 41 FR 14165, Apr. 2, 1976; 53 FR 36557, Sept. 21, 1988; 54 FR 8267, Feb. 28, 1989; 54 FR 25224, June 14, 1989 and 55 FR 1354, Jan. 14, 1990; 56 FR 20345, May 3, 1991; 58 FR 32050, June 8, 1993; 58 FR 32276, June 9, 1993; 64 FR 1502, Jan. 11, 1999]

APPENDIX A–1 TO SUBPART I OF PART 550—WINDCHILL CHART

WINDCHILL CHART IN METRIC UNITS

	Local Temperature (OC)										
Wind Speed (KPH)	0	-5	-10	-15	-20	-25	-30	-35	-40	-45	-50
Calm	0 C	-5	-10	-15	-20	-25	-30	-35	-40	-45	-50
8	-2	-7	-12	-17	-23	-28	-33	-38	-44	-49	-54
16	-8	-14	-20	-26	-32	-38	-44	-51	-57	-63	-69
24	-11	-18	-25	-32	-38	-45	-51	-58	-65	-72	-78
32	-14	-21	-28	-36	-42	-49	-57	-64	-71	-78	-85
40	-16	-23	-31	-39	-46	-53	-61	-68	-76	-83	-90
48	-17	-24	-33	-41	-48	-56	-63	-72	-78	-86	-94
56	-18	-26	-34	-42	-49	-57	-65	-73	-81	-88	-97
64	-19	-27	-35	-43	-51	-59	-66	-74	-82	-91	-98
72	-19	-28	-36	-43	-52	-59	-67	-76	-83	-91	-99
80	-20	-28	-36	-44	-52	-60	-68	-76	-84	-92	-100
	Little danger		Considerable danger			Very great danger					
	For properly clothed persons					Danger of freezing of exposed flesh					

WINDCHILL CHART IN NON-METRIC UNITS

APPENDIX A-1—WINDCHILL CHART

WINDCHILL CHART

Wind Speed (MPH)	Local Temperature (°F)										
	32	23	14	5	-4	-13	-22	-31	-40	-49	-58
Calm	32	23	14	5	-4	-13	-22	-31	-40	-49	-58
5	29	20	10	1	-9	-18	-28	-37	-47	-56	-65
10	18	7	-4	-15	-26	-37	-48	-59	-70	-81	-92
15	13	-1	-13	-25	-37	-49	-61	-73	-85	-97	-109
20	7	-6	-19	-32	-44	-57	-70	-83	-96	-109	-121
25	3	-10	-24	-37	-50	-64	-77	-90	-104	-117	-130
30	1	-13	-27	-41	-54	-68	-82	-97	-109	-123	-137
35	-1	-15	-29	-43	-57	-71	-85	-99	-113	-127	-142
40	-3	-17	-31	-45	-59	-74	-87	-102	-116	-131	-145
45	-3	-18	-32	-46	-61	-75	-89	-104	-118	-132	-147
50	-4	-18	-33	-47	-62	-76	-91	-105	-120	-134	-148
For Properly Clothed Persons	Little Danger		Considerable Danger			Very Great Danger					
	Danger From Freezing of Exposed Flesh										

[33 FR 12458, Sept. 4, 1968, as amended at 58 FR 32277, June 9, 1993]

Subpart J—Adjustment of Work Schedules for Religious Observances

AUTHORITY: 5 U.S.C. 5550a.

§550.1001 Coverage.

This subpart applies to each employee in or under an executive agency as defined by section 105 of title 5, United States Code.

[43 FR 46288, Oct. 6, 1978, and 51 FR 23036, June 25, 1986]

§550.1002 Compensatory time off for religious observances.

(a) These regulations are issued pursuant to title IV of Public Law 95–390, enacted September 29, 1978. Under the law and these regulations, an employee whose personal religious beliefs require the abstention from work during certain periods of time may elect to engage in overtime work for time lost for meeting those religious requirements.

(b) To the extent that such modifications in work schedules do not interfere with the efficient accomplishment of an agency's mission, the agency shall in each instance afford the employee the opportunity to work compensatory overtime and shall in each instance grant compensatory time off to an employee requesting such time off for religious observances when the employee's personal religious beliefs require that the employee abstain from work during certain periods of the workday or workweek.

(c) For the purpose stated in paragraph (b) of this section, the employee may work such compensatory overtime before or after the grant of compensatory time off. A grant of advanced compensatory time off should be repaid by the appropriate amount of compensatory overtime work within a reasonable amount of time. Compensatory overtime shall be credited to an employee on an hour for hour basis or authorized fractions thereof. Appropriate records will be kept of compensatory overtime earned and used.

(d) The premium pay provisions for overtime work in subpart A of part 550 of title 5, Code of Federal Regulations, and section 7 of the Fair Labor Standards Act of 1938, as amended, do not apply to compensatory overtime work performed by an employee for this purpose.

[43 FR 46288, Oct. 6, 1978, as amended at 51 FR 23036, June 25, 1986]

Subpart K—Collection by Offset From Indebted Government Employees

AUTHORITY: 5 U.S.C. 5514; sec. 8(1) of E.O. 11609; redesignated in sec. 2–1 of E.O. 12107.

SOURCE: 49 FR 27472, July 3, 1984, unless otherwise noted.

§550.1101 Purpose.

This subpart provides the standards to be used by Federal agencies to prepare regulations implementing 5 U.S.C. 5514 and by OPM to review and approve such agency regulations, and establishes procedural guidelines to recover debts from the current pay account of an employee when the employee's creditor and paying agencies are not the same.

§550.1102 Scope.

(a) *Coverage*. This subpart applies to agencies and employees defined by §550.1103.

(b) *Applicability*. This subpart and 5 U.S.C. 5514 apply in recovering certain debts by administrative offset, except where the employee consents to the recovery, from the current pay account of the employee. Because salary offset is a type of administrative offset, debt collection procedures for salary offset which are not specified in 5 U.S.C. 5514 and these regulations should be consistent with the provisions of the Federal Claims Collections Standards (FCCS) (dealing with administrative offset generally) and 31 CFR part 285 (dealing with centralized administrative offset under 31 U.S.C. 3716). Section 550.1108 addresses the use of centralized administrative offset procedures to effect salary offset. Generally, the procedures under §550.1109 should apply only when centralized administrative offset cannot be accomplished.

(1) *Excluded debts*. The procedures contained in this subpart do not apply to—

(i) Debts arising under the Internal Revenue Code (26 U.S.C. 1 *et seq.*);

(ii) Debts arising under the tariff laws of the United States;

(iii) Any case where collection of a debt by salary offset is explicitly provided for or prohibited by another statute (e.g., travel advances in 5 U.S.C. 5705 and employee training expenses in 5 U.S.C. 4108); or

(iv) Any other debt excluded by the FCCS or 31 CFR part 285.

(2) *Waiver requests*. This subpart does not preclude an employee from requesting waiver of an erroneous payment under 5 U.S.C. 5584, 10 U.S.C. 2774, or 32 U.S.C. 716, or in any way questioning the amount or validity of a debt, in the manner prescribed by the head of the responsible agency. Similarly, this subpart does not preclude an employee from requesting waiver of the collection of a debt under any other applicable statutory authority.

(3) *Compromise, suspension, or termination of collection actions*. This subpart does not preclude the compromise, suspension, or termination of collection actions, where appropriate, as provided in the FCCS (31 CFR 900.4) or the use of alternative dispute resolution methods if they are not inconsistent with agency-specific laws and regulations.

[49 FR 27472, July 3, 1984, as amended at 63 FR 72099, Dec. 31, 1998; 79 FR 530, Jan. 6, 2014]

§550.1103 Definitions.

For purposes of this subpart—

Agency means an executive department or agency; a military department; the United States Postal Service; the Postal Regulatory Commission; any nonappropriated fund instrumentality described in 5 U.S.C. 2105(c); the United States Senate; the United States House of Representatives; any court, court administrative office, or instrumentality in the judicial or legislative branches of the Government; or a Government corporation. If an agency under this definition is a component of an agency, the broader definition of *agency* may be used in applying the provisions of 5 U.S.C. 5514(b) (concerning the authority to prescribe regulations).

Creditor Agency means the agency to which the debt is owed, including a debt collection center when acting in behalf of a creditor agency in matters pertaining to the collection of a debt (as provided in § 550.1110).

Debt means an amount owed to the United States from sources which include loans insured or guaranteed by the United States and all other amounts due the United States from fees, leases, rents, royalties, services, sales of real or personal property, overpayments, penalties, damages, interest, fines and forfeitures (except those arising under the Uniform Code of Military Justice), and all other similar sources.

Debt collection center means the Department of the Treasury or other Government agency or division designated by the Secretary of the Treasury with authority to collect debts on behalf of creditor agencies in accordance with 31 U.S.C. 3711(g).

Disposable pay means that part of current basic pay, special pay, incentive pay, retired pay, retainer pay, or in the case of an employee not entitled to basic pay, other authorized pay remaining after the deduction of any amount required by law to be withheld (other than deductions to execute garnishment orders in accordance with parts 581 and 582 of this chapter). Among the legally required deductions that must be applied first to determine disposable pay are levies pursuant to the Internal Revenue Code (title 26, United States Code) and deductions described in § 581.105(b) through (f) of this chapter.

Employee means a current employee of an agency, including a current member of the Armed Forces or a Reserve of the Armed Forces (Reserves).

FCCS means the Federal Claims Collections Standards published in 31 CFR parts 900 through 904.

Paying agency means the agency employing the individual and authorizing the payment of his or her current pay.

Salary offset means an administrative offset to collect a debt under 5 U.S.C. 5514 by deduction(s) at one or more officially established pay intervals from the current pay account of an employee without his or her consent.

Waiver means the cancellation, remission, forgiveness, or non-recovery of a debt allegedly owed by an employee to an agency as permitted or required by 5 U.S.C. 5584, 10 U.S.C. 2774, or 32 U.S.C. 716, 5 U.S.C. 8346(b), or any other law.

[49 FR 27472, July 3, 1984, as amended at 51 FR 16670, May 6, 1986; 63 FR 72100, Dec. 31, 1998; 74 FR 23938, May 22, 2009; 79 FR 530, Jan. 6, 2014]

§ 550.1104 Agency regulations.

Under this subpart and 5 U.S.C. 5514, each creditor agency must issue regulations, subject to approval by the Office of Personnel Management (OPM), governing the collection of a debt by salary offset. Each agency is responsible for assuring that the regulations governing collection of internal debts are uniformly and consistently applied to all its employees. Agency regulations issued under authority of 5 U.S.C. 5514 must contain the following minimum provisions:

(a) *Applicability or scope.* Indicate whether regulations cover internal or Government-wide collections under 5 U.S.C. 5514, or both.

(b) *Entitlement to notice, hearing, written responses and decisions.* Identify when the employee is entitled to notice, when hearings will be offered, when the employee is entitled to a response or decision after exercising his or her rights under § 5514 and this subpart, and if the hearing official's decision is not in the employee's favor or the employee chooses not to request a hearing, what other rights and remedies are available under the statutes or regulations governing the program that requires the collection to be made. Except as provided in paragraph (c) of this section, each employee from whom the creditor agency proposes to collect a debt under this subpart is entitled to receive from the creditor agency—

(1) A written notice as described in paragraph (d) of this section;

(2) The opportunity to petition for a hearing and, if a hearing is given, to receive a written decision from the official holding the hearing on the following issues:

(i) The determination of the creditor agency concerning the existence or amount of the debt; and

(ii) The repayment schedule, if it was not established by written agreement between the employee and the creditor agency.

(c) *Exception to entitlement to notice, hearing, written responses, and final decisions.* In regulations covering internal collections, an agency must except from the provisions of paragraph (b) of this section—

(1) Any adjustment to pay arising out of an employee's election of coverage or a change in coverage under a Federal benefits program requiring periodic deductions from pay, if the amount to be recovered was accumulated over 4 pay periods or less;

(2) A routine intra-agency adjustment of pay that is made to correct an overpayment of pay attributable to clerical or administrative errors or delays in processing pay documents, if the overpayment occurred within the 4 pay periods preceding the adjustment and, at the time of such adjustment, or as soon thereafter as practical, the individual is provided written notice of the nature and the amount of the adjustment and point of contact for contesting such adjustment; or

(3) Any adjustment to collect a debt amounting to $50 or less, if, at the time of such adjustment, or as soon thereafter as practical, the individual is provided written notice of the nature and the amount of the adjustment and a point of contact for contesting such adjustment.

(d) *Notification before deductions begin.* Provide for notification before deductions begin. Except as provided in paragraph (c) of this section, deductions under the authority of 5 U.S.C. 5514 must not be made unless the head of the creditor agency (or authorized designee) provides the employee a written notice at least 30 days before any deduction begins. (For debts outstanding more than 10 years on or before June 11, 2009, see also 31 CFR 285.7(d) for additional notification requirements.) The written notice must state at a minimum:

(1) The creditor agency's determination that a debt is owed, including the origin, nature, and amount of that debt;

(2) The creditor agency's intention to collect the debt by means of deduction from the employee's current disposable pay account;

(3) The frequency and amount of the intended deduction (stated as a fixed dollar amount or as a percentage of pay, not to exceed 15 percent of disposable pay except as provided in paragraph (i) of this section) and the intention to continue the deductions until the debt is paid in full or otherwise resolved;

(4) An explanation of the creditor agency's policy concerning interest, penalties, and administrative costs, including a statement that such assessments must be made unless excused in accordance with the FCCS as defined in § 550.1103;

(5) The employee's right to inspect and copy Government records relating to the debt or, if employee or his or her representative cannot personally inspect the records, to request and receive a copy of such records;

(6) If not previously provided, the opportunity (under terms agreeable to the creditor agency) to establish a schedule for the voluntary repayment of the debt or to enter into a written agreement to establish a schedule for repayment of the debt in lieu of offset. The agreement must be in writing, signed by both the employee and the creditor agency; and documented in the creditor agency's files (see the FCCS);

(7) The employee's right to a hearing conducted by an official arranged by the creditor agency (an administrative law judge, or alternatively, a hearing official not under the control of the head of the agency) if a petition is filed as prescribed by the creditor agency;

(8) The method and time period for petitioning for a hearing;

(9) That the timely filing of a petition for hearing will stay the commencement of collection proceedings;

(10) That a final decision on the hearing (if one is requested) will be issued

at the earliest practical date, but not later than 60 days after the filing of the petition requesting the hearing unless the employee requests and the hearing official grants a delay in the proceedings;

(11) That any knowingly false or frivolous statements, representations, or evidence may subject the employee to:

(i) Disciplinary procedures appropriate under chapter 75 of title 5, United States Code, part 752 of title 5, Code of Federal Regulations, or any other applicable statutes or regulations;

(ii) Penalties under the False Claims Act, §§3729–3731 of title 31, United States Code, or any other applicable statutory authority; or

(iii) Criminal penalties under §§286, 287, 1001, and 1002 of title 18, United States Code or any other applicable statutory authority.

(12) Any other rights and remedies available to the employee under statutes or regulations governing the program for which the collection is being made; and

(13) Unless there are applicable contractual or statutory provisions to the contrary, that amounts paid on or deducted for the debt which are later waived or found not owed to the United States will be promptly refunded to the employee.

(e) *Petitions for hearing.* (1) Prescribe the method and time period for petitioning for a hearing. Ordinarily, a hearing may be requested by filing a written petition addressed to the appropriate creditor agency official stating why the employee believes the determination of the creditor agency concerning the existence or amount of the debt is in error.

(2) The employee's petition or statement must be signed by the employee and fully identify and explain with reasonable specificity all the facts, evidence and witnesses, if any, which the employee believes support his or her position.

(f) *Petitions for hearing made after time expires.* Prescribe the action to be taken on a petition for hearing made after the expiration of the period provided in the notice described in paragraph (d) of this section. Ordinarily a creditor agency should accept requests if the employee can show that the delay was because of circumstances beyond his or her control or because of failure to receive notice of the time limit (unless otherwise aware of it).

(g) *Form of hearings, written responses, and final decisions.* (1) Define the form and content of hearings, written responses, and written decisions to be provided when the employee exercises his or her rights under §5514 and this subpart.

(2) The form and content of hearings granted under this subpart will depend on the nature of the transactions giving rise to the debts included within each debt collection program. Agencies should refer to the FCCS for information on hearing form and content.

(3) Written decisions provided after a request for hearing must, at a minimum, state the facts purported to evidence the nature and origin of the alleged debt; the hearing official's analysis, findings and conclusions, in light of the hearing, as to the employee's and/or creditor agency's grounds, the amount and validity of the alleged debt and, where applicable, the repayment schedule.

(h) *Method and source of deductions.* Identify the method and source of deductions. At a minimum, agency regulations must identify the method of collection as salary offset and the source of deductions as current disposable pay, except as provided in paragraphs (l) and (m) of this section.

(i) *Limitation on amount of deductions.* Prescribe the limitations on the amount of the deduction. Ordinarily, the size of installment deductions must bear a reasonable relationship to the size of the debt and the employee's ability to pay (see the FCCS at 31 CFR 901.8). However, the amount deducted for any period under this subpart may not exceed 15 percent of the disposable pay from which the deduction is made, unless the employee has agreed in writing to the deduction of a greater amount or a higher deduction has been ordered by a court under section 124 of Public Law 97–276 (96 Stat.1195).

(j) *Duration of deductions.* Prescribe the duration of deductions under this subpart. Ordinarily, debts must be collected in one lump sum where possible. However, if the employee is financially unable to pay in one lump sum or the amount of the debt exceeds 15 percent of disposable pay (or other applicable limitation as provided in paragraph (i) of this section) for an officially established pay interval, collection must be made in installments. Such installment deductions must be made over a period not greater than the anticipated period of active duty or employment, as the case may be, except as provided in paragraphs (l) and (m) of this section.

(k) *When deductions may begin.* Prescribe when deductions will be scheduled to begin in internal agency collections.

(l) *Liquidation from final check.* Provide for offset under 31 U.S.C. 3716, if the employee retires or resigns or if his or her employment or period of active duty ends before collection of the debt is completed, from subsequent payments of any nature (e.g., final salary payment, lump-sum leave, etc.) due the employee from the paying agency as of the date of separation to the extent necessary to liquidate the debt.

(m) *Recovery from other payments due a separated employee* Provide for offset under 31 U.S.C. 3716 from later payments of any kind due the former employee from the United States, where appropriate, if the debt cannot be liquidated by offset from any final payment due the former employee as of the date of separation. (See the FCCS.)

(n) *Interest, penalties, and administrative costs.* Provide for the assessment of interest, penalties, and administrative costs on debts being collected under this subpart. These charges and the waiving of them must be prescribed in accordance with the FCCS.

(o) *Non-waiver of rights by payments.* Provide that an employee's involuntary payment, of all or any portion of a debt being collected under 5 U.S.C. 5514 must not be construed as a waiver of any rights which the employee may have under 5 U.S.C. 5514 or any other provision of contract or law, unless there are statutory or contractual provisions to the contrary.

(p) *Refunds.* (1) Provide for promptly refunding to the appropriate party, amounts paid or deducted under this subpart when—

(i) A debt is waived or otherwise found not owing to the United States (unless expressly prohibited by statute or regulation); or

(ii) The employee's paying agency is directed by an administrative or judicial order to refund amounts deducted from his or her current pay.

(2) Refunds do not bear interest unless required or permitted by law or contract.

[33 FR 12458, Sept. 4, 1968, as amended at 63 FR 72100, Dec. 31, 1998; 64 FR 69180, Dec. 10, 1999; 79 FR 530, Jan. 6, 2014]

§ 550.1105 Review and approval of agency regulations.

(a) *Initial OPM review of agency regulations.* (1) Creditor agencies must submit regulations to the Office of Personnel Management (OPM) for review in accordance with 5 U.S.C. 5514 and this subpart prior to publication of final regulations or prior to implementation, if intragency collection procedures are not published. Submissions must be for agency-wide and/or Government-wide collections.

(2) Creditor agency regulations must contain all provisions specified in § 550.1104. If agency regulations are incomplete, OPM will return them with information as to what must be done to obtain approval.

(b) *Proposed changes in salary offset regulations.* If a creditor agency proposes significant changes in the regulations covering provisions specified in § 550.1104, the proposed revisions must be submitted to OPM for review and approval prior to implementation.

(c) *Supplemental regulations.* When a creditor agency has issued approved regulations covering the provisions specified in § 550.1104, the agency may issue any supplemental regulations or instructions, consistent with its approved regulations, which are necessary for solely internal operations, without prior OPM approval.

§ 550.1106 Time limit on collection of debts.

Agencies may initiate salary offset to collect a debt without time limitations on any debt outstanding after the Government's right to collect the debt first accrued. (See §550.1108 for requirement when debts are delinquent over 180 days.)

[79 FR 530, Jan. 6, 2014]

§550.1107 Obtaining the services of a hearing official.

(a) When the debtor does not work for the creditor agency and the creditor agency cannot provide a prompt and appropriate hearing before an administrative law judge or before a hearing official furnished pursuant to another lawful arrangement, the creditor agency may contact an agent of the paying agency designated in appendix A of part 581 of this chapter to arrange for a hearing official, and the paying agency must then cooperate as provided by the FCCS as defined in §550.1103 and provide a hearing official.

(b) When the debtor works for the creditor agency, the creditor agency may contact any agent (of another agency) designated in appendix A of part 581 of this chapter to arrange for a hearing official. Agencies must then cooperate as required by the FCCS and provide a hearing official.

(c) The determination of a hearing official designated under this section is considered to be an official certification regarding the existence and amount of the debt for purposes of executing salary offset under 5 U.S.C. 5514. A creditor agency may make a certification to the Secretary of the Treasury under §550.1108 or a paying agency under §550.1109 regarding the existence and amount of the debt based on the certification of a hearing official. If a hearing official determines that a debt may not be collected via salary offset, but the creditor agency finds that the debt is still valid, the creditor agency may still seek collection of the debt through other means, such as offset of other Federal payments, litigation, etc.

[51 FR 16670, May 6, 1986, as amended at 63 FR 72100, Dec. 31, 1998]

§550.1108 Requesting recovery through centralized administrative offset.

Under 31 U.S.C. 3716, creditor agencies must notify the Secretary of the Treasury of all debts that are delinquent as defined in the FCCS (over 180 days) so that recovery may be made by centralized administrative offset. This includes those debts the agency seeks to recover from the pay account of an employee of another agency via salary offset. The Secretary of the Treasury and other Federal disbursing officials will match payments, including Federal salary payments, against these debts. Where a match occurs, and all the requirements for offset have been met, the payments will be offset to collect the debt. Prior to offset of the pay account of an employee, an agency must comply with the requirements of 5 U.S.C. 5514, this subpart, and agency regulations issued thereunder. Specific procedures for notifying the Secretary of the Treasury of a debt for purposes of collection by centralized administrative offset are contained in 31 CFR part 285 and the FCCS. At its discretion, a creditor agency may notify the Secretary of the Treasury of debts that have been delinquent for 180 days or less, including debts the agency seeks to recover from the pay account of an employee via salary offset.

[63 FR 72101, Dec. 31, 1998]

§550.1109 Requesting recovery when the current paying agency is not the creditor agency.

When possible, salary offset through the centralized administrative offset procedures in §550.1108 should be attempted before applying the procedures in this section.

(a) *Responsibilities of creditor agency.* Upon completion of the procedures established by the creditor agency under 5 U.S.C. 5514, the creditor agency must do the following:

(1) The creditor agency must certify, in writing, that the employee owes the debt, the amount and basis of the debt, the date on which payment(s) is due, the date the Government's right to collect the debt first accrued, and that the creditor agency's regulations implementing 5 U.S.C. 5514 have been approved by OPM.

(2) If the collection must be made in installments, the creditor agency also must advise the paying agency of the amount or percentage of disposable pay to be collected in each installment, and

if the creditor agency wishes, the number and the commencing date of the installments (if a date other than the next officially established pay period is required).

(3) Unless the employee has consented to the salary offset in writing or signed a statement acknowledging receipt of the required procedures and the written consent or statement is forwarded to the paying agency, the creditor agency also must advise the paying agency of the action(s) taken under 5 U.S.C. 5514 and give the date(s) the action(s) was taken.

(4) Except as otherwise provided in this paragraph, the creditor agency must submit a debt claim containing the information specified in paragraphs (a) (1) through (3) of this section and an installment agreement (or other instruction on the payment schedule), if applicable, to the employee's paying agency.

(5) If the employee is in the process of separating, the creditor agency must submit its debt claim to the employee's paying agency for collection as provided in § 550.1104(1). The paying agency must certify the total amount of its collection and notify the creditor agency and the employee as provided in paragraph (c)(1) of this section. If the paying agency is aware that the employee is entitled to payments from the Civil Service Retirement and Disability Fund, or other similar payments, it must provide written notification to the agency responsible for making such payments that the debtor owes a debt (including the amount) and that the provisions of this section have been fully complied with. However, the creditor agency must submit a properly certified claim to the agency responsible for making such payments before the collection can be made.

(6) If the employee is already separated and all payments due from his or her former paying agency have been paid, the creditor agency may request, unless otherwise prohibited, that money due and payable to the employee from the Civil Service Retirement and Disability Fund (5 CFR 831.1801 *et seq.*), or other similar funds, be administratively offset to collect the debt. (See 31 U.S.C. 3716 and the FCCS.)

(b) *Responsibilities of paying agency*—(1) *Complete claim.* When the paying agency receives a properly certified debt claim from a creditor agency, deductions should be scheduled to begin prospectively at the next officially established pay interval. The employee must receive written notice that the paying agency has received a certified debt claim from the creditor agency (including the amount) and written notice of the date deductions from salary will commence and of the amount of such deductions.

(2) *Incomplete claim.* When the paying agency receives an incomplete debt claim from a creditor agency, the paying agency must return the debt claim with a notice that procedures under 5 U.S.C. 5514 and this subpart must be provided and a properly certified debt claim received before action will be taken to collect from the employee's current pay account.

(3) *Review.* The paying agency is not required or authorized to review the merits of the determination with respect to the amount or validity of the debt certified by the creditor agency.

(c) *Employees who transfer from one paying agency to another.* (1) If, after the creditor agency has submitted the debt claim to the employee's paying agency, the employee transfers to a position served by a different paying agency before the debt is collected in full, the paying agency from which the employee separates must certify the total amount of the collection made on the debt. One copy of the certification must be furnished to the employee, another to the creditor agency along with notice of the employee's transfer. However, the creditor agency must submit a properly certified claim to the new paying agency before collection can be resumed.

(2) When an employee transfers to another paying agency, the creditor agency need not repeat the due process procedures described by 5 U.S.C. 5514 and this subpart to resume the collection. However, the creditor agency is responsible for reviewing the debt upon receiving the former paying agency's notice of the employee's transfer to make

sure the collection is resumed by the new paying agency.

[51 FR 21325, June 12, 1986. Redesignated and amended at 63 FR 72100, Dec. 31, 1998]

§ 550.1110 Debt collection centers.

A debt collection center may act in behalf of a creditor agency to collect claims via salary offset consistent with this section, subject to any limitations on its authority established by the creditor agency it represents or by the U.S. Department of the Treasury.

(a) A debt collection center may be authorized to enter into a written agreement with the indebted employee regarding the repayment schedule or, in the absence of such agreement, to establish the terms of the repayment schedule.

(b) A debt collection center may make certifications to the Secretary of the Treasury under § 550.1108 or to a paying agency under § 550.1109 based on the certifications it has received from the creditor agency or a hearing official.

(c) A debt collection center responsible for collecting a particular debt may not act in behalf of a creditor agency for the purpose of making determinations regarding the existence or amount of that debt.

(d) A debt collection center responsible for collecting a particular debt may arrange for a hearing on the existence or amount of the debt or the repayment schedule by an administrative law judge or, alternatively, another hearing official not under the supervision or control of the head of the creditor agency or the debt collection center.

[63 FR 72101, Dec. 31, 1998]

Subpart L—Lump-Sum Payment for Accumulated and Accrued Annual Leave

AUTHORITY: 5 U.S.C. 5553, 6306, and 6311.

SOURCE: 64 FR 36771, July 8, 1999, unless otherwise noted.

§ 550.1201 Purpose, applicability, and administration.

(a) *Purpose.* This subpart provides regulations to implement sections 5551, 5552, and 6306 of title 5, United States Code, and must be read together with those sections. Sections 5551 and 5552 provide for the payment of a lump-sum payment for accumulated and accrued annual leave when an employee:

(1) Separates from Federal service; or

(2) Enters on active duty in the armed forces and elects to receive a lump-sum payment for accumulated and accrued annual leave. Section 6306 requires that when an employee is reemployed in the Federal service prior to the expiration of the lump-sum period, he or she must refund an amount equal to the pay covering the period between the date of reemployment and the expiration of the period of annual leave (*i.e.*, the lump-sum leave period).

(b) *Applicability.* This subpart applies to—

(1) Any employee who separates, dies, or transfers under the conditions prescribed in § 550.1203; and

(2) Any employee or individual employed by a territory or possession of the United States who enters on active duty in the armed forces and who elects to receive a lump-sum payment for accumulated and accrued annual leave.

(c) *Administration.* The head of an agency having employees subject to this subpart is responsible for the proper administration of this subpart.

§ 550.1202 Definitions.

In this subpart—*Accumulated and accrued annual leave* means any annual leave accumulated and accrued, as these terms are defined in § 630.201 of this chapter, plus any annual leave credited to an employee under 5 U.S.C. 6304(c) and § 630.301(d) of this chapter and any annual leave restored under 5 U.S.C. 6304(d). Accumulated and accrued annual leave does not include annual leave received by a leave recipient under the voluntary leave transfer or leave bank programs established under subchapters III and IV of chapter 63 of title 5, United States Code, or annual leave advanced to an employee under 5 U.S.C. 6302(d).

Administrative workweek has the meaning given that term in § 610.102 of this chapter.

Agency means—(1) An executive agency and a military department as defined in sections 105 and 102 of title 5, United States Code, respectively; and

(2) A legislative or judicial agency or a unit of the legislative or judicial branch of the Federal Government that has positions in the competitive service.

Employee has the meaning given that term in 5 U.S.C. 2105.

Lump-sum payment means a final payment to an employee for accumulated and accrued annual leave.

Mixed tour of duty means a condition of employment for positions in which a fluctuating workload requires an employee to work full-time or part-time for a limited portion of the year and on an intermittent basis for the remainder of the year.

Rate of basic pay means the rate of pay fixed by law or administrative action for the position held by an employee, including any applicable locality payment under 5 CFR part 531, subpart F; special rate supplement under 5 CFR part 530, subpart C; or similar payment or supplement under other legal authority, before any deductions and exclusive of additional pay of any other kind.

Transfer means the movement of an employee to another position without a break in service of 1 workday or more.

[64 FR 36771, July 8, 1999, as amended at 70 FR 31314, May 31, 2005]

§550.1203 Eligibility.

(a) An agency must make a lump-sum payment for accumulated and accrued annual leave when an employee—

(1) Separates or retires from the Federal service;

(2) Dies; or

(3) Transfers to a position that is not covered by subchapter I of chapter 63 of title 5, United States Code, and his or her accumulated and accrued annual leave cannot be transferred, except as provided in paragraphs (c), (d), and (e) of this section.

(b) The Department of Defense (DOD) must make a lump-sum payment to an employee who has unused annual leave that was restored under 5 U.S.C. 6304(d)(3) when he or she transfers from a DOD installation undergoing closure or realignment to a position in any other department or agency of the Federal Government or moves to a position within DOD not located at an installation undergoing closure or realignment.

(c) An employee who enters on active duty in the armed forces may elect to receive a lump-sum payment for accumulated and accrued annual leave or may request to have the annual leave remain to his or her credit until return from active duty. However, an agency must make a lump-sum payment for any annual leave previously restored under 5 U.S.C. 6304(d) when the employee enters active duty. The agency may not recredit the restored leave when the employee returns to Federal service.

(d) An employee who transfers to a position in a public international organization under 5 U.S.C. 3582 may elect to retain accumulated and accrued annual leave to his or her credit at the time of transfer or receive a lump-sum payment for such annual leave under 5 U.S.C. 3582(a)(4). However, the agency must make a lump-sum payment for any annual leave previously restored under 5 U.S.C. 6304(d) when the employee transfers to the public international organization. The agency may not recredit the leave under these circumstances.

(e) An agency must make a lump-sum payment to an employee who transfers to a position excepted from subchapter I of chapter 63 of title 5, United States Code, by 5 U.S.C. 6301(2)(x)–(xiii) for any annual leave restored under 5 U.S.C. 6304(d) upon transfer to an excepted position. However, the agency may not make a lump-sum payment for any annual leave in the employee's regular leave account upon transfer to the excepted position. The agency must hold such annual leave in abeyance for recredit if the employee is subsequently reemployed without a break in service in a position to which his or her accumulated and accrued annual leave may be transferred. If the employee later becomes eligible for a lump-sum payment under the conditions specified in this section, the current employing agency must make a lump-sum payment for the annual leave held in abeyance. The agency must compute the lump-sum payment under §550.1205(b) based on the pay the employee was receiving immediately before the date of the transfer to the position excepted by 5 U.S.C. 6301(2)(x)–(xiii). An employee who elects to retain his or her leave benefits upon accepting a Presidential appointment, as permitted by 5 U.S.C. 3392(c), is not entitled to receive a lump-sum payment.

(f) In the case of an employee who transfers to a position that is not covered by subchapter I of chapter 63 of title 5, United States Code, and to which only a portion of his or her accumulated and accrued annual leave may be transferred, the agency must make a lump-sum payment for any remaining annual leave that cannot be transferred. The agency must compute the lump-sum payment under §550.1205(b) based on the pay the employee was receiving immediately before the date of the transfer to the position not covered by subchapter I of chapter 63 of title 5, United States Code. This does not apply to an employee transferring to an excepted position covered by paragraph (e) of this section.

(g) An agency must make a lump-sum payment for accumulated and accrued annual leave to an employee in a missing status (as defined in 5 U.S.C. 5561(5)) on or after January 1, 1965, or the employee may elect to have such leave restored in a separate leave account under 5 U.S.C. 6304(d)(2) upon his or her return to Federal service. The agency must compute the lump sum payment under §550.1205(b) based on the rate of pay in effect at the time the annual leave became subject to forfeiture under 5 U.S.C. 6304(a), (b), or (c).

(h) An agency may not make a lump-sum payment for accumulated or accrued annual leave to—(1) An employee who transfers between positions covered by subchapter I of chapter 63 of title 5, United States Code;

(2) An employee who transfers to a position not covered by subchapter I of chapter 63 of title 5, United States Code, but to which all of his or her accumulated and accrued annual leave may be transferred;

(3) An employee who transfers to the government of the District of Columbia or the U.S. Postal Service;

(4) A nonappropriated fund employee of the Department of Defense or the Coast Guard who moves without a break in service of more than 3 days to an appropriated fund position within the Department of Defense or the Coast Guard, respectively, under 5 U.S.C. 6308(b); or

(5) An employee who is concurrently employed in more than one part-time position and who separates from one of the part-time positions. Instead, the former employing agency must transfer the employee's accumulated and accrued annual leave to the current agency (if the part-time positions are in different agencies) or credit the employee's annual leave account in the current position (if the part-time positions are in the same agency).

(6) An employee who elects to retain his or her leave benefits upon accepting a Presidential appointment, as permitted by 5 U.S.C. 3392(c).

(i) An agency must establish a policy for determining when an employee in a continuing employment program with a mixed tour of duty will receive a lump-sum payment for annual leave. The agency may choose to pay an employee a lump-sum payment when he or she is assigned intermittent duty or hold the employee's annual leave in abeyance during intermittent duty and recredit it when the employee returns without a break in service to full-time or part-time employment. If the agency decides to hold the employee's annual leave in abeyance, it must also hold in abeyance the credit for any fractional pay period earned and recredit the annual leave on a pro rata basis, as provided in §630.204 of this chapter, when the employee returns to full-time or part-time employment. In developing its policy, each agency must consider the likelihood that the employee will return to work, as well as the agency's mission requirements and staffing needs. The agency's policy must ensure that employees are treated in a fair and equitable manner.

§550.1204 Projecting the lump-sum leave period.

(a) A lump-sum payment must equal the pay an employee would have received had he or she remained in the Federal service until the expiration of the accumulated and accrued annual leave to the employee's credit. The agency must project the lump-sum period leave beginning on the first workday (counting any holiday) occurring after the date the employee becomes eligible for a lump-sum payment under § 550.1203 and counting all subsequent workdays and holidays until the expiration of the period of annual leave. The period of leave used for calculating the lump-sum payment must not be extended by any holidays under 5 U.S.C. 6103 (or applicable Executive or administrative order) which occur immediately after the date the employee becomes eligible for a lump-sum payment under § 550.1203; annual leave donated to an employee under the leave transfer or leave bank programs under subparts I and J of part 630 of this chapter; unused compensatory time off earned under 5 U.S.C. 5543 and § 550.114(d) or § 551.531(d) or under 5 U.S.C. 5542(g) and § 550.1625; or credit hours accumulated under an alternative work schedule established under 5 U.S.C. 6126.

(b) For employees whose annual leave was held in abeyance immediately prior to becoming eligible for a lump-sum payment, the agency must project the lump-sum payment beginning on the first workday occurring immediately after the date the employee becomes eligible for a lump-sum payment under § 550.1203, consistent with paragraph (a) of this section.

[64 FR 36771, July 8, 1999, as amended at 80 FR 58112, Sept. 25, 2015]

§ 550.1205 Calculating a lump-sum payment.

(a) An agency must compute a lump-sum payment based on the types of pay listed in paragraph (b) of this section, as in effect at the time the affected employee becomes eligible for a lump-sum payment under § 550.1203 and any adjustments in pay included in paragraphs (b)(2), (3), and (4) of this section. The agency must calculate a lump-sum payment by multiplying the number of hours of accumulated and accrued annual leave by the applicable hourly rate of pay, including other applicable types of pay listed in paragraph (b) of this section, or by using a mathematically equivalent method, such as multiplying weeks of annual leave by the applicable weekly rate of pay. If the agency calculates a lump-sum payment using weekly rates, the number of weeks of annual leave must be rounded to the fourth decimal place (e.g., 0.4444). The agency must convert an annual rate of pay to an hourly rate of pay by dividing the annual rate of pay by 2,087 (or 2,756 for firefighters, if applicable) and rounding it to the nearest cent, counting one-half cent and over as the next higher cent.

(b) The agency must compute a lump-sum payment using the following types of pay and pay adjustments, as applicable:

(1) An employee's rate of basic pay (as defined in § 550.1202);

(2) Any statutory adjustments in pay or any general system-wide increases in pay, such as adjustments under sections 5303, 5304, 5305, 5318, 5362, 5363, 5372, 5372a, 5376, 5382, or 5392 of title 5, United States Code, that become effective during the lump-sum leave period. The agency must adjust the lump-sum payment to reflect the increased rate on and after the effective date of the pay adjustment.

(3) In the case of a prevailing rate employee, the agency must include in the lump-sum payment the scheduled rate of pay under 5 U.S.C. 5343, 5348, or 5349 and any applicable adjustments in rates that are determined under 5 U.S.C. 5343, 5348, or 5349 that become effective during the lump-sum leave period. The agency must adjust the lump-sum payment to reflect the increased prevailing rate on and after the effective date of the rate adjustment.

(4) A within-grade increase under 5 U.S.C. 5335 or 5343(e)(2) if the employee has met the requirements of § 531.404 or § 532.417 of this chapter prior to the date the employee becomes eligible for a lump-sum payment under § 550.1203.

(5) The following types of premium pay (to the extent such premium pay was actually payable to the employee):

(i) Night differential under 5 U.S.C. 5343(f) at the applicable percentage rate received by a prevailing rate employee for all regularly scheduled periods of night shift duty covered by the unused annual leave as if the employee had continued to work beyond the effective date of separation, death, or transfer. In the case of an employee who is assigned to a regular rotating schedule involving work on both day and night shifts, the night differential is payable for that portion of the lump-sum period that would have occurred when the employee was scheduled to work night shifts.

(ii) Premium pay under 5 U.S.C. 5545(c) or 5545a if the employee was receiving premium pay for the pay period immediately prior to the date the employee became eligible for a lump-sum payment under § 550.1203. The agency must base the lump-sum payment on the percentage rate received by the employee for the pay period immediately prior to the date the employee became eligible for a lump-sum payment under § 550.1203. In cases where the amount of premium pay actually payable in the final pay period was limited by a statutory cap, the agency must base the lump-sum payment on a reduced percentage rate that reflects the actual amount of premium pay the employee received in that pay period.

(iii) Overtime pay under 5 U.S.C. 5545b and § 550.1304 of this chapter for overtime hours in an employee's uncommon tour of duty (as defined in § 630.201 of this chapter), established in accordance with § 630.210 of this chapter. The uncommon tour of duty must be applicable to the employee for the pay period immediately prior to the date the employee became eligible for a lump-sum payment under § 550.1203. The agency must calculate overtime pay using the same methodology it used to calculate the employee's entitlement to overtime pay as provided in § 550.1304 of this chapter in the pay period immediately prior to the date the employee became eligible for a lump-sum payment under § 550.1203. An agency may not change an employee's work schedule for the sole purpose of avoiding or providing payment of premium pay under § 550.1205(b)(5)(i)–(iv) in a lump-sum payment.

(iv) An overtime supplement for regularly scheduled overtime within a Border Patrol agent's regular tour of duty under 5 U.S.C. 5550, as in effect immediately prior to the date the agent became eligible for a lump-sum payment under § 550.1203. The agency must base the lump-sum payment on the agent's assigned overtime supplement percentage. The assigned percentage will be considered fixed for the duration of the lump-sum annual leave projection period described in § 550.1204, even if an annual period for elections under 5 U.S.C. 5550 begins during that projection period. In cases where the amount of the overtime supplement actually payable in a pay period was limited by a statutory cap, the agency must base the lump-sum payment on a reduced percentage rate that reflects the actual amount of the overtime supplement the agent could receive in a pay period.

(6) Overtime pay under the Fair Labor Standards Act of 1938, as amended (FLSA), for overtime work that is regularly scheduled during an employee's established uncommon tour of duty, as defined in § 630.201(b)(1) of this chapter and established under § 630.210(a) of this chapter, for which the employee receives standby duty pay under 5 U.S.C. 5545(c)(1). The agency must include FLSA overtime pay in a lump-sum payment if an uncommon tour of duty was applicable to the employee for the pay period immediately prior to the date the employee became eligible for a lump-sum payment under § 550.1203. The agency must calculate FLSA overtime pay using the same methodology it used to calculate the employee's entitlement to FLSA overtime pay for the pay period immediately prior to the date the employee became eligible for a lump-sum payment under § 550.1203. An agency may not change an employee's work schedule for the sole purpose of avoiding or providing payment of FLSA overtime pay in a lump-sum payment.

(7) A supervisory differential under 5 U.S.C. 5755 based on the percentage rate (or dollar amount) received by the employee for the pay period immediately prior to the date the employee became eligible for a lump-sum payment under § 550.1203.

(8) A cost-of-living allowance and/or post differential in a nonforeign area under 5 U.S.C. 5941 if the employee's official duty station is in the nonforeign area when he or she becomes eligible for a lump-sum payment under § 550.1203.

(9) A post allowance in a foreign area under 5 U.S.C. 5924(1) and the *Standardized Regulations* (Government Civilians,

Foreign Areas) if the employee's official duty station is in the foreign area when he or she becomes eligible for a lump-sum payment under § 550.1203.

(c) The head of an agency must prescribe regulations or standards for the inclusion of any other kinds of pay authorized in statutes other than title 5, United States Code, in a lump-sum payment. Such regulations or standards must be consistent with 5 U.S.C. 5551, 5552, 6306, and other applicable provisions of law.

(d) A lump-sum payment may not include any other pay not specifically listed in paragraph (b) of this section, except as provided in paragraph (c) of this section.

(e) An employee may not earn leave for the period covered by a lump-sum payment.

(f) A lump-sum payment is not subject to deductions for retirement under the Civil Service Retirement System or the Federal Employees' Retirement System established by chapters 83 and 84 of title 5, United States Code, respectively; health benefits under the Federal Employees Health Benefits program established by chapter 89 of title 5, United States Code; life insurance under the Federal Employees' Group Life Insurance program established by chapter 87 of title 5, United States Code; and savings under the Thrift Savings Plan established by subchapter III of chapter 84 of title 5, United States Code.

(g) For a reemployed annuitant who becomes eligible for a lump-sum payment under § 550.1203, the agency must compute the lump-sum payment using the annuitant's pay before any reductions required under § 837.303 of this chapter.

(h) A lump-sum payment is subject to garnishment under parts 581 and 582 of this chapter and to administrative offset (for recovery of debts to the Federal Government) under 31 U.S.C. chapter 37.

[64 FR 36771, July 8, 1999, as amended at 70 FR 31314, May 31, 2005; 72 FR 12036, Mar. 15, 2007; 80 FR 58112, Sept. 25, 2015]

§ 550.1206 Refunding a lump-sum payment.

(a) When an employee who received a lump-sum payment for accumulated and accrued annual leave under 5 U.S.C. 5551 is reemployed in the Federal service prior to the end of the period covered by the lump-sum payment, the employee must refund to the employing agency an amount equal to the pay included in the lump-sum payment under § 550.1205(b) that covers the period between the date of reemployment and the expiration of the lump-sum leave period, except as provided in paragraphs (b) and (c) of this section. The agency must compute the refund based on the pay used to compute the lump-sum payment under § 550.1205(b). However, annual leave restored under 5 U.S.C. 6304(d) that was included in a lump-sum payment is not subject to refund if an agency reemploys the employee prior to the expiration of the lump-sum leave period. The agency must subtract such restored annual leave from the lump-sum leave period before calculating the refund. An agency may permit an employee to refund the lump-sum payment for annual leave in installments, but may not waive collection. If an agency permits the lump-sum refund to be paid in installments, the employee must refund the lump-sum payment in full within 1 year after the date of reemployment.

(b) An employee who is reemployed in a position listed in 5 U.S.C. 6301(2)(ii), (iii), (vi), or (vii) is not required to refund a lump-sum payment under paragraph (a) of this section.

(c) An employee who is reemployed in a position that has no leave system to which annual leave can be recredited is not required to refund a lump-sum payment under paragraph (a) of this section, except that individuals reemployed as Presidential appointees must refund a lump-sum payment and the annual leave will be held in abeyance, as provided in § 550.1207(e).

(d) An individual first hired by the District of Columbia government on or after October 1, 1987, who received a lump-sum payment upon separation from the District of Columbia government and who is employed by the Federal Government prior to the expiration of the lump-sum leave period must refund the lump-sum payment, and the agency must recredit the annual leave under § 550.1207.

(e) An employee who retired from the Federal Government and received a lump-sum payment under § 550.1203 of this chapter, and who is reemployed under a temporary appointment of less than 90 days prior to the expiration of the lump-sum leave period, is required to refund the lump-sum payment, and the agency must recredit the annual leave under § 550.1207. The employee may use the recredited annual leave during the temporary appointment.

§ 550.1207 Recrediting annual leave.

(a) When an employee pays a full refund to an agency under § 550.1206(a), the agency must recredit to the employee an amount of annual leave equal to the days or hours of work (including holidays) remaining between the date of reemployment and the expiration of the lump-sum period. The recredited annual leave is available for use by the employee on and after the date the annual leave is recredited. The agency must recredit annual leave as follows:

(1) When an employee is reemployed in the Federal service in a position covered by subchapter I of chapter 63 of title 5, United States Code, the employing agency must recredit an amount of annual leave equal to the days or hours of work (including holidays) remaining between the date of reemployment and the expiration of the lump-sum period.

(2) When an employee is reemployed in the Federal service in a position that is not covered by subchapter I of chapter 63 of title 5, United States Code, but is covered by a different leave system, the employing agency must recredit to the employee an amount of annual leave representing the days or hours of work (including holidays) remaining between the date of reemployment and the expiration of the lump-sum period, as determined under § 630.501(b) of this chapter. If the unexpired period of leave covers a larger amount of leave than can be recredited under the different leave system, the employee must refund only the amount that represents the leave that can be recredited.

(3) When an employee is reemployed prior to the expiration of the lump-sum leave period, the agency may not recredit to the employee the annual leave restored under 5 U.S.C. 6304(d) that was included in a lump-sum payment. The agency must subtract such restored annual leave from the lump-sum leave period before it determines the amount of annual leave to recredit under paragraph (a)(1) of this section.

(b) Any annual leave the agency recredits to the employee under paragraph (a) of this section is subject at the beginning of the next leave year to the maximum annual leave limitation established by 5 U.S.C. 6304(a), (b), (c), or (f), as appropriate, for the position in which the employee is reemployed, except as provided in paragraphs (c) and (d) of this section.

(c) If the amount of annual leave to be recredited under paragraph (a) of this section is more than the maximum annual leave limitation for the position in which reemployed, and the employee's former maximum annual leave limitation was established under 5 U.S.C. 6304(a), (b), (c), or (f), as appropriate, the agency must establish the employee's new maximum annual leave limitation on the date of reemployment as a personal leave ceiling equal to the amount of annual leave to be recredited under paragraph (a) of this section. The new maximum annual leave limitation is subject to reduction in the same manner as provided in 5 U.S.C. 6304(c) until the employee's accumulated annual leave is equal to or less than the maximum annual leave limitation for the position in which reemployed.

(d) If the amount of annual leave to be recredited under paragraph (a) of this section is more than the maximum annual leave limitation for the position in which the employee is reemployed, and the employee's former maximum annual leave limitation was established under an authority other than 5 U.S.C. 6304(a), (b), (c), or (f), as appropriate, the agency must establish the employee's new maximum annual leave limitation on the date of reemployment as a personal leave ceiling equal to the employee's former maximum annual leave limitation. The new maximum annual leave limitation is subject to reduction in the same manner as provided in 5 U.S.C. 6304(c) until the employee's accumulated annual leave is equal to or less than the maximum annual leave limitation for the position in which reemployed.

(e) When an employee is reemployed in a position listed in 5 U.S.C. 6301(2)(x)–(xiii), the agency must recredit and hold in abeyance the amount of annual leave that would have been recredited under paragraph (a) of this section. The agency must include unused annual leave in a lump-sum payment when the employee becomes eligible for a lump-sum payment under § 550.1203. If the employee transfers from a position listed in 5 U.S.C. 6301(2)(x)–(xiii) to a position covered by subchapter I of chapter 63 of title 5, United States Code, or to a position under a different formal leave system to which his or her annual leave can be recredited, the employing agency must recredit the annual leave to the employee's credit as provided in paragraph (a) of this section.

(f) An agency must document the calculation of an employee's lump-sum payment as provided in § 550.1205(b) so as to permit the subsequent calculation of any refund required under § 550.1206(a) and any recredit of annual leave required under this section.

Subpart M—Firefighter Pay

AUTHORITY: 5 U.S.C. 5545b, 5548, and 5553.

SOURCE: 63 FR 64593, Nov. 23, 1998, unless otherwise noted.

§ 550.1301 Purpose, applicability, and administration.

(a) *Purpose.* This subpart provides regulations governing the pay of covered Federal firefighters. It implements sections 5542(f) and 5545b of title 5, United States Code, as added by section 628 of section 101(h) of Pub. L. 105–277, and must be read together with those sections of law.

(b) *Applicability.* This subpart applies to any firefighter as defined in § 550.1302.

(c) *Administration.* The head of an agency having employees subject to this subpart is responsible for the proper administration of this subpart.

§ 550.1302 Definitions.

In this subpart:

Annual rate of basic pay (except as otherwise provided in §§ 550.1305 and 550.1308) means the annual rate fixed under the rate schedule applicable to the position held by the firefighter, including a locality rate schedule established under 5 U.S.C. 5304 or a special rate schedule established under 5 U.S.C. 5305, before any deductions and exclusive of additional pay of any other kind.

Basic 40-hour workweek means—

(1) A standard 40-hour workweek consisting of five 8-hour workdays that is part of the firefighter's regular tour of duty; or

(2) A designated block of hours within a firefighter's regular tour of duty that, on a fixed and recurring basis, consists of 40 hours of actual work during each administrative week (or 80 hours of actual work in each biweekly pay period), excluding sleep and standby duty hours, provided the regular tour of duty does not consist primarily of 24-hour shifts.

Firefighter means an employee—

(1) Whose regular tour of duty, as in effect throughout the year, averages at least 106 hours per biweekly pay period; and

(2) Who is in a position—

(i) Covered by the General Schedule and classified in the Fire Protection and Prevention Series, GS–0081, consistent with standards published by the Office of Personnel Management;

(ii) In a demonstration project established under chapter 47 of title 5, United States Code, or an alternative personnel system under a similar authority, which otherwise would be covered by the General Schedule, and which is classified in the Fire Protection and Prevention Series, GS–0081, consistent with standards published by the Office of Personnel Management, but only if application of 5 U.S.C. 5545b has not been waived; or

(iii) Covered by the General Schedule and classified in the GS–0099, General Student Trainee Series (as required by § 362.203(e) of this chapter), if the position otherwise would be classified in the GS–0081 series.

Firefighter hourly rate of basic pay means an hourly rate computed by dividing the applicable annual rate of basic pay by 2756 hours, as described in § 550.1303.

Irregular hours means hours of work that are outside a firefighter's regular tour of duty.

Overtime hours means hours of work in excess of 106 hours in a biweekly pay period, or, if the agency establishes a weekly basis for overtime pay computations, hours of work in excess of 53 hours in an administrative workweek.

Overtime pay means pay for overtime hours.

Regular tour of duty means a firefighter's official work schedule, as established by the employing agency on a regular and recurring basis (or on a temporary basis in cases where a temporary change in schedules results in a reduction in regular work hours or a change in the pay computation method used under § 550.1303). The tour of duty may consist of a fixed number of hours each week or a fixed recurring cycle of work schedules in which the number of hours per week varies in a repeating pattern. The regular tour of duty includes only those overtime hours that are part of the fixed recurring work schedule. However, irregular hours are deemed to be included in a firefighter's regular tour of duty if those hours are substituted for hours in the regular tour of duty for which leave without pay is taken, as provided in § 550.1303(d).

[63 FR 64593, Nov. 23, 1998, as amended at 67 FR 15466, Apr. 2, 2002; 77 FR 28223, May 11, 2012]

§ 550.1303 Hourly rates of basic pay.

(a) For firefighters with a regular tour of duty that does not include a basic 40-hour workweek (e.g., firefighters whose schedules generally consist of 24-hour shifts with a significant amount of designated standby and sleep time), the hourly rate of basic pay is computed by dividing the applicable annual rate of basic pay by 2756 hours. The resulting firefighter hourly rate of basic pay is multiplied by all nonovertime hours to determine the pay for those hours.

(b) For firefighters with a regular tour of duty that includes a basic 40-hour workweek, the hourly rate of basic pay is computed by dividing the applicable annual rate of basic pay by—

(1) 2087 hours, for hours within the basic 40-hour workweek (or 80-hour biweekly pay period); and

(2) 2756 hours, for any additional nonovertime hours.

(c) A firefighter's daily, weekly, or biweekly rate of basic pay must be computed using the applicable rates, as derived under paragraphs (a) and (b) of this section.

(d) If a firefighter takes leave without pay during his or her regular tour of duty, the agency shall substitute any irregular hours worked in the same biweekly pay period for those hours of leave without pay. (If a firefighter's overtime pay is computed on a weekly basis, the irregular hours must be worked in the same administrative workweek.) For firefighters whose regular tour of duty includes a basic 40-hour workweek, the agency shall first substitute irregular hours for hours of leave without pay in the basic 40-hour workweek, which are paid at an hourly rate based on the 2087 divisor. All other substituted hours are paid at an hourly rate based on the 2756 divisor, using the applicable overtime rate for overtime hours. The annual rate used to compute any such hourly rate is the annual rate in effect at the time the hour was actually worked.

[63 FR 64593, Nov. 23, 1998, as amended at 67 FR 15467, Apr. 2, 2002]

§ 550.1304 Overtime hourly rates of pay.

(a) For a firefighter who is covered by (*i.e.*, nonexempt from) the overtime provisions of the Fair Labor Standards Act (FLSA), the overtime hourly rate of pay equals 1½ times the firefighter hourly rate of basic pay for that firefighter, as established under § 550.1303(a) and (b)(2).

(b) For a firefighter who is exempt from the FLSA, the overtime hourly rate is computed as provided in § 550.113(e).

(c) For any firefighter, overtime pay for any pay period is derived by multiplying the applicable overtime hourly rate by all overtime hours within that period.

§ 550.1305 Treatment as basic pay.

(a) The sum of pay for nonovertime hours that are part of a firefighter's regular tour of duty (as computed under § 550.1303) and the straight-time portion of overtime pay for hours in a firefighter's regular tour of duty is treated as basic pay only for the following purposes:

(1) Retirement deductions and benefits under chapters 83 and 84 of title 5, United States Code;

(2) Life insurance premiums and benefits under chapter 87 of title 5, United States Code;

(3) Severance pay under section 5595 of title 5, United States Code;

(4) Cost-of-living allowances and post differentials under section 5941 of title 5, United States Code; and

(5) Advances in pay under section 5524a of title 5, United States Code.

(b) The straight-time portion of overtime pay for hours in a firefighter's regular tour of duty is derived by multiplying the applicable firefighter hourly rate of basic pay computed under § 550.1303(a) and (b)(2) by the number of overtime hours in the firefighter's regular tour of duty.

(c) Pay for any nonovertime hours outside a firefighter's regular tour of duty is computed using the firefighter hourly rate of basic pay as provided in § 550.1303(a) and (b)(2), but that pay is not considered basic pay for any purpose, except in applying §§ 550.105 and 550.106.

(d) For firefighters compensated under § 550.1303(b), pay for nonovertime hours within the regular tour of duty, but outside the basic 40-hour workweek, is basic pay only for the purposes listed in paragraph (a) of this section and for the purpose of applying § 410.402(b)(6) of this chapter and §§ 550.105 and 550.106.

(e) Locality pay under 5 U.S.C. 5304 is basic pay for firefighters only to the extent provided in this subpart, § 531.610 of this chapter, or other specific provision of law.

[63 FR 64593, Nov. 23, 1998, as amended at 67 FR 15467, Apr. 2, 2002; 70 FR 31314, May 31, 2005]

§ 550.1306 Relationship to other entitlements.

(a) A firefighter who is compensated under this subpart is entitled to overtime pay as provided under this subpart, but may not receive additional premium pay under any other provision of subchapter V of chapter 55 of title 5, United States Code, including night pay, Sunday pay, holiday pay, and hazardous duty pay. A firefighter is not entitled to receive paid holiday time off when not working on a holiday, but may be allowed to use annual or sick leave, as appropriate, or may be granted excused absence at the agency's discretion.

(b) A firefighter who is subject to section 7(k) of the Fair Labor Standards Act (FLSA) and who is subject to this subpart is deemed to be appropriately compensated under section 7(k) of the FLSA if the requirements of § 550.1304(a) are satisfied.

(c) In computing a lump-sum payment for accumulated annual leave under 5 U.S.C. 5551 and 5552 for firefighters with an uncommon tour of duty established under § 630.210 of this chapter for leave purposes, an agency must use the rates of pay for the position held by the firefighter that apply to hours in that uncommon tour of duty, including regular overtime pay for such hours.

(d) A firefighter compensated under this subpart shall receive basic pay and overtime pay for his or her regular tour of duty in any week in which attendance at agency-sanctioned training reduces the hours in the firefighter's regular tour of duty, as provided in § 410.402(b)(6) of this chapter.

(e) In applying the compensatory time off provision in § 550.114(c), compare the firefighter's annual rate of basic pay to the annual rate of basic pay for GS–10, step 10.

[63 FR 64593, Nov. 23, 1998, as amended at 67 FR 15467, Apr. 2, 2002]

§ 550.1307 Authority to regularize paychecks.

Upon a written request from the head of an agency (or designee), the Office of Personnel Management may approve an agency's plan to reduce or eliminate variation in the amount of firefighters' biweekly paychecks caused by work scheduling cycles that result in varying hours in the firefighters' tours of duty from pay period to pay period. Such a plan must provide that the total pay any firefighter would otherwise receive for regular tours of duty over the firefighter's entire work scheduling cycle must, to the extent practicable, remain the same.

Subpart N—Compensatory Time Off for Travel

AUTHORITY: 5 U.S.C. 5548(a).

SOURCE: 70 FR 3856, Jan. 27, 2005, unless otherwise noted.

§550.1401 Purpose.

This subpart contains OPM regulations implementing 5 U.S.C. 5550b, which establishes a separate type of compensatory time off. Subject to the conditions specified in this subpart, an employee is entitled to earn, on an hour-for-hour basis, compensatory time off for time in a travel status away from the employee's official duty station when the travel time is not otherwise compensable.

[70 FR 3856, Jan. 27, 2005, as amended at 72 FR 19098, Apr. 17, 2007]

§550.1402 Coverage.

This subpart applies to an employee as defined in 5 U.S.C. 5541(2) who is employed by an agency. In accordance with section 1111 of Public Law 110–181, an employee whose pay is fixed and adjusted from time to time in accordance with prevailing rates under subchapter IV of chapter 53 of title 5, United States Code, or by a wage board or similar administrative authority serving the same purpose, is covered by this subpart effective April 27, 2008.

[73 FR 30455, May 28, 2008]

§550.1403 Definitions.

In this subpart:

Accrued compensatory time off means the compensatory time off earned by an employee that has not been used or forfeited.

Agency means an Executive agency as defined in 5 U.S.C. 105.

Authorized agency official means the head of the agency or an official who is authorized to act for the head of the agency in the matter concerned.

Compensable refers to periods of time that are creditable as hours of work for the purpose of determining a specific pay entitlement, even when that work time may not actually generate additional compensation because of applicable pay limitations.

Compensatory time off means compensatory time off for travel that is credited under the authority of this subpart.

Official duty station means the geographic area surrounding an employee's regular work site that is the same as the area designated by the employing agency for the purpose of determining whether travel time is compensable for the purpose of determining overtime pay, consistent with the regulations in 5 CFR 550.112(j) and 551.422(d).

Regular working hours means the days and hours of an employee's regularly scheduled administrative workweek established under 5 CFR part 610.

Scheduled tour of duty for leave purposes means an employee's regular hours for which he or she may be charged leave under 5 CFR part 630 when absent. For full-time employees, it is the 40-hour basic workweek as defined in 5 CFR 610.102. For employees with an uncommon tour of duty as defined in 5 CFR 630.201, it is the uncommon tour of duty.

Travel means officially authorized travel—*i.e.*, travel for work purposes that is approved by an authorized agency official or otherwise authorized under established agency policies. Time spent traveling in connection with union activities is excluded.

Travel status means travel time as described in §550.1404 that is creditable in accruing compensatory time off for travel under this subpart, excluding travel time that is otherwise compensable under other legal authority.

[70 FR 3856, Jan. 27, 2005, as amended at 72 FR 19098, Apr. 17, 2007]

§550.1404 Creditable travel time.

(a) *General.* Subject to the conditions specified in this subpart, an agency must credit an employee with compensatory time off for time in a travel status if—

(1) The employee is required to travel away from the official duty station; and

(2) The travel time is not otherwise compensable hours of work under other legal authority.

(b)(1) *Travel status.* Time in a travel status includes the time an employee actually spends traveling between the official duty station and a temporary duty station, or between two temporary duty stations, and the usual waiting time that precedes or interrupts such travel, subject to the exclusion specified in paragraph (b)(2) of this section and the requirements in paragraph (c), (d) and (e) of this section. Time spent at a temporary duty station between arrival and departure is not time in a travel status. Time in a travel status ends when the employee arrives at the temporary duty worksite or his or her lodging in the temporary duty station, wherever the employee arrives first. Time in a travel status resumes when an employee departs from the temporary duty worksite or his or her lodging in the temporary duty station, from whichever the employee departs last. Travel time in connection with an employee's permanent change of station is not time in a travel status. Determinations regarding what is creditable as "usual waiting time" are within the sole and exclusive discretion of the employing agency.

(2) If an employee experiences an extended (*i.e.*, not usual) waiting time between actual periods of travel during which the employee is free to rest, sleep, or otherwise use the time for his or her own purposes, the extended waiting time is not creditable as time in a travel status.

(c) *Travel between home and a temporary duty station.* (1) If an employee is required to travel directly between his or her home and a temporary duty station outside the limits of the employee's official duty station, the travel time is creditable as time in a travel status if otherwise qualifying under this subpart. However, the agency must deduct from such travel hours the time the employee would have spent in normal home-to-work or work-to-home commuting.

(2) In the case of an employee who is offered one mode of transportation and who is permitted to use an alternative mode of transportation, or who travels at a time or by a route other than that selected by the agency, the agency must determine the estimated amount of time in a travel status the employee would have had if the employee had used the mode of transportation offered by the agency or traveled at the time or by the route selected by the agency. In determining time in a travel status under this subpart, the agency must credit the employee with the lesser of the estimated time in a travel status or the actual time in a travel status.

(3) In the case of an employee who is on a multiple-day travel assignment and who chooses, for personal reasons, not to use temporary lodgings at the temporary duty station, but to return home at night or on a weekend, only travel from home to the temporary duty station on the 1st day and travel from the temporary duty station to home on the last day that is otherwise qualifying as time in a travel status under this subpart is mandatorily creditable (subject to the deduction of normal commuting time). Travel to and from home on other days is not creditable travel time unless the agency, at its discretion, determines that credit should be given based on the net savings to the Government from reduced lodging costs, considering the value of lost labor time attributable to compensatory time off. The dollar value of an hour of compensatory time off for this purpose is equal to the employee's hourly rate of basic pay as defined in § 550.103.

(d) *Time spent traveling to or from a transportation terminal as part of travel away from the official duty station.* If an employee is required to travel between home and a transportation terminal (e.g., airport or train station) within the limits of his or her official duty station as part of travel away from that duty station, the travel time outside regular working hours to or from the terminal is considered to be equivalent to commuting time and is not creditable time in a travel status. If the transportation terminal is outside the limits of the employee's official duty station, the travel time to or from the terminal outside regular working hours is creditable as time in a travel status, but is subject to an offset for the time the employee would have spent in normal home-to-work or work-to-home commuting. If the employee travels between a worksite and a transportation terminal, the travel time outside regular working hours is creditable as time in a travel status, and no commuting time offset applies.

(e) *Travel involving two or more time zones.* When an employee's travel involves two or more time zones, the time zone from the point of first departure must be used to determine how many hours the employee actually spent in a travel status for the purpose of accruing compensatory time off.

[70 FR 3856, Jan. 27, 2005, as amended at 72 FR 19098, Apr. 17, 2007]

§ 550.1405 Crediting compensatory time off.

(a) Upon a request filed in accordance with the procedures established under paragraph (b) of this section, an employee is entitled to credit for compensatory time off for travel under the conditions specified in this subpart. The employing agency must credit an employee with compensatory time off for creditable time in a travel status as provided in § 550.1404. The agency may authorize credit in increments of one-tenth of an hour (6 minutes) or one-quarter of an hour (15 minutes). Agencies must track and manage compensatory time off granted under this subpart separately from other forms of compensatory time off.

(b) An employee must comply with his or her agency's procedures for requesting credit of compensatory time off under this section. Employees must file such requests within the time period required by the agency. An employee's request for credit of compensatory time off for travel may be denied if the request is not filed within the time period required by the agency.

[70 FR 3856, Jan. 27, 2005, as amended at 72 FR 19098, Apr. 17, 2007]

§ 550.1406 Use of accrued compensatory time off.

(a) An employee must request permission from his or her supervisor to schedule the use of his or her accrued compensatory time off in accordance with agency-established policies and procedures.

(b) Compensatory time off may be used when the employee is granted time off from his or her scheduled tour of duty established for leave purposes. An employee must use earned compensatory time off under this subpart in increments of one-tenth of an hour (6 minutes) or one-quarter of an hour (15 minutes). Agencies must charge compensatory time off in the chronological order in which it was earned, with compensatory time off earned first being charged first.

[70 FR 3856, Jan. 27, 2005, as amended at 72 FR 19098, Apr. 17, 2007]

§ 550.1407 Forfeiture of unused compensatory time off.

(a) *After 26 pay periods.* (1) Except as provided in paragraphs (a)(2) and (e) of this section, an employee must use accrued compensatory time off by the end of the 26th pay period after the pay period during which it was earned. If an employee fails to use the compensatory time off within 26 pay periods after it was earned, he or she must forfeit such compensatory time off.

(2) If an employee with unused compensatory time off separates from Federal service or is placed in a leave without pay status in the following circumstances and later returns to service with the same (or successor) agency, the employee must use all of the compensatory time off by the end of the 26th pay period following the pay period in which the employee returns to duty, or such compensatory time off will be forfeited:

(i) The employee separates or is placed in a leave without pay status to perform service in the uniformed services (as defined in 38 U.S.C. 4303 and 5 CFR 353.102) and later returns to service through the exercise of a reemployment right provided by law, Executive order, or regulation; or

(ii) The employee separates or is placed in a leave without pay status because of an on-the-job injury with entitlement to injury compensation under 5 U.S.C. chapter 81 and later recovers sufficiently to return to work.

(b) *Upon transfer to another agency.* When an employee voluntarily transfers to another agency (including a promotion or change to lower grade action), he or she must forfeit his or her unused compensatory time off.

(c) *Upon separation.* (1) When an employee separates from Federal service, any unused compensatory time off is forfeited, except as provided in paragraph (c)(2) of this section.

(2) Unused compensatory time off will not be forfeited but will be held in abeyance in the case of an employee who separates from Federal service and later returns to service with the same (or successor) agency under the circumstances described in paragraph (a)(2) of this section.

(d) *Upon movement to a noncovered position.* When an employee moves to a Federal position not covered by this subpart, he or she forfeits any unused compensatory time off. This requirement does not prevent an agency from using another legal authority to give the employee credit for compensatory time off equal to the forfeited amount.

(e) *Exception due to an exigency.* If an employee fails to use his or her compensatory time earned under § 550.1404(a) by the end of the 26th pay period after the pay period during which it was earned due to an exigency of the service beyond the employee's control, an authorized agency official, at his or her sole and exclusive discretion, may extend the time limit for using such compensatory time off for travel for up to an additional 26 pay periods.

[70 FR 3856, Jan. 27, 2005, as amended at 72 FR 19098, Apr. 17, 2007]

§ 550.1408 Prohibition against payment for unused compensatory time off.

As provided by 5 U.S.C. 5550b(b), an individual may not receive payment under any circumstances for any unused compensatory time off he or she earned under this subpart. This prohibition against payment applies to surviving beneficiaries in the event of the individual's death.

§ 550.1409 Inapplicability of premium pay and aggregate pay caps.

Accrued compensatory time off under this subpart is not considered in applying the premium pay limitations established under 5 U.S.C. 5547 and 5 CFR 550.105 through 550.107 or the aggregate limitation on pay established under 5 U.S.C. 5307 and 5 CFR part 530, subpart B.

Subpart O—Flag Recognition Benefit for Fallen Federal Civilian Employees

AUTHORITY: 5 U.S.C. 5570 note; also issued under Sec. 2 of Pub. L. 112–73, 125 Stat.784–785.

SOURCE: 79 FR 53602, Sept. 10, 2014, unless otherwise noted.

§ 550.1501 General.

(a) *Statutory authority.* This subpart implements the Civilian Service Recognition Act of 2011 (Public Law 112–73; December 20, 2011), reprinted as a note to 5 U.S.C.A. 5570, which authorizes agencies to give a flag of the United States to a beneficiary of a Federal civilian employee who dies of injuries incurred in connection with his or her employment with the Federal Government, under specific circumstances.

(b) *Eligibility.* Agencies may furnish a flag to the beneficiary (as defined in § 550.1503) of an eligible employee (as specified in § 550.1504) who died on or after December 20, 2011.

§ 550.1502 Coverage.

This subpart applies to—

(a) Executive agencies as defined in section 105 of title 5, United States Code, the United States Postal Service, and the Postal Regulatory Commission; and

(b) Employees as defined in section 2105 of title 5, United States Code; an officer or employee of the United States Postal Service; and an officer or employee of the Postal Regulatory Commission.

§ 550.1503 Definitions.

In this subpart—

Agency means an Executive agency as defined in 5 U.S.C. 105, the United

States Postal Service, or the Postal Regulatory Commission.

Authorized agency official means the head of an agency or an official who is authorized to act for the head of the agency in the matter concerned.

Beneficiary means the eligible person who may request the flag following the order of precedence specified in §550.1505.

Employee means an employee as defined in section 2105 of title 5, United States Code; an officer or employee of the United States Postal Service; and an officer or employee of the Postal Regulatory Commission.

Flag means a standard United States flag that is at least 3 feet by 5 feet.

§550.1504 Eligibility.

(a) An authorized agency official may, upon the request of a beneficiary, furnish one United States flag for an individual who—

(1) Was an employee of the agency at the time of death; and

(2) Died of injuries incurred in connection with such individual's employment with the Federal Government suffered as a result of—

(i) A criminal act;

(ii) An act of terrorism;

(iii) A natural disaster; or

(iv) Other circumstances, as determined by the President.

(b) An authorized agency official may not furnish a flag when the death is the result of—

(1) Unlawful or negligent action of the employee;

(2) Willful misconduct of the employee; or

(3) Activities unrelated to the employee's status as a Federal employee.

(c) The decision whether to furnish a flag to the beneficiary of an eligible employee is at the discretion of the agency. When an authorized agency official determines the agency will furnish a flag for a deceased eligible employee, the official must follow the order of precedence specified in §550.1505.

§550.1505 Order of precedence.

If the authorized agency official determines the agency will furnish a flag, it must be issued to one beneficiary pursuant to the following order of precedence—

(a) The widow or widower;

(b) If none, to a child (including step, foster, or adopted child), according to age (*i.e.*, oldest to youngest);

(c) If none, to a parent (including step, foster, or adoptive parent);

(d) If none, to a sibling (including step, half, or adopted sibling), according to age; (*i.e.*, oldest to youngest);

If none, to any individual related by blood or close family affiliation.

§550.1506 Beneficiary receipt of a flag.

One eligible beneficiary, following the order of precedence in §550.1505, may be provided a flag by the agency once the agency has—

(a) Documented the date and nature of death of the employee and certified that it conforms to the eligibility criteria in §550.1504;

(b) Received a request from a beneficiary; and

(c) Established the beneficiary's relationship to the deceased employee and determined whether the beneficiary may receive the flag, consistent with the order of precedence under 550.1505.

§550.1507 Agency responsibilities.

To efficiently and effectively implement the provisions of the law and these regulations, an agency that wishes to furnish a flag pursuant to this part must —

(a) Establish procedures for procuring and furnishing a flag, including reaching out to survivors of known eligible employees to provide information and offer assistance on obtaining a flag;

(b) Notify its employees of the flag benefit annually; and

(c) Disclose information necessary to prove that a deceased individual is an eligible employee as described in §550.1504 to the extent that such information is not classified and to the extent that such disclosure does not endanger the national security of the United States.

Subpart P—Overtime Pay for Border Patrol Agents

AUTHORITY: 5 U.S.C. 5548 and 5550(b)(1)(B) and (d)(1)(B); section 2(h), Pub. L. 113–277, 128 Stat. 3005.

SOURCE: 80 FR 58112, Sept. 25, 2015, unless otherwise noted.

GENERAL PROVISIONS

§ 550.1601 Purpose and authority.

This subpart contains OPM regulations to implement section 2 of the Border Patrol Agent Pay Reform Act of 2014 (Pub. L. 113–277), which added section 5550 in title 5, United States Code, and made related statutory amendments. The Act created a special overtime pay program for Border Patrol agents in the U.S. Customs and Border Protection component within the Department of Homeland Security. OPM has authority under 5 U.S.C. 5548(a) to regulate subchapter V (Premium Pay) of chapter 55 of title 5, United States Code, including section 5550 and the Act's amendments to sections 5542 and 5547. OPM was also granted broad authority to promulgate necessary regulations to carry out the Act and the amendments made by the Act under section 2(h) of the Act.

§ 550.1602 Coverage.

This subpart applies to an employee of the U.S. Customs and Border Protection component of the Department of Homeland Security (or any successor organization) who holds a position assigned to the Border Patrol Enforcement classification series 1896 or any successor series, consistent with classification standards established by OPM. Such an employee is referred to as a "Border Patrol agent" or "agent" in this subpart.

§ 550.1603 Definitions.

For the purpose of this subpart—

Advanced training means all training, other than initial training, provided on a whole-workday basis. Advanced training excludes training that covers only part of an 8-hour basic workday.

Agent means a Border Patrol agent.

Annual period means a 1-year period that begins on the first day of the first pay period beginning on or after January 1 of a given year and ends on the day before the first day of the first pay period beginning on or after January 1 of the next year. The term "year" in 5 U.S.C. 5550(b)(1)(A) and (C) and the term "leave year" in 5 U.S.C. 5542(g)(5)(A) are interpreted to be an annual period as defined here.

Basic regular tour of duty means an officially established weekly regular tour of duty consisting of five 8-hour workdays (including no overtime hours) for which no overtime supplement is payable.

Basic workday means the 8 nonovertime hours on a day within an agent's basic workweek.

Basic workweek, for full-time employees, means the 40-hour workweek established in accordance with 5 CFR 610.111.

Border Patrol agent means an employee to whom this subpart applies, as provided in § 550.1602.

CBP means the component of the Department of Homeland Security known as U.S. Customs and Border Protection (or any successor organization). When this term is used in the context of CBP making determinations or taking actions, it means management officials of CBP who are authorized to make the given determination or take the given action.

Hybrid pay period means a biweekly pay period within which—

(1) An agent has one type of established regular tour of duty for one part of the pay period and another type of regular tour of duty for a different part of the pay period; or

(2) An individual is employed as an agent for only a portion of the pay period.

Initial training means training for newly hired agents—including initial orientation sessions, basic training, and other preparatory activities—provided prior to the agent's first regular work assignment in which he or she will be authorized to make arrests and carry a firearm.

Irregular overtime work means officially ordered or approved overtime work that is not regularly scheduled overtime work—*i.e.*, overtime work that is not part of the agent's regularly scheduled administrative workweek.

Leave without pay means a period of time within an agent's basic workweek during which the agent is in nonpay status, including periods of unpaid voluntary absence with approval, absence without approval (AWOL), suspension, or furlough.

Level 1 regular tour of duty means an officially established weekly regular tour of duty generally consisting of five 10-hour workdays (including 2 overtime hours each workday) that provides entitlement to a 25 percent overtime supplement.

Level 2 regular tour of duty means an officially established weekly regular tour of duty generally consisting of five 9-hour workdays (including 1 overtime hour each workday) that provides entitlement to a 12.5 percent overtime supplement.

Obligated overtime hours means regularly scheduled overtime hours that an agent with a Level 1 or Level 2 regular tour of duty is obligated to work as part of the agent's regular tour of duty, if the agent performs any amount of work during regular time on same day, and that are converted into an overtime hours debt when the agent fails to work the hours.

Overtime hours debt means the balance of obligated overtime hours not worked for which the agent has not satisfied the hours obligation by applying compensatory time off hours or other overtime hours of work outside the agent's regular tour of duty.

Overtime supplement means a payment received (in addition to the regular amount of basic pay for nonovertime work) in exchange for regularly scheduled overtime work within an agent's Level 1 or Level 2 regular tour of duty. For an agent who is assigned a 10-hour workday as part of the agent's Level 1 regular tour of duty, the overtime supplement is 25 percent. For an agent who is assigned a 9-hour workday as part of the agent's Level 2 regular tour of duty, the overtime supplement is 12.5 percent. The overtime supplement is computed as provided in § 550.1621(a)(4) and (b)(4). For an agent with a Basic regular tour of duty, the overtime supplement is 0 percent.

Pay period means a 14-day biweekly pay period.

Rate of basic pay means the regular nonovertime rate of pay payable to an agent, excluding any overtime supplement, but including any applicable locality payment under 5 CFR part 531, subpart F; special rate supplement under 5 CFR part 530, subpart C; or similar payment or supplement under other legal authority, before any deductions and exclusive of additional pay of any other kind. An overtime supplement is included as part of an agent's rate of basic pay for purposes outside this subpart, as provided in § 550.1633.

Regularly scheduled administrative workweek, for a full-time employee, means the period within an administrative workweek, established in accordance with 5 CFR 610.111, within which the employee is regularly scheduled to work.

Regularly scheduled work means work (including overtime work) that is scheduled in advance of an administrative workweek under an agency's procedures for establishing workweeks in accordance with 5 CFR 610.111.

Regular time means the regular basic (nonovertime) hours within an agent's 8-hour basic workday within the 40-hour basic workweek.

Regular tour of duty means the basic 40-hour workweek plus any regularly scheduled overtime work hours that the agent is assigned to work as part of an officially established 5-day weekly work schedule generally consisting of—

(1) 10-hour workdays (including 2 overtime hours each workday) in exchange for a 25 percent overtime supplement (Level 1); or

(2) 9-hour workdays (including 1 overtime hour each workday) in exchange for a 12.5 percent overtime supplement (Level 2).

§ 550.1604 Authority of U.S. Customs and Border Protection.

Authorized management officials of U.S. Customs and Border Protection are responsible for determining the mission requirements and operational needs of the organization and have the right to assign scheduled and unscheduled work as necessary to meet those requirements and needs, regardless of an agent's officially established regular tour of duty. (See subsections (a) and (f)(1) of section 2 of Pub. L. 113–277 and 5 U.S.C. 5550(g).)

§ 550.1605 Interpretation instruction.

As required by section 2(f) of the Border Patrol Agent Pay Reform Act of 2014 (Public Law 113–277), nothing in section 2 of the Act or this subpart may be construed to require compensation of an agent other than for hours during which the agent is actually performing work or using approved paid leave or other paid time off. This section does not prevent CBP from granting paid excused absence from an agent's basic workweek under other authority.

ASSIGNMENT OF REGULAR TOUR OF DUTY AND OVERTIME SUPPLEMENT

§ 550.1611 Assignments for an annual period.

(a) *Annual period.* The assignment of a regular tour of duty and overtime supplement to an agent is in effect for a full annual period (or the portion of such period during which the individual is employed as an agent), except as otherwise provided in this subpart. The annual period is a 1-year period that begins on the first day of the first pay period beginning on or after January 1 of a given year and ends on the day before the first day of the first pay period beginning on or after January 1 of the next year.

(b) *Information regarding annual election opportunity.* No later than November 1 of each year, CBP must provide each currently employed agent with information regarding the opportunity to elect a regular tour of duty and corresponding overtime supplement for the next annual period. The information must include an explanation of election options and procedures. For an agent who will be in initial training status on the first day of the annual period, this paragraph is not applicable, and § 550.1612(a) and (b) will apply instead.

(c) *Annual election opportunity.* No later than December 1 of each year, an agent to whom paragraph (b) of this section is applicable may make an election among three options for the regular tour of duty and corresponding overtime supplement (as described in § 550.1621) that the agent wishes to be applicable to him or her during the next annual period.

(d) *Failure to make an election.* If an agent fails to make a timely election under paragraph (c) of this section, CBP must assign the agent a Level 1 regular tour of duty for the annual period (*i.e.*, deemed election) with a 25 percent overtime supplement, except as otherwise provided in paragraph (f) of this section or § 550.1622.

(e) *Effect of agent election.* CBP must assign an agent the regular tour of duty elected by the agent under paragraph (c) or (d) of this section unless CBP informs the agent of an alternative assignment, as provided under paragraph (f) of this section or § 550.1622. CBP may change the assignment during the annual period, as provided under § 550.1612(d). An annual election under paragraph (c) or (d) of this section that is superseded as provided under paragraph (f) of this section or § 550.1622 remains as the default election in the event that the superseding circumstances cease to be applicable, subject to § 550.1612(d).

(f) *Management assignment to tour.* CBP may assign a different regular tour of duty than that elected by the agent under paragraph (c) or (d) of this section for an upcoming annual period under the following circumstances:

(1) An agent who is assigned canine care duties must be assigned a Level 1 regular tour of duty, subject to § 550.1622(c);

(2) An agent who is unable to perform overtime on a daily basis, as determined by CBP, must be assigned a Basic regular tour of duty with no overtime supplement until such time as CBP determines the agent is able to perform the required overtime on a daily basis, subject to the rules in § 550.1612(e);

(3) An agent who holds a position at CBP headquarters, as a training instructor at a CBP training facility, or as a fitness instructor—or who holds another type of position that CBP has determined to be an administrative position— must be assigned a Basic regular tour of duty unless CBP determines a Level 1 or Level 2 regular tour of duty may be assigned to the agent based on a comprehensive staffing

analysis conducted for the agent's duty station as required by section 2(e) of the Border Patrol Agent Pay Reform Act of 2014 (Public Law 113–277);

(4) CBP determines that an agent must be assigned to a Level 1 regular tour of duty to ensure that not more than 10 percent (or higher percentage established under § 550.1614(b)) of agents stationed at a location are assigned to a Level 2 regular tour of duty or a Basic regular tour of duty, as required by 5 U.S.C. 5550(b)(1)(E) and § 550.1614; or

(5) CBP determines that assignment of a different regular tour of duty is necessary to comply with the pay assignment continuity provisions in 5 U.S.C. 5550(b)(1)(G) and § 550.1615, notwithstanding any other provision of law or this subpart (including paragraphs (f)(1) through (4) of this section).

(g) *Temporary detail.* If an agent is serving in a position under a temporary detail, that position may not be considered, for the purpose of applying paragraph (f)(3) of this section, to be the position held by the agent during the first 90 days of the detail. After completing 90 days under a temporary detail, an agent will be considered, for the purpose of applying paragraph (f)(3) of this section, to hold the position to which temporarily detailed for the remainder of the detail, notwithstanding the agent's official position of record.

§ 550.1612 Assignments made at other times.

(a) *Initial training period.* An individual who is newly hired as an agent must be assigned a Basic regular tour of duty during any period of initial training. After completing any period of initial training, an agent must be assigned a Level 1 regular tour of duty for any portion of the annual period remaining at that point, except under applicable circumstances described in paragraph (f) of § 550.1611 or paragraph (b) of this section.

(b) *Election by new agent.* An agent who would otherwise be assigned a regular tour of duty under paragraph (a) of this section may submit an election of a different regular tour of duty to be effective on a prospective basis for the remaining portion of the annual period. CBP must provide the agent with election information no later than the date the agent begins a regular work assignment (*i.e.*, after completing any period of initial training). CBP must assign an agent the regular tour of duty elected by the agent under this section unless CBP informs the agent of an alternative assignment based on the circumstances described in paragraph (f) of § 550.1611. Such election must be submitted to CBP no later than 30 days after the agent begins a regular work assignment and, if approved by CBP, is effective on the first day of the first pay period beginning on or after the later of—

(1) The date the election was submitted; or

(2) The date the agent completed initial training.

(c) *Belated election for new agent's first annual period.* An individual who is newly hired as an agent during the period beginning on November 2 and ending on the day before the first day of the next annual period may make an election to take effect at the beginning of the next annual period notwithstanding the normally applicable December 1 election deadline, if the agent will not be in initial training status on the first day of the annual period. Such election must be submitted no later than 30 days after receiving election information, but before the first day of the annual period. Such an election is subject to the same requirements and conditions that apply to an election for an annual period under paragraphs (e) and (f) of § 550.1611. If such election is not made, CBP must assign the agent a Level 1 regular tour of duty with a 25 percent overtime supplement for the next annual period, except under applicable circumstances described in paragraph (f) of § 550.1611.

(d) *Change in tour during annual period.* CBP may change an agent's assigned regular tour of duty during an annual period based on a change in the circumstances described in § 550.1611(f) or in § 550.1622. For example, an agent's regular tour of duty may be changed one or more times during an annual period as necessary to comply with the pay assignment continuity provision described in § 550.1611(f)(5). As provided in § 550.1611(e), an annual election under § 550.1611(c) or (d) that is superseded by operation of § 550.1611(f) or § 550.1622 remains as the default election and becomes effective in the event that § 550.1611(f) or § 550.1622 ceases to be applicable. A tour change under this paragraph is effective with the change in circumstances, as determined by CBP, except as otherwise provided in paragraph (e)(2) of this section and § 550.1622(c)(2).

(e) *Inability determination and effective date of tour change.* The action to assign a Basic regular tour of duty based on a determination that an agent is unable to perform overtime on a daily basis under § 550.1611(f)(2) is subject to the following rules:

(1) The inability determination may be made—

(i) When an agent's law enforcement authority is revoked (e.g., in connection with an investigation, loss of security clearance, or a suspension);

(ii) When an agent is unable to perform overtime duties for an extended period due to physical or health reasons; or

(iii) For any other appropriate reason, as determined by CBP, but excluding inability based on lack of work (as opposed to inability based on the employee's availability).

(2) The change to a Basic regular tour of duty is effective on the next workday following a CBP inability determination, except that—

(i) CBP may delay the effective date to coincide with the beginning of a week or a biweekly pay period;

(ii) CBP may delay the effective date as necessary to allow an agent who is able to work during regular time to exhaust a positive balance of unused compensatory time off (by applying that balance against the newly accruing overtime hours debt resulting from work during regular time);

(iii) CBP may delay the effective date as necessary to allow an agent to use accrued paid leave or other paid time off if the agent will be performing no work during regular time for a continuous period;

(iv) CBP may delay the effective date during a continuous period of leave without pay granted under 5 U.S.C. chapter 63, subchapter V (dealing with family and medical leave); and

(v) CBP must delay the effective date during any period of paid leave, continuation of pay, or leave without pay granted in connection with application of 5 U.S.C. chapter 81 (dealing with workers' compensation due to a job-related injury).

§ 550.1613 Selection of agents for assignment.

If application of paragraphs (f)(3) and (4) of § 550.1611 (or application of those paragraphs through § 550.1612) requires CBP to select agents for assignment to a particular regular tour of duty out of a pool of agents who prefer a different assignment, CBP must make any such selection consistent with an established written plan that includes the criteria that will be considered and the priority of those criteria. Such plan must be consistent with the requirements of this subpart.

§ 550.1614 Limit on percentage of agents who do not have a Level 1 regular tour of duty.

(a) CBP must take such action as is necessary, including unilateral assignment of agents to a Level 1 regular tour of duty, to ensure that not more than 10 percent of agents stationed at a location are assigned to a Level 2 regular tour of duty or a Basic regular tour of duty, as required by 5 U.S.C. 5550(b)(1)(E), notwithstanding any other provision of law or this subpart, except as provided by paragraphs (b), (c), and (d) of this section. For the purpose of this paragraph, the term "location" means a Border Patrol sector, which includes all subordinate organizational structures and related geographic areas within the sector (e.g., stations).

(b) CBP may waive the 10 percent limit in paragraph (a) of this section and apply a higher percentage limit if CBP determines it is able to adequately fulfill its operational requirements under that higher limit based on a comprehensive staffing analysis conducted for the agent's duty station under section 2(e) of the Border Patrol Agent Pay Reform Act of 2014 (Pub. L. 113–277).

(c) The 10 percent limit in paragraph (a) does not apply to agents working at

CBP headquarters or at a CBP training location.

(d) Regardless of the percentage limits set under this section, assignments of regular tours of duty to individual agents must be made consistent with the requirement to ensure pay assignment continuity under §550.1615.

§550.1615 Pay assignment continuity.

(a) *Plan.* (1) In consultation with OPM, CBP must develop and implement a plan to ensure, to the greatest extent practicable, that the assignment of a regular tour of duty to an agent during all consecutive 3-year periods within the control period specified in paragraph (b) of this section produces an average overtime supplement percentage (during each 3-year period) that is consistent with the agent's average overtime supplement percentage during the course of the agent's career prior to the beginning of that control period, subject to paragraph (c) of this section. The purpose of this plan is to protect the retirement fund and ensure that agents are not able to artificially enhance their retirement annuities during the period when the high-3 average pay may be determined (in accordance with 5 U.S.C. 8331(4) or 5 U.S.C. 8401(3)).

(2) In applying paragraph (a)(1) of this section, the career average overtime supplement percentage for an agent is the greater of—

(i) The average of overtime supplement percentages (25 percent, 12.5 percent, or 0 percent) assigned during service as an agent on or after January 10, 2016, that is prior to the beginning of the agent's control period (as specified in paragraph (b) of this section); or

(ii) The average of the overtime supplement percentages during all service as an agent that is prior to the beginning of the agent's control period (as specified in paragraph (b) of this section), with assigned overtime supplement percentages (25, 12.5, or 0 percent) assigned during service on or after January 10, 2016, and with assigned percentages of administratively uncontrollable overtime under 5 U.S.C. 5545(c)(2) treated as overtime supplement percentages for any period of service prior to January 10, 2016.

(3) In applying paragraph (a)(2) of this section, the assigned overtime supplement percentage is used regardless of whether or not the payable amount of the overtime supplement is limited by a premium pay cap.

(4) In applying paragraph (a)(2) of this section, if an agent's control period begins on January 10, 2016, as provided in paragraph (b), the agent's initially assigned overtime supplement percentage must be considered the agent's career average under paragraph (a)(2)(i).

(b) *Control period.* The period of time during which CBP must control an agent's assignment to a regular tour of duty (*i.e.*, the control period) begins on the date 3 years before the agent meets age and service requirements for an immediate retirement and remains in effect during all subsequent service in a Border Patrol agent position. If, as of January 10, 2016, the date that is 3 years before the agent first met age and service requirements for an immediate retirement has already passed, then the agent's control period is considered to have begun on January 10, 2016.

(c) *Consistency requirement.* (1) The consistency requirement in paragraph (a) of this section is considered to be met when the agent's average overtime supplement percentage during all consecutive 3-year periods within the control period specified in paragraph (b) of this section is within 2.5 percentage points of the agent's average overtime supplement percentage during the course of the agent's career prior to the beginning of that control period, except as provided in paragraph (c)(2) of this section.

(2) Notwithstanding the consistency requirement in paragraph (a) of this section, the CBP plan may allow an agent to be assigned a regular tour of duty that provides an overtime supplement percentage that is less than that necessary to produce an average percentage (during all consecutive 3-year periods within the control period specified in paragraph (b)) that is consistent with the agent's career average percentage if—

(i) The agent's overtime supplement is limited by the premium pay cap under §§550.105 and 550.107 and the agent voluntarily elects a regular tour of duty providing such a lesser overtime supplement percentage that is approved by CBP; or

(ii) CBP determines an agent is unable to perform overtime on a daily basis due to a physical or medical condition affecting the agent and assigns the agent a Basic regular tour of duty, as described in § 550.1611(f)(2), (but only if such assignment makes it impossible to satisfy the consistency requirement during any given consecutive 3-year period).

(d) *CBP authority.* (1) CBP may take such action as is necessary, including the unilateral assignment of a regular tour of duty to implement the plan described in paragraph (a) of this section, notwithstanding any other provision of law or this subpart, except as provided in paragraph (d)(2) of this section.

(2) Notwithstanding the requirements of 5 U.S.C. 5550(b)(1)(G) and this section, CBP is authorized to assign agents to regular tours of duty as necessary to meet operational requirements. Before exercising the authority to allow assignment of a regular tour of duty that does not comply with the plan described in paragraph (a) of this section, CBP must first determine that it cannot adequately address the specific operational requirements in question by other means, such as the assignment of overtime work outside the regular tour of duty to the affected agent or other agents. If this authority is exercised, CBP must return an affected agent to a regular tour of duty that complies with the plan described in paragraph (a) of this section as soon as possible.

(e) *Reporting requirements*—(1) *Annual data reporting for agents within their control period.* For each agent within the control period specified in paragraph (b) of this section, CBP must provide to OPM no later than March 30th of each year the following information (in a format specified by OPM) based on data compiled through the end of the most recent annual period:

(i) The date the agent became subject to controls on the assignment to a regular tour of duty;

(ii) The date the agent will become subject to mandatory separation under 5 U.S.C. 8335(b) or 5 U.S.C. 8425(b);

(iii) The service computation date based on eligibility under 5 U.S.C. 8336(c) or 5 U.S.C. 8412(d);

(iv) The average overtime supplement percentage during the course of the agent's career prior to the beginning of the control period specified in paragraph (b);

(v) The average overtime supplement percentage for the time period beginning with the date the agent became subject to controls on the assignment to a regular tour of duty and ending on the last day of the most recent annual period;

(vi) The average overtime supplement percentage for the last three annual periods (excluding any time that was not within a control period specified in paragraph (b) of this section);

(vii) The average overtime supplement percentage for the most recent annual period (excluding any time that was not within a control period specified in paragraph (b) of this section), and;

(viii) Any other information requested by OPM.

(2) *Annual data reporting for all agents.* No later than March 30th of each year, CBP must provide to OPM the following information (in a format specified by OPM) for each agent compiled for the preceding calendar year based on salary payments made during that year:

(i) The amount of earnings subject to retirement deductions, including overtime supplement payments, received during the most recent calendar year;

(ii) The amount of earnings subject to retirement deductions during the most recent calendar year minus the total amount of the overtime supplement payments during that year;

(iii) The service computation date computed as though law enforcement officer service is regular employee service (*i.e.*, the "regular" SCD);

(iv) The service computation date computed with credit for law enforcement officer service, and any other service creditable for eligibility under 5 U.S.C. 8336(c) or 5 U.S.C. 8412(d) (*i.e.*, the "LEO" SCD);

(v) Date of birth;

(vi) Gender;

(vii) Retirement system (e.g., CSRS, FERS, FERS–RAE, FERS–FRAE); and

(viii) Any other information requested by OPM.

(3) *Additional data.* CBP must provide additional data as requested by OPM at any time, including data on the percentage rate of administratively uncontrollable overtime under § 550.154 during the period before the annual period that begins in January 2016.

(f) *Corrective actions.* If it is determined that the consistency requirement described in paragraphs (a) and (c) of this section is not being met for a particular agent, CBP must document why the differential occurred and establish any necessary actions, including the modification of the plan described in paragraph (a) of this section, to ensure that the goal of pay assignment continuity is achieved going forward. Consistent with § 550.1616(b), CBP is not required to retroactively correct an agent's assigned tour or overtime supplement based on violation of the consistency requirement, except when CBP determines there exists, in connection with an agent's assigned overtime supplement, evidence of fraud, misrepresentation, fault, or lack of good faith on the part of that agent.

§ 550.1616 Corrective actions.

(a) Except at provided in paragraph (b) of this section, an error made in connection with the assignment of an agent's regular tour of duty (including any associated overtime supplement) must be corrected as soon as possible.

(b) A retroactive correction of a tour assignment (*i.e.*, actual assigned work schedule as opposed to an error in the payroll system) may not be made in the following circumstances, unless CBP determines there exists, in connection with an agent's assigned tour, evidence of fraud, misrepresentation, fault, or lack of good faith on the part of the affected agent:

(1) Correction of an error in applying the consistency requirement described in §§ 550.1611(f)(5) and 550.1615; and

(2) Correction of an error that caused an employee to have a Level 1 regular tour of duty based solely on misapplication of the applicable percentage limitation described in §§ 550.1611(f)(4) and 550.1614.

Treatment of Overtime Work

§ 550.1621 Rules for types of regular tour of duty.

(a) *Level 1 regular tour of duty.* For an agent with a Level 1 regular tour of duty and a 25 percent overtime supplement, the following rules apply:

(1) The agent has an officially established weekly regular tour of duty generally consisting of five 10-hour workdays (an 8-hour basic workday and 2 regularly scheduled overtime hours);

(2) The agent's 8-hour basic workday (regular time) may be interrupted by an unpaid off-duty meal break;

(3) The obligation to perform 2 hours of overtime work on a day including part of the agent's regular tour of duty does not apply if the agent performs no work during regular time on that day, subject to paragraph (e) of this section;

(4) As compensation for regularly scheduled overtime hours within the regular tour of duty, the agent is entitled to an overtime supplement equal to 25 percent of the agent's hourly rate of basic pay times the number of paid hours of regular time for the agent in the pay period (subject to the premium cap in §§ 550.105 and 550.107 and the restriction in § 550.1626(a)(5)), and no additional compensation or compensatory time off may be provided for such overtime hours;

(5) For any additional regularly scheduled overtime hours outside the regular tour of duty, the agent is entitled to overtime pay as provided in § 550.1624, except as otherwise provided by § 550.1626;

(6) For any irregular overtime hours, the agent is entitled to be credited with compensatory time off as provided in § 550.1625, except as otherwise provided by § 550.1626;

(7) The agent must be charged corresponding amounts of paid leave, compensatory time off, other paid time off, or time in nonpay status for each hour (or part thereof) the agent is absent from duty during regular time, as provided in § 550.1634, except as otherwise provided in § 550.1626(a); and

(8) If the agent is absent during regularly scheduled overtime hours within the agent's regular tour of duty that the agent is obligated to work, the agent accrues an obligation to perform

other overtime work for each hour (or part thereof) the agent is absent, and such obligation must be satisfied as provided in § 550.1626.

(b) *Level 2 regular tour of duty.* For an agent with a Level 2 regular tour of duty and a 12.5 percent overtime supplement, the following rules apply:

(1) The agent has an officially established weekly regular tour of duty generally consisting of five 9-hour workdays (an 8-hour basic workday and 1 regularly scheduled overtime hour);

(2) The agent's 8-hour basic workday (regular time) may be interrupted by an unpaid off-duty meal break;

(3) The obligation to perform 1 hour of overtime work on a day including part of the agent's regular tour of duty does not apply if the agent performs no work during regular time on that day, subject to paragraph (e) of this section;

(4) As compensation for regularly scheduled overtime hours within the regular tour of duty, the agent receives an overtime supplement equal to 12.5 percent of the agent's hourly rate of basic pay times the number of paid hours of regular time for the agent in the pay period (subject to the premium cap in §§ 550.105 and 550.107 and the restriction in § 550.1626(a)(5)), and no additional compensation or compensatory time off may be provided for such overtime hours;

(5) For any additional regularly scheduled overtime hours outside the regular tour of duty, the agent is entitled to overtime pay as provided in § 550.1624, except as otherwise provided by § 550.1626;

(6) For any irregular overtime hours, the agent is entitled to be credited with compensatory time off as provided in § 550.1625, except as otherwise provided by § 550.1626;

(7) The agent must be charged corresponding amounts of paid leave, compensatory time off, other paid time off, or time in nonpay status for each hour (or part thereof) the agent is absent from duty during regular time, as provided in § 550.1634, except as otherwise provided in § 550.1626(a); and

(8) If the agent is absent during regularly scheduled overtime hours within the agent's regular tour of duty that the agent is obligated to work, the agent accrues an obligation to perform other overtime work for each hour (or part thereof) the agent is absent, and such obligation must be satisfied as provided in § 550.1626.

(c) *Basic regular tour of duty.* For an agent with a Basic regular tour of duty that includes no scheduled overtime hours and provides no overtime supplement, the following rules apply:

(1) The agent has an officially established weekly regular tour of duty generally consisting of five 8-hour basic workdays;

(2) The agent's 8-hour basic workday (regular time) may be interrupted by an unpaid off-duty meal break;

(3) For any regularly scheduled overtime hours, the agent is entitled to overtime pay as provided in § 550.1624, except as otherwise provided by § 550.1626;

(4) For any irregular overtime hours, the agent is entitled to be credited with compensatory time off as provided in § 550.1625, except as otherwise provided by § 550.1626; and

(5) The agent must be charged corresponding amounts of paid leave, compensatory time off, other paid time off, or time in nonpay status for each hour (or part thereof) the agent is absent from duty during regular time, as provided in § 550.1634, except as otherwise provided in § 550.1626(a).

(d) *Effect of premium pay cap.* If a premium pay cap established under 5 U.S.C. 5547 and §§ 550.105 and 550.107 limits payment of an overtime supplement or regularly scheduled overtime pay, or limits crediting of compensatory time off, the affected agent is still required to perform assigned overtime work.

(e) *Meaning of "work".* In applying paragraphs (a)(3) and (b)(3) of this section, the term "work" refers to paid hours of work, consistent with § 550.112, except that paid leave and other paid time off when an agent is excused from duty are not considered to be work hours. Official time under 5 U.S.C. 7131 during regular time is considered to be paid hours of "work" during the time an employee otherwise would be in a duty status.

(f) *Approval of absences.* Any absence during obligated overtime hours (as described in paragraphs (a)(8) and (b)(8) of this section) is subject to management approval under CBP policies.

§550.1622 Circumstances requiring special treatment.

(a) *General.* The rules in paragraphs (b) and (c) of this section provide for special treatment based on specified circumstances and apply notwithstanding any other provision of this subpart.

(b) *Advanced training.* (1) During the first 60 days of advanced training in a calendar year, an agent's assigned regular tour of duty must be considered to continue and the agent must be deemed to have worked during any nonwork period within obligated overtime hours for the purpose of determining the agent's total hours to be compared to the applicable overtime threshold (as provided in §550.1623(a)(2)(iv)), except as provided under paragraph (b)(2) of this section.

(2) If an agent, during the period covered by paragraph (b)(1) of this section, performs creditable overtime work outside the agent's regular tour of duty on a day when the agent performed less than the required amount of obligated overtime work, the overtime work outside the regular tour of duty must be applied towards the obligated overtime hours, as provided in §550.1626(b). After any such substitution, CBP must credit the agent with hours of work for any remaining nonwork time during obligated overtime hours on the same day for the purpose of determining the agent's total hours to be compared to the applicable overtime threshold. For example, if an agent performs 2 creditable hours of regularly scheduled overtime work outside the agent's Level 1 regular tour of duty on a training day when the agent performed half an hour of work during the 2 hours of obligated overtime, CBP would substitute 1.5 hours of regularly scheduled overtime outside the regular tour of duty for 1.5 hours of obligated overtime when no work was performed. CBP would not provide the agent with any credit for nonwork hours under paragraph (b)(1) of this section, since the 0.5 hours of actual work plus the 1.5 substituted hours account for the entire 2-hour period. The agent would be paid for the unsubstituted half hour of creditable regularly scheduled overtime work under §550.1624.

(3) For days of advanced training in excess of 60 days in a calendar year, an agent must be assigned a Basic regular tour of duty and be treated accordingly. If this results in a hybrid pay period in which an agent has two types of regular tours of duty within the same biweekly pay period, CBP must determine the number of overtime hours outside the regular tour of duty as provided in §550.1623(c). For an agent who is assigned a Basic regular tour of duty during advanced training under this paragraph, CBP must change the agent's regular tour of duty to the type in effect before the Basic tour was assigned when the agent is no longer participating in advanced training.

(4) Paragraphs (b)(1) through (3) of this section apply solely to advanced training that is provided in whole-workday increments (*i.e.*, covering an entire 8-hour basic workday).

(c) *Canine care.* (1) For an agent assigned to provide care for a canine and assigned to the Level 1 regular tour of duty border patrol rate of pay, the combined sum of basic pay plus the 25 percent overtime supplement is considered to provide compensation for all canine care. Such an agent must be credited with 1 hour of regularly scheduled overtime work as part of the regular tour of duty on each day containing a part of that tour, without regard to the actual duration of such care or the time and day when such care was actually provided. That leaves the agent with an additional obligation to perform 1 other hour of regularly scheduled overtime work as part of the agent's regular tour of duty on any day containing a part of the employee's tour, if the agent performs work during regular time on that day and thus has obligated overtime hours. An agent may receive no other compensation or compensatory time off for hours of canine care beyond what is specifically provided under this paragraph.

(2) If an agent is generally assigned to provide care for a canine, but is temporarily relieved of that duty for any reason (e.g., no dog available), the agent may not receive the 1-hour credit for canine care on a day when the agent is relieved from providing canine care. If the period during which the

agent is temporarily relieved from providing canine care lasts more than two full pay periods, CBP must assign the agent's tour based on the agent's default election for the annual period as provided in § 550.1611(c) or (d) unless other circumstances described in paragraph (f) of § 550.1611 are applicable. For shorter periods, the Level 1 regular tour of duty assigned based on canine care responsibilities will continue unless the agent requests a different tour based on the agent's default election for the annual period.

§ 550.1623 Overtime work outside the regular tour of duty.

(a) *General.* (1) For the purpose of determining hours of overtime work outside an agent's regular tour of duty in order to apply §§ 550.1624, 550.1625, and 550.1626, CBP must apply the applicable biweekly overtime threshold prescribed in paragraphs (b) and (c) of this section. An agent's total hours of work (as determined under paragraph (a)(2) of this section) must be compared to the applicable threshold, and hours in excess of that threshold are overtime hours in applying §§ 550.1624, 550.1625, and 550.1626. The 8-hour daily and 40-hour weekly overtime thresholds under 5 U.S.C. 5542(a) and § 550.111 are not applicable to agents.

(2) An agent's total hours of work in a pay period for the purpose of applying applicable overtime thresholds is equal to the sum of:

(i) Time determined to be hours of work in duty status (regular time or overtime), subject to this subpart, 5 U.S.C. 4109 and 5 CFR 410.402 (related to training periods), and 5 U.S.C. 5542(b) and § 550.112 (establishing general rules), except that paragraphs (d) and (e) of § 550.112 are superseded by § 550.1626;

(ii) Paid leave or other paid time off during a period of nonduty status within an agent's regular time;

(iii) Obligated overtime hours during which no work is performed (creating a debt of hours) and for which no substitution is made under § 550.1626(b);

(iv) Nonwork hours deemed to be hours of work during obligated overtime hours on a day of advanced training under § 550.1622(b); and

(v) Overtime hours normally scheduled within an agent's regular tour of duty that an agent is not obligated to work because the agent performs no work during regular time on that day (as provided in paragraphs (a)(3) and (b)(3) of § 550.1621).

(b) *Overtime thresholds for standard tours.* (1) The applicable biweekly overtime threshold prescribed in paragraph (b)(2) of this section applies during a pay period to an agent whose regular tour of duty is fixed at one of the three standard tours for the entire pay period. (2) For an agent covered by paragraph (b)(1) of this section, the threshold used to determine whether an agent has performed overtime work outside the regular tour of duty in a given pay period is—

(i) 100 hours for a Level 1 regular tour of duty;

(ii) 90 hours for a Level 2 regular tour of duty; or

(iii) 80 hours for a Basic regular tour of duty.

(c) *Overtime threshold for hybrid pay period.* (1) For a hybrid pay period in which an agent has one type of regular tour of duty in effect for one part of the period and another type for another part of the period, the threshold used to determine whether an agent has performed overtime work outside the regular tour of duty in a given pay period is equal to the sum of the regular time hours (paid or unpaid) and the number of normally scheduled overtime hours within a regular tour of duty (whether obligated or not and whether worked or not) in the pay period. For example, if an agent has a Level 1 regular tour of duty in the first week of a pay period and a Level 2 regular tour of duty in the second week, the agent's regular time hours would be 40 in the first week and 40 in the second week and the normally scheduled overtime hours within a regular tour of duty would be 10 (5 days times 2 hours each day) in the first week and 5 (5 days times 1 hour each day) in second week, resulting in an biweekly overtime threshold of 95 hours.

(2) For a hybrid pay period in which an individual is employed as a Border Patrol agent for only part of the pay period, the threshold used to determine

whether an agent has performed overtime work outside the regular tour of duty in a given pay period is equal to the sum of the paid regular time hours (paid or unpaid) and the number of normally scheduled overtime hours within a regular tour of duty (whether obligated or not and whether worked or not) during the portion of the pay period the individual was employed as an agent. For example, if an individual is employed as an agent only during the second week of a pay period and has a Level 1 regular tour of duty, the overtime threshold would be 50 hours (40 regular time hours plus 10 normally scheduled overtime hours) in determining whether the agent has overtime hours in that week that are compensable under §§550.1624, 550.1625, and 550.1626.

§550.1624 Regularly scheduled overtime outside the regular tour of duty.

(a) *Coverage.* Any regularly scheduled overtime hours outside an agent's regular tour of duty, as specified in §550.1623, are covered by this section, except that such hours are excluded from coverage under this section when required by the superseding provisions in §550.1626.

(b) *Rates.* Agents receive overtime pay at the rates specified under 5 U.S.C. 5542(a) and §550.113 for regularly scheduled overtime hours covered by paragraph (a) of this section, subject to the premium pay limitation established under 5 U.S.C. 5547 and §§550.105 and 550.107. An agent's rate of basic pay (without any overtime supplement) is used in computing overtime pay for such hours.

(c) *Avoiding additional regularly scheduled overtime.* (1) As required by section 2(c)(2) of the Border Patrol Agent Pay Reform Act of 2014 (Public Law 113–277), CBP must, to the maximum extent practicable, avoid the use of regularly scheduled overtime work by agents outside of the regular tour of duty.

(2) Notwithstanding paragraph (c)(1) of this section, CBP may allow use of regularly scheduled overtime work outside an agent's regular tour of duty if an agent volunteers to perform such overtime (e.g., to reduce an overtime hours debt).

§550.1625 Irregular overtime and compensatory time off.

(a) *Coverage.* An agent is entitled to compensatory time off as provided in this section for irregular overtime hours outside an agent's regular tour of duty, as specified in §550.1623, except that such hours are excluded from coverage under this section (except paragraph (c) of this section) when required by the superseding provisions in §550.1626. The compensatory time off provisions in 5 U.S.C. 5543 and 5 CFR 550.114 are not applicable to an agent.

(b) *Earning on an hour-for-hour basis for irregular overtime.* Subject to the limitations specified in this section and the superseding provisions in §550.1626, an agent must receive compensatory time off for an equal amount of time spent performing irregular overtime work.

(c) *Call-back overtime work.* Notwithstanding paragraph (b) of this section, consistent with 5 U.S.C. 5542(b)(1) and §550.112(h), an agent must be deemed to have performed 2 hours of irregular overtime work for a lesser amount of irregular overtime work if—

(1) An agent is required perform such work on a day when the agent was not scheduled to work; or

(2) An agent is required to return to the agent's place of employment to perform such work.

(d) *Earning limited by premium pay cap.* An agent may not be credited with earning compensatory time off if the value of such time off would cause the sum of the agent's basic pay and premium pay in the given pay period to exceed the limitation established under 5 U.S.C. 5547 and §§550.105 and 550.107 in the period in which it was earned. The dollar value of compensatory time off for the purpose of this paragraph is the amount of overtime pay the agent would have received for the period during which compensatory time off was earned if the overtime had been regularly scheduled outside the agent's regular tour of duty.

(e) *Pay period limit.* (1) An agent may not earn more than 10 hours of compensatory time off during any pay period unless—

(i) CBP, as it determines appropriate, approves in writing a waiver of the 10-hour limit; and

(ii) Such waiver approval is executed in advance of the performance of any work for which compensatory time off is earned.

(2) If a waiver of the 10-hour limit described in paragraph (e)(1) of this section is not granted, the agent involved may not be ordered to perform the associated overtime work.

(f) *Annual period limit.* An agent may not earn more than 240 hours of compensatory time off during an annual period.

(g) *Usage.* (1) An agent may use compensatory time off by being excused from duty during regular time (in an amount equal to the compensatory time off being used) during the agent's basic workweek.

(2) An agent's balance of unused compensatory time off is used to satisfy an overtime hours debt, as provided in § 550.1626(c)(1).

(h) *Time limit for usage and forfeiture.* An agent must use any hours of compensatory time off not later than the end of the 26th pay period after the pay period during which the compensatory time off was earned. Any compensatory time off not used within that time limit, or prior to separation from an agent position, is forfeited and not available for any purpose, regardless of the circumstances. An agent may not receive any cash value for unused compensatory time off. An agent may not receive credit towards the computation of the agent's retirement annuity for unused compensatory time off.

§ 550.1626 Leave without pay during regular time and absences during obligated overtime hours.

(a) *Substitution for leave without pay during regular time.* (1) For any period of leave without pay during an agent's regular time (basic workweek), an equal period of work outside the agent's regular time in the same pay period must be substituted to the extent such work was performed. Any time substituted for leave without pay must be treated for all pay computation purposes as if it were regular time (except as provided in paragraph (a)(5) of this section) and may not be considered an overtime hour of work for any purpose, including §§ 550.1621(a)(4) and (b)(4), 550.1624, and 550.1625.

(2) Hours of work must be substituted for regular time work under paragraph (a)(1) of this section before being substituted for regularly scheduled overtime within the agent's regular tour of duty under paragraph (b) of this section.

(3) Hours used for substitution under paragraph (a)(1) of this section must be substituted in the following priority order: first, irregular overtime hours; second, regularly scheduled overtime hours outside the regular tour of duty; and third, regularly scheduled overtime hours within the regular tour of duty.

(4) The substitution of overtime hours for leave without pay is solely for pay computation purposes. The substitution does not change the hours of an agent's basic workweek or the fact that the agent was in a particular type of nonpay status during those hours. The hours that are substituted are considered to have been performed when they were worked, not during the leave without pay hours for which they are substituted. For example, if an agent performs 4 hours of overtime work outside the agent's regular tour of duty during the first week of a pay period and then is placed in leave without pay during the second week due to a shutdown furlough caused by a lapse in appropriations, the 4 hours must be substituted for furlough hours for the purpose of computing pay owed the agent for the week before the furlough began.

(5) If overtime hours are substituted for an absence without approval (AWOL) or a suspension, the basic pay for such substituted hours may not be used in computing an agent's overtime supplement.

(b) *Substitution for absences during obligated overtime hours within the regular tour of duty.* (1) For a period of absence during obligated overtime hours within an agent's regular tour of duty, an equal period of work outside the agent's regular tour of duty in the same pay period must be substituted to the extent such work was performed. Any time so substituted must be treated for all pay computation purposes as if it were obligated overtime work and may not be considered an overtime hour of work for any other purpose, including §§ 550.1624 and 550.1625.

(2) In substituting hours of work under paragraph (b)(1) of this section, work performed on the same day as the period of absence must be substituted first in circumstances described in § 550.1622(b)(2). Hours substituted under this paragraph must be substituted in the following priority order: first, irregular overtime hours; and second, regularly scheduled overtime hours outside the regular tour of duty.

(3) After substituting hours under paragraph (b)(2) of this section, any remaining hours used for substitution under paragraph (b)(1) of this section must be substituted in the following priority order: first, irregular overtime hours; and second, regularly scheduled overtime hours outside the regular tour of duty.

(4) The substitution of overtime hours outside the regular tour of duty for obligated overtime hours not worked is solely for pay computation purposes. The substitution does not change the hours of an agent's regular tour of duty. The hours that are substituted are considered to have been performed when they were worked, not during the obligated overtime hours for which they are substituted.

(c) *Application of compensatory time off or future overtime work to offset overtime hours debt.* (1) If a Border Patrol agent does not have sufficient additional work in a pay period to substitute for all periods of absence during obligated overtime hours within the agent's regular tour of duty for that pay period, any unused balance of compensatory time off hours previously earned under § 550.1625 must be applied towards the newly accrued overtime hours debt.

(2) If an agent has a remaining overtime hours debt after applying paragraphs (b) and (c)(1) of this section, any additional overtime work outside the agent's regular tour of duty in subsequent pay periods that would otherwise be credited under § 550.1624 or § 550.1625 must be applied towards the overtime hours debt until that debt is satisfied. The application of such hours must be done in the following priority order: first, irregular overtime hours; and second, regularly scheduled overtime hours outside the regular tour of duty. Any overtime hour applied under this paragraph (c)(2) may not be considered an overtime hour of work for any other purpose.

(d) *Unsatisfied overtime hours debt at movement to a non-agent position or separation.* (1) Any unsatisfied overtime hours debt that exists at the time of movement to a non-agent position or separation from Federal service must be recovered to the extent possible by offsetting the affected employee's positive balance (if any) of annual leave, time-off awards, or compensatory time off for travel. In cases where the offset will totally eliminate the debt, an agent's balances must be applied in the following order: first, the balance of annual leave; second, the balance of time-off awards; and third, the balance of compensatory time off for travel.

(2) Any unsatisfied overtime hours debt that exists at the time of movement to a non-agent position or separation from Federal service after applying paragraph (d)(1) of this section must be converted to a monetary debt equal to the result of multiplying the agent's hourly rate of basic pay at the time of movement to a non-agent position or separation by the number of hours in the overtime hours debt. CBP must follow standard debt collection procedures to recover any debt.

RELATIONSHIP TO OTHER PROVISIONS

§ 550.1631 Other types of premium pay.

(a) An agent may not receive premium pay for night, Sunday, or holiday work for hours of regularly scheduled overtime work within the agent's regular tour of duty.

(b) An agent may receive premium pay for night, Sunday, or holiday work, as applicable, for hours not covered by paragraph (a) of this section, in accordance with 5 U.S.C. 5545(a) and (b) and section 5546 and corresponding regulations, except that section 5546(d) does not apply. (For an agent, pay for overtime work on a Sunday or holiday is determined under 5 U.S.C. 5542(g), not under section 5546(d).) The agent's rate of basic pay (without any overtime supplement) must be used in computing such premium payments.

(c) An agent may not be paid standby duty premium pay under 5 U.S.C. 5545(c)(1) or administratively uncontrollable overtime pay under 5 U.S.C. 5545(c)(2).

§ 550.1632 Hazardous duty pay.

An agent is eligible for hazardous duty pay, subject to the requirements in 5 U.S.C. 5545(d) and subpart I of this part. The agent's rate of basic pay (without any overtime supplement) must be used in computing any hazardous duty pay.

§ 550.1633 Treatment of overtime supplement as basic pay.

Regularly scheduled overtime pay within an agent's regular tour of duty is treated as part of basic pay or basic salary only for the following purposes:

(a) 5 U.S.C. 5524a and 5 CFR part 550, subpart B, pertaining to advances in pay;

(b) 5 U.S.C. 5595(c) and 5 CFR part 550, subpart G, pertaining to severance pay;

(c) 5 U.S.C. 8114(e), pertaining to workers' compensation;

(d) 5 U.S.C. 8331(3) and 5 U.S.C. 8401(4) and related provisions that rely on the definition in those paragraphs, pertaining to retirement benefits;

(e) Subchapter III of chapter 84 of title 5, United States Code, pertaining to the Thrift Savings Plan;

(f) 5 U.S.C. 8704(c), pertaining to life insurance; and

(g) For any other purposes explicitly provided for by law or as the Office of Personnel Management may prescribe by other regulation.

§ 550.1634 Leave and other paid time off.

(a) An agent is subject to the rules governing leave accrual and usage under 5 U.S.C. chapter 63 on the same basis as other employees. The tour of duty for leave accrual and usage purposes is the basic workweek, which excludes regularly scheduled overtime hours within the regular tour of duty established under this subpart. The agent must be charged corresponding amounts of leave for each hour (or part thereof) the agent is absent from duty during regular time (except that full days off for military leave must be charged when required).

(b) An agent is subject to the normally applicable rules governing other types of paid time off (such as holiday time off under 5 U.S.C. chapter 61, compensatory time off for religious observances under subpart J of this part, or compensatory time off for travel under subpart N of this part) on the same basis as other covered employees. The tour of duty used in applying those rules is the basic workweek, which excludes regularly scheduled overtime hours within the regular tour of duty established under this subpart. The agent must be charged corresponding amounts of paid time off for each hour (or part thereof) the agent is absent from duty during regular time.

(c) In computing a lump-sum annual leave payment under 5 U.S.C. 5551–5552, an overtime supplement for an agent's regularly scheduled overtime hours within the agent's regular tour of duty is included, as provided in § 550.1205(b)(5)(iv).

§ 550.1635 Alternative work schedule.

An agent may not have a flexible or compressed work schedule under 5 U.S.C. chapter 61, subchapter II. The regular tour of duty established under this subpart is a special work schedule established under 5 U.S.C. 5550. CBP may allow flexible starting and stopping times for an agent's basic workday if it determines such flexibility is appropriate for the position in question.

§ 550.1636 Exemption from Fair Labor Standards Act.

The minimum wage and the hours of work and overtime pay provisions of the Fair Labor Standards Act do not apply to Border Patrol agents. (See also 5 CFR 551.217.)

§ 550.1637 Travel time.

(a) A Border Patrol agent's travel time to and from home and the agent's regular duty station (or to an alternative work location within the limits of the agent's official duty station, as defined in § 550.112(j)) may not be considered hours of work under any provision of law.

(b) Official travel time away from an agent's official duty station may be creditable hours of work as provided in

§ 550.112(g). When an agent travels directly between home and a temporary duty location outside the limits of the agent's official duty station (as defined in § 550.112(j)), the time the agent would have spent in normal home to work travel must be deducted from any creditable hours of work while traveling.

§ 550.1638 Official time.

An agent who uses official time under 5 U.S.C. 7131 may be assigned to a Level 1 or Level 2 regular tour of duty, but is required to perform agency work during obligated overtime hours or to accrue an overtime hours debt. Official time may be used during overtime hours only when, while the agent is engaged in the performance of agency work, an event arises incident to representational functions that must be immediately addressed during the overtime hours. CBP may excuse the agent from duty during scheduled obligated overtime hours if it determines that an agent's official time duties during the basic workday make it impracticable to perform agency work during the scheduled obligated overtime hours on that day. The agent will accrue an overtime hours debt for that excused time. If CBP excuses the agent in this manner, then it must provide the agent with an opportunity to eliminate the resulting overtime hours debt by performing agency work outside the agent's regular tour of duty at another time. As provided in § 550.1621(e), official time during regular time is considered to be "work" when an agent otherwise would be in a duty status in applying paragraphs (a)(3) and (b)(3) of § 550.1621.

PART 551—PAY ADMINISTRATION UNDER THE FAIR LABOR STANDARDS ACT

Subpart A—General Provisions

Subpart B—Exemptions and Exclusions

Subpart C—Minimum Wage Provisions

BASIC PROVISION

SUBMINIMUM WAGE

Subpart D—Hours of Work

GENERAL PROVISIONS

APPLICATION OF PRINCIPLES IN RELATION TO NORMAL WORKDAY

APPLICATION OF PRINCIPLES IN RELATION TO OTHER ACTIVITIES

SPECIAL SITUATIONS

Subpart E—Overtime Pay Provisions

BASIC PROVISIONS

AUTHORITY: 5 U.S.C. 5542(c); Sec. 4(f) of the Fair Labor Standards Act of 1938, as amended by Pub. L. 93–259, 88 Stat. 55 (29 U.S.C. 204f).

Subpart A—General Provisions

SOURCE: 72 FR 52762, Sept. 17, 2007, unless otherwise noted.

§551.101 General.

(a) The Fair Labor Standards Act of 1938, as amended (referred to as "the Act" or "FLSA"), provides minimum standards for both wages and overtime entitlements, and administrative procedures by which covered worktime must be compensated. Included in the Act are provisions related to child labor, equal pay, and portal-to-portal activities. In addition, the Act exempts specified employees or groups of employees from the application of certain of its provisions and prescribes penalties for the commission of specifically prohibited acts.

(b) This part contains the regulations, criteria, and conditions set forth by the Office of Personnel Management (OPM) as prescribed by the Act, supplements and implements the Act, and must be read in conjunction with it.

(c) OPM's administration of the Act must comply with the terms of the Act but the law does not require OPM's regulations to mirror the Department of Labor's FLSA regulations. OPM's administration of the Act must be consistent with the Department of Labor's administration of the Act only to the extent practicable and only to the extent that this consistency is required to maintain compliance with the terms of the Act. For example, while OPM's executive, administrative, and professional exemption criteria are consistent with the Department of Labor's exemption criteria, OPM does not apply the highly compensated employee criteria in 29 CFR 541.601 to determine FLSA exemption status.

§551.102 Authority and administration.

Section 3(e)(2) of the Act authorizes the application of the provisions of the Act to any person employed by the Government of the United States, as specified in that section.

(a) *Office of Personnel Management.* Section 4(f) of the Act authorizes the Office of Personnel Management (OPM) to administer the provisions of the Act. OPM is the administrator of the provisions of the Act with respect to any person employed by an agency, except as specified in paragraphs (b), (c), and (d) of this section.

(b) The *Equal Employment Opportunity Commission* administers the equal pay provisions contained in section 6(d) of the Act.

(c) The *Department of Labor* administers the Act for the government of the District of Columbia and the following United States Government entities:

(1) The Library of Congress;

(2) The United States Postal Service;

(3) The Postal Rate Commission; and

(4) The Tennessee Valley Authority.

(d) *Office of Compliance.* The Congressional Accountability Act of 1995, as amended, sections 1301 *et seq.* of title 2, United States Code, extends rights and protections of the FLSA to employees of the following United States Government entities, and assigns certain administrative responsibilities to the Office of Compliance:

(1) The United States House of Representatives;

(2) The United States Senate;

(3) The Capitol Guide Service;

(4) The Capitol Police;

(5) The Congressional Budget Office;

(6) The Office of the Architect of the Capitol;

(7) The Office of the Attending Physician; and

(8) The Office of Compliance.

§551.103 Coverage.

(a) *Covered.* Any employee of an agency who is not specifically excluded by another statute is covered by the Act. This includes any person who is:

(1) Defined as an employee in section 2105 of title 5, United States Code;

(2) A civilian employee appointed under other appropriate authority; or

(3) Suffered or permitted to work by an agency whether or not formally appointed.

(b) *Not covered.* The following persons are not covered by the Act:

(1) A person appointed under appropriate authority without compensation;

(2) A trainee;

(3) A volunteer; or

(4) A member of the Uniformed Services.

§551.104 Definitions.

In this part—

Act or *FLSA* means the Fair Labor Standards Act of 1938, as amended (29 U.S.C. 201 *et seq.*).

Administrative employee means an employee who meets the administrative exemption criteria in §551.206.

Agency means any instrumentality of the United States Government, or any constituent element thereof acting directly or indirectly as an employer, as this term is defined in section 3(d) of the Act and in this section, but does not include the entities of the United States Government listed in §551.102(c) for which the Department of Labor administers the Act or §551.102(d)(1) through (8), whose employees are covered by the Congressional Accountability Act of 1995, as amended, which makes applicable the rights and protections of the FLSA and assigns certain administrative responsibilities to the Office of Compliance.

Claim means a written allegation regarding a current or former employee concerning the employee's FLSA exemption status determination or entitlement to minimum wage or overtime pay for work performed under the Act. The term *claim* is used generically in subpart G and includes complaints under the child labor provisions of the Act.

Claim period means the time during which the cause or basis of the claim occurred.

Claimant means any party who files an FLSA claim.

Customarily and regularly means a frequency which must be greater than occasional but which may be less than constant. Tasks or work performed customarily and regularly includes work normally and recurrently performed every workweek. It does not include isolated or one-time tasks.

Directly and closely related means work that is directly and closely related to the performance of exempt work which is also considered exempt work. The phrase *directly and closely related* means tasks that are related to exempt duties and that contribute to or facilitate performance of exempt work. *Directly and closely related* work may include typically nonexempt tasks that arise out of and are integral to exempt duties. Those nonexempt tasks must be performed by the exempt employee to perform his or her exempt work. Work *directly and closely related* to the performance of exempt duties may also include recordkeeping; maintaining various records pertaining to workload or employee performance; monitoring and adjusting machinery; taking notes; using the computer to create documents or presentations; opening the mail for the purpose of reading it and making decisions; and using a photocopier or fax machine. Work which both workers and supervisors are required to perform is considered to be closely related to the primary duty of the position (for example, physical training during tours of duty for firefighting and law enforcement personnel) and is exempt work. Work is not *directly and closely* related if the work is remotely related or completely unrelated to exempt duties. The following examples illustrate the type of work that is and is not normally considered as *directly and closely related* to exempt work:

(1) Work is closely related to exempt supervisory work when it contributes to the effective supervision of subordinate workers, or the smooth functioning of the unit supervised, or both. A supervisor who spot checks and examines the work of subordinates to determine whether they are performing their duties properly, and whether the product is satisfactory, is performing work which is directly and closely related to managerial and supervisory functions, so long as the checking is distinguishable from the work ordinarily performed by a nonexempt inspector.

(2) Depending upon the nature of an organization, a supervisor who sets up a machine may be engaged in exempt work. In some cases the setup work, or adjustment of the machine for a particular job, is typically performed by the same employees who operate the machine. In such cases, setup work is part of the production operation and is not exempt. In other cases, the setting up of the work is a highly skilled operation which the ordinary production worker typically does not perform. In large plants, non-supervisors may perform such work. However, particularly in small plants, such work may be a regular duty of the executive employee and is directly and closely related to the executive employee's responsibility for the subordinates' work performance and for the adequacy of the final product. In addition, performing setup work that requires special skills typically is not performed by production employees in the occupation, and does not approach the volume that would justify hiring a specially trained employee to perform. Such closely related work may include performing infrequently recurring or one-time tasks which are impractical to delegate, because they would disrupt normal operations or take longer to explain than to perform. Under such circumstances, it is exempt work.

(3) A management analyst may take extensive notes recording the flow of work and materials through an organization; the analyst may personally use a computer to type a report and create a proposed table of organization. Standing alone, or separated from the primary duty, such note-taking and typing would not be exempt. However, because this work is necessary for analyzing the data and making recommendations (which is exempt work), it is directly and closely related to exempt work.

(4) A traffic manager in charge of planning an organization's transportation function, including identifying the most economical and quickest routes for shipping material to and from the activity, contracting for common-carrier and other transportation facilities, negotiating with carriers for adjustments for damages to material, and making the necessary rearrangements resulting from delays, damages or irregularities in transit, is performing exempt work. If the employee also spends part of the day taking telephone orders for local deliveries, such order-taking is a routine function and is not directly and closely related to the exempt work.

(5) An example of work directly and closely related to exempt professional duties is a chemist performing nonexempt tasks such as cleaning a test tube in the middle of an original experiment, even though such tasks can be assigned to laboratory assistants.

(6) A teacher performs work directly and closely related to exempt duties when, while taking students on a field trip, the teacher drives a school van or monitors the students' behavior in a restaurant.

Educational establishment means a nursery school, an elementary or secondary school system, an institution of higher education, other educational institutions, and in certain circumstances, training facilities. The term *other educational establishment* includes special schools for mentally or physically disabled or gifted children, regardless of any classification of such schools as elementary, secondary, or higher.

Emergency means a temporary condition that poses a direct threat to human life or safety, serious damage to property, or serious disruption to the operations of an activity, as determined by the employing agency.

Employ means to engage a person in an activity that is for the benefit of an agency, including any hours of work that are suffered or permitted.

Employee means a person who is employed—

(1) As a civilian in an Executive agency, as defined in section 105 of title 5, United States Code;

(2) As a civilian in a military department, as defined in section 102 of title 5, United States Code;

(3) In a nonappropriated fund instrumentality of an Executive agency or a military department;

(4) In a unit of the judicial branch of the Government that has positions in the competitive service; or

(5) In the Government Printing Office.

Employer, as defined in section 3(d) of the Act, means any person acting directly or indirectly in the interest of an employer in relation to an employee and includes a public agency, but does not include any labor organization (other than when acting as an employer) or anyone acting in the capacity of officer or agent of such labor organization.

Executive employee means an employee who meets the executive exemption criteria in §551.205.

Exempt area means any foreign country, or any territory under the jurisdiction of the United States, other than the following locations:

(1) A State of the United States;

(2) The District of Columbia;

(3) Puerto Rico;

(4) The U.S. Virgin Islands;

(5) Outer Continental Shelf Lands as defined in the Outer Continental Shelf Lands Act (67 Stat. 462);

(6) American Samoa;

(7) Guam;

(8) Commonwealth of the Northern Mariana Islands;

(9) Midway Atoll;

(10) Wake Island;

(11) Johnston Island; and

(12) Palmyra.

Filed means a claim has been properly submitted by the claimant. The claimant must deliver the claim to the appropriate office within the agency or OPM, whichever is deciding the FLSA claim. The claim must be postmarked or date-stamped in order to establish the time of delivery.

FLSA exempt means not covered by the minimum wage and overtime provisions of the Act.

FLSA exemption status means an employee's designation as either FLSA exempt or FLSA nonexempt from the minimum wage and overtime provisions of the Act.

FLSA nonexempt means covered by the minimum wage and overtime provisions of the Act.

FLSA overtime pay means overtime pay under this part.

FLSA pay claim means a claim concerning an employee's entitlement to minimum wage or overtime pay for work performed under the Act.

Formulate, affect, interpret, or implement management policies or operating practices means perform work that involves management policies or operating practices which range from specific objectives and practices of a small field office to broad national goals expressed in statutes or Executive orders. Employees performing such work make policy decisions or participate indirectly through developing or recommending proposals that are acted on by others. The work of employees who significantly affect the execution of management policies involves obtaining compliance with such policies by other individuals or organizations, within or outside of the Federal Government, or making significant determinations furthering the operation of programs and accomplishment of program objectives. Administrative employees engaged in such work typically perform one or more phases of program management (that is, planning, developing, promoting, coordinating, controlling, or evaluating operating programs of the employing organization or of other organizations subject to regulation or other controls).

Hours of work means all time spent by an employee performing an activity for the benefit of an agency and under the control or direction of the agency.

Hours of work are creditable for the purpose of determining overtime pay under subpart D of this part. Section 551.401 of subpart D further explains this term. However, whether time is credited as hours of work is determined by considering many factors, such as the rules in subparts D and E of this part, provisions of law, Comptroller General decisions, OPM decisions and policy guidance, agency policy, negotiated agreements, the rules in part 550 of this chapter (for hours of work for travel), and the rules in part 410 of this chapter (for hours of work for training).

Management means performing activities such as interviewing, selecting, and training of employees; setting and adjusting their rates of pay and hours of work; directing the work of employees; maintaining production or financial records for use in supervision or control; appraising employees' productivity and efficiency for the purpose of recommending promotions or other changes in status; handling employee complaints and grievances; disciplining employees; planning the work; determining the techniques to be used; apportioning the work among the employees; determining the type of materials, supplies, machinery, equipment, or tools to be used or merchandise to be bought, stocked and sold; controlling the flow and distribution of materials or merchandise and supplies; providing for the safety and security of the employees or the property; planning and controlling the budget; and monitoring or implementing legal compliance measures.

Nonexempt area means any of the following locations:

(1) A State of the United States;

(2) The District of Columbia;

(3) Puerto Rico;

(4) The U.S. Virgin Islands;

(5) Outer Continental Shelf Lands as defined in the Outer Continental Shelf Lands Act (67 Stat. 462);

(6) American Samoa;

(7) Guam;

(8) Commonwealth of the Northern Mariana Islands;

(9) Midway Atoll;

(10) Wake Island;

(11) Johnston Island; and

(12) Palmyra.

Official position means the position to which the employee is officially assigned by means of a personnel action authorized by the agency.

Perform work in connection with an emergency means perform work that is directly related to resolving or coping with an emergency, or its immediate aftermath, as determined by the employing agency.

Preserve the claim period means establish the period of possible entitlement to back pay by filing a written claim. The date the agency or OPM receives the claim preserves the claim period and is the date that determines the period of possible entitlement to back pay.

Primary duty typically means the duty that constitutes the major part (over 50 percent) of an employee's work. A duty constituting less than 50 percent of an employee's work (alternative primary duty) may be credited as the primary duty for exemption purposes provided that duty:

(1) Constitutes a substantial, regular part of the work assigned and performed;

(2) Is the reason for the existence of the position; and

(3) Is clearly exempt work in terms of the basic nature of the work, the frequency with which the employee must exercise discretion and independent judgment as discussed in §551.206, and the significance of the decisions made.

Professional employee means an employee who meets the professional exemption criteria in §551.207.

Reckless disregard of the requirements of the Act means failure to make adequate inquiry into whether conduct is in compliance with the Act.

Recognized organizational unit means an established and defined organizational entity which has regularly assigned employees and for which a supervisor is responsible for planning and accomplishing a continuing workload. This distinguishes supervisors from leaders of temporary groups formed to perform assignments of limited duration.

(1) The term *recognized organizational unit* is intended to distinguish between a mere collection of employees assigned from time to time to a specific job or series of jobs and a unit with

permanent status and function. A recognized organizational unit must have a permanent status and a continuing function. For example, a large human resources department might have subdivisions for labor relations, pensions and other benefits, equal employment opportunity, and recruitment and placement, each of which has a permanent status and function.

(2) A recognized organizational unit may move from place to place. The mere fact that the employee works in more than one location does not invalidate the exemption if other factors show that the employee is actually in charge of a recognized organizational unit with a continuing function in the organization.

(3) Continuity of the same subordinates is not essential to the existence of a recognized organizational unit with a continuing function. An otherwise exempt employee will not lose the exemption merely because the employee draws and supervises workers from a pool or supervises a team of workers drawn from other recognized organizational units, if other factors are present that indicate the employee is in charge of a recognized organizational unit with a continuing function.

Statute of limitations means the time frame within which an FLSA pay claim must be filed, starting from the date the right accrued. All FLSA pay claims filed on or after June 30, 1994, are subject to a 2-year statute of limitations, except in cases of willful violation where the statute of limitations is 3 years.

Suffered or permitted work means any work performed by an employee for the benefit of an agency, whether requested or not, provided the employee's supervisor knows or has reason to believe that the work is being performed and has an opportunity to prevent the work from being performed.

Title 5 overtime pay, for the purpose of §551.211, means overtime pay under part 550 of this chapter.

Trainee means a person who does not meet the definition of "employee" in this section and who is assigned or attached to a Federal activity primarily for training. A person who attends a training program under the following conditions is considered a trainee and is not a Federal employee for purposes of the Act:

(1) The training, even though it includes actual operation of the facilities of the Federal activity, is similar to that given in a vocational school or other institution of learning;

(2) The training is for the benefit of the individual;

(3) The trainee does not displace regular employees, but is supervised by them;

(4) The Federal activity which provides the training derives no immediate advantage from the activities of the trainee; on occasion its operations may actually be impeded;

(5) The trainee is not necessarily entitled to a job with the Federal activity at the completion of the training period; and

(6) The agency and the trainee understand that the trainee is not entitled to the payment of wages from the agency for the time spent in training.

Two or more other employees means the equivalent of two or more full-time employees. For the purpose of this definition, an employee is equal to a full-time equivalent (FTE). For example, one full-time and two half-time employees are equivalent to two full-time employees.

Volunteer means a person who does not meet the definition of *employee* in this section and who volunteers or donates his or her service, the primary benefit of which accrues to the performer of the service or to someone other than the agency. Under such circumstances there is neither an expressed nor an implied compensation agreement. Services performed by such a volunteer include personal services that, if left unperformed, would not necessitate the assignment of an employee to perform them.

Willful violation means a violation in circumstances where the agency knew that its conduct was prohibited by the Act or showed reckless disregard of the requirements of the Act. All of the facts and circumstances surrounding the violation are taken into account in determining whether a violation was willful.

Workday means the period between the commencement of the principal activities that an employee is engaged to perform on a given day and the cessation of the principal activities for that day. The term is further explained in § 551.411.

Worktime, for the purpose of determining FLSA exemption status, means time spent actually performing work. This excludes periods of time during which an employee performs no work, such as standby time, sleep time, meal periods, and paid leave.

Worktime in a representative workweek means the average worktime over a period long enough to even out normal fluctuations in workloads and is representative of the job as a whole.

Workweek means a fixed and recurring period of 168 hours—seven consecutive 24-hour periods. It need not coincide with the calendar week but may begin on any day and at any hour of a day. For employees subject to part 610 of this chapter, the workweek must be the same as the administrative workweek defined in § 610.102 of this chapter.

Workweek basis means the unit of time used as the basis for applying overtime standards under the Act and, for employees under flexible or compressed work schedules, under 5 U.S.C. 6121(6) or (7). The Act takes a single workweek as its standard (except for employees engaged in fire protection or law enforcement activities under section 7(k) of the Act) and does not permit the averaging of hours over two or more weeks, except for employees engaged in fire protection or law enforcement activities under section 7(k) of the Act.

Subpart B—Exemptions and Exclusions

SOURCE: 72 FR 52765, Sept. 17, 2007, unless otherwise noted.

§ 551.201 Agency authority.

The employing agency must review and make a determination on each employee's exemption status.

§ 551.202 General principles.

In all exemption determinations, the agency must observe the following principles:

(a) Each employee is presumed to be FLSA nonexempt unless the employing agency correctly determines that the employee clearly meets the requirements of one or more of the exemptions of this subpart and such supplemental interpretations or instructions issued by OPM. The agency must designate an employee FLSA exempt when the agency correctly determines that the employee meets the requirements of one or more of the exemptions of this subpart and such supplemental interpretations or instructions issued by OPM.

(b) Exemption criteria must be narrowly construed to apply only to those employees who are clearly within the terms and spirit of the exemption.

(c) The burden of proof rests with the agency that asserts the exemption.

(d) An employee who clearly meets the criteria for exemption must be designated FLSA exempt. If there is a reasonable doubt as to whether an employee meets the criteria for exemption, the employee will be designated FLSA nonexempt.

(e) While established position descriptions and titles may assist in making initial FLSA exemption determinations, the designation of an employee as FLSA exempt or nonexempt must ultimately rest on the duties actually performed by the employee.

(f) Although separate criteria are provided for the exemption of executive, administrative, and professional employees, those categories are not mutually exclusive. Employees who perform a combination of exempt duties set forth in this regulation may also qualify for exemption. For example, an employee whose primary duty involves a combination of exempt administrative and exempt executive work may qualify for exemption, *i.e.*, work that is exempt under one section of this part will not defeat the exemption under any other section.

(g) Failure to meet the criteria for exemption under what might appear to be the most obvious criteria does not preclude exemption under another category. For example, an engineering technician who fails to meet the professional exemption criteria may be performing exempt administrative work, or an administrative officer who fails to meet the administrative criteria may be performing exempt executive work.

(h) Although it is normally feasible and more convenient to identify a single exemption category, this is not always appropriate. An exemption may be based on a combination of functions, no one of which constitutes the primary duty, or the employee's primary duty may involve two categories which are intermingled and difficult to segregate. This does not preclude designating an employee FLSA exempt, provided the work as a whole clearly meets the other exemption criteria. The agency is responsible for showing and documenting that the work as a whole clearly meets one or more of the exemption criteria.

§551.203 Salary-based nonexemption.

(a) An employee, including a supervisory employee, whose annual rate of basic pay is less than $23,660 is nonexempt, unless:

(1) The employee is subject to §551.211 (Effect of performing different work or duties for a temporary period of time on FLSA exemption status); or

(2) The employee is subject to §551.212 (Foreign exemption criteria); or

(3) The employee is a professional engaged in the practice of law or medicine as prescribed in paragraphs (c) and (d) of §551.208.

(b) For the purpose of this section, "rate of basic pay" means the rate of pay fixed by law or administrative action for the position held by an employee, including any applicable locality payment under 5 CFR part 531, subpart F, special rate supplement under 5 CFR part 530, subpart C, or similar payment or supplement under other legal authority, before any deductions and exclusive of additional pay of any other kind, such as premium payments, differentials, and allowances.

§551.204 Nonexemption of certain employees.

(a) Certain nonsupervisory white-collar employees are FLSA nonexempt (unless the employees are subject to §551.211 (Effect of performing different work or duties for a temporary period of time on FLSA exemption status) or §551.212 (Foreign exemption criteria)) because they do not fit any of the exemption categories. They include:

(1) Employees in equipment operating and protective occupations, and most clerical occupations;

(2) Employees performing technician work in positions properly classified below GS–9 (or the equivalent level in other white-collar pay systems) and many, but not all, of those positions properly classified at GS–9 or above (or the equivalent level in other white-collar pay systems); and

(3) Employees at any grade, or equivalent level, in occupations requiring highly specialized, technical skills and knowledge that can be acquired only through prolonged job training and experience, such as in the Air Traffic Control series, or in the Aircraft Operations series unless such employees are performing predominantly administrative functions rather than the technical work of the occupation.

(b) Nonsupervisory employees in the Federal Wage System or in other comparable wage systems are nonexempt, unless the employees are subject to §551.211 (Effect of performing different work or duties for a temporary period of time on FLSA exemption status) or §551.212 (Foreign exemption criteria).

§551.205 Executive exemption criteria.

(a) An *executive employee* is an employee whose primary duty is management (as defined in §551.104) of a Federal agency or any subdivision thereof (including the lowest recognized organizational unit with a continuing function) and who:

(1) *Customarily and regularly directs* the work of two or more other employees. However, an employee who merely assists the manager of a particular department and supervises two or more employees only in the actual manager's absence does not meet this requirement. In addition, hours worked by an employee cannot be credited more than once for different executives. This takes into consideration those organizations that use matrix management, *i.e.*, a system of "shared" leadership, where supervision cuts across product and service lines in terms of accessing activities and advising top management on business operations, but where the supervisor/leader does not have the operating authority

over all employees. Thus, a shared responsibility for the supervision of the same two employees in the same recognized organizational unit does not satisfy this requirement. However, a full-time employee who works 4 hours for one supervisor and 4 hours for a different supervisor will be credited as a half-time employee for both supervisors; and

(2) Has the authority to hire or fire other employees or whose suggestions and recommendations as to the hiring, firing, advancement, promotion, or any other change of status of other employees, are given particular weight.

(b) *Particular weight.* Criteria to determine whether an employee's suggestions and recommendations are given particular weight by higher-level management include, but are not limited to: whether it is part of the employee's job duties to make such suggestions and recommendations; the frequency with which such suggestions and recommendations are made or requested; and the frequency with which the employee's suggestions and recommendations are relied upon. Generally, an executive's suggestions and recommendations must pertain to employees whom the executive customarily and regularly directs. Particular weight does not include consideration of an occasional suggestion with regard to the change in status of a co-worker. An employee's suggestions and recommendations may still be deemed to have particular weight even if a higher level manager's recommendation has more importance and even if the employee does not have authority to make the ultimate decision as to the employee's change in status.

§ 551.206 Administrative exemption criteria.

An *administrative employee* is an employee whose primary duty is the performance of office or non-manual work directly related to the management or general business operations, as distinguished from production functions, of the employer or the employer's customers and whose primary duty includes the exercise of discretion and independent judgment with respect to matters of significance.

(a) In general, the exercise of discretion and independent judgment involves the comparison and the evaluation of possible courses of conduct, and acting or making a decision after the various possibilities have been considered. The term "matters of significance" refers to the level of importance or consequence of the work performed.

(b) The phrase *discretion and independent judgment* must be applied in light of all the facts involved in the particular employment situation in which the question arises. Factors to consider when determining whether an employee exercises discretion and independent judgment with respect to matters of significance include, but are not limited to, whether the employee:

(1) Has authority to formulate, affect, interpret, or implement management policies or operating practices;

(2) Carries out major assignments in conducting the operations of the organization;

(3) Performs work that affects the organization's operations to a substantial degree, even if the employee's assignments are related to operation of a particular segment of the organization;

(4) Has authority to commit the employer in matters that have significant financial impact;

(5) Has authority to waive or deviate from established policies and procedures without prior approval;

(6) Has authority to negotiate and bind the organization on significant matters;

(7) Provides consultation or expert advice to management;

(8) Is involved in planning long- or short-term organizational objectives;

(9) Investigates and resolves matters of significance on behalf of management; and

(10) Represents the organization in handling complaints, arbitrating disputes, or resolving grievances.

(c) The exercise of discretion and independent judgment implies that the employee has authority to make an independent choice, free from immediate direction or supervision. However, an employee can exercise discretion and independent judgment even if the employee's decisions or recommendations are reviewed at a higher level. Thus, the term *discretion and independent judgment* does not require that decisions made by an employee have a finality that goes with unlimited authority and a complete absence of review. The decisions made as a result of the exercise of discretion and independent judgment may consist of recommendations for action rather than the actual taking of action. The fact that an employee's decision may be subject to review and that upon occasion the decisions are revised or reversed after review does not mean that the employee is not exercising discretion and independent judgment.

(d) An organization's workload may make it necessary to employ a number of employees to perform the same or similar work. The fact that many employees perform identical work or work of the same relative importance does not mean that the work of each such employee does not involve the exercise of discretion and independent judgment with respect to matters of significance.

(e) The exercise of discretion and independent judgment must be more than the use of skill in applying well-established techniques, procedures, or specific standards described in manuals or other sources.

(f) The use of manuals, guidelines, or other established procedures containing or relating to highly technical, scientific, legal, financial, or other similarly complex matters that can be understood or interpreted only by those with advanced or specialized knowledge or skills does not preclude exemption. Such manuals and procedures provide guidance in addressing difficult or novel circumstances and thus use of such reference material would not affect an employee's exemption status. However, employees who simply apply well-established techniques or procedures described in manuals or other sources within closely prescribed limits to determine the correct response to an inquiry or set of circumstances will be nonexempt.

(g) An employee does not exercise discretion and independent judgment with respect to matters of significance merely because the employer will experience financial losses if the employee fails to perform the job properly. For example, a messenger who is entrusted with carrying large sums of money does not exercise discretion and independent judgment with respect to matters of significance even though serious consequences may flow from the employee's neglect. Similarly, an employee who operates very expensive equipment does not exercise discretion and independent judgment with respect to matters of significance merely because improper performance of the employee's duties may cause serious financial loss to the employer.

(h) Employees in certain occupations typically assist and support line managers and assume facets of the overall management function. Neither the location of the work nor the number of employees performing the same or similar work turns such work into a production function. For example, independent agencies or agency components often provide centralized human resources, information systems, procurement and acquisition, or financial management services as support services to other agencies or agency components. However, this does not change the inherent administrative nature of the work performed to line or production work. Similarly, employees who develop, interpret, and oversee agency or Governmentwide policy are performing management support functions. Some of these activities may be performed by employees who would otherwise qualify under another exemption. Depending upon the purpose of the work and the organizational context, work in certain occupations may be either exempt or nonexempt. For example, criminal investigators who perform work directly related to the internal management of the agency and typically would be expected to provide recommendations of great significance based on the analysis of investigative findings would likely be considered as performing a staff function. In contrast, the performance of investigative and inspectional work to confirm whether specific regulatory requirements have been met for an investigative/inspectional component of any agency would likely be considered as performing a line rather than a staff function.

(i) An employee who leads a team of other employees assigned to complete major projects (such as acquisitions; negotiating real estate transactions or collective bargaining agreements; designing and implementing productivity improvements; oversight, compliance, or program reviews; investigations) generally meets the duties requirements for the administrative exemption, even if the employee does not have direct supervisory responsibility over the other employees on the team. An example is a lead auditor who oversees an audit team in an auditing agency and who is assigned responsibility for leading a major audit requiring the use of substantial agency resources. This auditor is responsible for proposing the parameters of the audit and developing a plan of action and milestones to accomplish the audit. Included in the plan are the methodologies to be used, the staff and other resources required to conduct the audit, proposed staff member assignments, etc. When conducting the audit, the lead auditor makes on-site decisions and/or proposes major changes to managers on matters of significance in accomplishing the audit, including deviations from established policies and practices of the agency.

(j) An executive assistant or administrative assistant to a high level manager or senior executive generally meets the duties requirements for the administrative exemption if such employee, without specific instructions or prescribed procedures, has been delegated authority regarding matters of significance.

(k) Human resources employees who formulate, interpret or implement human resources management policies generally meet the duties requirements for the administrative exemption. In addition, when interviewing and screening functions are performed by the human resources employee who makes the hiring decision or makes recommendations for hiring from a pool of qualified applicants, such duties constitute exempt work, even though routine, because this work is directly and closely related to the employee's exempt functions.

(l) Management analysts who study the operations of an organization and propose changes in the organization, program analysts who study program operations and propose changes to the program, and other management advisors generally meet the duties requirements for the administrative exemption.

(m) Acquisition employees with authority to bind the organization to significant purchases generally meet the duties requirements for the administrative exemption even if they must consult with higher management officials when making a commitment.

(n) Ordinary inspection work generally does not meet the duties requirements for the administrative exemption. Inspectors normally perform specialized work along standardized lines involving well-established techniques and procedures which may have been catalogued and described in manuals or other sources. Such inspectors rely on techniques and skills acquired by special training or experience. They have some leeway in the performance of their work but only within closely prescribed limits.

§ 551.207 Professional exemption criteria.

To qualify for the professional exemption, an employee's primary duty must be the performance of work requiring knowledge of an advanced type in a field of science or learning customarily acquired by a prolonged course of specialized intellectual instruction or requiring invention, imagination, originality or talent in a recognized field of artistic or creative endeavor. Learned professionals, creative professionals, and computer employees are described in §§ 551.208, 551.209, and 551.210, respectively.

§ 551.208 Learned professionals.

(a) To qualify for the learned professional exemption, an employee's primary duty must be the performance of work requiring advanced knowledge in a field of science or learning customarily acquired by a prolonged course of specialized intellectual instruction. The work must include the following three elements:

(1) The employee must perform work requiring advanced knowledge. Work

requiring advanced knowledge is predominantly intellectual in character and includes work requiring the consistent exercise of discretion and judgment, as distinguished from performance of routine mental, manual, mechanical or physical work. An employee who performs work requiring advanced knowledge generally uses the advanced knowledge to analyze, interpret or make deductions from varying facts or circumstances. Advanced knowledge cannot be attained at the high school level;

(2) The advanced knowledge must be in a field of science or learning which includes the traditional professions of law, medicine, theology, accounting, actuarial computation, engineering, architecture, teaching, various types of physical, chemical and biological sciences, pharmacy, and other similar occupations that have a recognized professional status as distinguished from the mechanical arts or skilled trades where in some instances the knowledge is of a fairly advanced type, but is not in a field of science or learning; and

(3) The advanced knowledge must be customarily acquired by a prolonged course of specialized intellectual instruction which restricts the exemption to professions where specialized academic training is a standard prerequisite for entrance into the profession. The best prima facie evidence that an employee meets this requirement is possession of the appropriate academic degree. However, the word "customarily" means that the exemption is appropriate for employees in such professions who have substantially the same knowledge level and perform substantially the same work as the degreed employees, but who attained the advanced knowledge through a combination of work experience and intellectual instruction. For example, the learned professional exemption is appropriate in unusual cases where a lawyer has not gone to law school, or a chemist does not possess a degree in chemistry. However, the learned professional exemption is not applicable to occupations that customarily may be performed with only the general knowledge acquired by an academic degree in any field, with knowledge acquired through an apprenticeship, or with training in the performance of routine mental, manual, mechanical, or physical processes. The learned professional exemption also does not apply to occupations in which most employees have acquired their skill by experience rather than by advanced specialized intellectual instruction. The position of Engineering Technician is an example of such an occupation where the employee collects, observes, tests and records factual scientific data within the oversight of professional engineers, and performs work using knowledge acquired through on-the-job and classroom training rather than by acquiring the knowledge through prolonged academic study.

(b) *Expansion of professional exemption.* The areas in which the professional exemption may be applicable are expanding. As knowledge is developed, academic training is broadened and specialized degrees are offered in new and diverse fields, thus creating new specialists in particular fields of science or learning. When an advanced specialized degree has become a standard requirement for a particular occupation, that occupation may have acquired the characteristics of a learned profession. Accrediting and certifying organizations similar to those listed in this section also may be created in the future. Such organizations may develop similar, specialized curriculums and certification programs which, if a standard requirement for a particular occupation, may indicate that the occupation has acquired the characteristics of a learned profession.

(c) *Practice of law.* (1) This exemption applies to an employee in a professional legal position requiring admission to the bar and involved in preparing cases for trial and/or the trial of cases before a court or an administrative body or persons having quasi-judicial power; rendering legal advice and services; preparing interpretive and administrative orders, rules, or regulations; drafting, negotiating, or examining contracts or other legal documents; drafting, preparing formal comments, or otherwise making substantive recommendations with respect to proposed legislation; editing and preparing for publication statutes enacted by Congress and opinions or decisions of a court, commission, or board; and drafting and reviewing decisions for consideration and adoption by agency officials.

(2) Section 551.203 (Salary-based nonexemption) does not apply to the employees described in this section.

(d) *Practice of medicine.* (1) An employee who holds a valid license or certificate permitting the practice of medicine or any of its branches and is actually engaged in the practice of the profession is exempt. The exemption applies to physicians and other practitioners licensed and practicing in the field of medical science and healing or any of the medical specialties practiced by physicians or practitioners. The term "physicians" includes medical doctors, including general practitioners and specialists, osteopathic physicians (doctors of osteopathy), podiatrists, dentists (doctors of dental medicine), and optometrists (doctors of optometry or bachelors of science in optometry).

(2) An employee who holds the required academic degree for the general practice of medicine and is engaged in an internship or resident program pursuant to the practice of the profession is exempt. Employees engaged in internship or resident programs, whether or not licensed to practice prior to commencement of the program, qualify as exempt professionals if they enter such internship or resident programs after the earning of the appropriate degree required for the general practice of their profession.

(3) Section 551.203 (Salary-based nonexemption) does not apply to the employees described in this section.

(e) *Accounting.* Certified public accountants generally meet the duties requirements for the learned professional exemption. An employee performing similar professional work in a position with a positive educational requirement and requiring the application of accounting theories, concepts, principles, and standards may qualify as an exempt learned professional. However, accounting clerks and technicians and other employees who normally perform a great deal of routine work generally will not qualify as exempt professionals.

(f) *Engineering.* Engineers generally meet the duties requirements for the learned professional exemption. Professional engineering work typically involves the application of a knowledge of such engineering fundamentals as the strength and strain analysis of engineering materials and structures, the physical and chemical characteristics of engineering materials such as elastic limits, maximum unit stresses, coefficients of expansion, workability, hardness, tendency to fatigue, resistance to corrosion, engineering adaptability, and engineering methods of construction and processing. Exempt professional engineering work includes equivalent work performed in any of the specialized branches of engineering (e.g., electrical, mechanical, or materials engineering). On unusual occasions, engineering technicians performing work comparable to that performed by professional engineers on the basis of advanced knowledge may also be exempt. In such instances, the employee actually is performing the work of an occupation that generally requires a specialized academic degree and is performing substantially the same work as the degreed employee, but has gained the same advanced knowledge through a combination of work experience and intellectual instruction which has provided both theoretical and practical knowledge of the specialty, including knowledge of related disciplines and of new developments in the field.

(g) *Architecture.* Architects generally meet the duties requirements for the learned professional exemption. Professional architectural work typically requires knowledge of architectural principles, theories, concepts, methods, and techniques; a creative and artistic sense; and an understanding and skill to use pertinent aspects of the construction industry, as well as engineering and the physical sciences related to the design and construction of new, or the improvement of existing, buildings.

(h) *Teachers.* A teacher is any employee with a primary duty of teaching, tutoring, instructing or lecturing in the activity of imparting knowledge and who is employed and engaged in this activity as a teacher in an educational establishment by which the employee is employed.

(1) A teacher performs exempt work when serving, for example, as a regular academic teacher; teacher of kindergarten or nursery school pupils; teacher of gifted or disabled children; teacher of skilled and semi-skilled trades and occupations; teacher engaged in automobile driving instruction; aircraft flight instructor; home economics teacher; or vocal or instrumental music instructor. A faculty member who is engaged as a teacher but also spends a considerable amount of time in extracurricular activities such as coaching athletic teams or acting as a moderator or advisor in such areas as drama, speech, debate, or journalism is engaged in teaching. Such activities are a recognized part of an educational establishment's responsibility in contributing to the educational development of the student. An instructor in an institution of higher education or another educational establishment whose primary duty is teaching, tutoring, instructing, or lecturing in the activity of imparting knowledge is also an exempt teacher.

(2) The possession of an elementary or secondary teacher's certificate provides a clear means of identifying the individuals contemplated as being within the scope of the exemption for teaching professionals. Teachers who possess a teaching certificate qualify for the exemption regardless of the terminology (e.g., permanent, conditional, standard, provisional, temporary, emergency, or unlimited) used by appropriate certifying entities. However, a teacher's certificate is not generally necessary for post-secondary educational establishments.

(3) Exempt teachers do not include teachers of skilled and semi-skilled trade, craft, and laboring occupations when the paramount knowledge is the knowledge of and the ability to perform the trade, craft, or laboring occupation. Conversely, if the primary requirement of the post-secondary education instructor is the ability to instruct, as opposed to knowledge of and ability to perform a trade, craft, or laboring occupation, then the position may be exempt.

(4) Section 551.203 (Salary-based nonexemption) does not apply to the employees described in this section.

(i) *Medical technologists.* Registered or certified medical technologists who have successfully completed 3 academic years of pre-professional study in an accredited college or university, plus a 4th year of professional course work in a school of medical technology approved by the Council of Medical Education of the American Medical Association, generally meet the duties requirements for the learned professional exemption.

(j) *Nurses.* Registered nurses who are registered by the appropriate State examining board generally meet the duties requirements for the learned professional exemption. Licensed practical nurses and other similar health care employees, however, generally do not qualify as exempt learned professionals because possession of a specialized advanced academic degree is not a standard prerequisite for entry into such occupations.

(k) *Dental hygienists.* Dental hygienists who have successfully completed 4 academic years of pre-professional and professional study in an accredited college or university approved by the Commission on Accreditation of Dental and Dental Auxiliary Educational Programs of the American Dental Association generally meet the duties requirements for the learned professional exemption.

(l) *Physician assistants.* Physician assistants who have successfully completed 4 academic years of pre-professional and professional study, including graduation from a physician assistant program accredited by the Accreditation Review Commission on Education for the Physician Assistant, and who are certified by the National Commission on Certification of Physician Assistants, generally meet the duties requirements for the learned professional exemption.

(m) *Paralegals.* Paralegals and legal assistants generally do not qualify as exempt learned professionals because an advanced, specialized academic degree is not a standard prerequisite for entry into the field. Although many paralegals possess general 4-year advanced degrees, most specialized paralegal programs are 2-year associate degree programs from a community college or equivalent institution. However, the learned professional exemption is applicable to paralegals who possess advanced, specialized degrees in other professional fields and apply advanced knowledge in that field in the performance of their duties. In addition, a paralegal who fails to meet the professional exemption criteria may be performing exempt administrative work, e.g., overseeing a full range of support services for a large legal office.

§ 551.209 Creative professionals.

(a) To qualify for the creative professional exemption, an employee's primary duty must be the performance of work requiring invention, imagination, originality, or talent in a recognized field of artistic or creative endeavor as opposed to routine mental, manual, mechanical, or physical work. The work performed must be "in a recognized field of artistic or creative endeavor," including such fields as music, writing, acting, and the graphic arts. The exemption does not apply to work which can be produced by a person with general manual or intellectual ability and training. The requirement of "invention, imagination, originality, or talent" distinguishes the creative professions from work that primarily depends on intelligence, diligence, and accuracy. The duties of employees vary widely, and exemption as a creative professional depends on the extent of the invention, imagination, originality, or talent exercised by the employee. Determination of exempt creative professional status must be made on a case-by-case basis. This requirement generally is met by actors, musicians, composers, conductors, and soloists; painters who at most are given the subject matter of their painting; and writers who choose their own subjects and hand in a finished piece of work to their employers. This requirement generally is not met by a person who is employed as a retoucher of photographs, since such work is not properly described as creative in character.

(b) Federal employees engaged in the work of newspapers, magazines, television, or other media are not exempt creative professionals if they only collect, organize, and record information that is routine or already public, or if they do not contribute a unique interpretation or analysis to a news product. For example, employees who merely rewrite press releases or who write standard recounts of public information by gathering facts on routine community events are not exempt creative professionals. Employees also do not qualify as exempt creative professionals if their work product is subject to substantial control by the organization. However, when the work requires invention, imagination, originality, or talent, as opposed to work which depends primarily on intelligence, diligence, and accuracy, such employees may qualify as exempt creative professionals if their primary duty is performing on the air in radio, television or other electronic media; conducting investigative interviews; analyzing or interpreting public events; writing editorials, opinion columns, or other commentary; or acting as a narrator or commentator. Work that does not fully meet the creative professional exemption criteria does not preclude exemption under another exemption category. For example, public affairs work under control of the organization that does not meet the creative professional exemption may meet the administrative exemption.

§ 551.210 Computer employees.

(a) Computer systems analysts, computer programmers, software engineers, or other similarly skilled workers in the computer field are eligible for exemption as professionals under section 13(a)(1) of the Act and under section 13(a)(17) of the Act. Because job titles vary widely and change quickly in the computer industry, job titles are not determinative of the applicability of this exemption.

(b) The exemption in section 13(a)(1) of the Act applies to any computer employee whose annual remuneration exceeds the salary-based nonexemption prescribed in § 551.203. The exemption in section 13(a)(17) applies to any computer employee compensated on an hourly basis at a rate of basic pay (as defined in § 551.203(b)) not less than

$27.63 an hour. In addition, these exemptions apply only to computer employees whose primary duties consist of:

(1) The application of systems analysis techniques and procedures, including consulting with users, to determine hardware, software or system functional specifications;

(2) The design, development, documentation, analysis, creation, testing or modification of computer systems or programs, including prototypes, based on and related to user or system design specifications;

(3) The design, documentation, testing, creation or modification of computer programs related to machine operating systems; or

(4) A combination of the aforementioned duties, the performance of which requires the same level of skills.

(c) *Computer manufacture and repair.* The exemption for employees in computer occupations does not include employees engaged in the manufacture or repair of computer hardware and related equipment. Employees whose work is highly dependent upon, or facilitated by, the use of computers and computer software programs (e.g., engineers, drafters and others skilled in computer-aided design software), but who are not primarily engaged in computer systems analysis and programming or other similarly skilled computer-related occupations as identified in paragraph (b) of this section, are also not exempt computer professionals.

(d) *Executive and administrative computer employees.* Computer employees within the scope of this exemption, as well as those employees not within its scope, may also have executive and administrative duties which qualify the employees for exemption under this subpart. For example, systems analysts and computer programmers generally meet the duties requirements for the administrative exemption if their primary duty includes work such as planning, scheduling, and coordinating activities required to develop systems to solve complex business, scientific or engineering problems of the organization or the organization's customers. Similarly, a senior or lead computer programmer who manages the work of two or more other programmers in a customarily recognized organizational unit, and whose recommendations regarding the hiring, firing, advancement, promotion, or other change of status of the other programmers are given particular weight, generally meets the duties requirements for the executive exemption. Alternatively, a senior or lead computer programmer who leads a team of other employees assigned to complete a major project that is directly related to the management or general business operations of the employer or the employer's customers generally meets the duties requirements for the administrative exemption, even if the employee does not have direct supervisory responsibility over the other employees on the team.

§551.211 Effect of performing different work or duties for a temporary period of time on FLSA exemption status.

(a) *Applicability.* Performing different work or duties for a temporary period of time may affect an employee's exemption status.

(1) *When applicable.* This section applies only when an employee must perform work or duties that are not consistent with the employee's primary duties for an extended period, that is, for more than 30 consecutive calendar days—the "30-day test." The period of performing different work or duties may or may not involve a different geographic duty location. The exemption status of an employee temporarily performing different work or duties must be determined as described in this section.

(2) *When not applicable.* This section does not apply when an employee is detailed to an identical additional position as the employee's position or to a position at the same level with the same basic duties and exemption status as the employee's position.

(b) An agency generally may not change an employee's exemption status based on a snapshot of the employee's duties during a particular week, unless the week involves emergency work under paragraph (f) of this section. An agency must:

(1) Assess an employee's temporary work or duties over a reasonable period

of time (the 30-day test), compare them with the primary duties upon which the employee's exemption status is based, and determine the employee's exemption status as described in §§ 551.203 through 551.210; and

(2) Ensure that it does not avoid reassessing, and perhaps changing, an employee's exemption status by breaking up periods of temporary work or duties with periods of having the employee perform his or her regular work or duties. For example, an agency may not assign exempt employees to perform nonexempt work or duties for 29 consecutive calendar days, return them to their exempt duties for two or three days, then assign them again to perform nonexempt work for another 29 days.

(c) Aggregation of more than 30 nonconsecutive calendar days over an extended period does not meet the 30-day test and may not be used to change an employee's exemption status. For example, if an exempt employee performs nonexempt duties 4 days in one week, 2 days in the following week, and so on over a period of weeks or months, the days of nonexempt work may not be aggregated for the purpose of changing the employee's exemption status.

(d) *Effect on nonexempt employees.* (1) A nonexempt employee who must temporarily perform work or duties that are different from the employee's primary duties remains nonexempt for the entire period of temporary work or duties unless both of the following conditions are met:

(i) The period of temporary work or duties exceeds 30 consecutive calendar days; and

(ii) The employee's primary duties for the period of temporary work are exempt as defined in this part.

(2) If a nonexempt employee becomes exempt under the criteria in paragraph (d)(1) of this section:

(i) The employee must be considered exempt for the entire period of temporary work or duties; and

(ii) If the employee received FLSA overtime pay for work performed during the first 30 calendar days of the temporary work or duties, the agency must recalculate the employee's total pay retroactive to the beginning of that period because the employee is no longer entitled to the FLSA overtime pay received but may be owed title 5 overtime pay, or its equivalent.

(e) *Effect on exempt employees.* (1) An exempt employee who must temporarily perform work or duties that are different from the employee's primary duties remains exempt for the entire period of temporary work or duties unless both of the following conditions are met:

(i) The period of temporary work or duties exceeds 30 consecutive calendar days; and

(ii) The employee's primary duties for the period of temporary work are not exempt as defined in this part.

(2) If an exempt employee becomes nonexempt under the criteria in paragraph (e)(1) of this section:

(i) The employee must be considered nonexempt for the entire period of temporary work or duties; and

(ii) If the employee received title 5 overtime pay, or its equivalent, for work performed during the first 30 consecutive calendar days of the temporary work or duties, the agency must recalculate the employee's total pay retroactive to the beginning of that period because the employee may no longer be entitled to some or all of the title 5, or equivalent, overtime pay received but may be owed FLSA overtime pay.

(f) *Emergency situation.* Notwithstanding any other provision of this section, and regardless of an employee's grade or equivalent level, the agency may determine that an emergency situation exists that directly threatens human life or safety, serious damage to property, or serious disruption to the operations of an activity, and there is no recourse other than to assign qualified employees to temporarily perform work or duties in connection with the emergency. In such a designated emergency:

(1) *Nonexempt employee.* A nonexempt employee remains nonexempt whether the employee performs nonexempt work or exempt work during the emergency; and

(2) *Exempt employee.* The exemption status of an exempt employee must be determined on a workweek basis. The

exemption status determination of exempt employees will result in the employee either remaining exempt or becoming nonexempt for that workweek, as described in paragraphs (f)(2)(i) and (f)(2)(ii) of this section.

(i) *Remain exempt.* An exempt employee remains exempt for any workweek in which the employee's primary duties for the period of emergency work are exempt as defined in this part.

(ii) *Become nonexempt.* An exempt employee becomes nonexempt for any workweek in which the employee's primary duties for the period of emergency work are nonexempt as defined in this part.

§551.212 Foreign exemption criteria.

Foreign exemption means a provision of the Act under which the minimum wage, overtime, and child labor provisions of the Act do not apply to any employee who spends all hours of work in a given workweek in an exempt area.

(a) *Application.* When the foreign exemption applies, the minimum wage, overtime, and child labor provisions of the Act do not apply to any employee who spends all hours of work in a given workweek in an exempt area. When an employee meets one of the two criteria in paragraph (b) of this section, the foreign exemption applies until the employee spends any hours of work in any nonexempt area as defined in §551.104.

(b) *Foreign exemption applies.* If an employee meets one of the two following criteria, the employee is subject to the foreign exemption of the Act and the minimum wage, overtime, and child labor provisions of the Act do not apply:

(1) The employee is permanently stationed in an exempt area and spends all hours of work in a given workweek in one or more exempt areas; or

(2) The employee is not permanently stationed in an exempt area, but spends all hours of work in a given workweek in one or more exempt areas.

(c) *Foreign exemption does not apply.* For any given workweek, the minimum wage, overtime, and child labor provisions of the Act apply to an employee permanently stationed in an exempt area who spends any hours of work in any nonexempt area. For that workweek, the employee is not subject to the foreign exemption, and the agency must determine the exemption status of such an employee as described in paragraphs (c)(1) and (c)(2) of this section. The foreign exemption does not resume until the employee again meets one of the criteria in paragraph (b) of this section.

(1) *Same duties.* If the duties performed during that workweek are consistent with the primary duties of the employee's official position, the agency must designate the employee the same FLSA exemption status as if the employee were permanently stationed in any nonexempt area.

(2) *Different duties.* If the duties performed during that workweek are not consistent with the primary duties of the employee's official position:

(i) The agency must first designate the employee the same FLSA exemption status as the employee would have been designated based on the duties included in the employee's official position if the employee was permanently stationed in any nonexempt area; and

(ii) The agency must determine the employee's exemption status for that workweek by applying §551.211.

(d) *Resumption of foreign exemption.* When an employee returns to any exempt area from performing any hours of work in any nonexempt area, the employee is not subject to the foreign exemption until the employee meets one of the criteria in paragraph (b) of this section.

§551.213 Exemption of employees receiving availability pay.

The following employees are exempt from the hours of work and overtime pay provisions of the Act:

(a) A criminal investigator receiving availability pay under §550.181(a) of this chapter, as provided in 29 U.S.C. 213(a)(16));

(b) A pilot employed by U.S. Customs and Border Protection or its successor who is a law enforcement officer as defined in section 5541(3) of title 5, United States Code, and who receives availability pay under section 5545a(i) of title 5, United States Code.

§551.214 Statutory exclusion.

A customs officer who receives overtime pay under subsection (a) or premium pay under subsection (b) of 19 U.S.C. 267 and under 19 CFR 24.16 for time worked may not receive pay or other compensation for that work under any other provision of law.

§551.215 Fire protection activities and 7(k) coverage for FLSA pay and exemption determinations.

(a) The Office of Personnel Management may determine that the provisions of section 7(k) of the Act apply to certain categories of fire protection employees based on appropriate factors, such as the type of premium payments they receive (see §551.501(a)(1) and (5) and §551.541).

(b) *Fire protection activities.* Fire protection activities involve the performance of functions directly concerned with the response to and the control and extinguishment of fires; or performance of inspection of facilities and equipment for the primary purpose of reducing or eliminating fire hazards by trained firefighters eligible for reassignment to fire control and suppression or prevention duties; or provision of the primary (*i.e.*, the first called) rescue and ambulance service in connection with fire protection functions.

(c) *Engaged in fire protection activities.* (1) An employee (including a firefighter, paramedic, emergency medical technician, rescue worker, ambulance personnel, or hazardous materials worker) is considered engaged in fire protection activities for the purpose of determining possible application of section 7(k) of the Act as provided for in §551.501(a)(1) and (5) and §551.541 if the employee:

(i) Is trained in fire suppression, has authority and responsibility to engage in fire suppression, and is employed by an organization with fire suppression as a primary mission; and

(ii) Is engaged in the prevention, control, and extinguishment of fires or response to emergency situations where life, property, or the environment is at risk.

(2) Subject to the requirements of paragraph (c)(1) of this section, the following types of employees are engaged in fire protection activities for the purpose of determining possible application of section 7(k) of the Act:

(i) Employees in positions properly classified in the Fire Protection and Prevention series, including any qualified firefighter who is assigned to perform support functions (e.g., communications or dispatching functions, equipment maintenance or repair) or who is transferred to an administrative or supervisory position within the fire protection activity, except when such administrative or supervisory work exempts the employee under executive, administrative, and professional considerations;

(ii) Employees in positions properly classified in other series, such as Forestry Technician, for whom fire protection functions constitute substantially full-time assignments throughout the year, or for the duration of a specified fire season within the year;

(iii) Temporary employees hired solely to perform fire suppression work on an as-needed basis;

(iv) Members of rescue and ambulance crews with fire suppression training, authority, and responsibility, who are part of a fire suppression organization, as described in paragraph (c)(1)(i) of this section; and

(v) Any other employee in any workweek in which the employee performs fire control or suppression work for 80 percent or more of the total hours worked.

(d) *Not engaged in fire protection activities.* Examples of types of employees who are not engaged in fire protection activities for the purpose of applying section 7(k) of the Act (as provided for in §551.501(a)(1) and (5) and §551.541) include the following:

(1) Professional engineers, engineering technicians, and similar employees involved in fire protection research or in the design and development of fire protection and prevention equipment and materials;

(2) Employees who perform functions that support fire protection activities but who are *not* trained, qualified firefighters eligible for reassignment to fire control and suppression or prevention duties. Supporting functions (such as maintenance of fire apparatus, equipment, alarm systems, etc., or communications and dispatching work

or preparation of records and reports) are included when performed by firefighters but are *not* included when performed by mechanics, communications systems and radio operators, clerks, or other employees;

(3) Employees whose primary duties are *not* related to fire protection but who perform fire control or suppression work on an as needed basis, *provided* that the fire control or suppression work constitutes less than 80 percent of the employees' hours of work within any workweek; and

(4) Employees on rescue and ambulance crews who:

(i) Are not trained in fire suppression;

(ii) Do not have fire suppression authority and responsibility; or

(iii) Are employed by an organization, such as a hospital, that does not have fire suppression as a primary mission.

§551.216 Law enforcement activities and 7(k) coverage for FLSA pay and exemption determinations.

(a) The Office of Personnel Management may determine that the provisions of section 7(k) of the Act apply to certain categories of law enforcement employees based on appropriate factors, such as the type of premium payments they receive (see §§551.501(a)(1) and (5) and 551.541).

(b) *Law enforcement activities.* Law enforcement activities involve work directly and primarily concerned with:

(1) Patrol and control functions that include patrolling an area to enforce law and order and to protect the lives, property, and civil rights of individuals through the prevention and detection of criminal acts; responding to complaints, violations, accidents, and emergencies; investigating for clues at the scene of a crime, interviewing witnesses, and evaluating evidence to locate suspects; and apprehending and arresting persons suspected of, or wanted for, criminal violations under a statutorily prescribed arrest authority;

(2) Executing the orders of a Federal court, including serving civil writs and criminal warrants issued by Federal courts; tracing and arresting persons wanted by warrants; and seizing and disposing of property under court orders;

(3) Planning and conducting investigations relating to alleged or suspected violations of criminal laws, including the arrest of suspected or wanted persons under a statutorily prescribed arrest authority;

(4) Security functions in a correctional institution involving direct custody and safeguarding of inmates charged with or convicted of violations of criminal laws; or

(5) Rescue and ambulance functions that provide the primary (*i.e.*, the first called) service in connection with law enforcement activities described above.

(c) *Engaged in law enforcement activities.* The following employees are engaged in law enforcement activities for the purpose of determining possible application of section 7(k) of the Act as provided for in §551.501(a)(1) and (5) and §551.541:

(1) Employees in positions properly classified in the Police series, and employees in positions that would be otherwise classifiable in that series if covered by classification criteria of chapter 51 of title 5, U.S. Code;

(2) Employees whose primary duties involve patrol and control functions performed for the purpose of detecting and apprehending persons suspected of violating criminal laws;

(3) Employees in positions properly classified in the U.S. Marshal series;

(4) Employees in positions properly classified in the Criminal Investigating series, and other employees performing criminal investigation as their primary duty, except as provided for in §551.213 (Exemption of employees receiving availability pay);

(5) Employees in positions properly classified in the Correctional Officer series, Guard series, or other series, whose primary duty is to maintain custody of inmates of a correctional institution; and

(6) Employees on rescue and ambulance crews that provide the primary service in connection with law enforcement functions, provided that crew members have received intensive training in specialized rescue and first aid procedures applicable to law enforcement emergencies (e.g., gunshot wounds, riot and accident victims) and

the crew responds to actual or potential law enforcement emergencies on a regular and recurring basis.

(d) *Not engaged in law enforcement activities.* The following employees are not engaged in law enforcement activities for the purpose of pay under section 7(k) of the Act as provided for in §§ 551.501(a)(1) and (5) and 551.541:

(1) Employees whose primary duties concern the protection of Government property from hazards such as sabotage, espionage, theft, fire, or accidental or willful damage and in so doing, control the movement of persons and protect the lives and property of persons on Government property (e.g., guards or other employees performing similar functions);

(2) Employees who perform work concerned with the determination of the applicability of or compliance with laws and regulations when the duties primarily involve:

(i) Examining or inspecting products, premises, property, or papers of persons or firms to enforce or obtain compliance with laws and regulations (e.g., immigration and customs examining or inspecting; mine safety and health examining or inspecting; alcohol, tobacco and firearms examining or inspecting; plant protection and quarantine examining or inspecting); or

(ii) Planning and conducting investigations covering the character, practices, suitability or qualifications of persons or organizations seeking, claiming or receiving Federal benefits, permits, or employment (e.g., general investigations work);

(3) Employees who work within correctional institutions but who do not have direct custody and safeguarding of inmates as their primary duty; and

(4) Members of rescue or ambulance crews that provide those services in connection with law enforcement activities only in unusual situations (e.g., when the primary crews are unavailable or when an emergency situation requires more crews than can be provided by the primary service).

[72 FR 52765, Sept. 17, 2007, as amended at 80 FR 58121, Sept. 25, 2015]

§ 551.217 Exemption of Border Patrol agents.

A Border Patrol agent (as defined in 5 U.S.C. 5550(a)(2) and 5 CFR 550.1603) is exempt from the minimum wage and the hours of work and overtime pay provisions of the Act.

[80 FR 58121, Sept. 25, 2015]

Subpart C—Minimum Wage Provisions

BASIC PROVISION

§ 551.301 Minimum wage.

(a)(1) Except as provided in paragraph (a)(2) of this section and § 551.311, an agency shall pay each of its employees wages at rates not less than the minimum wage specified in section 6(a)(1) of the Act for all hours of work as defined in subpart D of this part.

(2) The minimum wage provisions of the Act do not apply to a criminal investigator receiving availability pay under § 550.181.

(b) An employee has been paid in compliance with the minimum wage provisions of this subpart if the employee's hourly regular rate of pay, as defined in § 551.511(a) of this part, for the workweek is equal to or in excess of the rate specified in section 6(a)(1) of the Act.

[45 FR 85664, Dec. 30, 1980, as amended at 59 FR 66154, Dec. 23, 1994]

SUBMINIMUM WAGE

§ 551.311 Subminimum wage.

An agency may, if it meets certain criteria published by the Office of Personnel Management, employ certain groups of less than fully productive employees (e.g., handicapped patient workers) at rates less than the minimum wage specified in section 6(a)(1) of the Act.

[45 FR 85664, Dec. 30, 1980]

Subpart D—Hours of Work

SOURCE: 45 FR 85664, Dec. 30, 1980, unless otherwise noted.

GENERAL PROVISIONS

§551.401 Basic principles.

(a) All time spent by an employee performing an activity for the benefit of an agency and under the control or direction of the agency is "hours of work." Such time includes:

(1) Time during which an employee is required to be on duty;

(2) Time during which an employee is suffered or permitted to work; and

(3) Waiting time or idle time which is under the control of an agency and which is for the benefit of an agency.

(b) For an employee, as defined in 5 U.S.C. 5541(2), hours in a paid nonwork status (e.g., paid leave, holidays, compensatory time off, or excused absences) are "hours of work" under this part.

(c) Hours in an unpaid nonwork status (e.g., leave without pay, furlough, absence without leave) are not "hours of work" under this part.

(d) Time that is considered hours of work under this part shall be used only to determine an employee's entitlement to minimum wages or overtime pay under the Act, and shall not be used to determine hours of work for pay administration under title 5, United States Code, or any other authority.

(e) Irregular or occasional overtime work performed by an employee on a day on which work was not scheduled for that employee or for which the employee is required to return to his or her place of employment is deemed at least 2 hours in duration for the purpose of determining whether the employee may be entitled to overtime pay under this part, either in money or compensatory time off.

(f) For the purpose of determining hours of work in excess of 8 hours in a day under this part, agencies shall credit hours of work under §410.402 of this chapter, part 532 of this chapter and 5 U.S.C. 5544, and part 550 of this chapter, as applicable.

(g) For the purpose of determining hours of work in excess of 40 hours in a week or in excess of another applicable overtime work standard under section 7(k) of the Fair Labor Standards Act, agencies shall credit hours of work under §410.402 of this chapter, part 532 of this chapter and 5 U.S.C. 5544, and part 550 of this chapter, as applicable, that will not be compensated as hours of work in excess of 8 hours in a day, as well as any additional hours of work under this part.

(h) For the purpose of determining overtime pay for work in excess of 40 hours in a workweek under this part, time spent in a travel status is hours of work as provided in §551.422 of this part and §550.112(g) of this chapter or 5 U.S.C. 5544, as applicable.

[45 FR 85664, Dec. 30, 1980, as amended at 52 FR 47687, Dec. 16, 1987, and 53 FR 27147, July 19, 1988; 56 FR 20343, May 3, 1991; 57 FR 59279, Dec. 15, 1992; 64 FR 69180, Dec. 10, 1999]

§551.402 Agency responsibility.

(a) An agency is responsible for exercising appropriate controls to assure that only that work for which it intends to make payment is performed.

(b) An agency shall keep complete and accurate records of all hours worked by its employees.

APPLICATION OF PRINCIPLES IN RELATION TO NORMAL WORKDAY

§551.411 Workday.

(a) For the purposes of this part, *workday* means the period between the commencement of the principal activities that an employee is engaged to perform on a given day, and the cessation of the principal activities for that day. All time spent by an employee in the performance of such activities is hours of work. The workday is not limited to a calendar day or any other 24-hour period.

(b) Any rest period authorized by an agency that does not exceed 20 minutes and that is within the workday shall be considered hours of work.

(c) *Bona fide* meal periods are not considered hours of work, except for on-duty meal periods for employees engaged in fire protection or law enforcement activities who receive compensation for overtime hours of work under 5 U.S.C. 5545(c)(1) or (2) or 5545b. However, for employees engaged in fire protection or law enforcement activities who have periods of duty of more than 24 hours, on-duty meal periods may be excluded from hours of work by agreement between the employer and the employee, except as provided in § 551.432(e) and (f).

[45 FR 85664, Dec. 30, 1980, as amended at 48 FR 36805, Aug. 15, 1983; 57 FR 59279, Dec. 15, 1992; 67 FR 15467, Apr. 2, 2002]

§ 551.412 Preparatory or concluding activities.

(a)(1) If an agency reasonably determines that a preparatory or concluding activity is closely related to an employee's principal activities, and is indispensable to the performance of the principal activities, and that the total time spent in that activity is more than 10 minutes per workday, the agency shall credit all of the time spent in that activity, including the 10 minutes, as hours of work.

(2) If the time spent in a preparatory or concluding activity is compensable as hours of work, the agency shall schedule the time period for the employee to perform that activity. An employee shall be credited with the actual time spent in that activity during the time period scheduled by the agency. In no case shall the time credited for the performance of an activity exceed the time scheduled by the agency. The employee shall be credited for the time spent performing preparatory or concluding activities in accordance with paragraph (b) of § 551.521 of this part.

(b) A preparatory or concluding activity that is not closely related to the performance of the principal activities is considered a preliminary or postliminary activity. Time spent in preliminary or postliminary activities is excluded from hours of work and is not compensable, even if it occurs between periods of activity that are compensable as hours of work.

[48 FR 36805, Aug. 15, 1983]

Application of Principles in Relation to Other Activities

§ 551.421 Regular working hours.

(a) Under the Act there is no requirement that a Federal employee have a regularly scheduled administrative workweek. However, under title 5 United States Code, and part 610 of this chapter, the head of an agency is required to establish work schedules for his or her employees. In determining what activities constitute hours of work under the Act, there is generally a distinction based on whether the activity is performed by an employee during regular working hours or outside regular working hours. For purposes of this part, "regular working hours" means the days and hours of an employee's regularly scheduled administrative workweek established under part 610 of this chapter.

(b) [Reserved]

[45 FR 85664, Dec. 30, 1980, as amended at 48 FR 36806, Aug. 15, 1983]

§ 551.422 Time spent traveling.

(a) Time spent traveling shall be considered hours of work if:

(1) An employee is required to travel during regular working hours;

(2) An employee is required to drive a vehicle or perform other work while traveling;

(3) An employee is required to travel as a passenger on a one-day assignment away from the official duty station; or

(4) An employee is required to travel as a passenger on an overnight assignment away from the official duty station during hours on nonworkdays that correspond to the employee's regular working hours.

(b) An employee who travels from home before the regular workday begins and returns home at the end of the workday is engaged in normal "home to work" travel; such travel is not hours of work. When an employee travels directly from home to a temporary duty location outside the limits of his or her official duty station, the time the employee would have spent in normal home to work travel shall be deducted from hours of work as specified in paragraphs (a)(2) and (a)(3) of this section.

(c) An employee who is offered one mode of transportation, and who is permitted to use an alternative mode of transportation, or an employee who travels at a time other than that selected by the agency, shall be credited with the lesser of:

(1) The actual travel time which is hours of work under this section; or

(2) The estimated travel time which would have been considered hours of work under this section had the employee used the mode of transportation

offered by the agency, or traveled at the time selected by the agency.

(d) Except as provided in paragraph (b) of this section, an agency may prescribe a mileage radius of not greater than 50 miles to determine whether an employee's travel is within or outside the limits of the employee's official duty station for determining entitlement to overtime pay for travel under this part. However, an agency's definition of an employee's official duty station for determining overtime pay for travel may not be smaller than the definition of "official station and post of duty" under the Federal Travel Regulation issued by the General Services Administration (41 CFR 300–3.1).

[45 FR 85664, Dec. 30, 1980, as amended at 59 FR 66635, Dec. 28, 1994; 72 FR 12036, Mar. 15, 2007]

§551.423 Time spent in training or attending a lecture, meeting, or conference.

(a) Time spent in training, whether or not it is under the purview of part 410 of this chapter, shall be administered as follows:

(1) Time spent in training during regular working hours shall be considered hours of work.

(2) Time spent in training outside regular working hours shall be considered hours of work if:

(i) The employee is directed to participate in the training by his or her employing agency; and

(ii) The purpose of the training is to improve the employee's performance of the duties and responsibilities of his or her current position.

(3) Time spent in apprenticeship or other entry level training, or internship or other career related work study training, or training under the Veterans Recruitment Act (5 CFR part 307) outside regular working hours shall not be considered hours of work, provided no productive work is performed during such periods, except as provided by §410.402(b) of this chapter and paragraphs (f) and (g) of §551.401.

(4) Time spent by an employee performing work for the agency during a period of training shall be considered hours of work.

(b) The following phrases contained in paragraph (a) of this section, are further clarified:

(1) *Directed to participate* means that the training is required by the agency and the employee's performance or continued retention in his or her current position will be adversely affected by nonenrollment in such training. The fact that an agency pays for all or part of the expenses of training does not create an entitlement to overtime hours of work unless participation in the training is directed by the agency.

(2) Training "to improve the employee's performance * * * of his or her current position" is distinguished from upward mobility training or developmental training to provide an employee the knowledge or skills needed for a subsequent position in the same career field.

(c) Time spent by an employee within an agency's allowance of preparatory time for attendance at training shall be considered hours of work if such preparatory time is:

(1) During an employee's regular working hours; or

(2) Outside the employee's regular working hours, and the purpose of the training meets the requirements of paragraph (a)(2) of this section.

(d) Time spent attending a lecture, meeting, or conference shall be considered hours of work if attendance is:

(1) During an employee's regular working hours; or

(2) Outside an employee's regular working hours, and

(i) The employee is directed by an agency to attend such an event; or

(ii) The employee performs work for the benefit of the agency during such attendance.

[45 FR 85664, Dec. 30, 1980, as amended at 64 FR 69180, Dec. 10, 1999; 70 FR 72068, Dec. 1, 2005]

§551.424 Time spent adjusting grievances or performing representational functions.

(a) Time spent by an employee adjusting his or her grievance (or any appealable action) with an agency during the time the employee is required to be on the agency's premises shall be considered hours of work.

(b) "Official time" granted an employee by an agency to perform representational functions during those hours when the employee is otherwise in a duty status shall be considered hours of work. This includes time spent by an employee performing such functions during regular working hours (including regularly scheduled overtime hours), or during a period of irregular, unscheduled overtime work, provided an event arises incident to representational functions that must be dealt with during the irregular, unscheduled overtime period.

§ 551.425 Time spent receiving medical attention.

(a) Time spent waiting for and receiving medical attention for illness or injury shall be considered hours of work if:

(1) The medical attention is required on a workday an employee reported for duty and subsequently became ill or was injured;

(2) The time spent receiving medical attention occurs during the employee's regular working hours; and

(3) The employee receives the medical attention on the agency's premises, or at the direction of the agency at a medical facility away from the agency's premises.

(b) Time spent taking a physical examination that is required for the employee's continued employment with the agency shall be considered hours of work.

§ 551.426 Time spent in charitable activities.

Time spent working for public or charitable purposes at an agency's request, or under an agency's direction or control, shall be considered hours of work. However, time spent voluntarily in such activities outside an employee's regular working hours is not hours of work.

SPECIAL SITUATIONS

§ 551.431 Time spent on standby duty or in an on-call status.

(a)(1) An employee is on duty, and time spent on standby duty is hours of work if, for work-related reasons, the employee is restricted by official order to a designated post of duty and is assigned to be in a state of readiness to perform work with limitations on the employee's activities so substantial that the employee cannot use the time effectively for his or her own purposes. A finding that an employee's activities are substantially limited may not be based on the fact that an employee is subject to restrictions necessary to ensure that the employee will be able to perform his or her duties and responsibilities, such as restrictions on alcohol consumption or use of certain medications.

(2) An employee is not considered restricted for "work-related reasons" if, for example, the employee remains at the post of duty voluntarily, or if the restriction is a natural result of geographic isolation or the fact that the employee resides on the agency's premises. For example, in the case of an employee assigned to work in a remote wildland area or on a ship, the fact that the employee has limited mobility when relieved from duty would not be a basis for finding that the employee is restricted for work-related reasons.

(b) An employee will be considered off duty and time spent in an on-call status shall not be considered hours of work if:

(1) The employee is allowed to leave a telephone number or to carry an electronic device for the purpose of being contacted, even though the employee is required to remain within a reasonable call-back radius; or

(2) The employee is allowed to make arrangements such that any work which may arise during the on-call period will be performed by another person.

[45 FR 85664, Dec. 30, 1980, as amended at 64 FR 69180, Dec. 10, 1999]

§ 551.432 Sleep time.

(a) Except as provided in paragraph (b) of this section, *bona fide* sleep time that fulfills the following conditions shall not be considered hours of work if:

(1) The work shift is *24 hours or more;*

(2) During such time there are adequate facilities such that an employee may usually enjoy an uninterrupted period of sleep; and

(3) There are at least 5 hours available for such time during the sleep period.

(b) For employees engaged in law enforcement or fire protection activities who receive annual premium pay under 5 U.S.C. 5545(c)(1) or (2), the requirements of paragraph (a) of this section apply, except that on-duty sleep time may be excluded from hours of work only if the work shift is more than 24 hours.

(c) The total amount of bona fide sleep and meal time that may be excluded from hours of work may not exceed 8 hours in a 24-hour period.

(d) If sleep time is interrupted by a call to duty, the time spent on duty is considered hours of work.

(e) On-duty sleep and meal time during regularly scheduled hours for which standby duty premium pay under 5 U.S.C. 5545(c)(1) is payable may not be excluded from hours of work.

(f) For firefighters compensated under 5 U.S.C. 5545b, on-duty sleep and meal time may not be excluded from hours of work.

[45 FR 85664, Dec. 30, 1980, as amended at 57 FR 59279, Dec. 15, 1992; 64 FR 69180, Dec. 10, 1999]

Subpart E—Overtime Pay Provisions

SOURCE: 45 FR 85665, Dec. 30, 1980, unless otherwise noted.

BASIC PROVISIONS

§551.501 Overtime pay.

(a) An agency shall compensate an employee who is not exempt under subpart B of this part for all hours of work in excess of 8 in a day or 40 in a workweek at a rate equal to one and one-half times the employee's hourly regular rate of pay, except that an employee shall not receive overtime compensation under this part—

(1) On the basis of periods of duty in excess of 8 hours in a day when the employee receives compensation for that duty under 5 U.S.C. 5545(c)(1) or (2) or 5545b;

(2) On the basis of hours of work in excess of 8 hours in a day that are not overtime hours of work under §410.402 of this chapter, part 532 of this chapter and 5 U.S.C. 5544, or part 550 of this chapter;

(3) On the basis of hours of work in excess of 8 hours in a day for an employee covered by 5 U.S.C. 5544 for any hours in a standby or on-call status or while sleeping or eating;

(4) On the basis of hours of work in excess of 8 hours in a day for an individual who is not an employee, as defined in 5 U.S.C. 5541(2), for purposes of 5 U.S.C. 5542, 5543, and 5544;

(5) On the basis of hours of work in excess of 40 hours in a workweek for an employee engaged in fire protection or law enforcement activities when the employee is receiving compensation under 5 U.S.C. 5545(c)(1) or (2) or 5545b, or is not an employee (as defined in 5 U.S.C. 5541(2)) for the purposes of 5 U.S.C. 5542, 5543, and 5544;

(6) For hours of work that are not "overtime hours," as defined in 5 U.S.C. 6121, for employees under flexible or compressed work schedules;

(7) For hours of work compensated by compensatory time off under §551.531 of this part; and

(8) For fractional hours of work, except as provided in §551.521 of this part.

(b) An employee's "workweek" is a fixed and recurring period of 168 hours—seven consecutive 24-hour periods. It need not coincide with the calendar week but may begin on any day and at any hour of a day. For employees subject to part 610 of this chapter, the workweek shall be the same as the administrative workweek defined in §610.102 of this chapter.

(c) In this subpart, "irregular or occasional overtime work" is overtime work that is not scheduled in advance of the employee's workweek.

(d) The maximum earnings limitations described in §§550.105, 550.106, and 550.107 of this chapter do not apply to overtime pay due the employee under this subpart.

[45 FR 85665, Dec. 30, 1980, as amended at 56 FR 11060, Mar. 15, 1991; 56 FR 20343, May 3, 1991; 57 FR 59279, Dec. 15, 1992; 63 FR 64594, Nov. 23, 1998; 64 FR 69180, Dec. 10, 1999]

OVERTIME PAY COMPUTATIONS

§551.511 Hourly regular rate of pay.

(a) An employee's "hourly regular rate" is computed by dividing the total remuneration paid to an employee in the workweek by the total number of hours of work in the workweek for which such compensation was paid.

(b) "Total remuneration" includes all remuneration for employment paid to, or on behalf of, an employee except:

(1) Payments as rewards for service the amount of which is not measured by or dependent on hours of work, production, or efficiency (e.g., a cash award for a suggestion made by an employee and adopted by an agency);

(2) Reimbursements for travel expenses, or other similar expenses, incurred by an employee in furtherance of an agency's interest, which are not related to hours of work;

(3) Payments made in recognition of services performed during a given period, if both the fact that payment is to be made and the amount of the payment are determined at the sole discretion of the agency (*i.e.*, discretionary cash awards or bonuses);

(4) Contributions by an agency to a fund for retirement, insurance, or similar benefits;

(5) Extra compensation provided by a premium rate paid for hours of work performed by an employee in excess of eight in a day, or in excess of the normal workweek applicable to the employee;

(6) Extra compensation provided by a premium rate paid for hours of work performed by an employee on a Sunday or a holiday where such premium rate is at least one and one-half times the employee's rate of pay for work performed in nonovertime hours on other days; or

(7) Extra compensation provided by a premium rate paid for hours of work performed by an employee outside his or her regular working hours, where such premium rate is at least one and one-half times the employee's rate of pay for work performed in nonovertime hours.

[45 FR 85665, Dec. 30, 1980, as amended at 52 FR 47688, Dec. 16, 1987, and 53 FR 27147, July 19, 1988; 56 FR 20343, May 3, 1991; 64 FR 69180, Dec. 10, 1999]

§ 551.512 Overtime pay entitlement.

(a) An employee's overtime entitlement under this subpart includes:

(1) The straight time rate of pay times all overtime hours worked; plus

(2) One-half times the employee's hourly regular rate of pay times all overtime hours worked.

(b) An employee's "straight time rate of pay" is equal to the employee's rate of pay for his or her position (exclusive of any premiums, differentials, or cash awards or bonuses) except for an employee who is authorized annual premium pay under § 550.141 or § 550.151 of this chapter. For an employee who is authorized annual premium pay, straight time rate of pay is equal to basic pay plus annual premium pay divided by the hours for which the basic pay plus annual premium pay are intended.

(c) An employee has been paid in compliance with the overtime pay provisions of this subpart only if the employee has received pay at a rate at least equal to the employee's straight time rate of pay for all nonovertime hours of work in the workweek.

[45 FR 85665, Dec. 30, 1980, as amended at 64 FR 69181, Dec. 10, 1999]

§ 551.513 Entitlement to other forms of pay.

Overtime pay under this subpart shall be paid in addition to all pay, other than overtime pay, to which the employee is entitled under title 5, United States Code, or any other authority. An employee entitled to overtime pay under this subpart and overtime pay under any authority outside of title 5, United States Code, shall be paid under whichever authority provides the greater overtime pay entitlement in the workweek.

[57 FR 59280, Dec. 15, 1992]

§ 551.514 Nondiscretionary bonuses.

(a) When an employee earns a nondiscretionary cash award or bonus (as opposed to discretionary cash awards or bonuses as described in § 551.511(b)(3)), the bonus must be taken into account in determining overtime pay for the period of time during which the bonus was earned. An agency may meet the overtime pay requirements for the bonus period by using one of the procedures described in paragraphs (b) and (c) of this section. The procedures in paragraphs (b)(1) and (b)(2) of this section calculate the additional overtime pay the employee is due. The procedures in paragraphs (b)(3), (c)(2), and (c)(3) of this section describe methods where the overtime pay requirements are met in the calculation or distribution of the bonus itself.

(b) *Individual computation methods*—(1) *Week-by-week recomputation method.* The agency may compute the additional overtime pay owed an employee by allocating the nondiscretionary bonus payable under the agency bonus plan to the weeks or hours during which it was earned and recomputing the employee's total remuneration, hourly regular rate, and overtime pay for each applicable workweek in the bonus period.

(2) *Bonus hourly rate method.* The agency may assume that an equal amount of the nondiscretionary bonus applies to each hour worked during the bonus period and derive a bonus hourly rate by dividing the employee's total bonus by the total number of hours worked by the employee during the bonus period. Then the agency may compute the employee's additional overtime pay by multiplying one-half of that bonus hourly rate by the total number of overtime hours worked by the employee during the bonus period.

(3) *Percentage bonus method.* An agency may establish a nondiscretionary bonus as a fixed percentage of total pay (*i.e.*, pre-bonus total remuneration, including straight time pay for any overtime hours, plus any half-rate overtime pay under §551.512(a)(2)) to be earned by the employee during a future period of service. This method may not be used to circumvent any bonus limitations that might otherwise apply. At the agency's discretion, the portion of the bonus attributable to the employee's half-rate overtime pay under §551.512(a)(2) may be excluded in applying bonus limitations, since it can be viewed as constituting additional FLSA overtime pay. (This method does not apply to nondiscretionary bonuses established as a percentage of a segment of pay, such as ratings-based cash awards under §451.104(g) of this chapter that are expressed as a percentage of basic pay, excluding locality adjustments. To meet overtime pay requirements for these types of bonuses, use one of the methods described in paragraphs (b)(1) or (b)(2) of this section.)

(c) *Group-based bonus distribution methods.* (1) For employees who have earned nondiscretionary group cash awards or bonuses, payment of a bonus under one of the methods of distribution described in paragraphs (c)(2) and (c)(3) of this section is considered to be in full compliance with the overtime pay requirements of this subpart. These methods may not be used to circumvent any bonus limitations that might otherwise apply.

(2) *Percentage method.* (i) Identify the amount of the group bonus under the agency's bonus plan and the period of time during which it was earned;

(ii) Establish the group bonus as a percentage of the total pay (*i.e.*, total remuneration before considering the group bonus, including straight time pay for any overtime hours, plus any half-rate overtime pay under §551.512(a)(2)) earned by employees in the group during the bonus period; and (iii) Multiply the percentage in paragraph (c)(2)(ii) of this section times each individual employee's total pay earned during the bonus period to determine each employee's share of the group bonus.

(3) *Boosted hour method.* (i) Identify the amount of the group bonus under the agency's bonus plan and the period of time during which it was earned;

(ii) Determine the total number of boosted hours for all employees under the group bonus plan by adding up the total number of hours of work by those employees (nonovertime and overtime hours) and increasing that sum by one-half of the total number of overtime hours;

(iii) Divide the amount of the group bonus by the total number of boosted hours for all employees under the group bonus plan to determine the amount of the bonus allocable to each hour; and (iv) Multiply this hourly bonus amount by the number of boosted hours credited to each individual employee in the bonus period to determine each employee's share of the group bonus.

[64 FR 69181, Dec. 10, 1999]

FRACTIONAL HOURS OF WORK

§ 551.521 Fractional hours of work.

(a) An employee shall be compensated for every minute of regular overtime work.

(b) A quarter of an hour shall be the largest fraction of an hour used for crediting irregular or occasional overtime work under this subpart. When irregular or occasional overtime work is performed in other than the full fraction, odd minutes shall be rounded up or rounded down to the nearest full fraction of an hour used to credit overtime work.

[48 FR 36806, Aug. 15, 1983]

COMPENSATORY TIME OFF

§ 551.531 Compensatory time off.

(a) At the request of an employee who is not exempt under subpart B of this part, the head of an agency (or designee) may grant compensatory time off from an employee's tour of duty instead of payment under § 551.501 for an equal amount of irregular or occasional overtime work.

(b) At the request of an employee, as defined in 5 U.S.C. 2105, the head of an agency may grant compensatory time off from an employee's basic work requirement under a flexible work schedule under 5 U.S.C. 6122 instead of payment under § 551.501 of this part for an equal amount of overtime work, whether or not irregular or occasional in nature.

(c) An agency may not require that an employee be compensated for overtime work under this subpart with an equivalent amount of compensatory time off from the employee's tour of duty. An employee may not directly or indirectly intimidate, threaten, or coerce, or attempt to intimidate, threaten, or coerce any other employee for the purpose of interfering with such employee's rights to request or not to request compensatory time off in lieu of payment for overtime hours.

(d) If compensatory time off earned under paragraph (a) or (b) of this section is not taken within 26 pay periods after the pay period during which it was earned or if the employee transfers or separates from an agency before using the compensatory time, the employee must be paid for overtime work at the dollar value prescribed in paragraph (g) of this section.

(e) Compensatory time off to an employee's credit as of May 14, 2007 must be used by the end of the pay period ending 3 years after May 14, 2007. If the earned compensatory time off is not taken by the end of the pay period ending 3 years after May 14, 2007, the employee must be paid for overtime work at the dollar value prescribed in paragraph (g) of this section.

(f) If an employee with unused compensatory time off under paragraphs (a), (b), or (e) of this section separates from Federal service or is placed in a leave without pay status under the following circumstances, the employee must be paid for overtime work at the overtime rate at the dollar value prescribed in paragraph (g) of this section:

(1) The employee is separated or placed in a leave without pay status to perform service in the uniformed services (as defined in 38 U.S.C. 4303 and § 353.102); or

(2) The employee is separated or placed in a leave without pay status because of an on-the-job injury with entitlement to injury compensation under 5 U.S.C. chapter 81.

(g) The dollar value of compensatory time off when it is liquidated is the amount of overtime pay the employee otherwise would have received for hours of the pay period during which compensatory time off was earned by performing overtime work.

[56 FR 20343, May 3, 1991, as amended at 62 FR 28307, May 23, 1997; 64 FR 69181, Dec. 10, 1999; 72 FR 12036, Mar. 15, 2007]

SPECIAL OVERTIME PAY PROVISIONS

§ 551.541 Employees engaged in fire protection activities or law enforcement activities.

(a) An employee engaged in fire protection activities or law enforcement activities (as described in §§ 551.215 and 551.216, respectively) who receives compensation for those activities under 5 U.S.C. 5545(c)(1) or (2) or 5545b, or does not meet the definition of "employee" in 5 U.S.C. 5541(2) for the purposes of 5 U.S.C. 5542, 5543, and 5544, is subject to section 7(k) of the Act and this section.

(See §551.501(a)(1) and (5)). Such an employee shall be paid at a rate equal to one and one-half times the employee's hourly regular rate of pay for those hours in a tour of duty which exceed the overtime standard for a work period specified in section 7(k) of the Act.

(b) The tour of duty of an employee covered by paragraph (a) of this section shall include all time the employee is on duty. Meal periods and sleep periods are included in the tour of duty except as otherwise provided in §§551.411(c) and 551.432(b).

(c) Each agency shall establish the "work period" to be used for application of section 7(k) of the Act. The work period shall be at least seven days and not more than 28 days.

(d) A firefighter subject to section 7(k) of the Act who is compensated under part 550, subpart M, of this chapter is deemed to be appropriately compensated under section 7(k) of the Act and this part if the requirements of §550.1304(a) of this chapter are satisfied. (See 5 U.S.C. 5545b(d)(2).)

[45 FR 85665, Dec. 30, 1980, as amended at 57 FR 59280, Dec. 15, 1992; 63 FR 64595, Nov. 23, 1998; 64 FR 69181, Dec. 10, 1999; 72 FR 52773, Sept. 17, 2007]

Subpart F—Child Labor

SOURCE: 62 FR 67251, Dec. 23, 1997, unless otherwise noted.

§551.601 Minimum age standards.

(a) *16-year minimum age.* The Act, in section 3(l), sets a general 16-year minimum age, which applies to all employment subject to its child labor provisions, with certain exceptions not applicable here.

(b) *18-year minimum age.* The Act, in section 3(l), also sets an 18-year minimum age with respect to employment in any occupation found and declared by the Secretary of Labor to be particularly hazardous for the employment of minors of such age or detrimental to their health or well-being.

(c) All work in fire suppression is deemed hazardous for the employment of individuals under 18 years of age. All work in fire protection and prevention is particularly hazardous for the employment of individuals between 16 and 18 years of age, except the following:

(1) Work in offices or in repair or maintenance shops without exposure to hazardous materials;

(2) Work in the construction, operation, repair, or maintenance of living and administrative quarters in firefighting camps without exposure to hazardous materials;

(3) Work in forest protection, such as clearing fire trails or roads, piling and burning slash, maintaining firefighting equipment, or acting as fire lookout or fire patrolman away from the actual logging operations, provided that this provision shall not apply to the felling or bucking of timber, the collecting or transporting of logs, the operation of power-driven machinery, the handling or use of explosives, and work on trestles;

(4) Work in the clean-up service outside of a structure after a fire has been declared by the fire official in charge to be under control; and

(5) Work assisting in the administration of first aid.

[62 FR 67251, Dec. 23, 1997, as amended at 72 FR 52773, Sept. 17, 2007]

§551.602 Responsibilities.

(a) *Agencies* must remain cognizant of and abide by regulations and orders published in part 570 of title 29, Code of Federal Regulations, by the Secretary of Labor regarding the employment of individuals under the age of 18 years. These regulations and orders govern the minimum age at which persons under the age of 18 years may be employed and the occupations in which they may be employed. Persons under the age of 18 years must not be employed in occupations or engage in work deemed hazardous by the Secretary of Labor.

(b) *OPM* will decide complaints concerning the employment of persons under the age of 18 years. Complaints must be filed following the procedures set forth in subpart G of this part.

Subpart G—FLSA Claims and Compliance

SOURCE: 72 FR 52774, Sept. 17, 2007, unless otherwise noted.

§ 551.701 Applicability.

(a) *Applicable.* This subpart applies to *FLSA exemption status determination claims,* FLSA pay claims for minimum wage or overtime pay for work performed under the Act, and complaints arising under the child labor provisions of the Act.

(b) *Not applicable.* This subpart does not apply to claims or complaints arising under the equal pay provisions of the Act. The equal pay provisions of the Act are administered by the Equal Employment Opportunity Commission.

§ 551.702 Time limits.

(a) *Claims.* A claimant may at any time file a complaint under the child labor provisions of the Act or an FLSA claim challenging the correctness of his or her FLSA exemption status determination. A claimant may also file an FLSA claim concerning his or her entitlement to minimum wage or overtime pay for work performed under the Act; however, time limits apply to FLSA pay claims. All FLSA pay claims filed on or after June 30, 1994, are subject to a 2-year statute of limitations (3 years for willful violations).

(b) *Statute of limitations.* An FLSA pay claim filed on or after June 30, 1994, is subject to the statute of limitations contained in the Portal-to-Portal Act of 1947, as amended (section 255a of title 29, United States Code), which imposes a 2-year statute of limitations, except in cases of a willful violation where the statute of limitations is 3 years. In deciding a claim, a determination must be made as to whether the cause or basis of the claim was the result of a willful violation on the part of the agency.

(c) *Preserving the claim period.* A claimant or a claimant's designated representative may preserve the claim period by submitting a written claim either to the agency employing the claimant during the claim period or to OPM. The date the agency or OPM receives the claim is the date that determines the period of possible entitlement to back pay. The claimant is responsible for proving when the claim was received by the agency or OPM and for retaining documentation to establish when the claim was received by the agency or OPM, such as by filing the claim using certified, return receipt mail, or by requesting that the agency or OPM provide written acknowledgment of receipt of the claim. If a claim for back pay is established, the claimant will be entitled to pay for a period of up to 2 years (3 years for a willful violation) back from the date the claim was received.

§ 551.703 Avenues of review.

(a) *Negotiated grievance procedure (NGP) as exclusive administrative remedy.* If at any time during the claim period, a claimant was a member of a bargaining unit covered by a collective bargaining agreement that did not specifically exclude matters under the Act from the scope of the NGP, the claimant must use that NGP as the exclusive administrative remedy for all claims under the Act. There is no right to further administrative review by the agency or by OPM. The remaining sections in this subpart (that is, §§ 551.704 through 551.710) do not apply to such employees.

(b) *Non-NGP administrative review by agency or OPM.* A claimant may file a claim with the agency employing the claimant during the claim period or with OPM, but not both simultaneously, regarding matters arising under the Act if, during the entire claim period, the claimant:

(1) Was not a member of a bargaining unit, or

(2) Was a member of a bargaining unit not covered by a collective bargaining agreement, or

(3) Was a member of a bargaining unit covered by a collective bargaining agreement that specifically excluded matters under the Act from the scope of the NGP.

(c) *Judicial review.* Nothing in this subpart limits the right of a claimant to bring an action in an appropriate United States court. Filing a claim with an agency or with OPM does not satisfy the statute of limitations governing FLSA claims filed in court. OPM will not decide an FLSA claim that is in litigation.

§ 551.704 Claimant's representative.

A claimant may designate a representative to assist in preparing or presenting a claim. The claimant must designate the representative in writing. A representative may not participate in OPM interviews unless specifically requested to do so by OPM. An agency may disallow a claimant's representative who is a Federal employee in any of the following circumstances:

(a) When the individual's activities as a representative would cause a conflict of interest or position;

(b) When the designated representative cannot be released from his or her official duties because of the priority needs of the Government; or

(c) When the release of the designated representative would give rise to unreasonable costs to the Government.

§551.705 Filing an FLSA claim.

(a) *Filing an FLSA claim.* A claimant may file an FLSA claim with either the agency employing the claimant during the claim period or with OPM, but a claimant cannot pursue the same claim with both at the same time. OPM encourages a claimant to obtain a decision on the claim from the agency before filing the claim with OPM. However, this is a matter of personal discretion and a claimant is not required to do this; a claimant may use either avenue. A claimant who receives an unfavorable decision on a claim from the agency may still file the claim with OPM. However, a claimant may not file the claim with the agency after receiving an unfavorable decision from OPM. An OPM decision on a claim is final and is not subject to further administrative review.

(b) *FLSA claim filed with agency.* An FLSA claim filed with an agency should be made according to appropriate agency procedures. At the request of the claimant, the agency may forward the claim to OPM on the claimant's behalf. The claimant is responsible for ensuring that OPM receives all the information requested in paragraph (c) of this section.

(c) *FLSA claim filed with OPM.* An FLSA claim filed with OPM must be made in writing and must be signed by the claimant or the claimant's representative. Relevant information may be submitted to OPM at any time following the initial submission of a claim to OPM and prior to OPM's decision on the claim. The claim must include the following:

(1) The identity of the claimant (see §551.706(a)(2) regarding requesting confidentiality) and any designated representative, the agency employing the claimant during the claim period, the position (job title, series, and grade, or equivalent level) occupied by the claimant during the claim period, and the current mailing address, commercial telephone number, and facsimile machine number, if available, of the claimant and any designated representative;

(2) A description of the nature of the claim and the specific issues or incidents giving rise to the claim, including the time period covered by the claim;

(3) A description of actions taken by the claimant to resolve the claim within the agency and the results of any actions taken;

(4) A copy of any relevant decision or written response by the agency;

(5) Evidence available to the claimant or the claimant's designated representative which supports the claim, including the identity, commercial telephone number, and location of other individuals who may be able to provide information relating to the claim;

(6) The remedy sought by the claimant;

(7) Evidence, if available, that the claim period was preserved in accordance with §551.702. The date the claim is received by the agency or OPM becomes the date on which the claim period is preserved;

(8) A statement from the claimant that he or she was or was not a member of a collective bargaining unit at any time during the claim period;

(9) If the claimant was a member of a bargaining unit, a statement from the claimant that he or she was or was not covered by a negotiated grievance procedure at any time during the claim period, and if covered, whether that procedure specifically excluded the claim from the scope of the negotiated grievance procedure;

(10) A statement from the claimant that he or she has or has not filed an action in an appropriate United States court; and

(11) Any other information that the claimant believes OPM should consider.

§ 551.706 Responsibilities.

(a) *Claimant*—(1) *Providing information to OPM.* For all FLSA claims, the claimant or claimant's designated representative must provide any additional information requested by OPM within 15 workdays after the date of the request, unless the claimant or the claimant's representative requests additional time and OPM grants a longer period of time in which to provide the requested information. The disclosure of information by a claimant is voluntary. However, OPM may be unable to render a decision on a claim without the information requested. In such a case, the claim will be cancelled without further action being taken by OPM. In the case of an FLSA pay claim, it is the claimant's responsibility to provide evidence that the claim period was preserved in accordance with § 551.702 and of the liability of the agency and the claimant's right to payment.

(2) *Requesting confidentiality.* If the claimant wishes the claim to be treated confidentially, the claim must specifically request that the identity of the claimant not be revealed to the agency. Witnesses or other sources may also request confidentiality. OPM will make every effort to conduct its investigation in a way to maintain confidentiality. If OPM is unable to obtain sufficient information to render a decision and preserve the requested confidentiality, OPM will notify the claimant that the claim will be cancelled with no further action by OPM unless the claimant voluntarily provides written authorization for his or her name to be revealed.

(b) *Agency.* (1) In *FLSA exemption status determination claims,* the burden of proof rests with the agency that asserts the FLSA exemption.

(2) The agency must provide the claimant with a written acknowledgment of the date the claim was received.

(3) Upon a claimant's request, and subject to any Privacy Act requirements, an agency must provide a claimant with information relevant to the claim.

(4) The agency must provide any information requested by OPM within 15 workdays after the date of the request, unless the agency requests additional time and OPM grants a longer period of time in which to provide the requested information.

§ 551.707 Withdrawal or cancellation of an FLSA claim.

(a) *Withdrawal.* OPM may grant a request from the claimant or claimant's representative to withdraw an FLSA claim at any time before OPM issues its decision. The claimant or the claimant's representative must submit the request in writing to OPM.

(b) *Cancellation.* OPM may, at its discretion, cancel an FLSA claim if the claimant or the claimant's representative fails to provide requested information within 15 workdays after the date of the request, unless the claimant or the claimant's representative requests additional time and OPM grants a longer period of time in which to provide the requested information. OPM may, at its discretion, reconsider a cancelled claim on a showing that circumstances beyond the claimant's control prevented pursuit of the claim.

§ 551.708 Finality and effect of OPM FLSA claim decision.

(a) OPM will send an FLSA claim decision to the claimant or the claimant's representative and the agency. An FLSA claim decision made by OPM is final. There is no further right of administrative appeal. However, at its discretion, OPM may reconsider its FLSA claim decision when material information was not considered or there was a material error of law, regulation, or fact in the original decision. The request must be submitted in writing and received by OPM within 45 calendar days after the date of the decision. At its unreviewable discretion, OPM may waive the time limit.

(b) A decision by OPM under the Act is binding on all administrative, certifying, payroll, disbursing, and accounting officials of agencies for which OPM administers the Act.

(c)(1) Upon receipt of a decision, the agency employing the claimant during the claim period must take all necessary steps to comply with the decision, including adherence to compliance instructions provided with the decision. All compliance actions must be completed within the time specified in the decision, unless an extension of time is requested by the agency and granted by OPM.

(2) The agency should identify all similarly situated current and former employees to ensure that they are treated in a manner consistent with the decision on FLSA coverage, informing them in writing of their right to file an FLSA claim with the agency or OPM.

§551.709 Availability of information.

(a) Except when the claimant has requested confidentiality, the agency and the claimant must provide to each other a copy of all information submitted with respect to the claim.

(b) When a claimant has not requested confidentiality, OPM will disclose to the parties concerned the information contained in an FLSA claim file. When a claimant has requested confidentiality, OPM will delete any information identifying the claimant before disclosing the information in an FLSA claim file to the parties concerned. For the purposes of this subpart, "the parties concerned" means the claimant, any representative designated in writing, and any representative of the agency or OPM involved in the proceeding.

(c) Except when the claimant has requested confidentiality or the disclosure would constitute a clearly unwarranted invasion of personal privacy, OPM, upon a request which identifies the individual from whose file the information is sought, will disclose the following information from a claim file to a member of the public:

(1) Confirmation of the name of the individual from whose file the information is sought and the names of the other parties concerned;

(2) The remedy sought;

(3) The status of the claim;

(4) The decision on the claim; and

(5) With the consent of the parties concerned, other reasonably identified information from the file.

§551.710 Where to file an FLSA claim with OPM.

An FLSA claim must be filed with the OPM Classification Appeals and FLSA Program, 1900 E Street, NW., Washington, DC 20415–0001.

PART 553—REEMPLOYMENT OF CIVILIAN RETIREES TO MEET EXCEPTIONAL EMPLOYMENT NEEDS

Subpart A—General Provisions

Sec.

Subpart B—Special Provisions for Reemployment Without Penalty To Meet Exceptional Recruiting or Retention Needs

AUTHORITY: 5 U.S.C. 8344, 8468, Sec. 651, Pub. L. 106–65 (113 STAT. 664).

SOURCE: 56 FR 6206, Feb. 14, 1991, unless otherwise noted.

Subpart A—General Provisions

§553.101 Applicability.

This part applies to employment of civilian annuitants who would be subject to termination of annuity or annuity offset under 5 U.S.C. 8344 or 5 U.S.C. 8468. Agencies may request exceptions as provided in subpart B of this part from the reemployed annuitant provisions of 5 U.S.C. 8344 (for Civil Service Retirement System annuitants) or 8468 (for Federal Employees' Retirement System annuitants), as appropriate.

[65 FR 19644, Apr. 12, 2000]

§553.102 Definitions.

(a) *Agency*, as used in this part, means an executive agency as defined in 5 U.S.C. 105.

(b) *Annuitant*, as used in this part, refers to a current or former civilian employee who is receiving, or meets the legal requirements and is applying or has announced intention to apply for, an annuity under subchapter III of chapter 83 or chapter 84 of title 5, United States Code, based on his or her service.

(c) Retiree, as used in this part refers to an annuitant as defined in paragraph (b) of this section.

[56 FR 6206, Feb. 14, 1991, as amended at 65 FR 19644, Apr. 12, 2000]

§ 553.103 General policy.

(a) *Agency discretion and responsibility.* The decision to request an exception, or to grant an exception under delegated authority, for any individual under any of the provisions of this part will be at the discretion of the employing agency. A determination made in connection with one position does not require a like determination in connection with any other position. In deciding whether to request an exception or grant an exception under delegated authority, each agency is expected to weigh fiscal responsibility and employee equity and should consider such factors as availability of funds as well as the criteria set out in this part.

(b) *Application of exceptions.* An exception to the salary offset provisions of 5 U.S.C. 8344 or 8468 authorized by OPM or an agency under this part applies only to the particular individual for whom it was authorized and only while that individual continues to serve in the same or a successor position. The exception terminates upon the individual's assignment to a different position unless a new exception is authorized under the provisions of this part.

[56 FR 6206, Feb. 14, 1991, as amended at 65 FR 19644, Apr. 12, 2000]

Subpart B—Special Provisions for Reemployment Without Penalty To Meet Exceptional Recruiting or Retention Needs

§ 553.201 Requesting OPM approval for reemployment without reduction or termination of annuity in individual cases.

(a) *Request by agency head.* The head of an agency may request OPM to approve individual exceptions on a case-by-case basis to meet temporary hiring needs based on an emergency or other unusual circumstances or when the agency has encountered exceptional difficulty in recruiting or retaining a qualified candidate for a particular position. Authority to submit such a request may not be redelegated to an official below the agency's headquarters level.

(b) *Requirements for all requests.* (1) Each request must identify the individual for whom the exception is requested, the appointing authority to be used, and the position to which he or she will be appointed.

(2) The request must be submitted in accordance with the criteria set out in paragraphs (c), (d), (e), or (f) of this section.

(3) Unless the request is submitted in accordance with paragraph (e) of this section, the individual must be off the agency's rolls before submission.

(c) *Requests based on an emergency hiring need.* An agency may request reemployment without penalty for an individual whose services are needed on a temporary basis to respond to an emergency involving a direct threat to life or property. Requests submitted on that basis must meet the following criteria:

(1) *Nature of emergency.* Describe the military threat, natural disaster, or other unforeseen occurrence, the date it occurred, and the expected duration of the emergency response effort.

(2) *Need for the individual's services.* The agency must show either that the individual is uniquely qualified for the emergency response work to be done or that the number of positions to be filled and/or urgency of response justifies making the particular appointment without further delay. OPM will not approve reemployment without penalty under 5 U.S.C. 8344, or 8468 solely to meet normal seasonal workload fluctuations.

(d) *Requests based on severe recruiting difficulty.* Generally, requests for exception will be based on exceptional difficulty in recruiting a qualified candidate for a particular position. Requests submitted on this basis must include a description of the length, breadth, and results of the agency's recruiting efforts for the position and any other factors demonstrating that a legitimate recruiting need cannot be met without the requested waiver. These factors may include, but are not limited to, unusual qualification requirements or working conditions, possibility of job reengineering or contracting, or a need to fill the position without further delay.

(e) *Exceptions based on need to retain a particular individual.* In very rare cases, an exception may be appropriate when an agency needs to retain the services of a particular individual who is uniquely qualified for an ongoing project. Requests submitted on this basis must meet the following criteria:

(1) *Critical nature of project.* The agency must describe the importance of the project to the agency's mission, the potential costs of project failure or delay, legislative or Presidential deadlines, if any, and any other factors demonstrating that the project is unusually critical. Exceptions will not be approved under this paragraph merely to avoid delay in scheduled completion of ongoing work.

(2) *Candidate's unique qualifications.* The agency must describe the knowledges, skills, and abilities possessed by the individual that are essential for successful completion of the project and that could not be acquired by another appointee within a reasonable time.

(3) *Need for retention.* The agency must show good cause to believe that the employee will retire (or, in the case of an individual currently reemployed without an exception, will resign from that position) and that the agency will lose his or her services if the exception is not granted.

(4) *Other staffing options.* While an agency in this situation is not required to conduct outside recruiting, the request for exception must address why the work could not be assigned to other employees involved with the same project.

(f) *Requests based on other unusual circumstances.* An agency may request reemployment without penalty for an individual whose services are needed on a temporary basis due to other unusual circumstances. Agencies must provide justification describing the unusual circumstances.

(g) *Length of exceptions.* OPM may specify a time limit for reemployment without penalty of any individual approved under this subpart. If the agency wishes to continue the exception for an individual beyond the specified time, the request for renewal must demonstrate that the conditions justifying the initial exception still exist.

[56 FR 6206, Feb. 14, 1991, as amended at 57 FR 12406, Apr. 10, 1992; 65 FR 19644, Apr. 12, 2000; 72 FR 53412, Sept. 19, 2007]

§ 553.202 Request for delegation of authority to approve reemployment without reduction or termination of annuity in emergencies or other unusual circumstances.

(a) *Request by agency head.* The head of an agency may request OPM to delegate to the agency authority to approve individual exceptions on a case-by-case basis in specific circumstances. Authority to submit such a request may not be redelegated to an official below the agency's headquarters level (or, in the case of the Department of Defense, to an official below the headquarters level of the military department or Defense agency).

(b) *Content of request.* The request for delegation must include:

(1) Description of the situations for which authority is requested. The situation must result from emergencies posing immediate and direct threat to life or property or from other unusual circumstances.

(2) Identification of the occupations, grades, and locations of positions that might be filled under the delegated authority.

(3) Statement of the expected duration of the reemployment to be approved under the requested authority.

(c) *Delegation agreement.* OPM will set out the conditions for use of each authority that it delegates under the provisions of this section in a delegation agreement. The agreement will remain in effect without time limit unless OPM specifies a termination date in the agreement, or unless OPM withdraws the delegated authority upon finding that the circumstances justifying the delegation have changed substantially or that the agency has failed to manage the authority in accordance with the law, the regulations, and the agreement itself.

[56 FR 6206, Feb. 14, 1991, as amended at 57 FR 12406, Apr. 10, 1992; 72 FR 53412, Sept. 19, 2007]

§ 553.203 Status of individuals serving without reduction.

Annuitants reemployed with full salary and annuity under an exception granted in accordance with this part are not considered employees for purposes of subchapter III of chapter 83 or chapter 84 of title 5, United States Code. They may not elect to have retirement contributions withheld from their pay; they may not use any employment for which an exception is granted as a basis for a supplemental or recomputed annuity; and they may not participate in the Thrift Savings Plan.

[72 FR 53413, Sept. 19, 2007]

PART 572—TRAVEL AND TRANSPORTATION EXPENSES; NEW APPOINTEES AND INTERVIEWS

AUTHORITY: 5 U.S.C. 5706b and 5723.

SOURCE: 56 FR 6204, Feb. 14, 1991, unless otherwise noted.

§ 572.101 Agency authority.

(a) An agency may determine which positions qualify for the payment of a new appointee's travel expenses to the first post of duty. Payment of travel and transportation expenses will be in accordance with the Federal Travel Regulation (FTR) (41 CFR chapters 301–304).

(b) An agency may determine which interviewees are eligible for payment of pre-employment interview travel expenses. Payment of these travel expenses will be in accordance with the FTR.

[56 FR 28307, June 20, 1991]

§ 572.102 Agency discretion.

Payment of travel expenses for any individual candidate or appointee will be at the discretion of the employing agency. A decision by one agency that payment is appropriate for a particular position does not require a like determination by any other agency filling similar positions. A decision made in connection with one specific vacancy does not require a like decision in connection with future vacancies. In deciding to pay travel and transportation or interview expenses in filling any position, the agency should consider such factors as availability of funds as well as the desirability of conducting interviews for a particular job or offering a recruiting incentive to a particular candidate.

§ 572.103 Recordkeeping.

Each agency will maintain records of payments made under this authority and will make those records available to OPM on request.

PART 575—RECRUITMENT, RELOCATION, AND RETENTION INCENTIVES; SUPERVISORY DIFFERENTIALS; AND EXTENDED ASSIGNMENT INCENTIVES

Subpart A—Recruitment Incentives

Subpart B—Relocation Incentives

Subpart C—Retention Incentives

Subpart D—Supervisory Differentials

Subpart E—Extended Assignment Incentives

AUTHORITY: 5 U.S.C. 1104(a)(2) and 5307; subparts A and B also issued under 5 U.S.C. 5753; subpart C also issued under 5 U.S.C. 5754; subpart D also issued under 5 U.S.C. 5755; subpart E also issued under 5 U.S.C. 5757 and sec. 207 of Public Law 107–273, 116 Stat. 1780.

SOURCE: 56 FR 12838, Mar. 28, 1991, unless otherwise noted.

Subpart A—Recruitment Incentives

SOURCE: 70 FR 25740, May 13, 2005, unless otherwise noted.

§575.101 Purpose.

This subpart contains regulations implementing 5 U.S.C. 5753, which authorizes payment of recruitment incentives. An agency may pay a recruitment incentive to a newly appointed employee under the conditions specified in this subpart provided the agency has determined that the employee's position is likely to be difficult to fill in the absence of an incentive.

§575.102 Definitions.

In this subpart:

Agency means an executive agency or a legislative branch agency included in 5 U.S.C. 5102(a)(1).

Authorized agency official means the head of an agency or an official who is authorized to act for the head of the agency in the matter concerned.

Competencies means the knowledge, skills, abilities, behaviors, and other characteristics an individual needs to perform the duties of a position.

Employee has the meaning given that term in 5 U.S.C. 2105, except that the term also includes an employee described in 5 U.S.C. 2105(c). For the purpose of determining whether an individual was an employee of the Federal Government during the 90-day period referred to in the definition of *newly appointed*, *employee* also includes an employee described in 5 U.S.C. 2105(e). For the purpose of § 575.109(d), an *employee* means an individual not yet employed who has received a written offer to be newly appointed or reappointed and has signed the written service agreement required by § 575.110 before payment of the recruitment incentive.

Executive agency has the meaning given that term in 5 U.S.C. 105.

Federal Government means all entities of the Government of the United States, including the United States Postal Service and the Postal Regulatory Commission.

Newly appointed refers to—

(1) The first appointment, regardless of tenure, as an employee of the Federal Government;

(2) An appointment of a former employee of the Federal Government following a break in Federal Government service of at least 90 days; or

(3) An appointment of an individual in the Federal Government when his or her service in the Federal Government during the 90-day period immediately preceding the appointment was not in a position excluded by § 575.104 and was limited to one or more of the following:

(i) A time-limited appointment in the competitive or excepted service;

(ii) A non-permanent appointment in the competitive or excepted service;

(iii) Employment with the government of the District of Columbia (DC) when the candidate was first appointed by the DC government on or after October 1, 1987;

(iv) An appointment as an expert or consultant under 5 U.S.C. 3109 and 5 CFR part 304;

(v) Employment under a provisional appointment designated under 5 CFR 316.403;

(vi) Employment under an Internship Program appointment under § 213.3402(a) of this chapter; or

(vii) Employment as a Senior Executive Service limited term appointee or limited emergency appointee (as defined in 5 U.S.C. 3132(a)(5) and (a)(6), respectively).

OPM means the Office of Personnel Management.

Rate of basic pay means the rate of pay fixed by law or administrative action for the position to which an employee is or will be appointed before deductions and including any special rate under 5 CFR part 530, subpart C, or similar payment under other legal authority, and any locality-based comparability payment under 5 CFR part 531, subpart F, or similar payment under other legal authority, but excluding additional pay of any other kind. For example, a *rate of basic pay* does not include additional pay such as night shift differentials under 5 U.S.C. 5343(f) or environmental differentials under 5 U.S.C. 5343(c)(4).

Service agreement means a written agreement between an agency and an employee under which the employee agrees to a specified period of employment of not less than 6 months or more than 4 years with the agency in return for payment of a recruitment incentive.

[70 FR 25740, May 13, 2005, as amended at 72 FR 67837, Dec. 3, 2007; 77 FR 28223, May 11, 2012; 78 FR 49363, Aug. 14, 2013]

§ 575.103 Eligible categories of employees.

(a) Except as provided in § 575.104, an Executive agency may pay a recruitment incentive to an employee appointed or placed in the following categories of positions:

(1) A General Schedule position paid under 5 U.S.C. 5332 or 5305 (or similar special rate authority);

(2) A senior-level or scientific or professional position paid under 5 U.S.C. 5376;

(3) A Senior Executive Service position paid under 5 U.S.C. 5383 or a Federal Bureau of Investigation and Drug Enforcement Administration Senior Executive Service position paid under 5 U.S.C. 3151;

(4) A position as a law enforcement officer, as defined in 5 CFR 550.103;

(5) A position under the Executive Schedule paid under 5 U.S.C. 5311–5317 or a position the rate of pay for which is fixed by law at a rate equal to a rate for the Executive Schedule;

(6) A prevailing rate position, as defined in 5 U.S.C. 5342(a)(3); or

(7) Any other position in a category for which payment of recruitment incentives has been approved by OPM at the request of the head of an executive agency.

(b) Except as provided in §575.104, a legislative agency may pay a recruitment incentive to an employee appointed or placed in a General Schedule position paid under 5 U.S.C. 5332 or 5305 (or similar special rate authority).

[70 FR 25740, May 13, 2005, as amended at 72 FR 67837, Dec. 3, 2007]

§575.104 Ineligible categories of employees.

An agency may not pay a recruitment incentive to an employee in—

(a) A position to which an individual is appointed by the President, by and with the advice and consent of the Senate;

(b) A position in the Senior Executive Service as a noncareer appointee (as defined in 5 U.S.C. 3132(a)(7));

(c) A position excepted from the competitive service by reason of its confidential, policy-determining, policy-making, or policy-advocating character; or

(d) A position not otherwise covered by the exclusions in paragraphs (a), (b), and (c) of this section—

(1) To which an individual is appointed by the President without the advice and consent of the Senate, except a Senior Executive Service position in which the individual serves as a career appointee (as defined in 5 U.S.C. 3132(a)(4));

(2) Designated as the head of an agency, including an agency headed by a collegial body composed of two or more individual members;

(3) In which the employee is expected to receive an appointment as the head of an agency; or

(4) To which an individual is appointed as a Senior Executive Service limited term appointee or limited emergency appointee (as defined in 5 U.S.C. 3132(a)(5) and (a)(6), respectively) when the appointment must be cleared through the White House Office of Presidential Personnel.

[70 FR 25740, May 13, 2005, as amended at 78 FR 49363, Aug. 14, 2013]

§575.105 Applicability to employees.

(a) A recruitment incentive may be paid under the conditions prescribed in this subpart to an employee who is newly appointed to a position listed in §575.103 that is likely to be difficult to fill, as determined under §575.106.

(b)(1) An agency may target groups of similar positions (excluding positions covered by §575.103(a)(2), (a)(3), or (a)(5) or those in similar categories approved by OPM under §575.103(a)(7)) that have been difficult to fill in the past or that may be difficult to fill in the future and make the required determination to offer a recruitment incentive to newly-appointed employees on a group basis.

(2) An agency must define a targeted category of positions using factors that relate to the conditions described in §575.106(b). Factors that may be appropriate include the following: occupational series, grade level, distinctive job duties, unique competencies required for the positions, and geographic location.

(3) An agency must review each decision to target a group of similar positions for the purpose of granting a recruitment incentive at least annually to determine whether the positions are still likely to be difficult to fill. An authorized agency official must certify this determination in writing. If an agency determines the positions are no longer likely to be difficult to fill, the agency may not offer a recruitment incentive to newly-appointed employees in that group on a group basis.

(c) An agency may not commence a recruitment incentive service agreement during—

(1) A period of employment established under any service agreement required for a relocation incentive under 5 CFR part 575, subpart B, or

(2) A period of employment established under any service agreement required for a retention incentive or for which an employee receives retention incentive payments without a service agreement under 5 CFR part 575, subpart C.

[70 FR 25740, May 13, 2005, as amended at 72 FR 67838, Dec. 3, 2007; 78 FR 49363, Aug. 14, 2013]

§ 575.106 Authorizing a recruitment incentive.

(a) *Authority of authorized agency official.* An authorized agency official retains sole and exclusive discretion, subject only to OPM review and oversight, to—

(1) Determine when a position is likely to be difficult to fill under paragraph (b) of this section;

(2) Approve a recruitment incentive for an employee under § 575.105;

(3) Establish the criteria for determining the amount of a recruitment incentive and the length of a service period under §§ 575.109(a) and 575.110(a), respectively;

(4) Request a waiver from OPM of the limitation on the maximum amount of a recruitment incentive under § 575.109(c); and

(5) Establish the criteria for terminating a service agreement under § 575.111.

(b) *Factors for determining when a position is likely to be difficult to fill.* An agency in its sole and exclusive discretion, subject only to OPM review and oversight, may determine that a position is likely to be difficult to fill if the agency is likely to have difficulty recruiting candidates with the competencies required for the position (or group of positions) in the absence of a recruitment incentive. An agency must consider the following factors, as applicable to the case at hand, in determining whether a position (or group of positions) is likely to be difficult to fill in the absence of a recruitment incentive and in documenting this determination as required by § 575.108:

(1) The availability and quality of candidates possessing the competencies required for the position, including the success of recent efforts to recruit candidates for the position or similar positions using indicators such as offer acceptance rates, proportion of positions filled, and the length of time required to fill similar positions;

(2) The salaries typically paid outside the Federal Government for similar positions;

(3) Recent turnover in similar positions;

(4) Employment trends and labor-market factors that may affect the agency's ability to recruit candidates for similar positions;

(5) Special or unique competencies required for the position;

(6) Agency efforts to use non-pay authorities, such as special training and work scheduling flexibilities, to resolve difficulties alone or in combination with a recruitment incentive;

(7) The desirability of the duties, work or organizational environment, or geographic location of the position; and

(8) Other supporting factors.

(c) An agency may determine that a position (or group of positions) is likely to be difficult to fill if OPM has approved the use of a direct-hire authority applicable to the position (or group of positions) under 5 CFR part 337, subpart B.

[70 FR 25740, May 13, 2005, as amended at 72 FR 67838, Dec. 3, 2007]

§ 575.107 Agency recruitment incentive plan and approval levels.

(a) Before paying recruitment incentives under this subpart, an agency must establish a recruitment incentive plan. The plan must include the following elements:

(1) The designation of officials with authority to review and approve payment of recruitment incentives (subject to paragraph (b) of this section), including the circumstances under which an official has the authority to approve payment without higher-level approval under paragraph (b)(2) of this section, and the designation of officials with authority to waive the repayment of a recruitment incentive under § 575.111(h);

(2) The categories of employees who are prohibited from receiving recruitment incentives;

(3) Required documentation for determining that a position is likely to be difficult to fill;

(4) Any requirements for determining the amount of a recruitment incentive;

(5) The payment methods that may be authorized;

(6) Requirements governing service agreements, which, at a minimum, must include—

(i) The criteria for determining the length of a service period;

(ii) The conditions for terminating a service agreement; and

(iii) The obligations of the agency and the employee, as applicable, if an agency terminates a service agreement; and

(7) Documentation and recordkeeping requirements sufficient to allow reconstruction of the action and to fulfill the requirements of §§ 575.112 and 575.113.

(b)(1) Except as provided in paragraph (b)(2) of this section, an authorized agency official who is at least one level higher than the employee's supervisor must review and approve each determination to pay a recruitment incentive to a newly appointed employee, unless there is no official at a higher level in the agency. The authorized agency official must review and approve the recruitment incentive determination before the agency may pay the incentive to the employee.

(2) When necessary to make a timely offer of employment, an authorized agency official may establish criteria in advance for offering recruitment incentives to newly-appointed employees and may authorize an official who is not lower than a candidate's supervisor to use these criteria to offer a recruitment incentive (in any amount within a pre-established range) to a candidate without further review or approval.

(c) Unless the head of the agency determines otherwise, an agency recruitment incentive plan must apply uniformly across the agency.

[70 FR 25740, May 13, 2005, as amended at 72 FR 67838, Dec. 3, 2007]

§ 575.108 Approval criteria and written determination.

(a) For each determination to pay a recruitment incentive under this subpart, an agency must document in writing—

(1) The basis for determining that a position is likely to be difficult to fill, as determined under § 575.106;

(2) The basis for authorizing a recruitment incentive; and

(3) The basis for the amount and timing of the approved recruitment incentive payment and the length of the required service period.

(b) An agency must make the determination to pay a recruitment incentive before the prospective employee enters on duty in the position for which recruited.

§ 575.109 Payment of recruitment incentives.

(a) An authorized agency official must establish the criteria for determining the amount of a recruitment incentive. An agency may pay a recruitment incentive-(1) As an initial lump-sum payment at the commencement of the service period required by the service agreement or before the start of the service period, as authorized by paragraph (d) of this section;

(2) In installments throughout the service period required by the service agreement;

(3) As a final lump-sum payment upon the completion of the full service period required by the service agreement; or

(4) In a combination of these payment methods.

(b)(1) Except as provided in paragraph (c) of this section, the total amount of recruitment incentive payments paid to an employee in a service period may not exceed 25 percent of the annual rate of basic pay of the employee at the beginning of the service period multiplied by the number of years (including fractions of a year) in the service period (not to exceed 4 years).

(2) For hourly rate employees who do not have a scheduled annual rate of basic pay, compute the annual rate required for paragraph (b)(1) of this section by multiplying the applicable hourly rate in effect at the beginning of the service period by 2,087 hours.

(3) For the purpose of determining the number of years in a service period under paragraph (b)(1) of this section, divide the total number of calendar days in the service period by 365 and round the result to two decimal places. For example, a service period covering 39 biweekly pay periods equals 546 days, and 546 days divided by 365 days equals 1.50 years.

(c)(1) An authorized agency official may request that OPM waive the limitation in paragraph (b)(1) of this section for an employee or group of employees based on a critical agency need. The authorized agency official must determine that the competencies required for the position(s) are critical to the successful accomplishment of an important agency mission, project, or initiative (e.g., programs or projects related to a national emergency or implementing a new law or critical management initiative). Under such a waiver, the total amount of recruitment incentive payments paid to an employee in a service period may not exceed 50 percent of the employee's annual rate of basic pay at the beginning of the service period multiplied by the number of years (including fractions of a year) in the service period. However, in no event may a waiver provide total recruitment incentive payments exceeding 100 percent of the employee's annual rate of basic pay at the beginning of the service period.

(2) Waiver requests must include—

(i) A description of the critical agency need the proposed recruitment incentive would address;

(ii) The documentation required by § 575.108;

(iii) The proposed recruitment incentive payment amount and a justification for that amount;

(iv) The timing and method of making the recruitment incentive payments;

(v) The service period required; and

(vi) Any other information pertinent to the case at hand.

(d) An agency may pay a recruitment incentive to an employee who has not yet entered on duty once the employee has signed a service agreement established under § 575.110.

(e) A recruitment incentive is not part of an employee's rate of basic pay for any purpose.

(f) Payment of a recruitment incentive is subject to the aggregate limitation on pay under 5 CFR part 530, subpart B.

[70 FR 25740, May 13, 2005, as amended at 78 FR 49363, Aug. 14, 2013]

§ 575.110 Service agreement requirements.

(a) Before paying a recruitment incentive, an agency must require the employee to sign a written service agreement to complete a specified period of employment with the agency (or successor agency in the event of a transfer of function). An authorized agency official must establish the criteria for determining the length of a service period. The service period may not be less than 6 months and may not exceed 4 years.

(b)(1) The service agreement must include the commencement and termination dates of the required service period. Except as provided in paragraphs (b)(2) and (b)(3) of this section, the required service period must begin upon the commencement of service with the agency. The service period must terminate on the last day of a pay period.

(2) If service with the agency does not begin on the first day of a pay period, the agency must delay the service period commencement date so that a required service period begins on the first day of the first pay period beginning on or after the commencement of service in the agency.

(3) An agency may delay a service agreement commencement date until after the employee completes an initial period of formal training or required probationary period when continued employment in the position is contingent on successful completion of the formal training or probationary period. The agency must make the determination to pay a recruitment incentive before the employee enters on duty in the position. However, the service agreement must specify that if an employee does not successfully complete the training or probationary period before the service period commences, the agency is not obligated to pay any portion of the recruitment incentive to the employee.

(c) The service agreement must specify the total amount of the incentive, the method of paying the incentive, and the timing and amounts of each incentive payment, as established under § 575.109.

(d) The service agreement must include the conditions under which the agency must terminate the service agreement (*i.e.*, if an employee is demoted or separated for cause, receives a rating of record of less than "Fully Successful" or equivalent, or otherwise fails to fulfill the terms of the service agreement) and the conditions under which the employee must repay a recruitment incentive under § 575.111.

(e) The service agreement must include the conditions under which the agency may terminate the service agreement before the employee completes the agreed-upon service period. The service agreement must specify the effect of a termination under §575.111, including the conditions under which the agency will pay an additional recruitment incentive payment for partially completed service under §575.111(e) and (f).

(f) The service agreement may include any other terms or conditions that, if violated, will result in termination of the service agreement under §575.111(b). For example, the service agreement may specify the employee's work schedule, type of position, and the duties he or she is expected to perform. In addition, the service agreement may address the extent to which periods of time on detail, in a nonpay status, or in a paid leave status are creditable towards the completion of the service period.

§575.111 Termination of a service agreement.

(a) An authorized agency official may unilaterally terminate a recruitment incentive service agreement based solely on the management needs of the agency. For example, an agency may terminate a service agreement when the employee's position is affected by a reduction in force, when there are insufficient funds to continue the planned incentive payments, or when the agency assigns the employee to a different position (if the different position is not within the terms of the service agreement).

(b) An authorized agency official must terminate a recruitment incentive service agreement if an employee is demoted or separated for cause (*i.e.*, for unacceptable performance or conduct), if the employee receives a rating of record (or an official performance appraisal or evaluation under a system not covered by 5 U.S.C. chapter 43 or 5 CFR part 430) of less than "Fully Successful" or equivalent, or if the employee otherwise fails to fulfill the terms of the service agreement.

(c) The termination of a service agreement is not grievable or appealable.

(d) The agency must notify an employee in writing when it terminates a recruitment incentive service agreement.

(e) If an authorized agency official terminates a service agreement under paragraph (a) of this section, the employee is entitled to all recruitment incentive payments that are attributable to completed service and to retain any portion of a recruitment incentive payment he or she received that is attributable to uncompleted service.

(f) Except as provided in paragraph (j) of this section, if an authorized agency official terminates a service agreement under paragraph (b) of this section, the employee is entitled to retain recruitment incentive payments previously paid by the agency that are attributable to the completed portion of the service period. If the employee received recruitment incentive payments that are less than the amount that would be attributable to the completed portion of the service period, the agency is not obligated to pay the employee the amount attributable to completed service, unless the agency agreed to such payment under the terms of the recruitment incentive service agreement. If the employee received recruitment incentive payments in excess of the amount that would be attributable to the completed portion of the service period, he or she must repay the excess amount, except when an authorized agency official waives the requirement to repay the excess amount under paragraph (h) of this section.

(g) If an employee fails to reimburse the paying agency for the full amount owed under paragraph (f) of this section, the amount outstanding must be recovered from the employee under the agency's regulations for collection by offset from an indebted Government employee under 5 U.S.C. 5514 and 5 CFR part 550, subpart K, or through the appropriate provisions governing Federal debt collection if the individual is no longer a Federal employee.

(h) If an employee received recruitment incentive payments in excess of the amount that would be attributable to the completed portion of the service period under paragraph (f) of this section, an authorized agency official may waive the requirement to repay the excess amount when, in the judgment of the official, collection of the excess amount would be against equity and good conscience and not in the best interest of the United States.

(i) The full amount of the authorized recruitment incentive must be prorated across the length of the service period to determine the amount of the recruitment incentive attributable to completed service and uncompleted service under this section.

(j) Notwithstanding paragraph (f) of this section, if an agency terminates a service agreement under paragraph (b) of this section when an employee is separated as a result of material false or inaccurate statements or deception or fraud in examination or appointment, or as a result of failing to meet employment qualifications, the employee must repay all recruitment incentive payments received under that service agreement.

[70 FR 25740, May 13, 2005, as amended at 72 FR 67838, Dec. 3, 2007]

§ 575.112 Internal monitoring requirements and revocation or suspension of authority.

(a) Each agency must monitor the use of recruitment incentives to ensure that its recruitment incentive plan and the payment of recruitment incentives are consistent with the requirements and criteria established under 5 U.S.C. 5753 and this subpart.

(b) When OPM finds that an agency is not paying recruitment incentives consistent with the agency's recruitment incentive plan and the criteria established under 5 U.S.C. 5753 and this subpart or otherwise determines that the agency is not using this authority selectively and judiciously, OPM may—

(1) Direct the agency to revoke or suspend the authority granted to any organizational component in the agency and, with respect to any category or categories of employees, require that the component obtain approval from the agency's headquarters level before paying a recruitment incentive to such employees; or

(2) Revoke or suspend the authority granted to the agency under this subpart for all or any part of the agency and, with respect to any category or categories of employees, require that the agency obtain OPM's approval before paying a recruitment incentive to such employees.

§ 575.113 Records and reports.

Each agency must keep a record of each determination to pay a recruitment incentive and make such records available for review upon OPM's request.

[70 FR 25740, May 13, 2005, as amended at 78 FR 49363, Aug. 14, 2013]

Subpart B—Relocation Incentives

SOURCE: 70 FR 25743, May 13, 2005, unless otherwise noted.

§ 575.201 Purpose.

This subpart contains regulations implementing 5 U.S.C. 5753, which authorizes payment of relocation incentives. An agency may pay a relocation incentive to a current employee who must relocate to accept a position in a different geographic area under the conditions specified in this subpart provided the agency determines that the position is likely to be difficult to fill in the absence of an incentive.

§ 575.202 Definitions.

In this subpart:

Agency means an executive agency or a legislative branch agency included in 5 U.S.C. 5102(a)(1).

Authorized agency official means the head of an agency or an official who is authorized to act for the head of the agency in the matter concerned.

Competencies means the knowledge, skills, abilities, behaviors, and other characteristics an employee needs to perform the duties of a position.

Employee has the meaning given that term in 5 U.S.C. 2105, except that the term also includes an employee described in 5 U.S.C. 2105(c). For the purpose of determining whether an individual had status as an employee of the Federal Government immediately prior to the relocation (*i.e.*, in § 575.205(a)(2)), *employee* also includes an employee described in 5 U.S.C. 2105(e).

Executive agency has the meaning given that term in 5 U.S.C. 105.

Federal Government means all entities of the Government of the United States, including the United States Postal Service and the Postal Regulatory Commission.

OPM means the Office of Personnel Management.

Rate of basic pay means the rate of pay fixed by law or administrative action for the position to which the employee is relocated before deductions and including any special rate under 5 CFR part 530, subpart C, or similar payment under other legal authority, and any locality-based comparability payment under 5 CFR part 531, subpart F, or similar payment under other legal authority, but excluding additional pay of any other kind. For example, a *rate of basic pay* does not include additional pay such as night shift differentials under 5 U.S.C. 5343(f) or environmental differentials under 5 U.S.C. 5343(c)(4).

Service agreement means a written agreement between an agency and an employee under which the employee agrees to a specified period of employment of not more than 4 years with the agency at the new duty station to which relocated in return for payment of a relocation incentive.

[70 FR 25743, May 13, 2005, as amended at 72 FR 67838, Dec. 3, 2007]

§575.203 Eligible categories of employees.

(a) Except as provided in §575.204, an Executive agency may pay a relocation incentive to an employee in the following categories of positions:

(1) A General Schedule position paid under 5 U.S.C. 5332 or 5305 (or similar special rate authority);

(2) A senior-level or scientific or professional position paid under 5 U.S.C. 5376;

(3) A Senior Executive Service position paid under 5 U.S.C. 5383 or a Federal Bureau of Investigation and Drug Enforcement Administration Senior Executive Service position paid under 5 U.S.C. 3151;

(4) A position as a law enforcement officer, as defined in 5 CFR 550.103;

(5) A position under the Executive Schedule paid under 5 U.S.C. 5311–5317 or a position the rate of pay for which is fixed by law at a rate equal to a rate for the Executive Schedule;

(6) A prevailing rate position, as defined in 5 U.S.C. 5342(a)(3); or

(7) Any other position in a category for which payment of relocation incentives has been approved by OPM at the request of the head of an executive agency.

(b) Except as provided in §575.204, a legislative agency may pay a relocation incentive to an employee in a General Schedule position paid under 5 U.S.C. 5332 or 5305 (or similar special rate authority).

[70 FR 25743, May 13, 2005, as amended at 72 FR 67838, Dec. 3, 2007]

§575.204 Ineligible categories of employees.

An agency may not pay a relocation incentive to an employee in—

(a) A position to which an individual is appointed by the President, by and with the advice and consent of the Senate;

(b) A position in the Senior Executive Service as a noncareer appointee (as defined in 5 U.S.C. 3132(a)(7));

(c) A position excepted from the competitive service by reason of its confidential, policy-determining, policy-making, or policy-advocating character; or

(d) A position not otherwise covered by the exclusions in paragraphs (a), (b), and (c) of this section—

(1) To which an individual is appointed by the President without the advice and consent of the Senate, except a Senior Executive Service position in which the individual serves as a career appointee (as defined in 5 U.S.C. 3132(a)(4));

(2) Designated as the head of an agency, including an agency headed by a collegial body composed of two or more individual members;

(3) In which the employee is expected to receive an appointment as the head of an agency; or

(4) To which an individual is appointed as a Senior Executive Service limited term appointee or limited emergency appointee (as defined in 5 U.S.C. 3132(a)(5) and (a)(6), respectively) when the appointment must be cleared through the White House Office of Presidential Personnel.

[70 FR 25743, May 13, 2005, as amended at 78 FR 49363, Aug. 14, 2013]

§ 575.205 Applicability to employees.

(a) An agency may pay a relocation incentive under the conditions prescribed in this subpart to an employee who—

(1) Relocates to a different geographic area (permanently or temporarily) to accept a position listed in § 575.203 in an agency when the position is likely to be difficult to fill, as determined under § 575.206; and

(2) Is an employee of the Federal Government immediately before the relocation.

(b) An agency may pay a relocation incentive under paragraph (a) of this section when an employee must relocate to accept a position or assignment in a different geographic area. A position is considered to be in a different geographic area if the worksite of the new position is 50 or more miles from the worksite of the position held immediately before the move. If the worksite of the new position is less than 50 miles from the worksite of the position held immediately before the move, but the employee must relocate (*i.e.*, establish a new residence) to accept the position, an authorized agency official may waive the 50-mile requirement and pay the employee a relocation incentive subject to the requirements of this subpart. In all cases, the employee must establish a residence in the new geographic area before the agency may pay a relocation incentive to the employee. A relocation incentive may be paid only if the employee maintains residency in the new geographic area for the duration of the service agreement.

(c) A relocation incentive may be paid only when the employee's rating of record (or an official performance appraisal or evaluation under a system not covered by 5 U.S.C. chapter 43 or 5 CFR part 430) for the position held immediately before the move is at least "Fully Successful" or equivalent.

(d) An agency may not commence a relocation incentive service agreement during—

(1) A period of employment established under any service agreement required for a recruitment incentive under 5 CFR part 575, subpart A, or

(2) A period of employment established under any service agreement required for a relocation incentive previously authorized under this subpart.

(e) An agency may commence a relocation incentive service agreement during a period of employment established under a service agreement for a previously authorized retention incentive or for which an employee is receiving previously authorized retention incentive payments without a service agreement under 5 CFR part 575, subpart C. The service period under such a relocation incentive service agreement and the service period required by the retention incentive service agreement, if applicable, must be fulfilled concurrently.

[70 FR 25743, May 13, 2005, as amended at 72 FR 67838, Dec. 3, 2007; 78 FR 49364, Aug. 14, 2013]

§ 575.206 Authorizing a relocation incentive.

(a) *Authority of authorized agency official.* An authorized agency official retains sole and exclusive discretion, subject only to OPM review and oversight, to—

(1) Determine when a position is likely to be difficult to fill under paragraph (b) of this section;

(2) Approve a relocation incentive for an employee under § 575.205;

(3) Establish the criteria for determining the amount of a relocation incentive and the length of a service period under §§ 575.209 and 575.210, respectively;

(4) Request a waiver from OPM of the limitation on the maximum amount of a relocation incentive under § 575.209(c); and

(5) Establish the criteria for terminating a service agreement under § 575.211.

(b) *Factors for determining when a position is likely to be difficult to fill.* An agency in its sole and exclusive discretion, subject only to OPM review and oversight, may determine that a position is likely to be difficult to fill if the agency is likely to have difficulty recruiting candidates with the competencies required for the position (or group of positions) in the absence of a relocation incentive. An agency must consider the following factors, as applicable to the case at hand, in determining whether a position (or group of positions) is likely to be difficult to fill in the absence of a relocation incentive and in documenting this determination as required by §575.208:

(1) The availability and quality of candidates possessing the competencies required for the position, including the success of recent efforts to recruit candidates for the position or similar positions using indicators such as offer acceptance rates, proportion of positions filled, and the length of time required to fill similar positions;

(2) The salaries typically paid outside the Federal Government for similar positions;

(3) Recent turnover in similar positions;

(4) Employment trends and labor-market factors that may affect the agency's ability to recruit candidates for similar positions;

(5) Special or unique competencies required for the position;

(6) Agency efforts to use non-pay authorities, such as special training and work scheduling flexibilities, to resolve difficulties alone or in combination with a relocation incentive;

(7) The desirability of the duties, work or organizational environment, or geographic location of the position; and

(8) Other supporting factors.

(c) An agency may determine that a position (or group of positions) is likely to be difficult to fill if OPM has approved the use of a direct-hire authority applicable to the position (or group of positions) under 5 CFR part 337, subpart B.

[70 FR 25743, May 13, 2005, as amended at 70 FR 74996, Dec. 19, 2005; 72 FR 67839, Dec. 3, 2007]

§575.207 Agency relocation incentive plan and approval levels.

(a) Before paying relocation incentives under this subpart, an agency must establish a relocation incentive plan. This plan must include the following elements:

(1) The designation of officials with authority to review and approve payment of relocation incentives (subject to paragraph (b) of this section) and the designation of officials with authority to waive the repayment of a relocation incentive under §575.211(h);

(2) The categories of employees who are prohibited from receiving relocation incentives;

(3) Required documentation for determining that a position (or group of positions) is likely to be difficult to fill;

(4) Any requirements for determining the amount of a relocation incentive;

(5) The payment methods that may be authorized;

(6) Requirements governing service agreements which, at a minimum, must include—

(i) The criteria for determining the length of a service period under a service agreement;

(ii) The conditions for terminating a service agreement; and

(iii) The obligations of the agency and the employee, as applicable, if an agency terminates a service agreement; and

(7) Documentation and recordkeeping requirements sufficient to allow reconstruction of the action and fulfill the requirements of §§575.212 and 575.213.

(b)(1) Except as provided in paragraph (b)(2) of this section, an authorized agency official who is at least one level higher than the employee's supervisor must review and approve each determination to pay a relocation incentive, unless there is no official at a higher level in the agency. The authorized agency official must review and approve the relocation incentive determination before the agency pays the incentive to the employee.

(2) The higher level approval required by paragraph (b)(1) of this section is not needed when approving coverage of individual employees under a previously approved relocation incentive authorization if the case-by-case approval requirement is waived under §575.208(b).

(c) Unless the head of the agency determines otherwise, an agency relocation incentive plan must apply uniformly across the agency.

[70 FR 25743, May 13, 2005, as amended at 72 FR 67839, Dec. 3, 2007]

§575.208 Approval criteria and written determination.

(a)(1) For each determination to pay a relocation incentive under this subpart, an agency must document in writing—

(i) The basis for determining that a position is likely to be difficult to fill as determined under § 575.206;

(ii) The basis for authorizing a relocation incentive for an employee;

(iii) The basis for the amount and timing of the approved relocation incentive payments and the length of the required service period; and

(iv) That the worksite of the employee's new position is not in the same geographic area as the worksite of the position held immediately before the move (or that a waiver was approved under § 575.205(b)) and that the employee established a residence in the new geographic area, as required by § 575.205(b).

(2) Except as provided in paragraph (b) of this section, the agency must make each determination to pay a relocation incentive on a case-by-case basis for each employee.

(3) The agency must make the determination to pay a relocation incentive before the employee enters on duty in the position to which relocated.

(b)(1) An agency may waive the case-by-case approval requirement under paragraph (a) of this section when—

(i) The employee is a member of a group of employees subject to a mobility agreement and the agency determines that relocation incentives are necessary to retain employees subject to such an agreement to ensure continuation of operations; or

(ii) A major organizational unit of the agency is relocated to a new duty station and the agency determines that relocation incentives are necessary for a group of employees to ensure the continued operation of that unit without undue disruption of an activity or function that is deemed essential to the agency's mission or without undue disruption of service to the public.

(2) The written determination under paragraph (a) of this section must specify the group of employees covered by the case-by-case waiver, the conditions under which the waiver is approved, and the period of time for which the waiver may be applied.

§ 575.209 Payment of relocation incentives.

(a) An authorized agency official must establish the criteria for determining the amount of a relocation incentive. An agency may pay a relocation incentive—

(1) As an initial lump-sum payment at the commencement of the service period required by the service agreement;

(2) In installments throughout the service period required by the service agreement;

(3) As a final lump-sum payment upon the completion of the full service period required by the service agreement; or

(4) In a combination of these payment methods.

(b)(1) Except as provided in paragraph (c) of this section, the total amount of relocation incentive payments paid to an employee in a service period may not exceed 25 percent of the annual rate of basic pay of the employee at the beginning of the service period multiplied by the number of years (including fractions of a year) in the service period (not to exceed 4 years).

(2) For hourly rate employees who do not have a scheduled annual rate of basic pay, compute the annual rate required for paragraph (b)(1) of this section by multiplying the applicable hourly rate in effect at the beginning of the service period by 2,087 hours.

(3) For the purpose of determining the number of years in a service period under paragraph (b)(1) of this section, divide the total number of calendar days in the service period (as established under § 575.208) by 365 and round the result to two decimal places. For example, a service period covering 39 biweekly pay periods equals 546 days, and 546 days divided by 365 days equals 1.50 years.

(c)(1) An authorized agency official may request that OPM waive the limitation in paragraph (b)(1) of this section for an employee based on a critical agency need. The authorized agency official must determine that the competencies required for the position are critical to the successful accomplishment of an important agency mission, project, or initiative (e.g., programs or projects related to a national emergency or implementing a new law or critical management initiative). Under such a waiver, the total amount of relocation incentive payments paid to an employee in a service period may not exceed 50 percent of the annual rate of basic pay of the employee at the beginning of the service period multiplied by the number of years (including fractions of a year) in the service period. However, in no event may a waiver provide total relocation incentive payments exceeding 100 percent of the employee's annual rate of basic pay at the beginning of the service period.

(2) Waiver requests must include—

(i) A description of the critical agency need the proposed relocation incentive would address;

(ii) The documentation required by §575.208;

(iii) The proposed relocation incentive payment amount and a justification for that amount;

(iv) The timing and method for making the relocation incentive payments;

(v) The period of service required; and

(vi) Any other information pertinent to the case at hand.

(d) A relocation incentive is not part of an employee's rate of basic pay for any purpose.

(e) Payment of a relocation incentive is subject to the aggregate limitation on pay under 5 CFR part 530, subpart B.

§575.210 Service agreement requirements.

(a) Before paying a relocation incentive, an agency must require the employee to sign a written service agreement to complete a specified period of employment with the agency (or successor agency in the event of a transfer of function) at the new duty station. An authorized agency official must establish the criteria for determining the length of a service period. The service period may not exceed 4 years.

(b)(1) The service agreement must include the commencement and termination dates of the required service period. Except as provided under paragraphs (b)(2) and (b)(3) of this section, the required service period must begin upon the commencement of service at the new duty station. The service period must terminate on the last day of a pay period.

(2) If service at the new duty station does not begin on the first day of a pay period, the agency must delay the service period commencement date so that a required service period begins on the first day of the first pay period beginning on or after the commencement of service at the new duty station.

(3) An agency may delay a service agreement commencement date until after the employee completes an initial period of formal training when continued employment in the position is contingent on successful completion of the formal training. The agency must make the determination to pay a relocation incentive before the employee enters on duty in the position, as required by §575.208(a)(3). However, the service agreement must specify that if an employee does not successfully complete the training before the service period commences, the agency is not obligated to pay any portion of the relocation incentive to the employee.

(c) The service agreement must specify the total amount of the incentive, the method of paying the incentive, and the timing and amount of each incentive payment, as established under §575.209.

(d) The service agreement must include the conditions under which the agency must terminate the service agreement (*i.e.*, if an employee is demoted or separated for cause, receives a rating of record of less than "Fully Successful" or equivalent, fails to maintain residency in the new geographic area for the duration of the service agreement, or otherwise fails to fulfill the terms of the service agreement) and the conditions under which the employee must repay a relocation incentive under §575.211. An agency must define the limits of the new geographic area in the service agreement for the purpose of determining whether an employee maintains residency in that geographic area for the duration of the service agreement.

(e) The service agreement must include the conditions under which the agency may terminate the service agreement before the employee completes the agreed-upon service period. The service agreement must specify the effect of the termination under §575.211, including the conditions under which the agency will pay an additional relocation incentive payment for partially completed service under § 575.211(e) and (f).

(f) The service agreement may include any other terms or conditions that, if violated, will result in termination of the service agreement. For example, the service agreement may specify the employee's work schedule, type of position, and the duties he or she is expected to perform. In addition, the service agreement may address the extent to which periods of time on detail, in a nonpay status, or in a paid leave status are creditable towards the completion of the service period.

[70 FR 25743, May 13, 2005, as amended at 72 FR 67839, Dec. 3, 2007; 78 FR 49364, Aug. 14, 2013]

§ 575.211 Termination of a service agreement.

(a) An authorized agency official may unilaterally terminate a relocation incentive service agreement based solely on the management needs of the agency. For example, an agency may terminate a service agreement when the employee's position is affected by a reduction in force, when there are insufficient funds to continue the planned incentive payments, or when the agency assigns the employee to a different position (if the different position is not within the terms of the service agreement).

(b) An authorized agency official must terminate a relocation incentive service agreement if an employee is demoted or separated for cause (*i.e.*, for unacceptable performance or conduct), if the employee receives a rating of record (or an official performance appraisal or evaluation under a system not covered by 5 U.S.C. chapter 43 or 5 CFR part 430) of less than "Fully Successful" or equivalent, if the employee fails to maintain residency in the new geographic area for the duration of the service agreement, or if the employee otherwise fails to fulfill the terms of the service agreement.

(c) The termination of a service agreement is not grievable or appealable.

(d) The agency must notify an employee in writing when it terminates a relocation incentive service agreement.

(e) If an authorized agency official terminates a service agreement under paragraph (a) of this section, the employee is entitled to all relocation incentive payments attributable to completed service and to retain any portion of a relocation incentive payment he or she received that is attributable to uncompleted service.

(f) If an authorized agency official terminates a service agreement under paragraph (b) of this section, the employee is entitled to retain relocation incentive payments previously paid by the agency that are attributable to the completed portion of the service period. If the employee received relocation incentive payments that are less than the amount that would be attributable to the completed portion of the service period, the agency is not obligated to pay the employee the amount attributable to completed service, unless the agency agreed to such payment under the terms of the relocation incentive service agreement. If the employee received relocation incentive payments in excess of the amount that would be attributable to the completed portion of the service period, he or she must repay the excess amount, except when an authorized agency official waives the requirement to repay the excess amount under paragraph (h) of this section.

(g) If an employee fails to reimburse the paying agency for the full amount owed under paragraph (f) of this section, the amount outstanding must be recovered from the employee under the agency's regulations for collection by offset from an indebted Government employee under 5 U.S.C. 5514 and 5 CFR part 550, subpart K, or through the appropriate provisions governing Federal debt collection if the individual is no longer a Federal employee.

(h) If an employee received relocation incentive payments in excess of the amount that would be attributable to the completed portion of the service period under paragraph (f) of this section, an authorized agency official may waive the requirement to repay the excess amount when, in the judgment of the official, collection of the excess amount would be against equity and good conscience and not in the best interest of the United States.

(i) The full amount of the authorized relocation incentive must be prorated across the length of the service period to determine the amount of the relocation incentive attributable to completed service and uncompleted service under this section.

[70 FR 25743, May 13, 2005, as amended at 72 FR 67839, Dec. 3, 2007; 78 FR 49364, Aug. 14, 2013]

§ 575.212 Internal monitoring requirements and revocation or suspension of authority.

(a) Each agency must monitor the use of relocation incentives to ensure that the agency's relocation incentive plan and the payment of relocation incentives are consistent with the requirements and criteria established under 5 U.S.C. 5753 and this subpart.

(b) When OPM finds that an agency is not paying relocation incentives consistent with the agency's relocation incentive plan and the criteria established under this subpart or otherwise determines that the agency is not using this authority selectively and judiciously, OPM may—

(1) Direct the agency to revoke or suspend the authority granted to any organizational component in the agency and, with respect to any category or categories of employees, require that the component obtain approval from the agency's headquarters level before paying a relocation incentive to such employees; or

(2) Revoke or suspend the authority granted to the agency under this subpart for all or any part of the agency and, with respect to any category or categories of employees, require that the agency obtain OPM's approval before paying a relocation incentive to such employees.

§ 575.213 Records and reports.

Each agency must keep a record of each determination to pay a relocation incentive and make such records available for review upon OPM's request.

[70 FR 25743, May 13, 2005, as amended at 78 FR 49364, Aug. 14, 2013]

Subpart C—Retention Incentives

SOURCE: 70 FR 25747, May 13, 2005, unless otherwise noted.

§ 575.301 Purpose.

This subpart contains regulations implementing 5 U.S.C. 5754, which authorizes payment of retention incentives. An agency may pay a retention incentive to a current employee under the conditions specified in this subpart when an agency determines that the unusually high or unique qualifications of the employee or a special need of the agency for the employee's services makes it essential to retain the employee and that the employee would be likely to leave in the absence of an incentive.

[70 FR 25747, May 13, 2005, as amended at 72 FR 64527, Nov. 16, 2007]

§ 575.302 Definitions.

In this subpart:

Agency means an executive agency or a legislative branch agency included in 5 U.S.C. 5102(a)(1).

Authorized agency official means the head of an agency or an official who is authorized to act for the head of the agency in the matter concerned.

Competencies means the knowledge, skills, abilities, behaviors, and other characteristics an employee needs to perform the duties of a position.

Employee has the meaning given that term in 5 U.S.C. 2105, except that the term also includes an employee described in 5 U.S.C. 2105(c).

Executive agency has the meaning given that term in 5 U.S.C. 105.

OPM means the Office of Personnel Management.

Rate of basic pay means the rate of pay fixed by law or administrative action for the position to which an employee is appointed before deductions and including any special rate under 5 CFR part 530, subpart C, or similar payment under other legal authority, and any locality-based comparability payment under 5 CFR part 531, subpart F, or similar payment under other legal authority, but excluding additional pay of any other kind. For example, a *rate of basic pay* does not include additional pay such as night shift differentials under 5 U.S.C. 5343(f) or environmental differentials under 5 U.S.C. 5343(c)(4).

Service agreement means a written agreement between an agency and an employee under which the employee agrees to a specified period of employment with the agency in return for payment of a retention incentive.

§575.303 Eligible categories of employees.

(a) Except as provided in §575.304, an Executive agency may pay a retention incentive to a current employee who holds—

(1) A General Schedule position paid under 5 U.S.C. 5332 or 5305 (or similar special rate authority);

(2) A senior-level or scientific or professional position paid under 5 U.S.C. 5376;

(3) A Senior Executive Service position paid under 5 U.S.C. 5383 or a Federal Bureau of Investigation and Drug Enforcement Administration Senior Executive Service position paid under 5 U.S.C. 3151;

(4) A position as a law enforcement officer, as defined in 5 CFR 550.103;

(5) A position under the Executive Schedule paid under 5 U.S.C. 5311–5317 or a position the rate of pay for which is fixed by law at a rate equal to a rate for the Executive Schedule;

(6) A prevailing rate position, as defined in 5 U.S.C. 5342(a)(3); or

(7) Any other position in a category for which payment of retention incentives has been approved by OPM at the request of the head of an executive agency.

(b) Except as provided in §575.304, a legislative agency may pay a retention incentive to a current employee who holds a General Schedule position paid under 5 U.S.C. 5332 or 5305 (or similar special rate authority).

[70 FR 25747, May 13, 2005, as amended at 72 FR 67839, Dec. 3, 2007]

§575.304 Ineligible categories of employees.

An agency may not pay a retention incentive to an employee in—

(a) A position to which an individual is appointed by the President, by and with the advice and consent of the Senate;

(b) A position in the Senior Executive Service as a noncareer appointee (as defined in 5 U.S.C. 3132(a)(7));

(c) A position excepted from the competitive service by reason of its confidential, policy-determining, policy-making, or policy-advocating character; or

(d) A position not otherwise covered by the exclusions in paragraphs (a), (b), and (c) of this section—

(1) To which an individual is appointed by the President without the advice and consent of the Senate, except a Senior Executive Service position in which the individual serves as a career appointee (as defined in 5 U.S.C. 3132(a)(4));

(2) Designated as the head of an agency, including an agency headed by a collegial body composed of two or more individual members;

(3) In which the employee is expected to receive an appointment as the head of an agency; or

(4) To which an individual is appointed as a Senior Executive Service limited term appointee or limited emergency appointee (as defined in 5 U.S.C. 3132(a)(5) and (a)(6), respectively) when the appointment must be cleared through the White House Office of Presidential Personnel.

[70 FR 25747, May 13, 2005, as amended at 78 FR 49364, Aug. 14, 2013]

§575.305 Applicability to employees.

(a) An agency may pay a retention incentive to an individual employee under the conditions prescribed in this subpart when the agency determines that—

(1) The unusually high or unique qualifications (*i.e.*, competencies) of the employee or a special need of the agency for the employee's services makes it essential to retain the employee; and

(2) The employee would be likely to leave the Federal service in the absence of a retention incentive.

(b) Except as provided in paragraph (c) of this section, an agency may pay a retention incentive to a group or category of employees under the conditions prescribed in this subpart when the agency determines that—

(1) The unusually high or unique qualifications (*i.e.*, competencies) of

the group or category of employees or a special need of the agency for the employees' services makes it essential to retain the employees in that group or category; and

(2) There is a high risk that a significant number of the employees in the group would be likely to leave the Federal service in the absence of a retention incentive.

(c) An agency may not include in a group retention incentive authorization an employee covered by § 575.303(a)(2), (a)(3), or (a)(5) or those in similar categories of positions approved by OPM to receive retention incentives under § 575.303(a)(7).

(d) A retention incentive may be paid only when the employee's rating of record (or an official performance appraisal or evaluation under a system not covered by 5 U.S.C. chapter 43 or 5 CFR part 430) is at least "Fully Successful" or equivalent.

[70 FR 25747, May 13, 2005, as amended at 78 FR 49364, Aug. 14, 2013]

§ 575.306 Authorizing a retention incentive.

(a) *Authority of authorized agency official.* An authorized agency official retains sole and exclusive discretion, subject only to OPM review and oversight, to—

(1) Determine when the unusually high or unique qualifications (*i.e.*, competencies) of an employee or a special need of the agency for the employee's services makes it essential to retain the employee and when the employee would be likely to leave the Federal service in the absence of a retention incentive;

(2) Determine when a group or category of employees has unusually high or unique qualifications (*i.e.*, competencies) or when an agency has a special need for the employees' services that makes it essential to retain the employees in that group or category and when there is a high risk that a significant number of employees in the group would be likely to leave the Federal service in the absence of a retention incentive;

(3) Approve a retention incentive for an employee (or group or category of employees, except as prohibited by § 575.305(c)) in a position (or positions) listed in § 575.303;

(4) Establish the criteria for determining the amount of a retention incentive and the length of a service period under §§ 575.309 and 575.310, respectively;

(5) Request a waiver from OPM of the limitation on the maximum amount of a retention incentive for an employee (or group or category of employees) under § 575.309(e); and

(6) Establish the criteria for terminating a service agreement or retention incentive payments under § 575.311.

(b) *Factors for authorizing a retention incentive for an individual employee.* An agency must consider the following factors, as applicable to the case at hand, in determining whether the unusually high or unique qualifications of an employee or a special need of the agency for an employee's services makes it essential to retain the employee and that the employee would be likely to leave the Federal service in the absence of a retention incentive:

(1) Employment trends and labor market factors such as the availability and quality of candidates in the labor market possessing the competencies required for the position and who, with minimal training, cost, or disruption of service to the public, could perform the full range of duties and responsibilities of the employee's position at the level performed by the employee;

(2) The quality and availability of the potential sources of employees that are identified in any agency succession plan (e.g., succession plans required for leadership positions), who possess the competencies required for the position, and who, with minimal training, cost, and disruption of service to the public, could perform the full range of duties and responsibilities of the employee's position at the level performed by the employee;

(3) The success of recent efforts to recruit candidates and retain employees with competencies similar to those possessed by the employee for positions similar to the position held by the employee;

(4) Special or unique competencies required for the position;

(5) Agency efforts to use non-pay authorities to help retain the employee

instead of or in addition to a retention incentive, such as special training and work scheduling flexibilities or improving working conditions;

(6) The desirability of the duties, work or organizational environment, or geographic location of the position;

(7) The extent to which the employee's departure would affect the agency's ability to carry out an activity, perform a function, or complete a project that the agency deems essential to its mission;

(8) The salaries typically paid outside the Federal Government; and

(9) Other supporting factors.

(c) *Factors for authorizing a retention incentive for a group or category of employees.* (1) An agency must consider the factors in paragraph (b) of this section as they relate to determining whether a group or category of employees—

(i) Has unusually high or unique qualifications (*i.e.*, competencies) or that the agency has a special need for the employees' services that makes it essential to retain the employees in that category; and

(ii) That it is reasonable to presume that there is a high risk that a significant number of employees in the targeted category would be likely to leave the Federal service in the absence of a retention incentive.

(2) An agency must narrowly define a targeted category of employees using factors that relate to the conditions described in paragraph (c)(1) of this section. Factors that may be appropriate include the following: occupational series, grade level, distinctive job duties, unique competencies required for the position, assignment to a special project, minimum agency service requirements, organization or team designation, geographic location, and required rating of record. (While a rating of record of higher than the "Fully Successful" rating of record required by § 575.305(d) may be a factor used in defining the targeted category, a rating of record by itself is not sufficient to justify a retention incentive. A rating of record may function as a supporting factor in authorizing an incentive or setting the incentive rate only to the extent it directly relates to the conditions in paragraph (d) of this section.)

(d) An agency must document the determinations required under paragraphs (b) and (c) of this section as required by § 575.308.

[70 FR 25747, May 13, 2005, as amended at 78 FR 49364, Aug. 14, 2013]

§ 575.307 Agency retention incentive plan and approval levels.

(a) Before paying retention incentives under this subpart, an agency must establish a retention incentive plan. This plan must include the following elements:

(1) The designation of officials with authority to review and approve payment of retention incentives, subject to paragraph (b) of this section;

(2) The categories of employees who are prohibited from receiving retention incentives;

(3) Required documentation for determining that an employee would be likely to leave the Federal service;

(4) Any requirements for determining the amount of a retention incentive;

(5) The payment methods that may be authorized;

(6) Requirements governing service agreements which, at a minimum, must include—

(i) The criteria for determining the length of a service period under a service agreement;

(ii) The conditions for terminating a service agreement;

(iii) The obligations of the agency if the agency terminates a service agreement; and

(iv) The conditions for terminating retention incentive payments when no service agreement is required (see § 575.310(f)); and

(7) Documentation and recordkeeping requirements sufficient to allow reconstruction of the action and fulfill the requirements of §§ 575.312 and 575.313.

(b)(1) Except as provided in paragraph (b)(2) of this section, an authorized agency official who is at least one level higher than the employee's (or group of employees') supervisor must review and approve each determination to pay a retention incentive to an individual or group of employees, unless there is no official at a higher level in the agency. The authorized agency official must review and approve the retention incentive determination before the agency pays the incentive to the employee.

(2) The higher level approval required by paragraph (b)(1) of this section is not needed when approving coverage of individual employees under a previously approved group retention incentive authorization.

(c) Unless the head of the agency determines otherwise, an agency retention incentive plan must apply uniformly across the agency.

[70 FR 25747, May 13, 2005, as amended at 72 FR 67839, Dec. 3, 2007]

§575.308 Approval criteria and written determination.

(a) An agency in its sole and exclusive discretion, subject only to OPM review and oversight, may approve a retention incentive for an individual employee or group or category of employees using the approval criteria in §575.306.

(b) For each determination to pay a retention incentive under this subpart, an agency must document in writing—

(1) The basis for determining that the unusually high or unique qualifications of the employee (or group of employees) or a special need of the agency for the employee's (or group of employees') services makes it essential to retain the employee(s);

(2) The basis for determining that the employee (or a significant number of employees in a group) would be likely to leave the Federal service in the absence of a retention incentive; and

(3) The basis for establishing the amount and timing of the approved retention incentive payment and the length of the required service period.

§575.309 Payment of retention incentives.

(a) An authorized agency official must determine the criteria for determining the amount of a retention incentive. An agency must establish a single retention incentive rate for each individual or group of employees that is expressed as a percentage of the employee's rate of basic pay. Except as provided in paragraph (e) of this section, a retention incentive rate may not exceed—

(1) 25 percent, if authorized for an individual employee; or

(2) 10 percent, if authorized for a group or category of employees.

(b) An agency may pay a retention incentive in—

(1) Installments after the completion of specified periods of service; or

(2) A single lump-sum payment after completion of the full service period.

(c)(1) An installment payment is derived by multiplying the rate of basic pay the employee earned in the installment period by a percentage not to exceed the incentive percentage rate established for the employee under paragraph (a) of this section. For example, an agency establishes a retention incentive percentage rate of 10 percent for an employee. The employee has a service agreement that provides for a retention incentive installment payment after completion of 6 pay periods of service at the full percentage rate established for the employee. The employee earns $15,000 during the 6 pay periods of service ($2,500 biweekly rate of basic pay × 6). Upon completion of that service period, the employee will receive the accrued retention incentive installment payment of $1,500 ($15,000 × .10).

(2) If the retention incentive installment payment percentage is less than the full percentage rate established for the employee under paragraph (a) of this section, any accrued portion of the retention incentive that is not paid as an installment payment during the service period must be paid as part of a final installment payment to the employee after completion of the full service period under the terms of the service agreement established under §575.310. For example, an agency establishes a retention incentive percentage rate of 10 percent for an employee. The employee's service agreement provides for a 7 percent retention incentive installment payment after completion of 6 pay periods of service. The employee earns $15,000 during the 6 pay periods of service ($2,500 biweekly rate of basic pay × 6). Upon completion of that installment period, the employee accrues a retention incentive installment payment of $1,500 ($15,000 × .10). However,

under the terms of the service agreement, the employee will receive a $1,050 retention incentive installment payment ($15,000 × .07). The agency must pay the accrued but unpaid portion of the retention incentive payment of $450 ($1,500 − $1,050) as a final lump-sum payment upon completion of the full service period required by the service agreement.

(3) An agency may not pay a retention incentive as an initial lump-sum payment at the start of a service period or in advance of fulfilling the service period for which the retention incentive is being paid.

(d) A retention incentive payment paid as a single lump-sum payment upon completion of the full service period required by the service agreement is derived by multiplying the retention incentive percentage rate established under paragraph (a) of this section by the total basic pay the employee earned during the full service period. For example, an agency establishes a retention incentive percentage rate of 10 percent for an employee. The employee has a service agreement that provides for a single lump-sum retention incentive payment after completion of the full service period required by the service agreement (*i.e.*, 26 pay periods). The employee earns $65,000 during the 26 pay periods of service ($2,500 biweekly rate of basic pay × 26). Upon completion of the full service period, the employee will receive a single lump-sum retention incentive payment of $6,500 ($65,000 × .10).

(e)(1) An authorized agency official may request that OPM waive the limitation in paragraph (a) of this section and permit the agency to pay an individual employee or group of employees a retention incentive of up to 50 percent of the employee's basic pay based on a critical agency need. In addition to the determination required by § 575.308, the authorized agency official must determine that the employee's (or group of employees') unusually high or unique qualifications (*i.e.*, competencies) are critical to the successful accomplishment of an important agency mission, project, or initiative (e.g., programs or projects related to a national emergency or implementing a new law or critical management initiative).

(2) Waiver requests must include—

(i) A description of the employee's work requirements and responsibilities or, if requesting a group retention incentive, a description of the group or category of employees and the number of employees to be covered by the proposed retention incentive;

(ii) A description of the critical agency need the proposed retention incentive would address;

(iii) The written documentation required by § 575.308;

(iv) The proposed retention incentive percentage rate and a justification for that percentage;

(v) The timing and method of making the retention incentive payments;

(vi) The service period required; and

(vii) Any other information pertinent to the case at hand.

(3) OPM may require that waiver requests for groups or categories of employees be coordinated with other agencies having similarly situated employees in the same category.

(4) Notwithstanding § 575.310(f), an authorized agency official must require a signed written service agreement for any employee who may receive a higher retention incentive as a result of approval of a waiver of the maximum limit on the amount of a retention incentive under paragraph (e)(1) of this section.

(f) An agency may not offer or authorize a retention incentive for an individual prior to employment with the agency.

(g) An agency may not commence a group or individual retention incentive service agreement or provide a group or individual retention incentive without a service agreement under § 575.310(f) for any biweekly pay period during—

(1) A period of employment established under any service agreement required for the payment of a recruitment incentive under 5 CFR part 575, subpart A, or a relocation incentive under 5 CFR part 575, subpart B, (see 5 CFR 575.205(e) regarding the authority to commence a relocation incentive service agreement during a period of

employment established under a service agreement for a previously authorized retention incentive or for which an employee is receiving previously authorized retention incentive payments without a service agreement); or

(2) A period of employment established under a service agreement for a previously authorized retention incentive or for which an employee is receiving a previously authorized retention incentive without a service agreement under §575.310(f) (including a group retention incentive with or without a service agreement).

(h) A retention incentive is not part of an employee's rate of basic pay for any purpose.

(i) Payment of a retention incentive is subject to the aggregate limitation on pay under 5 CFR part 530, subpart B.

[70 FR 25747, May 13, 2005, as amended at 72 FR 67839, Dec. 3, 2007]

§575.310 Service agreement requirements.

(a) Before paying a retention incentive, an agency must require an employee, including each employee covered by a group retention incentive authorization and any employee who may receive a higher retention incentive as a result of an approved waiver of the maximum limit on the amount of a retention incentive under §575.309(e), to sign a written service agreement to complete a specified period of employment with the agency (or successor agency in the event of a transfer of function). An authorized agency official must determine the length of a service period. A written service agreement is not required under the condition described in paragraph (f) of this section.

(b) The service agreement must include the commencement and termination dates of the required service period. The service period must begin on the first day of a pay period and end on the last day of a pay period.

(c) The service agreement must specify the retention incentive percentage rate established under §575.309(a); whether the incentive will be paid in installments or in a lump-sum payment upon completion of the service period provided in the service agreement; whether any installment payments will be paid at less than the full retention incentive percentage rate established under §575.309(a), with the accrued but unpaid incentive payment being paid in a lump sum upon completion of the full service period required by the service agreement under §575.309(c)(2); and the timing of incentive payments.

(d) The service agreement must include the conditions under which the agency must terminate the service agreement before the employee completes the agreed-upon service period (*i.e.*, if an employee is demoted or separated for cause, receives a rating of record of less than "Fully Successful" or equivalent, or otherwise fails to fulfill the terms of the service agreement) under §575.311. The service agreement must specify the effect of a termination, including the conditions under which the agency will pay an additional retention incentive payment for partially completed service under §575.311(e) and (f).

(e) The service agreement may include any other terms or conditions that, if violated, will result in a termination of the service agreement under §575.311(b). For example, the service agreement may specify the employee's work schedule, type of position, and the duties he or she is expected to perform. In addition, the service agreement may address the extent to which periods of time on detail, in a nonpay status, or in paid leave status are creditable towards the completion of the service period.

(f) A written service agreement is not required if the agency—

(1) Pays the retention incentive in biweekly installments; and

(2) Sets each biweekly installment payment at the full retention incentive percentage rate established for the employee under §575.309(a).

[70 FR 25747, May 13, 2005, as amended at 70 FR 74996, Dec. 19, 2005]

§575.311 Continuation, reduction, and termination of retention incentives.

(a)(1) For each retention incentive that is subject to a service agreement, an authorized agency official must review the determination to pay a retention incentive at least annually to determine whether the original determination still applies or whether payment is still warranted as provided in paragraph (a)(2) of this section, and must certify this determination in writing.

(2) An authorized agency official must terminate a retention incentive service agreement when conditions change such that the original determination to pay the retention incentive no longer applies (e.g., when the agency assigns the employee to a different position that is not within the terms of the service agreement) or when payment is no longer warranted after considering factors such as—

(i) Whether a retention incentive is needed to retain the employee (or group of employees),

(ii) Whether labor-market factors make it more likely (or reasonably likely) to recruit a candidate with competencies similar to those possessed by the employee (or group of employees), or

(iii) Whether the agency's need for the services of the employee (or group or category of employees) has been reduced to a level that makes it unnecessary to continue paying a retention incentive.

(3) An authorized agency official may terminate unilaterally a retention incentive service agreement based solely on the management needs of the agency, even if the conditions giving rise to the original determination to pay the incentive still exist. For example, an agency may terminate a service agreement when there are insufficient funds to continue the planned retention incentive payments.

(b) An authorized agency official must terminate a retention incentive service agreement when—

(1) The employee is demoted or separated for cause (*i.e.*, for unacceptable performance or conduct);

(2) The employee receives a rating of record (or an official performance appraisal or evaluation under a system not covered by 5 U.S.C. chapter 43 or 5 CFR part 430) of less than "Fully Successful" or equivalent; or

(3) The employee otherwise fails to fulfill the terms of the service agreement.

(c) If an authorized agency official terminates a service agreement under paragraph (a) of this section, the employee is entitled to retain any retention incentive payments that are attributable to completed service and to receive any portion of a retention incentive payment owed by the agency for completed service.

(d) If an authorized agency official terminates a service agreement under paragraph (b) of this section, the employee is entitled to retain retention incentive payments previously paid by the agency that are attributable to the completed portion of the service period. If the employee received retention incentive payments that are less than the amount that would be attributable to the completed portion of the service period, the agency is not obligated to pay the employee the amount attributable to completed service, unless the agency agreed to such payment under the terms of the retention incentive service agreement.

(e) To determine the amount of retention incentive payments that may be owed to an employee for completed service under paragraphs (c) and (d) of this section, multiply the total rate of basic pay the employee earned during the completed portion of the service period by the retention incentive percentage rate established for the employee under § 575.309(a) and subtract the amount of retention incentive payments already paid to the employee from this product. The difference is the amount owed to the employee for completed service.

(f)(1) For retention incentives that are paid when no service agreement is required under § 575.310(f), an agency must review each determination to pay the incentive at least annually to determine whether payment is still warranted. An authorized agency official must certify this determination in writing.

(2) An agency may continue paying a retention incentive to an employee when no service agreement is required as long as the conditions giving rise to the original determination to pay the incentive still exist.

(3) An authorized agency official must reduce or terminate a retention incentive authorization when no service agreement is required whenever conditions change such that the original determination to pay the retention incentive no longer applies (e.g., when the agency assigns the employee to a different position that is not within the terms of the original determination) or when payment is no longer warranted at the level originally approved or at all after considering factors such as—

(i) Whether a lesser amount (or none at all) would be sufficient to retain the employee (or group or category of employees);

(ii) Whether labor-market factors make it more likely (or reasonably likely) to recruit a candidate with competencies similar to those possessed by the employee (or group or category of employees); or

(iii) Whether the agency's need for the services of the employee (or group or category of employees) has been reduced to a level that makes it unnecessary to continue payment at the level originally approved (or at all).

(4) An authorized agency official may terminate unilaterally a retention incentive authorization when no service agreement is required based solely on the management needs of the agency, even if the conditions giving rise to the original determination to pay the incentive still exist. For example, an agency may terminate a retention incentive when there are insufficient funds to continue the planned retention incentive payments.

(5) An authorized agency official must terminate a retention incentive authorization when no service agreement is required when—

(i) The employee is demoted or separated for cause (*i.e.*, for unacceptable performance or conduct), or

(ii) The employee receives a rating of record (or an official performance appraisal or evaluation under a system not covered by 5 U.S.C. chapter 43 or 5 CFR part 430) of less than "Fully Successful" or equivalent.

(g) The termination of a retention incentive service agreement or the reduction or termination of a retention incentive under this section is not grievable or appealable.

(h) If an agency terminates a retention incentive service agreement or reduces or terminates a retention incentive paid without a service agreement under this section, the agency must notify the employee in writing. When a retention incentive is terminated under paragraph (f) of this section, the employee is entitled to receive any scheduled incentive payments through the end of the pay period in which the written notice is provided or until the date of separation, if sooner.

[72 FR 67840, Dec. 3, 2007, as amended at 78 FR 49364, Aug. 14, 2013]

§575.312 Internal monitoring requirements and revocation or suspension of authority.

(a) Each agency must monitor the use of retention incentives to ensure that its retention incentive plan and the payment of retention incentives are consistent with the requirements and criteria established under 5 U.S.C. 5754 and this subpart.

(b) When OPM finds that an agency is not paying retention incentives consistent with the agency's retention incentive plan and the criteria established under 5 U.S.C. 5754 or this subpart or otherwise determines that the agency is not using this authority selectively and judiciously, OPM may—

(1) Direct the agency to revoke or suspend the authority granted to any organizational component of the agency and, with respect to any category or categories of employees, require that the component obtain approval from the agency's headquarters level before paying a retention incentive to such employees; or

(2) Revoke or suspend the authority granted to the agency under this subpart for all or any part of the agency and, with respect to any category or categories of employees, require that the agency obtain OPM's approval before paying a retention incentive to such employees.

§575.313 Records and reports.

Each agency must keep a record of each determination to pay a retention incentive and make such records available for review upon OPM's request.

[70 FR 25747, May 13, 2005, as amended at 78 FR 49364, Aug. 14, 2013]

§575.314 Retention incentives for employees likely to leave for a different position in the Federal service.

(a) *Authority*. (1) An agency in its sole and exclusive discretion, subject only to OPM review and oversight, may approve a retention incentive for an individual employee under the conditions prescribed in this section when the agency determines that—

(i) Given the agency's mission requirements and employee's competencies, the agency has a special need for the employee's services that makes it essential to retain the employee in his or her current position during a period of time before the closure or relocation of the employee's office, facility, activity, or organization; and

(ii) The employee would be likely to leave for a different position in the Federal service in the absence of a retention incentive.

(2) An agency in its sole and exclusive discretion, subject only to OPM review and oversight, may approve a retention incentive for a group or category of employees (subject to the exclusions in §575.305(c)) under the conditions prescribed in this section when the agency determines that—

(i) Given the agency's mission requirements and employees' competencies, the agency has a special need for the employees' services that makes it essential to retain the employees in their current positions during a period of time before the closure or relocation of the employees' office, facility, activity, or organization; and

(ii) There is a high risk that a significant number of the employees in the group would be likely to leave for different positions in the Federal service in the absence of a retention incentive.

(b) *Employee eligibility*. An agency may pay a retention incentive to an employee under this section when—

(1) The employee holds a position listed in §575.303, and is not excluded by §575.304;

(2) The employee's rating of record (or an official performance appraisal or evaluation under a system not covered by 5 U.S.C. chapter 43 or 5 CFR part 430) is at least "Fully Successful" or equivalent; and

(3) The agency has provided a general or specific written notice to the employee that his or her position may or would be affected by the closure or relocation of the employee's office, facility, activity, or organization (e.g., the employee's position may or would move to a new geographic location or the employee's position may or would be eliminated).

(c) *Retention incentive plan and approval levels*. Before authorizing a retention incentive under this section, an agency must include in its retention incentive plan established under §575.307(a) the conditions and requirements governing the use of retention incentives under this section for employees who would be likely to leave for a different position in the Federal service before the closure or relocation of the employees' office, facility, activity, or organization, including a designation of the authorized agency officials who may approve retention incentives under this section, consistent with the approval requirements in §575.307(b).

(d) *Approval criteria and written determination*. (1) For each determination to pay a retention incentive under this section, an agency must document in writing—

(i) The basis for determining the agency has a special need for the employee's (or group of employees') services that makes it essential to retain the employee(s), based on the agency's mission needs and the employee's (or group of employees') competencies, during a period of time before the closure or relocation of the employee's (or group of employees') office, facility, activity, or organization;

(ii) The basis for determining, in the absence of a retention incentive, the employee (or a significant number of employees in a group) would be likely to leave for a different position in the Federal service; and

(iii) The basis for establishing the amount and timing of the approved retention incentive payment and the length of the required service period.

(2) An agency must address the following factors when documenting the determination required by paragraph (a) of this section for an individual employee:

(i) The factors for authorizing a retention incentive for an individual employee described in § 575.306(b) as they relate to a determination made under paragraph (a)(1) of this section;

(ii) The extent to which the employee's departure for a different position in the Federal service would affect the agency's ability to carry out an activity, perform a function, or complete a project the agency deems essential to its mission before and during the closure or relocation period (e.g., the agency's need to retain the employee to ensure minimal disruption in the performance of mission-critical functions, continuity of key operations, or minimal disruption of service to the public before and during the closure or relocation; to train new employees who will move with the organization to the new geographic location; to assist with the actual closure or relocation of the office, facility, activity, or organization; or to perform similar mission-essential functions before or during the closure or relocation);

(iii) The competencies possessed by the employee that are essential to retain; and

(iv) The agency (which may be in the executive, judicial, or legislative branch) for which the employee would be likely to leave in the absence of the retention incentive.

(3) An agency must address the following factors when documenting the determination required by paragraph (a) of this section for a group or category of employees:

(i) The factors for authorizing a retention incentive for a group or category of employees described in § 575.306(c) as they relate to the determination made under paragraph (a)(2) of this section; and

(ii) The factors in paragraphs (d)(2)(ii) through (d)(2)(iv) of this section as they relate to the determination made under paragraph (a)(2) of this section for the group or category of employees.

(4) An agency must narrowly define a targeted category of employees using factors that relate to the conditions described in paragraph (a)(2) of this section. The factors that may be appropriate are described in § 575.306(c)(2), except that each group retention incentive authorized under this section may cover no more than one occupational series.

(e) *Payment of retention incentives.* (1) Except as provided in paragraph (e)(2) of this section, the provisions regarding computing and paying retention incentives under § 575.309 apply to computing and paying retention incentives under this section for employees who would be likely to leave for a different position in the Federal service before the closure or relocation of the their office, facility, activity, or organization.

(2) An agency may not pay retention incentives under this section in biweekly installments at the full retention incentive percentage rate established for the employee under § 575.309(a).

(f) *Service agreement requirements.* (1) The service agreement provisions in §§ 575.310(b) through 575.310(e) apply to retention incentive service agreements under this section, subject to the additional requirements in paragraphs (f)(2) through (f)(5) of this section.

(2) Before paying a retention incentive under this section, an agency must require an employee, including each employee covered by a group retention incentive authorization, to sign a written service agreement to complete a specified period of employment with the agency.

(3) In no event, may the service period under a service agreement established under this paragraph extend past the date on which the employee's position is actually affected by the relocation or closure of the employee's office, facility, activity, or organization (e.g., the date the employee's position moves to a new geographic location or the date the employee's position is eliminated).

(4) In addition to the terminating conditions in § 575.310(d) and (e), the service agreement must include the

conditions under which the agency must terminate the service agreement under paragraph (g) of this section, including the conditions under which the agency will pay an additional retention incentive payment for partially completed service under § 575.311.

(5) The service agreement must include a notification to the employee that the agency will review the determination to pay the retention incentive at least annually to determine whether payment is still warranted, as required by paragraph (g) of this section.

(g) *Termination of retention incentives.* (1) The provisions in § 575.311 regarding termination of retention incentive service agreements and paragraphs (g)(2) through (g)(4) of this section apply to the termination of retention incentives authorized under this section. Each determination to pay a retention incentive under this section must be reviewed at least annually to determine if payment is still warranted. An authorized agency official must certify this determination in writing.

(2) In addition to the terminating conditions in § 575.311(a) and (b), an authorized agency official must terminate a retention incentive service agreement under this section if—

(i) The closure or relocation is cancelled or no longer affects the employee's position;

(ii) The employee moves to another position not affected by the closure or relocation (including another position within the same agency);

(iii) For relocation situations, the employee accepts the agency's offer to relocate with his or her the office, facility, activity, or organization and, thus, the employee is no longer likely to leave for a different position in the Federal service; or

(iv) The employee moves to a different position in the same office, facility, activity, or organization subject to closure or relocation that is not covered by the employee's service agreement. In this situation, the agency may authorize a new retention incentive for the employee under this section, as appropriate.

(3) If an authorized agency official terminates a service agreement under paragraph (g)(2)(ii) or (iv) of this section in cases in which the employee's movement to another position is by management action and not at the employee's request or under paragraph (g)(2)(i) of this section, the employee is entitled to retain any retention incentive payments that are attributable to completed service and to receive any portion of a retention incentive payment owed by the agency for completed service.

(4) If an authorized agency official terminates a service agreement in termination actions under paragraph (g)(2) of this section that are not covered by paragraph (g)(3) of this section, the employee is entitled to retain retention incentive payments previously paid by the agency that are attributable to the completed portion of the service period. If the employee received retention incentive payments that are less than the amount that would be attributable to the completed portion of the service period, the agency is not obligated to pay the employee the amount attributable to completed service, unless the agency agreed to such payment under the terms of the retention incentive service agreement.

(h) *Monitoring requirements.* The monitoring requirements in § 575.312 apply to retention incentives authorized under this section.

(i) *Records and reports.* In addition to the recordkeeping requirements in § 575.313, each agency must submit a written report to OPM by March 31 of each year on the use of retention incentives under this section. Each report must include—

(1) A description of how the authority to pay retention incentives under this section was used in the agency during the previous calendar year;

(2) The number and dollar amount of retention incentives paid during the previous calendar year to individuals under this section by occupational series and grade, pay level, or other pay classification;

(3) The agency (which may be in the executive, judicial, legislative branch) to which each employee would be likely to leave in the absence of a retention incentive;

(4) Each employee's official worksite and the geographic location of the

agency (which may be in the executive, judicial, or legislative branch) for which each employee would be likely to leave in the absence of a retention incentive; and

(5) Other information, records, reports, and data as OPM may require.

[72 FR 64527, Nov. 16, 2007. Redesignated and amended at 78 FR 49364, Aug. 14, 2013]

Subpart D—Supervisory Differentials

SOURCE: 56 FR 20338, May 3, 1991, unless otherwise noted.

§ 575.401 Purpose.

This subpart provides regulations to implement 5 U.S.C. 5755, which authorizes payment of a supervisory differential to an employee under the General Schedule who has supervisory responsibility for one or more civilian employees not under the General Schedule if one or more of the subordinate civilian employees would, in the absence of such a differential, be paid more than the supervisory employee.

§ 575.402 Delegation of authority.

(a) The head of an agency may pay a supervisory differential to a supervisor who is—

(1) In a General Schedule position paid under 5 U.S.C. 5332; and

(2) Responsible for providing direct, technical supervision over the work of one or more civilian employees whose positions are not under the General Schedule if the continuing pay (as determined under § 575.405(d) of this part) of one or more of the subordinates would, in the absence of such a differential, be more than the continuing pay (as determined under § 575.405(c) of this part) of the supervisor.

(b) A supervisory differential may not be paid on the basis of supervising a civilian employee whose rate of basic pay exceeds the maximum rate of basic pay established for grade GS–15 on the pay schedule applicable to the GS supervisor, including a schedule for any applicable special rate under 5 CFR part 530, subpart C; locality-based comparability payment under 5 CFR part 531, subpart F; or similar payment or supplement under other legal authority.

[56 FR 20338, May 3, 1991, as amended at 57 FR 37394, Aug. 19, 1992; 58 FR 65537, Dec. 15, 1993; 61 FR 3543, Feb. 1, 1996; 70 FR 25751, May 13, 2005; 72 FR 67841, Dec. 3, 2007]

§ 575.403 Definitions.

In this subpart:

Agency has the meaning given that term in 5 U.S.C. 5102.

Continuing pay means the aggregate of all continuing payments and annual premium pay received by an employee at any one time.

Continuing payment means basic pay and any other form of pay that is paid in the same manner and at the same time as basic pay—*i.e.*, for periods during which an employee receives basic pay.

Employee has the meaning given that term in 5 U.S.C. 5102.

Head of agency means the head of an agency or an official who has been delegated the authority to act for the head of the agency in the matter concerned.

Rate of basic pay means the rate of pay fixed by law or administrative action for the position to which the employee is or will be appointed before deductions and including any special rate under 5 CFR part 530, subpart C; locality-based comparability payment under 5 CFR part 531, subpart F; or similar payment or supplement under other legal authority, but excluding additional pay of any other kind. For example, *rate of basic pay* excludes a night differential under 5 U.S.C. 5343(f), an environment differential under 5 U.S.C. 5343(c)(4), or a similar payment under other legal authority.

Supervisor has the meaning given that term in 5 U.S.C. 7103(a)(10).

[56 FR 20338, May 3, 1991, as amended at 57 FR 2435, Jan. 22, 1992; 61 FR 3543, Feb. 1, 1996; 70 FR 25751, May 13, 2005; 72 FR 67841, Dec. 3, 2007]

§ 575.404 Use of authority.

(a) Each determination to pay a supervisory differential shall be made in writing under procedures established by each agency.

(b) The procedures established by each agency under paragraph (a) of this section shall provide that—

(1) Each determination to pay a supervisory differential, including the amount of such differential, shall be reviewed and approved by an official of the agency who is at higher level than the official who made the initial decision, unless there is no official at a higher level in the agency; and

(2) In determining whether to use the authority under 5 U.S.C. 5755 and this subpart and in determining the amount of such differential, the relationship in pay among supervisors under the General Schedule in the same organizational component of the agency shall be considered, as well as the relationship in pay between the supervisor and his or her subordinate(s).

(3) Each determination to pay a supervisory differential shall be documented.

§ 575.405 Calculation and payment of supervisory differential.

(a) A supervisory differential shall be calculated as a percentage of the supervisor's rate of basic pay or as a dollar amount and shall be paid in the same manner and at the same time as the supervisor's basic pay—*i.e.*, the differential shall be paid at an hourly rate for each hour during which the supervisor receives basic pay.

(b) The amount of a supervisory differential shall not cause the supervisor's continuing pay, as determined under paragraph (c) of this section, to exceed the continuing pay of the highest paid subordinate not under the General Schedule, as determined under paragraph (d) of this section, by more than 3 percent.

(c) For purposes of comparing the continuing pay of a supervisor whose position is under the General Schedule with the continuing pay of a subordinate whose position is not under the General Schedule, the following payments shall be included in determining the amount of continuing pay received by the supervisor:

(1) Basic pay, including a retained rate of pay under 5 U.S.C. 5363 and part 536 of this chapter or other similar authority:

(2) Any other continuing payment, except night, Sunday, or holiday premium pay or a hazardous duty differential under chapter 55 of title 5, United States Code;

(3) Premium pay paid on an annual basis under 5 U.S.C. 5545(c); and

(4) Any other continuing payment, except night, Sunday, or holiday premium pay or hazardous duty pay under 5 U.S.C. chapter 55, subchapter V; recruitment or relocation incentives under 5 U.S.C. 5753; retention incentives under 5 U.S.C. 5754; or similar payments under other legal authority.

(d) For purposes of comparing the continuing pay of a supervisor whose position is under the General Schedule with the continuing pay of a subordinate whose position is not under the General Schedule, the following payments shall be included in determining the amount of continuing pay received by the subordinate:

(1) Basic pay, excluding a night or environmental differential under 5 U.S.C. 5343(f) or 5343(c)(4), respectively, or similar payment under other legal authority;

(2) Any other continuing payment, except Sunday or holiday pay under 5 U.S.C. chapter 55, subchapter V; recruitment or relocation incentives under 5 U.S.C. 5753; retention incentives under 5 U.S.C. 5754; or similar payments under other legal authority; and

(3) Premium pay paid on an annual basis under an authority similar to 5 U.S.C. 5545(c).

(e) For the purpose of making any of the comparisons required by this subpart, continuing pay shall be calculated on an annual basis for both the supervisor and the subordinate.

(f) Payment of a supervisory differential is subject to the aggregate limitation on pay under 5 U.S.C. 5307 and subpart B of part 530 of this chapter.

(g) A supervisory differential shall not be considered part of the supervisor's rate of basic pay for any purpose.

[56 FR 20338, May 3, 1991, as amended at 57 FR 2435, Jan. 22, 1992; 57 FR 37394, Aug. 19, 1992; 59 FR 66154, Dec. 23, 1994; 61 FR 3544, Feb. 1, 1996; 70 FR 25752, May 13, 2005; 72 FR 67841, Dec. 3, 2007]

§ 575.406 Adjustment or termination of supervisory differential.

(a) An agency may establish procedures that allow for adjusting or terminating a supervisory differential at any time the agency determines it is appropriate to do so.

(b) A supervisory differential shall be terminated when the continuing pay of the supervisor (not including the supervisory differential) exceeds the continuing pay of the highest paid subordinate whose position is not under the General Schedule.

(c) A supervisory differential shall be reduced or terminated, as appropriate, when the continuing pay of the supervisor (including the supervisory differential) exceeds the continuing pay of the highest paid subordinate whose position is not under the General Schedule by more than 3 percent.

(d) The effective date of a reduction or termination of a supervisory differential under paragraph (b) or (c) of this section shall be not later than 30 calendar days after the date on which the event that necessitates the reduction or termination occurs.

(e) Each determination to adjust a supervisory differential shall be made in writing under procedures established by each agency similar to those established under § 575.404 of this part.

(f) The reduction or termination of a supervisory differential may not be appealed. However, the preceding sentence shall not be construed to extinguish or lessen any right or remedy under subchapter II of chapter 12 of title 5, United States Code, or under any of the laws referred to in 5 U.S.C. 2302(d).

[56 FR 20338, May 3, 1991, as amended at 57 FR 37394, Aug. 19, 1992]

§ 575.407 Records.

(a) Each agency shall keep a record of each determination required by §§ 575.404(a) and 575.406(e) of this part. Each record shall contain sufficient information to allow reconstruction of the action, including the basis for determining the amount of the differential and the comparison of continuing pay required by § 575.405(b) of this part.

(b) Each agency shall promptly submit a report of each determination made to establish, adjust, or terminate a supervisory differential as a part of its regular submission to OPM's Central Personnel Data File.

Subpart E—Extended Assignment Incentives

SOURCE: 68 FR 53669, Sept. 12, 2003, unless otherwise noted.

§ 575.501 Purpose.

This subpart contains OPM regulations implementing 5 U.S.C. 5757, which authorizes the payment of extended assignment incentives. Subject to the requirements of this subpart, an agency may pay an extended assignment incentive to eligible Federal employees assigned to positions located in a territory or possession of the United States, the Commonwealth of Puerto Rico, or the Commonwealth of the Northern Mariana Islands who agree to complete a specified additional period of employment with the agency in that location.

§ 575.502 Definitions.

In this subpart:

Agency means an "Executive agency," as defined in 5 U.S.C. 105.

Authorized agency official means the head of an agency or an official who is authorized to act for the head of the agency in the matter concerned.

Employee means an employee of an agency who satisfies the definition of that term in 5 U.S.C. 2105.

Involuntarily reassigned refers to a reassignment initiated by an agency against an employee's will and without he employee's consent for reasons other than cause on charges of misconduct, delinquency, or inefficiency.

Involuntarily separated refers to a separation initiated by an agency against an employee's will and without the employee's consent for reasons other than cause on charges of misconduct, delinquency, or inefficiency. In addition, when an employee is separated because he or she declines to accept reassignment to another geographic area outside one of the covered locations, the separation is involuntary if the employee's position description or other written agreement does not provide for such reassignment. However, an employee's separation is not involuntary if, after such a written mobility agreement is added, the employee accepts one reassignment outside his or her particular territory, possession, or commonwealth, but subsequently declines another reassignment. An employee's separation as a result of disability retirement, a disability that prevents an employee from continuing Federal service or is the basis for separation by the agency as determined by acceptable medical evidence, or the death of an employee is considered to be an involuntary separation.

Rate of basic pay means the rate of pay fixed by law or administrative action for the position held by an employee, including any special rate under 5 CFR part 530, subpart C; locality-based comparability payment under 5 CFR part 531, subpart F; or similar payment under other legal authority, but before deductions and exclusive of additional pay of any other kind. For example, a *rate of basic pay* may not include nonforeign area cost-of-living allowances under 5 U.S.C. 5941, night shift differentials under 5 U.S.C. 5343(f), or environmental differentials under 5 U.S.C. 5343(c)(4).

Service agreement means a written agreement between an agency and an employee under which the employee agrees to a specified period of employment with the agency in a particular territory, possession, or commonwealth in return for payment of an extended assignment incentive.

Service period means an agreed-upon period of employment an employee is obligated to complete under a service agreement.

Territory, possession, or commonwealth means a territory or a possession of the United States, the Commonwealth of Puerto Rico, or the Commonwealth of the Northern Mariana Islands.

[68 FR 53669, Sept. 12, 2003, as amended at 70 FR 25752, May 13, 2005; 72 FR 67841, Dec. 3, 2007]

§ 575.503 Who may approve the payment of an extended assignment incentive?

An authorized agency official must review and approve the offer of an extended assignment incentive for an employee, including the amount of such incentive. The authorized agency official must be at a higher level than the official who made the initial decision to offer an extended assignment incentive, unless there is no official at a higher level in the agency.

§ 575.504 What requirements must an agency satisfy before authorizing the payment of an extended assignment incentive?

Before paying an extended assignment incentive under this subpart, an agency must establish an extended assignment incentive plan. This plan must include the following elements:

(a) The designation of authorized agency officials who must review and approve the payment of extended assignment incentives;

(b) The categories of employees which are prohibited from receiving an extended assignment incentive;

(c) The criteria that must be met or considered in authorizing extended assignment incentives, including criteria for determining the size of an incentive;

(d) The requirements governing service agreements, including the obligations of the agency and the employee when the service period is not completed;

(e) The procedures for paying extended assignment incentives; and

(f) Documentation and recordkeeping requirements sufficient to allow reconstruction of the action.

§ 575.505 What criteria must an agency use to determine who will receive an extended assignment incentive?

(a) An agency must base the payment of an extended assignment incentive on a written determination that—

(1) The eligible employee has completed at least 2 years of continuous service immediately before the commencement of the service agreement in one or more civil service positions located in a particular territory, possession, or commonwealth;

(2) It is in the best interest of the Government to encourage the employee to complete a specified additional period of employment with the agency in that location; and

(3) Replacing the employee with another employee possessing the required qualifications and experience would be difficult.

(b) In determining whether it is in the best interest of the Government to retain an employee under paragraph (a)(2) of this section, an agency may consider how the employee's departure would affect the agency's ability to operate effectively or to carry out an activity or perform a function which the agency deems essential to its mission.

(c) Any determination to approve an extended assignment incentive must be made on a case-by-case basis for each employee. However, an agency may consider common factors that apply to a category of employees, such as past recruitment and retention problems or the anticipation of such problems in the future.

§575.506 When is an agency prohibited from paying an extended assignment incentive?

(a) An extended assignment incentive may not be paid to the head of an agency, including an agency headed by a collegial body composed of two or more individual members.

(b) An agency may not begin paying an extended assignment incentive to an otherwise eligible employee who is receiving or fulfilling the requirements of a service agreement for the payment of a recruitment, relocation, or retention incentive. (See 5 CFR part 575, subparts A, B, and C.)

[68 FR 53669, Sept. 12, 2003, as amended at 70 FR 25752, May 13, 2005]

§575.507 What is the maximum extended assignment incentive that may be paid for a period of service?

(a) The total amount of extended assignment incentive payments that may be paid for a service period may not exceed the greater of—

(1) An amount equal to 25 percent of the annual rate of basic pay of the employee at the beginning of the service period times the number of years (including fractions of a year) in the service period; or

(2) $15,000 per year (including fractions of a year) in the service period.

(b) For hourly rate employees who do not have a scheduled annual rate of basic pay, the annual rate in paragraph (a) of this section is computed by multiplying the applicable hourly rate in effect at the beginning of the service period by 2,087 hours.

(c) The number of years in the service period is computed by dividing the total number of calendar days in the service period (as established under §575.510(a)) by 365 and rounding the result to two decimal places. For example, a service period covering 39 biweekly pay periods equals 546 days, and 546 days divided by 365 days equals 1.50 years.

§575.508 What is the maximum amount of service that may be covered by an extended assignment incentive?

An employee's total service under one or more extended assignment incentive service agreements with a particular agency for service in a particular territory, possession, or commonwealth may not exceed 5 years. For this purpose, a year is equal to 365 days, resulting in a total service limit of 1,825 days.

§575.509 Is an extended assignment incentive considered basic pay for any purpose?

No, an extended assignment incentive is not considered part of an employee's rate of basic pay for any purpose, nor is it included for the purpose of calculating a lump-sum payment for annual leave under 5 CFR 550.1205.

§575.510 What requirements are associated with service agreements?

(a) Before paying an extended assignment incentive, the agency must require the employee to sign a written service agreement to complete a specified period of employment with the agency in a particular territory, possession, or commonwealth. The service period must meet the following conditions:

(1) The service period must begin on the first day of a pay period and end on the last day of a pay period; and

(2) The service period must not cause an employee to exceed the 5-year lifetime limitation described in §575.508.

(b) In addition to the service requirement in paragraph (a) of this section, the service agreement may specify other terms and conditions of employment applicable to the employee. For example, the service agreement may specify the employee's work schedule, type of position, and performance level. In addition, the service agreement may address the extent to which periods of time on a detail, in a nonpay status, or in a paid leave status are creditable towards the completion of the service period.

(c) The service agreement must specify the method of payment of an extended assignment agreement. The agency may choose to pay an extended assignment incentive in an initial lump-sum payment at the beginning of the service period, in installments at the end of specified periods throughout the service period (biweekly, monthly, quarterly, etc.), in a lump-sum payment at the end of the entire service period, or through a combination of payment methods.

(d) The service agreement must include the conditions under which the employee would be required to repay an extended assignment incentive under § 575.513.

(e) The service agreement must specify the conditions under which the payment of an extended assignment incentive may be terminated by the agency under § 575.512.

(f) The service agreement must specify the conditions under which the agency may be obligated to pay an additional incentive payment for partially completed service, as provided in § 575.513(d).

(g) The service agreement must specify the conditions under which the agency may impose a repayment penalty under § 575.513(e) for an employee who fails to fulfill the terms of the service agreement.

(h) The service agreement must specify the conditions under which the agency may be obligated to pay an incentive payment attributable to some or all of the employee's *uncompleted* service for employees covered by § 575.511 or § 575.512.

§ 575.511 What happens when an employee is involuntarily separated or involuntarily reassigned prior to completion of the service period?

An employee who is involuntarily separated or is involuntarily reassigned to a position outside the particular territory, possession, or commonwealth involved is not indebted to the Federal Government for any extended assignment incentive payments he or she has received. The employee is entitled to keep all incentive payments received and, if applicable, is entitled to receive any additional amount representing the difference between the amount received and the prorated share of the total incentive attributable to completed service. The employee may receive a portion or all of the incentive payment attributable to uncompleted service only to the extent provided in the service agreement.

[68 FR 53669, Sept. 12, 2003; 68 FR 56665, Oct. 1, 2003]

§ 575.512 When may an agency terminate a service agreement?

(a) An agency may unilaterally terminate a service agreement based solely on the business needs of the agency. For example, an authorized agency official may terminate a service agreement when the employee's position is affected by a reduction in force or when there are insufficient funds to continue the planned incentive payments.

(b) If an agency terminates a service agreement under paragraph (a) of this section, the employee is entitled to keep all incentive payments received and, if applicable, is entitled to receive any additional amount representing the difference between the amount received and the prorated share of the total incentive attributable to completed service. The employee may receive a portion or all of the incentive payment attributable to uncompleted service only to the extent provided in the service agreement.

§ 575.513 What are the agency's and the employee's obligations when an employee fails to fulfill the terms of a service agreement?

(a) This section does not apply when an employee is involuntarily separated or involuntarily reassigned to a position outside the particular territory, possession, or commonwealth involved, as provided in § 575.511 or when an agency unilaterally terminates a service agreement under § 575.512.

(b) Except as provided in paragraph (g) of this section, an employee is indebted to the Federal Government and must repay the paying agency for an appropriate portion of an extended assignment incentive received by the employee if—

(1) The employee fails to complete the period of employment required in his or her service agreement; or

(2) The employee violates any other condition specified in the service agreement that would trigger termination of the agreement.

(c)(1) If an employee does not fulfill the terms of a service agreement under the circumstances prescribed in paragraph (b) of this section and has received incentive payments whose value as a percentage of the planned total sum of incentive payments for the entire service period exceeds the percentage reflecting the portion of the service period completed by the employee, he or she must repay the excess payment and any additional repayment penalty imposed by the agency under paragraph (e) of this section, except when an authorized agency official waives the requirement to repay the excess amount under paragraph (g) of this section.

(2) For example, consider an employee who signed a 364-day (26 pay period) service agreement and received the full amount of the extended assignment incentive as an initial lump-sum payment. If the employee voluntarily leaves after 20 pay periods (280 days), the employee will have received 100 percent of the total extended assignment incentive while completing only 76.9 percent (280/364) of the service period. The excess is 23.1 percent. Therefore, the employee must repay 23.1 percent (84/364) of the incentive. The employee is entitled to keep 76.9 percent of the incentive, unless the agency imposes an additional repayment penalty for failure to fulfill the service agreement under paragraph (e) of this section.

(d)(1) If an employee does not fulfill the terms of the service agreement under the circumstances prescribed in paragraph (b) of this section and has received incentive payments whose value as a percentage of the planned total sum of incentive payments for the entire service period is less than or equal to the percentage reflecting the portion of the service period completed by the employee, the employee has no repayment obligation unless the agency imposes an additional repayment penalty under paragraph (e) of this section. The agency may pay an additional incentive payment for some or all of the service completed by the employee if such additional payment is required by the service agreement. The total amount of incentive payments received by the employee may not exceed the prorated share of the planned incentive attributable to completed service.

(2) For example, consider an employee who signed a 364-day (26 pay period) service agreement to receive a total extended assignment payment of $24,501 in two equal installment payments—*i.e.*, $12,250.50 at the end of 13 pay periods of completed service and $12,250.50 at the end of the required service period. If the employee voluntarily leaves after 20 pay periods (280 days), the employee will have received only 50 percent of the total extended assignment incentive while completing 76.9 percent (280/364) of the service agreement. The agency may pay the employee an additional amount of up to 26.9 percent of the incentive payment that is attributable to completed service, as allowed under the terms of the service agreement, assuming the agency does not impose an additional repayment penalty for failure to fulfill the service period under paragraph (e) of this section.

(e) An agency may impose an additional repayment penalty on an employee who does not fulfill the terms of a service agreement. This repayment penalty is in addition to any repayment required by paragraph (c) of this section. The specific terms and conditions governing the repayment penalty must be included in the service agreement. For example, an agency may adopt a schedule or formula that provides for varying penalty amounts based on the portion of the service period completed by the employee.

(f) If an employee fails to reimburse the paying agency for the full amount owed under this section, the amount outstanding must be recovered from the employee under the agency's regulations for collection by offset from an indebted Government employee under 5 U.S.C. 5514 and 5 CFR part 550, subpart K, or through the appropriate provisions for debt collection if the individual is no longer a Federal employee.

(g) If an employee received extended assignment incentive payments in excess of the amount that would be attributable to the completed portion of the service period under paragraph (c) of this section, an authorized agency official may waive the requirement to repay the excess amount when, in the judgment of the official, collection of the excess amount would be against equity and good conscience and not in the best interest of the United States.

[68 FR 53669, Sept. 12, 2003, as amended at 69 FR 33536, June 16, 2004; 72 FR 67841, Dec. 3, 2007]

§ 575.514 What are an agency's monitoring responsibilities?

Each agency must monitor the use of extended assignment incentives to ensure that the agency's extended assignment incentive plan and the payment of extended assignment incentives are consistent with the requirements and criteria established under 5 U.S.C. 5757 and this subpart.

§ 575.515 What records and reports are required?

(a) Each agency must keep a record of each determination required by this subpart and make such records available for review upon OPM's request.

(b) Each agency must provide any information requested by OPM for its report to Congress, as required by 5 U.S.C. 5757(d). Before February 15, 2006, each agency must submit a written report to OPM on—

(1) The agency's use of extended assignment incentives by providing the data required in paragraph (c) of this section;

(2) Whether the use of extended assignment incentives influenced employees to stay longer than their initial tour of duty at their current duty stations; and

(3) The agency's recommendations for changes necessary to improve the effectiveness of extended assignment incentives.

(c) Each agency report must contain the following data for the period from May 2, 2003, to December 31, 2005:

(1) The number of extended assignment service agreements that commenced in each fiscal year;

(2) The dollar amount expended on extended assignment incentives in each fiscal year;

(3) The number of employees who declined an extended assignment incentive, by occupational series and geographic location;

(4) The number of employees who signed an extended assignment incentive service agreement, the total amount of the planned incentives, and the total number of years of agreed-upon service, by occupational series and geographic location;

(5) The number of employees whose service agreements were terminated before completion of the agreed-upon service period, with subcounts showing the number covered by §§ 575.511, 575.512, and 575.513, respectively.

(6) The number of employees who incurred a repayment debt under § 575.513 (including any repayment penalty under § 575.513(e)) and the total amount of repayment debt incurred; and

(7) The portion of the repayment debt that, as of December 31, 2005—

(i) Has been recovered;

(ii) Is subject to ongoing collection efforts; and

(iii) Has been waived or written off.

PART 576—VOLUNTARY SEPARATION INCENTIVE PAYMENTS

Subpart A—Voluntary Separation Incentive Payments

Subpart B—Waiver of Repayment of Voluntary Separation Incentive Payments

AUTHORITY: Sections 3521 through 3525 of title 5, United States Code.

SOURCE: 70 FR 3859, Jan. 27, 2005, unless otherwise noted.

Subpart A—Voluntary Separation Incentive Payments

§576.101 Definitions.

In this part:

Employee, as defined in 5 U.S.C. 3521, means an employee as defined under 5 U.S.C. 2105 employed by an agency and an individual employed by a county committee established under section 8(b)(5) of the Soil Conservation and Domestic Allotment Act (16 U.S.C. 590h(b)(5)) who—

(1) Is serving under an appointment without time limitation; and

(2) Has been currently employed for a continuous period of at least 3 years.

Specific designee means a senior officer or official within an agency who has been specifically designated to sign requests for authority to offer Voluntary Separation Incentive Payments for, or in place of, the head of the agency. Examples include the Chief Human Capital Officer, the Assistant Secretary for Administration, the Director of Human Resources Management, or a deputy of one of these persons.

§576.102 Voluntary Separation Incentive Payment implementation plans.

(a) In accordance with section 3522(b) of title 5, United States Code, a plan submitted by the head of an agency, or his or her specific designee, must include:

(1) Identification of the specific positions and functions to be reduced or eliminated, identified by organizational unit, geographic location, occupational series, grade level and any other factors related to the position;

(2) A description of the categories of employees who will be offered incentives identified by organizational unit, geographic location, occupational series, grade level and any other factors, such as skills, knowledge, or retirement eligibility (as discussed in implementing guidance);

(3) The time period during which incentives may be paid;

(4) The number and maximum amounts of Voluntary Separation Incentive Payments to be offered;

(5) A description of how the agency will operate without the eliminated or restructured positions and functions;

(6) A proposed organizational chart displaying the expected changes in the agency's organizational structure after the agency has completed the incentive payments;

(7) A short explanation of how Voluntary Early Retirement Authority will be used in conjunction with separation incentives, if the agency has requested, or will request, that authority; and

(8) A description of how Voluntary Separation Incentives offered under another statutory authority are being used, if the agency is offering incentives under any other statutory authority.

(b) When submitting a plan to OPM, the agency may submit either:

(1) A specific Voluntary Separation Incentive Payment implementation plan outlining the intended use of the incentive payments, or

(2) The agency's human capital plan, which outlines the intended use of the incentive payments and the expected changes in the agency's organizational structure after the agency has completed the incentive payments. If the human capital plan is submitted, it must include the information specified in paragraph (a) of this section.

(c) OPM will consult with the Office of Management and Budget regarding the plan and any subsequent modifications, and will notify the agency head in writing when the plan is approved. The review may include a consideration of costs and benefits associated with using the authority. If there are questions concerning the agency's plan, OPM reserves the right to contact the agency, inform agency staff of its concerns, and require that the agency revise the plan to bring it into conformance with these regulations. The agency must obtain OPM approval before offering incentives under this authority.

§ 576.103 Offering Voluntary Separation Incentive Payments to employees.

(a) Agencies may make offers of Voluntary Separation Incentive Payments to employees who agree to voluntarily separate by resignation, early retirement, or optional retirement.

(b) Each time an agency with authority to offer Voluntary Separation Incentive Payments establishes a window period for acceptance of Voluntary Separation Incentive applications, it may limit offers to its employees based on an established opening and closing date or the acceptance of a specified number of applications. However, at the time of the offer, the agency must notify its employees that it retains the right to limit the number of Voluntary Separation Incentive Payment offers by use of a specific closing date or by receipt of a specified number of applications.

(c) An agency's downsizing and/or reshaping strategy may change, necessitating a change in the offer notice to employees. If the amended notice includes a revised closing date, or a revised number of applications to be accepted, the new date or number of applications must be announced to the same group of employees included in the original announcement. If a new or separate notice includes a new window period with a new closing date, or a new instance of a specific number of applications to be accepted, the new window period or number of applications to be accepted may be announced to a different group of employees as long as the new group is covered by the approved Voluntary Separation Incentive Payment authority.

(d) Section 4311 of title 38, United States Code, requires that, for all practical purposes, agencies treat employees on military duty as though they were still on the job. Further, employees are not to be disadvantaged because of their military duty. In accordance with these provisions, employees on military duty who would otherwise be eligible for an offer of a Voluntary Separation Incentive Payment will have 30 days following their return to duty to either accept or reject an offer of a Voluntary Separation Incentive Payment. This is true even if the Voluntary Separation Incentive Payment authority provided by OPM has expired.

(e) An employee may separate from the service voluntarily, with a Voluntary Separation Incentive Payment, if, on the date of separation, the employee:

(1) Is serving in a position covered by a Voluntary Separation Incentive Payment offer; and

(2) Meets the definition of employee discussed in 5 U.S.C. 3521.

(f) Agencies are responsible for ensuring that employees are not coerced into accepting a Voluntary Separation Incentive Payment. If an agency finds any instances of coercion, it must take appropriate corrective action.

(g) An agency may not offer Voluntary Separation Incentive Payments beyond the stated expiration date of an authority or assign an effective date for a Voluntary Separation Incentive Payment that is beyond the time period for paying a Voluntary Separation Incentive Payment that was stated in the agency's approved Voluntary Separation Incentive Payment plan.

(h) An agency may not offer Voluntary Separation Incentive Payments to employees who are outside the scope of the Voluntary Separation Incentive Payment authority approved by OPM.

(i) OPM may amend, limit, or terminate Voluntary Separation Incentive Payment authority if it determines that the agency is no longer undergoing the condition(s) that formed the basis for its approval or to ensure that the law and regulations governing Voluntary Separation Incentive Payments, including the Voluntary Separation Incentive Payment usage reporting requirements, are being properly followed.

§ 576.104 Additional agency requirements.

After OPM approves an agency plan for Voluntary Separation Incentive Payments, the agency must immediately notify OPM of any subsequent changes in the conditions that served as the basis for the approval of the Voluntary Separation Incentive Payment authority.

[80 FR 75786, Dec. 4, 2015]

§ 576.105 Existing Voluntary Separation Incentive Payment authorities.

As provided in section 1313(a)(3) of Public Law 107–296, any agency exercising Voluntary Separation Incentive authority in effect on January 24, 2003, may continue to offer Voluntary Separation Incentives consistent with that authority until that authority expires. An agency that is eligible to offer Voluntary Separation Incentive Payments under this authority and under any other statutory authority may choose which authority it wishes to use, or offer incentives under both.

Subpart B—Waiver of Repayment of Voluntary Separation Incentive Payments

§ 576.201 Definitions.

'Employment' means employment with the Government of the United States, including employment under a personal services contract (or other direct contract) with the United States Government (other than an entity in the legislative branch) unless employed pursuant to § 576.203(a).

§ 576.202 Repayment requirement.

An executive branch employee who received a Voluntary Separation Incentive Payment as described in subpart A of this part and accepts any employment for compensation with the Government of the United States within 5 years after the date of the separation on which the payment is based must repay the entire amount of the Voluntary Separation Incentive Payment to the agency that paid it before the individual's first day of reemployment.

§ 576.203 Waivers of the Voluntary Separation Incentive Repayment requirement.

(a)(1) If the proposed reemployment is with an agency other than the Government Accountability Office, the United States Postal Service, or the Postal Rate Commission, the Director of the Office of Personnel Management may, at the request of the head of the agency, waive the repayment if—

(i) The individual involved possesses unique abilities and is the only qualified applicant available for the position; or

(ii) In case of an emergency involving a direct threat to life or property, the individual—

(A) Has skills directly related to resolving the emergency; and

(B) Will serve on a temporary basis only so long as that individual's services are made necessary by the emergency.

(2) If the proposed reemployment is with an entity in the legislative branch, the head of the entity or the appointing official may waive the repayment if the individual involved possesses unique abilities and is the only qualified applicant available for the position.

(3) If the proposed reemployment is with the judicial branch, the Director of the Administrative Office of the United States Courts may waive the repayment if the individual involved possesses unique abilities and is the only qualified applicant available for the position.

(4) The repayment waiver provisions under this section do not extend to a repayment obligation resulting from employment under a personal services contract or other direct contract.

(b) For a Voluntary Separation Incentive Payment made under statutory authority other than subpart A of this part, the agency should review the authorizing statute and, if a waiver is permitted, submit a request as specified by that statute.

[70 FR 3859, Jan. 27, 2005, as amended at 70 FR 46065, Aug. 9, 2005]

PART 581—PROCESSING GARNISHMENT ORDERS FOR CHILD SUPPORT AND/OR ALIMONY

Subpart A—Purpose and Definitions

Subpart B—Service of Process

Subpart C—Compliance With Process

Subpart D—Consumer Credit Protection Act Restrictions

Subpart E—Implementation by Governmental Entities

AUTHORITY: 42 U.S.C. 659; 15 U.S.C. 1673; E.O. 12105 (43 FR 59465 and 3 CFR 262)(1979). Secs. 581.102 and 581.306 also issued under 5 U.S.C. 8336a and 8412a.

SOURCE: 45 FR 85667, Dec. 30, 1980, unless otherwise noted.

Subpart A—Purpose and Definitions

§ 581.101 Purpose.

(a) Notwithstanding any other provision of law (including section 407 of title 42, United States Code, section 5301 of title 38, United States Code, and sections 8346 and 8470 of title 5, United States Code), section 659 of title 42, United States Code, as amended, provides that moneys, the entitlement to which is based upon remuneration for employment, due from, or payable by, the United States or the District of Columbia to any individual, shall be subject, in like manner and to the same extent as if the United States or the District of Columbia were a private person:

(1) To legal process for the enforcement of an obligor's legal obligations to provide child support, alimony, or both, resulting from an action brought by an individual obligee; and

(2) To withholding in accordance with State law enacted pursuant to subsections (a)(1) and (b) of section 666 of title 42, United States Code, and to regulations of the Secretary of Health and Human Services under such subsections, and to any other legal process brought by a State agency subject to regulations of the Secretary of Health and Human Services that is administering a program under an approved State plan to enforce the legal obligations of obligors to provide child support and alimony.

(b) Section 659 of title 42, United States Code, as amended, provides further that each governmental entity shall be subject to the same requirements as would apply if the governmental entity were a private person, except as set forth in this part.

[63 FR 14757, Mar. 26, 1998]

§ 581.102 Definitions.

In this part: (a) *The executive branch of the Government of the United States* means all "governmental entities" as defined in this section, including therein the territories and possessions of the United States, the United States Postal Service, the Postal Rate Commission, any wholly owned Federal corporation created by an Act of Congress, and the government of the District of Columbia.

(b) *Governmental entity* means each department, both civilian and military, agency, independent establishment, or instrumentality of the executive branch, including the United States Postal Service, the Postal Rate Commission, any wholly owned Federal corporation created by an Act of Congress, any office, commission, bureau, or other administrative subdivision or creature of the executive branch, and the governments of the District of Columbia and of the territories and possessions of the United States.

(c) *Private person* means a person who does not have sovereign or other special immunity or privilege which causes that person not be be subject to legal process.

(d) *Child support* means the amounts required to be paid for the support and maintenance of a child, including a child who has attained the age of majority under the law of the issuing State, or a child and the parent with whom the child is living, which provides for monetary support, health care, arrearages or reimbursement, and which may include other related costs and fees, interest and penalties, income withholding, attorney's fees, and other relief.

(e) *Alimony* means periodic payments of funds for the support and maintenance of the spouse (or former spouse) of the individual, and (subject to and in accordance with State law) includes separate maintenance, alimony pendente lite, maintenance, and spousal support, and includes attorney's fees, interest, and court costs when and to the extent that the same are expressly made recoverable as such pursuant to a decree, order, or judgment issued in accordance with applicable State law by a court of competent jurisdiction. *Alimony* does not include child support or any payment or transfer of property or its value by an individual to the spouse or a former spouse of the individual in compliance with any community property settlement, equitable distribution of property, or other division of property between spouses or former spouses.

(f) *Legal process* means any writ, order, summons, notice to withhold income pursuant to subsection (a)(1) or (b) of section 666 of title 42, United States Code, or other similar process in the nature of garnishment, which may include an attachment, writ of execution, court ordered wage assignment, or in the case where a child support order is submitted by a child support agency using the standard Order/Notice to withhold income for child support as required by section 324 of Pub. L. 104–193 and which—

(1) Is issued by:

(i) A court of competent jurisdiction, including Indian tribal courts, within any State, territory, or possession of the United States, or the District of Columbia;

(ii) A court of competent jurisdiction in any foreign country with which the United States has entered into an agreement that requires the United States to honor such process; or

(iii) An authorized official pursuant to an order of a court of competent jurisdiction or pursuant to State or local law; or

(iv) A State agency authorized to issue income withholding notices pursuant to State or local law or pursuant to the requirements of section 666(b) to title 42 of the United States Code; and

(2) Is directed to, and the purpose of which is to compel, a governmental entity, to make a payment from moneys otherwise payable to an individual, to another party to satisfy a legal obligation of the individual to provide child support, alimony or both.

(g) *Legal obligation* means an obligation to pay alimony and/or child support that is enforceable under appropriate State or local law. A legal obligation may include current as well as past due alimony and/or child support debts depending on the law in the jurisdiction from which the legal process was issued.

(h) *Obligor* means an individual having a legal obligation to pay alimony and/or child support.

(i) *Remuneration for employment* means compensation paid or payable for personal services, whether such compensation is denominated as wages, salary, commission, bonus, pay, or otherwise, and includes, but is not limited to, those items set forth in §581.103.

(j) *Party* means the person or persons to whom alimony and/or child support payments should be made, or, in the case of an agency established by State or local law, the agency which has been assigned, by law or by agreement, the right to receive such payment or payments.

(k) *Individual obligee* means any individual or entity other than a State agency authorized to issue income withholding notices pursuant to the requirements of section 666(b) to title 42 of the United States Code.

(l) *Phased retirement status* has the same meaning given that term in §838.103 of this chapter; and

(m) *Phased retirement annuity* has the same meaning given that term in § 838.103 of this chapter.

[45 FR 85667, Dec. 30, 1980, as amended at 48 FR 26279, June 7, 1983; 55 FR 1355, Jan. 16, 1990; 63 FR 14757, Mar. 26, 1998; 79 FR 46618, Aug. 8, 2014]

§ 581.103 Moneys which are subject to garnishment.

(a) For the personal service of a civilian employee obligor:

(1) Saved pay;

(2) Retained pay;

(3) Night differentials;

(4) Sunday and holiday premium pay;

(5) Overtime pay;

(6) Standby duty pay, administratively uncontrollable overtime pay, and availability pay;

(7) Environmental differentials;

(8) Hazardous duty pay;

(9) Tropical differentials;

(10) Recruitment incentives, recruitment and relocation bonuses and retention allowances;

(11) Equalization allowance;

(12) Any payment in consideration of accrued leave;

(13) Severance pay;

(14) Sick pay;

(15) Physicians comparability allowances;

(16) Special pay for physicians and dentists;

(17) Amounts paid pursuant to a personal services contract where the contractor recipient performed the services and received the payments in the capacity as a Federal employee;

(18) Merit pay;

(19) Incentive pay;

(20) Cash awards, including performance-based cash awards;

(21) Agency and Presidential incentive awards (except where such award is for making a suggestion);

(22) Senior Executive Service rank and performance awards;

(23) Moneys due for the services of a deceased employee obligor, including:

(i) Overtime or premium pay;

(ii) Amounts due as refunds of pay deductions for United States savings bonds;

(iii) Payments for accumulated and current accrued annual or vacation leave as provided for in section 5581 of title 5 of the United States Code;

(iv) Retroactive pay as provided for in section 5344(b)(2) of title 5 of the United States Code; and

(v) Amounts of checks drawn for moneys due which were not delivered by the governmental entity to the employee obligor prior to the employee obligor's death or which were not negotiated and returned to the governmental entity because of the death of the employee obligor, except those moneys due that are listed in § 581.104(i);

(24) Locality-based comparability payments or continued rate adjustments;

(25) Staffing differentials;

(26) Supervisory differentials;

(27) Special pay adjustments for law enforcement officers in selected cities;

(28) Advances in pay; and

(29) Voluntary separation incentive payments.

(b) For the personal service of an obligor in the uniformed services of the United States:

(1) Basic pay (including service academy cadet and midshipmen pay);

(2) Special pay (including enlistment and re-enlistment bonuses);

(3) Lump sum reserve bonus;

(4) Continuation pay for physicians and dentists;

(5) Special pay for physicians, dentists, optometrists, and veterinarians;

(6) Incentive pay;

(7) Variable incentive pay;

(8) Inactive duty training pay;

(9) Administrative duty pay;

(10) Academy official pay (other than personal money allowances);

(11) Any payments made in consideration of accrued leave (basic pay portion only);

(12) Readjustment pay;

(13) Disability retired pay;

(14) Severance pay (including disability severance pay);

(15) Cash awards (NOAA Corps);

(16) Special separation benefits; and

(17) Voluntary separation incentives.

(c) For obligors generally:

(1) Periodic benefits, including a periodic benefit as defined in section 428(h)(3) of title 42 of the United States Code, title II of the Social Security Act, to include a benefit payable in a

lump sum if it is commutation of, or a substitute for, periodic payments; or other payments to these individuals under the programs established by subchapter II of chapter 7 of title 42 of the United States Code (Social Security Act); and payments under chapter 9 of title 45 of the United States Code (Railroad Retirement Act) or any other system, plan, or fund established by the United States (as defined in section 662(a) of title 42 of the United States Code) which provides for the payment of:

(i) Pensions;

(ii) Retirement benefits;

(iii) Retired/retainer pay;

(iv) Annuities; and

(v) Dependents' or survivors' benefits when payable to the obligor;

(2) Refunds of retirement contributions where an application has been filed;

(3) Amounts received under any federal program for compensation for work injuries; and

(4) Benefits received under the Longshoremen's and Harbor Workers' Compensation Act.

(5) Compensation for death under any federal program, including death gratuities authorized under 5 U.S.C. 8133(f); 5 U.S.C. 8134(a); Pub. L. 103–332, section 312; and Pub. L. 104–208, section 651.

(6) Any payment under any federal program established to provide "black lung" benefits;

(7) Any payment by the Secretary of Veterans Affairs as compensation for a service-connected disability paid by the Secretary to a former member of the Armed Forces who is in receipt of retired or retainer pay if the former member has waived either the entire amount or a portion of the retired or retainer pay in order to receive such compensation. In such cases, only that part of the Department of Veterans Affairs payment that is in lieu of the waived retired pay or waived retainer pay is subject to garnishment.

[45 FR 85667, Dec. 30, 1980, as amended at 48 FR 26279, June 7, 1983; 55 FR 1356, Jan. 16, 1990; 56 FR 36723, Aug. 1, 1991; 58 FR 35846, July 2, 1993; 59 FR 66154, Dec. 23, 1994; 61 FR 3544, Feb. 1, 1996; 63 FR 14758, Mar. 26, 1998]

§581.104 Moneys which are not subject to garnishment.

(a) Payments made pursuant to the provisions of the Federal Tort Claims Act, as amended, sections 1346(b) and 2671 *et seq.*, of title 28 of the United States Code;

(b) Payments or portions of payments made by the Department of Veterans Affairs pursuant to sections 501–562 of title 38 of the United States Code, in which the entitlement of the payee is based on non-service-connected disability or death, age, and need;

(c) Refunds and other payments made in connection with overpayments or erroneous payments of income tax and other taxes levied under title 26 of the United States Code;

(d) Grants;

(e) Fellowships;

(f) Education and vocational rehabilitation benefits for veterans and eligible persons under chapters 30, 31, 32, 35, and 36 of title 38, United States Code, and chapters 106 and 107 of title 10, United States Code;

(g) Contracts, except where the contractor recipient performed personal services and received payments in his/her capacity as an employee of a governmental entity; and

(h) Reimbursement for expenses incurred by an individual in connection with his/her employment, or allowances in lieu thereof, and other payments and allowances, including, but not limited to:

(1) In the case of civilian employees:

(i) Uniform allowances;

(ii) Travel and transportation expenses (including mileage allowances);

(iii) Relocation expenses;

(iv) Storage expenses;

(v) Post differentials;

(vi) Foreign areas allowances;

(vii) Education allowances for dependents;

(viii) Separate maintenance allowances;

(ix) Post allowances and supplementary post allowances;

(x) Home service transfer allowances;

(xi) Quarters allowances;

(xii) Cost-of-living allowances (COLA), when applicable to an employee in a foreign area or an employee stationed outside of the continental United States or in Alaska;

(xiii) Remote worksite allowance; and

(xiv) Per diem allowances.

(2) In the case of members of the uniformed services:

(i) Position pay (Navy only);

(ii) Basic allowance for quarters;

(iii) Basic allowance for subsistence;

(iv) Station allowances;

(v) Armed Forces health professions scholarship stipends;

(vi) Public Health Service scholarship stipends;

(vii) Travel and transportation allowances;

(viii) Dislocation allowances;

(ix) Family separation allowances;

(x) ROTC subsistence allowance;

(xi) Allowance for recruiting expenses;

(xii) Education allowances for dependents;

(xiii) Clothing allowances for enlisted personnel;

(xiv) Uniform allowances; and

(xv) Personal money allowances for General and Flag officers, and for the Surgeon General of the United States.

(3) In the case of volunteers serving under either the Domestic Volunteer Service Act or the Peace Corps Act, all allowances, including, but not limited to, readjustment allowances, stipends, and reimbursements for out-of-pocket expenses.

(i) Moneys due a deceased employee obligor where the amounts are reimbursement for expenses incurred by the deceased employee in connection with his/her employment, or allowances in lieu thereof, including:

(1) Per diem instead of subsistence, mileage, and amounts due in reimbursement of travel expenses, including incidental and miscellaneous expenses in connection therewith;

(2) Allowances on change of official station;

(3) Quarters allowances; and

(4) Cost-of-living allowances (COLA), when applicable as a result of the deceased employee obligor's having been in a foreign area or stationed outside of the continental United States or in Alaska.

(j) Supplemental Security Income (SSI) payments made pursuant to sections 1381 *et seq.*, of title 42 of the United States Code (title XVI of the Social Security Act).

[45 FR 85667, Dec. 30, 1980, as amended at 48 FR 26280, June 7, 1983; 55 FR 1356, Jan. 16, 1990; 56 FR 36724, Aug. 1, 1991; 58 FR 35846, July 2, 1993; 60 FR 5044, Jan. 25, 1995; 63 FR 14758, Mar. 26, 1998]

§581.105 Exclusions.

In determining the amount of any "moneys due from, or payable by, the United States" to any individual, there shall be excluded amounts which:

(a) Are owed by the individual to the United States, except that an indebtedness based on a levy for income tax under section 6331 of title 26 of the United States Code, shall not be excluded in complying with legal process for the support of minor children if the legal process was entered prior to the date of the levy;

(b) Are required by law to be deducted from the remuneration or other payment involved, including, but not limited to:

(1) Amounts withheld from benefits payable under title II of the Social Security Act where the withholding is required by law;

(2) Federal employment taxes;

(3) Amounts mandatorily withheld for the United States Soldiers' and Airmen's Home;

(4) Fines and forfeitures ordered by a court-martial or by a commanding officer; and

(5) Amounts deducted for Medicare;

(c) Are properly withheld for Federal, State, or local income tax purposes, if the withholding of the amounts is authorized or required by law and if amounts withheld are not greater than would be the case if the individual claimed all dependents to which he/she were entitled. The withholding of additional amounts pursuant to section 3402(i) of title 26 of the United States Code may be permitted only when the individual presents evidence of a tax obligation which supports the additional withholding;

(d) Are deducted as health insurance premiums, including, but not limited to, amounts deducted from civil service annuities for Medicare where such deductions are requested by the Health Care Financing Administration;

(e) Are deducted as normal retirement contributions, not including amounts deducted for supplementary coverage. For purposes of this section, all amounts contributed under sections 8351 and 8432(a) of title 5 of the United States Code to the Thrift Savings Fund are deemed to be normal retirement contributions. Amounts withheld as Survivor Benefit Plan or Retired Serviceman's Family Protection Plan payments are considered to be normal retirement contributions. Except as provided in this paragraph, amounts voluntarily contributed toward additional retirement benefits are considered to be supplementary; or

(f) Are deducted as normal life insurance premiums from salary or other remuneration for employment, not including amounts deducted for supplementary coverage. Both Servicemen's Group Life Insurance and "Basic Life" Federal Employees' Group Life Insurance premiums are considered to be normal life insurance premiums; all optional Federal Employees' Group Life Insurance premiums and life insurance premiums paid for by allotment, such as National Service Life Insurance, are considered to be supplementary.

[45 FR 85667, Dec. 30, 1980, as amended at 48 FR 26280, June 7, 1983; 55 FR 1356, Jan. 16, 1990; 63 FR 14758, Mar. 26, 1998]

§581.106 Future payments.

Moneys paid by a governmental entity which may be due and payable to an individual at some future date, shall not be considered due the individual unless and until all of the conditions necessary for payment of the moneys to the individual have been met, including, but not limited to, the following conditions which might apply:

(a) Retirement;

(b) Resignation from a position in the Federal service; or

(c) Application for payment of moneys by the individual.

Subpart B—Service of Process

§581.201 Agent to receive process.

(a) Appendix A to this part lists agents designated to accept service of process.

(b) The head of each governmental entity shall submit to the Office of the General Counsel, Office of Personnel Management, 1900 E Street NW., Washington, DC 20415, for publication in appendix A to this part, the following information concerning the agent(s) designated to accept service of process:

(1) Title;

(2) Mailing address;

(3) Telephone number; and

(4) Geographical area or region, if applicable.

(c) United States Attorneys are not considered appropriate agents to accept service of process.

[45 FR 85667, Dec. 30, 1980, as amended at 55 FR 1356, Jan. 16, 1990]

§581.202 Service of process.

(a) A party using this part shall serve legal process on the agent designated in appendix A to this part, or if no agent has been designated for the governmental entity having payment responsibility for the moneys involved, then upon the head of that governmental entity, which has moneys due and payable to the obligor. Where the legal process is directed to, and the purpose of the legal process is to compel a governmental entity which holds moneys which are otherwise payable to an individual, to make a payment from such moneys in order to satisfy a legal obligation of such individual to provide child support or make alimony payments, the legal process need not expressly name the governmental entity as a garnishee.

(b) Service shall be accomplished pursuant to State procedures in effect pursuant to subsection (a)(1) or (b) of section 666 of title 42 of the United States Code. The designated agent shall note the date and time of receipt on the legal process. The governmental entity shall make every reasonable effort to facilitate proper service of process on its designated agent(s). If legal process is not directed to any particular official within the entity, or if it is addressed to the wrong individual, the recipient shall, nonetheless, forward the legal process to the designated agent. However, valid service is not accomplished until the legal process is received in the office of the designated agent. Moreover, the Government will not be liable for any costs or damages resulting from an agency's failure to timely serve process or to correct faulty service of process.

(c) Where it does not appear from the face of the process that it has been brought to enforce the legal obligation(s) defined in § 581.102(d) and/or (e), the process must be accompanied by a certified copy of the court order or other document establishing such legal obligations(s).

(d) Where the State or local law provides for the issuance of legal process without a support order, such other documentation establishing that it was brought to enforce legal obligation(s) defined in § 581.102(d) and/or (e) must be submitted.

(e) In order for the party who caused the legal process to be served to receive the additional five (5) percent provided for in either § 581.402(a) or (b), it must appear on the face of the legal process that the process was brought for the enforcement of a support order for a period which is twelve (12) weeks in arrears, or a certified copy of the support order, or other evidence acceptable to the head of the governmental entity, establishing this fact, must be submitted.

[45 FR 85667, Dec. 30, 1980, as amended at 48 FR 26280, June 7, 1983; 55 FR 1356, Jan. 16, 1990; 58 FR 35846, July 2, 1993; 63 FR 14758, Mar. 26, 1998]

§ 581.203 Information minimally required to accompany legal process.

(a) Sufficient identifying information must accompany the legal process in order to enable processing by the governmental entity named. Therefore, the following identifying information about the obligor, if known, is requested:

(1) Full name;

(2) Date of birth;

(3) Employment number, social security number, Department of Veterans Affairs claim number, or civil service retirement claim number;

(4) Component of the governmental entity for which the obligor works, and the official duty station or worksite; and

(5) Status of the obligor, e.g., employee, former employee, or annuitant.

(b) If the information submitted is not sufficient to identify the obligor, the legal process shall be returned directly to the court, or other authority, with an explanation of the deficiency. However, prior to returning the legal process, if there is sufficient time, an attempt should be made to inform the party who caused the legal process to be served, or the party's representative, that it will not be honored unless adequate identifying information is supplied.

[45 FR 85667, Dec. 30, 1980, as amended at 48 FR 26280, June 7, 1983; 55 FR 1357, Jan. 16, 1990]

Subpart C—Compliance With Process

§ 581.301 Suspension of payment.

Upon proper service of legal process, together with all supplementary documents and information as required by §§ 581.202 and 581.203, the head of the governmental entity, or his/her designee, shall identify the obligor to whom that governmental entity holds moneys due and payable as remuneration for employment and shall suspend, *i.e.*, withhold, payment of such moneys for the amount necessary to permit compliance with the legal process in accordance with this part.

[48 FR 26280, June 7, 1983]

§ 581.302 Notification of obligor.

(a) As soon as possible, but not later than fifteen (15) calendar days after the date of valid service of legal process, the agent designated to accept legal process shall send to the obligor, at his or her duty station or last known home address, written notice:

(1) That such process has been served, including a copy of the legal process, and, if submitted, such other documents as may be required by § 581.202;

(2) Of the maximum garnishment limitations set forth in § 581.402, with a request that the obligor submit supporting affidavits or other documentation necessary for determining the applicable percentage limitation;

(3) That by submitting supporting affidavits or other necessary documentation, the obligor consents to the disclosure of such information to the garnishor; and

(4) Of the percentage that will be deducted if he/she fails to submit the documentation necessary to enable the governmental entity to respond to the legal process within the time limits set forth in § 581.303.

(b) The governmental entity may provide the obligor with the following additional information:

(1) Copies of any other documents submitted in support of the legal process;

(2) That the United States does not represent the interests of the obligor in the pending legal proceedings;

(3) That the obligor may wish to consult legal counsel regarding defenses to the legal process that he or she may wish to assert; and

(4) That obligors in the uniformed services may avail themselves of the protections provided in sections 520, 521, and 523 of the Soldiers' and Sailors' Civil Relief Act of 1940 (50 U.S. Code App. 501 *et seq.*).

§ 581.303 Response to legal process or interrogatories.

(a) Whenever the designated agent is validly served with legal process pursuant to State procedures in effect pursuant to subjection (a)(1) or (b) of section 666 of title 42, United States Code, within 30 calendar days, or within such longer period as may be prescribed by applicable State law, the agent shall comply with all applicable provisions of section 666, including as follows:

(1) If an agent is served with notice concerning amounts owed by an obligor to more than one person, the agent shall comply with section 666(b)(7);

(2) Allocation of moneys due and payable to an individual under section 666(b) shall be governed by section 666(b) and the regulations prescribed under such section by the Secretary of Health and Human Services;

(3) Such moneys as remain after compliance with paragraphs (a)(1) and (a)(2) of this section shall be available to satisfy any other such legal process on a first-come, first-served basis, with any such legal process being satisfied out of such moneys as remain after the satisfaction of all such legal process which have been previously served.

(4) The agent or the agent's counsel or other designee shall respond within 30 calendar days to interrogatories which accompany legal process if the information sought in the interrogatory is not available to the entity to which it was sent, and the proper entity is known, the recipient shall forward the interrogatory to the appropriate entity in sufficient time to allow for a timely response.

(b) If State or local law authorizes the issuance of interrogatories prior to or after the issuance of legal process, the agent shall respond to the interrogatories within thirty (30) calendar days after receipt: *Provided*, That the document(s) required by § 581.202(c) have been presented.

[45 FR 85667, Dec. 30, 1980, as amended at 63 FR 14759, Mar. 26, 1998]

§ 581.304 Nonliability for disclosure.

(a) No Federal employee whose duties include responding to interrogatories pursuant to § 581.303(b), shall be subject to any disciplinary action or civil or criminal liability or penalty for any disclosure of information made by him/her in connection with the carrying out of any duties pertaining directly or indirectly to answering such interrogatories.

(b) However, a governmental entity would not be precluded from taking disciplinary action against an employee who consistently or purposely failed to provide correct information requested by interrogatories.

[45 FR 85667, Dec. 30, 1980, as amended at 48 FR 26280, June 7, 1983]

§ 581.305 Honoring legal process.

(a) The governmental entity shall comply with legal process, except where the process cannot be complied with because:

(1) It does not, on its face, conform to the laws of the jurisdiction from which it was issued;

(2) The legal process would require the withholding of funds not deemed moneys due from, or payable by, the United States as remuneration for employment;

(3) The legal process is not brought to enforce legal obligation(s) for alimony and/or child support;

(4) It does not comply with the mandatory provisions of this part; or

(5) An order of a court of competent jurisdiction enjoining or suspending the operation of the legal process has been served on the governmental entity.

(b) Where notice is received that the obligor has appealed either the legal process or the underlying alimony and/or child support order, payment of moneys subject to the legal process shall be suspended; *i.e.*, moneys shall continue to be withheld, but these amounts shall be retained by the governmental entity until the entity is ordered by the court, or other authority, to resume payments or otherwise disburse the suspended amounts. However, no suspension action shall be taken where the applicable law of the jurisdiction wherein the appeal is filed requires compliance with the legal process while an appeal is pending. Where the legal process has been issued by a court in the District of Columbia, a motion to quash shall be deemed equivalent to an appeal.

(c) Under the circumstances set forth in § 581.305 (a) or (b), or where the governmental entity is directed by the Justice Department not to comply with the legal process, the entity shall respond directly to the court, or other authority, setting forth its objections to compliance with the legal process. In addition, the governmental entity shall inform the party who caused the legal process to be served, or the party's representative, that the legal process will not be honored. Thereafter, if litigation is initiated or threatened, the entity shall immediately refer the matter to the United States Attorney for the district from which the legal process issued. To ensure uniformity in the executive branch, governmental entities which have statutory authority to represent themselves in court shall coordinate their representation with the United States Attorney.

(d) If a governmental entity is served with more than one legal process for the same moneys due or payable to an individual, the entity shall comply with § 581.303(a). *Provided,* That in no event will the total amount garnished for any pay or disbursement cycle exceed the applicable limitation set forth in § 581.402.

(e)(1) Neither the United States, any disbursing officer, nor any governmental entity shall be liable for any payment made from moneys due from, or payable by, the United States to any individual pursuant to legal process regular on its face, if such payment is made in accordance with this part.

(2) Neither the United States, any disbursing officer, nor any governmental entity shall be liable under this part to pay money damages for failure to comply with legal process.

(f) Governmental entities affected by legal process served under this part shall not be required to vary their normal pay or disbursement cycles to comply with the legal process. However, legal process, valid at the time of service, which is received too late to be honored during the disbursement cycle in which it is received, shall be honored to the extent that the legal process may be satisfied during the next disbursement cycle within the limits set forth in § 581.402. The fact that the legal process may have expired during this period would not relieve the governmental entity of its obligation to honor legal process which was valid at the time of service. If, in the next disbursement cycle, no further payment will be due from the entity to the obligor, the entity shall follow the procedures set forth in § 581.306.

(g) If a governmental entity receives legal process which, on its face, appears to conform to the laws of the jurisdiction from which it was issued, the entity shall not be required to ascertain whether the authority which issued the legal process had obtained personal jurisdiction over the obligor.

(h) A failure by the party bringing the garnishment action to comply with the provisions of the Uniform Reciprocal Enforcement of Support Act (URESA) or the Revised Uniform Reciprocal Enforcement of Support Act by itself shall not be a valid basis for a governmental entity to refuse to comply with legal process.

[45 FR 85667, Dec. 30, 1980, as amended at 48 FR 26280, June 7, 1983; 55 FR 1357, Jan. 16, 1990; 63 FR 14759, Mar. 26, 1998]

§ 581.306 Lack of moneys due from, or payable by, a governmental entity served with legal process; transfer of service of legal process to another governmental entity.

(a) When legal process is served on a governmental entity, and the individual identified in the legal process as the obligor is found not to be entitled to moneys (the entitlement to which is based upon remuneration for employment) due from, or payable by, the governmental entity, the entity shall follow the procedures set forth in the legal process for that contingency or, if no procedures are set forth therein, shall return the legal process to the court, or other authority from which it was issued, and advise the court, or other authority, that no moneys, the entitlement to which is based upon remuneration for employment, are due from, or payable by, the governmental entity to the named individual.

(b) Where it appears that remuneration for employment is only temporarily exhausted or otherwise unavailable, the court, or other authority, shall be fully advised as to why, and for how long, the remuneration will be unavailable, if that information is known by the governmental entity.

(c) In instances where an employee obligor separates from his/her employment with a governmental entity which is presently honoring a continuing legal process, the entity shall inform the party who caused the legal process to be served, or the party's representative, and the court, or other authority, that the payments are being discontinued. In cases where the obligor has a Thrift Savings Fund account, or has retired, or has separated and requested a refund of retirement contributions, or transferred, or is receiving benefits under the Federal Employees' Compensation Act, or where the employee obligor has been employed by either another governmental entity or by a private employer, and where this information is known by the governmental entity, the governmental entity shall provide the party with the designated agent for the new disbursing governmental entity or with the name and address of the private employer.

(d) In instances where an employee obligor, who is employed by a governmental entity which is honoring a continuing legal process, enters phased retirement status in accordance with part 831, subpart Q, and part 848 of this chapter, the entity must inform the party who caused the legal process to be served, or the party's representative, and the court or other authority, that remuneration for employment will continue at a reduced rate and that the employee obligor will be receiving a phased retirement annuity. The governmental entity must provide the party with the designated agent at the Office of Personnel Management who is responsible for the disbursement of retirement benefits.

[45 FR 85667, Dec. 30, 1980, as amended at 48 FR 26281, June 7, 1983; 55 FR 1357, Jan. 16, 1990; 58 FR 35846, July 2, 1993; 79 FR 46618, Aug. 8, 2014]

§ 581.307 Compliance with legal process requiring the payment of attorney fees, interest, and/or court costs.

Before complying with legal process that requires withholding for the payment of attorney fees, interest, and/or court costs, the governmental entity must determine that the legal process meets both of the following requirements:

(a) The legal process must expressly provide for inclusion of attorney fees, interest, and/or court costs as (rather than in addition to) child support and/or alimony payments;

(b) The awarding of attorney fees, interest, and/or court costs as child support and/or alimony must be within the authority of the court, authorized official, or authorized State agency that issued the legal process. It will be deemed to be within the authority of the court, authorized official, or authorized State agency to award attorney fees as child support and/or alimony if such order is not in violation of or inconsistent with State or local law, even if State or local law does not expressly provide for such an award.

[55 FR 1357, Jan. 16, 1990]

Subpart D—Consumer Credit Protection Act Restrictions

§ 581.401 Aggregate disposable earnings.

The "aggregate disposable earnings", when used in reference to the amounts due from, or payable by, the United States or the District of Columbia which are garnishable under the Consumer Credit Protection Act for child support and/or alimony, are the obligor's remuneration for employment less those amounts deducted in accordance with § 581.105.

§ 581.402 Maximum garnishment limitations.

(a) Except as provided in paragraph (b) of this section, pursuant to section 1673(b)(2) (A) and (B) of title 15 of the United States Code (the Consumer Credit Protection Act, as amended), unless a lower maximum garnishment limitation is provided by applicable State or local law, the maximum part of the aggregate disposable earnings subject to garnishment to enforce any support order(s) shall not exceed:

(1) Fifty percent of the obligor's aggregate disposable earnings for any workweek, where the obligor asserts by affidavit, or by other acceptable evidence, that he or she is supporting a spouse, a dependent child, or both, other than the former spouse, child, or both, for whose support such order is issued, except that an additional five percent will apply if it appears on the face of the legal process, or from other evidence submitted in accordance with § 581.202(d), that such earnings are to enforce a support order for a period which is 12 weeks prior to that workweek. An obligor shall be considered to be supporting a spouse, dependent child, or both, only if the obligor provides over half of the support for a spouse, dependent child or both.

(2) Sixty percent of the obligor's aggregate disposable earnings for any workweek, where the obligor fails to assert by affidavit or establishes by other acceptable evidence, that he or she is supporting a spouse, dependent child, or both, other than a former spouse, child, or both, with respect to whose support such order is issued, except that an additional five percent will apply if it appears on the face of the legal process, or from other evidence submitted in accordance with § 581.202(d), that such earnings are to enforce a support order for a period which is 12 weeks prior to that workweek.

(3) Where, under § 581.302(a)(2), an obligor submits evidence that he or she is supporting a second spouse, child, or both a second spouse and dependent child, copies of the evidence shall be sent by the governmental entity to the garnishor, or the garnishor's representative, as well as to the court, or other authority as specified in § 581.102(f)(1), together with notification that the obligor's support claim will be honored. If the garnishor disagrees with the obligor's support claim, the garnishor should immediately refer the matter to the court, or other authority, for resolution.

(b) In instances where an obligor is receiving remuneration from more than one governmental entity, an authority described in § 581.102(f)(1) may apply the limitations described in paragraph (a) of this section to the total remuneration, *i.e.*, to the combined aggregate disposable earnings received by the obligor.

[63 FR 14759, Mar. 26, 1998]

Subpart E—Implementation by Governmental Entities

§ 581.501 Rules, regulations, and directives by governmental entities.

Appropriate officials of all governmental entities shall, to the extent necessary, issue implementing rules, regulations, or directives that are consistent with this part or as are otherwise in accordance with statutory law.

[63 FR 14759, Mar. 26, 1998]

APPENDIX A TO PART 581—LIST OF AGENTS DESIGNATED TO ACCEPT LEGAL PROCESS

[This appendix lists the agents designated to accept legal process for the Executive Branch of the United States, the United States Postal Service, the Postal Rate Commission, the District of Columbia, American

Samoa, Guam, the Virgin Islands, and the Smithsonian Institution.]

I. DEPARTMENTS

Department of Agriculture

Office of the Secretary
Office of the Deputy Secretary
Office of the Under Secretaries
Office of the Assistant Secretaries
Director, Executive Resources and Services Division, Office of Personnel, Room 334 W—Administration Bldg., 14th St. and Independence Ave., SW., Washington, DC 20250, (202) 720–6047

Office of Inspector General

Chief Counsel to the Inspector General, Office of Inspector General, Room 27E—Administration Bldg., 14th St. and Independence Ave., SW., Washington, DC 20250, (202) 720–9110
Administration
Board of Contract Appeals
Chief Financial Officer
Judicial Officer
Office of Administrative Law Judges
Office of Budget and Program Analysis
Office of Civil Rights Enforcement
Office of Communications
Office of Congressional and Intergovernmental Relations
Office of the General Counsel
Office of Information and Resources Management
Office of Operations
Office of Personnel
Office of Small and Disadvantaged Business Utilization

Chief, Employment and Compensation Branch, Office of Personnel—POD, Room 31W—Administration Bldg., 14th St. and Independence Ave., SW., Washington, DC 20250–9630, (202) 720–7797

Chief Economist Office of risk Assessment and Cost-Benefit Analysis World Agricultural Outlook Board

Chief, Economics and Statistics Operations Branch, Human Resources Division, Agricultural Research Service, Room 1424—South Bldg., 14th St. and Independence Ave., SW., Washington, DC 20250, (202) 720–7657

Farm and Foreign Agricultural Services
Consolidated Farm Service Agency
Foreign Agricultural Service

Chief, Employee and Labor Relations Branch, Human Resources Division, Consolidated Farm Service Agency, Room 6732—South Bldg., PO Box 2415, Washington, DC 20013, (202) 720–5964

Federal Crop Insurance Corporation

Chief, Labor Relations Branch, Federal Crop Insurance Corporation, Consolidated Farm Service Agency, Room 6732—South Bldg., 14th St. and Independence Ave., SW., Washington, DC 20250, (202) 720–5964

Food, Nutrition, and Consumer Services
Food and Consumer Service

Senior Employee Relations Specialist, Employee Relations Division, Food and Consumer Service, 3101 Park Center Drive, Room 623, Alexandria, VA 22302, (703) 305–2374

Marketing and Regulatory Programs

Agricultural Marketing Service (except for employees of the Milk Marketing Administration)
Animal and Plant Health Inspection Service
Grain Inspection, Packers and Stockyards Administration

Chief, Human Resources, USDA, APHIS, Butler Square West, 5th Floor, 100 North 6th Street, Minneapolis, MN 55403, (612) 370–2107

Agricultural Marketing Service
Milk Marketing Employees

Personnel Management Specialist, Agricultural Marketing Service, DA, Room 2754—South Bldg., P.O. Box 96456, Washington, DC 20090–6456, (202) 720–7258

Food Safety and Inspection Service

Chief, Employee Relations Branch, Labor and Employee Relations Division, Food Safety and Inspection Service, Room 3175 South Building, 14th & Independence Avenue, SW., Washington, DC 20250–3700, 1–800–217–1886

Rural Development
Rural Housing Service
Rural Business-Cooperative Service
Rural Utilities Service

Chief, Human Resources Programs Branch, Human Resources, Rural Development, 1400 Independence Avenue, SW., Stop 0730, Washington, DC 20250–0730, (202) 692–0194

Rural Utilities Service

Chief, Rural Utilities Service, Personnel Operations Branch, Human Relations Division, Rural Housing and Community Development Service, Room 4031—South Bldg., 14th St. and Independence Ave., SW., Washington, DC 20250–1382, (202) 720–1382

Natural Resources and Environment
Forest Service
Washington Office

Director, Personnel Management, 900 RP-E, PO Box 96090, Washington, DC 20090–6090, (703) 235–8102

International Institute of Tropical Forestry

Director, Call Box 25000, UPR Experimental Station Grounds, Rio Piedras, PR 00928–2500, (809) 766–5335

Region 1

Regional Forester, Regional Office, Federal Bldg., PO Box 7669, Missoula, MT 59807, (406) 329–3003

Idaho

Clearwater—Forest Supervisor, 12730 Highway 12, Orofino, ID 83544, (208) 476–4541

Idaho Panhandle National Forests—Forest Supervisor, 1201 Ironwood Dr., Coeur d'Alene, ID 83814, (208) 765–7223

Nez Perce—Forest Supervisor, Rt. 2, Box 475, Grangeville, ID 83530, (208) 983–1950

Montana

Beaverhead—Forest Supervisor, 420 Barrett St., Dillon, MT 59725–3572, (406) 683–3900

Bitterroot—Forest Supervisor, 1801 N. 1st St., Hamilton, MT 59840, (406) 363–7121

Custer—Forest Supervisor, Box 2556, Billings, MT 59103, (406) 657–6361

Deerlodge—Forest Supervisor, Federal Bldg., Box 400, Butte, MT 59701, (406) 496–3400

Flathead—Forest Supervisor, 1935 3rd Ave., E., Kalispell, MT 59901, (406) 755–5401

Gallatin—Forest Supervisor, Federal Bldg., 10 E. Babcock Ave., Box 130, Bozeman, MT 59771, (406) 587–6701

Helena—Forest Supervisor, 2880 Skyway Dr., Helena, MT 59601, (406) 449–5201

Kootenai—Forest Supervisor, 506 Highway 2 W., Libby, MT 59923, (406) 293–6211

Lewis and Clark—Forest Supervisor, PO Box 869, 1101 15th St. N., Great Falls, MT 59403, (406) 791–7700

Lolo—Forest Supervisor, Bldg. 24, Ft. Missoula, Missoula, MT 59801, (406) 329–3750

Region 2

Regional Forester, Regional Office, 740 Simms St., Lakewood, CO 80255, (303) 275–5306

Colorado

Arapaho and Roosevelt—Forest Supervisor, 240 W. Prospect, Fort Collins, CO 80526, (303) 498–1100

Grand Mesa, Uncompahgre, and Gunnison—Forest Supervisor, 2250 Highway 50, Delta, CO 81416, (303) 874–7691

Pike and San Isabel—Forest Supervisor, 1920 Valley Dr., Pueblo, CO 81008, (719) 545–8737

Rio Grande—Forest Supervisor, 1803 West Highway 160, Monte Vista, CO 81144, (719) 852–5941

Routt—Forest Supervisor, 29587 W. US 40, Suite 20, Steamboat Springs, CO 80487–9550, (303) 879–1722

San Juan—Forest Supervisor, 701 Camino Del Rico, Room 301, Durango, CO 81301, (303) 247–4874

White River—Forest Supervisor, Old Federal Bldg., Box 948, Glenwood Springs, CO 81602, (303) 945–2521

Nebraska

Nebraska—Forest Supervisor, 125 N. Main St., Chadron, NE 69337, (308) 432–0300

South Dakota

Black Hills—Forest Supervisor, R.R. 2, Box 200, Custer, SD 57730–9504, (605) 673–2251

Wyoming

Bighorn—Forest Supervisor, 1969 So. Sheridan Ave., Sheridan, WY 82801, (307) 672–0751

Medicine Bow—Forest Supervisor, 2468 Jackson St., Laramie, WY 82070–6535, (307) 745–8971

Shoshone—Forest Supervisor, 808 Meadow Lane, Cody, WY 82414, (307) 527–6241

Region 3

Regional Forester, Regional Office, Federal Bldg., 517 Gold Ave., SW., Albuquerque, NM 87102, (505) 842–3380

Arizona

Apache—Sitgreaves—Forest Supervisor, Federal Bldg., Box 640, Springerville, AZ 85938, (602) 333–4301

Coconino—Forest Supervisor, 2323 E. Greenlaw Lane, Flagstaff, AZ 86004, (602) 527–3600

Coronado—Forest Supervisor, 300 W. Congress, Tucson, AZ 85701, (692) 670–4552

Kaibab—Forest Supervisor, 800 S. 6th St., Williams, AZ 86046, (602) 635–2681

Prescott—Forest Supervisor, 344 South Cortez, Prescott, AZ 86303, (602) 771–4700

Tonto—Forest Supervisor, 2324 E. McDowell Rd., Phoenix, AZ 85006, (602) 225–5200

New Mexico

Carson—Forest Supervisor, 208 Cruz Alta Rd., PO Box 558, Taos, NM 87571, (505) 758–6200

Cibola—Forest Supervisor, 2113 Osuna Rd., NE., Suite A, Albuquerque, NM 87113–1001, (505) 761–4650

Gila—Forest Supervisor, 3005 E. Camino del Bosque, Silver City, NM 88061, (505) 388–8201

Lincoln—Forest Supervisor, Federal Bldg., 1101 New York Ave., Alamogordo, NM 88310–6992, (505) 434–7200

Santa Fe—Forest Supervisor, 1220 St. Francis Dr., Santa Fe, NM 87504, (505) 988–6940

Region 4

Regional Forester, Regional Office, Federal Bldg., 324 25th St., Ogden, UT 84401, (801) 625–5298

Idaho

Boise—Forest Supervisor, 1750 Front Street, Boise, ID 83702, (208) 364–4100

Caribou—Forest Supervisor, 250 S. 4th Ave., Suite 282, Federal Bldg., Pocatello, ID 83201, (208) 236–7500

Challis—Forest Supervisor, HC 63 Box 1671, F.S. Bldg., Challis, ID 83226, (208) 879–2285
Payette—Forest Supervisor, Box 10206 or 106 W. Park, McCall, ID 83638, (208) 634–0700
Salmon—Forest Supervisor, P.O. Box 729, Salmon, ID 83467–0729, (208) 765–2215
Sawtooth—Forest Supervisor, 2647 Kimberly Rd. East, Twin Falls, ID 83301–7976, (208) 737–3200
Targhee—Forest Supervisor, 420 N. Bridge St., P.O. Box 208, St. Anthony, ID 83445, (208) 624–3151

Nevada

Humboldt—Forest Supervisor, 976 Mountain City Highway, Elko, NV 89801, (702) 738–5171
Toiyabe—Forest Supervisor, 1200 Franklin Way, Sparks, NV 89431, (702) 355–5300

Utah

Ashley—Forest Supervisor, 355 North Vernal Ave., Vernal, UT 84078, (801) 789–1181
Dixie—Forest Supervisor, 82 No. 100 E. St., P.O. Box 580, Cedar City, UT 84721–0580, (801) 865–3700
Fishlake—Forest Supervisor, 115 E. 900 N, Richfield, UT 84701, (801) 896–9233
Manti—La Sal—Forest Supervisor, 599 W. Price River Drive, Price, UT 84501, (801) 637–2817
Uinta—Forest Supervisor, 88 W. 100 N., Provo, UT 84601, (801) 342–5100
Wasatch—Cache—Forest Supervisor, 8236 Federal Bldg., 125 S. State St., Salt Lake City, UT 84138, (801) 524–5030

Wyoming

Bridger—Teton—Forest Supervisor, F.S. Bldg., 340 N. Cache, Box 1888, Jackson, WY 83001, (307) 739–5500

Region 5

Regional Forester, Regional Office, 630 Sansome St., San Francisco, San Francisco, CA 94111, (415) 705–2856

California

Angeles—Forest Supervisor, 701 N. Santa Anita Ave., Arcadia, CA 91006, (818) 574–1613
Cleveland—Forest Supervisor, 10845 Rancho Bernardo Rd., Suite 200, San Diego, CA 92127–2107, (619) 673–6180
Eldorado—Forest Supervisor, 100 Forni Rd., Placerville, CA 95667, (916) 622–5062
Inyo—Forest Supervisor, 873 North Main St., Bishop, CA 93514, (619) 873–2400
Klamath—Forest Supervisor, 1312 Fairlane Rd., Yreka, CA 96097, (916) 842–6131
Lassen—Forest Supervisor, 55 S. Sacramento St., Susanville, CA 96130, (916) 257–2151
Los Padres—Forest Supervisor, 6144 Calle Real, Goleta, CA 93117, (805) 683–6711
Mendocino—Forest Supervisor, 420 E. Laurel St., Willows, CA 95988, (916) 934–3316
Modoc—Forest Supervisor, 800 W. 12th St., Alturas, CA 96101, (916) 233–5811
Plumas—Forest Supervisor, 159 Lawrence St., Box 11500, Quincy, CA 95971–6025, (916) 283–2050
San Bernardino—Forest Supervisor, 1824 S. Commercenter Cir., San Bernardino, CA 92408–3430, (909) 383–5588
Sequoia—Forest Supervisor, 900 W. Grand Ave., Porterville, CA 93257–2035, (209) 784–1500
Shasta—Trinity—Forest Supervisor, 2400 Washington Ave., Redding, CA 96001, (916) 246–5222
Sierra—Forest Supervisor, 1600 Tollhouse Rd., Clovis, CA 93611, (209) 297–0706
Six Rivers—Forest Supervisor, 1330 Bayshore Way, Eureka, CA 95501–3834, (707) 441–3517
Stanislaus—Forest Supervisor, 19777 Greenley Rd., Sonora, CA 95370, (209) 532–3671
Tahoe—Forest Supervisor, 631 Coyote St., PO Box 6003, Nevada City, CA 95959–6003, (916) 265–4531

Region 6

Regional Forester, Regional Office, 333 S.W. 1st Ave., PO Box 3623, Portland, OR 97208, (503) 326–3630

Oregon

Deschutes—Forest Supervisor, 1645 Highway 20 E., Bend, OR 97701, (503) 388–2715
Fremont—Forest Supervisor, 524 North G St., Lakeview, OR 97630, (503) 947–2151
Malheur—Forest Supervisor, 139 NE Dayton St., John Day, OR 97845, (503) 575–1731
Mt. Hood—Forest Supervisor, 16400 Champion Way, Sandy, OR 97055, (503) 668–1613
Ochoco—Forest Supervisor, Box 490, Prineville, OR 97754, (503) 447–6247
Rogue River—Forest Supervisor, Federal Bldg., 333 W. 8th St., Box 520, Medford, OR 97501, (503) 776–3600
Siskiyou—Forest Supervisor, Box 440, Grants Pass, OR 97526, (503) 471–6500
Siuslaw—Forest Supervisor, Box 1148, Corvallis, OR 97339, (503) 750–7000
Umatilla—Forest Supervisor, 2517 SW Hailey Ave., Pendleton, OR 97801, (503) 278–3721
Umpqua—Forest Supervisor, Box 1008, Roseburg, OR 97470, (503) 672–6601
Wallowa—Whitman—Forest Supervisor, Box 907, Baker City, OR 97814, (503) 523–6391
Willamette—Forest Supervisor, Box 10607, Eugene, OR 97440, (503) 465–6521
Winema—Forest Supervisor, 2819 Dahlia, Klamath Falls, OR 97601, (503) 883–6714

Washington

Colville—Forest Supervisor, 765 S. Main, Colville, WA 99114, (509) 684–7000
Gifford Pinchot—Forest Supervisor, 6926 E. 4th Plain Blvd., Vancouver, WA 98668–8944, (206) 750–5000
Mt. Baker—Snoqualmie—Forest Supervisor, 21905 64th Avenue West, Mountlake Terrace, WA 98043, (206) 744–3200

Okanogan—Forest Supervisor, 1240 South Second Ave., Okanogan, WA 98840, (509) 826–3275

Olympic—Forest Supervisor, 1835 Black Lake Blvd., SW., Olympia, WA 98512, (206) 956–2300

Wenatchee—Forest Supervisor, 301 Yakima St., PO Box 811, Wenatchee, WA 98807, (509) 662–4335

Region 8

Regional Forester, Regional Office, 1720 Peachtree Rd., NW., Atlanta, GA 30367, (404) 347–3841

Alabama

National Forests in Alabama—Forest Supervisor, 2946 Chestnut St., Montgomery, AL 36107–3010, (205) 832–4470

Arkansas

Ouachita—Forest Supervisor, Box 1270, Federal Bldg., Hot Springs National Park, AR 71902, (501) 321–5200

Ozark—St. Francis—Forest Supervisor, 605 West Main, Box 1008, Russellville, AR 72801, (501) 968–2354

Florida

National Forests in Florida—Forest Supervisor, Woodcrest Office Park, 325 John Knox Rd., Suite F–100, Tallahassee, FL 32303, (904) 681–7265

Georgia

Chattahoochee and Oconee—Forest Supervisor, 508 Oak St., NW., Gainesville, GA 30501, (404) 536–0541

Kentucky

Daniel Boone—Forest Supervisor, 100 Vaught Rd., Winchester, KY 40391, (606) 745–3100

Louisiana

Kisatchie—Forest Supervisor, 2500 Shreveport Hwy., PO Box 5500, Pineville, LA 71361–5500, (318) 473–7160

Mississippi

National Forests in Mississippi—Forest Supervisor, 100 W. Capital St., Suite 1141, Jackson, MS 39269, (601) 965–4391

North Carolina

National Forests in North Carolina—Forest Supervisor, Post and Otis Streets, PO Box 2750, Asheville, NC 28802, (704) 257–4200

Puerto Rico and the Virgin Islands

Caribbean National Forest—Forest Supervisor, Call Box 25000, Rio Piedras, PR 00928–2500, (809) 766–5335

South Carolina

Francis Marion and Sumter National Forests—Forest Supervisor, 4923 Broad River Rd., Columbia, SC 29212, (803) 765–5222

Tennessee

Cherokee—Forest Supervisor, 2800 N. Ocoee St., NE., PO Box 2010, Cleveland, TN 37320, (615) 476–9700

Texas

National Forests in Texas—Forest Supervisor, Homer Garrison Federal Bldg., 701 N. First St., Lufkin, TX 75901, (409) 639–8501

Virginia

George Washington—Forest Supervisor, PO Box 233, Harrison Plaza, Harrisonburg, VA 22801, (703) 433–2491

Region 9

Regional Forester, Regional Office, 310 W. Wisconsin Ave., Room 500, Milwaukee, WI 53203, (414) 297–3674

Illinois

Shawnee—Forest Supervisor, 901 S. Commercial St., Harrisburg, IL 62946, (618) 253–7114

Indiana

Hoosier—Forest Supervisor, 811 Constitution Ave., Bedford, IN 47421, (812) 275–5987

Michigan

Hiawatha—Forest Supervisor, 2727 N. Lincoln Rd., Escanaba, MI 49829, (906) 786–4062

Huron—Manistee—Forest Supervisor, 421 S. Mitchell St., Cadillac, MI 49601, (616) 775–2421

Ottawa—Forest Supervisor, 2100 E. Cloverland Dr., Ironwood, MI 49938, (906) 932–1330

Minnesota

Chippewa—Forest Supervisor, Rt. 3 Box 244, Cass Lake, MN 56633, (218) 335–8600

Superior—Forest Supervisor, Box 338, Federal Bldg., 515 W. First St., Duluth, MN 55802, (218) 720–5324

Missouri

Mark Twain—Forest Supervisor, 401 Fairgrounds Rd., Rolla, MO 65401, (314) 364–4621

New Hampshire and Maine, White Mountain—Forest Supervisor, Federal Bldg., 719 Main St., PO Box 638, Laconia, NH 03247, (603) 528–8721

Ohio

Wayne—Forest Supervisor, 219 Columbus Rd., Athens, OH 45701–1399, (614) 592–6644

Pennsylvania

Allegheny—Forest Supervisor, 222 Liberty St., Box 847, Warren, PA 16365, (814) 723–5150

Vermont

Green Mountain and Finger Lakes—Forest Supervisor, 231 N. Main St., Rutland, NY 05701, (802) 747–6700

West Virginia

Monongahela—Forest Supervisor, USDA Bldg., 200 Sycamore St., Elkins, WV 26241–3962, (304) 636–1800

Wisconsin

Chequamegon—Forest Supervisor, 1170 4th Ave. South, Park Falls, WI 54552, (715) 762–2461

Nicolet—Forest Supervisor, Federal Bldg., 68 S. Stevens, Rhinelander, WI 54501, (715) 362–1300

Region 10

Regional Forester, Regional Office, Federal Office Bldg., Box 21628, Juneau, AK 99802–1628, (907) 586–8719

Alaska

Chugach—Forest Supervisor, 3301 C St., Suite 300, Anchorage, AK 99503–3998, (907) 271–2500

Tongass—Chatham Area—Forest Supervisor, 204 Siginaka Way, Sitka, AK 99835, (907) 747–6671

Tongass—Ketchikan Area—Forest Supervisor, Federal Bldg., Ketchikan, AK 99901, (907) 225–3101

Tongass—Stikine Area—Forest Supervisor, Box 309, Petersburg, AK 99833, (907) 772–3841

Forest and Range Experiment Stations

Intermountain Research Station, Director, 324 25th Street, Ogden, UT 84401, (801) 625–5412

North Central Forest Experiment Station, Director, 1992 Folwell Ave., St. Paul, MN 55108, (612) 649–5249

Northeastern Forest Experiment Station, Director, 5 Radnor Corporate Center, Suite 200, PO Box 6775, Radnor, PA 19087–8775, (610) 975–4017

Pacific Northwest Research Station, Director, PO Box 3890, Portland, OR 97208–3890, (503) 326–5640

Pacific Southwest Forest and Range Experiment Station, Director, 800 Buchanan St., West Building, Albany, CA 94710–0011, (510) 559–6310

Rocky Mountain Forest and Range Experiment Station, Director, 240 W. Prospect Rd., Fort Collins, CO 80526–2098, (303) 498–1126

Southeastern Forest Experiment Station, Director, 200 Weaver Blvd., PO Box 2680, Ashville, NC 28802, (704) 257–4300

Southern Forest Experiment Station, Director, T–10210, U.S. Postal Service Bldg., 701 Loyola Ave., New Orleans, LA 70113, (504) 589–3921

Forest Products Laboratory, Director, One Gifford Pinchot Dr., Madison, WI 53705–2398, (608) 231–9318

Northeastern Area State and Private Forestry, Director, 5 Radnor Corporate Center, Suite 200, PO Box 6775, Radnor, PA 19087–8775, (610) 975–4103

Natural Resources Conservation Service

Regional Administrative Officer, Natural Resources Conservation Service, Midwest Regional Office, 2820 Walton Commons West, Suite 123, Madison, WI 53704–6785, (608) 224–3000

Regional Administrative Officer, Natural Resources Conservation Service, West Regional Office, 650 Capitol Mall, Room 6072, Sacramento, CA 95814, (916) 498–5240

Regional Administrative Officer, Natural Resources Conservation Service, Southeast Regional Office, 1720 Peachtree Road, NW., Suite 716–N, Atlanta, GA 30309–2439, (404) 347–6153

Regional Administrative Officer, Natural Resources Conservation Service, East Regional Office, 11710 Beltsville Drive, Suite 100, Calverton Office Bldg., #2, Beltsville, MD 20705, (301) 586–1328

Regional Administrative Officer, Natural Resources Conservation Service, South Central Regional Office, PO Box 6459, Ft. Worth, TX 76115–0459, (817) 334–5258, ext. 3504

Regional Administrative Officer, Natural Resources Conservation Service, Northern Plains Regional Office, 100 Centennial Mall North, Room 152, Lincoln, NE 68508–3866, (402) 437–5315

Human Resources Officer, Natural Resources Conservation Service, National Business Management Center, Bldg. 23, 501 W. Felix Street, PO Box 6567, Ft. Worth, TX 76115, (817) 334–5427, ext. 3750

Human Resources Officer, Natural Resources Conservation Service, PO Box 2890, Room 5215-South Bldg., Washington, DC 20013–2890, (202) 720–4264

Human Resources Officer, Natural Resources Conservation Service, 665 Opelika Road, PO Box 311, Auburn, AL 36830–0311, (334) 887–4543

Human Resources Officer, Natural Resources Conservation Service, 3003 N. Central Ave., Suite 800, Phoenix, AZ 85012–2945, (602) 280–8800

Human Resources Officer, Natural Resources Conservation Service, 700 West Capitol Avenue, Federal Bldg., Room 5404, Little Rock, AR 72201–3225, (501) 324–5479

Human Resources Officer, Natural Resources Conservation Service, 2121–C 2nd Street, Davis, CA 95616, (916) 757–8294

Human Resources Officer, Natural Resources Conservation Services, 655 Parfet Street, Room E200C, Lakewood, CO 80215–5517, (303) 236–2891, ext. 219

Human Resources Officer, Natural Resources Conservation Service, 16 Professional Park Road, Storrs, CT 06268–1299, (860) 487–4034

Human Resources Officer, Natural Resources Conservation Service, 1203 College Park Drive, Suite 101, Dover, DE 19904–8713, (302) 678–4173

Human Resources Officer, Natural Resources Conservation Service, 2614 NW 43rd Street, Gainesville, FL 32606, (352) 338–9525

Human Resources Officer, Natural Resources Conservation Service, Federal Bldg., Box 13, 355 E. Hancock Avenue, Athens, GA 30601, (706) 546–2270

Human Resources Officer, Natural Resources Conservation Service, 300 Ala Moana Blvd., Rm 4316, PO Box 50004, Honolulu, HI 96850–0002, (808) 541–1896

Human Resources Officer, Natural Resources Conservation Service, 693 Federal Bldg., 210 Walnut Street, Des Moines, IA 50309, (515) 284–4588

Human Resources Officer, Natural Resources Conservation Service, 3244 Elder Street, Room 124, Boise, ID 83705–4711, (208) 378–5712

Human Resources Officer, Natural Resources Conservation Service, 1902 Fox Drive, Champaign, IL 61820, (217) 398–5288

Human Resources Officer, Natural Resources Conservation Service, 6013 Lakeside Blvd., Indianapolis, IN 46278, (317) 290–3207, ext. 335

Human Resources Officer, Natural Resources Conservation Service, 760 S. Broadway, Salina, KS 67401, (913) 823–4510

Human Resources Officer, Natural Resources Conservation Service, 771 Corporate Drive, Suite 110, Lexington, KY 40503–5479, (606) 224–7353

Human Resources Officer, Natural Resources Conservation Service, 3737 Government Street, Alexandria, LA 71302–3327, (318) 473–7786

Human Resources Officer, Natural Resources Conservation Service, 451 West Street, Amherst, MA 01002–2955, (413) 253–4353

Human Resources Officer, Natural Resources Conservation Service, John Hanson Business Center, 339 Busch's Frontage Road, Suite 301, Annapolis, MD 21401–5534, (410) 757–0861, ext. 337

Human Resources Officer, Natural Resources Conservation Service, 5 Godfrey Drive, Orono, ME 04473, (207) 866–7245

Human Resources Officer, Natural Resources Conservation Service, 1405 S. Harrison Road, Room 101, East Lansing, MI 48823–5243, (517) 337–6701, ext. 1233

Human Resources Officer, Natural Resources Conservation Service, 600 FCS Bldg., 375 Jackson St., St. Paul, MN 55101–1854, (612) 290–3678

Human Resources Officer, Natural Resources Conservation Service, 100 West Capitol Street, Federal Bldg., Suite 1321, Jackson, MS 39269, (601) 965–5183

Human Resources Manager, Natural Resources Conservation Service, 601 Business Loop 70 West, Parkade Center, Suite 250, Columbia, MO 65203, (573) 876–0904

Human Resources Manager, Natural Resources Conservation Service, Federal Building, Room 443, 10 East Babcock Street, Bozeman, MT 59715, (406) 587–6866

Human Resources Manager, Natural Resources Conservation Service, 4405 Bland Road, Suite 205, Raleigh, NC 27609, (919) 873–2108

Human Resources Manager, Natural Resources Conservation Service, 220 Rosser Avenue, P.O. Box 1458, Room 278, Bismarck, ND 58502–1458, (701) 250–4761

Human Resources Manager, Natural Resources Conservation Service, 100 Centennial Mall, N., Federal Bldg., Room 152, Lincoln, NE 68508–3866, (402) 437–4057

Human Resources Manager, Natural Resources Conservation Service, 2 Madbury Road, Federal Building, Durham, NH 03824–1499, (868) 686–7581

Human Resources Manager, Natural Resources Conservation Service, 1370 Hamilton Street, Somerset, NJ 08873, (908) 246–1171, ext. 166

Human Resources Manager, Natural Resources Conservation Service, 6200 Jefferson Street, NE., Albuquerque, NM 87109–3734, (505) 761–4409

Human Resources Manager, Natural Resources Conservation Service, 5301 Longley Lane, Bldg. F, Suite 201, Reno, NV 89511, (702) 784–5867

Human Resources Manager, Natural Resources Conservation Service, 441 South Salina Street, Suite 354, Syracuse, NY 13202–2450, (315) 477–6512

Human Resources Manager, Natural Resources Conservation Service, 200 North High Street, Room 522, Columbus, OH 43215, (614) 469–6977

Human Resources Manager, Natural Resources Conservation Service, 100 USDA, Suite 203, Stillwater, OK 74074–2655, (405) 742–1209

Human Resources Manager, Natural Resources Conservation Service, 101 SW Main Street, Suite 1300, Portland, OR 97204, (503) 414–3211

Human Resources Manager, Natural Resources Conservation Service, One Credit Union Place, Suite 340, Harrisburg, PA 17110–2993, (717) 782–3716

Human Resources Manager, Natural Resources Conservation Service, 1835 Assembly Street, Room 950, Columbia, SC 29201, (803) 253–3920

Human Resources Manager, Natural Resources Conservation Service, Federal

Bldg., 200 4th St., SW., Huron, SD 57350–2475, (605) 352–1224

Human Resources Manager, Natural Resources Conservation Service, 675 U.S. Courthouse, 801 Broadway, Nashville, TN 37203, (615) 736–5388

Human Resources Manager, Natural Resources Conservation Service, W.R. Poage Federal Bldg., 101 South Main St., Temple, TX 76501–7682, (817) 774–1246

Human Resources Manager, Natural Resources Conservation Service, 125 S. State Street, Room 4402, P.O. Box 11350, Salt Lake City, UT 84147, (801) 524–5068

Human Resources Manager, Natural Resources Conservation Service, 69 Union Street, Winooski, VT 05404–1999, (802) 951–6795, ext. 223

Human Resources Manager, Natural Resources Conservation Service, 1606 Santa Rosa Road, Culpeper Bldg., Suite 209, Richmond, VA 23229–5014, (804) 287–1625

Human Resources Manager, Natural Resources Conservation Service, Rock Pointe Tower II, W. 316 Boone Avenue, Suite 450, Spokane, WA 99201–2348, (509) 353–2333

Human Resources Manager, Natural Resources Conservation Service, 75 High Street, Room 301, Morgantown, WV 26505, (304) 291–4152, ext. 176

Human Resources Manager, Natural Resources Conservation Service, 6515 Watts Road, Suite 200, Madison, WI 53719–2726, (608) 264–5341, ext. 161

Human Resources Manager, Natural Resources Conservation Service, 100 East B Street, Room 3124, Casper, WY 82601–1911, (307) 261–6492

Research, Education, and Economics
Agricultural Research Service
Cooperative State Research, Education, and Extension Service
Economic Research Service
National Agricultural Statistics Service

Director, Human Resources Division, Administrative and Financial Management Staff, Agricultural Research Service, 5601 Sunnyside Avenue, Room 3–1145A, Beltsville, MD 20705–5101, (301) 504–1478

National Appeals Division

Administrative Officer, National Appeals Division, 3101 Park Center Drive, Room 1020, Alexandria, VA 22302, (703) 305–2566

Department of Commerce

1. Bureau of the Census and the Economics and Statistics Administration (ESA): For Census employee-obligors employed by Headquarters, a Regional Office, the Hagerstown Telephone Center and the Tucson Telephone Center; and for employee-obligors in ESA—Headquarters/Washington, DC offices only:

Bureau of the Census, Human Resources Division, ATTN: Chief, Pay, Processing and Systems Branch, FOB #3, Room 3254, Washington, DC 20233, (301) 457–3710

For employee-obligors employed by the Census Data Preparation Division:

Bureau of the Census, Data Preparation Division, ATTN: Chief, Human Resources Branch, Bldg. 66, Room 113, Jeffersonville, IN 47132, (812) 218–3323

2. Patent and Trademark Office (PTO): Human Resources Manager

U.S. Patent and Trademark Office, Box 3, Washington, DC 20231, (703) 305–8221

3. United States and Foreign Commercial Service (US&FCS): Personnel Officer

Office of Foreign Service Personnel, Room 3815, 14th & Constitution Avenue, NW., Washington, DC 20230, (202) 482–3133

4. International Trade Administration (ITA) (For employee-obligors of the Headquarters/Washington, DC offices only):

Human Resources Manager, Personnel Management Division, Room 4809, 14th & Constitution Avenue, NW., Washington, DC 20230, (202) 482–3438

5. National Institute of Standards and Technology (NIST), the Technology Administration (TA), and the National Technical Information Service (NTIS) (For NIST employee-obligors other than in Colorado and Hawaii; for employee-obligors employed by TA and NTIS):

Personnel Officer, Office of Human Resources Management, Administration Building, Room A–123, Gaithersburg, MD 20899, (301) 975–3000

6. Office of the Inspector General (OIG):

Human Resources Manager, Resource Management Division, Room 7713, 14th & Constitution Avenue, NW., Washington, DC 20230, (202) 482–4948

7. National Oceanic and Atmospheric Administration (NOAA) (For employee-obligors in the Headquarters/Washington, DC; the Silver Spring and Camp Springs, MD; and the Sterling, VA offices only): Chief

Human Resources Services Division, NOAA, 1315 East-West Highway, Room 13619, Silver Spring, MD 20910, (301) 713–0524

8. Office of the Secretary (O/S), Bureau of Economic Analysis (BEA), Bureau of Export Administration (BXA), Economic Development Administration (EDA), Minority Business Development Agency (MBDA), and National Telecommunications and Information Administration (NTIA) (For employee-obligors in Washington, DC metro area offices only):

Human Resources Manager, Office of Personnel Operations, Office of the Secretary, Room 5005, 14th and Constitution Avenue, NW., Washington, DC 20230, (202) 482–3827

9. Regional employees of NOAA, NIST, BXA, EDA, MBDA, ITA, NTIA, to the Human

Resources Manager servicing the region or State in which they are employed, as follows:

a. Central Region. For NOAA employee-obligors in the States of: Alabama, Arkansas, Florida, Georgia, Illinois, Indiana, Iowa, Kentucky, Louisiana, Michigan, Minnesota, Mississippi, Missouri, Ohio, Tennessee, and Wisconsin; for National Marine Fisheries Service employees in the states of North Carolina, South Carolina and Texas; and for National Weather Service employees in the States of Colorado, Kansas, Nebraska, North Dakota, South Dakota, and Wyoming; for employee-obligors in the BXA, EDA, MBDA, and ITA in the States of Alabama, Arkansas, Florida, Georgia, Illinois, Indiana, Iowa, Kansas, Kentucky, Louisiana, Michigan, Minnesota, Mississippi, Missouri, Nebraska, New York, Ohio, Oklahoma, Pennsylvania, South Carolina, South Dakota, Tennessee, Texas, and Wisconsin:

Human Resources Manager, Central Administrative Support Center (CASC), Federal Building, Room 1736, 601 East 12th Street, Kansas City, MO 64106, (816) 426–2056

b. Eastern Region. For NOAA employee-obligors in the States of: Connecticut, Delaware, Maine, Maryland, Massachusetts, New Hampshire, New Jersey, New York, North Carolina, Ohio, Pennsylvania, Rhode Island, South Carolina, Vermont, Virginia, West Virginia, Puerto Rico, and the Virgin Islands; for employee-obligors in the BXA, EDA, MBDA, and ITA in the States of Connecticut, Delaware, Maine, Maryland, Massachusetts, New Hampshire, New Jersey, New York, North Carolina, Pennsylvania, Rhode Island, South Carolina, Tennessee, Vermont, Virginia, Puerto Rico, and the Virgin Islands:

Human Resources Manager, Eastern Administrative Support Center (EASC), NOAA EC, 200 World Trade Center, Norfolk, VA 23510, (757) 441–6517

c. Mountain Region. For NOAA employee-obligors in the States of: Alaska, Colorado, Florida, Hawaii, Idaho, and Oklahoma, at the South Pole and in American Samoa; and for the National Weather Service employees in the States of Alabama, Arkansas, Florida, Georgia, Louisiana, Mississippi, New Mexico, Oklahoma, Tennessee, Texas and in Puerto Rico; for employee-obligors in BXA, EDA, MBDA, NIST, and NTIA in the States of Arkansas, Colorado, Hawaii, Iowa, Louisiana, Missouri, Montana, South Dakota, Texas, Utah and Wisconsin:

Human Resources Office, Mountain Administrative Support Center (MASC), MC22A, 325 Broadway, Boulder, CO 80303–3328, (303) 497–3578

d. Western Region. For NOAA employee-obligors in the States of Arizona, California, Montana, Nevada, Oregon, Utah, Washington, and the Trust Territories; for employee-obligors in BXA, EDA, MBDA, and ITA in the States of Arizona, California, Nevada, Oregon, Utah, Washington, and the Trust Territories:

Human Resources Manager, Western Administrative Support Center (WASC), NOAA WC2, 7600 Sand Point Way, NE., Bin C15700, Seattle, WA 89115–0070, (206) 526–6057

10. In cases where the name of the operating unit cannot be determined:

Director for Human Resources Management, U.S. Department of Commerce, 14th and Constitution Avenue, NW., Room 5001, (202) 482–4807

Department of Defense

Unless specifically listed below, all military members (active, retired, reserve, and national guard), and all civilian employees of the Department of Defense:

Assistant General Counsel for Garnishment Operations, Defense Finance and Accounting Service, Cleveland Center—Code L (DFAS-CL/L), P.O. Box 998002, Cleveland, OH 44199–8002, (216) 522–5301

Army

a. Civilian employees in Germany:

Commander, 266th Theater Finance Corps, Attention: AEUCF-CPF, Unit 29001, APO AE 09007, 011–49–6221–57–7977/6044

b. Nonappropriated fund civilian employees of the Army:

Post Exchanges

Army and Air Force Exchange Service, Attention: CM-C-RI, P.O. Box 660202, Dallas, TX 75266–0202, (214) 312–2011

Navy

a. Military Sealift Command Pacific Mariners:

Office of Counsel (Code N2), Military Sealift Command, Pacific, 280 Anchor Way, Suite 1W, Oakland, CA 94625–5010

b. Military Sealift Command Atlantic Mariners:

Office of Counsel, Military Sealift Command, Atlantic, Military Ocean Terminal, Building 42, Bayonne, NJ 07002–5399

c. Nonappropriated fund civilian employees of Navy Exchanges or related nonappropriated fund instrumentalities administered by the Navy Resale Systems Office:

Commanding Officer, Navy Exchange Service Command, 3280 Virginia Beach Blvd., Virginia Beach, VA 23452, (804) 631–3614

d. Nonappropriated fund civilian employees at Navy clubs, messes or recreational facilities:

Chief of Navy Personnel, Director, Morale, Welfare, and Recreation Division (MWR), Washington, DC 20370, (202) 433–3005

e. Nonappropriated fund personnel of activities that fall outside the purview of the Chief of Navy Personnel or the Commanding Officer of the Navy Exchange Service Command, such as locally established morale, welfare and other social and hobby clubs, such process may be served on the commanding officer of the activity concerned.

Marine Corps

Nonappropriated fund civilian employees, process may be served on the commanding officer of the activity concerned.

Air Force

a. Nonappropriated fund civilian employees of base exchanges:

Army and Air Force Exchange Service, Attention: FA-F/R, PO Box 650038, Dallas, TX 75265–0038, (214) 312–2119

b. Nonappropriated fund civilian employees of all other Air Force nonappropriated fund activities:

Office of Legal Counsel, Air Force Services Agency, 10100 Reunion Place, Suite 503, San Antonio, TX 78216–4138, (210) 652–7051

Department of Education

Assistant Secretary, Office of Management, FB–10, Room 2164, 600 Independence Avenue, SW., Washington, DC 20202–2110, (202) 401–0470

Department of Energy

Power Administration

1. Alaska Power Administration

Administrator, Alaska Power Administration, Department of Energy, PO Box 020050, Juneau, AK 99802–0050, (907) 586–7405

2. Bonneville Power Administration

Chief, Payroll Section DSDP, Bonneville Power Administration, Department of Energy, 905 NE. 11th Avenue, Portland, OR 97232, (503) 230–3203

3. Southeastern Power Administration

Chief, Payroll Branch, Department of Energy, Forrestal Building, Room 1E–184, 1000 Independence Avenue, SW., Washington, DC 20585, (202) 586–5581

4. Southwestern Power Administration

Chief Counsel, Southwestern Power Administration, Department of Energy, PO Box Drawer 1619, Tulsa, OK 74101, (918) 581–7426

5. Western Area Power Administration

General Counsel, Western Area Power Administration, Department of Energy, PO Box 3402, Golden, CO 80401, (303) 231–1529

Field Offices

1. Albuquerque Operations Office

Chief Counsel, Albuquerque Operations Office, Department of Energy, PO Box 5400, Albuquerque, NM 87115, (505) 844–7265

2. Chicago Operations Office

Chief Counsel, Chicago Operations Office, Department of Energy, 9800 South Cass Avenue, Argonne, IL 60439, (312) 972–2032

3. Idaho Operations Office

Financial Services Division-Payroll, 850 Energy Drive, Idaho Falls, ID 83401, (208) 526–0459

4. Nevada Operations Office

Chief, Payroll Branch, CR–431, Department of Energy, GTN Building, Room 259, Washington, DC 20585, (301) 903–4012

5. Oak Ridge Operations Office

Chief Counsel, Oak Ridge Operations Office, Department of Energy, P.O. Box 20001, Oak Ridge, TN 37831–8510, (615) 576–1200

6. Richland Operations Office

Chief Counsel, Richland Operations Office, Department of Energy, P.O. Box 550, Richland, WA 99352, (509) 376–7311

7. Oakland Operations Office

Director, Finance and Accounting Division, Department of Energy, 1301 Clay Street, Oakland, CA 94612–5208, (510) 637–1532

8. Savannah River Operations Office

Director, Financial Management and Program Support Division, Department of Energy, P.O. Box A, Aiken, SC 29802, (803) 725–5590

9. Washington DC Headquarters, Pittsburgh Naval Reactors Office, Schenectady Naval Reactors Office, and All Other Organizations Within the Department of Energy

Chief, Payroll Branch, CR–431, Department of Energy, GTN Building, Room E–259, Washington, DC 20585, (301) 903–4012

Department of Health and Human Services

Garnishment Agent, Office of General Counsel, Room 5362—North Building, 330 Independence Ave., SW., Washington, DC 20201, (202) 619–0150

Department of Housing and Urban Development

Director, Systems Support Division, Employee Service Center, 451 7th Street, SW., Room 2284, Washington, DC 20410, (202) 708–0241

Department of the Interior

Chief, Payroll Operations Division, Attn: Code D–2605, Bureau of Reclamation, Administrative Service Center, Department of the Interior, P.O. Box 272030, 7201 West Mansfield Avenue, Denver, CO 80227–9030, (303) 969–7739

Department of Justice

Offices, Boards, and Divisions

Personnel Group/Payroll Operations, 1331 Pennsylvania Avenue, NW., Suite 1170, Washington, DC 20530, (202) 514–6008

Office of the Inspector General

Personnel Division, 1425 New York Avenue, NW., Suite 7000, Washington, DC 20005, (202) 616–4501

For employees of any office of a United States Attorney and for employees of the Executive Office for United States Attorneys:

Assistant Director, Executive Office for United States Attorneys, Personnel Staff, Bicentennial Building, 600 E Street, NW., Room 8017, Washington, DC 20530

United States Marshals Service

Personnel Office, 600 Army Navy Drive, Room 850, Arlington, VA 22202–4210, (202) 307–9637

Office of Justice Programs

Office of Personnel, 633 Indiana Avenue, NW., Room 600, Washington, DC 20530, (202) 307–0730

U.S. Trustees Programs

Personnel Office, 901 E Street, NW., Room 770, Washington, DC 20530, (202) 616–1000

Drug Enforcement Administration

Office of Personnel, Employee Relations Unit, 700 Army Navy Drive, Room 3164, Arlington, VA 22202–4210, (202) 307–1222

Immigration and Naturalization Service

Personnel Support, Immigration and Naturalization Service, 425 I Street, NW., Room 2038, Washington, DC 20536, (202) 514–2525

Human Resources and Career Development, Immigration and Naturalization Service, One Federal Drive #400, Whipple Bldg., Fort Snelling, MN 55111, (612) 725–3211

Human Resources and Career Development, Immigration and Naturalization Service, 70 Kimball Avenue, South Burlington, VT 05403, (802) 660–5137

Human Resources and Career Development, Immigration and Naturalization Service, 7701 N. Stemmons Freeway, Dallas TX 75247, (214) 655–6032

Personnel Office, Immigration and Naturalization Service, P.O. Box 30070, Laguna Niguel, CA 92607, (714) 643–4934

Federal Prisons Systems, U.S. Penitentiary, Personnel Office, 1300 Metropolitan, Leavenworth, KS 66048, (913) 682–8700

Federal Correctional Institution, Personnel Office, Route 37, Danbury, CT 06811, (203) 743–6471

Personnel Office, 320 1st Street, NW., Room 161, Washington, DC 20534, (202) 307–3135

U.S. Penitentiary, Personnel Office, Highway 63 South, Terre Haute, IN 47808, (812) 238–1531

U.S. Penitentiary, Personnel Office, RD #5, Lewisburg, PA 17837, (717) 523–1251

Federal Correctional Institution, Personnel Office, P.O. Box 1000, Anthony, NM 88021, (915) 886–3422

Federal Correctional Institution, Personnel Office, Kettler River Road, Sandstone, MN 55072, (612) 245–2262

U.S. Penitentiary, Personnel Office, 601 McDonough Blvd., SE., Atlanta, GA 30315, (404) 622–6241

Federal Correctional Institution, Personnel Office, PO Box 9999, Milan, MI 48160, (313) 439–1511

Federal Correctional Institution, Personnel Office, PO Box 888, Ashland, KY 41105, (606) 928–6414

Federal Correctional Institution, Personnel Office, 501 Capital Cir., NE., Tallahassee, FL 32301, (904) 878–2173

Federal Correctional Institution, Personnel Office, Greenbag Road, Morgantown, WV 26505, (304) 296–4416

U.S. Medical Center, Federal Prison, Personnel Office, 1900 W. Sunshine, Springfield, MO 65808, (417) 862–7041

Federal Correctional Institution, Personnel Office, 2113 N. HWY 175, Seagoville, TX 75159, (214) 287–2911

Federal Correctional Institution, Personnel Office, 1000 River Road, Petersburg, VA 23804–1000, (804) 733–7881

Federal Prison Camp, Personnel Office, Glen Ray Road, Box B, Alderson, WV 24910 (304) 445–2901

U.S. Penitentiary, Personnel Office, 3901 Klein Blvd., Lompoc, CA 93436, (805) 735–3245

Federal Correctional Institution, Personnel Office, Highway 66 West, El Reno, OK 73036, (405) 262–4875

Federal Correctional Institution, Personnel Office, 9595 W. Quincy Avenue, Englewood, CO 80123, (303) 985–1566

Federal Correctional Institution, Personnel Office, 1299 Seaside Avenue, Terminal Island, CA 90731, (310) 831–8961

U.S. Penitentiary, Personnel Office, Rt. 5, P.O. Box 2000, Marion, IL 62959, (618) 964–1441

Federal Correctional Institution, Personnel Office, 3150 Norton Road, Fort Worth, TX 76119, (817) 535–2111

Metropolitan Correctional Center, Personnel Office, 150 Park Row, New York, NY 10007, (212) 791–9130

Federal Correctional Institution, Personnel Office, P.O. Box 1000, Butner, NC 27509, (919) 575–4541

Federal Correctional Institution, Personnel Office, RR #2, Box 820, Safford, AZ 85546, (602) 348–1337

Bureau of Prisons, South Central Regional Office, Personnel Office, 4211 Cedar Springs, Suite 300, Dallas, TX 75219, (214) 767–9700

Federal Correctional Institution, Personnel Office, Oxford, WI 53952, (608) 584–5511

Federal Medical Center, Personnel Office, 3301 Leestown Road, Lexington, KY 40511, (606) 255–6812

Federal Correctional Institution, Personnel Office, 5701 8th Street, Dublin, CA 94568, (510) 833–7500

Federal Correctional Institution, Personnel Office, 8901 S. Wilmot Road, Tucson, AZ 85706, (602) 574–7100

Bureau of Prisons, Personnel Office, SE Regional Office, 523 McDonough Blvd., SE., Atlanta, GA 30315, (404) 624–5252

Bureau of Prisons, North Central Regional Office, Personnel Office, 4th & State Avenue, 8th Floor—Tower II, Kansas City, KS 66101–2492, (913) 551–1144

Bureau of Prisons, Personnel Office, NE Region, U.S. Customs, 2nd & Chestnut, 7th Floor, Philadelphia, PA 19106, (215) 597–6302

Bureau of Prisons, Personnel Office, W. Regional Office, 7950 Dublin Blvd., 3rd Floor, Dublin, CA 94568, (510) 803–4710

Metropolitan Correctional Center, Personnel Office, 71 W. Van Buren Street, Chicago, IL 60605, (312) 322–0567

Metropolitan Correctional Center, Personnel Office, 808 Union Street, San Diego, CA 92101, (619) 232–4311

Metropolitan Correctional Center, Personnel Office, 15801 SW 137th Avenue, Miami, FL 33177, (305) 255–6788

Federal Correctional Institution, Personnel Office, 1101 John A. Denie Road, Memphis, TN 38134, (901) 372–2269

Federal Prison Camp, Personnel Office, P.O. Box 1000, Montgomery, PA 17752, (717) 547–1641

Federal Correctional Institution, Personnel Office, P.O. Box 730, HWY 95, Bastrop, TX 78602–0730, (512) 321–3903

Federal Prison Camp, Personnel Office, Eglin AFB, Eglin AFB, FL 32542, (904) 882–8522

Federal Correctional Institution, Personnel Office, 565 E Renfroe Road, Talladega, AL 35160, (205) 362–0410

Federal Prison Camp, Personnel Office, P.O. Box 500, Boron, CA 93516, (619) 762–5161

Federal Correctional Institution, Personnel Office, 1900 Simler Avenue, Big Spring, TX 79720, (915) 263–8304

Federal Correctional Institution, Personnel Office, P.O. Box 600, Otisville, NY 10963, (914) 386–5855

Federal Correctional Institution, Personnel Office, P.O. Box 300, Raybrook, NY 12977, (518) 891–5400

Federal Correctional Institution, Personnel Office, 37900 North 45th Avenue, Dept. 1680, Phoenix, AZ 85027, (602) 465–5112

Federal Correctional Institution, Personnel Office, P.O. Box 5050, Oakdale, LA 71463, (318) 335–4070

Federal Medical Center, Personnel Office, P.O. Box 4600, Rochester, MN 55903, (507) 287–0674

Federal Correctional Institution, Personnel Office, P.O. Box 1000, Loretto, PA 15940, (814) 472–4140

Federal Prison Camp, Personnel Office, Maxwell AFB, Montgomery, AL 36112, (205) 834–3681

Federal Correctional Institution, Personnel Office, 3625 FCI Road, Marianna, FL 32446, (904) 526–6377

Metropolitan Detention Center, Personnel Office, 535 N. Alameda Street, Los Angeles, CA 90012, (213) 485–0439

Federal Prison Camp, Personnel Office, P.O. Box 680, Yankton, SD 57078, (605) 665–3265

Federal Prison Camp, Personnel Office, Drawer 2197, Bryan, TX 77803, (409) 823–1879

Federal Prison Camp, Personnel Office, Saufley Field, Pensacola, FL 32509, (904) 457–1911

Federal Correctional Institution, Personnel Office, 3600 Guard Road, Lompoc, CA 93436, (805) 736–4154

Federal Correctional Institution, Personnel Office, Box 5000, Bradford, PA 16701, (814) 362–8900

Federal Prison Camp, Personnel Office, Seymour Johnson AFB, Goldsboro, NC 27533, (919) 735–9711

Federal Prison Camp, Personnel Office, Nellis AFB, Nellis, NV 89191, (702) 644–5001

Federal Correctional Institution, Personnel Office, P.O. Box 5001, Sheridan, OR 97378, (503) 843–4442

Federal Correctional Institution, Personnel Office, 2600 Highway 301 South, Jesup, GA 31545, (912) 427–0870

Federal Correctional Institution, Personnel Office, P.O. Box 280, Fairton, NJ 08320, (609) 453–4068

Federal Prison Camp, Personnel Office, P.O. Box 1400, Duluth, MN 55814, (218) 722–8634

Federal Prison Camp, Personnel Office, P.O. Box 16300, El Paso, TX 79906, (915) 540–6150

Federal Correctional Institution, Personnel Office, P.O. Box 4000, Three Rivers, TX 78071, (512) 786–3576

Federal Detention Center, Personnel Office, P.O. Box 5060, Oakdale, LA 71463, (318) 335–4070

Federal Prison Camp, Personnel Office, 6696 Navy Road, Millington, TN 38053, (901) 872–2277

Federal Medical Center, Personnel Office, P.O. Box 68, Carville, LA 70721, (504) 389–5044

Federal Correctional Institution, Personnel Office, P.O. Box 789, Minersville, PA 17954, (717) 544–7121

Federal Prison Camp, Personnel Office, Homestead, FL 33039, (305) 258–9676

Federal Prison Camp, Personnel Office, Box 40150, Tyndall AFB, FL 32403, (904) 286–6777

Metropolitan Detention Center, Personnel Office, P.O. Box 34028, Ft. Buchanan, PR 00934, (809) 749–4480

Bureau of Prisons #580, Personnel Office, Management & Specialist Training Center, 791 Chambers Road, Aurora, CO 80011, (303) 361–0567

LSCI, P.O. Box 1500, White Deer, PA 17887, (717) 547–1990

Federal Correctional Institution, Personnel Office, Rt. 8 Box 58, Fox Hollow Road, Manchester, KY 40962, (606) 598–4153

Metropolitan Detention Center, Personnel Office, 100 29th Street, Brooklyn, NY 11232, (718) 832–1039

U.S. Penitentiary-High, 5880 State Hwy, 67 South, Florence, CO 81226, (719) 784–9454

Federal Correctional Institution, Personnel Office, 5880 State Hwy, 67 South, Florence, Co 81226, (719) 784–9100

Federal Correctional Institution, Personnel Office, P.O. Box 699, Estill, SC 29918, (803) 625–4607

Federal Correctional Institution, Personnel Office, P.O. Box 2500, White Deer, PA 17887, (717) 547–7950

Federal Detention Center, Personnel Office, 1638, Northwest 82nd Avenue, Miami, FL 33126, (305) 597–4884

Bureau of Prisons, Personnel Office, Mid Atlantic Region, 10010 Junctions Dr., #100–N, Annapolis Junction, MD 20701, (301) 317–3199

U.S. Penitentiary, Personnel Office, P.O. Box 3500, White Deer, PA 17887, (717) 547–0963

North Central Regional Office, Personnel Office, 4th & State Ave., 8th Floor—Tower II, Kansas City, KS 66101–2492, (913) 551–1114

Federal Prison Camp, Personnel Office, Glen Ray Road—Box B, Alderson, WV 24910–0700, (304) 445–2901

Federal Correctional Complex, Personnel Office, P.O. Box 999, 904 NE 50th Way, Coleman, FL 33521–0999, (904) 748–0999

Federal Correctional Institution, Personnel Office, Fort Dix, P.O. Box 38, Trenton, NJ 08640, (609) 723–1100

Federal Medical Center, Personnel Office, P.O. Box 27066, J St., Bldg. 3000, Ft. Worth, TX 76127–7066, (817) 782–3834

Federal Bureau of Investigation

Chief, Payroll Administration and Processing Unit, Room 1885, 935 Pennsylvania Avenue, NW., Washington, DC 20535, (202) 324–5881.

Department of Labor

1. Payments to employees of the Department of Labor:

Director, Office of Accounting, Department of Labor, 200 Constitution Avenue, NW., Washington, DC 20210, (202) 219–8314

2. Process relating to those exceptional cases where there is money due and payable by the United States under the Longshoreman's Act should be directed to the:

Associate Director for Longshore and Harbor Worker's Compensation, Department of Labor, 200 Constitution Avenue, NW., Washington, DC 20210, (202) 219–8721

3. Process relating to benefits payable under the Federal Employees' Compensation Act should be directed to the appropriate district office of the Office of Workers' Compensation Programs:

District No. 1

District Director, Office of Workers' Compensation Programs, John F. Kennedy Building, Room 1800, Government Center, Boston, MA 12203, (617) 565–2137

Connecticut, Maine, Massachusetts, New Hampshire, Rhode Island, and Vermont

District No. 2

District Director, Office of Workers' Compensation Programs, 201 Varick Street, Room 750, P.O. Box 566, New York, NY 10014–0566, (212) 337–2075

New Jersey, New York, Puerto Rico, and the Virgin Islands

District No. 3

District Director, Office of Workers' Compensation Programs, Gateway Building, 3535 Market Street, Philadelphia, PA 19104, (215) 596–1457

Delaware, Pennsylvania, and West Virginia

District No. 6

District Director, Office of Workers' Compensation Programs, 214 N. Hogan Street, Suite 1026, Jacksonville, FL 32202, (904) 232–2821

Alabama, Florida, Georgia, Kentucky, Mississippi, North Carolina, South Carolina, and Tennessee

District No. 9

District Director, Office of Workers' Compensation Programs, 1240 East 9th Street, Cleveland, OH 44199, (216) 522–3800

Indiana, Michigan, and Ohio

District No. 10

District Director, Office of Workers' Compensation Programs, 230 S. Dearborn Street, 8th Floor, Chicago, IL 60604, (312) 353–5656

Illinois, Minnesota, and Wisconsin

District No. 11

Regional Director, Office of Workers' Compensation Programs, 1910 Federal Office Building, 911 Walnut Street, Kansas City, MO 64106, (816) 426–2195

Iowa, Kansas, Missouri, and Nebraska

District No. 12

District Director, Office of Workers' Compensation Programs, 1801 California Street, Suite 915, Denver, CO 80202, (303) 391–6000

Colorado, Montana, North Dakota, South Dakota, Utah, and Wyoming

District No. 13

District Director, Office of Workers' Compensation Programs, 71 Stevenson Street, 2nd Floor, P.O. Box 3769, San Francisco, CA 94119–3769, (415) 744–6610

Arizona, California, Hawaii, Guam, and Nevada

District No. 14

District Director, Office of Workers' Compensation Programs, 111 Third Avenue, Suite 615, Seattle, WA 98101, (206) 553–5508

Alaska, Idaho, Oregon, and Washington

District No. 16

District Director, Office of Workers' Compensation Programs, 525 Griffin Street, Room 100, Dallas, TX 75202, (214) 767–2580

Arkansas, Louisiana, New Mexico, Oklahoma, and Texas

District No. 25

District Director, Office of Workers' Compensation Programs, 800 N. Capitol Street, Room 800, Washington, DC 20211, (202) 724–0713

District of Columbia, Maryland, and Virginia

4. Process relating to claims arising out of the places set forth below and process seeking to attach Federal Employees' Compensation Act benefits payable to employees of the Department of Labor should be directed to the:

Regional Director, Office of Workers' Compensation Programs, 1910 Federal Office Building, 911 Walnut Street, Kansas City, MO 64106, (816) 426–2195

Department of State

Executive Director (L/EX), Office of the legal Adviser, Department of State, 22nd and C Streets, NW., Room 5519A, Washington, DC 20520, (202) 647–8323

Department of Transportation

Office of the Secretary

General Counsel, Department of Transportation, 400 7th Street, SW., Washington, DC 20590, (202) 366–4702

Agent designated to accept legal process issued by courts in the District of Columbia:

Assistant Chief Counsel, AGC–100, Department of Transportation, 701 Pennsylvania Avenue, NW., Suite 925, Washington, DC 20004, (202) 376–6416

Agent designated to accept legal process issued by courts in the District of Columbia:

Assistant Chief Counsel, MC–7, Department of Transportation, P.O. Box 25082, Oklahoma City, OK 73125, (405) 954–3296

Agent designated to accept legal process issued by courts in the State of New Jersey:

Assistant Chief Counsel, ACT–7, FAA Technical Center, Department of Transportation, Atlantic City, NJ 08405, (609) 485–7087

United States Coast Guard

Commanding Officer (LGL), Coast Guard Human Resources, Service and Information Center, 444 SE. Quincy Street, Topeka, KS 66683–3591, (785) 357–3595

Federal Aviation Administration

1. Headquarters (Washington, DC) and overseas employees:

Agent designated to accept legal process issued by courts in the District of Columbia:

Assistant Chief Counsel, AGC–100, General Legal Services Division, Federal Aviation Administration, 400 Seventh Street, SW., Suite PL-200A, Washington, DC 20590, (202) 366–4099.

Agent designated to accept legal process issued by courts in the State of Oklahoma:

Assistant Chief Counsel, AMC–7, Federal Aviation Administration, P.O. Box 25082, Oklahoma City, OK 73125, (405) 954–3296.

Agent designated to accept legal process issued by courts in the State of New Jersey:

Assistant Chief Counsel, ACT–7, FAA Technical Center, Federal Aviation Administration, Atlantic City, NJ 08405, (609) 485–7087

Agent designated to accept legal process issued by courts in the State of Alaska:

Assistant Chief Counsel, AAL–7, Federal Aviation Administration, 222 West 7th Avenue, #14, Anchorage, AL 99533, (907) 271–5269

Agent designated to accept legal process issued by courts in the States of Maine, New Hampshire, Vermont, Massachusetts, Rhode Island, and Connecticut:

Assistant Chief Counsel, ANE–7, Federal Aviation Administration, 12 New England Executive Park, Burlington, MA 01803, (617) 238–7040

Agent designated to accept legal process issued by courts in the States of New York, Pennsylvania, Maryland, West Virginia, Delaware, and Virginia:

Assistant Chief Counsel, AEA–7, Federal Aviation Administration, JFK International Airport, Fitzgerald Federal Building, Jamaica, NY 11430, (718) 553–1035

Agent designated to accept legal process issued by courts in the States of Kentucky, Tennessee, North Carolina, South Carolina, Georgia, Florida, Alabama, and Mississippi:

Assistant Chief Counsel, ASO–7, Federal Aviation Administration, P.O. Box 20636, Atlanta, GA 30320, (404) 763–7204

Agent designated to accept legal process issued by courts in the States of Louisiana, Arkansas, Texas, and New Mexico:

Assistant Chief Counsel, ASW–7, Federal Aviation Administration, 2601 Meacham Boulevard, Forth Worth, TX 76137–4298, (817) 222–5064

Agent designated to accept legal process issued by courts in the States of Nebraska, Iowa, Missouri, and Kansas:

Assistant Chief Counsel, ACE–7, Federal Aviation Administration, 601 East 12th Street, Federal Building, Kansas City, MO 64106, (816) 426–5446

Agent designated to accept legal process issued by courts in the State of Ohio, Indiana, Illinois, Michigan, Wisconsin, Minnesota, North Dakota, and South Dakota:

Assistant Chief Counsel, AGL–7, Federal Aviation Administration, O'Hare Lake Office Center, 2300 East Devon Avenue, Des Plaines, IL 60018, (708) 294–7108

Agent designated to accept legal process issued by courts in the States of Colorado, Utah, Wyoming, Montana, Idaho, Oregon, and Washington:

Assistant Chief Counsel, AMN–7, Federal Aviation Administration, 1601 Lind Avenue, SW., Renton, WA 98055–4056, (206) 227–2007

Agent designated to accept legal process issued by courts in the States of Hawaii, Arizona, Nevada, and California:

Assistant Chief Counsel, AWP, Federal Aviation Administration, PO Box 92007, World Postal Center, Los Angeles, CA 90009, (310) 297–1270

Department of the Treasury

(1) Departmental Offices

Assistant General Counsel (Administrative and General Law), Treasury Department, 1500 Pennsylvania Avenue, NW., Room 1410, Washington, DC 20220, (202) 622–0450

(2) Office of Foreign Assets Control

Chief Counsel, Second Floor, Treasury Annex, 1500 Pennsylvania Avenue, NW., Washington, DC 20220, (202) 622–2410

(3) Financial Management Service

Chief Counsel, Financial Management Service, 401 14th Street, SW., Room 531, Washington, DC 20227, (202) 874–6680

(4) Internal Revenue Service

Chief, Special Processing Unit, Garnishing Processing Center, 214 North Kanawha Street, Beckley, WV 25801, (304) 256–6200

(5) Bureau of Alcohol, Tobacco & Firearms

Chief Counsel, 650 Massachusetts Avenue, NW., Room 6100, Washington, DC 20226, (202) 927–7772

(6) Bureau of the Public Debt

Deputy Chief Counsel, Bureau of the Public Debt, Room 119, Hintgen Building, Parkersburg, WV 26106–1328, (304) 480–5192

(7) Secret Service

Legal Counsel, 1800 G Street, NW., Room 842, Washington, DC 20023, (202) 435–5771

(8) Bureau of Engraving & Printing

Legal Counsel, 14th & C Streets, NW., Room 306M, Washington, DC 20228, (202) 874–2500

(9) Office of the Comptroller of the Currency

Washington Headquarters.

Director of Litigation, Office of the Comptroller of the Currency, 250 E Street SW., Washington, DC 20219–0001, (202) 874–5280

District Offices

District Counsel, Office of the Comptroller of the Currency, Northeasten District, 1114 Avenue of the Americas, Suite 3900, New York, NY 10036–7730, (212) 790–4010

District Counsel, Office of the Comptroller of the Currency, Southeastern District, Marquis One Tower, Suite 600, 245 Peachtree

Center Ave., NE., Atlanta, GA 30303–1223, (404) 588–4520

District Counsel, Office of the Comptroller of the Currency, Central District, One Financial Place, Suite 2700, 440 South LaSalle St., Chicago, IL 60605–1073, (312) 663–8020

District Counsel, Office of the Comptroller of the Currency, Midwestern District, 2345 Grand Avenue, Suit 700, Kansas City, MO 64108–2683, (816) 556–1870

District Counsel, Office of the Comptroller of the Currency, Southwestern District, 1600 Lincoln Plaza, 500 North Akard Street, Dallas, TX 75201–3345, (214) 720–7012

District Counsel, Office of the Comptroller of the Currency, Western District, 50 Fremont Street, Suite 3900, San Francisco, CA 94105–2292, (415) 545–5980

(10) United States Mint

Chief Counsel, 633 3rd Street, NW., Room 733, Washington, DC 20220, (202) 874–6040

(11) Federal Law Enforcement Training Center

Legal Counsel, Building 69, Glynco, GA 31524, (912) 267–2100

(12) Customs Service

Assistant Chief Counsel, PO Box 68914, Indianapolis, IN 46278, (317) 298–1233

(13) Office of Thrift Supervision

Chief Counsel, 1700 G Street, NW., Fifth Floor, Washington, DC 20552, (202) 906–6251

Department of Veterans Affairs

The fiscal officer at each Department of Veterans Affairs (VA) facility shall be the designated agent for VA employee obligers at that facility. When a facility at which an individual is employed does not have a fiscal officer, the address and telephone number listed is for the fiscal officer servicing such a facility. In those limited cases where a portion of VA service-connected benefits may be subject to garnishment, service of process, unless otherwise indicated below, should be made at the regional office nearest the veteran obligor's permanent residence.

Alabama

Fiscal Officer, Birmingham Medical Center, Send to: Fiscal Officer, VA Medical Center, 215 Perry Hill Road, Montgomery, AL 36193, (205) 272–4670, ext. 4709

National Cemetery Area Office, 700 South 19th Street, Birmingham, AL 35233, (205) 939–2103

Mobile Outpatient Clinic Substation, Send to: Fiscal Officer, VA Medical Center, Gulfport, MS 39501, (601) 863–1972, ext. 225

Fiscal Officer, Montgomery Regional Office, 474 South Court Street, Montgomery, AL 36104, (205) 832–7172

Fiscal Officer Montgomery Medical Center, 215 Perry Hill Road, Montgomery, AL 36109, (205) 272–4670, ext. 204

Fiscal Officer, Tuscaloosa Medical Center, Tuscaloosa, AL 35401, (205) 553–3760

Fiscal Officer, Tuskegee Medical Center, Tuskegee, AL 36083, (205) 727–0550, ext. 0622

Alaska

Fiscal Officer, Anchorage Regional Office, Outpatient Clinic, 235 East 8th Avenue, Anchorage, AK 99501, (907) 271–2250

Juneau VA Office, Send to: Fiscal Officer, VA Regional Office, 235 East 8th Avenue, Anchorage, AK 99501, (907) 271–2250

Sitka National Cemetery Area Office, Send to: Fiscal Officer, VA Regional Office, 235 East 8th Avenue, Anchorage, AK 99501, (907) 271–2250

Arizona

Cave Creek National Cemetery Area Office, Send to: Fiscal Officer, VA Medical Center, Seventh Street & Indian School Road, Phoenix, AZ 85012, (602) 277–5551

Fiscal Officer, Phoenix Regional Office, 3225 North Central Avenue, Phoenix, AZ 85012, (606) 241–2735

Fiscal Officer, Phoenix Medical Center, Seventh Street & Indian School Road, Phoenix, AZ 85012, (602) 277–5551

Fiscal Officer, Prescott Medical Center, Prescott, AZ 86313, (602) 445–4860, ext. 264

Prescott National Cemetery Area Office, Send to: Fiscal Officer, VA Medical Center, Prescott, AZ 86313, (602) 445–4860, ext. 264

Fiscal Officer, Tucson Medical Center, Tucson, AZ 85723, (602) 792–1450, ext. 710

Arkansas

Fayetteville National Cemetery Area Office, Send to: Fiscal Officer, VA Medical Center, Fayetteville, AR 72701, (501) 443–4301

Fiscal Officer, Fayetteville Medical Center, Fayetteville, AR 72701, (501) 443–4301

Fort Smith National Cemetery Area Office, Send to: Fiscal Officer, VA Medical Center, Fayetteville, AR 72701, (501) 443–4301

Fiscal Officer, Little Rock Regional Office, 1200 W. 3d Street, Little Rock, AR 72201, (501) 378–5142

Fiscal Officer, John L. McClellan Memorial, Veterans Hospital, 4300 West 7th Street (04), Little Rock, AR 72205, (501) 661–1202, ext. 1310

Fiscal Officer, VA Regional Office, Send to: VA Medical Center, 11000 N. College Avenue, Fayetteville, AR 72701, (501) 444–5007

Fiscal Officer, VA Regional Office, Building 65, Fort Roots, PO Box 1280, North Little Rock, Little Rock, AR 72115, (501) 370–3741

California

Bell Supply Depot, Send to: Fiscal Officer, VA Supply Depot, PO Box 27, Hines, IL 60141, (312) 681–6800

Fiscal Officer, Fresno Medical Center, 2615 East Clinton Avenue, Fresno, CA 94703, (209) 225–6100

Fiscal Officer, Livermore Medical Center, Livermore, CA 94550, (415) 447–2560, ext. 317

Fiscal Officer, Loma Linda Medical Center, 11201 Benton Street, Loma Linda, CA 92357, (714) 825–7084, ext. 2550/2551

Fiscal Officer, Long Beach Medical Center, 5901 East Seventh Street, Long Beach, CA 90822, (213) 498–1313, ext. 2101

Fiscal Officer, Los Angeles Regional Office, Federal Building, 11000 Wilshire Blvd., Los Angeles, CA 90024, (213) 209–7565

Jurisdiction over the following counties in California: Inyo, Kern, Los Angeles, Orange, San Bernadino, San Luis Obispo, Santa Barbara and Ventura.

Los Angeles Data Processing Center, Send to: Fiscal Officer, VA Regional Office, Federal Bldg., 11000 Wilshire Blvd., Los Angeles, CA 90024, (213) 209–7565

Fiscal Officer, Los Angeles Medical Center—Brentwood Division, Los Angeles, CA 90073, (213) 478–3478

Fiscal Officer, Los Angeles Medical Center—Wadsworth Division, Los Angeles, CA 90073, (213) 478–3478

Fiscal Officer, Los Angeles Outpatient Clinic, 425 South Hill Street, Los Angeles, CA 90013, (213) 894–3870

Los Angeles Regional Office of Audit, Send to: Fiscal Officer, VA Medical Center—Brentwood Division, Los Angeles, CA 90073, (213) 824–4402

Los Angeles Field Office of Audit, Send to: Fiscal Officer, VA Medical Center—Wadsworth Division, Los Angeles, CA 90073, (213) 478–3478

Los Angeles National Cemetery Area Office, Send to: Fiscal Officer, VA Medical Center—Brentwood Division, Los Angeles, CA 90073, (213) 478–3478

Fiscal Officer, Martinez Medical Center, 150 Muir Rd., Martinez, CA 94553, (415) 228–6680, ext. 235

Fiscal Officer, Palo Alto Medical Center, 3801 Miranda Avenue, Palo Alto, CA 94304, (415) 493–5000, ext. 5643

Riverside National Cemetery Area Office, Send to: Fiscal Officer, VA Medical Center—Wadsworth Division, Los Angeles, CA 90073, (213) 478–3478

San Bruno National Cemetery Area Office, Send to: Fiscal Officer, VA Medical Center, 4150 Clement Street, San Bruno, CA 94121, (415) 221–4810, ext. 315/316

Fiscal Officer, San Diego Medical Center, 3350 La Jolla Village Drive, San Diego, CA 92161, (714) 453–7500, ext. 3351

San Diego Outpatient Clinic, Send to: Fiscal Officer, VA Medical Center, 3350 La Jolla Village Drive, San Diego, CA 92161, (714) 453–7500, ext. 3351

Fiscal Officer, San Diego Regional Office, 2022 Camino Del Rio North, San Diego, CA 92108, (714) 289–5703

Jurisdiction over the following counties in California: Imperial, Riverside and San Diego

San Francisco National Cemetery Area Office, Send to: Fiscal Officer, VA Medical Officer, 4150 Clement Street, San Francisco, CA 94121, (415) 556–0483

Fiscal Officer, San Francisco Regional Office, 211 Main Street, San Francisco, CA 94105, (415) 974–0160

Jurisdiction over all counties in California except Inyo, Kern, Los Angeles, Orange, San Bernardino, San Luis Obispo, Santa Barbara, Ventura, Imperial, Riverside, San Diego, Alpine, Lassen, Modoc and Mono.

Fiscal Officer, San Francisco Medical Center, 4150 Clement Street, San Francisco, CA 94121, (415) 221–4810, ext. 315/316

Fiscal Officer, Sepulveda Medical Center, 16111 Plummer Street, Sepulveda, CA 91343, (818) 891–2377

Colorado

Fiscal Officer, Denver Regional Office, Denver Federal Center, Building 20, Denver, CO 80225, (303) 234–3920

Fiscal Officer, Denver Medical Center, 1055 Clermont Street, Denver, CO 80220, (303) 393–2813

Denver National Cemetery Area Office, Send to: Fiscal Officer, VA Medical Center, 1055 Clermont Street, Denver, CO 80220, (303) 393–2813

Fort Logan National Cemetery Area Office, Send to: Fiscal Officer, VA Medical Center, 1055 Clermont Street, Denver, CO 80220, (303) 393–2813

Fort Lyon National Cemetery Area Office, Send to: Fiscal Officer, VA Medical Center, Fort Lyon, CO 81038, (719) 384–3987

Fiscal Officer, Fort Lyon Medical Center, Fort Lyon, CO 81038, (719) 384–3987

Fiscal Officer, Grand Junction Medical Center, 2121 North Avenue, Grand Junction, CO 81501, (303) 242–0731, ext. 275

Connecticut

Fiscal Officer, Hartford Regional Office, 450 Main Street, Hartford, CT 06103, (203) 244–3217

Fiscal Officer, Newington Medical Center, 555 Willard Avenue, Newington, CT 06111, (203) 666–6951, ext. 369

Fiscal Officer, West Haven Medical Center, 950 Campbell Avenue, West Haven, CT 06516, (203) 932–5711, ext. 859

Delaware

Fiscal Officer, Wilmington Medical and Regional Office Center, 1601 Kirkwood Highway, Wilmington, DE 19805, (302) 633–5432

District of Columbia

Finance Division Chief (047H), Washington Central Office, 810 Vermont Avenue, NW., Room C–50, Washington, DC 20420, (202) 233–3901

Washington Veterans Canteen Service Field Office, Send to: Finance Division Chief (047H), VA Central Office, 810 Vermont Avenue, NW., Room C–50, Washington, DC 20420, (202) 233–3901

Fiscal Officer, Washington Regional Office, 941 North Capitol Street, NE., Washington, DC 20421, (202) 208–1349

Jurisdiction over all foreign countries or overseas areas except Mexico, American Samoa, Guam, Midway, Wake, the Trust Territory of the Pacific Islands, the Virgin Islands and the Philippines. Also, jurisdiction over Prince George's and Montgomery Counties in Maryland; Fairfax and Arlington Counties and the cities of Alexandria, Fairfax and Falls Church in Virginia.

Fiscal Officer, Washington Medical Center, 50 Irving Street, NW., Washington, DC 20422, (202) 745–8229

Florida

Fiscal Officer, Bay Pines Medical Center, National Cemetery Area Office, Bay Pines, FL 33504, (813) 398–9321

Fiscal Officer, Gainesville Medical Center, Archer Road, Gainesville, FL 32601, (904) 376–1611, ext. 6685

Jacksonville Outpatient Clinic Substation, Send to: Fiscal Officer, VA Medical Center, 1601 SW. Archer Road, Gainesville, FL 32602, (904) 376–1611, ext. 6685

Jacksonville VA Office, Send to: Fiscal Officer, VA Regional Office, 144 First Avenue, South, St. Petersburg, FL 33731, (813) 893–3236

Fiscal Officer, Lake City Medical Center, 801 South Marion Street, Lake City, FL 32055, (904) 755–3016

Miami VA Office, Send to: Fiscal Officer, VA Regional Office, 144 First Avenue, South, St. Petersburg, FL 33731, (813) 893–3236

Fiscal Officer, Miami Medical Center, 1201 Northwest 16th Street, Miami, FL 33125, (305) 324–4284

Orlando Outpatient Clinic Substation, Send to: Fiscal Officer, VA Medical Center, 1300 North 30th Street, Tampa, FL 33612, (813) 971–4500

Fiscal Officer, James A. Haley Veterans' Hospital, 13000 Bruce B. Downs Blvd., Tampa, FL 33612, (813) 972–7501

Riviera Beach Outpatient Clinic Substation, Send to: Fiscal Officer, VA Medical Center, 1201 Northwest 16th Street, Miami, FL 33125, (305) 324–4284

Pensacola National Cemetery Area Office, Send to: Fiscal Officer, VA Medical Center, Gulfport, MS 39501, (601) 863–1972, ext. 225

St. Augustine National Cemetery Area Office, Send to: Fiscal Officer, VA Medical Center, Archer Road, Gainesville, FL 32602, (904) 376–1611, ext. 6685

Fiscal Officer, St. Petersburg Regional Office, 144 First Avenue, South, St. Petersburg, FL 33612, (813) 893–3236

Georgia

Fiscal Officer, Atlanta Regional Office, 730 Peachtree Street, NE., Atlanta, GA 30365, (404) 347–5008

Atlanta Veterans Canteen Service Field Office, Send to: Fiscal Officer, VA Medical Center, 1670 Clairmont Road, Decatur, GA 30033, (404) 321–6111

Atlanta National Cemetery Area Office, Send to: Fiscal Officer, VA Medical Office, 1670 Clairmont Road, Decatur, GA 30033, (404) 321–6111

Atlanta Field Office of Audit, Send to: Fiscal Officer, VA Regional Office, 730 Peachtree Street, NE., Atlanta, GA 30301, (404) 347–5008

Fiscal Officer, Augusta Medical Center, Augusta, GA 30904, (404) 733–4471, ext. 675/676

Fiscal Officer, VA Medical Center, 2460 Wrightsboro Road, Augusta, GA 30910, (404) 724–5116

Fiscal Officer, Decatur Medical Center, 1670 Clairmont Road, Decatur, GA 30033, (404) 321–6111, ext. 6320

Fiscal Officer, Dublin Medical Center, Dublin, GA 31021, (912) 272–1210, ext. 373

Marietta National Cemetery Area Office, Send to: Fiscal Officer, VA Medical Center, 1670 Clairmont Road, Decatur, GA 30033, (404) 321–6111

Hawaii

Fiscal Officer, Honolulu Regional Office, PO Box 50188, Honolulu, HI 96850, (808) 541–1490

Jurisdiction over Islands of American Samoa, Guam, Wake, Midway and Trust Territory of the Pacific Islands

Honolulu National Cemetery Area Office, Send to: Fiscal Officer, VA Regional Office, PO Box 50188, Honolulu, HI 96850, (808) 546–2109

Idaho

Fiscal Officer, Boise Medical Center, 500 West Fort Street, Boise, ID 83702, (208) 336–5100, ext. 7312

Fiscal Officer, Boise Regional Office, Federal Bldg. & U.S. Courthouse, 550 West Fort Street, Box 044, Boise, ID 83724, (208) 334–1009

Illinois

Alton National Cemetery Area Office, Send to: Fiscal Officer, VA Medical Center, St. Louis, MO 63125, (314) 894–4631

AMF O'Hare Field Office of Audit, Send to: Fiscal Officer, VA Medical Center, Hines, IL 60141, (312) 343–7200, ext. 2481

Fiscal Officer, Chicago Medical Center (Lakeside), 33 East Huron Street, Chicago, IL 60611, (312) 943–6600

Fiscal Officer, Chicago Medical Center (West Side), 820 South Damen Avenue, Chicago, IL 60612, (312) 666–6500, ext. 3338

Fiscal Officer, Chicago Regional Office, 536 South Clark Street, Chicago, IL 60680, (312) 886–9417

Fiscal Officer, Danville Medical Center, 1900 E. Main Street, Danville, IL 61832, (217) 442–8000

Danville National Cemetery Area Office, Send to: Fiscal Officer, VA Medical Center, 1900 E. Main Street, Danville, IL 61832, (217) 442–8000, ext. 210

Fiscal Officer, Hines Medical Center, Hines, IL 60141, (312) 343–7200, ext. 2481

Hines Marketing Center, Send to: Fiscal Officer, VA Supply Depot, PO Box 27, Hines, IL 60141, (312) 681–6800

Fiscal Officer, Hines Supply Depot, PO Box 27, Hines, IL 60141, (312) 681–6800

Fiscal Officer, Hines Data Processing Center, PO Box 66303, AMF O'Hare, Hines, IL 60666, (312) 681–6650

Fiscal Officer, Marion Medical Center, Marion, IL 62959, (618) 997–5311

Mound City National Cemetery Area Office, Send to: Fiscal Officer, VA Medical Center, 2401 West Main Street, Marion, IL 62959, (618) 997–5311

Fiscal Officer, North Chicago Medical Center, North Chicago, IL 60064, (312) 689–1900

Quincy National Cemetery Area Office, Send to: Fiscal Officer, VA Medical Center, Iowa City, IA 52240, (319) 338–0581, ext. 304

Rock Island National Cemetery Area Office, Send to: Fiscal Officer, VA Medical Center, Iowa City, IA 52240, (319) 338–0581, ext. 304

Springfield National Cemetery Area Officer, Send to: Fiscal Officer, VA Medical Center, 1900 E. Main Street, Danville, IL 61832, (217) 442–8000

Indiana

Evansville Outpatient Clinic Substation, Send to: Fiscal Officer, VA Medical Center, Marion, IL 62959, (618) 997–5311

Fiscal Officer, Fort Wayne Medical Center, 1600 Randalia Drive, Fort Wayne, IN 46805, (219) 426–5431

Fiscal Officer, Indianapolis Regional Office, 575 North Pennsylvania Street, Indianapolis, IN 46204, (317) 269–7840

Fiscal Officer, Indianapolis Medical Center, 1481 West 10th Street, Indianapolis, IN 46202, (317) 635–7401, ext. 2363

Indianapolis National Cemetery Area Office, Send to: Fiscal Officer, VA Medical Center, 1481 West 10th Street, Indianapolis, IN 46202, (317) 635–7401, ext. 2363

Fiscal Officer, Marion Medical Center, Marion, IN 46952, (317) 674–3321, ext. 214

Marion National Cemetery Area Office, Send to: Fiscal Officer, VA Medical Center, Marion, IN 46952, (317) 674–3321, ext. 211

New Albany National Cemetery Area Office, Send to: Fiscal Officer, VA Medical Center, 800 Zorn Avenue, Louisville, KY 40202, (502) 895–3401

Iowa

Fiscal Officer, Des Moines Regional Office, 210 Walnut Street, Des Moines, IA 50309, (515) 284–4220

Fiscal Officer, Des Moines Medical Center, 30th & Euclid Avenue, Des Moines, IA 50310, (515) 699–5999

Fiscal Officer, Iowa City Medical Center, Iowa City, IA 52246, (319) 338–0581, ext. 7702

Keokuk National Cemetery Area Office, Send to: Fiscal Officer, VA Medical Center, Iowa City, IA 52246, (319) 338–0581, ext. 7702

Keokuk National Cemetery Area Office, Send to: Fiscal Officer, VA Medical Center, Iowa City, IA 52246, (319) 338–0581, ext. 7702

Kansas

Ft. Leavenworth National Cemetery Area Office, Send to: Fiscal Officer, VA Medical Center, Leavenworth, KS 66048, (913) 682–2000, ext. 214

Ft. Scott National Cemetery Area Office, Send to: Fiscal Officer, VA Medical Center, Leavenworth, KS 66048, (913) 682–2000, ext. 214

Leavenworth National Cemetery Area Office, Send to: Fiscal Officer, VA Medical Center, Leavenworth, KS 66048, (913) 682–2000, ext. 214

Fiscal Officer, Leavenworth Medical Center, Leavenworth, KS 66048, (913) 682–2000, ext. 214

Fiscal Officer, Topeka Medical Center, 2200 Gage Blvd., Topeka, KS 66622, (913) 272–3111, ext. 521

Fiscal Officer, Wichita Medical Center, 5500 East Kellogg, Wichita, KA 67211 (316) 685–2221, ext. 256

Wichita Regional Office, Send to: VA Medical Center, 5500 East Kellogg, Wichita, KS 67211, (316) 685–2111, ext. 256

Process for VA service-connected benefits should also be sent to the Wichita Medical Center rather than to the Wichita Regional Office.

Fiscal Officer, VA Regional Office, 901 George Washington Blvd, Wichita, KS 67211, (316) 269–6813

Kentucky

Danville National Cemetery Area Office, Send to: Fiscal Officer, VA Medical Center, Lexington, KY 40507, (606) 223–4511

Fiscal Officer, Knoxville Medical Center, Knoxville, KY 50138, (515) 842–3101, ext. 241

Lebanon National Cemetery Area Office, Send to: Fiscal Officer, VA Medical Center, Lexington, KY 40507, (606) 233–4511

Lexington National Cemetery Area Office, Send to: Fiscal Officer, VA Medical Center, Lexington, KY 40507, (606) 233–4511

Fiscal Officer, Lexington Medical Center, Lexington KY 40507, (606) 233–4511

Fiscal Officer, Louisville Regional Office, 600 Federal Place, Louisville, KY 40202, (502) 582–6482

Fiscal Officer, Louisville Medical Center, 800 Zorn Avenue, Louisville, KY 40202, (502) 895–3401, ext. 241

Louisville National Cemetery Area Office (Zachry Taylor), Send to: Fiscal Officer, VA Medical Center, 800 Zorn Avenue, Louisville, KY 40202, (502) 895–3401, ext. 241

Louisville National Cemetery Area Office (Cave Hill), Send to: Fiscal Officer, VA Medical Center, 800 Zorn Avenue, Louisville, KY 40202, (502) 895–3401, ext. 241

Nancy National Cemetery Area Office, Send to: Fiscal Office, VA Medical Center, Lexington, KY 40507, (606) 233–4511

Nicholasville National Cemetery Area Office, Send to: Fiscal Officer, VA Medical Center, Lexington, KY 40507, (606) 233–4511

Perryville National Cemetery Area Office, Send to: Fiscal Officer, VA Medical Center, Lexington, KY 40507, (606) 233–4511

Louisiana

Fiscal Officer, Alexandria Medical Center, Alexandria LA 71303, (318) 473–0010, ext. 2281

Baton Rouge National Cemetery Area Office, Send to: Fiscal Officer, VA Medical Center, 1601 Perdido Street, New Orleans, LA 70146, (504) 568–0811

Fiscal Officer, New Orleans Regional Office, 701 Loyola Avenue, New Orleans, LA 70133, (504) 589–6604

Fiscal Officer, New Orleans Medical Center, 1601 Perdido Street, New Orleans, LA 70146, (504) 568–0811

Baton Rouge National Cemetery, 220 North 19th Street, Baton Rouge, LA 70806, (504) 389–0788

Pineville National Cemetery Area Office, Send to: Fiscal Officer, VA Medical Center, Alexandria, LA 71301, (318) 442–0251

Fiscal Officer, Shreveport Medical Center, 510 East Stoner Avenue, Shreveport, LA 71101, (318) 221–8411, ext. 722

Shreveport VA Office, Send to: Fiscal Officer, VA Regional Officer, 701 Loyola Avenue, New Orleans, LA 70113, (504) 589–6604

Port Hudson (Zachary) National Cemetery Area Office, Send to: Fiscal Officer, VA Medical Center, 1601 Perdido Street, New Orleans, LA 70146, (504) 568–0811

Maine

Portland VA Office, Send to: Fiscal Officer, VA Center, Togus, ME 04330, (207) 623–8411

Fiscal Officer, Togus Medical & Regional Office Center, Togus, ME 04330, (207) 623–8411

Togus National Cemetery Area Office, Send to: Fiscal Officer, VA Center, Togus, ME 04330, (207) 623–8411

Maryland

Annapolis National Cemetery Area Office, Send to: Fiscal Officer, VA Medical Center, 3900 Loch Raven Blvd., Baltimore, MD 21218, (301) 467–9932, ext. 5281/5282

Fiscal Officer, Baltimore Regional Office, Federal Bldg., 31 Hopkins Plaza, Baltimore, MD 21201, (301) 962–4410

Jurisdiction does not include Prince George's and Montgomery Counties which are included under the Washington, DC Regional Office

Baltimore Outpatient Clinic, Send to: Fiscal Officer, VA Medical Center, 3900 Loch Raven Blvd., Baltimore, MD 21218, (301) 467–9932, ext. 5281/5282

Fiscal Officer, Baltimore Medical Center, 3900 Loch Raven Blvd., Baltimore, MD 21218, (301) 467–9932, ext. 5281/5282

Baltimore National Cemetery Area Office (Loudon Park), Send to: Fiscal Officer, VA Medical Center, 3900 Loch Raven Blvd., Baltimore, MD 21218, (301) 467–9932, ext. 5281/5282

Fiscal Officer, Fort Howard Medical Center, Fort Howard, MD 21052, (301) 687–8768, ext. 328

Hyattsville Field Office of Audit, Send to: Fiscal Division Chief (047H), VA Central Office, Room C–50, 810 Vermont Avenue, Washington, DC 20420, (202) 389–3901

Fiscal Officer, Perry Point Medical Center, Perry Point, MD 21902, (301) 642–2411, ext. 5224/5225

Massachusetts

Fiscal Officer, Bedford Medical Center, 200 Springs Road, Bedford, MA 01730, (617) 275–7500

Fiscal Officer, Boston Regional Office, John F. Kennedy Bldg., Room 400C, Government Center, Boston, MA, (617) 565–2616

Jurisdiction over certain towns in Bristol and Plymouth Counties and the counties of Barnstable, Dukes and Nantucket is allocated to the Providence, Rhode Island Regional Office.

Boston Outpatient Clinic, Send to: Fiscal Officer, VA Medical Center, 150 South Huntington Avenue, Boston, MA 02130, (617) 232–9500, ext. 427/420

Fiscal Officer, Boston Medical Center, 150 South Huntington Avenue, Boston, MA 02130, (617) 232–9500, ext. 427/420

Bourne National Cemetery Area Office, Send to: Fiscal Officer, VA Medical Center, Brockton, MA 02401, (617) 583–4500, ext. 266

Fiscal Officer, Brockton Medical Center, Brockton, MA 02401 (617) 583–4500, ext. 266

Lowell Outpatient Clinic Substation, Send to: Fiscal Officer, VA Medical Center, 150 South Huntington Avenue, Boston, MA 02130 (617) 322–9500, ext 427/420

New Bedford Outpatient Clinic Substation, Send to: Fiscal Officer, VA Medical Center, Providence, RI 02908, (401) 273-7100

Fiscal Officer, Northampton Medical Center, Northampton, MA 01060, (413) 584-4040

Springfield Outpatient Clinic Substation, Send to: Fiscal Officer, VA Medical Center, Northampton, MA 01060, (413) 584-4040

Springfield VA Office, Send to: Fiscal Officer, VA Regional Office, John F. Kennedy Bldg., Room 400C, Government Center, Boston, MA 02203, (617) 565-2616

Fiscal Officer, West Roxbury Medical Center, 1400 Veterans of Foreign Wars Parkway, West Roxbury, MA 02132, (617) 323-7700, ext. 5650

Worcester Outpatient Clinic Substation, Send to: Fiscal Officer, VA Medical Center, 1400 Veterans of Foreign Wars Parkway, West Roxbury, MA 02132, (617) 323-7700, ext. 5650

Michigan

Fiscal Officer, Allen Park Medical Center, Allen Park, MI 48101, (313) 562-6000, ext. 535

Fiscal Officer, Ann Arbor Medical Center, 2215 Fuller Road, Ann Arbor, MI 48105, (313) 769-7100, ext. 288/289

Fiscal Officer, Battle Creek Medical Center, Battle Creek, MI 49016, (616) 966-5600, ext. 3566

Grand Rapids Outpatient Clinic Substation, Send to: Fiscal Officer, VA Medical Center, Battle Creek, MI 49016, (616) 966-5600, ext. 3566

Fiscal Officer, Detroit Regional Office, 477 Michigan Avenue, Detroit, MI 48226, (313) 226-4190

Fiscal Officer, Iron Mountain Medical Center, Iron Mountain, MI 49801, (906) 774-3300, ext. 308

Fiscal Officer, Saginaw Medical Center, 1500 Weiss Street, Saginaw, MI 48602, (517) 793-2340, ext. 3061

Minnesota

Fiscal Officer, Minneapolis Medical Center, 54th & 48th Avenue, South Minneapolis, MN 55417, (612) 725-6767, ext. 6311

Fiscal Officer, St. Cloud Medical Center, St. Cloud, MN 56301, (612) 252-1600, ext. 411

Fiscal Officer, St. Paul Center (Regional Office), Federal Building, Ft. Snelling, St. Paul, MN 55111, (612) 725-4075

Fiscal Officer, VA Medical Center, One Veterans Drive, Minneapolis, MN 55417, (612) 725-2150

Jurisdiction over the counties of Becker, Beltrami, Clay, Clearwater, Kittson, Lake of the Woods, Mahnomen, Marshall, Norman, Otter Tail, Pennington, Polk, Red Lake, Roseau and Wilkin is allocated to the Fargo, North Dakota Center.

St. Paul National Cemetery Area Office, Send to: VA Medical Center, 54th & 48th Avenue, South, Minneapolis, MN 55417, (612) 725-6767, ext. 6311

St. Paul Data Processing Center, Send to: Fiscal Officer, VA Center, Federal Building, Ft. Snelling, St. Paul, MN 55111, (612) 725-3075

St. Paul Outpatient Clinic, Send to: Fiscal Officer, VA Medical Center, 54th & 48th Avenue, Minneapolis, MN 55111, (612) 725-6767, ext. 6311

Mississippi

Biloxi National Cemetery Area Office, Send to: Fiscal Officer, VA Medical Center, Biloxi, MS 39531, (601) 863-1972, ext. 225

Fiscal Officer, Biloxi Medical Center, Biloxi, MS 39531, (601) 863-1972, ext. 225

Corrinth National Cemetery Area Office, Send to: Fiscal Officer, VA Medical Center, 1030 Jefferson Avenue, Memphis, TN 38104, (901) 523-8990

Fiscal Officer, Gulfport Medical Center, Gulfport, MS 39601, (601) 863-1972, ext. 225

Fiscal Officer, Jackson Medical Center, 1500 East Woodrow Wilson Drive, Jackson, MS 39216, (601) 362-4471, ext. 1281

Fiscal Officer, VA Regional Office, Federal Building, 100 W. Capitol St., Suite 207, Jackson, MS 39269, (601) 965-4853

Natchez National Cemetery, Send to: Fiscal Officer, VA Medical Center, 1500 E. Woodrow Wilson Dr., Jackson, MS 39216, (601) 362-4471, ext. 1281

Process for VA service-connected benefits should also be sent to the Jackson Medical Center rather than to the Jackson Regional Office.

Missouri

Fiscal Officer, Columbia Medical Center, 800 Stadium Road, Columbia, MO 62501, (314) 443-2511

Jefferson City National Cemetery Area Office, Send to: Fiscal Officer, VA Medical Center, 800 Stadium Road, Columbia, MO 65201, (314) 443-2511, ext. 6050

Fiscal Officer, Kansas City Medical Center, 4801 Linwood Blvd., Kansas City, MO 64128, (816) 861-4700, ext. 214

Fiscal Officer, Poplar Bluff Medical Center, Poplar Bluff, MO 63901, (314) 686-4151

St. Louis National Cemetery Area Office, Send to: Fiscal Officer, VA Medical Center, St. Louis, MO 63125, (314) 894-4931

Fiscal Officer, St. Louis Regional Office, 1520 Market Street, St. Louis, MO 63103, (314) 539-3112

Fiscal Officer, VA Medical Center, 1500 N. Westwood Blvd., Poplar Bluff, MO 63901, (314) 686-4151, ext. 265

St. Louis Veterans Canteen Service Field Office, Send to: Fiscal Officer, VA Medical Center, St. Louis, MO 63125, (314) 894-4631

Fiscal Officer, St. Louis Medical Center, St. Louis, MO 63125, (314) 894-4631

St. Louis Records Processing Center, Send to: Fiscal Officer, VA Regional Office, 1520 Market Street, St. Louis, MO 63103, (314) 539–3112

Springfield National Cemetery Area Office, Send to: Fiscal Officer, VA Medical Center, Fayetteville, AR 72701, (501) 443–4301

Montana

Fiscal Officer, Fort Harrison Medical & Regional Office Center, Fort Harrison, MT 59636, (406) 442–6410

Fiscal Officer, Mile City Medical Center, 210 N. Broadwell, Miles City, MT 59301, (406) 232–3060

Nebraska

Fiscal Officer, Grand Island Medical Center, 2201 N. Broadwell, Grand Island, NE 68801, (308) 382–3660, ext. 244

Fiscal Officer, Lincoln Regional Office, 100 Centennial Mall North, Lincoln NE 68510, (402) 437–5041

Fiscal Officer, Lincoln Regional Office, 600 South 70th Street, Lincoln NE 68510, (402) 489–3802, ext. 332

Maxwell National Cemetery Area Office, Send to: Fiscal Officer, VA Medical Center, Grand Island, NE 68801, (308) 382–3660, ext. 244

Fiscal Officer, Omaha Medical Center, 4101 Woolworth Avenue, Omaha, NE, (402) 346–8800, ext. 4538

Nevada

Las Vegas Outpatient Clinic, Send to: Fiscal Officer, VA Medical Center, 1000 Locust Street, Reno, NV 89250, (702) 786–7200, ext. 244

Fiscal Officer, Reno Regional Office, 1201 Terminal Way, Reno, NV (702) 784–5637

Jurisdiction over the following counties in California: Alpine, Lassen, Modoc and Mono.

Fiscal Officer, Reno Medical Center, 1000 Locust Street, Reno, NV 89520, (702) 786–7200, ext. 244

Henderson Outpatient Clinic, Send to: Fiscal Officer, Reno Medical Center, 1000 Locust Street, Reno, NV 89520, (702) 786–7200, ext. 244

New Hampshire

Fiscal Officer, Manchester Regional Office, 275 Chestnut Street, Manchester, NH 03103, (603) 666–7638

Fiscal Officer, Manchester Medical Center 718 Smyth Road, Manchester, NH 03104, (603) 624–4366

New Jersey

Beverly National Cemetery Area Office, Send to: Fiscal Officer, VA Medical Center, University and Woodland Avenues, Philadelphia, PA 19104, (215) 382–2400, ext. 291/292

Fiscal Officer, East Orange Medical Center, Tremont Avenue and So. Center Street, East Orange, NJ 07019, (201) 676–1000, ext. 1771

Fiscal Officer, Lyons Medical Center, Lyons, NJ 07939, (201) 647–0180, ext. 4302

Newark Outpatient Clinic, Send to: Fiscal Officer, VA Medical Center, Tremont Avenue and So. Center Street, East Orange, NJ 07019, (201) 676–1000, ext. 125

Fiscal Officer, Newark Regional Office, 20 Washington Place, Newark, NJ 07102, (201) 645–3507

Salem National Cemetery Area Office, Send to: Fiscal Officer, VA Center, 1601 Kirkwood Highway, Wilmington, DE 19805, (302) 994–2511

Fiscal Officer, Somerville Supply Depot, Somerville, NJ 08876, (210) 725–2540

New Mexico

Fiscal Officer, Albuquerque Regional Office, 500 Gold Avenue, SW., Albuquerque, NM 87102, (505) 766–2204

Fiscal Officer, Albuquerque Medical Center, 2100 Ridgecrest Drive, SE., Albuquerque NM 87108, (505) 265–1711

Santa Fe National Cemetery Area Office, Send to: Fiscal Officer, VA Medical Center, 2100 Ridgecrest Drive, SE., Albuquerque, NM 87108, (505) 265–1711, ext. 2214

New York

Fiscal Officer, Albany Medical Center, 113 Holland Ave., Albany, NY 12202, (518) 462–3311, ext. 355

Fiscal Officer, VA Medical Center, 800 Irving Center, Syracuse, NY 13210, (315) 476–7461, ext. 2358

Albany VA Office, Send to: Fiscal Officer, VA Regional Office, 252 Seventh Avenue & 24th Street, New York, NY 10001, (211) 620–6293

Fiscal Officer, Batavia Medical Center, Redfield Parkway, Batavia, NY 14020, (716) 345–7500, ext. 215

Fiscal Officer, Bath Medical Center, Bath, NY 14810, (607) 776–2111, ext. 1502

Fiscal Officer, Bronx Medical Center, 140 W. Kings Bridge Road, Bronx, NY 10408, (212) 584–9000, ext. 1502/1717

Fiscal Officer, Brooklyn Medical Center, 800 Poly Place, Brooklyn, NY 11209, (718) 630–3542

Brooklyn National Cemetery Area Office, Fiscal Officer, VA Medical Center, 800 Poly Place, Brooklyn, NY 11209, (718) 630–2541

Brooklyn Outpatient Clinic, Send to: Fiscal Officer, VA Medical Center, 800 Poly Place, Brooklyn, NY 11209, (718) 630–3542

Fiscal Officer, Buffalo Regional Office, 111 West Huron Street, Buffalo, NY 14202, (716) 846–5251

Brooklyn Outpatient Clinic, Send to: Fiscal Officer, VA Medical Center, 800 Poly Place, Brooklyn, NY 11209, (718) 630–3542

Fiscal Officer, Buffalo Regional Office, 111 West Huron Street, Buffalo, NY 14202, (716) 846–5251

Jurisdiction over all counties in New York not listed under the New York Regional Office.

Fiscal Officer, Buffalo Medical Center, 3495 Bailey Avenue, Buffalo, NY 14215, (716) 862–3335/(716) 834–9200, ext. 3335

Calverton National Cemetery Area Office, Send to: Fiscal Office, VA Medical Center, Northport, NY 11768, (516) 261–4400, ext. 7101/7103

Fiscal Officer, Canandiague Medical Center, Canandaigua, NY 14424, (716) 394–2000, ext. 3368

Fiscal Officer, Castle Point Medical Center, Castle Point, NY 12511, (914) 882–5404

Elmira National Cemetery Area Office, Send to: Fiscal Officer, VA Medical Center, Bath, NY 14810, (607) 776–2111

Farmingdale National Cemetery Area Office, Send to: Fiscal Officer, VA Medical Center, Northport, NY 11768, (516) 261–4400, ext. 2462/2463

Fiscal Officer, Montrose Medical Center, Montrose, NY 10548, (914) 737–4400, ext. 2463

Fiscal Officer, New York Medical Center, First Avenue at East 24th Street, New York, NY 10010, (212) 686–7320

New York Outpatient Clinic, Send to: Fiscal Officer, VA Medical Center, First Avenue at East 24th Street, New York, NY 10010, (212) 686–7320

New York Prosthetics Center, Send to: Fiscal Officer, VA Regional Office, 252 Seventh Avenue, New York, NY 10001, (212) 620–6293

Fiscal Officer, New York Regional Office, 252 Seventh Avenue at 24th Street, New York, NY 10001, (212) 620–6293

Jurisdiction over the following counties in New York: Albany, Bronx, Clinton, Columbia, Delaware, Dutchess, Essex, Franklin, Fulton, Greene, Hamilton, Kings, Montgomery, Nassau, New York, Orange, Otsego, Putnam, Queens, Rensselaer, Richmond, Rockland, Saratoga, Schenectady, Schharie, Suffolk, Sullivan, Ulster, Warren, Washington and Westchester.

New York Veterans Canteen Service Field Office, Send to: Fiscal Officer, VA Medical Center, First Avenue at East 24th Street, New York, NY 10010, (202) 686–7320

Fiscal Officer, Northport Medical Center, Northport, NY 11768, (516) 261–4400, ext. 2462/2463

Rochester VA Office, Send to: Fiscal Officer, VA Regional Office, 111 West Huron Street, Buffalo, NY 14202, (716) 846–5251

Rochester Outpatient Clinic Substation, Send to: Fiscal Officer, VA Medical Center, Batavia, NY 14020, (716) 343–7500, ext. 215

Fiscal Officer, Syracuse Medical Center, Irving Avenue & University Place, Syracuse, NY 13210, (315) 476–7461

Syracuse VA Office, Send to: Fiscal Officer, VA Regional Office, 111 West Huron Street, Buffalo, NY 14202, (716) 846–5251

North Carolina

Fiscal Officer, Asheville Medical Center, 1100 Tunnel Road, Asheville, NC 28801, (704) 298–7911, ext. 5616

Fiscal Officer, Durham Medical Center, 508 Fulton Street, Durham, NC 27705, (919) 671–6913

Fiscal Officer, Fayetteville Medical Center, 2300 Ramsey Street, Fayetteville, NC 28301, (919) 488–2120

New Bern National Cemetery Area Office, Send to: Fiscal Officer, VA Medical Center, 2300 Ramsey Street, Fayetteville, NC 28301, (919) 488–2120

Raleigh National Cemetery Area Office, Send to: Fiscal Officer, VA Medical Center, 508 Fulton Street, Durham, NC 27705, (919) 286–0411, ext. 6469

Fiscal Officer, Salisbury Medical Center, Salisbury, NC 28144, (704) 636–2351

Salisbury National Cemetery Area Office, Send to: Fiscal Officer, VA Medical Center, Salisbury, NC 28144, (704) 636–2351

Wilmington National Cemetery Area Office, Send to: Fiscal Officer, VA Medical Center, 2300 Ramsey Street, Fayetteville, NC 28301, (919) 488–2120

Fiscal Officer, Winston-Salem Regional Office, 251 North Main Street, Winston-Salem, NC 27102 (919) 761–3513

Winston-Salem Outpatient Regional Office, Send to: Fiscal Officer, VA Medical Center, Salisbury, NC 28144, (704) 636–2351

North Dakota

Fiscal Officer, Fargo Medical and Regional Office Center, 21st & Elm, Fargo, ND 58102, (701) 232–3241, ext. 249

See listing under the St. Paul, Minnesota Center for the names of the counties in Minnesota which come under the jurisdiction of the Fargo, North Dakota Center.

Ohio

Fiscal Officer, Chillicothe Medical Center, 17273 State Route 104, Chillicothe, OH 45601, (614) 773–1141, ext. 203

Fiscal Officer, Cincinnati Medical Center, 3200 Vine Street, Cincinnati, OH 45220, (513) 550–5040, ext. 4113

Fiscal Officer, VA Medical Center, 2090 Kenny Road, Columbus, OH 43221, (614) 469–6712

Cincinnati VA Office, Send to: Fiscal Officer, VA Regional Office, 1240 East Ninth Street, Cleveland, OH 44199, (216) 522–3540

Fiscal Officer, Cleveland Regional Office, 1240 East Ninth Street, Cleveland, OH 44199, (216) 522–3540

Fiscal Officer, Cleveland Medical Center, 10,000 Brecksville Rd, Brecksville, OH 44141, (216) 526–3030, ext. 7170

Fiscal Officer, Columbus Outpatient Clinic, 456 Clinic Drive, Columbus, OH 43210, (614) 469–6712

Columbus VA Office, Send to: Fiscal Officer, VA Regional Office, 1240 East Ninth Street, Cleveland, OH 44199, (216) 522–3540

Dayton National Cemetery Area Office, Send to: Fiscal Officer, VA Medical Center, Dayton, OH 45248, (513) 268–6511, ext. 262–2157

Fiscal Officer, VA Medical Center, 4100 W. Third Street, Dayton, OH 45428, (513) 262–2157

Oklahoma

Fort Gibson National Cemetery Area Office, Fiscal Officer, VA Medical Center, Memorial Station, Honor Heights Drive, Muskogee, OK 74401, (918) 683–3261, ext. 392

Fiscal Officer, Muskogee Regional Office, 125 South Main Street, Muskogee, OK 74401, (918) 687–2169

Fiscal Officer, Muskogee Medical Center, Memorial Station, Honor Heights Drive, Muskogee, OK 74401, (918) 683–3261, ext. 392

Fiscal Officer, Oklahoma City Medical Center, 921 Northeast 13th Street, Oklahoma, OK 73104, (405) 272–9876, ext. 500

Oklahoma City VA Office, Send to: Fiscal Officer, VA Regional Office, 125 South Main St., Muskogee, OK 74401, (908) 687–2169

Oregon

Portland National Cemetery Area Office, Send to: Fiscal Officer, VA Medical Center, 3710 SW U.S. Veterans Hospital Road, Portland, OR 97201, (503) 220–8262, ext. 6948

Fiscal Officer, Portland Regional Office, 1220 SW 3rd Avenue, Portland, OR 97204, (503) 221–2521

Fiscal Officer, Portland Medical Center, 3710 SW U.S. Veterans Hospital Road, Portland, OR 97201, (503) 220–8262, ext. 6948

Portland Outpatient Clinic, Send to: Fiscal Officer, VA Medical Center, 3710 SW U.S. Veterans Hospital Road, Portland, OR 97210, (503) 222–9221, ext. 6984

Fiscal Officer, VA Medical Center, Garden Valley Blvd., Roseburg, OR 97470, (503) 440–1000, ext. 4261

Roseburg National Cemetery Area Office, Send to: Fiscal Officer, VA Medical Center, Garden Valley Blvd., Roseburg, OR 97470, (503) 672–4411

Fiscal Officer, White City Domiciliary, White City, OR 97501, (503) 826–2111, ext. 241

White City National Cemetery Area, Send to: Fiscal Officer, VA Office, Domiciliary, White City, OR 97503, (503) 826–2111, ext. 241

Pennsylvania

Fiscal Officer, Altoona Medical Center, Altoona, PA 16603, (814) 943–8164, ext. 7046

Annville National Cemetery Area Office, Send to: Fiscal Officer, VA Medical Center, Lebanon, PA 17042, (717) 272–6621, ext. 229

Fiscal Officer, VA Medical Center, Butler, PA, 16001, (412) 287–4781, ext. 4505

Fiscal Officer, Coatsville Medical Center, Coatsville, PA 19320, (215) 384–7711, ext. 342

Fiscal Officer, Erie Medical Center, 135 East 38th Street, Erie, PA 16501, (814) 868–8661

Harrisburg Outpatient Clinic Substation, Fiscal Officer, VA Medical Center, Lebanon, PA 17042, (717) 272–6621, ext. 229

Fiscal Officer, Lebanon Medical Center, Lebanon Medical Center, Lebanon, PA, 17042, (717) 272–6621, ext. 229

Fiscal Officer, Philadelphia Center (Regional Office), PO Box 8079, Philadelphia, PA 19101, (215) 951–5321

Jurisdiction over the following counties in Pennsylvania: Adams, Berks, Bradford, Bucks, Cameron, Carbon, Centre, Chester, Clinton, Columbia, Cumberland, Dauphin, Delaware, Franklin, Juniata, Lackawanna, Lancaster, Lebanon, Lehigh, Luzerne, Lycoming, Mifflin, Monroe, Montgomery, Montour, Northampton, Northumberland, Perry, Philadelphia, Pike, Potter, Schuylkill, Snyder, Sullivan, Susquehanna, Tioga, Union, Wayne, Wyoming and York.

Philadelphia Data Processing Center, Send to: Fiscal Officer, VA Medical Center, P.O. Box 13399, Philadelphia, PA 19101, (215) 951–5321

Philadelphia National Cemetery Area Office, Send to: Fiscal Officer, VA Medical Center, University & Woodland Avenues, Philadelphia, PA 19104, (215) 951–5321

Fiscal Officer, VA Medical Center, University & Woodland Avenues, Philadelphia, PA 19104, (125) 951–5321

Fiscal Officer, Pittsburgh Regional Office, 1000 Liberty Avenue, Pittsburgh, PA 15222, (412) 644–4394

Jurisdiction over all of the counties in Pennsylvania that are not listed under the Philadelphia Center (Regional Office) and jurisdiction over the following counties in West Virginia: Brooke, Hancock, Marshall and Ohio.

Fiscal Officer, Pittsburgh Medical Center, Highland Drive, Pittsburgh, PA 15206, (412) 363–4900, ext. 4235

Fiscal Officer, Pittsburgh Medical Center, University Drive C, Pittsburgh, PA 15240 (412) 683–3000, ext. 675

Fiscal Officer, Wilkes-Barre Medical Center, 1111 East End Blvd., Wilkes-Barre, PA 18711, (717) 824–3521, ext. 7211

Philippines

Manila Regional Office Outpatient Clinic and Manila Regional Office Center

For either of the above, send to:

Director, Department of Veterans Affairs, APO, San Francisco, CA 96528, 011–632–521–7116, ext. 2560

Puerto Rico

Raymon National Cemetery Area Office, Send to: Fiscal Officer, VA Center, GPO, Box 4867, San Juan, PR 00936, (890) 766–5115

Hato Regional Office, GPO, Box 4867, San Juan, PR 00936, (809) 766–5115

Mayaguez Outpatient Clinic Substation, Send to: Fiscal Officer, VA Center, GPO, Box 4867, San Juan, PR 00936, (809) 763–0275

Rio Piedras Medical and Regional Office Center, Send to: Fiscal Officer, VA Center, GPO, Box 4867, San Juan, PR 00936, (809) 758–7575, ext. 4953

Fiscal Officer, VA Medical Center, One Veterans Plaza, San Juan, PR 00927–5800, (809) 766–5365/(809) 766–5953

Rhode Island

Fiscal Officer, Providence Regional Office, 321 South Main Street, Providence, RI 02903, (401) 528–4439

Jurisdication over the following towns and counties in Massachusetts: all towns in Bristol County except Mansfield and Easton, the towns of Lakeville, Middleboro, Carver, Rochester. Mattapoisett, Marion, and Wareham in Plymouth County; and the counties of Dukes, Nantucket and Barnstable.

Fiscal Officer, Providence Medical Center, Davis Park, Providence, RI 02908, (401) 475–3019

South Carolina

Beaufort National Cemetery Area Office, Send to: Fiscal Officer, VA Medical Center, 109 Bee Street, Charleston, SC 29403, (803) 577–5011, ext. 222

Fiscal Officer, Charleston Medical Center, 109 Bee Street, Charleston, SC 29403, (803) 577–5011, ext. 222

Fiscal Officer, Columbia Regional Office, 1801 Assembly Street, Columbia, SC 29201, (803) 765–5210

Fiscal Officer, Columbia Medical Center, Columbia, SC 29201, (803) 776–4000, ext. 150

Florence National Cemetery Area Office, Send to: Fiscal Officer, VA Medical Center, Columbia, SC 29201, (803) 776–4000, ext. 149

Greenville Outpatient Clinic Substation, Send to: Fiscal Officer, VA Medical Center, Columbia, SC 29201, (803) 776–4000, ext. 149

South Dakota

Fort Meade National Cemetery Area Office, Send to: Fiscal Officer, VA Medical Center, Fort Meade, SD 57741 (605) 347–2511, ext. 272

Fiscal Officer, VA Medical Center, Fort Meade, SD 57741 (605) 347–2511, ext. 272

Hot Springs National Cemetery Area Office, Fiscal Officer, VA Medical Center, Hot Springs, SD 57747 (605) 745–4101, ext. 246

Fiscal Officer, Hot Springs Medical Center, Hot Springs, SD 57747, (605) 745–4101

Fiscal Officer, Sioux Falls Medical and Regional Office Center, PO Box 5046, Sioux Falls, SD 57117, (605) 333–6823

Tennessee

Chattanooga Outpatient Clinic Substation, Send to: Fiscal Officer, VA Medical Center, 1310 24th Avenue, South, Nashville, TN 37203, (615) 327–4651

Chattanooga National Cemetery Area Office, Send to: Fiscal Officer, VA Medical Center, Murfreesboro, TN 37123, (615) 893–1360

Knoxville National Cemetery Area Office, Send to: Fiscal Officer, VA Medical Center, Mountain Home, TN 37684, (615) 926–1171, ext. 7601

Knoxville Outpatient Clinic Substation, Send to: Fiscal Officer, VA Medical Center, 1320 24th Avenue, South, Nashville, TN 37203, (615) 327–4651, ext. 553

Madison National Cemetery Area Office, Send to: Fiscal Officer, VA Medical Center, 1320 24th Avenue, South, Nashville, TN 37203, (615) 327–4651, ext. 553

Fiscal Officer, Memphis Medical Center, 1030 Jefferson Avenue, Memphis, TN 38104, (901) 523–8990, ext. 5838

Memphis National Cemetery Area Office, Send to: Fiscal Officer, VA Medical Center, 1030 Jefferson Avenue, Memphis, TN 38104, (901) 523–8990, ext. 5838

Fiscal Officer, Mountain Home Medical Center, Mountain Home, TN 37684, (615) 926–1171, ext. 7601

Mountain Home National Cemetery Area Office, Send to: Fiscal Officer, VA Medical Center, Mountain Home, TN 37684, (615) 926–1171

Fiscal Officer, Murfreesboro Medical Center, Murfreesboro, TN 37130, (615) 893–1360, ext. 3198

Fiscal Officer, National Regional Office, 110 Ninth Avenue South, Nashville, TN 37203, (615) 736–5352

Fiscal Officer, Medical Center, 1310 24th Avenue, South, Nashville, TN 37212, (615) 327–4751, ext. 5147

Texas

Fiscal Officer, Amarillo Medical Center, 6010 Amarillo Blvd. W., Amarillo, TX 79106, (806) 355–9703, ext. 7370

Fiscal Officer, Austin Data Processing Center, 1615 East Woodward Street, Austin, TX 78772, (512) 482–4028

Beaumont Outpatient Clinic Substation, Send to: Fiscal Officer, VA Medical Center, 2002 Holcombe Blvd., Houston, TX 77211, (713) 795–7493

Fiscal Officer, Big Spring Medical Center, Big Spring, TX 79720, (915) 263–7361, ext. 326

Fiscal Officer, Bonham Medical Center, East 96th & Lipscomb Street, Bonham, TX 75418, (218) 583–2111, ext. 240

Corpus Christi Outpatient Clinic Substation, Send to: Fiscal Officer, VA Medical Center,

7400 Merton Minter Blvd., San Antonio, TX 78284, (512) 696–9660, ext. 5871

Fiscal Officer, Dallas Medical Center, 4500 South Lancaster Road, Dallas, TX 75216, (214) 376–5451, ext. 5238

Dallas VA Office, Send to: Fiscal Officer, VA Regional Office, 1400 North Valley Mills Drive, Waco, TX 76799, (817) 757–6454

Fiscal Officer, El Paso Outpatient Clinic, 5919 Brook Hollow Drive, el Paso, TX 79925, (915) 579–7960

Fort Bliss National Cemetery Area Office, Send to: Fiscal Officer, VA Outpatient Clinic, 5919 Brook Hollow Drive, El Paso, TX 79925, (915) 579–7960

Fiscal Officer, Houston Medical Center, 2002 Holcombe Blvd., Houston, TX 77211, (713) 795–7493

Fiscal Officer, Houston Regional Office, 2515 Murworth Drive, Houston, TX 77054, (713) 660–4121

Jurisdiction over the country of Mexico and the following counties in Texas: Angelina, Aransas, Atascosa, Austin, Bandera, Bee, Bexar, Blanco, Brazoria, Brewster, Brooks, Caldwell, Calhoun, Cameron, Chambers, Colorado, Comal, Crockett, DeWitt, Dimmitt, Duval, Edwards, Fort Bend, Frio, Galveston, Gillespie, Goliad, Gonzales, Grimes, Guadalupe, Hardin, Harris, Hays, Hidalgo, Houston, Jackson, Jasper, Jefferson, Jim Hogg, Jim Wells, Karnes, Kenndall, Kennedy, Kerr, Kimble, Kinney, Kleberg, LaSalle, Lavaca, Liberty, Live Oak, McCulloch, McMullen, Mason, Matagorda, Maverick, Medina, Menard, Montgomery, Necogdoches, Newton, Nueces, Orange, Pecos, Polk, Real, Refugio, Sabine, San Augustine, San Jacinto, San Patrico, Schleicher, Shelby, Starr, Sutton, Terrell, Trinity, Tyler, Val Verde, Victoria, Walker, Waller, Washington, Webb, Wharton, Willacy, Wilson, Zapata and Zavala.

Houston National Cemetery Area Office, Send to: Fiscal Officer, VA Medical Center, 2002 Holcombe Blvd., Houston, TX 77211, (713) 795–7493

Fiscal Officer, Kerrville Medical Center, Kerrville, TX 78028, (512) 896–2020, ext. 300

Kerrville National Cemetery Area Office, Send to: Fiscal Officer, VA Medical Center, Kerrville, TX 78028, (512) 896–2020, ext. 300

Lubbock VA Office, Send to: Fiscal Officer, VA Regional Office, 1400 North Valley Mills Drive, Waco, TX 76799, (817) 657–6464, ext. 635

Fiscal Officer, Lubbock Outpatient Clinic, 1205 Texas Avenue, Lubbock, TX 79401, (806) 762–7209

Fiscal Officer, Marlin Medical Center, 1016 Ward Street, Marlin, TX 76661, (817) 883–3511, ext. 224

McAllen Outpatient Clinic Substation, Send to: Fiscal Officer, VA Medical Center, 7400 Merton Minter Blvd., San Antonio, TX 78284, (512) 696–9660, ext. 5871

Fiscal Officer, San Antonio Medical Center, 7400 Merton Minter Blvd., San Antonio, TX 78284, (512) 696–9660, ext. 5871

San Antonio VA Office, Send to: Fiscal Officer, VA Regional Office, 2515 Murworth Drive, Houston, TX 77054 (713) 226–4185

San Antonio National Cemetery Area Office, Send to: Fiscal Officer, VA Medical Center, 7400 Merton Minter Blvd., San Antonio, TX 78284, (512) 696–9660, ext. 5871

San Antonio National Cemetery Area Office, (Fort Sam Houston), Send to: Fiscal Officer, VA Medical Center, 7400 Merton Minter Blvd., San Antonio, TX 78284, (512) 696–9660, ext. 5871

Fiscal Officer, Temple Medical Center, Temple, TX 76501, (817) 778–4811

Fiscal Officer, Waco Regional Office, 1400 North Valley Mills Drive, Waco, TX 76799, (817) 756–6454

Jurisdiction over all counties in Texas not listed under the Houston Regional Office.

Fiscal Officer, Waco Medical Center, Memorial Drive, Waco, TX 76703, (817) 752–6581

Waco Outpatient Clinic, Send to: Fiscal Officer, VA Medical Center, Memorial Drive, Waco, TX 76703, (817) 752–6581

Utah

Fiscal Officer, Salt Lake City Regional Office, 125 South State Street, Salt Lake City, UT 84147, (801) 524–5361

Fiscal Officer, Salt Lake City Medical Center, 500 Foothill Blvd., Salt Lake City, UT 85148, (810) 584–1213

Vermont

Fiscal Officer, White River Junction, Medical and Regional Office Center, White River Junction, VT 05001, (802) 295–9363, ext. 1034

Virginia

Alexandria National Cemetery Area Office, Send to: Fiscal Officer, VA Medical Center, 50 Irving Street, NW., Washington, DC 20422, (202) 745–8228

Culpeper National Cemetery Area Office, Send to: Fiscal Officer, VA Medical Center, Martinsburg, WV 25401, (304) 263–0811, ext. 3176

Danville National Cemetery Area Office, Send to: Fiscal Officer, VA Medical Center, Salem, VA 24153, (703) 982–2463

Hopewell National Cemetery Area Office, Send to: Fiscal Officer, VA Medical Center, 1201 Broad Rock Road, Richmond, VA 23249, (804) 230–1304

Leesburg National Cemetery Area Office, Send to: Fiscal Officer, VA Medical Center, 50 Irving Street, NW., Washington, DC 20422, (202) 745–8228

Mechanicsville National Cemetery Area Office, Send to: Fiscal Officer, VA Medical Center, 1201 Broad Rock Road, Richmond, VA 23249, (804) 230–1304

Fiscal Officer, Hampton Medical Center, Hampton, VA 23667, (804) 722–9961

Hampton National Cemetery Area Office, Send to: Fiscal Officer, VA Medical Center, Hampton, VA 23667, (807) 722–9961

Quantico National Cemetery Area Office, Send to: Fiscal Officer, VA Medical Center, 50 Irving Street, NW., Washington, DC 20422, (202) 745–8228

Fiscal Officer, Richmond Medical Center, 1201 Broad Rock Road, Richmond, VA 23249, (804) 230–1304

Richmond National Cemetery Area Office, Send to: Fiscal Officer, VA Medical Center, 1201 Broad Rock Road, Richmond, VA 23249, (804) 230–1304

Fiscal Officer, Roanoke Regional Office, 210 Franklin Road, SW., Roanoke, VA 24011, (703) 982–6116

Jurisdiction over Fairfax and Arlington Counties and the cities of Alexandria, Fairfax, and Falls Church is allocated to the Washington, DC Regional Office.

Fiscal Officer, Salem Medical Center, Salem, VA 24153, (703) 982–2463

Sandston national Cemetery Area Office, Send to: Fiscal Officer, VA Medical Center, 1201 Broad Rock Road, Richmond, VA 23249, (804) 231–9011, ext. 205

Staunton National Cemetery Area Office, Send to: Fiscal Officer, VA Medical Center, Salem, VA 24135, (703) 982–2463

Winchester National Cemetery Area Office, Send to: Fiscal Officer, VA Medical Center, Martinsburg, WV 25401, (304) 263–0811, ext. 3176

Washington

Fiscal Officer, American Lake Medical Center, Tacoma, WA 98493, (206) 582–8440, ext. 6049

Fiscal Officer, Seattle Regional Office, 915 Second Avenue, Seattle, WA 98714, (206) 442–5025

Fiscal Officer, Seattle Medical Center, 1160 S. Columbian Way, Seattle, WA 98198, (206) 764–2226

Seattle Outpatient Clinic, Send to: Fiscal Officer, VA Medical Center, 1160 S. Columbia Way, Seattle, WA 98198, (206) 764–2226

Fiscal Officer, Spokane Medical Center—North, 4815 Assembly Street, Spokane, WA 99205, (509) 327–0283, ext. 286

Vancouver Medical Center, Send to: Fiscal Officer, VA Medical Center, 3710 SW U.S. Veterans Hospital Road, Portland, OR 97201, (503) 220–8262, ext. 6948

West Virginia

Fiscal Officer, Beckley Medical Center, 200 Veterans Avenue, Beckley, WV 25801, (304) 225–2121, ext. 4174

Fiscal Officer, Clarksburg Medical Center, Clarksburg, WV 26301, (304) 623–3461, ext. 3389

Grafton National Cemetery Area Office, Fiscal Officer, VA Medical Center, Clarksburg, WV 26301, (304) 623–3461, ext. 335

Fiscal Officer, Huntington Regional Office, 640 Fourth Avenue, Huntington, WV 25701, (304) 529–5477.

Jurisdiction over the counties of Brooke, Hancock, Marshall and Ohio is allocated to the Pittsburgh, Pennsylvania Regional Office.

Fiscal Officer, Huntington Medical Center, 1540 Spring Valley Drive, Huntington, WV 25704, (304) 429–6741, ext. 2422

Fiscal Officer, Martinsburg Medical Center, Martinsburg, WV 25401, (304) 263–0811, ext. 3176

Wheeling Outpatient Clinic Substation, Fiscal Officer, VA Medical Center, University Drive C, Pittsburgh, PA 15240, (412) 683–7675

Wisconsin

Fiscal Officer, Madison Medical Center, 2500 Overlook Terrace, Madison, WI 53705, (608) 262–7050

Fiscal Officer, Milwaukee (Wood) Regional Office, PO Box 6, Wood, WI 53193, (414) 671–8121

Fiscal Officer, Tomah Medical Center, Tomah, WI 54660, (608) 372–1786

Fiscal Officer, VA Medical Center, 5000 West National Avenue, Milwaukee, WI 53295, (414) 384–2000, ext. 2591

Wood National Cemetery Area Office, Fiscal Officer, VA Medical Center, 5000 West National Avenue, Milwaukee, WI 53295, (414) 384–2000, ext. 2591

Wyoming

Fiscal Officer, Cheyenne Medical & Regional, Office Center, 2360 East Pershing Blvd., Cheyenne, WY 82001, (307) 672–7339

Fiscal Officer, Sheridan Medical Center, Sheridan, WY 82801, (307) 672–3473

Social Security Administration

1. For the garnishment of the remuneration of employees:

Garnishment Agent, Office of the General Counsel, Room 611, Altmeyer Building, 6401 Security Blvd., Baltimore, MD 21235, (410) 965–4202

Effective March 30, 1998, garnishment orders for employees of the Social Security Administration should be sent to:

Chief, Payroll Operations Division, Attn.: Code D–2640, Bureau of Reclamation, Administrative Services Center, Department of the Interior, P.O. Box 272030, Denver, CO 80227–9030, (303) 969–7739

2. For the garnishment of benefits under Title II of the Social Security Act, legal process may be served on the office manager at any Social Security District or Branch Office. The addresses and telephone numbers of Social Security District and Branch Offices

may be found in the local telephone directory.

II. AGENCIES

(Unless otherwise indicated below, all agencies of the executive branch shall be subject to service of legal process brought for the enforcement of an individual's obligation to provide child support and/or make alimony payments where such service is sent by certified or registered mail, return receipt requested, or by personal service, upon the head of the agency.)

Agency for International Development

For employees of the Agency for International Development and the Trade and Development Program:

Payroll Division, Office of Financial Management (FM/P), U.S. Agency for International Development, Room 403 SA–2, Washington, DC 20523, (202) 663–2011, (fax) (202) 663–2354

Arms Control and Disarmament Agency

General Counsel, Arms Control and Disarmament Agency, 320 21st Street, NW., Washington, DC 20451, (202) 647–3596

Central Intelligence Agency

Office of Personnel Security, Attn: Chief, Special Activities Staff, Washington, DC 20505, (703) 482–1217

Commission on Civil Rights

Solicitor, Commission on Civil Rights, 624 9th Street, NW., Suite 632, Washington, DC 20425, (202) 376–8351

Commodity Futures Trading Commission

Director, Office of Personnel, Commodity Futures Trading Commission, Three Lafayette Center, Room 7200, 1155 21st Street, NW., Washington, DC 20581, (202) 418–5003

Consumer Product Safety Commission

(Mail Service), General Counsel, Consumer Product Safety Commission, Washington, DC 20207–0001, (202) 504–0980

(Personal Service), General Counsel, Consumer Product Safety Commission, 4330 East West Highway, Room 700, Bethesda, MD 20814–4408, (301) 504–0980

Environmental Protection Agency

Chief, Headquarters Accounting Operations Branch, Financial Management Division (3303), Environmental Protection Agency, 401 M Street, SW., Washington, DC 20460, (202) 260–5116

Export-Import Bank of the United States

General Counsel, Export-Import Bank of the United States, 811 Vermont Avenue, NW., Room 947, Washington, DC 20571, (202) 566–8334

Equal Employment Opportunity Commission

Director, Financial Management Division, 1801 L Street, NW., Room 2002, Washington, DC 20507, (202) 663–4224

Farm Credit Administration

Chief, Fiscal Management Division, Farm Credit Administration, 1501 Farm Credit Drive, McLean, VA 22102–5090, (703) 883–4122

Federal Deposit Insurance Corporation

Counsel, Federal Deposit Insurance Corporation, 550 17th Street, NW., Washington, DC 20429, (202) 898–3686

Federal Election Commission

Accounting Officer, Federal Election Commission, 999 E Street, NW., Washington, DC 20463, (202) 376–5270

Federal Emergency Management Agency

Office of General Counsel, General Law Division, 500 C Street, SW., Washington, DC 20472, (202) 646–4105

Federal Labor Relations Authority

Director of Personnel, Federal Labor Relations Authority, 607 14th Street, NW., Suite 430, Washington, DC 20424, (202) 482–6690

Federal Maritime Commission

Director of Personnel or Deputy Director of Personnel, Federal Maritime Commission, 800 North Capitol Street, NW., Washington, DC 20573, (202) 523–5773

Federal Mediation and Conciliation Service

General Counsel, Federal Mediation and Conciliation Service, 2100 K Street, NW., Washington, DC 20427, (202) 653–5305

Federal Retirement Thrift Investment Board

Payments to Board employees:

Director of Administration, Federal Retirement Thrift Investment Board, 1250 H Street, NW., Washington, DC 20005, (202) 942–1670

Benefits from the Thrift Savings Fund:

General Counsel, Federal Retirement Thrift Investment Board, 1250 H Street, NW., Washington, DC 20005, (202) 942–1662

Federal Trade Commission

Garnishment orders for employees of the Federal Trade Commission should be sent to:

Chief, Payroll Operations Division, Attn.: Code D–2605, Bureau of Reclamation, Administrative Services Center, Department of the Interior, 7201 West Mansfield Avenue, Denver, CO 80227–9030, (303) 969–7739

General Services Administration

Director, Kansas City Finance Division—6BC, 1500 East Bannister Road—Room 1107, Kansas City, MO 64131, (816) 926–7625.

Harry S. Truman Scholarship Foundation

Chief, Payroll Operations Division, Attention: Mail Code 2640, National Business Center, Department of the Interior, P.O. Box 272030, Denver, CO 80227–9030, (303) 969–7739

Institute of Peace

Garnishment orders for employees of the Institute of Peace should be sent to:

General Services Administration, Director, Finance Division—(6BC), 1500 E. Bannister Road, Room 1107, Kansas City, MO 64131, (816) 926–1666

International Trade Commission

Director, Office of Finance and Budget, 500 E Street, SW., Suite 316, Washington, DC 20436, (202) 205–2678

Merit Systems Protection Board

Director, Financial and Administrative, Management Division 1120 Vermont Avenue, NW., Washington, DC 20419, (202) 653–7263.

National Aeronautics and Space Administration

NASA Headquarters

Associate General Counsel (General), Attention: SN Code GG, NASA Headquarters, 300 E Street, SW., Washington, DC 20546, (202) 358–2465

NASA Field Installations

Chief Counsel, Ames Research Center, Moffett Field, CA 94035, (415) 694–5055

Chief Counsel, Dryden Flight Research Center, Edwards, CA 93523, (805) 258–2827

Chief Counsel, Goddard Space Flight Center, (including Wallops Flight Center), Greenbelt, MD 20771, (301) 286–9181

Chief Counsel, Johnson Space Center, Houston, TX 77058, (713) 483–3021

Chief Counsel, Kennedy Space Center, Kennedy Space Center, FL 32899, (407) 867–2550

Chief Counsel, Langley Research Center, Hampton, VA 23665, (804) 864–3221

Chief Counsel, Lewis Research Center, Cleveland, OH 44135, (216) 433–2318

Chief Counsel, Marshall Space Flight center, Marshall Space Flight Center, AL 35812, (205) 544–0012

Chief Counsel, John C. Stennis Space Center, Stennis Space Center, MS 39529–6000, (601) 688–2164

National Archives and Records Administration

General Counsel (NSL), Room 305 Archives Building, National Archives and Records Administration, 7th and Pennsylvania Avenue, NW., Washington, DC 20408, (202) 501–5535

National Capital Planning Commission

Administrative Officer, National Capital Planning Commission, 1325 G Street, NW., Washington, DC 20576, (202) 724–0170

National Credit Union Administration

General Counsel, Office of General Counsel, 1775 Duke Street, Alexandria, VA 22314–3428, (703) 518–6540

National Endowment for the Arts

General Counsel, National Endowment for the Arts, 1100 Pennsylvania Avenue, NW., Room 522, Washington, DC 20506, (202) 682–5418

National Endowment for the Humanities

General Counsel, National Endowment for the Humanities, Room 530, Old Post Office, 1100 Pennsylvania Avenue, NW., Washington, DC 20506, (202) 606–8322

National Labor Relations Board

Director of Personnel, National Labor Relations Board, 1099 14th Street, NW., Room 6700, Washington, DC 20570–0001, (202) 273–3904

National Mediation Board

Administrative Officer, National Mediation Board, 1301 K Street, NW., Suite 250 East, Washington, DC 20572, (202) 523–5950

National Railroad Adjustment Board

Staff Director/Grievances, National Railroad Adjustment Board, 175 West Jackson Boulevard, Chicago, IL 60604, (312) 886–7300

National Science Foundation

General Counsel, 4201 Wilson Boulevard, Arlington, VA 22230, (703) 306–1060

National Security Agency

General Counsel, National Security Agency, 9800 Savage Road, Ft. Meade, MD 20755–6000, (301) 688–6054

National Transportation Safety Board

Director, Personnel and Training Division, National Transportation Safety Board, 800 Independence Avenue, SW., Washington, DC 20594, ATTN: AD–30, (202) 382–6718

Navajo and Hopi Indian Relocation Commission

Attorney, Navajo and Hopi Indian Relocation Commission, 201 East Birch, Room 11,

P.O. Box KK, Flagstaff, AZ 86002, (602) 779–2721

Nuclear Regulatory Commission

Controller, Nuclear Regulatory Commission, Washington, DC 20555, (301) 492–4750

Office of Personnel Management

Payments to OPM employees:

General Counsel, Office of Personnel Management, 1900 E Street, NW., Washington, DC 20415, (202) 606–1700

Payments of retirement benefits under the Civil Service Retirement System and the Federal Employees Retirement System:

Associate Director for Retirement and Insurance, Office of Personnel Management, Court Ordered Benefits Branch, PO Box 17, Washington, DC 20044, (202) 606–0218,

Overseas Private Investment Corporation

Director, Human Resources Management, Overseas Private Investment Corporation, 1100 New York Avenue, NW., Washington, DC 20527, (202) 336–8524

Panama Canal Commission

Secretary, Office of the Secretary, International Square, 1825 I Street, NW., Suite 1050, Washington, DC 20006–5402, (202) 634–6441

Pension Benefit Guaranty Corporation

General Counsel or Deputy General Counsel, 1200 K Street, NW., Washington, DC 20005–4026, (202) 326–4020

Presidio Trust

Chief, Payroll Operations Division, Attention: Mail Code 2640, National Business Center, Department of the Interior, P.O. Box 272030, Denver, CO, 80227–9030, (303) 969–7739

Railroad Retirement Board

Deputy General Counsel, Bureau of Law, 844 North Rush Street, Chicago, IL 60611, (312) 751–4935

Securities and Exchange Commission

Branch Chief, Fiscal Operations, Office of the Comptroller, Securities and Exchange Commission, 450 Fifth Street, NW., Washington, DC 20549, (202) 942–0349

Selective Service System

General Counsel, 1515 Wilson Boulevard, Arlington, VA 22209–2425, (703) 235–2050,

Small Business Administration

District Director, Birmingham District Office, 908 South 20th Street, Birmingham, AL 35205, (205) 254–1344

District Director, Anchorage District Office, 1016 West 6th Avenue, Anchorage, AK 99501, (907) 271–4022

District Director, Phoenix District Office, 3030 North Central Avenue, Phoenix, AZ 85012, (602) 261–3611

District Director, Little Rock District Office, 611 Gaines Street, Little Rock, AR 72201, (501) 378–5871

District Director, Los Angeles District Office, 350 S. Figueroa Street, Los Angeles, CA 90071, (213) 688–2956

District Director, San Diego District Office, 880 Front Street, San Diego, CA 92188, (714) 291–5440

District Director, San Francisco District Office, 211 Main Street, San Francisco, CA 94105, (415) 556–7490

District Director, Denver District Office, 721 19th Street, Denver, CO 80202, (303) 837–2607

District Director, Hartford District Office, One Financial Plaza, Hartford, CT 06106, (203) 244–3600

District Director, Washington District Office, 1030 15th Street, NW., Washington DC 20417, (202) 655–4000

District Director, Jacksonville District Office, 400 West Bay Street, Jacksonville, FL 32202, (904) 791–3782

District Director, Miami District Office, 222 Ponce De Leon Blvd., Coral Gables, FL 33134, (305) 350–5521

District Director, Atlanta District Office, 1720 Peachtree Street, NW., Atlanta, GA 30309, (404) 347–2441

District Director, Honolulu District Office, 300 Ala Moana, Honolulu, HI 96850, (808) 546–8950

District Director, Boise District Office, 1005 Main Street, Boise, ID 83701, (208) 384–1096

District Director, Des Moines District Office, 210 Walnut Street, Des Moines, IA 50309, (515) 284–4433

District Director, Chicago District Office, 219 South Dearborn Street, Chicago, IL 60604, (312) 353–4528

District Director, Indianapolis District Office, 575 N. Pennsylvania Street, Indianapolis, IN 46204, (317) 269–7272

District Director, Wichita District Office, 110 East Waterman Street, Wichita, KS 67202, (316) 267–6571

District Director, Louisville District Office, 600 Federal Place, Louisville, KY 40201, (502) 582–5978

District Director, New Orleans District Office, 1001 Howard Avenue, New Orleans, LA 70113, (504) 589–6685

District Director, Augusta District Office, 40 Western Avenue, Augusta, ME 04330, (207) 622–6171

District Director, Baltimore District Office, 8600 LaSalle Road, Towson, MD 21204, (301) 862–4392

District Director, Boston District Office, 150 Causeway Street, Boston, MA 02114, (617) 223–2100

District Director, Detroit District, 477 Michigan Avenue, Detroit, MI 48116, (313) 226–6075

District Director, Minneapolis District Office, 12 South 6th Street, Minneapolis, MN 55402, (612) 725–2362

District Director, Jackson District Office, 101 West Capitol Street, Suite 400, Jackson, MS 39201, (601) 965–5371

District Director, Kansas City District Office, 1150 Grande Avenue, Kansas City, MO 64106, (816) 374–3416

District Director, St. Louis District Office, One Mercantile Center, St. Louis, MO 63101, (314) 425–4191

District Director, Helena District Office, 301 South Park Avenue, Helena, MT 59601, (406) 449–5381

District Director, Omaha District Office, 19th & Farnum Street, Omaha, NE 68102, (404) 221–4691

District Director, Las Vegas District Office, 301 East Stewart, Las Vegas, NV 89101, (702) 385–6611

District Director, Concord District Office, 55 Pleasant Street, Concord, NH 03301, (603) 224–4041

District Director, Newark District Office, 970 Broad Street, Newark, NJ 07102, (201) 645–2434

District Director, Albuquerque District Office, 5000 Marble Avenue, NE., Albuquerque, NM 87110, (505) 766–3430

District Director, New York District Office, 26 Federal Plaza, New York, NY 10007, (212) 264–4355

District Director, Syracuse District Office, 100 South Clinton Street, Syracuse, NY 13260, (315) 423–5383

District Director, Charlotte District Office, 230 South Tryon Street, Charlotte, NC 28202, (704) 371–6111

District Director, Fargo District Office, 657 2nd Avenue, North, Fargo, ND 58108, (701) 237–5771

District Director, Sioux Falls District Office, 101 South Main Avenue, Sioux Falls, SD 57102, (605) 336–2980

District Director, Cleveland District Office, 1240 East 9th Street, Cleveland, OH 44199, (216) 522–4180

District Director, Columbus District Office, 85 Marconi Boulevard, Columbus, OH 43215, (614) 469–6860

District Director, Oklahoma City District Office, 200 NW. 5th Street, Oklahoma City, OK 73102, (405) 231–4301

District Director, Portland District Office, 1220 SW. Third Avenue, Portland, OR 97204, (503) 221–2682

District Director, Philadelphia District Office, 231 St. Asaphs Road, Bala Cynwyd, PA 19004, (215) 597–3311

District Director, Pittsburgh District Office, 1000 Liberty Avenue, Pittsburgh, PA 15222, (412) 644–2780

District Director, Hato Rey District Office, Chardon & Bolivia Streets, Hato Rey, PR 00918, (809) 753–4572

District Director, Providence District Office, 57 Eddy Street, Providence, RI 02903, (401) 528–4580

District Director, Columbia District Office, 1835 Assembly Street, Columbia, SC 29201, (803) 765–5376

District Director, Nashville District Office, 404 James Robertson Parkway, Nashville, TN 37219, (615) 251–5881

District Director, Dallas District Office, 1100 Commerce Street, Dallas, TX 75242, (214) 767–0605

District Director, Houston District Office, 500 Dallas Street, Houston, TX 77002, (713) 226–4341

District Director, Lower Rio Grande Valley District Office, 222 East Van Buren Street, Harlingen, TX 78550, (512) 423–4534

District Director, Lubbock District Office, 1205 Texas Avenue, Lubbock, TX 79401, (806) 762–7466

District Director, San Antonio District Office, 727 East Durango Street, San Antonio, TX 78206, (512) 229–6250

District Director, Salt Lake City District Office, 125 South State Street, Salt Lake City, UT 84138, (314) 425–5800

District Director, Montpelier District Office, 87 State Street, Montpelier, VT 05602, (802) 229–0538

District Director, Richmond District Office, 400 North 8th Street, Richmond, VA 23240, (804) 782–2617

District Director, Seattle District Office, 915 Second Avenue, Seattle, WA 98174, (206) 442–5534

District Director, Spokane District Office, West 920 Riverside Avenue, Spokane, WA 99210, (509) 456–5310

District Director, Clarksburg District Office, 109 North 3rd Street, Clarksburg, WV 26301, (304) 623–5631

District Director, Madison District Office, 212 East Washington Avenue, Madison, WI 53703, (608) 264–5261

District Director, Casper District Office, 100 East B Street, Casper, WY 82602, (307) 265–5266

Tennessee Valley Authority

Payments to TVA employees:

Chairman, Board of Directors, Tennessee Valley Authority, 400 West Summit Hill Drive, Knoxville, TN 37902, (423) 632–2101

Payments of retirement benefits under the TVA Retirement System:

Chairman, Board of Directors, TVA Retirement System, 500 West Summit Hill Drive, Knoxville, TN 37902, (423) 632–0202

Trade and Development Agency

Effective August 3, 1998, garnishment orders for employees of the United States Trade and Development Agency should be sent to: Chief, Payroll Operations Division, Attn.: Code D–2640, Bureau of Reclamation, Administrative Services Center, Department of the Interior, P.O. Box 272030, Denver, CO 80227–9030, (303) 969–7739.

United States Information Agency

Counsel, U.S. Information Agency, 301 4th Street, SW., Washington, DC 20547, (202) 485–7976

United States Soldiers' & Airmen's Home

Assistant General Counsel for Garnishment Operations, Defense Finance and Accounting Service, Cleveland Center, Code L (DFAS—CL/L), PO Box 998002, Cleveland, OH 44199–8002, (216) 522–5301

III. UNITED STATES POSTAL SERVICE AND POSTAL RATE COMMISSION

United States Postal Service and Postal Rate Commission

Manager, Payroll Processing Branch, 1 Federal Drive, Ft. Snelling, MN 55111–9650, (612) 293–6300

IV. THE DISTRICT OF COLUMBIA, AMERICAN SAMOA, GUAM, AND THE VIRGIN ISLANDS

The District of Columbia

Assistant City Administrator for Financial Management, The District Building, Room 412, 14th and Pennsylvania Avenue, NW, Washington, DC 20004, (202) 727–6979

American Samoa

Director of Administrative Service, American Samoa government, Pago Pago, American Samoa 96799, (684) 633–4155

Guam

Attorney General, PO Box DA, Agana, Guam 96910, 472–6841 (Country Code 671)

The Virgin Islands

Attorney General, PO Box 280, St. Thomas, VI 00801, (809) 774–1163

V. INSTRUMENTALITY

Smithsonian Institution

For service of process in garnishment proceedings for child support and/or alimony of present Smithsonian Institution employees:

General Counsel, The Smithsonian Institution, MRC 012, 1000 Jefferson Drive, SW., Washington, DC 20560, (202) 357–2583

For service of process in garnishment proceedings for child support and/or alimony involving retirement annuities of former trust fund employees of the Smithsonian Institution:

General Counsel, Teachers Insurance and Annuity Association of America, College Retirement Equity Fund (TIAA/CREF), 730 Third Avenue, New York, NY 10017, (212) 490–9000

VI. EXECUTIVE OFFICE OF THE PRESIDENT

Executive Office of the President

Garnishment orders for civilian employees of the Executive Office of the President should be sent to: Assistant General Counsel for Garnishment Operations, Defense Finance and Accounting Service, Cleveland Center—Code L (DFAS-CL/L), P.O. Box 998002, Cleveland, OH 44199–8002, (216) 522–5301.

[63 FR 14759, Mar. 26, 1998; 63 FR 34777, June 26, 1998; 63 FR 56537, Oct. 22, 1998]

APPENDIX B TO PART 581—LIST OF AGENTS DESIGNATED TO FACILITATE THE SERVICE OF LEGAL PROCESS ON FEDERAL EMPLOYEES

(The agents designated to accept legal process for the garnishment of the remuneration for employment due from the United States are listed in appendix A to part 581. Appendix B to part 581 lists the agents designated to assist in the service of legal process in civil actions pursuant to orders of State courts to establish paternity and to establish or to enforce support obligations by making Federal employees and members of the Uniformed Services available for service of process, regardless of the location of the employee's workplace or of the member's duty station. Agents are listed in appendix B only for those executive agencies where the designations differ from those found in appendix A to part 581.)

Department of Defense

The Department of Defense officials identified pursuant to Executive Order 12953, section 302, shall facilitate an employee's or member's availability for service of process. Additionally, these officials shall be responsible for answering inquiries about their respective organization's service of process rules. Such officials are not responsible for actual service of process and will not accept requests to make such service.

Office of the Secretary of Defense

Personnel Management Specialist, DoD Civilian Personnel Management Service, 1400 Key Blvd., Level A, Arlington, VA 22209

Department of the Army

Members of the uniformed service, active, reserve, and retired.

Office of the Judge Advocate General, ATTN: DAJA-LA, 2200 Army Pentagon, Washington, DC 20310–2200, (703) 697–3170.

Federal civilian employees of the Army, both appropriated fund and nonappropriated fund.

Deputy Assistant Secretary, (Civilian Personnel Policy/Director of Civilian Personnel), 111 Army Pentagon, Washington, DC 20310–0111, (703) 695–4237

Active duty, reserve, and appropriated fund and nonappropriated fund employees of the Department of the Army employed within the United States.

Appropriated fund and nonappropriated fund Federal civilian employees employed in Panama.

Deputy Chief of Staff for Resource Management, U.S. Army Southern Command, Finance & Accounting Office, Civilian Personnel Section, ATTN: Unit 7153, SORM-FA-C, APO AA 34004

Department of the Navy

In order to locate, or determine the cognizant command and mailing address of a Navy Member:

Bureau of Naval Personnel, Worldwide Locator, (Pers 324D), 2 Navy Annex, Washington, DC 20370–3000, (703) 614–3155/5011

In order to obtain assistance in the service of legal process in civil actions pursuant to orders of State courts:

Bureau of Naval Personnel, Office of Legal Counsel (Pers 06), 2 Navy Annex, Washington, DC 20370–5006, (703) 614–4110

Members of the Marine Corps

Paralegal Specialist, Headquarters, U.S. Marine Corps (JAR), 2 Navy Annex, Washington, DC 20380–1775, (703) 614–2510

For assistance in service of process on Department of the Navy civilian employees:

Department of the Navy, Office of Civilian Personnel Mgmt., Office of Counsel (Code OL), 800 N. Quincy Street, Arlington, VA 2203, (703) 696–4717

Department of the Air Force

For all military and civilian personnel:

AFLSA/JACA, 1420 Air Force Pentagon, Washington, DC 20330–1420, (703) 695–2450

Defense Intelligence Agency

Defense Intelligence Agency, ATTN: Office of the General Counsel, The Pentagon—Room 2E–238, Washington, DC 20301-7400

Defense Mapping Agency

Defense Mapping Agency, Office of Legal Services, 3200 South Second Street, St. Louis, MO 63118

Defense Nuclear Agency

Associate General Counsel, Defense Nuclear Agency, 6801 Telegraph Road, Alexandria, VA 22310–3398, (703) 325–7681

On-Site Inspection Agency

General Counsel, Defense Nuclear Agency, 6801 Telegraph Road, Alexandria, VA 22310–3398, (703) 325–7681

Department of Housing and Urban Development

Headquarters

Chief, Systems Support Branch, Technology Support Division, 451 7th Street, SW., Room 2256, Washington, DC 20410, (202) 708–0241

New England (Massachusetts, Maine, Vermont, New Hampshire, Rhode Island, and Connecticut)

Human Resources Officer, Thomas P. O'Neill, Jr., Federal Building, 10 Causeway Street, Room 375, Boston, MA 02222, (617) 565–5435

New York, New Jersey

Human Resources Officer, 26 Federal Plaza, New York, NY 10278, (212) 264–0782

Mid-Atlantic (Pennsylvania, Maryland, Washington, DC, West Virginia, Virginia, and Delaware)

Human Resources Officer, The Wanamaker Building, 100 Penn Square East, Philadelphia, PA 19107, (215) 656–0593

Southwest (Georgia, North Carolina, Kentucky, Tennessee, South Carolina, Alabama, Mississippi, Puerto Rico, and Florida)

Human Resources Officer, Richard B. Russell Federal Building, 75 Spring Street, SW., Atlanta, GA 30303, (404) 331–4078

Midwest (Illinois, Minnesota, Wisconsin, Michigan, Ohio, and Indiana)

Human Resources Officer, Ralph H. Metcalfe Federal Building, 77 West Jackson Boulevard, Chicago, IL 60604, (312) 353–5960

Southwest (Texas, Oklahoma, Arkansas, Louisiana, and New Mexico)

Human Resources Officer, 1600 Throckmorton, Post Office Box 2905, Fort Worth, TX 76113, (817) 885–5471

Great Plains (Kansas, Missouri, Iowa, and Nebraska)

Human Resources Officer, Gateway Tower II, 400 State Avenue, Kansas City, KS 66101, (913) 551–5419

Rocky Mountain (Colorado, Montana, North Dakota, South Dakota, Wyoming, and Utah)

Human Resources Officer, First Interstate Tower North, 633 17th Street, Denver, CO 80202, (303) 672–5259

Pacific/Hawaii (California, Nevada, Arizona, and Hawaii)

Human Resources Officer, Phillip Burton Federal Building and U.S. Courthouse, 450 Golden Gate Avenue, Post Office Box 36003, San Francisco, CA 94102, (415) 556–7142

Northwest/Alaska (Washington, Oregon, Idaho, and Alaska)

Human Resources Officer, Federal Office Building, 909 First Avenue, Suite 200, Seattle, WA 98104, (206) 220–5125

Department of Transportation

HPT–1 (FHWA), Room 4317, Department of Transportation, Washington, DC 20590

G-PC (USCG), Room 4100E, CGHQ, Department of Transportation, Washington, DC 20590

RAD-10 (FRA), Room 8232, Department of Transportation, Washington, DC 20590

NAD-20 (NHTSA), Room 5306, Department of Transportation, Washington, DC 20590

TAD-30 (FTA), Room 7101, Department of Transportation, Washington, DC 20590

DMA-12 (RSPA), Room 8401, Department of Transportation, Washington, DC 20590

JM-20 (OIG), Room 7418, Department of Transportation, Washington, DC 20590

MAR-360 (MARAD), Room 8101, Department of Transportation, Washington, DC 20590

Personnel Officer (SLSDC), 180 Andrews Street, Masena, NY 13662–1763

AHR-1 (FAA), FOB–10A, Room 500E, Department of Transportation, Washington, DC 20590

Chief Counsel, Saint Lawrence Seaway Development Corporation, 400 Seventh St., SW., Room 5424, Washington, DC 20590

Department of Veterans Affairs

Alabama

Human Resources Management Officer, Birmingham Medical Center, 700 South 19th Street, Birmingham, AL 35233, (205) 933–4478

Montgomery Regional Office, Send to: VBA Southern Area Human Resources, Management Office, Human Resources Management Director, 6508 Dogwood Parkway, Suite E, Jackson, MS 39213, (601) 965–4140

Human Resources Management Officer, Montgomery Medical Center, 215 Perry Hill Road, Montgomery, AL 36109–3798, (334) 272–4670

Human Resources Management Officer, Tuskegee Medical Center, 2400 Hospital Road, Tuskegee, AL 36083–5001, (334) 727–0550

Human Resources Management Officer, Tuscaloosa Medical Center, 3701 Loop Road, Tuscaloosa, AL 35404, (205) 554–2000, ext. 2542

Fort Mitchell National Cemetery, Send to: Human Resources Management Officer, VA Medical Center, 2400 Hospital Road, Tuskegee, AL 36083–5001, (334) 727–0550

Mobile Outpatient Clinic Substation, Send to: Human Resources Management Officer, VA Medical Center, 400 Veterans Blvd., Biloxi, MS 39531, (601) 388–5541, ext. 5780

Alaska

Fort Richardson (Sitka) National Cemetery, Send to: Human Resources Management Officer, VA Medical Center & Regional Office, 2925 DeBarr Road, Anchorage, AK 99508–2989, (907) 257–4750

Human Resources Management Officer, Anchorage Medical Center & Regional Office, 2925 DeBarr Road, Anchorage, AK 99508–2989, (907) 257–4750

Arizona

Human Resources Management Officer, Prescott Medical Center, 500 N. Highway 89, Prescott, AZ 86313–5000, (520) 776–6015

Prescott National Cemetery Area Office, Send to: Human Resources Management Officer, VA Medical Center, 500 N. Highway 89, Prescott, AZ 86313–5000, (520) 776–6015

Human Resources Management Officer, Phoenix Medical Center, 650 E. Indian School Road, Phoenix, AZ 85012, (602) 277–5551, ext. 7594

Human Resources Management Officer, Tucson Medical Center, 3601 South Sixth Avenue, Tuscon, AZ 85723–0001, (520) 629–1803

Phoenix Regional Office, Send to: VBA Western Area Human Resources, Management Office, Human Resources Management Director, 126000 W. Colfax Ave., Suite C–300, Lakewood, CO 80215, (303) 231–5855

Arizona (Cave Creek) Memorial National Cemetery, Send to: Human Resources Management Officer, VA Medical Center, 650 E. Indian School Road, Phoenix, AZ 85012, (602) 277–5551, ext. 7594

Arkansas

Fayetteville National Cemetery, Send to: Human Resources Management Officer, VA Medical Center, 1100 N. College Avenue, Fayetteville, AR 72703, (501) 444–5020

Fort Smith National Cemetery, Send to: Human Resources Management Officer, VA Medical Center, 1100 N. College Avenue, Fayetteville, AR 72703, (501) 444–5020

Little Rock National Cemetery, Send to: Human Resources Management Officer, VA Medical Center, 4300 West 7th Street, Little Rock, AR 72114, (501) 370–6677

Little Rock Regional Office, Send to: VBA Southern Area Human Resources, Management Office, Human Resources Management Director, 6508 Dogwood Parkway, Suite E, Jackson, MS 39213, (601) 965–4140

Human Resources Management Officer, Little Rock Medical Center, 4300 West 7th Street, Little Rock, AR 72114, (501) 370–6677

Human Resources Management Officer, Fayetteville Medical Center, 1100 N. College Avenue, Fayetteville, AR 72703, (501) 444–5020

California

Human Resources Management Officer, Palo Alto Medical Center, 3801 Miranda Avenue, Palo Alto, CA 94304–1207, (415) 493–5000, ext. 5515

Human Resources Management Officer, Loma Linda Medical Center, 11201 Benton Street, Loma Linda, CA 92357–0002, (909) 825–7084, ext. 3058

San Diego Regional Office, Send to: VBA Western Area Human Resources, Management Office, Human Resources Management Director, 126000 W. Colfax Ave., Suite C–300, Lakewood, CO 80215, (303) 231–5855

Sepulveda VCS Western Region, Send to: Human Resources Management Officer, VA Medical Center, 16111 Plummer Street, Sepulveda, CA 91343–2099, (818) 895–9377

Human Resources Management Officer, San Francisco Medical Center, 4150 Clement Street, San Francisco, CA 94121–1598, (415) 750–2107

Human Resources Management Officer, Fresno Medical Center, 2615 E. Clinton Avenue, Fresno, CA 93703–2223, (209) 225–6100, ext. 5005

Human Resources Management Officer, San Diego Medical Center, 3350 La Jolla Village Drive, San Diego, CA 92161–0001, (619) 552–8585

Oakland Regional Office, Send To: VBA Western Area Human Resources, Management Office, Human Resources Management Director, 126000 W. Colfax Ave., Suite C–300, Lakewood, CO 80215, (303) 231–5855

Human Resources Management Officer, Sepulveda Medical Center, 16111 Plummer Street, Sepulveda, CA 91343–2099, (818) 895–9377

Human Resources Management Officer, Los Angeles, Medical Center, Wilshire & Sawtelle Blvds., Los Angeles, CA 90073, (310) 824–3153

Los Angeles Field Office of Audit, Send to: Human Resources Management Officer, VA Medical Center, Wilshire & Sawtelle Blvds., Los Angeles, CA 90073, (310) 824–3153

Los Angeles Regional Office of Audit, Send to: Human Resources Management Officer, VA Medical Center, Wilshire & Sawtelle Blvds., Los Angeles, CA 90073, (310) 824–3153

Human Resources Management Office, Los Angeles Outpatient Clinic, 351 E. Temple St., Los Angeles, CA 90012–3328, (213) 253–2677

Pleasant Hill Northern California System of Clinics, Human Resources Management Officer, 2300 Contra Costa Blvd., Suite 440, Pleasant Hills, CA 94523–3961, (510) 372–2008

Human Resources Management Officer, Long Beach Medical Center, 5901 E. Seventh Street, Long Beach, CA 90882–5201, (310) 494–5642

Los Angeles Regional Office, Send To: VBA Western Area Human Resources Management Office, Human Resources Management Director, 126000 W. Colfax Ave., Suite C–300, Lakewood, CO 80215, (303) 231–5855

San Bruno (Golden Gate) National Cemetery, Send to: Human Resources Management Officer, VA Medical Center, 4150 Clement Street, San Francisco, CA 94121–1598, (415) 750–2107

Fort Rosecrans National Cemetery, Send to: Human Resources Management Officer, VA Medical Center, 3350 La Jolla Village Drive, San Diego, CA 92161–0001, (619) 552–8585

Los Angeles National Cemetery, Send to Human Resources Management Office, VA Medical Center, Wilshire & Sawtelle Blvds., Los Angeles, CA 90073, (310) 824–3153

San Joaquin Valley National Cemetery, Send to: Human Resources Management Officer, VA Medical Center, 2615 E. Clinton Avenue, Fresno, CA 93703–2223, (209) 225–6100, ext. 5005

Riverside National Cemetery, Send to: Human Resources Management Officer, VA Medical Center, 11201 Benton Street, Loma Linda, CA 92357–0002, (909) 825–7084, ext. 3058

San Francisco National Cemetery, Send to: Human Resources Management Officer, VA Medical Center, 4150 Clement Street, San Francisco, CA 94121–1598, (415) 750–2107

San Diego Outpatient Clinic, Send to: Human Resources Management Officer, VA Medical Center, 3350 La Jolla Village Drive, San Diego, CA 92161–0001, (619) 552–8585

Colorado

Human Resources Management Officer, Grand Junction Medical Center, 2121 North Avenue, Grand Junction, CO 81501, (970) 252–0731, ext. 2062

Human Resources Management Officer, Denver Medical Center, 1055 Clermont Street, Denver, CO 80220–0166, (303) 393–2815

Denver Regional Office, Sent to: VBA Western Area Human Resources Management Office, Human Resources Management Director, 126000 W. Colfax Ave., Suite C–300, Lakewood, CO 80215, (303) 231–5855

Human Resources Management Officer, Fort Lyon Medical Center, Fort Lyon, CO 81038–5000, (719) 384–3190

Fort Logan National Cemetery, Send to: Human Resources Management Officer, VA

Medical Center, 1055 Clermont Street, Denver, CO 80220–0166, (303) 393–2815

Denver National Cemetery Area Office, Send to: Human Resources Management Officer, VA Medical Center, 1055 Clermont Street, Denver, CO 80220–0166, (303) 393–2815

VBA Western Area Human Resources Management Office, Human Resources Management Director, 12600, W. Colfax Ave., Suite C–300, Lakewood, CO 80215, (303) 231–5855

Denver Civilian Health and Medical Program (CHAMPVA), Human Resources Management Officer, 300 S. Jackson St., Denver, CO 80206, (303) 331–7514

Denver Distribution Center, Send to: VBA Western Area Human Resources, Management Office, Human Resources Management Director, 126000 W. Colfax Ave., Suite C–300, Lakewood, CO 80215 (303) 231–5855

Connecticut

Hartford Regional Office, Send to: Eastern Area Servicing Assistance Center, Human Resources Management Director, 31 Hopkins Plaza, Baltimore, MD 21202–2004, (410) 962–4090

Human Resources Management Officer, Newington Medical Center, 555 Willard Avenue, Newington, CT 06111, (203) 667–6710

Human Resources Management Officer, West Haven Medical Center, 950 Campbell Avenue, West Haven, CT 06516, (203) 932–5711

District of Columbia

Human Resources Management Officer, Washington DC Medical Center, 50 Irving Street, NW., Washington, DC 20422, (202) 745–8200

Director, Central Office Human Resources, Management Service, VA Central Office, 810 Vermont Ave., NW., Washington, DC 20420, (202) 273–4950

Washington DC Regional Office, Sent to: Eastern Area Servicing Assistance Center, Human Resources Management Director, 31 Hopkins Plaza, Baltimore, MD 21202–2004, (410) 962–4090

Delaware

Human Resources Management Officer, Wilmington Medical and Regional Office Center, 1601 Kirkwood Highway, Wilmington, DE 19805, (302) 633–5340

Florida

Pensacola (Barrancas) National Cemetery, Send to: Human Resources Management Officer, VA Medical Center, 400 Veterans Blvd., Biloxi, MS 39531, (601) 388–5541, ext. 5780

Human Resources Management Officer, Bay Pines Medical Center, 10000 Bay Pines Blvd., Bay Pines, FL 33504, (813) 398–6661, ext. 4116

Florida National Cemetery, Send to: Human Resources Management Officer, VA Medical Center, 13000 Bruce B. Downs Blvd., Tampa, FL 33612, (813) 972–7524

Riviera Beach Outpatient Clinic, Send to: Human Resources Management Officer, VA Medical Center, 1201 Northwest 16th Street, Miami, FL 33125, (305) 324–4455, ext. 3343

Orlando Outpatient Clinic, Send to: Human Resources Management Officer, VA Medical Center, 13000 Bruce B. Downs Blvd., Tampa, FL 33612, (813) 972–7524

Miami VA Office, Send to: VBA Southern Area Human Resources, Management Office, Human Resources Management Director, 6508 Dogwood Parkway, Suite E, Jackson, MS 39213, (601) 965–4140

Jacksonville VA Office, Send to: VBA Southern Area Human Resources, Management Office, Human Resources Management Director, 6508 Dogwood Parkway, Suite E, Jackson, MS 39213, (601) 965–4140

Jacksonville Outpatient Clinic, Send to: Human Resources Management Officer, VA Medical Center, 1601 SW Archer Road, Gainesville, FL 32608–1197, (904) 374–6045

Daytona Beach Outpatient Clinic, Send to: Human Resources Management Officer, VA Medical Center, 1601 SW Archer Road, Gainesville, FL 32608–1197, (904) 374–6045

Jacksonville Vet Center, Send to: Human Resources Management Officer,

VA Medical Center, 1601 SW Archer Road, Gainesville, FL 32608–1197, (904) 374–6045

Human Resources Management Officer, Tampa Medical Center, 13000 Bruce B. Downs Blvd., Tampa, FL 33612, (813) 972–7524

Bay Pines National Cemetery, Send to: Human Resources Management Officer, VA Medical Center, 10000 Bay Pines Blvd., Bay Pines, FL 33504, (813) 398–6661, ext. 4116

Human Resources Management Officer, Gainesville Medical Center, 1601 SW Archer Road, Gainesville, FL 32608–1197, (904) 374–6045

St. Petersburg Regional Office, Send to: VBA Southern Area Human Resources Management Office, 6508 Dogwood Parkway, Suite E, Jackson, MS 39213, (601) 965–4140

Human Resources Management Officer, Palm Beach Gardens Medical Center, P.O. Box 33207, Palm Beach Gardens, FL 33420, (407) 691–8251

Human Resources Management Officer, Miami Medical Center, 1201 Northwest 16th Street, Miami, FL 33125, (305) 324–4455, ext. 3343

Human Resources Management Officer, Lake City Medical Center, 801 S. Marion Street, Lake City, FL 32025–5898, (904) 755–3016

Georgia

Marietta National Cemetery, Send to: Human Resources Management Officer, VA Medical Center, 1670 Clairmont Road, Decatur, GA 30033, (404) 728–7636

Atlanta Veterans Canteen Service Field Office, Send to: Human Resources Management Officer, VA Medical Center, 1670 Clairmont Road, Decatur, GA 30033, (404) 728–7636

Human Resources Management Officer, Augusta Medical Center, 1 Freedom Way, Augusta, GA 30904–6285, (706) 823–3955

Human Resources Management Officer, Dublin Medical Center, 1826 Veterans Blvd., Dublin, GA 31021, (912) 277–2753

Atlanta Field Office of Audit, Send to: VBA Southern Area Human Resources Management Office, Human Resources Management Director, 6508 Dogwood Parkway, Suite E, Jackson, MS 39213, (601) 965–4140

Atlanta National Cemetery Area Office, Send to: Human Resources Management Officer, VA Medical Center, 1670 Clairmont Road, Decatur, GA 30033, (404) 728–7636

Human Resources Management Officer, Atlanta Medical Center, 1670 Clairmont Road, Decatur, GA 30033, (404) 728–7636

Income Verification Match Center, Send to: Human Resources Management Officer, VA Medical Center, 1670 Clairmont Road, Decatur, GA 30033, (404) 728–7636

Atlanta Regional Office, Send to: VBA Southern Area Human Resources, Management Office, Human Resources Management Director, 6508 Dogwood Parkway, Suite E, Jackson, MS 39213, (601) 965–4140

Hawaii

Human Resources Management Officer, Honolulu Medical and Regional Office Center, 300 Ala Moana Blvd., P.O. Box 50188, Honolulu, HI 96850, (808) 566–1470

Pacific Memorial National Cemetery, Send to: Human Resources Management Officer, VA Medical and Regional Office Center, 300 Ala Moana Blvd., P.O. Box 50188, Honolulu, HI 96850, (808) 566–1470

Idaho

Human Resources Management Officer, Boise Medical Center, 500 W. Fort Street, Boise, ID 83702–4598, (208) 338–7218

Boise Regional Office, Send to: VBA Western Area Human Resources, Management Office, Human Resources Management Director, 126000 W. Colfax Ave., Suite C–300, Lakewood, CO 80215, (303) 231–5855

Illinois

Human Resources Management Officer, North Chicago Medical Center, 3001 Green Bay Road, North Chicago, IL 60064, (708) 578–3763

Human Resources Management Office, Hines Medical Center, Edward Hines Jr. Hospital, 5th Avenue & Roosevelt Road, Hines, IL 60141, (708) 216–2601

Rock Island National Cemetery, Send to: Human Resources Management Officer, VA Medical Center, Highway 6 West, Iowa City, IA 52246, (319) 338–0581, ext. 7720

Danville National Cemetery, Send to: Human Resources Management Officer, VA Medical Center, 1900 E. Main Street, Danville, IL 61832, (217) 431–6548

Human Resources Management Officer, Chicago Lakeside Medical Center, 333 E. Huron Street, Chicago, IL 60611, (312) 943–6600

Camp Butler National Cemetery, Send to: Human Resources Management Officer, VA Medical Center, 1900 E. Main Street, Danville, IL 61832, (217) 431–6548

Hines Systems Delivery Center, Send to: Human Resources Management Officer, Hines Benefits Delivery Center, PO Box 27 (901A1), Hines, IL 60141, (708) 681–6680

Human Resources Management Officer, Chicago Medical Center, 820 South Damen Avenue, PO Box 8195, Chicago, IL 60680, (312) 633–2174

Chicago Regional Office, Send to: VBA Central Area Human Resources Management Office, Human Resources Management Director, 38701 Seven Mile Road, Suite 345, Livonia, MI 48152, (313) 953–8830

Human Resources Management Officer, Marion Medical Center, 2401 W. Main Street, Marion, IL 62959, (618) 997–5311, ext. 4116

Hines Finance Center, Send to: Human Resources Management Officer, Hines Benefits Delivery Center, PO Box 27 (901A1), Hines, IL 60141, (708) 681–6680

Human Resources Management Officer, Danville Medical Center, 1900 E. Main Street, Danville, IL 61832, (217) 431–6548

Hines National Acquisition Center, Send to: Human Resources Management Officer, Hines Benefits Delivery Center, PO Box 27 (901A1), Hines, IL 60141, (708) 681–6680

Hines Benefits Delivery Center, Human Resources Management Officer, PO Box 27 (901A1), Hines, IL 60141, (708) 681–6680

Alton National Cemetery Area Office, Send to: Human Resources Management Officer, VA Medical Center, Jefferson Barracks, St. Louis, MO 63106, (314) 894–6620

Mound City National Cemetery Area Office, Send to: Human Resources Management Officer, VA Medical Center, 2401 W. Main Street, Marion, IL 62959, (618) 997–5311, ext. 4116

Quincy National Cemetery Area Office, Send to: Human Resources Management Officer, VA Medical Center, Highway 6 West, Iowa City, IA 52246, (319) 338–0581, ext. 7720

Indiana

Marion National Cemetery, Send to: Human Resources Management Officer, VA Medical Center, 1700 East 38th, Marion, IN 46953–4589, (317) 677–3101

Human Resources Management Officer, Marion Medical Center, 1700 East 38th, Marion, IN 46953–4589, (317) 677–3101

Human Resources Management Officer, Indianapolis Medical Center, 1481 West 10th Street, Indianapolis, IN 46202, (317) 267–8758
Human Resources Management Officer, Fort Wayne Medical Center, 2121 Lake Avenue, Fort Wayne, IN 46805–5100, (219) 460–1342
Indianapolis Regional Office, Send to: VBA Central Area Human Resources Management Office, Human Resources Management Director, 38701 Seven Mile Road, Suite 345, Livonia, MI 48152, (313) 953–8830
New Albany National Cemetery, Send to: Human Resources Management Officer, VA Medical Center, 800 Zorn Avenue, Louisville, KY 40206, (502) 895–3401, ext. 5866
Evansville Outpatient Clinic Substation, Send to: Human Resources Management Officer, VA Medical Center, 2401 W. Main Street, Marion, IL 62959, (618) 997–5311, ext. 4116
Indianapolis National Cemetery Area Office, Send to: Human Resources Management Officer, VA Medical Center, 1481 West 10th Street, Indianapolis, IN 46202, (317) 267–8758

Iowa

Des Moines Regional Office, Send to: VBA Central Area Human Resources Management Office, Human Resources Management Director, 38701 Seven Mile Road, Suite 345, Livonia, MI 48152, (313) 953–8830
Keokuk National Cemetery, Send to: Human Resources Management Officer, VA Medical Center, Highway 6 West, Iowa City, IA 52246, (319) 338–0581, ext. 7720
Human Resources Management Officer, Knoxville Medical Center, 1515 W. Pleasant Street, Knoxville, IA 50138, (515) 842–3101, ext. 6219
Human Resources Management Officer, Des Moines Medical Center, 3600 30th Street, Des Moines, IA 50310, (515) 271–5812
Human Resources Management Officer, Iowa City Medical Center, Highway 6 West, Iowa City, IA 52246, (319) 338–0581, ext. 7720

Kansas

Human Resources Management Officer, Topeka Medical Center, 2200 Gage Blvd., Topeka, KS 66622, (913) 271–4310
Human Resources Management Officer, Leavenworth Medical Center, 4101 S. 4th St. Trafficway, Leavenworth, KS 66048, (913) 682–2000, ext. 2500
Leavenworth National Cemetery, Send to: Human Resources Management Officer, VA Medical Center, 4101 S. 4th St. Trafficway, Leavenworth, KS 66048, (913) 682–2000, ext 2500
Human Resources Management Officer, Wichita Medical and Regional Office Center, 901 George Washington Blvd., Wichita, KS 67211, (316) 651–3625
Fort Scott National Cemetery, Send to: Human Resources Management Officer, VA Medical Center, 4101 S. 4th St. Trafficway, Leavenworth, KS 66048, (913) 682–2000, ext. 2500
Ft. Leavenworth National Cemetery Area Office, Send to: Human Resources Management Officer, VA Medical Center, 4101 S. 4th St. Trafficway, Leavenworth, KS 66048, (913) 682–2000, ext. 2500

Kentucky

Nicholasville (Camp Nelson) National Cemetery Area Office, Send to: Human Resources Management Officer, VA Medical Center, 2250 Leestown Road, Lexington, KY 40511–1093, (606) 281–3924
Zachary Taylor National Cemetery Area Office, Send to: Human Resources Management Officer, VA Medical Center, 800 Zorn Avenue, Louisville, KY 40206, (502) 895–3401, ext. 5866
Human Resources Management Officer, Louisville Medical Center, 800 Zorn Avenue, Louisville, KY 40206, (502) 895–3401, ext. 5866
Lebanon National Cemetery Area Office, Send to: Human Resources Management Officer, VA Medical Center, 800 Zorn Avenue, Louisville, KY 40206, (502) 895–3401, ext. 5866
Louisville Regional Office, Send to: VBA Central Area Human Resources Management Office, Human Resources Management Director, 38701 Seven Mile Road, Suite 345, Livonia, MI 48152, (313) 953–8830
Cave Hill National Cemetery Area Office, Send to: Human Resources Management Officer, VA Medical Center, 800 Zorn Avenue, Louisville, KY 40206, (502) 895–3401, ext. 5866
Human Resources Management Officer, Lexington Medical Center, 2250 Leestown Road, Lexington, KY 40511–1093, (606) 281–3924
Danville National Cemetery Area Office, Send to: Human Resources Management Officer, VA Medical Center, 2250 Leestown Road, Lexington, KY 40511–1093, (606) 281–3924
Lexington National Cemetery Area Office, Send to: Human Resources Management Officer, VA Medical Center, 2250 Leestown Road, Lexington, KY 40511–1093, (606) 281–3924
Nancy National Cemetery Area Office, Send to: Human Resources Management Officer, VA Medical Center, 2250 Leestown Road, Lexington, KY 40511–1093, (606) 281–3924
Perryville National Cemetery Area Office, Send to: Human Resources Management Officer, VA Medical Center, 2250 Leestown Road, Lexington, KY 40511–1093, (606) 281–3924

Louisiana

Human Resources Management Officer, New Orleans Medical Center, 1601 Perdido Street, New Orleans, LA 70146, (504) 568–0811

Port Hudson (Zachary) National Cemetery, Send to: Human Resources Management Officer, VA Medical Center, 1601 Perdido Street, New Orleans, LA 70146, (504) 568–0811

Human Resources Management Officer, Alexandria Medical Center, Highway 171, Alexandria, LA 71301, (318) 473–0010, ext. 2262

Human Resources Management Officer, Shreveport Medical Center, 510 E. Stoner Avenue, Shreveport, LA 71101–4295, (318) 424–6028

Alexandria (Pinesville) National Cemetery, Send to: Human Resources Management Officer, VA Medical Center, Highway 171, Alexandria, LA 71301, (318) 473–0010, ext. 2262

New Orleans Regional Office, Send to: VBA Southern Area Human Resources Management Office, Human Resources Management Director, 6508 Dogwood Parkway, Suite E, Jackson, MS 39213, (601) 965–4140

Baton Rouge National Cemetery Area Office, Send to: Human Resources Management Officer, VA Medical Center, 1601 Perdido Street, New Orleans, LA 70146, (504) 568–0811

Shreveport VA Office, Send to: VBA Southern Area Human Resources Management Office, Human Resources Management Director, 6508 Dogwood Parkway, Suite E, Jackson, MS 39213, (601) 965–4140

Maine

Human Resources Management Officer, Togus Medical and Regional Office Center, Togus, ME 04330, (207) 623–5713

Portland VA (Vet Center) Office, Send to: Human Resources Management Officer, VA Medical and Regional Office Center, Togus, ME 04330, (207) 623–5713

Togus National Cemetery Area Office, Send to: Human Resources Management Officer, VA Medical and Regional Office Center, Togus, ME 04330, (207) 623–5713

Maryland

Human Resources Management Officer, Ft. Howard Medical Center, 9600 N. Point Road, Ft. Howard, MD 21052, (410) 687–8343

Ft. Howard VCS Eastern Region, Send to: Human Resources Management Officer, VA Medical Center, 9600 N. Point Road, Ft. Howard, MD 21052, (410) 687–8343

Baltimore Regional Office, Send to: Eastern Area Servicing Assistance Center, Human Resources Management Director, 31 Hopkins Plaza, Baltimore, MD 21202–2004, (410) 962–4090

Human Resources Management Officer, Baltimore Medical Center, 10 N. Greene Street, Baltimore, MD 21201, (410) 605–7200

Baltimore National Cemetery, Send to: Human Resources Management Officer, VA Medical Center, 10 N. Greene Street, Baltimore, MD 21201, (410) 605–7200

Eastern Area Servicing Assistance Center, Human Resources Management Director, 31 Hopkins Plaza, Baltimore, MD 21202–2004, (410) 962–4090

Human Resources Management Officer, Perry Point Medical Center, Building 101, Perry Point, MD 21902, (410) 642–2411, ext. 5193

Baltimore Rehabilitation, Research and Development Center, Send to: Human Resources Management Officer, VA Medical Center, 10 N. Greene Street, Baltimore, MD 21201, (410) 605–7200

Annapolis National Cemetery Area Office, Send to: Human Resources Management Officer, VA Medical Center, 10 N. Greene Street, Baltimore, MD 21201, (410) 605–7200

Baltimore Outpatient Clinic, Send to: Human Resources Management Officer, VA Medical Center, 10 N. Greene Street, Baltimore, MD 21201, (410) 605–7200

Hyattsville Field Office of Audit, Send to: Director, CO Human Resources Management Service, VA Central Office, 810 Vermont Ave., NW., Washington, DC 20420, (202) 273–4950

Massachusetts

Human Resources Management Officer, Boston Medical Center, 150 S. Huntington Ave., Boston, MA 02130, (617) 232–9500, ext. 5561

Human Resources Management Officer, Northampton Medical Center, Northampton, MA 01060–1288, (413) 582–3027

Boston Regional Office, Send to: Eastern Area Servicing Assistance Center, Human Resources Management Director, 31 Hopkins Plaza, Baltimore, MD 21202–2004, (410) 962–4090

Human Resources Management Officer, Bedford Medical Center, 200 Springs Road, Bedford, MA 01730, (617) 275–7500, ext. 2367

Bourne National Cemetery, Send to: Human Resources Management Officer, VA Medical Center, 940 Belmont Street, Brockton, MA 02401, (508) 583–4500, ext. 3260

Human Resources Management Officer, Brockton Medical Center, 940 Belmont Street, Brockton, MA 02401, (508) 583–4500, ext. 3260

Boston Outpatient Clinic, Send to: Human Resources Management Officer, VA Medical Center, 150 S. Huntington Ave., Boston, MA 02130, (617) 232–9500, ext. 5561

Lowell Outpatient Clinic, Send to: Human Resources Management Officer, VA Medical Center, 150 S. Huntington Ave., Boston, MA 02130, (617) 232–9500, ext. 5561

New Bedford Outpatient Clinic, Send to: Human Resources Management Officer, VA Medical Center, 830 Chalkstone Avenue, Providence, RI 02908–4799, (401) 457–3072

Springfield Outpatient Clinic, Send to: Human Resources Management Officer, VA Medical Center, Northampton, MA 01060–1288, (413) 582–3027

Springfield VA Office, Send to: Eastern Area Servicing Assistance Center, Human Resources Management Director, 31 Hopkins Plaza, Baltimore, MD 21202–2004, (410) 962–4090

West Roxbury Medical Center, Send to: Human Resources Management Officer, VA Medical Center, 940 Belmont Street, Brockton, MA 02401, (508) 583–4500, ext. 3260

Worchester Outpatient Clinic Substation, Send to: Human Resources Management Officer, VA Medical Center, 940 Belmont Street, Brockton, MA 02401, (508) 583–4500, ext. 3260

Michigan

Fort Custer National Cemetery, Send to: Human Resources Management Officer, VA Medical Center, 5500 Armstrong Rd., Battle Creek, MI 49016, (616) 966–5600, ext. 3600

Grand Rapids Outpatient Clinic, Send to: Human Resources Management Officer, VA Medical Center, 5500 Armstrong Rd., Battle Creek, MI 49016, (616) 966–5600, ext. 3600

Detroit Regional Office, Send to: VBA Central Area Human Resources Management Office, Human Resources Management Director, 38701 Seven Mile Road, Suite 345, Livonia, MI 48152, (313) 953–8830

Human Resources Management Officer, Battle Creek Medical Center, 5500 Armstrong Rd., Battle Creek, MI 49016, (616) 966–5600, ext. 3600

Human Resources Management Officer, Saginaw Medical Center, 1500 Weiss Street, Saginaw, MI 48602, (517) 793–2340, ext. 3070

VBA Central Area Human Resources Management Office, Human Resources Management Director, 38701 Seven Mile Road, Suite 345, Livonia, MI 48152, (313) 953–8830

Human Resources Management Officer, Iron Mountain Medical Center, H Street, Iron Mountain, MI 49801, (906) 774–3300, ext. 2280

Human Resources Management Officer, Ann Arbor Medical Center, 2215 Fuller Rd., Ann Arbor, MI 28105, (313) 761–7938

Human Resources Management Officer, Allen Park Medical Center, Southfield & Outer Drive, Allen Park, MI 48101, (313) 562–6000, ext. 3323

Minnesota

St. Paul Regional Office and Insurance Center, Send to: VBA Central Area Human Resources, Management Office, Human Resources Management Director, 38701 Seven Mile Road, Suite 345, Livonia, MI 48152, (313) 953–8830

Fort Snelling National Cemetery, Send to: Human Resources Management Officer, VA Medical Center, One Veterans Drive, Minneapolis, MN 55417, (612) 725–2061

Fort Snelling Debt Management Center, Send to: VBA Central Area Human Resources Management Office, Human Resources Management Director, 38701 Seven Mile Road, Suite 345, Livonia, MI 48152, (313) 953–8830

Human Resources Management Officer, Minneapolis Medical Center, One Veterans Drive, Minneapolis, MN 55417, (612) 725–2061

Human Resources Management Officer, St. Cloud Medical Center, 4801 8th Street North, St. Cloud, MN 56303, (612) 255–6301

St. Paul Outpatient Clinic, Send to: Human Resources Management Officer, VA Medical Center, One Veterans Drive, Minneapolis, MN 55417, (612) 725–2061

Mississippi

Corinth National Cemetery, Send to: Human Resources Management Officer, VA Medical Center, 1030 Jefferson Avenue, Memphis, TN 38104, (901) 523–8990, ext. 5928

VBA Southern Area Human Resources Management Office, Human Resources Management Director, 6508 Dogwood Parkway, Suite E, Jackson, MS 39213, (601) 965–4140

Human Resources Management Officer, Biloxi Medical Center, 400 Veterans Blvd., Biloxi, MS 39531, (601) 388–5541, ext. 5780

Biloxi National Cemetery, Human Resources Management Officer, VA Medical Center, 400 Veterans Blvd., Biloxi, MS 39531, (601) 388–5541, ext. 5780

Jackson Regional Office, Send to: VBA Central Area Human Resources Management Office, Human Resources Management Director, 6508 Dogwood Parkway, Suite E, Jackson, MS 39213, (601) 965–4140

Human Resources Management Officer, Jackson Medical Center, 1500 E. Woodrow Wilson Blvd., Jackson, MS 39216, (601) 364–1239

Natchez National Cemetery, Send to: Human Resources Management Officer, VA Medical Center, 1500 E. Woodrow Wilson Blvd., Jackson, MS 39216, (601) 364–1239

Missouri

Human Resources Management Officer, St. Louis Medical Center, Jefferson Bks., St. Louis, MO 63106, (314) 894–6620

Human Resources Management Officer, Poplar Bluff Medical Center, 1500 N. Westwood Blvd., Poplar Bluff, MO 63901, (314) 686–4151, ext. 328

St. Louis Records Processing Center, Send to: VBA Central Area Human Resources Management Office, Human Resources Management Director, 38701 Seven Mile Road, Suite 345, Livonia, MI 48152, (313) 953–8830

Human Resources Management Officer, Kansas City Medical Center, 4801 Linwood Blvd., Kansas City, MO 64128, (816) 861–4700, ext. 6926

Jefferson Barracks National Cemetery, Send to: Human Resources Management Officer, VA Medical Center, 800 Hospital Drive, Columbia, MO 65201, (314) 443–2511, ext. 6261

Human Resources Management Officer, Columbia Medical Center, 800 Hospital Drive, Columbia, MO 65201, (314) 443–2511, ext. 6261

St. Louis Regional Office, Send to: VBA Central Area Human Resources, Management Office, Human Resources Management Director, 38701 Seven Mile Road, Suite 345, Livonia, MI 48152, (313) 953–8830

Veterans Canteen Service Field Office, Send to: Human Resources Management Officer, VA Medical Center, Jefferson Barracks, St. Louis, MO 63106, (314) 894–6620

Springfield National Cemetery, Send to: Human Resources Management Officer, VA Medical Center, 1100 N. College Avenue, Fayetteville, AR 72703, (501) 444–5020

Montana

Human Resources Management Officer, Fort Harrison Medical Center and Regional Office, Fort Harrison, MT 59636, (406) 447–7933

Human Resources Management Officer, Miles City Medical Center, 210 South Winchester, Miles City, MT 59301–4798, (406) 232–8287

Nebraska

Lincoln Regional Office, Send to: VBA Central Area Human Resources, Management Office, Human Resources Management Director, 38701 Seven Mile Road, Suite 345, Livonia, MI 48152, (313) 953–8830

Human Resources Management Officer, Lincoln Medical Center, 600 South 70th Street, Lincoln, NE 68510, (402) 489–3802, ext. 7819

Human Resources Management Officer, Grand Island Medical Center, 2201 N. Broadwell Ave., Grand Island, NE 68803, (308) 389–5177

Maxwell (Fort McPherson) National Cemetery, Send to: Human Resources Management Officer, VA Medical Center, 2201 N. Broadwell Ave., Grand Island, NE 68803, (308) 389–5177

Human Resources Management Officer, Omaha Medical Center, 4101 Woolworth Avenue, Omaha, NE 68105, (402) 449–0614

Nevada

Human Resources Management Officer, Reno Medical Center, 1000 Locust Street, Reno, NV 89520–0111, (702) 328–1260

Reno Regional Office, Send to: VBA Western Area Human Resources Management Office, Human Resources Management Director, 126000 W. Colfax Ave., Suite C–300, Lakewood, CO 80215, (303) 231–5855

Las Vegas Outpatient Clinic, Send to: Human Resources Management Officer, VA Medical Center, 1000 Locust Street, Reno, NV 89520–0111, (702) 328–1260

Henderson Outpatient Clinic, Send to: Human Resources Management Officer, VA Medical Center, 1000 Locust Street, Reno, NV 89520–0111, (702) 328–1260

New Hampshire

Manchester Regional Office, Send to: Eastern Area Servicing Assistance Center, Human Resources Management Director, 31 Hopkins Plaza, Baltimore, MD 21202–2004, (410) 962–4090

Human Resources Management Officer, Manchester Medical Center, 718 Smyth Road, Manchester, NH 03104, (603) 624–4366, ext. 6608

New Jersey

Beverly National Cemetery, Send to: Human Resources Management Officer, VA Medical Center, University & Woodland Avenues, Philadelphia, PA 19104, (215) 823–4088

New Regional Office, Send to: Eastern Area Servicing Assistance Center, Human Resources Management Director, 31 Hopkins Plaza, Baltimore, MD 21202–2004, (410) 962–4090

Human Resources Management Officer, East Orange Medical Center, 385 Tremont Avenue, East Orange, NJ 07018–0195, (201) 676–1000, ext. 1366

James J. Howard Outpatient Clinic, Send to: Human Resources Management Officer, VA Medical Center, 385 Tremont Avenue, East Orange, NJ 07018–0195, (201) 676–1000, ext. 1366

Newark Outpatient Clinic, Send to: Human Resources Management Officer, VA Medical Center, 385 Tremont Avenue, East Orange, NJ 07018–0195, (201) 676–1000, ext. 1366

Human Resources Management Officer, Lyons Medical Center, Knollcroft Road, Lyons, NJ 07939, (908) 647–0180, ext. 4002

New Mexico

Albuquerque Regional Office, Send to: VBA Western Area Human Resources Management Office, Human Resources Management Director, 126000 W. Colfax Ave., Suite C–300, Lakewood, CO 80215, (303) 231–5855

Santa Fe National Cemetery, Send to: Human Resources Management Officer, VA Medical Center, 2100 Ridgecrest Dr., SE., Albuquerque, NM 87108–5138, (505) 256–5702

New York

Human Resources Management Officer, Bath Medical Center, Bath, NY 14810, (607) 776–2111, ext. 1239

Human Resources Management Officer, Brooklyn Medical Center, 800 Poly Place, Brooklyn, NY 11209, (718) 630–3660

Human Resources Management Officer, Montrose Medical Center, P.O. Box 100, Montrose, NY 10548–0100, (914) 737–4400, ext. 2553

Human Resources Management Officer, Syracuse Medical Center, 800 Irving Avenue, Syracuse, NY 13210–2799, (315) 477–4531

Human Resources Management Officer, Bronx Medical Center, 130 W. Kingsbridge

Road, Bronx, NY 10468, (718) 584–9000, ext. 6590

Human Resources Management Officer, New York Medical Center, 423 East 23rd Street, New York, NY 10010, (212) 686–7500, ext. 7635

Human Resources Management Officer, Castle Point Medical Center, Route 9D, Castle Point, NY 12511, (914) 831–2000, ext. 5405

Human Resources Management Officer, Northport Medical Center, 79 Middleville Road, Northport, NY 11768, (516) 261–4400, ext. 2715

Human Resources Management Officer, Albany Medical Center, 113 Holland Avenue, Albany, NY 12208, (518) 462–3311, ext. 2231

Calverton National Cemetery, Send to: Human Resources Management Officer, VA Medical Center, 79 Middleville Road, Northport, NY 11768, (516) 261–4400, ext. 2715

Human Resources Management Officer, Buffalo Medical Center, 3495 Bailey Avenue, Buffalo, NY 14215, (716) 862–3605

New York Regional Office, Send to: Eastern Area Servicing Assistance Center, Human Resources Management Director, 31 Hopkins Plaza, Baltimore, MD 21202–2004, (410) 962–4090

Human Resources Management Officer, Batavia Medical Center, 222 Richmond Ave., Batavia, NY 14020, (716) 343–7500, ext. 7272

Bath (Elmira) National Cemetery, Send to: Human Resources Management Officer, VA Medical Center, Bath, NY 14810, (607) 776–2111, ext 1239

Long Island National Cemetery, Send to: Human Resources Management Officer, VA Medical Center, 79 Middleville Road, Northport, NY 11768, (516) 261–4400, ext. 2715

Albany VA (Vet Center) Office, Send to: Human Resources Management Officer, VA Medical Center, 113 Holland Avenue, Albany, NY 12208, (518) 462–3311, ext. 2231

Brooklyn National Cemetery Area Office, Send to: Human Resources Management Officer, VA Medical Center, 800 Poly Place, Brooklyn, NY 11209, (718) 630–3660

Brooklyn Outpatient Clinic, Send to: Human Resources Management Officer, VA Medical Center, 800 Poly Place, Brooklyn, NY 11209, (718) 630–3660

New York Outpatient Clinic, Send to: Human Resources Management Officer, VA Medical Center, 423 East 23rd Street, New York, NY 10010, (212) 686–7500, ext. 7635

New York Prosthetics Center, Send to: Human Resources Management Officer, VA Medical Center, 423 East 23rd Street, New York, NY 10010, (212) 686–7500, ext. 7635

New York Veterans Canteen Service Field Office, Send to: Human Resources Management Officer, VA Medical Center, 423 East 23rd Street, New York, NY 10010, (212) 686–7500, ext. 7635

Rochester VA (Vet Center) Office, Send to: Human Resources Management Officer, VA Medical Center, 222 Richmond Ave., Batavia, NY 14020, (716) 343–7500, ext. 7272

Buffalo Regional Office, Send to: Eastern Area Servicing Assistance Center, Human Resources Management Director, 31 Hopkins Plaza, Baltimore, MD 21202–2004, (410) 962–4090

Rochester Outpatient Clinic Substation, Send to: Human Resources Management Officer, VA Medical Center, 222 Richmond Ave., Batavia, NY 14020, (716) 343–7500, ext. 7272

Human Resources Management Officer, Canandaigua Medical Center, Canandaigua, NY 14424, (716) 394–2000, ext. 3700

Syracuse VA Office, Send to: Eastern Area Servicing Assistance Center, Human Resources Management Director, 31 Hopkins Plaza, Baltimore, MD 21202–2004, (410) 962–4090

North Carolina

Human Resources Management Officer, Fayetteville Medical Center, 2300 Ramsey Street, Fayetteville, NC 28301, (919) 822–7055

Raleigh National Cemetery, Send to: Human Resources Management Officer, VA Medical Center, 508 Fulton Street, Durham, NC 27705, (919) 286–6901

Human Resources Management Officer, Durham Medical Center, 508 Fulton Street, Durham, NC 27705, (919) 286–6901

Human Resources Management Officer, Asheville Medical Center, 1100 Tunnell Road, Asheville, NC 28805, (704) 299–2535

New Bern National Cemetery, Send to: Human Resources Management Officer, VA Medical Center, 2300 Ramsey Street, Fayetteville, NC 28301, (919) 822–7055

Salisbury National Cemetery, Send to: Human Resources Management Officer, VA Medical Center, 1601 Brenner Avenue, Salisbury, NC 28144, (704) 638–3432

Winston-Salem Regional Office, Send to: VBA Southern Area Human Resources Management Office, Human Resources Management Director, 6508 Dogwood Parkway, Suite E, Jackson, MS 39213, (601) 965–4140

Human Resources Management Officer, Salisbury Medical Center, 1601 Brenner Avenue, Salisbury, NC 28144, (704) 638–3432

Wilmington National Cemetery Area Office, Send to: Human Resources Management Officer, VA Medical Center, 2300 Ramsey Street, Fayetteville, NC 28301, (919) 822–7055

Winston-Salem Outpatient Regional Office, Send to: Human Resources Management Officer, VA Medical Center, 1601 Brenner Avenue, Salisbury, NC 28144, (704) 638–3432

North Dakota

Human Resources Management Officer, Fargo Medical and Regional Office Center, 655 First Avenue, Fargo, ND 58102, (701) 232–3241

Ohio

Human Resources Management Officer, Columbus Outpatient Clinic, 2090 Kenny Road, Columbus, OH 43221, (614) 257–5501

Cleveland Regional Office, Send to: VBA Central Area Human Resources Management Office, Human Resources Management Director, 38701 Seven Mile Road, Suite 345, Livonia, MI 48152, (313) 953–8830

Dayton National Cemetery, Send to: Human Resources Management Officer, VA Medical Center, 4100 W. Third Street, Dayton, OH 45428, (513) 262–2107

Human Resources Management Officer, Cincinnati Medical Center, 3200 Vine Street, Cincinnati, OH 45220, (513) 559–5051

Cincinnati VA Office, Send to: VBA Central Area Human Resources Management Office, Human Resources Management Director, 38701 Seven Mile Road, Suite 345, Livonia, MI 48152, (313) 953–8830

Columbus VA Office, Send to: VBA Central Area Human Resources Management Office, Human Resources Management Director, 38701 Seven Mile Road, Suite 345, Livonia, MI 48152, (313) 953–8830

Human Resources Management Officer, Dayton Medical Center, 4100 W. Third Street, Dayton, OH 45428, (513) 262–2107

Human Resources Management Officer, Cleveland Medical Center, 10000 Brecksville Rd., Brecksville, OH 44141, (216) 526–3030, ext. 7900

Human Resources Management Officer, Chillicothe Medical Center, 17273 State Route 104, Chillicothe, OH 45601, (614) 773–1141, ext. 7538

Oklahoma

Fort Gibson National Cemetery, Send to: Human Resources Management Officer, VA Medical Center, Honor Heights Drive, Muskogee, OK 74401, (918) 683–3261, ext. 404

Human Resources Management Officer, Oklahoma City Medical Center, 921 NE 13th Street, Oklahoma City, OK 73104, (405) 270–5157

Muskogee Regional Office, Send to: VBA Southern Area Human Resources Management Office, Human Resources Management Director, 6508 Dogwood Parkway, Suite E, Jackson, MS 39213, (601) 965–4140

Human Resources Management Officer, Muskogee Medical Center, Honor Heights Drive, Muskogee, OK 74401, (918) 683–3261, ext. 404

Oklahoma City VA Office, Send to: VBA Southern Area Human Resources Management Office, Human Resources Management Director, 6508 Dogwood Parkway, Suite E, Jackson MS 39213, (601) 965–4140

Oregon

Portland Regional Office, Send to: VBA Western Area Human Resources Management Office, Human Resources Management Director, 126000 W. Colfax Ave., Suite C–300, Lakewood, CO 80215, (303) 231–5855

Human Resources Management Officer, White City Medical Center, 8495 Craterlake Highway, White City, OR 97503–1088, (503) 826–2111, ext. 3204

Human Resources Management Officer, Roseburg Medical Center, 913 NW Garden Valley Blvd., Roseburg, OR 97470–6153, (503) 440–1260

Human Resources Management Officer, Portland Medical Center, 3710 SW US Veterans Hospital Rd., Portland, OR 97207–1034, (503) 220–3403

Eagle Point National Cemetery, Send to: Human Resources Management Officer, VA Medical Center, 8495 Craterlake Highway, White City, OR 97503–1088, (503) 826–2111, ext. 3204

Williamette National Cemetery, Send to: Human Resources Management Officer, VA Medical Center, 3710 SW US Veterans Hospital Rd., Portland, OR 97207–1034, (503) 220–3403

Pennsylvania

Human Resources Management Officer, Pittsburgh Medical Center, University Drive C, Pittsburgh, PA 15240, (412) 692–3240

Philadelphia Benefits Delivery Center, Send to: Human Resources Management Liaison, VA Regional Office, 5000 Wissahickon Avenue, P.O. Box 13399, Philadelphia, PA 19101, (215) 951–5534

Human Resources Management Officer, Wilkes-Barre Medical Center, 1111 East End Boulevard, Wilkes-Barre, PA 18711, (717) 821–7209

Philadelphia Systems Development Center, Send to: Human Resources Management Liaison, VA Regional Office, 5000 Wissahickon Avenue, P.O. Box 13399, Philadelphia, PA 19101, (215) 951–5534

Philadelphia National Cemetery Area Office, Send to: Human Resources Management Officer, VA Medical Center, University & Woodland Avenues, Philadelphia, PA 19104, (215) 823–4088

Annville (Indiantown Gap) National Cemetery, Send to: Human Resources Management Officer, VA Medical Center, 1700 S. Lincoln Avenue, Lebanon, PA 17042, (717) 272–6621, ext. 4055

Human Resources Management Officer, Philadelphia Medical Center, University & Woodland Avenues, Philadelphia, PA 19104, (215) 823–4088

Human Resources Management Officer, Altoona Medical Center, 2907 Pleasant Valley Blvd., Altoona, PA 16602–4377, (814) 943–8164, ext. 7039

Human Resources Management Officer, Lebanon Medical Center, 1700 S. Lincoln Avenue, Lebanon, PA 17042, (717) 272–6621, ext. 4055

Harrisburg Outpatient Clinic Substation, Send to: Human Resources Management

Officer, VA Medical Center, 1700 S. Lincoln Avenue, Lebanon, PA 17042, (717) 272–6621, ext. 4055

Human Resources Management Officer, Coatesville Medical Center, 1400 BlackHorse Hill Rd., Coatesville, PA 19320–2096, (610) 383–0234

Human Resources Management Officer, Pittsburgh (HD) Medical Center, 7180 Highland Drive, Pittsburgh, PA 15206–1297, (412) 365–4755

Human Resources Management Officer, Butler Medical Center, 325 New Castle Road, Butler, PA 16001–2480, (412) 477–5051

Pittsburgh Regional Office, Send to: Eastern Area Servicing Assistance Center, Human Resources Management Director, 31 Hopkins Plaza, Baltimore, MD 21202–2004, (410) 962–4090

Philadelphia Regional Office, Human Resources Management Liaison, 5000 Wissahickon Avenue, P.O. Box 13399, Philadelphia, PA 19101, (215) 951–5534

Human Resources Management Officer, Erie Medical Center, 135 East 38th Street, Erie, PA 16504, (814) 868–6205

Philippines

Manila Regional Office Outpatient Clinic, Manila Regional Office Center, Send to: Director, Department of Veterans Affairs, APO, San Francisco, CA 96528, 011–632–521–7116

Puerto Rico

Puerto Rico National Cemetery, Send to: Human Resources Management Officer, VA Medical Center, One Veterans Plaza, San Juan, PR 00927–5800, (809) 766–5485

Human Resources Management Officer, San Juan Medical Center, One Veterans Plaza, San Juan, PR 00927–5800, (809) 766–5485

Mayaguez Outpatient Clinic Substation, Send to: Human Resources Management Officer, VA Medical Center, One Veterans Plaza, San Juan, PR 00927–5800, (809) 766–5485

San Juan Regional Office, Send to: VBA Southern Area Human Resources Management Officer, Human Resources Management Director, 6508 Dogwood Parkway, Suite E, Jackson, MS 39213, (601) 965–4140

Rhode Island

Human Resources Management Officer, Providence Medical Center, 830 Chalkstone Avenue, Providence, RI 02908–4799, (401) 457–3072

Providence Regional Office, Send to: Eastern Area Servicing Assistance Center, Human Resources Management Director, 31 Hopkins Plaza, Baltimore, MD 21202–2004, (410) 962–4090

South Carolina

Florence National Cemetery, Send to: Human Resources Management Officer, VA Medical Center, 6439 Garners Ferry Rd., Columbia, SC 29201–1639, (803) 695–6835

Human Resources Management Officer, Columbia Medical Center, 6439 Garners Ferry Rd., Columbia, SC 29201–1639, (803) 695–6835

Greenville Outpatient Clinic Substation, Send to: Human Resources Management Officer, VA Medical Center, 6439 Garners Ferry Rd., Columbia, SC 29201–1639, (803) 695–6835

Human Resources Management Officer, Charleston Medical Center, 109 Bee Street, Charleston, SC 29401–5799, (803) 577–5011, ext. 7610

Beaufort National Cemetery, Send to: Human Resources Management Officer, VA Medical Center, 109 Bee Street, Charleston, SC 29401–5799, (803) 577–5011, ext. 7610

Columbia Regional Office, Send to: VBA Southern Area Human Resources Management Office, Human Resources Management Director, 6508 Dogwood Parkway, Suite E, Jackson, MS 39213, (601) 965–4140

South Dakota

Human Resources Management Officer, Hot Springs Medical Center, 500 North 5th Street, Hot Springs, SD 57747, (605) 745–2018

Hot Springs National Cemetery, Send to: Human Resources Management Officer, VA Medical Center, 500 North 5th Street, Hot Springs, SD 57747, (605) 745–2018

Human Resources Management Officer, Fort Meade Medical Center, 113 Comanche Road, Fort Meade, SD 57741, (605) 347–7090

Fort Meade (Black Hills) National Cemetery, Send to: Human Resources Management Officer, VA Medical Center, 113 Comanche Road, Fort Meade, SD 57741, (605) 347–7090

Human Resources Management Officer, Sioux Falls Medical and Regional Office Center, PO Box 5046, 2501 W. 22nd St., Sioux Falls, SD 57117, (605) 333–6852

Tennessee

Mountain Home National Cemetery, Send to: Human Resources Management Officer, VA Medical Center, Johnston City, Mountain Home, TN 37684, (615) 926–1171, ext. 7181

Nashville (Madison) National Cemetery, Send to: Human Resources Management Officer, VA Medical Center, 1310 24th Avenue South, Nashville, TN 37212–2637, (615) 327–5381

Chattanooga National Cemetery, Send to: Human Resources Management Officer, VA Medical Center, 3400 Lebanon Road, Murfreesboro, TN 37129–1236, (615) 893–1360, ext. 3317

Knoxville National Cemetery, Send to: Human Resources Management Officer, VA Medical Center, Johnston City, Mountain Home, TN 37684, (615) 926–1171, ext. 7181

Memphis National Cemetery, Send to: Human Resources Management Officer, VA Medical Center, 1030 Jefferson Avenue, Memphis, TN 38104, (901) 523–8900, ext. 5928

Human Resources Management Officer, Memphis Medical Center, 1030 Jefferson Avenue, Memphis, TN 38104, (901) 523–8990, ext. 5928

Human Resources Management Officer, Mountain Home Medical Center, Johnston City, Mountain Home, TN 37684, (615) 926–1171, ext. 7181

Human Resources Management Officer, Nashville Medical Center, 1310 24th Avenue South, Nashville, TN 37212–2637, (615) 327–5381

Knoxville Outpatient Clinic Substation, Send to: Human Resources Management Officer, VA Medical Center, 1310 24th Avenue South, Nashville, TN 37212–2637, (615) 327–5381

Nashville Regional Office, Send to: VBA Southern Area Human Resources Management Office Human Resources Management Officer, Human Resources Management Director, 6508 Dogwood Parkway, Suite E, Jackson, MS 39213, (601) 965–4140

Texas

Human Resources Management Officer, San Antonio Medical Center, 7400 Merton Minter Blvd., San Antonio, TX 78284, (210) 617–5300, ext. 6732

Corpus Christi Outpatient Clinic, Send to: Human Resources Management Officer, VA Medical Center, 7400 Merton Minter Blvd., San Antonio, TX 78284, (210) 617–5300, ext. 6732

McAllen Outpatient Clinic Substation, Send to: Human Resources Management Officer, VA Medical Center, 7400 Merton Minter Blvd., San Antonio, TX 78284, (210) 617–5300, ext. 6732

Human Resources Management Officer, Temple Medical Center,1901 S. 1st Street, Temple, TX 76504, (817) 778–4811, ext. 4429

Human Resources Management Officer, Austin Automation Center, 1615 E. Woodard Street, Austin, TX 78772, (512) 326–6054

Human Resources Management Officer, Waco Medical Center, 4800 Memorial Drive, Waco, TX 76711, (817) 752–6581, ext. 6346

Waco Outpatient Clinic, Send to: Human Resources Management Officer, VA Medical Center, 4800 Memorial Drive, Waco, TX 76711, (817) 752–6581, ext. 6346

Human Resources Management Officer, Dallas Medical Center, 4500 S. Lancaster Road, Dallas, TX 75216, (214) 372–7032

Human Resources Management Officer, Houston Medical Center, 2002 Holcombe Blvd., Houston, TX 77030, (713) 794–7458

Beaumont Outpatient Clinic Substation, Send to: Human Resources Management Officer, VA Medical Center, 2002 Holcombe Blvd., Houston, TX 77030, (713) 794–7458

Lufkin Outpatient Clinic, Send to: Human Resources Management Officer, VA Medical Center, 2002 Holcombe Blvd., Houston, TX 77030, (713) 794–7458

Human Resources Management Officer, Waco Medical Center, 4800 Memorial Drive, Waco, TX 76711, (817) 752–6581, ext. 6346

Human Resources Management Officer, El Paso Outpatient Clinic, 5919 Brook Hollow Drive, El Paso, TX 79925, (915) 540–7878

Fort Bliss National Cemetery, Send to: Human Resources Management Officer, El Paso Outpatient Clinic, 5919 Brook Hollow Drive, El Paso, TX 79925, (915) 540–7878

Houston Regional Office, Send to: VBA Southern Area Human Resources Management Office, Human Resources Management Director, 6508 Dogwood Parkway, Suite E, Jackson, MS 39213, (601) 965–4140

San Antonio VA Office, Send to: VBA Southern Area Human Resources Management Office, Human Resources Management Director, 6508 Dogwood Parkway, Suite E, Jackson, MS 39213, (601) 965–4140

Human Resources Management Officer, Big Spring Medical Center, 2400 Gregg St., Big Spring, TX 79720, (915) 264–4820

Austin Systems Development Center, Send to: Human Resources Management Officer, Austin Automation Center, 1615 E. Woodard Street, Austin, TX 78772, (512) 326–6054

Human Resources Management Officer, Amarillo Medical Center, 6010 Amarillo Blvd. West, Amarillo, TX 79106, (806) 354–7827

Houston National Cemetery, Send to: Human Resources Management Officer, VA Medical Center, 2002 Holcombe Blvd., Houston, TX 77030, (713) 794–7458

San Antonio National Cemetery Area Office, Send to: Human Resources Management Officer, VA Medical Center, 7400 Merton Minter Blvd., San Antonio, TX 78284, (210) 617–5300, ext. 6732

Fort Sam Houston National Cemetery, Send to: Human Resources Management Officer, VA Medical Center, 7400 Merton Minter Blvd., San Antonio, TX 78284, (210) 617–5300, ext. 6732

Human Resources Management Officer, Kerrville Medical Center, 3600 Memorial Blvd., Kerrville, TX 78028, (210) 792–2518

Kerrville National Cemetery Area Office, Send to: Human Resources Management Officer, VA Medical Center, 3600 Memorial Blvd., Kerrville, TX 78028, (210) 792–2518

Human Resources Management Officer, Marlin Medical Center, 1016 Ward Street, Marlin, TX 76661, (817) 883–3511, ext. 4702

Human Resources Management Officer, Bonham Medical Center, East Ninth & Lipscomb Street, Bonham, TX 75418–4091, (903) 583–2111, ext. 6331

Waco Regional Office, Send to: VBA Southern Area Human Resources Management

Office, Human Resources Management Director, 6508 Dogwood Parkway, Suite E, Jackson, MS 39213, (601) 965–4140

Dallas VA Office, Send to: VBA Southern Area Human Resources Management Office, Human Resources Management Director, 6508 Dogwood Parkway, Suite E, Jackson, MS 39213, (601) 965–4140

Lubbock VA Office, Send to: VBA Southern Area Human Resources Management Office, Human Resources Management Director, 6508 Dogwood Parkway, Suite E, Jackson, MS 39213, (601) 965–4140

Lubbock Outpatient Clinic, Send to: Human Resources Management Office, VA Medical Center, 6010 Amarillo Blvd. West, Amarillo, TX 79106, (806) 354–7827

Austin Finance Center, Send to: Human Resources Management Officer, Austin Automation Center, 1615 E. Woodard Street, Austin, TX 78772, (512) 326–6054

Utah

Salt Lake City Regional Office, Send to: VBA Western Area Human Resources Management Office, Human Resources Management Director, 126000 W. Colfax Ave., Suite C–300, Lakewood, CO 80215, (303) 231–5855

Human Resources Management Officer, Salt Lake City Medical Center, 500 Foothill Blvd., Salt Lake City, UT 84148–0001, (801) 584–1284

Vermont

Human Resources Management Officer, White River Junction Medical and Regional Office Center, White River Junction, VT 05009, (802) 295–9363, ext. 5350

Virginia

Human Resources Management Officer, Richmond Medical Center, 1201 Broad Rock Blvd., Richmond, VA 23249, (804) 230–1305

Human Resources Management Officer, Hampton Medical Center, 100 Emancipation Road, Hampton, VA 23667, (804) 722–9961, ext. 3160

Richmond National Cemetery, Send to: Human Resources Management Officer, VA Medical Center, 1201 Broad Rock Blvd., Richmond, VA 23249 (804) 230–1305

Quantico National Cemetery, Send to: Human Resources Management Officer, VA Medical Center, 50 Irving Street, NW., Washington, DC 20422, (202) 745–8200

Hampton National Cemetery, Send to: Human Resources Management Officer, VA Medical Center, 100 Emancipation Road, Hampton, VA 23667, (804) 722–9961, ext. 3160

Culpepper National Cemetery, Send to: Human Resources Management Officer, VA Medical Center, Route 9, Martinsburg, WV 25401, (304) 263–0811, ext. 3237

Roanoke Regional Office, Send to: Eastern Area Servicing Assistance Center, Human Resources Management Director, 31 Hopkins Plaza, Baltimore, MD 21202–2004, (410) 962–4090

Human Resources Management Officer, Salem Medical Center, 1970 Roanoke Blvd., Salem, VA 24153, (703) 982–2463, ext. 2812

Danville National Cemetery Area Office, Send to: Human Resources Management Officer, VA Medical Center, 1970 Roanoke Blvd., Salem, VA 24153, (703) 982–2463, ext. 2812

Alexandria National Cemetery Area Office, Send to: Human Resources Management Officer, VA Medical Center, 50 Irving Street, NW., Washington, DC 20422, (202) 745–8200

Leesburg National Cemetery Area Office, Send to: Human Resources Management Officer, VA Medical Center, 50 Irving Street, NW., Washington, DC 20422, (202) 745–8200

Mechanicsville National Cemetery Area Office, Send to: Human Resources Management Officer, VA Medical Center, 1201 Broad Rock Blvd., Richmond, VA 23249, (804) 230–1305

Sandston National Cemetery Area Office, Send to: Human Resources Management Officer, VA Medical Center, 1201 Broad Rock Blvd., Richmond, VA 23249, (804) 230–1305

Hopewell National Cemetery Area Office, Send to: Human Resources Management Officer, VA Medical Center, 1201 Broad Rock Blvd., Richmond, VA 23249 (804) 230–1305

Staunton National Cemetery Area Office, Send to: Human Resources Management Officer, VA Medical Center, 1970 Roanoke Blvd., Salem, VA 24153, (703) 982–2463, ext. 2812

Winchester National Cemetery Area Office, Send to: Human Resources Management Officer, VA Medical Center, Route 9, Martinsburg, WV 25401, (304) 263–0811, ext. 3237

Washington

Seattle Regional Office, Send to: VBA Western Area Human Resources, Management Office, Human Resources Management Director, 126000 W. Colfax Ave., Suite C–300, Lakewood, CO 80215, (303) 231–5855

Human Resources Management Officer, Walla Walla Medical Center, 77 Wainwright Drive, Walla Walla, WA 99362–3975, (509) 527–3453

Human Resources Management Officer, Seattle Medical Center, 1660 S. Columbian Way, Seattle, WA 98108–1597, (206) 764–2135

Seattle Outpatient Clinic (Vet Center), Send to: Human Resources Management Officer, VA Medical Center, 1660 S. Columbian Way, Seattle, WA 98108–1597, (206) 764–2135

Human Resources Management Officer, Tacoma Medical Center, American Lake, Tacoma, WA 98493, (206) 582–8440, ext. 6054

Human Resources Management Officer, Spokane Medical Center, 4815 North Assembly

Street, Spokane, WA 99205–6197, (509) 327–0242

West Virginia

Human Resources Management Officer, Huntington Medical Center, 1540 Spring Valley Road, Huntington, WV 25704, (304) 429–6755, ext. 2343

Human Resources Management Officer, Beckley Medical Center, 200 Veterans Avenue, Beckley, WV 25801, (304) 255–2121, ext. 4461

Human Resources Management Officer, Clarksburg, Medical Center, 1 Medical Center Dr., Clarksburg, WV 26301, (304) 623–7697

Human Resources Management Officer, Martinsburg Medical Center, Route 9, Martinsburg, WV 25401, (304) 263–0811, ext. 3237

West Virginia (Grafton) National Cemetery, Send to: Human Resources Management Officer, VA Medical Center, 1 Medical Center Dr., Clarksburg, WV 26301, (304) 623–7697

Huntington Regional Office, Send to: Eastern Area Servicing Assistance Center, Human Resources Management Director, 31 Hopkins Plaza, Baltimore, MD 21202–2004, (410) 962–4090

Wisconsin

Wood National Cemetery, Send to: Human Resources Management Officer, VA Medical Center, 5000 W. National Avenue, Milwaukee, WI 53295, (414) 384–2000

Milwaukee Regional Office, Send to: VBA Central Area Human Resources Management Office, Human Resources Management Director, 38701 Seven Mile Road, Suite 345, Livonia, MI 48152, (313) 953–8830

Human Resources Management Officer, Milwaukee Medical Center, 5000 W. National Avenue, Milwaukee, WI 53295, (414) 384–2000, ext. 2930

Human Resources Management Officer, Tomah Medical Center, 500 E. Veterans Street, Tomah, WI 54660, (608) 372–1636

Human Resources Management Officer, Madison Medical Center, 2500 Overlook Terrace, Madison, WI 53705, (608) 262–7026

Wyoming

Human Resources Management Officer, Sheridan Medical Center, 1898 Fort Road, Sheridan, WY 82801–8320, (307) 672–1673

Human Resources Management Officer, Cheyenne Medical and Regional Office Center, 2360 East Pershing Blvd., Cheyenne, WY 82001, (307) 778–7331

II. AGENCIES

American Battle Monuments Commission

Chief, Administration, Room 5127, Pulaski Building, 20 Massachusetts Avenue, NW., Washington, DC 20314–0001, (202) 761–0533

Architectural and Transportation Barriers Compliance Board

General Counsel, 1331 F Street, NW., #1000, Washington, DC 20004–1111, (202) 272–5434, ext. 16

Equal Employment Opportunity Commission

Management Director, Office of Management, 1801 L Street, NW., Washington, DC 20507, (202) 663–4411

Export-Import Bank of the United States

Associate General Counsel, 811 Vermont Avenue, NW., Room 955, Washington, DC 20571, (202) 565–3432

Farm Credit Administration

Chief, Human Resources Division, Farm Credit Administration, 1501 Farm Credit Drive, McLean, VA 22102–5090, (703) 883–4122

Federal Communications Commission

Chief, Payroll/Personnel Support Branch, 1919 M Street, NW., Room 212, Washington, DC 20554, (202) 481–0136

Federal Deposit Insurance Corporation

Chief, Operations Section, Office of Personnel Management, 550 17th Street, NW., PA–1730–5018, Washington, DC 20429, (202) 942–3401

Federal Election Commission

Assistant General Counsel—Administrative Law, 999 E Street, NW., Washington, DC 20463, (202) 219–3690

Federal Energy Regulatory Commission

Chief, Payroll Branch, Department of Energy, GTN Building, Room E–259, Washington, DC 20585, (301) 903–4012

Federal Housing Finance Board

Federal Housing Finance Board, 1777 F Street, NW., Washington, DC 20006, (202) 408–2685 or (202) 408–2686

Federal Retirement Thrift Investment Board

Director of Personnel, 1250 H Street, NW., Suite 400, Washington, DC 20005, (202) 942–1680

Federal Trade Commission

Director, Division of Personnel, 6th Street & Pennsylvania Avenue, NW., Room H–148, Washington, DC 20580, (202) 326–2022

General Accounting Office

Comptroller General, Attention: Chief, Payroll/Personnel Systems Branch, Personnel, Room 1180, 441 G Street, NW., Washington, DC 20415, (202) 512–5811

Institute of Peace

Personnel and Benefits Manager, 1550 M Street, NW., Suite 700, Washington, DC 20005, (202) 429–3801

Inter-American Foundation

General Counsel, 901 N. Stuart Street, 10th Floor, Arlington, VA 22203, (703) 841–3894

JFK Assassination Records Review Board

General Counsel, 600 E Street, NW., Washington, DC 20530

National Archives & Records Administration

Supervisory Personnel Staffing Specialist, Personnel Operations Branch, 9700 Page Avenue, Room 2002, St. Louis, MO 63132, (314) 538–4953

National Capital Planning Commission

General Counsel, 801 Pennsylvania Avenue, NW, Suite 301, Washington, DC 20576, (202) 724–0174

Nuclear Regulatory Commission

Chief, Policy and Labor Relations, Office of Personnel, Washington, DC 20555, (301) 415–7526

Nuclear Waste Technical Review Board

Administrative Officer, 1100 Wilson Blvd., Suite 910, Arlington, VA 22209, (703) 235–4473

Office of Special Counsel

Director of Management and Associate Special Counsel for Planning and Advice, 1730 M Street, NW., Suite 201, Washington, DC 20036–4505, (202) 653–9485

Peace Corps

Associate General Counsel, 1990 K Street, NW., Room 8300, Washington, DC 20526, (202) 606–3114

Resolution Trust Corporation

Payroll Specialist/Paralegal Specialist, 1717 H Street, NW., Washington, DC 20434, (202) 736–3095

Securities and Exchange Commission

Personnel Management Specialist, Office of Administrative & Personnel Management, 450 5th Street, NW. (Stop 2–3), Washington, DC 20549

Small Business Administration

Chief, Personnel/Payroll Systems Branch or Payroll Analyst, 409 3rd Street, SW., Suite 4200, Washington, DC 20416, (202) 205–6148 or (202) 205–6213

III. UNITED STATES POSTAL SERVICE

United States Postal Service

The United States Postal Service will cooperate with process servers in the service of process regarding private civil or criminal matters only when service is attempted in person on the subject employee at the employee's place of employment, in accordance with the provisions of 39 CFR 243.2(g). Service of summonses and complaints, in prviate matters, by mail to either the agent or employees at their workstations is not permitted.

The Postal Service agent will attempt to facilitate and assist personnel of child support enforcement agencies within the limitations imposed by the Privacy Act, 5 U.S.C. 552a and relevant Postal regulations. The requester must furnish the name and social security number of the person who is the subject of the inquiry.

Manager, Payroll Processing Branch, 1 Federal Drive, Ft. Snelling, MN 55111–9650, (612) 293–6300

[63 FR 14777, Mar. 26, 1998; 63 FR 34777, June 26, 1998; 63 FR 56537, Oct. 22, 1998]

PART 582—COMMERCIAL GARNISHMENT OF FEDERAL EMPLOYEES' PAY

Subpart A—Purpose, Definitions, and Exclusions

Subpart B—Service of Legal Process

Subpart C—Compliance With Legal Process

Subpart D—Consumer Credit Protection Act Restrictions

Subpart E—Implementation by Agencies

AUTHORITY: 5 U.S.C. 5520a; 15 U.S.C. 1673; E.O. 12897; Sec. 582.102 also issued under 5 U.S.C. 8336a and 8412a.

SOURCE: 60 FR 13030, Mar. 10, 1995, unless otherwise noted.

Subpart A—Purpose, Definitions, and Exclusions

§ 582.101 Purpose.

Section 5520a of title 5 of the United States Code provides that with certain exceptions set forth in this part, pay from an agency to an employee is subject to legal process in the same manner and to the same extent as if the agency were a private person. The purpose of this part is to implement the objectives of section 5520a as they pertain to each executive agency of the United States Government, except with regard to employees of the United States Postal Service, the Postal Rate Commission, and the General Accounting Office.

§ 582.102 Definitions.

In this part—(1) *Agency* means each agency of the executive branch of the Federal Government, excluding the United States Postal Service, the Postal Rate Commission, and the General Accounting Office; *agency* does not include the government of the District of Columbia or the territories and possessions of the United States. (Section 5520a(j)(1) of title 5 of the United States Code provides that separate implementing regulations shall be promulgated by the legislative branch and the judicial branch; section 5520a(k) provides that separate implementing regulations shall be promulgated with regard to members of the uniformed services; and Executive Order 12897 provides that separate implementing regulations shall be promulgated with regard to employees of the United States Postal Service. The regulations promulgated for employees of the United States Postal Service also apply to employees of the Postal Rate Commission.)

(2) *Employee or employee-obligor* means an individual who is employed by an *agency* as defined in this section, including a reemployed annuitant, an individual engaged in phased employment as defined in part 831, subpart Q, and part 848 of this chapter, and a retired member of the uniformed services who is employed by an agency. *Employee* does not include a retired employee, a member of the uniformed services, a retired member of the uniformed services, or an individual whose service is based on a contract, including an individual who provides personal services based on a contract with an agency.

(3) *Legal process* means any writ, order, summons, or other similar process in the nature of garnishment, which may include an attachment, writ of execution, court ordered wage assignment, or tax levy from a State or local government, which—

(i) Is issued by:

(A) A court of competent jurisdiction, including Indian tribal courts, within any State, territory, or possession of the United States, or the District of Columbia. As stated in § 582.101, pay is subject to legal process in the same manner and to the same extent as if the agency were a private person. There is, therefore, no requirement in this part that, for example, legal process be signed by a Judge; or.

(B) An authorized official pursuant to an order of a court of competent jurisdiction or pursuant to State or local law; or

(C) A State agency authorized to issue income withholding notices pursuant to State or local law; and

(ii) Orders an agency to withhold an amount from the pay of an employee-obligor and to make a payment of such withholding to a *person*, for a specifically described satisfaction of a legal debt of the employee-obligor, or recovery of attorney fees, interest, or court costs;

(4) *Person* may include an individual, partnership, corporation, association, joint venture, private organization or other legal entity, and includes the plural of that term; *person* may include any of the entities that may issue *legal*

process as set forth in §582.102(3)(i) (A), (B), and (C), and a State or local government as well as a foreign entity or a foreign governmental unit, but does not include the United States or an agency of the United States.

(5) In conformance with 5 U.S.C. 5520a, *pay* means basic pay; premium pay paid under chapter 55, subchapter V, of title 5 of the United States Code; any payment received under chapter 55, subchapters VI, VII, and VIII, of title 5 of the United States Code; severance pay and back pay under chapter 55, subchapter IX, of title 5 of the United States Code; sick pay, and any other paid leave; incentive pay; locality pay (including special pay adjustments for law enforcement officers and locality-based comparability payments); back pay awards; and any other compensation paid or payable for personal services, whether such compensation is denominated as pay, wages, salary, lump-sum leave payments, commission, bonus, award, or otherwise; but does not include amounts received under any Federal program for compensation for work injuries; awards for making suggestions, reimbursement for expenses incurred by an individual in connection with employment, or allowances in lieu of thereof as determined by the employing agency.

[60 FR 13030, Mar. 10, 1995, as amended at 61 FR 3544, Feb. 1, 1996; 79 FR 46618, Aug. 8, 2014]

§582.103 Exclusions.

In determining the amount of pay subject to garnishment under this part, there shall be excluded amounts which:

(a) Are owed by the employee-obligor to the United States;

(b) Are required by law to be deducted from the employee-obligor's pay, including, but not limited to amounts deducted in compliance with the Federal Insurance and Contributions Act (FICA), including amounts deducted for Medicare and for Old Age, Survivor, and Disability Insurance (OASDI);

(c) Are properly withheld for Federal, State, or local income tax purposes, if the withholding of the amounts is authorized or required by law and if amounts withheld are not greater than would be the case if the employee-obligor claimed all dependents to which the employee-obligor were entitled. The withholding of additional amounts pursuant to section 3402(i) of title 26 of the United States Code may be permitted only when the employee-obligor presents evidence of a tax obligation which supports the additional withholding;

(d) Are deducted as health insurance premiums;

(e) Are deducted as normal retirement contributions, not including amounts deducted for supplementary coverage. For purposes of this section, all amounts contributed under sections 8351 and 8432(a) of title 5 of the United States Code to the Thrift Savings Fund are deemed to be normal retirement contributions. Except as provided in this paragraph, amounts voluntarily contributed toward additional retirement benefits are considered to be supplementary;

(f) Are deducted as normal life insurance premiums from salary or other remuneration for employment, not including amounts deducted for supplementary coverage. Federal Employees' Group Life Insurance premiums for "Basic Life" coverage are considered to be normal life insurance premiums; all optional Federal Employees' Group Life Insurance premiums and any life insurance premiums paid for by allotment are considered to be supplementary.

(g) Amounts withheld in compliance with legal process based on child support and/or alimony indebtedness are not exclusions.

Subpart B—Service of Legal Process

§582.201 Agent to receive process.

(a) Except as provided in appendix A to this part, appendix A to 5 CFR part 581 lists agents designated to accept service of process under part 581 and this part.

(b) United States Attorneys are not considered appropriate agents to accept service of process.

§582.202 Service of legal process.

(a) A person using this part shall serve interrogatories and legal process on the agent to receive process as explained in §582.201. Where the legal process is directed to an agency, and the purpose of the legal process is to compel an agency to garnish an employee's pay, the legal process need not expressly name the agency as a garnishee.

(b) Service of legal process may be accomplished by certified or registered mail, return receipt requested, or by personal service only upon the agent to receive process as explained in § 582.201, or if no agent has been designated, then upon the head of the employee-obligor's employing agency. The designated agent shall note the date and time of receipt on the legal process.

(c) Parties bringing garnishment actions shall comply with the service of process provisions in this section. Service will not be effective where parties fail to comply with the service of process provisions of this section, notwithstanding whether the person bringing the garnishment action has complied with the service of process requirements of the jurisdiction issuing the legal process.

§ 582.203 Information minimally required to accompany legal process.

(a) Sufficient identifying information must accompany the legal process in order to enable processing by the agency. Parties seeking garnishment actions, therefore, should provide as many of the following identifying pieces of information concerning the employee-obligor as possible:

(1) Full name;

(2) Date of birth;

(3) Employment number or social security number;

(4) Component of the agency for which the employee-obligor works;

(5) Official duty station or worksite; and

(6) Home address or current mailing address.

(b) If the information submitted is not sufficient to identify the employee-obligor, the legal process shall be returned directly to the court, or other authority, with an explanation of the deficiency. However, prior to returning the legal process, if there is sufficient time prior to the time limits imposed in § 582.303, an attempt should be made to inform the person who caused the legal process to be served, or the person's representative, that it will not be honored unless adequate identifying information is supplied.

§ 582.204 Electronic disbursement.

The party designated to receive the garnished funds may forward a written request to the garnishing agency to have the funds remitted by electronic funds transfer, rather than by paper check. The request shall include the designated party's name, address, and deposit account number, and the name, address, and 9-digit routing transit number of the designated party's financial institution. Written requests accompanying service of process will be honored beginning with the first remission of garnished funds. Written requests received by the agency subsequent to service of process will be honored in as timely a manner as the agency deems feasible.

Subpart C—Compliance With Legal Process

§ 582.301 Suspension of payment.

Upon proper service of legal process as specified in §§ 582.202 and 582.203, the agency shall suspend, *i.e.*, withhold, payment of such moneys for the amount necessary to permit compliance with the legal process in accordance with this part.

§ 582.302 Notification of employee-obligor.

(a) As soon as possible, but not later than 15 calendar days after the date of valid service of legal process, the agent designated to accept legal process shall send to the employee-obligor, at his or her duty station or last known home address, written notice that such process has been served, including a copy of the legal process;

(b) The agency may provide the employee-obligor with the following additional information:

(1) Copies of any other documents submitted in support of or in addition to the legal process;

(2) Notice that the United States does not represent the interests of the employee-obligor in the pending legal proceedings; and

(3) Advice that the employee-obligor may wish to consult legal counsel regarding defenses to the legal process that he or she may wish to assert.

§ 582.303 Response to legal process or interrogatories.

(a) Whenever the designated agent is validly served with legal process, the agent shall respond within 30 calendar days after receipt, or within such longer period as may be prescribed by applicable State or local law. The agent shall also respond within this time period to interrogatories which accompany legal process. Notwithstanding State law, an agent need only respond once to legal process.

(b) If State or local law authorizes the issuance of interrogatories prior to or after the issuance of legal process, the agent shall respond to the interrogatories within 30 calendar days after being validly served, or within such longer period as may be prescribed by applicable State or local law.

§ 582.304 Nonliability for disclosure.

(a) No agency employee whose duties include responding to interrogatories pursuant to § 582.303(b), shall be subject to any disciplinary action or civil or criminal liability or penalty for any disclosure of information made in connection with the carrying out of any duties pertaining directly or indirectly to answering such interrogatories.

(b) However, an agency would not be precluded from taking disciplinary action against an employee who consistently or purposely failed to provide correct information requested by interrogatories.

§ 582.305 Honoring legal process.

(a) The agency shall comply with legal process, except where the process cannot be complied with because:

(1) It is not regular on its face.

(2) The legal process would require the withholding of funds not deemed pay as described in § 582.102(a)(5).

(3) It does not comply with section 5520a of title 5 of the United States Code or with the mandatory provisions of this part; or

(4) An order of a court of competent jurisdiction enjoining or suspending the operation of the legal process has been served on the agency.

(b) While an agency will not comply with legal process which, on its face, indicates that it has expired or is otherwise no longer valid, legal process will be deemed valid notwithstanding the fact that the underlying debt and/or the underlying judgment arose prior to the effective date of section 5520a of title 5 of the United States Code.

(c)(1) The filing of an appeal by an employee-obligor will not generally delay the processing of a garnishment action. If the employee-obligor establishes to the satisfaction of the employee-obligor's agency that the law of the jurisdiction which issued the legal process provides that the processing of the garnishment action shall be suspended during an appeal, and if the employee-obligor establishes that he or she has filed an appeal, the employing agency shall comply with the applicable law of the jurisdiction and delay or suspend the processing of the garnishment action.

(2) Notwithstanding paragraph (c)(1) of this section, the employing agency shall not be required to establish an escrow account to comply with the legal process even if the applicable law of the jurisdiction requires private employers to do so.

(d) Under the circumstances set forth in § 582.305 (a) or (b), or where the agency is directed by the Justice Department not to comply with the legal process, the agency shall respond directly to the court, or other authority, setting forth its reasons for non-compliance with the legal process. In addition, the agency shall inform the person who caused the legal process to be served, or the person's representative, that the legal process will not be honored. Thereafter, if litigation is initiated or appears imminent, the agency shall immediately refer the matter to the United States Attorney for the district from which the legal process issued. To ensure uniformity in the executive branch, agencies which have statutory authority to represent themselves in court shall coordinate their representation with the United States Attorney.

(e) In the event that an agency is served with more than one legal process or garnishment order with respect to the same payments due or payable to the same employee, the agency shall satisfy such processes in priority based on the time of service: *Provided*, That in no event will the total amount garnished for any pay or disbursement cycle exceed the applicable limitation set forth in § 582.402. *Provided further*, That processes which are not limited in time shall preserve their priority based on time of service until fully satisfied. Generally, a modified order will retain its original priority while a time limited order will lose its priority after it has expired.

(f) Legal process to which an agency is subject under sections 459, 461, and 462 of the Social Security Act (42 U.S.C. 659, 661, and 662) for the enforcement of an employee's legal obligation to provide child support or to make alimony payments, including child support or alimony arrearages, shall have priority over any legal process to which an agency is subject under this part. In addition to having priority, compliance with legal process to which an agency is subject under sections 459, 461, and 462 of the Social Security Act may exhaust the moneys available for compliance with legal process under this part. See § 582.402(a).

(g)(1) Neither the United States, and executive agency, nor any disbursing officer shall be liable for any payment made from moneys due from, or payable by, the United States to any individual pursuant to legal process regular on its face, if such payment is made in accordance with this part.

(2) Neither the United States, an executive agency, nor any disbursing officer shall be liable under this part to pay money damages for failure to comply with the legal process.

(h) Agencies affected by legal process served under this part shall not be required to vary their normal pay or disbursement cycles to comply with the legal process. However, legal process, valid at the time of service, which is received too late to be honored during the disbursement cycle in which it is received, shall be honored, to the extent that the legal process may be satisfied, during the next disbursement cycle within the limits set forth in § 582.402. The fact that the legal process may have expired during this period would not relieve the agency of its obligation to honor legal process which was valid at the time of service. If, in the next disbursement cycle, no further payment will be due from the agency to the employee-obligor, the agency shall follow the procedures set forth in § 582.306.

(i) Agencies need not establish escrow accounts in order to comply with legal process. Therefore, even if the amount garnished by an agency in one disbursement cycle is not sufficient to satisfy the entire indebtedness, the agency need not retain those funds until the amount retained would satisfy the entire indebtedness. On the contrary, agencies will, in most instances, remit the garnished amount after each disbursement cycle. Agencies need not pro-rate payments for less than a full disbursement cycle.

(j) If an agency receives legal process which is regular on its face, the agency shall not be required to ascertain whether the authority which issued the legal process had obtained personal jurisdiction over the employee-obligor.

(k) At the discretion of the executive agency, the agency's administrative costs in executing a garnishment may be added to the garnishment amount and the agency may retain costs recovered as offsetting collections. To facilitate recovery of these administrative costs, an administrative fee may be assessed for each legal process that is received and processed by an agency, provided that the fee constitutes the agency's administrative costs in executing the garnishment action.

(l) Where an employee-obligor has filed a bankruptcy petition under section 301 or 302 of title 11 of the United States Code, or is the debtor named in an involuntary petition filed under section 303 of title 11, the agency must cease garnishment proceedings affected by the automatic stay provision, section 362(a) of title 11. Upon filing a petition in bankruptcy or upon learning that he or she is the debtor named in an involuntary petition, the employee-obligor should immediately notify the agency. To enable the agency to determine if the automatic stay applies, the employee-obligor should provide the agency with a copy of the filing or a letter from counsel stating that the petition was filed and indicating the court and the case number, the chapter under which the petition was filed, whether State or federal exemptions were elected, and the nature of the claim underlying the garnishment order.

(m) Within 30 days following the collection of the amount required in the garnishment order, the creditor may submit a final statement of interest that accrued during the garnishment process, and the employing agency shall process the statement for payment, provided the garnishment order authorizes the collection of such interest. This final statement of interest should be accompanied by a statement of account showing how the interest was computed.

[60 FR 13030, Mar. 10, 1995, as amended at 63 FR 14787, Mar. 26, 1998]

§ 582.306 Lack of entitlement by the employee-obligor to pay from the agency served with legal process.

(a) When legal process is served on an agency and the individual identified in the legal process as the employee-obligor is found not to be entitled to pay from the agency, the agency shall follow the procedures set forth in the legal process for that contingency or, if no procedures are set forth therein, the agency shall return the legal process to the court, or other authority from which it was issued, and advise the court, or other authority, that the identified employee-obligor is not entitled to any pay from the agency.

(b) Where it appears that the employee-obligor is only temporarily not entitled to pay from the agency, the court, or other authority, shall be fully advised as to why, and for how long, the employee-obligor's pay will not be garnished, if that information is known by the agency and if disclosure of that information would not be prohibited.

(c) In instances where an employee-obligor separates from employment with an agency that had been honoring a continuing legal process, the agency shall inform the person who caused the legal process to be served, or the person's representative, and the issuing court, or other authority, that the garnishment action is being discontinued. In cases where the employee-obligor has been employed by either another agency or by a private employer, and where this information is known by the agency, the agency shall provide the person with the designated agent for the new employing agency or with the name and address of the private employer.

Subpart D—Consumer Credit Protection Act Restrictions

§ 582.401 Aggregate disposable earnings.

In accordance with the Consumer Credit Protection Act, the *aggregate disposable earnings* under this part are the employee-obligor's pay less those amounts excluded in accordance with § 582.103.

§ 582.402 Maximum garnishment limitations.

Pursuant to section 1673(a)(1) of title 15 of the United States Code (the Consumer Credit Protection Act, as amended) and the Department of Labor regulations to title 29, Code of Federal Regulations, part 870, the following limitations are applicable:

(a) Unless a lower maximum limitation is provided by applicable State or local law, the maximum part of an employee-obligor's aggregate disposable earnings subject to garnishment to enforce any legal debt other than an order for child support or alimony, including any amounts withheld to offset administrative costs as provided for in § 582.305(k), shall not exceed 25 percent of the employee-obligor's aggregate disposable earnings for any workweek. As appropriate, State or local law should be construed as providing a lower maximum limitation where legal process may only be processed on a one at a time basis. Where an agency is garnishing 25 percent or more of an employee-obligor's aggregate disposable earnings for any workweek in compliance with legal process to which an agency is subject under sections 459, 461, and 462 of the Social Security Act, no additional amount may be garnished in compliance with legal process under this part. Furthermore, the following dollar limitations, which are contained in title 29 of the Code of Federal Regulations, part 870, must be applied in determining the garnishable amount of the employee's aggregate disposable earnings:

(1) If the employee-obligor's aggregate disposable earnings for the workweek are in excess of 40 times the Fair Labor Standards Act (FLSA) minimum hourly wage, 25 percent of the employee-obligor's aggregate disposable earnings may be garnished. For example, effective September 1, 1997, when the FLSA minimum wage rate is $5.15 per hour, this rate multiplied by 40 equals $206.00 and thus, if an employee-obligor's disposable earnings are in excess of $206.00 for a workweek, 25 percent of the employee-obligor's disposable earnings are subject to garnishment.

(2) If the employee-obligor's aggregate disposable earnings for a workweek are less than 40 times the FLSA minimum hourly wage, garnishment may not exceed the amount by which the employee-obligor's aggregate disposable earnings exceed 30 times the current minimum wage rate. For example, at an FLSA minimum wage rate of $5.15 per hour, the amount of aggregate disposable earnings which may not be garnished is $154.50 [$5.15 × 30]. Only the amount above $154.50 is garnishable.

(3) If the employee-obligor's aggregate disposable earnings in a workweek are equal to or less than 30 times the FLSA minimum hourly wage, the employee-obligator's earnings may not be garnished in any amount.

(b) There is no limit on the percentage of an employee-obligor's aggregate disposable earnings that may be garnished for a Federal, State or local tax obligation or in compliance with an order of any court of the United States having jurisdiction over bankruptcy cases under Chapter 13 of title 11 of the United States Code. Orders from courts having jurisdiction over bankruptcy cases under Chapter 7 or Chapter 11 of the United States Code are subject to the maximum garnishment restrictions in § 582.402(a).

[60 FR 13030, Mar. 10, 1995, as amended at 63 FR 14788, Mar. 26, 1998]

Subpart E—Implementation by Agencies

§ 582.501 Rules, regulations, and directives by agencies.

Appropriate officials of all agencies shall, to the extent necessary, issue implementing rules, regulations, or directives that are consistent with this part or as are otherwise in accordance with statutory law.

[63 FR 14788, Mar. 26, 1998]

Appendix A to Part 582—List of Agents Designated To Accept Legal Process

NOTE: The agents designated to accept legal process are listed in appendix A to part 581 of this chapter. This appendix A to part 582 provides listings only for those executive agencies where the designations differ from those found in appendix A to part 581 of this chapter.

I. Departments

Department of Defense. Defense Finance and Accounting Service, Cleveland Center, Office of General Counsel, Attention: Code L, P.O. Box 998002, Cleveland, OH 44199–8002, (216) 522–5301.

Agents for receipt of all legal process for all Department of Defense civilian employees except where another agent has been designated as set forth below.

For requests that apply to employees of the Army and Air Force Exchange Service or to civilian employees of the Defense Contract Audit Agency (DCAA) and the Defense Logistics Agency (DLA) who are employed outside the United States: See appendix A to part 581 of this chapter.

For requests that apply to civilian employees of the Army Corps of Engineers, the National Security Agency, the Defense Intelligence Agency, and non-appropriated fund civilian employees of the Air Force, serve the following offices:

Army Nonappropriated Fund Employees in Europe. Commander, 266th Theater Finance Command, NAF Payroll, Unit #29001–07, APO AE 09007–0137, 011–49–6221–57–7752, DSN 379–7752.

National Security Agency. General Counsel, National Security Agency/Central Security Service, 9800 Savage Rd., Ft. George G. Meade, MD 20755–6000, (301) 688–6705.

Defense Intelligence Agency. Office of General Counsel, Defense Intelligence Agency, Pentagon, 2E238, Washington, DC 20340–1029, (202) 697–3945.

Air Force Nonappropriated Fund Employees. Office of General Counsel, Air Force Services Agency, 10100 Reunion Place, Suite 503, San Antonio, TX 78216–4138, (210) 652–7051.

For civilian employees of the Army, Navy and Marine Corps who are employed outside the United States, serve the following offices:

Army Civilian Employees in Europe. Commander, 266th Theater Finance Command, ATTN: AEUCF-CPF, APO AE 09007–0137, 011–49–6221–57–6303/2136, DSN 370–6303/2136.

Army Civilian Employees in Japan. Commander, U.S. Army Finance and Accounting Office, Japan, ATTN: APAJ-RM-FA-E-CP, Unit 45005, APO AP 96343–0087, DSN 233–3362.

Army Civilian Employees in Korea. Commander, 175th Finance and Accounting Office, Korea, ATTN: EAFC-FO (Civilian Pay), Unit 15300, APO AP 96205–0073, 011–822–791–4599, DSN 723–4599.

Army Civilian Employees in Panama. DCSRM Finance & Accounting Office, ATTN: SORM-FAP-C, Unit 7153, APO AA 34004–5000, 011–507–287–6766, DSN 287–5312.

Navy and Marine Corps Civilian Employees Overseas. Director of the Office of Civilian Personnel Management, Office of Counsel, Office of Civilian Personnel Management (OCPM-OL), Department of the Navy, 800 N. Quincy Street, Arlington, VA 22203–1990, (703) 696–4717.

Navy and Marine Corps Nonappropriated Fund Employees. The agents are the same as those designated to receive garnishment orders of Navy and Marine Corps nonappropriated fund personnel for the collection of child support and alimony, published at 32 CFR part 734 (1994 ed.), except as follows:

For non-civil service civilian personnel of the Navy Exchanges or related nonappropriated fund instrumentalities administered by the Navy Exchange Service Command: Commander, Navy Exchange Service Command, ATTN: Human Resources Beverly Building, 3280 Virginia Beach Boulevard, Virginia Beach, VA 23453–5274, (804) 631–3675.

For non-civil service civilian personnel of Marine Corps nonappropriated fund instrumentalities, process may be served on the Commanding Officer of the employing activity ATTN: Morale, Welfare and Recreation Director.

Department of the Interior. Chief, Payroll Operations Division Attn: Code: D–2605, Bureau of Reclamation. Administrative Service Center, Department of the Interior, P.O. Box 272030, 7201 West Mansfield Avenue, Denver, CO 80227–9030, (303) 969–7739.

PART 591—ALLOWANCES AND DIFFERENTIALS

Subpart A—Uniform Allowances

Sec.

Subpart B—Cost-of-Living Allowance and Post Differential—Nonforeign Areas

COST-OF-LIVING ALLOWANCES AND POST DIFFERENTIALS

COST-OF-LIVING ALLOWANCES

Subpart C—Allowance Based on Duty at Remote Worksites

Subpart D—Separate Maintenance Allowance for Duty at Johnston Island

Subpart A—Uniform Allowances

AUTHORITY: 5 U.S.C. 5903; E.O. 12748, 3 CFR 1991 Comp., p. 316.

SOURCE: 59 FR 43705, Aug. 25, 1994, unless otherwise noted.

§591.101 Purpose.

This subpart prescribes the regulations authorized by section 5903 of title 5, United States Code, for the payment of uniform allowances.

§591.102 Definitions.

Agency means an "Executive agency," as defined in 5 U.S.C. 105.

Employee means an employee in or under an agency.

Category of employees means any group of employees designated by an agency that has the same basic uniform requirements.

Head of agency means the head of an agency or an official who has been delegated the authority to act for the head of the agency in the matter concerned.

Uniform means a specified article or articles of clothing that may include, but is not limited to, such items as shoes, boots, hats, shirts, slacks, skirts, or outerwear an employee is required by an agency to wear to provide a distinctive and easily identifiable appearance in performing his or her job.

A "uniform" does not include protective equipment required for the employee's safety under 5 U.S.C. 7903 or normal business or work attire purchased at the discretion of the employee.

Year means any period of 12 consecutive months designated by an agency as the basis for applying the maximum uniform allowance rates established under this part.

§591.103 Governmentwide maximum uniform allowance rate.

Unless a higher initial maximum uniform allowance rate is payable under §591.104 to an employee who is required by statute, regulation, or an agency's written administrative procedures to wear a uniform, the head of each agency concerned, out of funds available, shall—

(a) Pay an allowance for a uniform not to exceed $800 a year; or

(b) Furnish a uniform at a cost not to exceed $800 a year.

(c) Any agency which provides a uniform allowance under paragraph (a) of this section must establish policies to administer the uniform allowance program, including uniform standards acceptable to the agency.

[59 FR 43705, Aug. 25, 1994, as amended at 72 FR 20702, Apr. 26, 2007]

§591.104 Higher initial maximum uniform allowance rate.

(a) The head of an agency may establish one or more initial maximum uniform allowance rates greater than the Governmentwide maximum uniform allowance rate established under §591.103.

(b) A higher initial maximum uniform allowance rate established under this section may not exceed the average total uniform cost for the minimum basic uniform for the affected employees and, except as provided in paragraph (c) of this section, applies only to the year in which the employee becomes subject to a requirement to wear the uniform.

(c) An agency that establishes one or more higher initial maximum uniform allowance rates under this section may divide the cost of the minimum basic uniform and continue a higher initial maximum uniform allowance for the year following the year the employee first becomes subject to the requirement to wear the uniform, provided the agency publishes a notice of its intention to continue such payments in the FEDERAL REGISTER for notice and comment.

(d) Before establishing a higher initial maximum uniform allowance rate under this section, an agency shall publish in the FEDERAL REGISTER for notice and comment—

(1) A description and justification of the circumstances requiring a higher initial maximum uniform allowance rate;

(2) An estimate of the number of employees affected;

(3) The specific items required for the basic uniform and the average total uniform cost for the affected employees;

(4) The amount of the proposed higher initial maximum uniform allowance rate to be paid during the year the employee first becomes subject to the uniform requirement;

(5) The proposed effective date of the higher initial maximum uniform allowance rate; and,

(6) The intent of the agency (if any) to divide the cost of a minimum basic uniform and continue to make higher initial maximum basic uniform allowance payments in the year following the year the employee first becomes subject to the uniform requirement.

(e) So that OPM can evaluate agencies' use of this authority and provide the Congress and others with information regarding the use of a higher initial maximum uniform allowance rate, each agency concerned shall maintain such other records and submit to OPM such other reports and data as OPM shall require.

(f) When OPM determines that an agency is using this authority inappropriately, OPM may require its prior approval before that agency establishes any future higher initial maximum uniform allowance rate.

(g) An agency may increase a higher initial maximum uniform allowance rate only as a result of an increase in the average total uniform cost for the affected employees. Before effecting an increase under this paragraph, an agency shall follow the notice and comment procedures required by paragraph (d) of this section.

(h) To establish a higher initial maximum uniform allowance rate applicable to the initial year a new style or type of minimum basic uniform is required for a category of employees, an agency shall use the higher initial maximum uniform allowance procedures provided under this section.

Subpart B—Cost-of-Living Allowance and Post Differential—Nonforeign Areas

AUTHORITY: 5 U.S.C. 5941; E.O. 10000, 3 CFR, 1943–1948 Comp., p. 792; and E.O. 12510, 3 CFR, 1985 Comp., p. 338.

SOURCE: 67 FR 22340, May 3, 2002, unless otherwise noted.

EDITORIAL NOTE: Nomenclature changes to subpart B of part 591 appear at 70 FR 31313, May 31, 2005.

§591.201 Definitions.

In this subpart—

Agency means an Executive agency as defined in section 105 of title 5, United States Code, but does not include Government-controlled corporations.

Bureau of Labor Statistics (BLS) means the Bureau of Labor Statistics of the Department of Labor.

Commonwealth of the Northern Mariana Islands (CNMI) means the Commonwealth of the Northern Mariana Islands, which is part of the Guam/CNMI COLA area.

Consumer Expenditure Survey (CES) means the BLS survey of consumers and their expenditures.

Consumer Price Index (CPI) means the BLS survey of the change of consumer prices over time.

Cost-of-living allowance (COLA) means an allowance that the Office of Personnel Management (OPM) establishes under 5 U.S.C. 5941 at a location in a nonforeign area where living costs are substantially higher than in the Washington, DC, area.

Cost-of-living allowance area means a geographic area for which OPM has authorized a COLA. COLA areas are listed in §591.207.

Detailed Expenditure Category (DEC) means the lowest level of expenditure shown in tabulated nationwide CES data.

Major Expenditure Group (MEG) means one of the nine major groups into which OPM categorizes expenditures. These categories are food, shelter and utilities, clothing, transportation, household furnishings and supplies, medical, education and communication, recreation, and miscellaneous.

Nonforeign area means one of the areas listed in §591.205.

Office of Personnel Management (OPM) means the Office of Personnel Management.

Official worksite means the official location of an employee's position of record as determined under 5 CFR 531.605.

Position of record means an employee's official position (defined by grade, occupational series, employing agency, law enforcement officer status, and any other condition that determines coverage under a pay schedule (other than official worksite)), as documented on the employee's most recent Notification of Personnel Action (Standard Form 50 or equivalent) and the current position description, excluding any position to which the employee is temporarily detailed. For an employee whose change in official position is followed within 3 workdays by a reduction in force resulting in the employee's separation before he or she is required to report for duty in the new position, the position of record in effect immediately before the position change is deemed to remain the position of record through the date of separation.

Post differential means an allowance OPM establishes under 5 U.S.C. 5941 at a location in a nonforeign area where conditions of environment differ substantially from conditions of environment in the contiguous United States and warrant its payment as a recruitment incentive.

Post differential area means a geographic area for which OPM authorizes a post differential. Post differential areas are listed in §591.231.

Primary Expenditure Group (PEG) means one of approximately 40 expenditure groups into which OPM categorizes expenditures. A PEG is the first level of categorization under the MEG.

Rate of basic pay means the rate of pay fixed by statute for the position held by an individual, including any supplement included as part of basic pay under this subpart by law or regulation (e.g., a special rate supplement under 5 CFR part 530, subpart C), before any deductions and exclusive of additional pay of any other kind, such as overtime pay, night differential, extra pay for work on holidays, or other allowances and differentials. For firefighters covered by 5 U.S.C. 5545b, straight-time pay for regular overtime hours is basic pay, as provided in §550.1305(b) of this chapter.

Washington, DC, area or *DC area* means the District of Columbia; Montgomery County, MD; Prince Georges County, MD; Arlington County, VA; Fairfax County, VA; Prince William County, VA; and the independent cities of Alexandria, Fairfax, Falls Church, Manassas, and Manassas Park, Virginia; and in the context of certain survey items, includes additional geographic locations beyond these jurisdictions.

[67 FR 22340, May 3, 2002, as amended at 69 FR 59762, Oct. 6, 2004; 70 FR 31314, May 31, 2005]

Cost-of-Living Allowances and Post Differentials

§591.202 Why does the Government pay COLAs?

The Government pays COLAs as additional compensation to certain civilian Federal employees in specified nonforeign areas in consideration of higher living costs in the local area compared with living costs in the Washington, DC, area.

§591.203 Why does the Government pay post differentials?

The Government pays post differentials to certain civilian Federal employees in specified nonforeign areas as a recruitment incentive based on conditions of environment in the local area compared with conditions in the continental United States. Post differentials are designed to attract persons from outside the area to work for the Federal Government in the post differential area.

§591.204 Who can receive COLAs and post differentials?

(a) Agencies pay COLAs and post differentials authorized under this subpart to civilian Federal employees whose rates of basic pay are fixed by statute. The following pay plans are covered by this subpart:

(1) General Schedule,

(2) Veterans Health Administration (Department of Veterans Affairs),

(3) Foreign Service (including the Senior Foreign Service),

(4) Postal Service (where applicable under title 39, United States Code),

(5) Administrative law judges paid under 5 U.S.C. 5372,

(6) Senior Executive Service (including the Federal Bureau of Investigation and Drug Enforcement Administration Senior Executive Service),

(7) Senior-level and scientific or professional positions paid under 5 U.S.C. 5376, and

(8) Administrative appeals judges paid under 5 U.S.C. 5372b.

(b) At its sole discretion and consistent with the intent of 5 U.S.C. 5941, an agency may apply this subpart to other positions authorized by specific law.

(c) Agencies pay COLAs to employees covered by paragraphs (a) or (b) of this section and whose official worksite is in a COLA area as defined in §591.207.

(d) Agencies pay post differentials to employees covered by paragraphs (a) or (b) of this section whose official worksite or detail to temporary duty is in a post differential area as defined in §591.231 and who are eligible to receive a post differential under §591.233.

§591.205 Which areas are nonforeign areas?

(a) The nonforeign areas are States, commonwealths, territories, and possessions of the United States outside the 48 contiguous United States and any additional areas the Secretary of State designates as being within the scope of Part II of Executive Order 10000, as amended.

(b) The following areas are nonforeign areas:

(1) State of Alaska;

(2) State of Hawaii;

(3) American Samoa (including the island of Tutuila, the Manua Islands, and all other islands of the Samoa group east of longitude 171 degrees west of Greenwich, together with Swains Island);

(4) Commonwealth of Puerto Rico;

(5) Commonwealth of the Northern Mariana Islands;

(6) Howland, Baker, and Jarvis Islands;

(7) Johnston Atoll;

(8) Kingman Reef;

(9) Midway Atoll;

(10) Navassaa Island;

(11) Palmyra Atoll;

(12) Territory of Guam;

(13) United States Virgin Islands;

(14) Wake Atoll;

(15) Any small guano islands, rocks, or keys that, in pursuance of action taken under the Act of Congress, August 18, 1856, are considered as pertaining to the United States; and

(16) Any other islands outside of the contiguous 48 states to which the U.S. Government reserves claim.

COST-OF-LIVING ALLOWANCES

§ 591.206 How does OPM establish COLA areas?

(a) OPM designates, within nonforeign areas, areas where agencies pay employees a COLA by virtue of living costs that are substantially higher than those in the Washington, DC, area. In establishing the boundaries of COLA areas, OPM considers—

(1) The existence of a well-defined economic community,

(2) The availability of consumer goods and services,

(3) The concentration of Federal employees covered by this subpart, and

(4) Unique circumstances related to a specific location.

(b) If a department or agency wants OPM to consider establishing or revising the definition of a COLA area, the head of the department or agency or his or her designee must submit a request in writing to OPM.

§ 591.207 Which areas are COLA areas?

OPM has established the following COLA areas:

(a) City of Anchorage, AK, and 80-kilometer (50-mile) radius by shortest route using paved roads when available, as measured from the Federal courthouse to the official duty station;

(b) City of Fairbanks, AK, and 80-kilometer (50-mile) radius by shortest route using paved roads when available, as measured from the Federal courthouse to the official duty station;

(c) City of Juneau, AK, and 80-kilometer (50-mile) radius by shortest route using paved roads when available, as measured from the Federal courthouse to the official duty station;

(d) Rest of the State of Alaska;

(e) City and County of Honolulu, HI;

(f) County of Hawaii, HI;

(g) County of Kauai, HI;

(h) County of Maui (including Kalawao County), HI;

(i) Commonwealth of Puerto Rico;

(j) Territory of Guam and Commonwealth of the Northern Mariana Islands; and

(k) U.S. Virgin Islands.

[67 FR 22340, May 3, 2002, as amended at 73 FR 65245, Nov. 3, 2008]

§ 591.208 How does OPM establish COLA rates?

OPM establishes COLA rates based on price differences between the COLA area and the Washington, DC, area, plus an adjustment factor. OPM expresses price differences as indexes.

(a) OPM computes price indexes for various categories of consumer expenditures.

(b) OPM combines the price indexes using Consumer expenditure weights to produce an overall price index for the COLA area.

(c) To combine overall price indexes for COLA areas with multiple survey areas, OPM uses employment weights to combine overall price indexes by survey area for COLA areas. The COLA areas that have multiple survey areas are listed in § 591.215(b).

(d) OPM adds an adjustment factor to the overall price index for the COLA area.

§ 591.209 What is a price index?

(a) The price index is the COLA area price divided by the DC area price and multiplied by 100.

(b) Example:

COLA Area Average Price for Item A = $1.233

DC Area Average Price for Item A = $1.164

Computation:

$1.233/$1.164 = 1.0592783

1.0592783 × 100 = 105.92783.

(c) In the case of the final index, OPM rounds the index to two decimal places.

§ 591.210 What are weights?

(a) A weight is the relative importance or share of a subpart of a group compared with the total for the group. A weight is frequently expressed as a percentage. For example, in a pie chart, each wedge has a percentage that represents its relative importance or the size of the wedge compared with the whole pie.

(b) OPM uses two kinds of weights: Consumer expenditure weights and employment weights.

(1) *Consumer expenditure weights.* The consumer expenditure weight for a category of expenditures (e.g., Food) is the relative importance or share (often expressed as a percentage) of that category in terms of total consumer expenditures. OPM derives consumer expenditure weights from the tabulated results of the Bureau of Labor Statistics (BLS) Consumer Expenditure Survey (CES).

(2) *Employment weights.* The employment weight is the relative employment population of the survey area compared with the employment population of the COLA area as a whole. OPM uses the number of General Schedule employees in the survey area to compute employment weights. OPM uses these employment weights as described in § 591.216(b).

§ 591.211 What are the categories of consumer expenditures?

OPM uses three different types of categories: Major expenditure groups, primary expenditure groups, and detailed expenditure categories.

(a) *Major expenditure groups.* OPM groups expenditures into nine major expenditure groups (MEGs). These categories are food, shelter and utilities, clothing, transportation, household furnishings and supplies, medical, education and communication, recreation, and miscellaneous.

(b) *Primary expenditure groups.* OPM subdivides each MEG into primary expenditure groups (PEGs). There are approximately 40 PEGs.

(c) *Detailed expenditure categories.* OPM further subdivides each PEG into other categories down to the detailed expenditure categories (DECs), which are generally equivalent to the most detailed level of tabulated CES categories. OPM classifies each DEC into one of the PEGs to aggregate DECs with similar demand and cost characteristics into PEGs. Alternatively, OPM may remove the DEC entirely from the list of expenditures. Therefore, the classification of the DECs into PEGs and sub-PEGs does not necessarily follow that used in published CES tables.

§ 591.212 How does OPM select survey items?

(a) OPM selects a sufficient number of items to represent PEGs and reduce overall price index variability. In selecting these items, OPM applies the following guidelines. The item should be—

(1) Relatively important (*i.e.*, represent a DEC with a relatively large weight) within the PEG;

(2) Relatively easy to find in both COLA and DC areas;

(3) Relatively common, *i.e.*, what people typically buy;

(4) Relatively stable over time, e.g., not a fad item; and

(5) Subject to similar supply and demand functions.

(b) To the extent practical, the items OPM surveys in the COLA area must be identical to the items that OPM surveys in the DC area or be of closely similar quality and quantity, with quantity adjustments as necessary. An example of a quantity adjustment is converting prices for 10 and 12 oz. packages to a price per pound.

(c) Within any DEC, OPM may specify items that differ in quality and quantity from other items specified for the same DEC. However, when OPM compares prices for such items between the COLA area and the DC area, OPM compares prices of like products.

§ 591.213 What prices does OPM collect?

(a) OPM surveys the price charged to the consumer at the time of the survey. The price includes any sales, excise, or general business tax passed on to the consumer at the time of sale and any discounts, mark-downs, or "sales" in progress at the time the price was collected.

(b) *Exceptions:* (1) OPM does not collect coupon prices, clearance prices, going-out-of-business prices, or area-wide distress sale prices.

(2) OPM prices automobiles at dealers and obtains the sticker (*i.e.*, non-negotiated) price for the model and specified options. The prices are the manufacturer's suggested retail price (including options), destination charges, additional shipping charges, appropriate dealer-added items or options, dealer mark-up, and taxes.

(3) OPM estimates prices for selected items, such as health insurance and K–12 education, based on employee usage of the item. For example, OPM estimates health insurance prices based on the employee's share of the premium costs and weights reflecting Federal enrollment, as reported in OPM's Central Personnel Data File, in the various plans available to Federal employees in each area.

[67 FR 22340, May 3, 2002, as amended at 69 FR 59762, Oct. 6, 2004]

§ 591.214 How does OPM collect prices?

(a) OPM collects most prices by visiting or calling retail outlets in each survey area and observing or verbally obtaining the item prices.

(b) OPM prices some items by catalog, Internet, or a similar source. Other items, not normally sold within an area, may be priced in a different area. In either case, the price of such items includes any applicable taxes, shipping, and handling charges. When an item is normally sold within an area but is not available at the time of survey, OPM may, on a case-by-case basis, use the price of the item in a neighboring survey or COLA area.

§ 591.215 Where does OPM collect prices in the COLA and DC areas?

(a) *Survey areas.* Each COLA area has one survey area, except Hawaii County, HI, and the U.S. Virgin Islands COLA areas. Hawaii County has two survey areas: the Hilo area and the Kailua Kona/Waimea area. The U.S. Virgin Islands also has two survey areas: the Island of St. Croix and the Islands of St. Thomas and St. John. The Washington, DC, area has three survey areas: the District of Columbia, the Maryland suburbs of the District of Columbia, and the Virginia suburbs of the District of Columbia. OPM collects non-housing data throughout the survey area, and for selected items such as golf, snow skiing, and air travel, OPM collects non-housing data in additional geographic locations. OPM may collect housing data throughout the survey area or in specific housing data collection areas. The following table shows the survey areas:

SURVEY AREAS

COLA and reference areas	Survey areas and geographic coverage
Anchorage	City of Anchorage. [1]
Fairbanks	Fairbanks/North Pole area. [1]
Juneau	Juneau/Mendenhall/Douglas area. [1]
Rest of Alaska	See paragraph (c) of this section.
Honolulu	City and County of Honolulu.
Hawaii County	Hilo area. [1]
	Kailua Kona/Waimea area.
Kauai	Kauai Island.
Maui	Maui Island.
Guam & CNMI	Guam.
Puerto Rico	San Juan/Caguas area. [2]
U.S. Virgin Islands	St. Croix.
	St. Thomas/St. John area. [3]
Washington, DC-DC	District of Columbia. [1]
Washington, DC-MD.	Montgomery County and Prince Georges County. [1]
Washington, DC-VA	Arlington County, Fairfax County, Prince William County, City of Alexandria, City of Fairfax, City of Falls Church, City of Manassas, and City of Manassas Park. [1]

[1] For selected items, such as golf, snow skiing, and air travel, these survey areas may include additional geographic locations beyond these jurisdictions.

[2] OPM may collect housing data in other areas in Puerto Rico that have a significant concentration of Federal employees stationed in those areas.

[3] OPM collects housing data in St. John. OPM also may collect non-housing data from selected outlets in St. John.

(b) *Rest of the State of Alaska COLA area.* OPM may collect survey data onsite, use alternative indicators of relative living costs (e.g., price and cost information published by the University of Alaska), or both. If the use of alternative indicators would result in a

COLA rate reduction, OPM will conduct onsite surveys in one or more locations in the Rest of the State of Alaska COLA area, before making a reduction, to ensure that the reduction is warranted.

(c) *Determining Survey Coverage.* To aid OPM in determining survey coverage, OPM may from time to time conduct surveys of Federal employees in the COLA areas and/or the Washington, DC, area to determine where employees shop and what they spend on certain goods or services and to collect other information related to the price surveys and the calculation of price indexes.

[67 FR 22340, May 3, 2002, as amended at 69 FR 59762, Oct. 6, 2004]

§591.216 How does OPM combine survey data for the DC area and for COLA areas with multiple survey areas?

(a) *Washington, DC, area.* For each survey item except shelter, OPM averages separately the prices collected in each of the DC survey areas identified in §591.215(a) and then averages these average prices together using equal weights to compute an overall average by item for the DC area.

(b) *COLA areas with multiple survey areas.* OPM computes weighted average indexes at the item, PEG, MEG, and/or overall level by using the corresponding indexes and Federal employment weights from each survey area within the COLA area.

[67 FR 22340, May 3, 2002, as amended at 69 FR 59763, Oct. 6, 2004]

§591.217 In which outlets does OPM collect prices?

OPM collects prices in popular outlets in each survey area. OPM selects these outlets based on their proximity to the housing data collection areas, accessibility by road, physical size, advertising, and other characteristics that reflect sales volume. To the extent practical, OPM prices like items in the same types of outlets in the COLA areas and the Washington, DC, area. As warranted, OPM also may conduct point-of-purchase surveys and select outlets based on the results of those surveys.

§591.218 How does OPM compute price indexes?

Except for shelter and energy utilities, OPM averages by item the prices collected in each survey area. For the Washington, DC, area, OPM computes a simple average for each item based on the average prices from each DC survey area. On an item-by-item basis, OPM divides the COLA survey area average price by the DC average price and produces a price index.

§591.219 How does OPM compute shelter price indexes?

(a) In addition to rental and rental equivalence prices and/or estimates, OPM obtains for each unit surveyed information about the important characteristics of the unit, such as size, number of bathrooms, and other amenities that reflect the quality of the unit.

(b) OPM then uses these characteristics and rental prices and/or estimates in hedonic regressions (a type of multiple regression) to compute for each COLA survey area the price index for rental and/or rental equivalent units of comparable quality and size between the COLA survey area and the Washington, DC, area.

[67 FR 22340, May 3, 2002, as amended at 69 FR 59763, Oct. 6, 2004]

§591.220 How does OPM calculate energy utility cost indexes?

(a) OPM calculates energy utility cost indexes based on the relative cost of maintaining a standard size dwelling in each area at a given ambient temperature and the cost of other energy uses. Although the dwelling size may vary from one COLA survey area to another, OPM compares the utility cost for the same size dwelling in the COLA survey area and the Washington, DC, area.

(b) OPM applies the following six-step process to compute a cost index(es) for heating and cooling a standard home to a given ambient temperature and to combine the cost index(es) by energy type (e.g., electricity and natural gas) with cost indexes for other energy uses.

(1) *Step 1.* OPM obtains technical information about the requirements by major energy type for heating and cooling a standard size dwelling, built

according to current local building practices and codes in each area, given local climatic conditions (e.g., seasonal temperature and humidity). OPM also obtains similar information for use of energy types in other household operations (e.g., hot water, cooking, cleaning, recreation).

(2) *Step 2.* OPM obtains from the shelter survey, a survey of Federal employees, or other appropriate sources, information on dwelling size and the types and prevalence of heating and cooling equipment and energy types (e.g., electricity, gas, and oil) in each area.

(3) *Step 3.* OPM computes estimates of total home energy requirements by energy type attributable to heating and cooling plus all other household energy uses for the COLA survey area and the Washington, DC, area.

(4) *Step 4.* OPM surveys utility prices for each major energy type appropriate to the area.

(5) *Step 5.* OPM combines the above data to produce for each COLA survey area the cost of maintaining the standard size dwelling at a given ambient temperature and the cost of other household energy uses.

(6) *Step 6.* OPM compares the COLA survey area cost with the DC area cost to produce a price index.

§ 591.221 How does OPM compute the consumer expenditure weights it uses to combine price indexes?

OPM uses the following ten-step process to compute consumer expenditure weights:

(a) *Step 1.* OPM obtains the latest BLS tabulated CES data nationwide and for the Washington, DC, area.

(b) *Step 2.* In both the nationwide and DC area tabulated data, OPM replaces the homeowners' expenditures for shelter with estimated rental values of owned homes that are available elsewhere in tabulated CES data. Note: These replacements are consistent with the rental equivalence approach described in § 591.219.

(c) *Step 3.* OPM selects the central income groups in the nationwide CES tabulation.

(d) *Step 4.* OPM calculates the expenditure shares (*i.e.*, percentages) for each central income group by dividing each of its DEC expenditures by total expenditures for the income group. OPM also calculates expenditure shares for total nationwide expenditures by dividing each nationwide DEC expenditure by total nationwide expenditures.

(e) *Step 5.* OPM computes a democratic distribution of expenditure shares by averaging the central income groups' shares at each DEC and higher level of aggregation.

(f) *Step 6.* OPM computes a set of ratios by dividing each expenditure share of the nationwide democratic distribution by the corresponding expenditure share of the total national distribution.

(g) *Step 7.* OPM computes estimated expenditures for Washington DC for each DC DEC and higher level of aggregation that BLS reported by multiplying the reported expenditure by the corresponding ratio derived in Step 6.

(h) *Step 8.* For each DC DEC and higher level of aggregation that BLS did not report, OPM computes expenditures for DC by distributing the DC expenditure calculated in step 7 using the distribution of expenditure shares derived in step 5.

(i) *Step 9.* As described in § 591.211(c), OPM classifies each DEC and aggregate into PEGs.

(j) *Step 10.* OPM computes expenditure weights by dividing each DEC or aggregate by the total expenditure derived from the DC expenditure computed in step 8. Therefore, the sum of the MEGs, PEGs, and DECs, will separately total 100, *i.e.*, so that all consumer expenditures in the original tabulation are accounted for.

§ 591.222 How does OPM use the expenditure weights to combine price indexes?

OPM uses a three-step process to combine price indexes.

(a) *Step 1.* For each DEC represented by one or more items for which OPM could make valid price comparisons (e.g., OPM was able to collect representative prices in both the COLA and DC areas), OPM computes the unweighted geometric average (the *nth* root of the product of *n* numbers) of the price index(es) of all item(s) representing the DEC.

(b) *Step 2.* OPM multiplies the price index for each DEC by its expenditure weight, sums the cross products, and divides by the sum of the weights used in the calculation. This produces a price index for the level of aggregation (e.g., PEG or sub-PEG) in which the DEC is categorized.

(c) *Step 3.* OPM repeats the process described in Step 2 at each level of aggregation within the PEG to produce a price index for the PEG, at the PEG level to produce an index for the MEG, and at the MEG level to produce the overall price index for the COLA area.

[67 FR 22340, May 3, 2002, as amended at 69 FR 59763, Oct. 6, 2004]

§591.223 When does OPM conduct COLA surveys?

(a) OPM conducts a survey in each COLA area once every 3 years on a rotational basis and surveys the Washington, DC, area concurrently with each COLA area survey. The order of the COLA area surveys is as follows:

(1) *Year 1.* All COLA areas in the Commonwealth of Puerto Rico and the U.S. Virgin Islands.

(2) *Year 2.* All COLA areas in the State of Alaska, except as provided in paragraph (b)(2) of this section.

(3) *Year 3.* All COLA areas in the State of Hawaii and the Territory of Guam and CNMI.

(b) *Exceptions:*

(1) Nothing in this subpart precludes OPM from conducting interim surveys or implementing some other change in response to conditions caused by a natural disaster or similar emergency, provided OPM publishes a notice or rule in the FEDERAL REGISTER explaining the change and the reason(s) for it.

(2) As provided in §591.215(c), OPM does not conduct surveys in the Rest of the State of Alaska COLA area unless COLA rate reductions appear warranted.

§591.224 How does OPM adjust price indexes between surveys?

(a) OPM adjusts price indexes between the triennial surveys in each COLA area that is not surveyed in that year. To do this, OPM uses the annual or biennial change in the Consumer Price Index (CPI) for the COLA area relative to the annual or biennial change in the CPI for the Washington, DC, area. OPM uses the annual change for those areas surveyed the preceding year. OPM uses the biennial change for those areas surveyed 2 years before.

(b) Paragraph (a) of this section applies beginning with the effective date of the results of the 2005 survey conducted in Puerto Rico and the U.S. Virgin Islands.

(c) Based on additional housing data that may be collected before the 2005 survey conducted in Puerto Rico and the U.S. Virgin Islands, OPM will adjust as warranted the price indexes and COLA rates for Puerto Rico, the U.S. Virgin Islands, and the COLA areas in the State of Alaska. OPM will implement any such adjustments on a one-time basis on the effective date of the results of the 2004 surveys conducted in Hawaii and Guam/CNMI, and subject to §591.228. OPM will publish such adjustments as provided in §591.229.

[67 FR 22340, May 3, 2002, as amended at 69 FR 59763, Oct. 6, 2004]

§591.225 Which CPIs does OPM use?

OPM uses the following CPIs:

(a) For the Washington, DC, area—the BLS Consumer Price Index, All Urban Consumers (CPI-U);

(b) For all COLA areas in the State of Alaska—the BLS CPI-U for Anchorage, AK;

(c) For all COLA areas in the State of Hawaii and for Guam and the CNMI—the BLS CPI-U for Honolulu, HI; and

(d) For Puerto Rico and the U.S. Virgin Islands—the Puerto Rico CPI as produced by the Puerto Rico Department of Work and Human Resources.

§591.226 How does OPM apply the CPIs?

(a) OPM uses a three-step process to adjust price indexes by relative annual or biennial changes in the CPIs. For steps 1 and 2, OPM computes the annual change by dividing the CPI from 1 year after the survey by the CPI from the time of the survey. OPM computes the biennial change by dividing the CPI from 2 years after the survey by the CPI from the time of the survey.

(1) *Step 1.* OPM computes the annual or biennial CPI change for the COLA area.

(2) *Step 2.* OPM computes the annual or biennial CPI change for the DC area.

(3) *Step 3.* OPM multiplies the COLA area price index from the last survey by the COLA area CPI change computed in step 1 divided by the DC area CPI change computed in step 2. The adjusted price index is rounded to the second decimal place.

(b) *Example:*

	2008	2009
COLA Area CPI	172.2	174.7
DC Area CPI	159.7	161.9
COLA Area Survey Index	117.33	([1])
COLA Area CPI Adjusted Index	([2])	117.42

[1] No survey.
[2] N/A

Computation:
117.33 × (174.7/172.2)/(161.9/159.7) = 117.4159, which would round to 117.42.

§ 591.227 What adjustment factors does OPM add to the price indexes?

OPM adds to the price index an adjustment factor that reflects differences in need, access to and availability of goods and services, and quality of life in the COLA area relative to the DC area. The following table shows the adjustment factor for each area:

COLA area	Amount
Anchorage, AK	7.0
Fairbanks, AK	9.0
Juneau, AK	9.0
Rest of the State of Alaska	9.0
City and County of Honolulu, HI	5.0
Hawaii County, HI	7.0
Kauai County, HI	7.0
Maui County, HI	7.0
Guam and CNMI	9.0
Commonwealth of Puerto Rico	7.0
U.S. Virgin Islands	9.0

[1] Amount added to the price index.

§ 591.228 How does OPM convert the price index plus adjustment factor to a COLA rate?

(a) OPM converts the price index plus the adjustment factor to a COLA rate as shown in the following table:

Price index plus adjustment factor	COLA rate subject to paragraph (b) of this section
Equal to or greater than 124.50.	25 percent.
Equal to or greater than 102.00 but less than 124.50.	Price index plus the adjustment factor, minus 100, expressed to the nearest whole percent.
Less than 102.00	0 percent.

(b) This section is applicable on an area-by-area basis beginning with the effective date of the results of the first survey conducted in each area.

(c) OPM may reduce the COLA rate in any area by no more than 1 percentage point in any 12-month period. Any reduction in the COLA rate for any COLA area cannot be effective until the effective date of the first survey conducted in Hawaii and Guam and CNMI under these regulations.

§ 591.229 How does OPM inform agencies and employees of COLA rate changes?

OPM publishes COLA area survey summary reports, MEG and PEG indexes, and COLA rates in the FEDERAL REGISTER. OPM makes survey data and other information available to the public to the extent authorized by the Freedom of Information Act and the Privacy Act.

POST DIFFERENTIALS

§ 591.230 When does OPM establish post differential areas?

(a) OPM establishes post differential areas in response to agency requests when—

(1) Conditions of environment within the post differential area differ substantially from conditions of environment in the continental United States, and

(2) The major Federal employers within the area believe payment of a post differential is warranted as a recruitment incentive to attract candidates from outside the post differential area to work for the Government in the post differential area.

(b) If a department or agency wants OPM to consider establishing or revising the definition of a post differential area, the head of the department or agency or his or her designee must submit a request in writing to OPM.

§ 591.231 Which areas are post differential areas?

OPM has established the following post differential areas:

(a) American Samoa as defined in § 591.205,

(b) Territory of Guam,

(c) Commonwealth of the Northern Mariana Islands,

(d) Johnston Atoll (including Sand Island),

(e) Midway Atoll, and

(f) Wake Atoll.

§591.232 How does OPM establish and review post differentials?

(a) OPM establishes a post differential by rulemaking if Government agencies require it for recruitment purposes and if one or more of the following conditions exist:

(1) Extraordinarily difficult living conditions,

(2) Excessive physical hardship, and/or

(3) Notably unhealthful conditions.

(b) OPM periodically reviews with Federal agencies whether conditions of environment have changed in the post differential areas and whether payment of the post differential continues to be warranted as a recruitment incentive.

§591.233 Who can receive a post differential?

An employee must meet all of the following conditions to be eligible to receive a post differential:

(a) The employee must be a citizen or national of the United States,

(b) The employee's official worksite or detail to temporary duty must be in the post differential area, and

(c) Immediately prior to being assigned to duty in the post differential area, the employee must have maintained his or her actual place(s) of residence outside the post differential area for an appropriate period of time (generally at least 1 year or more), except as provided in §591.234.

§591.234 Under what circumstances may people recruited locally receive a post differential?

(a) Current residents of the area qualify for a post differential if they were originally recruited from outside the differential area and have been in substantially continuous employment by the United States or by U.S. firms, interests, or organizations.

(b) Examples of persons recruited locally but eligible to receive a post differential include, but are not limited to—

(1) Those who were originally recruited from outside the area and have been in substantially continuous employment by other Federal agencies, contractors of Federal agencies, or international organizations in which the U.S. Government participates and whose conditions of employment provide for their return transportation to places outside the post differential area,

(2) Those who are temporarily present in the post differential area for travel or formal study at the time they are hired and have maintained actual places of residence outside the area for an appropriate period of time, and

(3) Those who are discharged from U.S. military service in the differential area to accept employment with a Federal agency and have maintained actual places of residence outside the differential area for an appropriate period of time.

PROGRAM ADMINISTRATION

§591.235 When do COLA and post differential payments begin?

(a) Agencies begin paying an employee a COLA or post differential on the effective date of the change in the employee's official worksite to an official worksite within the COLA or post differential area or, in the case of local recruitment, on the effective date of the appointment.

(b) For an employee detailed to temporary duty in a post differential area and who is otherwise eligible for a post differential, agencies must begin paying a post differential after 42 consecutive calendar days of temporary duty in the post differential area.

§591.236 When do COLA and post differential payments end?

Subject to §591.237(a), agencies stop paying an employee a COLA or post differential on—

(a) Separation,

(b) The effective date of assignment or transfer to a new official worksite outside the COLA or post differential area, or

(c) In the case of an employee on detail to temporary duty in a post differential area, the ending date of the detail.

§591.237 Under what circumstances may employees on leave or travel receive a COLA and/or post differential?

(a) An employee on leave or travel may receive a COLA or post differential only if the agency anticipates that the employee will return to duty in the area. *Exceptions:* If the employee does not return to duty in the area, the agency may still pay a COLA and/or a post differential for the period of leave or travel, subject to paragraph (b) of this section, if the agency determines that—

(1) It is in the public interest not to return the employee to the official worksite, or

(2) The employee will not return because of compelling personal reasons or circumstances over which the employee has no control.

(b) *Post differentials.* Agencies may pay a post differential to an employee only during the employee's first 42 consecutive calendar days of absence from the post differential area.

§591.238 How do agencies pay COLAs and post differentials?

(a) Agencies pay COLAs and post differentials as a percentage of an employee's hourly rate of basic pay, including a retained rate of pay under 5 U.S.C. 3594(c) or 5363, for those hours during which the employee receives basic pay. This includes all periods of paid leave, detail, or travel status outside the COLA or post differential area.

(b) Agencies pay employees eligible for both a COLA and a post differential the full amount of the COLA, plus so much of the post differential as will not cause the combined total of the COLA and post differential to exceed 25 percent of the hourly rate of basic pay.

§591.239 How do agencies treat COLAs and post differentials for the purpose of overtime pay and other entitlements?

(a) Agencies include COLAs in the employee's straight time rate of pay and include COLAs and post differentials in an employee's regular rate of pay for computing overtime pay entitlements for nonexempt employees under the Fair Labor Standards Act of 1938, as amended.

(b) Agencies may not include a COLA or post differential as part of an employee's rate of basic pay for the purpose of computing entitlements to overtime pay, retirement, life insurance, or any other additional pay, COLA, or post differential under title 5, United States Code.

(c) Payment of a COLA or post differential is not an equivalent increase in pay within the meaning of 5 U.S.C. 5335.

§591.240 How are agency and employee representatives involved in the administration of the COLA and post differential programs?

(a) OPM may establish a COLA Advisory Committee in each COLA survey area. The committees are composed of agency and employee representatives from the COLA survey area and one or more representatives from OPM.

(b) To the extent practical, the COLA Advisory Committees coordinate and work with the Survey Implementation Committee established pursuant to *Caraballo, et al.* v. *United States,* No. 1997–0027 (D.V.I).

§591.241 What are the key activities of the COLA Advisory Committees?

(a) The COLA Advisory Committees may—

(1) Advise and assist OPM in planning living-cost surveys;

(2) Provide or arrange for observers for data collection during living-cost surveys;

(3) Advise and assist OPM in the review of survey data;

(4) Advise OPM on its administration of the COLA program, including survey methodology; and

(5) Assist OPM in disseminating information to affected employees about the living-cost surveys and the COLA program.

(b) The committees also may advise OPM on special situations or conditions, such as hurricanes and earthquakes, as they relate to OPM's authority under §591.223(b) to conduct interim surveys or implement some other change in response to conditions caused by a natural disaster or similar emergency.

§ 591.242 What is the tenure of a COLA Advisory Committee?

OPM may establish a COLA Advisory Committee in each area prior to each living-cost survey conducted in that area. OPM will appoint committee members for 3-year renewable terms. To the extent practical, the committee will continue to exist between surveys, but OPM may periodically review with the committee whether there is a continuing need for the committee.

§ 591.243 How many members are on each COLA Advisory Committee?

A COLA Advisory Committee has up to 12 members composed of OPM representatives and other agency and employee representatives, unless OPM determines that the committee should be larger. In determining the number of committee members, OPM considers the amount of work the committee is likely to be requested to do (based on the size and complexity of the local living-cost survey) and the availability of employee and agency representatives to participate as committee members.

§ 591.244 How does OPM select COLA Advisory Committee members?

(a) In establishing a COLA Advisory Committee, OPM invites local agencies and employee organizations to nominate committee members. OPM also invites COLA Defense Corporations and the local Federal Executive Board or Federal Executive Association each to nominate committee members. Subject to § 591.243, OPM selects committee members from these nominations in a manner designed to achieve a balanced representation that is reflective of agencies and employee organizations in the area. In consultation with the committee, OPM may select additional nominees to serve as alternates to the primary committee members. OPM designates not more than two OPM representatives to serve on each committee.

(b) Each Executive agency, as defined in 5 U.S.C. 105, must cooperate and release appointed employees for committee proceedings and activities unless the agency can demonstrate that exceptional circumstances directly related to accomplishing the mission of the employee's work unit require his or her presence on the job. Executive agency employees serving as committee members are considered to be on official assignment to an interagency function, rather than on leave, and are eligible to receive reimbursement for authorized travel expenses from their respective agencies.

APPENDIX A TO SUBPART B OF PART 591—PLACES AND RATES AT WHICH ALLOWANCES ARE PAID

This appendix lists the places approved for a cost-of-living allowance and shows the authorized allowance rate for each area. The allowance rate shown is paid as a percentage of an employee's rate of basic pay. The rates are subject to change based on the results of future surveys.

Geographic coverage	Allowance rate (percent)
State of Alaska:	
City of Anchorage and 80-kilometer (50-mile) radius by road	23
City of Fairbanks and 80-kilometer (50-mile) radius by road	23
City of Juneau and 80-kilometer (50-mile) radius by road	23
Rest of the State	25
State of Hawaii:	
City and County of Honolulu	25
Hawaii County, Hawaii	18
County of Kauai	25
County of Maui and County of Kalawao	25
Territory of Guam and Commonwealth of the Northern Mariana Islands	25
Commonwealth of Puerto Rico	14
U.S. Virgin Islands	25

[74 FR 7777, Feb. 20, 2009]

APPENDIX B TO SUBPART B OF PART 591—PLACES AND RATES AT WHICH DIFFERENTIALS ARE PAID

This appendix lists the places where a post differential has been approved and shows the differential rate to be paid to eligible employees. The differential percentage rate shown is paid as a percentage of an employee's rate of basic pay.

Geographic coverage	Percentage differential rate
American Samoa (including the island of Tutuila, the Manua Islands, and all other islands of the Samoa group east of longitude 171° west of Greenwich, together with Swains Island)	25.0
Johnston Atoll	25.0
Midway Atoll	25.0
Territory of Guam and Commonwealth of the Northern Mariana Islands	20.0
Wake Atoll	25.0

Subpart C—Allowance Based on Duty at Remote Worksites

AUTHORITY: 5 U.S.C. 5942; sec. 8, E.O. 11609, 3 CFR 1971–1975 Comp., p. 591; 5 U.S.C. 1104, Pub. L. 95–454, 92 Stat. 1120 and Sec. 3(5) of Pub. L. 95–454; 92 Stat. 1120.

SOURCE: 44 FR 55134, Sept. 25, 1979, unless otherwise noted.

§ 591.301 Purpose.

This subpart prescribes the regulations required by section 5942 of title 5, United States Code, for the payment of an allowance based on duty at remote worksites.

§ 591.302 Coverage.

(a) *Agencies.* This subpart applies to executive departments as defined in section 101 of title 5, United States Code, and to independent establishments as defined in section 104 of title 5, United States Code, but does not apply to Government corporations as defined in section 103 of title 5, United States Code.

(b) *Employee.* This subpart applies to each employee assigned to a permanent duty station at or within a designated remote duty post, except an employee who is a permanent or temporary resident at the remote duty post, and except foreign nationals employed at remote duty posts in foreign countries.

§ 591.303 Responsibilities of agencies and the Office of Personnel Management.

(a) Each agency is responsible for:

(1) Establishing and subsequently adjusting, in accordance with the provisions of this subpart, an allowance for each remote duty post at which the agency has employees and which meets the criteria in paragraph (a)(1) of § 591.304, as restricted by paragraph (b) of § 591.304;

(2) Advising the Office of Personnel Management of each establishment or adjustment of an allowance under paragraph (a)(1) of this section, and of the basis for such establishment or adjustment;

(3) Submitting a recommendation to the Office of Personnel Management to establish or adjust an allowance for each remote duty post at which the agency has employees and which meets the criteria in paragraph (a)(2) or (a)(3) or paragraph (c) of § 591.304; and

(4) Advising the Office of Personnel Management in a timely manner of any changes in a duty post or commuting conditions or other factors that may affect an allowance that has been authorized by the Office of Personnel Management under paragraph (b) of this section.

(b) The Office of Personnel Management is responsible for:

(1) Establishing and subsequently adjusting, in accordance with the provisions of this subpart, an allowance for each remote duty post which does not meet the criteria in paragraph (a)(1) of § 591.304, but does meet the criteria in paragraph (a)(2) or (a)(3) or paragraph (c) of § 591.304;

(2) Reviewing each establishment or adjustment of an allowance by an agency under paragraph (a)(1) of this section to determine if such establishment or adjustment is in accordance with the provisions of this subpart; and

(3) Directing the termination or adjustment of any allowance determined by the Office to be not in accordance with the provisions of this subpart, which termination or adjustment shall be implemented by the agency without delay.

(c) Each allowance which has been authorized by the Office of Personnel Management or the Civil Service Commission on or before February 1, 1979, and which is authorized for a remote duty post which meets the criteria in paragraph (a)(1) of § 591.304, shall be subject to further adjustment by the agency under paragraph (a)(1) of this section as if such allowance had been initially authorized by the agency under that paragraph.

§ 591.304 Criteria for determining remoteness.

(a) Except as provided by paragraphs (b) and (c) of this section, a duty post shall be determined to be a remote duty post for basic allowance eligibility purposes when:

(1) Normal ground transportation (e.g., automobile, train, bus) is available on a daily basis and the duty post is 80 kilometers (50 miles), or more, one way from the nearest established community or suitable place of residence.

Distance shall be computed in road or rail kilometers (miles) over the most direct route traveled from the center of the city, or other appropriate point for large cities or areas; or

(2) Daily commuting is impractical because the location of the duty post and available transportation are such that agency management requires employees to remain at the duty post for their workweek as a normal and continuing part of the conditions of employment; or

(3) Transportation may be accomplished only by boat, aircraft, or unusual conveyance, or under extraordinary conditions, and the distance, time, and commuting conditions result in expense, inconvenience, or hardship significantly greater than that encountered in metropolitan area commuting. A determination may only be made on an individual location basis.

(b) Except when the criteria in paragraph (a)(2) or (3) of this section are met, the criteria in paragraph (a)(1) of this section are not met:

(1) When the duty post is within the boundary of a metropolitan area, a developed urban area, or community of sufficient size to provide adequate consumer facilities; and

(2) When the duty post is within 80 kilometers (50 miles) of the center of, or other appropriate point for large cities or areas, a metropolitan area, a developed urban area, or community of sufficient size to provide adequate consumer facilities. (This generally excludes a post of duty within 80 kilometers (50 miles) of any city of 5,000 or more population.)

(c) A determination of remoteness for a duty post outside the 50 United States will be made on an individual location basis, taking into consideration the distance, time, and commuting conditions, and the extent to which these factors result in significant expense, inconvenience, or hardship.

[44 FR 55134, Sept. 25, 1979, as amended at 58 FR 32278, June 9, 1993]

§ 591.305 Allowance rates.

(a) *General.* An allowance rate may not exceed $10 a day. An allowance rate shall be established for each post of duty determined to be remote under § 591.304, and shall be terminated or adjusted as warranted. In determining the amount of the allowance rate, the following shall be considered:

(1) Transportation expenses incurred in commuting to the remote post of duty as compared to transportation expenses (including cost of public transportation service) representative of those incurred in metropolitan areas within the United States or overseas as appropriate as periodically determined by the Office of Personnel Management.

(2) Expenses incurred for lodging, meals, other services, and miscellaneous expenses when it is not feasible for an employee to commute daily as at duty posts determined under § 591.304(a)(2).

(3) Inconvenience or hardship associated with commuting to the remote duty post taking into account such factors as travel time, road conditions and terrain, type and quality of vehicle, and climate conditions, and conditions that exist at those duty posts determined by the Office of Personnel Management to meet the criteria in § 591.304(a)(2).

(4) Operational or workload demands, weather conditions, or other situations which require an employee to report to or remain at this post of duty substantially beyond his or her normal arrival or departure time with respect to those duty posts meeting the criteria in § 591.304(a)(2).

(b) *Authorized allowance rates.* Each authorized allowance rate for each duty post may consist of up to three parts, separately stated as appropriate, and the authorized allowance rate shall be paid as provided in § 591.306, but no employee may be paid more than $10 a day. The parts which make up the authorized allowance rate are:

(1) *Transportation allowance*—(i) *Commuting by private motor vehicle.* A transportation allowance schedule showing the daily transportation expense rate to be paid under the distances and conditions described, when commuting by private motor vehicle is set out as appendix A to this subpart and is incorporated in and made part of this section.

(ii) *Travel by commercial or Government-provided transportation.* The transportation allowance shall be limited to the cost of the service less normal cost for public transportation service in metropolitan areas.

(2) *Inconvenience or hardship allowance.* An allowance rate to compensate for hardship or inconvenience may not be considered unless the travel time normally exceeds one hour one way between the closest established community or suitable place or residence and the remote duty post. An allowance schedule covering land travel by motor vehicle, showing the daily rates to be paid under the time factors and conditions described, for inconvenience or hardship combined, is set out as appendix B to this subpart and is incorporated in and made part of this section.

(3) *Other commuting situations.* Notwithstanding paragraphs (b)(1) and (b)(2) of this section, when commuting is by boat, aircraft or an unusual conveyance, or under extraordinary conditions by motor vehicle, or involving factors or conditions unique to the duty post, the Office of Personnel Management shall establish the allowance based on the facts and circumstances of that individual remote duty post.

(4) *Miscellaneous.* When daily commuting is impractical as determined under §591.304(a)(2):

(i) The Office of Personnel Management may authorize a miscellaneous allowance, the amount to depend on such factors as miscellaneous expenses, living conditions that exist at the duty post, or inconvenience or hardship that may be associated with this type of employment environment. When employees are required to pay a fee for lodging, meals, or other services at the remote duty post, the miscellaneous allowance shall at least equal the amount charged for the use of facilities and services.

(ii) On those days when operational or workload demands, weather conditions, or other situations result in employees reporting to or remaining at the remote duty post substantially beyond normal arrival or departure time, the maximum daily allowance rate of $10 shall be paid.

§591.306 Employee eligibility for an allowance.

(a) An authorized allowance rate shall be paid to each employee with a permanent duty station at or within a remote post of duty approved under §591.304, regardless of type of appointment or work schedule, only (1) when the employee travels the prescribed minimum distance and time, or is subject to prescribed minimum inconvenience or hardship factors, while commuting from the nearest established community or suitable place of residence and the remote duty post, or (2) the employee remains at the worksite at the direction of management because daily commuting is impractical.

(b) An employee shall be paid an authorized allowance rate for those days on which he or she incurs unusual expense in commuting to a remote post of duty or for those days on which he or she is subject to extraordinary inconvenience or hardship during the commuting.

(c) An employee who resides permanently, or temporarily for his or her own convenience at a remote duty post is not eligible for an authorized allowance rate during his or her period of residence.

§591.307 Payment of allowance rate.

(a) An authorized allowance rate is earned on a daily basis; however, where appropriate for administrative convenience, the rate may be averaged taking into consideration the number of non-commuting days over a period of time, and paid for each workday, excluding days in a nonpay status and period of extended absence.

(b) The transportation allowance is paid only when expense is incurred and at the lowest rate consistent with available transportation.

(c) The inconvenience or hardship allowance is paid regardless of eligibility for the transportation expense part of the allowance rate when the employee is otherwise eligible.

(d) Except as provided under §591.305(b)(4)(ii), when the necessity for remaining at the post of duty for the workweek is the basis for the allowance under §591.304(a)(2), the allowance rate is paid for each full day, or prorated for each part of a day, that the employee remains at the duty post.

(e) The transportation allowance prescribed by paragraph (b)(1)(i) of § 591.305, or other allowance as may be prescribed for commuting by private motor vehicle, may not be paid unless the officially approved work schedule of the employee precludes use of the transportation services that may be available at lower cost.

(f) An employee, who normally commutes on a daily basis, will not be disqualified from receiving an authorized allowance when he or she is officially required to remain overnight at the remote duty post, for one or more days on a temporary basis, because of the schedule of operations or the nature of assigned work.

(g) When a remote duty post is determined by the Office of Personnel Management under paragraph (a)(3) or (c) of § 591.304 as being basically eligible for an allowance, the Office of Personnel Management will determine the basis for payment of the allowance rate taking into consideration the facts and circumstances associated with commuting to the remote duty post.

§ 591.308 Relationship to additional pay payable under other statutes.

An allowance authorized under this subpart is in addition to any additional pay or allowances payable under other statutes. It shall not be considered part of the employee's rate of basic pay in computing additional pay or allowances payable under other statutes.

§ 591.309 Effective date for payment of allowances.

When an allowance is authorized for a remote duty post, the authorization shall specify the effective date that an agency shall begin paying the allowance to its employees, except that a date earlier than January 8, 1971, may not be specified.

§ 591.310 Effect of regulations in this subpart on allowances established under previous statutes.

Regulations in this subpart do not require a reduction in the allowance rates authorized under previous statutes unless an adjustment is determined to be warranted on the basis of a change in facts and circumstances on which that previous allowance was established.

Appendix A to Subpart C of Part 591—Daily Transportation Allowance Schedule, Commuting Over Land by Private Motor Vehicle to Remote Duty Posts

Schedule I—Effective January 8, 1971, Through July 12, 1975

Round trip distance in excess of 50 miles	Degree A commuting conditions	Degree B commuting conditions	Degree C commuting conditions
up to 9 miles	$0.20	$0.22	$0.24
10 to 19	.70	.77	.84
20 to 29	1.20	1.32	1.44
30 to 39	1.70	1.87	2.04
40 to 49	2.20	2.42	2.64
50 to 59	2.70	2.97	3.24
60 to 69	3.20	3.52	3.84
70 to 79	3.70	4.07	4.44
80 to 89	4.20	4.62	5.04
90 to 99	4.70	5.17	5.64
100 to 109	5.20	5.72	6.24
110 to 119	5.70	6.27	6.84
120 to 129	6.20	6.82	7.44
130 to 139	6.70	7.37	8.04
140 to 149	7.20	7.92	8.64
150 to 159	7.70	8.47	9.24
160 to 169	8.20	9.02	9.84
170 and over	8.70	9.57	[1] 10.00

[1] See footnote at end of Schedule II.

Schedule II—Effective on or After July 13, 1975

Round trip distance in excess of 50 miles	Degree A commuting conditions	Degree B commuting conditions	Degree C commuting conditions
up to 9 miles	$0.30	$0.32	$0.34
10 to 19	1.05	1.12	1.19
20 to 29	1.80	1.92	2.04
30 to 39	2.55	2.72	2.89
40 to 49	3.30	3.52	3.74
50 to 59	4.13	4.32	4.68
60 to 69	4.80	5.12	5.44
70 to 79	5.55	5.92	6.29
80 to 89	6.30	6.72	7.14
90 to 99	7.05	7.52	7.99
100 to 109	7.80	8.32	8.84
110 to 119	8.55	9.12	9.69
120 to 129	9.30	9.92	[1] 10.00
130 to 139	[1] 10.00	[1] 10.00	[1] 10.00
140 to 149	[1] 10.00	[1] 10.00	[1] 10.00
150 to 159	[1] 10.00	[1] 10.00	[1] 10.00
160 to 169	[1] 10.00	[1] 10.00	[1] 10.00
170 and over	[1] 10.00	[1] 10.00	[1] 10.00

[1] Under the statute, $10 a day is the maximum allowance.

SCHEDULE III—EFFECTIVE ON OR AFTER DECEMBER 28, 1980

Round-trip distance in excess of 80 kilometers (50 miles)	Degree A commuting conditions	Degree B commuting conditions	Degree C commuting conditions
Up to 15 km (up to 9 mi)	$0.40	$0.42	$0.44
16 to 31 km (10 to 19 mi)	1.40	1.47	1.54
32 to 47 km (20 to 29 mi)	2.40	2.52	2.64
48 to 63 km (30 to 39 mi)	3.40	3.57	3.74
64 to 79 km (40 to 49 mi)	4.40	4.62	4.84
80 to 95 km (50 to 59 mi)	5.40	5.67	5.94
96 to 111 km (60 to 69 mi)	6.40	6.72	7.04
112 to 127 km (70 to 79 mi)	7.40	7.77	8.14
128 to 144 km (80 to 89 mi)	8.40	8.82	9.24
145 to 160 km (90 to 99 mi)	9.40	9.87	10.00
161 to 176 km (100 to 109 mi)	10.00	10.00	10.00
177 to 192 km (110 to 119 mi)	10.00	10.00	10.00
193 to 208 km (120 to 129 mi)	10.00	10.00	10.00
209 to 224 km (130 to 139 mi)	10.00	10.00	10.00
225 to 240 km (140 to 149 mi)	10.00	10.00	10.00
241 to 256 km (150 to 159 mi)	10.00	10.00	10.00
257 to 272 km (160 to 169 mi)	10.00	10.00	10.00
273 km and over (170 mi and over)	10.00	10.00	10.00

Under the statute, $10 a day is the maximum allowance.

Degree A Commuting Conditions

Good paved roads; climatic conditions cause intermittent driving difficulty.

Degree B Commuting Conditions

Roads typically fair but may be good for part of distance or may be unpaved for short distances; climatic conditions during part of a season, in relation to terrain, contribute to additional cost.

Degree C Commuting Conditions

Fair to poor roads; unpaved for part of distance, or travel over range; hilly or mountainous terrain; climatic conditions during most of a season contribute to additional cost.

[44 FR 55134, Sept. 25, 1979, as amended at 45 FR 76087, Nov. 18, 1980; 58 FR 32278, June 9, 1993]

APPENDIX B TO SUBPART C OF PART 591—DAILY INCONVENIENCE OR HARDSHIP ALLOWANCE SCHEDULE, COMMUTING OVER LAND BY MOTOR VEHICLE TO REMOTE DUTY POSTS

Round trip distance in excess of 2 hours	Degree A commuting conditions	Degree B commuting conditions	Degree C commuting conditions
up to 15 minutes	$0.50	$0.63	$0.75
16 to 30	1.00	1.25	1.50
31 to 45	1.50	1.88	2.25
46 to 60	2.00	2.50	3.00
61 to 75	2.50	3.13	3.75
76 to 90	3.00	3.75	4.50
91 to 105	3.50	4.38	5.25
106 to 120	4.00	5.00	6.00
121 to 135	4.50	5.63	6.75
136 to 150	5.00	6.25	7.50
151 to 165	5.50	6.88	8.25
166 to 180	6.00	8.13	9.00

Degree A Commuting Conditions

Good paved roads; climatic conditions, in relation to type and quality of vehicle, cause minimal discomfort during trip.

Degree B Commuting Conditions

Roads typically fair, but may be good for part of distance and possibly unpaved for short distances; climatic conditions during part of a season, in relation to type and quality of vehicle, result in moderate discomfort during trip.

Degree C Commuting Conditions

Fair to poor roads, unpaved for part of distance, climatic conditions during most of a season, in combination with such factors as type and quality of vehicle and terrain, result in unusual discomfort during trip.

Subpart D—Separate Maintenance Allowance for Duty at Johnston Island

AUTHORITY: 5 U.S.C. 5942a(b); E.O. 12822, 3 CFR, 1992 Comp., p. 325

SOURCE: 58 FR 51566, Oct. 4, 1993, unless otherwise noted.

§ 591.401 Purpose and applicability.

(a) *Purpose.* This subpart prescribes the regulations required by section

5942a of title 5, United States Code, to authorize payment of a separate maintenance allowance to assist an employee assigned to Johnston Island to meet the additional expenses of maintaining family members elsewhere who would normally reside with him or her because they cannot accompany the employee to Johnston Island. This subpart provides rules for determining which employees are eligible to receive the separate maintenance allowance, who qualifies as family members under the program, the method of payment, and payment amounts.

(b) *Applicability.* This subpart applies to an employee (as defined in 5 U.S.C. 2105) in an executive department (as defined in section 101 of title 5, United States Code) or an independent establishment (as defined in section 104 of title 5, United States Code) who is assigned to a post of duty at Johnston Island.

[58 FR 51566, Oct. 4, 1993, as amended at 61 FR 27244, May 31, 1996]

§591.402 Definitions.

Adult, a term used in the Department of State *Standardized Regulations (Government Civilians, Foreign Areas)*, means a family member who is 21 years of age or older.

Domestic partner means a person in a domestic partnership with an employee or annuitant of the same sex.

Domestic partnership means a committed relationship between two adults of the same sex in which the partners—

(1) Are each other's sole domestic partner and intend to remain so indefinitely;

(2) Maintain a common residence, and intend to continue to do so (or would maintain a common residence but for an assignment abroad or other employment-related, financial, or similar obstacle);

(3) Are at least 18 years of age and mentally competent to consent to contract;

(4) Share responsibility for a significant measure of each other's financial obligations;

(5) Are not married or joined in a civil union to anyone else;

(6) Are not the domestic partner of anyone else;

(7) Are not related in a way that, if they were of opposite sex, would prohibit legal marriage in the U.S. jurisdiction in which the domestic partnership was formed;

(8) Are willing to certify, if required by the agency, that they understand that willful falsification of any documentation required to establish that an individual is in a domestic partnership may lead to disciplinary action and the recovery of the cost of benefits received related to such falsification, as well as constitute a criminal violation under 18 U.S.C. 1001, and that the method for securing such certification, if required, will be determined by the agency; and

(9) Are willing promptly to disclose, if required by the agency, any dissolution or material change in the status of the domestic partnership.

Family member means one or more of the following relatives of an employee who would normally reside with the employee except for circumstances warranting the granting of a separate maintenance allowance, but who does not receive from the Government an allowance similar to that granted to the employee and who is not deemed to be a family member of another employee for the purpose of determining the amount of a separate maintenance allowance or similar allowance:

(1) Children who are unmarried and under 21 years of age or who, regardless of age, are incapable of self-support, including natural children, step and adopted children, and those under legal guardianship or custody of the employee, or of the employee's spouse or domestic partner, when they are expected to be under such legal guardianship or custody at least until they reach 21 years of age and when dependent upon and normally residing with the guardian;

(2) Parents (including step and legally adoptive parents) of the employee, or of the employee's spouse or domestic partner, when such parents are at least 51 percent dependent on the employee for support;

(3) Sisters and brothers (including step or adoptive sisters and brothers) of the employee, or of the employee's spouse or domestic partner, when such

sisters and brothers are at least 51 percent dependent on the employee for support, unmarried and under 21 years of age, or regardless of age, are incapable of self-support;

(4) Spouse, excluding a spouse independently entitled to and receiving a similar allowance; or

(5) Domestic partner, excluding a domestic partner independently entitled to and receiving a similar allowance.

Johnston Island, also called Johnston Atoll, is a possession of the United States located 717 nautical miles southwest of Honolulu, Hawaii.

Separate maintenance allowance means an allowance to assist an employee assigned to Johnston Island who is compelled by reason of dangerous, notably unhealthful, or excessively adverse living conditions at Johnston Island, or for the convenience of the Government, to meet the additional expense of maintaining family members at a location other than Johnston Island.

[61 FR 27244, May 31, 1996, as amended at 77 FR 42905, July 20, 2012]

§591.403 Amount of payment.

(a) The annual rate of the separate maintenance allowance paid to an employee is determined by the number of individuals, including a spouse, a domestic partner, and/or one or more other family members, who are maintained at a location other than Johnston Island.

(b) The annual rates for the separate maintenance allowance paid to employees assigned to Johnston Island shall be the same as the annual rates for the separate maintenance allowance established by the Department of State in its *Standardized Regulations (Government Civilians, Foreign Areas)*. The annual rates shall not vary by location of the separate household.

(c) The annual rates of the separate maintenance allowance shall be adjusted on the first day of the first pay period beginning on or after July 1, 1996 and, subsequently, on the first day of the first pay period beginning on or after the effective date established for adjustment of annual rates for the separate maintenance allowance in the *Standardized Regulations (Government Civilians, Foreign Areas)*.

[61 FR 27244, May 31, 1996, as amended at 77 FR 42905, July 20, 2012]

§591.404 Method of payment.

(a) Separate maintenance allowance rates are paid from the employee's date of arrival at Johnston Island to the employee's date of departure from Johnston Island. No deductions are necessary for details away from Johnston Island or for partial days. The separate maintenance allowance shall be computed and paid at daily rates as follows:

(1) Divide the annual rate of payment by the number of days in the applicable calendar year to obtain a daily rate (counting one half-cent and over as a whole cent);

(2) Multiply the daily rate by 14 to obtain a biweekly rate; and

(3) Multiply the daily rate by the number of days involved to obtain the rate for any period.

(b) A separate maintenance allowance is not part of an employee's rate of basic pay for any purpose.

(c) The rate for any pay period shall be computed at the daily rate applicable on the first day of that pay period.

§591.405 Responsibilities of agencies.

Agencies with employees stationed at Johnston Island may require reasonable verification of relationship and dependency.

[61 FR 27244, May 31, 1996]

§591.406 Records and reports.

So that the Office of Personnel Management can evaluate agencies' use of this authority and provide the Congress and others with information regarding the use of a nonforeign separate maintenance allowance, each agency shall maintain such records and submit to the Office of Personnel Management reports and data as requested.

PART 595—PHYSICIANS' COMPARABILITY ALLOWANCES

Sec.

AUTHORITY: 5 U.S.C. 5948; E.O. 12109, 44 FR 1067, Jan. 3, 1979.

SOURCE: 44 FR 40876, July 13, 1979, unless otherwise noted.

§ 595.101 Purpose.

Section 5948 of title 5, United States Code, authorizes the payment of allowances to certain eligible Federal physicians who enter into service agreements with their agencies. These allowances are paid only to categories of physicians for which the agency is experiencing recruitment and retention problems and are fixed at the minimum amounts necessary to deal with such problems. The President has delegated regulatory responsibility for this program to the Director of OPM, acting in consultation with the Office of Management and Budget. This part contains the regulations, criteria and conditions which the Director of OPM, in consultation with the Director of the Office of Management and Budget, has prescribed for the administration of the physicians' comparability allowance program. This part supplements and implements 5 U.S.C. 5948 and should be read together with that section of law.

[69 FR 27817, May 17, 2004]

§ 595.102 Who is covered by this program?

(a) This program covers individuals employed as physicians under the Federal pay systems listed in 5 U.S.C. 5948(g)(1), except as provided in 5 U.S.C. 5948(b). For the purposes of this part, an individual is *employed as a physician* only if he or she is serving in a position the duties and responsibilities of which could not be satisfactorily performed by an incumbent who is not a physician.

(b) Section 5948(b) of title 5, United States Code, prohibits the payment of physicians' comparability allowances to certain physicians, including physicians who are reemployed annuitants. For the purpose of applying this prohibition, *reemployed annuitant* means an individual who is receiving or has title to and has applied for an annuity under any retirement program of the Government of the United States, or the government of the District of Columbia, on the basis of service as a civilian employee.

(c) Physicians employed and paid under title 38, United States Code, and Commissioned Corps officers of the Public Health Service under title 42, United States Code, are not eligible for physicians' comparability allowances.

[44 FR 40876, July 13, 1979, as amended at 58 FR 65537, Dec. 15, 1993; 64 FR 72458, Dec. 28, 1999; 69 FR 27817, May 17, 2004]

§ 595.103 What requirements must agencies establish for determining which physician positions are covered?

(a) The head of each agency must determine categories of physician positions for which there is a significant recruitment and retention problem, and physicians' comparability allowances may be paid only to physicians serving in positions in such categories.

(b) In determining categories of physician positions, the head of each agency must, as a minimum, establish as separate categories the following types of positions:

(1) Positions primarily involving the practice of medicine or direct service to patients, involving the performance of diagnostic, preventive, or therapeutic services to patients in hospitals, clinics, public health programs, diagnostic centers, and similar settings, but not including positions described in paragraph (b)(3) of this section;

(2) Positions primarily involving the conduct of medical research and experimental work, including the conduct of medical work pertaining to food, drugs, cosmetics, and devices (or the review or evaluation of such medical research and experimental work), or the identification of causes or sources of disease or disease outbreaks;

(3) Positions primarily involving the evaluation of physical fitness, or the provision of initial treatment of on-the-job illness or injury, or the performance of preemployment examinations, preventive health screenings, or fitness-for-duty examinations; and

(4) Positions not described by paragraph (b) (1), (2), or (3) of this section, including positions involving disability evaluation and rating, the performance of medicolegal autopsies, training activities, or the administration of medical and health programs, including the administration of patient care or medical research and experimental programs.

(c) The agency head may establish as separate categories any additional subdivisions of these four categories of positions, based on any factors the agency head determines relevant. These may include such factors as the location, grade or level, and medical specialization of the positions, and the level of qualifications sought by the agency for physicians in the category.

[44 FR 40876, July 13, 1979, as amended at 69 FR 27817, May 17, 2004]

§ 595.104 What criteria are used to identify a recruitment and retention problem?

The head of each agency may determine that a significant recruitment and retention problem exists for each category of physician position established under § 595.103 only if the following conditions are met with respect to the category:

(a) Such evidence as vacant positions, an unacceptably high turnover rate, or other positive evidence indicates that the agency is unable to recruit and retain physicians for the category;

(b) The qualification requirements being used as a basis for considering candidates for the vacant positions in the category do not exceed the qualifications that are actually necessary for successful performance of the work of the positions in the category;

(c) The agency has made efforts to recruit qualified candidates for any vacant positions in the category and to retain physicians presently employed in positions in the category; and

(d) A sufficient number of qualified candidates is not available to fill the existing vacancies in the category at the rate of pay the agency may offer if no comparability allowance is paid.

[44 FR 40876, July 13, 1979, as amended at 69 FR 27817, May 17, 2004]

§ 595.105 What criteria must be used to determine the amount of a physicians' comparability allowance?

(a) The amount of the comparability allowance payable for each category of physician positions established under § 595.103 must be the minimum amount necessary to deal with the recruitment and retention problem identified under § 595.104 for that category of positions. In determining this amount, the agency head must consider the relative earnings, responsibilities, expenses, workload, working conditions, conditions of employment, and personnel benefits for physicians in each category and for comparable physicians inside and outside the Federal Government.

(b) Agencies may not pay a physicians' comparability allowance in excess of $14,000 annually to a physician with 24 months or less of service as a Government physician. Agencies may not pay a physicians' comparability allowance in excess of $30,000 annually to a physician with more than 24 months of service as a Government physician.

(c) In determining length of service as a Government physician, agencies must exclude periods of leave without pay. However, agencies may credit any prior service as a Government physician, including—

(1) Prior service as a physician under sections 7401 and 7405 of title 38, United States Code; and

(2) Prior active service as a medical officer in the Commissioned Corps of the Public Health Service under title II of the Public Health Service Act (42 U.S.C. chapter 6A).

(d) A physician who is employed on a regularly scheduled part-time basis of half-time or more is eligible to receive a physicians' comparability allowance, but any such allowance must be prorated according to the proportion of the physicians' work schedule to full-time employment. A physician who is employed on less than a half-time or intermittent basis is excluded from the physicians' comparability allowance program.

(e) A physician who is serving with the Government under a loan repayment program must have the amount of any loan being repaid deducted from any physicians' comparability allowance for which he or she is eligible and may receive only that portion of such allowance which exceeds the amount of the loan being repaid during the period of employment required by the service agreement under the student loan repayment program.

[44 FR 40876, July 13, 1979, as amended at 53 FR 8141, Mar. 14, 1988, and 53 FR 24011, June 27, 1988; 64 FR 72458, Dec. 28, 1999; 69 FR 27817, May 17, 2004]

§ 595.106 What termination and refund provisions are required?

Each service agreement entered into by an agency and a physician under the comparability allowance program must prescribe the terms under which the agreement may be terminated and the amount of allowance, if any, required to be refunded by the physician for each reason for termination. In the case of each service agreement covering a period of service of more than 1 year, the service agreement must include a provision that, if the physician completes more than 1 year of service pursuant to the agreement, but fails to complete the full period of service specified in the agreement either voluntarily or because of misconduct by the physician, the physician must refund the amount of allowance he or she has received under the agreement for the 26 weeks of service immediately preceding the termination (or for a longer period, if specified in the agreement).

[69 FR 27818, May 17, 2004]

§ 595.107 What are the requirements for implementing a physicians' comparability allowance program?

(a) An agency may not enter into any service agreement under 5 U.S.C. 5948 until the agency's plan for implementing the physicians' comparability allowance program has been submitted to and approved by the Office of Management and Budget in accordance with this section and such instructions as the Office of Management and Budget may prescribe.

(b) The agency must submit to the Office of Management and Budget a complete description of its plan for implementing the physicians' comparability allowance program, including the following:

(1) An identification of the categories of physician positions the agency has established under § 595.103, and of the basis for such categories;

(2) An explanation of the determination that a recruitment and retention problem exists for each such category, in accordance with the criteria in § 595.104; and

(3) An explanation of the basis for the amount of comparability allowance determined necessary for each category of physician position under § 595.105.

(c) The Office of Management and Budget (OMB) will review each agency's plan for implementing the physicians' comparability allowance program and determine whether the plan is consistent with 5 U.S.C. 5948 and the requirements of this part. The Office of Management and Budget will advise the agency within 45 calendar days after receipt of the plan as to whether the plan is consistent with 5 U.S.C. 5948 and this part or what changes need to be made.

[44 FR 40876, July 13, 1979, as amended at 53 FR 8142, Mar. 14, 1988, and 53 FR 24011, June 27, 1988; 69 FR 27818, May 17, 2004]

PART 610—HOURS OF DUTY

Subpart A—Weekly and Daily Scheduling of Work

Subpart B—Holidays

Subpart C—Administrative Dismissals of Daily, Hourly, and Piecework Employees

Subpart D—Flexible and Compressed Work Schedules

SOURCE: 33 FR 12474, Sept. 4, 1968, unless otherwise noted.

Subpart A—Weekly and Daily Scheduling of Work

AUTHORITY: 5 U.S.C. 6101; sec. 1(1) of E.O. 11228, 3 CFR, 1964–1965 Comp., p. 317.

§ 610.101 Coverage.

This subpart applies to each employee to whom subpart A of part 550 applies and to each employee whose pay is fixed and adjusted from time to time under section 5343 or 5349 of title 5, United States Code, or by a wage board or similar administrative authority serving the same purpose.

[42 FR 3297, Jan. 18, 1977]

§ 610.102 Definitions.

In this subpart:

Administrative workweek means any period of 7 consecutive 24-hour periods designated in advance by the head of the agency under section 6101 of title 5, United States Code.

Agency means an Executive agency and a military department as defined by sections 105 and 102 of title 5, United States Code.

Basic workweek, for full-time employees, means the 40-hour workweek established in accordance with § 610.111.

Employee means an employee of an agency to whom this subpart applies.

Head of agency means the head of an agency or an official who has been delegated the authority to act for the head of the agency in the matter concerned.

Regularly scheduled administrative workweek, for a full-time employee, means the period within an administrative workweek, established in accordance with § 610.111, within which the employee is regularly scheduled to work. For a part-time employee, it means the officially prescribed days and hours within an administrative workweek during which the employee is regularly scheduled to work.

Regularly scheduled work means work that is scheduled in advance of an administrative workweek under an agency's procedures for establishing workweeks in accordance with § 610.111.

Tour of duty means the hours of a day (a daily tour of duty) and the days of an administrative workweek (a weekly tour of duty) that constitute an employee's regularly scheduled administrative workweek.

(5 U.S.C. 5548 and 6101(c))

[33 FR 12474, Sept. 4, 1968, as amended at 48 FR 3934, Jan. 28, 1983; 60 FR 67287, Dec. 29, 1995; 64 FR 69182, Dec. 10, 1999]

WORKWEEK

§ 610.111 Establishment of workweeks.

(a) The head of each agency, with respect to each full-time employee to whom this subpart applies, shall establish by a written agency policy statement:

(1) A basic workweek of 40 hours which does not extend over more than 6 of any 7 consecutive days. Except as provided in paragraphs (b), (c), and (d) of this section, the written agency policy statement shall specify the days and hours within the administrative workweek that constitute the basic workweek.

(2) A regularly scheduled administrative workweek that consists of the 40-hour basic workweek established in accordance with paragraph (a)(1) of this section, plus the period of regular overtime work, if any, required of each employee. Except as provided in paragraphs (b), (c), and (d) of this section,

the written agency policy statement, for purposes of leave and overtime pay administration, shall specify by days and hours of each day the periods included in the regularly scheduled administrative workweek that do not constitute a part of the basic workweek.

(b) When it is impracticable to prescribe a regular schedule of definite hours of duty for each workday of a regularly scheduled administrative workweek, the head of an agency may establish the first 40 hours of duty performed within a period of not more than 6 days of the administrative workweek as the basic workweek. A first 40-hour tour of duty is the basic workweek without the requirement for specific days and hours within the administrative workweek. All work performed by an employee within the first 40 hours is considered regularly scheduled work for premium pay and hours of duty purposes. Any additional hours of officially ordered or approved work within the administrative workweek are overtime work.

(c) (1) When an employee is paid additional pay under section 5545(c)(1) of title 5, United States Code, his regularly scheduled administrative workweek is the total number of regularly scheduled hours of duty a week.

(2) When an employee has a tour of duty which includes a period during which he remains at or within the confines of his station in a standby status rather than performing actual work his regularly scheduled administrative workweek is the total number of regularly scheduled hours of duty a week, including time in a standby status except that allowed for sleep and meals by a written agency policy statement.

(d) When the head of an agency establishes a flexible or compressed work schedule under section 6122 or section 6127 of title 5, United States Code, he or she shall establish a basic work requirement for each employee as defined in section 6121 of title 5, United States Code. A flexible or compressed work schedule is a scheduled tour of duty and all work performed by an employee within the basic work requirement is considered regularly scheduled work for premium pay and hours of duty purposes.

(5 U.S.C. 5548 and 6101(c))

[33 FR 12474, Sept. 4, 1968, as amended at 48 FR 3934, Jan. 28, 1983; 48 FR 44060, Sept. 27, 1983; 64 FR 69182, Dec. 10, 1999]

WORK SCHEDULES

§610.121 Establishment of work schedules.

(a) Except when the head of an agency determines that the agency would be seriously handicapped in carrying out its functions or that costs would be substantially increased, he or she shall provide that—

(1) Assignments to tours of duty are scheduled in advance of the administrative workweek over periods of not less than 1 week;

(2) The basic 40-hour workweek is scheduled on 5 days, Monday through Friday when possible, and the 2 days outside the basic workweek are consecutive;

(3) The working hours in each day in the basic workweek are the same;

(4) The basic nonovertime workday may not exceed 8 hours;

(5) The occurrence of holidays may not affect the designation of the basic workweek; and

(6) Breaks in working hours of more than 1 hour may not be scheduled in a basic workday.

(b)(1) The head of an agency shall schedule the work of his or her employees to accomplish the mission of the agency. The head of an agency shall schedule an employee's regularly scheduled administrative workweek so that it corresponds with the employee's actual work requirements.

(2) When the head of an agency knows in advance of an administrative workweek that the specific days and/or hours of a day actually required of an employee in that administrative workweek will differ from those required in the current administrative workweek, he or she shall reschedule the employee's regularly scheduled administrative workweek to correspond with those specific days and hours. The head of the agency shall inform the employee of the change, and he or she shall record the change on the employee's

time card or other agency document for recording work.

(3) If it is determined that the head of an agency should have scheduled a period of work as part of the employee's regularly scheduled administrative workweek and failed to do so in accordance with paragraphs (b) (1) and (2) of this section, the employee shall be entitled to the payment of premium pay for that period of work as regularly scheduled work under subpart A of part 550 of this chapter. In this regard, it must be determined that the head of the agency: (i) Had knowledge of the specific days and hours of the work requirement in advance of the administrative workweek, and (ii) had the opportunity to determine which employee had to be scheduled, or rescheduled, to meet the specific days and hours of that work requirement.

(5 U.S.C. 5548 and 6101(c))

[48 FR 3935, Jan. 28, 1983]

§ 610.122 Variations in work schedules for educational purposes.

(a) Notwithstanding § 610.121, the head of an agency may authorize a special tour of duty of not less than 40 hours to permit an employee to take one or more courses in a college, university, or other educational institution when it is determined that:

(1) The courses being taken are not training under chapter 41 of title 5, United States Code;

(2) The rearrangement of the employee's tour of duty will not appreciably interfere with the accomplishment of the work required to be performed;

(3) Additional costs for personal services will not be incurred; and

(4) Completion of the courses will equip the employee for more effective work in the agency.

(b) The agency may not pay to the employee any premium pay solely because the special tour of duty authorized under this section causes the employee to work on a day, or at a time during the day, for which premium pay would otherwise be payable.

(c) OPM may from time to time request an agency to report on the use of this authority.

§ 610.123 Travel on official time.

Insofar as practicable travel during nonduty hours shall not be required of an employee. When it is essential that this be required and the employee may not be paid overtime under § 550.112(e) of this chapter the official concerned shall record his reasons for ordering travel at those hours and shall, upon request, furnish a copy of his statement to the employee concerned.

Subpart B—Holidays

AUTHORITY: 5 U.S.C. 6101; sec. 1(1) of E.O. 11228, 3 CFR, 1964–1965 Comp., p. 317.

§ 610.201 Identification of holidays.

Agencies determine holidays under section 6103 of title 5, United States Code, and Executive Order 11582 of February 11, 1971.

[65 FR 48135, Aug. 7, 2000]

§ 610.202 Determining the holiday.

For purposes of pay and leave, the day to be treated as a holiday is determined as follows:

(a) Except when employees are entitled to a different holiday under 5 U.S.C. 6103(b)(3), an employee's holiday is the day designated by 5 U.S.C. 6103(a) whenever part of the employee's basic workweek (as defined in § 610.102) or basic work requirement (as defined in 5 U.S.C. 6121(3)) is scheduled on that day.

(b) When a holiday falls on a nonworkday outside an employee's basic workweek, the day to be treated as his or her holiday is determined in accordance with sections 6103 (b) and (d) of title 5, United States Code, and Executive Order 11582.

(c) When an agency determines the holiday in accordance with section 6103(d) of title 5, United States Code, for an employee under a compressed work schedule, the agency shall select a workday for the holiday that is in the same biweekly pay period as the date of the actual holiday designated under 5 U.S.C. 6103(a) or in the biweekly pay period immediately preceding or following that pay period.

(d) The provisions of section 6103(b)(3) of title 5, United States Code, on determining holidays for certain employees at duty posts outside the United States apply to covered employees who are working outside the United States at a permanent or temporary station or under travel orders. For the purpose of section 6103(b)(3), *United States* includes—

(1) A State of the United States;

(2) The District of Columbia;

(3) Puerto Rico;

(4) The U.S. Virgin Islands;

(5) Outer Continental Shelf Lands, as defined in the Outer Continental Shelf Lands Act (67 Stat. 462);

(6) American Samoa;

(7) Guam;

(8) Midway Atoll;

(9) Wake Island;

(10) Johnston Island; and

(11) Palmyra.

[42 FR 3297, Jan. 18, 1977, as amended at 60 FR 67287, Dec. 29, 1995; 62 FR 28308, May 23, 1997; 64 FR 72458, Dec. 28, 1999; 65 FR 48136, Aug. 7, 2000]

Subpart C—Administrative Dismissals of Daily, Hourly, and Piecework Employees

AUTHORITY: 5 U.S.C. 6104; E.O. 10552, 3 CFR, 1954–1958 Comp., p. 201.

§ 610.301 Purpose.

The purpose of this subpart is to provide uniform and equitable standards under which regular employees paid at daily, hourly, or piecework rates may be relieved from duty with pay by administrative order.

§ 610.302 Policy statement.

The authority in this subpart may be used only to the extent warranted by good administration for short periods of time not generally exceeding 3 consecutive work days in a single period of excused absence. This authority may not be used in situations of extensive duration or for periods of interrupted or suspended operations such as ordinarily would be covered by the scheduling of leave, furlough, or the assignment of other work. Insofar as practicable, each administrative order issued under this subpart shall provide benefits for regular employees paid at daily, hourly, or piecework rates similar to those provided for employees paid at annual rates.

§ 610.303 Definitions.

In this subpart:

Administrative order means an order issued by an authorized official of an agency relieving regular employees from active duty without charge to leave or loss of pay.

Regular employees means employees paid at daily, hourly, or piecework rates who have a regular tour of duty, and whose appointments are not limited to 90 days or less or who have been currently employed for a continuous period of 90 days under one or more appointments without a break in service.

[33 FR 12474, Sept. 4, 1968, as amended at 34 FR 2479, Feb. 21, 1969; 60 FR 67287, Dec. 29, 1995]

§ 610.304 Coverage.

This subpart applies to regular employees of the Federal Government paid at daily, hourly, or piecework rates. This subpart does not apply to experts and consultants.

§ 610.305 Standards.

An administrative order may be issued under this subpart when:

(a) Normal operations of an establishment are interrupted by events beyond the control of management or employees;

(b) For managerial reasons, the closing of an establishment or portions thereof is required for short periods; or

(c) It is in the public interest to relieve employees from work to participate in civil activities which the Government is interested in encouraging.

(d) The circumstances are such that an administrative order under paragraph (a), (b), or (c) of this section is not appropriate and the agency under its regulations excuses, or is authorized to excuse, without charge to leave or loss of pay, employees paid on an annual basis.

[33 FR 12474, Sept. 4, 1968, as amended at 34 FR 2479, Feb. 21, 1969]

§ 610.306 Supplemental regulations.

Each agency is authorized to issue supplemental regulations not inconsistent with this subpart.

[33 FR 12474, Sept. 4, 1968, as amended at 34 FR 2479, Feb. 21, 1969]

Subpart D—Flexible and Compressed Work Schedules

AUTHORITY: 5 U.S.C. 6133(a).

SOURCE: 48 FR 44060, Sept. 27, 1983, unless otherwise noted.

§ 610.401 General.

This subpart contains regulatory requirements prescribed by the Office of Personnel Management to implement certain provisions of subchapter 11 of chapter 61 of title 5, United States Code. These regulations supplement that subchapter and must be read together with it.

§ 610.402 Coverage.

The regulations contained in this subpart apply only to flexible work schedules and compressed work schedules established under subchapter 11 of chapter 61 of title 5, United States Code.

§ 610.403 Definitions.

In this subpart, *Agency*, *Credit Hours*, and *Employee* have the meaning given these terms in section 6121 of title 5, United States Code.

[58 FR 58262, Nov. 1, 1993]

§ 610.404 Requirement for time-accounting method.

An agency that authorizes a flexible work schedule or a compressed work schedule under this subpart shall establish a time-accounting method that will provide affirmative evidence that each employee subject to the schedule has worked the proper number of hours in a biweekly pay period.

§ 610.405 Holiday for part-time employees on flexible work schedules.

If a part-time employee is relieved or prevented from working on a day within the employee's scheduled tour of duty that is designated as a holiday by Federal statute or Executive order, the employee is entitled to basic pay with respect to the holiday for the number of hours the employee is scheduled to work on that day, not to exceed 8 hours. When a holiday falls on a nonworkday of a part-time employee, he or she is not entitled to an in-lieu-of day for that holiday.

§ 610.406 Holiday for employees on compressed work schedules.

(a) If a full-time employee is relieved or prevented from working on a day designated as a holiday by Federal statute or Executive order, the employee is entitled to basic pay for the number of hours of the compressed work schedule on that day.

(b) If a part-time employee is relieved or prevented from working on a day within the employee's scheduled tour of duty that is designated as a holiday by Federal statute or Executive order, the employee is entitled to basic pay for the number of hours of the compressed work schedule on that day. When a holiday falls on a nonworkday of a part-time employee, he or she is not entitled to an in-lieu-of day for that holiday.

§ 610.407 Premium pay for holiday work for employees on compressed work schedules.

(a) An employee on a compressed schedule who performs work on a holiday is entitled to basic pay, plus premium pay at a rate equal to basic pay, for the work that is not in excess of the employee's compressed work schedule for that day. For hours worked on a holiday in excess of the compressed work schedule, a full-time employee is entitled to overtime pay under applicable provisions of law and a part-time employee is entitled to straight time pay or overtime pay, depending on whether the excess hours are nonovertime hours or overtime hours.

(b) An employee on a compressed work schedule is not entitled to holiday premium pay while engaged in training, except as provided in § 410.402 of this chapter.

[48 FR 44060, Sept. 27, 1983, as amended at 64 FR 69182, Dec. 10, 1999]

§ 610.408 Use of credit hours.

Members of the Senior Executive Service (SES) may not accumulate credit hours under an alternative work schedule. Any credit hours accumulated in the SES prior to December 1, 1993, must be used within 6 months of that date.

[58 FR 58262, Nov. 1, 1993]

PART 630—ABSENCE AND LEAVE

Subpart A—General Provisions

Subpart B—Definitions and General Provisions for Annual and Sick Leave

Subpart C—Annual Leave

Subpart D—Sick Leave

Subpart E—Recredit of Leave

Subpart F—Home Leave

Subpart G—Shore Leave

Subpart H—Funeral Leave

Subpart I—Voluntary Leave Transfer Program

Subpart J—Voluntary Leave Bank Program

Subpart K—Emergency Leave Transfer Program

Subpart L—Family and Medical Leave

Subpart M—Disabled Veteran Leave

AUTHORITY: 5 U.S.C. 6311; § 630.205 also issued under Pub. L. 108–411, 118 Stat 2312; § 630.301 also issued under Pub. L. 103–356, 108 Stat. 3410 and Pub. L. 108–411, 118 Stat 2312; § 630.303 also issued under 5 U.S.C. 6133(a); §§ 630.306 and 630.308 also issued under 5 U.S.C. 6304(d)(3), Pub. L. 102–484, 106 Stat. 2722, and Pub. L. 103–337, 108 Stat. 2663; subpart D also issued under Pub. L. 103–329, 108 Stat. 2423; § 630.501 and subpart F also issued under E.O. 11228, 30 FR 7739, 3 CFR, 1974 Comp., p. 163; subpart G also issued under 5 U.S.C. 6305; subpart H also issued under 5 U.S.C. 6326; subpart I also issued under 5 U.S.C. 6332, Pub. L. 100–566, 102 Stat. 2834, and Pub. L. 103–103, 107 Stat. 1022; subpart J also issued under 5 U.S.C. 6362, Pub. L 100–566, and Pub. L. 103–103; subpart K also issued under Pub. L. 105–18, 111 Stat. 158; subpart L also issued under 5 U.S.C. 6387 and Pub. L. 103–3, 107 Stat. 23; and subpart M also issued under section 2(d) of Pub. L. 114–75, 129 Stat. 640.

SOURCE: 33 FR 12475, Sept. 4, 1968, unless otherwise noted.

Subpart A—General Provisions

§ 630.101 Responsibility for administration.

The head of an agency having employees subject to this part is responsible for the proper administration of this part so far as it pertains to employees under his jurisdiction, and for maintaining an account of leave for each employee in accordance with methods prescribed by the General Accounting Office.

[34 FR 13655, Aug. 26, 1969]

Subpart B—Definitions and General Provisions for Annual and Sick Leave

§630.201 Definitions.

(a) In section 6301(2)(iii) of title 5, United States Code, the term *temporary employee engaged in construction work at an hourly rate* means an employee hired on a temporary basis solely for the purpose of work on a specific construction project and paid on an hourly rate.

(b) In subparts B through G of this part:

Accrued leave means the leave earned by an employee during the current leave year that is unused at any given time in that year.

Accumulated leave means the unused leave remaining to the credit of an employee at the beginning of the leave year.

Agency means an Executive agency, as defined in 5 U.S.C. 105, and any other entity of the Federal Government that employs officers and employees to whom subchapter I of chapter 63 of title 5, United States Code, applies.

Committed relationship means one in which the employee, and the domestic partner of the employee, are each other's sole domestic partner (and are not married to or domestic partners with anyone else); and share responsibility for a significant measure of each other's common welfare and financial obligations. This includes, but is not limited to, any relationship between two individuals of the same or opposite sex that is granted legal recognition by a State or by the District of Columbia as a marriage or analogous relationship (including, but not limited to, a civil union).

Domestic partner means an adult in a committed relationship with another adult, including both same-sex and opposite-sex relationships.

Employee means an employee to whom subchapter I of chapter 63 of title 5, United States Code, applies.

Family member means an individual with any of the following relationships to the employee:

(1) Spouse, and parents thereof;

(2) Sons and daughters, and spouses thereof;

(3) Parents, and spouses thereof;

(4) Brothers and sisters, and spouses thereof;

(5) Grandparents and grandchildren, and spouses thereof;

(6) Domestic partner and parents thereof, including domestic partners of any individual in paragraphs (2) through (5) of this definition; and

(7) Any individual related by blood or affinity whose close association with the employee is the equivalent of a family relationship.

Health care provider has the meaning given that term in §630.1202.

Leave year means the period beginning with the first day of the first complete pay period in a calendar year and ending with the day immediately before the first day of the first complete pay period in the following calendar year.

Medical certificate means a written statement signed by a registered practicing physician or other practitioner certifying to the incapacitation, examination, or treatment, or to the period of disability while the patient was receiving professional treatment.

Parent means—

(1) A biological, adoptive, step, or foster parent of the employee, or a person who was a foster parent of the employee when the employee was a minor;

(2) A person who is the legal guardian of the employee or was the legal guardian of the employee when the employee was a minor or required a legal guardian;

(3) A person who stands *in loco parentis* to the employee or stood *in loco parentis* to the employee when the employee was a minor or required someone to stand *in loco parentis;* or

(4) A parent, as described in paragraphs (1) through (3) of this definition, of an employee's spouse or domestic partner.

Serious health condition has the meaning given that term in §630.1202.

Son or daughter means—

(1) A biological, adopted, step, or foster son or daughter of the employee;

(2) A person who is a legal ward or was a legal ward of the employee when that individual was a minor or required a legal guardian;

(3) A person for whom the employee stands *in loco parentis* or stood *in loco parentis* when that individual was a

minor or required someone to stand *in loco parentis;* or

(4) A son or daughter, as described in paragraphs (1) through (3) of this definition, of an employee's spouse or domestic partner.

Uncommon tour of duty means an established tour of duty that exceeds 80 hours of work in a biweekly pay period, provided the tour—

(1) Includes hours for which the employee is compensated by standby duty pay under 5 U.S.C. 5545(c)(1) and § 550.141 of this chapter;

(2) Is a regular tour of duty (as defined in § 550.1302 of this chapter) established for firefighters compensated under 5 U.S.C. 5545b and part 550, subpart M, of this chapter; or

(3) Is authorized for a category of employees by the Office of Personnel Management.

United States means the several States and the District of Columbia.

[61 FR 64450, Dec. 5, 1996, as amended at 63 FR 64595, Nov. 23, 1998; 65 FR 37239, June 13, 2000; 71 FR 54570, Sept. 18, 2006; 75 FR 33495, June 14, 2010]

§ 630.202 Full biweekly pay period; leave earnings.

(a) *Full-time employees.* A full-time employee earns leave during each full biweekly pay period while in a pay status or in a combination of a pay status and a nonpay status.

(b) *Part-time employees.* Hours in a pay status in excess of an agency's basic working hours in a pay period are disregarded in computing the leave earnings of a part-time employee.

[33 FR 12475, Sept. 4, 1968, as amended at 55 FR 6595, Feb. 26, 1990]

§ 630.203 Pay periods other than biweekly.

An employee paid on other than a biweekly pay period basis earns leave on a pro rata basis for a full pay period.

§ 630.204 Fractional pay periods.

When an employee's service is interrupted by a non-leave-earning period, he earns leave on a pro rata basis for each fractional pay period that occurs within the continuity of his employment.

§ 630.205 Credit for prior work experience and experience in a uniformed service for determining annual leave accrual rate.

(a) The head of an agency or his or her designee may, at his or her sole discretion, provide credit for service that otherwise would not be creditable under 5 U.S.C. 6303(a) for the purpose of determining the annual leave accrual rate of an individual receiving his or her first appointment (regardless of tenure) as a civilian employee of the Federal Government or an employee who is reappointed following a break in service of at least 90 calendar days after his or her last period of civilian Federal employment. The head of the agency or his or her designee must determine that the skills and experience the employee possesses are—

(1) Essential to the new position and were acquired through performance in a prior position having duties that directly relate to the duties of the position to which he or she is being appointed; and

(2) Necessary to achieve an important agency mission or performance goal.

(b) Notwithstanding 5 U.S.C. 6303(a), the head of an agency or his or her designee may, at his or her sole discretion, provide credit for active duty uniformed service that otherwise would not be creditable under 5 U.S.C. 6303(a) for the purpose of determining the annual leave accrual rate of an employee who is a retired member of a uniformed service as defined by 38 U.S.C. 4303. The head of the agency or his or her designee must determine that the skills and experience the employee possesses are—

(1) Essential to the new position and were acquired through performance in a position in the uniformed services having duties that directly relate to the duties of the position to which he or she is being appointed; and

(2) Necessary to achieve an important agency mission or performance goal.

(c) When the head of an agency or his or her designee makes a determination to provide service credit for prior work experience or active duty in the uniformed services under paragraph (a) or

(b) of this section, he or she must determine the amount of service that will be credited. The amount of service credited may not exceed the actual amount of service during which the employee performed duties directly related to the position to which the employee is being appointed.

(d) An employee must provide written documentation, acceptable to the agency, of his or her prior work experience. An employee must provide written documentation from the military, acceptable to the agency, of his or her uniformed service. The head of an agency or his or her designee must make the determination to approve an employee's qualifying prior work experience before the employee enters on duty.

(e) The agency must establish documentation and recordkeeping procedures sufficient to allow reconstruction of each action.

(f)(1) Credit for prior work experience or experience in a uniformed service under paragraphs (a) and (b) of this section is granted to the employee upon the effective date of his or her initial appointment to the agency or reappointment after a 90-day break in service and remains creditable for annual leave accrual purposes thereafter unless the employee fails to complete 1 full year of continuous service with the appointing agency.

(2) If an employee is placed in a leave without pay status during the 1-year period of continuous service required by paragraph (f)(1) of this section, the 1-year period of continuous service must be extended by the amount of time in a leave without pay unless—

(i) The employee separates or is placed in a leave without pay status to perform service in the uniformed services (as defined in 38 U.S.C. 4303 and 5 CFR 353.102) and later returns to civilian service through the exercise of a reemployment right provided by law, Executive order, or regulation; or

(ii) The employee separates or is placed in a leave without pay status because of an on-the-job injury with entitlement to injury compensation under 5 U.S.C. chapter 81 and later recovers sufficiently to return to work.

(g) If an employee separates from Federal service or transfers to another agency before completing 1 full year of continuous service with the appointing agency—

(1) Any credit under paragraph (a) or (b) of this section must be subtracted from the employee's total creditable service before the employee transfers or separates, and the agency must establish a new service computation date for leave accrual purposes under 5 U.S.C. 6303(a);

(2) Any annual leave accrued or accumulated by an employee as a result of receiving credit for service under paragraph (a) or (b) of this section remains to the credit of the employee; and

(3) The agency must—

(i) Transfer the annual leave balance to the new employing agency under 5 CFR 630.501 if the employee is transferring to a position to which annual leave may be transferred; or

(ii) Make a lump-sum payment under 5 CFR 550.1205 for any unused annual leave if the employee is separating from Federal service or moving to a position to which annual leave cannot be transferred.

[70 FR 22246, Apr. 29, 2005, as amended at 71 FR 54570, Sept. 18, 2006]

§ 630.206 Minimum charge.

(a) Unless an agency establishes a minimum charge of less than one hour, or establishes a different minimum charge through negotiations, the minimum charge for leave is one hour, and additional charges are in multiples thereof. If an employee is unavoidably or necessarily absent for less than one hour, or tardy, the agency, for adequate reason, may excuse him without charge to leave.

(b) When an employee is charged with leave for an unauthorized absence or tardiness, the agency may not require him to perform work for any part of the leave period charged against his account.

[33 FR 12475, Sept. 4, 1968, as amended at 38 FR 18446, July 11, 1973; 38 FR 26601, Sept. 24, 1973]

§ 630.207 Travel time.

The travel time granted an employee under section 6303(d) of title 5, United States Code, is inclusive of the time necessarily occupied in traveling to and from his post of duty and (a) the United States, or (b) his place of residence, which is outside the area of employment, in the Commonwealth of Puerto Rico or the territories or possessions of the United States. The employee shall designate his place of residence in his request for leave under section 6303(d) of title 5, United States Code.

§ 630.208 Reduction in leave credits.

(a) When the number of hours in a nonpay status in a full-time employee's leave year equals the number of basepay hours in a pay period, the agency shall reduce his credits for leave by an amount equal to the amount of leave the employee earns during the pay period. When the employee's number of hours of nonpay status does not require a reduction of leave credits, the agency shall drop those hours at the end of the employee's leave year. For the purpose of determining the reduction of leave credits under this paragraph when an employee has one or more breaks in service during a leave year, the agency shall include all hours in a nonpay status (other than nonpay status during a fractional pay period when no leave accrues) for each period of service during the leave year in which annual leave accrued.

(b) An employee who is in a nonpay status for his entire leave year does not earn leave.

(c) When a reduction in leave credits results in a debit to an employee's annual leave account at the end of a leave year, the agency shall:

(1) Carry the debit forward as a charge against the annual leave to be earned by the employee in the next leave year; or

(2) Require the employee to refund the amount paid him for the period covering the excess leave that resulted in the debit.

(d) A period covered by an employee's refund for unearned advanced leave is deemed not a nonpay status under this section.

§ 630.209 Refund for unearned leave.

(a) When an employee who is indebted for unearned leave is separated, the agency shall:

(1) Require him to refund the amount paid him for the period covering the leave for which he is indebted; or

(2) Deduct that amount from any pay due him.

An employee who enters active military service with a right of restoration is deemed not separated for the purpose of this paragraph.

(b) This section does not apply when an employee:

(1) Dies;

(2) Retires for disability; or

(3) Resigns or is separated because of disability which prevents him from returning to duty or continuing in the service, and which is the basis of the separation as determined by his agency on medical evidence acceptable to it.

§ 630.210 Uncommon tours of duty.

(a) An agency may require that an employee with an uncommon tour of duty accrue and use leave on the basis of that uncommon tour of duty. The leave accrual rates for such employees shall be directly proportional (based on the number of hours in the biweekly tour of duty and the accrual rate of the corresponding leave category) to the standard leave accrual rates for employees who accrue and use leave on the basis of an 80-hour biweekly tour of duty. One hour (or appropriate fraction thereof) of leave shall be charged for each hour (or appropriate fraction thereof) of absence from the uncommon tour of duty.

(b) When an employee is converted to a different tour of duty for leave purposes, his or her leave balances shall be converted to the proper number of hours based on the proportion of hours in the new tour of duty compared to the former tour of duty.

(c) An agency shall establish an uncommon tour of duty for each firefighter compensated under part 550, subpart M, of this chapter. The uncommon tour of duty shall correspond directly to the firefighter's regular tour of duty, as defined in § 550.1302 of this chapter, so that each firefighter accrues and uses leave on the basis of that tour.

[59 FR 66635, Dec. 28, 1994, as amended at 63 FR 64595, Nov. 23, 1998; 67 FR 15467, Apr. 2, 2002]

§630.211 Exclusion of Presidential appointees.

(a) *Authority.* (1) Section 6301(2)(xi) of title 5, United States Code, authorizes the President to exclude certain Presidential appointees in the executive branch or the government of the District of Columbia from the annual and sick leave provisions of subchapter I of chapter 63 of title 5, United States Code, and from the related provisions of this part.

(2) The President, by Executive Order 10540, as amended, has delegated to the Office of Personnel Management the responsibility for making exclusions under section 6301(2)(xi), and the Office of Personnel Management has delegated responsibility to the head of each agency consistent with the provisions of this section.

(3) Presidential appointees in positions where the rate of basic pay is equal to or exceeds the rate for level V of the Executive Schedule are already excluded from the annual and sick leave provisions by 5 U.S.C. 6301(2)(x). Therefore, no further action by an agency is necessary to exclude these appointees.

(b) *Criteria for exclusions.* The head of an agency may exclude an officer in the agency from the annual and sick leave provisions only if the officer meets all of the following criteria:

(1) The officer is a Presidential appointee;

(2) The officer is not a United States attorney or United States marshal; and

(3) The officer's responsibilities for carrying out the duties of the position continue outside normal duty hours and while away from the normal duty post.

(c) *Revocation of exclusion.* The head of an agency may revoke an exclusion from the annual and sick leave provisions which was made under this section.

(d) *Reports.* The head of an agency must report any exclusion, or revocation of an exclusion, authorized under this section to the Office of Personnel Management.

(e) *Continuation of previous authorizations.* Any officer in an agency who was excluded by action of the President or the Civil Service Commission prior to February 15, 1979, from the annual and sick leave provisions under the authority of 5 U.S.C. 6301(2)(xi) shall continue to be excluded from annual and sick leave unless the exclusion is revoked by the agency under the provisions of this section.

[44 FR 54694, Sept. 21, 1979, as amended at 56 FR 18663, Apr. 23, 1991]

§630.212 Use of annual leave to establish initial eligibility for retirement or continuation of health benefits.

(a) An employee may elect to use annual leave and remain on the agency's rolls in order to establish initial eligibility for immediate retirement under 5 U.S.C. 8336, 8412, or 8414, and/or to establish initial eligibility under 5 U.S.C. 8905 to continue health benefits coverage into retirement, as provided in:

(1) Section 351.606(b)(1) for an employee who would otherwise have been separated by reduction in force procedures under part 351 of this chapter; or

(2) Section 351.606(b)(2) of this chapter for an employee who would otherwise have been separated by adverse action procedures under authority of part 752 of this chapter because of the employee's decision to decline relocation (including transfer of function).

(b)(1) Annual leave that may be used for the purposes described in paragraph (a) of this section includes all accumulated, accrued, and restored annual leave to the employee's credit prior to the effective date of the reduction in force or relocation (including transfer of function) and annual leave earned by an employee while in a paid leave status after the effective date of the reduction in force or relocation (including transfer of function).

(2) Annual leave that is advanced to an employee under 5 U.S.C. 6302(d), including any advance annual leave that may be credited to an employee's leave account after the effective date of the reduction in force or relocation (including transfer of function), may not be used for purpose of this section.

(3) For purposes of this section, the employing agency may approve the use of any or all annual leave donated to an employee under part 630, subpart I, of this chapter (Voluntary Leave Transfer Program), or made available to the employee under part 630, subpart J, of this chapter (Voluntary Leave

Bank Program), as of the effective date of the reduction in force or relocation.

[62 FR 10683, Mar. 10, 1997]

Subpart C—Annual Leave

§ 630.301 Annual leave accrual and accumulation—Senior Executive Service, Senior-Level, and Scientific and Professional Employees.

(a) Annual leave accrues at the rate of 1 day (8 hours) for each full biweekly pay period for an employee who is covered by 5 U.S.C. 6301, who is employed for the full pay period, and who—

(1) Holds a position in the Senior Executive Service (SES) which is subject to 5 U.S.C. 5383; or

(2) Holds a senior-level (SL) or scientific or professional (ST) position which is subject to 5 U.S.C. 5376.

(b) The head of an agency may request that OPM authorize an annual leave accrual rate of 1 full day (8 hours) for each biweekly pay period for additional categories of employees who are covered by 5 U.S.C. 6301 and who hold positions that are determined by OPM to be equivalent to positions subject to the pay systems under 5 U.S.C. 5383 or 5376. Such a request must include documentation that the affected pay system is equivalent to the SES or SL/ST pay system because it meets all three of the following conditions:

(1) Pay rates are established under an administratively determined (AD) pay system that was created under a separate statutory authority. If an AD position has a single rate of pay established under an authority outside of 5 U.S.C. chapters 51 and 53, that single rate (excluding locality pay) must be higher than the rate for GS–15, step 10 (excluding locality pay). If an AD position is paid within a rate range established under an authority outside of 5 U.S.C. chapters 51 and 53, the minimum rate of the rate range (excluding locality pay) must be at least equal to the minimum rate for the SES and SL/ST pay systems (120 percent of the rate for GS–15, step 1, excluding locality pay), and the maximum rate of the rate range (excluding locality pay) must be at least equal to the rate for level IV of the Executive Schedule;

(2) Covered positions are equivalent to a "Senior Executive Service position" as defined in 5 U.S.C. 3132(a)(2), a senior-level position (*i.e.*, a non-executive position that is classified above GS–15, such as a high-level special assistant or a senior attorney in a highly-specialized field who is not a manager, supervisor, or policy advisor), or a scientific or professional position as described in 5 U.S.C. 3104; and

(3) Covered positions are subject to a performance appraisal system established under 5 U.S.C. chapter 43 and 5 CFR part 430, subparts B and C, or other applicable legal authority, for planning, monitoring, developing, evaluating, and rewarding employee performance.

(c) If OPM approves an agency's request to cover additional categories of employees, the higher annual leave accrual rate will become effective for the pay period during which OPM approves the agency's request. Agencies must credit annual leave at the 8-hour accrual rate for affected employees who are employed for the full pay period.

(d) An employee who moves to a position not covered by this section will no longer be entitled to the higher annual leave accrual rate established under paragraph (a) or (b) of this section, except as provided in 5 U.S.C. 6303(a). Upon movement to a noncovered position, an employee's annual leave accrual rate must be determined based on his or her years of creditable service, as provided in 5 U.S.C. 6303(a).

(e) Unused annual leave accrued by an employee while serving in a position subject to one of the pay systems under 5 U.S.C. 5383 (Senior Executive Service) or 5 U.S.C. 5376 (Senior-Level and Scientific or Professional) or 10 U.S.C. 1607(a) (Intelligence Senior Level), shall accumulate for use in succeeding years until it totals not more than 90 days (720 hours) at the beginning of the first full biweekly pay period (or corresponding period for an employee who is not paid on the basis of biweekly pay periods) occurring in a calendar year.

(f) When an employee in a position outside of those listed in paragraph (e) of this section moves to a position covered by paragraph (e) of this section, any annual leave accumulated prior to movement shall remain to the employee's credit.

(1) Annual leave accumulated prior to movement to a position covered by paragraph (e) of this section that is in excess of the amount allowed for the former position by 5 U.S.C. 6304(a), (b), or (c) and that is not used by the beginning of the first full biweekly pay period in the next leave year shall be subject to forfeiture.

(2) If an employee serves less than a full pay period in a position listed in paragraph (e) of this section, only that portion of accrued annual leave that is attributable to service in such a position shall be subject to the 90-day (720-hour) limitation on accumulation of annual leave. Annual leave accrued during the remainder of the pay period shall be subject to the limitations in 5 U.S.C. 6304(a), (b), and (c), as appropriate.

(g) When an employee covered by paragraph (e) of this section moves to a position not covered by paragraph (e) of this section, any annual leave accumulated while serving in the former position that is in excess of the amount allowed for the position by 5 U.S.C. 6304(a), (b), or (c) shall remain to the employee's credit and shall be subject to reduction under procedures identical to those described in 5 U.S.C. 6304(c).

(h) An employee in the Senior Executive Service who, as of the first day of the first pay period beginning after October 13, 1994, has accumulated annual leave in excess of 90 days (720 hours) is entitled to retain that leave as a personal leave ceiling. The leave shall be credited to the employee and shall be subject to reduction in the following manner:

(1) Annual leave credited to an employee shall be based on the amount of annual leave accumulated by the employee as of the end of the pay period preceding the first pay period beginning after October 13, 1994. The credited leave shall exclude—

(i) Any annual leave restored to the employee under 5 U.S.C. 6304(d); and

(ii) Any annual leave advanced to the employee under 5 U.S.C. 6302(d) that had not yet been earned.

(2) Annual leave credited to an employee that is in excess of 90 days (720 hours) shall be subject to reduction in the same manner as provided in 5 U.S.C. 6304(c) until the employee's accumulated annual leave is equal to or less than 90 days (720 hours). For the 1994 leave year, 5 U.S.C. 6304(c) shall be applied only for leave earned and used between the start of the first pay period beginning after October 13, 1994, and the end of the 1994 leave year.

(i) Agencies shall notify affected employees and maintain records on the accumulated annual leave credited to each employee under paragraph (h) of this section and on any reductions in the credited annual leave made under 5 U.S.C. 6304(c). If the employee transfers to another agency, such records shall be provided to the gaining agency.

[59 FR 65705, Dec. 21, 1994, as amended at 60 FR 33328, June 28, 1995; 70 FR 13344, 13345, Mar. 21, 2005; 71 FR 61634, Oct. 19, 2006; 73 FR 18943, Apr. 8, 2008]

§ 630.302 Maximum annual leave accumulation—forty-five day limitation.

(a) The effective date on which an employee (otherwise eligible thereunder) becomes subject to section 6304(b) of title 5, United States Code, is the:

(1) Date of his entry on duty when he is employed locally;

(2) Date of his arrival at a post of regular assignment for duty; or

(3) Date on which he begins to perform duty in an area outside the United States and the area of recruitment or from which transferred, when the employee is required to perform duty en route to his post of regular assignment for duty.

(b) Subject to section 6304(c) of title 5, United States Code, the maximum amount of annual leave that may be carried forward into the next leave year by an employee who is transferred or reassigned to a position in which he is no longer subject to section 6304(b) of that title is determined as follows:

(1) When, on the date prescribed by paragraph (c) of this section, the amount of an employee's accumulated and accrued annual leave is 30 days or less, he may carry forward the amount prescribed by section 6304(a) of title 5, United States Code;

(2) When, on the date prescribed by paragraph (c) of this section, the amount of an employee's accumulated and accrued annual leave is more than 30 days but not more than 45 days, he

may carry forward the full amount thereof that is unused at the end of the current leave year;

(3) When, on the date prescribed by paragraph (c) of this section, the amount of an employee's accumulated and accrued annual leave is more than 45 days, he may carry forward the amount of unused annual leave to his credit at the end of the current leave year that does not exceed:

(i) 45 days, if he is not entitled to a greater accumulation under section 6304(c) of title 5, United States Code; or

(ii) The amount he is entitled to accumulate under section 6304(c) of that title, if that amount is greater than 45 days.

(c) For the purposes of paragraph (b) of this section, an agency shall determine the amount of an employee's accumulated and accrued annual leave at the end of the pay period which includes:

(1) The date on which the employee departs from his post of regular assignment for transfer or reassignment, except that when the employee is required to perform duty en route in an area in which he would be subject to section 6304(b) of title 5, United States Code, if assigned there, it is the date on which he ceases to perform the duty; or

(2) The date on which final administrative approval is given to effect a change in the employee's duty station when he is on detail or leave in the United States, or in an area (the Commonwealth of Puerto Rico or a territory or possession of the United States) from which he was recruited or transferred.

§ 630.303 Part-time employees; earnings.

A part-time employee for whom there has been established in advance a regular tour of duty on 1 or more days during each administrative workweek, and a part-time employee on a flexible work schedule for whom there has been established only a biweekly work requirement, earn annual leave as follows:

(a) An employee with less than 3 years of service earns 1 hour of annual leave for each 20 hours in a pay status.

(b) An employee with 3 but less than 15 years of service earns 1 hour of annual leave for each 13 hours in a pay status.

(c) An employee with 15 years or more of service earns 1 hour of annual leave for each 10 hours in a pay status.

[33 FR 12475, Sept. 4, 1968, as amended at 48 FR 44061, Sept. 27, 1983]

§ 630.304 Accumulation limitation for part-time employees.

A part-time employee may accumulate not more than 240 or 360 hours' annual leave on the same basis that a full-time employee may accumulate not more than 30 or 45 days' annual leave.

§ 630.305 Designating agency official to approve exigencies.

Before annual leave may be restored under 5 U.S.C. 6304, the determination that an exigency is of major importance and that therefore annual leave may not be used by employees to avoid forfeiture must be made by the head of the agency or someone designated to act for him or her on this matter. Except where made by the head of the agency, the determination may not be made by any official whose leave would be affected by the decision.

[53 FR 42933, Oct. 25, 1988]

§ 630.306 Time limit for use of restored annual leave.

(a) Except as otherwise authorized under paragraphs (b) and (c) of this section or other regulation, annual leave restored under 5 U.S.C. 6304(d) must be scheduled and used not later than the end of the leave year ending 2 years after:

(1) The date of restoration of the annual leave forfeited because of administrative error; or

(2) The date fixed by the agency head, or his or her designee, as the termination date of the exigency of the public business that resulted in forfeiture of the annual leave; or,

(3) The date the employee is determined to be recovered and able to return to duty if the leave was forfeited because of sickness.

(b) Annual leave restored to an employee under 5 U.S.C. 6304(d)(3) must be scheduled and used within the time limits prescribed in paragraphs (b)(1) and (b)(2) of this section:

(1) A full-time employee shall schedule and use excess annual leave of 416 hours or less by the end of the leave year in progress 2 years after the date the employee is no longer subject to 5 U.S.C. 6304(d)(3). The agency shall extend this period by 1 leave year for each additional 208 hours of excess annual leave or any portion thereof.

(2) A part-time employee shall schedule and use excess annual leave in an amount equal to or less than 20 percent of the number of hours in the employee's scheduled annual tour of duty by the end of the leave year in progress 2 years after the date the employee is no longer subject to 5 U.S.C. 6304(d)(3). The agency shall extend this period by 1 leave year for each additional number of hours of excess annual leave, or any portion thereof, equal to 10 percent of the number of hours in the employee's scheduled annual tour of duty.

(c) The time limits established under paragraphs (a) and (b) of this section for using restored annual leave accounts shall not apply for the entire period during which an employee is subject to 5 U.S.C. 6304(d)(3). When coverage under 5 U.S.C. 6304(d)(3) ends, a new time limit shall be established under paragraph (b) of this section for all annual leave restored to an employee under 5 U.S.C. 6304(d).

[59 FR 62972, Dec. 7, 1994]

§ 630.307 Time limit for use of restored annual leave—former missing employees.

Annual leave restored under section 5562 of title 5, United States Code, shall be used within a time limit to be prescribed by the Office of Personnel Management in each case taking into consideration the amount of the restored leave and other relevant factors.

[39 FR 1575, Jan. 11, 1974]

§ 630.308 Scheduling of annual leave.

(a) Except as provided in paragraph (b) of this section and §§ 630.310 and 630.311, before annual leave forfeited under 5 U.S.C. 6304 may be considered for restoration under that section, use of the annual leave must have been scheduled in writing before the start of the third biweekly pay period prior to the end of the leave year.

(b) The requirement for advance scheduling of annual leave in paragraph (a) of this section shall not apply to an employee who is covered by 5 U.S.C. 6304(d)(3). When coverage under 5 U.S.C. 6304(d)(3) terminates during a leave year, the employee shall make a reasonable effort to comply with the scheduling requirement in paragraph (a) of this section. The head of the agency or his or her designee may exempt employees from the advance scheduling requirement in paragraph (a) of this section if coverage under 6304(d)(3) terminated during the leave year and the employee was unable to comply with the advance scheduling requirement due to circumstances beyond his or her control.

[59 FR 62973, Dec. 7, 1994; 59 FR 65839, Dec. 21, 1994, as amended at 64 FR 46258, Aug. 25, 1999; 66 FR 55558, Nov. 2, 2001]

§ 630.309 Time limit for use of restored annual leave—extended exigency of the public business.

(a) Annual leave restored under 5 U.S.C. 6304(d)(1)(B) because of an extended exigency, as defined in paragraph (b) of this section, must be scheduled and used within a time period that equals twice the number of full calendar years, or parts thereof, that the exigency existed. This time period begins at the beginning of the leave year following the leave year in which the exigency is declared to be ended.

(b) An *extended exigency* means an exigency of such significance as to—

(1) Threaten the national security, safety, or welfare;

(2) Last more than 3 calendar years;

(3) Affect a segment of an agency or occupational class; and

(4) Preclude subsequent use of both restored and accrued annual leave within the time limit specified in § 630.306.

[50 FR 29937, July 23, 1985]

§ 630.310 [Reserved]

§ 630.311 Scheduling of annual leave by employees determined necessary to respond to the "National Emergency by Reason of Certain Terrorist Attacks."

(a) The "National Emergency by Reason of Certain Terrorist Attacks" (Presidential Proclamation of September 14, 2001) is deemed to be an exigency of the public business for the purpose of restoring annual leave forfeited under 5 U.S.C. 6304.

(b) For any employee who forfeits annual leave under 5 U.S.C. 6304 at the beginning of a leave year because the agency determined the employee's services were required in response to the national emergency, the forfeited annual leave is deemed to have been scheduled in advance for the purpose of 5 U.S.C. 6304(d)(1)(B) and § 630.308.

(c) Annual leave restored under 5 U.S.C. 6304(d) because of the national emergency must be scheduled and used within the time limits prescribed in paragraphs (c)(1) and (c)(2) of this section:

(1) A full-time employee must schedule and use excess annual leave of 416 hours or less by the end of the leave year in progress 2 years after the date the employee's services are no longer required by the national emergency. The agency must extend this period by 1 leave year for each additional 208 hours of excess annual leave or any portion thereof.

(2) A part-time employee must schedule and use excess annual leave in an amount equal to or less than 20 percent of the number of hours in the employee's scheduled annual tour of duty by the end of the leave year in progress 2 years after the date the employee's services are no longer required by the national emergency. The agency must extend this period by 1 leave year for each additional number of hours of excess annual leave, or any portion thereof, equal to 10 percent of the number of hours in the employee's scheduled annual tour of duty.

(d) The time limits established under paragraphs (c)(1) and (c)(2) of this section for using restored annual leave accounts do not apply for the entire period during which an employee's services are required for the national emergency. When coverage under paragraphs (a) and (b) of this section ends, a new time limit will be established under paragraph (c) of this section for all annual leave restored to an employee under 5 U.S.C. 6304(d).

(e) An employee whose services were determined essential during the national emergency, but who subsequently moves to a position not considered essential, must make a reasonable effort to comply with the scheduling requirement in § 630.308(a). The head of the agency or his or her designee may exempt such an employee from the advance scheduling requirement in § 630.308(a) if coverage under paragraphs (a) and (b) of this section terminated during the leave year and the employee can demonstrate that he or she was unable to comply with the advance scheduling requirement due to circumstances beyond his or her control.

[66 FR 55558, Nov. 2, 2001]

Subpart D—Sick Leave

SOURCE: 71 FR 47695, Aug. 17, 2006, unless otherwise noted.

§ 630.401 Granting sick leave.

(a) Subject to paragraphs (b) through (e) of this section, an agency must grant sick leave to an employee when he or she—

(1) Receives medical, dental, or optical examination or treatment;

(2) Is incapacitated for the performance of his or her duties by physical or mental illness, injury, pregnancy, or childbirth;

(3) Provides care for a family member—

(i) Who is incapacitated by a medical or mental condition or attends to a family member receiving medical, dental, or optical examination or treatment;

(ii) With a serious health condition; or

(iii) Who would, as determined by the health authorities having jurisdiction or by a health care provider, jeopardize the health of others by that family member's presence in the community because of exposure to a communicable disease;

(4) Makes arrangements necessitated by the death of a family member or attends the funeral of a family member;

(5) Would, as determined by the health authorities having jurisdiction or by a health care provider, jeopardize the health of others by his or her presence on the job because of exposure to a communicable disease; or

(6) Must be absent from duty for purposes relating to his or her adoption of a child, including appointments with adoption agencies, social workers, and attorneys; court proceedings; required travel; and any other activities necessary to allow the adoption to proceed.

(b) The amount of sick leave granted to an employee during any leave year for the purposes described in paragraphs (a)(3)(i), (a)(3)(iii), and (a)(4) of this section may not exceed a total of 104 hours (or, for a part-time employee or an employee with an uncommon tour of duty, the number of hours of sick leave he or she normally accrues during a leave year).

(c) The amount of sick leave granted to an employee during any leave year for the purposes described in paragraph (a)(3)(ii) of this section may not exceed a total of 480 hours (or, for a part-time employee or an employee with an uncommon tour of duty, an amount of sick leave equal to 12 times the average number of hours in his or her scheduled tour of duty each week), subject to the limitation found in paragraph (d) of this section.

(d) If, at the time an employee uses sick leave to care for a family member with a serious health condition under paragraph (c) of this section, he or she has used any portion of the sick leave authorized under paragraph (b) of this section during that leave year, the agency must subtract that amount from the maximum number of hours authorized under paragraph (c) of this section to determine the total amount of sick leave the employee may use during the remainder of the leave year to care for a family member with a serious health condition. If an employee has previously used the maximum amount of sick leave permitted under paragraph (c) of this section in a leave year, he or she is not entitled to use additional sick leave under paragraph (b) of this section.

(e) If the number of hours in the employee's tour of duty is changed during the leave year, his or her entitlement to use sick leave for the purposes described in paragraphs (a)(3) and (4) of this section must be recalculated based on the new tour of duty.

[71 FR 47695, Aug. 17, 2006, as amended at 75 FR 75372, Dec. 3, 2010]

§ 630.402 Advanced sick leave.

(a) At the beginning of a leave year or at any time thereafter when required by the exigencies of the situation, an agency may grant advanced sick leave in the amount of:

(1) Up to 240 hours to a full-time employee—

(i) Who is incapacitated for the performance of his or her duties by physical or mental illness, injury, pregnancy, or childbirth;

(ii) For a serious health condition of the employee or a family member;

(iii) When the employee would, as determined by the health authorities having jurisdiction or by a health care provider, jeopardize the health of others by his or her presence on the job because of exposure to a communicable disease;

(iv) For purposes relating to the adoption of a child; or

(v) For the care of a covered servicemember with a serious injury or illness, provided the employee is exercising his or her entitlement under 5 U.S.C. 6382(a)(3).

(2) Up to 104 hours to a full-time employee—

(i) When he or she receives medical, dental or optical examination or treatment;

(ii) To provide care for a family member who is incapacitated by a medical or mental condition or to attend to a family member receiving medical, dental, or optical examination or treatment;

(iii) To provide care for a family member who would, as determined by the health authorities having jurisdiction or by a health care provider, jeopardize the health of others by that family member's presence in the community because of exposure to a communicable disease; or

(iv) To make arrangements necessitated by the death of a family member or to attend the funeral of a family member.

(b) Two hundred forty hours is the maximum amount of advanced sick leave an employee may have to his or her credit at any one time. For a part-time employee (or an employee on an uncommon tour of duty), the maximum amount of sick leave an agency may advance must be prorated according to the number of hours in the employee's regularly scheduled administrative workweek.

[75 FR 75373, Dec. 3, 2010]

§ 630.403 Substitution of sick leave for unpaid family and medical leave to care for a covered servicemember.

The amount of accumulated and accrued sick leave an employee may substitute for unpaid family and medical leave under 5 U.S.C. 6382(a)(3) for leave to care for a covered servicemember may not exceed a total of 26 administrative workweeks in a single 12-month period (or, for a part-time employee or an employee with an uncommon tour of duty, an amount of sick leave equal to 26 times the average number of hours in his or her scheduled tour of duty each week).

[75 FR 75373, Dec. 3, 2010]

§ 630.404 Requesting sick leave.

An employee must file an application—written, oral, or electronic, as required by the agency—for sick leave within such time limits as the agency may require. The employee must request advance approval for sick leave for the purpose of receiving medical, dental, or optical examination or treatment and, to the extent possible, for the purposes described in § 630.401(a)(3), (4), and (6).

[71 FR 47695, Aug. 17, 2006. Redesignated at 75 FR 75373, Dec. 3, 2010]

§ 630.405 Supporting evidence for the use of sick leave.

(a) An agency may grant sick leave only when the need for sick leave is supported by administratively acceptable evidence. An agency may consider an employee's self-certification as to the reason for his or her absence as administratively acceptable evidence, regardless of the duration of the absence. An agency may also require a medical certificate or other administratively acceptable evidence as to the reason for an absence for any of the purposes described in § 630.401(a) for an absence in excess of 3 workdays, or for a lesser period when the agency determines it is necessary.

(b) An employee must provide administratively acceptable evidence or medical certification for a request for sick leave no later than 15 calendar days after the date the agency requests such medical certification. If it is not practicable under the particular circumstances to provide the requested evidence or medical certification within 15 calendar days after the date requested by the agency despite the employee's diligent, good faith efforts, the employee must provide the evidence or medical certification within a reasonable period of time under the circumstances involved, but no later than 30 calendar days after the date the agency requests such documentation. An employee who does not provide the required evidence or medical certification within the specified time period is not entitled to sick leave.

(c) An agency may require an employee requesting sick leave to care for a family member under § 630.401(a)(3)(ii) to provide an additional written statement from the health care provider concerning the family member's need for psychological comfort and/or physical care. The statement must certify that—

(1) The family member requires psychological comfort and/or physical care;

(2) The family member would benefit from the employee's care or presence; and

(3) The employee is needed to care for the family member for a specified period of time.

[71 FR 47695, Aug. 17, 2006. Redesignated at 75 FR 75373, Dec. 3, 2010]

§ 630.406 Use of sick leave during annual leave.

Subject to § 630.401(b) through (e), an agency may grant sick leave to an employee during a period of annual leave for any of the purposes described in §630.401(a).

[71 FR 47695, Aug. 17, 2006. Redesignated at 75 FR 75373, Dec. 3, 2010]

§630.407 Sick leave used in the computation of an annuity.

Sick leave used in the computation of an annuity is charged against an employee's sick leave account and may not thereafter be used, transferred, or recredited. All sick leave to the credit of an employee as of the date of his or her retirement (or death) and reported to OPM for credit towards the calculation of an annuity is considered used.

[71 FR 47695, Aug. 17, 2006. Redesignated at 75 FR 75373, Dec. 3, 2010]

§630.408 Records on the use of sick leave.

An agency must maintain records of the amount of sick leave used by an employee for family care purposes and to make arrangements for or attend the funeral of a family member under §630.401(a)(3) and (4). The records must be sufficient to ensure that an employee does not exceed the limitations in §630.401(b) and (c).

[71 FR 47695, Aug. 17, 2006. Redesignated at 75 FR 75373, Dec. 3, 2010]

Subpart E—Recredit of Leave

§630.501 Annual leave recredit.

(a) When an employee transfers between positions under subchapter I of chapter 63 of title 5, United States Code, the agency from which he transfers shall certify his annual leave account to the employing agency for credit or charge.

(b) When annual leave is transferred between different leave systems under section 6308 of title 5, United States Code, or is recredited under a different leave system as the result of a refund under section 6306 of that title, 7 calendar days of annual leave are deemed equal to 5 workdays of annual leave.

[35 FR 18581, Dec. 8, 1970]

§630.502 Sick leave recredit.

(a) When an employee transfers between positions under subchapter I of chapter 63 of title 5, United States Code, the agency from which the employee transfers shall certify his or her sick leave account to the employing agency for credit or charge.

(b) Except as provided in §630.407 and in paragraph (c) of this section, an employee who has had a break in service is entitled to a recredit of sick leave (without regard to the date of his or her separation), if he or she returns to Federal employment on or after December 2, 1994, unless the sick leave was forfeited upon reemployment in the Federal Government before December 2, 1994.

(c) Except as provided in §630.407, an employee of the government of the District of Columbia who was first employed by the government of the District of Columbia before October 1, 1987, and who has had a break in service is entitled to a recredit of sick leave (without regard to the date of his or her separation) if he or she returns to Federal employment on or after December 2, 1994, unless the sick leave was forfeited upon reemployment in the Federal Government before December 2, 1994.

(d) When sick leave is transferred between different leave systems under section 6308 of title 5, United States Code, 7 calendar days of sick leave are deemed equal to 5 workdays of sick leave.

(e) An employee who transfers to a position under a different leave system to which he or she can transfer only a part of his or her sick leave is entitled to a recredit of the untransferred sick leave (without regard to the date of the original transfer) if the employee returns to the leave system under which it was earned on or after December 2, 1994.

(f) An employee who transfers to a position to which he or she cannot transfer his or her sick leave is entitled to a recredit of the untransferred sick leave (without regard to the date of the original transfer) if the employee returns to the leave system under which it was earned on or after December 2, 1994.

(g) The recredit of sick leave under this section shall be supported by written documentation available to the employing agency in its official personnel records concerning the employee, the official records of the employee's former employing agency, copies of contemporaneous earnings and leave statement(s) provided by the employee, or copies of other contemporaneous written documentation acceptable to the agency.

(h) The sick leave to be recredited under this section must have been accrued under 5 U.S.C. 6307 or transferred to the employee's credit under 5 U.S.C. 6308 (or the corresponding provisions of prior statutes).

[59 FR 62271, Dec. 2, 1994, as amended at 74 FR 10165, Mar. 10, 2009; 75 FR 75373, Dec. 3, 2010]

§ 630.503 Leave from former leave systems.

An employee who earned leave under the leave acts of 1936 or any other leave system merged under subchapter I of chapter 63 of title 5, United States Code, is entitled to a recredit of that leave under that subchapter if he would have been entitled to recredit for it on reentering the leave system under which it was earned. However, this section does not revive leave already forfeited.

§ 630.504 Reestablishment of leave account after military service.

(a) When an employee leaves his or her civilian position to enter the military service, the employing agency shall certify his or her leave account for credit or charge.

(b) If the employee returns to a civilian position following military service, the agency to which the employee returns shall reestablish the certified leave account as a credit or charge (without regard to the date he or she left the civilian position) when the employee is—

(1) Restored in accordance with a right of restoration after separation from active military duty or hospitalization continuing thereafter as provided by law or in accordance with the mandatory provisions of a statute, Executive order, or regulation; or

(2) Reemployed in a position under subchapter I of chapter 63 of title 5, United States Code, on or after December 2, 1994.

(c) For the purpose of documenting a returning employee's entitlement to a recredit of sick leave under this section, the documentation criteria established in § 630.502(g) shall apply.

[59 FR 62272, Dec. 2, 1994]

§ 630.505 Restoration after appeal.

When an employee is restored to an agency as a result of an appeal, the agency shall reestablish his leave account as a credit or charge as it was at the time of separation.

§ 630.506 Minimum unit.

(a) When an employee moves between positions under subchapter I of chapter 63 of title 5, United States Code, in different agencies, only his leave in whole hour units may be transferred.

(b) When an employee moves between positions under subchapter I of chapter 63 of title 5, United States Code, covered by different leave charging systems within the same agency, his leave is transferable in accordance with paragraph (a) of this section, unless the agency establishes a different policy making fractions of an hour of leave transferable.

[38 FR 18446, July 11, 1973; 38 FR 26601, Sept. 24, 1973]

Subpart F—Home Leave

§ 630.601 Definitions.

In this subpart:

Home leave means leave authorized by section 6305(a) of title 5, United States Code, and earned by service abroad for use in the United States, in the Commonwealth of Puerto Rico, or in the territories or possessions of the United States.

Month means a period which runs from a given day in 1 month through the date preceding the numerically corresponding day in the next month.

Service abroad means service on and after September 6, 1960, by an employee at a post of duty outside the United States and outside the employee's place of residence if his place of residence is in the Commonwealth of Puerto Rico or a territory or possession of the United States.

[33 FR 12475, Sept. 4, 1967, as amended at 60 FR 67287, Dec. 29, 1995]

§ 630.602 Coverage.

An employee who meets the requirements of section 6304(b) of title 5, United States Code, for the accumulation of a maximum of 45 days of annual leave earns and may be granted home leave in accordance with section 6305(a) of that title and this subpart.

§ 630.603 Computation of service abroad.

For the purpose of this subpart, service abroad:

(a) Begins on the date of the employee's arrival at a post of duty outside the United States, or on the date of his entrance on duty when recruited abroad;

(b) Ends on the date of the employee's departure from the post for separation or for assignment in the United States, or on the date of his separation from duty when separated abroad; and

(c) Includes (1) absence in a nonpay status up to a maximum of 2 workweeks within each 12 months of service abroad, (2) authorized leave with pay, (3) time spent in the Armed Forces of the United States which interrupts service abroad (but only for eligibility, not leave-earning, purposes), and (4) a period of detail.

In computing service abroad, full credit is given for the day of arrival and the day of departure.

[33 FR 12475, Sept. 4, 1968, as amended at 35 FR 14763, Sept. 23, 1970]

§ 630.604 Earning rates.

(a) For each 12 months of service abroad, an employee earns home leave at the following rate:

(1) An employee who accepts an appointment to, or occupies, a position for which the agency has prescribed the requirement that the incumbent accept assignments anywhere in the world as the needs of the agency dictate—15 days.

(2) An employee who is serving with a U.S. mission to a public international organization—15 days.

(3) An employee who is serving at a post for which payment of a foreign or nonforeign (but not a tropical) differential of 20 percent or more is authorized by law or regulation—15 days.

(4) An employee not included in paragraph (a) (1), (2), or (3) of this section who is serving at a post for which payment of a foreign or territorial (but not a tropical) differential of at least 10 percent but less than 20 percent is authorized by law or regulation—10 days.

(5) An employee not included in paragraph (a) (1), (2), (3), or (4) of this section—5 days.

(6) An employee included under (a) (1) through (5) of this section whose civilian service abroad is interrupted by a tour of duty in the Armed Forces of the United States, for the duration of such tour—0 (zero) days.

(b) An agency shall credit home leave to an employee's leave account, as earned, in multiples of 1 day.

[33 FR 12475, Sept. 4, 1968, as amended at 35 FR 14763, Sept. 23, 1970]

§ 630.605 Computation of home leave.

(a) For each month of service abroad, an employee earns home leave under the rates fixed by § 630.604(a) in the amounts set forth in the following table:

HOME LEAVE-EARNING TABLE

[Days earned]

Months of service abroad	Earning rate (days for each 12 months)		
	15	10	5
1	1	0	0
2	2	1	0
3	3	2	1
4	5	3	1
5	6	4	2
6	7	5	2
7	8	5	2
8	10	6	3
9	11	7	3
10	12	8	4
11	13	9	4
12	15	10	5

(b) When an employee moves between different home leave-earning rates during a month of service abroad, or when a change in the differential during a month of service abroad results in a different home leave-earning rate, the agency shall credit the employee with the amount of home leave for the month at the rate to which he was entitled before the change in his home leave-earning rate.

§ 630.606 Grant of home leave.

(a) *Entitlement.* Except as otherwise authorized by statute, an employee is entitled to home leave only when he has completed a basic service period of 24 months of continuous service abroad. This basic service period is terminated by (1) a break in service of 1 or more workdays, or (2) an assignment (other than a detail) to a position in which an employee is no longer subject to section 6305(a) of title 5, United States Code.

(b) *Agency authority.* A grant of home leave is at the discretion of an agency. An agency may grant home leave in combination with other leaves of absence in accordance with established agency policy.

(c) *Limitations.* An agency may grant home leave only:

(1) For use in the United States, the Commonwealth of Puerto Rico, or a territory or possession of the United States; and

(2) During an employee's period of service abroad, or within a reasonable period after his return from service abroad when it is contemplated that he will return to service abroad immediately or on completion of an assignment in the United States.

Home leave not granted during a period named in paragraph (c)(2) of this section may be granted only when the employee has completed a further substantial period of service abroad. This further substantial period of service abroad may not be less than the tour of duty prescribed for the employee's post of assignment, except when the agency determines that an earlier grant of home leave is warranted in an individual case.

(d) *Charging of home leave.* The minimum charge for home leave is 1 day and additional charges are in multiples thereof.

(e) *Refund for home leave.* An employee is indebted for the home leave used by him when he fails to return to service abroad after the period of home leave, or after the completion of an assignment in the United States. However, a refund for this indebtedness is not required when (1) the employee has completed not less than 6 months' service in an assignment in the United States following the period of home leave; (2) the agency determines that the employee's failure to return was due to compelling personal reasons of a humanitarian or compassionate nature, such as may involve physical or mental health or circumstances over which the employee has no control; or (3) the agency which granted the home leave determines that it is in the public interest not to return the employee to his overseas assignment.

§ 630.607 Transfer and recredit of home leave.

An employee is entitled to have his home leave account transferred or recredited to his account when he moves between agencies or is reemployed without a break in service of more than 90 days.

Subpart G—Shore Leave

AUTHORITY: 5 U.S.C. 6305.

§ 630.701 Coverage.

This subpart applies to an employee as defined in section 6301 of title 5, United States Code, who is regularly assigned to duties aboard an oceangoing vessel. An employee is considered to be regularly assigned when his continuing duties are such that all or a significant part of them require that he serve aboard an oceangoing vessel. Temporary assignments of a shore-based employee, such as for limited work projects or for training, do not constitute a regular assignment.

§ 630.702 Definitions.

Extended voyage means a voyage of not less than 7 consecutive calendar days duration.

Oceangoing vessel means a vessel in use on the high seas or the Great Lakes; but does not include a vessel which operates primarily on rivers, other lakes, bays, sounds or within the 3-nautical-mile limit of the coastal area of the 48 contiguous States, except when used in mapping, charting, or surveying operations or when in or sailing to or from foreign, territorial, Hawaiian, or Alaskan waters, or waters outside its normal area of operations or outside the 3-nautical-mile limit.

Shore leave means leave authorized by section 6305(c) of title 5, United States Code, and this subpart.

Voyage means the sailing of an oceangoing vessel from one port and its return to that port or the final port of discharge.

[33 FR 12475, Sept. 4, 1968, as amended at 60 FR 67287, Dec. 29, 1995]

§ 630.703 Computation of shore leave.

(a) An employee earns shore leave at the rate of 1 day of shore leave for each 15 calendar days of absence on one or more extended voyages.

(b) (1) For an employee who is an officer or crewmember, a voyage begins either on the date he assumes his duties aboard an oceangoing vessel to begin preparation for a voyage or on the date he comes aboard when a voyage is in progress. The voyage terminates on the date he ceases to be an officer or crewmember of the oceangoing vessel or on the date on which he is released from assignment of his duties relating to that voyage aboard the oceangoing vessel at the port of origin or port of final discharge, whichever is earlier.

(2) For an employee other than an officer or crewmember, a voyage begins on the date of sailing and terminates on the date the oceangoing vessel returns to a port at which the employee will disembark in completion of his assignment aboard the vessel, or on the date he is released from his assignment aboard the vessel, whichever is earlier.

(c) In computing days of absence, an agency shall include (1) the beginning date of a voyage and the termination date of a voyage; (2) the days an employee spends traveling to join an oceangoing vessel to which assigned when the vessel is at a place other than the port of origin; (3) the days an employee spends traveling between oceangoing vessels when the employee is assigned from one vessel to another; (4) the period representing the number of days within which an employee is reasonably expected to return to the port of origin when his oceangoing vessel's voyage is terminated, or his employment as an officer or crewmember is terminated, at a port other than the port of origin; (5) for an employee who is an officer or crewmember, the days on which he is on sick leave when he becomes sick during a voyage (whether or not continued as a member of the crew) but not beyond the termination date of the voyage of the oceangoing vessel or his repatriation to the port of origin, whichever is earlier; (6) for an employee other than an officer or crewmember, the days on which he is carried on sick leave but not beyond the date on which he returns to the port of origin or the termination date of the voyage, whichever is earlier; and (7) the days of approved leave from a vessel (paid or unpaid) during a voyage.

§ 630.704 Granting shore leave.

(a) *Authority.* (1) An employee has an absolute right to use shore leave, subject to the right of the head of the agency to fix the time at which shore leave may be used.

(2) Shore leave may be granted during a voyage only when requested by an employee.

(3) An employee shall submit his request for shore leave in writing and whenever an employee's request for shore leave is denied, the denial shall be in writing.

(b) *Accumulation.* Shore leave is in addition to annual leave and may be accumulated for future use without limitation.

(c) *Charge for shore leave.* The minimum charge for shore leave is one day and additional charges are in multiples thereof.

(d) *Lump-sum payment.* Shore leave may not be the basis for lump-sum payment on separation from the service.

(e) *Terminal leave.* (1) Except as provided by paragraph (e)(2) of this section, an agency shall not grant shore leave to an employee as terminal leave. For the purpose of this paragraph terminal leave is approved absence immediately before an employee's separation when an agency knows the employee will not return to duty before the date of his separation.

(2) An agency shall grant shore leave as terminal leave when the employee's inability to use shore leave was due to circumstances beyond his control and not due to his own act or omission.

(f) *Forfeiture of shore leave.* Shore leave not granted before (1) separation from the service, or (2) official assignment (other than by temporary detail) to a position in which the employee does not earn shore leave, is forfeited. When an official assignment will result in forfeiture of shore leave, the agency to the extent administratively practicable shall give an employee an opportunity to use the shore leave he has to his credit either before the reassignment or not later than 6 months after the date of his reassignment when the agency is unable to grant the shore leave before the reassignment.

Subpart H—Funeral Leave

SOURCE: 34 FR 13655, Aug. 26, 1969, unless otherwise noted.

§ 630.801 Applicability.

This subpart and section 6326 of title 5, United States Code, apply to the granting of funeral leave to an employee in connection with the funeral of, or memorial service for, his immediate relative who died as a result of wounds, disease, or injury incurred while serving as a member of the armed forces in a combat zone.

§ 630.802 Coverage.

This subpart applies to:

(a) An employee as defined in section 2105 of title 5, United States Code, who is employed by an executive agency as defined in section 105 of title 5, United States Code; and

(b) An individual who is employed by the government of the District of Columbia.

§ 630.803 Definitions.

Armed forces means the Army, Navy, Air Force, Marine Corps, and Coast Guard.

Combat zone means those areas determined by the President in accordance with section 112 of the Internal Revenue Code.

Committed relationship means one in which the employee, and the domestic partner of the employee, are each other's sole domestic partner (and are not married to or domestic partners with anyone else); and share responsibility for a significant measure of each other's common welfare and financial obligations. This includes, but is not limited to, any relationship between two individuals of the same or opposite sex that is granted legal recognition by a State or by the District of Columbia as a marriage or analogous relationship (including, but not limited to, a civil union).

Domestic partner means an adult in a committed relationship with another adult, including both same-sex and opposite-sex relationships.

Employee means an employee or individual covered by § 630.802.

Funeral leave means leave authorized by section 6326 of title 5, United States Code, and this subpart.

Immediate relative means an individual with any of the following relationships to the employee:

(1) Spouse, and parents thereof;

(2) Sons and daughters, and spouses thereof;

(3) Parents, and spouses thereof;

(4) Brothers and sisters, and spouses thereof;

(5) Grandparents and grandchildren, and spouses thereof;

(6) Domestic partner and parents thereof, including domestic partners of any individual in paragraphs (2) through (5) of this definition; and

(7) Any individual related by blood or affinity whose close association with the employee is the equivalent of a family relationship.

Parent means—

(1) A biological, adoptive, step, or foster parent of the employee, or a person who was a foster parent of the employee when the employee was a minor;

(2) A person who is the legal guardian of the employee or was the legal guardian of the employee when the employee was a minor or required a legal guardian; or

(3) A person who stands *in loco parentis* to the employee or stood *in loco parentis* to the employee when the employee was a minor or required someone to stand *in loco parentis*.

(4) A parent, as described in paragraphs (1) through (3) of this definition, of an employee's spouse or domestic partner.

Son or daughter means—

(1) A biological, adopted, step, or foster son or daughter of the employee;

(2) A person who is a legal ward or was a legal ward of the employee when that individual was a minor or required a legal guardian;

(3) A person for whom the employee stands *in loco parentis* or stood *in loco parentis* when that individual was a minor or required someone to stand *in loco parentis;* or

(4) A son or daughter, as described in paragraphs (1) through (3) of this definition, of an employee's spouse or domestic partner.

[34 FR 13655, Aug. 26, 1969, as amended at 60 FR 67287, Dec. 29, 1995; 75 FR 33496, June 14, 2010]

§ 630.804 Granting of funeral leave.

(a) An agency shall grant an employee such funeral leave as is needed and requested by him, not to exceed 3 workdays, without loss of or reduction in pay, leave to which he is otherwise entitled, or credit for time or service, and without adversely affecting his performance or efficiency rating. Funeral leave is granted to allow an employee to make arrangements for, or to attend, the funeral or memorial service for an immediate relative who died as the result of a wound, disease, or injury incurred while serving as a member of the armed forces in a combat zone. The 3 days need not be consecutive but if not, the employee shall furnish the approving authority satisfactory reasons justifying a grant of funeral leave for nonconsecutive days.

(b) An agency may grant funeral leave only from a prescribed tour of duty, including regularly scheduled overtime, or, in the case of a substitute employee in the postal field service, from a period during which, except for absence on funeral leave, the employee would have worked.

Subpart I—Voluntary Leave Transfer Program

SOURCE: 59 FR 67125, Dec. 29, 1994, unless otherwise noted.

§ 630.901 Purpose and applicability.

(a) *Purpose.* The purpose of this subpart is to set forth procedures and requirements for a voluntary leave transfer program under which the unused accrued annual leave of one agency officer or employee may be transferred for use by another agency officer or employee who needs such leave because of a medical emergency.

(b) *Applicability.* This subpart applies to officers and employees to whom subchapter I of chapter 63 of title 5, United States Code, applies.

§ 630.902 Definitions.

Agency means—

(a) An *Executive agency,* as defined in 5 U.S.C. 105;

(b) A *military department,* as defined in 5 U.S.C. 102; or

(c) Any other entity of the Federal Government that employs officers or employees to whom subchapter I of chapter 63 of title 5, United States Code, applies. *Agency* does not include the Central Intelligence Agency; the Defense Intelligence Agency; the National Security Agency; the Federal Bureau of Investigation; or any other Executive agency or unit thereof, as determined by the President, whose principal function is the conduct of foreign intelligence or counterintelligence activities.

Available paid leave means accrued or accumulated annual or sick leave under subchapter I of chapter 63 of title 5, United States Code, and recredited and restored annual or sick leave under subpart E of this part. *Available paid leave* does not include annual or sick leave advanced to an employee under 5 U.S.C. 6302(d) or 6307(c) or any annual or sick leave accrued under § 630.907(a) that has not been transferred to the appropriate leave account under § 630.907(c).

Committed relationship means one in which the employee, and the domestic partner of the employee, are each other's sole domestic partner (and are not married to or domestic partners with anyone else); and share responsibility for a significant measure of each other's common welfare and financial obligations. This includes, but is not limited to, any relationship between two individuals of the same or opposite sex that is granted legal recognition by a State or by the District of Columbia as a marriage or analogous relationship (including, but not limited to, a civil union).

Domestic partner means an adult in a committed relationship with another adult, including both same-sex and opposite-sex relationships.

Employee has the meaning given that term in 5 U.S.C. 6301(2), except an individual employed by the government of the District of Columbia.

Family member means an individual with any of the following relationships to the employee:

(1) Spouse, and parents thereof;

(2) Sons and daughters, and spouses thereof;

(3) Parents, and spouses thereof;

(4) Brothers and sisters, and spouses thereof;

(5) Grandparents and grandchildren, and spouses thereof;

(6) Domestic partner and parents thereof, including domestic partners of any individual in paragraphs (2) through (5) of this definition; and

(7) Any individual related by blood or affinity whose close association with the employee is the equivalent of a family relationship.

Leave donor means an employee whose voluntary written request for transfer of annual leave to the annual leave account of a leave recipient is approved by his or her own employing agency.

Leave recipient means a current employee for whom the employing agency has approved an application to receive annual leave from the annual leave accounts of one or more leave donors.

Medical emergency means a medical condition of an employee or a family member of such employee that is likely to require an employee's absence from duty for a prolonged period of time and to result in a substantial loss of income to the employee because of the unavailability of paid leave.

Paid leave status under subchapter I means the administrative status of an employee while the employee is using annual or sick leave accrued or accumulated under subchapter I of chapter 63 of title 5, United States Code.

Parent means—

(1) A biological, adoptive, step, or foster parent of the employee, or a person who was a foster parent of the employee when the employee was a minor;

(2) A person who is the legal guardian of the employee or was the legal guardian of the employee when the employee was a minor or required a legal guardian; or

(3) A person who stands *in loco parentis* to the employee or stood *in loco parentis* to the employee when the employee was a minor or required someone to stand *in loco parentis*.

(4) A parent, as described in paragraphs (1) through (3) of this definition, of an employee's spouse or domestic partner.

Shared leave status means the administrative status of an employee while the employee is using transferred leave under this subpart or leave transferred from a leave bank under subpart J of this part.

Son or daughter means—

(1) A biological, adopted, step, or foster son or daughter of the employee;

(2) A person who is a legal ward or was a legal ward of the employee when that individual was a minor or required a legal guardian;

(3) A person for whom the employee stands *in loco parentis* or stood *in loco parentis* when that individual was a minor or required someone to stand *in loco parentis;* or

(4) A son or daughter, as described in paragraphs (1) through (3) of this definition, of an employee's spouse or domestic partner.

[59 FR 67125, Dec. 29, 1994, as amended at 75 FR 33496, June 14, 2010]

§ 630.903 Administrative procedures.

Each Federal agency shall establish and administer procedures to permit the voluntary transfer of annual leave consistent with this subpart.

§ 630.904 Application to become a leave recipient.

(a) An employee may make written application to his or her employing agency to become a leave recipient. If an employee is not capable of making application on his or her own behalf, a personal representative of the potential leave recipient may make written application on his or her behalf.

(b) Each application shall be accompanied by the following information concerning each potential leave recipient:

(1) The name, position title, and grade or pay level of the potential leave recipient;

(2) The reasons transferred leave is needed, including a brief description of the nature, severity, and anticipated duration of the medical emergency, and if it is a recurring one, the approximate frequency of the medical emergency affecting the potential leave recipient;

(3) Certification from one or more physicians, or other appropriate experts, with respect to the medical emergency, if the potential leave recipient's employing agency so requires; and

(4) Any additional information that may be required by the potential leave recipient's employing agency.

(c) If the potential leave recipient's employing agency requires that a potential leave recipient obtain certification from two or more sources under paragraph (b)(3) of this section, the potential leave recipient's employing agency shall ensure, either by direct payment to the expert involved or by reimbursement, that the potential leave recipient is not required to pay for the expenses associated with obtaining certification from more than one source.

§ 630.905 Approval of application to become a leave recipient.

(a) The potential leave recipient's employing agency shall review an application to become a leave recipient under procedures established by the employing agency for the purpose of determining that the potential leave recipient is or has been affected by a medical emergency.

(b) Before approving an application to become a leave recipient, the potential leave recipient's employing agency shall determine that the absence from duty without available paid leave because of the medical emergency is (or is expected to be) at least 24 hours (or, in the case of a part-time employee or an employee with an uncommon tour of duty, at least 30 percent of the average number of hours in the employee's biweekly scheduled tour of duty).

(c) In making a determination as to whether a medical emergency is likely to result in a substantial loss of income, an agency shall not consider factors other than whether the absence from duty without available paid leave is (or is expected to be) at least 24 hours (or, in the case of a part-time employee or an employee with an uncommon tour of duty, at least 30 percent of the average number of hours in the employee's biweekly scheduled tour of duty).

(d) If the application is approved, the employing agency shall notify the leave recipient (or the personal representative who made application on behalf of the leave recipient), within 10 calendar days (excluding Saturdays, Sundays, and legal public holidays) after the date the application was received (or the date the employing agency established its administrative procedures, if that date is later), that—

(1) The application has been approved; and

(2) Other employees of the leave recipient's employing agency may request the transfer of annual leave to the account of the leave recipient.

(e) If the application is not approved, the employing agency shall notify the applicant (or the personal representative who made application on behalf of the potential leave recipient), within 10 calendar days (excluding Saturdays, Sundays, and legal public holidays) after the date the application was received (or the date the employing agency established its administrative procedures, if that date is later)—

(1) That the application has not been approved; and

(2) The reasons for its disapproval.

[59 FR 67125, Dec. 29, 1994, as amended at 60 FR 26979, May 22, 1995; 61 FR 64451, Dec. 5, 1996]

§ 630.906 Transfer of annual leave.

(a) An employee may submit a voluntary written request to his or her own employing agency that a specified number of hours of his or her accrued annual leave be transferred from his or her annual leave account to the annual leave account of a specified leave recipient. Except as provided in paragraph (f) of this section, annual leave may be transferred only to a leave recipient employed by the leave donor's employing agency.

(b) Except as provided in paragraph (d) of this section and subject to the limitations on the amount of annual leave that may be donated by a leave donor under § 630.908, all or any portion of the annual leave requested under paragraph (a) of this section may be transferred to the annual leave account of the specified leave recipient under procedures established by the leave recipient's employing agency.

(c) An agency having employees who earn and use annual leave on the basis of an uncommon tour of duty shall establish procedures for administering the transfer of annual leave to or from such employees under this subpart.

(d) A leave recipient's employing agency shall not transfer annual leave to a leave donor's immediate supervisor.

(e) Annual leave transferred under this section may be substituted retroactively for period of leave without pay (LWOP) or used to liquidate an indebtedness for advanced annual or sick leave granted on or after a date fixed by the leave recipient's employing agency as the beginning of the period of medical emergency for which LWOP or advanced annual or sick leave was granted.

(f) A leave recipient's employing agency shall accept the transfer of annual leave from leave donors employed by one or more other agencies when—

(1) A family member of a leave recipient is employed by another agency and requests the transfer of annual leave to the leave recipient;

(2) In the judgment of the leave recipient's employing agency, the amount of annual leave transferred from leave donors employed by the leave recipient's employing agency may not be sufficient to meet the needs of the leave recipient; or

(3) In the judgment of the leave recipient's employing agency, acceptance of leave transferred from another agency would further the purpose of the voluntary leave transfer program.

(g) The employing agency of a leave donor who wishes to donate annual leave to a leave recipient in another agency shall verify the availability of annual leave in the leave donor's annual leave account, determine that the amount of annual leave to be donated does not exceed the limitations in § 630.908, and ascertain that the leave recipient's employing agency has made any determination that may be required under paragraph (f) of this section. Upon satisfying these requirements, the leave donor's employing agency shall—

(1) Reduce the amount of annual leave credited to the leave donor's annual leave account, as appropriate; and

(2) Notify the leave recipient's employing agency in writing of the amount of annual leave to be credited to the leave recipient's annual leave account.

§ 630.907 Accrual of annual and sick leave.

(a) Except as otherwise provided in this section, while an employee is in a shared leave status, annual and sick leave shall accrue to the credit of the employee at the same rate as if the employee where then in a paid leave status under subchapter I of chapter 63 of title 5, United States Code, except that—

(1) The maximum amount of annual leave that may be accrued by an employee while in a shared leave status in connection with any particular medical emergency may not exceed 40 hours (or, in the case of a part-time employee or an employee with an uncommon tour of duty, the average number of hours in the employee's weekly scheduled tour of duty); and

(2) The maximum amount of sick leave that may be accrued by an employee while in a shared leave status in connection with any particular medical emergency may not exceed 40 hours (or, in the case of a part-time employee or an employee with an uncommon tour of duty, the average number of hours in the employee's weekly scheduled tour of duty).

(b) Any annual or sick leave accrued by an employee under this subpart and subpart J of this part—

(1) Shall be credited to an annual or sick leave account, as appropriate, separate from any leave account of the employee under subchapter I of chapter 63 of title 5, United States Code; and

(2) Shall not become available for use by the employee and may not otherwise be taken into account under subchapter I of chapter 63 of title 5, United States Code, until it is transferred to the appropriate leave account of the employee under subchapter I of chapter

63 of title 5, United States Code, as provided in paragraph (c) of this section.

(c) Any annual or sick leave accrued by an employee under this section shall be transferred to the appropriate leave account of the employee under subchapter I of chapter 63 of title 5, United States Code, and shall become available for use—

(1) As of the beginning of the first pay period beginning on or after the date on which the employee's medical emergency terminates as described in §630.910(a)(2) or (3); or

(2) If the employee's medical emergency has not yet terminated, once the employee has exhausted all leave made available to such employee under this subpart or subpart J of this part.

(d) If the leave recipient's employing agency advances at the beginning of the leave year the amount of annual leave the employee normally would accrue during the entire leave year under 5 U.S.C. 6302(d)—

(1) The leave recipient's employing agency shall establish procedures to ensure that 40 hours (or, in the case of a part-time employee or an employee with an uncommon tour of duty, the average number of hours in the employee's weekly scheduled tour of duty) of annual leave are placed in a separate annual leave account and made available for use by the employee as described in paragraph (c) of this section; and

(2) The employee shall continue to accrue annual leave while in a shared leave status to the extent necessary for the purpose of reducing any indebtedness caused by the use of annual leave advanced at the beginning of the leave year.

(e) If the employee's medical emergency terminates as described in §630.910(a)(1), no leave shall be credited to the employee under this section.

[59 FR 67125, Dec. 29, 1994, as amended at 60 FR 26979, May 22, 1995; 61 FR 64451, Dec. 5, 1996]

§630.908 Limitations on donation of annual leave.

(a) In any one leave year, a leave donor may donate no more than a total of one-half of the amount of annual leave he or she would be entitled to accrue during the leave year in which the donation is made.

(b) In the case of a leave donor who is projected to have annual leave that otherwise would be subject to forfeiture at the end of the leave year under 5 U.S.C. 6304(a), the maximum amount of annual leave that may be donated during the leave year shall be the lesser of—

(1) One-half of the amount of annual leave he or she would be entitled to accrue during the leave year in which the donation is made; or

(2) The number of hours remaining in the leave year (as of the date of the transfer) for which the leave donor is scheduled to work and receive pay.

(c) Each agency shall establish written criteria for waiving the limitations on donating annual leave under paragraphs (a) and (b) of this section. Any such waiver shall be documented in writing.

(d) The limitations in this section shall apply to the total amount of annual leave donated or contributed under subparts I and J of this part.

§630.909 Use of transferred annual leave.

(a) A leave recipient may use annual leave transferred to his or her annual leave account under §630.906 only for the purpose of a medical emergency for which the leave recipient was approved.

(b) Except as provided in §630.907, during each biweekly pay period that a leave recipient is affected by a medical emergency, he or she shall use any accrued annual leave (and sick leave, if applicable) before using transferred annual leave.

(c) The approval and use of transferred annual leave shall be subject to all of the conditions and requirements imposed by chapter 63 of title 5, United States Code, part 630 of this chapter, and the employing agency on the approval and use of annual leave accrued under 5 U.S.C. 6303, except that transferred annual leave may accumulate without regard to the limitation imposed by 5 U.S.C. 6304(a).

(d) Transferred annual leave may be substituted retroactively for any period of leave without pay or used to liquidate an indebtedness for any period of advanced leave that began on or after the date fixed by the agency as the beginning of the medical emergency.

(e) Transferred annual leave may not be—

(1) Transferred to another leave recipient under this subpart, except as provided in § 630.911(e)(3);

(2) Included in a lump-sum payment under 5 U.S.C. 5551 or 5552; or

(3) Made available for recredit under 5 U.S.C. 6306 upon reemployment by a Federal agency.

§ 630.910 Termination of medical emergency.

(a) The medical emergency affecting a leave recipient shall terminate—

(1) When the leave recipient's Federal service is terminated;

(2) At the end of the biweekly pay period in which the leave recipient's employing agency receives written notice from the leave recipient or from a personal representative of the leave recipient that the leave recipient is no longer affected by a medical emergency;

(3) At the end of the biweekly pay period in which the leave recipient's employing agency determines, after written notice from the agency and an opportunity for the leave recipient (or, if appropriate, a personal representative of the leave recipient) to answer orally or in writing, that the leave recipient is no longer affected by a medical emergency; or

(4) At the end of the biweekly pay period in which the leave recipient's employing agency receives notice that the Office of Personnel Management has approved an application for disability retirement for the leave recipient under the Civil Service Retirement System or the Federal Employees' Retirement System.

(b) The leave recipient's employing agency shall continuously monitor the status of the medical emergency affecting the leave recipient to ensure that the leave recipient continues to be affected by a medical emergency.

(c) When the medical emergency affecting a leave recipient terminates, no further requests for transfer of annual leave to the leave recipient may be granted, and any unused transferred annual leave remaining to the credit of the leave recipient shall be restored to the leave donors under § 630.911.

(d) An agency may deem a medical emergency to continue for the purpose of providing a leave recipient an adequate period of time within which to receive donations of annual leave.

§ 630.911 Restoration of transferred annual leave.

(a) Under procedures established by the leave recipient's employing agency, any transferred annual leave remaining to the credit of a leave recipient when the medical emergency terminates shall be restored, as provided in paragraphs (b) and (c) of this section and to the extent administratively feasible, by transfer to the annual leave accounts of leave donors who, on the date leave restoration is made, are employed by a Federal agency and subject to chapter 63 of title 5, United States Code.

(b) The amount of unused transferred annual leave to be restored to each leave donor shall be determined as follows:

(1) Divide the number of hours of unused transferred annual leave by the total number of hours of annual leave transferred to the leave recipient;

(2) Multiply the ratio obtained in paragraph (b)(1) of this section by the number of hours of annual leave transferred by each leave donor eligible for restoration under paragraph (a) of this section; and

(3) Round the result obtained in paragraph (b)(2) of this section to the nearest increment of time established by the leave donor's employing agency to account for annual leave.

(c) If the total number of eligible leave donors exceeds the total number of hours of annual leave to be restored, no unused transferred annual leave shall be restored. In no case shall the amount of annual leave restored to a leave donor exceed the amount transferred to the leave recipient by the leave donor.

(d) If the leave donor retires from Federal service, dies, or is otherwise separated from Federal service before the date unused transferred annual leave can be restored, the employing agency of the leave recipient shall not restore the unused transferred annual leave.

(e) At the election of the leave donor, unused transferred annual leave restored to the leave donor under paragraph (a) of this section may be restored by—

(1) Crediting the restored annual leave to the leave donor's annual leave account in the current leave year;

(2) Crediting the restored annual leave to the leave donor's annual leave account effective as of the first day of the first leave year beginning after the date of election; or

(3) Donating such leave in whole or part to another leave recipient.

(f) If a leave donor elects to donate only part of his or her restored leave to another leave recipient under paragraph (e)(3) of this section, the donor may elect to have the remaining leave credited to the leave donor's annual leave account under paragraph (e)(1) or (e)(2) of this section.

(g) Transferred annual leave restored to the account of a leave donor under paragraph (e) (1) or (2) of this section shall be subject to the limitation imposed by 5 U.S.C. 6304(a) at the end of the leave year in which the restored leave is credited to the leave donor's annual leave account.

(h) If a leave recipient elects to buy back annual leave as a result of claim for an employment-related injury approved by the Office of Workers' Compensation Programs under 20 CFR 10.202 and 10.310, and the annual leave was leave transferred under § 630.906, the amount of annual leave bought back by the leave recipient shall be restored to the leave donor(s).

[59 FR 67125, Dec. 29, 1994, as amended at 61 FR 64451, Dec. 5, 1996]

§ 630.912 Prohibition of coercion.

(a) An employee may not directly or indirectly intimidate, threaten, or coerce, or attempt to intimidate, threaten, or coerce, any other employee for the purpose of interfering with any right such employee may have with respect to donating, receiving, or using annual leave under this subpart.

(b) For the purpose of paragraph (a) of this section, the term "intimidate, threaten, or coerce" includes promising to confer or conferring any benefit (such as an appointment or promotion or compensation) or effecting or threatening to effect any reprisal (such as deprivation of appointment, promotion, or compensation).

§ 630.913 Records and reports.

(a) Each agency shall maintain records concerning the administration of the voluntary leave transfer program and may be required by the Office of Personnel Management to report any information necessary to evaluate the effectiveness of the program.

(b) Agencies shall maintain the following information:

(1) The number of applications approved for medical emergencies affecting the employee and the number of applications approved for medical emergencies affecting an employee's family member;

(2) The grade or pay level of each leave recipient and leave donor, the gender of each leave recipient, and the total amount of transferred annual leave used by each leave recipient; and

(3) Any additional information OPM may require.

Subpart J—Voluntary Leave Bank Program

SOURCE: 59 FR 67129, Dec. 29, 1994, unless otherwise noted.

§ 630.1001 Purpose and applicability.

(a) *Purpose*. The purpose of this subpart is to establish procedures and requirements for a voluntary leave bank program under which the unused accrued annual leave of an employee may be contributed to a leave bank for use by a leave bank member who needs such leave because of a medical emergency.

(b) *Applicability*. This subpart applies to officers and employees—

(1) To whom subchapter I of chapter 63 of title 5, United States Code applies; and

(2) Who are employed in agencies and their organizational subunits operating a voluntary leave bank program under this subpart.

§ 630.1002 Definitions.

Agency means an "Executive agency," as defined in 5 U.S.C. 105, or a "military department," as defined in 5 U.S.C. 102. "Agency" does not include the Central Intelligence Agency, the Defense Intelligence Agency, the National Security Agency, the Federal Bureau of Investigation, or any other Executive agency or subunit thereof, as determined by the President, whose principal function is the conduct of foreign intelligence or counterintelligence activities.

Available paid leave has the meaning given that term in subpart I of this part.

Committed relationship has the meaning given that term in subpart I of this part.

Domestic partner has the meaning given that term in subpart I of this part.

Employee has the meaning given that term in subpart I of this part.

Family member has the meaning given that term in subpart I of this part.

Leave bank means a pooled fund of annual leave established by an agency under § 630.1003.

Leave bank member means a leave contributor who has contributed, in an open enrollment period (or individual enrollment period, as applicable) of the current leave year, at least the minimum amount of annual leave required by § 630.1004.

Leave contributor means an employee who contributes annual leave to a leave bank under § 630.1004.

Leave recipient means a leave bank member whose application to receive contributions of annual leave from a leave bank has been approved under § 630.1007.

Medical emergency has the meaning given that term in subpart I of this part.

Paid leave status under subchapter I has the meaning given that term in subpart I of this part.

Parent has the meaning given that term in subpart I of this part.

Shared leave status has the meaning given that term in subpart I of this part.

Son or daughter has the meaning given that term in subpart I of this part.

[59 FR 67129, Dec. 29, 1994, as amended at 75 FR 33496, June 14, 2010]

§ 630.1003 Establishing leave banks and leave bank boards.

(a) Each agency that participates in the voluntary leave bank program shall, in accordance with this subpart—

(1) Develop written policies and procedures for establishing and administering leave banks and leave bank boards;

(2) Establish one or more leave bank boards to perform the duties authorized by this subpart; and

(3) Establish and begin operating one or more leave banks.

(b) No more than one leave bank board may be established for each leave bank.

(c) Each leave bank board shall consist of three members. At least one member shall represent a labor organization or employee group.

(d) Each leave bank board shall—

(1) Establish its internal decision-making procedures;

(2) Review and approve or disapprove each application to become a leave contributor under § 630.1004 and a leave recipient under §§ 630.1006 and 630.1007;

(3) Monitor the status of each leave recipient's medical emergency;

(4) Monitor the amount of leave in the leave bank and the number of applications to become a leave recipient;

(5) Maintain an adequate amount of annual leave in the leave bank to the greatest extent practicable in accordance with § 630.1004; and

(6) Perform other functions prescribed in this subpart.

(e) Annual leave may not be borrowed, contributed, or otherwise transferred between leave banks.

§ 630.1004 Application to become a leave contributor and leave bank member.

(a) An employee may make voluntary written application to the leave bank board to become a leave contributor. The application shall specify the number of hours of annual leave to be contributed and any other information the leave bank board may reasonably require.

(b) An employee may request that annual leave be contributed to a specified bank member other than the leave contributor's immediate supervisor.

(c) A leave contributor shall become a leave bank member for a particular leave year if he or she submits an application meeting the requirements of this section during an open enrollment period established by the leave bank board under paragraphs (d) and (e) of this section (or where applicable, during an individual enrollment period established under paragraph (f) of this section).

(d) The leave bank board shall establish at least one open enrollment period for each leave year of leave bank operation.

(e) An open enrollment period shall last at least 30 calendar days. The agency shall take appropriate action to inform employees of each open enrollment period.

(f) An employee entering the agency or participating organizational subunit or returning from an extended absence outside an open enrollment period may become a leave bank member for the leave year by submitting an application meeting the requirements of this section during an individual enrollment period lasting at least 30 calendar days, beginning on the date the employee entered or returned to the agency or organizational subunit.

(g) Except as provided in paragraph (h) of this section, the minimum contribution required to become a leave bank member for a leave year shall be—

(1) 4 hours of annual leave for an employee who has less than 3 years of service at the time he or she submits an application to contribute annual leave;

(2) 6 hours of annual leave for an employee who has at least 3, but less than 15, years of service at the time he or she submits an application to contribute annual leave; and

(3) 8 hours of annual leave for an employee who has 15 or more years of service at the time he or she submits an application to contribute annual leave.

(h) The leave bank board may—

(1) Decrease the minimum contribution required by paragraph (g) of this section for the following leave year when the leave bank board determines that there is a surplus of leave in the bank;

(2) Increase the minimum contribution required by paragraph (g) of this section for the following leave year when the leave bank board determines that such action is necessary to maintain an adequate balance of annual leave in the leave bank; or

(3) Eliminate the requirement for a minimum contribution under paragraph (g) of this section when a leave bank member transfers within his or her employing agency to an organization covered by a different leave bank.

(i) If a leave recipient does not have sufficient available accrued annual leave to his or her credit to make the full minimum contribution required by this section, he or she shall be deemed to have made the minimum contribution.

(j) The leave bank board shall deposit all contributions of annual leave under this subpart in the leave bank. Except as provided in § 630.1016(c), the leave bank board may not return a contribution of annual leave to a leave contributor after deposit in the leave bank.

(k) A leave bank member may apply to contribute additional annual leave at any time. An employee who is not a leave bank member may apply to become a leave contributor at any time.

§ 630.1005 Limitations on contribution of annual leave.

(a) In any one leave year, a leave contributor may contribute no more than a total of one-half of the amount of annual leave he or she would be entitled to accrue during the leave year in which the contribution is made.

(b) In the case of a leave contributor who is projected to have annual leave that otherwise would be subject to forfeiture at the end of the leave year under 5 U.S.C. 6304(a), the maximum amount of annual leave that may be contributed during the leave year shall be the lesser of—

(1) One-half of the amount of annual leave he or she would be entitled to accrue during the leave year in which the contribution is made; or

(2) The number of hours remaining in the leave year (as of the date of the contribution) for which the leave contributor is scheduled to work and receive pay.

(c) The agency shall establish written criteria permitting a leave bank board to waive the limitations on contributing annual leave under paragraphs (a) and (b) of this section. Any such waiver shall be documented in writing.

(d) The limitations in this section shall apply to the total amount of annual leave donated or contributed during the leave year under subparts I and J of this part.

§ 630.1006 Application to become a leave recipient.

(a) A leave bank member may make written application to the leave bank board to become a leave recipient. If a leave bank member is not capable of making application on his or her own behalf, a personal representative may make written application on his or her behalf.

(b) The leave bank board may require leave bank members to submit applications under this section within a prescribed period of time following the termination of a medical emergency.

(c) An application by a leave bank member to become a leave recipient shall be accompanied by the following information concerning the potential leave recipient:

(1) The leave bank member's name, position title, and grade or pay level;

(2) The reasons leave is needed, including a brief description of the nature, severity, anticipated duration, and if it is a recurring one, the approximate frequency of the medical emergency affecting the leave bank member;

(3) Certification from one or more physicians, or other appropriate experts, with respect to the medical emergency, if the leave bank board so requires; and

(4) Any additional information that may be required by the leave bank board.

(d) If the leave bank board requires a leave bank member to submit certification from two or more sources under paragraph (b)(3) of this section, the agency shall ensure, either by direct payment to the expert involved or by reimbursement, that the leave bank member is not required to pay for the expenses associated with obtaining certification from more than one source.

§ 630.1007 Approval of application to become a leave recipient.

(a) The leave bank board shall review an employee's application to become a leave recipient under procedures established by the agency for the purpose of determining whether the employee is a leave bank member who is or has been affected by a medical emergency.

(b) Before approving an application to become a leave recipient, the leave bank board shall determine that the absence from duty without available paid leave because of the medical emergency is (or is expected to be) at least 24 hours (or, in the case of a part-time employee or an employee with an uncommon tour of duty, at least 30 percent of the average number of hours in the employee's biweekly scheduled tour of duty).

(c) In making a determination as to whether a medical emergency is likely to result in a substantial loss of income, the leave bank board shall not consider factors other than whether the absence from duty without available paid leave is (or is expected to be) at least 24 hours (or, in the case of a part-time employee or an employee with an uncommon tour of duty, at least 30 percent of the average number of hours in the employee's biweekly scheduled tour of duty).

(d) The leave bank board shall provide timely written notification to the applicant of the action taken on the application. If the leave bank board disapproves the application, notification shall include the reasons for disapproval.

(e) The leave bank board may establish written policies limiting the amount of annual leave that may be granted to a leave recipient.

[59 FR 67125, Dec. 29, 1994, as amended at 60 FR 26979, May 22, 1995]

§ 630.1008 Accrual of annual and sick leave.

(a) Except as otherwise provided in this section, while an employee is in a shared leave status, annual and sick leave shall accrue to the credit of the employee at the same rate as if the employee were then in a paid leave status under subchapter I of chapter 63 of title 5, United States Code, except that—

(1) The maximum amount of annual leave that may be accrued by a leave recipient while in a shared leave status in connection with any particular medical emergency may not exceed 40 hours (or, in the case of a part-time employee or an employee with an uncommon tour of duty, the average number of hours in the employee's weekly scheduled tour of duty); and

(2) The maximum amount of sick leave that may be accrued by a leave recipient while in a shared leave status in connection with any particular medical emergency may not exceed 40 hours (or, in the case of a part-time employee or an employee with an uncommon tour of duty, the average number of hours in the employee's weekly scheduled tour of duty).

(b) Any annual or sick leave accrued by an employee under this subpart and subpart I of this part—

(1) Shall be credited to an annual or sick leave account, as appropriate, separate from any leave account of the employee under subchapter I of chapter 63 of title 5, United States Code; and

(2) Shall not become available for use by the employee and may not otherwise be taken into account under subchapter I of chapter 63 of title 5, United States Code, until it is transferred to the appropriate leave account of the employee under subchapter I of chapter 63 of title 5, United States Code, as provided in paragraph (c) of this section.

(c) Any annual or sick leave accrued by an employee under this section shall be transferred to the appropriate leave account of the employee under subchapter I of chapter 63 of title 5, United States Code, and shall become available for use—

(1) As of the beginning of the first pay period beginning on or after the date on which the employee's medical emergency terminates as described in §630.1010(a)(3) or (4); or

(2) If the employee's medical emergency has not yet terminated, once the employee has exhausted all leave made available to such employee under this subpart of subpart I of this part.

(d) If the leave recipient's employing agency advances at the beginning of the leave year the amount of annual leave the employee normally would accrue during the entire leave year under 5 U.S.C. 6302(d)—

(1) The leave recipient's employing agency shall establish procedures to ensure that 40 hours (or, in the case of a part-time employee or an employee with an uncommon tour of duty, the average number of hours in the employee's weekly scheduled tour of duty) of annual leave are placed in a separate annual leave account and made available for use by the employee as described in paragraph (c) of this section; and

(2) The employee shall continue to accrue annual leave while using annual leave withdrawn from a leave bank to the extent necessary for the purpose of reducing an indebtedness caused by the use of annual leave advanced at the beginning of the leave year.

(e) If the leave recipient's medical emergency terminates as described in §630.1010(a)(1), no leave shall be credited to the employee under this section.

[59 FR 67125, Dec. 29, 1994, as amended at 60 FR 26979, May 22, 1995]

§630.1009 Use of annual leave withdrawn from a leave bank.

(a) A leave recipient may use annual leave withdrawn from a leave bank only for the purpose of medical emergency for which the leave recipient was approved.

(b) Except as provided in §630.1008, during each biweekly pay period that a leave recipient is affected by a medical emergency, he or she shall use any accrued annual leave (and sick leave, if applicable) before using annual leave withdrawn from a leave bank.

(c) The approval and use of annual leave withdrawn from a leave bank shall be subject to all of the conditions and requirements imposed by chapter 63 of title 5, United States Code, part 630 of this chapter, and the agency on the approval and use of annual leave accrued under 5 U.S.C. 6303, except that annual leave withdrawn from a leave bank may accumulate without regard to any limitation imposed by 5 U.S.C. 6304(a).

(d) Annual leave withdrawn from a leave bank may be substituted retroactively for any period of leave without pay or used to liquidate an indebtedness for any period of advanced leave that began on or after the date fixed by the leave bank board as the beginning of the medical emergency.

(e) Annual leave withdrawn from a leave bank may not be—

(1) Included in a lump-sum payment under 5 U.S.C. 5551 or 5552; or

(2) Made available for recredit under 5 U.S.C. 6306 upon reemployment by a Federal agency.

(f) An agency having employees who earn and use annual leave on the basis of an uncommon tour of duty shall establish procedures for administering the contribution and withdrawal of annual leave by such employees under this subpart.

§ 630.1010 Termination of medical emergency.

(a) The medical emergency affecting a leave recipient shall terminate—

(1) When the leave recipient's Federal service terminates;

(2) When the leave recipient leaves the agency or participating organizational subunit, if the bank board so determines;

(3) At the end of the biweekly pay period in which the leave bank board receives written notice from the leave recipient or from a personal representative of the leave recipient that the leave recipient is no longer affected by a medical emergency;

(4) At the end of the biweekly pay period in which the leave bank board determines, after written notice from the bank board and an opportunity for the leave recipient (or, if appropriate, a personal representative of the leave recipient) to answer orally or in writing, that the leave recipient is no longer affected by a medical emergency; or

(5) At the end of the biweekly pay period in which the agency receives notice that the Office of Personnel Management has approved an application for disability retirement for the leave recipient under the Civil Service Retirement System or the Federal Employees Retirement System.

(b) The leave bank board shall ensure that annual leave withdrawn from the leave bank and not used before the termination of a leave recipient's medical emergency shall be returned to the leave bank.

(c) The leave bank board may deem a medical emergency to continue for the purpose of providing a leave recipient an adequate period of time within which to receive contributions of annual leave.

(d) If a leave recipient elects to buy back annual leave as a result of a claim for an employment-related injury approved by the Office of Workers' Compensation Programs under 20 CFR 10.202 and 10.310, the amount of annual leave withdrawn from the leave bank that is bought back by the leave recipient shall be restored to the leave bank.

[59 FR 67129, Dec. 29, 1994, as amended at 61 FR 64451, Dec. 5, 1996]

§ 630.1011 Prohibition of coercion.

(a) An employee may not directly or indirectly intimidate, threaten, or coerce, or attempt to intimidate, threaten, or coerce, any other employee for the purpose of interfering with any right such employee may have with respect to contributing, withdrawing, or using annual leave under this subpart.

(b) For the purpose of paragraph (a) of this section—

(1) The term "employee" has the meaning given that term in 5 U.S.C. 6301(2), excluding an individual employed by the District of Columbia; and

(2) The term "intimidate, threaten, or coerce" includes promising to confer or conferring any benefit (such as an appointment or promotion or compensation) or effecting or threatening to effect any reprisal (such as deprivation of appointment, promotion, or compensation).

[59 FR 67125, Dec. 29, 1994, as amended at 60 FR 26979, May 22, 1995]

§ 630.1012 Records and reports.

(a) Each agency shall maintain records concerning the administration of the voluntary leave bank program and may be required by the Office of Personnel Management to report any information necessary to evaluate the effectiveness of the program.

(b) An agency shall maintain the following information for each leave bank:

(1) The number of leave bank members for each leave year;

(2) The number of applications approved for medical emergencies affecting the employee and the number of applications approved for medical emergencies affecting an employee's family member;

(3) The grade or pay level of each leave contributor and the total amount of annual leave he or she contributed to the bank;

(4) The grade or pay level and gender of each leave recipient and the total amount of annual leave he or she actually used; and

(5) Any additional information OPM may require.

§630.1013 Participation in voluntary leave transfer and leave bank programs.

(a) If an agency or organizational subunit establishes a voluntary leave bank program under this subpart—

(1) A covered employee may also participate in a voluntary leave transfer program under subpart I of this part;

(2) Except as provided in paragraphs (b) and (c) of this section, any annual leave previously transferred to an employee under the voluntary leave transfer program shall remain to the credit of the employee who later becomes a leave recipient in a leave bank and shall become subject to the agency's policies and procedures for administering this subpart; and

(3) The agency or organizational subunit shall establish policies or procedures governing the use of donated or transferred leave for any leave recipient who receives leave under both a voluntary leave transfer program and a voluntary leave bank program for the same medical emergency.

(b) Upon termination of a leave recipient's medical emergency, any annual leave previously transferred under the voluntary leave transfer program and remaining to the credit of a leave recipient shall be restored under §630.911(a) through (d).

(c) Transferred annual leave restored to the account of a leave donor under paragraph (b) of this section shall be subject to the limitation imposed by 5 U.S.C. 6304(a) at the end of the leave year in which the annual leave is restored.

§630.1014 Movement between voluntary leave bank programs.

If an employee moves between an agency or organizational subunit operating a leave bank to an agency or organizational subunit operating a different leave bank, the following procedures shall apply:

(a) On the date of the employee's move, he or she shall become subject to the policies and procedures of the voluntary leave bank program of the new agency or organizational subunit; and

(b) Nothing in §630.1010(a)(2) or (b) shall interfere with the employee's right to submit an application to become a leave contributor or leave recipient in accordance with the policies and procedures of the voluntary leave bank program of the new agency or organizational subunit.

§630.1015 Movement between voluntary leave bank and leave transfer programs.

If an employee moves between an agency or organizational subunit covered by a voluntary leave bank program under this subpart and an agency or organizational subunit covered by a voluntary leave transfer program under subpart I of this part, the following procedures shall apply.

(a) On the date of the employee's move, he or she shall become subject to the policies and procedures of the voluntary leave transfer and voluntary leave bank program (if applicable) of the new agency or organizational subunit; and

(b) Nothing in §630.1010(a)(2) or (b) shall interfere with the employee's right to submit an application to become a leave donor (or leave contributor, as applicable) or leave recipient under the voluntary leave transfer or voluntary leave bank program (as applicable) of the new agency or organizational subunit.

§630.1016 Termination of a voluntary leave bank program.

(a) An agency may terminate a voluntary leave bank program only after it gives at least 30 calendar days advance written notice to current leave bank members.

(b) If an agency terminates a voluntary leave bank program before the termination of the medical emergency affecting a leave bank recipient, annual leave transferred to a leave bank recipient shall remain available for use under the rules set forth in subpart I of this part.

(c) An agency that terminates a voluntary leave bank program shall make provisions for the timely and equitable distribution of any leave remaining in the leave bank. The agency may allocate the leave to current leave recipients, recredit the leave to the accounts of the voluntary leave bank members, or a combination of both. The agency may distribute the leave immediately or may delay the distribution, in whole or part, until the beginning of the following leave year.

Subpart K—Emergency Leave Transfer Program

SOURCE: 73 FR 65500, Nov. 4, 2008, unless otherwise noted.

§ 630.1101 Purpose, applicability, and administration.

(a) *Purpose.* This subpart provides regulations to implement section 6391 of title 5, United States Code, and must be read together with section 6391. Section 6391 of title 5, United States Code, provides that in the event of a major disaster or emergency, as declared by the President, that results in severe adverse effects for a substantial number of employees, the President may direct the Office of Personnel Management (OPM) to establish an emergency leave transfer program under which an employee may donate unused annual leave for transfer to employees of his or her agency or to employees in other agencies who are adversely affected by such disaster or emergency.

(b) *Applicability.* This subpart applies to any individual who is defined as an "employee" in 5 U.S.C. 6331(1) and who is employed in—

(1) An Executive agency; or

(2) The Judicial branch.

(c) *Administration.* The head of each agency having employees subject to this subpart is responsible for the proper administration of this subpart. Each Federal agency must establish and administer procedures to permit the voluntary transfer of annual leave consistent with this subpart.

§ 630.1102 Definitions.

In this subpart:

Agency means—

(1) An "Executive agency," as defined in 5 U.S.C. 105; or

(2) A Judicial branch entity.

Committed relationship has the meaning given that term in subpart I of this part.

Disaster or emergency means a major disaster or emergency, as declared by the President, that results in severe adverse effects for a substantial number of employees (e.g., loss of life or property, serious injury, or mental illness as a result of a direct threat to life or health).

Domestic partner has the meaning given that term in subpart I of this part.

Emergency leave donor means a current employee whose voluntary written request for transfer of annual leave to an emergency leave transfer program is approved by his or her employing agency.

Emergency leave recipient means a current employee for whom the employing agency has approved an application to receive annual leave under an emergency leave transfer program.

Emergency leave transfer program means a program established by OPM that permits Federal employees to transfer their unused annual leave to other Federal employees adversely affected by a disaster or emergency, as declared by the President.

Employee means—

(1) An employee as defined in 5 U.S.C. 6331(1); or

(2) An employee of a Judicial branch entity.

Family member has the meaning given that term in § 630.902.

Leave year has the meaning given that term in § 630.201.

Parent has the meaning given that term in subpart I of this part.

Son or daughter has the meaning given that term in subpart I of this part.

Transferred annual leave means donated annual leave credited to an approved emergency leave recipient's annual leave account.

[73 FR 65500, Nov. 4, 2008, as amended at 75 FR 33497, June 14, 2010]

§ 630.1103 Establishment of an emergency leave transfer program.

(a) When directed by the President, OPM will establish an emergency leave transfer program that permits an employee to donate his or her accrued annual leave to employees of the same or other agencies who are adversely affected by a disaster or emergency as defined in § 630.1102. In certain situations, OPM may delegate to an agency the authority to establish an emergency leave transfer program.

(b) OPM will notify agencies of the establishment of an emergency leave transfer program for a specific disaster or emergency, as declared by the President. Once notified, each agency affected by the disaster or emergency is authorized to do the following:

(1) Determine whether, and how much, donated annual leave is needed by affected employees;

(2) Approve emergency leave donors and/or emergency leave recipients within the agency, as appropriate;

(3) Facilitate the distribution of donated annual leave from approved emergency leave donors to approved emergency leave recipients within the agency; and

(4) Determine the period of time for which donated annual leave may be accepted for distribution to approved emergency leave recipients.

§ 630.1104 Donations from a leave bank to an emergency leave transfer program.

A leave bank established under subchapter IV of chapter 63 of title 5, United States Code, and subpart J of part 630 may, with the concurrence of the leave bank board established under § 630.1003, donate annual leave to an emergency leave transfer program administered by its own agency, or, during a Governmentwide transfer of emergency leave coordinated by OPM, to an emergency leave transfer program administered by another agency. Donated annual leave not used by an emergency leave recipient must be returned to the leave bank as provided in § 630.1117.

[74 FR 10166, Mar. 10, 2009]

§ 630.1105 Application to become an emergency leave recipient.

(a) An employee who has been adversely affected by a disaster or emergency may make written application to his or her employing agency to become an emergency leave recipient. If an employee is not capable of making written application, a personal representative may make written application on behalf of the employee.

(b) An employee who has a family member who has been adversely affected by a disaster or emergency also may make written application to his or her employing agency to become an emergency leave recipient. An emergency leave recipient may use donated annual leave to assist an affected family member, provided such family member has no reasonable access to other forms of assistance.

(c) For the purpose of this subpart, an employee is considered to be adversely affected by a major disaster or emergency if the disaster or emergency has caused the employee, or a family member of the employee, severe hardship to such a degree that his or her absence from work is required.

(d) The employee's application must be accompanied by the following information:

(1) The name, position title, and grade or pay level of the potential emergency leave recipient;

(2) A statement describing his or her need for leave from the emergency leave transfer program; and

(3) Any additional information that may be required by the potential leave recipient's employing agency.

(e) An agency may determine a time period by which an employee must apply to become an emergency leave recipient after the occurrence of a disaster or emergency, as defined in § 630.1102.

§ 630.1106 Agency review of an application to become an emergency leave recipient.

An agency must review an application to become an emergency leave recipient under procedures the agency has established for the purpose of determining that a potential leave recipient is or has been affected by a disaster or emergency, as defined in § 630.1102.

§ 630.1107 Notification of approval or disapproval of an application to become an emergency leave recipient.

Once the employee's application to become an emergency leave recipient is either approved or disapproved, the agency must notify the employee (or his or her personal representative who made application on the employee's behalf) within 10 calendar days (excluding Saturdays, Sundays, and legal public holidays) after the date the application was received (or the date established by the agency, if that date is later). If disapproved, the agency must give the reason for its disapproval.

§ 630.1108 Use of available paid leave.

An approved emergency leave recipient is not required to exhaust his or her accrued annual and sick leave before receiving donated leave under the emergency leave transfer program and the recipient is eligible to be placed in a paid leave status using transferred annual leave.

§ 630.1109 Donating annual leave.

An employee may voluntarily submit a written request to his or her agency that a specified number of hours of his or her accrued annual leave, consistent with the limitations in § 630.1110, be transferred from his or her annual leave account to an emergency leave transfer program established under § 630.1103. An emergency leave donor may not donate annual leave for transfer to a specific emergency leave recipient under this subpart. Donated annual leave not used by an emergency leave recipient must be returned to the emergency leave donor(s) and/or leave banks as provided in § 630.1117.

§ 630.1110 Limitation on the amount of annual leave donated by an emergency leave donor.

(a) An emergency leave donor may not contribute less than 1 hour or more than 104 hours of annual leave in a leave year to an emergency leave transfer program. Each agency may establish written criteria for waiving the 104-hour limitation on donating annual leave in a leave year.

(b) Annual leave donated to an emergency leave transfer program may not be applied against the limitations on the donation of annual leave under the voluntary leave transfer or leave bank programs established under 5 U.S.C. 6332 and 6362, respectively.

§ 630.1111 Limitation on the amount of donated annual leave received by an emergency leave recipient.

An emergency leave recipient may receive a maximum of 240 hours of donated annual leave at any one time from an emergency leave transfer program for each disaster or emergency. After taking into consideration the amount of donated annual leave available to all approved emergency leave recipients and the needs of individual emergency leave recipients, an employing agency may allow an employee to receive additional disbursements of donated annual leave based on the employee's continuing need. Each disbursement of transferred annual leave may not exceed 240 hours.

§ 630.1112 Transferring donated annual leave between agencies.

(a) If an agency does not receive sufficient amounts of donated annual leave to meet the needs of approved emergency leave recipients within the agency, the agency may contact OPM to obtain assistance in receiving donated annual leave from other agencies. The agency must notify OPM of the total amount of donated annual leave needed for transfer to the agency's approved emergency leave recipients. OPM will solicit and coordinate the transfer of donated annual leave from other Federal agencies to affected agencies who may have a shortfall of donated annual leave. OPM will determine the period of time for which donations of accrued annual leave may be accepted for transfer to affected agencies.

(b) Each Federal agency OPM contacts for the purpose of providing donated annual leave to an agency in need must—

(1) Approve emergency leave donors under the conditions specified in §§630.1109 and 630.1110 and determine how much donated annual leave is available for transfer to an affected agency;

(2) Maintain records on the amount of annual leave donated by each emergency leave donor to the emergency leave transfer program (for the purpose of restoring unused transferred annual leave under §630.1117(b)).

(3) Report the total amount of annual leave donated to the emergency leave transfer program to OPM; and

(4) When OPM has accepted the donated annual leave, debit the amount of annual leave donated to the emergency leave transfer program from each emergency leave donor's annual leave account.

(c) OPM will notify each affected agency of the aggregate amount of donated annual leave that will be credited to it for transfer to its approved emergency leave recipient(s). The affected agency will determine the amount of donated annual leave to be transferred to each emergency leave recipient (an amount that may vary according to individual needs).

(d) The affected agency must credit the annual leave account of each approved emergency leave recipient as soon as possible after the date OPM notifies the agency of the amount of donated annual leave that will be credited to the agency under paragraph (c) of this section.

§630.1113 Using donated annual leave.

(a) Any donated annual leave an emergency leave recipient receives from an emergency leave transfer program may be used only for purposes related to the disaster or emergency for which the emergency leave recipient was approved. Each agency is responsible for ensuring that annual leave donated under the emergency leave transfer program is used appropriately.

(b) Annual leave transferred under this subpart may be—

(1) Substituted retroactively for any period of leave without pay used because of the adverse effects of the disaster or emergency; or

(2) Used to liquidate an indebtedness incurred by the emergency leave recipient for advanced annual or sick leave used because of the adverse effects of the disaster or emergency. The agency may advance annual or sick leave, as appropriate (even if the employee has available annual and sick leave), so that the emergency leave recipient is not forced to use his or her accrued leave before donated annual leave becomes available.

§630.1114 Accrual of leave while using donated annual leave.

While an emergency leave recipient is using donated annual leave from an emergency leave transfer program, annual and sick leave continue to accrue to the credit of the employee at the same rate as if he or she were in a paid leave status under 5 U.S.C. chapter 63, subchapter I, and will be subject to the limitations imposed by 5 U.S.C. 6304(a), (b), (c), and (f) at the end of the leave year in which the transferred annual leave is received.

§630.1115 Limitations on the use of donated annual leave.

Donated annual leave transferred to a leave recipient under this subpart may not be—

(a) Included in a lump-sum payment under 5 U.S.C. 5551 or 5552;

(b) Recredited to a former employee who is reemployed by a Federal agency; or

(c) Used to establish initial eligibility for immediate retirement or acquire eligibility to continue health benefits into retirement under 5 U.S.C. 6302(g).

§630.1116 Termination of a disaster or emergency.

The disaster or emergency affecting the employee as an emergency leave recipient terminates at the earliest occurrence of the following conditions.

(a) When the employing agency determines that the disaster or emergency has terminated;

(b) When the employee's Federal service terminates;

(c) At the end of the biweekly pay period in which the employee, or his or her personal representative, notifies the emergency leave recipient's agency that he or she is no longer affected by such disaster or emergency;

(d) At the end of the biweekly pay period in which the employee's agency determines, after giving the employee or his or her personal representative written notice and an opportunity to answer orally or in writing, that the employee is no longer affected by such disaster or emergency; or

(e) At the end of the biweekly pay period in which the employee's agency receives notice that OPM has approved an application for disability retirement for the emergency leave recipient under the Civil Service Retirement System or the Federal Employees' Retirement System, as appropriate.

§ 630.1117 Procedures for returning unused donated annual leave to emergency leave donors and leave banks.

(a) When a disaster or emergency is terminated, any unused annual leave donated to the emergency leave transfer program must be returned by the employing agency to the emergency leave donors, and if annual leave was donated by any leave bank(s) it must be returned to the leave bank(s).

(b) Each agency must determine the amount of annual leave to be restored to any leave bank and/or to each of the emergency leave donors who, on the date leave restoration is made, is employed in the Federal service. The amount of unused annual leave to be returned to each emergency leave donor and/or leave bank must be proportional to the amount of annual leave donated by the employee or the leave bank to the emergency leave transfer program for such disaster or emergency, and must be returned according to the procedures outlined in § 630.911(b). Any unused annual leave remaining after the distribution will be subject to forfeiture.

(c) Annual leave donated to an emergency leave transfer program for a specific disaster or emergency may not be transferred to another emergency leave transfer program established for a different disaster or emergency.

(d) At the election of the emergency leave donor, the employee may choose to have the agency restore unused donated annual leave by crediting the restored annual leave to the emergency leave donor's annual leave account in either the current leave year or the first pay period of the following leave year.

§ 630.1118 Protection against coercion.

(a) An employee may not directly or indirectly intimidate, threaten, or coerce, or attempt to intimidate, threaten, or coerce, any emergency leave donor or emergency leave recipient for the purpose of interfering with any right such employee may have with respect to donating, receiving, or using annual leave under this subpart.

(b) For the purpose of paragraph (a) of this section, the term "intimidate, threaten, or coerce" includes promising to confer or conferring any benefit (such as appointment or promotion or compensation) or effecting or threatening to effect any reprisal (such as deprivation of appointment, promotion, or compensation).

Subpart L—Family and Medical Leave

SOURCE: 58 FR 39602, July 23, 1993, unless otherwise noted.

§ 630.1201 Purpose, applicability, and administration.

(a) *Purpose.* This subpart provides regulations to implement sections 6381 through 6387 of title 5, United States Code. This subpart must be read together with those sections of law. Sections 6381 through 6387 of title 5, United States Code, provide a standard approach to providing family and medical leave to Federal employees by prescribing an entitlement to a total of 12 administrative workweeks of unpaid leave during any 12-month period for certain family and medical needs, as specified in § 630.1203(a) of this part.

(b) *Applicability.* (1) Except as otherwise provided in this paragraph, this subpart applies to any employee who—

(i) Is defined as an "employee" under 5 U.S.C. 6301(2), excluding employees covered under paragraph (b)(2) of this section; and

(ii) Has completed at least 12 months of service (not required to be 12 recent or consecutive months) as—

(A) An employee, as defined under 5 U.S.C. 6301(2), excluding any service as an employee under paragraph (b)(2) of this section;

(B) An employee of the Veterans Health Administration appointed under title 38, United States Code, in occupations listed in 38 U.S.C. 7401(1);

(C) A "teacher" or an individual holding a "teaching position," as defined in section 901 of title 20, United States Code; or

(D) An employee identified in section 2105(c) of title 5, United States Code, who is paid from nonappropriated funds.

(2) This subpart does not apply to—

(i) An individual employed by the government of the District of Columbia;

(ii) An employee serving under a temporary appointment with a time limitation of 1 year or less;

(iii) An intermittent employee, as defined in 5 CFR 340.401(c); or

(iv) Any employee covered by Title I or Title V of the Family and Medical Leave Act of 1993 (Pub. L. 103-3, February 5, 1993). The Department of Labor has issued regulations implementing Title I at 29 CFR part 825.

(3) For the purpose of applying sections 6381 through 6387 of title 5, United States Code—

(i) An employee of the Veterans Health Administration appointed under title 38, United States Code, in occupations listed in 38 U.S.C. 7401(1) is be governed by the terms and conditions of regulations prescribed by the Secretary of Veterans Affairs;

(ii) A "teacher" or an individual holding a "teaching position," as defined in section 901 of title 20, United States Code, shall be governed by the terms and conditions of regulations prescribed by the Secretary of Defense; and

(iii) An employee identified in section 2105(c) of title 5, United States Code, who is paid from nonappropriated funds shall be governed by the terms and conditions of regulations prescribed by the Secretary of Defense or the Secretary of Transportation, as appropriate.

(4) The regulations prescribed by the Secretary of Veterans Affairs, Secretary of Defense, or Secretary of Transportation under paragraph (b)(3) of this section shall, to the extent appropriate, be consistent with the regulations prescribed in this subpart and the regulations prescribed by the Secretary of Labor to carry out Title I of the Family and Medical Leave Act of 1993 at 29 CFR part 825.

(c) *Administration.* The head of an agency having employees subject to this subpart is responsible for the proper administration of this subpart.

[58 FR 39602, July 23, 1993, as amended at 61 FR 64451, Dec. 5, 1996; 65 FR 26486, May 8, 2000]

§ 630.1202 Definitions.

In this subpart:

Accrued leave has the meaning given that term in § 630.201 of this part.

Accumulated leave has the meaning given that term in § 630.201 of this part.

Administrative workweek has the meaning given that term in § 610.102 of this chapter.

Adoption refers to a legal process in which an individual becomes the legal parent of another's child. The source of an adopted child—e.g., whether from a licensed placement agency or otherwise—is not a factor in determining eligibility for leave under this subpart.

Covered active duty or *call to covered active duty status* means—

(1) In the case of a member of a regular component of the Armed Forces, duty during the deployment of the member with the Armed Forces to a foreign country under a call or order to active duty (or notification of an impending call or order to active duty); and

(2) In the case of a member of a reserve component of the Armed Forces, duty during the deployment of the member with the Armed Forces to a foreign country under a call or order to active duty (or notification of an impending call or order to active duty) in support of a contingency operation pursuant to any of the following sections of title 10, United States Code, or any other provision of law during a war or during a national emergency declared by the President or Congress:

(i) Section 688, which authorizes ordering to active duty retired members of the Regular Armed Forces and members of the Retired Reserve retired after 20 years for length of service, and members of the Fleet Reserve or Fleet Marine Corps Reserve;

(ii) Section 12301(a), which authorizes ordering all reserve component members to active duty in the case of war or national emergency declared by Congress, or when otherwise authorized by law;

(iii) Section 12302, which authorizes ordering any unit or unassigned member of the Ready Reserve to active duty in time of national emergency declared by the President after January 1, 1953, or when otherwise authorized by law;

(iv) Section 12304, which authorizes ordering any unit or unassigned member of the Selected Reserve and certain members of the Individual Ready Reserve to active duty;

(v) Section 12305, which authorizes the suspension of promotion, retirement, or separation rules for certain Reserve components;

(vi) Section 12406, which authorizes calling the National Guard into Federal service in certain circumstances; or

(vii) Chapter 15, which authorizes calling the National Guard and State militia into Federal service in the case of insurrections and national emergencies.

Covered military member means the employee's spouse, son, daughter, or parent on covered active duty or call to covered active duty status.

Employee means an individual to whom this subpart applies.

Essential functions means the fundamental job duties of the employee's position, as defined in 29 CFR 1630.2(n). An employee who must be absent from work to receive medical treatment for a serious health condition is considered to be unable to perform the essential functions of the position during the absence for treatment.

Family and medical leave means an employee's entitlement to 12 administrative workweeks of unpaid leave for certain family and medical needs, as prescribed under sections 6381 through 6387 of title 5, United States Code.

Foster care means 24-hour care for children in substitution for, and away from, their parents or guardian. Such placement is made by or with the agreement of the State as a result of a voluntary agreement by the parent or guardian that the child be removed from the home, or pursuant to a judicial determination of the necessity for foster care, and involves agreement between the State and foster family to take the child. Although foster care may be with relatives of the child, State action is involved in the removal of the child from parental custody.

Health care provider means—

(1) A licensed Doctor of Medicine or Doctor of Osteopathy or a physician who is serving on active duty in the uniformed services and is designated by the uniformed service to conduct examinations under this subpart;

(2) Any health care provider recognized by the Federal Employees Health Benefits Program or who is licensed or certified under Federal or State law to provide the service in question;

(3) A health care provider as defined in paragraph (2) of this definition who practices in a country other than the United States, who is authorized to practice in accordance with the laws of that country, and who is performing within the scope of his or her practice as defined under such law;

(4) A Christian Science practitioner listed with the First Church of Christ, Scientist, in Boston, Massachusetts; or

(5) A Native American, including an Eskimo, Aleut, and Native Hawaiian, who is recognized as a traditional healing practitioner by native traditional religious leaders who practices traditional healing methods as believed, expressed, and exercised in Indian religions of the American Indian, Eskimo, Aleut, and Native Hawaiians, consistent with Public Law 95–314, August 11, 1978 (92 Stat. 469), as amended by Public Law 103–344, October 6, 1994 (108 Stat. 3125).

In loco parentis refers to the situation of an individual who has day-to-day responsibility for the care and financial support of a child or, in the case of an employee, who had such responsibility for the employee when the employee was a child. A biological or legal relationship is not necessary.

Incapacity means the inability to work, attend school, or perform other regular daily activities because of a serious health condition or treatment for or recovery from a serious health condition.

Intermittent leave or leave taken intermittently means leave taken in separate blocks of time, rather than for one continuous period of time, and may include leave periods of 1 hour to several weeks. Leave may be taken for a period of less than 1 hour if agency policy provides for a minimum charge for leave of less than 1 hour under § 630.206(a).

Leave without pay means an absence from duty in a nonpay status. Leave without pay may be taken only for those hours of duty comprising an employee's basic workweek.

Parent means a biological, adoptive, step, or foster father or mother, or any individual who stands or stood in loco parentis to an employee meeting the definition of son or daughter below. This term does not include parents "in law."

Reduced leave schedule means a work schedule under which the usual number of hours of regularly scheduled work per workday or workweek of an employee is reduced. The number of hours by which the daily or weekly tour of duty is reduced are counted as leave for the purpose of this subpart.

Regularly scheduled has the meaning given that term in § 610.102 of this chapter.

Regularly scheduled administrative workweek has the meaning given that term in § 610.102 of this chapter.

Serious health condition. (1) Serious health condition means an illness, injury, impairment, or physical or mental condition that involves—

(i) Inpatient care (*i.e.*, an overnight stay) in a hospital, hospice, or residential medical care facility, including any period of incapacity or any subsequent treatment in connection with such inpatient care; or

(ii) Continuing treatment by a health care provider that includes (but is not limited to) examinations to determine if there is a serious health condition and evaluations of such conditions if the examinations or evaluations determine that a serious health condition exists. Continuing treatment by a health care provider may include one or more of the following—

(A) A period of incapacity of more than 3 consecutive calendar days, including any subsequent treatment or period of incapacity relating to the same condition, that also involves—

(*1*) Treatment two or more times by a health care provider, by a health care provider under the direct supervision of the affected individual's health care provider, or by a provider of health care services under orders of, or on referral by, a health care provider; or

(*2*) Treatment by a health care provider on at least one occasion which results in a regimen of continuing treatment under the supervision of the health care provider (e.g., a course of prescription medication or therapy requiring special equipment to resolve or alleviate the health condition).

(B) Any period of incapacity due to pregnancy or childbirth, or for prenatal care, even if the affected individual does not receive active treatment from a health care provider during the period of incapacity or the period of incapacity does not last more than 3 consecutive calendar days.

(C) Any period of incapacity or treatment for such incapacity due to a chronic serious health condition that—

(*1*) Requires periodic visits for treatment by a health care provider or by a health care provider under the direct supervision of the affected individual's health care provider,

(*2*) Continues over an extended period of time (including recurring episodes of a single underlying condition); and

(*3*) May cause episodic rather than a continuing period of incapacity (e.g., asthma, diabetes, epilepsy, etc.). The condition is covered even if the affected individual does not receive active treatment from a health care provider during the period of incapacity or the period of incapacity does not last more than 3 consecutive calendar days.

(D) A period of incapacity which is permanent or long-term due to a condition for which treatment may not be effective. The affected individual must be under the continuing supervision of, but need not be receiving active treatment by, a health care provider (e.g., Alzheimer's, severe stroke, or terminal stages of a disease).

(E) Any period of absence to receive multiple treatments (including any period of recovery) by a health care provider or by a provider of health care services under orders of, or on referral by, a health care provider, either for restorative surgery after an accident or other injury or for a condition that would likely result in a period of incapacity or more than 3 consecutive calendar days in the absence of medical intervention or treatment (e.g., chemotherapy/radiation for cancer, physical therapy for severe arthritis, dialysis for kidney disease).

(2) (Serious health condition does not include routine physical, eye, or dental examinations; a regimen of continuing treatment that includes the taking of over-the-counter medications, bed-rest, exercise, and other similar activities that can be initiated without a visit to the health care provider; a condition for which cosmetic treatments are administered, unless inpatient hospital care is required or unless complications develop; or an absence because of an employee's use of an illegal substance, unless the employee is receiving treatment for substance abuse by a health care provider or by a provider of health care services on referral by a health care provider. Ordinarily, unless complications arise, the common cold, the flu, earaches, upset stomach, minor ulcers, headaches (other than migraines), routine dental or orthodontia problems, and periodontal disease are not serious health conditions. Allergies, restorative dental or plastic surgery after an injury, removal of cancerous growth, or mental illness resulting from stress may be serious health conditions only if such conditions require inpatient care or continuing treatment by a health care provider.)

Son or daughter means a biological, adopted, or foster child; a step child; a legal ward; or a child of a person standing *in loco parentis* who is—

(1) Under 18 years of age; or

(2) 18 years of age or older and incapable of self-care because of a mental or physical disability. A son or daughter incapable of self-care requires active assistance or supervision to provide daily self-care in three or more of the "activities of daily living" (ADL's) or "instrumental activities of daily living" (IADL's). Activities of daily living include adaptive activities such as caring appropriately for one's grooming and hygiene, bathing, dressing, and eating. Instrumental activities of daily living include cooking, cleaning, shopping, taking public transportation, paying bills, maintaining a residence, using the telephones and directories, using a post office, etc. A "physical or mental disability" refers to a physical or mental impairment that substantially limits one or more of the major life activities of an individual as defined in 29 CFR 1630.2 (h), (i) and (j).

Son or daughter on covered active duty or call to covered active duty status means the employee's biological, adopted, or foster child, stepchild, legal ward, or a child for whom the employee stood in loco parentis, who is on covered active duty or call to covered active duty status, and who is of any age.

Spouse, as defined in the statute, means a husband or wife. For purposes of this definition, husband or wife refers to the other person with whom an individual entered into marriage as defined or recognized under State law for purposes of marriage in the State where the marriage was entered into or, in the case of a marriage entered into outside of any State, if the marriage is valid in the place where entered into and could have been entered into in at least one State. This definition includes an individual in a same-sex or common law marriage that either:

(1) Was entered into in a State that recognizes such marriages, or

(2) If entered into outside of any State, is valid in the place where entered into and could have been entered into in at least one State.

State means any State of the United States or the District of Columbia or any Territory or possession of the United States.

Tour of duty has the meaning given that term in § 610.102 of this chapter.

[58 FR 39602, July 23, 1993, as amended at 60 FR 67287, Dec. 29, 1995; 61 FR 64451, Dec. 5, 1996; 65 FR 37240, June 13, 2000; 76 FR 60704, Sept. 30, 2011; 81 FR 20524, Apr. 8, 2016]

§ 630.1203 Leave entitlement.

(a) An employee shall be entitled to a total of 12 administrative workweeks of unpaid leave during any 12-month period for one or more of the following reasons:

(1) The birth of a son or daughter of the employee and the care of such son or daughter;

(2) The placement of a son or daughter with the employee for adoption or foster care;

(3) The care of a spouse, son, daughter, or parent of the employee, if such spouse, son, daughter, or parent has a serious health condition; or

(4) A serious health condition of the employee that makes the employee unable to perform any one or more of the essential functions of his or her position.

(5) Any qualifying exigency arising out of the fact that the employee's spouse, son, daughter, or parent is a covered military member on covered active duty (or has been notified of an impending call or order to covered active duty) in the Armed Forces.

(b) An employee must invoke his or her entitlement to family and medical leave under paragraph (a) of this section, subject to the notification and medical certification requirements in §§ 630.1207 and 630.1208. An employee may not retroactively invoke his or her entitlement to family and medical leave. However, if an employee and his or her personal representative are physically or mentally incapable of invoking the employee's entitlement to FMLA leave *during the entire period* in which the employee is absent from work for an FMLA-qualifying purpose under paragraph (a) of this section, the employee may retroactively invoke his or her entitlement to FMLA leave within 2 workdays after returning to work. In such cases, the incapacity of the employee must be documented by a written medical certification from a health care provider. In addition, the employee must provide documentation acceptable to the agency explaining the inability of his or her personal representative to contact the agency and invoke the employee's entitlement to FMLA leave during the entire period in which the employee was absent from work for an FMLA-qualifying purpose. An employee may take only the amount of family and medical leave that is necessary to manage the circumstances that prompted the need for leave under paragraph (a) of this section.

(c) The 12-month period referred to in paragraph (a) of this section begins on the date an employee first takes leave for a family or medical need specified in paragraph (a) of this section and continues for 12 months. An employee is not entitled to 12 additional workweeks of leave until the previous 12-month period ends and an event or situation occurs that entitles the employee to another period of family or medical leave. (This may include a continuation of a previous situation or circumstance.)

(d) The entitlement to leave under paragraphs (a)(1) and (2) of this section shall expire at the end of the 12-month period beginning on the date of birth or placement. Leave for a birth or placement must be concluded within this 12-month period. Leave taken under paragraphs (a)(1) and (2) of this section, may begin prior to or on the actual date of birth or placement for adoption or foster care, and the 12-month period, referred to in paragraph (a) of this section begins on that date.

(e) Leave under paragraph (a) of this section is available to full-time and part-time employees. A total of 12 administrative workweeks will be made available equally for a full-time or part-time employee in direct proportion to the number of hours in the employee's regularly scheduled administrative workweek. The 12 administrative workweeks of leave will be calculated on an hourly basis and will equal 12 times the average number of hours in the employee's regularly scheduled administrative workweek. If the number of hours in an employee's workweek varies from week to week, a weekly average of the hours scheduled over the 12 weeks prior to the date leave commences shall be used as the basis for this calculation. Any holidays authorized under 5 U.S.C. 6103 or by Executive order and nonworkdays established by Federal statute, Executive order, or administrative order that occur during the period in which the employee is on family and medical leave may not be counted toward the 12-week entitlement to family and medical leave.

(f) If the number of hours in an employee's regularly scheduled administrative workweek is changed during the 12-month period of family and medical leave, the employee's entitlement to any remaining family and medical leave will be recalculated based on the number of hours in the employee's current regularly scheduled administrative workweek.

(g) Each agency shall inform its employees of their entitlements and responsibilities under this subpart, including the requirements and obligations of employees.

(h) An agency may not put an employee on family and medical leave and may not subtract leave from an employee's entitlement to leave under paragraph (a) of this section unless the agency has obtained confirmation from the employee of his or her intent to invoke entitlement to leave under paragraph (b) of this section. An employee's notice of his or her intent to take leave under § 630.1207 may suffice as the employee's confirmation.

[58 FR 39602, July 23, 1993, as amended at 61 FR 64452, Dec. 5, 1996; 65 FR 26486, May 8, 2000; 76 FR 60704, Sept. 30, 2011]

§ 630.1204 Qualifying exigency leave.

(a) An employee may take FMLA leave while the employee's spouse, son, daughter, or parent (the "covered military member") is on covered active duty or call to covered active duty status for one or more of the following qualifying exigencies:

(1) *Short-notice deployment.* To address any issue that arises from the fact that a covered military member is notified of an impending call or order to covered active duty 7 or fewer calendar days prior to the date of deployment. Leave taken for this purpose can be used for a period of up to 7 calendar days beginning on the date a covered military member is notified of an impending call or order to covered active duty.

(2) *Military events and related activities.* (i) To attend any official ceremony, program, or event sponsored by the military that is related to the covered active duty or call to covered active duty status of a covered military member; and

(ii) To attend family support or assistance programs and informational briefings sponsored or promoted by the military, military service organizations, or the American Red Cross that are related to the covered active duty or call to covered active duty status of a covered military member.

(3) *Childcare and school activities.* (i) To arrange for alternative childcare when the covered active duty or call to covered active duty status of a covered military member necessitates a change in the existing childcare arrangement for a child;

(ii) To provide childcare on an urgent, immediate need basis (but not on a routine, regular, or everyday basis) when the need to provide such care arises from the covered active duty or call to covered active duty status of a covered military member for a child;

(iii) To enroll in or transfer to a new school or day care facility a child, when enrollment or transfer is necessitated by the covered active duty or call to covered active duty status of a covered military member; and

(iv) To attend meetings with staff at a school or a daycare facility, such as meetings with school officials regarding disciplinary measures, parent-teacher conferences, or meetings with school counselors, for a child when such meetings are necessary due to circumstances arising from the covered active duty or call to covered active duty status of a covered military member.

(v) For purposes of paragraphs (a)(3)(i) through (a)(3)(iv) of this section, "child" means a biological, adopted, or foster child, a stepchild, or a legal ward of a covered military member, or a child for whom a covered military member stands in loco parentis, who is either under age 18, or age 18 or older and incapable of self-care because of a mental or physical disability at the time the FMLA leave is to commence.

(4) *Financial and legal arrangements.* (i) To make or update financial or legal arrangements to address the covered military member's absence while on covered active duty or call to covered active duty status, such as preparing

and executing financial and health care powers of attorney, transferring bank account signature authority, enrolling in the Defense Enrollment Eligibility Reporting System (DEERS), obtaining military identification cards, or preparing or updating a will or living trust; and

(ii) To act as the covered military member's representative before a Federal, State, or local agency for purposes of obtaining, arranging, or appealing military service benefits while the covered military member is on covered active duty or call to covered active duty status, and for a period of 90 days following the termination of the covered military member's covered active duty status.

(5) *Counseling.* To attend counseling provided by someone other than a health care provider for oneself, for the covered military member, or for a child as defined in paragraph (a)(3)(v) of this section, provided that the need for counseling arises from the covered active duty or call to covered active duty status of a covered military member.

(6) *Rest and recuperation.* To spend time with a covered military member who is on short-term, temporary, rest and recuperation leave during the period of deployment. Eligible employees may take up to 5 days of leave for each instance of rest and recuperation.

(7) *Post-deployment activities.* (i) To attend arrival ceremonies, reintegration briefings and events, and any other official ceremony or program sponsored by the military for a period of 90 days following the termination of the covered military member's covered active duty status; and

(ii) To address issues that arise from the death of a covered military member while on covered active duty status, such as meeting and recovering the body of the covered military member and making funeral arrangements.

(8) *Additional activities.* To address other events that arise out of the covered military member's covered active duty or call to covered active duty status, provided that the agency and employee agree that such leave qualifies as an exigency, and that they agree to both the timing and duration of such leave.

(b) An employee is eligible to take FMLA leave because of a qualifying exigency when the covered military member is on covered active duty or call to covered active duty status as a member of a regular component of the Armed Forces, or when the covered military member is on covered active duty or call to covered active duty status in support of a contingency operation pursuant to one of the provisions of law identified in the definition of *covered active duty or call to covered active duty status* as either a member of the reserve components (Army National Guard of the United States, Army Reserve, Navy Reserve, Marine Corps Reserve, Air National Guard of the United States, Air Force Reserve, and Coast Guard Reserve), or a retired member of the Regular Armed Forces or Reserve.

(c) For those called to covered active duty status in support of a contingency operation—

(1) A call to active duty for purposes of leave taken because of a qualifying exigency refers to a Federal call to active duty. State calls to active duty are not covered unless under order of the President of the United States pursuant to one of the provisions of law identified in paragraph (b) of this section in support of a contingency operation.

(2) For such members, the active duty orders of a covered military member will generally specify whether the servicemember is serving in support of a contingency operation by citation to the relevant section of title 10 of the United States Code or by reference to the specific name of the contingency operation, or both. A military operation qualifies as a contingency operation if it:

(i) Is designated by the Secretary of Defense as an operation in which members of the Armed Forces are or may become involved in military actions, operations, or hostilities against an enemy of the United States or against an opposing military force; or

(ii) Results in the call or order to, or retention on, active duty of members of the uniformed services under section 688, 12301(a), 12302, 12304, 12305, or 12406, or chapter 15 of title 10 of the United States Code, or any other provision of law during a war or during a national emergency declared by the President or Congress. (See 10 U.S.C. 101(a)(13).)

[76 FR 60704, Sept. 30, 2011]

§ 630.1205 Intermittent leave or reduced leave schedule.

(a) Leave under § 630.1203(a) (1) or (2) of this part shall not be taken intermittently or on a reduced leave schedule unless the employee and the agency agree to do so.

(b) Leave under § 630.1203(a)(3) or (4) may be taken intermittently or on a reduced leave schedule when medically necessary, subject to §§ 630.1207 and 630.1208 (b)(6). Leave under § 630.1203(a)(5) may be taken on an intermittent or reduced leave schedule basis, subject to §§ 630.1207 and 630.1209.

(c) If an employee takes leave under § 630.1203(a) (3) or (4) of this part intermittently or on a reduced leave schedule that is foreseeable based on planned medical treatment or recovery from a serious health condition, the agency may place the employee temporarily in an available alternative position for which the employee is qualified and that can better accommodate recurring periods of leave. Upon returning from leave, the employee is entitled to be returned to his or her permanent position or an equivalent position, as provided in § 630.1210(a) of this part.

(d) For the purpose of applying paragraph (c) of this section, an alternative position need not consist of equivalent duties, but must be in the same commuting area and must provide—

(1) An equivalent grade or pay level, including any applicable locality payment under 5 CFR part 531, subpart F; special rate supplement under 5 CFR part 530, subpart C; or similar payment or supplement under other legal authority;

(2) The same type of appointment, work schedule, status, and tenure; and

(3) The same employment benefits made available to the employee in his or her previous position (e.g., life insurance, health benefits, retirement coverage, and leave accrual).

(e) The agency shall determine the available alternative position that has equivalent pay and benefits consistent with Federal laws, including the Rehabilitation Act of 1973 (29 U.S.C. 701) and the Pregnancy Discrimination Act of 1978 (42 U.S.C. 2000e).

(f) Only the amount of leave taken intermittently or on a reduced leave schedule, as these terms are defined in § 630.1202, shall be subtracted from the total amount of leave available to the employee under § 630.1203 (e) and (f).

[58 FR 39602, July 23, 1993, as amended at 61 FR 3544, Feb. 1, 1996; 61 FR 64453, Dec. 5, 1996; 70 FR 31314, May 31, 2005. Redesignated and amended at 76 FR 60704, 60705, Sept. 30, 2011]

§ 630.1206 Substitution of paid leave.

(a) Except as provided in paragraph (b) of this section, leave taken under § 630.1203(a) of this part shall be leave without pay.

(b) An employee may elect to substitute the following paid leave for any or all of the period of leave without pay to be taken under § 630.1203(a)—

(1) Accrued or accumulated annual or sick leave under subchapter I of chapter 63 of title 5, United States Code, consistent with current law and regulations governing the granting and use of annual or sick leave;

(2) Advanced annual or sick leave approved under the same terms and conditions that apply to any other agency employee who requests advanced annual or sick leave; and

(3) Leave made available to an employee under the Voluntary Leave Transfer Program or the Voluntary Leave Bank Program consistent with subparts I and J of part 630 of this chapter.

(c) An agency may not deny an employee's right to substitute paid leave under paragraph (b) of this section for any or all of the period of leave without pay to be taken under § 630.1203(a), consistent with current law and regulations.

(d) An agency may not require an employee to substitute paid leave under paragraph (b) of this section for any or all of the period of leave without pay to be taken under § 630.1203(a).

(e) An employee shall notify the agency of his or her intent to substitute paid leave under paragraph (b) of this section for the period of leave without pay to be taken under § 630.1203(a) prior to the date such paid leave commences. An employee may not retroactively substitute paid leave for leave without pay previously taken under § 630.1203(a)

[58 FR 39602, July 23, 1993, as amended at 61 FR 64453, Dec. 5, 1996. Redesignated at 76 FR 60704, Sept. 30, 2011]

§ 630.1207 Notice of leave.

(a) If leave taken under § 630.1203(a) of this part is foreseeable based on an expected birth, placement for adoption or foster care, or planned medical treatment, the employee shall provide notice to the agency of his or her intention to take leave not less than 30 calendar days before the date the leave is to begin. If the date of birth or placement or planned medical treatment requires leave to begin within 30 calendar days, the employee shall provide such notice as is practicable.

(b) If leave taken under § 630.1203(a) (3) or (4) of this part is foreseeable based on planned medical treatment, the employee shall consult with the agency and make a reasonable effort to schedule medical treatment so as not to disrupt unduly the operations of the agency, subject to the approval of the health care provider. The agency may, for justifiable cause, request that an employee reschedule medical treatment, subject to the approval of the health care provider.

(c) If the need for leave taken under § 630.1203(a)(5) is foreseeable, the employee must provide notice as soon as practicable, regardless of how far in advance the leave is being requested.

(d) If the need for leave is not foreseeable—e.g., a medical emergency or the unexpected availability of a child for adoption or foster care, and the employee cannot provide 30 calendar days' notice of his or her need for leave, the employee shall provide notice within a reasonable period of time appropriate to the circumstances involved. If necessary, notice may be given by an employee's personal representative (e.g., a family member or other responsible party). If the need for leave is not foreseeable and the employee is unable, due to circumstances beyond his or her control, to provide notice of his or her need for leave, the leave may not be delayed or denied.

(e) If the need for leave is foreseeable, and the employee fails to give 30 calendar days' notice with no reasonable excuse for the delay of notification, the agency may delay the taking of leave under § 630.1203(a) of this part until at least 30 calendar days after the date the employee provides notice of his or her need for family and medical leave.

(f) An agency may waive the notice requirements under paragraph (a) of this section and instead impose the agency's usual and customary policies or procedures for providing notification of leave. The agency's policies or procedures for providing notification of leave must not be more stringent than the requirements in this section. However, an agency may not deny an employee's entitlement to leave under § 630.1203(a) of this part if the employee fails to follow such agency policies or procedures.

(g) An agency may require that a request for leave under § 630.1203(a) (1) and (2) be supported by evidence that is administratively acceptable to the agency.

[58 FR 39602, July 23, 1993, as amended at 59 FR 62274, Dec. 2, 1994; 61 FR 64453, Dec. 5, 1996; 65 FR 26487, May 8, 2000. Redesignated and amended at 76 FR 60704, 60705, Sept. 30, 2011]

§ 630.1208 Medical certification.

(a) An agency may require that a request for leave under § 630.1203(a) (3) or (4) be supported by written medical certification issued by the health care provider of the employee or the health care provider of the spouse, son, daughter, or parent of the employee, as appropriate. An agency may waive the requirement for an initial medical certificate in a subsequent 12-month period if the leave under § 630.1203(a) (3) or (4) is for the same chronic or continuing condition.

(b) The written medical certification shall include—

(1) The date the serious health condition commenced;

(2) The probable duration of the serious health condition or specify that the serious health condition is a chronic or continuing condition with an unknown duration and whether the patient is presently incapacitated and the likely duration and frequency of episodes of incapacity;

(3) The appropriate medical facts within the knowledge of the health care provider regarding the serious health condition, including a general statement as to the incapacitation, examination, or treatment that may be required by a health care provider;

(4) For the purpose of leave taken under § 630.1203(a)(3) of this part—

(i) A statement from the health care provider that the spouse, son, daughter, or parent of the employee requires psychological comfort and/or physical care; needs assistance for basic medical, hygienic, nutritional, safety, or transportation needs or in making arrangements to meet such needs; and would benefit from the employee's care or presence; and

(ii) A statement from the employee on the care he or she will provide and an estimate of the amount of time needed to care for his or her spouse, son, daughter, or parent;

(5) For the purpose of leave taken under § 630.1203(a)(4), a statement that the employee is unable to perform one or more of the essential functions of his or her position or requires medical treatment for a serious health condition, based on written information provided by the agency on the essential functions of the employee's position or, if not provided, discussion with the employee about the essential functions of his or her position; and

(6) In the case of certification for intermittent leave or leave on a reduced leave schedule under § 630.1203(a) (3) or (4) for planned medical treatment, the dates (actual or estimates) on which such treatment is expected to be given, the duration of such treatment, and the period of recovery, if any, or specify that the serious health condition is a chronic or continuing condition with an unknown duration and whether the patient is presently incapacitated and the likely duration and frequency of episodes of incapacity.

(c) The information on the medical certification shall relate only to the serious health condition for which the current need for family and medical leave exists. The agency may not require any personal or confidential information in the written medical certification other than that required by paragraph (b) of this section. If an employee submits a completed medical certification signed by the health care provider, the agency may not request new information from the health care provider. However, a health care provider representing the agency, including a health care provider employed by the agency or under administrative oversight of the agency, may contact the health care provider who completed the medical certification, with the employee's permission, for purposes of clarifying the medical certification.

(d) If the agency doubts the validity of the original certification provided under paragraph (a) of this section, the agency may require, at the agency's expense, that the employee obtain the opinion of a second health care provider designated or approved by the agency concerning the information certified under paragraph (b) of this section. Any health care provider designated or approved by the agency shall not be employed by the agency or be under the administrative oversight of the agency on a regular basis unless the agency is located in an area where access to health care is extremely limited—e.g., a rural area or an overseas location where no more than one or two health care providers practice in the relevant specialty, or the only health care providers available are employed by the agency.

(e) If the opinion of the second health care provider differs from the original certification provided under paragraph (a) of this section, the agency may require, at the agency's expense, that the employee obtain the opinion of a third health care provider designated or approved jointly by the agency and the employee concerning the information certified under paragraph (b) of this section. The opinion of the third health care provider shall be binding on the agency and the employee.

(f) To remain entitled to family and medical leave under § 630.1203(a) (3) or (4) of this part, an employee or the employee's spouse, son, daughter, or parent must comply with any requirement from an agency that he or she submit to examination (though not treatment) to obtain a second or third medical certification from a health care provider other than the individual's health care provider.

(g) If the employee is unable to provide the requested medical certification before leave begins, or if the agency questions the validity of the original certification provided by the employee and the medical treatment requires the leave to begin, the agency shall grant provisional leave pending final written medical certification.

(h) An employee must provide the written medical certification required by paragraphs (a), (d), (e), and (g) of this section, signed by the health care provider, no later than 15 calendar days after the date the agency requests such medical certification. If it is not practicable under the particular circumstances to provide the requested medical certification no later than 15 calendar days after the date requested by the agency despite the employee's diligent, good faith efforts, the employee must provide the medical certification within a reasonable period of time under the circumstances involved, but no later than 30 calendar days after the date the agency requests such medical certification.

(i) If, after the leave has commenced, the employee fails to provide the requested medical certification, the agency may—

(1) Charge the employee as absent without leave (AWOL); or

(2) Allow the employee to request that the provisional leave be charged as leave without pay or charged to the employee's annual and/or sick leave account, as appropriate.

(j) At its own expense, an agency may require subsequent medical recertification on a periodic basis, but not more than once every 30 calendar days, for leave taken for purposes relating to pregnancy, chronic conditions, or long-term conditions, as these terms are used in the definition of *serious health condition* in § 630.1202. For leave taken for all other serious health conditions and including leave taken on an intermittent or reduced leave schedule, if the health care provider has specified on the medical certification a minimum duration of the period of incapacity, the agency may not request recertification until that period has passed. An agency may require subsequent medical recertification more frequently than every 30 calendar days, or more frequently than the minimum duration of the period of incapacity specified on the medical certification, if the employee requests that the original leave period be extended, the circumstances described in the original medical certification have changed significantly, or the agency receives information that casts doubt upon the continuing validity of the medical certification.

(k) To ensure the security and confidentiality of any written medical certification under § 630.1208 or 630.1210(h) of this part, the medical certification is subject to the provisions for safeguarding information about individuals under subpart A of part 293 of this chapter.

[58 FR 39602, July 23, 193, as amended at 61 FR 64453, Dec. 5, 1996; 65 FR 26487, May 8, 2000; 65 FR 38409, June 21, 2000. Redesignated and amended at 76 FR 60704, 60705, Sept. 30, 2011]

§ 630.1209 Certification for leave taken because of a qualifying exigency.

(a) *Active duty orders.* The first time an employee requests leave because of a qualifying exigency arising out of the covered active duty or call to covered active duty status of a covered military member, an agency may require the employee to provide a copy of the covered military member's active duty orders or other documentation issued by the military that indicates the covered military member is on covered active duty or call to covered active duty status, and the dates of the covered military member's active duty service. This information need only be provided to the agency once. A copy of new active duty orders or other documentation issued by the military must be provided to the agency if the need for leave because of a qualifying exigency arises out of a different covered active duty or call to covered active duty status of the same or a different covered military member.

(b) *Required information.* An agency may require that leave for any qualifying exigency specified in § 630.1204 be supported by a certification from the employee that sets forth the following information:

(1) A statement or description, signed by the employee, of appropriate facts regarding the qualifying exigency for which FMLA leave is requested. The facts must be sufficient to support the need for leave. Such facts include the type of qualifying exigency for which leave is requested and any available written documentation that supports the request for leave, such as a copy of a meeting announcement for informational briefings sponsored by the military, a document confirming an appointment with a counselor or school official, or a copy of a bill for services for the handling of legal or financial affairs;

(2) The approximate date on which the qualifying exigency commenced or will commence;

(3) If an employee requests leave because of a qualifying exigency for a single, continuous period of time, the beginning and end dates for such absence;

(4) If an employee requests leave because of a qualifying exigency on an intermittent or reduced leave schedule basis, an estimate of the frequency and duration of the qualifying exigency; and

(5) If the qualifying exigency involves meeting with a third party, appropriate contact information for the individual or entity with whom the employee is meeting (such as the name, title, organization, address, telephone number, fax number, and e-mail address) and a brief description of the purpose of the meeting.

(c) *Verification.* If an employee submits a complete and sufficient certification to support his or her request for leave because of a qualifying exigency, the agency may not request additional information from the employee. However, the agency may verify the information described in paragraphs (c)(1) and (c)(2) of this section and does not need the employee's permission to do so.

(1) If the qualifying exigency involves meeting with a third party, the agency may contact the individual or entity with whom the employee is meeting for purposes of verifying a meeting or appointment schedule and verifying the information provided in the employee's statement under paragraph (b)(1) of this section regarding the meeting between the employee and the specified individual or entity. No additional information may be requested by the agency.

(2) An agency may contact an appropriate unit of the Department of Defense to request verification that a covered military member is on covered active duty or call to covered active duty status. No additional information may be requested by the agency.

[76 FR 60705, Sept. 30, 2011]

§630.1210 Protection of employment and benefits.

(a) Any employee who takes leave under §630.1203(a) of this part shall be entitled, upon return to the agency, to be returned to—

(1) The same position held by the employee when the leave commenced; or

(2) An equivalent position with equivalent benefits, pay, status, and other terms and conditions of employment.

(b) For the purpose of applying paragraph (a)(2) of this section, an equivalent position must be in the same commuting area and must carry or provide at a minimum—

(1) The same or substantially similar duties and responsibilities, which must entail substantially equivalent skill, effort, responsibility, and authority;

(2) An equivalent grade or pay level, including any applicable locality payment under 5 CFR part 531, subpart F; special rate supplement under 5 CFR part 530, subpart C; or similar payment or supplement under other legal authority;

(3) The same type of appointment, work schedule, status, and tenure;

(4) The same employment benefits made available to the employee in his or her previous position (e.g., life insurance, health benefits, retirement coverage, and leave accrual);

(5) The same or equivalent opportunity for a within-grade increase, performance award, incentive award, or other similar discretionary and nondiscretionary payments, consistent with applicable laws and regulations; however, the entitlement to be returned to an equivalent position does not extend to intangible or unmeasurable aspects of the job;

(6) The same or equivalent opportunity for premium pay consistent with applicable law and regulations under 5 CFR part 550, subpart A, or 5 CFR part 551, subpart E; and

(7) The same or equivalent opportunity for training or education benefits consistent with applicable laws and regulations, including any training that an employee may be required to complete to qualify for his or her previous position.

(c) As a result of taking leave under § 630.1203(a) of this part, an employee shall not suffer the loss of any employment benefit accrued prior to the date on which the leave commenced.

(d) Except as otherwise provided by or under law, a restored employee shall not be entitled to—

(1) The accrual of any employment benefits during any period of leave; or

(2) Any right, benefit, or position of employment other than any right, benefit, or position to which the employee would have been entitled had the employee not taken the leave.

(e) For the purpose of applying paragraph (d) of this section, the same entitlements and limitations in law and regulations that apply to the position, pay, benefits, status, and other terms and conditions of employment of an employee in a leave without pay status shall apply to any employee taking leave without pay under this part, except where different entitlements and limitations are specifically provided in this subpart.

(f) An employee is not entitled to be returned to the same or equivalent position under paragraph (a) of this section if the employee would not otherwise have been employed in that position at the time the employee returns from leave.

(g) An agency may not return an employee to an equivalent position where written notification has been provided that the equivalent position will be affected by a reduction in force if the employee's previous position is not affected by a reduction in force.

(h) As a condition to returning an employee who takes leave under § 630.1203(a)(4), an agency may establish a uniformly applied practice or policy that requires all similarly-situated employees (*i.e.*, same occupation, same serious health condition) to obtain written medical certification from the health care provider of the employee that the employee is able to perform the essential functions of his or her position. An agency may delay the return of an employee until the medical certification is provided. The same conditions for verifying the adequacy of a medical certification in § 630.1208(c) apply to the medical certification to return to work. No second or third opinion on the medical certification to return to work may be required. An agency may not require a medical certification to return to work during the period the employee takes leave intermittently or under a reduced leave schedule under § 630.1205.

(i) If an agency requires an employee to obtain written medical certification under paragraph (h) of this section before he or she returns to work, the agency shall notify the employee of this requirement before leave commences, or to the extent practicable in emergency medical situations, and pay the expenses for obtaining the written medical certification. An employee's refusal or failure to provide written medical certification under paragraph (h) of this section may be grounds for appropriate disciplinary or adverse action, as provided in part 752 of this chapter.

(j) An agency may require an employee to report periodically to the agency on his or her status and intention to return to work. An agency's policy requiring such reports must take into account all of the relevant facts and circumstances of the employee's situation.

(k) An employee's decision to invoke FMLA leave under § 630.1203(a) does not prohibit an agency from proceeding with appropriate actions under part 432 or part 752 of this chapter.

(l) An employee who does not comply with the notification requirements in § 630.1207 and does not provide medical certification signed by the health care provider that includes all of the information required in § 630.1208(b) is not entitled to family and medical leave.

[58 FR 39602, July 23, 1993, as amended at 61 FR 3544, Feb. 1, 1996; 61 FR 64453, Dec. 5, 1996; 65 FR 26487, May 8, 2000; 70 FR 31314, May 31, 2005. Redesignated at 76 FR 60704, Sept. 30, 2011 and further redesignated and amended at 76 FR 60705, 60706, Sept. 30, 2011]

§ 630.1211 Health benefits.

An employee enrolled in a health benefits plan under the Federal Employees Health Benefits Program (established under chapter 89 of title 5, United States Code) who is placed in a leave without pay status as a result of entitlement to leave under § 630.1203(a) of this part may continue his or her health benefits enrollment while in the leave without pay status and arrange to pay the appropriate employee contributions into the Employees Health Benefits Fund (established under section 8909 of title 5, United States Code). The employee shall make such contributions consistent with 5 CFR 890.502.

[58 FR 39602, July 23, 1993. Redesignated at 76 FR 60704, Sept. 30, 2011, and further redesignated at 76 FR 60705, Sept. 30, 2011]

§ 630.1212 Greater leave entitlements.

(a) An agency shall comply with any collective bargaining agreement or any agency employment benefit program or plan that provides greater family or medical leave entitlements to employees than those provided under this subpart. Nothing in this subpart prevents an agency from amending such policies, provided the policies comply with the requirements of this subpart.

(b) The entitlements established for employees under this subpart may not be diminished by any collective bargaining agreement or any employment benefit program or plan.

(c) An agency may adopt leave policies more generous than those provided in this subpart, except that such policies may not provide entitlement to paid time off in an amount greater than that otherwise authorized by law or provide sick leaved in any situation in which sick leave would not normally be allowed by law or regulation.

(d) The entitlements under sections 6381 through 6387 of title 5, United States Code, and this subpart do not modify or affect any Federal law prohibiting discrimination. If the entitlements under sections 6381 through 6387 of title 5, United States Code, and this subpart conflict with any Federal law prohibiting discrimination, an agency must comply with whichever statute provides greater entitlements to employees.

[58 FR 39602, July 23, 1994, as amended at 61 FR 64454, Dec. 5, 1996. Redesignated at 76 FR 60704, Sept. 30, 2011, and further redesignated at 76 FR 60705, Sept. 30, 2011]

§ 630.1213 Records and reports.

(a) So that OPM can evaluate the use of family and medical leave by Federal employees and provide the Congress and others with information about the use of this entitlement, each agency shall maintain records on employees who take leave under this subpart and submit to OPM such records and reports as OPM may require.

(b) At a minimum, each agency shall maintain the following information concerning each employee who takes leave under this subpart:

(1) The employee's rate of basic pay, as defined in 5 CFR 550.103;

(2) The occupational series for the employee's position;

(3) The number of hours of leave taken under § 630.1203(a), including any paid leave substituted for leave without pay under § 630.1206(b); and

(4) Whether leave was taken—

(i) Under § 630.1203(a) (1), (2) or (3) of this part; or

(ii) Under § 630.1203(a)(4) of this part.

(c) When an employee transfers to a different agency, the losing agency shall provide the gaining agency with information on leave taken under § 630.1203(a) of this part by the employee during the 12 months prior to the date of transfer. The losing agency shall provide the following information:

(1) The beginning and ending dates of the employee's 12-month period, as determined under § 630.1203(c) of this part; and

(2) The number of hours of leave taken under § 630.1203(a) of the part during the employee's 12-month period,

as determined under § 630.1203(c) of this part.

[58 FR 39602, July 23, 1993, as amended at 60 FR 67288, Dec. 29, 1995; 61 FR 64454, Dec. 5, 1996. Redesignated at 76 FR 60704, Sept. 30, 2011, and further redesignated and amended at 76 FR 60705, 60706, Sept. 30, 2011]

Subpart M—Disabled Veteran Leave

SOURCE: 81 FR 51779, Aug. 5, 2016, unless otherwise noted.

§ 630.1301 Purpose and authority.

This subpart implements 5 U.S.C. 6329, which establishes a leave category, to be known as "disabled veteran leave," for an eligible employee who is a veteran with a service-connected disability rated at 30 percent or more. Such an employee is entitled to this leave for purposes of undergoing medical treatment for such disability. Disabled veteran leave must be used during the 12-month period beginning on the first day of employment. OPM's authority to regulate section 6329 is found in section 2(d) of Public Law 114–75.

§ 630.1302 Applicability.

This subpart applies to an employee who is a veteran with a service-connected disability rated at 30 percent or more, subject to the conditions specified in this subpart. This subpart does not apply to employees of the United States Postal Service or the Postal Regulatory Commission who are subject to regulations issued by the Postmaster General under section 2(d)(2) of Public Law 114–75. This subpart applies only to an employee who is hired on or after November 5, 2016.

§ 630.1303 Definitions.

In this subpart:

12-month eligibility period means the continuous 12-month period that begins on the first day of employment. For an employee who was eligible (or later determined to have been eligible) for disabled veteran leave as an employee of the United States Postal Service or the Postal Regulatory Commission and who subsequently commences employment covered by this subpart, the 12-month eligibility period is the period that began on the first day of employment with the United States Postal Service or the Postal Regulatory Commission (as determined under regulations issued by the Postmaster General to implement 5 U.S.C. 6329).

Agency means an agency of the Federal Government. In the case of an agency in the Executive branch, it means an Executive agency as defined in 5 U.S.C. 105. When the term "agency" is used in the context of an agency making determinations or taking actions, it means management officials of the agency who are authorized by the agency head to make the given determination or take the given action.

Employee has the meaning given that term in 5 U.S.C. 2105.

Employment means service as an employee during which the employee is covered by a leave system under which leave is charged for periods of absence. This excludes service in a position in which the employee is not covered by 5 U.S.C. 6329 due to application of another statutory authority.

First day of employment means the first day of service that qualifies as employment that occurs on the later of—

(1) The earliest date an employee is hired after the effective date of the employee's qualifying service-connected disability, as determined by the Veterans Benefits Administration; or

(2) The effective date of the employee's qualifying service-connected disability, as determined by the Veterans Benefits Administration.

Health care provider has the meaning given that term in § 630.1202.

Hired means the action of—

(1) Receiving an initial appointment to a civilian position in the Federal Government in which the service qualifies as employment under this subpart;

(2) Receiving a qualifying reappointment to a civilian position in the Federal Government in which the service qualifies as employment under this subpart; or

(3) Returning to duty status in a civilian position in the Federal Government in which the service qualifies as employment under this subpart, when such return immediately followed a

break in civilian duty (with the employee in continuous civilian leave status) to perform military service.

Medical certificate means a written statement signed by a health care provider certifying to the treatment of a veteran's qualifying service-connected disability.

Medical treatment means any activity carried out or prescribed by a health care provider to treat a veteran's qualifying service-connected disability.

Military service means "active military, naval, or air service" as that term is defined in 38 U.S.C. 101(24).

Qualifying reappointment means an appointment of a former employee of the Federal Government following a break in employment of at least 90 calendar days.

Qualifying service-connected disability means a veteran's service-connected disability rated at 30 percent or more by the Veteran Benefits Administration, including a combined degree of disability of 30 percent or more that reflects the combined effect of multiple individual disabilities, which resulted in the award of disability compensation under title 38, United States Code. A temporary disability rating under 38 U.S.C. 1156 is considered a valid rating in applying this definition for as long as it is in effect.

Service-connected has the meaning given such term in 38 U.S.C. 101(16).

Veteran has the meaning given such term in 38 U.S.C. 101(2).

Veterans Benefits Administration means the Veterans Benefits Administration of the Department of Veterans Affairs.

§ 630.1304 Eligibility.

(a) An employee who is a veteran with a qualifying service-connected disability is entitled to disabled veteran leave under this subpart, which will be available for use during the 12-month eligibility period beginning on the first day of employment. For each employee, there is a single first day of employment.

(b) In order to be eligible for disabled veteran leave, an employee must provide to the agency documentation from the Veterans Benefits Administration certifying that the employee has a qualifying service-connected disability. The documentation should be provided to the agency—

(1) Upon the first day of employment, if the employee has already received such certifying documentation; or

(2) For an employee who has not yet received such certifying documentation from the Veterans Benefit Administration, as soon as practicable after the employee receives the certifying documentation.

(c) Notwithstanding paragraph (b) of this section, an employee may submit certifying documentation at a later time, including after a period of absence for medical treatment, as described in § 630.1306(c). The 12-month eligibility period is fixed based on the first day of employment and is not affected by the timing of when certifying documentation is provided.

(d) If an employee's service-connected disability rating is decreased or discontinued during the 12-month eligibility period such that the employee no longer has a qualifying service-connected disability—

(1) The employee must notify the agency of the effective date of the change in the disability rating; and

(2) The employee is no longer eligible for disabled veteran leave as of the effective date of the rating change.

§ 630.1305 Crediting disabled veteran leave.

(a) Upon receipt of the certifying documentation under § 630.1304, an agency must credit 104 hours of disabled veteran leave to a full-time, nonseasonal employee or a proportionally equivalent amount for employees with part-time, seasonal, or uncommon tours of duty, except as otherwise provided in this section.

(b) The proportional equivalent of 104 hours for a full-time employee is determined for employees with other schedules as follows:

(1) For an employee with a part-time work schedule, the 104 hours is prorated based on the number of hours in the part-time schedule (as established for leave charging purposes) relative to a full-time schedule (e.g., 52 hours for a half-time schedule);

(2) For an employee with a seasonal work schedule, the 104 hours is prorated based on the total projected

hours to be worked in an annual period of 52 weeks (based on the seasonal employee's seasonal work periods and full-time or part-time schedule during those periods) relative to a full-time work year of 2,080 hours (e.g., 52 hours for a seasonal employee who works full-time for half a year); and

(3) For an employee with an uncommon tour of duty (as defined in § 630.201 and described in § 630.210), 104 hours is proportionally increased based on the number of hours in the uncommon tour relative to the hours in a regular full-time tour (e.g., 187 hours for an employee with a 72-hour weekly uncommon tour of duty.)

(c) When an employee is converted to a different tour of duty for leave purposes, the employee's balance of unused disabled veteran leave must be converted to the proper number of hours based on the proportion of hours in the new tour of duty compared to the former tour of duty. For seasonal employees, hours must be annualized in determining the proportion.

(d) The amount of disabled veteran leave initially credited to an employee under paragraphs (a) and (b) of this section must be offset by the number of hours of sick leave an employee has credited to his or her account as of the first day of employment. For example, if an employee is being reappointed and having sick leave recredited upon such reappointment, the amount of disabled veteran leave must be reduced by the amount of such recredited sick leave. Similarly, if an employee is returning to civilian duty status after a period of leave for military service, that employee may have a balance of sick leave, which must be used to offset the disabled veteran leave.

(e)(1) An employee who was previously employed by an agency whose employees were not subject to 5 U.S.C. 6329 must certify, at the time the employee is hired in a position subject to 5 U.S.C. 6329, whether or not that former agency provided entitlement to an equivalent disabled veteran leave benefit to be used in connection with the medical treatment of a service-connected disability rated at 30 percent or more. The employee must certify the date he or she commenced the period of eligibility to use disabled veteran leave in the former agency.

(2) If 12 months have elapsed since the commencing date referenced in paragraph (e)(1) of this section, the employee will be considered to have received the full amount of an equivalent benefit and no benefit may be provided under this subpart.

(3) If the employee is still within the 12-month period that began on the commencing date referenced in paragraph (e)(1) of this section, the employee must certify the number of hours of disabled veteran leave used at the former agency. The gaining agency must offset the number of hours of disabled veteran leave to be credited to the employee by the number of such hours used by the employee at such agency, while making no offset under paragraph (d) of this section. If the employee had a different type of work schedule at the former agency, the hours used at the former agency must be converted before applying the offset, consistent with § 630.1305(c).

§ 630.1306 Requesting and using disabled veteran leave.

(a) An employee may use disabled veteran leave only for the medical treatment of a qualifying service-connected disability. The medical treatment may include a period of rest, but only if such period of rest is specifically ordered by the health care provider as part of a prescribed course of treatment for the qualifying service-connected disability.

(b)(1) An employee must file an application—written, oral, or electronic, as required by the agency—to use disabled veteran leave. The application must include a personal self-certification by the employee that the requested leave will be (or was) used for purposes of being furnished medical treatment for a qualifying service-connected disability. The application must also include the specific days and hours of absence required for the treatment. The application must be submitted within such time limits as the agency may require.

(2) An employee must request approval to use disabled veteran leave in advance unless the need for leave is critical and not foreseeable—e.g., due

to a medical emergency or the unexpected availability of an appointment for surgery or other critical treatment. The employee must provide notice within a reasonable period of time appropriate to the circumstances involved. If the agency determines that the need for leave is critical and not foreseeable and that the employee is unable to provide advance notice of his or her need for leave, the leave may not be delayed or denied.

(c)(1) When an employee did not provide the agency with certification of a qualifying service-connected disability before having a period of absence for treatment of such disability, the employee is entitled to substitute approved disabled veteran leave retroactively for such period of absence (excluding periods of suspension or absence without leave (AWOL), but including leave without pay, sick leave, annual leave, compensatory time off, or other paid time off) in the 12-month eligibility period. Such retroactive substitution cancels the use of the original leave or paid time off and requires appropriate adjustments. In the case of retroactive substitution for a period when an employee used advanced annual leave or advanced sick leave, the adjustment is a liquidation of the leave indebtedness covered by the substitution.

(2) An agency may require an employee to submit the medical certification described in § 630.1307(a) before approving such retroactive substitution.

§ 630.1307 Medical certification.

(a) In addition to the employee's self-certification required under § 630.1306(b)(1), an agency may additionally require that the use of disabled veteran leave be supported by a signed written medical certification issued by a health care provider.

(b) When an agency requires a signed written medical certification by a health care provider, the agency may specify that the certification include—

(1) A statement by the health care provider that the medical treatment is for one or more service-connected disabilities of the employee that resulted in 30 percent or more disability rating;

(2) The date or dates of treatment or, if the treatment extends over several days, the beginning and ending dates of the treatment;

(3) If the leave was not requested in advance, a statement that the treatment required was of an urgent nature or there were other circumstances that made advanced scheduling not possible; and

(4) Any additional information that is essential to verify the employee's eligibility.

(c)(1) An employee must provide any required written medical certification no later than 15 calendar days after the date the agency requests such medical certification, except as otherwise allowed under paragraph (c)(2) of this section.

(2) If the agency determines it is not practicable under the particular circumstances for the employee to provide the requested medical certification within 15 calendar days after the date requested by the agency despite the employee's diligent, good faith efforts, the employee must provide the medical certification within a reasonable period of time under the circumstances involved, but no later than 30 calendar days after the date the agency requests such documentation.

(3) An employee who does not provide the required evidence or medical certification within the specified time period is not entitled to use disabled veteran leave, and the agency may, as appropriate and consistent with applicable laws and regulations—

(i) Charge the employee as absent without leave (AWOL); or

(ii) Allow the employee to request that the absence be charged to leave without pay, sick leave, annual leave, or other forms of paid time off.

§ 630.1308 Disabled veteran leave forfeiture, transfer, reinstatement.

(a) Disabled veteran leave not used during the 12-month eligibility period may not be carried over to subsequent years and must be forfeited.

(b) If a change in the employee's disability rating during the 12-month eligibility period causes the employee to no longer have a qualifying service-connected disability (as described in

§630.1304(d)), any unused disabled veteran leave to the employee's credit as of the effective date of the rating change must be forfeited.

(c) When an employee with a positive disabled veteran leave balance transfers between positions in different agencies, or transfers from the United States Postal Service or Postal Regulatory Commission to a position in another agency, during the 12-month eligibility period, the agency from which the employee transfers must certify the number of unused disabled veteran leave hours available for credit by the gaining agency. The losing agency must also certify the expiration date of the employee's 12-month eligibility period to the gaining agency. Any unused disabled veteran leave will be forfeited at the end of that eligibility period. For the purpose of this paragraph, the term "transfers" means movement from a position in one agency (or the United States Postal Service or Postal Regulatory Commission) to a position in another agency without a break in employment of 1 workday or more in circumstances where service in both positions qualifies as employment under this subpart.

(d)(1) An employee covered by this subpart, or an employee of the United States Postal Service or Postal Regulatory Commission, with a balance of unused disabled veteran leave who has a break in employment of at least 1 workday during the employee's 12-month eligibility period, and later recommences employment covered by 5 U.S.C. 6329 within that same eligibility period, is entitled to a recredit of the unused balance.

(2) When an employee has a break in employment as described in paragraph (d)(1) of this section, the losing agency must certify the number of unused disabled veteran leave hours available for recredit by the gaining agency. The losing agency must also certify the expiration date of the employee's 12-month eligibility period. Any unused disabled veteran leave must be forfeited at the end of that eligibility period.

(3) In the absence of the certification described in paragraph (d)(2) of this section, the recredit of disabled veteran leave may also be supported by written documentation available to the employing agency in its official personnel records concerning the employee, the official records of the employee's former employing agency, copies of contemporaneous earnings and leave statement(s) provided by the employee, or copies of other contemporaneous written documentation acceptable to the agency.

(e) An employee may not receive a lump-sum payment for any unused disabled veteran leave under any circumstance.

PARTS 631–699 [RESERVED]

FINDING AIDS

A list of CFR titles, subtitles, chapters, subchapters and parts and an alphabetical list of agencies publishing in the CFR are included in the CFR Index and Finding Aids volume to the Code of Federal Regulations which is published separately and revised annually.

Table of CFR Titles and Chapters

(Revised as of January 1, 2018)

Title 1—General Provisions

Title 2—Grants and Agreements

Title 2—Grants and Agreements—Continued

Title 3—The President

Title 4—Accounts

Title 5—Administrative Personnel

Title 5—Administrative Personnel—Continued

Title 6—Domestic Security

Title 7—Agriculture

Title 8—Aliens and Nationality

Title 9—Animals and Animal Products

Title 10—Energy

Title 11—Federal Elections

Title 12—Banks and Banking

Title 12—Banks and Banking—Continued

Title 13—Business Credit and Assistance

Title 14—Aeronautics and Space

Title 15—Commerce and Foreign Trade

Title 15—Commerce and Foreign Trade—Continued

Title 16—Commercial Practices

Title 17—Commodity and Securities Exchanges

Title 18—Conservation of Power and Water Resources

Title 19—Customs Duties

Title 20—Employees' Benefits

Title 20—Employees' Benefits—Continued

Title 21—Food and Drugs

Title 22—Foreign Relations

Title 23—Highways

Title 23—Highways—Continued

Chap.

II National Highway Traffic Safety Administration and Federal Highway Administration, Department of Transportation (Parts 1200—1299)

III National Highway Traffic Safety Administration, Department of Transportation (Parts 1300—1399)

Title 24—Housing and Urban Development

SUBTITLE A—OFFICE OF THE SECRETARY, DEPARTMENT OF HOUSING AND URBAN DEVELOPMENT (PARTS 0—99)

SUBTITLE B—REGULATIONS RELATING TO HOUSING AND URBAN DEVELOPMENT

I Office of Assistant Secretary for Equal Opportunity, Department of Housing and Urban Development (Parts 100—199)

II Office of Assistant Secretary for Housing-Federal Housing Commissioner, Department of Housing and Urban Development (Parts 200—299)

III Government National Mortgage Association, Department of Housing and Urban Development (Parts 300—399)

IV Office of Housing and Office of Multifamily Housing Assistance Restructuring, Department of Housing and Urban Development (Parts 400—499)

V Office of Assistant Secretary for Community Planning and Development, Department of Housing and Urban Development (Parts 500—599)

VI Office of Assistant Secretary for Community Planning and Development, Department of Housing and Urban Development (Parts 600—699) [Reserved]

VII Office of the Secretary, Department of Housing and Urban Development (Housing Assistance Programs and Public and Indian Housing Programs) (Parts 700—799)

VIII Office of the Assistant Secretary for Housing—Federal Housing Commissioner, Department of Housing and Urban Development (Section 8 Housing Assistance Programs, Section 202 Direct Loan Program, Section 202 Supportive Housing for the Elderly Program and Section 811 Supportive Housing for Persons With Disabilities Program) (Parts 800—899)

IX Office of Assistant Secretary for Public and Indian Housing, Department of Housing and Urban Development (Parts 900—1699)

X Office of Assistant Secretary for Housing—Federal Housing Commissioner, Department of Housing and Urban Development (Interstate Land Sales Registration Program) (Parts 1700—1799)

XII Office of Inspector General, Department of Housing and Urban Development (Parts 2000—2099)

XV Emergency Mortgage Insurance and Loan Programs, Department of Housing and Urban Development (Parts 2700—2799) [Reserved]

XX Office of Assistant Secretary for Housing—Federal Housing Commissioner, Department of Housing and Urban Development (Parts 3200—3899)

Title 25—Indians

Title 26—Internal Revenue

Title 27—Alcohol, Tobacco Products and Firearms

Title 28—Judicial Administration

Title 29—Labor

Chap.

SUBTITLE A—OFFICE OF THE SECRETARY OF LABOR (PARTS 0—99)

SUBTITLE B—REGULATIONS RELATING TO LABOR

I National Labor Relations Board (Parts 100—199)

II Office of Labor-Management Standards, Department of Labor (Parts 200—299)

III National Railroad Adjustment Board (Parts 300—399)

IV Office of Labor-Management Standards, Department of Labor (Parts 400—499)

V Wage and Hour Division, Department of Labor (Parts 500—899)

IX Construction Industry Collective Bargaining Commission (Parts 900—999)

X National Mediation Board (Parts 1200—1299)

XII Federal Mediation and Conciliation Service (Parts 1400—1499)

XIV Equal Employment Opportunity Commission (Parts 1600—1699)

XVII Occupational Safety and Health Administration, Department of Labor (Parts 1900—1999)

XX Occupational Safety and Health Review Commission (Parts 2200—2499)

XXV Employee Benefits Security Administration, Department of Labor (Parts 2500—2599)

XXVII Federal Mine Safety and Health Review Commission (Parts 2700—2799)

XL Pension Benefit Guaranty Corporation (Parts 4000—4999)

Title 30—Mineral Resources

I Mine Safety and Health Administration, Department of Labor (Parts 1—199)

II Bureau of Safety and Environmental Enforcement, Department of the Interior (Parts 200—299)

IV Geological Survey, Department of the Interior (Parts 400—499)

V Bureau of Ocean Energy Management, Department of the Interior (Parts 500—599)

VII Office of Surface Mining Reclamation and Enforcement, Department of the Interior (Parts 700—999)

XII Office of Natural Resources Revenue, Department of the Interior (Parts 1200—1299)

Title 31—Money and Finance: Treasury

SUBTITLE A—OFFICE OF THE SECRETARY OF THE TREASURY (PARTS 0—50)

SUBTITLE B—REGULATIONS RELATING TO MONEY AND FINANCE

I Monetary Offices, Department of the Treasury (Parts 51—199)

II Fiscal Service, Department of the Treasury (Parts 200—399)

IV Secret Service, Department of the Treasury (Parts 400—499)

V Office of Foreign Assets Control, Department of the Treasury (Parts 500—599)

Title 31—Money and Finance: Treasury—Continued

Title 32—National Defense

Title 33—Navigation and Navigable Waters

Title 34—Education

Title 34—Education—Continued

Title 35 [Reserved]

Title 36—Parks, Forests, and Public Property

Title 37—Patents, Trademarks, and Copyrights

Title 38—Pensions, Bonuses, and Veterans' Relief

Chap.

Chap.	
I	Department of Veterans Affairs (Parts 0—199)
II	Armed Forces Retirement Home (Parts 200—299)

Title 39—Postal Service

Chap.	
I	United States Postal Service (Parts 1—999)
III	Postal Regulatory Commission (Parts 3000—3099)

Title 40—Protection of Environment

Chap.	
I	Environmental Protection Agency (Parts 1—1099)
IV	Environmental Protection Agency and Department of Justice (Parts 1400—1499)
V	Council on Environmental Quality (Parts 1500—1599)
VI	Chemical Safety and Hazard Investigation Board (Parts 1600—1699)
VII	Environmental Protection Agency and Department of Defense; Uniform National Discharge Standards for Vessels of the Armed Forces (Parts 1700—1799)
VIII	Gulf Coast Ecosystem Restoration Council (Parts 1800—1899)

Title 41—Public Contracts and Property Management

Chap.	
	SUBTITLE A—FEDERAL PROCUREMENT REGULATIONS SYSTEM [NOTE]
	SUBTITLE B—OTHER PROVISIONS RELATING TO PUBLIC CONTRACTS
50	Public Contracts, Department of Labor (Parts 50-1—50-999)
51	Committee for Purchase From People Who Are Blind or Severely Disabled (Parts 51-1—51-99)
60	Office of Federal Contract Compliance Programs, Equal Employment Opportunity, Department of Labor (Parts 60-1—60-999)
61	Office of the Assistant Secretary for Veterans' Employment and Training Service, Department of Labor (Parts 61-1—61-999)
62—100	[Reserved]
	SUBTITLE C—FEDERAL PROPERTY MANAGEMENT REGULATIONS SYSTEM
101	Federal Property Management Regulations (Parts 101-1—101-99)
102	Federal Management Regulation (Parts 102-1—102-299)
103—104	[Reserved]
105	General Services Administration (Parts 105-1—105-999)
109	Department of Energy Property Management Regulations (Parts 109-1—109-99)
114	Department of the Interior (Parts 114-1—114-99)
115	Environmental Protection Agency (Parts 115-1—115-99)
128	Department of Justice (Parts 128-1—128-99)
129—200	[Reserved]
	SUBTITLE D—OTHER PROVISIONS RELATING TO PROPERTY MANAGEMENT [RESERVED]

Chap.	
	SUBTITLE E—FEDERAL INFORMATION RESOURCES MANAGEMENT REGULATIONS SYSTEM [RESERVED]
	SUBTITLE F—FEDERAL TRAVEL REGULATION SYSTEM
300	General (Parts 300–1—300–99)
301	Temporary Duty (TDY) Travel Allowances (Parts 301–1—301–99)
302	Relocation Allowances (Parts 302–1—302–99)
303	Payment of Expenses Connected with the Death of Certain Employees (Part 303–1—303–99)
304	Payment of Travel Expenses from a Non-Federal Source (Parts 304–1—304–99)

Title 42—Public Health

I	Public Health Service, Department of Health and Human Services (Parts 1—199)
ii—III	[Reserved]
IV	Centers for Medicare & Medicaid Services, Department of Health and Human Services (Parts 400—699)
V	Office of Inspector General-Health Care, Department of Health and Human Services (Parts 1000—1099)

Title 43—Public Lands: Interior

	SUBTITLE A—OFFICE OF THE SECRETARY OF THE INTERIOR (PARTS 1—199)
	SUBTITLE B—REGULATIONS RELATING TO PUBLIC LANDS
I	Bureau of Reclamation, Department of the Interior (Parts 400—999)
II	Bureau of Land Management, Department of the Interior (Parts 1000—9999)
III	Utah Reclamation Mitigation and Conservation Commission (Parts 10000—10099)

Title 44—Emergency Management and Assistance

I	Federal Emergency Management Agency, Department of Homeland Security (Parts 0—399)
IV	Department of Commerce and Department of Transportation (Parts 400—499)

Title 45—Public Welfare

	SUBTITLE A—DEPARTMENT OF HEALTH AND HUMAN SERVICES (PARTS 1—199)
	SUBTITLE B—REGULATIONS RELATING TO PUBLIC WELFARE
II	Office of Family Assistance (Assistance Programs), Administration for Children and Families, Department of Health and Human Services (Parts 200—299)

Title 45—Public Welfare—Continued

Chap.

III Office of Child Support Enforcement (Child Support Enforcement Program), Administration for Children and Families, Department of Health and Human Services (Parts 300—399)

IV Office of Refugee Resettlement, Administration for Children and Families, Department of Health and Human Services (Parts 400—499)

V Foreign Claims Settlement Commission of the United States, Department of Justice (Parts 500—599)

VI National Science Foundation (Parts 600—699)

VII Commission on Civil Rights (Parts 700—799)

VIII Office of Personnel Management (Parts 800—899)

IX Denali Commission (Parts 900—999)

X Office of Community Services, Administration for Children and Families, Department of Health and Human Services (Parts 1000—1099)

XI National Foundation on the Arts and the Humanities (Parts 1100—1199)

XII Corporation for National and Community Service (Parts 1200—1299)

XIII Administration for Children and Families, Department of Health and Human Services (Parts 1300—1399)

XVI Legal Services Corporation (Parts 1600—1699)

XVII National Commission on Libraries and Information Science (Parts 1700—1799)

XVIII Harry S. Truman Scholarship Foundation (Parts 1800—1899)

XXI Commission of Fine Arts (Parts 2100—2199)

XXIII Arctic Research Commission (Part 2301)

XXIV James Madison Memorial Fellowship Foundation (Parts 2400—2499)

XXV Corporation for National and Community Service (Parts 2500—2599)

Title 46—Shipping

I Coast Guard, Department of Homeland Security (Parts 1—199)

II Maritime Administration, Department of Transportation (Parts 200—399)

III Coast Guard (Great Lakes Pilotage), Department of Homeland Security (Parts 400—499)

IV Federal Maritime Commission (Parts 500—599)

Title 47—Telecommunication

I Federal Communications Commission (Parts 0—199)

II Office of Science and Technology Policy and National Security Council (Parts 200—299)

III National Telecommunications and Information Administration, Department of Commerce (Parts 300—399)

Title 48—Federal Acquisition Regulations System

Chap.	
54	Defense Logistics Agency, Department of Defense (Parts 5400—5499)
57	African Development Foundation (Parts 5700—5799)
61	Civilian Board of Contract Appeals, General Services Administration (Parts 6100—6199)
99	Cost Accounting Standards Board, Office of Federal Procurement Policy, Office of Management and Budget (Parts 9900—9999)

Title 49—Transportation

	SUBTITLE A—OFFICE OF THE SECRETARY OF TRANSPORTATION (PARTS 1—99)
	SUBTITLE B—OTHER REGULATIONS RELATING TO TRANSPORTATION
I	Pipeline and Hazardous Materials Safety Administration, Department of Transportation (Parts 100—199)
II	Federal Railroad Administration, Department of Transportation (Parts 200—299)
III	Federal Motor Carrier Safety Administration, Department of Transportation (Parts 300—399)
IV	Coast Guard, Department of Homeland Security (Parts 400—499)
V	National Highway Traffic Safety Administration, Department of Transportation (Parts 500—599)
VI	Federal Transit Administration, Department of Transportation (Parts 600—699)
VII	National Railroad Passenger Corporation (AMTRAK) (Parts 700—799)
VIII	National Transportation Safety Board (Parts 800—999)
X	Surface Transportation Board (Parts 1000—1399)
XI	Research and Innovative Technology Administration, Department of Transportation (Parts 1400—1499) [Reserved]
XII	Transportation Security Administration, Department of Homeland Security (Parts 1500—1699)

Title 50—Wildlife and Fisheries

I	United States Fish and Wildlife Service, Department of the Interior (Parts 1—199)
II	National Marine Fisheries Service, National Oceanic and Atmospheric Administration, Department of Commerce (Parts 200—299)
III	International Fishing and Related Activities (Parts 300—399)
IV	Joint Regulations (United States Fish and Wildlife Service, Department of the Interior and National Marine Fisheries Service, National Oceanic and Atmospheric Administration, Department of Commerce); Endangered Species Committee Regulations (Parts 400—499)
V	Marine Mammal Commission (Parts 500—599)

Alphabetical List of Agencies Appearing in the CFR

(Revised as of January 1, 2018)

Agency	CFR Title, Subtitle or Chapter
Administrative Committee of the Federal Register	1, I
Administrative Conference of the United States	1, III
Advisory Council on Historic Preservation	36, VIII
Advocacy and Outreach, Office of	7, XXV
Afghanistan Reconstruction, Special Inspector General for	5, LXXXIII
African Development Foundation	22, XV
Federal Acquisition Regulation	48, 57
Agency for International Development	2, VII; 22, II
Federal Acquisition Regulation	48, 7
Agricultural Marketing Service	7, I, IX, X, XI
Agricultural Research Service	7, V
Agriculture Department	2, IV; 5, LXXIII
Advocacy and Outreach, Office of	7, XXV
Agricultural Marketing Service	7, I, IX, X, XI
Agricultural Research Service	7, V
Animal and Plant Health Inspection Service	7, III; 9, I
Chief Financial Officer, Office of	7, XXX
Commodity Credit Corporation	7, XIV
Economic Research Service	7, XXXVII
Energy Policy and New Uses, Office of	2, IX; 7, XXIX
Environmental Quality, Office of	7, XXXI
Farm Service Agency	7, VII, XVIII
Federal Acquisition Regulation	48, 4
Federal Crop Insurance Corporation	7, IV
Food and Nutrition Service	7, II
Food Safety and Inspection Service	9, III
Foreign Agricultural Service	7, XV
Forest Service	36, II
Grain Inspection, Packers and Stockyards Administration	7, VIII; 9, II
Information Resources Management, Office of	7, XXVII
Inspector General, Office of	7, XXVI
National Agricultural Library	7, XLI
National Agricultural Statistics Service	7, XXXVI
National Institute of Food and Agriculture	7, XXXIV
Natural Resources Conservation Service	7, VI
Operations, Office of	7, XXVIII
Procurement and Property Management, Office of	7, XXXII
Rural Business-Cooperative Service	7, XVIII, XLII
Rural Development Administration	7, XLII
Rural Housing Service	7, XVIII, XXXV
Rural Telephone Bank	7, XVI
Rural Utilities Service	7, XVII, XVIII, XLII
Secretary of Agriculture, Office of	7, Subtitle A
Transportation, Office of	7, XXXIII
World Agricultural Outlook Board	7, XXXVIII
Air Force Department	32, VII
Federal Acquisition Regulation Supplement	48, 53
Air Transportation Stabilization Board	14, VI
Alcohol and Tobacco Tax and Trade Bureau	27, I
Alcohol, Tobacco, Firearms, and Explosives, Bureau of	27, II
AMTRAK	49, VII
American Battle Monuments Commission	36, IV
American Indians, Office of the Special Trustee	25, VII

Agency	CFR Title, Subtitle or Chapter
Animal and Plant Health Inspection Service	7, III; 9, I
Appalachian Regional Commission	5, IX
Architectural and Transportation Barriers Compliance Board	36, XI
Arctic Research Commission	45, XXIII
Armed Forces Retirement Home	5, XI
Army Department	32, V
Engineers, Corps of	33, II; 36, III
Federal Acquisition Regulation	48, 51
Bilingual Education and Minority Languages Affairs, Office of	34, V
Blind or Severely Disabled, Committee for Purchase from People Who Are	41, 51
Broadcasting Board of Governors	22, V
Federal Acquisition Regulation	48, 19
Career, Technical and Adult Education, Office of	34, IV
Census Bureau	15, I
Centers for Medicare & Medicaid Services	42, IV
Central Intelligence Agency	32, XIX
Chemical Safety and Hazardous Investigation Board	40, VI
Chief Financial Officer, Office of	7, XXX
Child Support Enforcement, Office of	45, III
Children and Families, Administration for	45, II, III, IV, X, XIII
Civil Rights, Commission on	5, LXVIII; 45, VII
Civil Rights, Office for	34, I
Council of the Inspectors General on Integrity and Efficiency	5, XCVIII
Court Services and Offender Supervision Agency for the District of Columbia	5, LXX
Coast Guard	33, I; 46, I; 49, IV
Coast Guard (Great Lakes Pilotage)	46, III
Commerce Department	2, XIII; 44, IV; 50, VI
Census Bureau	15, I
Economic Analysis, Bureau of	15, VIII
Economic Development Administration	13, III
Emergency Management and Assistance	44, IV
Federal Acquisition Regulation	48, 13
Foreign-Trade Zones Board	15, IV
Industry and Security, Bureau of	15, VII
International Trade Administration	15, III; 19, III
National Institute of Standards and Technology	15, II; 37, IV
National Marine Fisheries Service	50, II, IV
National Oceanic and Atmospheric Administration	15, IX; 50, II, III, IV, VI
National Technical Information Service	15, XI
National Telecommunications and Information Administration	15, XXIII; 47, III, IV
National Weather Service	15, IX
Patent and Trademark Office, United States	37, I
Secretary of Commerce, Office of	15, Subtitle A
Commercial Space Transportation	14, III
Commodity Credit Corporation	7, XIV
Commodity Futures Trading Commission	5, XLI; 17, I
Community Planning and Development, Office of Assistant Secretary for	24, V, VI
Community Services, Office of	45, X
Comptroller of the Currency	12, I
Construction Industry Collective Bargaining Commission	29, IX
Consumer Financial Protection Bureau	5, LXXXIV; 12, X
Consumer Product Safety Commission	5, LXXI; 16, II
Copyright Royalty Board	37, III
Corporation for National and Community Service	2, XXII; 45, XII, XXV
Cost Accounting Standards Board	48, 99
Council on Environmental Quality	40, V
Court Services and Offender Supervision Agency for the District of Columbia	5, LXX; 28, VIII
Customs and Border Protection	19, I
Defense Contract Audit Agency	32, I
Defense Department	2, XI; 5, XXVI; 32, Subtitle A; 40, VII
Advanced Research Projects Agency	32, I

Agency	CFR Title, Subtitle or Chapter
Presidential Documents	3
Science and Technology Policy, Office of	32, XXIV; 47, II
Trade Representative, Office of the United States	15, XX
Export-Import Bank of the United States	2, XXXV; 5, LII; 12, IV
Family Assistance, Office of	45, II
Farm Credit Administration	5, XXXI; 12, VI
Farm Credit System Insurance Corporation	5, XXX; 12, XIV
Farm Service Agency	7, VII, XVIII
Federal Acquisition Regulation	48, 1
Federal Aviation Administration	14, I
Commercial Space Transportation	14, III
Federal Claims Collection Standards	31, IX
Federal Communications Commission	5, XXIX; 47, I
Federal Contract Compliance Programs, Office of	41, 60
Federal Crop Insurance Corporation	7, IV
Federal Deposit Insurance Corporation	5, XXII; 12, III
Federal Election Commission	5, XXXVII; 11, I
Federal Emergency Management Agency	44, I
Federal Employees Group Life Insurance Federal Acquisition Regulation	48, 21
Federal Employees Health Benefits Acquisition Regulation	48, 16
Federal Energy Regulatory Commission	5, XXIV; 18, I
Federal Financial Institutions Examination Council	12, XI
Federal Financing Bank	12, VIII
Federal Highway Administration	23, I, II
Federal Home Loan Mortgage Corporation	1, IV
Federal Housing Enterprise Oversight Office	12, XVII
Federal Housing Finance Agency	5, LXXX; 12, XII
Federal Housing Finance Board	12, IX
Federal Labor Relations Authority	5, XIV, XLIX; 22, XIV
Federal Law Enforcement Training Center	31, VII
Federal Management Regulation	41, 102
Federal Maritime Commission	46, IV
Federal Mediation and Conciliation Service	29, XII
Federal Mine Safety and Health Review Commission	5, LXXIV; 29, XXVII
Federal Motor Carrier Safety Administration	49, III
Federal Prison Industries, Inc.	28, III
Federal Procurement Policy Office	48, 99
Federal Property Management Regulations	41, 101
Federal Railroad Administration	49, II
Federal Register, Administrative Committee of	1, I
Federal Register, Office of	1, II
Federal Reserve System	12, II
Board of Governors	5, LVIII
Federal Retirement Thrift Investment Board	5, VI, LXXVI
Federal Service Impasses Panel	5, XIV
Federal Trade Commission	5, XLVII; 16, I
Federal Transit Administration	49, VI
Federal Travel Regulation System	41, Subtitle F
Financial Crimes Enforcement Network	31, X
Financial Research Office	12, XVI
Financial Stability Oversight Council	12, XIII
Fine Arts, Commission of	45, XXI
Fiscal Service	31, II
Fish and Wildlife Service, United States	50, I, IV
Food and Drug Administration	21, I
Food and Nutrition Service	7, II
Food Safety and Inspection Service	9, III
Foreign Agricultural Service	7, XV
Foreign Assets Control, Office of	31, V
Foreign Claims Settlement Commission of the United States	45, V
Foreign Service Grievance Board	22, IX
Foreign Service Impasse Disputes Panel	22, XIV
Foreign Service Labor Relations Board	22, XIV
Foreign-Trade Zones Board	15, IV
Forest Service	36, II
General Services Administration	5, LVII; 41, 105

Agency	CFR Title, Subtitle or Chapter
Indian Arts and Crafts Board	25, II
Indian Health Service	25, V
Industry and Security, Bureau of	15, VII
Information Resources Management, Office of	7, XXVII
Information Security Oversight Office, National Archives and Records Administration	32, XX
Inspector General	
Agriculture Department	7, XXVI
Health and Human Services Department	42, V
Housing and Urban Development Department	24, XII, XV
Institute of Peace, United States	22, XVII
Inter-American Foundation	5, LXIII; 22, X
Interior Department	2, XIV
American Indians, Office of the Special Trustee	25, VII
Endangered Species Committee	50, IV
Federal Acquisition Regulation	48, 14
Federal Property Management Regulations System	41, 114
Fish and Wildlife Service, United States	50, I, IV
Geological Survey	30, IV
Indian Affairs, Bureau of	25, I, V
Indian Affairs, Office of the Assistant Secretary	25, VI
Indian Arts and Crafts Board	25, II
Land Management, Bureau of	43, II
National Indian Gaming Commission	25, III
National Park Service	36, I
Natural Resource Revenue, Office of	30, XII
Ocean Energy Management, Bureau of	30, V
Reclamation, Bureau of	43, I
Safety and Enforcement Bureau, Bureau of	30, II
Secretary of the Interior, Office of	2, XIV; 43, Subtitle A
Surface Mining Reclamation and Enforcement, Office of	30, VII
Internal Revenue Service	26, I
International Boundary and Water Commission, United States and Mexico, United States Section	22, XI
International Development, United States Agency for	22, II
Federal Acquisition Regulation	48, 7
International Development Cooperation Agency, United States	22, XII
International Joint Commission, United States and Canada	22, IV
International Organizations Employees Loyalty Board	5, V
International Trade Administration	15, III; 19, III
International Trade Commission, United States	19, II
Interstate Commerce Commission	5, XL
Investment Security, Office of	31, VIII
James Madison Memorial Fellowship Foundation	45, XXIV
Japan–United States Friendship Commission	22, XVI
Joint Board for the Enrollment of Actuaries	20, VIII
Justice Department	2, XXVIII; 5, XXVIII; 28, I, XI; 40, IV
Alcohol, Tobacco, Firearms, and Explosives, Bureau of	27, II
Drug Enforcement Administration	21, II
Federal Acquisition Regulation	48, 28
Federal Claims Collection Standards	31, IX
Federal Prison Industries, Inc.	28, III
Foreign Claims Settlement Commission of the United States	45, V
Immigration Review, Executive Office for	8, V
Independent Counsel, Offices of	28, VI
Prisons, Bureau of	28, V
Property Management Regulations	41, 128
Labor Department	2, XXIX; 5, XLII
Employee Benefits Security Administration	29, XXV
Employees' Compensation Appeals Board	20, IV
Employment and Training Administration	20, V
Employment Standards Administration	20, VI
Federal Acquisition Regulation	48, 29
Federal Contract Compliance Programs, Office of	41, 60

Agency	CFR Title, Subtitle or Chapter
Federal Procurement Regulations System	41, 50
Labor-Management Standards, Office of	29, II, IV
Mine Safety and Health Administration	30, I
Occupational Safety and Health Administration	29, XVII
Public Contracts	41, 50
Secretary of Labor, Office of	29, Subtitle A
Veterans' Employment and Training Service, Office of the Assistant Secretary for	41, 61; 20, IX
Wage and Hour Division	29, V
Workers' Compensation Programs, Office of	20, I, VII
Labor-Management Standards, Office of	29, II, IV
Land Management, Bureau of	43, II
Legal Services Corporation	45, XVI
Library of Congress	36, VII
Copyright Royalty Board	37, III
U.S. Copyright Office	37, II
Local Television Loan Guarantee Board	7, XX
Management and Budget, Office of	5, III, LXXVII; 14, VI; 48, 99
Marine Mammal Commission	50, V
Maritime Administration	46, II
Merit Systems Protection Board	5, II, LXIV
Micronesian Status Negotiations, Office for	32, XXVII
Military Compensation and Retirement Modernization Commission	5, XCIX
Millennium Challenge Corporation	22, XIII
Mine Safety and Health Administration	30, I
Minority Business Development Agency	15, XIV
Miscellaneous Agencies	1, IV
Monetary Offices	31, I
Morris K. Udall Scholarship and Excellence in National Environmental Policy Foundation	36, XVI
Museum and Library Services, Institute of	2, XXXI
National Aeronautics and Space Administration	2, XVIII; 5, LIX; 14, V
Federal Acquisition Regulation	48, 18
National Agricultural Library	7, XLI
National Agricultural Statistics Service	7, XXXVI
National and Community Service, Corporation for	2, XXII; 45, XII, XXV
National Archives and Records Administration	2, XXVI; 5, LXVI; 36, XII
Information Security Oversight Office	32, XX
National Capital Planning Commission	1, IV, VI
National Commission for Employment Policy	1, IV
National Commission on Libraries and Information Science	45, XVII
National Council on Disability	5, C; 34, XII
National Counterintelligence Center	32, XVIII
National Credit Union Administration	5, LXXXVI; 12, VII
National Crime Prevention and Privacy Compact Council	28, IX
National Drug Control Policy, Office of	2, XXXVI; 21, III
National Endowment for the Arts	2, XXXII
National Endowment for the Humanities	2, XXXIII
National Foundation on the Arts and the Humanities	45, XI
National Geospatial-Intelligence Agency	32, I
National Highway Traffic Safety Administration	23, II, III; 47, VI; 49, V
National Imagery and Mapping Agency	32, I
National Indian Gaming Commission	25, III
National Institute of Food and Agriculture	7, XXXIV
National Institute of Standards and Technology	15, II; 37, IV
National Intelligence, Office of Director of	5, IV; 32, XVII
National Labor Relations Board	5, LXI; 29, I
National Marine Fisheries Service	50, II, IV
National Mediation Board	29, X
National Oceanic and Atmospheric Administration	15, IX; 50, II, III, IV, VI
National Park Service	36, I
National Railroad Adjustment Board	29, III
National Railroad Passenger Corporation (AMTRAK)	49, VII
National Science Foundation	2, XXV; 5, XLIII; 45, VI

Agency	CFR Title, Subtitle or Chapter
Federal Acquisition Regulation	48, 25
National Security Council	32, XXI
National Security Council and Office of Science and Technology Policy	47, II
National Telecommunications and Information Administration	15, XXIII; 47, III, IV, V
National Transportation Safety Board	49, VIII
Natural Resources Conservation Service	7, VI
Natural Resource Revenue, Office of	30, XII
Navajo and Hopi Indian Relocation, Office of	25, IV
Navy Department	32, VI
Federal Acquisition Regulation	48, 52
Neighborhood Reinvestment Corporation	24, XXV
Northeast Interstate Low-Level Radioactive Waste Commission	10, XVIII
Nuclear Regulatory Commission	2, XX; 5, XLVIII; 10, I
Federal Acquisition Regulation	48, 20
Occupational Safety and Health Administration	29, XVII
Occupational Safety and Health Review Commission	29, XX
Ocean Energy Management, Bureau of	30, V
Oklahoma City National Memorial Trust	36, XV
Operations Office	7, XXVIII
Overseas Private Investment Corporation	5, XXXIII; 22, VII
Patent and Trademark Office, United States	37, I
Payment From a Non-Federal Source for Travel Expenses	41, 304
Payment of Expenses Connected With the Death of Certain Employees	41, 303
Peace Corps	2, XXXVII; 22, III
Pennsylvania Avenue Development Corporation	36, IX
Pension Benefit Guaranty Corporation	29, XL
Personnel Management, Office of	5, I, XXXV; 5, IV; 45, VIII
Human Resources Management and Labor Relations Systems, Department of Homeland Security	5, XCVII
Federal Acquisition Regulation	48, 17
Federal Employees Group Life Insurance Federal Acquisition Regulation	48, 21
Federal Employees Health Benefits Acquisition Regulation	48, 16
Pipeline and Hazardous Materials Safety Administration	49, I
Postal Regulatory Commission	5, XLVI; 39, III
Postal Service, United States	5, LX; 39, I
Postsecondary Education, Office of	34, VI
President's Commission on White House Fellowships	1, IV
Presidential Documents	3
Presidio Trust	36, X
Prisons, Bureau of	28, V
Privacy and Civil Liberties Oversight Board	6, X
Procurement and Property Management, Office of	7, XXXII
Public Contracts, Department of Labor	41, 50
Public and Indian Housing, Office of Assistant Secretary for	24, IX
Public Health Service	42, I
Railroad Retirement Board	20, II
Reclamation, Bureau of	43, I
Refugee Resettlement, Office of	45, IV
Relocation Allowances	41, 302
Research and Innovative Technology Administration	49, XI
Rural Business-Cooperative Service	7, XVIII, XLII
Rural Development Administration	7, XLII
Rural Housing Service	7, XVIII, XXXV
Rural Telephone Bank	7, XVI
Rural Utilities Service	7, XVII, XVIII, XLII
Safety and Environmental Enforcement, Bureau of	30, II
Saint Lawrence Seaway Development Corporation	33, IV
Science and Technology Policy, Office of	32, XXIV
Science and Technology Policy, Office of, and National Security Council	47, II
Secret Service	31, IV

Agency	CFR Title, Subtitle or Chapter
Securities and Exchange Commission	5, XXXIV; 17, II
Selective Service System	32, XVI
Small Business Administration	2, XXVII; 13, I
Smithsonian Institution	36, V
Social Security Administration	2, XXIII; 20, III; 48, 23
Soldiers' and Airmen's Home, United States	5, XI
Special Counsel, Office of	5, VIII
Special Education and Rehabilitative Services, Office of	34, III
State Department	2, VI; 22, I; 28, XI
Federal Acquisition Regulation	48, 6
Surface Mining Reclamation and Enforcement, Office of	30, VII
Surface Transportation Board	49, X
Susquehanna River Basin Commission	18, VIII
Tennessee Valley Authority	5, LXIX; 18, XIII
Thrift Supervision Office, Department of the Treasury	12, V
Trade Representative, United States, Office of	15, XX
Transportation, Department of	2, XII; 5, L
Commercial Space Transportation	14, III
Emergency Management and Assistance	44, IV
Federal Acquisition Regulation	48, 12
Federal Aviation Administration	14, I
Federal Highway Administration	23, I, II
Federal Motor Carrier Safety Administration	49, III
Federal Railroad Administration	49, II
Federal Transit Administration	49, VI
Maritime Administration	46, II
National Highway Traffic Safety Administration	23, II, III; 47, IV; 49, V
Pipeline and Hazardous Materials Safety Administration	49, I
Saint Lawrence Seaway Development Corporation	33, IV
Secretary of Transportation, Office of	14, II; 49, Subtitle A
Transportation Statistics Bureau	49, XI
Transportation, Office of	7, XXXIII
Transportation Security Administration	49, XII
Transportation Statistics Bureau	49, XI
Travel Allowances, Temporary Duty (TDY)	41, 301
Treasury Department	2, X;5, XXI; 12, XV; 17, IV; 31, IX
Alcohol and Tobacco Tax and Trade Bureau	27, I
Community Development Financial Institutions Fund	12, XVIII
Comptroller of the Currency	12, I
Customs and Border Protection	19, I
Engraving and Printing, Bureau of	31, VI
Federal Acquisition Regulation	48, 10
Federal Claims Collection Standards	31, IX
Federal Law Enforcement Training Center	31, VII
Financial Crimes Enforcement Network	31, X
Fiscal Service	31, II
Foreign Assets Control, Office of	31, V
Internal Revenue Service	26, I
Investment Security, Office of	31, VIII
Monetary Offices	31, I
Secret Service	31, IV
Secretary of the Treasury, Office of	31, Subtitle A
Thrift Supervision, Office of	12, V
Truman, Harry S. Scholarship Foundation	45, XVIII
United States and Canada, International Joint Commission	22, IV
United States and Mexico, International Boundary and Water Commission, United States Section	22, XI
U.S. Copyright Office	37, II
Utah Reclamation Mitigation and Conservation Commission	43, III
Veterans Affairs Department	2, VIII; 38, I
Federal Acquisition Regulation	48, 8
Veterans' Employment and Training Service, Office of the Assistant Secretary for	41, 61; 20, IX
Vice President of the United States, Office of	32, XXVIII
Wage and Hour Division	29, V
Water Resources Council	18, VI

Agency	CFR Title, Subtitle or Chapter
Workers' Compensation Programs, Office of	20, I, VII
World Agricultural Outlook Board	7, XXXVIII

List of CFR Sections Affected

All changes in this volume of the Code of Federal Regulations (CFR) that were made by documents published in the FEDERAL REGISTER since January 1, 2013 are enumerated in the following list. Entries indicate the nature of the changes effected. Page numbers refer to FEDERAL REGISTER pages. The user should consult the entries for chapters, parts and subparts as well as sections for revisions.

For changes to this volume of the CFR prior to this listing, consult the annual edition of the monthly List of CFR Sections Affected (LSA). The LSA is available at *www.fdsys.gov*. For changes to this volume of the CFR prior to 2001, see the "List of CFR Sections Affected, 1949–1963, 1964–1972, 1973–1985, and 1986–2000" published in 11 separate volumes. The "List of CFR Sections Affected 1986–2000" is available at *www.fdsys.gov*.

2013

5 CFR

78 FR Page

Chapter I

213 Authority citation revised 12220
213.3102 (u) revised 12220
531.212 (a)(1)(ii) amended; (a)(3) revised; (a)(5) added 49362
531.602 Amended 5115
531.609 (d) revised 5115
532 Technical correction 1
532.213 Table amended 58153
532.267 (c)(1) table amended 58154
532.285 (c)(1) table amended 58154
532.201—532.285 (Subpart B) Appendix A amended 21515
Appendix B amended; interim 29612
Appendix C amended 21515, 29612
Appendix D amended; interim 29612
Appendix D amended 60181, 60182
Regulation at 78 FR 29612 confirmed 60182
532.313 (a) table amended 58154
575 Authority citation revised 49363
575.102 (3) amended 49363
575.104 (d)(1) revised; (d)(2) and (3) amended; (d)(4) added 49363
575.105 (b) revised 49363
575.109 (c)(1) revised 49363
575.113 (b) and (a) designation removed 49363
575.114 Removed 49363
575.204 (d)(1) revised; (d)(2) and (3) amended; (d)(4) added 49363
575.205 (b) amended 49364
575.210 (d) revised 49364

5 CFR—Continued

78 FR Page

Chapter I—Continued

575.211 (b) revised 49364
575.213 (b) and (a) designation removed 49364
575.214 Removed 49364
575.304 (d)(1) revised; (d)(2) and (3) amended; (d)(4) added 49364
575.305 (c) revised 49364
575.306 (b)(2) through (b)(8) redesignated as (b)(3) through (b)(9); new (b)(2) added 49364
575.311 (a)(1) and (2) redesignated as (a)(2) and (3); new (a)(1) added 49364
575.313 (b) and (a) designation removed 49364
575.314 Removed; new section redesignated from 575.315; new (i)(2) removed; new (i)(1) introductory text and new (i)(1)(i) through (i)(1)(v) redesignated as new (i) introductory text and new (i)(1) through (i)(5); new (i) introductory text revised 49364
575.315 Redesignated as 575.314 49364

2014

5 CFR

79 FR Page

Chapter I

151 Authority citation revised 25484
151.101 (b) and (d) revised 25484
151.121 (c) revised 25484

5 CFR—Continued

79 FR Page

Chapter I—Continued
151.122 (c) revised 25484
179.401 (Subpart D) Added 29072
211 Revised; interim 77835
300 Authority citation revised 43922
300.102 (c) revised 43922
300.103 (c) revised 43922
300.104 (c)(1) revised 43922
315 Authority citation revised 43922
315.806 (d) revised 43922
335 Authority citation revised 43922
335.103 (b)(1) revised 43922
410 Authority citation revised 43923
410.302 (a)(1) revised 43923
532.201—532.285 (Subpart B) Appendix C corrected; CFR correction 74585
532.287 Added 22765
532.313 (a) corrected 21121
534 Authority citation revised 12357
534.404 (c)(3)(v) and (e)(2) removed 12357
534.501—534.511 (Subpart E) Revised 12357
537 Authority citation revised 43923
537.105 (d) revised 43923
550.1102 (b)(1) revised; (b)(3) added 530
550.1103 Amended 530
550.1104 (d) introductory text, (3), (i) and (j) revised 530
550.1106 Revised 530
550.1501—550.1507 (Subpart O) Added 53602
581 Authority citation revised 46618
581.102 (l) and (m) added 46618
581.306 Heading revised; (d) added 46618
582 Authority citation revised 46618
582.102 (2) revised 46618

2015

5 CFR

80 FR Page

Chapter I
337.305 Removed; eff. 1–4–16 75786
410.402 (b)(8) added 58111
430.301—430.314 (Subpart C) Revised 57694
531.403 Amended; CFR correction 76629
531.602 Amended 65610
531.603 (b) revised 65611
532.289 Added 61277
532.201—532.289 (Subpart B) Appendix C amended 5451, 15147, 17307, 40895, 74673

5 CFR—Continued

80 FR Page

Chapter I—Continued
534.505 (c)(1) revised 57698
550.101—550.187 (Subpart A) Authority citation revised 58111
550.103 Amended 58111
550.107 (a)(3) and (4) amended; (a)(5) added 58111
550.111 (j) added 58111
550.122 (e) added 58111
550.132 (d) added 58111
550.172 Existing text designated as (a); (b) added 58111
550.201—550.206 (Subpart B) Authority citation revised 58111
550.202 Amended 58111
550.703 Amended 58112
550.1204 (a) amended 58112
550.1205 (b)(5)(ii) amended; (b)(5)(iv) added 58112
550.1601—550.1638 (Subpart P) Added 58112
551.216 (c)(2) revised 58121
551.217 Added 58121
576 Authority citation revised; eff. 1–4–16 75786
576.104 Revised; eff. 1–4–16 75786

2016

5 CFR

81 FR Page

Chapter I
185 Authority citation revised 46828
185.103 (a) introductory text and (f)(2) amended; interim 46828
211 Revised 83109
211.102 (d) introductory text revised; interim 94909
250.201—250.209 (Subpart B) Revised; eff. 4–11–17 89364
250.301—250.303 (Subpart C) Revised; eff. 4–11–17 89367
315.201 (a) and (b) revised 78498
330.1300 Added; eff. 1–3–17 86561
532.211 (f) added 86249
532.201—532.289 (Subpart B) Appendix D amended 8639
Appendices A and C amended 24455
Appendix C amended 57745, 86250, 86562
630 Authority citation revised 51778
630.310 Removed 51779
630.1202 Amended 20524
630.1301—630.1308 (Subpart M) Revised 51779

2017

5 CFR

82 FR Page

Chapter I

330 Authority citation revised........ 5339
330.104 (c) added; interim 5339
332 Authority citation revised........ 5339
332.408 Added; interim 5339
337 Authority citation revised........ 5340
337.304 Revised; interim 5340

5 CFR—Continued

82 FR Page

Chapter I—Continued

339 Revised 5350
Regulation at 82 FR 5350 eff. date delayed to 3–21–17 10959
532.201—532.289 (Subpart B) Appendix D amended ... 6197, 24825, 40669, 41321
Appendix C amended; CFR Correction 29699, 50801

www.ingramcontent.com/pod-product-compliance
Lightning Source LLC
LaVergne TN
LVHW052202200926
848481LV00001B/12
9781640242487